ENCYCLOPEDIA OF

HUMAN

BEHAVIOR

EDITOR-IN-CHIEF

V. S. Ramachandran

University of California, San Diego
La Jolla, California

VOLUME 3   J-P

ACADEMIC PRESS

San Diego New York Boston London Sydney Tokyo Toronto

This book is printed on acid-free paper. ∞

Academic Press, Inc.
A Division of Harcourt Brace & Company
525 B Street, Suite 1900, San Diego, California 92101-4495

United Kingdom Edition published by
Academic Press Limited
24–28 Oval Road, London NW1 7DX

Library of Congress Cataloging-in-Publication Data

Encyclopedia of human behavior / edited by V. S. Ramachandran.
        p.   cm.
    Includes index.
    ISBN 0-12-226920-9 (set). -- ISBN 0-12-226921-7 (v. 1)
    ISBN 0-12-226922-5 (v. 2) -- ISBN 0-12-226923-3 (v. 3)
    ISBN 0-12-226924-1 (v. 4).
    1.   Psychology--Encyclopedias.   I.   Ramachandran, V. S.
BF31.E5   1994
150'.3--dc20   93-34371
                                                    CIP

PRINTED IN THE UNITED STATES OF AMERICA
   95 96 97 QW 9 8 7 6 5 4 3 2

CONTENTS

O

P

JEALOUSY

Peter N. Stearns
Carnegie Mellon University

Glossary

Constructivism Theory of emotion that argues all emotions are constructed by society according to its fundamental needs at the time.
Courtly love Literary praise for platonic love, in the 14th to 15th centuries.
Darwinian psychology Study of emotions from perspective of evolutionary utility.
Dating Informal courtship associated with entertainment outside the home; began to become common, particularly in the United States, after about 1918.
Early modern period 16th to 18th centuries in European history.
Freudian psychology Psychology based on the theories of Freud, emphasizing unconscious impulses and their conscious control.
Honor Code of conduct demanded of worthy people.
Open marriage Marriage with approval of multiple sexual partners.
Prescriptive literature Books or articles written to advise people on proper standards of behavior, family life, etc.
Siblings Brothers and/or sisters.

Spock, Dr. Benjamin The leading popular writer on childrearing in the second half of the 20th century.
Unwritten law Idea that a man has a right to attack a wife's or fiancée's lover.
Victorian Middle-class culture in 19th century Europe and the United States.

JEALOUSY constitutes the emotional reaction to a real or imagined loss or threat of loss of a valued object, quality or person, to a rival. It is most commonly seen, in modern West European and United States society, in terms of sexual or love relationships, when individuals become jealous of a partner's interest in or involvement with someone else. Jealousy can also arise simply because such interest and involvement are imagined, in which case the emotion helps cause the perception as well as resulting from it. Another common instance of jealousy involves relationships among children. At least some forms of sibling rivalry stem from a child's jealous response to the attentions lavished on a new baby, which seem to constitute a loss of parental love for the child himself or herself.

I. PROBLEMS IN DEFINING JEALOUSY

Jealous responses vary greatly among individuals in a given culture. Many studies of jealousy, for example among American college students, reveal such variations. Clinicians, such as marriage counselors dealing with jealousy as a problem in couples, note such variations as well, not only in the United States but also in Germany and elsewhere. A lover's flirtation may be easily tolerated by one partner, while provoking an intensely jealous reaction in another. Some psychological studies in the 1930s hypothesized that variations in jealousy stemmed from different childhood experiences, depending on whether earlier threats of loss were cushioned by emotional support. Many psychoanalysts continue to argue that jealousy experiences in childhood are absolutely unavoidable, but that many individuals suffer losses without support while others learn that loss—for example, a parent's death or a separation from a close friend or relative—may be compensated by other fruitful relationships. Individuals in this second category, according to this argument, will be able to deal with adult threats to affection with little or no jealousy. The explanation is plausible, and many therapists explore childhood background in dealing with intense jealousy. But no rigorous or systematic correlations have been demonstrated.

Recent psychological research, paying renewed attention to jealousy, has discounted the explicit childhood origins of jealousy. Differences among individuals are vitally important, and indeed new categories extend the differentiation. Thus "suspicious jealousy," provoking jealous reactions because of internal pressures within an individual, is distinguished from "reactive jealousy," which responds to a definite threat. But why some individuals are suspicious, and why some react more than others to the same threat, is attributed to broader personality factors and to an overall emotional style that is not easy to explain. Jealousy often results from a larger sense of personal insecurity, an older belief reemphasized in recent research, but here too the ultimate causation problem is pushed back more than accounted for save insofar as it clearly depends on more general traits.

Jealousy is a social emotion. That is, it arises in interactions among people and it affects the way people operate in social situations. Jealousy also depends to some degree on social sanctions. Some cultures tolerate or even encourage jealousy, while other cultures disapprove. The social aspects of jealousy and its dependence on particular cultural contexts have determined much recent research on the emotion, bent on determining jealousy's results in interpersonal relationships and on understanding why jealousy varies and changes depending on place and time. Even psychologists who assume fairly standard emotional reactions thus note different triggers and different responses (jealous Frenchmen get angry, jealous Dutch get sad) depending on cultures.

The most obvious difficulties in pinpointing jealousy, however, arise from the fact that it is an amalgam of a number of emotions, or as one psychologist puts it, serves as a "blended emotion." Only a few recent definitions argue that it is a basic emotion. While animals may display something like jealousy—for example, the pet that mopes at the arrival of a new baby or another pet in the household because of a resentment against deprivation of attention, or the male animal that displays aggression against a sexual rival—it is not clear how useful it is to perceive jealousy in humans as an innate response. Again, the considerable variations among individuals and differences in cultural guidelines complicate the issue. Jealousy, when it is intensely experienced, expresses a sense of grief at loss plus anger at the individual seen as responsible for the loss (a lover's lover, for example). It may involve not only anger but also aggression, when the cause of jealousy is attacked either outright or in imagination. Or, like grief, it may occasion passivity, sadness, and self-doubt. Perceived or anticipated jealousy may also embody fear of impending loss. The mixture of emotions and responses involved complicates any easy definition of jealousy itself.

Jealousy is also close to envy. Technically, to be sure, the two emotions are quite different: jealousy involves reactions to loss or threat of loss, and envy a desire to have what someone else has. Envy may lead someone to take something belonging to another, thus causing jealousy. In practice, jealousy and envy are not always distinguishable, and some scholars have found in the 20th century United States a growing confusion of the two terms. Most Americans, thus, while able to define envy, rarely use the word, terming themselves jealous instead. Teenagers who say they are jealous of so-and-so's hairdo are in fact envious. Their use of the term jealous, however, may be revealing of some new emotional configurations, and thus may be open to explanation. Both envy and jealousy involve hostility, and one major study finds the only emotional difference between them is that jealousy is more intense. The proximity between the terms and the experiences of jealousy and envy unquestionably add another complication to any definition; again, jealousy is an amalgamated emotional experience.

Jealousy is normally defined as an unpleasant emotion. Certainly it is so regarded in contemporary Western culture. A German therapist writes in the 1980s of "how agonizing, how galling, how unbearable even 'completely normal' jealousy can be. Anxiety, disquiet, and an incessant compulsion to brood about the immediate situation endanger, even prevent, one's ability to conduct one's life as usual." Most commentators on jealousy have similarly noted its potentially consuming qualities. In some cultures, however, jealousy's pain is accompanied by a feeling of invigoration, and jealousy is not regarded simply as disagreeable. Recent psychological research, turning to the coping mechanisms jealousy generates, begins to turn from the dysfunctional, often violent results of the emotion in certain instances, to potentially constructive translations. Thus jealous individuals have more stable marriages on average than less jealous because they learn how to win the commitment that will allow them to avoid emotional pain. Here too, basic definitions are complex.

II. MEANINGS OF JEALOUSY AND METHODS FOR ITS STUDY

Some of the complexity of jealousy as an emotional response and potential spur to behavior emerges from consideration of its various meanings. The word in English derived from the same Greek stem as the word for zeal, and at least until recently elements of this definitional linkage persisted. The Christian God, in the West European language versions of the Bible, was a jealous god, which implied resentment of any threats to position—worship of false idols, for example—but also a vigorous defense of legitimate prerogatives. Attached to the divinity, jealousy has obvious positive connotations. Similarly, references to a jealous defense of rights suggested a commendable and justifiable energy, not a narrow unwillingness to share. Jealousy as a goad to righteous and useful action enters into the usage of the word in many circumstances, although it no longer forms the dominant evaluation.

Jealousy also early acquired its more common meaning, of possessive alertness and response to threat. Jealousy in love was a prominent theme in the courtly literature of late-medieval Europe. Part of the enthrallment with a highly stylized love, according to the troubadours, involved subjection to the woes of jealousy, as suitors (by implication usually male) fended off rivals and coped with the flirtations of their adored.

Jealousy's meaning has also embraced implications of both strength and weakness. Jealous defense of rights, honor, or property—including God's jeal-

ous wrath against impure worship—generated strength. Jealousy in these areas was indeed a motivation for forceful action and could be associated with larger virtues of manhood. Jealousy played a considerable role in inspiring defenses of family honor, when men sought to avenge an insult or sexual transgression against a wife or sister which caused the family to lose its appropriate control over female virtue. On the other hand, jealousy has often been associated with pettiness and weakness. Here, the emotion can appear as a last-ditch attempt by enfeebled people to cling to some object or relationship. Natalie Davis, a historian of France in the 16th century, has noted that, in appeals for official pardon after a conviction of crime, men often argued that they had acted in anger—a clearly aggressive emotion associated with power—whereas women more commonly pleaded that they had been overwhelmed by jealousy, a reaction more suitable for the less powerful gender. In this category too, word usages suggest a considerable range for jealousy's interpretation by individuals invoking the emotion and by other people observing a jealous response.

Jealousy has long served as a literary theme, because of its relations to honor and love and because of its capacity to consume those who experience it and on occasion drive them to extreme acts. The dramatic quality of the emotion, in Western culture, extends from the Old Testament to contemporary American films. A mixture of jealousy and envy frequently turned brothers against each other in the stories of the ancient Jews. Shakespeare's *Othello* focused entirely on the insane frenzy generated by groundless jealousy, a cautionary tale against the uncontrollable qualities of the emotion in those whose folly made them susceptible. Some of the same qualities made jealousy a frequent subject for comment by moral philosophers. Thus, the French aphorist La Rochefoucauld opined, in discussing the links between jealousy and love: "It resembles hate more than friendship." Alexander Pope termed the emotion "hateful," following the much earlier lead of St. Paul who condemned the effects of selfish jealousy in his comments on marriage.

Other, more scientific vantagepoints for examining jealousy began to emerge only in the later 19th century, as an outgrowth of Darwinian interest in considering the evolutionary implications of common emotions. A number of Darwinian psychologists, including G. Stanley Hall in the United States, studied jealous reactions among children or adolescents. The studies generated significant data on jealous responses. They also produced some general claims about jealousy's functions. Most evolutionary theorists argued that jealousy served a purpose in helping to form and defend families, converting romantic or sexual interests into definite commitment because of a fear of rivals or because of reaction to a partner's expressions of jealous concern. Some popularizers added that jealousy helped turn love into marriage. This evolutionary school generally contended that women displayed more jealousy than men, because of their role in forming and protecting families from outside threat and because of their own dependence on family for survival.

The rise of Freudian psychology created a second general approach to jealousy, though relatively few Freudians directly commented on the emotion. Freudian beliefs in inevitable competition for parental affection, including the famous Oedipal conflict between a child and his same-sex parent, called attention mainly to aggression and withdrawal. Freudian concern for the early stages of childhood did encourage more direct studies of jealous interactions among young children themselves, though not cast in an explicitly Freudian mold. Further, one writer, Melanie Klein, wrote about the inherent envy of infants toward the mother as giver or withdrawer of breast, formulating a generalized psychological dynamic relevant to presumably universal manifestations of jealousy. Other scattered psychological research has studied displays of childhood jealousy, seeking to define inherent components across cultures.

The rise of sibling studies in the 1920s and 1930s formed the next major empirical approach to jealousy, focused of course on jealous disputes among young children over parental attention and related material possessions provided by adults. A large number of observations on interactions among siblings and young children piled up empirical evidence about the frequency of sibling jealousy, though one study argued that it was far from normal; more general findings indicated a slight preponderance of girls over boys in sibling strife. The sibling studies related to a larger psychological literature that assumed the necessity of successful management of sibling disputes, on the assumption that these disputes were dangerous to young children themselves and, if unresolved, could produce distorted jealous personalities in later life, incapable of successful personal or work relationships. These extensions of the sibling studies were not, however, scientifically researched. Finally, while sibling research trailed off after the

1930s a renewed set of studies in the 1980s disputed many earlier findings, calling the research into question methodologically and contesting the findings of frequency. Recent sibling research argues that severe jealousy is far from common among siblings, who often bond quite positively. According to some recent research, the relationship that most regularly produces sibling rivalry (though technically envy more than jealousy) occurs when the oldest child in a boy. Otherwise patterns are quite random and unpredictable and, as noted earlier, not necessarily significant in late adult response.

After the more concentrated spate of sibling studies in the 1930s, jealousy research has become increasingly fragmented, with few clear lines of inquiry and relatively little theoretical structure. Essays on jealousy have reemerged, particularly from scattered feminists ruminating over their tense relationships with mothers or lovers.

These aside, the most frequent inquiries into jealousy in the past 30 years have emphasized its social context or its psychological components, with insufficient bridging between the two approaches. On the social side, some anthropologists have inquired into jealousy patterns in different cultures, though this has not been a major emphasis. Several social psychologists have compared jealousy reactions in various societies on the basis of questionnaire research. Questionnaire research also figured strongly, even before the 1970s, in inquiries into male and female jealousy in dating contexts, particularly among American college students. In the 1970s, when jealousy standards were undergoing considerable revision, both social psychologists and a new breed of sociologists of emotion looked into standard definitions of jealousy, through questionnaires but also inquiries in special settings such as communes and other centers of experimental sexuality. The result of this research has been a considerable exploration of widely accepted norms concerning jealousy, and also the tensions these norms can produce in contemporary settings. Finally, two publications in recent years have explored jealousy from a historical standpoint—another largely social approach, though one focused on changes over time rather than simply contemporary social and cultural context—and problems of jealousy as a vital theme in modern marriage counseling.

Psychological research has reflected concern for social context; recognizing jealousy as a genuine if blended emotion brings attention to cognitive appraisals of jealousy-producing situations, which in turn involves cultural standards. The surge of psychological interest involves more attention to how jealousy fits with other models of emotion, why and how individuals differ, and what strategies are used to deal with jealousy once experienced. Psychological studies of jealousy focus almost exclusively on romance, which raises questions about the emotion's broader scope. They rely heavily on questionnaires administered in laboratory settings, which produce replicable results but also raise questions about actual experience in lived relationships. Some follow-ups on correlations between jealous personalities and marital history begin to bridge this gap in part. In addition to distinguishing among types of jealousy and insisting on the links between jealousy and other emotional responses in an individual personality, the psychological research traces the emotional channels jealousy may take once aroused—anger, withdrawal, embarrassment—and the overall intensities involved. As they move beyond classification schemes, recent studies particularly emphasize the importance of jealousy in producing coping strategies and the potentially fruitful nature of some of these strategies. Jealousy, in other words, remains an active emotion, shaping individual lives and contacts with others. While some responses can be quite dysfunctional, leading to violence or to devastating emotional collapse, others work well in causing individuals to reassess problems, including lack of self-confidence, or in inducing their partners to provide needed reassurance.

Jealousy, in sum, is only beginning to command the kind of scientific interest devoted to a number of other emotions. It has been part of several theoretical frameworks, and research has generated important (though sometimes also disputed) data. The current emphasis on jealousy as part of social interactions lacks large claims about jealousy's theoretical place in a larger emotional arsenal, but it has produced growing understanding about the evolution of contemporary standards in relation to functional results of jealousy in interpersonal contacts—particularly, in terms of recent literature, among adult lovers, married or otherwise.

III. JEALOUSY IN COMPARATIVE PERSPECTIVE

One of the huge gaps in current knowledge involves any systematic sense of differences in evaluation and uses of jealousy from one culture to the next.

Yet the fact of such variation is well established, and several larger possibilities invite attention. Jealousy seems particularly attached to cultures that place strong emphasis on possession of property and, by extension, on women treated as property. Less property-conscious societies, such as certain Eskimo groups or the Tahitians, manifest a willingness to share possessions, children (as in common adoption practices with parental consent), even sexual partners (before and sometimes after marriage) in ways that reflect either an unusual absence of jealousy or a distinctive targeting of the emotion. The connection between jealousy and possessiveness is obvious, but what cultural and historical circumstances generated a rather low level of both have not been probed. Possibly jealousy, for all its potential intensity, is a culturally constructed emotional amalgam that developed rather late in human prehistory—a line of argument that, though speculative, would bear some interesting relationship to a larger constructivist approach to emotions.

Among propertied societies, cultures that generate a particular attachment to personal honor also generate unusually fierce versions of jealousy. Jealousy serves as an emotion that motivates defense of honor against threat, and also revenge when honor has been violated. In some instances, it seems more freely indulged in upper classes, where honor codes may relate to family power and military prowess, than in the population at large. In other instances, however, jealousy and honor concepts alike spread widely. This seems particularly true in Mediterranean cultures (both Muslim and Christian) and in some of the American cultures heavily influenced by Spain. Thus, a jealous response to affronts to honor or to the sexual purity of a family's women remains particularly vivid in these cultural areas. The quick jealousy of Arab men has often been noted (though not systematically studied), and the frequency of jealousy-derived crimes of passion, directed against sexual rivals, contributes to unusually high murder rates in a number of Latin American and Caribbean societies. Though slightly less marked, a disproportionate rate of jealousy-induced murders in the American South (compared to other regions of the United States, in the 19th and 20th centuries alike) reflects a similar cultural complex. Emphasis on honor generates particular social utility for jealousy. Jealousy, in turn, helps create both the emotional vividness often associated with attacks on rivals and the sustained grievance essential to longer-term campaigns for revenge. Some of these same cultures that elevate jealousy also attempt particular arrangements of controlled seclusion for women, as in traditional Arab cities, in order to express the legitimacy of possessiveness in social habits but also to reduce the occasions for active exercise of jealousy in day-to-day routine.

Opportunities for more extensive and focused comparative research, that would more fully explain cross-cultural differentials in promptings toward jealousy while also exploring jealousy's role in motivating social patterns, are obviously considerable. A wide-ranging anthropology of jealousy has yet to be offered.

IV. JEALOUSY AND THE LAW

One potential focus, relevant to comparative analysis of jealousy's social functions, has already attracted some attention. Legal treatment of jealousy, closely related to jealousy's presumed role in actual crime, is an important variable. Informal notions that jealousy's consuming qualities might excuse certain crimes seem to have developed early in Western culture; the link between jealousy and weakness also might have legal relevance.

French courts long accepted jealousy as an excuse for what would otherwise be murder, on the part of men and women alike. The American legal culture of jealousy was slightly different. In the United States, formal allowance for jealousy in the law emerged after 1850. Between 1859 and 1900 about 30 homicide cases invoked what was called the "unwritten law" in defense of a jealousy-inspired murder of the lover of a fiancée or wife. With urbanization, community sanctions against adultery declined. This provided a context for ingenious lawyers to argue that jealous outrage so legitimately and intensely consumed an offended husband that he was rendered temporarily insane and so not responsible for his acts. As one attorney argued in 1870, "For jealousy is the rage of a man; therefore he will not spare in the day of vengeance. . . . Those who dishonor husbands are here warned of their doom. . . . Jealousy . . . enslaves the injured husband, and vents itself in one result, which seems to be inevitable and unavoidable." Several trials invoking this new defense were highly publicized, and acquittals often produced extensive popular approval from men and women alike. Women were not allowed the defense; only men could be swept away by this uncontrollable

passion, in the eyes of the law. Nevertheless, the new interest in jealousy as a legal excuse shows an important connection between law and emotional norms, in a society that was developing new concerns about appropriate sexual behavior particularly for women.

Equally important, however, was the fact that this connection did not prove permanent. By 1900 many state courts were rejecting unwritten law defenses, on grounds that they merely encouraged violence. Jealousy could and should be restrained, according to this new thinking. Some states experimented with compromises between old and new, holding that killings committed in the "heat of passion" should be regarded as manslaughter, not murder. Several southern states, particularly, continued to grant some tolerance to murders resulting from momentary but blinding jealousy. But by the 1970s even southern states were moving away from this thinking. A 1977 Georgia ruling argued that

> In this day of no-fault, on-demand divorce, when adultery is merely a misdemeanor . . . any idea that a spouse is ever justified in taking the life of another—adulterous spouse or illicit lover—to prevent adultery is uncivilized. This is murder; and henceforth, nothing more appearing, an instruction on justifiable homicide may not be given.

Clearly, in less than a century, jealousy in the United States had moved from serving as a logical response to sexual infidelity on the part of women, to becoming (if not suitably restrained) uncivilized. This example shows the potential importance of jealousy in influencing not only social norms but also criminal jurisprudence; it also demonstrates the possibility of substantial change, with jealousy open to redefinition depending on larger cultural norms.

V. JEALOUSY IN SOCIAL HISTORY: TRADITIONAL TO VICTORIAN

Much recent work on jealousy, by sociologists, social psychologists, and historians, uses changes in social standards concerning jealousy as a basic frame of reference for dealing with the emotion. Particular attention rivets on the widespread disavowal of the legitimacy of jealousy by the vast majority of middle-class Americans by the 1970s.

This disavowal was important, even if a number of the people questioned admitted problems in living up to the standards they believed in. The disavowal was also new, which meant that its emergence requires some essentially historical treatment and explanation.

The earlier history of jealousy in Western society is by no means entirely clear. The emotion had acknowledged function, in relationship to defense of honor and of rights. Its danger was also widely noted, for the potential intensity of jealous passion was extensively criticized. The result, studied most clearly in work on French literature in the early modern period, was a definite ambivalence. While many authors and essayists highlighted the risks of jealousy, others noted its importance to love. As a French courtly love author put it: "Real jealousy always increases the feelings of love. . . . Jealousy, and therefore love, are increased when one suspects his beloved." For many West European dramatists in the 17th and 18th centuries, jealous wiles formed an uncomfortable but diverting thread in romance, so long as they were kept within bounds. A few religious writers, finally, tried to reconcile the ambivalence: "There is a just and an unjust jealousy. Just, is with married partners, who mutually love each other; there is with them a just and prudent zeal lest their conjugal love be violated." Unjust love, in contrast, involved loss of control or a suspiciousness totally out of proportion to any real threat.

The standards of 19th century middle-class society in Western Europe and the United States were more clear-cut, though the existence of legal allowance for jealous crimes indicates some ongoing ambivalence. Because concepts of honor declined in middle-class culture, and because greater emphasis was placed on romantic love, jealousy was rethought—and in principle condemned. True love was not supposed to involve jealousy, for the latter was a selfish and possessive passion that would only sully the high ground of real romance. Women, particularly, were warned against jealousy, not only of other people but of their husband's work. At the same time, however, jealousy was not seen as a major problem in most instances, and some prescriptive literature recognized that modest expressions of jealousy (mainly from women, now assumed to be particularly liable to jealous reactions) could usefully recall men to their proper attentiveness. Women's focus on domesticity, part of Victorian emphases on "respectability," also reduced active concern about jealousy.

VI. THE 20TH CENTURY DYNAMIC: THE SIBLING JEALOUSY CRISIS

Jealousy began to assume problem proportions early in the 20th century, and it was at this point that the essential background to contemporary standards started to take shape. The outpouring of concern about sibling rivalry that emerged by around 1920 was one index of the new identification of jealousy as a major emotional issue. The leading child-rearing manuals routinely advised that "Few emotions are experienced . . . which from a social point of view are more important than jealousy. . . . The jealous person becomes an object of dislike." A few advice manuals retained a vestige of older attitudes, in urging that a bit of jealousy could be useful as motivation for children. In general, however, the overwhelming message stressed dire warning. "Unless the parents recognize that jealousy will normally appear, and are prepared for it, strong feelings of hostility often develop which continue to make life miserable for both [rivalrous] children over many years," one popular pamphlet intoned.

The same child-rearing materials recommended a number of remedies. Dr. Spock's 1945 bestseller, urging that "a lot of effort" was essential, summed up the standard advice. Prepare a child for a new baby carefully. Spend extra money on a separate room for each child, and on separate toys and clothes, to reduce jealous potential. Teach grandparents and other visitors not to make a fuss over a new baby, but rather to pay greater attention to the older, jealous sibling. Above all, in various ways, reassure of love, while conveying understanding of any feelings of hostility. "I know how you feel, dear. Come on over and I'll give you a hug and we'll see if that doesn't help." Or, in a similar recommended parental antidote: "I know how you feel; you wish there were no baby; I love you just as always." The goals of these strategies were to prevent outright conflict among children themselves, now assumed to be natural enemies because of inevitable jealousy, and to use wise management of sibling jealousy to prevent jealous personalities in adulthood. These twin goals, regarded as difficult but essential, gave urgency to the parental task. Large numbers of American parents, by the 1930s, dutifully listed their concern about sibling rivalry as one of their chief worries.

The rise of the sibling jealousy campaign is a fascinating chapter in the history of jealousy. The emotion was hardly new, but it had never before been identified with such anxious fervor. Two factors prompted the change in outlook. First, shifts in family life may actually have heightened jealousy among young children. The decline in the birth rate, the disappearance of adults other than parents from the normal household, and emphasis on intense maternal affection may well have created more childish anxiety about the arrival of a new sibling than had been common before. Even more obviously, adults grew more hostile to the potential impacts of jealousy in their lives, and more impatient with signs of the emotion in their children. Hence, the acceptance of a major socialization effort. The sibling campaign itself became more routine by about the 1940s in the United States. The inevitability of traumatic jealousy among young children was downplayed, but at the same time more parents took for granted the need for some of the reassurances that their own parents needed to be taught. Efforts to prevent jealous personalities through careful child-rearing on the whole continued.

The sibling jealousy crisis forms a vital link in examinations of jealousy that blend an understanding of common emotional tensions with cultural context. Although contemporary psychological experts are confident that their more relaxed view of sibling jealousy is more accurate than the near-hysteria of the 1930s, full exploration of sibling interactions remains to be accomplished. Also important, and as yet undone, is comparative work. There is evidence that large families generate less sibling rivalry than small, because in the former children band together against parents rather than competing with each other for parental favor. This finding has both cross-cultural and historical significance, given changes and variations in birth rates and family size.

VII. ADULT JEALOUSY: NEW STANDARDS

In the United States and Western Europe, concern about sibling jealousy was closely linked to an unprecedented attack on the emotion in adult relationships. Marriage counselors, for example, almost uniformly urged against jealousy by the 1920s. "Jealousy kills love. It is a symptom of weakness and of selfishness. Wanting a suitor, or a wife, or a husband to pay exclusive attention to one has nothing in common with real devotion." Or in another marriage-expert sally: "We may even blight and blacken our happiness by jealousy, which is really an admission of our own inferiority, of our own cowardice and conceit." Accepted wisdom now held that adult jealousy, almost exclusively defined from the 1920s onward in terms of love relationships, resulted from inadequate childhood socialization: jealousy was immature.

These new standards had two major sources. First, while their intensity of concern and the attribution of immaturity were new in the 20th century, the idea that jealousy marred love had developed in the 19th century, with some roots even earlier in Western culture. Second, the growing attention paid to jealousy followed from a decline in the domestic seclusion of women. With women participating increasingly in coeducational schools, politics, work (albeit as inferiors to men in most respects), and leisure activities, jealousy reactions almost had to relax in Western Europe and the United States. Add to the increasing interaction between men and women a growing interest in sexual expression—another development taking shape in the 1920s—the need to encourage adults to play down jealousy became virtually essential from a functional standpoint. Young men and women who began to date fairly regularly, with a considerable variety of partners, were thus urged to avoid jealousy or to conceal it if avoidance broke down. Married couples who began to socialize more informally, with more interactions with the spouses of others, earned the same advice. Here was the context for the considerable outpouring of popularized advice, in books directed toward young people and in popular magazines: "Jealousy is a terrible emotion, one of the extreme forms of psychological cruelty." This was the context, also, for the shifts in criminal law, which assumed that jealousy could and should be controlled even in extreme provocation.

The general trend toward firm prescriptions against jealousy gained additional ground in the 1960s, when sexual standards in Western society loosened further. Many experimental sexual situations, including "open marriage," were predicated explicitly on an ability to keep jealousy under wraps. Urging a variety of sexual partners, advocates of open marriages noted that "Jealousy has no place in open marriage. The fact that it is so prevalent in closed marriage does not mean that love and sex must always be accompanied by this dark shadow." Couples in open marriages or visiting promiscuous resorts—couples interested in what 1960s Americans called "swinging"—were taught strategies to deal with unwanted jealous impulses, including wishing their partner a good time as he or she went off for an evening with someone else. Jealousy workshops opened in several American cities, directed to the upper middle class and designed, according to their founders, for "those who are strongly motivated to outgrow jealousy."

Most adults in the West did not, of course, participate in the most extreme sexual experiments. Some of those who did found themselves sorely tested, caught between their cognitive belief that jealousy was immature and the fact that they felt very uncomfortable with a partner's "swinging." Jealousy increasingly produced shame: one woman told a sociologist, "I think it comes from possessiveness and I'm trying to grow away from that." Most middle-class Americans, if they felt jealousy at all—and polls taken in the 1970s suggested that about a third really did not experience much sexual jealousy—sought to minimize it or to deny it. A comparative study revealed that Americans were far more likely to try to conceal jealousy than were West Indians, Asians, or Africans. Women were a bit franker than men in discussing jealousy problems that cropped up despite good intentions. American male culture urged at least a claim of superiority to jealousy, along with vigorous resentment against jealous, nagging women. Women's culture was a bit more ambivalent, and concern about men's infidelity was correspondingly considerable. The vast majority of middle-class Americans, both male and female, professed to find jealousy uncivilized and unacceptable. There was no significant gap between the standards urged in emotional advice literature, and those disclosed by adults. And while American jealousy was particularly examined in this regard, every indication suggests that a similar middle-class culture had developed in Britain, Germany, and elsewhere. Indeed, the proscriptions against admitting jealousy even in cases of outright adultery may have been even greater in European society than in the United States, in the wake of the sexual revolution of the 1960s.

The development of new and strongly disapproving standards for jealousy, and indications that many people internalized these standards, colors most of the research and comment on jealousy in recent years. The historical approach permits some understanding not just of what the current standards are, but also of how they developed and what caused them. The current standards themselves, however, raise at least four additional questions essential to a wider understanding of jealousy as a social emotion:

1. Has the evolution of jealousy standards in the West been matched by changes in other cultures? The scant comparative work available suggests that contemporary Western efforts to evade jealousy are unusual, but no full exploration has been ventured. A few psychologists claim to find basic uniformities in sexual jealousy across culture, but the data are limited.

2. Within Western society itself, have the jealousy standards been as widely accepted in fact as in principle? Here the answer is clearly negative. Groups outside the middle class may not fully accept the disapproval of jealousy in the first place—though subcultural differentiation has not been explored systematically. Gender differences are also salient. American women more often use jealousy to terminate a relationship than men do, who (surprisingly) more commonly seek to reinforce loyalties to deal with their jealousy. A variety of evidence suggests that many middle-class people themselves of both genders experience a jealousy of which they disapprove. Their guilt or embarrassment in some instances actually complicates their reaction, making constructive adjustments more difficult. This is an important theme in marriage therapy, and it is a struggle that a number of individual writers (mainly women) have also documented, in dealing with their extremely complex reactions to what is even by itself a troubling emotion. It is probable that fewer people feel intense jealousy than was the case a century ago, at least in comparable behavioral circumstances; altered standards do correspond in part to altered emotional experience. Nevertheless, the very disapproval of jealousy makes reactions to it—always somewhat diverse—both subtle and difficult.

3. Has the 20th century attack on the acceptability of romantic jealousy persisted into the 1980s and 1990s? Some popularized literature by the 1980s, at least in the United States where fear of AIDS and correspondingly enhanced sexual conservatism ran particularly strong, suggested that jealousy might again become more acceptable as an emotion useful in defending sexual fidelity. Psychological research on jealous personalities and on successful coping strategies returns attention to the important role jealousy can play in mature relationships. It is certainly possible, given what we know about the frequent oscillations in cultural standards applied to

jealousy and their dependence on larger social functions, that more public acknowledgment of at least limited utility for jealousy is developing. But the prospect, however logical, remains uncertain.

4. What has happened to jealousy in other contexts? Modern Western culture, beginning in the 19th century, increasingly associated jealousy with love—love for parent and expectation of parental love in return, love of suitor or spouse. The decline of explicit recognition of jealousy in relation to wider concepts such as honor paralleled this narrower definition. But jealousy relates to other relationships as well, and here scattered findings suggest some interesting manifestations in recent decades. It is, further, possible (though not proved) that as jealousy was combatted in romance individuals who experienced it might seek other outlets. Jealous children, for example, were urged explicitly to turn their attention to a new toy or some other material possession. This could serve as the basis for later jealous competitiveness in consumer interests, with individuals relieving an unacknowledged jealousy by trying to surpass others through acquisitions. Jealousy in school and work formed other expressions, providing emotional spur to a sense of rivalry. Many school children, eager to claim in interviews that they had outgrown sibling jealousy at home, more freely expressed jealousy of classmates' looks, athletic prowess, or good grades. Work authorities generally urged that jealousy be downplayed in the interests of smooth bureaucratic functioning, but jealous rivalries were common. [See LOVE AND INTIMACY.]

None of this was necessarily novel, and again a full exploration of contemporary jealousy outside romance has not been attempted. The apparently growing confusion, in normal speech, between envy and jealousy was nevertheless significant in this context. The jealousy that was most freely admitted—of school or work rivals—was in fact primarily envy—that is, resentment of something someone else possessed. But perhaps because Americans sought outlets for jealousy, perhaps because they viewed certain expectations such an intimate part of their person that another's achievement provoked a sense of threat or loss, and hence real jealousy, the increasing confusion of envy with jealousy was exceedingly suggestive. Here, evaluation of the meaning of jealousy may be a central ingredient in understanding contemporary emotional life and

definitions of self. In using the term jealousy for their reactions, some Americans may have heightened the emotional charge of their reactions to other people's possessions or attributions.

VIII. CONCLUSION

Jealousy is a complex emotional amalgam. It can be overpoweringly intense, even compulsive in some instances, particularly in societies that find some jealousy functional and that value emotional intensity generally. It plays a direct role in motivating certain behaviors, including violence, and several forms of rivalry. It may also motivate a desire to excel competitively, though this is not clearly acknowledged in contemporary American culture. The emotion is social, in that it takes shape in social relationships. It is also social in its dependence on social or cultural norms for its frequency, its vigor, and its manifestations. Variations in jealousy, ranging from qualified approval to blanket hostility, form a vital part of understanding the emotion in terms of particular cultures and also in terms of significant changes over time. It is also true, however, that within any given culture jealousy is clearly variable from one individual to the next. Societies that encourage some jealousy encounter diverse response, with some individuals being less jealous and more forgiving than they are "supposed" to be. Contemporary Western society, that rigorously discountenances the emotion at least in love relationships, certainly generates variety, from individuals who apparently experience no sexual jealousy, to people who experience jealousy but manage to conceal or displace it, to people profoundly troubled by their inability to live up to what they recognize is a widely shared emotional norm.

Clearly an emotional variable, jealousy can be understood in large part through the various social functions it serves, and the disadvantages it entails. Cultural divergences and significant changes in these social formulas provide the most explicit entry to jealousy's meaning beyond their purely individual level. Jealousy's obvious mixture of several discrete emotions helps explain the different roles it can provide, and the different kinds of action—from dire revenge to embarrassed self-doubt to a recementing of a threatened relationship—it can generate.

Bibliography

Baumgart, H. (1990). "Jealousy: Experiences and Solutions" (translated by Manfred and Evelyn Jacobson). University of Chicago Press, Chicago.

Bertrand, M. (1981). "La jalousie dans la litterature au temps de Louis XIII." Droz, Geneva.

Chapsal, M. (1977). "La jalousie." Presses Universitaires, Paris.

Clanton, G., and Smith, L. G. (Eds.) (1977). "Jealousy." Prentice Hall, Englewood Cliffs, NJ.

Clanton, G. (1989). Jealousy in american culture, 1945–1985: Reflections from popular literature. In "The Sociology of Emotions" (D. Franks and E. D. McCarthy, Eds.). JAI Press, Greenwich, CT.

Dunn, J. and Kendrick, C. (1982). "Siblings: Love, Envy and Understanding." Harvard University Press, Cambridge, MA.

Klein, M. (1977). "Envy, Gratitude and Other Works." Harper and Row, New York.

Pines, A., and Aronson, E. (1983). Antecedents, correlations and consequences of sexual jealousy." J. Pers. 51, 126–40.

Ruack, L. T. (1980). Jealousy, anxiety and loss. In "Exploring Emotions" (A. O. Rortz, Ed.), pp. 457–483. University of California Press, Berkeley.

Salovey, Peter, (Ed.) (1991). "The Psychology of Jealousy and Envy." Guilford Press, New York.

Stearns, P. N. (1989). "Jealousy: The Evolution of an Emotion in American History." New York University Press, New York.

White, Gregory L. and Paul E. Mullen (1989). "Jealousy: Theory, Research and Clinical Strategies." Guilford Press, New York.

JUNGIAN PERSONALITY TYPES

Irving F. Tucker
Shepherd College

Terence Duniho
Life Patterns Institute

Glossary

Arational (A) Mental emphasis on acceptance of one's sensed or intuited perception of context, situation, or idea. No inherent need to "double check" initial sense of certainty experienced with perception. "Trust perceptions." People who use sensing or intuition as their dominant way to deal with life are called arational types (Jung referred to them as "irrational").

Extraversion (E) An attitude that places primary emphasis on the importance of people and things (i.e., objects outside oneself are the primary focus). Importance of self is dependent on right relationship to the object(s). Breadth (dealing with things across the board) is preferred over depth (selectively focusing in one area over an extended period of time). When extraverting, one asks, "*How* am I in relationship to *that* (people, things, events)?" rather than, "Do I relate?" External requirements determine and limit self-interest. Energized by involvement with external happenings.

Feeling (F) One of two ways to reach closure (judge). Feeling decisions are made reactively as a result of one's sense of a situation or idea in the context of one's emotional state. The decisions reflect the person's emotional priorities, whether one has conscious awareness of those priorities or not. A concern for closure that honors the emotional assessment. Feeling decisions are often unconsciously made. May be accompanied by conscious denial that decision is influenced emotionally. Nonlogical.

Introversion (I) An attitude placing primary emphasis on the importance of self or self's interests. Importance of the objects is dependent on their relatedness to self or self's interests. Depth is preferred over breadth. "Does that relate to *my interests?*" Internal requirements determine and limit one's public interest. Energized by focus on internal happenings.

Intuition (N) One of two ways to perceive. Use of intellect to see meaning (interpretation) of information. Emphasis on "invisible" information (i.e., possibilities; relations between objects or ideas). Abstract. "Things can be made better than they've been." Importance of "invisible" (intuited) information determined by degree of certainty that is felt to accompany it. "What if?"

Judgment (J) Making decisions about information. Emphasis on closure, certainty, structure, and goals. "Follow the plan." Resists unanticipated change. Not focused on new input. Means adjust to end goal. Judgment is of two kinds: thinking and feeling.

Perception (P) Taking in information. Emphasis on being open to new data, experiences, meanings, interpretations, or relations between things and ideas. "Flexing the plan." Adapt to change. Not focused on closure or follow-through. End goal adjusts to fit appropriate means. Perception is of two kinds: sensing and intuition.

Rational (R) Mental emphasis on need to consciously determine one's assessment of (and, therefore mentally have control over) context, situation, or idea. Inherent need to "double check" initial sense of certainty experienced with perception. "Trust judgments." People who use feeling or thinking as their dominant way to deal with life are called rational types.

Sensing (S) One of two ways to perceive. Use of five senses to take in information. Emphasis on "visible" information (i.e., that which can be perceived with the five senses). Concrete. Sensing resists changing things already experienced or ideas already accepted. Important information for sensing comes from past and present experience. "What is."

Thinking (T) One of two ways to reach closure (judge). Thinking decisions are made proactively as a result of one's awareness of cause/effect and consequences. The decision accords with what makes logical sense. A concern for closure that honors the intellectual assessment. Thinking decisions are more often consciously made. May be accompanied by unconscious denial of affective influences.

JUNGIAN PERSONALITY TYPES are an approach to the understanding of personality structure, human differences, and lifespan development that emphasizes the neither good nor bad ways in which we naturally prefer to function. In Jung's words, they reflect "the psychology of consciousness . . . the polarity and dynamics of the psyche." They are mainly concerned with the opposite ways in which people process and respond to information. The most common formulation of Jungian types posits 16 different personality structures or *patterns*, created because of the interplay between the need for wholeness or balance (both/and) and the need for fundamental preferences (either/or) in one's conscious orientation to life. Two attitudes (extraversion [E] and introversion [I]), two orientations (perceiving [P] and judging [J]), two ways to perceive (sensing [S] and intuition [N]), and two ways to judge or reach closure (feeling [F] and thinking [T]) are logically interwoven to create these 16 patterns. Jungian typology considers (a) the differing needs, strengths, and vulnerabilities that result from each preference; (b) the path each pattern follows to achieve a healthy balance between opposites; and (c) the ways stress interacts with each pattern to create the individual.

I. AN OVERVIEW

As we near the end of the 20th century, many of the disparate areas in which knowledge of human personality has been developing are coming together in mind/body syntheses. Sigmund Freud recognized the influence of the unconscious and the many ways in which our drive toward maturity can be thwarted, especially in early childhood. Carl Jung observed that for most people the conscious self has been cut off from the unconscious; he believed the conscious and unconscious selves need to maintain an intimate dialogue with each other if we are to become all we are meant to be. His work was constantly concerned with what he called "the problem of opposites." So he wrote much not only about the unconscious, but also about its opposite, consciousness (psychological types). Jung also saw that the first half of life is meant to have a very different agenda than the second half, thus emphasizing the importance of lifespan development.

R. W. Sperry, Michael Gazzaniga, and others, through split-brain research, have discussed much about how the left hemisphere of the cortex generally performs quite different functions than the right. Their work, along with that of Alexander Luria, has led to wide recognition among neuropsychologists of a "three-axis model of the brain." Research with identical twins, especially those raised apart, has made it clear that genetics play an essential role in forming personality.

Isabel Briggs Myers, through development of the Myers–Briggs Type Indicator, has done much to popularize Jung's theory of the conscious self, thus stimulating considerable thinking, research, and applications of Jung's personality theory. Many of those influenced by her have seen value in a model that organizes Jung's four functions in a hierarchy where two functions are extraverted and the other two introverted (the "2 in, 2 out" or "2 and 2" model, now called Life Patterns; so named by Terence Duniho). James Newman has created a synthesis from his knowledge of Jungian types, neuropsychology, and neurophysiology that points us toward a cognitive psychology of type. Duniho has developed a lifespan development model that shows, for each pattern, how the four functions differentiate as one moves toward wholeness. Duniho's explication of Life Patterns integrates the work of Newman, Myers, and Jung, with additional contributions from other sources.

Since 1983, Duniho has repeatedly emphasized the importance of first determining the "actual type" or Life Pattern of the individual and has made it an essential component in his work as a counselor and human resource consultant. Whether one's focus is on affirming and reinforcing wellness or assessing pathology and determining treatment, three components first need to be known about the individual: the natural cognitive pattern of their brain, their developmental history, and their current stage of development as seen in relation to their pattern.

The next section provides a framework in which these three components can be considered. It integrates Jungian personality theory with the three-axis neuropsychological model and Duniho's lifespan development approach. Following that section, we step back to consider the history of how this integration became possible. Then three major theoretical approaches now in common use are reviewed. Next, methods for testing and measuring Jungian personality preferences are described. At that point, having considered the conscious psychology of the 16 patterns, we look at the patterns in relation to depth psychology and the unconscious.

II. A NEUROPSYCHOLOGICAL MODEL OF PERSONALITY

A. Three-Axis Model of the Brain

During the last 10 years or more, neuropsychologists have evolved a three-axis model of the brain to study the interplay of psychological functioning: up/down (the reticular activating system), back/front (the sensory and motor systems), and right/left (the two hemispheres of the cerebral cortex). Derived from the work of Luria and the split-brain research of Sperry and others, this model provides the skeletal framework to link Jung's attitudes, orientations, and functions to the workings of the brain. According to Newman, the up/down axis corresponds to introversion/extraversion, and back/front to perceiving/judging. When considered in combination with the back/front axis, the right and left hemispheres of the cortex are actually "four quadrants of specialization" corresponding to Jung's four functions.

1. Up/Down—Introversion/Extraversion

According to S. J. Dimond, a British neuropsychologist, "the action of [the reticular system] is to change the whole relationship which the individual holds to the environment." It has a "tendency . . . to move from a sporadic externally controlled firing to internally controlled cycles of regular action." In the words of Newman, "extraversion and introversion [are] mechanisms of *attention* and *arousal*." These two attitudes determine whether one's focus is on external events or inner, subjective "states of mind." These are "inner ideas and imagery, 'self' awareness, emotions and moods, and unconscious processes." The process of extraverting focuses attention on happenings in the external world. "It is

characterized by rapid and effective responsiveness to immediate contingencies . . . [and] tends to 'short-circuit' the elaboration of affective and subjective reactions associated with introversion." [*See* EXTRAVERSION–INTROVERSION.]

There are two arousal systems, one located in the lower portion (reticular formation) of the RAS, the other mainly in the thalmic/limbic regions. The reticular formation receives stimuli from the outside world and mediates an "orienting reflex": to orient reflexively to external stimuli is the essence of extraverting. The limbic system, especially the thalamus, is "intimately involved in the generation of internal brain states" and maintains the organism's internal economy. When one is internally focused, the cortex "recruits" pertinent stimuli as they come into the limbic system, filtering out anything that is not related to the internal focus of the moment. This is introversion, according to Newman. [*See* LIMBIC SYSTEM.]

2. Back/Front—Perceiving/Judging

According to Jane Holmes Bernstein, a neuropsychologist at Children's Hospital in Boston, "the back of the brain is like the symphony orchestra . . . the front is Seiji Osawa. You've got to have somebody to get the full orchestration of this wonderful system out in all its glory. [The front] is the primary regulator, organizer, planner, general fine tuner of the system. The back . . . basically deals in the reception, coding, storage of information—[it is] the receiver of the information." In Jungian terms, the back is perceiving and the front is judging.

3. Right/Left—Attached/Detached

The right hemisphere is attached to the information it processes; it is the "experiential sphere." Emotion, sensory reactions, and the nonverbal experience of life are processed in the right half-brain. It deals with the "wholeness" of everything and is called a parallel processor. Emotional and relatively unconscious, it is mainly concerned with experiencing and reacting to life with the senses and emotions. It emphasizes how things look, that is, the appearance of things.

The left hemisphere maintains detachment from the information it processes; it is the "intellectual sphere." Speech and all complex language are processed in the left half-brain. It divides everything into parts and is more serial in its processing. Unemotional and more conscious than the right half-brain, it is mainly concerned with intellectual interpretation and logical control. It emphasizes what works, that is, how things function.

B. Four Quadrants of Specialization (Jung's Four Functions)

Combining the left–right and back–front axes, we have four quadrants of specialization in the cerebral cortex: attached input, attached output, detached input, and detached output. Newman has identified these, respectively, as analogous to Jung's four functions: sensate perception and feeling judgment, right–brain; intuitive perception and thinking judgment, left.

Duniho has consistently observed that one only uses sensing, feeling, intuition, and thinking when extraverting or introverting, never simply by themselves apart from one or another of these two attitudes. Because, in a sense, the four functions do not exist apart from extraverting and introverting, we can legitimately speak of eight functions instead of four: IS, ES, IF, EF, IN, EN, IT, and ET, corresponding to Jung's eight types. In normal development, four of the eight usually become consciously preferred, at least to some degree, while their opposites do not.

Two factors influence which four become part of one's conscious orientation and, therefore, which do not: (1) the need to be clear on which of the four functions (S, F, N, T) is most preferred, second most, etc., and (2) the need to know in which attitude (I or E) one prefers to use each function. These two needs establish the functional hierarchy and determine how each function is normally used. Though these two factors are characterized here as "needs," they are probably determined genetically; regardless, effective functioning for most, if not in fact all, people requires this degree of consistency. If "home-base" is firmly established, then doing that which is not part of one's usual or preferred approach becomes all the easier.

C. Chronological Development

Duniho has observed that there seem to be ways in which most people shift priorities as they age; he sees these shifts as rhythmic 7-year cycles (0–7, 7–14, 14–21, etc.). Beginning with the focus on self (I), somewhere around age 7 a shift to dealing primarily with the external world occurs (E). Then, as one moves into adolescence, the emphasis is once again on self (I). But, with the onset of young adult-

hood, the importance of finding one's fit "out there" takes priority (E). And on it goes. The descriptions that follow are adapted from Duniho's *Wholeness Lies Within* and cover development up to age 56. However, it is important to recognize that this model is equally helpful in understanding the issues and priorities of those older than 56. [*See* PERSONALITY DEVELOPMENT.]

1. 0–7, Unconscious Wholeness (Emphasis on Introverting)

We begin life with an undifferentiated, mainly unconscious emphasis on "how does that relate to me?" Gradually a limited awareness of self/not-self emerges. One's needs are mainly those of self rather than the needs of others. Because the four functions have not begun to differentiate, they work as one, producing what Howard Gardner, in *Art, Mind and Brain*, calls "a golden age of creativity, a time when every child sparkles with artistry."

2. 7–14, The Literal Years (Emphasis on Extraverting)

Gardner has called these years the literal stage, a time when children have "heightened awareness of, and concern with, the standards of their culture." Creativity for most disappears, because it requires all four functions, and now one's energies are devoted to differentiating (making conscious) one of the four in order to cope with "the big world." Extraverts begin differentiating their dominant function; introverts, their auxiliary.

3. 14–21, Trying on Different Hats (Emphasis on Introverting)

During these years a strong focus on self is apparent in the majority. One's interests are on choosing friends, hobbies, or interests that please "me." It is often a confusing time of "who am I" and "who am I going to become." Extraverts shift to developing their auxiliary; introverts, to their dominant. As a result, this is often a more difficult time for extraverts than for introverts.

4. 21–28, Paying Our Dues (Emphasis on Extraverting)

Once again the focus is on fitting with the external world. We are trying to function as adults and find a role to play in society. One's own priorities are often set aside so as to meet others' expectations. The two functions that had begun to differentiate from 7 to 21 contribute to one's style and priorities, but to some extent are often at odds with what is required by one's job, family, etc.

5. 28–35, Owning Who You Really Are (Emphasis on Introverting)

This is the "me generation." Dreams that we thought would be realized by the time we reached 30 are too often still more fantasy than reality. Now is when people usually feel permission to make adjustments (job, home, marriage, geography, etc.) that bring their lives into better alignment with the priorities of their dominant and auxiliary functions.

6. 35–42, Changing Who We Are (Emphasis on Extraverting)

As soon as we have developed some level of comfort in living in alignment with our Life Pattern, things change again. What can I *do* in this world that will make a difference? This is also the stage where the tertiary function begins to differentiate. After using the dominant and auxiliary together since about age 14, one's psyche begins to explore the potential of directly combining the dominant and tertiary. For a time, the auxiliary is pushed aside; many priorities can radically change during this time. But the purpose of this mid-life disruption is to prepare one for the greater challenges of the second half of life. If sensing is tertiary, the person becomes more grounded; if intuition is, the person becomes more desirous of change; if feeling is, the person becomes more directly concerned with quality relationships; if thinking is, the person asserts more logical control over life.

7. 42–49, Taking Off! (Emphasis on Introverting)

This can be a time of much productivity, a celebration of self, a giving of what one *wants* to give, a time of empowerment and creative expression. Now the dominant, auxiliary, and tertiary are working together—with the dominant more able to lead than was possible before. The dominant can do this because the auxiliary and tertiary functions are now working together to support the dominant's priorities, needs, and goals.

8. 49–56, Conscious Wholeness (Emphasis on Extraverting)

This is the time of life when one's desire for dynamic balance, for the integration of the four functions, comes into the foreground. We now learn to live life from our fourth function: for those whose dominant is sensing, openness to possibilities (N) permeates activities; for intuition, living just this moment (S); for feeling, owning their ability to control life (T); for thinking, doing what feels right and building caring relationships (F). This is often when true humility takes hold and the spiritual life becomes essential.

9. The Other Stages and Other Models

The 7-year cycling between introverting and extraverting continues. The stages from age 56 on, though not described here, are equally important to understand. People continue to experience major shifts in their orientation as long as they live. Each developmental model provides a different lens for looking at changes that occur over the lifespan. Abraham Maslow, Erik Erikson, and many others have made important contributions to our ongoing effort to understand how and why we change as we age. Much more can and will be learned, deduced, and written that further clarifies and deepens our knowledge of human development. Even much of what is presented here, though based on experience and the observation of many people, should be taken as suggestive of research that needs to be designed, carried out, and replicated.

D. The Patterns of Freud and Jung

To illustrate the basics of the Life Patterns model, an interpretation is offered here of the personalities and relationship of Freud and Jung, based on our assessment of their patterns. An argument for the accuracy of their patterns as presented here is made by Duniho in *Freud and Jung: Patterns in Conflict*.

Freud appears to have been best developed in generating theoretical possibilities; he trusted these to a marked degree. This fits well with dominant introverted intuition. Freud was very much focused on his own interests (introverted). His use of logic was determinedly focused on the object (auxiliary extraverted thinking). His feelings were a very private affair and, even at an older age, not highly developed (tertiary introverted feeling). His orientation toward the senses (e.g., sex) was decidedly obsessive, generalized, and primitive (fourth function extraverted sensing). This gives us the following pattern:

$$e: s \, T \, J$$
$$I: \underline{N} \, f \, p$$

Intuition (N̲) is capitalized and underlined to show that, of the four functions, it is dominant; it is placed below the line to indicate its preference when introverting. Thinking (T) is capitalized but not underlined to show that it is auxiliary; its placement above the line indicates that it is preferred when extraverting. Feeling (**f**) is lowercase and boldfaced to show that it is tertiary; it is below the line to show it is introverted. Sensing (s) is lowercase, not boldfaced, to show that it is least preferred of the four; it is above the line to show it is extraverted. Though Freud preferred introverting and was actually quite flexible intellectually (intuitive perception), changing much about his theories over time, he dealt with the external world in an organized, decisive, and logical manner (thinking judgment). Thus, the J above the line reminds us that thinking judgment was preferred more than sensing perception when extraverting. The p below the line reminds us that he preferred intuitive perceiving over feeling judgments when introverting.

Jung had a rigorously logical mind, geared to understanding things theoretically (introverted thinking judgment), that wanted a degree of certainty and clarity beyond that needed by Freud. Jung observed that "when [Freud] had thought something then it was settled" (i.e., Freud trusted his perceptions—arational), whereas Jung was "doubting all along the line." However, Jung dealt with the external world very flexibly, with endless curiosity, drawing on the endless diversity of reality to illustrate and expand his studies (auxiliary extraverted intuitive perception). His senses were quite intense and selective, and underdeveloped, especially until mid-life, at which point he became intensively involved with the sensate realm (tertiary introverted sensing perception). The area in which he was most vulnerable was that of his feelings toward others generally and toward humankind as a whole (fourth function extraverted feeling judgment). His pattern looks like this:

$$e: \text{N} \textbf{f} \text{P}$$
$$\text{I: s} \underline{\text{T}} \text{j}$$

Jung usually appeared to others as quite flexible and endlessly curious about new possibilities and the meaningful connections between things (extraverted intuition). But if something had mainly to do with the ordering of his own conduct or priorities, this was decided logically and firmly (introverted thinking judgment). He was highly selective in the use of his five senses (introverted sensing perception, and

often exhibited a child-like quality in his emotional relationships to others that could be in turn endearing, needlessly disruptive, or even destructive (fourth function feeling). He was very open with his feelings, seemed to genuinely like nearly everyone, and had a decided tendency to place blame outside himself, though of course he could do this very intelligently and with apparent objectivity (extraverted feeling, with introverted thinking).

Careful observation and analysis of the two "type fractions" above reveals that Freud and Jung were alike in certain important ways (both being I, N, and T). But the hierarchy of their four functions was irritatingly different, with Freud preferring N–T–F–S and Jung T–N–S–F.

Freud	Jung
N (i)	(i) T
T (e)	(e) N
F (i)	(i) S
S (e)	(e) F

This difference caused many miscommunications between them. Freud easily trusted his own intuition (N, introverted) but expressed himself in a quite decisive manner most of the time (T, extroverted). Jung kept his conclusions more for himself (T, introverted) and was continually open and inquiring when in dialogue with others (N, extraverted). Jung was a "pure" thinker, preferring to use thinking without it being colored by feeling (T #1, F #4), but Freud usually combined thinking and feeling (T #2, F #3) in a way that was inherently unnatural for Jung. Freud's thinking and feeling served his intuitive focus; Jung's sensing and intuition served his thinking. Freud was often surprised by facts he had failed to consider (N #1), or could simply ignore contrary facts (S #4); Jung combined his curiosity (N #2) with his concern for getting the facts right (S #3).

Much more needs to be written on the relationship of Jung and Freud utilizing the Life Patterns model. It allows for a high degree of sophistication in the analysis of personality, development, and relationships. We have considered briefly an example of how the Life Patterns model encourages more sophisticated analyses, but how did we reach this level of complexity in understanding the psyche? The next section answers that question.

III. HISTORICAL PERSPECTIVE

Personality psychology in the United States has been dominated by trait approaches. The present article focuses on an equally useful, though quite different, approach to the study of personality—that of types. Traits are generally compared to one norm ("one size should fit all"), with about 68% of those tested scoring in a middle ("normal") range and 16% scoring above and 16% below the mid-range (often referred to as the "bell curve"). [*See* TRAITS.]

Trait theorists consistently tend toward a + vs − pole evaluation of major traits (e.g., extroversion—spelled with an "o"—is "confident," "dominant," "outgoing," etc., and introversion is "reclusive," "subdued," "shy," etc.). In type theory, extraversion—spelled with an "a"—and introversion, are opposite but equally useful ways of being in the world.

Type theories distinguish people from each other qualitatively. Where traits can be the result of either nature or nurture, types are considered to be the result of nature, therefore neither good nor bad. Type theories establish several qualitatively different (though equally acceptable) norms of preferred ways of being and of functioning.

With the publication of *Psychological Types* by Jung in 1921, an approach to the understanding of personality began that is currently more widely accepted and variously applied than any other personality theory. It is not possible, within this article, to cover even one-fourth of the theoretical variations and practical applications that have resulted from or been substantially influenced by that one book. This article is mainly about the theoretical approaches and applications linked in some way to the work of Myers and the uses of the Myers–Briggs Type Indicator for two reasons: (1) because Myers' work has had more impact by far on the practical use of Jungian typology than any other formulation of Jungian types, and (2) because this is the area within which the present authors are engaged. The MBTI is the most widely used instrument for assessing normal personality in the world with over two million answer sheets sold each year since 1985.

A. Sigmund Freud and Carl Jung

1. Psychological Types

Research for and the writing of *Psychological Types* resulted directly from Jung's relationship to Freud and their painful split. Freud had not only been Jung's friend, colleague, and mentor. Nineteen years Jung's senior, Freud was like a father to him; also, Freud saw Jung as his "heir apparent" in the psychoanalytic movement. Jung's father, with whom he had never had a satisfactory relationship,

died when Jung was 19. In 1905, at age 30, he initiated what became a voluminous correspondence with Freud, lasting until 1914—9 years. They first met in 1907, talking "without pause" for 13 hours. This meeting began a personal friendship that ended in 1913. In Jung's words, "Freud was the first man of real importance" he had encountered. In *Memories, Dreams, Reflections*, his autobiography, Jung refers to Freud more than twice as often as he does any other person.

This rupture in their relations, occurring at age 38, when he was dealing with "a mass of doubts" and difficult developmental changes, helped to focus him on the "need to define the ways in which my outlook differed from Freud's. . . ." *Psychological Types* was the result. Although he wrote very little that specifically addresses the impact of their type preferences on their relationship, he did lay the groundwork on which our current understanding has been able to build.

2. The Four Psychological Functions

Jung identified four psychological functions: two ways to perceive and two ways to judge. The perceiving functions he called sensation and intuition; the judging functions, thinking and feeling. He also recognized two attitudes, one focusing on the object as primary (extraversion) and the other on the subject (introversion). (Note the use of the letter "a" in extraversion, rather than "o.") By linking the two attitudes with the four functions, he was able to identify and describe eight "types": the extraverted sensation type, the introverted sensation type, etc. These eight provide the foundation on which nearly everyone who uses Jungian typology or the MBTI has built. His eight types are the same as the eight dominants identified by Myers.

B. Johannes H. van der Hoop and *Conscious Orientation*

1. van der Hoop and Jung

One of the more important early contributions to our understanding of the psychological dynamics of consciousness is a book by Dr. J. H. van der Hoop, first published in German in 1937, then in 1939 in English: *Conscious Orientation: A Study of Personality Types in Relation to Neurosis and Psychosis*. One of several innovative clarifications is his use of the word "instinct" in place of "sensation." Beginning in the autumn of 1913, van der Hoop began to study psychoanalysis with Jung in Zurich and was analyzed by him for 6 months. The conflicts between Jung and Freud were "a matter of lively interest" to him and "formed the main theme" of his first book, *Character and the Unconscious,* which appeared the same year as *Psychological Types* (1921).

2. The Auxiliary Function

Though Jung focused almost entirely on what is now seen as the first-preferred or "dominant" function, thus identifying and describing eight types, he also indicated that "another function of secondary importance . . . is constantly present, and is a relatively determining factor." In *Conscious Orientation,* van der Hoop placed special emphasis on this: "The subsidiary [auxiliary] function frequently tends to control adaptation in the direction towards which the dominant function is not orientated." This addition of a second preferred function results in 16 types. For example, introverted sensation types are of two kinds: (1) introverted sensation with extraverted thinking or (2) introverted sensation with extraverted feeling. It remained for others to clarify and extend this refinement on Jung's original eight types.

C. Katharine Briggs and Isabel Briggs Myers

1. Briggs and Jung

In the United States, Katharine Briggs, born the same year as Jung (1875), was also interested in understanding personality differences. A well-educated woman, she was married to Lyman Briggs, a physicist and head of the National Bureau of Standards. Her deep, life-long interest in character analysis resulted in a manuscript entitled "Notes on the Art of Creating Characters" in which she described her own approach to analyzing character in writing fiction. Then she discovered Jung's book *Psychological Types.*

In 1923, when Jung's work on types appeared in English translation Briggs immediately adapted her approach to Jung's. From 1927 to 1936 she corresponded with Jung "sporadically." In 1937, when Jung came to the United States to give the Terry lectures at Yale, she arranged to meet him in New York. Her daughter, Isabel, went with her. Briggs and Jung were 62; Myers was 40. Several years later, when asked what Jung and her mother talked about, she said, "I don't know. I didn't listen."

2. Myers and the MBTI

It was not until 5 years later (1942) when Myers read about the "Humm–Wadsworth Temperament

Scale" in *Reader's Digest* that she became personally interested in work closely connected to her mother's life-long interests. Securing a position with the Pennsylvania Co. for Banking and Trusts through their personnel officer, E. N. Hay, she began rescoring all the Humm–Wadsworth scales for several hundred employees. Finding the results "not useful," she was soon hard at work developing a "people-sorting test."

By late 1943, she had completed the first version of the Myers–Briggs Type Indicator or MBTI. All versions of the MBTI have questions that require the answerer to choose between word pairs or phrase pairs that, based on Myers' extensive observation and analysis, reflect extraversion (E) or introversion (I), sensing (S) or intuition (N), etc. Choices are scored so that one has a higher score for E or I, S or N, etc. Thus, 16 types are possible (e.g., ISTJ, ISFP, ENFJ, ENTJ, etc.). The fourth letter is supposed to show which function one prefers to extravert; thus, for extraverts, J indicates that a judging function (thinking or feeling) is dominant, while P indicates that a perceiving function (sensing or intuition) is dominant. For introverts, this is reversed: I--Js have a dominant introverted perceiving function, I--Ps a dominant introverted judging function. The MBTI is not explicitly designed to measure one's dominant function, the hierarchy of the four functions, or whether a function is extraverted or introverted.

By 1959, Form F of the MBTI was "developed and ready for use" under the auspices of Educational Testing Service. In late 1969, Myers and Mary McCaulley, then on the faculty of the University of Florida in the Department of Clinical Psychology, first met. This began a collaboration that has born much fruit. By 1974, they had realized their dream of establishing a center for research on the MBTI. Initially associated with the University of Florida, it was called the "Typology Laboratory." In 1975 it became the Center for Applications of Psychological Type (CAPT) of which McCaulley is president. CAPT was the first organization to provide MBTI training.

3. CPP and APT

By September 1975, CAPT had contracted with Consulting Psychologists Press (CPP) in Palo Alto, California, as publisher of the MBTI and related materials. That relationship continues to this day. The next month, in Gainesville, Florida (home of CAPT), the first national MBTI conference was held. Two years later (1977), in Lansing, Michigan, the second national MBTI conference took place. Form G of the MBTI was published by CPP in 1978. In 1979, the idea to create a membership organization of MBTI users and researchers took form. In Philadelphia that year, at the third national MBTI conference, which began on October 18th, Myers' 82nd birthday, 150 people became charter members of the Association for Psychological Type (APT). Kathy Myers, wife of Myers' only son, Peter, was their first president. APT has continued to hold conferences every other year. A book that Myers had been writing for nearly 20 years, *Gifts Differing*, was finally published in 1980, shortly after her death.

D. David Keirsey and Temperament Theory

In 1978, *Please Understand Me: An Essay on Temperament Styles*, by Keirsey and Marilyn Bates, was published. The next year, Keirsey was the keynote speaker at the biennial APT Conference; he was at that time chair of the counseling/school psychology department at California State University, Fullerton. Beginning in 1955, Keirsey had adopted Jung's typology and Myers' method for measuring type for use in his clinical practice. Although his book deals with all 16 MBTI types, Keirsey takes the position that four temperaments (SJ, SP, NF, and NT) come before and are more fundamental than Jung's 8 or Myers' 16 types. He links these with the four temperaments of Hippocrates (a Greek physician, ca. 400 B.C.).

E. James Newman and "A Cognitive Psychology of Type"

Since 1981, Newman, a clinical psychologist, has written several papers based on his study of psychological type, neuropsychology, and neurophysiology. His work is a sound beginning toward the development of a cognitive psychology based in Jung's psychological types. Since everything psychological can be assumed to have a physiological correlate in the working of the brain, any effort to assess the relative merits of the various theoretical approaches to type will do well to begin with as much understanding of brain/personality relationships as is available.

Newman's work not only builds on the work of Jung, Myers, and van der Hoop, but he also draws extensively from the split-brain research of R. W. Sperry and others, Luria's "three principal functional units," and numerous other sources independent of those that deal specifically with Jungian typology. In correspondence with Duniho, Newman makes reference to a talk by Jane Holmes (now Bernstein), "Normal Neuropsychological Development," presented at a symposium on developmental neuropsychology in San Francisco in 1982. As a result of Newman's work, these sources and many more have provided crucial pieces of the brain/personality puzzle in relationship to type.

Newman emphasizes that all four functions are cognitive in nature, and offers both evidence and persuasive argument to show that they can be associated with four quadrants of specialization in the cerebral cortex. Ned Hermann and others have assumed that sensing and feeling correlate with the more primitive parts of the brain: for example, sensing with the cerebellum and brain stem, and feeling with the limbic system. But Newman's work clearly shows that sensing and feeling are as complex, cerebral, and involved in cognition as are intuition and thinking.

The Jungian perceptual processes (S and N) correspond mainly to the functions of the posterior half of the cortex with the judging processes (F and T) being associated mainly with prefrontal systems. Intuition (which Jung called passive or undirected thinking: "prethinking") and thinking are left-brain, intellectual functions; sensing and feeling are right-brain, experiential functions. This may appear to be at odds with the popular conception of intuition as a right-brain function. But associating intuition with left hemisphere processing results from (1) clarifying definitions by emphasizing intuition's oppositeness to sensing and (2) considering the particularly strong correlations between MBTI scores on intuition and scores from other instruments that measure verbal and mathematical abilities (clearly left-brain) as documented in the manual for the MBTI.

F. Terence Duniho and Life Patterns

In early 1980, Duniho was introduced to the MBTI and Jungian typology. As a career counselor he was very interested in adult development theories. To better understand the relationships among type, lifespan development, and life/work choices, he began to read Jung, Myers, Keirsey, and others. But it was *Facing Your Type* by George Schemel and James Borbely in which Duniho first saw a model of type showing two functions as extraverted and two as introverted. He was persuaded that their explanation of the dynamic relationship of the four functions within each type made both logical and intuitive sense. The validity of their approach has been repeatedly and consistently borne out by direct observation. Instead of focusing on each person's type in an either/or manner as the MBTI does (you are either an E or an I, an S or an N, etc.), Schemel and Borbely were emphasizing a both/and way to think about type (e.g., you use both S and N, but prefer to use them in different ways [E or I], with one being preferred fundamentally over the other). From this point forward, Duniho has continually thought about type "three-dimensionally" (dynamically) as patterns, considering how all four functions operate within each person. He has developed several visual representations to illustrate how each type uses the functions according to a logically derived pattern, including the "type fraction" (see Table I), and has written extensively on the types as patterns.

The "type fraction" extends the four capital letters in Myers' system of 16 types. Whatever is introverted is below the line, while that which is extraverted is above the line. Because the fourth capital letter in her system indicates one's preferred *extraverted* orientation, it is always above the line (extraverted). The colon after "e" (for introverts) or "E" (for extraverts) indicates that when the person of that pattern is focused on the object as primary (extraversion), he or she triggers the use of the functions or orientation represented by the letters above the line. The colon after "i" (for extraverts) or "I" (for introverts) indicates that the functions or orientation below the line are triggered when focused on the subject—self or self's interests (introverting). The dominant function is underlined, while the tertiary is boldfaced.

Convinced that there must be a relationship between the brain and the Life Patterns model, Duniho began reading books and articles that report brain research. In 1989, at the 6th International Conference of the Association for Psychological Type, in Evanston, Illinois, he attended a presentation by Newman. Newman's ideas, data, and conclusions provided many answers to questions Duniho's reading had generated. That evening Newman and Duniho discussed matters on type from 6 PM until 2 AM. This began an extensive correspondence between the two. Newman continues to be one of a handful doing serious research on the brain/type relationship. Currently he is the Consultant for Psychological Theory on APT's Communication and Education Council.

Duniho has written extensively on Life Patterns, integrating mainly his understanding of the work of Jung, van der Hoop, Myers, and Newman in the context of the "2 and 2" model of type. In 1992 Life Patterns Institute, a nonprofit corporation, was formed in Providence, Rhode Island, to promote research and education relating to those aspects of personality that influence human development throughout life and function according to a meaningful, dynamic pattern. The Institute is concerned with the study of the patterns of personality that begin to manifest at and even before birth, and how these patterns interact with environmental influences to create who and what we become. Although centered on the Life Patterns model—especially as conceptualized and explained through Duniho's writings on personality—LPI is mainly interested in increasing our understanding of *whatever is true* about personality and *what works* in practical applications. In this spirit, LPI affirms and is interested in research involving other models not directly influenced by Jung, as they complement and improve our knowledge of personality.

TABLE I

Duniho's Type Fractions for All 16 Life Patterns

ISTJ	ISFJ	INFJ	INTJ
e: n T J / I: <u>S</u> f p	e: n F J / I: <u>S</u> t p	e: s F J / I: <u>N</u> t p	e: s T J / I: <u>N</u> f p
ISTP	**ISFP**	**INFP**	**INTP**
e: <u>S</u> f P / I: **n** <u>T</u> j	e: <u>S</u> t P / I: **n** <u>F</u> j	e: <u>N</u> t P / I: **s** <u>F</u> j	e: <u>N</u> f P / I: **s** <u>T</u> j
ESTP	**ESFP**	**ENFP**	**ENTP**
E: <u>S</u> f P / i: n T j	E: <u>S</u> t P / i: n F j	E: <u>N</u> t P / i: s F j	E: <u>N</u> f P / i: s T j
ESTJ	**ESFP**	**ENFJ**	**ENTJ**
E: **n** <u>T</u> J / i: S f p	E: **n** <u>F</u> J / i: S t p	E: **s** <u>F</u> J / i: N t p	E: **s** <u>T</u> J / i: N f p

IV. THEORETICAL APPROACHES

Three major approaches to the explication and use of type dynamics have developed in the United States alongside each other. One is tied to the "letter" of Jung's work, another to its "spirit," and a third takes the position that Keirsey's four temperaments are more fundamental than Jungian types.

A. Type and the "Letter" of Jung
(the "1 and 3" Model)

Throughout Jung's works, one reads continually of opposites. Perhaps the most consistent theme in his thinking is what he called "the problem of opposites." He strongly believed that "the problem of opposites . . . should be made the basis for a critical psychology." However, he did not really think through many of the implications of his observations on type. Almost all that he wrote on type deals with "the most highly differentiated function," the dominant or "typical" function. But, in at least two places, he indicated that the other three functions operate in the opposite attitude to the dominant. For example, if sensing is dominant and introverted, then intuition, thinking, and feeling would all be extraverted. Myers, and McCaulley after her, accepted this view. In the first three editions of Myers' *Introduction to Type,* discussion is limited to how the 16 types each prefer two functions: if one of the two is extraverted, the other will be introverted; if one is a perceiving function, the other will be judging; and vice versa. But, the fourth edition, revised by Allen Hammer, provides a chart that illustrates this view in accord with the two statements in Jung's work (quoted in Myers' *Gifts Differing*), placing three functions in one attitude if the dominant is in the other. Although frequently discussed, nothing has been written (of which the present authors are aware) that provides practical or applied discussion using this "1 and 3" model.

B. Keirsey and His Temperament Theory

At an all-day presentation in 1985, at the 6th APT Conference (available on tape), David Keirsey said that he believes introversion and extraversion do not actually exist. If he is right, the position that his four temperaments (SJ, SP, NF, and NT) are fundamental would be reinforced, since his temperaments do not depend on the attitudes. In *Please Understand Me,* Keirsey says, ". . . in the temperament hypothesis we must abandon Jung's idea of 'functions.'" This is immediately followed with "But in giving up Jung's 'function' we must not abandon his behavior descriptions." And then, ". . . so it is not so much that the 'function type' is abandoned but rather subordinated to the concept of 'temperament,' the latter having a much wider range of convenience as an explainer of behavior." Keirsey further believed that "the Jungian types

emerge from temperaments by way of differentiation."

He thought that "Jungian typology must undergo some rearrangement to conform to these temperaments." However, it is easier to fit temperament theory with Jungian typology than the other way around. It makes more sense to understand temperaments in light of Life Patterns, because Life Patterns explain far more of the data we have on personality.

According to Duniho, the first function to differentiate for introverts is the auxiliary; the first for extraverts is the dominant. This happens because between ages 7 and 14 everyone has to begin learning how to deal effectively with the extraverted aspects of life. This first step in differentiation of the functions does indeed create four "temperaments" (SP, NP, TJ, and FJ), but only one of these fits with Keirsey's four. Using Myers' letter system, SPs are those who use sensing as the main way to deal with the extraverted side, NPs use intuition as their primary extraverting mode, etc.

Nevertheless, Keirsey's way of condensing the 16 patterns to four categories works quite well for many purposes. It is very useful, and often easier, to identify people as one of Keirsey's four temperaments (SP/SJ/NF/NT), but not because his temperaments are more fundamental than Jungian typology. In addition to Keirsey's 4, there are 13 other logical and equally useful ways to consolidate the 16 types into groupings of 4, depending on one's purpose. For example, 4 that are often used are IS/IN/ES/EN, IJ/IP/EP/EJ, ST/SF/NF/NT, and SJ/FP/NJ/TP. When one sees that Life Patterns are the natural ways in which the brain processes information, it becomes clear why Jungian types are more fundamental than any four-part personality model could be.

C. Type and the Spirit of Jung
(the "2 and 2" Model)

This approach to type recognizes that opposite functions truly oppose each other, a fact that Jung saw clearly and emphasized repeatedly throughout his writings. Even though he did not realize that "the problem of opposites" also applied to each pair of functions, Jung did observe that if the dominant (#1) function is both extraverted and perceptive (sensing or intuition), then the auxiliary (#2) function will be introverted and judging (thinking or feeling). If #1 is extraverted and judging, #2 will be introverted and perceiving. (Likewise, for introverts: if #1 is introverted and judging, #2 will be extraverted and perceiving; if #1 is introverted and perceptive, #2 will be extraverted and judging.)

For exactly the same reasons, it would appear that if a function (e.g., feeling) is introverted (no matter whether #1, #2, #3, or #4) then its opposite (in this case, thinking) would necessarily be extraverted. Defining extraversion and introversion as Jung did (with the emphasis on object vs subject), Duniho and many others have consistently found this to be the case. The Life Patterns model, which reflects this spirit of Jung's work, has two essential elements:

1. The four functions are organized according to a hierarchy. Either the dominant (#1) and fourth (#4) will both be perceiving functions and the auxiliary (#2) and tertiary (#3) both judging, or vice versa.

2. Two functions are preferred when extraverting and their opposites when introverting. For extraverts the dominant (#1) and tertiary (#3) are extraverted, and the auxiliary (#2) and fourth (#4) are introverted. These numbers are reversed for introverts: #1 and #3 are introverted; #2 and #4 are extraverted.

V. TESTS AND MEASUREMENTS

Ideally, determination of an individual's type preferences (i.e., "true type," "actual type," or Life Pattern) involves (A) clear definitions of terms, (B) thorough understanding of type dynamics, developmental changes, and the numerous consequences of various combinations of stress and one's vulnerabilities, (C) objective observation, (D) questioning and dialogue (preferably in the context of educating the individual about definitions, dynamics, development, and stress), and (E) mutual confirmation between the professional and the individual.

(A) emphasizes the need for clarity (thinking), (C) the need for fact gathering (sensing), (B) and (D) the need to understand possibilities and relationships (intuition), and (D) and (E) the need to involve the individual (feeling). The effectiveness of paper-and-pencil questionnaires or any other standardized methods of measuring or assessing preferences depends on (A) and (B). However, no standardized measurement is sufficient in itself, because (C), (D), and (E) require a professional with sufficient knowl-

edge and understanding to observe and preferably dialogue with the individual.

There are different schools of thought on the ethics of assessing preferences without (a) using the MBTI or some other valid and reliable instrument and/or without (b) being able to directly observe, educate, question, and dialogue with the person being assessed. More than one school of thought is inevitable, given the many ways in which we differ one from the other. It should, however, be recognized that if neither (a) nor (b) is possible, the resulting assessment should be seen as tentative at best. If only (a) or (b) is possible, we believe that the results of *informed* observation, etc., are preferable to those of a standardized method that does not involve human interaction.

A. Nonpsychometric Measurements

Jung and van der Hoop did not rely on standardized measuring devices to assess or to help them assess the preferences of their patients or others with whom they used their knowledge of type. Jung said,

It is not the purpose of a psychological typology to classify human beings into categories. . . . Its purpose is rather to provide a critical psychology which will make a methodical investigation and presentation of the empirical material possible . . . it is a great help in understanding the wide variations that occur among individuals. . . . [and] Last but not least, it is an essential means for determining the 'personal equation' of the practising psychologist, who, armed with an exact knowledge of his differentiated and inferior functions, can avoid many serious blunders in dealing with his patients.

In a letter commenting on the statistical evaluation of types, he said,

My book . . . was written to demonstrate the structural and functional aspect of certain typical elements of the psyche. That such a means of communication and explanation could be used also as a means of classification was an aspect which I was rather afraid of, since the intellectually detached classifying point of view is just the thing to be avoided by the therapist. . . . I admit that your statistical line of research is perfectly legitimate but it certainly does not coincide with the purpose of my book.

If professionals are going to use any of the several instruments now available, they should at least recognize that *prior* emphasis is needed on (a) sufficient theoretical understanding and (b) knowledge of self. *After* testing, and preferably before results are revealed, there needs to be equal emphasis given to observation, dialogue, and independent determination of preferences. None of the instruments currently available directly assess which function is dominant (or auxiliary, tertiary, or fourth) or which functions are introverted or extraverted. Even if they did, the *primary* method to determine one's preferences should still depend on observation, interpretation, and discussion.

1. Duniho's Method for Determining One's Actual Life Pattern

Beginning in 1983, Duniho designed, began using, and has continually refined a 10-part interview that combines questions, education, and dialogue to independently determine an individual's Life Pattern. These questions not only deal with extraversion–introversion, sensing–intuition, thinking–feeling, and judging–perceiving, but they also address rational–arational, introverted vs extraverted use of the four functions, and the hierarchical relationship of the four. After the MBTI has been administered, but before the results have been shared, 2 hours is spent one-on-one to go through the 10-part interview. This provides an opportunity to observe, educate, question, and dialogue to mutually determine one's preferences. The results of the interview are then compared with the results from the MBTI and any variations interpreted and discussed with the client in light of knowledge developed during the interview. Occasionally, far more than 2 hours is required to make a dependable determination.

2. Other Approaches to Determining Type

Several others have also been concerned with the inevitable inadequacies of standardized instruments, including the MBTI. For example, William Jeffries, among others, has addressed this problem by writing *True to Type*. It is subtitled "Answers to the Most Commonly Asked Questions about Interpreting the Myers-Briggs Type Indicator." He asks and answers 50 such questions. However, though some of the approaches used to determine type recognize that the hierarchy and attitudinal preference for each function must be clearly determined, none of these approaches recognize the dynamics of Life Patterns or systematically address each polarity of those dynamics.

B. Psychometric Instruments

Besides the most used version of the MBTI (Form G, 126 items), there are several other psychometric instruments currently available that measure one's type preferences. They include the Gray–Wheelwright Test (also known as the Jungian Type Survey), the Singer–Loomis Inventory of Personality, Forms K (131 items, 20 subscales) and J (290 items, 27 subscales) of the MBTI, and the Murphy–Meisgeier Type Indicator for Children. In addition to these, the Duniho/Duniho Life Pattern Indicator (DDLI) is currently under development by Fergus Duniho (a Ph.D. candidate at University of Rochester) and Terence Duniho. Unlike the other instruments, it will directly measure type dynamics. [*See* PERSONALITY ASSESSMENT.]

1. Gray–Wheelwright Test

This test measures one's preference for extraversion or introversion, sensing or intuition, and thinking or feeling. It does not explicitly consider judging or perceiving. However, one's preference for either of these can be inferred from the strength of the sensing, intuition, thinking, or feeling scores. If the sensing or intuition score is highest, this implies that one prefers perceiving over judging; if thinking or feeling, then a preference for judging is implied.

It should be noted that the types identified by the MBTI as I -- J or I -- P (and therefore called by MBTI users "judgers" or "perceivers," respectively) would be called perceivers or judgers, respectively, by users of the Gray–Wheelwright. This occurs because the MBTI is referring to how one prefers to orient toward the external world, while the Gray–Wheelwright is considering the dominant as determining whether one is fundamentally a perceiver or judger (therefore, for users of the Gray-Wheelwright, perceiver is synonymous with arational and judger with rational).

For example, the dominant of an I -- J is either sensing or intuition (a perceiving function); but the I -- J prefers either thinking or feeling for extraverting. So the world sees the I -- J as a judger. However, since the I -- J's dominant is a perceiving function, the I -- J could be referred to as a *closet P* (i.e., fundamentally preferring perceiving, though only exhibiting this preference in situations where he or she feels that introverted behavior is appropriate or safe. Likewise, I -- Ps are *closet Js*.

2. The Singer–Loomis Inventory of Personality (SLIP)

Developed by June Singer and Mary Loomis, SLIP is an attempt to measure Jung's eight types or "cognitive modes," not dynamically (i.e., how they function in relationship with each other) but independently, suggesting the relative preference of all eight modes for the respondent. The SLIP is experimental and requires cautious interpretation by experienced clinicians.

3. Form K, MBTI (Expanded Analysis Report—EAR)

Based on research originally inspired by Briggs and done by Myers, the EAR was developed by David R. Saunders, a psychometrician who worked with Myers while he was at Educational Testing Service from 1956 until her death. The EAR provides scores for the same four scales as Form G (EI, SN, TF, JP). In addition, 20 subscales are provided: 5 each for the four usual scales. These subscales are intended to be seen as neither good nor bad and are meant to provide further differentiation (for example, what *kind* of extravert one is or in what *way* one is extraverted). The EAR also does not directly assess type dynamics.

4. Form J, MBTI (Type Differentiation Indicator—TDI)

Based on 290 items drawn mainly from the several versions of the MBTI developed by Myers, the TDI provides experienced users of the MBTI with "more comprehensive scoring and interpretive applications." A "C" level instrument, the TDI user must have an advanced degree, licensure or certification and/or membership in a professional association requiring the ethical and competent use of psychological tests. In addition to the 20 subscales of the EAR, 7 more scales are added that are not directly tied to the 4 primary scales. Also, unlike the other 20 subscales, these 7 are meant to be interpreted as "good vs bad."

5. The Kiersey Temperament Sorter

The Kiersey Temperament Sorter (KTS) involves 70 questions with content similar to the MBTI. It is available to the general public without the kinds of quality control required of users of the MBTI, such

as certification through participation in special training seminars or possession of an advanced professional degree. Irving Tucker and Bonnie Gillespie have shown that the correlations between corresponding subcategories of the KTS and the group form of the MBTI (Form G) are high enough for the two tests to be considered to be measuring the same constructs. In fact, the pattern of intercorrelations were comparable to the test–retest reliability coefficients reported for the original version of the MBTI. Tucker and Gillespie also found this to be true of Kiersey's computer version of the KTS, called Please Understand Me (PUM). This latter version allows the test taker to omit up to ten items which he or she might consider ambiguous, and it provides the option of electing to be given a more elaborate explanation of each item. It was also found that test takers who were given both Form G of the MBTI and PUM preferred taking PUM.

6. Murphy–Meisgeier Type Indicator for Children (MMTIC)

The MMTIC has 70 items. It measures the same four scales as the MBTI. Developed by Charles Meisgeier and Elizabeth Murphy, it is intended for use with children in the second through eighth grades as a method for identifying the learning styles of students.

7. The Duniho–Duniho Life Pattern Indicator (DDLI)

Fergus Duniho, a Ph.D. candidate and T. A. in the philosophy department at the University of Rochester, and T. Duniho's eldest son, began developing the DDLI in 1992. Unlike the other questionnaires designed to measure type preferences, the DDLI has questions that reflect the 10-part interview that T. Duniho has been conducting with clients since 1983. The DDLI is experimental, currently consists of about 95 items, and will not be available for general use until at least 1995.

VI. UNCONSCIOUS FUNCTIONS AND DEPTH PSYCHOLOGY

Of the eight functions (IS, ES, IN, EN, IT, ET, IF, EF), the four that are most preferred form one's conscious orientation; the other four are primarily unconscious.

For example, the type fraction for the ESTP is as follows:

$$\frac{E: S\,f\,P}{i: n\,T\,j}$$

The hierarchy of the ESTP's four functions is "ES, IT, EF, IN." From one moment to the next, any one or more of these functions may be used with conscious or unconscious awareness. But the ESTP generally acknowledges that each of them is part of who he or she is. However, he or she would not normally recognize the other four (IS, ET, IF, EN) as "natural," at least for self.

Since these patterns are largely concerned with the placement and displacement of psychic energy, we can determine the hierarchy of the four unconscious functions by considering which of the conscious four have the most psychic energy, second most, etc. Since extraverted sensing (ES) has the most, its opposite (IS) will have the least of all eight. (Notice that the opposite of sensing is intuition, but the opposite of extraverted sensing is introverted sensing.) The opposite of ET (IT) will have the second least, etc. So the hierarchy for all eight is as follows:

#1-ES, #2-IT, #3-EF, #4-IN, #5-EN, #6-IF, #7-ET, #8-IS.

This hierarchy reveals the ease, or difficulty, in accessing each of the eight functions. Each function takes on a different "look," depending on its position in the hierarchy and the individual's overall attitude toward it. A promising start in the direction of correlating each function at each level with the various archetypes identified by depth psychologists has been made by John Beebe of the San Francisco Jung Institute. Table II shows the eight functions for all 16 patterns.

Although this approach to the human psyche may seem relatively simple, the letters and numbers used in looking at Jungian personality types act as a "doorway" into a much more complex understanding of the psyche and its endless diversity and potential. Without the knowledge of the unconscious developed by depth psychologists, one's use of type is bound to be relatively shallow. Likewise, without the firm footing provided by sufficient knowledge of the 16 basic patterns and their involvement in establishing our conscious orientation toward life, it is far too easy and quite common to lose one's way in exploring the murky depths of the unconscious. Knowledge of the brain and how it processes information, when understood in conjunction with typology and depth psychology, gives us the most solid footing of all.

Many have been working for many years to understand the psyche from different angles (the unconscious, depth psychologists; the conscious, typologists; and the brain, neuropsychologists); now their separate perspectives are beginning to come together. The holistic marriage and consequent applications of these and many other legitimate though partial perspectives is the next frontier. The new civilization that needs to be built on that frontier will be concerned with the development of treatment strategies that recognize the natural diversity of our life patterns.

Human beings are infinitely complex. That complexity can be much better understood through Jungian personality types, when they are seen holistically, developmentally, and dynamically as the natural patterns the brain uses to process information. At their core, these patterns show us the how and why of what motivates each person, no matter who they are or how they behave. In other words,

TABLE II
The Hierarchy for All Eight Functions for Each Pattern

	ISTJ	ESTJ	ISTP	ESTP	ISFJ	ESFJ	ISFP	ESFP	INFJ	ENFJ	INFP	ENFP	INTJ	ENTJ	INTP	ENTP
1	IS	ET	IT	ES	IS	EF	IF	ES	IN	EF	IF	EN	IN	ET	IT	EN
2	ET	IS	ES	IT	EF	IS	ES	IF	EF	IN	EN	IF	ET	IN	EN	IT
3	IF	EN	IN	EF	IT	EN	IN	ET	IT	ES	IS	ET	IF	ES	IS	EF
4	EN	IF	EF	IN	EN	IT	ET	IN	ES	IT	ET	IS	ES	IF	EF	IS
5	IN	EF	IF	EN	IN	ET	IT	EN	IS	ET	IT	ES	IS	EF	IF	ES
6	EF	IN	EN	IF	ET	IN	EN	IT	ET	IS	ES	IT	EF	IS	ES	IF
7	IT	ES	IS	ET	IF	ES	IS	EF	IF	EN	IN	EF	IT	EN	IN	ET
8	ES	IT	ET	IS	ES	IF	EF	IS	EN	IF	EF	IN	EN	IT	ET	IN

the Life Patterns of Jungian typology are motivation maps to help us understand who people are, how they grow, how they dysfunction, and how they heal. As Jung understood so well, we first need to thoroughly understand the natural motivations that create our own views, priorities, and behaviors. Next we need to understand how others differ in natural ways from each other. Without this knowledge, no matter what else we know, we are inevitably going to be controlled by unexamined biases, projections, and naive assumptions.

Bibliography

Duniho, T. (1983; revised 1988). "Freud and Jung: Patterns in Conflict." Life Patterns Institute, Providence, RI.

Duniho, T. (1985). "Patterns of Preference: A Brief Introduction to the Life Patterns Model." Life Patterns Institute, Providence, RI.

Duniho, T. (1986). "Wholeness Lies Within: Sixteen Natural Paths to Spirituality." Type and Temperament, Inc., Gladwyne, PA.

Duniho, T. (1987). "Our Brain, Life Patterns, and the Myers-Briggs: Observations and Applications." Life Patterns Institute, Providence, RI.

Duniho, T. (1988). "Actual Type: Determining Your Life Pattern." Life Patterns Institute, Providence, RI.

Duniho, T. (1989). "Personalities at Risk: Addiction, Codependency and Psychological Type." Type and Temperament, Gladwyne, PA.

Jung, C. G. (1921). "Psychological Types" (revision by R. F. C. Hull, 1971; H. G. Baynes, tr.). Princeton University Press, Princeton, NJ.

Keirsey, D., and Bates, M. (1978). "Please Understand Me: An Essay on Temperament Styles." Prometheus Nemesis Books, Del Mar, CA.

Myers, I. B., and Myers, P. B. (1980). "Gifts Differing." Consulting Psychologists Press, Palo Alto, CA.

Myers, I. B. (1962, 1970, 1976). "Introduction to Type." Center for Applications of Psychological Type, Gainesville, FL.

Myers, I. B., and McCaulley, M. H. (1985). "Manual: A Guide to the Development and Use of the Myers-Briggs Type Indicator." Consulting Psychologists Press, Palo Alto, CA.

Myers, I. B., Hammer, A. L., and McCaulley, M. H. (1987). "Introduction to Type," 4th ed. Center for Applications of Psychological Type, Gainesville, FL.

Newman, J. (1990). "A Cognitive Perspective on Jungian Typology." Center for Applications of Psychological Type, Gainesville, FL.

Schemel, G. J., and J. A. Borbely (1982). "Facing Your Type." Typrofile Press, Wernersville, PA.

Tucker, I. F. and Gillespie, B. V. (1993). Correlations among three measures of personality type. *Perceptual and Motor Skills* **77,** 650.

van der Hoop, J. H. (1937). "Conscious Orientation: A Study of Personality Types in Relation to Neurosis and Psychosis." Harcourt, Brace and Company, New York.

JURY PSYCHOLOGY

Allen J. Hart
University of Iowa

Glossary

Challenge for cause Counsel's opportunity to exclude potential jurors from service because they may be biased, prejudiced, or possess some conflict of interest.

Judge's instruction The description of the responsibilities, legal definitions, and criteria that must be met in order to reach a verdict, given by the judge to the jury prior to deliberations (alternatively called jury, pattern, model, or standard instructions).

Leniency bias The belief that juries are more likely to acquit defendants than are judges.

Limiting instruction Judge's instruction during the trial admonishing the jury to disregard certain remarks, testimony, or evidence.

Peremptory challenge Counsel's opportunity to exclude a potential juror from the jury without having to give any reasons.

Representativeness The goal of selecting juries so as not to systematically eliminate or underrepresent any subgroups of the population.

Scientific jury selection The systematic use of surveys and other "scientific" techniques to detect bias in potential jury populations.

Standards of proof The standards by which the juror must be satisfied that the evidence is sufficient to prove the defendant's culpability (e.g., beyond a reasonable doubt).

Voir dire The time after a panel of jurors are assembled during which either the judge or the attorneys may present questions to the panel to uncover any biases or prejudgments.

IN ANY TRIAL, civil or criminal, two opposing viewpoints are put forth, with each touted as "the truth." Both prosecution and defense are quite naturally likely to be concerned with the make-up of the jury. Aware that different sets of 12 jury members may well arrive at different verdicts—even when faced with the same arguments and evidence—each litigant hopes to be heard by a sympathetic jury. Given the high stakes in a jury trial, neither side is willing to gamble with jury sentiment. Hence, the emergence of a relatively new research focus in psychology—jury psychology. It is the result of research devoted to turning the aforementioned hope for a sympathetic jury into informed selection by design. The psychology of how juries are selected and issues affecting how they reach their decisions are discussed here.

I. PSYCHOLOGY AND THE LAW

Many people argue that the jury, although once a vital component of the criminal justice system, is no longer important. They point out that juries currently decide only about 8% of all criminal cases, with the rest resolved by a judge (called a bench trial) or through plea-bargaining. Opponents of trial by jury have major questions about the competence and fairness of jurors. One critic has described the jury as, at best, 12 people of average ignorance. The eminent judge Jerome Frank complained that juries apply law that they do not understand to facts that they cannot get straight.

Proponents of trial by jury argue that even though the jury decides only a small proportion of cases, it has important effects on the entire criminal justice system, both philosophical and practical. On the one

Encyclopedia of Human Behavior, Volume 3

hand, the jury seems somehow to encapsulate what is special about the United States' legal system. On the other hand, the prosecutor's decision to charge someone with a crime and the defendant's willingness to plea-bargain depend upon their views of how likely they are to win their case before a jury. Studies of jurors themselves have shown that participating on a jury both educates and enhances regard for our system of justice. Verdicts by representative juries, especially in controversial trials, increase the legitimacy of the process in the public's eyes, because jury verdicts are trusted to represent the community more than are verdicts by judges. Proponents of trial by jury maintain that juries are competent and not prejudiced, or at least no more prejudiced than judges. Furthermore, because juries deliberate in secret and need not give reasons for their verdicts as judges must, they retain a flexibility denied judges: the ability to bend the law to achieve justice in individual cases.

Who is right? Over the last several decades, researchers have subjected the jury to systematic and scientific inquiry. This article synthesizes what has been learned about how the institution of trial by jury operates in our society. This knowledge comes from many different sources: archives, court documents, appellate opinions, research studies on jury selection, and jury decision making, and from actual jurors who wrote books or granted interviews about their experiences. This article draws most heavily from the relevant psychological research, but other sources will be discussed.

We begin by examining the key issues of jury selection, including its underlying assumptions, the procedures required by the courts to select unbiased jurors, and the recent trend toward "scientific jury selection." From there we will take an in-depth look at jury decisions and how jurors combine their individual perspectives into a single verdict. We address three central criticisms: that the jury is incompetent, that the jury is prejudiced, and that the jury ignores the law. Recent changes in jury size and the requirements for unanimous verdicts are also considered. Then we will focus on the jury in controversial cases where the defendant raises the insanity defense. The article concludes with an endorsement of the competence of the jury system and a call for continued research into the psychology of the jury.

II. JURY SELECTION: REPRESENTATIVENESS AND BIAS

In the United States, the foundation for the criminal jury's composition is contained in the Sixth Amend-ment to the Constitution. A similar guarantee for the civil jury appears in the Seventh Amendment. From these amendments, and subsequent decisions by the U.S. Supreme Court, three general principles for the selection and make-up of the jury have emerged. First, the jury must be drawn from a representative cross-section of the community. Second, the trial should be held in the district in which the crime was committed. Third, the jurors must be impartial: Potential jurors who are unable to judge the facts with an open mind may be rejected from the jury.

History has shown that the jury as a group can reach a balanced result only if it reflects the different beliefs and attitudes of the community. As Justice Thurgood Marshall once wrote, "When any large and identifiable segment of the community is excluded from jury service, the effect is to remove from the jury room qualities of human nature and varieties of human experience, the range of which is unknown and perhaps unknowable." There is no absolute requirement that each jury must represent all groups in the community. In fact, this is not possible in a 12-person jury given the diversity of our society. Rather, no "perceivable" group may be systematically excluded from the jury panel from which the jury is drawn.

Supporters of the representative jury argue that a jury composed of individuals with a variety of experiences, backgrounds, and knowledge is more likely to perceive and interpret the facts from a variety of perspectives. More thorough deliberations are consequently more likely to occur.

Drawing the jury from a representative cross-section may also increase the legitimacy of the jury system and jury verdicts. For example, if African Americans (or any other minority group) suspect that they as a group are underrepresented on juries, they may feel that verdicts are biased reflections of community sentiment rather than fair judgments.

Another principle of jury selection is that the jury should be drawn from the community in which the offense occurred. This rule goes almost unnoticed until trial participants fear that a fair trial cannot be had in the community and demand that it be held elsewhere. When trials are moved to another jurisdiction to increase the chances for a fair jury this is called a change of venue.

The principles of jury selection are designed to assemble juries that will reflect the range of voices in the community and decide cases in an unbiased way. Yet, even if the jury pool is representative, and the community as a whole is relatively unbiased, there is no guarantee that the people selected for the jury will be free from prejudice. That is the problem we consider next.

The voir dire presents an opportunity to learn about existing prejudices on the part of prospective jurors. During the voir dire, the trial judge and attorneys ask questions of prospective jurors to determine their qualifications for jury service, their knowledge of the defendant and the case, and attitudes toward issues or individuals in the case that could bias their views of the trial evidence. Questions may be wide-ranging or more specifically related to the case, depending on what the trial judge allows. On the basis of prospective jurors' responses to these questions, the trial judge may determine that they would have difficulty being fair and impartial jurors, and may dismiss them with a challenge for cause. At one time, if prospective jurors asserted that they could judge the case impartially, they were taken at their word unless they had an obvious interest in the outcome of the case. Today many judges tend to grant dismissals on somewhat broader grounds, partly because they have become increasingly knowledgeable about psychological research on the effects of unconscious biases in jurors. Often, however, attorneys feel that prospective jurors whom the judge does not dismiss for cause are, nevertheless, likely to view their side unfavorably. Such people may be eliminated from the jury through the use of peremptory challenges. Peremptory challenges are solely the prerogative of the attorneys, and may be exercised without providing reasons. Both sides are given a limited number of these challenges (often referred to as "pre-empts"). The exact number is dependent on the jurisdiction and the type of case. A typical number is 6 for civil disputes and many criminal misdemeanor matters, and 12 or more for very serious crimes.

III. SCIENTIFIC JURY SELECTION

Scientific jury selection is a jury selection technique that primarily takes advantage of community surveys to identify which demographic characteristics of jurors are related to their being sympathetic to one side in the case. The centerpiece of scientific or systematic jury selection is a public opinion survey of citizens from the area of the trial. Often a large survey is conducted by telephone, in efforts to obtain a random selection of the voting residents. The telephone surveys are frequently supplemented by longer face-to-face interviews with selected participants to explore issues in greater detail.

The surveys contain information relevant to the case. Specific questions about the trial are asked rather than more general questions because psychological research indicates that more specific questions are better indicators of what individuals will actually do in a specific case. While the particular questions about each trial vary, respondents are always asked to provide demographic information about themselves such as age, sex, race, education, occupation, religion, and political party.

The data obtained from the community survey serve a number of functions. Most important, the pattern of differential opinions in the community is used to construct profiles of "good" and "bad" jurors. Community surveys provide other valuable information to attorneys, giving them leads in formulating questions to ask during the voir dire and in determining what trial tactics are likely to be effective with the jury.

An intriguing new development in jury research involves the use of ghost juries—groups of individuals thought to mirror the characteristics of the jury that will actually hear the case. The phrase "ghost jury" should not be confused with the phrase "mock jury." The phrase "mock jury" is the more encompassing term which includes all trial simulation participants. The phrase "ghost jury" refers to a special case when a group of mock jurors are assembled in an actual courtroom and shadow the actual jury hearing a particular case. Prior to a trial, ghost juries are typically presented with an abbreviated version of the case that the actual jury will hear. The ghost jurors then deliberate to a group verdict. The deliberations are observed and often taped, and members of the ghost juries are interviewed after they reach a decision in the case. Their responses are used to predict what types of jurors are likely to produce the desired verdict. The selection of jurors, what kinds of jurors to seek or to challenge and what trial tactics will be most effective with the different types of jurors, is then based on the outcome of the ghost jury proceedings.

There are good reasons to be skeptical about claims for the effectiveness of scientific jury selection. The success rate in such cases may not be due to the jury selection techniques but rather to other features of the cases. First, in many of the most highly publicized cases where scientific jury selection was used, the evidence against the defendant was weak. Second, many professionals believe that an attorney that has the inclination and resources to use scientific jury selection probably has prepared other aspects of their cases exceptionally well. Outstanding case preparation rather than scientific jury selection techniques may be responsible for the favorable results. The critical issue is whether scientific jury selection techniques by themselves are more effective than a good, experienced attorney using traditional selection techniques. Since trials are not subject to experimental manipulation, it is doubtful that we will ever have a definitive answer to this key question.

IV. JURY COMPETENCE AND JURY INSTRUCTIONS

In the 1950s, the University of Chicago Law School's Jury Project undertook the task of assessing jury effectiveness by investigating if and how juries differed from judges. The logic of their research strategy was simple; since judges preside over the trial and hear the same evidence as the jury, one need only to ask the judge how she or he would have decided the case and then compare the judges' hypothetical verdict with the actual decision of the jury. The results show that in their sample of 3576 trials, the judge and the jury agreed 78% of the time. A further analysis showed that in 64% of the cases both judge and jury agreed that the defendant was guilty, and in 14% they agreed that the defendant should be acquitted. But these figures mean that the judge and the jury disagreed on the remaining 22% of cases. The nature of the disagreement was further examined. It was found that the judges would have found the defendant guilty in 19% of the trials when the jury acquitted. Whereas, in only 3% of the cases did the jury convict when the judge would have acquitted. These two results are indicative of a leniency bias.

Whereas the overall report card on jury competence may be fairly good, other research suggests that jurors may have trouble with the judge's instructions. During the judge's instructions, the judge describes the responsibilities, legal definitions, and criteria that must be met in order for the jury to reach a verdict. More than once it has been noted that jurors are treated like children during the testimony and like accomplished law school graduates during the judge's instructions. Research has shown that juror comprehension of the judge's instructions and their performance on vocabulary tests including words drawn from the judge's instructions are somewhat limited.

There is a research literature that suggests disturbingly low comprehension levels (about 50%) by jurors of pattern (or model or standard) instructions. Bruce Sales and his colleagues have shown that jurors' misunderstanding of the pattern instructions can lead juries to discuss legally inappropriate issues, ignore legally relevant facts, and be unduly influenced by jurors who mistakenly claim expertise based on previous jury duty experience. Three remedies have been suggested to combat these tendencies: changing the content and vocabulary of the instructions, providing written copies of the instructions, and presenting the standard of proof in probability terms. In experimental settings, each of these remedies have been able to reduce jurors' uncertainty, increase comprehension, and produce the expected results, assuming juror comprehension. Ironically, many of the legal objections to these revisions are based on the precision of the measures. The objections include the following: there are situations that are imprecise and representing them precisely would be misleading; most people feel more comfortable and more competent dealing with words than numbers; and furthermore, these probability levels are somewhat arbitrarily assigned.

It is also true that jurors may have difficulty with specific instructions. During the course of a trial, jurors often hear testimony that is later deemed inadmissible or is meant only to be used to judge credibility and not guilt. In those instances, jurors are admonished to disregard the testimony, that is, to act as if the information were never given. For example, whenever the defendant takes the stand his or her prior criminal record may be admitted to judge his or her trustworthiness, but should not be considered to reach the final verdict. Research has shown that jurors have a difficult time following these so-called limiting instructions. In fact, under these conditions a type of psychological reactance often ensues, that is, after being instructed to disregard testimony jurors may actually emphasize that bit of information while making their final verdict decision.

Several studies have found that jury verdicts are usually based upon the amount of evidence brought forth at trial, and that juries discriminate between various types of evidence. However, occasionally, and only under special circumstances, juries depart from the judge's instructions. For example, empirical research has shown that when the cases involved a serious offense, a young victim, or an unemployed defendant, mock juries often deviate from the prescribed decision criteria offered in the judge's instructions. Their departures from the law tended to be infrequent and not due to incompetence but rather the jurors' sentiments of what was fair and just.

Closer scrutiny of jury decision-making processes addresses the jury's strength as a fact finder. In one jury simulation study it was discovered that, individually, jurors' memories were only moderate. However, the jury's collective memory was fairly impressive. As groups, juries remembered nearly 90% of the evidence and 80% of the judge's instructions correctly. Part of the reason for the jury's competence, then, may be its ability to combine information, primarily the individual memories and perspectives of jurors.

In about 5% of all jury trials, the primary evidence against the defendant is an eyewitness who makes a positive identification of the defendant. The ability of jurors to evaluate and accurately consider the impact of an eyewitness identification also bears on the discussion of jurors' competence to make legally appropriate decisions. Psychologists have investigated the accuracy of eyewitness identifications, have documented the limited reliability of such identifications, and have assessed its impact on jurors. The legal issue centers around the jury's ability to discriminate between accurate and inaccurate identifications and weigh that information accordingly. Psychologists have shown that jurors often place a great deal of importance on a single eyewitness, even if that eyewitness' testimony seems unreliable. Further, the research has shown that jurors tend to persevere in their reliance on the eyewitness to the extent that even after an eyewitness account has been discredited, it may still influence jurors' decisions.

The impact of eyewitness identification and its seemingly large influence on juror decision making bears more directly on the legal issue regarding jurors' ability to discriminate between reliable and unreliable eyewitnesses. Jurors are greatly influenced by the confidence with which an eyewitness makes an identification. Eyewitness accounts are most influential when individuals are confident in their identifications of the defendant. Unfortunately, psychological research has shown that there is little or no relationship between the eyewitness' confidence in their identification and the accuracy of that identification. Put another way, jurors rely on the eyewitness' confidence to assess his or her reliability when in fact there is no relationship between confidence and accuracy.

It should be noted that there is also a sizeable research literature in psychology that identifies the conditions under which eyewitness identifications are most reliable. When these conditions are met, confidence may accurately predict an eyewitness' accuracy. [*See* EYEWITNESS TESTIMONY.]

Simulation research has also shown that mock jurors may be influenced by judicial behavior and opinion. A series of studies of mock trials have suggested that even though jurors are admonished to disregard the judge's behavior and form their own opinions, that judges' opinion as assessed through their nonverbal behavior can influence jury verdict decisions. In these studies, judicial behavior seems especially influential on jurors who had not previously served on a jury.

V. JURY SIZE AND DECISION RULE

When Americans hear the phrase "trial by jury," we tend to picture a group of 12 individuals who witness legal proceedings and are then sequestered until they can reach a unanimous verdict. The source of this model is unknown. In fact, all English and American law juries took this form for hundreds of years until 1966 in England and 1970 in the United States. Similarly, the justification for having exactly 12 jurors rather than any other number has not been ascertained. Some have speculated that the origin of the 12-person jury is mystical: the 12 months of the year or the 12 apostles or the 12 tribes of Israel. Whatever the origin, the size and decision rule are elements of contemporary juries which have come under scrutiny and, in many jurisdictions, are changing. It is interesting to note that even though the justification for the 12-person jury remains elusive, whenever smaller juries are assembled, they frequently comprise panels of 6 jurors, half of 12.

The first appearance of the legalized use of majority rule was in England in 1966. Initially, the majority called for was 10 of 12. Simultaneously in the United States there was a movement in support of smaller juries and decision rules requiring only a majority. Legal scholars have attributed much of the United States' sentiment to practical considerations: the rising crime rate which led to increasing case loads for the courts, and concern about the appropriateness of jury decisions. Florida, Georgia, Louisiana, and Oregon went ahead with using 6-person juries in some cases, but the constitutionality of the four states' changes was questioned (several convicted individuals took their appeals all the way to the Supreme Court).

Four years after English law legalized a majority rule, the Supreme Court began to issue a series of decisions regarding jury size and decision rule, the first of which was *Williams v. Florida*. The Supreme Court noted that the Constitution made no direct reference to jury size and verdict rule and decided to assess whether these changes might produce jury decisions that were "functionally equivalent" to 12-member juries. Functional equivalency was defined along the following criteria: Is the probability of reaching a correct verdict the same for a 6-person jury as for a 12-person jury? Under a majority decision rule, are the opinions of the minority less likely to be considered? How representative can a smaller jury be of the community from which it is drawn? And, in a smaller jury, will the conformity pressure to reach unanimity be more pronounced? These questions aside, it became clear very early that smaller juries had two distinct advantages to the traditional 12-person jury—smaller juries take less time to deliberate and cost the legal system less money. In that sense smaller juries were responsive to the practical issues which gave rise to their consideration, at least in the United States.

Representativeness is a key characteristic of a jury, as prescribed by the Sixth Amendment. Most jurisdictions try to sample their population of potential jurors as nearly at random as possible, usually from telephone directories, voter registration rolls, or the United States census. These methods are used by some marketing opinion researchers and political pollsters, who face the same problem of determining how many people must be selected (or "sampled") in order to be considered representative. The answer depends on the heterogeneity of the original population. Relatively smaller samples may still produce representativeness if they are drawn from relatively homogeneous populations. One general conclusion is known: All else being equal, the smaller the random sample drawn, the less likely it is to be representative of the original population. Michael Saks, a psychologist and law professor, offers the following empirical support: Suppose African Americans account for 10% of a community's population, and we draw many random samples of 12 people from this community: Then 72% of these potential juries would be expected to be represented by at least 1 African American juror. If we were to draw random samples of size 6 from that same community, however, we would expect only 47% of these smaller juries to have African American representation.

In this case, the Supreme Court's logic is flawed by something decision-science researchers call "the law of small numbers." In this particular example, the court overestimated the degree to which juries of 6 would be representative of the population from which they are drawn. Research in sampling theory has shown that many people (sometimes even mathematicians) believe that a relatively small sample, if it is drawn at random, will replicate all the essential features of the larger population.

Conformity pressure was another functional equivalency criteria used to assess juries of fewer than 12 persons and juries that were not required to reach unanimous verdicts. Ideally, each side's arguments are considered fully before a verdict is reached. Partially due to conformity pressure, we know that jury decisions deviate from this rational ideal. Psychological research has shown that the majority has some power to influence the perceptual judgments of the minority, at least the public reporting of those judgments. It is also known that small minorities in juries sometimes agree to go along with a verdict, thus making it unanimous, even though they have not been persuaded that it is the correct decision. [*See* OBEDIENCE AND CONFORMITY.]

When jury size is reduced from 12, there is reason to believe that the ability of a minority to maintain its position in the face of the majority is adversely affected. Both mock trial and psychological research have shown that in a 12-person jury a minority of 2 can resist (to some degree) the pressure to conform to the majority. That scenario may be very different in smaller juries primarily depending upon how that comparison is made. For example, in a 6-person jury, a 2-person minority will also be able to resist the majority. However, the proper comparison is probably with a 1-person minority and 5 in the majority. The random process that produces a minority of 2 in a group of 12 is likely to yield a minority of 1 in a group of 6. Therefore, the essential question is whether a minority of 1 can resist the conformity pressure of 5 to the same degree as 2 persons can resist 10.

In 1970, the Florida State Court ruled that "jurors in the minority on the first ballot are likely to be influenced by the proportional size of the majority aligned against them." If in fact the pressure exerted on those holding the minority opinion is proportional to the ratio of the majority to the minority, then the influence of 10 jurors on 2 dissenting jurors would be exactly the same as that of 5 on 1 in a smaller jury. Research conducted by Solomon Asch argues that conformity pressure would be greater in the 5 to 1 case than in the 10 to 2 case. In Asch's basic experiments a minority of 1 confronted unanimous majorities which varied in size. Asch found that in about 35% of the trials when individuals were asked to make objectively easy visual judgments the person in the minority agreed with the objectively false observation reported by the majority. Further, Asch found that nearly 65% of all individuals conformed to the majority opinion at least once. When, however, Asch changed the situation so that the individual was confronted with an objectively false majority position *and* a single respondent who answered truthfully, instances of conformity were greatly reduced. When respondents saw even one other person disagree with the majority they were better able to resist the pressure to conform. Conformity was almost negligible even when the dissenter gave an incorrect response, suggesting that the dissension was the important factor for breaking the conformity pressure rather than the correct answer. Given Asch's results, the conformity pressure of the majority on the minority was certainly not solely a function of the proportional size of the majority; 1 person against 5 is not in the same situation as 2 persons against 10, but the single dissenter is in a distinctly weaker position. From Asch's work and sampling theory, the court should have ruled that using a 6-person jury would offer more occasions in which a dissenter would acquiesce to conformity pressure and align with the majority than would a 12-person jury.

In 1970, when the Supreme Court ruled that 6-person juries could be used in criminal cases, the available social psychological research permitted the court to say that the smaller juries would be less representative and more prone to the effects of conformity pressure than 12-person juries would be. The available social psychological research in 1970, however, did not permit the court to conclude that the verdicts reached by the smaller juries would be any less fair or that their deliberation processes would be marred in any way relative to those of the larger juries. The real issue concerned the extent to which reduced representativeness and increased risk of conformity pressure would affect jury deliberations or verdicts.

In 1972, the Supreme Court found that juries operating under majority rule (as opposed to unanimity) could be used constitutionally in state but not federal criminal trials. Cases in Oregon and Louisiana were especially illustrative because the opposing opinions were based on very different beliefs about juror attitudes and behavior. The majority of the Supreme Court judges assumed that jurors act conscientiously. That is, even with a single dissenting juror, serious and fair consideration of opposing points of view would continue even after there was a majority large enough to reach a verdict. Such jurors' primary concern is with serving justice, not with just reaching a decision. In that case, relaxing the decision rule would have little or no effect on the deliberation process. Whereas, the minority opinion argued that since a majority rule meant that jurors were not required to deliberate after a majority was attained, there would be no incentive for them to do so, and deliberation would cease at that instant. The discrepancy between the two opinions centered around the quality and the quantity of deliberation in the two cases. That is, will less than unanimous juries deliberate beyond the point when a majority is reached and as earnestly as unanimous juries? These were both empirical questions and social psychologists took up the charge to resolve the issues.

Reid Hastie and his colleagues conducted a large jury simulation study examining three decision rules: 12 of 12, 10 of 12, 8 of 12. In an effort to achieve external validity, they tried to make the simulation as realistic as possible. Despite their efforts, the limitations of simulation research still applied—with the largest restriction being that mock jurors know that their verdict does not have real consequences. Given those limitations, the research showed that unanimous juries required more time to complete deliberations. Further analyses revealed that unanimous juries and majority juries go through much the same phases, in the same sequence, in the decision-making process, only the majority juries do so more quickly. The research found that the pattern of verdict decisions were indistinguishable between unanimous and majority juries. Lastly, the research showed that all jurors (both the prevailing majority and the minority) in majority juries were less satisfied with the deliberation process than were members of unanimous decision-rule juries. Part of the jurors' satisfaction resulted from the fact that in unanimous juries small minorities were more likely to speak, thus ensuring that opposing points of view would be heard. In majority juries, the opinions of small minorities had relatively little impact on the deliberation process since ultimately their votes might not have affected the final verdict. Because of this tendency for minorities in unanimous juries to speak out, first-ballot reversals were more likely to occur in unanimous-rule juries. From this set of results, Hastie and his colleagues concluded that the evidence argues that the unanimous-rule jury best realizes due process—defined as hearing a variety of community sentiments.

VI. JURIES AND THE DEFENSE OF INSANITY

On June 21, 1982, John Hinckley was cleared of 13 charges stemming from the attempted assassination of President Reagan. John Hinckley was found *not guilty by reason of insanity*. Much of the ensuing controversy stemmed from the legal system's belief that individuals should not be held accountable for crimes committed as a function of one's mental incompetence—which is legally determined by one of several standards. The McNaughtan rule, sometimes called the right–wrong test, is employed to this day as the standard in many insanity trials in Britain and the United States. The rule reads as follows: "At the time of committing the act, the party accused was laboring under such a defect of reason from disease of the mind as not to know the nature and quality of the act he was doing, or if he did know it, that he did not know what he was doing was wrong." The Durham rule, proposed in 1954 in response to criticisms of the McNaughtan rule, states that: "An accused is not criminally responsible if his unlawful act was the product of mental disease or mental defect."

The Durham rule, used in some jurisdictions, broadened the grounds for an insanity verdict. No longer did the defense have to prove the narrow right versus wrong criterion of the McNaughtan rule. Under Durham, it was sufficient merely to establish that criminal conduct was produced by mental disease. The Durham rule was problematic because mental disease criteria were difficult for juries to apply consistently, and psychiatric evidence was often too technical and confusing to clarify the judgment criteria. In some jurisdictions, the Durham rule was replaced with the American Law Institute's (ALI) Model Penal Code definition of legal insanity. The ALI Rule states that "A person is not responsible for criminal conduct if at the time of such conduct as a result of mental disease or defect he lacks substantial capacity to appreciate the wrongfulness of his conduct or to conform his conduct to the require-

ments of the law." This definition was employed in the Hinckley case.

The unpopularity of the Hinckley decision has contributed to the debate of what actions ought to be excusable by reason of insanity. Psychological research has focused on two aspects of how jurors respond in insanity cases. First, researchers were interested in whether jurors responded differently to different legal definitions of insanity. The research evidence, primarily from jury simulation studies, suggests that the importance of the wording of legal instruction in insanity cases tends to be overstated. That is to say, that verdicts rendered in jury simulation studies tend not to vary systematically with respect to the legal standard of insanity. Reasons why the specific form of legal instruction has relatively little impact include: jurors do not understand the subtle differences in the instructions, jurors understand the instructions but ignore them, and the people found insane under one rule meet the criteria for all standards. The research is far from conclusive, but suggests that each of these factors has a role in minimizing the effects of different legal standards of insanity. Largely due to the issues surrounding the assessment of mental disease, psychiatrists and clinical psychologists became in great demand, since their testimony was necessary to provide the existence of mental disease.

The second area of concern focused on jurors' evaluation of psychiatric testimony. The opposing sides argue either that juries cannot understand psychiatric testimony and therefore do not give it enough consideration or that juries are so impressed by the psychiatrists' credentials that they give their testimony too much weight. The research has not demonstrated that juries' evaluations of psychiatric testimony are inappropriate. Additionally, many legal scholars feel that the adversarial system may be the best forum for the airing of honest differences of opinion.

VII. SUMMARY

In conclusion, critics have argued that the jury system fails on many grounds, primarily because juries are judged to be incompetent, prejudiced, and unreliable. Our best research refutes those claims. The data from hundreds of jury trials, empirical studies, jury simulations, and archival searches suggest that juries are not incompetent. There are instances when judges and juries have disagreed, but these disagreements are more often attributable to factors other than juror incompetence. In those cases where juries deviate from what the judge would have decided, that deviation usually results from the jury's different sense of justice rather than from jury incompetence. Admittedly, there are limitations to simulated jury research: volunteer subjects may not be representative of actual juries, mock trials usually involve simulated trials or condensed transcripts and may not be representative of actual trials, and mock trials do not involve the real consequences of an actual trial. Despite the legal, ethical, and practical constraints inherent in jury psychology research, laboratory research continues to be relevant and useful.

In fact, field and experimental research offer the best opportunities to improve our understanding of the dynamics of jury psychology.

Bibliography

Fukurai, H., Butler, E. W., and Krooth, R. (1993). ''Race and the Jury.'' Plenum, New York.

Hans, V. P., and Vidmar, N. (1986). ''Judging the Jury.'' Plenum, New York.

Loftus, E., and Ketcham, K. (1991). ''Witness for the Defense: The Accused, the Eyewitness, and the Expert Who Puts Memory on Trial.'' St. Martin's Press, New York.

Tyler, T. (1990). ''Why People Obey the Law.'' Yale University Press, New Haven.

LANGUAGE DEVELOPMENT

Rose A. Sevcik and Mary Ann Romski

Georgia State University

Glossary

Grammar Composed of morphology (the study of the smallest units of meaning) and syntax (the rules governing the ordering of elements into phrases, clauses, and sentences).

Phonology Study of speech sounds, their production, and how they function in the language system.

Pragmatics Study of rules governing the use of language in context.

Semantics Study of meaning (i.e., the relationship between a speaker's language and his or her perception of reality).

LANGUAGE is a socially shared code or conventional system for representing concepts through the use of arbitrary symbols and rule-governed combinations of symbols. It is typically divided into four components: grammar (comprising morphology and syntax), phonology, pragmatics, and semantics. For decades behavioral and biological disciplines alike have focused investigative energies on the study of language, its origins, and its development. In this article the varied aspects of language that have been addressed during the last two decades are highlighted.

I. LANGUAGE DEVELOPMENT THEORIES

The modern study of child language development has focused on exploring the processes by which children acquire language. The theories that account for development have generated a significant amount of lively debate.

A. Traditional Perspectives

The theories of language acquisition proposed by Skinner, a behaviorist, and his contemporary, Chomsky, a linguist, in the late 1950s provided a foundation for debates about how language is acquired. Skinner's original theory argued vigorously that adult language skills were shaped almost solely by the environment. Chomsky's theory, on the other hand, emphasized the importance of linguistic structure and asserted that language (i.e., linguistic structure) was an innate capacity unique to humans. A child, he argued, was born with a biological capacity for learning rules for combining words. For Chomsky the environment played a relatively minor role in the way children learned to speak in sentences. Piaget, a Swiss genetic epistemologist, offered a third account of language development. His theory placed language development within a more general framework of cognitive development and suggests that children map language onto what they already know about their world conceptually. Many alternative explanations have since been advanced to prove, disprove, or modify these theories to some degree.

B. Contemporary Accounts

In the early 1970s many scholars objected to the intense emphasis on formal linguistic structure, particularly in relation to the way it accounted for initial language development. The primacy of syntax gave way to a broadening interest in the early acquisition of words themselves and the communicative context in which children learned to talk. It was argued that the meanings of words and the social conventions for using language played roles as important as learning the rules for combining words. The 1970s saw a proliferation of empirical studies that sought to resolve some of these issues.

More recently, there has been a renewed interest in linguistic structure and its learnability. Chomsky's earlier notions have been refined in the form of learnability theory. This theory asserts that if language is acquired by learning syntactic rules, then those rules must, in some sense, be grasped from the linguistic data provided by the child's environment. A trend toward an examination of children's lexicons, with an emphasis on verbs and their role in learnability, is apparent in the current literature.

A contemporary competing viewpoint to language learnability theory, which accounts for the social component of language, is derived from the parallel distributed processing informational model. This model emphasizes both structural and social functions in language learning. The proponents argue that linguistic structure emerges from the communicative function served by the structure. In this model, the only innate structure necessary is the powerful parallel distributed processing learning mechanism.

Theories that account for the emergence of a competent adult language user are plentiful. However, the explorations of language learning are far from complete. For every argument there is a counterargument with contradictory evidence. Theoretical as well as empirical investigations of the language acquisition process will most definitely continue to generate significant debate as scientists wrestle with the explanations for our complex system of communication.

II. BIOLOGICAL BASES OF LANGUAGE DEVELOPMENT

Implicit within the theories that include an innate component is the notion of the biological base for language development. Two broad issues emerge concerning the biological foundations: the relationship between language and its correlates in the brain,

as observed during human discourse, and the potential biological uniqueness of language to our species.

A. Neurological Correlates

While language itself is an observable phenomenon, a large quantity of research has focused on specifying the relationships between the actual behavior and its correlates in the brain. It is estimated that in about 85% of the population language resides in the left cerebral hemisphere of the brain. The most common method of investigating language laterality has been dichotic listening. In this experimental paradigm, different auditory material is simultaneously presented to each ear, and differences in response or error rate are noted. Research findings suggest a right ear, or left hemisphere, advantage for the processing of linguistic information. Specific structures in the human cerebral cortex (e.g., Broca's area, Wernicke's area) are also known to be associated with particular aspects of adult language. Recent evidence suggests that the right hemisphere of the brain also plays a role in controlling language, most likely the emotional dimensions.

In the late 1960s it was proposed that there is a critical period during which language development could occur. Lateralization for language would take place by puberty, and after that language could no longer be acquired. Recent advances in technology have permitted more sophisticated investigations of brain–language behavior relationships during the developmental process. Using electrophysiological procedures (i.e., auditory-evoked potentials), it was shown that children as young as 16 months can discriminate known from unknown spoken words and that these effects are lateralized in the brain.

The use of such refined methodologies suggests that language lateralization under typical conditions takes place well before puberty, or, in fact, is probably complete at birth. In the late 1970s, the language development of an adolescent named Genie, who had spent her childhood isolated in a small room in her parents' home, was examined. Even given intense instruction, Genie, an adolescent, did not master more advanced language structures typical of young children. These findings provided additional support for the early lateralization of language. Even though brain–behavior research has advanced considerably over the last two decades, understanding of the relationship between the brain and observable language behavior will continue to evolve as our methodologies become more sophisticated.

B. Language Origins

Questions about the biological bases of language development have generated two lines of inquiry about its origins. Some scientists have examined the natural communication systems of other creatures to provide a comparative perspective about the evolution of our auditory language system. Another area of investigation that has received intense scrutiny in the last two decades is language training research with marine animals and great apes.

Research has explored the natural communication systems of a wide range of animals. While earlier work focused on bee communication and bird song, more recently scientists have studied the vocalization systems of lower primates. It was found that the alarm calls of the vervet monkey (*Cercopithecus aethiops*) in the natural environment convey specific information about either the type of predator that is nearby or the type of evasive action the monkey should take to avoid the specific predator. Such findings suggest that animals have elaborate systems of natural communication that facilitate survival in their respective habitats.

A second route for studying animal communication has been to teach components of human language and communication to marine animals and great apes. It has been possible to teach bottlenose dolphins (*Tursiops truncatus*) to carry out complex commands presented via either computer-generated acoustic signals or a gestural language. These dolphins were able to carry out novel auditory or visual commands. Two California sea lions (*Zalophus californianus*) were taught a gestural language similar to the one used with bottlenose dolphins. Here, too, carrying out commands was the desired response. At the end of 2 years, the sea lions had learned approximately 20 gestures and were responding to them by carrying out three-item commands. While these studies, in concert, suggest that marine animals are capable of responding to gestural or acoustic patterns, the animals themselves did not generate spontaneous linguistic communication as we know it.

Young common chimpanzees (*Pan troglodytes*) do not have the specialized physical mechanisms necessary to produce speech. However, they have the capacity to learn alternative communication systems, such as complex manual signs or computer-based visual-graphic symbols.

In the late 1970s new research sparked debate concerning the earlier findings on the language abilities of the great ape and whether other explanations could account for these findings. While questions were raised as to the apes grasp of syntax, convincing evidence was obtained that two common chimpanzees could acquire word meanings and use computer-based visual-graphic symbols to convey information to humans as well as to each other.

Recently, research efforts have focused on the language learning abilities of the rare bonobo or pygmy chimpanzee (*Pan paniscus*). Findings from a young male bonobo have revealed that he learned symbols via observation rather than through intense training efforts like those used in earlier studies. In addition, he demonstrated understanding of spoken words. A recent study further revealed that this young male bonobo also understands novel combinatorial information and suggests that the bonobo's speech comprehension skills could far exceed their symbol production abilities. These findings have been replicated with additional infant bonobos and suggest that the capacities for auditory language comprehension might not be completely unique to humans.

The compelling findings of the last decade, then, suggest that great apes share at least some of the components that permit the emergence of language competence in humans. The future should reveal more detailed explanations about the origins of language, as well as the differential capacities of various mammalian species to learn language.

III. CURRENT PERSPECTIVES ABOUT THE LANGUAGE DEVELOPMENT PROCESS

Anyone observing a child beginning to talk will agree that it is a most remarkable process. While one might receive the impression that the child becomes a competent communicator overnight, a careful review of the evidence suggests that this perception is misleading.

A. Language in Infancy

Infants actually begin communicating very early. Research over the last decade suggests that the stage for language development emerges from birth. Advances in methodologies have permitted scientists to measure changes in the physiological state (e.g., heart rate) and correlate them with environmental changes (e.g., the mother's voice versus a stranger's voice). Mothers seem to interpret what their infants want from early in the infant's life. Thus, even though infants are not talking, their behaviors are interpreted as communication by their mothers. As infants proceed through their first year, they begin to perceive speech sounds and later to comprehend speech in the context of intonational, gestural, and facial cues. Concurrently, infants proceed through a series of stages during which their vocal abilities become more complex. Before youngsters are 9 months of age, they are using their vocalizations and gestures to communicate a variety of intents to their caregivers.

B. Development of Meaning

Infant communicative interactions lead to the use of first words and to examinations of what these words mean. Of all of the language subsystems, semantics is most closely tied to cognitive development and what a child knows about his or her world. The conceptual basis of a child's early word meanings has generated considerable debate in the language acquisition literature. A semantic feature theory suggested that early word acquisition is based on perceptual attributes. For example, the word "doggie" might be used to refer to all four-legged animals, based on the four legged characteristic of dogs, cats, cows, and the like. A relational theory argued that the child's meaning of words is initially based on functional relationships, followed by a perceptual analysis. According to a prototype theory, semantic categories are not organized by a single defining feature, but by categories occurring at both a basic object level and a superordinate level. [See CATEGORIZATION; SEMANTICS.]

More contemporary debate has focused on the findings of systematic experimental studies, as well as the methodological issues related to the way children use words, especially concrete words, such as nouns. Recently, some attention has been given to the role of relational words and verbs in the language acquisition process as well.

Children's vocabularies expand at an amazingly rapid rate. By the time they reach school age, children have acquired vocabularies of more than 8000 words. One recent theoretical explanation for this remarkable process is described as fast mapping. Researchers have hypothesized that children quickly recognize a word as a word, know something about its grammatical role, and have a partial sense of the word's meaning after only brief exposure to it. While learning individual words is a continuing process throughout the lifespan, children quickly learn to combine words to create more complex communications.

For some time television was not thought to have a significant role in language learning. With the impact of television on modern society, empirical studies are suggesting that some types of television viewing could facilitate the language acquisition process. For example, novel words can be learned via viewing some specially designed children's television sequences. Investigations in this area are continuing.

C. Syntactic Development

Because syntax has been central to linguistic theories of language acquisition, intense emphasis has been placed on studying the unfolding of syntactic skills. Empirical data have advanced significantly since the pioneering research of Roger Brown, who studied the early language development of three young children. Brown provided a detailed analysis of their early development of grammatical morphemes (e.g., present progressive tense marker "-ing"), which has served as a basis for much of the later empirical work in this area of investigation. Brown devised a measure, termed mean length of utterance in morphemes, to serve as an index of early syntactic growth. When children produce longer sentences, the type and the complexity of the sentences expand as well. As syntactic development continues into the school years, the production of more complex grammatical constructions (e.g., passive constructions, coordinations, and relative clauses) emerge.

Traditionally, the empirical study of syntax has focused on spontaneous speech production skills, with relatively minimal attention on comprehension. In a few studies the production of sentences actually preceded comprehension of them. Using a creative behavioral testing methodology, it has been shown that infants as young as 17 months of age might comprehend word order before they even begin to produce two-word utterances. Such findings suggest that the young child is absorbing a large amount of sophisticated linguistic information at a very young age, and perhaps such comprehension is setting the stage for later productive syntactic abilities. [See SENTENCE PROCESSING; SYNTAX.]

D. Later Development of Oral and Written Language

As the child progresses through school, important syntactic and vocabulary skills continue to develop.

Not until adolescence are some figurative language concepts (e.g., metaphors and idioms) completely mastered.

Oral language skills are the basis from which literacy skills emerge. The development of literacy skills is now thought to be a gradual process that begins in infancy, when most infants and toddlers enjoy book reading. Long before some children begin school, they are immersed in activities that permit the development of an awareness of print uses and conventions.

Literacy has multiple interwoven dimensions, from reading comprehension to the mechanisms of written language production (e.g., spelling and punctuation), which must be in place to produce a literate individual. The development of reading skills is thought to result from a synthesis of a complex network of perceptual and cognitive acts along a continuum from word recognition and decoding skills to comprehension and integration. Writing skills include the development of the mechanics of written productions as well as expository writing skills. [See PHONOLOGICAL PROCESSING AND READING; READING.]

Literacy is a dominant social policy issue today. Efforts are under way to increase literacy awareness in general. Because a large number of adults are functionally illiterate, special attention is being given to adult literacy. While some individuals have not had adequate instruction or opportunity to learn to read, others show evidence of developmental dyslexia. This term refers to the continuum of impairments in the acquisition and development of reading and writing skills despite instruction and opportunity. The scientific study of these impairments offers valuable insight into the developmental reading process.

E. Language Learning through the Lifespan

While it was once thought that language learning was complete by the end of childhood, current views suggest that learning language is an evolving process that continues and changes, albeit subtly, across the lifespan. Adolescents and adults can acquire a variety of language skills, coherent writing skills, and social polite language conventions. These skills are typically not formally learned, but instead are acquired in context.

The multicultural nature of society highlights the consideration of second language acquisition across the lifespan. Children exposed to two languages during early childhood appear to learn both languages with a minimum of delay. The key to their bilingual development seems to be the pattern of use within the language community. Even young monolingual children can learn a second language relatively easily, and the sequence of second language development mirrors that found in the acquisition of the initial language. Second language learning is sometimes not as facile for adolescents and adults as it is for young children. [See BILINGUALISM.]

Another multicultural issue that emerges during the school years and continues into adulthood is dialect. Dialects are associated with relatively stable characteristics of the speaker (e.g., race, gender, age, social class, and geographic origin). Adults' language use can be greatly influenced by the social contexts in which they communicate. While some speakers use one dialect exclusively during their lifetime, others might find it necessary to learn more than one dialect. Variations in language use might also take place in business and social situations. For example, a speaker might use different registers in conversation based on the gender of the listener.

With an aging population, changes that take place in language as a part of the natural aging process are becoming an increasing focus of investigation. Access to the vocabulary frequently described as "word finding" becomes more difficult as we age. Changes in the ability to understand complex linguistic materials and to use complex syntactic forms also occur. While we currently know little about the effects the typical aging process has on language, the shifting population dynamics will likely result in continued emphasis on this particular area of investigation.

IV. LANGUAGE DEVELOPMENT AND BREAKDOWN IN SPECIAL POPULATIONS

Given the importance placed on language by society, it is of particular consequence when language is in some way impaired, be it at birth or after it has already been acquired. Studying the language patterns of these special populations provides scientists with a unique route for understanding the language learning process and the relationship between the brain and behavior.

A. Congenital Language Disabilities

Researchers have estimated that 8–10% of school-aged children demonstrate patterns of language development that might be termed "delayed" or "disordered." Any number of congenital disabilities can contribute to an impairment of language, including autism, cerebral palsy, mental retardation, sensory impairments (i.e., deafness), and specific language impairment. Each of these disabilities may have a unique detrimental effect on language acquisition. The type of impairment, its severity, the age of the child at the time of detection, and the child's environment interact to determine the seriousness of the language impairment across the lifespan.

Intervention research has advanced the treatment of congenital language disabilities considerably. Children who, 20 years ago, were not given an optimistic prognosis for language development are now making impressive gains in learning to communicate. One of the most significant advances of this decade relates to the integration of advancing computer technology into treatment approaches for severe congenital language disabilities.

Augmentative communication systems permit children who have not learned to speak (e.g., those with cerebral palsy or mental retardation) to communicate via alternative output modes. Advances in synthetic speech intelligibility have provided an interface between their means of communication and our otherwise auditory world. When technology is paired with experimentally validated treatment approaches, children who were previously unable to communicate develop functional means of language expression.

B. Acquired Language Disabilities

After an individual has developed language, a variety of events, including strokes, progressive neurological diseases, and traumatic brain injuries, can impair language skills. Characterizing the language deficits associated with these various acquired disorders has been a focus of considerable investigation. Research with human adult brains that have suffered cerebral insults clearly indicates that specific areas of the cerebral cortex are associated with specific aspects of adult language. Loss of previously acquired language due to brain damage, known as aphasia, has been divided into several types, based on the site of lesion and the person's residual receptive and productive language skills. For example, Broca's aphasia is primarily an impairment of ex-

pressive grammatical abilities associated with frontal lobe damage specifically to Broca's area. Specific language disorders associated with dementing diseases (e.g., Alzheimer's disease) frequently resemble aphasia during the early stages. As the dementia progresses, the language disturbance is much different from aphasia, as it is the result of more widespread damage to the brain. Advancing diagnostic tools permit scientists to gain an increasingly sophisticated understanding of neurological impairment and language breakdown. [*See* ALZHEIMER'S DISEASE; APHASIA.]

V. CONCLUSIONS

In conclusion, language development is an amazing and extremely complex process that unfolds not only in infancy, but over the course of the lifespan. Our collective knowledge about the biological bases of language, the process of language development in children, and the language of special populations has advanced significantly over the last two decades. Probing and creative questions, coupled with more sophisticated methodologies, frequently using advanced computer technology, have permitted scientists to uncover previously unattainable information. Even so, the theoretical and empirical data bases are far from complete. Scientific investigation about language processes should easily continue into the 21st century.

Acknowledgments

The preparation of this article was supported by National Institute of Child Health and Human Development Grant 06016, which supports the Language Research Center, Georgia State University.

Bibliography

Adamson, L. B. (in press). "Communication Development during Infancy." Brown & Benchmark, Madison, WI.
Berko-Gleason, J. (1989). "The Development of Language." Merrill, Columbus, OH.
Kaiser, A., and Gray, D. (1992). "Enhancing Children's Communication: Research Foundations for Intervention." Paul H. Brookes, Baltimore, MD.
Savage-Rumbaugh, E. S., Murphy, J., Sevcik, R. A., Brakke, K., Williams, S., and Rumbaugh, D. (1993). Language comprehension in ape and child. *Monogr. Soc. Res. Child Dev.* (Serial No. 233) **58**(3–4).

LEADERSHIP

Martin M. Chemers
Claremont McKenna College

Glossary

Charisma A leader's ability to appear extraordinarily gifted.

Contingency theory Approach that argues that the relationship between the leader's behavior and group performance depends on situational characteristics.

Expectancy theory Theory of motivation stressing the individual's perception that effort will result in the attainment of desirable outcomes.

Idiosyncrasy credit Status credit that a group member earns by demonstrating task-related competence and loyalty to group norms and values.

Implicit leadership theory Observers have unstated assumptions about the nature of leadership that influence their judgments of leaders.

Intrinsic motivation Motivational properties inherent in a task, but not influenced by external rewards.

Values Orientations toward what is considered desirable by social actors.

LEADERSHIP can be described as a process of social influence through which a person can enlist the aid of others in attaining a goal or accomplishing a mission. Effective leadership involves the ability to gain the trust and enthusiastic support of followers and the ability to direct follower effort toward objectives. Apparent contradictions and inconsistencies in contemporary views of leadership are discussed, and a functional approach to theoretical integration is offered.

I. INTRODUCTION

It is an axiom in the study of group effectiveness that groups are less efficient than individuals working alone. These inefficiencies, sometimes called "coordination decrements," result from the fact that for groups to achieve their full potential, that is to utilize all the talents and resources available to them, a number of crucial processes must be maintained. Group members must be motivated to engage in goal-directed activity. Members must communicate with one another to share information. Finally, the activities of individual members must be coordinated toward goal attainment. Each of these processes requires time and energy. [*See* GROUP DYNAMICS.]

Given the costs of maintaining effective groups, it is clear that the major reason for composing groups is that the tasks confronting an organization or society cannot be accomplished by individuals. However, once individuals have been collected into groups and groups into larger organizations, the success of these aggregations depends upon the fulfillment of two vital functions.

The first of these functions is directed toward maintaining the internal integrity of the group and can be called *internal maintenance*. The objectives of internal maintenance are to develop an orderliness in group activities that facilitates the motivation, communication, and coordination of group member activities. These objectives are realized in terms of (1) reliability, i.e., ensuring that key group tasks and procedures are carried out in a uniform manner; (2) predictability, i.e., allowing members to anticipate one another's actions; and (3) accountability, i.e., providing a mechanism for rewarding appropriate or correcting inappropriate actions. The focus of the internal maintenance function is necessarily on standardization and conformity.

The second crucial function of effective organization is directed toward making the group responsive to changing conditions in the surrounding environment. This function, *external adaptability*, is concerned with (1) sensitivity, i.e., the ability of the group to notice changes in important external elements; (2) flexibility, i.e., the capability of the group to modify its goals and procedures; and (3) responsiveness, i.e., the propensity to align internal goals and processes to external environmental demands. For example, a manufacturing organization might develop new products in the face of changes in demand or the availability of supplies.

It is a sad and often ignored fact of organizational life that these two functions are contradictory and oppositional. Factors which help to make a group more orderly and reliable reduce its flexibility and responsiveness and vice versa. The survival and success of an organization depend on its ability to balance these two functions, choosing the trade-off between stability and change that is appropriate for the group's goals and the demands of the environment.

The organizational answer to this dilemma is leadership. The function of leaders is to help the group or organization manage the balance between internal maintenance and external adaptability. When groups differentiate their members according to status, they do so in order to place the most competent members of the group in positions of greatest responsibility. This is an attempt to align the group's resources, i.e., talents, with the demands of its tasks and environment. Leaders are then usually given authority commensurate with their responsibilities. This provides the leader with a mechanism to influence other members of the group to enhance motivation, communication, and coordination. Typically, leaders are also given rewards to compensate them for the extra effort involved in responsible activities and to encourage them to accept leadership positions.

The rewards and power that the leader is given enhance visibility and focus follower attention. The leader can serve as a role model for others in the group. Thus, the leader's behavior helps to define normative group behavior. The leader's ability to organize and direct the work of followers and to provide a standard for behavior helps to ensure commonality of action and promotes the orderliness necessary for internal maintenance.

However, the bases for status bestowal are rooted in the past. Individuals are accorded status for evidence of competence on tasks that have confronted the group in the past and for conformity to the group's values, norms, and traditions. The focus on past performance and conformity has the tendency

to encourage stability and even stagnation. Groups must also build into their operational processes mechanisms by which innovation can be introduced to ensure external adaptability. As Edwin Hollander's idiosyncrasy credit model has shown, status enhancement, i.e., leadership, is again the process through which this function is accomplished. Individuals who have been recognized for their competence and their loyalty to group values gain increased influence that allows them to introduce new ideas and behaviors into the group's repertoire.

The positive aspects of status and leadership, then, include the harnessing of competent individuals to important group activities, the distribution of authority and reward to enhance leader influence, the role modeling of normative behavior, and the facilitation of innovation and change. Unfortunately, the positive potential of leadership status is matched by a negative side.

The rewards and satisfactions associated with high status, whether material or psychological, can create anxiety about the loss of status or a preoccupation with increasing one's status and attendent benefits. Status anxiety can lead to a number of maladaptive group phenomena. Individuals may try to manipulate perceptions of their competence and contributions to group success. Status differentials in groups can distort communication systems, resulting in the reduction in the accuracy or distribution of critical information.

Those in positions of power can abuse their authority to maintain or enhance their power and solidify their position of privilege. Such activities divert energy away from goal accomplishment and can suborn the processes of status systems to identify and elevate the most competent group members. Some authors have referred to some of these negative aspects of leadership as "the dark side of charisma."

Truly effective leadership, leadership that serves the interests of the group and organization, represents a balance between a number of opposing functions. The needs for stability, predictability, and order must be balanced against the need for change, responsiveness, and innovation. In accomplishing these contradictory objectives, the leader must, on one hand, motivate and direct followers to carry out assigned tasks, and on the other hand, create an environment where information and debate can enhance decision making and creativity. To accomplish this tall order the leader must also balance the positive uses of authority and influence with the dangerous, self-serving potential inherent in positions of power and persuasion.

Understanding the nature of the complexity of effective leadership requires a broad theoretical sweep buttressed by sound empirical evidence. The sections that follow will present an overview of the major streams of research and theorizing on leadership. Finally, a functional model of leadership will be offered in an attempt to identify the common themes in the literature.

II. HISTORICAL REVIEW

Social theorists and philosophers have long recognized the importance of leadership to successful organizational performance. The scientific, empirical study of leadership, however, dates from the early part of the 20th century. The initial approaches tended to be, understandably, somewhat simplistic and not very productive.

A. Traits

The earliest approach to leadership emergence and effectiveness was rooted in the view that leadership was something that people (mostly men) "had." Philosophical views had expounded the notion of the "Great Man" as leader, rising to positions of prominence and influence based on inborn capabilities manifested regardless of time or place. The translation of these assumptions into a research methodology resulted in the search for the trait or constellation of traits that would differentiate leaders from nonleaders and effective from ineffective leaders. [*See* TRAITS.]

In 1948, Stogdill reviewed the results of three decades of research comprising over 100 studies of leadership traits. He concluded that while some traits, like intelligence, were frequently associated with leadership (i.e., about half the studies show significant differences in intelligence between leaders and followers), no trait was universally associated with leadership. Subsequent reviews reached similar conclusions.

Stogdill's analysis had a chilling effect on personality research related to leadership, in part because students of the field failed to pay close enough attention to what Stogdill actually said. He did not say that personality traits or other stable aspects of the individual played no role in leadership, but rather that the effects of traits needed to be considered in interaction with situational aspects, such as group composition, tasks, and authority relations.

It should be noted that more recent research on trait effects in leadership has shown that stable aspects of individual personality have reliable, long-lasting, and nontrivial effects on leadership behavior or managerial performance. These findings do not, however, bear directly on the intent of those early researchers to find a trait, that not only affected leadership, but defined it.

B. Behaviors

Following World War II, interest in social psychology became focused on observable behavior more than on internal traits or processes. In leadership work, behavioral research attempted to identify what it was that leaders actually did. A variety of approaches were taken.

At Ohio State University, scales were developed to measure the incidence of and relationships among various leader behaviors. Research with the leader behavior description questionnaire (LBDQ) revealed that a large percentage of leadership behavior fell into two distinct categories or factors. *Consideration* behaviors reflected the leader's attempts to maintain a congenial relationship with subordinates and a positive social atmosphere in the work group. This factor included behaviors like being friendly and considerate of feelings and looking out for the welfare of subordinates. The other major factor, *initiation of structure*, included leader behaviors intended to move the work group toward task completion by direction and exhortation. Behaviors related to assigning job duties and monitoring their completion fell into this category of behavior.

Interview studies conducted by scientists at the University of Michigan under the direction of Rensis Likert found that descriptions of first line supervisors by their subordinates could be grouped into two general types. "Employee-centered" bosses were described as sociable types who looked out for their workers, while "job-centered" supervisors emphasized high productivity and spent much of their time planning and organizing the work. The parallels between the supervisory styles observed in the Michigan studies and the LBDQ factors were apparent.

Using yet another methodology, Bales and his colleagues at Harvard observed and coded the behavior of college students in problem-solving groups. They identified two types of individuals who played active and influential roles in the groups. One type, labeled "socio-emotional specialists" made comments aimed at maintaining a positive climate in the groups and encouraging participation by all members. "Task-specialists" spent more time focusing on getting the group's task accomplished. The extent to which these studies and others seemed to yield similar results was heartening to researchers seeking some common ground on which to build research and theory.

Unfortunately, attempts to relate task and relationship directed behaviors to important group or organizational outcomes yielded decidedly mixed results. In retrospect, we can see that this approach to leadership while moving in more productive directions was still somewhat simplistic. Since leadership involves a task to be accomplished and people with whom to work, it seems logical that leader behavior would include aspects directed toward task concerns and aspects related to interpersonal or morale issues. However, investigators were still failing to attend to Stogdill's admonition to include situational factors in explanations of leadership effects. Behaviors, like the traits that spawn them, do not operate in a vacuum.

C. Situational Factors

While most of the early research was focused on the leader, a few studies of situational variables were conducted. These studies were not organized into a coherent body of work, but revealed some strong effects.

A number of studies showed that spatial factors, whether physical or psychological, could affect leader emergence and influence. Laboratory studies of communication networks reported that centrality was associated with perceived influence. A similar finding was reported for position in the communication networks of military crews and other types of teams. Several studies indicated that spatial arrangement of persons sitting at a discussion table affected leadership emergence. Again, centrality, whether in terms of ability to make eye contact with more group members or a central seat at the table, resulted in greater probability of emergent leadership. In a comprehensive review of small group research published in 1966, McGrath and Altman pointed out that the most powerful way of changing a leader's behavior was to change the task on which the group was working.

Not surprisingly, another very powerful factor affecting leadership process is the nature of the followers. Studies have shown that the personality or attitudes of group members affected their choice of or

satisfaction with leaders. The amount of support that followers give to a leader's influence attempts has strong effects on subsequent leader behavior.

The situational studies, while interesting and informative, did not provide a sufficient rubric to take leadership theory to its next explanatory plateau. Dissatisfaction with the trait and behavioral approaches, however, made the field ripe for a new theoretical paradigm. The modern era of leadership research dawned with the publication of the exciting and controversial "contingency" theories.

III. CONTEMPORARY APPROACHES

The period from the middle 1960s to the present, while marked by several shifts and changes in emphasis, maintains a continuity of research approach. The theories and empirical work during the last three decades will be reviewed here by topical area. Five major approaches will be discussed. These include the contingency, transactional, transformational, cognitive, and cultural/gender theoretical approaches. The final section of the article will present a model for integrating the contemporary approaches in terms of the major functions associated with effective leadership.

A. Contingency Approaches

1. The Contingency Model

A dramatic shift in approach was instigated by the publication in 1967 of Fred Fiedler's work on the "contingency model of leadership effectiveness." This model, which stressed the interaction of leader personality and situational characteristics, was inductively derived from the results of an extensive research program. The centerpiece of the program was a measure, the "least preferred co-worker" (LPC) scale that assessed the degree of pervasive negativity in a person's rating of the most unproductive co-worker with whom they had ever worked.

A considerable body of research evidence suggests that the measure taps into the relative importance that the respondent places on task versus relationship success in group activities. Raters who reveal an intensely negative reaction to the poor co-worker tend to value task success and respond very favorably to the orderly situations and cooperative co-workers who help to ensure that success. Raters who give a more favorable rating to the least preferred co-worker derive satisfaction and esteem from the positive regard of and harmonious relationships with co-workers.

When Fiedler found that the relative success of these leader types shifted from one study to another (a finding quite in keeping with the historical problem of this area), he followed Stogdill's admonition and sought to identify situational modifiers of the relationship between leader motivation and group performance. He found that three characteristics of the leader's situation could be combined into a dimension reflecting the degree of predictability, certainty, and control that the situation offered to the leader. These three factors, in order of importance, were (1) the cooperation and support of followers, (2) the degree of clarity and structure in the group's task, and (3) the leader's formal authority. The dimension, labeled originally "situational favorableness" and subsequently "situational control" provided a reliable moderator of leadership effects. Task-motivated leaders, with their emphasis on orderly procedures and somewhat directive style, were associated with high group productivity in highly controllable situations, where a predictable environment made orderly procedures efficient, and in extremely uncontrollable situations, in which a directive style helped to provide a basis for at least minimal goal-directed group activity. The relationship-motivated leaders, employing a more considerate and participative style, were at their best in situations of moderate control. In moderate control situations, the ambiguities created by a vague and unstructured task or a recalcitrant group of followers benefitted from an approach likely to generate a more harmonious environment conducive to creativity and problem solving.

Compelling support has been provided for the predictive validity of the model. Using meta-analysis to combine the results of over 100 tests of the model, Strube and Garcia reported extremely strong statistical support for the model's predictions. In another, somewhat more conservative meta-analysis, Peters, Hartke, and Pohlmann reached similar conclusions. Recently, research has shown that the predictions of the model with respect to group task productivity also hold for subordinate satisfaction and leader satisfaction, stress, and stress-related illness.

While the predictive validity of the model seems well supported, the most important area of omission for the contingency model is a clear explanation of the causal processes that result in differential performance and satisfaction across situations. Other leadership models, however, took the contingency approach in somewhat different directions in an attempt to explain leadership effectiveness.

2. Vroom and Yetton's Normative Decision Theory

The normative model of leadership decision making developed in 1973 by Victor Vroom and Phillip Yetton, combined the group performance work of Norman Maier with an emphasis on organizational efficiency. Maier had shown that when group members are allowed to participate in group decision making a number of positive outcomes ensue. The members are more motivated to engage in group activities and more committed to group action. This is sometimes referred to as the "subordinate acceptance" issue. Also, when more people are included in the decision-making process the amount of information and creative input is enhanced, referred to as the "quality issue."

However, as was pointed out in the first section of this article, groups are less efficient than individuals in analyzing problems and reaching decisions. The more democratic and participative the decision procedures are the greater is the potential for costly coordination decrements to encumber the process. The normative decision model attempts to balance the relative costs and benefits of participative procedures.

The model identifies three general classes of decision strategies: *autocratic,* in which the leader makes the decision alone either without seeking any information from subordinates (autocratic I) or with information (autocratic II); *consultative,* in which the leader makes the decision after sharing the problem and obtaining advice from subordinates, either individually (consultative I) or in a group setting (consultative II); and *group,* in which the leader and the group make the decision through participation and consensus (group II).

The situational contingencies that guide the choice of decision strategy include attributes that assess the leader's knowledge and understanding of the problem parameters, the supportiveness and reliability of the subordinates, and the relationships among the subordinates. A number of decision rules are promulgated to protect against making a decision that will be difficult to implement because of lack of follower support or cooperation or due to failure to have enough information to generate a high-quality (i.e., correct or creative) decision or solution. Finally, the time to make the decision is considered, and the most efficient strategy is chosen from among those strategies that protect other concerns.

Thus, if the leader is assured of making a good decision (knowledge and structure are adequate) and can count on united follower support, a relatively autocratic decision style is appropriate, because it is the most efficient. If the leader lacks important knowledge, a consultative style that elicits broader follower input and advice is warranted. When follower support is not assured, a participative style is chosen to increase subordinate commitment. When conflict among subordinates is likely, the model suggests that conflicts be discussed before making a decision, calling for a group meeting in the consultative II or group II style.

Although the normative decision model has not generated as much empirical validation research as Fiedler's contingency model, carefully done studies have found support for the model's predictions. Some field studies have been completed. In these studies, leaders were asked to specify which decision style they would use in response to 30 decision problems varying in situational characteristics. Leaders whose responses were consistent with the normative prescriptions of the model had significantly more productive and satisfied subordinates. The methodology in these field studies often suffers from the failure to assure that the styles that leaders say they use are indeed the same as they use in practice. However, laboratory experiments in which leaders were instructed as to which decision style to use also supported the model's predictions.

Certain parallels exist between the contingency model and the normative decision model. Both include situational variables reflecting the leader's support from followers and the leader's job-related knowledge and understanding. Both predict that when situations are relatively predictable, the more directive leaders fare well. In situations of greater ambiguity, lacking either subordinate commitment or task structure, more consultative and participative styles are suggested. The models diverge in the lowest control situations when both follower support and job knowledge are lacking. Here Fiedler predicts task-oriented, directive leadership while Vroom and Yetton favor participative procedures. This difference may be based on a short-term versus long-term perspective. Fiedler's data come primarily from group performance measures with a short time perspective in which directive action may help to forestall crisis, while Vroom and Yetton's theory is more concerned with long-range group and organizational success.

3. House's Path–Goal Theory

The third major contingency approach was developed by Robert House and his associates. Path–goal theory represented an amalgam of two streams of research, the Ohio State LBDQ studies of structuring and considerate leader behavior and the expectancy theory approach to motivation.

Path–goal theory hypothesized that leader behavior would have a positive effect on the psychological states of subordinates (i.e., motivation and satisfaction) to the extent that the behavior clarified and reinforced the paths to the subordinate's goals, i.e., by making the subordinate see how effort would result in good performance and desirable rewards. The type of leader behavior that would be effective was determined by characteristics of the subordinates and the task situation in which the subordinate was working.

The leader's function is a complementary one. Leader behaviors are considered to be beneficial to the extent that they replace factors missing in the subordinate's environment. In most research with this theory, the focus has been on the degree of structure provided in the subordinate's task. When the task lacks structure, structuring behaviors by the leader are expected to have positive effects; but when structure is present in the job, additional structuring by the leader is seen as overly close monitoring or production push and is expected to have a negative effect on subordinates. Considerate leader behavior is expected to have a positive effect when the subordinate's job is aversive or boring, but not when it is interesting and absorbing.

Empirical support for path–goal theory has been mixed. Research with this theory typically suffers from some common methodological problems. Frequently ratings of leader behavior and subordinate satisfaction are taken from the same person, the subordinate, and are subject to consistency or demand effects. Also, specifications of the situational characteristics have been quite inconsistent, including such disparate variables as job level, role ambiguity, or rated task structure.

Judith Komaki has argued that a problem with many theories of supervision or coaching is that the specification of what the leader actually should do to direct the work of a subordinate is far too vague. Growing out of reinforcement theory, Komaki's operant model of leadership specifies what good leaders must do. Several careful studies have shown that leaders who closely *monitor* subordinate performance and provide direct and meaningful *conse-*

quences for that performance have more productive subordinates.

Another potential reason for inconsistent results with path–goal theory may be that while the theory's exposition emphasized subordinate characteristics, most of the early research did not. However, a study by Griffin in 1981 showed that the subordinate's desire for an interesting and challenging job moderated the effects of leader behavior. Subordinates with strong growth needs did not find the leader's structuring behavior beneficial under any job characteristics, highlighting the importance of personal characteristics in the leader–follower relationship.

The contingency model, normative decision theory, and path–goal theory are the three most influential of the contingency theories, although other less well researched models offer similar theoretical formulations. All of these theories relate the leader's task or relationship orientation to the degree of clarity or predictability in the leadership situation.

An examination of the contingency theories reveals certain important differences as well as similarities. Two important distinctions are whether the leader is seen as capable of changing behavior or decision styles at will, as in normative decision theory and path–goal theory, or is constrained by personality predispositions as in the contingency model. This question is important, because there is evidence that leaders may have strong propensities toward a particular style or set of styles.

A second very significant contrast regards who is affected by the degree of structure and certainty in the environment. In the supervisory models that are focused on the subordinate, such as path–goal theory, it is the subordinate who has either sufficient or insufficient levels of structure. The supervisor is assumed always to have relevant job knowledge to dispense. However, in the more leader-oriented models of Vroom and Yetton and Fiedler, the degree of structure refers to the leader's knowledge and understanding. In the former case, we are talking about coaching, while in the latter, problem solving.

B. Transactional Approaches

1. Hollander's Idiosyncrasy Credit Theory

Predating the contingency theories, but still an important and relevant aspect of contemporary leadership theorizing are approaches that address the relationship between leader and led. Hollander's work on leader legitimacy indicates that follower judgments of the leader's competency, i.e., the leader's

past and future capability of moving the group toward its goal, and the leader's commitment and loyalty to group values, play a major role in the leader's latitude to influence follower attitudes and behavior. When leaders are seen as competent, loyal, and fair, their influence extends beyond simply inducing followers to expend effort on behalf of the group's mission. Enhanced influence adds to the leader's ability to introduce new ideas and innovations into the group's life. Recently, Hollander has shown how many contemporary theories of leadership that stress attributions about the leader's competency and charisma are rooted in leader legitimation concepts.

2. Graen's Vertical Dyad Linkage Model

In an attempt to explain the way that roles and responsibilities develop in organizational units, George Graen and his associates focus on the leader–subordinate dyad as the most prevalent and important building block. Vertical dyad linkage (VDL) theory argues that these dyadic relationships can vary in quality from high level exchanges, in which leader and follower function as partners, to very low level exchanges, in which the subordinate is treated like a "hired hand" and largely denied participation in decisions and opportunities for personal growth and development. Research has shown that better exchanges result in subordinates who are more satisfied, motivated, and committed to the organization.

The notion of a transactional relationship or exchange between leader and followers has also been developed in theories that address leader–follower relationships that transcend our ordinary notions of motivation and legitimacy. Such theories involve charismatic and transformational characteristics.

C. Transformational Approaches

In a biographical and philosophical analysis of several great leaders, historian and political scientist James McGregor Burns raised the distinction between "transactional" and "transformational" leaders. Transactional leaders motivated subordinates through quid pro quos that exchanged benefits like pay and promotion for subordinate effort and loyalty. Transformational leadership, however, was thought to transcend bargains and transformed subordinates into truly committed, intrinsically motivated contributors to the organizational mission. Burn's idea of the transformational leader was similar to Max Weber's notion of "charismatic" leader, which helped encourage and coalesce interest around the concept.

1. Charismatic Leadership

House's theory of charismatic leadership, first published in 1977, restated many of Weber's ideas in psychological terms emphasizing motivational constructs. House applied his model to historical leaders like Gandhi and Martin Luther King, Jr. In House's model, the charismatic leader's self-confidence and use of image management techniques establish legitimacy; and the leader's role modeling and high expectations for followers generate high levels of follower motivation.

A number of other theorists have addressed the concept of charismatic, visionary, or transformational leadership. These theories share many common notions. Transformational leaders demonstrate extremely high levels of competence and trustworthiness, in keeping with Hollander's idiosyncrasy credit notions. They behave in ways that reveal them to be extraordinarily committed to a well-articulated vision, self-confident and confident in others, and leading followers to goals that are of overarching and transcendant importance. Two of the most comprehensive and thoroughly developed of the transformational approaches, Bass' transformational leadership theory and House and Shamir's recently presented self-concept theory, will be dealt with in greater detail.

Unlike most transformational leadership theorists, Bass and his colleagues initially approached the construct from an inductive direction, amassing followers' descriptions of outstanding leaders in their experience. From these data, the multifactor leadership questionnaire (MLQ) was developed to differentiate aspects of transactional and transformational leadership.

The Bass model identifies seven leadership behavior factors that range from passive to active levels of involvement. The seven include three transactional factors—*laissez-faire* (do nothing) management; *management by exception*, in which leaders act only to correct mistakes; *contingent reward*, exchanges in which leaders provide appropriate tangible rewards for subordinate effort and accomplishment—and four transformational factors—*individualized consideration*, in which the leader provides specially targeted support and encouragement dependent on the needs of the subordinate (reminiscent of Graen's "high quality dyadic exchanges"); *intellectual stimulation*, in which followers are encouraged to grow and change; *inspirational vision*, i.e., emotionally appealing goal descriptions; and *idealized influence* or charisma, in which followers are induced to identify with the leader and the mission.

Data from a number of studies support the notion that while contingent reward and other active transactional leader behaviors can have beneficial effects on follower motivation, satisfaction, and performance, the truly exceptional effects are associated with the transformational factors. The body of evidence supporting tranformational leadership theory is quite impressive, but a few problems of interpretation remain. One question is whether the tranformational behaviors might simply reflect extremely effective manifestations of the more mundane transactional behavior like contingent reward and the LBDQ factors of structuring and consideration. Another problem shared by many descriptive models of leadership concerns the extent to which the behaviors attributed to outstanding leaders are accurate descriptions of specific behaviors or simply idealized responses to leaders who are liked and admired.

In an elegant attempt to go beyond description of the behaviors that are ascribed to transformational leaders and to explain the psychological processes that underlie charismatic leadership effects, Robert House and Boas Shamir have presented a self-concept theory. Building on path–goal theory's emphasis on aligning the followers' expectancies with the leader's or organization's mission, self-concept theory argues that transformational leaders induce their followers to attach their own self-concepts to the leader's goals. Followers then seek to enhance their own self-esteem through achievement of the mission, bringing to bear all the self-regulating, self-directing power of intrinsic motivation. Transformational leaders achieve this goal by heightening the salience of the follower's collective or group identity and meshing self-concept with collective accomplishment.

The leader augments followers' intrinsic motivation by employing motive arousal techniques that raise specific motives essential to mission accomplishment. The "larger-than-life" leader uses his or her salience to manipulate symbols with motivational properties. Thus, Mother Theresa's selflessness arouses affiliative motives in her followers, while General Patton's aggressive symbolism arouses power motivation in his.

D. Cognitive Approaches

Leadership is an interpersonal process in which perceptions, thoughts, and judgments play an important role. Increasing attention has been paid to cognitive factors in recent years. A number of studies reported that ratings of leader behavior were affected by knowledge of the group's performance. Subsequent research supported the finding, and the role of perception and judgment in leadership effects became an important area of study.

1. Implicit Theories

Some theorists have argued that the entire concept of leadership was flawed by the fact it had to be inferred from behavior open to multiple interpretations and was, therefore, more of an attribution than a reality. In an extensive program of research, Robert Lord and his associates have developed the idea that individuals hold implicit theories about the nature of social relationships like leadership and about social objects like leaders. The implicit theories include prototypes of what kinds of traits and behaviors are associated with leaders of different types. These prototypes affect how we judge whether an individual is or is not a leader and affect what we notice and remember about the behavior of leaders. Since much of leadership research relies on reports of leader behavior from followers or observers, these cognitive biases raise troubling questions about the validity of such studies.

Recently, James Meindl and his associates have argued that people also hold implicit theories of organization and those implicit theories assign great causal importance to the effects of leadership on organizational functioning. Meindl calls this strong belief in the efficacy of leaders "the romance of leadership," and he argues that it leads to an overemphasis on the importance of leaders and insufficient attention, both popular and scientific, to the importance of followers in group and organizational outcomes.

The evidence is quite clear that our perceptions of leaders are influenced by cognitive biases, and there is strong evidence that we probably do exaggerate the effects of leadership. Nonetheless, there is also considerable evidence that leadership does, indeed, play a significant role in group performance. Furthermore, the perceptions of leadership and the leader's ability to influence those perceptions are an important aspect of the leader's ability to exert influence, i.e., to lead.

2. Leaders' Perceptions of Subordinates

The roles of cognition and judgment are not confined to the perceptions of leaders by others, but are also significant in the leader's perceptions of subordinates. The ways in which a leader interprets the behavior and performance of subordinates determines the leader's subsequent actions toward those subordinates. Terence Mitchell and his colleagues have shown that supervisors are naturally prone to ascribe the responsibility for failure to internal factors, such as ability or effort, rather than factors external to the subordinate, such as insufficient training or support. This tendency to make internal attributions is exacerbated when the outcomes of subordinates' actions are severe.

Karen Brown has also pointed out that since the supervisor bears responsibility for the subordinate's work environment and support, attributions to internal characteristics of the subordinate protect the supervisor from accountability for the subordinate's failure. She argues that when entire groups or teams perform poorly, the threat to the supervisor strongly encourages these self-serving judgments. Clearly, then, leadership effectiveness will be affected by the judgments made of the leader and by the leader. The interpretation and evaluation of behavior are strongly determined by the expectations and values that observers hold. Expectations and values are the central aspects of the study of cultural differences.

3. Cognitive Resource Theory (CRT)

While most cognitively oriented leadership theories are focused on perception and judgment, Fred Fiedler and his associates have tried to understand the role of cognitive resources, like intelligence and knowledge. A number of empirical studies have found that a leader's intelligence and experience based knowledge are assets that may not always result in high performance. A critical determinant is the level of stress under which the leader is functioning. Highly intelligent leaders are best able to make use of their intellectual abilities when they are not under stress. High levels of stress interfere with intellectural functioning, however, and the leader's experience is then a better predictor of performance. Cognitive resource theory, like other contingency approaches, reveals that the path from leader attributes to leader behavior and on to group performance may not be a simple or direct one.

E. Cultural Approaches

Much of the previous discussion in this essay has shown the moderating effects of followers' needs and expectations on the effectiveness of various types of leader behavior or style. What people value, need, and expect vary from one culture to another. A full understanding of leadership must take cultural differences into account. Cross-cultural research on leadership was sporadic, but has begun to coalesce in the last 15 years.

1. Work-Related Values

Some of the first cross-cultural work in organizational psychology compared values across different cultures. In a comprehensive survey study of work-related values, Dutch psychologist Geert Hofstede collected data from managers of 40 nationalities employed by a large, multinational corporation. Factor analyses yielded four value dimensions: (1) *power distance*, i.e., the degree of acceptance of large power differentials within groups; (2) *uncertainty avoidance*, i.e., need for order and structure and desire to avoid ambiguous or unpredictable situations; (3) *individualism–collectivism*, i.e., the relative emphasis placed on self-reliance and individual achievement versus social responsibility and dependence; and (4) *masculinity–femininity*, i.e., the relative emphasis on "masculine" concerns with achievement, strength, and aggressiveness versus quality of life, nurturance, and passivity. Based on the great differences he found across nationalities, Hofstede argued that what constitutes effective leadership, motivation, or organizational design will vary from country to country.

2. Leader Behaviors

A number of researchers have partially supported Hofstede's point while revealing some universal aspects to effective leadership. Inspired by research with North American leader behavior measures, Jyuji Misumi developed a similar questionnaire and conducted a 25-year program of research on leadership effectiveness of Japanese managers. Japanese leader behavior fell into two general categories emphasizing task performance (P) or the maintenance of positive morale (M). Japanese leaders who are associated with productive work groups and satisfied subordinates are described by those subordinates as exhibiting high levels of both types of behavior while the worst leaders were low on both.

Subsequent cross-national research with Misumi's measure found the same performance and maintenance factors in the behavior of leaders from the United States, England, Hong Kong, and Japan, but also found that the specific behaviors that were associated with each factor varied from nation to nation, i.e., a meld of cultural specificity and universality. For example, while a factor of considerate leader behavior is found in all four cultures, a specific behavior (such as telling a subordinate's co-workers that the subordinate is performing poorly) loads positively on the factor in some cultures and negatively in others.

3. Contingency Effects

In a program of research undertaken in part to test the cross-cultural validity of Fiedler's contingency model, Roya Ayman and Martin Chemers have also reported a mix of specific and universal effects. For example, the interaction of leadership orientation and situational control predicted by the contingency model is found, but its effects are weakened by strong cultural norms that limit the freedom of a leader to express a personal style. In so-called "tight" cultures, the expression of a person's internal characteristics, such as motivations or personality, is diminished by normative expectations for behavior.

4. Gender Effects

A prevalent question in the contemporary leadership literature concerns whether differences in socialization and role between men and women have resulted in sex differences in leadership style or effectiveness.

Comparisons of the leader behavior ratings of men and women managers, by subordinates, peers, or superiors have shown few differences. Although a few studies have shown such differences, those studies primarily used college students as subjects or measures of leadership that were quite vague. In organizational studies employing specific behavioral measures, very few differences in leader behavior, decision strategy, or problem-solving style have been found.

Recently, Kay Deaux reviewed the various approaches to understanding gender differences in social psychological phenomena. She concluded that gender seems to have its strongest effect as a social category affecting the stereotypes that influence expectations and attributions about men and women. In an analysis compatible with Deaux's, Ayman outlined the cognitive discontinuities that are caused by differences in the prototypes that we hold for men, women, and "managers." The North American cultural stereotype of a manager includes traits like decisive, forceful, and analytic; quite compatible with the masculine prototype, but very different from the feminine prototype of nurturant, passive, and emotional. While the actual observed differences between men and women are quite small, the expectations and stereotypes are quite divergent. Thus, when sex is made salient in a leadership context, it affects the perceptions that leader and followers hold about themselves and about others. [*See* PREJUDICE AND STEREOTYPES.]

IV. A FUNCTIONAL INTEGRATION

The foregoing review of leadership theory and research confronts the reader with a number of apparent contradictions. Transformational models seem to identify a leadership approach appropriate to every situation, while the contingency theories emphasize the role of context. Some cognitive theorists argue that leadership is a fabrication of our imagination, while other theories treat leadership effects as real, powerful, and pervasive. Some theories focus heavily on the leader, while others focus on the follower.

The parable of the blind men examining the elephant seems apt here. First, when scrutinizing a complex phenomenon, perspective becomes very important. Second, different parts of the elephant, for example the trunk and the legs, have different functions for the animal and are, not surprisingly, differently formed and configured. The same holds true for leadership. Effective leadership has more than one aspect with more than one function. Effective leaders are competent at moving the group toward the accomplishment of its mission, loyal to the values of the organization or society, and fair and honorable in their relationships with others.

In order to fulfill these requirements, leaders must attend to three aspect of leadership: (1) *image management*, fulfilling the prototypical expectations that others hold for a good leader; (2) *relationship development*, establishing and maintaining an exchange with followers that motivates and directs; and (3) *resource utilization*, deploying the knowledge, talents, and energies of self and followers effectively for goal attainment. The characteristics of the leader that are most important vary for each of these aspects.

A. Image Management

Hollander's work showed that in order for leaders to gain the legitimate power to influence others, they must be seen as competent and loyal to group values and goals. Under many circumstances, it is not possible for followers to gain direct and objective evidence of competence and loyalty. In such cases, those characteristics are judged by comparing the leader with implicit theories and prototypes of what a leader should be. Lord points out that leaders can enhance their fit with implicit theories by behaving in ways that are expected (e.g., by acting decisive, concerned, and serious) and by associating themselves with successful accomplishments (and by avoiding association with failures). When leaders carry off this image management at very high levels, observers attribute extraordinary qualities to them, and they are seen as visionary and charismatic.

As the "implicit leadership" theorists have pointed out, images can be manipulated and observers' inferences can be exaggerated. Image management, then, is an aspect of leadership that is very susceptible to social construction. Still, the accuracy of leadership judgments is likely to be improved by the continued close scrutiny of followers over extended periods of time.

B. Relationship Development

The theories of supervision and coaching (e.g., path–goal theory, the operant model of leadership, vertical dyad linkage theory, and transformational leadership) coalesce to identify the critical functions of this aspect. An effective leader–follower relationship involves giving the follower appropriate direction and emotional support. What is appropriate (i.e., what the follower *needs*) depends on the follower's task, background, and personality. The effective leader must be able discern these needs by accurate attribution based on careful observation. This is most effective when the leader is able to provide direction and concern in an individualized manner that helps the subordinate to grow and develop.

Further, the exchange must be seen as fair and equitable by both leader and follower. This is dependent, in part, on the nature of their particular relationship and, in part, on the cultural expectations of what an appropriate exchange relationship is supposed to be. The essence of relationship development, then, is effective coaching and guidance, buttressed by good communication and attribution, in a context of equity and fairness, that results in the personal and professional growth of the subordinate. When those functions are fulfilled exceptionally well, the relationship between the parties is transformed from one of calculated exchange to one of true commitment.

C. Resource Utilization

If the first two functions of leadership have been fulfilled such that the leader's positive image has resulted in legitimacy and the exchange relationship has developed leader and follower into a highly motivated team, a third element is still required for effective leadership. The team's resources must be properly used to accomplish the mission of the group. A highly motivated team without appropriate coordination may resemble a runaway stage coach hurtling off the cliff after the driver has fallen off.

Resource utilization depends on the contingency relationship between leader and situation. On an individual level, when the match between leadership pattern and situational demand is appropriate, leaders perform confidently and enthusiastically. At the team level, the choice of problem solving or decision strategies determines effectiveness. As the contingency model, normative decision theory, and cognitive resource theory make clear, the group's resources must be managed in a manner appropriate to the situation.

When tasks are complex and ambiguous, greater informational input and creative analysis are required. However, the group's interpersonal characteristics (i.e., cooperation and harmony) influence the most appropriate manner for the leader to gain subordinate input. Using a decision strategy or organizational structure unsuited to the internal or external environment of the group will result in the dissipation of the group's resources of talent, knowledge, and energy.

When viewed from a functional perspective, the contradictions between well-tested theories are more apparent than real. Although subjective aspects of leadership are important in the image management and relationship development aspects, they are much less so in the area of resource utilization. While specifications of effective leadership (e.g., transformational leadership characteristics) may seem universal from one perspective or level of analysis (e.g., follower perceptions), contingency processes may be more important when viewed from another perspective (e.g., objective team performance). Attention to function and level of analysis allows for the integration of many good theories and points the way toward models of training and development of effective leaders and productive organizations.

Bibliography

Chemers, M. M., and Ayman, R. (Eds.) (1993). "Leadership Theory and Research: Perspectives and Directions." Academic Press, New York.

Eagley, A. H., and Johnson, B. T. (1991). Gender and leadership style: A meta-analysis. *Psychol. Bull.* **108**, 233–256.

Fiedler, F. E. (1967). "A Theory of Leadership Effectiveness." McGraw–Hill, New York.

Fiedler, F. E., and Garcia, J. E. (1987). "New Approaches to Effective Leadership: Cognitive Resources and Organizational Performance." Wiley, New York.

Hofstede, G. (1981). "Culture's Consequences: International Differences in Work-Related Values." Sage, Beverly Hills, CA.

Hollander, E. P. (1958). Conformity, status, and idiosyncrasy credit. *Psychol. Rev.* **65**, 117–127.

House, R. J., and Dessler, G. (1974). The Path-Goal theory of leadership: Some post-hoc and a priori tests. In "Contingency Approaches to Leadership." (J. G. Hunt and L. L. Larson, Eds.), Southern Illinois University Press, Carbondale.

Komaki, J. L. (1986). Toward effective supervision. *J. Appl. Psychol.* **71**, 270–279.

Lord, R. G., and Mahar, K. J. (1989). Perceptions of leadership and their implications in organizations. In "Applied Social Psychology in Buisness Organizations (J. Carroll, Ed.), Erlbaum, Hillside, NJ.

Meindl, J. R. (1990). On leadership: An alternative to the conventional wisdom. In "Research in Organizational Behavior" (B. A. Shaw, Ed.) Vol. 12. JAI Press, New York.

Misumi, J., and Peterson, M. F. (1985). The Performance-Maintenance (PM) theory of leadership: Review of Japanese research program. *Administrative Sci. Quart.* **30**, 198–223.

Peters, J. H., Hartke, D. D., and Pohlman, J. T. (1985). Fiedler's contingency theory of leadership: An application of the meta-analytic procedures of Schmidt and Hunter. *Psychol. Bull.* **97**, 274–285.

Stogdill, R. M. (1948). Personal factors associated with leadership. *J. Psychol.* **25**, 35–71.

Vroom, V. H., and Yetton, P. W. (1973). "Leadership and Decision-Making." University of Pittsburgh Press, Pittsburgh, PA.

LEARNED HELPLESSNESS

Christopher Peterson
University of Michigan

Glossary

Attributional reformulation Elaboration of the learned helplessness model which proposes that the extent of deficits following experience with uncontrollable events is influenced by how the individual explains them.

Attributional Style Questionnaire ASQ, questionnaire for assessing explanatory style.

CAVE technique Content Analysis of Verbatim Explanations; content analysis procedure for assessing explanatory style from written or spoken material.

Explanatory style A cognitive personality variable: how someone habitually explains the causes of bad events involving the self.

Learned helplessness Disruptions in motivation, cognition, and emotion that follow experience with uncontrollable events; also, the explanation of these deficits in cognitive terms.

Triadic design In learned helplessness research, an experimental design that separates the effects of uncontrollability from those of trauma per se.

THE LEARNED HELPLESSNESS phenomenon is the set of motivational, cognitive, and emotional disruptions that follow experience with uncontrollable events. The learned helplessness model explains these disruptions in terms of a learned expectation that responses and outcomes are independent of one another. Learned helplessness exists in both animals and people. In people, their causal explanations for the uncontrollable events influence the nature and extent of the ensuing helplessness. Learned helplessness is involved in a variety of problems entailing maladaptive passivity, including depression and illness.

I. THE MEANING OF LEARNED HELPLESSNESS

Learned helplessness was first discovered in an animal learning laboratory in the 1960s. Dogs were immobilized and given a brief series of electrical shocks—painful yet not damaging—which they could neither avoid nor escape. Twenty-four hours later, these dogs were again exposed to shock, this time in a situation in which a simple response would terminate it. The typical animal in this situation readily learns the appropriate response. However, the dogs previously shocked simply sat still and endured the shock. When they occasionally made the response which terminated the shock, they were unlikely to profit from this experience. At the next shock, they again were likely to sit still and endure it.

Researchers Steven Maier and Martin Seligman proposed that when the dogs were exposed to shocks they could neither avoid nor escape, they learned that the shocks were independent of their responses. In other words, because the shocks occurred regardless of what they did or did not do, the animals in effect learned that they were helpless; nothing they did mattered. According to Maier and Seligman, the dogs mentally represented this learning as an expectation of response–outcome independence. This expectation was generalized to new situations where it produced several sorts of difficulties. These included a motivational deficit (the failure of the dogs to initiate escape responses), a cognitive interference (the failure of the dogs to learn from their occasionally successful responses), and an emotional passivity (the absence of whimpering and other signs of emotionality).

The difficulties following experience with uncontrollable events have come to be known as the learned helplessness phenomenon. The explanation of these difficulties in terms of a learned expectation has come to be known as the learned helplessness model. In the decades since the phenomenon was discovered and the explanation proposed, learned helplessness has been the subject of extensive research and theorizing. Learned helplessness has been documented in a variety of species, including human beings. It has been implicated in numerous failures of adaptation, notably depression and physical illness. At present, learned helplessness encompasses disparate lines of investigation.

Common to all these lines of work is a conception of learned helplessness as entailing three critical features. The first is maladaptive passivity. The helpless person or animal fails through inactivity to control important outcomes that indeed can be influenced by behavior. The second feature is a history of uncontrollable events preceding the observed passivity. Trauma per se may or may not be present, but uncontrollability is the active ingredient in producing learned helplessness. And the third feature is cognitive mediation. It is the person or animal's expectation of response–outcome independence that causes helplessness deficits.

These critical features deserve emphasis because learned helplessness has become quite popular within psychology, particularly its applications. Some theorists applying these ideas have done so promiscuously, arguing for the role of learned helplessness in given phenomena despite the absence of evidence for one or more of its critical features. These applications should be regarded as incomplete cases. They have value, to be sure, in directing future research, but they should not be confused with examples of helplessness in which all three critical features have been documented.

II. LEARNED HELPLESSNESS IN ANIMALS

Learned helplessness research with animals first occurred in the 1960s, at a time when stimulus–response (S-R) conceptions of learning dominated theorizing. According to S-R accounts, learning entails the acquisition of particular responses in particular situations. The learned helplessness model is very much at odds with this view, because it pro-

poses that the helpless animals learn not specific responses but rather general expectations affecting responses across a variety of situations. The helplessness model is a cognitive account of learning, and in the 1960s, it was a radical theory in a field long dominated by strict behaviorism.

Accordingly, much of the early interest in learned helplessness stemmed from its clash with the tenets of traditional S-R theories of learning. Alternative accounts of learned helplessness were proposed by theorists who saw no need to invoke mentalistic constructs. Different alternatives were proposed, but many emphasized an incompatible motor response learned when animals were first exposed to uncontrollable shock. This response was presumably generalized to the second situation where it interfered with performance at the test task. Said another way, the learned helplessness phenomenon is produced by an inappropriate *response* learned in the originial situation rather than an inappropriate *expectation* (of response–outcome independence). For example, perhaps the dogs learned that holding still when shocked somehow decreased pain. If so, then they hold still in the second situation as well, because this response was previously reinforced.

Steven Maier, Martin Seligman, and others conducted a series of studies testing between the learned helplessness model and the incompatible motor response alternatives. In a way, the learned helplessness advocates had an easier time, because the helplessness model does not deny the possibility that incompatible motor responses may play some role in passivity. Their point was merely that expectations play a role as well. The advocates of incompatible motor responses, in contrast, categorically denied any role of expectations in producing the helplessness phenomenon.

Several lines of research implied that expectations were operative. Perhaps the most compelling argument comes from the so-called triadic design, a three-group experimental design which shows that the uncontrollability of shocks is responsible for ensuing deficits. So, animals in one group are exposed to shock which they are able to terminate by making some response. Animals in a second group are "yoked" to those in the first group, exposed to the identical shocks, the only difference being that animals in the first group control their offset whereas those in the second do not. Animals in a third group are exposed to no shock at all in the original situation. All animals are then given the same test task.

Animals with control over the initial shocks typically show no helplessness when subsequently tested. They act just like animals with no prior exposure to shock. Animals without control become helpless. Whether shocks are controllable is not a property of the shocks per se, but rather of the relationship between the animal and the shocks. That animals are sensitive to the link between responses and outcomes implies that they must be able to detect and represent contingencies. A cognitive explanation of this ability is more parsimonious than one phrased in terms of incompatible motor responses.

Also arguing in favor of a cognitive interpretation of helplessness effects are studies showing that an animal can be "immunized" against the debilitating effects of uncontrollability by first exposing it to controllable events. Presumably, the animal learns during immunization that events can be controlled, and *this* expectation is sustained during exposure to uncontrollable events. Learned helplessness is thus precluded.

Along these same lines, other studies show that learned helplessness deficits can be undone by forcibly exposing a helpless animal to the contingency between behavior and outcome. In other words, the animal is forced to make an appropriate response at the test task, by pushing or pulling it into action. After several such trials, the animal "notices" that escape is possible and begins to respond on its own. Again, the presumed process at work is a cognitive one. The animal's expectation of response–outcome independence is challenged during the "therapy" experience, and hence learning occurs.

In an elegant experiment, Steven Maier took literally the claims of the incompatible motor response theories. If holding still is indeed what is learned during helplessness pretreatment, then why not explicitly train the animal to do so, and then see what happens during the test task? He arranged the original pretreatment so that the response which allowed the animal to terminate shock was not moving for several seconds. Any movement allowed the shock to continue. His research animals readily learned not to move. But when later tested in a situation in which moving was the appropriate response to terminate shock, these animals had no difficulty learning what to do. The "incompatible" motor response they had previously acquired proved no impediment.

The studies described so far exposed animals to aversive stimuli (i.e., shocks). But it is also possible to produce helplessness by providing uncontrollable appetitive stimuli: food or water regardless of re-

sponses. Here an explanation in terms of incompatible motor responses becomes quite difficult to support. What is gained by holding still in response to food or water? Certainly not the reduction of pain.

Research into helplessness among animals was dominated over the years by attempts on the part of learned helplessness theorists to argue against these peripheralist alternatives. Accordingly, a great deal of research pitted the two accounts against one another. Because the cognitive explanation eventually proved more satisfactory, more recent research has tried to understand better just what happens when an animal "learns" that it is helpless. The exact nature of the cognitive representation of helplessness has begun to be studied, and it is still not clear just how the animal detects and represents the lack of dependence between responses and outcomes. Complicating this line or research is evidence that animals exposed to uncontrollable shocks become more fearful and anxious than animals without this experience. At least some helplessness deficits may be produced by fear and anxiety—not directly by expectations of response–outcome independence.

Also influencing research was Martin Seligman's proposal that learned helplessness in animals was analogous to depression in people. Numerous studies therefore sought to establish parallels between learned helplessness on the one hand and depression on the other. These studies are discussed in a later section.

III. THE BIOLOGY OF LEARNED HELPLESSNESS

Uncontrollable events, particularly shock, have biological effects on the organism which experiences them, and these biological effects are related to the sorts of behaviors that ensue. At one time, such biological effects were regarded as alternatives to the cognitive mediation proposed by the learned helplessness model. But rather than regarding these effects as an alternative, it is probably more reasonable to regard them as the biological substrate of operative cognitive processes. Indeed, upon close examination, cognitive versus biological explanation is a false dichotomy, a holdover from the mind–body dualism that has dominated Western thinking since at least the time of Descartes.

As it turns out, the biology of learned helplessness proves quite complex. One reason is that the uncontrollable stressors used to induce helplessness in animals are typically potent enough to alter a variety of brain chemicals. Because these effects are so widespread, almost any brain chemical becomes a plausible mediator of the effects of uncontrollability.

Studies take a few basic forms. First, they show that uncontrollable shocks affect the amount and/ or activity of some brain chemical. Second, they show that a direct manipulation of the chemical in question produces helplessness deficits in the absence of uncontrollability. Third, they show that a manipulation which precludes changes in the chemical of interest interferes with the production of helplessness deficits by uncontrollability. When studies of these types converge to implicate a given brain chemical, there is good reason to believe that it is involved in learned helplessness.

However, no given brain chemical proves to be *the* single biological mediator of the learned helplessness phenomenon. Several have been well documented, and they mutually influence one another. For example, the neurotransmitter norepinephrine (NE) was the first potential mediator that was studied. Among the reasons for studying NE was a procedural one—a great deal was already known about how to assay it in the brain. There was also a theoretical reason—depression entails a deficiency in NE, and as already noted, learned helplessness had been proposed as analogous to depression.

Researchers showed that NE was reduced by uncontrollable shock, and that NE depletion resulted not only in motor deficits but also in psychological processes related to attention and vigilance. Here we have a plausible account of the biochemical basis of learned helplessness deficits.

But an equally plausible case can be made for the involvement of another neurotransmitter: γ-aminobutyric acid (GABA). GABA is the major inhibitory transmitter of the brain, and it is importantly involved in counteracting sympathetic arousal. (Tranquilizers such as Valium reduce anxiety by encouraging GABA activity.) Uncontrollable shock depletes GABA, producing a more fearful and anxious organism. We have already mentioned that fear and anxiety may be involved in the learned helplessness phenomenon, so perhaps GABA figures in this involvement.

Also influenced by uncontrollable shocks are the endorphins: brain substances with actions similar to opioids such as morphine. Research suggests that endorphins modulate pain at both brain and spinal levels. Further, exposure to uncontrollable stressors activates this analgesic system. Applied to the learned helplessness phenomenon, this argument has an intuitive appeal. If one can control an aversive event, then it makes sense to be active and attempt control. However, when an event is uncontrollable, then it makes sense to conserve energy and withdraw from the event as much as possible: i.e., to display the learned helplessness phenomenon. Reduction of pain certainly facilitates conservation and withdrawal.

Exposure to uncontrollable shocks creates in animals as potent an analgesic state as moderately large doses of morphine. Decreased sensitivity to pain following uncontrollable shocks lingers as long as 48–72 hr. Subsequent research suggests that at least part of this analgesic effect is due to the stimulation of endorphins. Part of the learned helplessness effect may be brought about by decreased sensitivity to aversive stimuli.

Other studies have implicated as well neurotransmitters such as acetylcholine, serotonin, and dopamine, as well as hormones such as the adrenal corticosteroids. As noted, the biology of learned helplessness proves complex, and we are far from understanding what—if anything—links together all these biological responses to uncontrollability. One candidate is corticotrophin releasing factor, a hormone manufactured in the hypothalamus that interacts with all of the other biological processes so far discussed. However, much further work needs to be done in order to map out the biological route entailed in moving from uncontrollability to helplessness.

IV. LEARNED HELPLESSNESS IN PEOPLE

Shortly after learned helplessness was described in animals, researchers wondered if a similar phenomenon existed in people. The first learned helplessness studies using human research subjects were modeled closely on the animal example. The triadic design was employed. Sometimes inescapable bursts of noise were used as the uncontrollable event; sometimes problems without solutions were used. Subjects were then tested on a different test task, typically a series of solvable anagrams. The finding, in literally hundreds of investigations, was that experience with uncontrollable events interfered with the ability to solve subsequent problems.

Other studies further attested to the similarity between the animal phenomenon and what was produced in the human laboratory. Uncontrollability made anxiety and depression more likely. Previous exposure to controllable events immunized human subjects against learned helplessness. Similarly, exposure to contingencies reversed helplessness deficits.

Two aspects of human helplessness have no obvious counterpart among animals. First is what can be termed vicarious helplessness. Problem-solving difficulties can be produced in people who do not directly experience uncontrollable events if they simply see someone else exposed to uncontrollability. The significance of vicarious helplessness is that it greatly extends the potential ways in which helpless might be produced in the natural world. News stories, for example, often feature uncontrollable events imposed upon other people. The full parameters of this phenomenon have not been investigated, and it is of obvious interest whether we can immunize people against vicarious helplessness or undo its effects via therapy.

Second is the fact that small groups can be made helpless by exposure to uncontrollable events. In other words, when a group works at an unsolvable problem, it later shows group problem-solving deficits relative to another group with no previous exposure to uncontrollability. Interestingly, group level helplessness is not simply a function of individual helplessness produced among group members. Rather, it exists at the group level, characterizing group efforts at future tasks but *not* individual efforts. Again, the real-life implications of this phenomenon are intriguing, and future research into this phenomenon seems indicated.

Learned helplessness in humans has not been without its critics. Helplessness produced in the human laboratory is not as general as the helplessness model implies. Remember that generality of deficits is a critical prediction of the cognitive explanation. Yet research with humans showed that generality sometimes occurred across time and situation, and sometimes did not.

Learned helplessness in people proves more complex than the animal-based theory allows. (Helplessness in animals is also more complex, but this point was not fully appreciated when the anomalous data with human subjects were first reported.) Something was occurring beyond the simple learning of response–outcome independence in one situation and its generalization to other situations. One reaction to this complexity was an attempt to specify factors influencing the boundary conditions of

learned helplessness in people. We discuss this reaction in the next section.

But other reactions to the complexity of human helplessness occurred as well, with theorists arguing that altogether different processes were entailed than those proposed by the learned helplessness model. It is interesting to juxtapose these alternative explanations with those inspired by the learned helplessness phenomenon in animals. In animals, the alternatives stressed either incompatible motor responses or biochemical alteration—peripheral processes as opposed to the central, cognitive account contained in the learned helplessness account. But in people, the alternatives were cognitive as well. No theorist proposed that helplessness produced in the human laboratory was the result of peripheral processes. Rather, the resulting difference of opinion was over just which cognitive process might be responsible for mediating the link between uncontrollability and helplessness deficits.

Here are thumbnail sketches of some of the more important of these alternative cognitive explanations:

1. *Hypothesis testing.* When trying to solve problems, people proceed by successively proposing and testing various hypotheses, presumably moving to increasingly complex possibilities. Uncontrollable events result in people discarding as useless hypotheses later necessary for the solution of the test task.

2. *Egotism.* People give up following uncontrollable problems not because they believe in response–outcome independence but in order to save face. *Not* trying at a task protects their ego from the consequences of trying and then failing.

3. *State orientation.* Uncontrollable problems produce in a person a marked self-consciousness of his or her own psychological state: past, present, and future. "How am I feeling?" "Why am I having trouble?" "What does this experience imply about my well-being?" This state orientation does not help the person solve the problem at hand, and if the task is sufficiently difficult, state orientation interferes with problem solution, producing "helplessness" in the absence of the processes proposed by the learned helplessness model.

4. *Cognitive exhaustion.* Yet another alternative explanation of the learned helplessness phenomenon in people starts with the assumption

that uncontrollability initially elicits a great deal of cognitive activity on the part of the person trying to make sense of it. However, this activity does not continue indefinitely. The individual eventually stops thinking, succumbing to cognitive exhaustion. It is obvious that cognitive exhaustion leads to difficulties at the subsequent test task.

5. *Secondary control.* A final alternative interpretation of the learned helplessness phenomenon starts with a distinction between people's primary control over events—the literal ability to influence their onset and offset—versus secondary control—the ability to make some sense of them. Both forms of control are beneficial. Different strategies of secondary control exist, and some may strike the onlooker as passive. For example, people may align themselves with fate or chance. In so doing, they look listless and fatalistic. However, this "passivity" is a way to gain secondary control over events that elude their primary control.

All of these alternative explanations have supporting data, so we can conclude that each—at least occasionally—is an account of how people respond to uncontrollable events. Unfortunately, the pertinent studies have not always explicitly pitted these explanations against the learned helplessness model. No studies have tested the alternatives against one another. As noted previously, the learned helplessness account does not claim to specify the only process triggered by uncontrollability. To date, an extensive study of when these different alternatives apply and when they do not has yet to be undertaken.

It is clear that not all can apply simultaneously. After all, the state orientation hypothesis attributes helplessness deficits to too much thinking, whereas the cognitive exhaustion hypothesis implicates too little thinking! The best we can say at present is that the cognitive mediation of learned helplessness effects is not well understood. Perhaps what is needed is a series of studies that take time into account, because most of the alternative explanations hypothesize about processes that unfold as experience with uncontrollability increases. Until this happens, the biggest unknown of human helplessness will remain the details of what and how the helpless person thinks.

V. THE ATTRIBUTIONAL REFORMULATION

As noted, researchers investigating the learned helplessness phenomenon in people concluded that a more complex account was needed. In particular, it seemed to many researchers that one should take into account how the helpless individual interpreted the causes of the original uncontrollability. Here learned helplessness research made contact with the social psychology field of attribution theory, a collection of approaches concerned with the how people explain events. Attribution theory represents a cognitive view of human nature, one that accords great importance to how and what people think. Subsequent emotions, motivation, and behavior are presumably under the sway of causal explanations. [*See* ATTRIBUTION.]

In what has come to be known as the attributional reformulation of helplessness theory, Lyn Abramson, Martin Seligman, and John Teasdale incorporated attributional notions into the learned helplessness model. The original theory was not replaced by the attributional reformulation but rather elaborated in attributional terms. So, the theory still proposed that uncontrollable events lead to passivity through expectations of response–outcome independence. However, the nature and extent of induced helplessness is influenced by how people explain the causes of uncontrollability.

The attributional reformulation proposes that when confronted by uncontrollable events, people ask themselves "why?" Their particular answer influences the expectations they form and hence their reactions to these events. Three dimensions of causal explanations are deemed important.

First, a causal explanation can be stable, implicating a long-lasting cause, or unstable, pointing to a transient cause. According to theory, stable causes are more likely than unstable ones to produce long-lasting deficits, in accordance with the induced expectation.

Second, a causal explanation can be global, a factor that influences numerous outcomes, or it can be specific, a cause that influences just the events on immediate focus. Global explanations presumably lead to pervasive helpless deficits, whereas specific explanations result only in circumscribed deficits.

Third, a causal explanation may point to an internal factor, something about the individual, or to an external factor such as other people, circumstances, or fate. Uncontrollable events explained with internal causes are thought to result in a loss of self-esteem, whereas those explained with external causes do not.

So, to the degree that uncontrollable events are explained with stable, global, and internal causes ("it's me; it's going to last forever; it's going to undermine everything I do''), helplessness following uncontrollability is more striking and serious.

The particular cause that someone entertains for an uncontrollable event has several determinants. The most obvious is the reality of the event itself. Although ''attribution'' has connotations of projection, people do take into account the actual causal texture of the world in offering attributions. They may not be perfectly accurate, but nonetheless, they are influenced by the event itself and surrounding circumstances (''I failed, but so did everyone else''). Relatedly, there may exist consensus within a given culture about the way certain events are caused, and people may draw on these widely held notions in making attributions.

Nonetheless, in other cases, what appears to be the same event is explained differently by different people, which leads to an interest in styles of causal explanation. People have habitual explanations on which they rely when reality and/or social consensus does not dictate a particular cause. Explanatory style is thus an individual difference, a cognitive personality variable, that influences how people explain events. According to the helplessness reformulation, explanatory style is therefore a distal influence on induced helplessness. Explanatory style pertains to any and all behaviors in which learned helplessness in involved.

Explanatory style has become one of the most frequently investigated individual differences in part because methods were devised for measuring it. The Attributional Style Questionnaire (ASQ) presents respondents with a series of hypothetical events that involve themselves, good or bad. For example, ''you cannot get all the work done that your employer requires.'' Respondents are asked to imagine this event happening, and then to write its ''one major cause'' if it were to happen. Then the cause is rated on 7-point scales along the dimensions deemed important by the helplessness reformulation. That is, respondents rate the cause as internal versus external, as stable versus unstable, and as global versus specific.

Ratings are averaged across different events, separately for good events and bad events, to yield explanatory style scores. Sometimes scores for internality, stability, and globality are averaged together, yielding a composite explanatory style score. Internal, stable, and global explanations for bad events taken together are referred to as a helpless or pessimistic explanatory style.

The ASQ has been translated from its original English into several languages, including Spanish, German, Chinese, Russian, and Armenian. Versions exist for children, as well as special populations such as athletes, medical patients, the elderly, and so on. The questionnaire proves reliable, particularly newer versions that increase the number of events for which attributions are offered.

One consistent finding is that stability and globality of explanatory style are substantially entwined. Although these dimensions can be distinguished conceptually, when people actually offer causal attributions, stable explanations are invariably global ones, and vice versa. Perhaps there are really but two dimensions of explanatory style: internality and generality, which subsumes stability and globality.

The second way in which explanatory style is measured is with a content analysis procedure called the CAVE technique, an acronym for Content Analysis of Verbatim Explanations. Written or spoken material in which an individual explains events involving the self are suitable for CAVEing, and the strategy has been used with letters, diaries, interviews, political speeches, song lyrics, and the like. A researcher reads the relevant material on the lookout for causal explanations of good or bad events. When these are encountered, they are copied down on a separate page. Other researchers then rate the extracted cause along 7-point scales according to its internality, stability, and globality. Obviously, the CAVE technique is modeled on the ASQ format, and the chief difference is that the researcher uses the rating scales rather than the respondent. But scores are treated in the same way.

The CAVE technique proves reliable and valid, although care must be taken not to study events for which there is no variation in how they are explained. The more events that are studied, the more likely a psychologically meaningful style will be apparent. The CAVE technique is obviously more painstaking than the ASQ, but its notable virtue is that research subjects not accessible with the questionnaire can be studied. Individuals unwilling or unable to complete questionnaires can be studied, so long as they have left behind a verbal record.

Research into explanatory style has been devoted mainly to showing that a pessimistic explanatory style characterizes those with depression. This hypothesis has received ample support and is discussed shortly. Other studies show that explanatory style relates to the actual explanations that people offer in everyday life, that it is stable across time—in some cases even decades, and that it relates to outcomes entailing passivity and demoralization.

Other aspects of the helplessness reformulation have been comparatively neglected by researchers.

For instance, the helplessness reformuation is a diathesis–stress model, proposing that deficits ensue only when a stressful event occurs *and* is processed through a pessimistic explanatory style. Most researchers have not measured stress, and when studies do look at stress, there is inconsistent support for the diathesis–stress model. Evidence is much better that explanatory style has a "direct" effect on negative outcomes, and perhaps a pessimistic view on the causes of events is upsetting whether or not actual bad events are encountered. [*See* STRESS.]

Along these lines, researchers have also neglected the claim of the reformulation that causal explanations affect the nature of helplessness through their influence on expectations about response–outcome independence. This is a central claim of the theory, but its status is mostly unknown, perhaps because the availability of a questionnaire to measure explanatory style led researchers to focus on the distal influences on helplessness (explanatory style) instead of the proximal ones (causal explanations and expectations).

VI. APPLICATIONS OF LEARNED HELPLESSNESS

From the very first, the learned helplessness model attracted the interest of applied researchers trying to make sense of people's passivity. Although in some cases, passivity is clearly produced by direct reward and punishment, in other cases, it is puzzling why someone does not attempt to influence outcomes that seem, objectively, to be controllable. The learned helplessness model provides a ready answer: the person has learned in a previous situation that responses and outcomes are unrelated; if this learning is represented as an expectation of future response–outcome independence and generalized to a new situation, then passivity results, whether or not the new situation warrants it.

How can we tell that learned helplessness is at work in a given instance of passivity? Remember the meaning of learned helplessness. The researcher wishing to document the presence of learned helplessness in a possible example must show that: (a) the passivity is *not* instrumental, i.e., *not* maintained by locally prevailing rewards and/or punishments; (b) a history of uncontrollable events precedes the passivity; and (c) expectations of uncontrollability mediate the passivity.

These criteria seem straightforward enough, but many supposed demonstrations of learned helplessness fall short of showing that all three criteria are present. There are understandable reasons for these partial demonstrations. The ideal demonstrations would follow people over time, yet longitudinal research is more difficult than the more common cross-sectional strategy, in which, for example, explanatory style is merely correlated with passive coping. And even if traumatic events clearly foreshadow passivity, it may be difficult to show that their uncontrollability is the critical factor.

Applied psychologists have used learned helplessness ideas to explain literally dozens of real-life problems that entail passivity. Only a handful of these applications have been attentive to the three necessary criteria. The typical application documents one or two, then assumes the existence of those that remain. We regard these applications as incomplete, not necessarily wrong, but needing further investigation.

Because interventions to prevent or undo passivity can be derived from the helplessness model, it is important that this further investigation eventually takes place. It would be a grievous error, for example, to regard passivity as learned helplessness when in actuality it is maintained by the immediate environment. Trying to change people's perceptions of control is apt to be ineffective at best and cruel at worst. Energy would better be spent changing the world in which these people live.

Good examples of learned helplessness include thwarted academic achievement, burnout among social service providers, behavioral reactions to crowding and noise, and, in some cases, the response of ethnic minorities to discrimination. It is worth emphasizing, though, that even for these good examples, all that has been shown is that learned helplessness plays *some* role. It is not the only reason, or even the most important reason, why individuals act passively.

A. Depression

One of the very best applications of learned helplessness is to depression. Let us see how depression satisfies the three criteria. To start, depression involves passivity; this is part of its very definition. Depression also follows bad events, particularly those that people judge to be uncontrollable. And depression is mediated by cognitions of helplessness, hopelessness, and pessimism. Explanatory style is a consistent correlate of depressive symptoms, as well as a demonstrable risk factor. [*See* Depression.]

Cognitive therapy for depression, which is highly effective, explicitly targets helpless expectations and pessimistic attributions. And research suggests that cognitive therapy may work precisely because it changes these cognitions. Improvement in depression goes lockstep with changes in attributions for bad events from internal, stable, and global to external, unstable, and specific. An intriguing possibility is that the encouragement of an optimistic explanatory style might prevent depression. [*See* Cognitive Behavior Therapy.]

Questions remain about the use of the helplessness model to make sense of depression. One concerns the issue of whether depression is continuous versus discontinuous across its mild and severe forms. Are these essentially the same, differing only in degree, or do mild depression and severe depression differ in kind? The learned helplessness model takes the strong position of continuity, but the other position has its advocates as well.

Another issue concerns the fine detail of the mechanism that leads from helplessness constructs to the symptoms of depression. The typical study in support of the model demonstrates distant links, typically between pessimistic explanatory style and depressive symptoms. What transpires in between? Do expectations of helplessness set off by uncontrollability and influenced by explanatory style bear the sole mediating burden? Some research suggests that people's tendencies to ruminate about bad events and their causes are also important in determining who becomes depressed. Perhaps so too are people's tendencies to be self-conscious and to infer negative consequences from setbacks. Further work, with a closer look at mechanisms, is needed to evaluate the specific process hypthesized by the helplessness model.

One more issue about the use of the helplessness model to explain depression comes from laboratory investigations by Lauren Alloy and Lyn Abramson showing that nondepressed people perceive more control over events than they actually have. Depressives, in contrast, perceive control realistically, which is to say, without the illusory boost that characterizes nondepressive thinking. This "sadder but wiser" effect is an intriguing one, implying that the helplessness account may be wrong in charactering depressive cognitions about control as distorted. [*See* Control.]

B. Illness

Another well-known application of helplessness ideas is to physical illness, although here the supporting evidence is more preliminary than in the case of depression. Again, let us ask how the three criteria of learned helplessness have been documented. First, "passivity" refers not to behavior but to the individual's ability to maintain physical health. Second, research with both animals and people shows that uncontrollable stress foreshadows poor health. However, this research has not always shown that uncontrollability is the critical reason why stressful life events can produce poor health. Third, explanatory style has been found to correlate with such indices of health as duration of symptom reports, physician exams, medical tests, longevity, and survival time following the diagnosis of serious diseases such as cancer. Pessimistic people have worse health than their optimistic counterparts. Many of these correlations have been established in longitudinal studies, where baseline measures of physical health are taken into account.

How strong is the correlation between pessimistic explanatory style and poor health? Most studies report correlation coefficients in the .20 to .30 range, which are moderate in size and typical of correlations in psychological research. At the same time, it is clear that explanatory style is but one influence on physical well-being.

Why does learned helplessness influence health? Several processes have been implicated. There may be an immunological pathway, because animal studies imply that uncontrollable stress can suppress aspects of immune functioning. However, it should be noted that these findings are highly complex, and one should offer broad generalizations about immune functioning only with caution. [*See* Stress and Illness.]

Another pathway may be emotional. As described, learned helplessness is involved in depression, and epidemiologists have shown that depressed individuals are at increased risk for morbidity and mortality. So, perhaps learned helplessness influences health in part because of its role in depression.

Several studies attest to a behavioral pathway. People with a pessimistic explanatory style tend to neglect the basics of health care, and when they fall ill, they tend not to do the sorts of things that might speed recovery. As these failures to promote health through one's actions accumulate, what may result is the observed link between explanatory style and illness.

A final possibility is that helpless people fall ill because they are socially estranged. Rich and supportive relationships with others are a well-demonstrated correlate of good health. To the degree that helpless people do not partake of social support—and studies show that they indeed do not—then poor health is an unsurprising result.

VII. CONCLUSIONS

How has the learned helplessness model fared since proposed in the 1960s? It has not only survived but flourished, which is striking because the half-life of most psychological theories is quite brief. In conclusion, therefore, it may be instructive to consider why the learned helplessness model has been as popular as it has.

One reason is that it was proposed precisely as the cognitive revolution in psychology began. The "radical" statements of the helplessness model soon became the readily accepted form of psychological explanation. Other reasons for the popularity of helplessness research are that it spans both animal and human work, that it rests on simple and reliable research techniques that investigators can readily master, and that it tries to speak to human problems and their solution.

Perhaps most profoundly, the learned helplessness model has been popular because it concerns itself with personal control, one of the central issues of our contemporary world. In a society like our own that stresses individuality and choice, a theory that looks at the effects of control and its lack necessarily has wide applicability and garners much attention.

Bibliography

Abramson, L. Y., Metalsky, G. I., and Alloy, L. B. (1989). Hopelessness depression: A theory-based subtype of depression. *Psychol. Rev.* **96,** 358–372.
Buchanan, G., and Seligman, M. E. P. (Eds.) (in press). "Explanatory Style." Erlbaum, Hillsdale, NJ.
Maier, S. F. (1989). Coping and learned helplessness: Some theoretical and pharmacological considerations. In "Adaptation and Affect" (J. Madden, S. Matthysee, and J. D. Barchas, Eds.). Raven Press, New York.
Maier, S. F. (1989). Learned helplessness: Event co-variation and cognitive changes. In "Contemporary Theories of Learning" (S. B. Klein and R. R. Mowrer, Eds.). Erlbaum, Hillsdale, NJ.
Peterson, C. (1991). The meaning and measurement of explanatory style. *Psychol. Inquiry* **2,** 1–10.
Peterson, C., and Bossio, L. M. (1991). "Health and Optimism." Free Press, New York.
Peterson, C., Maier, S. F., and Seligman, M. E. P. (1993). "Learned Helplessness: A Theory for the Age of Personal Control." Oxford, New York.
Seligman, M. E. P. (1990). "Learned Optimism." Knopf, New York.

LIMBIC SYSTEM

R. Joseph

Neurobehavioral Center
and Palo Alto Veterans Affairs Medical Center

Glossary

Adipsia A failure to drink and lack of thirst.

Agnosia An inability to recognize or to achieve understanding.

Aphagia A failure to eat and lack of hunger.

Cognition A mental process involved in speech, thought, and achieving knowledge.

Enkephalins Opiate-like chemical substances.

Evoked potentials Electrical activity of the brain elicited in response to flashes of light or sounds, which is then measured and detected by electrodes placed in the brain or on the surface of the skull.

Neural ganglia A collection of nerve cells (neurons) which perform similar functions.

Neuron A cell specialized to receive, process, or express sensory or motor information.

Nuclei A collection of nerve cells which perform similar functions.

Pheromone A chemical substance secreted by glands in the skin and detected by specialized neurons and which can indicate one's sexual, social, and emotional status.

THE LIMBIC SYSTEM is buried within the depths of the cerebrum and consists of a collection of ancient brain structures which are preeminent in the mediation and expression of emotional, motivational, sexual, and social behavior. The limbic system is involved in learning and the formation of new memories, monitors internal homeostasis and basic needs such as hunger and thirst, controls the secretion of hormones involved in pregnancy and reactions to stress, and even makes possible the ability to experience orgasm, depression, fear, rage, and love.

Broadly, these limbic system nuclei include the hypothalamus, amygdala, hippocampus, septal nuclei, and cingulate gyrus (see Fig. 1). Also related to limbic system functioning are portions of the reticular activating system, the orbital frontal and inferior temporal lobes, as well as parts of the thalamus and cerebellum. The limbic system is exceedingly ancient and originally provided the foundation for the development and evolution of much of the brain. [*See* BRAIN.]

I. THE EVOLUTION OF THE OLFACTORY/ LIMBIC SYSTEM

About 700 million years ago a cellular metamorphosis of paramount importance resulted in the creation of a completely unique type of cell, the neuron. These nerve cells in turn were especially responsive to light as well as chemical (olfactory and pheromonal) messages. Over the course of evolution, as the number of secreting and transmitting nerve cells that a creatures possessed increased, a network of interlinked neurons, called the "nerve net" was fashioned. Soon tiny neural ganglia, composed of colonies of similarly functioning nerve cells began to form in the anterior head region of various ancient and primitive creatures.

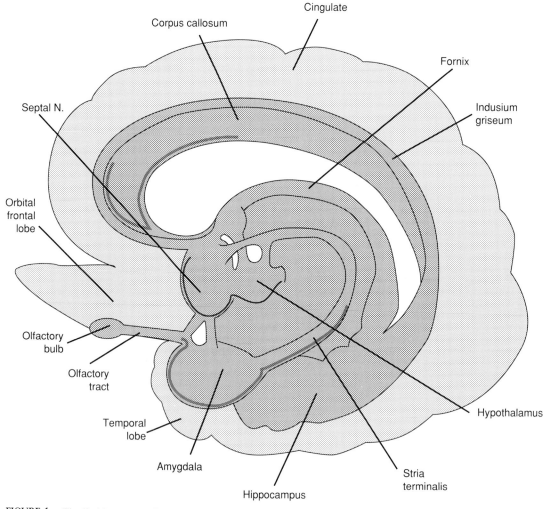

FIGURE 1   The limbic system: the amygdala, septal nuclei, hippocampus, hypothalamus, and cingulate gyrus. [Reproduced with permission from Joseph, R. (1990). ''Neuropsychology, Neuropsychiatry, Behavioral Neurology.'' Plenum, New York.]

By time the first vertebrates and fish began to swim the oceans, around 500 million years ago, the first primitive lobes of the brain had also become fashioned through the collectivization of these neural ganglia. This included the olfactory–limbic lobe (the forebrain), which was concerned with the detection of olfactory/pheromonal chemicals that might betray the presence of predators, prey, or a mate; the optic lobe/tectum of the midbrain which was responsive to visual messages; and the hindbrain which was concerned with movement. By 450,000 years ago, the first sharks had acquired a limbic system, which they, like modern humans, still possess today.

II. HYPOTHALAMUS

The hypothalamus is an exceedingly ancient structure and unlike most other brain regions it has maintained a striking similarity in structure throughout phylogeny and apparently over the course of evolution. The hypothalamus is fully functional at birth and is highly involved in all aspects of endocrine, hormonal, visceral, and autonomic functions and mediates or exerts controlling influences on eating, drinking, and the experience of pleasure, rage, and aversion. The hypothalamus is the central core from which all emotions derive their motive force. The hypothalamus is also sexually differentiated. That is, structurally and functionally the hypothalamus of men and women is sexually dissimilar. [*See* HYPOTHALAMUS.]

A. Lateral and Ventromedial Hypothalamic Nuclei

Although the hypothalamus consists of several distinct regions and subgroups, the lateral and medial (ventromedial) hypothalamic nuclei play particularly important roles in almost all aspects of emotion and internal homeostasis. They also appear to share a somewhat antagonistic relationship and act to exert counterbalancing influences on each other.

For example, the medial hypothalamus controls parasympathetic activities (e.g., reduction in heart rate, increased peripheral circulation) and exerts a dampening effect on certain forms of emotional/motivational arousal. The lateral hypothalamus mediates sympathetic activity (increasing heart rate, elevation of blood pressure) and is involved in controlling the metabolic and somatic correlates of heightened emotionality.

B. Hunger and Thirst

The lateral and medial region are highly involved in monitoring internal needs such as hunger and thirst. For example, both nuclei contain receptors which are sensitive to the body's fat content (lipostatic receptors) and to circulating metabolites such as glucose, which together indicate the need for food and nourishment. The lateral hypothalamus also appears to contain osmoreceptors which determine if water intake should be altered. Both hypothalamic nuclei also become highly active immediately prior to and while the organism is eating or drinking.

For example, the lateral region alters its activity when the subject is hungry and simply looking at food. If the lateral hypothalamus is electrically stimulated a compulsion to eat and drink results. Conversely, if the lateral area is destroyed there results aphagia and adipsia so severe animals will die of starvation. If the medial hypothalamus is surgically destroyed, inhibitory influences on the lateral region appear to be abolished such that hypothalamic hyperphagia and severe obesity result.

Overall, it appears that the lateral hypothalamus is involved in the initiation of eating and acts to maintain a lower weight limit such that when the limit is reached the organism is stimulated to eat. Conversely, the medial regions seem to be involved

in setting a higher weight limit such that when these levels are approached it triggers the cessation of eating. That is, the medial area seems to act as a satiety center; but, a center that can be overridden. In part, these nuclei exert these differential influences on eating and drinking via motivational/emotional influences they exert on other brain nuclei (e.g., via reward or punishment). [*See* APPETITE.]

C. Pleasure and Reward

In 1952, R. G. Heath reported what was then considered remarkable. Electrical stimulation near the septal nuclei elicited feelings of pleasure in human subjects: "I have a glowing feeling. I feel good!" Subsequently, in 1954 James Olds and Peter Milner reported that rats would tirelessly press a lever in order to receive electrical stimulation via tiny electrodes planted in this same region. Olds and Milner, in fact, concluded that stimulation in this region of the brain "has an effect which is apparently equivalent to that of a conventional primary reward." Even hungry animals would demonstrate a preference for self-stimulation over food.

Feelings of pleasure have since been obtained following electrical excitation to a number of diverse limbic areas including the olfactory bulbs, amygdala, hippocampus, cingulate gyrus, the basal ganglia, thalamus, reticular formation, medial forebrain bundle, and orbital frontal lobes. However, the greatest area of concentration and the highest rates of self-stimulatory activity were found to occur in the lateral hypothalamus. Indeed, according to Olds, animals "would continue to stimulate as rapidly as possible until physical fatigue forced them to slow or to sleep."

More recently, the lateral hypothalamus (as well as the amygdala and other limbic nuclei) have been found to have nerve cells which produce and are responsive to opiate-like substances, i.e., enkephalins. Hence, when an individual is injected with various narcotic substances, it is these limbic nuclei which respond with feelings of pleasure.

In contrast to the lateral hypothalamus and its involvement in pleasurable self-stimulation, activation of the medial hypothalamus is so aversive that subjects will work to reduce it—apparently so as to obtain relief (e.g., active avoidance). In this regard, when considering behavior such as eating, it might be postulated that when upper weight limits (or nutritional requirements) are met, the medial hypothalamus becomes activated which in turn leads to behavior which terminates its activation (e.g., cessation of eating). In fact, it is probably in this manner that the hypothalamus is able to exert considerable influence on a variety of behaviors, acting either to reward one's actions or to generate feelings of aversion so that one is less likely to act in a similar manner in the future.

D. Emotional Incontinence: Laughter and Rage

Although highly involved in all aspects of emotion and motivational functioning, the emotional states elicited by the hypothalamus are very primitive, diffuse, undirected, and unrefined, being limited to pleasure in general, or aversion/unpleasure in general. It is for this reason that ancient and primitive animals are also very limited in their ability to express and perceive emotion. Higher order emotional reactions (e.g., desire, love, hate, etc.) require the involvement of other limbic regions as well as the participation of the more recently evolved regions of the brain, the neocortex (i.e., "new brain").

Nevertheless, due to its involvement in the generation of positive and negative emotions, not surprisingly, when the hypothalamus has been injured or is made to function abnormally, extremely positive or negative reactions can also be elicited, including rage and uncontrolled laughter. For example, laughter has been noted to occur with hilarious or obscene speech—usually as a prelude to stupor or death—in cases where tumor has infiltrated the hypothalamus. In several instances it has been reported that in the course of neurosurgery involving the hypothalamus, patients "became lively, talkative, joking, and whistling each time the hypothalamus was manipulated." In one case, the patient became excited and began to sing. Some individuals with hypothalamic damage have in fact died laughing. However, such patients claim that their laughter does not reflect their true feelings. Hence, laughter in these instances has been referred to as "sham mirth." Moreover, the type of emotional reaction elicited is dependent on which region of the hypothalamus has been injured or activated.

Stimulation of the lateral hypothalamus, for example, can induce extremes in emotionality, including intense attacks of rage accompanied by biting and attack upon any moving object. If this nucleus is destroyed, aggressive and attack behavior is abolished. Hence, the lateral hypothalamus is responsible for rage and aggressive behavior, including attack and predatory actions, which coincides with its involvement with eating. In contrast, stimulation of the medial region counters the lateral hypothalamus such that rage reactions are reduced or eliminated. If the medial region is destroyed there results lateral hypothalamic release and the triggering of extreme savagery. [See AGGRESSION.]

Nevertheless, like "sham mirth," rage reactions elicited in response to direct electrical activation of the hypothalamus immediately and completely dissipate when the stimulation is removed. As such, these outbursts have been referred to as "sham rage."

III. PSYCHOLOGICAL MANIFESTATIONS OF HYPOTHALAMIC ACTIVITY

Phylogenetically and from an evolutionary perspective, the appearance and development of the hypothalamus predates the emergence and differentiation of all other limbic nuclei, e.g., amygdala, septal nucleus, hippocampus. It constitutes the most primitive, archaic, reflexive, and purely biological aspect of the psyche.

Biologically the hypothalamus serves the body tissues by attempting to maintain internal homeostasis and by providing for the immediate discharge of tensions in an almost reflexive manner. Hence, as based on studies of lateral and medial hypothalamic functioning, it appears to act reflexively, in an almost on/off manner so as to seek or maintain the experience of pleasure and escape or avoid unpleasant, noxious conditions. [See HOMEOSTASIS.]

Emotions elicited by the hypothalamus are largely undirected, short-lived, and unconnected with events occurring within the external environment, being triggered reflexively and without concern or understanding regarding consequences. Direct contact with the real world is quite limited and almost entirely indirect as the hypothalamus is largely concerned with the internal environment of the organism. It has no sense of morals, danger, values, logic, etc., and cannot feel or express love or hate. Although quite powerful, hypothalamic emotions are largely undifferentiated, consisting of feelings such as pleasure, unpleasure, aversion, rage, hunger, thirst, etc.

As the hypothalamus is concerned with the internal environment much of its activity occurs outside conscious–awareness. Moreover, being involved in maintaining internal homeostasis, via, for example, its ability to reward or punish the organism with feelings of pleasure or aversion, it tends to serve what Sigmund Freud described as the "pleasure principle."

IV. AMYGDALA

In contrast to the primitive hypothalamus, the amygdala is preeminent in the control and mediation of all higher order emotional and motivational activities, including the capacity to form emotional attachments and to feel love. Neurons located in the amygdala are able to monitor and abstract from the sensory array stimuli that are of motivational significance so as to organize and express appropriate feelings and behaviors. This includes the ability to discern and express even subtle social–emotional nuances such as friendliness, fear, affection, distrust, anger, etc., and at a more basic level, determine if something might be good to eat. In fact, amygdaloid neurons respond selectively to the flavor of certain preferred foods, as well as to the sight or sound of something that might be especially desirable to eat.

Moreover, some neurons located in the amygdala are responsive to faces and facial emotions conveyed by others. Many neurons are also able to respond to visual, tactual, olfactory, and auditory stimuli simultaneously. Hence, many amygdaloid neurons are predominantly polymodal, responding to a variety of stimuli from different modalities. It is in this manner that the amygdala has come to be involved not only in emotion, but attention, and learning and memory, for multimodal assimilation of various sensory impressions occurs in this region.

A. Medial and Lateral Amygdala Nuclei

The amygdala is buried within the depths of the anterior–inferior temporal lobe and consists of two major nuclear groups. These are a phylogenetically ancient anteromedial group (or medial amygdala) which is involved in olfaction, pheromonal perception, and motor activity (via rich interconnections with the basal ganglia), and a relatively newer basolateral division (lateral amygdala) which is maximally developed among humans.

Like the lateral and medial hypothalamus, the medial and lateral amygdala are rich in opiate receptors and cells containing enkephalins and both subserve different functions. For example, the medial amygdala is highly involved in motor, olfactory, and sexual functioning, whereas the lateral division is intimately involved in all aspects of higher order emotional activity including the generation of selective attention. That is, the amygdala acts to perform environmental surveillance and can trigger orienting responses as well as mediate the maintenance of attention if something of interest or importance were to appear. Hence, electrical stimulation of the lateral division can initiate quick and/or anxious glancing and searching movements of the eyes and head such that the organism appears aroused and highly alert as if in expectation of something that is going to happen.

Indeed, via its rich interconnections with the inferior, middle, and superior temporal lobes, as well as other neocortical regions, the lateral amygdala is able to sample and influence the auditory, somesthetic, and visual information being received and processed in these areas, as well as scrutinize this information for motivational and emotional significance. It is through the lateral division that emotional meaning and significance can be assigned to as well as extracted from that which is experienced.

B. The Amygdala and Hypothalamus

The amygdala, overall, maintains a functionally interdependent relationship with the hypothalamus. It is able to modulate and even control rudimentary emotional forces governed by the hypothalamic nucleus. However, it also acts as the behest of hypothalamically induced drives. For example, if certain nutritional requirements need to be meet, the hypothalamus signals the amygdala which then surveys the external environment for something good to eat. On the other hand, if the amygdala via environmental surveillance were to discover a potentially threatening stimulus such as a predator, it acts to excite and drive the hypothalamus as well as the motor centers, so that the organism is mobilized to take appropriate action. When the hypothalamus is activated by the amygdala, instead of responding in an on/off manner, cellular activity continues for an appreciably longer time period. The amygdala can tap into the reservoir of emotional energy mediated by the hypothalamus so that certain ends may be attained.

C. Fear, Rage, and Aggression

Initially, electrical stimulation of the amygdala produces sustained attention and orienting reactions. If the stimulation continues fear and/or rage reactions are elicited. When fear follows the attention response, the pupils dilate and the subject will cringe, withdraw, and cower. This cowering reaction in turn may give way to extreme fear and/or panic such that the animal will attempt to take flight.

Among humans, the fear response is one of the most common manifestations of amygdaloid electrical stimulation. Moreover, unlike hypothalamic on/off emotional reactions, attention and fear reactions can last up to several minutes after the stimulation is withdrawn. In addition to behavioral manifestations of heightened emotionality, amygdaloid stimulation can also result in intense changes in emotional facial expression. This includes facial contortions, baring of the teeth, dilation of the pupils, widening or narrowing of the eye-lids, flaring of the nostrils, tearing, as well as sniffing, licking, and chewing. In fact, epileptic seizure activity in this area (i.e., temporal lobe epilepsy) often induces involuntary chewing, and smacking of the lips and licking. [See Anxiety and Fear.]

In many intances, rather than fear, stimulation of the amygdala results in anger, irritation, and rage which seems to gradually build up until finally the animal or human will attack. Unlike hypothalamic "sham rage," amygdaloid activation results in attacks directed at something real, or, in the absence of an actual stimulus, at something imaginary. Moreover, rage and attack will persist well beyond the termination of the electrical stimulation of the amygdala. In fact, the amygdala remains electrophysiologically active for long time periods even after a stimulus has been removed (be it external–perceptual or internal–electrical) such that it appears to continue to process—in the abstract—information even when that information is no longer observable. Moreover, tumors in this area can trigger violent rage attacks. A famous example of this is Charles Whitman, who in 1966 climbed a tower at the University of Texas carrying a high powered hunting rifle and for the next 90 minutes shot at everything that moved, killing 14, wounding 38. Postmortem autopsy of his brain revealed a glioblastoma multiformed tumor the size of a walnut compressing the amygdaloid nucleus. [See Anger.]

D. Social–Emotional Agnosia

Among primates and mammals, bilateral destruction of the amygdala significantly disturbs the ability to determine and identify the motivational and emotional significance of externally occurring events, to discern social–emotional nuances conveyed by others, or to select what behavior is appropriate given a specific social context. Bilateral destruction of both amygdalas (located in the right and left temporal lobe) usually results in increased tameness, docility, and reduced aggressiveness in cats, monkeys, and other animals and humans. It also lowers responsiveness to aversive and social stimuli, and reduces fearfulness, competitiveness, dominance, and social interest. Indeed, this condition is so pervasive that subjects seem to have tremendous difficulty discerning the meaning or recognizing the significance of even common objects—a condition sometimes referred to as "psychic blindness," or the "Kluver–Bucy syndrome." However, it is important to note that although Drs. Kluver and Bucy reported this in 1937, this condition had first been reported in 1888 by Drs. Brown and Shaefer.

Like an infant (who similarly is without a fully functional amygdala), individuals with bilateral amygdala destruction engage in extreme orality and will indiscriminately pick up various objects and place them in their mouth regardless of its appropriateness. There is a repetitive quality to this behavior, for once they put it down they seem to have *forgotten* that they had just *explored* it, and will immediately pick it up and place it again in their mouth as if it were a completely unfamiliar object.

Hence, humans as well as animals with bilateral amygdala destruction, although able to see and interact with their environment, respond in an emotionally blunted manner, and seem unable to recognize what they see, feel, and experience. Things seem stripped of meaning. This condition pervades all aspects of higher level social–emotional functioning including the ability to appropriately interact with loved ones. As might be expected, maternal behavior is severely affected. According to Dr. A. Kling, mothers will behave as if their "infant were a strange object to be mouthed, bitten and tossed around as though it were a rubber ball."

Among primates who have undergone bilateral amygdaloid removal, once they are released from captivity and allowed to return to their social group, a social–emotional agnosia becomes readily apparent as they no longer respond to or seem able to appreciate or understand emotional or social nuances. Indeed, they appear to have little or no interest in social activity and persistently attempt to avoid contact with others. If approached they withdraw, and if followed they flee. Indeed, they behave as if they have no understanding of what is expected of them or what others intend or are attempting to convey, even when the behavior is quite friendly and concerned. Among adults with bilateral lesions, total isolation seems to be preferred.

It is thus apparent that the amygdala, in conjunction with other limbic tissue, such as septal nuclei and the more recently evolved transitional limbic cortex, the cingulate gyrus, is highly involved in all aspects of social and emotional functioning. It has been argued that the differential maturation of these limbic structures, in particular, that of the amygdala, septal nuclei, and cingulate gyrus, is responsible for seeking contact comfort and forming of emotional and loving attachments during infancy. [*See* SOCIO-EMOTIONAL DEVELOPMENT.]

V. SEPTAL NUCLEI

The septal nuclei appears to develop out of the hypothalamus. Phylogenetically and presumably, ontogenetically, it seems to mature following the development of the amygdala, but at about the same time as the hippocampus, a limbic system structure involved in the formation of memory. The septal nuclei also increases in relative size and complexity as we ascend the ancestral tree, attaining its greatest degree of development in humans.

The septal nuclei lies in the medial portions of the hemispheres, just anterior to the hypothalamus, and maintains rich interconnections with all regions of the limbic system. Unfortunately, unlike other limbic tissue, the functioning of the septal nuclei is still not well understood. Nevertheless, it appears to maintain a complementary relationship with the hippocampus, but an oppositional, and sometimes antagonistic relationship with the amygdala. For example, the amygdala appears to act so as to either facilitate or inhibit septal functioning whereas septal influences on the amygdala are largely inhibitory. However, in large part, the amygdala and septal nuclei appear to exert the majority of their counterbalancing influences on the emotional functioning of the hypothalamus with which they both maintain rich interconnections.

A. Rage and Quiescence

A primary activity of the septal nucleus appears to be that of reducing extremes in emotionality and arousal, and maintaining the organism in state of quiescence and readiness to respond. Stimulation of the septum acts to reduce blood pressure and heart rate, induces andrenocortical secretion, counters lateral hypothalamic self-stimulatory activity, inhibits aggressive behavior and suppresses the expression of rage reactions following hypothalamic stimulation.

If the septal nucleus is destroyed, these counterbalancing influences are removed such that initially there results dramatic increases in aggressive behavior. In fact, bilateral lesions of the septal nuclei can trigger explosive emotional reactivity to tactile, visual, or auditory stimulation such that the animal may attempt to attack or run away. However, if the amygdala is subsequently destroyed, the septal rage and emotional reactivity are completely attenuated. However, when the amygdala remains intact, septal lesions appear to result in a loss of modulatory and inhibitory restraint.

B. Contact Comfort and Septal Social Functioning

Although initially destruction of the septal nuclei results in rage reactions, within a few weeks this aggressiveness subsides and/or completely disappears. However, a generalized tendency to overrespond and a generalized failure to inhibit emotional responsiveness persists, and animals so affected tend to demonstrate an extreme and indiscriminate need for social and physical contact. That is, in contrast to amygdaloid lesions which produce a severe social–emotional agnosia and social avoidance, septal lesions produce a dramatic and persistent increase in social cohesiveness.

These findings suggest that the normal, intact amygdala appears to promote social behavior whereas the septal nucleus seems to counter socializing tendencies. Hence, with destruction of the septal nuclei (which results in a release of the amygdala), the drive for social contact appears to be irresistible such that persistent attempts to make physical contact occurs—even with species quite unlike their own.

For example, septal lesioned rats, unlike normals, will readily seek out mice (to which they are normally indifferent) or rabbits (which they usually avoid). If presented with a choice of an empty (safe) chamber or one containing a cat, septal lesioned rats persistently attempt to huddle and crawl upon this normally feared creature, even when the cat is acting perturbed. If a group of septally lesioned animals are placed together, extreme huddling results. So intense is this need for contact comfort following septal lesions, that if other animals are not available they will seek out blocks of wood, old rags, bare wire frames, or walls.

Among humans with right-sided or bilateral disturbances in septal functioning (such as due to seizure activity being generated in this region), a behavior referred to as "stickiness" is sometimes observed. Such individuals seek to make repeated, prolonged, and often inappropriate contact with anyone who is available or who happens to be near by so as to tell them stories, jokes, or merely pass the time. Moreover, they refuse to take a "hint," and do not depart unless given a direct request to do so.

VI. EMOTIONAL ATTACHMENT AND AMYGDALA–SEPTAL INTERACTIONS

Physical, social, and emotional interaction and contact during infancy is critically important to the child's well-being as well as his or her neurological, sensory, cognitive, intellectual, social, and emotional development. Indeed, babies need their "mamas" and all the love and attendant physical and emotional interaction they can get. The more an infant is held, stroked, and spoken to, and the greater the visual divergence of his surroundings, the greater will be its resilience and capability to adapt to negative emotional and physical onslaughts and to withstand stressful extremes later in life. In fact, the very cells of the nervous system will prosper by growing larger and more complex.

So great is the need for stimulation that until 6–7 months of age most children will eagerly and indiscriminately seek social and physical contact from anyone including complete strangers. Indiscriminate social interaction is not merely a manifestation of friendliness but serves a specific purpose: it maximizes opportunities for social and physical contact and interaction. Like hunger and the desire for food (which is mediated by the hypothalamus) there is a physical drive and hunger for social, emotional, and physical stimulation (which is mediated by the amygdala).

At about 7 months of age the infant becomes more discriminate in his or her interactions and it is during this time period that a very real and specific attachment (e.g., to one's mother) becomes progressively more intense and stable. This does not mean that prior to this period the mother is not highly important to the infant, but rather maximal social interaction

takes precedence during the first critical months of life. Often a baby needs more contact than a single mother is capable of providing.

After these specific attachments such as to mother have been formed, most children increasingly begin to show anxiety, fear, and even flight reactions at the approach of a stranger. By 1 year of age 90% of children respond aversively to strangers. This also serves a purpose for it maximizes the bond with mother and ensures that a child who can crawl and maneuver through space does not indiscriminately attach to and wander off with a stranger.

Thus, the infant's initial seeking of indiscriminate social contact is followed at a later age by progressively narrowed contact seeking. According to a theory developed by Dr. R. Joseph, these stages of emotional development coincide with the maturation of different nuclei in the limbic system of the brain; the amygdala, septal nuclei, and cingulate gyrus.

As noted, the septal nucleus and amygdala often act in balanced opposition. That is, the septal nuclei appears to be highly involved in social and intimate contact seeking, but in a fashion quite different from the amygdala. The *normal* amygdala, which matures before the septal region promotes social contact seeking, whereas the *normal, undamaged* septal nuclei, which matures later, acts to inhibit and restrict these tendencies so that they are directed and focused (such as upon one person), rather than being generalized and indiscriminate. These two regions of the brain, in conjunction with the cingulate gyrus, are highly interactive and crucially important in the formation of our first and earliest attachments, as well as those later in life.

It is these same limbic nuclei which later in life are involved in the ability to feel love (as well as hate and anger) for, and attachment to, a loved one. That is, the limbic system controls the basic aspects of emotion, such as love, hate, anger, rage, fear, pleasure, the desire to bond together, as well as biological drives, including hunger, thirst, and even the capacity to experience orgasm during sex. Often all these impulses and needs at one time or another becomes associated with mother or the primary caretaker, and later in life (to a considerable degree), with a spouse. Even the presence or absence of mother can at one time or another elicit these responses (e.g., rage when the infant is not being held or fed).

Similarly, due to limbic attachment, the rejecting actions of a mate elicit limbic reactions including infantile feelings of rage and abandonment. That is, the amygdala striving to maintain the bonds of love responds with rage when the bond is severed, and the hypothalamus, feeling likewise, responds similarly. Even the murderous desire to kill one's spouse can be elicited. Indeed, loss of love, such as occurs when a relationship ends, seconded only by jealously and money, is a prime elicitor of such murderous feelings and is due to the high involvement of the limbic system in all affairs of the heart.

A. Limbic Abnormalities in Love and Socialization Skills

If contact with others is restricted during the early phases of infant development, then the ability to interact successfully with others at a later stage of life is retarded. That is, the infant and child must experience love and nurturance during this time period, otherwise these limbic nuclei will not develop and interact normally. If these interactional needs are not met during this critical period of development, gross abnormalities can result. Children will lose the ability to form emotional attachments with others, sometimes for the rest of their lives.

This is even true among non-human animals. Kittens which are not handled or stroked by humans soon become "wild" and unapproachable even when they have otherwise been exposed to people on a daily basis. Similarly, young children and infants who are separated from their parents and who fail to receive necessary loving and social stimulation are also affected adversely. They have difficulty forming emotional attachments and even their brains may not properly develop. If not adequately physically and emotionally stimulated, the child may even die.

In other words, if a child is not firmly attached to a mother figure and has been neglected early in life, the ability to form attachments increasingly narrows and then disappears, possibly forever. The child becomes attached to no one and its ability to form loving attachments later in life will be abnormal if drastic countermeasures are not taken. This is because cells in the amygdala, not receiving sufficient and appropriate stimulation begin to die and atrophy from disuse; just like a muscle if unused: "Use it or lose it." Once these limbic neurons die or if certain interconnections between different regions are not maintained, they are no longer able to respond appropriately to physical, emotional, and social interaction.

VII. THE CINGULATE GYRUS

A. The Evolution of Maternal Care

As noted, most creatures, including sharks, amphibians, reptiles, and fish, possess a limbic system, consisting of an amygdala, hippocampus, hypothalamus, and septal nuclei. It is these limbic nuclei which enable a group of fish to congregate together, i.e., to school, or for reptiles (creatures who first began to roam the planet about 300 million years ago) to form territories and very loosely organized social aggregates consisting of an alpha male and female, several subfemales, and a few juveniles. Such creatures, however, although sometimes showing parental investment, generally do not provide long-term care for their young and do not produce complex meaningful vocalizations, although, like amphibians they do produce very limited socially meaningful sounds, which in turn appear to be generated and perceived by limbic nuclei such as the amygdala.

Nevertheless, although in possession of a limbic system, reptiles and other non-mammalian species are lacking the more recently acquired cingulate cortex which appears to have begun to evolve around 250 million years ago when reptiles diverged to form repto-mammals (the therapsids) who in turn evolved into mammals and then primates. It was with the appearance of the repto-mammals that the first evidence of suckling of infants and long-term maternal care came into being. Indeed, it has been postulated by Paul Maclean (who in fact coined the term "limbic system"), as well as by Dr. R. Joseph, that the cingulate (in conjunction with the amygdala and septal nuclei) is largely responsible for the appearance of maternal feelings and the evolution of the family.

However, primates and other mammals, in addition to limbic and transitional limbic cingulate cortex, are also equipped with the six- to seven-layered neocortex which evolved approximately 100 million years ago and which covers the old brain like a shroud. However, like the amygdala, the cingulate has reached its maximal size among humans and maintains rich interconnections with the neocortex as well as with the older portions of the limbic system such as the amygdala and hippocampus. [*See* NEO-CORTEX.]

Among humans and lower mammals, destruction of the anterior cingulate results in a loss of fear, lack of maternal responsiveness, and severe alterations in socially appropriate behavior. Humans will often become initially mute and socially unresponsive, and when they speak, their vocal melodic–inflectional patterns and the emotional sounds they produce sound abnormal. Animals, such as monkeys who have suffered cingulate destruction will also become mute, will cease to groom or show acts of affection, and will treat their fellow monkeys as if they were inanimate objects. For example, they may walk upon and over them as if they were part of the floor or some obstacle rather than a fellow being. In other words, their behavior is more typical of a reptile than a primate. Maternal behavior is also abolished following cingulate destruction, and the majority of infants soon die from lack of care.

More importantly, when the cingulate cortex is electrically stimulated, the separation cry, similar if not identical to that produced by an infant, is elicited. In fact, it appears that the cingulate, in conjunction with the amygdala and other limbic tissue, is responsible for not only the development of long-term infant care, but also the initial production of what would become language. This has been referred to by Joseph as "limbic language." In fact, be it humans or reptiles the limbic system is preeminent in the mediation, production, and comprehension of emotional–social sounds, including sex differences in their production.

VIII. LIMBIC LANGUAGE

Phylogenetically and ontogenetically, the original impetus to vocalize springs forth from roots buried within the depths of the ancient "limbic lobe" a term coined by Paul Broca in the 1800s. Although non-humans do not have the capacity to speak, they still vocalize, and these vocalizations are primarily limbic in origin being evoked in situations involving sexual arousal, terror, anger, flight, helplessness, and separation from the primary caretaker when young.

The first vocalizations of human infants are similarly emotional in origin and limbically mediated, consisting predominantly of sounds indicative of pleasure and displeasure. Indeed, these sounds and cries are produced soon after birth, indicating they are innate, and are produced even by infants born deaf and blind. Similarly, apes and monkeys reared in isolation or with surgically muted mothers also produce appropriately sounding complex emotional calls in order to convey a wealth of information, including the presence of danger. Moreover, they will respond to these same calls with appropriate

reactions, even when they had never before been heard.

A. Limbic Localization of Emotional Sound Production

Emotional cries and warning calls have been produced via electrode stimulation of wide areas throughout the limbic system. Nevertheless, the type of cry elicited, in general, depends upon which limbic nuclei has been activated. For example, portions of the septal nuclei, hippocampus, and medial hypothalamus have been repeatedly shown to be generally involved in the generation of negative and unpleasant mood states, whereas the lateral hypothalamus and amygdala, and portions of the septal nuclei, are associated with pleasureable feelings. Not surprisingly, areas associated with pleasurable sensations often give rise, when sufficiently stimulated, to pleasurable calls, whereas those linked to negative mood states will trigger cries of alarm and shrieking. However, of all limbic nuclei, the amygdala and cingulate gyrus appear to be the most vocal.

In humans and animals a wide range of emotional sounds have been evoked through amygdala activation, including those indicative of pleasure, sadness, happiness, and anger. Conversely, in humans, destruction limited to the amygdala, the right amygdala in particular, has abolished the ability to sing, convey melodic information, or enunciate properly via vocal inflection and can result in great changes in pitch and the timbre of speech. Even the capacity to perceive and respond appropriately to social–emotional cues is abolished.

However, in the cingulate gyrus, completely different emotional calls can be elicited from electrodes which are immediately adjacent, and the calls do not always correlate with the mood state. This suggests considerable flexibility within the cingulate which also appears to have the capability of producing emotional sounds that are not reflective of mood. This suggests a high degree of voluntary control within the cingulate. However, of the many sounds produced, the separation cry of the infant is one of the most significant, particularly in regard to the evolution of language. It is from the cingulate where the separation cry is most frequently elicited.

B. Limbic Language and Mother–Infant Vocalization

Among social terrestrial vertebrates the production of sound is very important in regard to infant care, for if an infant becomes lost, separated, or in danger, a mother would have no way of quickly knowing this by smell alone. Such information would have to be conveyed via a cry of distress or a sound indicative of separation fear and anxiety. It would be the production of these sounds which would cause a mother to come running to the rescue. Hence, the first forms of limbic social–emotional communication was probably produced in a maternal context.

Indeed, considerable vocalizing typically occurs between human and non-human mammalian mothers and their infants, and the infants of many species, including primates, will often sing along or produce sounds in accompaniment to those produced by their mothers. In fact, among primates, females are more likely to vocalize and utter alarm calls when they are near their infants versus non-kin, and vice versa, and adult males are more likely to call or cry when in the presence of their mother or an adult female vs an adult male. Similarly, infant primates will loudly protest when separated from their mother so long as she is in view and will quickly cease to vocalize when isolated. It thus appears that the purpose of these vocalizations are to elicit a response from the mother.

Hence, the production of emotional sounds appears to be limbically linked and associated with maternal–infant care, and with interactions with an adult female. In fact, human females in general tend to vocalize more so than males and their speech tends to be perceived as friendlier and more social.

It is important to note, however, that the hypothalamus, septal nuclei, and the periquaductal gray (which is located in the midbrain) are also important components in the formulation of limbic language. Given the role of these limbic nuclei in sex related differences in cognition and behavior, it is perhaps highly likely that they may contribute to sex differences in language as well.

IX. SEXUAL DIFFERENTIATION OF THE HYPOTHALAMUS AND AMYGDALA

As is well known, sexual differentiation is strongly influenced by the presence or absence of gonadal androgen hormones during certain critical periods of prenatal development in many species including humans. However, not only are the external genitalia and other physical features sexually differentiated but certain regions of the brain have also been found to be sexually dimorphic and differentially sensitive to steroids, particularly the amygdala and the preoptic area and medial nucleus of the hypothalamus. Specifically, the presence or absence of the male hormone, testosterone, during this critical neonatal period directly affects and determines the pattern of interconnections between the amygdala and hypothalamus, between axons and dendrites in these nuclei, and thus the organization of specific neural circuits. In the absence of testosterone, the female pattern of neuronal development occurs.

That various limbic regions, such as the preoptic and medial (ventromedial) hypothalamus are sexually differentiated is not surprising in that it has long been known that this area is extremely important in controlling the basal output of gonadotrophins in females prior to ovulation and is heavily involved in mediating cyclic changes in hormone levels (e.g., estrogen, progesterone). Chemical and electrical stimulation of these nuclei also triggers sexual behavior and even sexual posturing in females and males. Moreover, in primates, electrical stimulation of the preoptic area increases sexual behavior in males, and significantly increases the frequency of erections, copulations, and ejaculations, as well as pelvic thrusting followed by an explosive discharge of semen even in the absence of a mate. Conversely, lesions to these nuclei eliminate male sexual behavior and result in gonadal atrophy.

Similarly, electrical stimulation of the amygdala, the medial division in particular, results in sex related behavior and activity. In females this includes ovulation, uterine contractions, and lactogenetic responses, and in males penile erections.

Conversely, damage to the amygdala bilaterally, often results in heightened and indiscriminate sexual activity. For example, primates and other animals (while in captivity) will engage in excessive masturbation and genital manipulation and will repeatedly attempt to copulate even with species other than their own (e.g., a cat with a dog, a dog with a turtle, etc.) regardless of their sex. Hence, with bilateral destruction, animals are not only overly active sexually, but also unable to identify appropriate partners. Conversely, with abnormal activity involving the amygdala, such as due to temporal lobe epilepsy, sensations of sexual excitement, and even sexual behavior sometimes leading to orgasm, may also occur as a function of seizures originating in the temporal lobe.

A. Sex Differences in Language and Cognition

Hence, it thus appears that the limbic system not only is involved in all aspects of emotion, including sexual behavior and the production of emotional speech, but that these same limbic nuclei may be responsible for sex differences in thought, feeling, and even language. For example, it has been argued by that sex differences in language, emotion, and cognitive capability may represent the differential effects of early hormonal influences on various limbic system nuclei as well as within the neocortex. Indeed, the administration of testosterone to females during these early critical periods or the castration of males will completely reverse sex differences in behavior and cognition.

For example, it is well known that men, boys, and even male rats demonstrate superior spatial-perceptual abilities, such as in maze learning, as compared to females. If testosterone is not present during these early critical periods, these superiorities are reversed. On the other hand, women and young girls have shown some superiority in regard to various aspects of language, including those related to social and emotional functioning. It may be that these results are also related to early hormonal influences on limbic organization.

Consider for example intonation and pitch. Women tend to employ five to six different variations and to utilize the higher registers when conversing. They are also more likely to employ glissando or sliding effects between stressed syllables, and they tend to talk faster as well. Men tend to be more monotone, employing two to three variations on average, most of which hovers around the lower registers. Even when trying to emphasize a point males are less likely to employ melodic extremes but instead tend to speak louder.

B. Sex Differences in Emotion

As has been demonstrated in a number of recent studies, women are also more emotionally expressive, and are more perceptive in regard to comprehending emotional verbal nuances. This superior female sensitivity even includes the comprehension of emotional faces, and the ability to feel and express empathy. In fact, from childhood to adulthood women appear to be much more emotionally expressive than males in general. Indeed, given woman's role in rearing children, and the role of the limbic system in promoting maternal care and communication, it seems rather natural that they are much more sensitive to and expressive of these nuances. These

differences may reflect sex-related differences in the structure and function of the male vs female limbic system.

Indeed, although sex differences in the structure of the cingulate have not yet been reported, consider for example, the anterior commissure, a bundle of fibers which acts to interconnect the two amygdalas and inferior temporal lobes. This fiber pathway is 18% larger in the female vs the male brain. Given the preimmanent role of the amygdala in emotionality and sound production, as well as evidence indicating that this nuclei is sexually dimorphic, this latter finding of an enlargement in the anterior commissure may be yet another reason why females are more emotionally expressive, receptive, and tend to employ a wider range of melodic pitch when they speak. Moreover, given the intimate role of the amygdala with the hippocampus, it is possible that sexual differentiation of this and other limbic nuclei may be responsible for sex differences in spatial–perceptual abilities and other cognitive differences as well.

X. HIPPOCAMPUS

A. Arousal, Attention, and Inhibition

The hippocampus is an elongated structure located within the inferior medial wall of the temporal lobe, posterior to the amygdala, and is shaped somewhat like a telephone receiver. It consists of an anterior and posterior region, and is richly interconnected with the septal nuclei (which in some ways acts as a relay nucleus for the hippocampus), as well as the cingulate gyrus and amygdala. Among animals it has also been found to be sexually differentiated. [See HIPPOCAMPAL FORMATION.]

Various authors have assigned the hippocampus a major role in information processing, including memory, new learning, spatial mapping of the environment, and voluntary movement toward a goal, as well as in attention and behavioral arousal. For example, hippocampal cells greatly alter their activity in response to certain spatial correlates, particularly as an animal moves about in its environment. It is also intimately involved in the encoding and memory storage of spatial, as well as verbal, emotional, and other forms of information. However, few studies have implicated the hippocampus in emotional functioning per se, although responses such as "anxiety" or "bewilderment" have been observed when directly electrically stimulated.

Over the course of evolution the hippocampus has become modified and many of its functions have come to be hierarchically mediated, controlled, or at least, influenced by activity occurring within the neocortex, with which it maintains rich interconnections. Due to this interrelationship the hippocampus is able to monitor as well as exert reciprocal influences over neocortical functioning which it monitors.

For example, when the neocortex becomes highly activated, the hippocampus functions at a much lower level of arousal in order not to become overwhelmed. When the neocortex is not highly aroused, the hippocampus presumably compensates by increasing its own level of arousal so as to tune in to information that is being processed at a low level of neocortical intensity. However, in situations where both the neocortex and the hippocampus become highly aroused and activated, the individual becomes easily distracted, hyperresponsive, and overwhelmed, confused, and disoriented. Attention, learning, and memory functioning are also decreased due to this interference in the ability to selectively maintain attention. Situations such as this sometimes occur when individuals are highly anxious or upset.

There is also evidence to suggest that the hippocampus may act so as to reduce extremes in neocortical arousal. For example, whereas stimulation of the reticular activating system augments cortical arousal and EEG evoked potentials, hippocampal stimulation reduces or inhibits these potentials such that cortical responsiveness and arousal are dampened.

On the other hand, if neocortical arousal is at a low level, hippocampal stimulation often results in an augmentation of the neocortical evoked EEG potential, thus increasing arousal levels. It is presumably in this manner that the hippocampus can exert influence on what is being processed in the neocortex so as to control selective attention and maintain concentration. Again, this aids in learning and the retention of significant information via selective attention or the filtering of irrelevant forms of input that might otherwise become processed and attended to.

The hippocampus thus prevents the neocortex from becoming overwhelmed or inattentive, and may act to increase neocortical arousal so that it is sufficiently activated. This is because very high or very low states of excitation are incompatible with alertness and selective attention as well as the ability to learn and retain information. When the hippocampus is damaged or destroyed, animals have great difficulty inhibiting behavioral responsiveness or shifting attention. The ability to shift from one set of perceptions to another or to change behavioral patterns is disrupted and the organism becomes overwhelmed by a particular mode of input. Learning, memory, and attention, are greatly compromised.

B. Learning and Memory

The hippocampus is thus associated with learning and memory encoding (e.g., long-term storage and retrieval of newly learned information), particularly the anterior regions. Of course, many other brain areas such as the mammillary bodies, dorsal medial nucleus of the thalamus, etc., are also important in memory functioning. Nevertheless, the hippocampus, in conjunction with the amygdala, appears to be preeminent in this regard.

It is now well known that bilateral destruction of the anterior hippocampus results in striking and profound disturbances involving memory and new learning, i.e., anterograde amnesia. For example, one such individual who underwent bilateral destruction of this nuclei (H.M.) was subsequently found to have almost completely lost the ability to recall anything experienced after surgery. If you introduced yourself to him, left the room, and then returned a few minutes later he would have no recall of having met or spoken to you. Dr. Brenda Milner has worked with H.M. for almost 20 years and yet she is an utter stranger to him. However, events that occurred for up to 2 years before his surgery were also somewhat disrupted. [See AMNESIA.]

Nevertheless, H.M. is in fact so amnesic for everything that has occurred since his surgery that every time he rediscovers that his favorite uncle died (years after his surgery) he suffers the same grief as if he had just been informed for the first time. Even so, although without memory for new (nonmotor) information, H.M. has adequate intelligence, is painfully aware of his deficit, and constantly apologizes for his problem. "Right now, I'm wondering" he once said, "Have I done or said anything amiss?" You see, at this moment everything looks clear to me, but what happened just before? That's what worries me. It's like waking from a dream. I just don't remember. . . . Every day is alone in itelf, whatever enjoyment I've had, and whatever sorrow I've had . . . I just don't remember.''

As noted above, presumably the hippocampus acts to protect memory and the encoding of new information during the storage and consolidation phase via the gating of afferent streams of information and the filtering/exclusion (or dampening) of irrelevant and interfering stimuli. When the hippocampus is damaged there results input overload, the brain is overwhelmed by irrelevant stimuli, and the consolidation phase of memory is disrupted such that relevant information is not properly stored or even attended to. Consequently, the ability to form associations (e.g., between stimulus and response) or to alter preexisting schemas (such as occurs during learning) is attenuated.

C. Hippocampal and Amygdaloid Interactions: Memory

The amygdaloid nucleus via its rich interconnections with other brain regions is able to sample and influence activity occurring in other parts of the cerebrum and add emotional color to one's perceptions. As such it is highly involved in the assimilation and association of divergent emotional, motivational, somesthetic, visceral, auditory, visual, motor, olfactory, and gustatory stimuli. Thus, it is very concerned with learning, memory, and attention, and can generate reinforcement for certain behaviors. Moreover, via reward or punishment it can promote the encoding, storage, and later retrieval of particular types of information. That is, learning often involves reward and it is via the amygdala (in concert with other nuclei) that emotional consequences can be attributed to certain events, actions, or experiences, as well as extracted from the world of possibility so that it can be attended to and remembered. Indeed, the amygdala, in conjunction with the hippocampus, is extremely important in learning and memory, and both are richly interconnected.

The amygdala thus seems to reinforce and maintain hippocampal activity via the identification of motivationally and emotionally significant information and the generation of pleasurable rewards (through action on the lateral hypothalamus). This is because reward increases the probability of attention being paid to a particular stimulus or conse-

quence as a function of its association with reinforcement. As such, events which are positively or negatively reinforced are more likely to be remembered.

Hence, the hippocampus acts to reduce or enhance extremes in arousal associated with information reception and storage in memory, whereas the amygdala acts to identify the social–emotional–motivational characteristics of the stimuli as well as to generate (in conjunction with the hippocampus) appropriate emotional rewards so that learning and memory will be reinforced. Thus, we find that when both the amygdala and hippocampus are damaged, striking and profound disturbances in memory functioning result.

D. Visual and Verbal Memory

It is now very well known that lesions involving the inferior temporal lobes and the amygdala/hippocampus of the left cerebral hemisphere typically produce significant disturbances involving verbal memory. Left-sided damage disrupts the ability to recall simple sentences and complex verbal narrative passages or to learn verbal paired-associates or a series of digits.

In contrast, right temporal amygdala–hippocampal destruction typically produces deficits involving visual and spatial memory, such as the learning and recall of geometric patterns, visual mazes, human faces, or even where some object was placed the night before. Right-sided damage also disrupts the ability to recall olfactory stimuli, emotional sounds and passages, or sounds from the environment.

Hence, the left amygdala/hippocampus is highly involved in processing and/or attending to verbal information, whereas the right amygdala/hippocampus is more involved in the learning, memory, and recollection of nonverbal, visual–spatial, environmental, emotional, motivational, and facial information. However, as noted above, the limbic system, including the hippocampus, is sexually differentiated, which in turn appears to affect the ability to attend to and recall spatial vs emotional and verbal information. In this regard, the male limbic system appears to have conferred an advantage in the processing of spatial information, whereas the female limbic system is more adept at expressing, processing, and possibly recalling emotionally laden visual and verbal stimuli.

Bibliography

Gerall, A. A., Molttz, H., and Ward, I. L. (Eds.) (1992). "Sexual Differentiation." Plenum, New York.

Joseph, R. (1990). "Neuropsychology, Neuropsychiatry, and Behavioral Neurology." Plenum, New York.

Joseph, R. (1992). The limbic system: Emotion, laterality, and unconscious mind. *Psychoanal. Rev.* **79,** 405–456.

Joseph, R. (1992). "The Right Brain and the Unconscious." Plenum, New York.

Joseph, R. (1993). "The Naked Neuron: Evolution and the Languages of the Body and Brain." Plenum, New York.

Kling, A. S., Lloyd, R. L., and Perryman, K. M. (1987). Slow wave changes in amygdala to visual, auditory, and social stimuli following lesions of the inferior temporal cortex in squirrel monkey. *Behav. Neural Biol.* **47,** 54–72.

MacLean, P. (1990). "The Triune Brain in Evolution." Plenum, New York.

Olds, M. E., and Forbes, J. L. (1981). The central basis of motivation: Intracranial self-stimulation studies. *Annu. Rev. Psychol.* **32,** 523–574.

Steklis, H. D., and Kling, A. (1985). Neurobiology of affiliative behavior in nonhuman primates. In "The Psychobiology of Attachment and Separation." (M. Reite and T. Field, Eds.). Academic Press, Orlando.

LOGIC

Jonas Langer
University of California at Berkeley

Glossary

Combinativity structures Comprised of composing, decomposing, and reforming (plus derivatives such as recomposing and attaching) operations that produce elements and sets. To illustrate, reforming a malleable ring alters its intensive properties (e.g., the shape of the ring) while keeping its extensive properties (e.g., its quantity) constant.

Concrete operations *Intra*propositional reasoning about apparent phenomena (e.g., observable causal variables) marked by inverse *or* reciprocal relations not yet coordinated by reversibility.

Formal operations *Inter*propositional reasoning about hypotheticodeductive phenomena (e.g., nonobservable causal variables) marked by necessity, sufficiency, and reversibility between inverse *and* reciprocal relations.

Heterochrony Phylogenetic change in the ontogenetic timing or rate at which features develop in relation to each other.

Part–whole transformation A basic mapping form by which subjects structure their interactions with the environment to construct logical cognition. These transformations are the source of operations (e.g., composing and negating) that produce necessary extensive (e.g., equivalence) and intensive (e.g., identity) relations.

LOGICAL COGNITION is an evolutionary and developmental product. Like many other natural cognitive phenomena, its phylogenetic and ontogenetic roots predate the acquisition of language. However, its systematic formalization, even in the natural reasoning by adults who are not logicians, requires symbolic notation. Hence, we will trace the development of natural logical cognition from its roots in prelinguistic actions and perceptions to its instantiation in natural formal reasoning by (nonlogician) adults.

Recently, attention is beginning to be given to studying the roots of logical cognition in human infancy and even in phylogeny. In part this has come about because traditional assumptions about logical cognition are no longer universally accepted. Maximally, it has been assumed that logical cognition is about valid inferences framed in formal symbolic language. Minimally, it has been assumed that verbal language was required. Animals and human infants do not have a verbal let alone a formal symbolic language. Therefore, they cannot have any logical cognition. Often, this conclusion led to the further presumption that logical cognition is an advanced human cultural product transmitted to prelogical children when they begin to be ready to manipulate verbal and formal symbols, probably beginning during late childhood and early adolescence.

Similar but more cautious views have been proposed in historical analyses of the rise of logic from their Sumerian and Babylonian manifestations onward. These analyses assume that the introduction of special systems of arbitrary symbols to represent objects, quantities, variables, operations, etc., led to the initial great advances in logic and mathematics. It has not been denied that the rudiments of logic, upon which these advances were built, were constructed in ordinary language. Further, the issue of prelinguistic antecedents of logic has not yet been addressed in historical analyses.

Questioning the traditional assumptions about logical cognition, comparative developmental psychology seeks the roots of logical cognition in the preverbal behavior of animals and human infants. Further, it aims to recover the initial advances in logical cognition in the developments during childhood when verbal language is available but without the assistance of formal systems of symbolic notation. Moreover, deaf adolescents deprived of any verbal language nevertheless develop advanced formal logical operations that, we shall see in Section III, are characteristic of normal adolescents. Accordingly, we sketch the main developments in logical cognition from its preverbal origins in human infancy to its culmination in formal logical operations during adolescence and adulthood. We conclude by considering the evolution of logical cognition in primates.

I. THE ORIGINS OF LOGIC IN INFANCY

Newborns behave. But their acts may be nothing more than agnostic movements; not all behaviors produce knowledge, let alone logical knowledge. Here we are only concerned with infants' gnostic acting that produces logical knowledge. Infants' gnostic range spans receptive, perceptual to constructive, sensorimotor acting.

A variety of different roles have been ascribed to receptive perception in the origins of logical cognition. The minimalist supposition is that perception is a necessary but not sufficient condition for the origins of logical operations. To emerge, logical operations require the re-representation of perceptual knowledge in culturally transformed and communicable forms. The maximalist supposition is that logical knowledge is nothing but the cultural explication by productive thinking of implicit configurational principles prefigured in perception. Thus, both traditional minimalist and maximalist perceptual views assume that logical cognition is derivative (secondary), not original (primary).

Both derivationalist hypotheses remained plausible as long as no contrary data emerged on the logical development of infants. Thus, even Piaget's pioneering research only discovered the origins of physical concepts (of objects, space, causality, and time) in infants. Our research, however, is advancing a third alternative, the originalist hypothesis that logical cognition is not a derivative ontogenetic development but an original development during infancy. Our originalist hypothesis takes its cue from earlier discoveries of sensorimotor seriating and classifying by infants. Classes and relations, it should be remembered, have long been proposed as generative structures of logical cognition (beginning at least with the logicians Boole and DeMorgan, and formulated more recently and comprehensively by Piaget).

Our originalist hypothesis is that infants' gnostic actions generate elementary logical, or more accurately protological, cognition. A corollary is that language is not even necessary for, let alone constitutive of, the origins of logical cognition. The originalist hypothesis does not rule out the possibility that receptive forms of gnostic acting, particularly perception, contribute to the origins of logical cognition. But, constructive sensorimotor activity is the main source of logical cognition's origins.

The next section outlines some representative findings on infants' developing logical cognition. They provide empirical support for the originalist hypothesis. Then we turn to the possible role that infants' perception plays.

A. Constructive Sensorimotor Activity

Logical cognition is structureless unless (a) one or more operations and/or relations are defined, and (b) the elements of cognition are constant. We have proposed three types of operations that provide sufficient foundational structures to generate the fundamentals of logical cognition: (1) combinativity structures of pragmatic composing, decomposing, and deforming; (2) relational structures of pragmatic adding, subtracting, multiplying, and dividing; and (3) conditional structure of pragmatic correspondence, exchange (including commuting and associativity), and negating. The foundational elements of infants' cognition are objects, collections, and series.

These foundational operations (e.g., composing) and elements (e.g., collections) of cognition are inherent in infants' constructive sensorimotor activity (e.g., touching one object to another). The reason is that constructive activity maps part–whole transformations onto objects and events (e.g., construct collections or sets of objects where there were none). These foundational operations and elements are therefore sufficient to the development of logical cognition. Most importantly, this includes progressively coming to know about necessary (a) equivalence, both quantitative (equality) and qualitative (identity); (b) ordered nonequivalence, both quantitative (inequality) and qualitative (difference); and (c) reversibility by negation.

1. The Initial Elements

The elements of infants' logical cognition are initially constructed by infants themselves. Infants' combinativity operations are fundamental to constructing these elements (i.e., objects, collections, series, and eventually mappings). For instance, at least as early as age 6 months, infants consistently compose discrete objects by uniting them into collections or sets. Infants first compose minimal and unstable elements, that should probably be called proto-elements (e.g., the sets usually comprise no more than the minimum of two objects). Progressively, they construct ever more extensive and stable elements that increasingly approximate, but never achieve, the status of fully formed constant givens for logical operations. Thus, infants compose ever larger sets during their second year (e.g., more than half of their collections exceed the minimum of two objects). Still, infants rarely combine even intermediate numbers of 5 to 7 objects into sets by age 24 months.

Single-set composing characterizes infants' constructions during their first year. A very small but not unimportant percentage of infants' constructions begin to comprise two contemporaneous sets of objects generated and preserved in partial or total temporal overlap. During their second year infants increasingly construct two or more contemporaneous sets. By their third year, children mainly construct contemporaneous sets. These compositions become progressively powerful elements for logical operations since they increasingly exceed two sets at a time (e.g., four separate stacks of blocks).

2. The Initial Operations

Logical operations, like the elements onto which they are mapped, are initially constructed by infants themselves. As the elements progressively approximate constant givens, they open up new and ever-growing possibilities for infants' operations. These operations map qualitative or intensive (e.g., classifying objects within a collection) and quantitative or extensive (e.g., commuting objects within a collection) part–whole transformations onto the elements infants construct. At first infants construct elementary and weak operations that should probably be called proto-operations. Progressively they become ever more complex and powerful mappings that increasingly approximate, but never achieve, the status of fully formed logical operations during infancy. We refer to the former as first-order operations, since they comprise direct elementary mappings, and to the latter as second-order operations, since they comprise mappings upon mappings.

Infants begin to map quantitative or extensive transformations by exchanging (substituting, replac-

ing, and commuting) objects in sets. Parallel development marks all three operations in human infancy (but not all primates, we shall soon see). So I illustrate with findings on substituting only. Only one-third of infants at age 6 months produce quantitative equivalence within single sets by substituting objects. These are limited to the minimum of substituting objects within two-object sets without any inversion. While still limited to single sets, by age 12 months all infants substitute and invert objects within two-object sets, and 50% of infants already extend substituting objects to three-object sets. Progress in first-order substituting continues during infants' second year. Most notably, some infants begin substituting within single four- to eight-object sets.

Another type of fundamental operation that infants begin to construct, albeit in rudimentary form, is classificatory. These operations map qualitative or intensive transformations onto sets to produce similarity, identity, and difference relations. Surprisingly, at age 6 months infants consistently couple objects from different classes with each other when presented with two contrasting classes of two objects. For example, 6 month olds consistently pair crosses with triangles, rather than crosses with crosses or triangles with triangles. At ages 8 and 10 months, infants no longer consistently couple objects from different classes with each other. Instead, their couplings are random. Thus, for example, infants this age are equally likely to pair crosses with triangles as they are to pair crosses with crosses and triangles with triangles. By age 12 months, infants begin to couple identical objects with each other (e.g., red crosses with red crosses), but only infrequently. By age 15 months, infants begin to couple consistently similar (e.g., red with blue crosses) as well as identical (e.g., red with red crosses) objects with each other.

While elementary first-order operations such as substituting and classifying mark infants' logical constructions during their first year, they no longer do so during their second year. The rudiments of more advanced operations originate toward the end of their first year and develop rapidly during their second year. These more advanced second-order operations are the developmental products of infants' integrating their elementary first-order operations.

The major new feature marking the development of second-order substituting consists of exchanges involving two contemporaneous sets. In about half of these constructions, older infants first map 1-to-1 correspondence onto two sets by, for example, composing two sets of 1-spoon-in-1-cup. Then they use these equivalent sets as the elements for mapping equivalence by substituting between the two collections (e.g., by substituting the spoons for each other). The quantitative product of mapping substituting onto correspondences is equivalences upon equivalences.

An important cognitive consequence of developing second-order operations is that infants try them out in situations for which they were not initially constructed. This opens up myriad possibilities for constructing new and more powerful cognitions. To illustrate, toward the end of their second year, infants begin to apply second-order substituting to classifying objects. This includes beginning to correct nonverbal counterconditions posed to them. To illustrate, one countercondition presents infants with two alignments of four ring shapes each in which one alignment comprises three circular rings and one square ring and the other alignment comprises three square rings and one circular ring. Beginning at the end of the second year, some infants correct the classificatory errors by substituting the singular square and circular rings for each other. At the same time, infants begin to develop a more direct way of constructing second-order classifying. They simply compose two contemporaneous sets in which the membership of each set is identical or similar objects, while the membership of the two sets is different objects.

Logical classifying does not merely reflect another, perhaps a cognitively primary way of naturally partitioning objects into "basic level" prototype-based categories. If it is more natural, then basic level categorizing should precede logical classifying in infant ontogeny. However, if anything, logical classifying develops before basic level categorizing during infancy. [See CATEGORIZATION.]

Parallel development marks infants' initial ordering operations. Briefly, during their first year infants begin to construct unidirectional (increasing or decreasing) series, usually of no more than two objects but occasionally already of three objects, as long as the ordering is pragmatic and physically constrained, such as nesting a smaller in a larger cup where it is, of course, impossible to nest a larger in a smaller cup. Infants extend first-order unidirectional seriating to as many as four or five objects during their second year. The main advance, however, is in the development of rudimentary bidirectionally ordered pragmatic increasing and decreasing series and in the origins of constructing two minimal co-seriated pragmatic orderings.

B. Receptive Perceptual Activity

Perceiving is undoubtedly a rich means by which infants acquire and process logical information. The relations between receptive perceptual acting and constructive sensorimotor acting in the origins of infants' cognition have been little explored. To begin to analyze this problem requires examining logical phenomena that have apparent counterparts in infants' receptive and constructive activity. Infants' developing cognition of classes serves as an especially good exemplar for at least three reasons. Classifying is a fundamental component of logical knowledge, It comes with relatively well-documented data bases, and it is perhaps the only logical phenomenon for which there is substantial evidence on infants' perceptual activity.

Perceptual categorizing is an apparent receptive counterpart during infancy of the constructive sensorimotor classifying outlined in the previous section. A growing body of research using perceptual habituation–dishabituation procedures finds that infants can be familiarized with a variety of single categories of similar stimuli, such as orientations, forms, and schematic faces, so that they will recognize them. Moreover, infants also habituate to two categories of contrasting stimuli (i.e., squares and triangles) at the same time. The onset ages for both single- and two-category perception are controversial. Most likely infants recognize single categories by age 7 months and two categories by age 10 months.

The comparative developmental picture that emerges is complex. Given the disagreements about the onset ages for receptive perceptual categorizing, there is no simple way to compare its ontogenetic trajectory with that of constructive sensorimotor classifying outlined in the previous section. So we will consider two prime theoretical alternatives, modularity and interdependence. Perceptual categorizing and sensorimotor classifying may be segregated, separate, and noninteractive cognitive modules that follow independent developmental trajectories during infancy without any flow of information between them. Alternatively, perceptual categorizing and sensorimotor classifying may be differentiated but related and interactive cognitive processes that follow interdependent developmental trajectories during infancy with information flow between them. Analyses of our ongoing research suggest that the relation is mainly modular during infants' first year.

II. CHILDHOOD DEVELOPMENT FROM INTUITIVE FUNCTIONS TO CONCRETE LOGICAL OPERATIONS

Logical development is multifaceted and expands rapidly. Nevertheless, its base generative structures continue to include classifying and ordering. These structures, we have seen, originate in infancy. We will therefore trace their progressive development, beginning with classifying.

A. Classifying

Young children (ages 2 to 4 years) build upon their infantile classifying of objects into simple sets by identity, similarity, and differences only. Their advances include beginning to relate classes of the same rank as complements (e.g., that red and green apples are different kinds of apples). This advance is limited to generating complementary relations between simple sets that comprise very few classes, very few objects per class, equal number of objects per class, etc. With such simple sets, young children begin to use an overlapping procedure of switching back and forth between classes into which they spontaneously sort objects; and they correctly exchange classificatory misplacements.

None of this requires hierarchizing classes into superordinates and subordinates. Nor does it exceed classifying minimal sets of objects into complementary classes of the same rank. Young children generate unorganized heaps or figural collections such as symmetrical configurations that do not take into account the class properties of objects when dealing with more complex sets (e.g., where the number of classes is numerous and not symmetrical and the number of objects per class is numerous and unequal).

Middle age children (ages 4 to 7 years) progress markedly even when classifying complex sets. They sort objects by their identity, difference, and similarity properties; and they construct complementary relations between classes of the same rank. Most strikingly, they begin to hierarchize classes into superordinates and subordinates by simple class addition and subtraction. These are simple one-way hier-

archical operations. Thus, middle age children compose concrete classes and their complements of the same lower rank to form a higher rank class (e.g., putting together apples, oranges, grapes, etc., makes up a basket of fruit). They also decompose higher rank concrete classes into complementary classes at the same lower rank (e.g., taking away apples from a basket of fruit leaves oranges, grapes, etc.).

It is therefore expectable that middle age children already decompose the part–whole relations that obtain within objects and collections. So, by age 5 years, children answer correctly inclusion questions that can be solved by visualizing that a whole object is greater than any of its parts. For example, they answer "the butterfly" when asked about an outline drawing of a butterfly with large wings and a small body: "Who would have more to color, someone who colored the wings or someone who colored the butterfly?" So, too, 5 year olds answer correctly inclusion questions that can be solved by visualizing that a whole collection is greater than any of its parts. For example, they correctly answer "the class" when asked about a collection of boy and girl dolls: "Here are kindergarten children. These are the boys and these are the girls and these are the children. Who would have a bigger birthday party, someone who invited the boys or someone who invited the class?"

This has led to the further claim that 5 year olds who do not conserve number will do so when collection terms are used. The idea is that collection labels enable young children to recognize that qualitative transformations do not change the quantity of objects in sets. However, repeated replication attempts have failed.

Middle age children do not yet grasp the class inclusion relations that obtain between hierarchical classes. Presented, for example, with a bouquet of flowers that includes more primulas than roses, middle age children assert both (a) that the primulas and the roses make up the flowers and (b) that if one takes away the primulas, then flowers remain, the roses. Still, the same children assert that there are more primulas than flowers. They cannot coordinate their one-way class addition and subtraction functions to conclude that the superordinate class necessarily includes its subordinate classes and is, therefore, greater.

In sum, middle age children know about object inclusion and collection inclusion, but not class inclusion. Note in this regard that the structure of objects and collections is that of well-formed experiential configurations. To illustrate, a collection such as an ''army'' evokes considerations of a numerous or very numerous assemblage. Armies do not comprise no members, a single member, or even a small number of members; no soldiers, one soldier, or a small band of soldiers is not an army. While comprising large numbers, an army is finite; armies are never infinite. In sharp contrast, the structure of classes such as ''flowers'' or ''soldiers'' is that of a logical relation. A class, may be null, singular, small or large, finite or infinite. The differences between objects and collections, on the one hand, and classes, on the other hand, are not merely verbal. They are fundamental structural differences such that only class-inclusion relations are about logical functions.

By late childhood, around age 8 years, some aspects of class inclusion relations begin to be construed as necessary, e.g., that subordinate classes cannot be larger than their superordinates. Inhelder and Piaget, who discovered this development in logical cognition, have offered a structural developmental theory to account for this as well as the logical developments to be reviewed in the next section. The basic idea is that older children begin to compose their previously developed one-way addition and subtraction functions by negation to form two-way reversible operations.

While already reversible, these inverse operations are referred to as concrete operations for a number of theoretical and empirical reasons. These include the fundamental limitation that the reversible operations generated by older children are not yet fully integrated to form a closed comprehensive system in which all the relations are necessary and that their application is limited to nonformal empirical elements. Thus, for example, older children who correctly solve class-inclusion problems often believe that it is still possible to modify a subordinate class to make it become larger than its superordinate.

B. Ordering

Parallel development continues to mark children's ordering operations. Building upon their ability to compose rudimentary bidirectional as well as unidirectionally orderings by late infancy, young children generate some basic ordering operations as long as the series are simple (e.g., a set of nested cups that only comprises very few graded objects, where the gradations are very marked and obvious perceptu-

ally and the ordering is functional and physically constrained). This includes occasionally intercollating intermediate objects into functional series that are physically constrained to unidirectional ordering such as nested cups.

Intercollated ordering is prerequisite to forming reciprocal operations. Young children begin to construct reciprocal relations as long as the orderings are pragmatic and symmetrical (such as container: contained relations), the number of elements is very small, and the graded differences are very large. Under these limiting conditions they may even manifest other fundamental properties entailed by reciprocal operations, such as transitivity between a very few ordered elements.

When ordering less functional and physically constrained series of objects (e.g., 10 slightly graded sticks), however, young children only compose small series (e.g., couples and triples) or categorize the objects (e.g., into small vs big). At most, they produce one-sided series. For example, they arrange graded sticks so that their tops form a staircase-like arrangement while ignoring the actual length of each stick. So a medium-size stick might be followed by a long stick followed by a short stick, and so on, as long as their tops form an ascending order.

Middle age children seriate such series of objects but by trial and error. Moreover, they cannot intercollate correctly intermediate steps into their constructed series when they are not physically constrained to unidirectional orderings. Whether they also make transitive inferences about more simple orders remains controversial. Older children correctly intercollate intermediate steps into ordered series, including multiplicatively coseriated orders, and make transitive inferences about them. Thus, older children construct reversible relations between concrete reciprocal orderings of series of objects.

III. THE ORIGINS OF FORMAL LOGICAL OPERATIONS IN ADOLESCENCE AND ADULTHOOD

Formal thinking begins to develop during early adolescence, between ages 11 and 14 years. No longer limited to reasoning about concrete empirical phenomena, logical thought becomes progressively hypotheticodeductive and necessary. Moreover, this level of reasoning is progressively applied to physical phenomena as well. [See REASONING.]

Consider first the elements of logical thought. They begin to include formal relations. To illustrate, young adolescents realize that subordinate classes cannot be made to become larger than their superordinates. They now know that the relation—superordinates include their subordinates—is fully necessary, not empirical. So, the class elements about which they reason become formal relations such as necessary inclusion relations.

Logical thought operations themselves also just begin to be formal. A prime, perhaps the prime manifestation is that reasoning is beginning to include reversible operations that are mapped onto other reversible operations. Thus, previously reversible but unrelated negation operations, such as inverse classifying and reciprocal ordering, are themselves now reversibly integrated with each other. This forms a closed formal system of second-order reversible operations. Natural formal logical thinking, then, progresses to include the rudiments of systematic thinking about thinking or mapping operations onto operations. Logical reasoning is becoming *inter-* as well as *intra*propositional.

Consider the developing hypotheticodeductive operations required to reversibly relate inverse classifying to reciprocal ordering (as expressed formally in DeMorgan's duality principle applied to the inclusion of complementary classes). As already noted in the previous section, older children already conclude correctly, for example, (a) that there are more birds than ducks, (b) that if one kills all the ducks, other birds and animals remain, and (c) that if one kills all the birds only other animals remain. Nevertheless, they do not know that it necessarily follows that there are more living things that are not ducks than not birds. Young adolescents begin to deduce that there are more living things that are not ducks than living things that are not birds. This requires reversibly relating the proposition that there are more birds than ducks ($A < B$) to the proposition that there are more nonduck than nonbird living things ($\overline{A} > \overline{B}$).

Reversibly relating inverse to reciprocal negation indicates interpropositional reasoning marked by mutual implication. Thus, if ($A < B$) is true, then ($\overline{A} > \overline{B}$) is necessarily true, and, reciprocally, if ($\overline{A} > \overline{B}$) is true, then ($A < B$) is necessarily true. This reversible interpropositional structure of hypotheticodeductive operations seems to be general. For instance, it underlies adolescents' beginning constructions of correlational relations as the sum of reciprocal associations minus the sum of inverse associations.

Sufficiency, Piaget discovered, also begins to be linked to necessity during early adolescence. To illustrate, subjects were presented with two envelopes and told that one contained 10 blue chips while the other contained 5 blue and 5 white chips. They were asked how many chips must be drawn from one envelope in order to identify its contents. Most young adolescents correctly concluded that drawing 6 chips from one envelope is both necessary and sufficient. Not only did younger children (ages 7 to 10 years) not know that 6 chips were necessary but they concluded that the greater the number of chips drawn the greater the certainty. So one is surest if one draws 10 chips.

Adolescents begin to extend their hypotheticodeductive interpropositional reasoning to understanding physical phenomena, such as causal events. For example, adolescents begin to systematically control and test the effects of independent on dependent variables. To illustrate, they begin to correctly vary only one variable at a time when trying to determine what causes phenomena such as the oscillatory rate of a pendulum. Thereby they determine that if the length of the pendulum changes then the oscillatory rate changes. Therefore, they begin to infer that the necessary reciprocal implication follows that if the oscillatory rate changes then the length of the pendulum must have been changed. Inclusion of the causal variable, length, is complemented by systematic exclusion of noncausal variables such as of weight and of force exerted in starting the pendulum. Finally, they begin to infer that therefore the correlative follows that whether or not the oscillatory rate changes then noncausal variables (such as weight and force) may or may not have changed. [*See* ADOLESCENCE.]

Formal reversible operations permit adolescents to begin to infer nonobservable causal variables. This enables some of them, for example, to deduce aspects of the conservation of motion. First, these adolescents determine that traveling bodies (e.g., balls launched along a track) are slowed down and stopped by a number of variables (such as friction, air resistance, and surface irregularities in the track). Inversely, they then begin to deduce that if all the causal variables are negated (i.e., by eliminating friction, air resistance, etc.) then traveling bodies would not slow down or stop (e.g., the balls would continue moving indefinitely). The structure of such adolescent formal hypotheticodeductive operations, then, takes the following form. First, slowing down or stopping implies that the balls met friction *or* air resistance *or* etc.; that is, $p \supset (q \vee r \vee s \vee t \vee \ldots)$. Second, by inverse reversibility, it necessarily follows that if friction *and* air resistance *and* etc. are negated, then slowing down or stopping will be eliminated; that is, $(\bar{q} \cdot \bar{r} \cdot \bar{s} \cdot \bar{t} \cdot \ldots) \supset \bar{p}$.

While originating in early adolescence, hypotheticodeductive reasoning develops throughout young adulthood. An extensive intergenerational study examined the development of formal operational reasoning about problems such as the correlation between associated classes. Predominantly formal reasoning was produced by 53% of the young adolescents (ages 10–15 years), increased to 60% by the older adolescents (ages 16–20 years), and increased further to 79% by the young adults (ages 21–30 years). The percentage slipped a bit, but not significantly, to 70% by the parents (ages 45–50 years).

To account for the development of formal operations, Piaget proposed that its generative structure comprises a four-group (of identity, negation, reciprocal, and correlative operations) marked by properties of closure, associativity, etc. Then, and only then, are reciprocal and inverse forms of formal negation operations composed by reversibility. Further, the group structure of adolescent formal interpropositional thought grows out of the generative structure of concrete operations developed by older children. The latter intrapropositional thought comprises groupings (approximately, degenerate groups) in which reciprocal and inverse forms of concrete negation operations are not yet related to each other.

The formalization of this structural developmental theory has both critics and supporters. Additionally, it has been claimed that it overestimates the competence of adolescents and adults. This seems unlikely in light of the intergenerational data cited above. Moreover, detailed analyses readily reveal at least components of spontaneous formal operational reasoning that increase with age in adolescence and young adulthood. It has also been argued that the theory underestimates the extralogical features involved in ordinary or natural reasoning performance, such as its argumentative structure and the semantic procedures that form subjects' mental models when reasoning. Nevertheless, to date, Piaget's theory remains the only comprehensive, formal, and unified account. It comprehends developments from one-way functions in early childhood to two-way concrete operations in late childhood to reversibly integrated formal operations in adolescence and adulthood. Moreover, it is a very heuristic theory that is generating substantial empirical research. [*See* COGNITIVE DEVELOPMENT.]

IV. COMPARATIVE LOGICAL DEVELOPMENT

Most research seeks the origins and development of natural logical cognition in human ontogeny. With increasing recognition that it need not require language, the quest for the evolutionary origins of logical cognition has turned to comparative research on nonhuman primate ontogeny. Nonverbal techniques used with human infants and young children have been adapted to study childhood and adolescent development in nonhuman primates. The aim is to compare the origins and development of natural logical cognition in different primate species.

Nonhuman primates develop the basic components comprising logical cognition, including elementary classifying and ordering. Monkeys (*Cebus apella* and *Macaca fasciculeris*) develop first-order but not second-order logical operations outlined under Section IA. Chimpanzees (*Pan troglodytes*) develop rudimentary second-order logical operations as well.

While sharing a common foundation for logical cognition, primates vary markedly in the onset, offset, rate, extent, sequencing, and organization of their developing operations. Contrary to much persistent speculation, humans' logical cognition develops most rapidly during infancy. The onset or origins of logical operations are earliest in humans; and the velocity of its subsequent development is fastest, that is, comparatively accelerated.

The offset in adulthood and ultimate developmental extent of formal logical operations, outlined under Section III, far exceeds that developed or acquired by any other species. Both accelerated rate and surpassing extent of humans' developing logical cognition can be readily glimpsed from one simple fact. Only by age 5 years do chimpanzees develop rudimentary second-order operations comparable to those that human infants already develop by age 18 months.

Sequencing of logical operations differs significantly between primate species. To illustrate, recall that first-order classifying by human infants forms a four-stage sequence: consistently by differences at age 6 months, inconsistently or random classifying at ages 8 and 10 months, consistently by identities at age 12 months, and consistently by similarities at age 15 months. In comparison, the sequence for cebus monkeys is: inconsistently or random classifying at age 16 months, consistently by differences at age 36 months, and consistently by both identities and similarities at age 48 months. Note the sharp differences in onset and velocity as well as order of development illustrated by this comparison.

Primates' developing organizations of logical cognition differ as well. This is necessarily so because of the just noted variations in developmental sequencing. But their developing organizations also differ even when their sequencing does not. For instance, first-order exchange operations of substituting, commuting, and replacing develop in synchrony in human infants but not in cebus monkeys. So by age 48 months the organization of cebus' exchange operations amalgamates operations that are out of phase with each other, i.e., an organization comprising primitive first-order substituting with more advanced first-order commuting and replacing.

Thus, the ontogeny of humans' logical cognition does not recapitulate its phylogeny in other primate species. Instead, it seems likely that heterochronic mechanisms of evolution are at play. Our heterochronic hypothesis is that structural realignments in phylogenesis of logical operations due to accelerated onset and rate, delayed offset, and sequential reorganization are integral to the evolution of intelligence including the uniquely human development of formal logical operations.

Bibliography

Antinucci, F. (Ed.) (1989). "Cognitive Structure and Development of Nonhuman Primates." Erlbaum, Hillsdale, NJ.

Bornstein, M. (1984). A descriptive taxonomy of psychological categories used by infants. In "Origins of Cognitive Skills" (C. Sophian, Ed.), Erlbaum, Hillsdale, NJ.

Breslow, L. (1981). Reevaluation of the literature on the development of transitive inferences. *Psychol. Bull.* **89,** 325–351.

Furth, H. (1971). Linguistic deficiency and thinking. *Psychol. Bull.* **76,** 58–72.

Fuson, K. C., Lyons, B. G., Pergament, G. G., Hall, J. W., and Kwon, Y. (1988). Effects of collection terms on class-inclusion and on number tasks. *Cog. Psychol.* **20,** 96–120.

Inhelder, B., and Piaget, J. (1958). "The Growth of Logical Thinking from Childhood to Adolescence." Basic Books, New York.

Inhelder, B., and Piaget, J. (1964). "Early Growth of Logic in the Child: Classification and Seriation." Harper & Row, New York.

Kuhn, D., Langer, J., Kohlberg, L., and Haan, N. S. (1977). The development of formal operations in logical and moral judgment. *Genet. Psychol. Monogr.* **95,** 97–188.

Langer, J. (1980). "The Origins of Logic: Six to Twelve Months." Academic Press, New York.

Langer, J. (1986). "The Origins of Logic: One to Two Years." Academic Press, New York.

Langer, J. (1994). From acting to understanding: The comparative development of meaning. In "The Nature and Ontogeny of Meaning" (W. F. Overton and D. S. Palermo, Eds.), Erlbaum, Hillsdale, NJ.

Mays, W. (1992). Piaget's logic and its critics: A deconstruction. *Arch. Psychol.* **60,** 45–70.

Neimark, E. (1982). Adolescent thought: Transition to formal operations. In "Handbook of Developmental Psychology" (B. Wolman, Ed.), Prentice Hall, Engelwood Cliffs, NJ.

Overton, W. F. (Ed.) (1990). "Reasoning, Necessity, and Logic: Developmental Perspectives." Erlbaum, Hillsdale, NJ.

Piaget, J. (1987). "Possibility and Necessity," Vol. 2. University of Minnesota Press, Minneapolis.

◆

LOVE AND INTIMACY

Elaine Hatfield and Richard L. Rapson
University of Hawaii at Manoa

Glossary

Attachment An emotional bond between infants and their caretakers. Infants are considered to be attached to their caretakers if they appear to be comfortable in their presence, cling to them when threatened, and become anxious if they are separated.

Commitment Decision/commitment refers, in the short term, to a couple's decision that they love one another, and in the long term, to their commitment to maintain that love.

Companionate love The affection and tenderness men and women feel for those with whom their lives are deeply entwined. Companionate love is a complex functional whole including appraisals or appreciations, subjective feelings, expressions, patterned physiological processes, action tendencies, and instrumental behaviors.

Intimacy A process in which couples, who feel close and who trust one another, reveal personal information and feelings to one another and, as a consequence, come to feel cared for, known, and validated.

Passionate love A state of intense longing for union with another. Reciprocated love (union with the other) is associated with fulfillment and ecstasy. Unrequited love (separation) with emptiness, anxiety, or despair. Passionate love is a complex functional whole including appraisals or appreciations, subjective feelings, expressions, patterned physiological processes, action tendencies, and instrumental behaviors.

SCIENTISTS distinguish between two forms of love—passionate love and companionate love. Both kinds of love are based, in part, on the parent/child attachment experience. Researchers interested in passionate love tend to focus on infants' attachments to their caretakers as the prototype of later passionate attachments. Those interested in companionate love tend to focus on maternal and parental attachments to one another and their children as the prototype of companionate love. Of course, love relationships can involve both passion and companionship.

I. DEFINING AND MEASURING LOVE

Love is a basic emotion. It comes in a variety of forms. Most scientists distinguish between two kinds of love—passionate love and companionate love. *Passionate love* is a "hot," intense emotion. It is sometimes also labeled obsessive love, puppy love, a crush, lovesickness, infatuation, or being-in-love. It has been defined as

A state of intense longing for union with another. Reciprocated love (union with the other) is associated with fulfillment and ecstasy. Unrequited love (separation) with emptiness, anxiety, or despair. Passionate love is a complex functional whole including appraisals or appreciations, subjective feelings, expressions, patterned physiological processes, action tendencies, and instrumental behaviors. (Hatfield and Rapson, 1993)

The Passionate Love Scale was developed to assess the cognitive, emotional, and behavioral components of such love.

Companionate love is a "cooler," far less intense emotion. It is sometimes also called true love or conjugal love. It combines feelings of deep attachment, commitment, and intimacy. It has been defined as

The affection and tenderness people feel for those with whom their lives are deeply entwined. Companionate love is a complex functional whole including appraisals or appreciations, subjective feelings, expressions, patterned physiological processes, action tendencies, and instrumental behaviors. (Hatfield and Rapson, 1993)

Psychologists have used a variety of scales to measure companionate love. One of the most popular scales is the measure of Companionate Love, which includes measures of commitment and intimacy.

Social psychologists have observed that in close, companionate, relationships, couples' thoughts, emotions, actions, and lives are profoundly linked. The close relationship is one of strong, frequent, and diverse interdependence that lasts over a considerable period of time. Researchers have developed scales to measure how close couples are—i.e., how closely linked their organized action sequences are.

Other scientists have proposed still other typologies of love. Some scientists contended that people could adopt any of six different styles of loving. The Love Attitudes Scale was designed to measure these love styles: *Eros* (passionate, intense, disclosing love), mania (obsessive, dependent, insecure love), *storge* (friendship-based, steady, secure love), *pragma* (practical, logical love), *agape* (altruistic, giving, spiritual love), and *ludis* (game-playing, cool, playful love). Robert Sternberg proposed a triangular model of love. He argued that the different kinds of love differ in how much of three different components—passion, intimacy, and the decision/commitment to stay together—they possess. Passionate love (which he labeled infatuation), for example, involves intense passionate arousal but little intimacy or commitment. Companionate love involves less passion but far more intimacy and commitment. The most complete form of love is consummate love, which combines passion, intimacy, and commitment.

II. PASSIONATE LOVE

A. Predictors of Romantic Attraction

Researchers have identified four factors which affect couples' interactions: "person" factors, "other" factors, "person × other" factors, and "environmental" factors. Let us consider how the first two

factors can affect men's and women's readiness for love and their preferences for various kinds of partners. [*See* INTERPERSONAL ATTRACTION AND PERSONAL RELATIONSHIPS.]

1. "Person" Factors

There is evidence that certain kinds of people, at certain times, are especially susceptible to passionate love.

a. Attachment Theory and Passionate Love

Mary Ainsworth observed that infants and toddlers form different kinds of attachments to their caretakers. Some infants are securely attached. They are tightly bonded to their mothers. They feel comfortable in her presence. They are confident that she will be there when they need her; that she will support them when they feel brave enough to explore the world. (These infants may also be genetically predisposed to have an even temperament.) Other infants possess an anxious/ambivalent attachment to their caretakers. Their mothers may have been more responsive to her own rhythms than to their infants'. As a consequence, sometimes they "smother" their infants with unwanted affection; sometimes they ignore them. Since these infants have learned they cannot count on their mothers, they tend to be anxious and uncertain in their interactions with her. (Of course, some infants are simply born with a fearful disposition.) Finally, some infants develop an avoidant attachment with their caretakers. Perhaps their mothers generally ignored them. Perhaps the infants were simply lacking whatever it takes to form close relationships with *anyone*. In any case, such infants are unemotional and unresponsive.

Social psychologists proposed that children's early patterns of attachment should influence their adult attachments. They found that children who were securely attached did tend to mature into adults who were able to trust and depend on those they cared for and who were comfortable with intimacy. Those who were anxious/ambivalent tended to fall in love easily, seek extreme levels of closeness, worry that they would be abandoned, and have short-lived love affairs in later life. The avoidant tended to become adults who were uncomfortable getting too close and who had difficulty depending on others. There is considerable evidence that childhood attachments do serve as a model for later passionate love relationships.

If passionate love is rooted in childhood attachments, it follows that anything that makes adults feel as helpless and dependent as they were as children, anything that makes them fear separation and loss, should increase their passionate craving to merge with others. There is some evidence that this is so. For example, researchers have found that when men and women's self-esteem is threatened, when they are anxious and afraid, when they feel insecure or are dependent on others, they tend to be especially vulnerable to falling in love.

b. Additional Person Factors

There are other "Person" factors that affect susceptibility to passionate love. For example, in love, timing is often everything. There are certain times when people are ready for love; times when they are not. If young people are not in a romantic relationship and wish they were, they are especially vulnerable to potential romantic partners. Conversely, if they are already dating someone, they are unlikely to feel much attraction toward others; they may even devalue others in order not to be tempted.

2. "Other" Factors

Most people prefer dates and mates who are reasonably good looking, personable, warm and intelligent, and similar to themselves in background characteristics (such as age, race, socio-economic class, religion, and educational level), as well as in attitudes and values, and perhaps even more. People reject potential dates who are arrogant, conceited, rude, boring, or consistently make life difficult. [See MATE SELECTION.]

B. The Emotional Consequences of Falling in Love

The previous section, dealing with the roots of passion, has painted a somewhat dismal picture. It focused on the bruised self-esteem, the dependence, and the insecurity that make people hunger for love. When people fall in love with someone and feel loved in return, however, they may well experience intense happiness and excitement. Interviews with lovers suggest that they may experience five kinds of rewards. Moments of passionate bliss; feeling understood and accepted; sharing a sense of union; feeling secure and safe; and transcendence. Of course, passionate love may have its costs too. When hopes are dashed, or relationships fall apart,

people's self-esteem may be shattered; they may feel lonely and miserable and may experience intense jealousy.

All in all, for most people, passionate love is a bittersweet experience. People from individualistic studies (such as America and Western Europe), which tend to idealize passionate love, generally have an fairly optimistic view of passionate love. They expect it to go well. People from collectivistic societies (such as Eastern Europe, Asia, and the Middle Eastern countries), generally assume "unrestrained" love is a threat to social order. They tend to be more pessimistic about the possibilities of passionate love.

C. How Long Does Passionate Love Last?

Passionate love is generally fleeting. Researchers surveyed dating couples, newlyweds, and couples married varying lengths of time to ascertain how passionately they loved one another. Initially, it was often passion that drew men and women together. As the relationship matured, however, passion began to fade into the background. After a while, what seemed to matter most was companionate love, commitment, and intimacy.

III. COMPANIONATE LOVE

A. Evolutionary Antecedents

Theorists have often taken an evolutionary approach to explain the origins of companionate love. They argued that emotional "packages" are inherited, adaptive patterns of emotional experience, physiological reaction, and behavior. At every phylogenetic level, they pointed out, organisms face the same problems. If they are to survive and reproduce they must find food, avoid being killed, mate, and reproduce. Many theorists believe that companionate love is built on the ancient circuitry evolved to ensure that animals mate, reproduce, and care for their young. Recently neuroscientists, anthropologists, and developmentalists have begun to learn more about companionate love.

1. The Chemistry of Love

Neuroscientists have begun to speculate about the biological bases of companionate love and tenderness. They have identified a hormone, oxytocin, which seems to promote sexual and reproductive behavior and to facilitate affectionate, nurturant, close, intimate bonds between caretakers (usually mothers) and their infants. [See HORMONES AND BEHAVIOR.]

2. The Looks, Sounds, and Postures of Love

Some theorists have argued that love's ancient heritage can be read today in the looks, gazes, and sounds of companionate love. Emotions researchers have found that the universal emotions—such as joy, love, sadness, fear, and anger—reveal themselves in certain characteristic facial expressions. Some speculate that when men and women are feeling companionate love and tenderness they tend to display traces of the the expressions caretakers often instinctively display when they are gazing happily and tenderly at their young infants. They gaze downward (at the child). Their faces soften, and a slight, tender smile may play about their lips. [See FACIAL EXPRESSIONS OF EMOTION.]

French psychophysiologists have argued that companionate love is associated with certain breathing patterns and sounds. Mothers often coo or croon softly with their mouths held near the infant's head. They speculated that such tender maternal sounds become the forerunners of the breathing patterns associated with companionate love and tenderness.

Desmond Morris argued that after birth, mothers instinctively try to recreate the security of the womb. They kiss, caress, fondle, and embrace their infants; they cradle them in their arms. In the womb, neonates hear the steady beat of the mothers' hearts—pulsing at 72 beats per minute. After birth, mothers instinctively hold their babies with their heads pressed against their left breasts, closest to the maternal heart. When their infants fret, mothers rock them at a rate of between 60 and 70 rocks per minutes, the rate that is most calming to infants. Morris points out: "It appears as if this rhythm, whether heard or felt, is the vital comforter, reminding the baby vividly of the lost paradise of the womb." Of course, in adulthood, these same kisses, tender caresses, and embraces continue to provide security for men and women—unconscious of their early origins.

Anthropologists have observed that that primate mothers and infants and adults in all cultures reveal their close attachments in much the same ways. For instance, newborn infants rhythmically rotate their heads from side to side as they root for their mothers' nipples. As adults playfully nuzzle someone they love, they sometimes find themselves using motions,

rhythms, and gestures from the distant past: holding the beloved's head and rubbing their lips against the other's cheek with a sideways movement of their head. They argue that such primitive kissing, mutual feeding, and embracing bonds people together.

Now that we have discussed the antecedents of companionate love, let us focus on what scientists have learned about three of its components—affection and liking, intimacy, and commitment.

B. Affection and Liking

1. Reinforcement Theory

Many psychologists use reinforcement theory principles to explain why people love and like others. According to reinforcement theory, men and women come to care for those who provide them with important rewards and dislike those who punish them. They also come to feel the same way about people who are merely associated with pleasure or pain. For example, people judged members of the other sex to be more physically attractive if they made their assessments while they were listening to pleasant rock music rather than harsh avant-garde tones. Both men and women were more attracted to people they met in pleasant surroundings than to those they met in rooms that were too hot or too cold, too humid or too dry, crowded, or dirty.

Social psychologists contrasted the behavior of happily married couples with those who were distressed. Happy couples generally had positive exchanges. They smiled, nodded, and made eye contact. They spoke to each other in soft, tender, happy voices. They leaned forward to catch one another's words. Distressed couples had corrosive patterns of interacting. They tried to bludgeon one another into agreements by complaints and punishment. They sneered, cried, and frowned at one another. Their voices were tense, cold, impatient, whining. They made rude gestures, pointed, jabbed, and threw up their hands in disgust; or they simply ignored one another. As soon as one partner resorted to these tactics, the other began to respond in the same way, leading to an escalation of reciprocal aversiveness.

Unfortunately, as couples settle into a routine, kind words are often replaced by harsh evaluations, thoughtful courtesies by neglect. For some reason, married couples frequently treat one another worse than they treat strangers.

2. Equity Theory

Couples care both about how rewarding their relationships are *and* how fair they seem to be.

A few theorists have argued that lovers and marital partners do not really care very much about fairness. A few social psycholigists, for example, asserted that couples have very different ideas as to the nature of appropriate behavior in *communal* relationships (such as love relationships, family relationships, or close friendships) as opposed to *exchange* relationships (such as encounters with strangers or business associates). In communal relationships, they argued, couples feel responsible for one another's well-being. They wish to show their love and affection; to help those they love. They expect nothing in return. In exchange relationships, on the other hand, acquaintances do not feel particularly responsible for one another. They care very much about "what's in it for me?"

Most theorists, however, take the equity perspective. Elaine Hatfield and her colleagues, for example, assumed that couples must be careful to ensure that their partners feel loved, rewarded, and fairly treated. Otherwise, love relationships will suffer and possibly dissolve. Persons generally believe that if their partners loved them they would *wish* to treat them fairly; but it doesn't always work that way. If men and women get too much or too little from their relationships for too long a time it leads to serious trouble. In a number of studies, equity considerations have been found to be important in determining who gets into relationships in the first place, how those relationships go, and how likely they are to endure. Researchers have found that couples in equitable relationships are more likely to fall in love and become sexually involved. When couples who were sexually intimate were asked why they had decided to have sexual relations, those in equitable relationships were most likely to say that *both* of them wanted to have sexual intercourse. Couples in inequitable relationships were more likely to admit that sex had not been a mutual decision; often, one person had pressured the other into having sexual relations. It is not surprising then, that couples in equitable relationships had more satisfying sexual lives. [*See* EQUITY.]

Equitable relationships tended to be happier and more satisfying. When researchers interviewed dating couples, newlyweds, and couples married for various lengths of time, they found that equitable relations were the most comfortable relations at every stage. If lovers gave too much and received nothing in return (not even gratitude), they eventually began to feel uneasy. Did the other really love *them*? If so, why didn't he or she seem to appreciate their sacrifices? The selfish usually began to have their doubts too. What kind of men or women would allow themselves to be made a doormat? Didn't they have any pride? Not surprisingly, those who feel they were receiving less than they deserved from their dating relationships and marriages were especially dissatisfied.

Couples were most committed to their relationships when they felt equitably treated. When undergraduates were asked to write an essay on "Why we broke up," 12% of them mentioned the lack of equity as a precipitating factor. Women were most likely to mention inequity as the reason they wanted out. (Perhaps many women keenly feel the injustice of having to work outside the home and then coming home to work a "second shift" cooking, shopping, doing housework, and caring for children.) Equitably treated men and women have also been found to be especially reluctant to risk their marriages by getting sexually and emotionally involved with someone else.

Researchers disagree as to how important equity is in determining whether couples remain together, separate, or divorce. Most agree, however, that it plays at least some part in such decisions.

C. Intimacy

The word intimacy is derived from *intimus,* the Latin term for "inner" or "inmost." Scientists reviewed the way most theorists have used this term. They found that almost all of them assumed that intimate relationships involved affection and warmth, self-disclosure, and closeness and interdependence. Most people mean much the same thing by intimacy. Some scientists asked college men and women to tell them about times when they felt especially intimate with (or distant from) someone they cared about. For most people, intimate relations were associated with feelings of affection and warmth, with happiness and contentment, talking about personal things, and sharing pleasurable activities. What sorts of things put an inpenetrable wall between couples? For most, distant relationships were associated with anger, resentment, and sadness as well as criticism, insensitivity, and inattention. Men and women seemed to mean something slightly different by "intimacy." Women tended to focus primarily on love and affection and the expression of warm feelings when recounting "intimate moments." They rarely mentioned sex. For men, a key feature of intimacy was sex and physical closeness.

Clinical psychologists developed the Personal Assessment of Intimacy in Relationships (PAIR) to measure intimacy. They identified five types of intimacy: Emotional, social, intellectual, sexual, and recreational intimacy.

1. The Components of Intimacy

The threads of intimacy—affection, trust, emotional expressiveness, communication, and sex—are so entwined that it is almost impossible to tease them apart.

a. Love and Affection

Men and women generally feel more love and affection for their intimates than for anyone else; such mutual affection is probably the first condition of intimacy.

b. Trust

People seldom risk exposing their dreams or fears unless they know it is safe to do so.

c. Self-Disclosure

When men and women are able to reveal their inner feelings and experiences to others, relationships bloom. Caring and trust may be the soil in which self-disclosure thrives, but self-disclosure, in turn, nourishes love, liking, caring, trust and understanding.

Researchers reviewed a series of studies on the "social penetration process." They made two major discoveries: (1) intimacy takes time. As couples began to get better acquainted, they began to disclose more. (2) Acquaintances tend to match one another in how intimate their disclosures are. In some relationships, both partcipants are willing to reveal a great deal about themselves. In others, both confine themselves to small talk.

Intimates confide two very different kinds of information—feelings and facts—to one another. On a first encounter, acquaintances usually reveal only the bare facts of their lives; they talk little about their feelings. New acquaintances are careful not to reveal too much too soon and not to reveal much more than their partners do. Daters tend to warm up fairly quickly, however. After 6 weeks or so, people are already confiding in one another at about as high a level as they ever will. It is in long-term love relationships that intimates can be *most* relaxed and trusting. Once couples know each other well, the recital of mere facts counts for little; it is the communication of feelings that is critical to dating and marital satisfaction. In long-term relationships, moment-to-moment reciprocity becomes unimport-

ant. Things can wait. When relationships are about to end, however, the pattern of self-disclosure changes. Now, words can be used to wound. In terminal relationships, couples often begin to spew out the ugly accusations that they have kept hidden. They begin to spill out years of hatred, anger, and exaggerated grievances. Couples may begin to talk through the night, trying to figure out what went wrong and if there is any chance to set things right.

d. Nonverbal Communication

Intimates feel comfortable in close physical proximity. They sneak little looks at their mates to convey shared understandings, gaze at one another, touch, stand close, and even lean on one another. Of course, people can reveal how alienated and distant they feel from one another via the flip side of these same techniques. If a person feels that a potential date they have just met is moving too fast and they are starting to feel cornered, they can reduce intimacy in several ways—by averting their gaze, shrinking back, shifting their body orientation, or simply by changing the subject and steering clear of intimate topics. We all know how enemies behave when they want to sever all contact. They glare, clench their jaws, sigh in disgust, or walk on ahead. [*See* NONVERBAL BEHAVIOR.]

2. Perspectives on Intimacy

Theorists have taken a trio of approaches to intimacy:

a. Life-Span Developmental Models

Developmental theorists have observed that young people must learn how to be intimate. Erik Erikson pointed out that infants, children, adolescents, and adults face a continuing series of developmental tasks. If loved and nurtured, infants develop a basic trust in the universe. They develop the ability to hope. In early, middle and late childhood, children learn to be autonomous, to take initiative, and to be industrious. The develop a will of their own, a sense of purpose, and a belief in their own competence. The next two stages are those in which we are primarily interested. In adolescence, teenagers must develop some sense of their own identity. Only when adolescents have formed a relatively stable, independent identity are they able to master their next "crisis"—to learn how to become intimate with someone, to learn how to love. Mature relationships, then, according to Erikson, involve an ability to balance intimacy and independence.

b. Motivational Approaches

Psychiatrists and psychologists have pointed out that people are *motivated* to be intimate. Developmental psychologists point out that some people are high in intimacy motivation. They tend to be more loving and affectionate, warmer, more egalitarian, less self-centered, and less dominant than their peers. They spend more time thinking about people and relationships, more time talking and writing to others; they are more tactful and less outspoken. They stand closer to others. Not surprisingly, others like them, too. [*See* MOTIVATION.]

c. Equilibrium Models

Researchers point out that people prefer an optimal level of intimacy. Too much or too little intimacy makes everyone uncomfortable. When people get close to us, we become physiologically aroused. If we feel positive about this arousal we will move closer to them. If it is "too much" we will back off. We literally back up when someone gets too close too fast. We move forward when they seem to be slipping away. Two features of this model are worth noting. First, researchers view intimacy from a dialectical perspective. They see people as constantly adjusting the level of their intimate encounters. Second, they point out that once the intimacy equilibrium has been disturbed, any of several different techniques can be used to set things right. People differ markedly in how much intimacy they desire. Attaining the "right degree" of intimacy often requires a delicate balancing act.

3. Why People Seek Intimacy

It seems a bit odd to ask *why* people wish for intimacy. When scientists ask men and women what they most desire in life, they generally mention a close intimate relationship. People can feel sad and lonely for two very different reasons. Some lonely people are experiencing *emotional loneliness;* they hunger for one special intimate. Others are experiencing *social loneliness;* they merely lack friends and casual acquaintances. Of the two, it is emotional loneliness that is the more painful. Contentment is better predicted by the existence of intimacy (i.e., lack of loneliness) than popularity, the frequency of contact with friends, or the amount of time spent with acquaintances. Theorists contend that intimacy has the three following major beneficial effects.

a. Its Intrinsic Appeal

If people were happily in love, over 90% of them were also "very happy in general." If they were generally unhappy, most thought that love was the one thing that they needed to be happy. So people long for intimacy in and of itself.

b. Its Links to Psychological Well-Being

A number of studies document that intimacy and psychological health seem to go hand-in-hand. Intimacy has been shown to be associated with happiness, contentment, and a sense of well-being. Happy (intimate) marriages provide social support.

c. Its Links to Mental and Physical Well-Being

A number of medical researchrs have confirmed that intimacy and mental and physical well-being are connected. Intimate relationships apparently buffer the impact of stress. Intimacy problems are closely linked to many mental health disorders. If persons have a chance to disclose emotionally upsetting material to someone who seems to care, they exhibit improved mental and physical health in follow-up physical examinations. Most of our knowledge about the ties between intimate relationships and physical health comes from studies of the impact of a husband or wife's death on the survivor's mental and physical health. Investigators find that bereavement increases the likelihood of a host of mental and physical problems. Bereavement increases vulnerability to mental illness; produces a variety of physical symptoms (these include migraines, headaches, facial pain, rashes, indigestion, peptic ulcers, weight gain or loss, heart palpitations, chest pain, asthma, infections, and fatigue); aggravates existing illnesses; causes physical illness; predisposes a person to engage in risky behaviors—such as smoking, drinking, and drug use; and increases the likelihood of death. Of course, a "close" relationship filled with hatred and strife can be worse than no relationship at all for couples' mental and physical health. [*See* STRESS AND ILLNESS.]

4. Why People Avoid Intimacy

Given all the advantages of intimate relationships, why would people ever be reluctant to become intimate with others? Men and women admit that they are hesitant to get too deeply involved with others for a variety of reasons: Some people feared that if they get too close to someone they will end up "stuck" with them; having to take care of someone worse off than themselves. Some people fear that if they begin to confide in others, they will end up feeling worse—aware of how sad, frightened, or angry they really are. Some fear that if they reveal too much about themselves, others will criticize them, be disappointed in them, or get angry at them. Some worried that if a relationship were to end, vindictive dates or mates would confide the innermost details of their lives to subsequent dates, mates, or business associates. Close relationship researchers developed the Perceptions of Risk in Intimacy scale to measure people's fear of intimacy.

5. Are There Gender Differences in Intimacy?

Researchers have observed that there is a gap between men's and women's ideas of what constitutes intimacy. Researchers interviewed 130 married couples at the University of Texas. They found that for the wives, intimacy meant talking things over. The husbands, by and large, were more interested in action. They thought that if they did things (took out the garbage, for instance) and if they engaged in some joint activities, that should be enough. Huston found that during courtship men were willing to spend a great deal of time in intimate conversation. But after marriage, as time went on, they reduced the time for close marital conversation while devoting increasingly greater time to work or hanging around with their own friends. Ted Huston observed:

> Men put on a big show of interest when they are courting, but after the marriage their actual level of interest in the partner often does not seem as great as you would think, judging from the courtship. The intimacy of courtship is instrumental for the men, a way to capture the woman's interest. But that sort of intimacy is not natural for many men. Women complain about men's "emotional stingyness."

Huston suggested a compromise: Couples should try to engage in the sort of intimate conversation which springs spontaneously from shared interests. This requires, of course, that couples share some interests—that they read books, or watch films, or plan trips to Europe together, and so forth.

Researchers pointed out that men are taught to take pride in being independent while women take pride in being close and nurturant. Erik Erikson contended that as men mature, they find it easy to achieve an independent identity; they experience more difficulty in learning to be intimate with those they love. Women have an easy time learning to be close to others; they have more trouble learning how to be independent. There is considerable evidence that men are less comfortable with intimacy than women.

Researchers find that in casual encounters, women disclose far more to others than do men. In our culture, women have traditionally been encouraged to show feelings. Men have been taught to hide their emotions and to avoid displays of weakness. In a study of college students, social psychologists found that women's friendships were more deeply intimate than were men's. Women placed great emphasis on talking and emotional sharing in their relationships. Men tended to emphasize shared activities; they generally limited their conversations to sports, money, and sex.

In their deeply intimate relationships, however, men and women differ little, if at all, in how much they are willing to reveal to one another. Researchers, for example, asked dating couples how much they had revealed to their steady dates. Did they talk about their current relationships? previous affairs? their feelings about their parents and friends? their self-concepts and life views? their attitudes and interests? their day-to-day activities? Overall, men and women did not differ in how much they were willing to confide to their partners. They did differ, however, in the kinds of things they shared. Men found it easy to talk about politics; women found it easy to talk about people. Men found it easy to talk about their strengths; women found it easy to talk about their own fears and weaknesses. Interestingly enough, traditional men and women were most likely to limit themselves to stereotyped patterns of communication. More modern men and women were more relaxed about talking about all sorts of intimate matters—politics, friends, their strengths and their weaknesses.

Women receive more disclosures than do men. This is not surprising in view of the fact that the amount of information people reveal to others has an enormous impact on the amount of information they receive in return. In any case, both men and women seem to feel most comfortable confiding in women. Modern tradition dictates that women should be the "intimacy experts."

Some authors have observed that currently neither men nor women may be getting exactly the amount of intimacy they would like. Women tend to desire more intimacy than they are getting; men may prefer more privacy and distance. Couples tend to negotiate a pattern of self-disclosure that is bearable to both. Unfortunately, this may ensure that neither of them gets what they really want. Of course, as men and women's roles become more alike, this double standard of intimacy might be expected to decline.

6. A Prescription for Intimacy

Most humans appear to flourish in a warm intimate relationship. Yet, intimacy is risky. What then is the solution? What advice do social psychologists give as to how to secure the benefits of deep commitment without being engulfed by its dangers? A variety of therapists and researchers have developed programs to teach young people intimacy skills. Generally, they focus on teaching men and women four types of skills: (1) encouraging people to accept themselves as they are; (2) encouraging people to recognize their intimates for what they are; (3) encouraging people to express themselves; and (4) teaching people to deal with their intimate's reactions.

D. Commitment

1. Perspectives on Commitment

It is not always easy for people to know how comitted they and others are to one another. Researchers have begun to elaborate on how the commitment process works. Researchers proposed that a close relationship's cohesiveness (stability) can be defined as "the total field of forces which act" on the pair to keep them in the marriage." There are three kinds of forces that influence cohesiveness: (1) Attractiveness of the relationship. Is the relationship more (or less) rewarding than the couple expected? The more rewarding and the less costly the relationship, the more stable it will be. (2) Alternative attractions. Is this relationship more attractive than other relationships or than living alone? The more attractive the alternatives, the more likely the marriage is to dissolve. (3) Barriers against leaving the relationship. These are the "psychological restraining forces" that keep people in marriages. They include religious, legal, economic, and social barriers as well as responsibilities to children. Other researchers proposed a similar model to explain who likely will persevere in a relationship as opposed to those most likely to separate or divorce. They argued that the more satisfied couples are, the more eager they will be to preserve their relationships; the more they

have invested in their relationships (in time, money, and effort) and the more limited their alternatives, the more reluctant they will be to sacrifice everything by leaving.

Recently, scientists attempted to test the relative importance of the factors that attract people to relationships (love and reward) versus the factors that prevent them from leaving (feelings of commitment and a knowledge that they have invested a great deal in the relationship) in keeping couples together in times of stress. They found that although love and rewards are important, even more important are the commitments couples feel they have made to the relationship and the practical investments they have made in it.

E. How Long Does Companionate Love Last?

Researchers have studied the fate of passionate and companionate love. One researcher interviewed couples married one month to 36 years. Initially, it was passion that drew men and women to one another. As the relationship matured, passion began to fade into the background. "Passion is the quickest to develop, and the quickest to fade," he observed. After a while, what mattered most was companionate love—which comprises commitment and intimacy. It took longer for couples to feel fully committed to their marriages and to become intimate with one another, but in love, these were the things that seemed to last.

Bibliography

Ainsworth, M. D. S. (1989). Attachments beyond infancy. *Amer. Psychol.* **44,** 709–716.
Erikson, E. (1982). "The Life Cycle Completed: A Review." Norton, New York.
Gottman, J., Notarius, C., Gonso, J., and Markman, H. (1976). "A Couple's Guide to Communication." Research Press, Champaign, IL.
Hatfield, E., and Rapson, L. R. (1993). "Love, Sex, and Intimacy: Their Psychology, Biology, and History." HarperCollins, New York.
Kelley, H. H., Berscheid, E., Christensen, A., Harvey, J. H., Huston, T. L., Levinger, G., McClintock, E., Peplau, L. A., and Peterson, D. R. (Eds.) (1983). "Close Relationships." Freeman, New York.
Morris, D. (1971). "Intimate Behavior." Triad: Grafton Books, London.
Shaver, P. R., and Hazan, C. (1988). A biased overview of the study of love. *J. Soc. Pers. Relationships,* **5,** 474–501.
Sternberg, R. J., and Barnes, M. L. (Eds.) (1988). "The Psychology of Love." Yale University Press, New Haven.

MARITAL DYSFUNCTION

Gary R. Birchler and William S. Fals-Stewart
University of California at San Diego

Glossary

Character The aggregate of features and traits that form the individual nature of a person.

Commitment The state of having pledged, devoted, or obligated oneself to another; to be involved, remain loyal, and maintain the relationship over time.

Constructive communication Open and honest sharing of information between two people; when the message intended and sent by the speaker is exactly the same as the message heard or received by the listener.

Contract An explicit agreement between two people for the doing or not doing of something specified. In relationships, this is more often a set of implicit expectations which partners have concerning how they will define the relationship and interact with another.

Marital life cycle A set of developmental stages through which a typical marriage passes, from the time of the wedding until the death of one spouse.

Mid-life crisis Within an individual approaching or in mid-life, a condition of instability and significant concern about one's identity, the purpose and meaning of life and insecurities about past and future accomplishments.

MARITAL DYSFUNCTION is a state of matrimony in which there has been a significant and persistent breakdown in partners' effective interaction and their experience of relationship quality.

I. INTRODUCTION AND CONTEXT

The subject of marital dysfunction is not new, nor is it peculiar to our age. The breakdown of marriage, along with explicit provisions for divorce, is a phenomenon recognized in ancient Greek, Hebrew, Babylonian, and Roman law. The notion of a lifelong, indissoluble marriage evolved during the rise of Christianity in Western civilization. The subsequent religious, societal, and legal barriers to divorce that eventually emerged served to mask marital problems and helped to perpetuate the myth of a man and a woman marrying and "living happily ever after." Although this idealized romantic image of marriage persists, there is longitudinal evidence indicating that there is an ever widening gulf between this expectation and reality. In the United States, the divorce rate in 1860 was approximately 2%; by 1960, this rate had increased to 17%. At present, the average marriage in the United States lasts 9.4 years; marital divorce affects more than two million adults a year and over 50% of first marriages now end in divorce. [*See* DIVORCE.]

However, divorce is only one of several possible reactions to marital dysfunction. The behavioral responses of dissatisfied partners can lie along any one of four primary dimensions—voice, loyalty, exit, and neglect. Voice (e.g., discussing problems, compromising, and expressing concern) and loyalty (e.g., being committed and supportive) are considered constructive responses, intended to maintain and repair a dysfunctional relationship. Exit (e.g., desertion, separation, and divorce) and neglect (e.g., refusing to discuss problems, spending less time together, mistreating the partner emotionally or physically) are considered destructive responses, which tend to break up the relationship.

Thus, using divorce rates as the sole indicator of the prevalence of marital dysfunction underestimates the magnitude of the total problem. These figures do not include temporary and permanent separations, or acute or protracted marital discord which persists while spouses continue to live under the same roof. Some studies suggest that of those couples who do not divorce, roughly 10% will informally or legally separate, another 10% of couples will seek conjoint therapy to address relationship problems, while another 10–15% will suffer through prolonged periods of relationship disruptions without seeking professional help. Coupled with the divorce figures, only 10–15% of newlywed couples can expect to remain happily married throughout the course of their relationships. Given that well over 90% of men and women marry at least once, most adults will suffer through disruptive discord over the course of their marital relationships.

II. DETERMINANTS OF MARITAL SATISFACTION OVER THE LIFE CYCLE

The life span perspective of marriage becomes broader and more complicated as time goes on. The significantly shrinking numbers of "nuclear" families, the increasing economic necessity to two-worker households, increased longevity, and the changing role of women all have become important factors in determining the level of marital stability and satisfaction for a given couple. Unfortunately, theories of the determinants of marital satisfaction are much more prevalent than substantiating empirical research. However, among family sociologists and researchers there is emerging consensus regarding positive and negative *pre*marital and *post*marriage factors which can account for marital satisfaction and stability.

A. Premarital Factors

Obviously, mate selection can be a critical prerequisite to a happy marriage. In particular, marital suc-

cess is relatively more assured to the extent that partners are similar in background and status on the following variables: education, socio-economic status, race, religion, age, culture, physique, physical attraction, and values. Interestingly, for decades, research on the importance of similarities and differences in partners' personality variables has been inconclusive. In contrast, there is relatively recent evidence that a couple's joint effectiveness in basic communication skills predicts later marital satisfaction. [*See* MATE SELECTION.]

Concerning negative premarital factors, it is believed that all too frequently people get married for the wrong reasons: to escape from an unpleasant home life, to cure severe psychological deficits, or to meet the expectations of friends, families, or community. In addition, marital adjustment problems seem to occur frequently if a person marries after the loss of a significant other, marries before age 20, marries before an acquaintanceship of 6 months or after 3 years, marries after getting pregnant, becomes fully dependent on one's family for housing or financial support, or lives too close or too far from an extended family. Clearly, even before the act of marriage itself, many obstacles must be avoided or overcome in order to have a chance at long-term marital quality and intimacy.

B. Factors Affecting Marital Satisfaction at Different Marital Stages

The family literature includes articles describing from 3 to 24 marriage and family life cycle stages. Indeed, in contemporary society there are many variations to the basic nuclear family model. However, for purposes of brevity and conceptual clarity, we will outline 5 basic marital life cycle stages representing the course of events for a basic family unit, comprising father, mother, and one or more children.

1. New Couple

Excitement and *adjustment* are the basic characteristics of the new couple stage. Ironically, while in general, marital satisfaction is never again higher than during this first stage of the marital life cycle, the first 2 years of marriage also are marked by the highest divorce rates. Partners must make adjustments to many of the disconcerting "premarital" factors noted above and face the sometimes harsh reality of the myth of romance. Idealization of marriage (and one's partner) often is followed by the disappointment and disillusionment inherent in the task at hand: the "hard work" of developing a successful marital partnership!

Typical responsibilities and adjustments during the new couple stage include finding work and establishing viable economic resources; establishing a home; revising friend and family relationships; establishing a satisfying sexual relationship; accommodating to one another's personal habits and activity preferences; developing workable patterns of communication, decision making, and conflict resolution. Each of these tasks can be formidable and failure to negotiate one or more of them can result in varying levels of marital dysfunction. However, a good majority of new couples survive this stage and face a most important decision in Stage II: To be or not to be parents.

2. Parental: To Be or Not to Be

The transition to parenthood lasts basically from the birth of the first child until the first child reaches adolescence. If the decision is made *not* to have children, the developmental markers are less clear; the stage generally concludes after the wife has passed childbearing age. Exerting a definite influence on marital satisfaction, three basic developmental tasks are implicated during this stage: to have or not have a family; a lasting commitment to careers and work inside or outside the home; working through the inevitable power struggles caused by identity and role changes associated with individual development and the marriage up to this time. Typically, during this stage there is a generalized erosion of spousal emotional attachment; there is no evidence that having children prevents this phenomenon from occurring. In fact, for many couples the adjustments associated with child-rearing result in the lowest level of marital satisfaction experienced throughout the marital life cycle. Young mothers, in particular, may feel stressed during this time and financial and division-of-labor issues may stress both parents during the early part of the parental stage. There is some evidence that childless couples do better during these early years, but in general, any deterioration in marital satisfaction solely attributable to the advent of children seems to disappear after about 7 years of marriage. [*See* PARENTING.]

Similarly, available research evidence is mixed regarding whether marital satisfaction is enchanced or deteriorates if the wife works. Young mothers have more difficulty working than mothers with older children. Basically, most studies show that if

(a) the woman wants to work, (b) she gets satisfaction from her work, (c) satisfactory child care arrangements can be made, and (d) she has the support of her husband, then marital satisfaction is maintained or enhanced. In contrast, full-time housewives generally experience somewhat lower marital satisfaction than their working counterparts, unless they personally prefer to stay home. As a group, wives who choose homemaking are somewhat happier than the average working wives.

The notorious "7-year itch" has some basis in fact. Marital problems and related power struggles tend to be at their peak as early child-rearing responsibilities, increased career pressures, and the age 30 developmental transitions for the two individuals all exacerbate the interdependency requirements of marriage and the inequalities often associated with traditional sex roles. Couples who do well during this stage have developed supportive caring behaviors, communication and problem-solving skills, and effective mechanisms to resolve the inherent conflicts. Almost as many of their counterparts struggle passively and aggressively to determine who is in charge; indeed, too many couples do not resolve their individual differences well enough to maintain the marriage. During the parental stage, significant marital dysfunction and frequent marriage failures are indicated by the second highest divorce rate, resulting in the unprecedented numbers of single-parent and blended families. In an alternative pattern, many other partners begin to drift apart gradually over the years. These covertly dissatisfied couples go on to join the many relatively satisfied couples entering the mid-life adolescence stage of development.

3. Mid-Life Adolescence

The mid-life adolescence stage is the period between when the first child reaches adolescence and the last child leaves home. Ironically, the name of this stage refers to the *adult's* level of development, not the children's. The majority of the couples have been married between 15 and 30 years and are between their mid-30s and early 50s—prime time for the classic identity struggles of the adolescent to be revisited. Couples in this stage may experience a "mid-life crisis," including insecurities concerning self-identity, independence–dependence on family relationships, vocational accomplishments, sexual fulfillment, and perhaps premature health problems.

Men and women may experience this stage somewhat differently. Typical but not universal, many men have worked for over two decades, the better part of life has passed, they experience their minds and bodies as perceptively slower, their adolescent children are raising hell, and their marriage and sex life may be stale. In the early part of this stage some men are more unhappy and confused than ever before in their lives. Like the adolescent, they may act out in many different ways—in ways which are potentially devastating to the marital relationship (e.g., major depression or alcoholism, quitting their jobs, having an affair, severe workaholism, abandon the family, etc). For women, the early part of this stage also can be very stressful, especially if her job is burdensome or unrewarding or there are deteriorating bonds between her and the children and between her and the husband. This is the most difficult stage in the parenting process. The frequently disruptive distancing of the adolescents puts a significant pressure on the parents to be supportive of one another. If the marital relationship is not strong, coping can be miserable; talk of separation and divorce may surface for the first time. Partners are questioning and examining the meaning of life and their personal prospects for the future.

In contrast, for those couples well-prepared and so motivated, the mid-life adolescence stage can be one of redefinition, reorganization, and renewed commitment to the marriage. Personal independence and the development of autonomy reach a healthy balance with relationship dependence and the gratifications of affiliation as the couple reconnects and reorganizes in the wake of departing adolescents. The various inevitable insecurities mentioned above are discussed, shared, and largely resolved. The successful relationship has now passed through the romance and power struggle phases and reaches a point of acceptance and stability. Interestingly, for many couples, some aspects of gender role reversal occur. In lieu of vocational preoccupations, husbands now turn more attention to intra-family matters; many wives (free from full-time mothering) become more active outside of the home and family, and may go back to school or start careers. Role reversal may also take place in the area of sexual interaction, with husbands less energetic and demanding and wives now more active and enthusiastic. During this challenging stage, a collaborative relationship and open communication are required to make the necessary life-style adjustments. If successful, the foundation is now laid for the newest stage of the marital life cycle, the long haul: The postparental stage.

4. Postparental

The postparental stage begins when the last child leaves home and ends when the husband and/or the wife retires. While this stage may last as little as a few months, more typically today, it can last 15–20 years because longevity and working years have increased. The path taken by couples seems to be bifurcated. The potential for marital dysfunction can increase significantly if any of the following occur: (a) either partner going through the climacteric, (b) men are still encountering their mid-life crises, (c) mothers have overly invested in their children to the detriment of the marriage, (d) there is a physiological or psychological loss of sexual interest and performance, in men especially, (e) there is development of such rigid personalities and sex-role structures that partners cannot negotiate diverging interests and role changes, (f) there is inattention and gradual deterioration of the marital relationship over the years to the point that the marriage is devitalized. Couples who seek treatment at this stage of life are suffering frequently from one or more of the above problems.

On the other hand, evidence exists that most couples do relatively well during the postparental stage. In fact, some studies suggest that the level of marital satisfaction reached by many couples in this time of life is surpassed only during the new couple stage. The positive potential of renewed and deepened commitment is realized. Sufficient resources and good health are available after the children leave that spouses lead active and pleasurable lives together. Partners regroup to cope with the many changes and challenges at this time, for example, children leaving home, significant others sick and dying, the diminution of mental and physical abilities, career plateaus, and even more pronounced sex-role reversals, etc. To maintain a positive marriage during the postparental stage, all these challenges must be identified, shared, and met as the couple prepares for the final stage: culmination.

5. Culmination

The culmination stage is defined as the period of marriage between retirement and the death of one spouse. It may last from a few weeks to 10–15 years. Fortunately, most couples have become pretty good partners by this time of life. This is the least studied stage of marriage. Our best information to date suggests that couples in the culmination stage enjoy a level of marital satisfaction just below that of the postparental stage. Typically these elderly spouses must rely heavily upon one another for emotional and physical support. They tend to have a solid companionship and relative contentment with one another. The major tasks include adjusting to retirement and preparing for the loss of one's spouse. Retirement brings on major adjustments, both practically and psychologically. Daily living is the central focus. As well as any other variables, partners' health and vigor, and adequate financial resources seem to predict their level of personal and marital satisfaction. For some, especially men, retirement can be stressful; power and sex-role relationships can be altered significantly. Unfortunately, significant physical and mental health problems increase for many people at this time of life. In particular, depression, dementias, heart disease, lung disease, organ dysfunctions, cancers, and other maladies can not only affect the identified patients, but also increase the stress on spouses as caretakers. Caretakers are known to suffer significantly from depression, loneliness, and fatigue. Suicide and depression rates do increase for men at this time of life. Couples who do the best in the culmination stage have learned to communicate openly about their concerns, to be flexible in sex-role assignments, and have maintained good health and adequate financial resources. While those couples who do separate and divorce at this time are tragic to contemplate, their counterparts who reach "golden anniversaries" are often delightful to behold.

III. CRITICAL ASPECTS OF MARITAL SATISFACTION: THE SEVEN "C's"

The institution of marriage is most confounding and complex. While it would be extremely difficult to find perfect agreement among family therapists and researchers, there is reasonable consensus regarding certain fundamental requisites for a satisfactory long-term intimate marriage. These basic components are called by various names throughout the marital and family literature, but they can be subsumed under the rubric of "The Seven 'C's' ": Commitment, Caring, Communication, Conflict Resolution, Character, Culture, and Contract. This section will describe these important aspects of marital satisfaction along with comments regarding their relevance for marital therapy.

A. Commitment

Commitment is essential for the development and maintenance of a quality marriage. Without it, there will probably be insufficient trust and faith in the security and stability of the relationship to foster the development of long-term intimacy. Commitment is largely a motivational variable, born of past and present interpersonal relationships. Couples who can live up to their wedding vows of "meet whatever challenges together, through thick and thin, 'til death do us part" stand a significantly better chance of avoiding marital dysfunction than many contemporary couples who both fear abandonment and threaten relationship dissolution at the first sign of discord and failed expectations.

Unfortunately, as more and more children become products of broken homes and/or are subjected to destructive or abusive family interactions, the more tenuous is their commitment as adults to their mates. The increased divorce rate tends to feed on itself; children of divorce (and dysfunctional families) are more likely to become divorced themselves. Couples who have the ability and willingness to "commit" to a relationship for the long term and to do the ongoing work that is necessary to resolve the inevitable problems are known to have a better prognosis for satisfaction and stability. This is also true when couples enter marital therapy. An important early determination is: Are the partners committed to one another in this marriage? If not, the prognosis for a positive therapeutic outcome is poor and the lack of commitment tends to obstruct any other progress. When present, commitment combines with caring to form the motivational foundation for marital satisfaction.

B. Caring

Needless to say, caring behaviors are critical to a truly intimate relationship. Interestingly, caring behaviors derive from both motivational and instrumental (i.e., skill acquisition) determinants. Caring behaviors encompass not only sex and affection (i.e., love behaviors) but also the development of mutually rewarding activities, quality time together, and a real friendship experience offering interpersonal support and understanding. Marital dysfunction results when partners are deficient in the skills of expressing love and affection or, just as likely, they fail to sufficiently maintain formerly expressed caring behaviors. That is, partners take one another for granted, become preoccupied with other tasks, become disillusioned and uninvolved, or withhold caring behaviors in a punitive fashion. Marital therapy is most successful when the process is capable of modifying both the motivational and instrumental determinants of caring. Unfortunately, however, there are limits to partners' abilities to recover positive, intimate feelings for one another once too much damage has been done to the basic fabric of caring. Even a solid commitment/intention to stay together, without caring, sets the stage for an empty and lonely experience. Commitment and caring together provide the heart and soul of marital satisfaction. [*See* LOVE AND INTIMACY.]

C. Communication

Beyond the basics of caring and commitment, a necessary vehicle for expressing these values, for building friendship, and for identifying and understanding important relationship issues is marital communication. While the *will* to communicate is an important motivational variable, we believe that the *skill* to communicate significantly helps or hinders most couples in their pursuit of an intimate relationship.

Communication is a nebulous concept to define. Operationally speaking, in the context of a marriage, constructive communication can be defined as: When the message intended and sent by either spouse is exactly the same as the message received and understood by the other spouse. Good fidelity in this process requires not only an effective speaker but just as important is an effective listener. Naturally, communication is more difficult when the content of the message is confusing and unclear or in any way emotionally laden with negative affect (e.g., blame, criticism, sadness, anger, resentment, frustration, etc.). Distressed partners are known to be selective in their attention to the negative versus the positive components of messages and then to respond with negative behaviors in return. This self-fulfilling process frequently results in a pattern of reciprocally negative exchanges, including various criticisms and personal attacks. Interestingly, some couples also have considerable difficulty sending or receiving positive messages (e.g., compliments, enjoyment, love and affection, etc.). Failure in active, open, and accurate communication is one of the most frequent complaints of dysfunctional couples seeking marital therapy. Effective communication is critical for long-term marital satisfaction; it is the necessary (but not by itself sufficient) requisite for sharing the positive and understanding the negative aspects of marital interaction. [*See* INTERPERSONAL COMMUNICATION.]

D. Conflict Resolution

Effective communication may help couples to identify and understand their problems, but often, more than communication and understanding are required for effective resolution of the problems. Since conflict is inevitable in marriage, couples must possess (or soon develop) conflict resolution skills in order to manage their anger and resolve their conflicts. Otherwise, unresolved problems tend to accumulate and eventually damage other important aspects of their relationship. Two aspects of conflict resolution are important: (1) general problem-solving and joint decision-making skills generally employed *before* high conflict is reached, and (2) anger/conflict management and resolution skills which need to be employed *after* high conflict is encountered. [*See* CONFLICT COMMUNICATION.]

Effective problem solving is facilitated by the development of a focused and mutually accepted agenda, an open process of sharing each partner's perspective on the problem, non-judgemental creative problem-solution generation process (i.e., brainstorming), a comprehensive plan for implementation of the agreed upon solution, and evaluation of the effectiveness (or modification) of the solution. Anger and conflict management skills include learning how to identify and anticipate anger-arousing situations and physiological cues, developing individual and interpersonal prevention behaviors to avert the anger escalation process, and later stage time-out and conflict de-escalation techniques. Some fortunate couples develop both sets of skills, some are good at one but not the other, and the most dysfunctional couples are deficient in both. [*See* ANGER.]

E. Character

From a bio-psycho-social perspective, individuals must grow and develop to the point where each has whatever essential personal resources are required to establish and to maintain a healthy relationship. The combinations of individual personalities (i.e., characters) in marriages can be quite diverse. Each partner comes with a different personal history and personality style, and, based on a developmental combination of biological and environmental factors, spouses can have tremendously varying levels of "character psychopathology." For example, one's "premarital" character can be influenced significantly by medical, psychiatric, or substance abuse problems, legal difficulties, or traumatic sexual experiences. One's experiences and responses to such problems can severely impact marital quality. Indeed, just as the number of cases where there have been previous marriages and blended families has grown dramatically, the likelihood of significant psychopathology in one or both partners has increased. More than ever, it is important to understand what past experiences and expectations each individual brings into the current relationship, especially any traumatic legacies from one's family of origin or from previous formative relationships. Past experiences can influence significantly partners' current behavioral patterns, cognitions, and affective perspectives.

There is little doubt that if one partner is experiencing a major depression, an anxiety disorder, active substance abuse, a significant personality disorder, or a psychosis, for example, that these aspects of "character" will significantly impact marital satisfaction. In fact, there is known to be a strong bidirectional link between partners' levels of depression and their experience of marital satisfaction. Research indicates that throughout the marital life cycle about half of the clinically distressed marriages include one or more depressed partners and about half of the married patients who are treated for depression have distressed marriages. In sum, failure to adequately recognize and treat these types of individual disorders will almost surely result in marital dysfunction and distressed marital interaction often exacerbates individual dysfunction. [*See* DEPRESSION.]

F. Culture

"Culture," in the broadest sense of the seven C's, refers to the influences on the marriage from traditional family, ethnic, religious, community, and even national sources. It is well known among family sociologists and family practitioners that these factors can be significant and even dominant in an individual's physical and psychological development.

The very prospect of a new marriage is shaped, for better or for worse, by the forces of surrounding culture. For example, since the beginning of the institution of marriage, well meaning (and not so well meaning) parents and other relatives, in defending traditional, religious, ethnic, or socio-economic boundaries, have prevented, pressured, and otherwise adversely affected the establishment and development of certain marriages. Similarly, whether being upheld or contradicted, religious values, community standards, peer pressures, national movements, and economical cycles, all these cultural forces have significantly influenced many marriages. [*See* MARRIAGE.]

It is incumbent on those who propose to get married, and on those who hope to help distressed marriages after the fact, to be aware and knowledgeable of the important cultural variables which can support or destroy a new relationship. For example, it can be more difficult to treat a distressed marriage where the partners and the therapist all come from different ethnic or fundamental religious backgrounds from one another. Partners may also have very divergent family interactional traditions and styles, socioeconomic standards and expectations, or orientations as to sexuality or violence. Effective treatment may require special interventions or consultations to take into account these cultural factors.

G. Contract

The notion of "contract" derives from the expectations which partners have about one another and the marriage. Typically, one's expectations of a mate are formed by virtue of past experiences in one's family of origin or in other significant developmental relationships, including previous marriages. Interestingly, these expectations frequently are implicit, perhaps out of conscious awareness. Inherent and unspoken expectations can be profound criteria for marital happiness. Unfortunately, as well, one's expectations of a mate or about a marriage can be quite demanding; even unrealistic or unhealthy. For example, some people expect their mates to behave toward them and to meet the same needs as did their mothers or fathers. Yet they may marry people who have personality traits and behavioral dispositions quite different from their parents. Other people expect too much from their spouses, for example, as if they can and should provide for all of their emotional or financial support. Alternatively, one might expect to get (and therefore will give) very little to the relationship. In this case, what one spouse provides the other may fall far short of the recipient's expectations and discord will result.

More recently, in the face of ever-increasing second and third marriages, partners are developing more explicit marriage contracts. These so-called "prenuptial agreements" are usually designed to protect significant assets one partner has acquired prior to the marriage. However, it is less clear that contemporary newlyweds are any better at explicating other contractual features of their relationships. Emotional, behavioral, and nonfinancial security arrangements are very difficult for "people in love" to address prior to marriage. However, this does not mean that they do not have fairly significant, sometimes even rigid, expectations in these areas of interaction. Clearly marital satisfaction is impacted by the implicit and explicit contracts which partners may believe to exist. Unfulfilled or dashed expectations can form the basis for severe marital conflict. It is important for couples to have the will (based on commitment and caring) and the competence (i.e., communication and conflict resolution skills) both to identify and to resolve various contractual disputes which may be due to unclear or contradictory expectations of one another.

In summary, many, if not most, of the ingredients important to a long-term intimate relationship can be accounted for by the seven C's: (1) Loyalty to the marriage with a long-term perspective and the will to work out the inevitable problems (i.e., *commitment*) in the context of (2) love, affection, and emotional support (i.e., *caring*) combined with (3) open and effective *communication* and (4) *conflict resolution* skills given (5) wholesome personal values and a healthy personality (i.e., *character*) plus (6) strong family traditions and compatible *cultural backgrounds*, and finally, (7) a marital *contract*, which offers viable expectations that can be specified, negotiated, and modified as the marriage develops over time. Once again, approximately one-fifth of all newly married couples are able naturally to develop and maintain the seven C's sufficiently to enjoy a high-quality long-term intimate relationship. On the other hand, the majority of all couples run into significant difficulties. Presumably, they could benefit from professional diagnosis of their problems and such assistance as might take place in marital therapy. Unfortunately, only a small minority of couples seek out and take advantage of these professional services.

IV. TREATMENT OF MARITAL DYSFUNCTION: APPROACHES TO THERAPY

There are many thousands of therapists in the United States who practice marital therapy. Married individuals and couples are either self-referred or re-ferred to these therapists by their physicians and clergymen, or by their friends and family members. Typically, a therapist is trained primarily in one theoretical approach. However, since no one approach is a panacea, in practice, most therapists are rather eclectic in their treatment of marital dysfunction. Many practitioners learn to incorporate certain aspects of three basic theoretical approaches: family systems, cognitive–behavioral, and psychodynamic.

In general, family systems and cognitive–behavioral approaches are similar in that they focus on (a) the marital relationship, (b) behaviors and interactions which take place in the present, and (c) attempting to modify the dysfunctional manner in which partners communicate and behave toward one another. Family systems and cognitive–behavioral approaches differ primarily in that the cognitive–behavioral approach is designed to obtain quantifiable assessments of (i.e., data pertaining to) the current dysfunctions, and to modify partners' specific cognitions and behaviors based on empirically derived, skill-oriented technologies. In contrast, family systems therapists are somewhat more diverse in their theoretical backgrounds, tend not to be as objective or "data-driven," and employ many system-oriented interventions designed to change partners' dysfunctional patterns of interaction. Typically, in using structural or strategic interventions, the purposes of the interventions are much less obvious to the clients than is the case in the cognitive–behavioral approach. [See COGNITIVE BEHAVIOR THERAPY.]

In considerable contrast to the approaches mentioned above, some of the psychodynamic approaches feature considerably more work with the individual partners, presuming on a theoretical basis that developmental factors and intrapsychic conflicts are more accountable for the couples' presenting problems than present behavioral interactions. Psychodynamic approaches focus more on individuals' conscious and unconscious thought patterns and unexpressed feelings, which are the residuals of prior significant relationships and which are imported into the present marriage to cause (or to perpetuate) interpersonal problems. It should be noted that while these approaches can be quite different from one another, so far none, in isolation, has demonstrated conclusively that it is superior to the other approaches. However, it should also be noted that only the behaviorally oriented practitioners have offered replicated empirical evidence of the effectiveness of their approach, based on a number of controlled scientific investigations over the past two decades.

In brief, the following description is offered to give the reader an idea of what might transpire should a distressed couple present to a contemporary cognitive–behavioral marital therapist. The first task, which takes from 2 to 4 weeks, is to complete a comprehensive evaluation of the marriage and the various contributions of its partners. Typically, during the first session, introductions occur and an administrative discussion takes place concerning such items as the therapist's policies on fees, confidentiality, length of sessions, office hours, etc. The bulk of the first meeting is devoted to hearing each partner's presenting complaints (i.e., what brings them to therapy?), their goals and expectations for treatment (i.e., who and what do they want changed?), and perhaps a brief developmental history concerning when and why they got married, and their experiences during the early course of the relationship, etc. The first session typically ends with a discussion about whether to meet again, and if so, what the next steps are to further evaluate the current status of the marriage and the prospects for therapy.

The subsequent one–three evaluation sessions are designed to complete the comprehensive assessment process. Many therapists employ both individual and relationship-oriented paper and pencil questionnaires to help them assess various levels of dissatisfaction and dysfunction and to ascertain the marital system's assets and strengths. The couple may even be asked to provide a sample of their problem-solving communication so that the therapist can actually observe their basic communication and conflict resolution skills. Also, in some settings, a combination of conjoint (i.e., including both partners) and individual (i.e., private meeting) sessions may be conducted to learn about pertinent aspects of past and present problems.

Thus, after several hours of discussion, the completion of questionnaires, and possibly an observed sample of communication, the evaluation is completed. Our program, as one example, features a final evaluation phase feedback session, where the therapist integrates all of the multimodal assessment information, formulates the problems, and outlines suggested goals for treatment. Based on this presentation, all parties discuss the findings and then decide whether to enter into marital therapy. Sometimes

the nature of the problem is such that engaging in marital therapy is not advised. In such cases, one or both partners may be referred for *individual* therapy to work on certain personal issues.

The length and course of marital therapy are quite variable. Couples typically meet for $1-1\frac{1}{2}$ hours weekly for 10 to 20 weeks, but, of course, some couples terminate prematurely and others make slow but steady progress for over a year, and longer. The length of treatment depends, in part, on the number and severity of the problems, whether improvement/modification is needed in one or more of the seven C's, and on the basic motivation and intelligence levels of the partners and the therapist. Not infrequently, partners have conflicted or hidden agendas as they enter marital therapy. Helping couples to work effectively as a team toward open, agreeable, and attainable goals can take considerable time, especially if spouses have spent many years entrenching themselves in disparate and unrewarding patterns of interaction.

The general interventions and specific techniques employed by therapists to help couples reach their treatment goals also are highly variable. Cognitive–behavioral marital therapists typically feature: (a) certain interventions and homework exercises designed to strengthen commitment and caring, (b) psycho-educational, experiential training in communication and conflict resolution skills, (c) a review of partners' expectations and beliefs and modification of any negative or otherwise dysfunctional thoughts which may impede the processes of acceptance or change, and (d) specific negotiated behavior-change strategies, designed to help people modify maladaptive relationship behaviors. Specific intervention procedures include: videotape feedback, role-playing, therapist coaching and modeling, communication exercises, lots of homework, and keeping track of self- and spouse-observed cognitive and behavioral variables, and reading assignments. After treatment is completed, it is hoped that couples share maximum abilities to accept and be tolerant of certain aspects of their relationship and to effectively identify and modify those behaviors and interactions which are maladaptive or destructive. Also, many therapists recommend booster sessions (i.e., follow-up meetings) in order to help couples maintain the gains made earlier in treatment. A healthy marriage may be best conceptualized as compared to dental hygiene or the maintenance of a well-running vehicle or a functional household. They do not work optimally without good maintenance and periodic check-ups. Booster sessions have been shown to prolong and to help stabilize the improved ways of interacting which are learned in marital therapy.

V. OUTCOME OF MARITAL DISTRESS: TREATED AND UNTREATED

Several factors account for considerable difficulty in stating, definitively, what the outcome prospects are once a couple enters and completes marital therapy: (a) There is debate regarding what the criteria should be for a positive outcome. Should the criteria include subjective satisfaction, various improvement scores, measures of specific problem behaviors (those identified by the couple or by the therapist), increased skills, or therapist estimates of change, etc.? (b) When should these measures be taken? Should they be obtained immediately at the end of therapy, after 3 months, after a year, etc.? (c) To date there are a couple dozen well-controlled scientific studies designed to measure the effectiveness of marital therapy (compared to no treatment at all), and most of them have been done by practitioners of one basic approach: behavioral marital therapy. (d) There have been even fewer well-controlled comparative studies, which compare the effectiveness of one type of treatment to another. Finally, (e) can there be a "positive outcome" to marital therapy when a hopelessly destructive marriage is terminated in divorce? These and other factors force us to estimate overall results from many different studies and to generalize from a number of specific and mixed findings across investigations.

In general, based on couples' responses to measures of marital satisfaction, based on certain increased skills in communication and problem solving and based on reductions in the intensity and amounts of couple-identified problem behaviors at the end of treatment, there is consistent evidence that the behavioral approach to marital dysfunction is significantly more effective than no treatment at all. One-half to two-thirds of the dysfunctional couples who come in for help experience substantial improvement in their marriage; about half of these couples achieve the "happy marriage" level of satisfaction. Unfortunately, however, after about 2 years, one-third of the former successes have relapsed back into marital distress. These particular couples have been unable to sustain the gains made in short-term therapy over an extended period of time.

Essentially, there are two lessons to be learned here. First, if a couple is experiencing marital distress or dysfunction, they would be wise to seek treatment. Based on existing data, treatments (a) which are designed to improve dyadic communication and problem-solving skills, (b) which assist couples to enrich affective or emotional involvement with one another, and (c) which seek to develop and validate a balance of autonomous and affiliative behaviors in both partners would seem to be the most effective in improving the relationships long term. If dysfunctional couples do not seek treatment, the relationship likely will remain unsatisfactory or deteriorate. Once a marriage is clinically distressed, without help there is only about a 10% chance of improvement.

Second, 10–15 weeks of treatment (i.e., the typical amount provided in the scientific studies) seems to have a short-term effect for a third of the treated couples. Therefore, periodic "booster" sessions are recommended for all treated couples to provide for maintenance of the gains they make in therapy.

Clearly, the scientific investigation of marital dysfunction will continue to determine which types of treatments are best for which types of couples. Also, efforts are under way to increase the overall therapeutic success rate above two-thirds and to reduce the relapse rate below one-third. Many investigators around the world are working on these problems.

VI. CONCLUSION

The reader has been introduced to the topic of "marital dysfunction." Marital distress, separation, and divorce have proliferated during the last several decades and have significantly affected the vast majority of individuals, couples, and families in our country. During the past two decades, in particular, marriage and family investigators have been able to increase the amount and sophistication of the information about how marriage works and what factors contribute to its dysfunction. This article has presented a discussion of what factors impact marital satisfaction at different stages of marital development and has suggested that there are seven critical aspects of marital relationships. In large measure, the seven C's account for the basic quality of marriage over the long run. Basic approaches to the treatment of marital dysfunction were discussed briefly, along with a short description of how at least one therapeutic approach might address the marital problems. Finally, issues related to the importance and success of marital therapy were discussed.

Bibliography

Birchler, G. R. (1992). Marriage. In "Handbook of Social Development: A Lifespan Perspective" (V. B. Van Hasselt and M. Hersen, Eds.), pp. 397–419. Plenum, New York.

Birchler, G. R., and Schwartz, L. (in press). Marital dyads. In "Diagnostic Interviewing" (M. Hersen and S. Turner, Eds.), 2nd ed. Plenum, New York.

Carter, B., and McGoldrick, M. (1988). "The Changing Family Life Cycle" 2nd ed. Gardner Press, New York.

Jacobson, N. S., and Addis, M. E. (1993). Research on couples and couples therapy. *J. Consult. Clin. Psychol.* **61,** 85–93.

Markman, H. J. (1981). Prediction of marital distress: A 5-year follow-up. *J. Consult. Clin. Psychol.* **49,** 760–762.

Rusbult, C. E., and Zembrodt, I. M. (1983). Responses to dissatisfaction in romantic involvements: A multidimensional scaling analysis. *J. Exp. Soc. Psychol.* **19,** 273–293.

◆

MARRIAGE

Norman Epstein, Lynda Evans, and John Evans
University of Maryland at College Park

Glossary

Companionate love Love based on deep attachment and affection, developed from a couple's history of shared positive and negative life experiences.

Complementarity Mate selection concept that people tend to choose mates whose characteristics compensate for each other's deficiencies.

Family life cycle Ordered sequence of changes over time in the structure and roles within the family, as adaptations to evolving needs of family members, the expansion and contraction of the nuclear family, and the demands of society.

Heterogamy Mate selection concept that people tend to marry people with dissimilar characteristics.

Homogamy Mate selection concept that people tend to marry others whose characteristics are similar to their own.

Intimacy A sense of closeness between two people based on sharing of ideas, emotions, and life experiences.

Negative reciprocity The tendency for one person in a relationship to respond to the other's negative behavior by reciprocating with negative behavior.

Romantic love Love characterized by strong caring and a need for the other person's presence, positive and negative mood swings, and persistent thoughts of the loved person.

Triangulation When one person in a dyad draws a third person into the relationship as an ally against the partner.

MARRIAGE is one of the most fundamental and enduring social institutions. Marriage has a long and rich history with so many divergent forms that it is difficult to render one definition that accommodates all of the variations. The prevalent American marital form is a legal, ostensibly lifelong sexually exclusive relationship between one adult man and one adult woman who typically have children together. Although the vast majority of Americans enter into this type of marital relationship at some point in their lifetimes, this definition fails to account for nontraditional adult relationship arrangements such as open marriages, swinging, coprimary relationships (also known as man sharing), cohabitation, homosexual relationships, or multiadult relationships such as communes or planned communes. The following discussion provides a historical perspective of the purposes, functions, and characteristics of the institution of marriage. It then describes the developmental issues of the marital relationship, from mate selection through dissolution, and it examines the interpersonal processes that can contribute to a successful or problematic marital relationship.

I. A HISTORICAL PERSPECTIVE ON MARRIAGE

A. Marriage in Early Societies

An understanding of modern marriage requires an appreciation of the evolutionary characteristics, purposes, and functions of the institution. There is evidence that even pre-Homo sapien hominids organized themselves into kinship-recognizing bands. There was consortship between mating partners, but it remains unclear whether the pair shared child care and socialization tasks or if these functions were fulfilled by the community. Sometime after 10,000 B.C., the hunter–gatherer societies began to store food for later consumption and soon thereafter began stationary dwelling and agriculture.

The early agricultural villages of the Middle East began separating their huts by function. Around

9000 B.C. these agricultural societies reserved one hut for community sleeping and another for community food storage. This living arrangement changed by 7000 B.C. when each family unit had their own individual hut where each family slept and stored their own food. This separation of family from the band placed a larger responsibility on the marital pair. They were responsible for providing food and shelter for themselves and their offspring as well as performing child care and socialization tasks.

Resources shifted from community shared goods to family owned goods. Cultivation rights became very important as did the inheritance of those cultivation rights and stored goods. The agricultural societies generally used matrilineal or patrilineal inheritance patterns.

The establishment of permanent dwellings in the agricultural villages invited the domestication of animals, and pastoral/herding societies evolved. Increased labor demands on the agricultural wife and the advent of feeding children animal milk and cereal grains allowed the mother to wean the child sooner and free her for work in the garden. The resultant shorter lactation period increased fertility rates and soon the numbers of children within the family increased. Marital pairs were required to take care of their dependent aging parents in exchange for the inherited agricultural/grazing rights and to care for more dependent, closely spaced children. This increased dependency load changed the form of marriage. More adults capable of work were brought into the marriage in the form of polygyny (more than one wife) and polyandry (more than one husband) and extended families were encouraged to live and work together.

B. Evolving Functions of Marriage

The purposes and functions of marriage changed as the needs and demands of the different society structures changed. Since property and wealth were controlled by marriage, families had much concern and influence over who married whom. The marriage contract was a private contract between families as far back as the Roman Empire. Early Christians and philosophers became concerned that sexual chaos would result if familial control lapsed, so the ability to change or dissolve marital contracts was forbidden. Marriage became a sacrament with God, thus ensuring that the institution of marriage would survive and fulfill the responsibilities necessary to the continuation of that society.

The view of marriage solely as a sacrament changed with King Henry VIII, who wished to divorce and remarry. The Catholic church was divided on the issue, which contributed to the weakening of religious control over governmental matters. Although the record is not clear, sometime between 1660 and 1857 the English Parliament passed the Matrimonial Causes Act making divorce possible by private acts of parliament, thus making marriage a status with the government instead of the church. The government was now responsible for protecting the marital entity.

Government-regulated marriage remained virtually unchanged as America became a nation. Since the time of inheritable property, marriage has been a highly regulated institution, controlled by families, the church, the state or any combination of the three. Modern American marriage is a status or special legal entity. The marital laws of each state codify the rights and obligations of the parties to a marriage contract. In addition, each individual state determines who can marry, the age of eligibility, the effect on property rights, and the grounds necessary for the dissolution of the marriage contract.

C. Legal Aspects of Marriage

State marital laws have typically not kept pace with changing social trends and values. Currently, any unmarried adult, or minors with parental consent, can enter at will into marriage with another unmarried adult of the opposite sex. However, when two individuals marry, the marital laws of their state apply to their marriage whether the individuals agree with them or not. Generally speaking, marital statutes in most states follow traditional gender roles, considering the husband to be the head of the household and holding him responsible for support of his wife and children. The wife is viewed as responsible for domestic roles that include nurturance, affection, sexual companionship, household services, and childcare. These roles are inconsistent with the trend toward more egalitarian relationships now typical of a large majority of married couples. Sexual exclusivity has been legally expected, but violation of this standard is rarely prosecuted today due to new divorce laws that allow for a "no-fault" dissolution of the marriage. Although marital laws have been slow to change, courts are making relatively rapid changes in their handling of divorce. The courts have begun to respect individual couples' marital contracts that differ somewhat from the codified traditional gender roles in marital obligations and responsibilities, which in effect partially shifts the responsibility of defining the rights and obligations of the marital contract from the government to the individual marital pair. Nevertheless, the government still maintains control over parental duties and attempts to have the parents fulfill their societal responsibilities for child maintenance and socialization, regardless of the status of the marital bond itself.

Thus, the structure and functions of marriage have undergone many changes over time, and it is reasonable to expect that the characteristics of marriage will continue to evolve in the future. This broad overview of the evolution of the institution of marriage sets the stage for a closer examination of the characteristics of American marriage.

II. MARITAL DEMOGRAPHICS

A. Trends in Marriage

The characteristics of American marriages can be illustrated by examining the demographics of marriage and how they have changed over time. Although concerns have been voiced that the institution of marriage is on the decline and that the traditional values of marriage and family are at risk, marriage has in fact remained an enduring social entity. There have been some changes in marital trends, but there are some indicators that have remained relatively stable over time. On the one hand, due in large part to a significant rise in the divorce rate, the two-parent biological nuclear family is no longer the majority family form, and a variety of other family structures (e.g., single-parent families, stepfamilies) have become increasingly common. On the other hand, the proportion of people getting married has remained fairly constant, and the proportion of married couples choosing to have children has remained essentially the same over time.

The vast majority of Americans (90%) marry at some point in their lives. The age at first marriage declined steadily from the turn of the century until a reverse in the 1960s, with notable dips during the 1940s and 1950s. The average age at first marriages for males currently is approximately 23 while the average age for females is approximately 21. The most striking change has been in the marriage behavior of men and women under 24 years of age. Among individuals between the ages of 20 and 24, there has

been a drop from 170 to 80 per 1000 marriages for men and a drop from 261 to 123 per 1000 marriages for women since 1960. Similarly, teenage marriage rates have fallen since 1970, from 1 in 40 to 1 in 200 male teens, and from 1 in 10 to 1 in 40 female teens. Increased academic goals for women and female participation in the labor market are among the social factors that have been cited as underlying these age trends.

As stated earlier, the number of married couples having children (approximately 95%) has essentially not changed over time. The most significant change has been in the number and timing of children. The birth rate in America has steadily dropped, with the exception of an unusual peak in the late 1950s. At that time the birth rate was 3.5 children per woman, but the previous steady decline resumed to a current birth rate of approximately 2 children per woman. Married women are waiting longer to have those children, and some social scientists have predicted that the women born in the late 1950s will surpass all previous cohorts in delaying the birth of their children.

B. Trends in Marital Dissolution and Remarriage

The total proportion of marital dissolutions by death, desertion, or divorce has remained relatively stable. However, this is due to a decrease in dissolutions by death, because of increased life expectancies, and a substantial increase in the number of divorces. In 1860, the number of marital dissolutions was 33.3 per 1000 marriages, 32.1 due to death and 1.2 due to divorce. In contrast, in 1970 the marital dissolution rate was 34.5 per 1000 marriages, 19.3 due to death and 15.2 due to divorce. Thus, although the marital dissolution rate has remained relatively constant, the percentage of those dissolutions due to divorce changed drastically between 1860 and 1970, from 3.5 to 44%. On the one hand, the escalation in the divorce rate during recent decades has been attributed to increased stresses (e.g., spouses' higher expectations that marriage will provide satisfaction of their needs for intimacy, companionship, and personal growth; the strain of trying to balance career and family demands in dual-worker marriages). On the other hand, divorce increasingly has been viewed as an option as women have become more independent economically, as the social stigma of divorce has decreased, and as divorce laws have become more flexible. [See DIVORCE.]

Divorce statistics reveal that 16.3% of first-time marriages and 23.6% of remarriages end in divorce by the fifth anniversary. After 10 years, 30% of first marriages and 36.4% of remarriages have ended in divorce. The rate of divorce steadily decreases for each successive year, but by the 50th anniversary date, 47.3% of all first marriages and 48.9% of all remarriages have ended in divorce.

It was feared during the social changes of the 1960s that people no longer believed in marriage and that the increasing divorce rate was evidence that marriage as an institution was in decline. However, statistics show that 77% of everyone who divorces will enter another marriage, with only 13% of those who divorce dropping out of the marriage pool. Although the majority of current marriages (58%) are still first-time marriages for both the bride and the groom, 22% of all marriages are remarriages for both the bride and groom, 10% involve first-time brides and previously married grooms, and 8% include first-time grooms marrying previously married brides. Apparently, marriage is not on the way out; rather, it is merely changing, and the frequency of remarriage suggests that "serial marriage" has become an acceptable pattern for a significant number of individuals. Nevertheless, those entering either a first marriage or a remarriage still typically hope to achieve a permanent relationship. The following section addresses the questions of how all of these people select mates.

III. MATE SELECTION

A. The History of Mate Selection

Historically, the important decision of who marries whom was not left to the young individuals. Parents made the decision for them, because marriage was and is the link between kin lines where property, power, lineage, and honor are passed through the spouses to their offspring. Rationality in choosing the best spouse to preserve inheritances was the basis for marriage and was promoted in the 17th and 18th centuries. Marital experts denounced passion and emotional satisfaction as a basis for marriage, and passionate love did not generally lead to marriage even as late as 19th century.

The end of the 19th century brought an increase in individualism in America. Men and women worked side by side, were educated together, and had the opportunity to become companions. Urbanization increased the contact between the sexes and widened the field of eligible mates. Love as a basis for marriage between equals became common in the literature of the early 20th century. Most industrialized nations now support individual freedom of choice in marriage partners. Parentally arranged marriages still exist in some cultures, but American parents cannot legally prevent or require their children to marry, with the exception of parental consent usually being required for weddings involving minors.

Although parents can no longer directly enforce an arranged marriage for their offspring, they still figure quite prominently in the mate selection process. Recent research supports the notion that parents directly and indirectly influence their children's mate selection beginning in childhood. Significant adults transmit values and provide role models that help to ensure homogamy or sameness in marital partners. For example, adults can effectively restrict potential mates by choosing schools and neighborhoods to limit propinquity as a means of ensuring that the available courtship pool is acceptable. Nevertheless, individuals are likely to meet potential mates while away from their neighborhoods, such as at work or while attending college. Furthermore, the basis for marriage generally has changed from the rationally arranged relationship for the preservation of property, power, and lineage of the past to a marriage based on romantic love and companionship. Although love still does not always lead to marriage, love is widely touted as the prerequisite to Western marriage.

B. Theories of Mate Selection

Several concepts have been offered in an attempt to explain how people select mates. *Homogamy* reflects the old adage that "birds of a feather flock together" or that people tend to marry others who are similar to themselves. *Heterogamy* reflects the adage "opposites attract" or that people tend to marry people who have dissimilar characteristics. Some theorists emphasized *complementarity,* in which people select mates whose characteristics compensate for each other's deficiencies. Other writers have emphasized that this form of mate selection may not be based on a process of compensating for deficiencies, but rather a meshing of two people's strengths. In fact, recent thinking about complementary needs involves a combination of homogamy and social exchange ideas. Homogamy is considered an important factor in this theory, in that research has indicated that individuals tend to marry someone who shares a similar education, socioeconomic status, race, religion, age, and culture. However, these homogamous variables serve as screening factors by defining the eligible pool of potential spouses. Then, according to social exhange theory, from the pool of potential mates who share basic characteristics with the individual, a particular partner is selected based on complementary needs. For example, two individuals may be attracted to each other both because they have similar backgrounds and because one person has a need to be nurtured whereas the other person has a need to be nurturant. These needs are complementary in that meeting the nurturing need of one individual simultaneously meets the need of the other individual: a social exchange wherein both parties benefit.

Process theorists assert that mate selection cannot be understood by merely observing the traits in the individuals, but it depends on the interaction or process between two people. The stimulus-value-role (SVR) theory is a well-researched three-stage process theory based on exchanges between people. Attraction and continued interaction depend on the exchange value of the assets and liabilities that each party brings to the relationship. Each person attempts to maximize their profits in the interaction. The stimulus stage is the initial period when the parties generally know little about each other, and continued interaction depends on adequate attractiveness, including physical characteristics, socioeconomic standing, educational experiences, status, etc. If each potential mate feels that the rewards and costs of a continued relationship are profitable, the interactions will continue and the pair will proceed to the second stage of value comparison by gathering more information about each other. Values are compared, and consensus on important values such as world views and religious beliefs is required for the relationship to continue.

In the third and most intimate stage of mate selection, partners gather information regarding role compatibility, which takes precedence over attractiveness and value consensus. This role stage is a time of evaluating expected behaviors with actual behaviors for the role of husband and the role of wife. The two individuals evaluate not only their own but also their partners' expected versus actual behaviors in the dyadic relationship. The exchange must be considered profitable to both members of the dyad for the relationship to continue. It is at this

point that the couple examines and negotiates roles for an intimate, committed relationship, often leading to marriage. The remainder of this discussion is devoted to the exploration of the marital relationship beyond the mate selection phase. [*See* INTERPERSONAL ATTRACTION AND PERSONAL RELATIONSHIPS; MATE SELECTION.]

IV. DEVELOPMENTAL ASPECTS OF MARRIAGE

A. Marriage as a Process

Marriage is a long-term process rather than a static entity. The individuals in a marital dyad must cope with the changes in structure and function that occur in the relationship as it endures a continuous evolution in their physical, emotional, and social environments. People age and mature, families expand and contract, roles shift, and the demands of the physical and social milieu fluctuate. Although there are endless variations possible, many of these changes come in a predictable sequence and are shared to some extent by most married couples. In order to understand marriage and family experiences as a process, social scientists have viewed relationship changes over time, using a developmental perspective.

The study of marital developmental issues includes the effects of changes in the number of family members, the relative ages of the members, individual developmental processes, the balance of economic resources and demands on the relationship, and the effects of the fluctuations in academic, social, and occupational roles of the participants. This discussion will focus on the structural and functional roles within the marriage, career issues, and family economics, as well as the impact of parenting issues and individual development on the marriage throughout its course. An advantage of this approach is that it provides a more comprehensive view of a system of individuals across time, and considers how changes in various subunits of the system affect each individual as well as the entire system.

B. Family Life Cycle Theory

Because the vast majority of marriages eventually become systems of procreation, the study of marital development has been done almost exclusively within the realm of nuclear family development over time, commonly known as *the family life cycle*. The family life cycle is defined as the process of an ordered sequence of changes in the structure and roles within the family that occur across time as an adaptation to the evolving needs of the family members, the expansion and contraction of the nuclear family, and the demands of society. Theorists have selected various event common to families' experiences and have described phenomena typical of these different stages. Perhaps the greatest contribution of this literature is not the labeling of stages or the prediction of a particular sequence, but the recognition that the transition from one phase to the next involves changes in family roles, structure, and function, and that there is a resultant stress that married couples and other family members must cope with.

Family life cycle theory is based on some fundamental ideas about the nature of families. These are: (1) the family is an interdependent system, in which behavior of any single member affects all the others; (2) the family has a structure, with members having positions and roles within the system, and norms for behavior in those roles; and (3) the structure and functions of the family change in a sequence over time to adapt to external and internal events. Family development is thus a process of progressive transformation of the structure and activities of the family, which requires the acquisition and discarding of roles by family members as they adapt to changing demands of their situation. [*See* FAMILY SYSTEMS.]

Family life cycle theory is also based on the idea that there are certain tasks or functions common to all families: (1) the physical maintenance of its members, (2) the socialization of family members for their roles in the family and the larger social milieu, (3) the maintenance of members' motivation to perform familial and other roles, (4) the exertion of social control within the family and between family members and the social environment, and (5) the addition of family members and their release when mature. Over time, the behaviors required to successfully accomplish these tasks will vary, and the study of family development can predict many of these changes that are bound to occur as the family strives to adapt.

Different theorists disagree on their demarcation of the life cycle stages, ranging from 5 stages to as many as 24. However, most models include the following: (1) the initial establishment of the marriage, (2) the transition into parenthood, (3) the children's entry into school and/or adolescence, (4) the launching of children into their own adult lives, and (5) the postparental or retirement phase. Obviously there can be many variations on this sequence such as divorce, remarriage, or death of family members.

The establishment of marriage implies a joining of two previously separate individuals into a new interpersonal unit with its own unique identity. Each spouse expands his or her interpersonal world dramatically by creating an interpersonal system with new boundaries that separate the marital dyad from their family of origin; a new social subsystem of a larger family system. If the boundary between the new couple and their families of origin remains ambiguous, as when the spouses share personal information about marital concerns with their parents and other relatives, significant marital conflict can arise.

Each partner takes on new roles as spouse, and these roles vary based on the interaction of the couple and their expectations of conjugal behavior. Their first tasks are to establish a satisfactory arrangement of domestic and occupational roles, and to develop procedures for making decisions and resolving conflicts. The couple also must develop or adjust their sexual relationship within the context of a committed long-term relationship, and their ability to do so can have a major impact on the quality of the marriage as a whole.

Marital satisfaction is often especially high during the early "honeymoon" stage of the relationship, when the spouses commonly discount the significance of existing conflicts and have high hopes for happiness in the future. Cohesion and sharing of power are typically higher during this phase than during the parental phase, and the partners usually look to each other for the meeting of their emotional needs. Dual employment is likely, especially in recent years, although for young couples the income derived from their employment may be low. Career demands are often high, as younger employees often work longer hours for less pay than their more experienced counterparts. The financial demands are less at this time, and couples without children can be more flexible in their choices of housing and lifestyle, making adaptation to circumstances easier.

The relationship between employment and marital adjustment is complex. On the one hand, an increasing percentage of wives work, for a variety of reasons (e.g., personal growth, financial necessity, financial independence), with dual-worker couples now representing the majority of marriages. There is evidence that employed wives enjoy better physical and psychological health than wives who do not work outside the home. However, employed wives also commonly experience stress from combining their work responsibilities with their typically large share of household and childcare responsibilities. Furthermore, some husbands express ambivalence about their wives working, on the one hand enjoying the income but on the other hand resenting the limited attention from their spouses, as well as the sharing of the breadwinner role. Women whose husbands are supportive of their employment tend to cope better with their competing role demands and have higher satisfaction in both their work and family lives. For both spouses, it is not working per se that affects marital satisfaction, but rather the positive or negative quality of each person's work experiences, including job stresses themselves and strains between work and family relationships.

As the realities of everyday life, including the awareness of spouses' differences in values, preferences, and personal habits impinge on the partners' possibly unrealistic positive expectations of marriage, the potential for disillusionment develops. Spouses who previously focused on each other's positive qualities may become distressed at what they perceive as the drawbacks of the marriage. Research has indicated that spouses are more distressed about their marriages when they are not satisfied with how their personal standards about the ways their marriage ''should'' be are being met. For many couples, the disillusionment is alleviated through acceptance of ways in which the realities of their marriages fall short of their ideals, as well as through collaborative problem-solving efforts that resolve some conflicts. However, for other couples the disillusionment leads to escalation of conflict and distress, and the potential for divorce. [See MARITAL DYSFUNCTION.]

The greatest single developmental change in marriage typically occurs when the couple begins their role as parents. The addition of a new member into the nuclear family, particularly one who demands such a great investment of emotional and physical energy, forces the couple to expand their boundaries and reprioritize their own needs. Domestic and financial demands increase markedly, while the ability to gain income is diminished due to the necessity of providing continual childcare. The couple is faced with the need to renegotiate their roles, as the number of dyadic relationships in their nuclear family unit has increased from one to three, and the allotment of the roles of companion, nurturer, and provider shift and expand. Decisions must be made as

to whose employment might be sacrificed, and how domestic duties and leisure pursuits can be accommodated. Research studies have indicated that even in couples where the husbands espouse nontraditional gender roles and where both spouses work full time, wives commonly have the large majority of household and childcare responsibilities. When the arrival of children leads to more traditional gender division of household labor, there tends to be an increase in marital stress.

New infants and young children also impinge on the couple's amount of rest, as well as the time and energy available for emotional and sexual intimacy. The presence of children has been found to decrease spouses' time together and increase the incidence of marital conflict. When the spouses do have time to communicate, their conversations tend to focus on the children rather than on their own relationship. These and other factors combine to make the transition to parenthood stressful, and research studies have indicated a common decrease in marital satisfaction during this stage of family life. Family therapists also have noted that in some marriages with underlying conflicts there is the danger that spouses will attempt to ''triangulate'' a child, using the child as an ally against their partner. Such triangles are not only very stressful for the children, but they also reduce the probability that the couple will resolve their marital conflicts. Nevertheless, it is important to note that the negative effects of children on marital satisfaction are only modest in degree, and many couples report positive effects of having children.

As children get older and enter school, the need for childcare diminishes, but the parents must cope with an expansion of their roles to accommodate the demands of the school system and the widening social circle of the child. Each year the child's peer relationships assume greater importance, and the parents must adapt to this change, as well as deal with teachers, coaches, and others whose behavior affects the life of their child. While family income typically is greater as time passes, the amount of career responsibility brought to bear on one or both partners may increase, adding to the complexity of roles and functions of the family as a whole.

The onset of adolescence brings a further increase in the complexity of the family system. The child or children are in a state of rapid physical and emotional growth, and the boundaries of the family must become more flexible to adapt to the teenager's increasing need for autonomy, personal responsibility and peer involvement. In addition, it is often during this time that one or both members of the couple experience personal stresses associated with middle age, such as concerns about whether they have achieved the career and financial goals that they expected for themselves by this stage of life. To further complicate the life circumstances facing the couple, their aging parents may develop an increasingly greater need for physical or financial support, and accommodations must be made to care for them. Unfortunately, it typically falls upon the female member of the couple to provide much of the caretaking functions for aging parents.

Marital roles and family structure shift again in a dramatic way as children leave home to establish independent adult lives and the couple experiences an "empty nest." As parenting roles diminish, the amount of stress on the couple is typically reduced. The parent–child relationships must change to allow the grown children to assume contol of their own lives, and as grandchildren are born, the older couple takes on a different type of nurturing role primarily as grandparents rather than parents. There also is a greater emphasis on the couple's own relationship, as the family structure within the household returns to a dyad for the first time in several decades. This might bring on difficulties, depending on the underlying quality of the marital relationship itself. Without the buffering effect of parental roles, inadequacies in the marriage may become more obvious. On the other hand, many couples experience a renewal of pleasure in their marriage as the stress of full-time parenting is relieved.

There are limited longitudinal data as yet on retired couples, because it has only been in the past few decades that life expectancy has increased enough for partners to reach retirement age together. On the one hand, retirement may decrease marital stress by eliminating job pressures and allowing a couple significantly more time for shared leisure activities. On the other hand, some individuals find it difficult to relinguish familiar work roles that constituted an important part of their self-concept, and couples who shared few interests over the years may experience discomfort at the prospect of spending much more time together. Furthermore, couples commonly must learn to cope with a reduction in income, as well as the physical restrictions of aging. The onset of chronic illness can also have a dramatic impact on the structure and function of the couple, as one or both partners may be forced to become more dependent on others (including each other) for physical care, and on their children for support.

Thus, the quality of this stage of marital life can vary greatly, depending on factors of health, finances, and relationship strengths or weaknesses.

Across the stages of the marital and family life cycle, one also must consider the degree to which the two individuals' needs and personality development mesh at any particular point. A disparity in personal characteristics and needs can lead to marital conflict and dissatisfaction. For example, if one spouse is focusing on building a career and expresses a need for an increased degree of autonomy during this period, there may or may not be serious conflict, depending on how much autonomy or intimacy is required by the other spouse during this time. Some other marriages develop problems over time if the spouses' characteristics meshed well initially (see the earlier discussion of homogamy and complementarity), but the individuals' interests and needs developed in different directions or at different paces.

Family life cycle theory provides a paradigm for understanding the process of marriage. There are certain limitations in this approach, however. Although there has been an increase in the number of couples who never have children (by choice or not), there is currently little theoretical and empirical literature on the developmental course of these marriages. Another limitation of the life cycle model is that it does not adequately consider larger social, economic, and political forces affecting marital relationships (e.g., changes in divorce laws; economic shifts making it difficult for couples to live comfortably without two incomes; increased mobility of the population, resulting in many couples living far from their own parents and their children). Nevertheless, an understanding of the basic principles of family life cycle development can give the social scientist insight into the types of adaptations that must be made to the various normative and nonnormative stressors encountered during the course of a marriage.

V. INTERPERSONAL PROCESSES IN MARRIAGE

As noted earlier, marriage is a dynamic process of interaction between two people (also influenced by others, such as children and extended family members), rather than a static entity. The ability of two individuals to meet each other's personal needs (e.g., for love, companionship, physical security, self-esteem) depends on the particular ways in which the spouses interact with each other. Marital satisfaction is a subjective state that includes both an individual's cognitive evaluation of the degree to which the relationship meets his or her standards for a "good" marriage, as well as the associated degree of emotional happiness the person experiences. Research on marriage has indicated that satisfaction depends on the kinds of behaviors exchanged by spouses, as well as the partners' cognitions (i.e., thinking) about those behaviors. The following is a discussion of behavioral and cognitive factors that tend to influence marital satisfaction.

A. Communication and Conflict Resolution

Quality of communication tends to be the most frequently cited determinant of marital satisfaction, and research studies consistently demonstrate differences in the communication behaviors of happy versus distressed couples. The quality of couples' communication not only is associated with their current marital satisfaction, but it also has been shown to predict satisfaction and marital stability (versus divorce) several years into the future. The quality of marital communication can be evaluated in terms of (a) whether the spouses send and receive information clearly and accurately, (b) whether the messages they send are pleasing (e.g., compliments, approval) or displeasing (e.g., criticism, threats) to each other, (c) whether the sharing of information increases or decreases a sense of intimacy between the spouses, and (d) whether the information exchanged helps or hinders the couple's ability to solve problems together and meet each other's needs. [See INTERPERSONAL COMMUNICATION; INTERPERSONAL PERCEPTION AND COMMUNICATION.]

Partners' mutual self-disclosure of their thoughts and emotions (especially positive ones) tends to be associated with marital satisfaction, and it seems likely that the positive impact of self-disclosure is due to its constructive contributions to all four of the above functions of communication. However, a number of authors have warned, and research findings have indicated, that full disclosure and an absence of tact can be hurtful and destructive. Thus, open communication is important for marital success, but it can be overdone.

Research on marital communication has indicated that members of distressed couples are more likely than happy spouses to exchange negative messages such as criticisms, disagreements, complaints and threats, whereas happy couples are more likely to

agree and communicate approval of each other. Distressed couples also express more negative feelings toward each other nonverbally (e.g., through facial expressions and posture) than do nondistressed couples. Furthermore, distressed couples are more likely to exhibit negative reciprocity, in which one partner's negative message is followed by a negative message from the other person, and so on. Marital researchers have noted that such reciprocity produces a destructive escalation of conflict. Members of happy couples are more likely to limit conflict escalation either by failing to reciprocate a negative response or by proposing a solution to the issue that has produced the conflict. The amount of negative communication has been found to differentiate distressed from happy couples more than the amount of positive communication in their relationships, suggesting that unpleasant, painful experiences with a spouse have greater impacts on partners' overall feelings about their marriages. Consequently, marital therapists commonly strive to decrease negative interactions between spouses and to substitute positive patterns of behavior. They teach distressed couples more constructive communication skills, which focus on clear, assertive (rather than aggressive) expression of thoughts and emotions, good listening skills, and systematic problem solving. [See CONFLICT COMMUNICATION.]

It also has been found that members of happy couples exchange higher ratios of pleasant than unpleasant "noncommunication" behaviors (i.e., doing nice things for and with each other) than do distressed couples. Whether unhappy spouses share relatively few positive experiences due to intentional avoidance of each other or due to the impact of busy and stressful lives, marital theorists and therapists have emphasized the importance of helping them shift this pattern and find ways of exchanging positive behaviors.

When asked to describe their relationships, couples generally report that they have egalitarian patterns of power in their marriages (e.g., equal influence in decision making). However, in studies where researchers observe spouses' specific communication behaviors it is clear that partners frequently attempt to exert control over each other. Efforts to exert power can be considered a normal aspect of interpersonal relationships of all kinds, and they are not necessarily problematic, but there is the potential for trouble if there is a significant power imbalance in a couple's marriage, or if spouses use negative means to gain control. In other words, the outcomes of marital decision making may be unbalanced, such that one spouse gets his or her way much more often than the other does, or the process by which spouses act toward each other to influence the outcomes of decisions may involve destructive forms of communication. An example of a negative decision-making process is the individual who uses coercive communication (e.g., threats, put-downs) to influence a spouse, and who alienates the spouse and elicits reciprocal aggression. Marital researchers have emphasized the advantages of assertive communication, where a spouse expresses his or her preferences clearly but does not attempt to coerce the partner into compliance. Concerning the outcomes of decision making, some marital scholars have suggested that women who are in low-power positions in their marriages are at risk for depression. Marital satisfaction does not necessitate absolute equality and compromise between spouses on all issues, but it appears to be important for both partners to perceive the balance of power in their marriage as equitable or fair.

B. Cognitive Factors in Marital Interaction

It is inevitable that at least some conflict will arise between two people who live together in a close relationship over time, because no marital pair is likely to have identical needs and preferences at all times. The degree to which spouses will be satisfied with their marital interactions will be determined not only by the positive versus negative quality of their communicaton and other behavioral exchanges, but also by the ways in which they think about those behaviors (i.e., their cognitions). For example, some marital conflicts arise from selective perceptions in which the spouses notice and remember different aspects of their interactions (e.g., one spouse notices all of the positive things that he or she does to contribute to the marriage, whereas the partner tends to notice the things that the person has failed to do). Marital satisfaction also is influenced by the attributions that spouses make concerning the causes of positive and negative events in their relationships. For example, research has indicated that happy spouses are likely to attribute positive marital events (e.g., a compliment from their mate) to positive stable and global causes (e.g., traits of the mate that are likely to persist into the future), whereas unhappy spouses are more likely to discount positive events, attributing them to unstable causes (i.e., a "fluke"). In contrast, unhappy

spouses are more likely than happy ones to attribute negative marital events (e.g., a partner forgetting their birthday) to global, stable traits (e.g., "She doesn't love me"). [See ATTRIBUTION.]

Marital researchers also have found that marital satisfaction is affected when spouses hold extreme or unrealistic assumptions about the characteristics of intimate relationships and standards about how marriage "should" be, presumably because their own marriages fail to match such beliefs. For example, spouses who believe that they should be able to read each other's mind and not have to communicate their thoughts and emotions may become distressed when their partners fail to sense all of their needs. Individuals commonly enter marriage with many pre-existing beliefs about a good relationship, and it is important that they communicate these to each other, so that they may determine how they may best meet each other's realistic assumptions and standards, and how they can revise the unrealistic ones.

C. Gender Differences in Marital Interaction

Although the patterns of interaction described above tend to hold equally for wives and husbands, some gender differences also have been identified. For example, wives tend to react to marital conflicts with more negative communication than husbands do, and thus they have been referred to as "barometers" of distress in their marriages. In contrast, husbands have been found to withdraw more behaviorally than wives when couples have conflicts, apparently in an attempt to avoid overt conflict. Despite the fact that wives send more negative messages to their partners than husbands do, it also has been found that wives are more effective than husbands in sending positive messages. The latter finding is consistent with the idea that males have been socialized less than females to express positive feelings such as love and affection.

D. Intimacy and Cohesion

One of the major reasons why individuals choose to marry is to meet their needs for intimacy and emotional support. Couples whose relationships are characterized by greater levels of cohesion (closeness, support, and commitment) are more satisfied with their marriages. Although research studies have found that the more cohesion there is among family members, the more satisfied and the less depressed they are, marital and family theorists have hypothesized that healthy intimate relationships are characterized by a balance between togetherness and autonomy.

Intimacy between spouses comprises a number of ways in which the partners share in each other's life. Sexual intimacy can be a source of great pleasure and comfort, but it also has the potential to be a source of stress in a couple's relationship. Stress can arise when the spouses hold unrealistic standards concerning their own or their partner's sexual behavior, when poor communication or lack of sexual knowledge leads to unsatisfying sexual experiences, or when specific sexual dysfunctions (e.g., low sexual desire; erectile dysfunction) go untreated. The quality of a couple's overall marital relationship and the quality of their sexual relationship commonly have mutual influences on each other.

Other important forms of marital intimacy include emotional intimacy (experiencing and disclosing feelings of warmth and closeness), intellectual intimacy (discussing and demonstrating respect of each other's ideas), the sharing of activities (recreation, daily chores, work), and spiritual intimacy (sharing religion and values). It is common for these forms of intimacy to grow and broaden over the course of a marriage, as the spouses' initially intense romantic love fades and develops into companionate love. *Romantic love* is characterized by a strong need of the partner's presence, mood swings (including anxiety as well as joy), and persistent thoughts of the loved individual. *Companionate love* involves less intense emotion but deep attachment and caring associated with a history of sharing ideas and experiences. Couples can keep elements of romantic love alive in their marriages; yet it appears to be companionate love that contributes more to the long-term stability of marital relationships. [*See* LOVE AND INTIMACY.]

E. The Relationship between Marital Interaction and Individual Psychopathology

There is considerable evidence that stress in marital relationships has an impact on spouses' development of psychological problems such as depression and anxiety, and vice versa. For example, episodes of clinical depression and anxiety are commonly preceded by significant marital conflict, and individuals are less likely to benefit from treatments for these psychological problems when they have conflictual marriages. In turn, symptoms of depression and anxiety (e.g., unpleasant mood states, self-critical talk, worry) can interfere with couples' intimacy and sharing of positive life experiences, thereby eliciting marital distress. The communication between depressed individuals and their spouses has been found to be a mixture of caring messages and hostility. Consequently, it now is common for people suffering from such psychological disorders to receive both individual treatment and marital therapy with their spouses. [*See* ANXIETY DISORDERS; DEPRESSION.]

Bibliography

Carter, B., and McGoldrick, M. (Eds.) (1989). "The Changing Family Life Cycle." Allyn and Bacon, Boston.
Coleman, J. C. (1988). "Intimate Relationships, Marriage, and Family," 2nd ed. Macmillan, New York.
Cowan, P. A., and Hetherington, M. (Eds.) (1991). "Family Transitions." Erlbaum, Hillsdale, NJ.
Fincham, F. D., and Bradbury, T. N. (1990). "The Psychology of Marriage: Basic Issues and Applications." Guilford, New York.
Fitzpatrick, M. A. (1988). "Between Husbands and Wives: Communication in Marriage." Sage, Newbury Park, CA.
L'Abate, L. (Ed.). (1985). "The Handbook of Family Psychology and Therapy." Dorsey Press, Homewood, IL.
Quayle, G. R. (1988). "A History of Marriage Systems." Greenwood Press, New York.
Sussman, M. A., and Steinmetz, S. K. (Eds.) (1987), "Handbook of Marriage and the Family." Plenum, New York.
Whyte, M. K. (1990). "Dating, Mating, and Marriage." Aldine de Gruyter, New York.

MATE SELECTION

Adriana Balaguer
Long Island Jewish Hospital

Howard Markman
University of Denver

Glossary

Communication The exchange of thoughts, messages, or ideas between individuals.

Conflict Controversy or opposition between individuals based on differing and, at times, mutually exclusive desires, impluses, views, or tendencies.

Heterogamy Selection of a mate with differing characteristics from the self. Includes such factors as ethnic, racial, age, or educational status.

Homogamy Mate selection based on similarity of characteristics between partners. Includes factors such as ethnic, racial, age, or educational status.

Interactive networks The networks of persons with whom an individual interacts.

Marital choice The choosing of a partner with whom to enter into a marital union.

Mate selection The formation of a close personal relationship that may result in a long-term union such as marriage.

Monogamy The custom or condition of only having one mate at any given time.

Psychological networks The networks of persons who are close and important to an individual such as family members and close friends.

LOVE AND MATE SELECTION are far from being a random process in American society. In fact, an entire body of literature has developed around how, when, and why individuals come together to form close relationships. The term *mate selection,* as used in this article, refers to the formation of close personal relationships, many of which will result in a long-term union such as marriage. Because mate selection has taken on somewhat different forms historically, we will begin by discussing changing trends in dating and mate selection that have occurred over the last decades. Second, we will review some of the major structural, contextual, and personal factors that have been found to exert significant influence on the mate selection process. We will also give an overview of current models used to study and understand relationship satisfaction and success. We will focus on contextual models, investment models, and problem solving/communication models in particular. Finally, we will examine mate selection and relationship success among gay and lesbian couples, including how selection and success factors differ in homosexual versus heterosexual relationships.

I. CHANGING TRENDS IN MATE SELECTION

Dating and mate selection have changed considerably in the United States during the last two decades. Consequently, much of the research on mate choice in the 1980s has focused on identifying the changes that have occurred. Most intriguing for researchers have been emerging trends such as postponement in the decision to wed, increases in premarital intimacy and cohabitation, and greater heterogamy in mate selection.

A. The Postponement of Marriage

One of the most striking trends in mate choice in recent decades has been the increasing delay in individuals' decision to marry. In 1988, the estimated median age at first marriage was 23.6 years for women and 25.9 years for men, the highest since the turn of the century. In fact, marriages among those in their teens have declined by an average of 50% between 1970 and 1985, and marriages before age 25 have decreased by 24%. Nonetheless, the declines in marriage before age 25 are not as large as those before age 20, indicating that some of the decline in teenage marriages represents a postponement into the early 20s. Interestingly, the increase in the median age of marrying has been greater for women than for men, thus causing women's age at first marriage to become more similar to men's. [*See* MARRIAGE.]

The postponement of marriage has also been found to be more pronounced among blacks than whites. Teenage marriages declined by 75% for blacks between 1970 and 1985 as compared to 46% for whites. Likewise, the number of blacks marrying before the age of 25 decreased 40% during that time period as compared to 23% for white marriages. By 1988, the median age for first marriage for black women was approximately 3 years older than for white women. Similar discrepancies in the propensity to marry have also been found for older blacks and whites.

B. Cohabitation

Although some speculate that the postponement of marriage is indicative of a more general disinterest in close or committed relationships, the research on cohabitation suggests that this is not entirely the case. While rates of legal marriage have decreased during the last two decades, nonmarital unions have emerged as an important new trend in the mate selection process. The U.S. Bureau of the Census in 1988 estimated the number of unmarried couples living together at 2.6 million. This indicated a 63% increase between 1980 and 1988. When cohabitation is considered, the increases in couples living together compensate for the declines in marriage rates to a large extent. For example, whereas the decline in evermarried at the age of 20 between 1970 and 1985 was 49%, the percentage decline for those ever in a union (either cohabitation or marriage) was only 20%. The gap was even smaller by age 25. The percentage decline in marriages by age 25 was 24% between 1970 and 1985, while for unions it was only 6%.

Changes in the prevalence of cohabitation have led many to conclude that living together has become a customary step in the mating process. Yet, little is known about the particular role that cohabitation plays in relationship formation. The general treatment of cohabitation has focused on college graduates or college students. Thus, the impression was that cohabitation had begun as a college student phenomenon that had then spread to the rest of the population. Yet, the data indicate that cohabitation has compensated least for declining marriage rates among persons who have attended college, and that cohabitation is actually inversely related to education. While the college-educated group did experience a surge in cohabitation rates during the 1970s, so did all other groups. Currently, cohabitation rates continue to rise for those with 12 years of school or less, but have slowed or stopped among those with one or more years of college.

Who are the people who cohabit, then? They are mostly young adults, 68% under age 35, 53% of which have never been married, and 34% of which have been divorced. Cohabitation rates have been found to be higher for women than for men, for blacks than for whites, and as mentioned previously, for the less educated rather than the better educated. Four out of ten cohabiting couples have children. This proportion includes one-third of never-married individuals and almost half of previously married individuals. Cohabitors are likely to be homogamous in terms of race, age, and education. Compared with noncohabitors, cohabitors were found to express more liberal attitudes regarding family life and were generally less conventional in such areas as religion and division of labor.

Despite the prevalence of cohabitation as a feature of the lifecourse for individuals, cohabitation tends to be a short-lived state. Only approximately 1 in 10 individuals remain in cohabiting relationships beyond 5 years without either marrying or breaking up. Among men, two-thirds of their cohabitation relationships were dissolved within 2 years. Of those, 40% terminated without marriage and 23% involved transition into marriage. Among women, 60% of unions ended within 2 years, 23% through dissolution of the relationships, and 37% through marriage to the partner. Recent studies on cohabitation have also begun to clarify the associations between cohabitation and marital success, since cohabitation is often considered a testing ground for marriage. In general, such studies have demonstrated cohabitation to be positively related to rates of marital dissolution and divorce. Marriages that follow cohabitation have been found to have 50% higher disruption rates than marriages where the partners did not live together prior to marrying.

Several possible reasons have been cited for the increase in disruption associated with cohabitation previous to marriage. Some have suggested that personal traits such as lower religiosity and conventionality which are associated with cohabitation may contribute to marital instability by also making divorce or separation a more acceptable solution to marital distress. Second, there may also be selection into cohabitation of persons more tentative about their relationship. Researchers have found that a majority of cohabiting couples cited testing for compatibility as an important reason for living together. Cohabitors were also twice as likely as married individuals to report that their relationship had been in trouble over the past year.

Nevertheless, the data on cohabitation do indicate that cohabitation encompasses a large variety of relationship experiences. These include short-term unions that either dissolve or result in marriage, long-term unions or "common law" marriages that may last many years and include the presence of children, and unions following divorce or separation that take the place of remarriage. Consequently, further research will be necessary in order to fully understand how cohabitation fits into the process of dating and courtship. At present, however, it is apparent that cohabitation without marriage must be considered, at minimum, an important transitional state in the courtship process for a large fraction of the population in the United States, and a critical factor in future studies on mate selection.

C. Premarital Sex

As with cohabitation, the last decades have witnessed a steady rise in premarital sexual activity, thus making permarital sex a normative part of the current dating and mate selection process in the United States. A study of mate choice and marriage involving 500 women from the Detroit area found a 64% increase in women who had engaged in premarital sex between 1924 and 1984. The trend was even more striking for those married between 1965 and 1984. The percentage of women who had premarital sexual experiences among those married between 1965 and 1969 was 56%. Rates of premarital sexual activity rose to 67% for those married 1970–1974, 85% for 1975–1979, and 88% for 1980–1984. In addition, women were found to engage in sexual activities at earlier ages and to be involved with a greater number of sexual partners before marriage.

Despite a growing awareness in recent years of the problems of unintended pregnancy, sexually transmitted diseases, and the human immunodeficiency virus (HIV), sexual activity, particularly among teenagers, continues to rise. Data from the National Survey of Family Growth indicate that between 1982 and 1988, the number of women ages 15–19 who reported having had sexual intercourse grew from 47 to 53%. Furthermore, among women ages 15–44 in 1988 who had ever had intercourse, 67% reported having had two or more sexual partners in their lifetime. The proportion was highest among 20- to 34-year-old women with an incidence of 70%. While only 58% of sexually active teenagers reported having had two or more sexual partners, the incidence remains high considering that teenagers would have been sexually active for a relatively short period of time.

Among males, sexual activity for those ages 17–19 grew from 66% in 1979 to 76% in 1988. Moreover, 25% of men ages 18–44 surveyed in 1988–1989 reported two or more sexual partners in that time period. Of men 18–19 years of age, 50% had had multiple partners in a 1-year period. These increases, representing more individuals (particularly teenagers) at risk for unwanted pregnancy and disease, represent a significant change in the dating and mate selection process and a cause for alarm. More comprehensive data will be necessary beyond simple prevalence rates of sexual activity in order to understand the full implications of the data for sexual behavior.

For example, current data on contraceptive use suggest that a shift in contraceptive behavior among teenagers may have already occurred. Between 1982 and 1988 the use of condoms at first heterosexual intercourse more than doubled among both males and females. Likewise, even though the data indicate high levels of sexual activity among both males and females, closer inspection of numbers of partners and incidence of intercourse suggests relatively low levels of activity. According to recent studies, once young men have their first sexual experience, the majority do not continue to be sexually active on a regular basis. In fact, sexually active respondents reported spending about half of the last year without sexual partners. The common pattern appears to be one of a series of monogamous relationships that follow one another. This pattern is interpreted by some researchers as representing a process in which deeper levels of intimacy are reached more rapidly in a variety of relationships, but where the ultimate goal of establishing an exclusive long-term union remains virtually unchanged.

D. Homogamy

Despite the increased intimacy and variety of premarital relationships, formation of homogamous marriages and unions (unions among partners with similar characteristics) continues to be the norm in the United States today. This is particularly true for homogamy with respect to age and race. In general, marriages still tend to occur within the same racial group and with age differences of no more than 3 or 4 years. Heterogamy, however, has been increasingly common in terms of religious denomination, ethnic background, mother tongue, and education. Interracial marriages were found to be more common among non-blacks than blacks, with a preference for black grooms. Age heterogamy was more common among blacks. When spouses deviated from educational homogamy, the trend had been for women to marry up, although this has recently decreased. Overall, then, the declining strength of some of the status criteria for mate selection does represent a broadening of options in the process of mate selection. Nevertheless, the most common pattern is still for most couples to come from similar social backgrounds.

II. FACTORS INFLUENCING MATE SELECTION

Despite the broadening of options and the substantial changes in dating practices noted thus far, the mate selection process remains very different from the random "love conquers all" pattern in which many Americans would like to believe. How is this possible? The research on mate selection has been able to identify both distal and proximal factors that significantly influence mate choice. Those factors have generally been divided into structural, contextual, and psychological factors. Structural factors are factors that originate in the larger societal context, such as demographic trends and social norms. Contextual factors refer to the immediate social context within which mate selection occurs. Contextual factors include factors related to the social networks within which relationships form. Finally, psychological factors pertain to specific characteristics of the individuals, as well as the attributions those individuals make during the mate selection process. It is important to remember, however, that the factors that bring people together are not the same factors that necessarily predict relationship success. [*See* INTERPERSONAL ATTRACTION AND PERSONAL RELATIONSHIPS; LOVE AND INTIMACY.]

A. Structural Factors

One line of research on structural factors in mate selection focuses on the composition of the population in terms of characteristics that make individuals within that population desirable spouses. A classic example is the research that has been conducted on sex ratios. Sex ratios in this case are conceptualized as the ratio of the number of unmarried men of marriageable age to unmarried women of marriageable age. In the 1970s, researchers began studying the effects of the oversupply of women born during the baby boom that were competing for a limited amount of older, marriageable men. Such researchers hypothesized that such competition should be associated with higher rates of singlehood and divorce among women, later age at first marriage, a lower proportion of remarriages, and less traditional roles for women. These hypotheses have been confirmed. From 1980 and through the turn of the century, it will be men who will face an undersupply of women as the baby boom males reach marriageable age. It is expected then, that the oversupply of men will be associated with relatively low age at first marriage and relatively high marriage rates among men.

Structural factors such as sex ratios may also impact groups differently at different times. For example, a study of white women who delay marriage after age 30 tested the hypothesis that due to the shrinking pool of eligible men, older women would shift to atypical marriage markets. The study found that older women were more likely to marry partners with a significant age difference, to marry previously married men, and to marry men with a lower educational status. Interestingly, crossing racial boundaries was not a common alternative. Rather, interracial mixing was more likely to be fostered by spatial proximity than by shortage of homogamous partners.

A second line of research focuses on population size and composition in terms of how those factors impact the amount of interaction between social groups. This research tests the hypothesis that individuals marry outside their social group, not out of preference, but because of the degree of interaction they have with other groups. Consequently, the size of a group possessing a certain characteristic should be inversely related to the rate of marriage outside it. In other words, if the group were large enough, those within the group would marry others of the same group who shared similar characteristics. Marriages outside the group occur more prevalently in smaller groups, in more heterogeneous groups, and in groups that intersect with a variety of other groups. Apparently, heterogeneity and social intersection facilitate marriage outsides one's group by providing opportunities to meet and stay in contact with others who are dissimilar. Unclear, however, is to what extent individuals deliberately determine the extent to which they interact with diverse groups. As mentioned earlier, homogamy remains the predominating trend in the United States, thus suggesting that individuals tend to associate with and select mates from within their own social group.

B. Contextual Factors

The research on contextual factors in the mate selection process has focused primarily on the effects of social support and interference in the context of social networks. An individual's social network consists of his or her associates and the interrelationships among those associates. Researchers distinguish between ''interactive networks'' and ''psychological networks.'' Interactive networks are made up of those with whom the individual interacts. Psychological networks, on the other hand, consist of those who are close or important to an individual, namely the significant others. With regards to social support and interference, the evidence indicates that psychological networks have greater impact on relationship formation than do interactive networks. In particular, it is the perceived subjective reaction of important individuals that is most influential, even more so than interfering or supportive actions on the part of those individuals. In other words, most often, it is the reaction that an individual anticipates or imagines from those close to him or her that most influences relationship choice and development.

Researchers have found that individual's reports of romantic involvement (i.e., love, commitment, time spent with partner) were positively related to support from the individual's and the partner's networks. This was evident for both adolescent dating relationships and college-age relationships. Furthermore, support from one's own and the partner's networks was found to predict the stability of a relationship over a 3-month period, while interference predicted declines in dating involvement. Likewise, efforts at support or interference became more salient as relationship seriousness increased, but decreased during the engagement period when opposition would be likely to alienate the couple.

C. Psychological Factors

Personality and individual difference variables have also been identified as important factors in the mate selection process. Psychological factors that have been studied in the mate selection and relationship satisfaction literature include personal characteristics such as emotional expressivity, attentional processes, locus of control, and ability to self-monitor. In addition, attitudes and attributions have been found to play important roles in mate selection. These include attitudes toward love, beliefs about appropriate behavior in a relationship, expectations about relationship success, and perceived similarity between partners. Finally, other psychological factors such as chronic depression can significantly impact relationship formation.

Certain theorists emphasize personal characteristics as being important in whether they make a particular match between two partners either stable or unstable. Such theorists have found characteristics like neuroticism, psychopathology, fearfulness, and poor social adjustment to be indicative of future instability in a union. In addition, impulsivity on the part of men, measured by such indices as irregular employment, aggressive and domineering social behavior, and levels of premarital sexual activity, have been associated with negative marital outcomes. Extraversion on the part of individuals, however, has been generally associated with relationship success. Likewise, individuals who describe themselves as more feminine have been found to form more positive intimate relationships. Levels of masculinity, however, had no association with relationship satisfaction.

A second approach to studying psychological factors in mate selection and relationship success focuses on the compatibility of partners. Research on compatibility has considered similarity of partners on a variety of personality and background characteristics as a predictor of relationship success. In general, the results have indicated a positive relationship between partner similarity and relationship satisfaction. Success based on similarity makes intuitive sense in that couples who are more similar in attitudes, personality, and background are likely to have fewer issues to disagree about and fewer conflicts to negotiate. Nevertheless, similarity alone falls short of being able to account for either mate choice or relationship success. This is particularly true since mate selection is often based on *perceived similarity* by the partners rather than on actual compatibility. Such perceived similarity is likely to lead to the blurring or ignoring of real differences that then come back to haunt the couple later on.

One final approach to understanding the role of psychological factors in the mate selection focuses on relationship beliefs. According to this approach, beliefs regarding relationship development and success are thought to play a critical role in relationship formation. For example, recent research indicates that individuals who hold unrealistic beliefs about how relationships should function (e.g., that partners should be able to sense each others needs and moods without having to say anything) have greater difficulty in forming successful relationships.

Unfortunately, most of the research on psychological factors has tended to consider specific psychological factors individually, thus leading to a disjointed and incomplete understanding of the factors that influence mate selection. Further research is needed to study how the factors that influence mate selection interact, and how those interactions ultimately impact the formation of close relationships.

III. MODELS OF RELATIONSHIP SATISFACTION AND SUCCESS

In addition to examining particular factors that influence relationship formation, researchers have also developed several models to explain and predict satisfaction and success in intimate relationships. We will focus on contextual models, investment models, and problem solving/communication models in particular.

A. Contextual Model

The contextual model, summarized by Bradbury and Fincham, represents one model that attempts to consider different individual difference variables and their interactions in determining relationship formation and success. The contextual model suggests that individual appraisals of relationship satisfaction are dependent on individual difference variables that filter relationship satisfaction in two contexts. First, in the proximal context, individual difference variables impact the individual's subjective state immediately prior to a relationship interaction and impact his or her interpretation of that interaction. Second, in the distal context, individual difference variables that are relatively stable and related to interpersonal competence, such as expressiveness or sex role characteristics, impact general relationship satisfaction and success.

Bradbury and Fincham found that both proximal *and* distal variables were crucial in understanding relationship satisfaction and success. In other words, both general characteristics of a person that impact their interpersonal competence and personal characteristics that impact specific interactions with the partner must be considered in order to obtain a fuller understanding of factors influencing relationship satisfaction.

B. Investment Model

The investment model, proposed by Rusbult, does not focus on individual characteristics as the determinants of relationship success. Instead, the investment model states that relationship satisfaction and success are based on the individual's assessment of the rewards associated with the relationship, the costs of being in the relationship, and how the relationship compares to an internal standard of what a good relationship should be. The model also proposes that satisfaction and commitment have different predictors. Specifically, satisfaction increases when rewards are greater and costs are fewer than what the individual feels they deserve. In other words, it is based on a comparison with an internal standard. Commitment, however, is based on the degree of satisfaction, on investment in the relationship, and on an assessment of possible alternatives to the relationship.

Studies that have assessed the investment model have supported the importance of perceived rewards and the assessment of alternatives as related to both satisfaction and commitment. Higher reward levels were found to predict greater satisfaction and greater commitment to relationships. Likewise, more satisfied partners have been demonstrated to have a higher level of commitment, and commitment increased with greater investment and decreased as alternatives became more attractive. Surprisingly, however, costs of the relationship were generally not found to be related to decreased relationship satisfaction or commitment. Rather, in some cases higher costs were related to increased commitment.

Further research will be needed in order to further refine the investment model and test its applicability across groups and types of relationships.

C. Problem Solving/Communication Model

The problem solving/communication model suggests that marital success and satisfaction are related to communication and problem-solving strategies used by the couple and that relationship satisfaction can often be predicted from early on in the relationship. More specifically, these models have proposed that communication and problem-solving strategies used in conflict resolution are particularly important to relationship satisfaction and success. In other words, what is important for relationship success is not the existence of differences or conflict, but how such differences are handled. [See INTERPERSONAL COMMUNICATION; PROBLEM SOLVING.]

Researchers using such models have found that among couples seriously considering marriage, what distinguished between those who remained together and those who eventually broke up was the ability to constructively handle negative affect as assessed in their initial interactions. More specifically, those couples that were able to discuss conflict and express negative feelings without defensiveness, counterattacks, and withdrawal, were more likely to experience greater marital satisfaction and stability over time.

Interestingly, positive communication was not found to have strong associations to future relationship satisfaction. Namely, couples who were positive, supportive, and validating, did not necessarily have more successful or satisfying relationships. Thus, it is not what couples are doing right that appears to be crucial, but what they are doing wrong that counts most. For example, Markman and colleagues, found that when partners who are expecting validation in a relationship receive validation, it does not predict relationship success. Yet if partners receive invalidation, when they are expecting validation, the impact is profound and has been found to predict marital distress and divorce with great accuracy. In fact, using communication variables, Markman and colleagues were able to obtain 93% predictability of marital success.

Overall, then, it appears that mate selection and relationship satisfaction are determined by many intrapersonal, as well as, interpersonal factors. Furthermore, the factors that have been found to predict mate selection are not necessarily the same factors that predict future relationship satisfaction. The focus on particular factors, thus, has been largely dependent on the theoretical perspective used to examine relationship development and the stage of the relationship being examined. More complex theoretical models are increasingly necessary to fully understand the inter-relationship among specific factors and their roles in relationship development and success.

IV. MATE SELECTION IN GAY AND LESBIAN RELATIONSHIPS

The present discussion of mate selection and relationship success has up to this point been limited to heterosexual relationships and unions. Yet, a growing body of literature exists regarding homosexual relationships that provide a unique and important perspective on relationship formation and the societal, personal, and interpersonal factors involved.

A. Characteristics of Gay and Lesbian Relationships

Contrary to popular myths, most lesbians and gay men say that they very much want enduring close relationships. In a study on close relationships, 24% of lesbians and 14% of gay men described cohabitation with an intimate homosexual partner as the most important priority for them. Likewise, 35% of lesbians and 28% of gay men said a permanent close relationship was very important and only 13% of lesbians and 19% of gay men said such a relationship was not important at all.

Studies of intimate relationships among gays and lesbians have found that approximately 40–60% of gay men and 45–80% of lesbians were currently involved in steady relationships. Estimates of cohabitation suggest that about half of all gay male couples live together and that about three-quarters of lesbian couples cohabit. Little is known at present as to what leads certain homosexual couples to live together and others to live apart.

Some data are available, however, on the longevity of homosexual partnerships. Among couples followed over an 18-month period, Blumstein and Schwartz found that break-ups in couples that had been together for more than 10 years were rare (6% for lesbians, 4% for gay men). For couples that had been together for 2 years or less, less than one relationship in five ended during the 18-month period of the study. In fact, only 22% of lesbian relationships were dissolved and only 16% of relationships among gay men. Other studies that have focused on older lesbians and gay men have found that relationships lasting 20 years or more are not uncommon.

Good information is not yet available on how factors such as age, ethnicity, or social class influence the formation of intimate gay and lesbian relationships. Some research, however, does suggest that the principle of homogamy, or selecting a mate that is similar to oneself, is active in homosexual as well as in heterosexual coupling. Findings indicate that both gay and lesbian cohabiting couples tend to be similar on demographic and other relationship-oriented variables. Furthermore, no differences were found between gay and lesbian relationships or between short- and long-term relationships as to degree of homogamy.

Gay and lesbian relationships are unique in that they do not lend themselves readily to gender-linked roles. Historical accounts of homosexual relationships often emphasized the taking on of masculine and feminine roles in the selection of a mate. Current research, however, shows that most gays and lesbians actively reject husband–wife roles. Instead, most gay and lesbian relationships consist of dual-worker relationships in which partners are financially independent, and specialization of activities is based on more individualistic factors such as skills or interests rather than gender roles. In fact, most relationships among lesbians and gay men are described according to a friendship model where partners tend to be similar in age, and the focus of the relationship is on companionship, sharing, and equality. [See SEX ROLES.]

A second unique factor of gay and lesbian mate selection and relationship development is that these partnerships are generally not sanctioned by society, and often face hostility and resistance. All gay men and lesbians grow up in a society which is basically homophobic and, as a result, to some degree internalize negative feelings about themselves. Reaching a level of comfort with self becomes an important part of relationship development and stability. In addition, because homosexuality is not an apparent feature of the individual and is not often openly acknowledged, the identification of possible mates can be further complicated.

Similarly, since homosexual couples have few legal sanctions to be together, each couple has to define a way of being together outside of the traditional roles and structures (such as marriage) that are available to heterosexual couples. Most couples find ways and reasons for staying together such as shared groups of friends and social activities, shared property and personal belongings, shared finances and investments, and possibly children.

Yet despite the lack of societal sanctions for homosexual relationships, gays and lesbians have been found to have satisfying social networks. Studies of social support among gays and lesbians indicate that reported levels of support and satisfaction with support did not differ among gays and lesbians or between homosexual and heterosexual respondents. The sources of support, however, differed somewhat. Gays and lesbians were more likely to depend more on their partner and on friends while heterosexuals depended more on family. Nevertheless, 81% of gay men and 86% of lesbians cited a member of their family as a source of support.

B. Relationship Satisfaction and Success

In general, studies focusing on relationship satisfaction and success in homosexual relationships have found that most gays and lesbians describe their intimate relationships as satisfying and emotionally close. No significant differences were found between homosexual and heterosexual couples on measures of levels of love, satisfaction, expression of affection, or cohesion. Homosexual couples have been found to have slightly lower measures of couple consensus than heterosexual couples. Nevertheless, homosexual couples' reports of the best and worst aspects of their relationships are strikingly similar to reports of heterosexual couples.

Research looking at differences in relationship formation and satisfaction between gay and lesbian couples has found few differences between the two groups. In general, similar factors have been associated with relationship satisfaction in both gay and lesbian couples. These factors include trust in the partner, shared decision making, good communication, high motivation to be in the relationship, low autonomy, and few beliefs that disagreement is destructive to the relationship. Lesbian relationships, however, do appear to have a greater interpersonal focus than relationships between gay men. They are often characterized as more focused on emotional expressivity and equality, while male relationships focus more on reciprocity and autonomy.

Another difference between gay and lesbian relationships has been found in the area of sexual exclusivity versus openness. In general lesbians have been found to be more supportive of sexual monogamy in relationships than are gay men. While 71% of lesbians reported believing that sexual monogamy was important, only 35% of gay men viewed sexual exclusivity as important. Furthermore, gay men are more likely than lesbians to engage in sexual encounters outside their primary relationship. This is not to say, however, that nonmonogamy reflects problems or dissatisfaction with the primary relationship.

In fact, current research did not find sexual exclusivity/nonexclusivity to be related to relationship satisfaction among gays and lesbians. In addition, the current impact of possible HIV infection on the gay community has led to a decrease in the number of encounters gay men are having with new partners, particularly among those in close relationships.

In addition to specific factors related to relationship satisfaction and success in gay and lesbian couples, researchers have also examined the applicability of the contextual, investment, and problem-solving communication models of relationship success to homosexual relationships. Overall, the findings support the usefulness of such models in predicting relationship success for gay and lesbian relationships, and may point to the existence of general processes that underlie a variety of close relationships. Most researchers, however, point to the danger of studying gay and lesbian relationships exclusively using theories originally developed for the study of heterosexual relationships. They emphasize the need to develop theories that emerge originally from the gay and lesbian experience of relationship formation.

V. CONCLUSIONS AND FUTURE DIRECTIONS

In reviewing the process of mate selection and relationship formation what becomes most strikingly apparent is the incredible variety and diversity in the particular forms that close relationships take. Such diversity poses a challenge for future research on close relationships.

First, future research on mate selection will need to include an expanded view of what the term intimate relationship means including both short- and long-term unions, cohabiting and noncohabiting couples, first-time unions and unions following divorce, and homosexual as well a heterosexual relationships. Second, greater efforts will be needed to include a wider diversity of ethnic, social, racial, and age groups in research on relationship formation. Finally, researchers will need to consider both short-term and long-term effects of relationship development factors, since those factors that predict mate selection often differ from the factors that predict relationship success.

Nevertheless, the increased complexity and variety of today's relationships should not deter researchers from attempting to identify universal patterns in mate selection and relationship development. Recent models that reflect the complexity of relationships and the impact of multiple interacting influences on relationship formation show great promise. Pursuit of such models should continue in order to promote a fuller understanding of the processes and interactions in the mate selection.

Bibliography

Bradbury, T. N., and Fincham, F. D. (1988). Individual difference variables in close relationships: A contextual model of marriage as an integrative framework. *J. Pers. Soc. Psychol.* **54,** 713–721.

Gottman, J. M., and Krokoff, L. J. (1989). Marital interaction and satisfaction: A longitudinal view. *J. Consult. Clin. Psychol.* **54,** 47–52.

Kelly, L. E., and Conley, J. J. (1987). Personality and compatibility: A prospective analysis of marital stability and marital satisfaction. *J. Pers. Soc. Psychol.* **52,** 27–40.

Kurdek, L. A. (1991). Correlates of relationship satisfaction in cohabiting gay and lesbian couples: Integration of contextual, investment, and problem-solving models. *J. Pers. Soc. Psychol.* **61,** 910–922.

Markman, H. J., FLoyd, F., Stanley, S., and Storaasli, R. (1988). The prevention of marital distress: A longitudinal perspective. *J. Consul. Clin. Psychol.* **56,** 210–217.

Peplau, L. A., and Cochran, S. D. (1990). A relationship perspective on homosexuality. In "Homosexuality/Heterosexuality: Concepts of Sexual Orientation" (D. P. McWhirter, S. A. Sanders, and J. M. Reinisch, Eds.), Oxford University Press, New York.

Surra, C. A. (1990). Research and theory on mate selection and premarital relationships in the 1980's. *J. Marriage Family* **52,** 844–864.

Thorton, A. (1988). Cohabition and marriage in the 1980's. *Demography* **25,** 497–508.

Whyte, M. K. (1990). "Dating, Mating, and Marriage." Gruyter, New York.

MEMORY

Gabriel A. Radvansky
University of Notre Dame

Robert S. Wyer, Jr.
University of Illinois at Urbana-Champaign

Glossary

Category An organized set of conceptual entities (objects, events, concepts, etc.) that are similar to one another in some respect.

Episodic memory The memory system that contains knowledge concerning events from a person's life. Episodic memories are localized in time and place, and often include a representation of oneself as either a participant or observer of the events.

Explicit memory Memory processes that operate through a deliberate and conscious act of remembering (e.g., recognition and recall).

Implicit memory Memory processes that operate through unconscious mechanisms.

Long-term memory A large-capacity portion of the memory system where information is stored in a highly organized fashion for long periods of time, possibly lasting a lifetime.

Memory The mental systems, representations, and processes that are involved in the retention of information.

Procedural memory The memory system that contains memories of performance activities, including stimulus–response associations (e.g., knowledge of how to ride a bike or drive a car).

Schema General world knowledge structures of well-defined common human experiences used to organize new information and reconstruct information that may have been forgotten.

Semantic memory The memory system that contains encyclopedic general world knowledge which does not refer to a specific event in the individual's life.

Short-term memory A limited capacity portion of the memory system where information enters, but lasts for only a short period of time before being either transmitted to long-term memory or discarded. Sometimes referred to as working memory.

Spreading activation The notion that the activation or availability of one conceptual entity spreads to other related conceptual entities through a complex of associative pathways.

MEMORY refers to the mental systems, representations, and processes that are involved in the retention of information. The ability to remember the information one has accumulated plays an integral role in the comprehension of new experiences as well as in judgment and behavioral decision making. Indeed, the loss of memory (through amnesia, Alzheimer's disease, or other disabilities) is one of the most dehumanizing of experiences. This article provides a brief overview of some of the more important topics in current memory research, particularly from the area of cognitive psychology, with respect to how memory operates and has an influence in shaping our lives.

I. INTRODUCTION

Several characteristics of human memory are of interest to psychologists. The issues of concern include (a) the specification of different types of memory structures and processes, (b) whether memories are permanent or, alternatively, whether they eventually fade away and disappear entirely, and (c) how aspects of memory impact on people's daily lives. These issues are not mutually exclusive. For clarity of expression, however, they will be considered separately.

II. TYPES OF MEMORY

A. Memory Models as Metaphors

Human memory is a repository for information as widely varied as images of people's faces, knowledge of how to drive a stick shift, phone numbers, how much money is in your checking account, the names of the countries of Europe, and the smells of good home cooking. A complete account of human memory must specify the structure of the mental representations formed for these types of information, their organization in relation to one another, and the processes that are involved in retrieving them. Because the structure of memory and the processes involved in its use cannot be directly observed, theoretical accounts of them make use of metaphors. In the earlier 20th century, models of memory used metaphors such as a filing cabinet or bin system. Later, with the expansion of telephone systems, memory was referred to as though it were a telephone operator's switch board. With the advent of the digital computer in the late mid-century, models of memory during the cognitive revolution adopted a computer metaphor, which relied on the way in which computers represent information, and the processes involved in encoding, storing, retrieving, and operating on information. This metaphor was especially important because of its separation of physical and mental states (the hardware versus the software). More recently, in an effort to consider how information might be represented neurally, some researchers have been calling for a brain metaphor, despite the oxymoron.

People exhibit different memory characteristics under different sorts of conditions. For instance, a person might forget the names of most of his high school classmates after 10 years, but might remember how to ride a bicycle throughout his life. Recognition of this fact has led to the postulation of different memory systems and different types of mental representations.

B. Short-Term and Long-Term Memory

Many metaphorical conceptualizations distinguish between long-term and short-term memory. Long-term memory contains a lasting record of the information one receives. In contrast, short-term memory, which is typically viewed as the place where information enters the information processing system, is assumed to last for only a short period of time before its contents are either transmitted to long-term memory or discarded. Whereas long-term memory contains information that has accumulated over a lifetime, short-term memory is of limited capacity, being able to retain only a small set of information chunks. However, this "physical" distinction between short-term and long-term memory is by no means universally assumed. In some theories, short-term memory is viewed merely as the portion of long-term memory that is currently active rather than as a separate memory system itself. In these theories, the limit on short-term memory capacity simply depends on the amount of information from long-term memory that can be called into consciousness at any one time.

Short-term memory is thought to be where information processing occurs. Because of this, it is sometimes referred to as working memory, and is even thought of by some researchers as the seat of consciousness in the memory system. On occasion researchers consider working memory itself as divided into subcomponents. These subcomponents include an articulatory loop, which handles linguistic information, a visual–spatial sketchpad for handling visual–spatial information, and a central executive which controls the processing of information. These subsystems are generally thought of as being semiautonomous. Thus, while one subsystem is actively processing information, another might be available for performing other tasks. For example, it is easier to read a paragraph (a linguistic task) if one is simultaneously trying to remember the location of a dot on a screen (using the visual–spatial sketchpad) than if one is trying to remember a set of words (using the articulatory loop).

In general, information remains in short-term memory until something comes to force it out. Because the capacity of short-term memory is limited, new information that enters the memory system is likely to push out the old, leaving only the most recently encountered information available. This property of short-term memory leads to what is referred to as the recency effect in which the recently acquired information is more available than earlier information. (For example, if a person is given a list of names and is then asked to recall them immediately afterward, the names at the end of the list will have a better chance of being remembered because they will still be in short-term memory.)

Most research and theory on memory, however, has focused on the structure and content of long-term memory, and the storage and retrieval processes associated with it. The remaining discussion will focus on these matters.

C. Analogue versus Propositional Representation

Memory theories often distinguish between information that is coded propositionally and information that is coded in an analogue fashion. In the propositional form, memory is thought to rely on a small set of very simple idea units. The structured complex of these idea units serves to represent more complex notions. In the analogue form, memory is thought to rely on representational structures that directly conform, in some way, to the outside world, such as a mental image.

These different types of memory representations predict different types of processing mechanisms and memory storage operations. For example, propositional representations convey information directly in terms of the idea units that are incorporated in the mental structure. Furthermore, propositions can be linked together to form a large associative network. Analogue representations convey not only the information that was originally directly encoded, but also any emergent properties that derive from the information (e.g., features and relations of the described information that are unmentioned). Several representations might contain similar sorts of information, organized in different ways.

Theories of memory often make different assumptions about the extent to which different representational formats are used. Some theories argue that all information is represented propositionally and that any apparent analogue aspects of human cognition, such as imagery, are merely epiphenominal. Others take the position that both types of representational formats are used, although at different levels of the memory system. Still others postulate two separate memory systems, one for handling propositional information and one for handing analogue information. According to this view, information is understood in terms of either one or both of these systems, depending on its nature.

III. ORGANIZATION OF LONG-TERM MEMORY

Information in memory is often assumed to be organized on the basis of both its content and the context in which the information was presented. However, not all types of information are represented in the same way. Theories of long-term memory often postulate different systems and subsystems, each of which is dedicated to the representation and processing of different types of information, and each of which exhibits properties that are not found in the others. Endel Tulving's monohierarchy of memory systems provides a particularly useful framework for conceptualizing how different types of information are organized and remembered. Other types of memory organization will be considered at the point in which they conform to the different levels of this hierarchy.

A. Tulving's Monohierarchy

Tulving's monohierarchy is a three-level organization, with one system occupying each level, and each of the higher systems being dependent on the lower ones. These systems are denoted procedural, semantic, and episodic and are each considered in turn.

1. Procedural Memory

The procedural memory system, which is at the most basic level of the monohierarchy, contains memories of performance activities, including stimulus–response associations. Examples of procedural memories include knowledge of how to ride a bike or drive a car, how to play the drums, how to solve a puzzle, and how to walk. The procedures contained in this memory system can potentially be activated without conscious awareness of their features. Thus, the procedural knowledge that governs driving a car is applied with minimal attention to the specific sequence of steps involved in this activity. As this observation implies, the information stored in procedural memory is often difficult to articulate, but typically lasts for quite a long time. In addition, procedural knowledge is relatively resistant to deliberate changes to add, modify, or rearrange various components of the memory. A person who needs to acquire some new form of procedural skill may gain some savings in learning from previous knowledge. Nevertheless, the person must go through an extensive learning process to acquire the new information.

2. Semantic Memory

The semantic memory system, which is at the second level of Tulving's monohierarchy, contains general knowledge of the world that does not refer to a specific event in the individual's life. As such it is an encyclopedia of facts about the world. The content of semantic memory, like that of procedural memory, is retained for quite a long time. Semantic memory differs from procedural memory, however, in that people can often effectively articulate the information that is stored. Semantic memory is typically conceptualized as a highly integrated system in which related concepts are stored together. This organizational structure of the memory can be seen in how general world knowledge is used. For example, semantic memory exhibits effects of relatedness. Information is identified faster if it is preceded by information that has similar content. Semantic memory also exhibits effects of ordered structure. For example, it takes longer to identify the order of two items in an ordered sequence (e.g., size) if they are close together than if they are far apart, because they are less discriminable in the former case.

Several theories conceptualize semantic memory as an associative network of concepts. Each concept represents a separate entity that is associatively linked to other entities by pathways connecting them. Concepts that are more similar to one another are more closely associated in the network. So, when information from one concept is used, other concepts that are associated with it are also brought to mind. (This type of process will be discussed in more detail in the section on spreading activation and reminding.) Two types of mental representations contained in the semantic system, schemas and categories, are worth noting. [*See* SEMANTIC MEMORY.]

a. Schemas

Schemas are general world knowledge structures that help people to organize new information that they encounter and reconstruct information that they may have forgotten. Each schema is a structured representation of all the easily articulated information that a person has referring to a well-defined domain of common human experience, such as washing a car, getting a promotion, or reading a newspaper.

The way that schematic knowledge helps to encode information to make it more easy to remember was demonstrated by Bransford and Johnson. Subjects were given passages to read of the following form:

The procedure is actually quite simple. First you arrange things into different groups. Of course, one pile may be sufficient depending on how much there is to do. If you have to go somewhere else due to a lack of facilities, this is the next step; otherwise you are pretty well set. It is important not to overdo things. That is, it is better to do too few things at once than to do too many. In the short run this may not seem important, but complications can easily arise. A mistake can be expensive as well. At first the whole procedure will seem complicated. Soon, however, it becomes another facet of life. It is difficult to foresee any end to the necessity for this task in the immediate future, but then one can never tell. After the procedure is completed, one arranges the materials into different groups again. Then they can be put into their appropriate places. Eventually they will be used once more, and the whole cycle will have to be repeated. However, this is part of life. (Bransford and Johnson, 1972, p. 722)

Although the individual sentences composing this paragraph are meaningful, the passage as a whole is very difficult to understand out of context. In the study, half of the subjects were given a title before reading each passage (''washing clothes'' in the above example), whereas the remaining subjects were not. Subjects who were given a title had substantially better memory for what they had read than those that were not. This is because the former group of subjects were able to organize the incoming information with reference to a ''clothes washing'' schema that helped them to remember it later. In contrast, subjects who were not given a title could not identify a schema that would permit them to understand and organize the information, and so they had a more difficult time remembering it.

Schemas can also help people figure out things that they may have temporarily or permanently forgotten, or even missed entirely. Anyone who has begun watching a television show or movie from the middle of the story has had the experience of being able to figure out what has gone on previously without having actually seen it. People essentially fill in the gaps with what they know about similar situations. This reconstructive process can sometimes lead people astray. In James Bartlett's famous work on schemas, students in England were given an American Eskimo folktale to read. This folktale possessed a structure quite different from the stories of English culture. Bartlett found that as time passed, the students forgot more and more of the details and structure of the original story. The portions that they forgot were replaced with ideas that were Westernized transformations of the story. The students had filled in the gaps in their memory with schematic knowledge of what they knew about folktales and the topics covered in the folktale.

The organization of a schema's features may be spatial (as in a human face), temporal (as in a sequence of events), or logical (as in a syllogism). A special type of event schema, denoted a *script*, describes a temporally ordered sequence of events (or "frames") that frequently occur in the real world and can be used both to explain new events one encounters and to predict future consequences of the event. Moreover, they can be used as behavioral guides. For example, "Asking for a menu" is a frame in a "restaurant" script that precedes frames that pertain to ordering, eating, and paying the bill. Therefore, the determinants and consequences of a particular individual's request for a menu can be inferred on the basis of the additional frames of the script that are used to interpret it. Moreover, one's own decision to leave a tip at a restaurant may be based on the perception that this behavior is appropriate, as implied by the same script.

b. Categories

People can also organize information into mental categories. Each category is made up of a set of conceptual entities (objects, events, concepts, etc.) that are in some respects similar to one another. Categories help to organize the various entities that are encountered in the world.

There are several different classes of theories of how the categorization process is accomplished, and the representations of knowledge that result from it. A threefold classification of these theories was proposed by Douglas Medin. According to the classical view, categorization is accomplished by identifying a set of necessary and sufficient features or properties that correspond to the nature of the category. Entities either have these features or do not, and therefore either belong or do not belong to the category in question.

According to the probabilistic view, categorization is also accomplished with reference to a set of features or properties. However, these features are not all necessary and sufficient. Entities vary with respect to the number and pervasiveness of their features. Therefore, some entities are more well endowed than others, leading to a graded category structure. The defining features for each category

are either contained in a representation of the prototypical member (real or not) or are derived from an average of all of the separate exemplars of the category.

The third class of theories is knowledge-based. In a lot of ways, this view is similar to schemia theories. According to this view, the organization of concepts into some categorical structure is based on knowledge of the world, and how the various members function or operate in the world. In other words, entities are organized into categories in the sense that they are used in similar ways to explain things about the world. This is in contrast to the other two classes of theories which regard the presence or absence of various features or properties as the basis for categorization. For example, the category "things to take out of the house in a fire" would be composed of things that are combustible, easily transportable, and difficult or impossible to replace. This would include such diverse things as family members, money, photos, and pets, which do not share features that would cause them to be classified together a priori except for the knowledge that they conform to a common goal. [See CATEGORIZATION.]

3. Episodic Memory

Episodic memory, which is at the highest level of Tulving's monohierarchy, is like semantic memory in that the information that is stored in memory is easily articulated. However, episodic memory differs from semantic memory in that the subject matter which composes its content is concerned with events from a person's life rather than general world knowledge. Thus, episodic memories are localized in time and place, and often include a representation of oneself as either a participant or observer of the events that compose them. For example, general knowledge of police work is the domain of semantic memory, whereas knowledge of a particular incident in which one receives a speeding ticket is the domain of episodic memory. Episodic memories, unlike procedural and semantic memories, are more influenced by the passage of time. That is, they exhibit the classical exponential forgetting curve outlined by Hermann Ebbinghaus at the end of the 19th century. In the absence of maintenance procedures, such as the repeated recall and rehearsal of the features of an event, memory for the features of the event, if not the event itself, appears to decrease over time. Episodic memories also differ from procedural and semantic memories in the fact that the retrieval of one episodic memory is less likely to influence the retrieval of other episodes. Two specific theories that relate to Tulving's conception of an episodic memory system—mental models and autobiographical knowledge—are worth special attention. [*See* EPISODIC MEMORY.]

a. Mental Models

Whereas schemas, scripts, and categories refer to generalized knowledge structures, mental models are representations of specific situations in the world. A conception of these representations has been developed most fully by Philip Johnson-Laird. Mental models are organized representations of specific situations that directly model the functional relations of these situations. This construction often involves general world knowledge, possibly in the form of schemas. Consequently, the structure and organization of mental models are likely to resemble the structure and organization of one or more of the schemas used to construct them. The mental models that are formed could represent either simple mundane event descriptions or more complex life experiences. For example the statement "the book is on the table" may simulate the construction of a mental model based on a spatially organized schema concerning the physical location of objects on a table top. Alternatively, the model of a friend's story about the circumstances surrounding her divorce might be constructed on the basis of several different schemas or scripts, each of which is applied to a different sequence of events in the narrative.

Despite their similarity in structure to general world knowledge, mental models are distinguished from semantic knowledge in that they are stored and retrieved relatively independently of one another. For example, a set of related information (e.g., knowing about a group of people and the locations they are in) that refers to several different situations is stored in several mental models in memory and produces interference during retrieval. This is because the related mental models interfere with one another during retrieval. However, there is no interference for a similar set of information that refers to general knowledge (e.g., knowing about a group of people and the places they can be). In this case, there are no separate representations competing when someone is trying to remember something. Instead, everything is stored in a single, highly integrated representation, resulting in no interference at retrieval.

The mental models that are constructed in the course of processing information are likely to depend on the purpose for which the information is to be used. A person who receives information for the purpose of making a judgment or behavioral decision, for example, may form a different mental representation of the information than a person whose objective is to remember or comprehend it. The role of processing objectives in the construction of mental representations of information has been a particularly important consideration in research in social cognition. Social cognition research is concerned with the way people respond to information that they receive for the purpose of attaining objectives that do not necessarily require learning and remembering it (e.g., the goal of forming a general impression of a person or object, explaining the occurrence of social experience, or predicting a future event).

b. Autobiographical Memory

The information from which mental models are constructed can concern people, objects, and events that are not related to oneself except insofar as one is aware of receiving the information and comprehending its implications. Much of the information one receives, however, more directly involves oneself as an active participant in the experience that occurs. This self-knowledge, or autobiographical memory, composes a large share of the episodic information that people accumulate.

Autobiographical knowledge is presumably distributed throughout the episodic memory system. Representations of this knowledge, like other episodic representations, may initially be formed at different points in time and initially stored independently of one another. Nevertheless, these separate representations are often retrieved later and integrated into a single representation that describes the sequence of events that occurred over a period of days, weeks, or even years. Thus, a person might construct a representation of the events leading up to and following his marriage, based on pieces of episodic knowledge that were initially stored separately in memory at the time they first occurred. These constructive processes underlie the construction of mental models more generally. The reconstructive process also has some systematic effects on the memories for the event. For example, these memories tend to be remembered as closer in time to major events in a person's life, such as the start of a semester, losing a job, or the birth of a child. Once formed, these representations constitute "theories" about oneself and one's behavior in the situations in question. [*See* AUTOBIOGRAPHICAL REMEMBERING AND SELF-KNOWLEDGE.]

c. Temporal Dating

If episodic memories of events are stored independently of one another, how do people determine the temporal order in which these events occurred? It seems unlikely that people always store the day, month, and year of an event in the representation they form of it. How, then, might they determine whether John Lennon's death occurred before or after the eruption of Mt. Saint Helen's if these events have never been previously been considered in relation to one another? Sometimes this is done by relating each event to a "landmark" event relative to which the events being judged can be compared. Alternatively, people sometimes compute the recency of an event from the amount of knowledge they can retrieve about it, inferring that events they remember the best have occurred more recently. However, the computational process that underlie temporal dating, and when they are applied, have not been completely identified.

B. Relations among Memory Systems

Although episodic and semantic memory systems are assumed to function independently, it is clear that episodic and semantic memories can play similar roles in cognitive functioning. Moreover, semantic representations may be formed on the basis of episodic ones and vice versa. A man who is asked directions to a restaurant might respond on the basis of an episodic memory of how he drove there the previous day, or on the basis of more general knowledge that is not temporally localized and is not based on personal experience at all. In some instances, semantic memories may simply be episodic representations (e.g., mental models) in which situation-specific features denoting the time and place of occurrences (and of oneself as the experiencing agent) have somehow been forgotten. Consequently, the distinction between episodic and semantic memory is not quite as clear as Tulving's monohierarchical system might suggest.

C. Reminding

One intriguing aspect of memory is the fact that when people think of one thing, they are often reminded of some other similar thing. These remindings are often of either information of similar content that the person may know or earlier experiences that are in some way similar to the current situation. The use of free association to bring other-wise unaccessible memories into consciousness is based on the notion that the information currently being processed not only draws on the most direct sources in memory to understand the information, but can also remind the person of related pieces of knowledge that are more remotely associated with it.

1. Spreading Activation and Priming

The most popular mechanism that memory researchers use to describe the reminding process is spreading activation. The notion of spreading activation assumes that memory has the form of a network with concepts being connected through a complex of associative links. When information from the network is used in some way, those concepts that are used are energized or activated. This activation spreads along the associative pathways emanating from each of the activated concepts to other concepts, and when the activation building up at these concepts exceeds some threshold value, they are activated as well. The activation from the original concepts is theoretically distributed over the pathways connected to it. This means that the greater the number of concepts that are independently associated with an originally activated concept, the less likely it is that a related concept is activated as a result of thinking about it.

This activation process is generally thought to be able to occur for both general world knowledge and event-specific knowledge. For example, if you were in a conversation and someone brought up the topic of fire trucks, your concepts for fire trucks would become activated in long-term memory. The activation would also spread to related general world knowledge concepts that are related to fire trucks, such as red, emergency, and dalmatians. This activation could also spread to event-specific knowledge, such as a memory that the last time you saw a speeding fire truck, you were in your neighbor's Volvo and the engine conked out in the middle of a busy intersection.

This spreading activation process is generally thought of as largely automatic. That is, it proceeds without any deliberate intention to do so. However, spreading activation can be controlled to some extent. When related information is deemed to be irrelevant, or the activation has been spreading for some time with no benefit to the current processing goals, it can be dampened, so that activation resources can be directed elsewhere. This serves to help people pursue their current processing goals, and keep them from constantly rattling through an endless series of irrelevant associative meanderings.

The effects of spreading activation have been investigated in many experiments. In a typical study, people are asked to decide whether each of several letter strings are words or nonwords. People can identify "nurse" more quickly after seeing the word "doctor" than after seeing the work "bread." Presumably, encountering the word "doctor" and accessing its meaning in memory caused activation to spread to the concepts related to it, including "nurse," thus making "nurse" easier to identify. In other words, "nurse" was primed by the word "doctor."

D. Explicit and Implicit Memory

Recently, much interest in memory research has been focused on the distinction between explicit and implicit memory. Explicit memory processes operate through the conscious action of remembering. These processes are used deliberately and, therefore, generally involve conscious awareness. Recognition and recall memory tasks, in which a person deliberately tries to remember something, are salient examples of tasks that rely heavily on explicit memory. In contrast, implicit memory processes operate through unconscious mechanisms. Typical tests of implicit memory involve the assessment of the unconscious influence of previous encountered information on an ostensibly unrelated task. For example, subjects in a test of implicit memory might read a list of words, one of which is "memoirs." Later, they might perform a task that does not involve conscious recollection, such as a word stem completion task in which the subject is asked to complete a word stem such as MEM___ with the first word that comes to mind. People are more likely to complete the word stems with words that they had seen earlier than are people who were not exposed to the original list.

Explicit memory and implicit memory respond to different sorts of influences. For example, performance on explicit memory tasks tends to be affected by conceptually driven strategies, imposed by the individual, that help to organize the information. Conversely, implicit memory performance is affected by factors that govern more data-driven strategies that rely on the physical properties of the stimulus and are likely to be invariant over stimulus situations. Some theories argue that explicit and implicit memory are two distinct systems containing different representations and different processes.

Advocates of these theories point to evidence that people can sometimes show deficits in explicit memory but not implicit memory. However, other theories assume that explicit memory and implicit memory reflect two different types of processing mechanisms that operate independently on a common memory representation. Proponents of these theories point to studies in which the two processes have been put in competition. For example, suppose some subjects in a word-stem completion task are asked to try to complete the stems with words that they saw earlier, whereas others are asked to complete the stems with words they did not see. The differential rate of completing the stems with earlier seen items provides an index of the use of explicit and implicit memory processes. This rate varies with the sort of tasks and the conditions in which they are performed, suggesting that different processing strategies are at work rather than different memory systems. [See IMPLICIT MEMORY.]

E. Evidence from Amnesia

A great deal of knowledge about how information in memory is organized, and the possible existence of different memory systems, has come from studies working with anterograde amnesics. These individuals have suffered some brain injury, typically due to head trauma, surgical mishaps, or chronic alcohol abuse. Such individuals usually have difficulty remembering information they have received after the time that the injury occurred. (Some of the more severe cases need to be reintroduced to their doctors if they leave the room for a few minutes because they have no memory of them.) Although amnesics are unable to recollect some types of information, they retain other types quite well. For example, severe amnesics who show a deficit in semantic and episodic memories appear to have intact procedural memories. Amnesics, who knew how to play the piano before their injury, could be taught to play a new song. When asked if they know how to play the song they would report no memory of it, yet they would be able to play it successfully if coaxed into trying. Amnesics also show deficits in explicit memory tasks, such as recognition and recall, which require active remembering, but show memory performance similar to that of normal people in implicit memory tasks, such as word-stem completion. [See AMNESIA.]

F. Alternative Types of Memory Models

Associative network models of the sort described in the section on spreading activation provide only one of the several possible theoretical accounts of how information is represented in memory. Two other types are noteworthy.

Multiple trace memory models assume that information is stored in memory as a series of distinct traces. Each trace is theoretically composed of a set of features and properties that, in combination, represent a different episode, concept, or some other coherent mental structure. These traces are relatively independent of one another. There is generally little or no structure which organizes these traces. When information needs to be retrieved from long-term memory, a probe composed of the desired set of features and properties is compared with all of the traces in memory. Traces that are more similar to the probe will "resonate" with it more than traces that have little to do with the memory probe. These related memory traces are then made available for further processing. For example, if one were trying to remember what was eaten on his last birthday, all of the memory traces relating to eating, possibly cake, birthday, and the previous year would be activated. Those traces containing more features would be activated more, and the trace that contains the desired information would receive the most activation. This information would be what was actually retrieved from memory.

Unlike multiple trace memory models, distributive memory models assume that large amounts of information are stored using a rather limited set of structures. This limited structure might take the form of vectors of features in some holographic memory system. An alternative representation is assumed by connectionist models of memory, which are currently an area of great interest. In these models, information is represented in a massive assemblage of simple units and connections in which all of the units are connected to most if not all of the other units at a series of computational levels. Information is represented as a pattern of activation across a series of these units and connections. An attractive feature of distributive memory models is that information does not need to be represented in a single location in memory. So, if one portion of the memory network is damaged, the information may be available at other areas, since it is distributed throughout the memory system.

IV. PERMANENCE OF MEMORIES

People encounter a great deal of information in their lifetime. They see lots of things, meet many people,

read many things, and have lots of experiences. What happens to all of this information? Is all of it remembered forever, such that a person needs only to figure out how to bring the information to consciousness? Or is it the case that once information has been lost from memory it is lost forever, and will never again be recovered and play a role in influencing behavior?

A. Evidence for the Permanence of Memory

One position is that everything that is ever encountered and stored in long-term memory remains there permanently. This permanent store of information either can be actively retrieved into consciousness and/or exerts an unconscious influence on behaviors and ideas through the lifespan. Stronger positions of this view claim that absolutely anything ever encountered in life is permanently stored in long-term memory, although one may have difficulty activating the information at any given point in time. Less strong positions claim that only certain things actually have an opportunity to be stored in long-term memory; however, once there, they remain permanently.

1. Penfield

A well-known and seemingly powerful source of evidence for the permanence of memory comes from the work of the neurosurgeon Wilder Penfield. During the 1950s, he performed operations that involved cutting away part of a patient's brain in the treatment of some ailment. Before actually removing part of the cortex, Penfield stimulated various areas with a mild electrical charge to determine what functions the areas were in charge of so as not to remove any vital functions. Sometimes the patient reported having vivid experiences, such as: "Yes, sir, I think I heard a mother calling her little boy somewhere" (Penfield, 1955, p. 54). These experiences, because of their mundane nature, led Penfield to suggest that the electrical stimulations caused a re-emergence of previously forgotten memories from the person's distant past. Such evidence seemed to suggest that everything that a person had ever experienced was stored somewhere in long-term memory, and that all that is needed is for some way to get the information out; electrical stimulation of the cortex in this case.

However, despite how convincing this finding seems, there are some serious considerations against it. First of all, only about 25% of Penfield's patients actually reported having some experience, and only

3–7% of these reports were sufficiently clear to suggest that the patients were actually re-experiencing a previous life event. Finally, there is no independent source of evidence that these experiences actually happened to the patients providing the reports.

2. Permastore

While Penfield's account of long-term memory as being a repository for the continuous stream of consciousness, other positions have been put forward in support of some version of permanent long-term memory storage. In this section, we consider Harry Bahrick's permastore idea. According to this position, when information is first encoded into long-term memory, initially there is some forgetting over time. However, at some point, the amount of forgetting ceases and the amount of information retained from the original time period remains constant over long periods of time. The information that remains is said to be in a permastore where it does not decay.

In one study, Bahrick has been able to show this with people's memory of Spanish after college. For the first 3 years after college, there is a drop in the amount of information remembered by the students. However, the amount of information stored remains relatively constant for the next 40 years or so, regardless of the student's initial level of performance and other factors. The drop off did appear to resume again in later years, possibly reflecting more global changes in memory that occur at that time.

3. Reasons for Forgetting in a Permanent Memory System

Under some theories, memories are thought to be permanently stored in the long-term memory system. If this is the case, then there must be some account of why forgetting would occur in such a system. Two of the more prominent reasons considered here are the lack of sufficient retrieval cues and retrieval interference.

a. Retrieval Cues

Although information may be stored in memory, it may be destined for some dark and dusty corner of the system if the person cannot get at it. One often cited reason for this inability is the idea that the person does not have the proper retrieval cues for accessing the information. Retrieval cues are the set of features or properties that allow for the appropriate selection and retrieval of the memory. If these cues are not available, the memory cannot be retrieved. A common metaphor that is used to describe this process is that of a library. A book may be stored somewhere on the library shelves, and if it can be gotten, all of the information in it would be available. However, if its entry in the card catalog is missing, it becomes very difficult to retrieve, and might even be said not to exist in the library at all.

i. Depth of Processing   One of the factors that can influence the ability to remember information at a later point in time is the amount of processing that the information had received when it was first encountered. Basically, the more time and effort that a person expends processing newly encountered information through elaboration or association with previously known information, the more likely that the person will be able to remember that information at a later point in time. This is referred to as the level of processing hypothesis. According to this position, information that is processed at a deeper level is remembered better because there are more cues that can be used to retrieve the information. For example, is a person were to scan a newspaper article for certain letters, it is unlikely that much would be remembered. Whereas, if a person were to read the article in detail, thinking of related stories that have been reported earlier, or to other related topics, much of the information in the newspaper article would be remembered.

Recently, there has also been a lot of investigation on the related topic of the generation effect. Basically, information that was generated by a person is remembered better than information that is presented to the person. This presumably occurs because all of the processing involved in the generation of the information is somehow associated with it in memory, thus allowing for a richer set of retrieval cues to access the information.

ii. Flashbulb Memories   An extreme example of a depth of processing effect is what are referred to as "flashbulb" memory. Flashbulb memories are typically thought to occur in situations of extreme surprise, shock, or other events that have a strong emotional impact. Common examples of flashbulb memories are highly detailed memories of what a person was doing, who they were with, what they were wearing, etc., when some surprising and important news was heard, such as the assassination of President Kennedy, or the explosion of the space shuttle Challenger. It is as though a picture of the situation had been taken, hence the name flashbulb memory. The high degree of detail encoded in them would make them highly accessible because there would be many cues to retrieve them. However, other possible explanations for flashbulb memories, besides being highly detailed permanent memories is that the facts that are associated with flashbulb memories are retrieved over and over again. This constant usage of information is what allows it to be easily retrieved. This is basically a use-it or lose-it theory of memory. There is also some evidence that the information stored in flashbulb memories is often incomplete and inaccurate.

iii. Encoding Specificity In a more mundane vein, more accurate information retrieval has been shown to occur by providing the same sorts of contextual cues that were available when the information was first learned. This effect is known as encoding specificity. Contextual factors that can influence memory can be just about anything, including the person's mood, the room that the information was learned in, the person from whom the information was originally learned from, and so on. The effects of encoding specificity can be seen in daily life. How often have you thought of doing something when you were in one room of your home, and walked into another room to act on it and then you can't remember why you went in there. So, you return to the room in which you started and, all of a sudden, you remember why you went to the other room in the first place. This remembering presumably occurs because the room in which the original idea occurred presumably provides a sufficient number of retrieval cues to access the information.

b. Retrieval Interference

Another reason for forgetting things that are actually stored in memory is retrieval interference. When a large number of pieces of information about an object are acquired at different points in time, they are stored independently of one another. In some cases, the more recent information appears to "bury" the earlier information, making it more difficult to recall. This referred to as retroactive interference. In other cases, the earlier information makes it difficult to remember subsequent information. This is referred to as proactive interference. Both types of interference are more pronounced when the memories contain content information that is similar and possibly conflicting. Then, the stronger memories are typically recalled instead of the weaker ones. Thus, the weaker memories appear to have been forgotten despite the fact they still exist in memory. For exam-

ple, when people move, it may be difficult after a period of time to remember some of the streets in the town they lived in previously. This is because the names of the streets in the new town interfere with the retrieval of the street names in the old town.

B. Evidence for the Nonpermanence of Memory

The arguments for permanent memories can be quite convincing. However, there is good reason to consider the possibility that, while some information may be retained throughout a person's lifetime, due to frequent use or strong encoding, most information is removed from long-term memory after a period of disuse. Two sources of evidence for the nonpermanence of memory considered here are reconstructive processing and misleading postevent information.

1. Reconstructive Processing

Reconstructive processing refers to situations where people have been presented with a set of information that they do not know that they will need to remember. When the people actually do recall the information, they have often forgotten various details of the original set of information and substituted other pieces of information. Much of the research on schema and script usage has shown that these gaps in memory are filled in with information that is consistent with the original source of information in terms of the gist of the originally presented facts, but nevertheless, is inaccurate. Even though gaps in one's knowledge have been filled in with unoriginal information, people express high confidence that the reported information was actually presented to them.

However, it could also be argued that although the schema-enhanced report did contain some reconstructed inaccuracies, the original information was retained. In such a case the general world knowledge was used as a crutch to avoid an extensive and effortful memory search. Some memory research has shown that if people are encouraged to adopt a perspective that is different from the one they originally adopted during encoding, their ability to recall the original information accurately improves. At first, this seems to run counter to the encoding specificity effects described earlier. However, in this case, people are able to access the information in memory. Rather than expending all the effort needed to retrieve that information, they choose to reconstruct the more detailed aspects of the memory by assuming various defaults for the type of situation that is being remembered. In the case of encoding specificity, the nature of the information is unavailable to the person, not the details.

2. Misleading Postevent Information

Other evidence that the information stored in memory is not permanent comes from research on misleading postevent information. In studies investigating this topic, people often watch a series of events, such as a scenario of a car accident, in a slide-show or videotape. After seeing the situation, people are presented with some description that provides misleading information. In the case of the car accident, for example, people might be asked whether one of the cars stopped before the yield sign, when in fact the sign in the scenario was a stop sign. Later, people are likely to report that the features of the postevent information were actually part of the original event they observed. This could occur because the more recent information contains features that were never observed, but were added to the original representation after it had been formed. Or, it could occur because the more recently described features actually replaced the original features in the representation, thus modifying it forever. This second possibility suggests that information in long-term memory will be discarded if it is superceded by other relevant and more recent information.

The question of how postevent information can affect memory is especially important outside the laboratory, for example, in trial cases involving eyewitness testimony. One problem is that over time, the information in the memory of an event may decay, be difficult to retrieve, be interfered with, and perhaps be reconstructed. The additional possibility that the information a person may encounter subsequent to an event can actually change the eyewitness's memory has enormous legal ramifications. Eyewitness testimony is often thought of as one of the most valuable sources of evidence. However, the fragility of memory contents questions this assumption, as demonstrated by the fact that leading statements or questions by other people could cause the eyewitness to incorporate additional and extraneous information into their memory representation, thus corrupting their memory of the event. [*See* EYEWITNESS TESTIMONY.]

V. SUMMARY

Human memory is a complex storage system. Information entering it is subject to different types of processing depending on whether it is in short-term or long-term storage. The question of how long information that is successfully stored in long-term memory will remain there is uncertain: it could remain throughout one's lifetime, or fade away permanently if it does not get used. Information is stored in different ways in memory depending on the type of information it is (whether it is knowledge of skilled action, general world knowledge, or knowledge of one's own life events). Information stored in memory has different effects on current processing goals depending on whether it was explicitly retrieved or whether it has an influence on behavior through some unconscious process.

Acknowledgment

This article was prepared while the first author was supported by a National Institute of Mental Health Quantitative Training Grant MH14257 at the University of Illinois.

Bibliography

Alba, J. W., and Hasher, L. (1983). Is memory schematic? *Psychol. Bull.* **93**, 203–231.

Anderson, J. R. (1983). "The Architecture of Cognition." Harvard University Press, Cambridge, MA.

Bahrick, H. P. (1984). Semantic memory content in permastore: Fifty years of memory for Spanish learned in school. *J. Exp. Psychol. Gen.* **113**, 1–29.

Bransford, J. D., and Johnson, M. K. (1972). Contextual prerequisites for understanding: Some investigations of comprehension and recall. *J. Verbal Learning Verbal Behav.* **11**, 717–726.

Craik, F. I. M., and Lockhart, R. S. (1972). Levels of processing: A framework for memory research. *J. Verbal Learning Verbal Behav.* **11**, 671–684.

Hintzman, D. L. (1988). Judgments of frequency and recognition memory in a multiple-trace memory model. *Psychol. Rev.* **95**, 528–551.

Johnson-Laird, P. N. (1989). Mental models, In "Foundations of Cognitive Science" (M. I. Posner, Ed.). MIT Press, Cambridge, MA.

Medin, D. L. (1989). Concepts and conceptual structure. *Am. Psychol.* **44**, 1469–1481.

Rumelhart, D. E., and McClelland, J. L. (1986). "Parallel Distributed Processing: Explorations in the Microstructure of Cognition." MIT Press, Cambridge, MA.

Tulving, E. (1985). How many memory systems are there? *Am. Psychol.* **40**, 385–398.

MEMORY, NEURAL SUBSTRATES

Daniel Tranel
University of Iowa

Glossary

Agnosia A condition in which familiar stimuli cannot be recognized, despite normal perception; agnosia for faces is known as prosopagnosia.

Amnesia Memory impairment; especially an inability to acquire new information (anterograde amnesia) or recall previously learned knowledge (retrograde amnesia).

Hippocampus A neuroanatomical structure in the mesial temporal lobe that is critical for memory.

Lesion method A method of scientific investigation of brain–behavior relationships, in which neuropsychological functions of subjects with focal brain lesions are studied with controlled experiments.

Long-term memory Information that can be retrieved for long periods of time (days, years, decades) after initial learning; huge capacity.

Memory Knowledge stored in the brain, and the processes used to acquire and retrieve that knowledge.

Rehearsal Processing information over and over, to facilitate its transfer to and maintenance in long-term memory.

Retrieval Remembering information through recall or recognition.

Short-term memory A transient type of memory, lasting about 30–45 seconds and with capacity limited to about 7 "chunks" of information.

Temporal lobes Lobes of the brain located laterally and inferiorly, which contain many structures important for memory; on the left, there is specialization for verbal information; on the right, there is specialization for nonverbal and visuospatial information.

MEMORY is the knowledge stored in our brains, and the processes used to acquire and retrieve that knowledge. Memory is critical for virtually all aspects of human behavior. Human brains have evolved a tremendous capacity for memory, and many structures in the brain are dedicated to various subtypes of memory and memory processing. The hippocampus, in the mesial temporal region, is important for acquiring new information. Neural structures in the lateral and inferior temporal lobe, and in various association regions of the brain, are important for maintenance and retrieval of long-term memories. The basal ganglia are important for learning new motor skills. Regions in the thalamus and basal forebrain provide important neurotransmitters for memory. The ventromedial frontal region provides a link between memory and emotions. Research aimed at understanding how various brain structures subserve memory is a central part of modern neuroscience.

I. INTRODUCTION

The importance of memory for human behavior can hardly be overemphasized. In fact, it is hard to think of many mental functions that do not involve memory—functions such as language, planning, and problem solving all rely on memory. Over the course of a lifetime, a person will acquire a tremendous amount of information—knowledge about the outside world, about the self, and about relationships between the self and the outside world. Our brains are capable of storing and retrieving an enormous amount of information, provided they are in good health and are given sufficient opportunity to learn and rehearse. In fact, an upper limit on the extent of information our brains can acquire and maintain has yet to be established. [*See* MEMORY.]

What biological machinery subserves memory? What are the brain mechanisms that allow us to learn facts (e.g., the U.S. state capitols), visual patterns (e.g., the faces of our classmates), and motor skills (e.g., skating, skiing)? In recent decades, intensive scientific investigation of these questions has provided several preliminary answers. For example, we know that there is a structure called the hippocampus, buried deep in the middle part of the temporal lobes of the brain, that is critical for *acquiring new information*. We know that there are neural systems in the lateral parts of the temporal lobes that are critical for *retrieving conceptual knowledge*. And structures such as the basal ganglia and cerebellum play an important role in the *acquisition of new motor skills*. In fact, it is becoming apparent that many brain structures have a role in memory—it could be argued that in a broad sense, virtually the entire brain is concerned with memory of some form or another.

The objective of this article is to provide an overview of the current state of understanding regarding the neural substrates of memory. The focus is on adult humans. Although much of our understanding of memory has come from studies involving nonhuman animals, this work will not be covered here except when it bears directly on a point at hand. Also, it should be noted that there are several "levels" in neuroscience that deal with the neural basis of memory; for example, some scientists study the molecular basis of memory, others study memory at a cellular level, and others study various neural systems, that is, groups of neuroanatomical structures, each comprising many thousands of brain cells that function together as units. The focus here is on neural systems and how these subserve different aspects of memory function in the adult human.

II. TERMS AND PARADIGMS

A. Definition and Basic Terms

Memory refers to information that is stored in the brain, and to the processes of acquiring and retrieving such information. The process of getting information into a permanent memory store involves three basic steps: (1) acquisition, (2) consolidation, and (3) storage. Acquisition refers to the process of bringing information into the brain and into a first-stage memory "buffer," via sensory organs and pri-

mary sensory cortices. For example, you have just met a new person. In order to acquire knowledge about the face of that person, you bring into your brain the visual pattern of that face via your eyes and primary visual cortex in the occipital lobes. Consolidation is the process of rehearsing information and building a robust representation of it in the brain. Storage refers to the creation of a more or less permanent "memory trace" or "record" of information in the brain. In learning a new face, for example, you would consolidate the visual pattern information, and then create a relatively permanent record of this pattern, a record which would be connected to other pertinent information (e.g., the person's name, facts about the situation in which you first met the person, how you felt). Our brains use *dynamic* records, rather that static, immutable memory traces. For example, the "record" of the face you learned in the example above is a set of linked neuronal activations, rather than a "picture" that is stored somewhere in the brain. Dynamic records can be changed, updated, and otherwise modified to provide the most efficient and economical means of storing and retrieving information.

Retrieval is the process of reactivating information in such a way that it can be brought into consciousness (into our "mind's eye") or into a form that can be translated into a motor output (an action of movement, speech, or autonomic activity). Retrieval takes place via several mechanisms: (1) Recall is a process in which we deliberately conjure up information from our brains. For example, you may bring into your consciousness the image of the face of the person you met. (2) Recognition refers to encountering a previously learned stimulus, and realizing (recognizing) that there is a "match" between that stimulus and information in our brains. For example, you run into a group of people at a party, one of whom happens to be the person you met before, and you recognize the person's face because it "matches" the visual pattern you learned previously. (3) Retrieval also operates via motor outputs, although these are not actually brought into consciousness. For example, when we lace on a pair of skates and take to the ice after a long summer layoff, we automatically "retrieve" the pertinent motor skills that were learned previously for this activity.

B. Paradigms

Investigation of the neural basis of human memory has utilized several paradigms. Foremost among these is the lesion method, which refers to the study of cognitive functions in individuals with focal brain injuries. In fact, detailed investigations of a few subjects with rare patterns of brain damage have provided much of the current knowledge regarding the neural substrates of human memory. Two subjects in particular have been intensively studied. One is a man known as "H.M.," who developed a severe inability to acquire new information following bilateral resection of the mesial temporal lobes to control seizures. The other, a man known as "Boswell," is an individual who suffered extensive damage to the limbic system (including most of both temporal lobes) following herpes simplex encephalitis. Boswell lost his capacity to acquire new information and to retrieve previously learned knowledge of many types. Both subjects are remarkable for the fact that their profound memory disturbance occurs in the setting of otherwise well preserved cognitive functioning—for example, they have normal language, basic intellectual abilities, perception, and attention. The two provide an ideal contrast because in H.M., the memory impairment is confined to new learning (anterograde memory), whereas in Boswell, both new learning and previously acquired knowledge (retrograde memory) are affected.

The lesion method is a time-honored tradition of investigating the neural basis of mental functions, and in fact, the initial studies of H.M. began nearly four decades ago. However, recent advances in the capacity of imaging the living human brain have contributed major breakthroughs in the experimental power of the lesion method. First was the arrival of computed tomography (CT) in the mid 1970s; this was followed by magnetic resonance imaging (MRI) about a decade later. These techniques have permitted *in vivo* visualization of brain structures with a degree of detail many orders of magnitude greater than that available previously. Coupled with advances in experimental neuropsychology, which provided well-controlled, standardized methods of measuring memory and other cognitive functions, the neuroimaging techniques have facilitated a fine-grained analysis of neural correlates of complex human functions.

Other methods are currently being developed. Positron emission tomography, known as PET, involves the measurement of brain cell activity, such as glucose metabolism and local blood flow. In the PET paradigm, it is possible to study which brain regions are active during particular cognitive tasks (and which ones are not), allowing inferences about how certain neural units are related to certain mental

functions. Another new technique is functional magnetic resonance imaging (fMRI). Similar to PET, functional MRI can be used to measure levels of activity in various brain regions during cognitive tasks, permitting inferences about how neural units relate to mental activity. PET and fMRI will likely become powerful techniques leading to many new discoveries about the neural basis of memory and other higher-order mental functions.

III. MEMORY DICHOTOMIES

A number of subdivisions are generally applied to the domain of memory, many of which form basic dichotomies regarding different types of memory processes and information. Major dichotomies are defined below (summarized in Table I) and where relevant, basic neural correlates have been briefly specified. More detail regarding neural substrates of various types of memory is provided in Section IV.

A. Short-Term and Long-Term Memory

1. Short-Term Memory

Short-term memory refers to the brief period of time, in the vicinity of 30 to 45 seconds, during which a limited amount of information can be held without rehearsal. Our brains acquire information and hold it in a short-term store, whereafter, unless we rehearse the information and make a deliberate effort to retain it, most or all will be lost. For example, when we look up the phone number for a music store in town, so that we can check to see if the new compact disc from our favorite artist has arrived yet, we find the number, read it, and place it in short-term memory. Within a few seconds, we dial the number, and then promptly forget it. If we wait too long before dialing, more than a half-minute or so, we will not remember the number. Another characteristic of short-term memory is that is has a limited capacity, in the neighborhood of about 7 "chunks" of information (e.g., about what is in a 7-digit phone number). This capacity is commonly referred to as "7 plus or minus 2," which reflects the fact that the variation in normal persons in short-term memory capacity is between about 5 and 9 "chunks" of information.

2. Long-Term Memory

Long-term memory refers to information that is recorded in more or less permanent fashion (albeit dynamically) in our brain, and is retrievable for long periods of time (days, months, years) after initial

TABLE I
Subdivisions of Memory

Dichotomy	Characteristics
Short term	Ephemeral (30–45 seconds); limited capacity (7 ± 2)
Long term	Permanent; unlimited capacity
Declarative	Information that can be brought into consciousness; "declared"
Nondeclarative	Performance-based; motor output; habits; automatic tendencies
Verbal	Words, names, verbally coded facts; word-based material
Nonverbal	Faces, geographic routes, complex melodies; spatially based material
Retrograde	Previous learning; material acquired prior to onset of brain injury
Anterograde	New learning; material acquired after onset of brain injury
Unique	Information belonging to class of one; proper names, familiar faces
Nonunique	Information from classes larger than one; animals, fruits, tools
Retrospective	Memory for the past; what happened before
Prospective	Memory for the future; what will happen

learning. Information that is rehearsed and consolidated is transferred from short-term to long-term memory, where it can remain for considerable periods of time. In fact, with occasional rehearsal, information can be maintained indefinitely in long-term memory. Also, unlike short-term memory, the capacity of long-term memory is enormous; in fact, the upper limit on this capacity has not been discovered.

Structures in the mesial temporal region, especially the hippocampus, are critical for nonephemeral acquistion of new information, i.e., the process whereby information begins to be transferred from short-term to long-term memory. Short-term memory per se does not require mesial temporal structures, and patients with extensive bilateral damage to this region (such as H.M. and Boswell) can still perform normally on tasks such as digit and sentence repetition (i.e., immediate reproduction of spans that have 7 plus or minus 2 pieces of information). As long-term memories are consolidated, however, they too become relatively independent of hippocampus and related mesial temporal structures. This independence is achieved when such memories are recorded in neocortices, according to modality (see Section IV).

B. Declarative and Nondeclarative Memory

1. Declarative Memory

This term denotes information in memory that can be brought to mind and consciously inspected, or "declared." Examples include words, facts, faces, and specific events. These types of information can be conjured up in our "mind's eye" and held in consciousness as propositions or images.

2. Nondeclarative Memory

Nondeclarative memory, on the other hand, comprises various types of memory that are expressed in performance but cannot be brought to mind and held in consciousness. A variety of skills, especially motor skills (e.g., skating, dancing), fall under the domain of nondeclarative memory; such abilities can be acquired, improved through practice, and expressed in performance, but they cannot be brought to mind or "declared." Other types of memory that have been designated as nondeclarative include automatic dispositions to respond in a certain way to particular stimuli (e.g., putting your foot on the brake at a red light), habits, and certain types of autonomic responses (e.g., producing an electrodermal response to an emotionally charged picture). In general, nondeclarative memory comprises information that depends on a motor output, via either the voluntary-skeletal or autonomic systems, for its expression. The neural correlates of declarative and nondeclarative memory are discussed in Section IV.

C. Verbal and Nonverbal Memory

Verbal memory refers to information that is verbal in form (i.e., names, words, lyrics, and facts stated

TABLE II
Hemispheric Specialization of Memory Systems

Left	Right
Verbal	Nonverbal
Words	Patterns
Names	Faces
Stories	Geographic routes
Lyrics	Complex melodies
Sequential; feature-based	Holistic; gestalt-based
Lexical retrieval	Unique personal knowledge

in verbal terms). Nonverbal memory, by contrast, comprises information that is not coded by words. Examples include faces, geographic routes, and complex melodies.

The distinction between verbal and nonverbal memory has been useful in understanding the neural basis of memory function, because in general, the brain's memory systems follow basic organizational principles of brain–behavior relationships (see Table II). That is, left-hemisphere memory systems, in concert with the language dominant nature of the left hemisphere, are dedicated primarily to verbal memory. Conversely, right-hemisphere memory systems are specialized for nonverbal memory, again in concert with the nonverbal, spatially dominant nature of the right hemisphere.

D. Retrograde and Anterograde Memory

This designation is used to divide memories according to whether they were acquired prior to (retrograde) or subsequent to (anterograde) the onset of brain injury. Anterograde memory, the acquisition of new information, is highly dependent upon the hippocampus and other structures in the mesial aspect of the temporal lobes. Even mild damage to this region, such as that produced by the early-stage pathology of Alzheimer's disease or by brain anoxia/ischemia (e.g., from sudden cardiac arrest), can produce marked impairments in anterograde memory. By contrast, retrograde memory remains well preserved even with major damage to the hippocampus, reflecting the fact that retrieval of information from the past is *not* dependent upon mesial temporal memory systems.

E. Unique and Nonunique Memory

1. Unique Memory

Unique memory refers to information that belongs to a class of one. It can be divided further into unique–personal (e.g., your daughter's face; your wedding date) and unique–public (e.g., Willie Nelson's face; the date of the Japanese attack on Pearl Harbor).

2. Nonunique Memory

Nonunique memory includes information that belongs to a class larger than one. Examples include animals, fruits and vegetables, and tools and utensils—all of these classes have numerous members that we learn as exemplars of a type (e.g., groundhog, corn, hammer), but not as individuals. Other examples, paralleling the unique exemplars mentioned above but falling at the level of nonunique, include human faces, anniversaries, country music singers, and famous dates in history. Nonunique material is *not* dependent upon the context or timing of specific learning episodes; in fact, terms such as "nonepisodic" or "semantic" have been used to designate the same types of information referred to here as "nonunique." The neuroanatomical correlates of unique and nonunique memory are reviewed in Section IV.

F. Retrospective and Prospective Memory

Another distinction is between memories for the past (retrospective memory) and memories for the future (prospective memory). The division is straightforward: retrospective memories are events, facts, and motor actions that have already happened, whereas prospective memories are events, facts, and behaviors that have yet to happen. For example, if asked to recall what you did yesterday, those memories would be retrospective. By contrast, recalling the things that you have planned for later today, and for tomorrow, would constitute prospective memory.

Neural correlates of retrospective and prospective memory have not been established. There is some preliminary evidence that retrospective memory may be linked primarily to the temporal lobes, while prospective memory is linked primarily to the ventromedial and mesial parts of the frontal lobes (the orbitofrontal cortex, lower mesial frontal cortices, anterior cingulate gyrus and perhaps basal forebrain). It has been noted, for example, that patients with damage to the ventromedial frontal region and anterior cingulate have a tendency to "forget to remember." The patients have a normal fund of information, but they fail to recall information at appropriate times in the ongoing course of their lives. For example, they may forget to keep appointments, take medications, or set the VCR to tape a TV program.

IV. MEMORY SYSTEMS IN THE HUMAN BRAIN

We turn now to a more detailed discussion of the principal neuroanatomical regions which subserve memory.

A. Systems in the Temporal Lobe

The temporal lobes contain a number of anatomical units that are important for memory (Fig. 1). In fact, with the exception of the superior temporal gyrus located in the upper part of the temporal lobe (which mainly subserves auditory perception and comprehension), most structures in the temporal lobe have key roles in various aspects of memory. One set of structures, located in the mesial aspect of the temporal lobes (Figs. 2 and 3), plays a crucial role in the *acquisition of new information*. Another set of structures, located in anterior, inferior, and lateral aspects of the temporal lobes, plays a major role in the retrieval of knowledge from long-term memory.

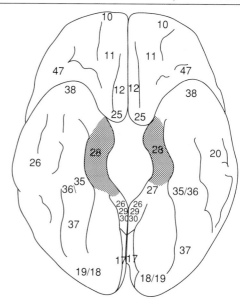

FIGURE 2   The inferior aspect of the hemispheres (the left hemisphere is on the right side, and vice versa). The mesial location of the hippocampal-bound memory system is shaded. The system comprises the amygdala, entorhinal and perirhinal cortices, hippocampus, and parahippocampal gyrus. The parahippocampal gyrus (area 28) shows in this view; the hippocampus itself, however, is buried deep within this region.

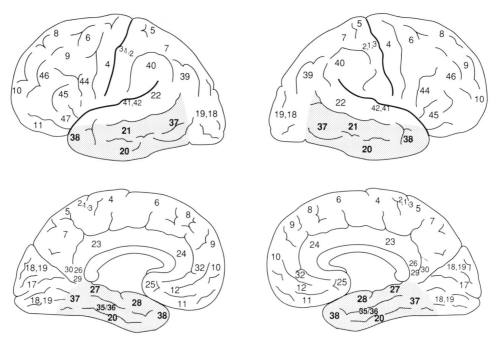

FIGURE 1   The lateral (upper) and mesial (lower) aspects of the left (left side of figure) and right (right side of figure) cerebral hemispheres. The regions of the temporal lobes which contain neural structures critical for memory are shaded.

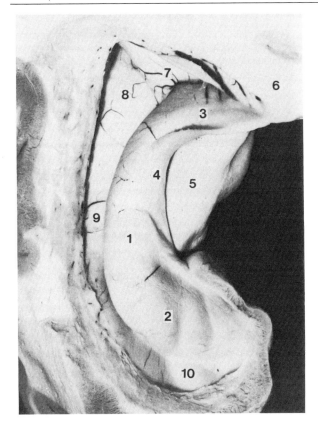

FIGURE 3   The hippocampus (Nos. 1–3) and related structures (Nos. 4–10). [Adapted from Duvernoy, 1988.]

1. The Hippocampal-Bound System

a. Anatomy

The mesial temporal lobe memory system includes the amygdala, entorhinal and perirhinal cortices, hippocampus, and parahippocampal gyrus (Figs. 2 and 3). As far as memory is concerned, the hippocampus is the most important structure in this system; thus, the term hippocampal-bound memory system. The structures of the hippocampal-bound system are highly interconnected, and they contain a number of local neuroanatomical circuits, providing a substrate for the types of recursive processing that are needed for rehearsal and consolidation.

The hippocampal-bound system is also extensively interconnected with virtually all major sensory regions of the brain, especially unimodal and polymodal association cortices (unimodal association cortices process information from one sensory modality; polymodal association cortices provide higher-order processing of information from more than one sensory modality). The entorhinal and per-

irhinal cortices, and parahippocampal gyrus, have extensive two-way connections with visual, auditory, and somatosensory association cortices, and with polymodal association cortices in the parietal and frontal lobes that are concerned with integration of information from multiple sensory modalities. This relationship is diagramed in Figure 4. Thus, hippocampal-bound memory structures have access to, and influence over, information from throughout the brain. The system is thus in a position to communicate directly with all major sensory modalities. This anatomical arrangement provides the substrate for the types of memory functions subserved by the hippocampal-bound system. For example, the system can create records that bind together various aspects of memory experiences, including visual, auditory, and somatosensory information. [See HIPPOCAMPAL FORMATION.]

b. Principal Function

As noted previously, the principal function of the hippocampal-bound system is the acquisition of new information. The system is specialized for making records of information acquired from the world outside, records that bind information together in such a way as to permit (1) more or less permanent storage of the information, and (2) coherent retrieval of memory experiences at a later time. The ability of the brain to acquire new information is of obvious importance in numerous aspects of everyday life, and disruption of this function, such as occurs frequently in Alzheimer's disease, head injury, certain types of brain infections, and conditions of extended deprivation of oxygen to the brain (anoxia), can have devastating consequences for afflicted patients.

c. The Left (Verbal) and Right (Nonverbal) Systems

There are two hippocampal-bound memory systems, one in the left hemisphere and one in the right. Anatomically, the two systems are roughly equivalent, but there are major differences in their functional roles. The two hippocampal systems are specialized for different types of information in a manner that parallels the overall arrangement of the brain, in which most individuals develop left-hemisphere specialization for speech and other verbal functions, and right-hemisphere specialization for spatial and other nonverbal abilities (Table II). Specifically, the left-sided system is dedicated primarily to verbal material—words, names, stories,

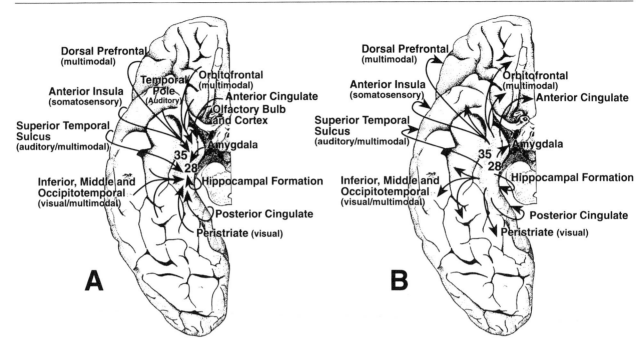

FIGURE 4 The neuroanatomical connectivity between the hippocampal-bound memory system (in particular, the entorhinal and perirhinal cortices) and various parts of the cerebral cortices. The system has extensive two-way connections with unimodal and polymodal association cortices throughout the brain. The figure shows ventral views of the human brain depicting likely input and output relationships of the entorhinal (area 28) and perirhinal (area 35) cortices as gleaned from nonhuman primate neuroanatomical research. These areas probably receive extensive direct or indirect sensory-specific (unimodal) association input (olfactory, auditory, somatosensory, and visual) as well as multimodal sensory input from the prefrontal, superior temporal and occipitotemporal regions of the cortex. Limbic system input from the amygdala, hippocampal formation, temporal polar, and cingulate areas is also a probable neuroanatomical feature. In all instances, the input structures receive direct or indirect feedback from areas 28 and 35. The powerful interconnections between the entorhinal/perirhinal cortices and the hippocampal formation assure widespread cortical and hippocampal interactions in a multitude of neural systems.

and the numerous other types of material that come to us in verbal (word-coded) form. The hippocampal system on the right, on the other hand, is specialized for nonverbal material—visual patterns (e.g., faces, geographical routes), melodies, spatial information, and other types of complex material that arrive in our brains in nonverbal form.

Normally, both systems participate in the acquisition of new information, and much of the information that we eventually commit to long-term memory arrives in our brains initially in both verbal and nonverbal form. For example, when we meet a new person, we are provided both a visual pattern (the face) and a verbal label (the name). Because the two sides of the brain (including the mesial temporal regions) are connected (mainly via the corpus callosum), we can retrieve nonverbal information given a verbal prompt, or vice versa. For example, given the name of someone we know well, we can conjure up an image of that person's face; conversely, presented

with the face of an acquaintance, we can recall the name. When one of the hippocampal-bound systems is damaged, however, the capacity to acquire the portion of information that is reliant upon the damaged system is lost. After damage to the left hippocampus, for example, an individual may lose the ability to learn new names and verbal facts, even though the person remains capable of learning new faces and spatial arrangements.

d. Involvement in Declarative Memory

Another feature of the hippocampal-bound memory system is that it is dedicated primarily to declarative forms of memory. It has a much lesser role in nondeclarative memory; in fact, there are several types of nondeclarative learning and retrieval that are entirely independent of hippocampal function. Thus, the learning of new facts, words, names, faces, and other declarative material is dependent upon mesial temporal structures, but learning of motor skills, habits, and other nondeclarative memories is not linked to the hippocampal system.

e. Involvement in Anterograde Memory

As noted above, the key function of the hippocampal-bound memory system is the acquisition of new information (anterograde memory). By contrast, the system does not have a crucial role in retrieval of previously learned knowledge (retrograde memory). Extensive bilateral damage to the hippocampus spares entirely the capacity to retrieve information from the past, even when new learning has been rendered virtually impossible. This principle is illustrated in compelling fashion in patient H.M., who despite complete bilateral removal of the hippocampus, can remember information that he had acquired prior to his surgery. Also, in patients with moderate or even advanced Alzheimer's disease, in whom hippocampal pathology is extensive and learning of new information has been reduced virtually to zero, there may remain a surprising degree of accurate recall of information from the past; in fact, it is often the case that the farther back in time one goes, the better the patient's recall is.

2. The Nonmesial Temporal System

We turn now to memory-related regions of the temporal lobe that are outside the mesial, hippocampal-bound system. These structures, collectively termed the nonmesial temporal system, comprise anatomical units in anterior, inferior, and lateral portions of the temporal lobe (Fig. 5). The system includes cortices in the temporal pole (Brodmann area 38), the inferotemporal region (Brodmann areas 20/21), and the transition region between the posterior temporal lobe and the inferior occipital lobe (Brodmann area 37). Details of brain–behavior relationships regarding this region are less well understood than those of the mesial, hippocampal-bound system. Some of the better known findings regarding the role of nonmesial temporal structures in memory are reviewed below.

a. Role in Retrograde Memory

In a general sense, structures in the nonmesial temporal region are important for the retrieval of previously learned knowledge, i.e., retrograde memory. Damage to the nonmesial system can impair significantly the capacity to retrieve previously

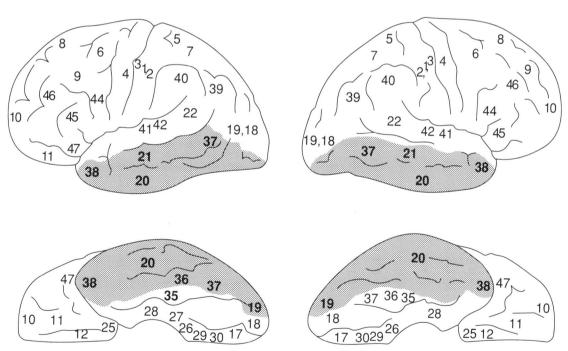

FIGURE 5   Lateral (upper) and inferior (lower) views of the left (left side of figure) and right (right side of figure) cerebral hemispheres. The regions formed by areas 38, 20/21, 37, and ventral 18/19 are important for long-term memory. The posterior part of the region (occipitotemporal system) supports conceptual knowledge related to unique entities (e.g., familiar faces), while the more anterior part, including the inferotemporal region (IT), supports knowledge related to nonunique entities (e.g., animals).

learned information. When the damage is bilateral, in fact, retrograde memory may be severely compromised for a wide array of different types of information. Patient Boswell, one of the few well-studied cases with extensive bilateral nonmesial temporal destruction, has lost nearly all capacity to retrieve information about his past. Outside of a few shreds of general information regarding his hometown, his parents, and his former occupation, he can recall virtually nothing regarding important events of his past life—for example, he cannot remember details about his spouse, his children, places he has lived, or his educational history.

b. The Left- and Right-Sided Systems

In general, the nonmesial temporal region follows the same organizational principles as other part of the brain, i.e., the left side is specialized for verbal material, and the right for nonverbal information (see Table II). For example, the left nonmesial structures play a key role in the retrieval of lexical information, particularly common and proper nouns that denote various nonunique and unique entities. The right-sided structures, on the other hand, are specialized for information such as faces and geographical routes.

c. Unique and Nonunique Knowledge

There is considerable subspecialization within the nonmesial temporal region for unique and nonunique types of knowledge. The posterior part of the system, particularly the region formed by the lower portion of the visual association cortices in the inferior occipital lobe (ventral Brodmann's areas 18/19) and the occipitotemporal transition zone (part of area 37), is involved in the retrieval of unique conceptual information, i.e., information about stimuli such as familiar faces and well-known geographical landmarks. To recognize a familiar face or a famous building, we call on information that is supported by structures in the occipitotemporal region. Bilateral damage to this region can produce a condition in which affected individuals lose their ability to recognize familiar faces (prosopagnosia) and other stimuli that are normally recognized at unique level (e.g., the White House, Devil's Tower).

Another subunit in the nonmesial temporal system is the inferotemporal region, known as IT. This region is formed primarily by the lateral and inferior aspects of areas 20/21 and 37 (Fig. 5). The IT region has a role in the retrieval of conceptual knowledge related to nonunique entities, e.g., animals, fruits

and vegetables, and other items that are normally recognized at a basic object level (e.g., a "raccoon" or an "eggplant"), but not more specifically (not as individual members of the class). Thus, recognition of various nonunique entities depends on retrieval of conceptual information (knowledge regarding physical and functional attributes) supported by neural systems in IT.

There is some degree of left–right specialization of the IT and occipitotemporal systems, although much of this remains to be explored. With regard to face recognition, for example, the right-hemisphere part of the system uses a more holistic, gestalt-based method of analysis, while the left-hemisphere system operates with a more sequential, feature-based method. Damage restricted to one of the two systems (confined to the left or right side) usually does not produce full-blown defects in face recognition, and it is patients with bilateral damage who manifest the most profound forms of prosopagnosia.

There is strong left-sided specialization for the retrieval of lexical items (words) that denote various entities. Thus, retrieval of the names that go with nonunique and unique entities depends on neural structures in the left nonmesial temporal region. More specifically, the retrieval of common nouns, which denote nonunique concrete entities (animals, fruits/vegetables, tools/utensils, etc.), depends on the anterior part of the IT system on the left. Retrieval of proper nouns, which denote unique entities such as faces and landmarks, depends on the anteriormost part of the nonmesial temporal region, including area 38 located in the pole of the temporal lobe.

The right nonmesial temporal system does not play a role in lexical retrieval; however, the anterior part of this system may be important for the retrieval of unique personal knowledge, i.e., information about various entities and events that comprise the autobiography of an individual. Thus, if you were asked to remember your graduation from high school, your wedding, or the birth of your first child, you would utilize information that is supported by neural systems in the right anterolateral temporal region.

B. Higher-Order Sensory Association Cortices

Each of the primary sensory modalities (visual, auditory, somatosensory) has associated with it a band of adjacent cortex that is termed an association area, and these association regions have important roles in memory. In the visual modality, for example, the cortex in the lingual gyrus, immediately adjacent to primary visual cortex in the inferior mesial occipital lobe, contains important neural units for the mapping of basic information about color (Fig. 6). Other visual association cortices in this region (in the lingual and fusiform gyri) are important for the mapping of form (shape) information. In an intriguing design feature that is only beginning to be understood, it appears that the same association cortices that are called into play when we *perceive* various information are used when we *recall* that information. For example, consider a well-known place, such as your bedroom. In the many times that you have looked at your bedroom, information regarding color, shape, and texture was processed by visual association cortices. Now, when you attempt to imagine your bedroom, to bring it into your mind's eye without being there to look at it, you can conjure up lots of details about the place, including information about color and form. The color and form information comes from the same neural structures that were used to perceive the information in the first place, i.e., visual association regions in the inferior occipital lobes.

This neural design is probably repeated in other sensory modalities, so that association regions for each modality map basic information related to the sensory modality, and support the retrieval of that information in recall. For audition, this includes information about various auditory features of a stimulus or event, such as the blend of sounds, the pitches, melodies, acoustic word-forms, and other aural patterns. The association cortices connected to the somatosensory modality contain neural units used in the perception and recall of information regarding texture, weight, smoothness, and other tactile percepts.

C. Memory-Related Neural Systems in Frontal Lobe

There are several memory-related neural systems in the frontal lobes, including the basal forebrain, ventromedial frontal region, and dorsolateral frontal region (Fig. 7).

1. Basal Forebrain

The basal forebrain is formed by a set of bilateral paramidline gray nuclei that includes the septal nuclei, the diagonal band of Broca, and the substantia innominata. One of the principal functions of this region is to deliver the critical neurotransmitter acetylcholine to the hippocampus and many regions of the cerebral cortex. The basal forebrain also delivers

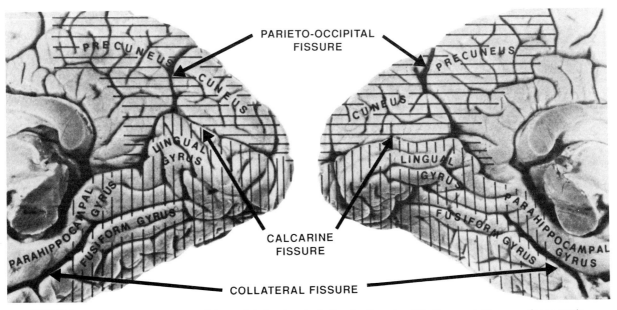

FIGURE 6 The mesial components of the occipital region, including the lingual and fusiform gyri. These cortices contain neural structures dedicated to processing basic visual information, such as color and form. The processing occurs here both during perception (of stimuli in the outside world) and imagery (bringing information into the "mind's eye"). [Adapted from A. R. Damasio, 1985.]

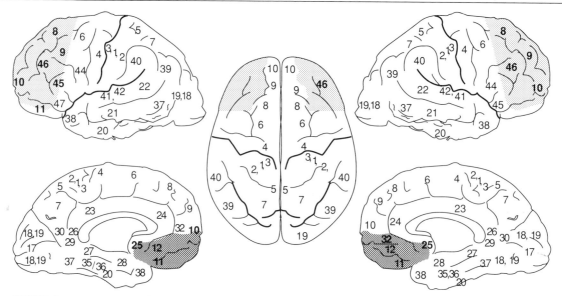

FIGURE 7   Lateral (upper), mesial (lower), and superior (center) views of the cerebral hemispheres (left hemisphere is on right side of picture, and vice versa). Regions of the frontal lobes that are involved in various memory processes include the ventromedial frontal region (dark gray), the dorsolateral frontal region (light gray), and the basal forebrain (located just posterior to the orbital cortices in the inferior aspect of the frontal lobes).

to various parts of the cerebral cortex other important neurotransmitters such as dopamine, norepinephrine, and serotonin. When the delivery of these neurotransmitters is disrupted by damage in basal forebrain, defects in memory can result. The memory impairment, however, is much different from that produced by lesions in the mesial temporal, hippocampal-bound system.

The basal forebrain appears to contribute to the *binding together of different modal components of a particular memory*. That is, different pieces of modal information that belong together in a memory "set" are linked together in a coherent fashion by the influence of neuronal units in the basal forebrain. Consider the following example: We are watching a program on television about a small-country dictator who has gone on a rampage to destroy all persons of a certain ethnic origin. During the program, we learn (1) the face and general appearance of the dictator; (2) his name; (3) the accent he has when speaking English; and (4) various facts about his regime. The basic learning of these pieces of information is dependent upon the mesial temporal (hippocampal-bound) system, as discussed previously. However, the basal forebrain plays a key role in the *binding together* of these pieces of information, so that they form a set in recall. For example, when we recall the name of the dictator, we will also recall the nature of his speech accent and specific information about his activities.

When the basal forebrain is functioning improperly or not at all, the capacity to keep various components of memorial episodes linked together in coherent sets is lost. In the example above, the name of the dictator may be recalled, but it will be put together with an incorrect name, an incorrect speech accent, or incorrect factual information about his activities. This modal mismatching of information can affect retrograde as well as the anterograde recall. For example, a patient may remember various facts about an occupation from 10 years previously, but link these facts with the wrong business name and wrong geographical location. The following quote from a patient illustrates this problem: "I used to work on an assembly line (correct) putting metal rings on the legs of frozen turkeys (correct), at the Hawkeye Packing Plant (incorrect) in the southwest part of town (incorrect)."

2. Ventromedial Frontal Region

The ventromedial frontal region comprises (1) the orbital cortices in the ventral and lower mesial part of the frontal lobe, including Brodmann areas 11 and 12, and (2) parts of areas 32 and 10 in the lower mesial aspect of the frontal lobe (Fig. 7). Related nearby neural units include the posterior aspect of the orbital region (area 25) and the anterior cingulate gyrus (area 24). This region has interesting anatomical connections with other parts of the brain. It receives projections from all sensory modalities, either directly or indirectly, including vision, audition, and touch. It also is a source of projections from frontal regions to central autonomic control structures. In addition, the ventromedial cortices have extensive bidirectional connections with the hippocampus and amygdala. Thus, the ventromedial region has direct influence over basic autonomic functions including various patterns of visceral and musculoskeletal activity that are involved in emotional processing (e.g., feelings of fear, anger, happiness, surprise). At the same time, the region is privy to information hailing from all major sensory modalities.

In keeping with this anatomical arrangement, the ventromedial frontal region has an important memory function that pertains to the relationship between memory and emotion. The region provides neural units that help link memorial information to pertinent feeling states (emotions), or what have been termed "somatic markers." For example, many learning experiences take place in the context of particular emotions, and a certain feeling may be an important part of the overall memory episode. Consider an example in which a child learns the relationship between the size of flame in the woodstove and the temperature of the chimney pipe (onto which the child puts her hand). Learning that a large flame predicts a red-hot stovepipe will be accompanied by a strong somatic marker, namely, the feeling of pain (burned hand); in fact, the feeling may be sufficiently strong that a single learning trial will establish the association firmly and permanently in the child's brain.

Learning experiences of this type, in which a distinct somatic marker is part of the set of memorial information, are at the crux of the socialization process. We learn that certain stimulus configurations are associated with certain feeling states, and we behave accordingly. This information helps us guide our social behavior in a fashion that is in our overall best interest, in both the short and long term. Behaving appropriately in a particular social situation, for example, will facilitate the development of friendships and other positive relationships that will lead to reinforcing feeling states.

Neural units in the ventromedial frontal lobe provide the support for linking various stimuli with various feeling states, thus helping us make decisions that are in our best interest. When these neural units are damaged, individuals develop patterns of maladaptive social behavior and decision making. They behave as if they have no regard for potential punishment. Such persons, in fact, may become frankly psychopathic. Also, improper early development of critical neural units in the ventromedial frontal region, which would deprive the individual of the opportunity to establish links between various stimulus configurations and various feeling states, could lead to a life-long pattern of psychopathy (antisocial personality disorder). [See ANTISOCIAL PERSONALITY DISORDER.]

As noted in Section III, the ventromedial frontal region may also play a role in prospective memory, the capacity of "remembering in the future." Take as an example the following scenario. I am supposed to remember to call my spouse at around mid-day, to arrange plans for picking up children from school. I can appose a "somatic marker" to this stimulus configuration, so that when noon-time arrives, I am "reminded" by my brain (via a signal from the ventromedial frontal region, which may come as the feeling that "something needs to be done") to call my spouse and make a plan. What if I "forget to remember?" The more time that elapses without my accomplishing the behavior, the more salient the feeling of "forgetting something" becomes; finally, I remember what the "something" is, and the salient feeling dissipates (or is replaced by another strong feeling, such as "Now I'm in trouble!").

3. Dorsolateral Frontal Region

A curious form of memory capacity has been linked to the dorsolateral sector of the frontal lobes, i.e., the expanse of cortex and attendant white matter that comprises the prefrontal region on the convexity of the hemispheres (Fig. 7). This is a type of memory in which we are called upon to estimate the number of times that a particular event has occurred (frequency judgment), or how long ago something took place (recency judgment). For example, if you were asked, "How many times did you look at your watch yesterday?", you would form an estimate by searching back through your memories of yesterday, bringing to mind the events of the day, what you were doing, and so on. Answering the question requires a judgment or estimate of frequency. A similar capacity is called for when you are asked a question such as, "When was the last time you talked to your mother on the phone?" The answer may be anywhere from minutes to years. Estimating the recency of a behavior such as this is another capacity that requires a type of memory that has been linked to the dorsolateral sector of the frontal lobes.

In general, there may be some degree of hemispheric specialization for recency/frequency judgments, whereby the left dorsolateral region is dominant for verbally coded information, while the right is dominant for nonverbal, visuospatial information (in keeping with the overall hemispheric specialization of the brain). It should be noted, though, that there are very few studies of this topic, and the neuroanatomical basis of recency/frequency judgments must be considered tentative.

One other type of memory, known as working memory, should be mentioned. Working memory refers to a transient type of memory processing, on the order of seconds and minutes in which we can hold "on-line" the relevant stimuli, rules, and mental representations that are needed to execute a particular task. In particular, working memory is used to bridge temporal gaps, that is, to hold representations in a mental workspace long enough so that we can make appropriate responses to stimulus configurations or contingencies in which some, or even all, of the basic ingredients are no longer extant in perceptual space. The concept of working memory has some overlap with short-term memory, as defined in Section III above—both are relatively transient and of limited capacity.

The reason for mentioning working memory in the current section is because this memory function has been linked to the prefrontal region of the brain, i.e., part of the dorsolateral frontal lobe that comprises the anterior convexity of the cerebral hemispheres. However, most of the studies of working memory have been done in nonhuman primates, making it difficult to draw direct neuroanatomical comparisons to humans. Nonetheless, there is strong evidence in nonhuman primates that the prefrontal region plays a crucial role in working memory, and it is likely that this relationship will apply to humans as well, at least to some extent.

D. Basal Ganglia and Cerebellum

The basal ganglia are a set of gray-matter nuclei buried deep at the base of the cerebral hemispheres. They include the caudate nucleus, the putamen, the globus pallidus, and the subthalamic nucleus. Although the principal function of these structures is motor control, recent evidence suggests that they also have some important memory functions. Specifically, the basal ganglia have been linked to various forms of nondeclarative memory, particularly those types of memory that are dependent upon a motor act for their realization, or what has been termed procedural memory (e.g., riding a bicycle,

skating). The cerebellum, another motor-related structure situated behind the brainstem at the base of the brain, participates along with the basal ganglia in many types of procedural learning and memory. [See CEREBELLUM.]

The roles of the basal ganglia and cerebellum in procedural memory, on the one hand, and the mesial temporal (hippocampal-bound) region in declarative memory, on the other, are quite independent. Damage to one system may have little or no effect on the capacities of the other. For example, the severe neuropathology in the mesial temporal region caused by Alzheimer's disease may spare entirely the integrity of the basal ganglia and cerebellum; as a consequence, many patients with Alzheimer's remain fully capable of performing complex motor activities such as dancing or playing golf, and such patients may even be able to acquire new motor skills. In fact, patients with virtually complete destruction of the mesial temporal region, such as H.M. and Boswell, are capable of learning new motor skills, even when they cannot remember where, when, or any other factual (declarative) information about the context in which those skills were acquired. The reverse situation occurs when disease strikes the basal ganglia, but spares the hippocampal-bound system. For example, in patients with Parkinson's or Huntington's disease, in whom neuropathology affects the basal ganglia but not the mesial temporal region, the retrieval and learning of motor skills may be severely impaired, while memory for declarative knowledge is spared. Damage to the cerebellum can also produce motor learning defects while sparing declarative memory. [See ALZHEIMER'S DISEASE.]

The caudate nucleus, which together with the putamen forms the striatal component of the basal ganglia, may have nondeclarative memory functions that have to do with the development of habits and other "nonconscious" response tendencies. The tendencies we develop to respond to certain situations in certain ways, behaviors such as following the same route home each day, or repeatedly seeking out a particular person for moral support and encouragement, are examples of habits and response tendencies that we engage on a fairly automatic basis, with little or no conscious deliberation. These types of "memory" behavior have been linked to the striatum, and in particular, the caudate nucleus.

E. Thalamus

Similar to the basal ganglia, the principal functions of the thalamus are outside the domain of memory;

however, parts of the thalamus and related diencephalic structures do have important roles in memory. Structures that have been consistently linked to memory include the dorsomedial and anterior nuclei of the thalamus, the mammillary bodies, and two related fiber tracts—the mammillothalamic tract, which connects the mesial temporal hippocampal-bound system to the anterior nuclei of the thalamus, and the ventroamygdalofugal pathway, which connects the amygdala to the dorsomedial nuclei.

The precise roles of these diencephalic structures in memory are not well specified, but in general, they support memory capacities in a manner that supplements the support of the mesial temporal system. In particular, structures in the diencephalon contribute to the acquisition of new declarative information. They are less involved in retrieval of previously learned knowledge, and they do not appear to support nondeclarative memory. Anterior parts of the thalamus may make an important contribution to the temporal sequencing of memories, i.e., situating memories in correct temporal context. Also, the thalamus appears to have material-specific functions that parallel those of the mesial temporal memory system: left-sided thalamic nuclei are specialized for verbal information, while right-sided nuclei are specialized for nonverbal, visuospatial material.

The diencephalon gives rise to a number of important neurochemical systems that innervate widespread regions of cerebral cortex. Thus, structures such as the mammillary bodies and certain thalamic nuclei may provide to the cortex important neurotransmitters that are needed for normal memory function. It follows that damage to the diencephalon may not only disrupt important neuroanatomical connections between limbic regions (including the hippocampal-bound system) and the neocortex, but it might also interfere with memory-related neurochemical influences on cortex.

V. CLOSING COMMENT

To provide a reasonable summary of the neural substrates of human memory, it is necessary to review a large number and variety of neural structures. In fact, it could be argued that virtually the entire human brain is concerned with memory, of one kind or another, at one level or another. Certainly one of the prime accomplishments of our brains has been the development of higher-order memory function—the potential to store vast amounts of information; to maintain knowledge so that it can be retrieved in a timely fashion; the ability to use representational thought to consider future events; the capacity to learn myriad names, numbers, faces, and facts. The importance of memory is underscored further when one considers the devastation and suffering caused by neurological conditions that rob persons of their memory, such as Alzheimer's disease, head injury, anoxia, and certain types of strokes and brain infections.

From a scientific perspective, the pursuit of understanding of the manner in which neural structures subserve human memory remains a central question in neuroscience. A tremendous amount of progress has been realized since the days when notable researchers threw up their hands in despair and declared that memory "traces" could not be found in the brain. However, much remains to be learned, and many contemporary researchers would agree that we have only just begun to unravel some of mysteries of how our brains subserve memory.

Acknowledgments

Supported by Program Project Grant NINDS 19632. I thank Gary Van Hoesen, Ph.D., for his kind assistance with the figures.

Bibliography

Butters, N., and Stuss, D. T. (1989). Diencephalic amnesia. In "Handbook of Neuropsychology" (F. Boller and J. Grafman, Eds.), Vol. 3, pp. 107–148. Elsevier, Amsterdam.

Corkin, S. (1984). Lasting consequences of bilateral medial temporal lobectomy: Clinical course and experimental findings in H. M. *Semin. Neurol.* **4,** 249–259.

Damasio, A. R. (1989). Time-locked multiregional retroactivation: A systems-level proposal for the neural substrates of recall and recognition. *Cognition* **33,** 25–62.

Damasio, A. R., Tranel, D., and Damasio, H. (1989). Amnesia caused by herpes simplex encephalitis, infarctions in basal forebrain, Alzheimer's disease, and anoxia. In "Handbook of Neuropsychology" (F. Boller and J. Grafman, Eds.), Vol. 3, pp. 149–166. Elsevier, Amsterdam.

Milner, B. (1972). Disorders of learning and memory after temporal lobe lesions in man. *Clin. Neurosurg.* **19,** 421–446.

Mishkin, M. (1978). Memory in monkeys severely impaired by combined but not separate removal of amygdala and hippocampus. *Nature* **273,** 297–298.

Squire, L. R. (1992). Memory and the hippocampus: A synthesis from findings with rats, monkeys, and humans. *Psychol. Rev.* **99,** 195–231.

MENTAL IMAGERY

Kevin N. Ochsner and Stephen M. Kosslyn
Harvard University

Glossary

Image generation Mental images are not always present, but rather occur only after visual information is activated. Unless an image is formed by retaining perceptual input on-line, it is formed by (a) activating stored representations of objects and their parts, and (b) mentally placing these parts in relation to each other.

Image maintenance Once generated, images fade quickly. To be retained, they must be actively regenerated. But at best, mental images are transitory.

Image scanning Attention can be shifted over objects in mental images, and more time is required to scan farther distances across the object—even though one's eyes may be closed.

Image transformation Once generated, objects in images can be rotated, expanded, and otherwise manipulated. Most image transformations are analogous to the corresponding physical transformations.

Mental rotation People can imagine objects rotating, and more time is required to imagine greater amounts of rotation. When mentally turning an object upside-down, we "see" it pass through intermediate positions; and the farther we have to turn it, the longer the transformation takes to accomplish.

Visual buffer A functionally defined structure that corresponds to a set of spatially organized visual processing regions in the brain. During perception, patterns of activation in the visual buffer represent surface properties of viewed objects. During imagery, patterns of activation represent a mental image. The visual buffer functions as the "mental screen" upon which mental images are "displayed."

A MENTAL IMAGE is a transient perceptual representation that is in short-term memory. It can be formed by briefly retaining (over a few seconds) perceptual input or by activating stored information. A percept, in contrast, is the representation that is evoked on-line while one is in the act of perceiving a stimulus. Imagery is similar to perception experientially, and also shares many of the same underlying brain systems. Both imagery and perception are accomplished through the cooperative actions of a number of specialized subsystems. Patterns of activity in sensory cortex that correspond to percepts either can be created by immediate external sensory input (in perception) or can be evoked via efferent connections from higher order cortical centers (in imagery). Although many people report experiencing mental imagery in all sensory modalities, we focus primarily on visual imagery because most research has been devoted to its study.

I. Historical Overview

The subjective experience of "seeing with the mind's eye" has been a topic of heated debate at least since Plato, who characterized mental images as patterns etched in a block of wax. Although classical philosophers, such as Locke and Hobbes, and early psychologists, such as James and Wundt, often assigned mental imagery a central role in their theorizing, the spread of Behaviorism banished these unobservable phenomena from the realm of empirical discourse. It was not until the early 1970s, buoyed by the rise of cognitive psychology, that mental imagery again came to the fore. Paivio and his colleagues showed that imagery is a potent force in helping one to remember new information, and Shepard and his colleagues demonstrated highly systematic and reliable similarities between imagery and perception. Indeed, perhaps the most important aspect of the pioneering studies of Shepard and his colleagues was that the nature of mental images, although inherently subjective and inaccessible, could be studied scientifically.

In following years a debate ensued concerning the nature of representations underlying mental images. This debate focused on the nature of the internal representations that underlie the experience of imagery, not whether people have such experiences. The central issue was whether the image representations used in information processing are abstract and language-like ("propositional") or percept-like and "quasi-pictorial" ("depictive").

This debate has subsided in the wake of recent evidence confirming that visual mental imagery depends upon spatially organized regions of the brain that are also used in visual perception. For example, it is known that primary visual cortex in humans is spatially organized. Each neuron in visual cortex is sensitive to visual cues at a specific location in the visual field, and the arrangement of these neurons corresponds to (roughly) the spatial relations among these locations. There is, in a sense, a "map" of the visual field on visual cortex. Input from the high-resolution central part of the retina (the *fovea*) reaches the posterior part of primary visual cortex, and input from increasingly peripheral (*parafoveal*) regions reaches progressively anterior parts of visual cortex. Thus, it is of interest that when people close their eyes and visualize letters, not only does visual cortex become activated, but the focus of activation depends on the size of the mental image. When objects are imaged so that they seem to cover small regions of space, the posterior part of visual cortex is most strongly activated; in contrast, when objects are imaged so that they seem to cover larger regions of the visual field, activation in the brain shifts toward the anterior part (which represents the periphery) of this structure—just as is found when one views larger objects. [*See* VISUAL PERCEPTION.]

II. PURPOSES OF IMAGERY: WHEN DO WE USE MENTAL IMAGERY?

In this section we discuss the purposes of imagery and the contexts in which imagery tends to be used spontaneously.

A. Forecasting Outcomes

At some point you may have wondered what would happen if you pulled a tablecloth out from under a set of dishes—but then decided not to give it a yank after you imagined the consequences. This example illustrates one primary purpose of mental imagery: Aiding reasoning and problem solving by forecasting the outcome of an action. Using imagery, you can create hypothetical scenarios and "observe" what takes place.

For example, Albert Einstein claimed that he gained his initial insights into the theory of relativity when he imagined what he would "see" if he matched the speed of a beam of light. Physical theory at that time predicted that from his parallel vantage point, Einstein should have "seen" an electromagnetic wave of a particular type. However, the wave he saw did not conform to accepted theory. Thus an imaginal observation planted the seed for the development of relativity theory.

B. Mental Models

In a similar fashion we can use imagery to help reason symbolically. Consider the following problem: Bill is smarter than John, and George is dumber than John. Who is the smartest? One way to answer the question easily is by imagining a line with dots placed upon it that represent each person. If you order the dots from left to right in terms of relative intelligence, answering the question becomes a matter of simply "observing" which dot is placed farthest to the right. Such processes may play a role in language comprehension when one visualizes a "model" of what is said as part of the process of comprehending a description.

C. Retrieval and Visualization of Memories

Is a frozen pea darker than a Christmas tree? Do a German Shepherd's ears rise above the top of its head? Chances are, you (like the subjects who participated in formal experiments using such stimuli) used imagery to answer these questions. Indeed, a major function of imagery is to help one recall information that may have been noticed only incidentally, and not considered in detail at the time it was stored in memory. Thus, when asked, "How many windows are there in your living room?" one is unlikely to have thought explicitly about this before. Consequently, one does not already have the answer stored either verbally or in another explicit manner.

Rather, the information is implicit in an image, and we use imagery to retrieve the information from memory. Once we form an image, we "inspect" it to find the answer. As discussed below, this process of "inspecting" an imaged object apparently uses many of the same mechanisms that are used in actual perception. [See MEMORY.]

Because imagery and perception share common mechanisms, it is not surprising that people sometimes cannot determine whether a memory was formed on the basis of imagined rather than experienced events. In fact, recent research suggests that such deficits in such "reality monitoring" may underlie aspects of certain psychiatric syndromes.

D. Learning

The ancient Greeks discovered that imagery can help one to memorize a list of objects. For example, in the "method of loci" one first memorizes locations along a familiar route (e.g., through your house). When one later wants to remember a list of items (e.g., of things to get at the market), one visualizes walking along the route and "leaving" an image of an item in each successive location (such as a loaf of bread in the hallway, some soap on the chair in the den, some sponges on the rug, etc.). To recall the items subsequently, one needs only to visualize the route, image walking along it, and "see" what was stored at each location. In general, visualizing objects as if they were interacting in some way facilitates recall the most: In addition to the names and images of the objects, one can also use the associations among them to aid subsequent retrieval.

The memory and extrapolative aspects of imagery can also aid learning of skills: We can replay the actions of an instructor and "obseve" his or her actions in order to improve our own. What's more, by imagining yourself performing an action and "observing" your performance, you can "hone" the same memory that is used to direct actual performance of that action.

E. Wool Gathering

In a recent survey of how people use imagery, the authors were surprised to discover that most imagery was not directed toward any specific purpose. Rather, people most often used imagery to daydream. But even such apparently aimless wanderings could have productive consequences: Subjects sometimes reported being reminded of an important errand or having "an idea" when noticing something in their imagery. These moments of epiphany are a direct consequence of the fact that visual mental images unpack information that is only implicit in long-term memory. That is why one must form an image to answer a question like "how many windows are there in your house?" The information is in long-term memory, but not in a form that is immediately accessible. By visualizing objects and events, one can notice features and relations that previously were not considered, which sometimes has important consequences.

III. INSPECTING IMAGED OBJECTS

If one could not "see" objects and their properties in mental images, then for all intents and purposes they would not exist. The ability to inspect imaged objects is central to all uses of imagery.

A. Imagery and Perception

The idea that visual imagery relies on mechanisms used in visual perception has a long history, and has received much support. For example, visual images can interfere with visual perception more than with auditory perception, but vice versa for auditory images. In addition, various visual illusions are evident in imagery. Moreover, brain-damaged patients with lesions of right parietal lobe sometimes ignore ("neglect") objects in the half of space on the opposite side from their lesion. A patient who can not attend to the left half of a building when standing in front of it also cannot attend to the left side when asked to form an image of the building from memory. However, if the patient is asked to "turn" so that the formerly neglected side is now in the half of space that the patient can perceive, the patient can now "see" the formerly neglected side of the object—both in perception and in imagery.

It may at first seem paradoxical to speak of "seeing" objects in mental images with "the mind's eye." After all, there is no homunculus inside our heads that "observes" imaged objects for us. This apparent paradox is put to rest by the realization that visual mental imagery employs many of the brain systems used in visual perception. Just as one does not need to invoke a "little man in the head" to explain how we perceive objects and events, one also need not evoke such a little man to explain how we inspect their imaged counterparts.

In recent years increasing use of brain imaging technology has spurred progress toward explaining how the brain forms and uses mental images. Like other complex mental functions, mental imagery is the product of the operation of a host of specialized subsystems. Converging evidence suggests that these subsystems are instantiated in localized areas of the brain.

Specifically, during perception, information traveling from the eyes first sets up a pattern of neural activity in the *visual buffer*. This structure corresponds to spatially organized areas of the brain (including the human equivalents of areas V1 and V2 of the monkey, and possibly other related areas as well). The visual buffer functions as if it were a sort of "screen" on which information can be displayed and viewed. Visual mental images consist of depictive representations in these spatially organized areas. One might think of the visual buffer as a screen used to display both input from a camera (perception) and stored information from a VCR (imagery). But this screen is active: it computes edges and organizes regions of objects, it is not simply a passive receptacle of information.

The idea that imagery uses a perceptual "screen" is plausible because virtually every visual area that sends information to another visual area also receives information from that area. During imagery, higher cortical areas presumably use such *reciprocal connections* to create patterns of activity in the visual buffer; these patterns correspond to imaged objects.

We "see" objects in visual images with the mind's eye precisely because images exist as patterns of activation in the cortical areas used in visual perception. Indeed, positron emission tomography (PET) has shown that several spatially organized areas, which together may correspond to the visual buffer, are activated during imagery. PET scanning relies on the fact that the more a specific brain area is active, the more blood it requires. Water that contains radioactive oxygen is introduced into the bloodstream (either by injection or via breathing radioactive carbon dioxide), and hence the more blood that is required in a given brain area, the more radioactivity is present in that area. Thus, by measuring the amount of radioactivity in different brain areas while a person performs a given task, one can discover which areas are used for such processing. In addition, when a patient loses a part of occipital cortex and thus part of his or her visual buffer (see Fig. 1), the "size" of the "imagery space" available for visualizing objects is narrowed.

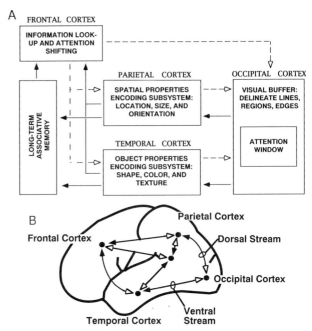

FIGURE 1   Subsystems in the visual system involved in generating and transforming visual images. Solid arrowheads depict projections from areas early in the visual processing system to areas later in the system. Open arrowheads depict projections from higher to lower cortical centers. These connections are used to evoke patterns of activation in the visual buffer that correspond to visual images. (A) Schematic layout of proposed subsystems. Each box represents an individual subsystem with its anatomical location noted above the box. Note that, in addition to frontal cortex, a variety of other areas are involved in shifting attention, including the parietal lobes and the superior colliculus. (B) Lateral view of left hemisphere of brain. The dots indicate the approximate locations of cortex that is maximally activated when the visual buffer, dorsal system, ventral system, and information-lookup subsystem are used.

B. Scanning Images

During perception, the visual buffer contains more information than can be processed in detail at one time. Therefore, when viewing or imagining a complex scene we must have some mechanism for selecting some of the information present for further processing. We call this mechanism the *attention window*, and its location can be shifted in the visual buffer, thereby allowing one to make covert shifts of attention across perceived and imagined objects. Hence, the time to scan across an imaged scene increases with the distance covered. For example, in one experiment subjects memorized the locations of different objects (e.g., a palm tree or a hut) on a drawing of an island. They then visualized the island and focused on a specific location. Shortly thereafter, they heard the name of another object, which may or may not have been on the map. The subjects were to "look" for the object on the imaged map (with their eyes closed). As predicted, the farther apart objects were on the island, the longer it took subjects to scan between them.

Such shifts of attention are apparently one mechanism that underlies our ability to scan imaged objects, but cannot be the only one: we can scan continuously around the walls of an imaged room, without "bumping into the edge" of the visual buffer. Some types of scanning apparently also involve shifting the imaged pattern across the visual buffer, just as would occur on a television screen when a camera is panned across a scene.

Posner and his colleagues have described three mechanisms that are responsible for shifting the location of the attention window within the visual buffer; each mechanism is dependent upon discrete brain regions. The first disengages attention from an initial location; the second shifts attention to the proper place; and the last engages attention at the new location. As is discussed below, these mechanisms may also allow us to generate "attention-based images."

IV. GENERATING IMAGES

We do not have a given image in mind all the time. Rather, either on-line perceptual information must be encoded and repeatedly re-activated in order to be retained or information in long-term memory must be activated in order to form an image. The process of forming an image from information in long-term memory is called "image generation."

A. Wholes and Parts

We can generate images of the overall shape of an object, its parts, or a combination of the two, thereby fleshing out an image of an object's general shape by adding high-resolution details about its parts. One reason that we can form such images lies in the limitations of our ability to attend to objects. When we pay attention to an entire object, we will not encode its parts as sharply as when we pay attention to the parts themselves. Thus, we will encode different kinds of information when we interact with an object in different ways. For example, when walking around an object, we may encode only its global shape, but when picking it up, we will encode at least some of its parts.

Consequently, if one needs high-resolution details in an image, then the image must be formed by activating more than one stored visual memory: Both the whole and the parts must be activated. Furthermore, one must also organize the activated parts in the appropriate way. Because the process of positioning parts is distinct from the process of activating them, one sometimes may visualize parts of an object in the wrong locations.

Research on the neural substrate of object recognition has provided insights into the mechanisms underlying image generation. This research has demonstrated that information in the visual buffer flows into separate dorsal (running along the top of brain) and ventral (running along the bottom of brain) processing streams, shown in Figure 1. These streams are specialized for processing spatial properties and object properties, respectively. The dorsal "spatial-properties encoding" pathway relies on parietal cortex and encodes information about object size, orientation, and location. In contrast, the ventral "object-properties encoding" pathway relies on temporal cortex and encodes information about object color, shape, and texture. [See SPATIAL PERCEPTION.]

To generate an image of a single shape, one need only activate stored memories in the ventral system. Upon activating this information, a pattern of activity can be imposed on the visual buffer, and this pattern of activation is the image itself. This type of image generation is apparently related to the kind of "priming" that occurs when one anticipates seeing a specific shape, and hence can encode it more easily. The crucial difference is that during imagery, the "priming" is so intense that, rather than simply facilitating encoding of a perceptual pattern, the expected pattern of activation is actually created.

In contrast, when one visualizes an object with many details, the dorsal and ventral systems work together in concert. If one wants to include a high-resolution image of a cat's claws on its paws, for example, one needs not only to activate the stored memories, but also to place the imaged claws in the correct locations relative to the paws. In such cases mental images are built up a part at a time, which requires the combined use of both the object-properties encoding system (to image the parts) and the spatial-properties encoding system (to place them in proper locations).

These conclusions are drawn, in part, from the results of a relatively simple experiment. On each trial, the subjects viewed a lowercase script letter printed underneath a 4 × 5 grid; shortly thereafter, an X mark appeared in one cell (see Fig. 2). The task was to visualize in the grid the corresponding uppercase block version of the script letter, and then decide whether that letter would have covered the X mark if it were actually in the grid. The X mark appeared in different positions in the grid on different trials; it could fall on or near the letter segment that was typically drawn first, second, third, and so on. Subjects required the least amount of time to make their decision when the X fell on a segment that was typically drawn first, more time for segments drawn second, yet more time for segments

drawn third, and so on. Overall, response times were predicted well by the number of segments one would have had to draw to reach the location of the X. In contrast, if subjects were allowed to finish forming the image before an X was presented, or actually saw a light gray letter in the grids, then there was no effect on response times of where the X was located.

These results indicate that subjects formed the images a segment at a time. As was expected, PET scanning during this task revealed not only that spatially organized visual cortex was activated during imagery, but also that the ventral (object-properties encoding) and dorsal (spatial-properties encoding) systems were active as well. To form an image of a letter the subjects apparently first activated stored representations of the letter segments and then placed them in proper relations to one another. Furthermore, parts of the frontal lobes were also activated. The frontal lobes apparently are involved in decision making and control of sequential activity, and presumably play a role in coordinating activation of visual memories and the processes that adjust where parts will appear in the image.

B. Two Kinds of Imagery

The two visual pathways can be used independently to form images. Indeed, when used independently, each pathway appears to subserve generation of different types of images: Patients who have damage to temporal cortex may have great difficulty visualizing objects, but can visualize spatial relations; in contrast, patients who have damage to parietal cortex may have great difficulty visualizing spatial relations, but can visualize objects.

These findings suggest that one can form images not only by activating stored visual memories but also by allocating attention over a region of the visual buffer. For example, by activating stored visual memories, one can visualize one's mother's face, but by allocating attention to the appropriate rows and columns, one can image letters in grids. People commonly report that they can look at a tiled floor and "see" geometric patterns by attending to specific rows and columns of tiles. PET imaging studies have shown that when subjects are led to form such attention-based images, although there is no activation in the temporal lobes, there is activation of a structure (the pulvinar nucleus of the thalamus, a subcortical mass of cells) known to be involved in

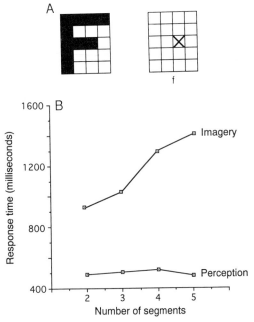

FIGURE 2   Stimuli and results of image generation experiment described in text. (A) (*Left*) An uppercase block letter formed by selectively filling in cells of a matrix. (*Right*) In the imagery task, subjects were shown lowercase cue and instructed to form an image of the corresponding uppercase block letter in the grid. An X mark then appeared in the grid and subjects decided whether the imaged block letter would occupy the grid cell containing the X. In the perception task, a light gray uppercase block letter and X mark were presented simultaneously on the screen. (B) The mean time to evaluate probe X marks in the imagery and perception tasks when the probe mark was on the second, third, fourth, or fifth letter segment typically drawn. In the imagery task, only 500 msec was allowed between presentation of the lowercase cue and X mark, which is not enough time to read the cue and finish forming the image. Hence, the decision times reflect in part the time to form an image, segment by segment, in the grid. In contrast, response times in the perception task did not vary as a function of probe location. [Adapted from S. M. Kosslyn, C.B. Cave, D. A. Provost, and S. M. von Gierke (1988). *Cognitive Psychol.* **20,** 39–343.]

engaging visual attention. Furthermore, there is no activation in the parietal lobes, which is especially intriguing because Posner and his colleagues have suggested that the parietal lobes are used to disengage attention prior to moving it. Thus, it appears that in attention-based imagery one does not disengage attention from each successive set of attended locations; rather, one forms the image by engaging and distributing attention over a pattern.

C. Image Generation in the Cerebral Hemispheres

About 5 years ago, a review of the neuropsychological literature would probably have suggested that only damage to the posterior left hemisphere disrupts image generation. For example, various researchers found that the left hemispheres of split-brain patients (who for medical reasons have had the fiber bundle connecting the hemispheres severed) were better able to generate images of multi-part objects than were the right hemispheres. In keeping with this assessment, scalp-electrode recording techniques also indicated a left posterior foci of activity during image generation.

However, there were some notable exceptions to this overall pattern. For example, some research with split-brain patients showed that although the left hemisphere excelled at tasks that required building an image from multiple stored parts, both hemispheres could form images of global shapes with equal efficacy. To complicate matters further, results from research with normal subjects then showed that the right hemisphere was better than the left at certain imagery tasks. For example, in one experiment, subjects viewed uppercase letters and were asked to decide whether the corresponding lowercase letters were "short" or "tall" (e.g., "a" versus "b"). The subjects responded more quickly when the letter cues were presented in the left visual field and hence were seen first by the right cerebral hemisphere.

Recently it has become clear that both hemispheres can generate images of multi-part objects, but apparently do so in different ways. A number of researchers have shown that the dorsal ("where") system in the right hemisphere encodes precise, coordinate spatial relations more efficiently than the corresponding dorsal system in the left hemisphere. Moreover, Kosslyn and his colleagues have shown that the right hemisphere can use such precise spatial relations more effectively than the left hemisphere

to arrange parts into an image. In contrast, the dorsal system in the left hemisphere encodes categorical spatial relations (such as on/off, above/below, and left/right) more efficiently than the dorsal system in the right hemisphere. And the left hemisphere can use such categorical relations more effectively than the right hemisphere to arrange parts into an image.

This conclusion has been supported by results from a variant of the block-letter imaging task described above. In this version of the task, subjects formed images either after memorizing a description of how segments were arranged to form an overall shape or after viewing the individual segments, one at a time, arranged in the proper spatial relations. In both cases the overall imaged pattern was constructed by mentally "gluing together" parts, but different methods were used for this process: In the first case, subjects had to rely on encoded categorical spatial relations, whereas in the second they had to rely on encoded metric spatial relations. Subjects also learned to associate each pattern with a number, and the numbers were later used to cue image generation of the appropriate letter. In the task itself, a grid with an X mark was presented briefly in one visual half-field, ensuring that it was seen first by only one hemisphere. Immediately prior to presentation of the grid, subjects saw one of the number cues. They were to visualize the corresponding pattern in the grid and decide whether it covered the X mark. If the associated pattern had been learned by connecting parts with categorical relations, the subjects subsequently could visualize it faster if the cue was presented to the left hemisphere than if it was presented to the right hemisphere. But if the pattern had been learned by connecting parts with metric spatial relations, the subjects subsequently could visualize it faster if the cue was presented first to the right hemisphere.

Together with results discussed above, this demonstration suggests that there may be at least four ways to generate images: by activating visual memories of parts or by attending to specific regions, and in either case, arranging the parts using categorical or metric spatial relations.

V. TRANSFORMING IMAGES

Most uses of imagery in reasoning rely on the ability to manipulate the form and size of imagined objects. This ability has been studied experimentally, and researchers have demonstrated that people can transform imaged objects in numerous ways, such as rotating complex three-dimensional forms and mentally folding paper to form cubes. Indeed, people can translate and rearrange imaged objects in arbitrary ways. For example, visualize an uppercase version of the letter "j" positioned beneath an uppercase version of the "d" that has been rotated 90° counterclockwise. What pattern have you formed? Many people report "seeing" an umbrella.

Just as people require more time to scan across greater distances of imaged objects, so too do they require more time to transform objects greater amounts. Indeed, Shepard and colleagues showed that more time is required to rotate an imaged object greater amounts, and the time to fold a cube increases linearly with the number of sides that must be moved. Such results suggest that images are transformed in small increments. One possible reason for this is that images are transformed by visualizing what one would see if one actually manipulated an object in some way. Such findings make sense if images are formed by the same processes that "prime" the object-properties or spatial-properties systems to better encode a stimulus that one anticipates seeing. During transformation of imaged objects, one is not simply "primed" to see an object, one is anticipating what one would see if an object were manipulated in some way.

This line of reasoning leads us to expect the motor system, which guides actual use and manipulation of objects, to play an important role in priming the visual system to "expect" certain transformations. In fact, recent PET imaging studies have shown that motor cortex is active during both actual and imagined writing. In addition, there is evidence from single unit recording studies in monkeys that the motor system coordinates movements by programming muscles to move limbs through trajectories. These programs could be used to prime sensory systems during image transformation.

Such processing would cause the image transformation process to mimic the corresponding physical transformation: Because one must move one's limbs through a trajectory, one anticipates seeing one's limbs (or objects manipulated by them) move in this way. As one would expect from this inference, it is easier to imagine movements that the motor system can easily program, such as a hand rotating about the wrist, than it is to imagine movements that are difficult to program, such as a hand rotating about

an arbitrary point. Similarly, people report that rotation of heavy objects takes more time than mental rotation of light objects. In fact, when mentally rotating a hammer about the center point of its handle, people often report that it seems to move more quickly as the head passes through the bottom of the trajectory.

It is important to note that there is no physical reason why imaged objects must pass through a trajectory during transformation—unlike actual objects, which cannot instantaneously change locations but rather must pass through a trajectory. However, the fact that image transformations are typically incremental is consistent with at least two other types of theories: One class posits that natural selection has shaped the brain so that mental processes "internalized" physical properties of the world, which allows one to model physical events in their absence. Thus, for example, internalization of physical laws governing the motion of objects is thought to constrain the way we image them. The other class of theories posits computational processes that allow one to shift through intermediate orientations more easily than to erase an initial image and in one step form a new image at a different orientation. It is possible that different mechanisms transform images in different circumstances, and that different theories account for the different mechanisms.

VI. MAINTAINING IMAGES

During perception, information in the visual buffer should not be retained for long periods of time, lest it be "smeared" with the new input that arises every time we move our head or eyes. Although this property is good for perception, it apparently has less salubrious consequences for imagery: Because the visual buffer does not retain patterns of activation for very long, one must continually re-activate the image in order to retain it. In fact, recent PET studies suggest that in some circumstances primary visual cortex can be more active during imagery than during perception.

One can improve one's ability to hold information in an image by organizing patterns into relatively few "chunks," thereby reducing the number of elements that need to be refreshed individually. Consider the following example: A group of college students were asked to listen to a set of directions, such as "north-west, south, east . . .,'' and to imagine a 1-in. line segment for each direction, laying segments end to end, building up a path. When later asked to recall the sequence of directions, over 90% of the subjects who recalled the entire sequence had noticed that the segments depicted four repeating shapes. These subjects used these shapes to aid retention, apparently refreshing each as a unit. The people who did not notice these units tried to retain individual line segments, and recalled far fewer of them. [See Chunking.]

VII. INDIVIDUAL DIFFERENCES

In the early days of imagery research, various measures of imagery ability were created. These measures were not strongly correlated, and eventually it became clear that imagery ability is not a single entity. Indeed, most imagery processes are independent: A measure of the efficiency of one process is not good a predictor of measures of the efficiency of other processes. Because mental imagery relies upon various processes, imagery ability as revealed by one task, requiring use of one set of processes, need not bear on how well a person can perform a second task, which requires use of different processes. For example, some people may be quite good at generating images but not at rotating them, others may be good at inspecting objects in images but not at maintaining them, and so on.

VIII. CONCLUSIONS AND FUTURE PROSPECTS

Visual mental imagery, like other cognitive abilities, is not accomplished by a single process. Rather, it is the product of a host of distinct processes. The fact that imagery shares mechanisms with like-modality perception has helped researchers to discover the nature of these processes, and will continue to do so. As our knowledge of the mechanisms underlying visual perception improves, so too will the hypotheses about the nature of imagery. We expect that these hypotheses will become increasingly neuropsychological, and techniques such as PET scanning will play an invaluable role in testing them.

Bibliography

Farah, M. H. (1988). Is visual imagery really visual? Overlooked evidence from neuropsychology. *Psychol. Rev.* **95**, 30–37.
Finke, R. A. (1989). ''Principles of Mental Imagery.'' MIT Press, Cambridge, MA.
Kosslyn, S. M. (1994). ''Image and Brain: The Resolution of the Imagery Debate.'' MIT Press, Cambridge, MA.
Kosslyn, S. M., and Koenig, O. (1992). ''Wet Mind: The New Cognitive Neuroscience.'' Free Press, New York.
Paivio, A. (1971). ''Imagery and Verbal Processes.'' Holt, Rinehart and Winston, New York.
Paivio, A. (1986). ''Mental Representations.'' Oxford University Press, New York.
Shepard, R. N., and Cooper, L. A. (1982). ''Mental Images and Their Transformations.'' MIT Press, Cambridge.

MENTAL RETARDATION

Robert M. Hodapp

University of California, Los Angeles

Glossary

Adaptive behavior Everyday behaviors required for personal and social sufficiency.

Double ABCX model Model used to understand the retarded child as a stressor in the family system.

Down syndrome and fragile X syndrome The two most common genetic disorders of mental retardation; each shows unique genetic, physical, behavioral, and developmental features.

Normalization Movement to make as normal as possible the lives of retarded persons; sometimes extended to service delivery.

Similar sequence hypothesis Prediction that retarded children will develop in order along Piagetian and other universal sequences of development.

Similar structure hypothesis Prediction that, when matched on overall mental age, retarded children will perform equal to nonretarded children on cognitive or linguistic tasks.

Two-group approach Classificatory scheme that separates retarded population into those who do and do not show clear organic cause for their mental retardation.

MENTAL RETARDATION refers to the population of individuals with significantly subaverage levels of intelligence, deficits in adaptive behavior, and onset during the childhood years. Prevalence is between 1 and 3% of the general population. Individu-

als with mental retardation can be differentiated by level of impairment or by etiology and can be examined using developmental, behaviorist, sociological, information-processing, or biomedical perspectives. Schooling and living arrangements have changed greatly over the past several decades.

I. ISSUES OF DEFINITION AND PREVALENCE

Mental retardation has received widespread attention over many centuries. For most of this time, an ambivalent attitude has persisted toward persons with retardation. On one hand, these individuals have been considered innocent, unpretentious, clear-sighted, or even blessed by God (the French expression *"les enfants du bon Dieu"*). At the same time, there has been a widespread fear of retarded persons, with Luther and others condemning such individuals.

Some of this ambivalence is due to the confusion of mental retardation with mental illness. Only in the late 18th century did John Locke emphasize the distinction between mental retardation and mental illness, noting that "Herein seems to lie the difference between idiots and madmen, that madmen put wrong ideas together and reason from them, but idiots make very few propositions and reason scarce at all." Even today, one can find articles and news reports that interchangeably use the terms mental illness and mental retardation.

With the growth of scientific psychology over the past 100 years, more objective definitions of mental retardation are now possible. Both the American Association on Mental Retardation (AAMR) and the American Psychiatric Association currently employ a three-factor definition of mental retardation. According to these groups, "mental retardation refers to significantly subaverage intellectual functioning resulting in or associated with impairments in adaptive behavior and manifested during the developmental period."

This definition has three criteria. First, persons with mental retardation must show significantly *subaverage intellectual functioning*. Although the cutoff score for mental retardation has changed over the years, subaverage intellectual functioning is currently defined as an IQ score below 70 on standardized psychometric instruments such as the Stanford-Binet or Wechsler-based IQ tests. [*See* INTELLIGENCE.]

The second factor involves *impairments in adaptive behavior*. Adaptive behavior has not always been easy to measure, but the term refers to communicating with others, performing activities of daily living, and being socialized to follow rules and get along with others. At present, the criteria for adaptive deficits are somewhat vague (including clinical judgment), but with new tests such as the Vineland Adaptive Behavior Scales and the AAMR's Adaptive Behavior Scale, we are increasingly able to accurately assess this construct.

The third criterion of mental retardation involves an onset of problems *during the childhood years*. This criterion is less discussed than IQ or social adaptation, but excludes from the retarded population individuals whose disabilities are caused by Alzheimer's disease or head trauma occurring in adulthood.

Although this three-factor definition has generally been accepted, some workers have questioned one or more of these components. The vicissitudes of IQ tests—particularly for minority groups—have received most notice, yet there continues to be no better way than IQ to measure intellectual abilities. Social adaptation also receives criticism, particularly in that social adaptation is equally weighted to intellectual impairment in the current definition.

These definitional issues also affect prevalence rates, or how many persons are diagnosed as having mental retardation. The issue has generally been referred to as the "3% versus 1%" debate, with the more standard view being that about 3% of the general population has mental retardation. This 3% figure is derived by adding those persons (about 2.25%) who are two or more standard deviations below the mean of the normal distribution of intelligence to some "extra" persons who will be discussed below.

The 3% position does, however, involve several questionable assumptions. For example, the 3% figure assumes either that a subaverage IQ is the sole criterion of mental retardation or that IQ and social adaptation are equal and perfectly correlated. Unfortunately, the exact relationship between IQ and social adaptation is difficult to determine. At more severe levels of impairment, the two seem highly correlated: for example, most persons who are extremely impaired intellectually also cannot dress, toilet, or feed themselves independently. Yet at lesser degrees of impairment the relationship varies widely. Some individuals with IQs in the 50 to 70 range live independently, hold jobs, marry, and their status as retarded persons may be little known. Others with the same degree of intellectual impairment are more dependent in living, school, or work settings.

Another questionable assumption of the 3% figure is that equal percentages of persons will be diagnosed as having mental retardation throughout the lifespan. Even if approximately 3% of persons are diagnosed as mentally retarded at any one age, the overall prevalence rate will be lower if rates are lower at other ages. Prevalence rates do indeed vary across ages, with the highest prevalence rates of mental retardation occurring from approximately 6 to 16 years, or the period of formal schooling. Schools place the highest intellectual demands on children, clarifying (and testing) when a child is significantly behind intellectually compared to same-aged peers.

Before the school years, only the most severely impaired children are diagnosed. Approximately 0.4% of children have IQs below 50, with most of these children diagnosed in the preschool years. Similarly, children with clearly identified conditions (e.g., Down syndrome) are also diagnosed during this period. In contrast, many children with lesser degrees of impairment or those without clear organic causes for their mental retardation are not identified early on; only during the school years do many of these children receive the diagnosis of mental retardation.

Just as less impaired children are not diagnosed before the school years, so too are many children no longer diagnosed during the postschool years (a phenomenon called "decertification"). For example, even despite a growth in the number of technological jobs in recent years, many retarded persons with lesser degrees of intellectual impairment can still adequately perform many unskilled and semi-skilled jobs. Particularly from approximately IQ 50 upward, postschool adjustment is determined not by IQ per se, but instead by the ability to hold a job, to not be depressed, and to get along with others.

A final factor lowering prevalence from the 3% estimate is differential death rates. On average, persons with mental retardation do not live as long as nonretarded persons and certain etiologies of mental retardation are much more prone to health-related symptoms. Examples include the frequent heart defects and respiratory problems found in Down syndrome and the extreme obesity of Prader-Willi syndrome. While mortality rates have gradually improved, individuals of several etiologies usually do not live beyond their 50s or 60s. Even more at-risk for early deaths are those persons with the most profound and multiple impairments; persons who are nonambulatory and extremely impaired intellectually often do not live past their late teens or early 20s.

What then is the prevalence of mental retardation? Given the inaccuracy of several assumptions underlying the 3% figure, the prevalence rate must be below 3%, although a 1% prevalence rate seems too low. A rate somewhere in the 2% range seems likely. Whatever the true prevalence rate, the 3% versus 1% debate shows many of the complex issues in the field of mental retardation.

II. DIFFERENTIATING INDIVIDUALS WITH MENTAL RETARDATION

In discussing the definition and prevalence of mental retardation, it becomes obvious that all retarded persons are not alike. Some individuals with retardation live independent or relatively independent lives, blending in with the nonretarded population. Conversely, others require intensive care over many years. Issues of both level of impairment and of the exact cause of the person's mental retardation have been briefly touched on to explain these differences, but these now receive more in-depth attention.

The most common system of differentiation involves level of intellectual impairment (neither social adaptation nor age of onset has historically played a role in the differentiation process). The following is the general format of such differentiation by level of impairment:

Mild mental retardation—IQs from 55 to 69. Individuals with mild mental retardation form the largest subgroup among the retarded population. These individuals are often not diagnosed until the school years and are often "decertified" in adulthood. Adaptive functioning varies widely, with some persons requiring supervised school, living, or work

arrangements, others functioning totally independently in each of these settings.

Moderate mental retardation—IQs from 40 to 54. These individuals comprise the second largest group of persons with mental retardation. Although some individuals with moderate mental retardation live independently, most require at least some degree of supervision in school, work, or living settings. In contrast to those with mild mental retardation—many of whom show no clear cause for their retardation—many persons in the moderate range show retardation due to a particular organic etiology.

Severe mental retardation—IQs from 25 to 39. Although severely retarded individuals often achieve the basic, everyday self-help and communication skills, most require some help and supervision throughout life. As adults, many of these individuals do well in group home settings, although some continue to live in larger facilities. Workshop and other supervised work settings are also within the capabilities of many persons with severe mental retardation. The majority of severely retarded individuals show one or more clear organic causes for their mental retardation.

Profound mental retardation—IQs below 20 to 25. These persons are the most impaired intellectually and adaptively; in addition, physical deformities and health problems often accompany their intellectual impairments. Although advances have been made in teaching self-help skills to individuals with profound mental retardation, most require life-long care and supervision.

This grouping of mild, moderate, severe, and profound levels of retardation is the most widely used system of classification within the mental retardation field. It tells the interventionist or researcher approximately how intellectually impaired the individual is; but particularly at the higher levels of retardation, the classification scheme is only slightly predictive of any individual's adaptive functioning or potential.

Classifying by level of impairment also does not consider the cause of the individual's mental retardation. Partly in response to this lack of attention to etiology and partly to an overabundance of persons with severe and profound mental retardation than predicted by the normal or Gaussian distribution, researchers from the 1930s on have postulated what has been called the "two-group approach" to mental retardation. This approach notes that there are two types of persons with mental retardation, those who show no evidence of organicity (and form the lower tail of the normal distribution of intelligence), and those who do show a clear organic cause for their mental retardation, forming an extra "bump" in the curve somewhere in the severely retarded range of IQ.

The first group—those without clear organic cause—comprise somewhat over half of the retarded population and are referred to by a variety of names: familial mental retardation; cultural–familial mental retardation; sociocultural familial mental retardation; mental retardation due to environmental deprivation; nonspecific mental retardation; even "garden variety" mental retardation. As this listing of terms indicates, we do not understand why persons in this group are mentally retarded. These individuals may have received a poor polygenetic "draw" for intelligence from their parents, be environmentally deprived, or have some combination of polygenetic and environmental factors causing their lower levels of intelligence. Whatever the cause of this type of mental retardation, most individuals with familial mental retardation are mildly retarded (some are moderately retarded), many have family members who are retarded or have lower IQs, and many come from impoverished environments. In physical features and in behavior, familial retarded persons are not qualitatively different from individuals whose IQs are in the nonretarded range of intelligence.

A second group comprises those individuals who do show a clear organic cause for their mental retardation. This cause may be prenatal, perinatal, or postnatal in origin. Prenatal causes include all of the genetic disorders, thalidomide, and accidents *in utero*. Perinatal causes include prematurity, anoxia, and other birth-related disorders, whereas postnatal causes include diseases such as meningitis and childhood accidents causing head trauma. IQ levels of persons with organic mental retardation vary widely, but organically retarded persons predominate at the severe and profound levels of mental retardation. Pre-, peri-, and postnatal causes now number approximately 300, with new genetic disorders discovered at the rate of 5–10 per year.

Although there are many types of organic mental retardation, two disorders—Down syndrome and fragile X syndrome—deserve special mention. These disorders illustrate mental retardation's most recent biological and behavioral advances.

A. Down Syndrome

First identified as a clinical entity in the late 1860s by Langdon Down, Down syndrome is the most common genetic form of mental retardation, with a prevalence rate of approximately 1.2 per every 1000 live births. Mothers who are older are at greater risk of having Down syndrome babies, and for this reason amniocentisis is routinely performed on expectant mothers over the age of 30 to 35 years. In the large majority of cases, Down syndrome is caused by trisomy 21, a genetic anomaly such that there are three chromosomes instead of two at the 21st pair.

As the original name for the syndrome—mongolism—suggests, persons with Down syndrome have facial features that include epicanthal folds around the eyes, giving them an oriental appearance. Other physical features include short, stubby fingers, a "blocky" body-build, and a thick tongue that often contributes to articulation difficulties. Congenital heart defects are also common, although these defects are now correctable through surgery. There is also a long-suspected relationship between Down syndrome and Alzheimer's disease, with Down syndrome adults showing Alzheimer's (upon autopsy) in the young adult and middle-age years. But none of these physical features and problems occurs in every person with Down syndrome, and those that occur vary in prominence at different chronological ages.

Although the severity of impairment in Down syndrome varies widely, IQ levels of approximately 50–55 are common. Particularly during the infancy years, those children with Down syndrome who are most hypotonic—that is, those who have the weakest muscle tone—are the most impaired intellectually. Also during these early years, abilities in several areas appear to be highly correlated; thus, the Down syndrome child at a particular level of symbolic play has a corresponding level of linguistic and cognitive development.

But whatever the child's IQ during the early years, this level usually declines with increasing chronological age. Before 12 months of age, many children who will eventually become severely or profoundly retarded progress at normal or near-normal rates, but development slows over time. This slowing seems caused both by task-related and age-related factors. Early on, these children have task-related difficulties accomplishing many of the qualitative "leaps" of development required in various Piagetian sensorimotor and grammatical stages. Later, especially between the ages of 6 and 11 years, age-related plateaus occur. During this later period many (not all) Down syndrome children temporarily slow in their development of grammar, intelligence, and adaptive behavior. This mixture of task-related and age-related slowing combines to produce increasingly lower levels of IQ as these children get older.

Etiology-specific strengths and weaknesses also occur in this syndrome. Compared to other abilities, Down syndrome children are good at pragmatics, or the uses of language. They take their turns appropriately in conversations and are able to maintain a conversational topic. These children also appear to have increased abilities in receptive as opposed to expressive language skills. Their major weaknesses include articulation and linguistic grammar. Indeed, weaknesses in grammar along with difficulties in counting, adding, and other early mathematical abilities have led several researchers to suggest that the manipulation of symbols (linguistic, mathematical, or other) is a particular problem for individuals with this syndrome.

B. Fragile X Syndrome

In contrast to the long history of Down syndrome, fragile X syndrome is a recently discovered type of mental retardation. Reports suggesting X-linked mental retardation date from the 1940s on, but it was not until the late 1960s that Herbert Lubs identified a "fragile site" (a thin, threadlike segment) on the X-chromosome of affected males. Lubs' discovery could not be replicated until the mid-1970s, when researchers realized that the fragile site only appears when chromosomal analyses are performed using a medium that lacks folate.

Since the mid-1970s, fragile X syndrome has attracted widespread attention due to its prevalence and its interesting genetics. Fragile X syndrome is the second most common genetic and most common hereditary form of mental retardation (as Down syndrome is rarely passed from generation to generation). The prevalence rate is approximately 0.73 to 0.93 per 1000 live births. As a sex-linked disorder on the X-chromosome, boys are most often affected, with fragile X syndrome accounting for 2 to 5% of all retarded males (partly accounting for the overabundance of males as opposed to females with mental retardation). As a syndrome that runs in families, fragile X syndrome also decreases the number of individuals formerly thought to have familial or nonspecific mental retardation.

The genetics of fragile X have been described as "peculiar" or "bizarre." In most X-linked disorders such as color-blindness or hemophilia, females are carriers who pass the disorder on to their sons, but they themselves are not affected. In fragile X, however, approximately one-third of carrier females

show either mental retardation or learning disabilities. Conversely, there are occasional reports of males who show the fragile site for fragile X syndrome, but who do not appear to have mental retardation or learning problems. Whether such "nonpenetrant males" are indeed unaffected remains unclear, but the genetics of fragile X syndrome will surely receive increased study in future years.

As in Down syndrome, there is also a particular physical phenotype in fragile X syndrome. Males with this disorder generally have long, thin faces and big ears. After puberty, these males also have large testes. Height and weight are increased during the prepubertal years, but decreased relative to same-aged peers in adolescence and adulthood. There is also an avoidance of eye contact by many fragile X males.

In addition to these physical features, certain behavioral features characterize the syndrome. Males with fragile X syndrome are mildly retarded or of borderline intelligence (IQs from 70 to 85) during the early childhood years, but are often severely and profoundly retarded as adults. Unlike Down syndrome, however, the declines in IQ appear at later ages, approximately from the age of 10 to 15 years. Controversy continues about why males with fragile X syndrome slow in development during this period, but developmental plateaus may be tied to neurobiological changes related to puberty. Such slowing or even stopping occurs in the development of both intellectual and adaptive skills, and affects most boys with the disorder.

Etiology-specific strengths and weaknesses are also present in fragile X syndrome. Males with the disorder show extreme deficits in sequential processing, or the ability to remember and recall items presented in temporal or serial order. These children thus have difficulties in digit-span tasks or on tasks requiring the replication of a series of hand movements in the order presented by the experimenter. Other abilities, such as tasks requiring simultaneous (i.e., holistic) processing and achievement are less difficult for these individuals. The deficits in sequential processing also become more pronounced as these children reach their adolescent and early adult years. As opposed to children with Down syndrome, pragmatic abilities of fragile X males may be both delayed and deviant, featuring repetition and perseveration of words, phrases, or topics. In adaptive behavior, strengths are evident in daily living skills relative to abilities in communication and socialization.

Fragile X males also seem prone to certain types of psychopathology. Up to three-fourths of these children have hyperactivity and attentional problems, which may be related to their sequential deficits. Some have also suggested a connection between fragile X syndrome and autism; others feel that these children are socially avoidant, but not autistic. The relationship of hyperactivity and autism to fragile X syndrome continues to be debated.

III. DEVELOPMENTAL APPROACH TO MENTAL RETARDATION

In discussing the levels of impairment and etiology-based differentiation of mental retardation, we are reminded that mental retardation is a population of people that is open to a variety of perspectives. In the pages below, one of these perspectives, the developmental approach, is described at length. Other approaches will then be briefly outlined before a final discussion of educational and residential issues affecting persons with mental retardation.

A. Overview of Developmental Approach

In its most general sense, the developmental approach to mental retardation applies the theories, findings, and approaches used in normal development to understand and intervene with children with mental retardation. This approach has its beginnings over 50 years ago, when the most famous names in developmental psychology—Heinz Werner, Jean Piaget, and Lev Vygotsky—first attempted to apply their theories of development to children with mental retardation.

But a more formal developmental approach to mental retardation only came about in the work of Edward Zigler in the late 1960s. At that time, Zigler hypothesized that retarded children progress through the same sequences of development (in the same order) as do nonretarded children and that, when matched on overall level of cognitive functioning, these children would perform equally on cognitive or linguistic tasks to nonretarded children. Zigler also emphasized a series of personality–motivational factors affecting functioning in persons with mental retardation. [See COGNITIVE DEVELOPMENT.]

In much of this work, the developmental approach was limited to familial retarded children and to those aspects of development (e.g., sequences and stages) that concerned the development of the individual child. Since that time, various workers have attempted to extend developmental analyses to Down syndrome, fragile X syndrome, and other organically impaired groups; at the same time, these workers have attempted to broaden their focus to include mother–child interaction, families, and the environments in which children develop. The review below examines sequences and structures in both familial and organically retarded groups, then continues with issues of mother–child interaction and families for all children with mental retardation.

B. Similar Sequence Hypothesis

Central to virtually every developmental approach is the idea of sequences, that nonretarded children progress in invariant order through a series of developments. Sequential development may be due to biological tendencies in human development, to logic (later-occurring behaviors often combine two or more earlier behaviors), or to certain universally present environments, but the sequential development of nonretarded children is the hallmark of development in most developmental theories.

In the developmental approach to mental retardation, the prediction is that children with mental retardation will also progress through developmental sequences in the same invariant order. This prediction has been borne out in a variety of cross-sectional and longitudinal studies of many different Piagetian and other developmental progressions. In addition, the prediction of sequential development holds for children with both familial and organic mental retardation. The few exceptions occur in children with extreme seizure disorders (where accurate testing is difficult) and in certain social and social-cognitive developments in autism. Apart from these rare exceptions, all retarded children, of whatever etiology, seem to progress along the same course of development as seen in nonretarded children.

The importance of sequential development in retarded groups cannot be overemphasized. Given that children with mental retardation proceed in order along the same sequences as shown by nonretarded children, various assessment and intervention programs based on normal sequences of development have now been developed. Particularly in the areas of sensorimotor cognitive and early language development, such interventions appear useful for a variety of retarded children.

C. Similar Structure Hypothesis and Cross-Domain Relations

The similar structure hypothesis is the prediction that, when matched on overall level of intellectual functioning (i.e., mental age, or MA), retarded and nonretarded children will perform equally on any cognitive or linguistic task. In the original developmental approach, this hypothesis had two sources: the idea that familial retarded children did not suffer from attentional, linguistic, or other "defects" causing their mental retardation; and the stage notion of flat or horizontally organized development from one domain to another.

To date, the similar structure hypothesis has held up reasonably well for children with familial mental retardation, not so well for children with organic mental retardation. For all of the many Piagetian tasks, familial retarded children have performed equally to MA-matched nonretarded children. Some information-processing tasks are questionable in this regard, with familial retarded children sometimes performing less well than nonretarded children. In contrast to familial retarded children, virtually all groups of children with organic mental retardation perform below MA-matched nonretarded children on Piagetian and other cognitive or linguistic tasks.

Although studies continue on the original similar structure hypothesis, there is a movement away from the idea of perfect horizontal organization across domains for either retarded or nonretarded children. But there may still be certain, more limited types of interdomain organization. For example, different behaviors that rely on the same underlying concept develop at or around the same time (these are called "local homologies"). The infant's ability to uncover an object hidden under a cloth (sensorimotor Stage IV object permanence), to cry when the mother leaves the room, and to uncover the mother and laugh in a peek-a-boo game all appear to develop near the same ages—all imply a knowledge that objects continue to exist when out of sight. In addition, there may be limits to how far advanced an individual's strengths can be relative to overall functioning, or how far below overall functioning one's weaknesses can be. Both local homologies and limits provide a more complex sense to the organization of development from one domain to another.

For the most part, children with mental retardation—both familial and organic—show these more complicated senses of interdomain organization. Behaviors reflecting the same underlying mental scheme do appear at approximately the same ages, just as there are limits to strengths and weaknesses in retarded as well as nonretarded children.

There are, however, a few exceptions that deserve notice. A select few individuals with severe–profound mental retardation (who are often autistic) show what have been called savant behaviors, or extremely high-level behaviors in circumscribed areas (e.g., memory for dates; understanding of prime numbers). Equally interesting is new work on Williams syndrome, a rare, presumably genetic, disorder. In this disorder, children demonstrate very high levels of grammatical, vocabulary, and narrative abilities in the absence of corresponding levels of intelligence. In essence, behavior in Williams syndrome provides developmental researchers a case of "language in the (relative) absence of thought." Behaviors of both savants and Williams syndrome children challenge current ideas about cross-domain organization.

D. Mother–Child Interactions

Beginning in the 1970s, developmental psychology began to examine not only the child's development but also changes over time in the environments in which those children develop. Much of this work was inspired by Richard Bell's concept of "interaction," the idea that children and parents mutually affect one another. This sense of interaction, combined with more recent studies of how adults promote the child's development and about the perceptions of both children and adults, has led to much work on caretaker (usually mother)–child interaction in nonretarded child–mother pairs. More recently, this interest has spread to the nature of interactions between mothers and their children with mental retardation.

Across many studies, interactions between mothers and their retarded children are "the same but different" compared to mother–nonretarded child pairs. Compared to mothers of nonretarded children at the same level of development, mothers of retarded children act much the same in the basic structure of their interactions. These mothers shorten their speech to their children, emphasize and repeat the key words, and in other ways provide the "motherese" common in mother–nonretarded child interactions. Yet at the same time, mothers of retarded children differ stylistically from mothers of nonretarded children. These mothers are much more didactic, more intrusive, and more directive than are mothers of nonretarded children.

Differences in style but not structure may have several explanations. Mothers of retarded children must "mourn"—as in a death—the loss of the idealized normal child, and the emotional reaction of mourning may lead to a different maternal style of interaction. Related to maternal emotional reactions are the very realistic concerns these mothers have about the development of their children. Mothers of Down syndrome and other retarded children may rarely "just play" with their infants; issues of teaching, learning, and intervention may always be present. Conversely, some children with retardation might require a more intrusive maternal style; the problems with muscle tone and the relationship between increased hypotonia and lower IQ in young Down syndrome children here come to mind. We do not as yet know why mothers of retarded children are the same in structure but different in the style of their interactions, nor do we know which styles of interaction best promote development in children with different types of mental retardation.

E. Families of Children with Mental Retardation

Related to mother–child interaction is the issue of families. Although families of retarded children have been studied for many years, a renewed interest has recently occurred due to developmental psychology's expansion to include the environments or ecologies of child development.

To summarize this work, raising a retarded child has profound effects on mothers, fathers, siblings, and the family as a whole, but the effects vary widely from family to family. Considering siblings as an example, some siblings as adults feel that they have benefitted greatly from growing up with a retarded sibling: these children feel more empathic and tolerant of human differences. Other siblings feel angry, citing a lack of attention and affection from parents who were preoccupied with caring for the child with handicaps. Similar effects are found for couples: whereas divorce rates may be higher in families with handicapped members, many couples note that raising a retarded child has brought them closer together.

These different outcomes relate to characteristics of the child and to the family's internal and external resources. For example, mothers feel less stress when children are younger, less impaired, have fewer associated physical or medical disabilities, and have clearly diagnosed syndromes (as opposed to nonspecific mental retardation). Families with two parents (especially those in good marriages), more money, and more external supports (extended family, friends) do better than do families who are less well-off in each of these areas.

These findings relate to earlier work in other fields on the effects of stress. According to this perspec-

tive, the retarded child can be considered a stressor on the family system, a stressor that may produce either good or bad effects. The so-called Double ABCX model is one example of a recent stress-coping model used to conceptualize functioning in families with a retarded member. According to this model, the initial crisis (X) is dependent on the specific characteristics of the retarded child (the "stressor event," or A), mediated by the family's internal and external resources (B) and by the family's perceptions of the child (C). But as the child develops, new stressors (A'), resources (B'), and perceptions (C') arise and change over time. [*See* STRESS.]

While general, this Double ABCX model has recently served to tell us much about the effects of the retarded child on the family. It explains why both good and bad effects occur and why some families that cope well at one time have difficulties later on. The model also begins to identify families and individual family members that might be at risk for problems. In addition, the Double ABCX model moves family research in mental retardation from the earlier, more psychopathology-based perspective to a view that focuses on stress and coping in these families. The model thus provides a more positive—albeit realistic—sense of raising a child with mental retardation.

IV. OTHER APROACHES TO MENTAL RETARDATION

A. Sociological Approach

Mental retardation can be considered a sociological phenomenon, a role that the individual plays in the society. Social roles may most apply to familial retarded individuals at mild or borderline levels of intellectual impairment. These individuals vary widely in adaptive functioning and are often only identified during the school years, not before or after. Some have even asserted that schools create a "6-hr retarded child," a child who is labeled (and acts) retarded only during the school day. The extreme form of this social roles–labeling argument is that "mental retardation exists only to the extent that some people persist in calling other people retarded."

Consistent with role theory is the phenomenon of "passing," or attempting to hide one's status as a retarded person. Several studies have documented that many mildly retarded individuals go to great lengths to hide their retardation and histories of living in institutions.

Besides studies of how retarded persons avoid the retarded role, research has also begun on the roles that are played by retarded persons. Each of us assumes a variety of roles in everyday life: we are simultaneously spouse, offspring, sibling, employee, supervisor, churchgoer, commuter, sports fan, jogger, political party member, etc. Participation in these many roles provides diverse emotional outlets. But retarded persons—even those living in the community—may not partake in as many social roles, and their lives may be impoverished as a result.

B. Behaviorist Approach

The behaviorist or functional approach has long focused on intervention with retarded individuals. Such intervention has centered on the three areas of teaching adaptive behavior, eliminating maladaptive behavior, and teaching parents of retarded persons how to manage their children's behavior.

Behaviorist techniques have been extremely successful in teaching the most severely and profoundly retarded individuals to perform everyday self-help behaviors. Through careful and closely followed regimens of rewards, shaping, and chaining, interventionists have been able to teach retarded persons to brush their teeth, to be toilet trained, to eat using utensils, and to bathe, groom, and dress themselves. Vocational skills have also been successfully taught using behavior modification techniques. [See OPERANT LEARNING.]

Behaviorists have also had great success in eliminating maladaptive behaviors. Again through the careful application of behavior modification principles, interventionists have been able to eliminate head banging, biting, and assaultive behavior. The role of aversives has here received wide attention, with experts divided on their usefulness and humaneness. Overall, though, behaviorists have in a humane way been successful in controlling maladaptive behaviors that had previously been considered intractable.

A final area of behaviorist interventions involves teaching parents the techniques of behavior management. One of the hardest issues for many parents is how to handle difficult-to-manage retarded children, and problems become more difficult as the child gets older. This work transfers the techniques used by behaviorally oriented interventionists; parents themselves become the interventionists who help their retarded children to acquire adaptive behaviors and to eliminate maladaptive behaviors.

C. Information-Processing Approaches

If behaviorist approaches have been most successful with those retarded persons who are most severely and profoundly affected, information-processing strategies have been most successful with more mildly impaired individuals. This approach features identifying the nature of a particular problem, breaking the problem down into its component parts, developing and following a particular plan of problem-solving, examining the success of this plan (feedback), and modifying one's strategies until appropriate solutions emerge.

In information-processing interventions, retarded persons are explicitly taught such principles. The retarded person must then approach a given problem with this problem-solving strategy, often explicitly verbalizing each component. Success is measured by the degree to which retarded persons solve problems before and after being taught these problem-solving strategies.

To date, interventions based on these models have been tried with mildly retarded persons and persons at borderline levels of intelligence. Although several interventions have claimed remarkable successes, further work is needed.

D. Biomedical Approaches

In contrast to other perspectives, the biomedical approach incorporates work from medicine, psychiatry and child psychiatry, neuropsychology, genetics, and clinical psychology. The approach has several emphases, including the issue of dual diagnosis and drug treatments, brain–behavior relationships, and genetics.

Although mental retardation's recent history began with the distinction between mental retardation and mental illness, the two can co-occur to produce a "dually diagnosed" retarded person. To date, most studies have shown that retarded persons are particularly prone to psychoses and to acting out behaviors. Prevalence rates of depression in retarded groups have often been shown to be lower than rates in nonretarded samples, but higher and equal rates have sometimes been noted. Confusion exists partly because depression in retarded persons may be masked by other symptoms, partly because retarded persons often have difficulty in providing self-reports of their symptoms and feelings. It is also possible that, to many service professionals, mental retardation "overshadows" depression (thereby sometimes leading to lower prevalence rates of depression in retarded populations). [*See* DEPRESSION.]

Given that many retarded persons suffer from emotional disorders, various therapies have been attempted. Several decades ago, little effort was made to provide psychotherapy to retarded persons, who were thought to lack psychological insight. Currently, however, a variety of treatment modalities are used to help retarded persons with emotional disorders. These treatments run the gamut from ecological and educational interventions, to behavioral approaches, to individual, family, and group psychotherapy, to psychopharmacological approaches (e.g., psychotropics, antidepressants). Future years promise a clearer specification of the relationship between etiology of mental retardation and psychopathology, as several etiological groups seem especially prone to specific pathologies (e.g., hyperactivity, possibly autism, in fragile X syndrome). [*See* PSYCHOTHERAPY.]

The relationship of brain and behavior is another topic within biomedical approaches. Recent studies suggest impaired functioning of the prefrontal cortex as the possible underlying mechanism for the sequential processing deficits in fragile X syndrome, and other disorders are also receiving attention. Most links between neurology and behavior remain speculative, but the area is receiving increased attention.

A final topic within the biomedical perspective involves genetics. The peculiar genetics of fragile X syndrome are discussed above, but other syndromes have also received attention. Most notable here is the relationship between Prader-Willi syndrome and Angelman's syndrome. Prader-Willi syndrome is a disorder involving mild mental retardation, short stature, and extreme obesity, whereas Angelman's Syndrome involves severe and profound mental retardation and no food or obesity problems. But recent findings show that both disorders arise from defective genetic material on the same portion of the 15th chromosome. When the defective genetic material comes from the father, the child has Prader-Willi syndrome; when the defective material comes from the mother, the child has Angelman's. As a rare case in which the nature and severity of the disorder seem determined by the particular parent

from whom the child receives the defective gene(s), Prader-Willi and Angelman's are changing our views of the relationship between genetic characteristics and resultant handicapping conditions.

V. EDUCATIONAL AND RESIDENTIAL ISSUES IN MENTAL RETARDATION

In addition to the many issues relating to definition, prevalence, differentiation, and the various research approaches, mental retardation is also a social policy issue. Specifically, recent years have witnessed great changes in educational and living environments for individuals with mental retardation.

Many of these changes have occurred under the aegis of normalization. As originally described by Nirje and other Scandinavian workers, normalization is the idea that all retarded persons should enjoy a "normal" lifestyle within their culture: to go to work or school, to enjoy weekends and vacations, etc. Recently, normalization has subtly changed to emphasize service delivery. Group homes have been built and community living is common for the large majority of retarded individuals; those institutional facilities that remain have been made smaller and more humane. The number of special classes and schools is decreasing, with mainstream placement of retarded children alongside nonhandicapped children becoming the norm.

Many of these changes are obviously beneficial. In contrast to only 30 years ago, we now realize that even many severely and profoundly retarded individuals can live in group home or more community-based settings. Similarly, for many mildly retarded children, mainstreamed class placements are beneficial, especially if these children receive needed special services.

Still, concern has been expressed about some changes brought about by normalization. For instance, not all group homes are promoting living settings that truly integrate residents into the community and, for the most impaired and behaviorally disruptive individuals, larger facilities may always be needed (though these need not be as big or impersonal as the large institutions of the 1960s). There have also been occasional reports of abuses within group homes in certain areas.

In the same way, not all children benefit from placement in mainstreamed classrooms. Although in theory it may be possible to provide special services within regular classrooms, it is uncertain in practice how often these services are actually provided.

Some experts fear that mainstreaming may be becoming a cheap, expedient, "politically correct" way to avoid special education services (and costs) in the education of retarded children. If so, the field will need to modify a practice that can be beneficial to many children with mental retardation.

In both research and service delivery, then, the field of mental retardation has come a long way. Granted, we continue to disagree about many aspects of definition, prevalence, and differentiation. We also need to better understand the development of retarded children and their environments. Similarly, much of the work on sociological, behaviorist, information-processing, and biomedical approaches is just beginning, and residential and educational issues also persist. Still, across many areas and in the many professions dealing with the population of mentally retarded persons, great strides have already been made. Even greater advances are expected in the years to come.

Bibliography

Bregman, J. D. (1991). Current developments in the understanding of mental retardation. II. Psychopathology. *J. Am. Acad. Child Adolescent Psych.* **30,** 861–872.

Cicchetti, D., and Beeghly, M. (Eds.) (1990). "Children with Down Syndrome: A Developmental Approach." Cambridge University Press, New York.

Dykens, E. M., Hodapp, R. M. and Leckman, J. F. (1994). "Behavior and Development in Fragile X Syndrome." Sage, Newbury Park, CA.

Hodapp, R. M., Burack, J. A., and Zigler, E. (Eds.) (1990). "Issues in the Developmental Approach to Mental Retardation." Cambridge University Press, New York.

Krauss, M. W., Simeonsson, R., and Ramey, S. L. (Eds.) (1989). Special issues on research on families. *Am. J. Mental Retardation* **94** (3).

Luckasson, R. (Ed.) (1993). "Classification in Mental Retardation." American Association on Mental Retardation, Washington, DC.

Marfo, K. (Ed.) (1988). "Parent–Child Interaction and Developmental Disabilities." Praeger, New York.

Matson, J. L. (Ed.) (1990). "Handbook of Behavior Modification with the Mentally Retarded," 2nd ed. Plenum, New York.

Ross, R. T., Begab, M. J., Dondis, E. H., Giampiccolo, J. S., and Meyers, C. E. (1985). "Lives of the Retarded: A Forty-Year Follow-up Study." Stanford University Press, Stanford, CA.

Scheerenberger, R. C. (1987). "A History of Mental Retardation: A Quarter Century of Progress." Brookes, Baltimore.

Vitello, S. J., and Soskin, R. M. (1985). "Mental Retardation: Its Social and Legal Context." Prentice–Hall, Englewood Cliffs, NJ.

Zigler, E., and Hodapp, R. M. (1986). "Understanding Mental Retardation." Cambridge University Press, New York.

METACOGNITION

Thomas O. Nelson
University of Washington

Glossary

Ease-of-learning judgment A person's judgment of how easy or difficult the items will be to acquire.

Feeling-of-knowing judgment A person's prediction of whether he or she will eventually remember an answer that he or she currently does not recall.

Judgment of learning A person's evaluation of how well he or she has learned a given item.

Metacognition The scientific study of an individual's cognitions about his or her own cognitions.

Metamemory The monitoring and control of one's own memory.

Source information Information about when and where a person learned a given item.

METACOGNITION is defined as the scientific study of an individual's cognitions about his or her own cognitions. What makes it scientific is that the theories of metacognition attempt to account for empirical data about metacognition. The two broad subdivisions of metacognition are (1) metacognitive knowledge (what do people know about their own cognitions as based on their life history?) and (2) on-going metacognitive monitoring and control of one's own cognitions. The first of those subdivisions includes autobiographical facts such as "I learn things easier when I hear them than when I see them" or "I can solve problems better if I think about them in a distributed fashion rather than trying to solve them all at once." The second subdivision, which is currently a very exciting area of research in psychology, involves questions about the way in which people monitor their on-going cognitions and also the way in which people control their on-going cognitions. Thus, the notion of voluntary learn-

ing—in contrast to incidental learning—fits well within the domain of metacognition.

One of the most heavily researched areas of metacognition is the portion of metacognition pertaining to learning and memory. It is called *metamemory* and refers to the monitoring and control of one's own memory during the acquisition of new information and during the retrieval of previously acquired information. Metamemory has been investigated by psychologists for less than 40 years, prior to which the researchers conceptualized people as blank slates, and the way that acquisition was believed to occur was that the individual was assumed to be passive and to have little or no control over his or her own acquisition. Since the 1950s, researchers have conceptualized the individual as having substantial control over acquisition and as being active rather than passive, both during the acquisition of new information and during the retrieval of previously learned information. [*See* MEMORY.]

An example might help us become aware of some of the aspects of metamemory during acquisition and retrieval. Suppose that a student is studying for an examination that will occur tomorrow on French–English vocabulary such as *chateau–castle*. Imagine the monitoring and control processes that occur while the student learns the new vocabulary and while the student attempts to retrieve the answers during the subsequent examination. Some of those monitoring and control processes are discussed in the next section, and a theoretical framework that integrates all of these processes into an overall system can be found in an article by Nelson and Narens.

I. METACOGNITIVE MONITORING

Various kinds of monitoring processes are differentiated by when they occur during acquisition and retrieval, especially in terms of whether they pertain to the person's future performance (prospective monitoring) or the person's past performance (retrospective monitoring). These are discussed separately.

A. Prospective Monitoring

1. Ease-of-Learning Judgments

When someone is getting ready to learn new information, even prior to the beginning of acquisition some metacognitive monitoring occurs. An *ease-of-learning judgment* is the person's judgment of how easy or difficult the items will be to acquire. For instance, the person might believe that the overall set of items will take such-and-such amount of time to learn and that *chateau–castle* will be more difficult to learn than *boite–box*. In 1966, Underwood showed that people are somewhat accurate—not perfectly, but well above chance—at predicting which items would be easiest to learn. People's predictions of how easy it would be to learn each item, which were made in advance of acquisition, were moderately correlated with subsequent recall after a constant amount of study time on every item: The items people predicted would be easiest to learn had a greater subsequent likelihood of being recalled than items people predicted would be hardest to learn.

2. Judgments of Learning

The next kind of monitoring occurs during or soon after acquisition. The person's *judgment of learning* is the person's evaluation of how well he or she has learned a given item. It is a prediction of the likelihood that the item will be remembered correctly on a future test. In 1969, Arbuckle and Cuddy showed that the predictive accuracy of people's judgments of learning is above chance but far from perfect, similar to the situation for ease-of-learning judgments. Research by Leonesio and Nelson (1990) showed that judgments of learning are more accurate than ease-of-learning judgments for predicting eventual recall, probably because in contrast to ease-of-learning judgments, people's judgments of learning can be based on what the learner notices about how well he or she is mastering the items during acquisition. Most recently, Nelson and Dunlosky showed an especially interesting situation in which people's judgments of learning can be extremely accurate, if not perfectly accurate. This occurs when people make the judgment of learning not immediately after studying a given item but rather after a short delay; accordingly this is called the delayed-JOL effect

(where "JOL" stands for judgment of learning). Subsequent research by Dunlosky and Nelson showed that the delayed-JOL effect occurs if and only if the cue for the judgments is the stimulus alone rather than the stimulus–response pair (e.g., it occurs if the cue for the judgment about *chateau–castle* is *"chateau?"* but not if the cue is *"chateau–castle"*). This delayed-JOL effect is exciting because it shows that under the proper conditions, people can monitor their learning extremely accurately.

3. Feeling-of-Knowing Judgments

These are people's prediction of whether they will eventually remember an answer that they currently do not recall. This was the first metamemory judgment examined in the laboratory to assess whether it was accurate at predicting subsequent performance. In 1965, the pioneering researcher Joseph Hart found that feeling-of-knowing judgments were somewhat accurate at predicting subsequent memory performance. In particular, the likelihood of correctly recognizing a nonrecalled answer was higher for nonrecalled items people said were stored in memory than for nonrecalled items people said were not stored in memory. But people often did not recognize answers that they had claimed that they would recognize, and people sometimes did recognize answers that they had claimed they would not recognize; the latter is less critical than the former because the latter may be due to chance factors that always occur during recognition tests. Subsequently, the accuracy of predicting other kinds of memory performance such as relearning was investigated by Nelson *et al.* who also offered several theoretical explanations for how people might make their feeling-of-knowing judgments.

B. Retrospective Confidence Judgments

In contrast to the previous metamemory monitoring judgments, in which people attempted to predict their future memory performance, retrospective confidence judgments occur after someone recalls or recognizes an answer, either correctly or incorrectly. They are judgments of how confident the person is that his or her answer was correct. For instance, if someone were asked to recall the English equivalent of *chateau*, the person might say "castle" (the correct answer) or might say "red" (the incorrect answer), after which he or she would make a confidence judgment about the likelihood that the recalled answer was correct. Fischhoff *et al.* discovered that these retrospective confidence judgments had substantial accuracy, but there was a reliable and strong tendency for people to be overconfident, especially when the test was one of recognition. For instance, for the items that people had given a confidence judgment of "90% likely to be correct," the actual percentage of correct recognition was substantially below that.

C. Source Monitoring and Reality Monitoring

In addition to the aforementioned kinds of monitoring that pertain to a person's knowledge of a particular item, people also monitor information about when and where they learned a given item (called "source information"). People who are unable to remember the source of when and where the acquisition occurred are said to have source amnesia. One useful distinction in terms of the source of prior acquisition is whether the item occurred externally to the person (e.g., from someone else saying it to the person) or occurred internally in the person (e.g., in a dream). The ability to distinguish between those two possibilities for a given item is called reality monitoring and has been investigated by Johnson and Raye.

II. METACOGNITIVE CONTROL

The fact that people can monitor their progress during acquisition and retrieval is interesting, but it is little more than a curiosity if it has no other role in the overall memory system. Fortunately, people can also control aspects of their acquisition and retrieval. First, let us consider what people can control during self-paced acquisition and then consider what they can control during retrieval.

A. Control during Self-Paced Acquisition

1. Allocation of Self-Paced Study Time during Acquisition

Someone who is learning foreign-language vocabulary can choose to allocate various amounts of study time to each item and can allocate even more extra study time during subsequent study trials to some items. In 1978, the researchers Bisanz, Voss, and Vesonder found that the allocation of study time

may occur in conjunction with people's judgments of learning. Bisanz *et al.* discovered that learners in the early years of primary school make accurate judgments of learning but will not utilize those judgments when allocating additional study time across the items, whereas slightly older children will utilize those judgments when allocating additional study time. The older children allocated extra study time to items that they judged to have not yet learned and did not allocate extra study time to items that they judged to have learned. However, the younger children were not systematic in allocating extra study time primarily to the unlearned items.

2. Strategy Employed during Self-Paced Study

Not only can people control how much study time they allocate to various items, but they can also control which strategy they use during that study time. There usually are strategies that are more effective than rote repetition, but do people know what they are? People's utilization of a mnemonic strategy for the acquisition foreign-language vocabulary was investigated by Pressley *et al.* After people had learned some foreign-language vocabulary by rote and other foreign-language vocabulary by the mnemonic strategy, they were allowed a choice of using whichever strategy they wanted for a final trial of learning some additional foreign-language vocabulary. Only 12% of the adults chose the mnemonic strategy if they had not received any test trials during the earlier phase, whereas 87% of them chose the mnemonic strategy if they had received test trials during the earlier acquisition phase. Thus, test trials help people to realize the effectiveness of different strategies for acquisition. When the subjects were children instead of adults, then they not only needed test trials, but they also needed to have feedback after those test trials to tell them how well they had done on the rote-learned items versus the mnemonic-learned items; without both the test trials and the feedback, the children were unlikely to adopt the advantageous mnemonic strategy.

B. Control during Retrieval

1. Control of Initiating One's Retrieval

Immediately after someone is asked a question and before attempting to search memory for the answer, a metacognitive decision is made about whether the answer is likely to be found in memory. If you were asked what the telephone number is for your mailman, you probably would decide immediately that the answer is not in your memory. Notice that you do not need to search through all the telephone numbers that you know, nor do you need to search through all the information you have stored in your memory about your mailman. Therefore, you do not initiate protracted attempts to retrieve that answer. Consider how different that situation is from one in which you are asked the telephone number of one of your friends.

This initial feeling-of-knowing judgment that precedes an attempt to retrieve an answer was investigated by Reder. An especially interesting finding was that people are faster at making a feeling-of-knowing decision about whether they know the answer to a general-information question (e.g., "What is the capital of Finland?") than they are at answering that question (e.g., saying "Helsinki"). This demonstrates that the metacognitive decision is made prior to (rather than after) retrieving the answer. Only if people feel that they know the answer will they continue their attempts to retrieve the answer. When they feel they do not know the answer, they do not even attempt to search memory (as in the aforementioned example of your mailman).

2. Control of the Termination of Extended Attempts at Retrieval

People may initially believe that they know an answer and begin searching memory for the answer, but after extended attempts at retrieval without producing the answer, they eventually terminate searching for the answer. The metacognitive decision to terminate such an extended search of memory was investigated by Nelson *et al*. They found that the amount of time elapsing before someone gives up searching memory for a nonretrieved answer is greater when the person's on-going feeling of knowing for the answer is high rather than low.

As an example, someone might spend a long time during an examination attempting to retrieve the English equivalent of *chateau* (which the person studied the night before) but little or no time attempting to retrieve the English equivalent of *cheval* (which the person did not study previously). The megacognitive decision to continue versus terminate attempts at retrieving an answer from memory may of course also be affected by other factors, such as the total amount of time available during the examination.

Most of the research articles cited above have been reprinted (with discussion to tie them together and with additional articles for further reading) in a recent book by Nelson.

Bibliography

Dunlosky, J., and Nelson, T. O. (1992). Importance of the kind of cue for judgments of learning (JOL) and the delayed-JOL effect. *Memory Cog.* **20**, 374–380.

Fischhoff, B., Slovic, P., and Lichtenstein, S. (1977). Knowing with certainty: The appropriateness of extreme confidence. *J. Exp. Psychol. Hum. Percep. Perform.* **3**, 552–564.

Johnson, M. K., and Raye, C. L. (1981). Reality monitoring. *Psychol. Rev.* **88**, 67–85.

Leonesio, R. J., and Nelson, T. O. (1990). Do different measures of metamemory tap the same underlying aspects of memory? *J. Exp. Psychol. Learning, Memory, Cog.* **16**, 464–470.

Nelson, T. O., and Dunlosky, J. (1991). The delayed-JOL effect: When delaying your judgments of learning can improve the accuracy of your metacognitive monitoring. *Psychol. Sci.* **2**, 267–270.

Nelson, T. O. (1992). "Metacognition: Core Readings." Allyn & Bacon, Boston.

Nelson, T. O., Gerler, D., and Narens, L. (1984). Accuracy of feeling-of-knowing judgments for predicting perceptual identification and relearning. *J. Exp. Psychol. Gen.* **113**, 282–300.

Nelson, T. O., and Narens, L. (1990). Metamemory: A theoretical framework and new findings. In "The Psychology of Learning and Motivation" (G. H. Bower, Ed.), Academic Press, San Diego.

Pressley, M., Levin, J. R., and Ghatala, E. (1984). Memory strategy monitoring in adults and children. *J. Verbal Learning Verbal Behav.* **23**, 270–288.

Reder, L. M. (1987). Strategy selection in question answering. *Cog. Psychol.* **19**, 90–138.

MILITARY PSYCHOLOGY

Henry L. Taylor
University of Illinois at Urbana-Champaign

Earl A. Alluisi
Institute for Defense Analyses

Glossary

Classification The use of aptitude tests to determine which military personnel should be assigned to specific military occupations.

Cohesion Military unit solidarity.

Human resources engineering Consideration during weapon system design of the impact of human resources over the life cycle of the system.

Human-systems development The design of systems based on estimated requirements for personnel to operate and maintain the system and for training needed compared to the availability of personnel and training resources.

Morale The U.S. Army defines morale as the soldiers' mental, emotional, and spiritual condition; it is how the soldier feels.

Personnel subsystem Military personnel constitute a subsystem in the design, development, and use of weapon systems.

Selection Mental tests designed to indicate those individuals qualified to perform military service.

MILITARY PSYCHOLOGY is an applied area of psychology that focuses on the study and application of relevant psychological principles to military problems. The *practice* of military psychology involves research and development (R&D) and applications. The focus of this article is on the *experimental* aspects of military psychology and not on its clinical (medical or psychological treatment) aspects. Fol-

lowing a brief historical overview, the article addresses five areas, the first two in considerable detail, and the final three only briefly. The five areas are as follows: (a) selection, classification, and assignment; (b) human factors engineering and human performance research and development (R&D); (c) environmental factors and performance; (d) leadership and performance; and (e) individual and group behavior.

I. HISTORICAL OVERVIEW

A. World War I

In the United States, military psychology began during World War I. During 1917 and 1918, American military psychologists developed two group mental tests: (a) the *Army Alpha* for English-language literates, and (b) the *Army Beta* for English-language illiterates. These were the first tests widely used for the selection and classification of military personnel—i.e., used to help identify individuals who would be trainable for military jobs (and therefore qualified for military service), and to help determine the best training assignments for specific individuals.

These tests were administered to 1,726,966 men between 1917 and the end of the war in 1918, primarily in mental testing units organized by military psychologists for personnel classification in 35 Army training camps. Military psychologists also assisted in development battalions organized to determine if low-scoring individuals could be trained to contribute to the war effort. As a result of the special training, over half of the 230,000 men who received the special training were then qualified for military assignments.

In the personnel and training areas, in addition to their development of group mental tests for selection and classification, and to their contributions to training in the development battalions, military psychologists (a) provided useful psychological consultant services (such as interpreting the test scores and providing advice regarding their proper use in classification, assignment, and personnel matters), (b) served on recruit examining boards and disability boards, (c) constructed special examinations for selecting personnel for special assignments such as officers' training camps, and (d) developed guidelines for making final selections for commissions.

In their human performance work, they developed practical methods to demonstrate how the shooter's trigger squeeze and breathing contributed to the accuracy of rifle marksmanship, and from these studies, they developed rifle-firing practice techniques that improved accuracy.

As part of a committee on psychological problems of aviation, military psychologists selected a number of tests, and developed optimum weights for the separate test scores, to provide a practical method of predicting aptitude for learning to fly. When the test results were compared with the actual success of pilots in learning to fly, they were found to be valid. This appears to be the first widely applied test battery for selecting personnel for tasks requiring special aptitudes.

In other work, a general methodology was developed to use continuous tasks to investigate performance deficits due to altitude-related oxygen deprivation. It was suggested as early as 1918 that these methods could be used to study problems of the effects of drugs and of fatigue on human performance—a suggestion that forecasted the development of dose–response curves by the drug industry decades later.

B. 1921–1939

The period between the two world wars was one of little activity in military psychology. Some aviation psychologists were involved in the collection and analysis of data from pilots who were exposed to the physical, physiological, and psychological stresses related to the expanding aviation environment. These tests were conducted both in the aircraft and in the laboratory.

Others were involved in the design and test of protective equipment for pilots in order to protect them from the hazards of the flight environment. The goal was to determine the natural limitations of the pilot and to develop equipment to extend the pilot's capabilities or to adapt the design of future

aircraft to conform better to human capabilities and limitations. Their work influenced the design and operation of military aircraft in World War II.

C. World War II

During World War II, from 1939 to 1945, military psychologists made major contributions to the war efforts. In the U.S. Army, multiple forms of a new selection and classification test, the Army General Classification Test (AGCT), were developed, as were mechanical and clerical tests, trade tests, and nonlanguage tests for illiterates. By the end of the war, the AGCT in its various forms had been administered to over 13,000,000 persons in the selection, classification, training, and assignment of personnel in all the military services, and in counseling veterans in separation centers, including over 9,000,000 men in the Army alone. R&D on psychomotor selection devices for test pilot candidates were conducted.

In another area, military aviation psychologists developed what is probably still the most successful test battery of all times, the Air-Crew Classification Test Battery consisting of 20 tests—6 apparatus tests of coordination and speed of decision, and 14 printed tests measuring intellectual aptitude and abilities, perception and visualization, and temperament and motivation. More than 600,000 men took this comprehensive battery of tests, which was demonstrated to be of high predictive value especially for pilot and navigator training success, and to be significantly correlated with measures of success in operational training and in combat.

In still other areas, military psychologists applied their skills to the full range of war-time needs. For example, they established the usefulness of clinical psychology in military medical and hospital settings, and by July 1945 there were 250 clinical psychology officers providing neuro-psychiatric services in Army Hospitals. Perhaps even more importantly, they applied the methods and knowledge of experimental psychology to military problems of all sorts, and they developed an entirely new technology and field of R&D—human factors engineering, and engineering psychology. The activities and successes of military psychologists during the war profoundly influenced the rapid expansion and further development of both the science and the profession of psychology during the postwar years and subsequent decades, even down to the present.

II. SELECTION, CLASSIFICATION, AND ASSIGNMENT

A. Personnel Assessment and Assignment

The principles of personnel selection and classification had been well established by military psychologists at the end of World War II. Procedures for implementing these principles had also been systematically tested.

1. The AFQT and the ASVAB

Until 1950, military psychologists developed selection and classification tests for their specific service. However, in that year, the Armed Forces Qualification Test (AFQT) was installed in the principal recruiting offices in the United States and became the first mental test with a cutoff score that was mandated by the U.S. Congress. This test was also the first Department of Defense (all-service) screening test implemented by the U.S. Military Departments. The AFQT continues to serve as the selection test in the United States, but its scores are now derived from the Armed Services Vocational Aptitude Battery (ASVAB)—the test battery that is currently used for all military personnel screening.

2. Computer Adaptive Testing (CAT)

One recent new trend has been the R&D on experimental computerized versions of the ASVAB. A specific focus of the work by military psychologists has been on computerized adaptive testing (CAT). In CAT, the next test item to be administered is selected from a large pool based on (a) a prediction of the testee's aptitudes or abilities as calculated from his previous responses on the test, and (b) the item's difficulty level. The testee will eventually reach a point at which the CAT model predicts a final test score at a given (specified) level of confidence, and testing ceases.

Among the more recent studies of CAT-ASVAB technology are the following: (a) initial aptitude estimates, (b) algorithms for item selection, (c) termination rules, (d) test item pool development and calibration, (e) validation, and (f) scaling.

Current tests at the Military Entrance Processing Stations (MEPS) are being conducted to determine the extent to which use of the CAT would be cost-effective. It has already been demonstrated that CAT improves test efficiency by reducing test errors and testing time, as well as easing the requirements for technical supervision and test security.

3. Person–Job Matching

The optimum assignment of military personnel to jobs (i.e., person–job matching) has a long R&D history in military psychology. For example, the U.S. Air Force job analysis system, the Comprehensive Occupational Data Analysis Program (CODAP), was developed and implemented in the late 1960s. This system uses a series of job analysis surveys that are completed by current job incumbents to determine task importance, criticality, difficulty, and frequency of performance. The surveys can subsequently be analyzed for factors such as experience level.

Proper assignments are obviously essential for optimizing individual career development, and personnel managers need maangement tools such as those provided by the computer-based person–job matching programs. Obviously, computers have come to be used extensively in the Military Departments to maximize the efficiency of person–job matching. [See CAREER DEVELOPMENT.]

B. Pilot Selection

R&D on pilot selection have been especially emphasized by military psychologists because of their potentially high payoff, given the costs of training pilots and, therefore, of the losses incurred when candidate pilots fail in their training—losses that approach hundreds of thousands of dollars for each pilot-trainee who "washes out."

At the beginning of World War II, the Army Air Force established a large military psychology program to conduct R&D on pilot selection for both flight training and operational flying. Their R&D led to two examining procedures: (a) a 150-item screening examination called the AAF Qualifying Examination, use of which rejected between a quarter and a half of the more than one million aircrew applicants, and (b) the *Air-Crew Classification Test Battery* (which was previously mentioned under Historical Overview). The latter consisted of 20 tests—6 apparatus tests of coordination and speed of decision, and 14 printed tests measuring intellectual aptitude and abilities, perception and visualization, and temperament and motivation.

1. Stanines

Test-battery performance was recorded in terms of a nine-category standard score, called a stanine, with a mean of 5.0 and standard deviation of about 2.0. Testees were assigned stanines scores for the various aircrew specialities. More than 600,000 men took this battery of tests during the war. The stanines were found to have high predictive value especially for pilot and navigator training success, and to be significantly correlated with measures of success in operational training and in combat. By the end of the war, pilot selection methods were well established, especially in the Army Air Force. However, the stanines were abandoned after World War II, primarily because of "difficulties" in maintaining in good working condition the apparatus for the six performance tests, given the postwar drawdown of the Services' personnel and funding.

2. Reemergence of Performance Tests

During recent years, as computers have become more plentiful, powerful, and economical, the R&D trend in pilot selection has been increasingly toward the use of apparatus-based performance tests. The role of pilots in military aircraft has also changed from a relative emphasis on manual control to one of cockpit-resource management. Many of the flight-control functions are automated in today's high technology cockpit, and this, combined with the increasing use of cathode ray tubes (CRTs) for displays and fly-by-wire systems for aircraft control, has dramatically changed the flight tasks of pilots. Thus, performance tests are viewed as more likely to improve the validity of any new pilot-selection battery, especially since most military psychologists agree it is extremely unlikely that the predictive value of intelligence and aptitude-type paper-and-pencil tests can be substantially increased above that of the currently available tests.

III. HUMAN FACTORS ENGINEERING AND HUMAN PERFORMANCE R&D

The objective of human factors engineering and human performance R&D in the U.S. military establishment is to improve military combat performance. In peacetime, this objective is met in terms of the increased combat readiness of military units—that is, the predicted increase in the probability of their success were they to be engaged in combat.

Human factors engineering, broadly defined, means to include in the design of a weapon system considerations of all aspects of the human beings who will be called upon to operate and maintain the system once it is fielded. These human factors considerations include the relevant aspect of mili-

tary leadership, training, past experience, organization factors, motivation, morale, and discipline—all of which can influence the effectiveness with which the weapon system will be employed in combat.

A. Human–Machine Systems

A human–machine system consists of the things, people, and ideas that are interfaced with each other and integrated into a single whole that is maintained and operated to accomplish certain specified tasks. The *things* (hardware and software) are the weapon system parts usually acquired from industry; but these *things* must interface and take into account properly the ideas (military operational concepts) and people (military personnel and units) with which they constitute a weapon system. Otherwise they run the danger of ending up as just so much useless material.

Human factors applications to system design are usually called human factors engineering, but other names have also been used (e.g., ergonomics, human engineering, or, simply, human factors). Supporting these applications are the data and methods devised through R&D in an area commonly known as engineering psychology, but also sometimes called applied experimental psychology, ergonomics research, or human performance R&D.

The involvement of military psychologists in human factors engineering is generally accepted as beginning in the early 1940s when they were called upon to investigate cockpit design and layout. By 1945, they had assisted engineers in the design of a great variety of military equipment for all Services—for example, aircraft cockpits, combat information centers, instrument displays and dials, radar consoles, gunsights, controls, synthetic training devices, underwater sound-detection systems, and voice communication systems.

1. An Early Handbook

In the late 1940s and early 1950s, the U.S. Navy sponsored the development of a handbook—the *Handbook of Human Engineering Data for Design Engineers* (the "Tufts Handbook")—that was prepared at the Tufts College Institute for Applied Experimental Psychology under contract support from the Special Devices Center, Office of Naval Research, and published first in 1949. The handbook included chapters on audition, environmental factors, learning, motor coordination, muscle sensitivity, reaction time, and vision. The purpose of the handbook was to present and summarize the data on human capabilities and limitations in a way that would be relevant to, and usable in, the applications of human factors engineering. It was the first of its genre, excellent in its coverage, and useful in its presentations. It was likely to be found in the libraries (if not the hands) of all practising engineering psychologists and human factors engineers of the day.

2. The Personnel Subsystem

In the 1950s, military psychologists were advocating that considerations of interactions of the human and equipment components of any new weapon system, the availability of personnel, their skill and experience level, and their trainability needed to be considered at all stages of the weapon system's design and planned miantenance and use. In the mid-1950s, the U.S. Air Force first developed the personnel subsystem as an approach to weapon system design. The approach called for consideration of the manpower and personnel, training, and human factors engineering components and requirements to be factored into the design and evaluation of new weapon systems at each stage of the acquisition process.

Although no longer considered a formal subsystem requirement after the mid-1960s, the personnel-subsystem concept has been absorbed into the acquisition processes of all three U.S. military departments. For example, during the early 1970s, the U.S. Air Force adapted a Monte Carlo computer simulation program, the Logistic Composite model, to estimate maintenance manpower requirements during the development and validation phases of aircraft weapon system acquisition programs. Then, in 1977, the U.S. Navy began a program known as Hardware Procurement U.S. Military Manpower (HARDMAN), which it first applied in its fleet modernization program. Later, during the 1980s, the U.S. Army initiated a manpower and personnel integration (MANPRINT) program that made it a requirement to consider human resources in the design, development, and use of weapon systems. By the 1990s, the Office of the Secretary of Defense had mandated a Human Systems Integration (HSI) program for all future Defense acquisitions.

The centers of human factors engineering and engineering psychology R&D in the Services have traditionally been (a) the U.S. Army Human Engineering Laboratory, Aberdeen Proving Ground, Maryland, (b) the Engineering Psychology Division, Crew Systems Directorate, (U.S. Air Force) Arm-

strong Laboratory, Wright-Patterson Air Force Base, Ohio, and (c) the Naval Training Equipment Center, Orlando, Florida, as well as the several systems commands of the U.S. Navy (e.g., Naval Air Systems Command and Naval Sea Systems Command). In the United Kingdom, the Applied Psychology Unit at Cambridge University began work early in the war and continued for decades afterward as one of the world's centers of human performance R&D.

B. Training and Simulation

As far back as World War I, military psychologists working for the U.S. Navy produced successful naval gunnery simulators for training. During World War II, with the problems of mobilizing and training a much larger force placing an even greater demand for effective training devices, many specialists in electronics, hydraulics, mechanics, optics, and other phases of the engineering sciences joined with military psychologists and trainers to create numerous training devices. These devices simulated tasks such as airborne flexible gunnery, celestial navigation, instrument flying, and submarine warfare. The job of the military psychologist was typically to apply their experimental and quantitative skills to ensure that the training devices would have the highest feasible levels of reliability and validity, as well as other desired characteristics such as objective scoring, adjustable task difficulty, and other important psychological features.

During World War II and immediately afterward, both the U.S. Army and Navy provided contract support for engineering psychology research at universities (e.g., Berkeley, Harvard, Johns Hopkins, and Maryland, among others), and at the Psychological Corporation, where Jack Dunlap had set up a Biomechanics Division for engineering psychology R&D. That division later became Dunlap and Associates, probably the first consulting and R&D organization exclusively devoted to human performance R&D.

Relatively large simulator-based engineering psychology R&D programs were established in the late 1940s, by the U.S. Air Force at the Laboratory of Aviation Psychology of The Ohio State University, and by the U.S. Navy at the Aviation Psychology Laboratory of the University of Illinois. The former conducted R&D aimed to guide the direction of future design efforts for radar air traffic control centers through use of an impressively large and effective simulator, in addition to supporting laboratory research and other R&D such as on the effectiveness of a F-86D fire-control simulator for part-task training.

At the University of Illinois, with Navy sponsorship, the effective use of flight simulators was demonstrated in 1949 with what are generally considered the first carefully controlled flight-simulator transfer-of-training studies ever conducted. The findings demonstrated quantitatively and conclusively that training in a ground-based flight simulator could be employed to reduce the time required for training in flying actual aircraft.

1. The Advanced Simulator for Pilot Training (ASPT)

During the 1970s, a major thrust in training and simulation was the development and use of a state-of-the art R&D simulator for pilot training, the Advanced Simulator for Pilot Training (ASPT). Initially used for R&D on undergraduate (beginning) pilot training, its focus was later shifted from the training of basic-flying skills to air-combat skills. When first installed and operated at Williams Air Force Base, Arizona, in 1976, this simulator presented the most capable wide-angle (nearly 360°) visual scene available for R&D on the training of pilots in air combat. Although the low-intensity monochromatic scene limited to 2500 edges is quite primitive by todays standards, the ASPT had the most advanced computer image generating (CIG) visual system for flight simulators in existence at that time.

The R&D experience with the ASPT over the decade of the mid-1970s to the mid-1980s demonstrated that flight simulators built with wide-angle visual capabilities could be used to increase the efficiently and effectiveness not only of undergraduate pilot training, but also of transition and continuation training. The later studies demonstrated that such devices could also be used to increase the combat effectiveness of aircrews—not only in the training of generic air combat skills, but also with the potential of providing for situational awareness, mission planning, and mission rehearsal in actual combat situations during time of war.

This line of development in military psychology has been advanced to a major R&D thrust to develop further the capabilities of synthetic environments ("virtual world" simulations) as one of seven major thrusts announced in July 1992 by the Director of Defense Research and Engineering. The creation of that thrust was based in large measure on the successful SIMNET demonstrations of what the technology could do for U.S. Army training if properly developed and implemented.

2. Simulator Networking (SIMNET)

Specifically, in 1983 a project on simulator networking (SIMNET) was initiated at the Department of Defense's Advanced Research Projects Agency (ARPA). The objective of the project was to demonstrate the utility of an interactive simulator network for real-time, human-in-the-loop, battle-engagement simulation and war-gaming aimed at the training of combat skills in military units from mechanized platoons up to battalions. ARPA received considerable U.S. Army support to develop and demonstrate SIMNET.

Since SIMNET and SIMNET-based follow-ons are still being expanded and developed, descriptions of SIMNET capabilities necessarily have to be fixed at a given point in time. Thus, in January 1990, SIMNET consisted of 260 tank, fighting-vehicle, and aircraft simulators, with the associated command posts, and data processing and communication facilities, distributed among 11 sites, 7 of which were in the United States and 4 of which were at U.S. Army facilities in Europe.

The largest SIMNET site was at Fort Knox, Kentucky, with 72 ground vehicle simulators, 4 aircraft simulators, 1 tactical operations center at battalion task-force level, and other support elements such as a administrative-logistic operating center, command and control, artillery and motor, and close air support control elements—all operating on a single local area network.

All SIMNET sites can be "connected" through communications networks, so that troops at the 11 locations can be engaged in a single battle on the same simulated terrain, which, in turn, can be at any location on the earth (real or imagined), in any season of the year, under any weather and battlefield conditions, etc.—limited only by SIMNET's digital terrain and environmental databases.

SIMNET was developed to have considerable flexibility. As additional modules (tank or other simulators) are developed, they can be added to the interactive net. In the future, a planned feature includes the capability of using SIMNET to test new weapons system concepts with real troops trained to use the new system and interacting in real time on simulated battlefields—all prior to a decision being made to develop the new system or not. Changes in proposed new systems, or proposed modifications in existing weapon systems, can also be tested in simulated form before commitments are made to build or modify any hardware. Likewise, SIMNET can be used to develop, test, and evaluate new tactics and doctrine. Finally, SIMNET technology has the capability of supporting situational awareness, mission rehearsal, and even battlefield-management functions in time of war, as well as real-time training in these functions with a realism never before achieved during peacetime.

3. Other Computer Applications to Training

By the early 1980s, all three military departments were developing and demonstrating effective computer-based adaptive instructional systems. The focus covered the range of adaptations of mainframe, mini-, and micro- (i.e., the rapidly evolving desk-top) computers to instructional and training domains. During the mid-1980s, numerous training technologies were being investigated by military psychologists. These included technologies such as training systems design, part-task trainers, simulators for training (as well as for tactics development, mission planning, situational awareness, and mission rehearsal), aircrew performance measurement, on-the-job training, expert systems, computer-based training, and training management decision aiding. An impressively broad range, indeed!

The attention to this breadth of R&D and applications topics was stimulated, beginning in the mid-1970s, by a mandate from the Office of the Secretary of Defense that a sharpened focus and increased attention be given by military psychologists to the productivity of training. It was during that time that cost-effectiveness analyses were developed in order that valid evaluations could be made of alternative methods of training, uses of training devices and simulators, and new technologies to improve training. Studies conducted within the Department of Defense during this period emphasized the need to develop analytic capabilities to make cost-effectiveness analyses of training technologies, and to develop further and use those found to be most cost-effective.

IV. ENVIRONMENTAL FACTORS AND HUMAN PERFORMANCE

Advances in weapon-system technology, tied in with increasingly demanding requirements for military forces to perform in extremely hostile environments, have provided numerous challenges to military psychologists to expand the environmental conditions under which troops can perform effectively, and to protect them from the health hazards intrinsic to environmental extremes such as those of heat, cold, and altitude.

In many situations, troops must perform while encapsulated in protective clothing (e.g., a chemical-warfare protective ensemble) and operate in a hot environment—a combination that may produce substantial heat stress. Military psychologists have worked on interdisciplinary R&D teams that include physiologists, physicians, engineers, computer specialists, and others, to devise methods to obviate the deleterious effects of such stress. Successful developments have included the design and use of (a) cooling vests that lower heat stress and body temperature, (b) protocols to train troops in the proper donning and use of protective clothing and gear, and (c) behavioral actions that can be taken to minimize the performance and health effects of heat stress. This entire area is likely to be a continuing focus of military psychology R&D.

A. Sustained Human Performance in Continuous Operations

Advances in the technologies of night vision devices and battlefield sensors have given military field commanders capabilities of conducting continuous operations—that is, of maintaining a maximum of fire power on the line 24 hours a day for periods of 30 days or more. This represents a change in the way ground warfare has been conducted down through the ages. Until now, battles have been fought during daylight hours, with relatively little action at night. A move to implement continuous operations requires, among other things, the development of new military concepts and doctrine, tactics, logistic processes and plans, and even battle management techniques.

In many cases, military personnel may be required to operate for extended periods without what in the past has been regarded as "adequate" rest or relief. Army field studies of continuous operations have indicated that a platoon can operate for 9 days with 3 hours of sleep per night. If the platoon is permitted no sleep, they become ineffective after 3 days. If sleep is limited to 1.5 hours per night, a platoon becomes ineffective after 6 days. Thus, it has been demonstrated that the combined effects of stress, sleep loss, and fatigue can lead to relatively poor performances by both individuals and units—reductions that will be reflected in lower combat effectiveness.

In addition, certain tasks are especially sensitive to the length of time they are performed continuously. R&D conducted by military psychologists on the topic of vigilance, monitoring, or watch-keeping behavior have indicated that the ability to sustain attention to task demands decreases rapidly with time or task. For example, although many military duties involve monitoring tasks requiring watch-keeping performances that are continued for 2 hours or more without a break, such performances typically deteriorate substantially after only 20 minutes. This knowledge is factored into the design of new weapon systems and even to the operational procedures that are employed with existing systems.

B. Human Performance in Noise Environments

In military operations, personnel are often exposed to a wide range of intense noises. The exposure duration and the frequency range of the sounds vary considerably depending on the type of military operation. Exposures to intense noise environments result in hearing losses. Noise is a health hazard from which troops need protection, and noisy environments usually lower human performances in ways similar to those of other environmental stresses.

C. Human Performance in Acceleration Environments

Exposure to acceleration and vibration conditions occurs in air, sea, and ground-based military operations. Maneuvers performed in a high performance combat fighter can expose a pilot to sustained accelerations of up to 7 or 8 g (7 or 8 times the earth's gravitational field). Low-altitude, high-speed flight and air turbulence result in exposure of military pilots to severe vibrations. Military psychologists have investigated environmental stresses such as these through the use of subjective reports, physiological techniques, and behavioral measures.

Early studies during the late 1940s used responses to visual stimuli under various g loads as measures of human performance. Detection thresholds, errors in reading cockpit displays, and both simple and choice reaction times have been found to increase with increased positive g. In the 1960s, numerous studies indicated memory impairment at high positive g (forces greater than 7 g), and manual control

studies have indicated that performance rapidly decreases above 6 g.

R&D findings to date consistently indicate that controlled motions, manual dexterity, speech, vision, vestibular orientation, cardiovascular output, and respiratory volume are adversely affected at and above levels of 3 to 4 positive g. For example, the unprotected human will have zero blood pressure to his eyes when exposed to a positive force of 4.5 g or greater. As an aircraft pilot approaches this level, he will experience progressively (a) "grayout" (diminishing of vision), (b) "blackout" (complete, but temporary, loss of vision), and (c) g-induced loss of consciousness. To protect the pilot (modern fighter and attack aircraft can pull well in excess of 8 g), much of the R&D in this area has focussed on the design and use of anti-g flight suits, and on the development of and training of pilots in the use of an active straining maneuver. Both R&D products have been found to increase human tolerance to the effects of exposure to high positive g.

D. Human Performance in Vibration Environments

Many of the negative effects of vibration on military performances are well understood. Vibrations are generally associated with their greatest performance decrements at those frequencies where whole-body resonances occur. However, decrements also occur at other frequencies—for example, decreased abilities to read displays have been found as functions of vibratory frequency and amplitude. Also, low-frequency vibrations have not generally been found to reduce performances on tests of mental addition, pattern recognition, or pattern matching. Performances of manual control tasks are most affected by vibrations between 3 to 8 Hz in frequency. Performance degradations attributable to vibration environments have been substantially reduced by military psychologists though use of their R&D-based inputs to the designs of protective equipment and of controls and displays.

V. LEADERSHIP AND HUMAN PERFORMANCE

Military psychologists have conducted extensive empirical leadership R&D since the end of World War II. Most of the R&D in the decade that immediately followed the war was concerned with leader behavior and leadership skills. The results provided convincing evidence that leader effectiveness is in great measure a function of situational factors. Consequently, a trend that has emerged during the last four decades has been a uniting of leadership and organizational theory. It is recognized today that the construct of leadership must include indirect as well as direct (face-to-face) influences. [*See* LEADERSHIP.]

Current organizational theories are based on three levels of operation as follows: (a) lower level or production activiites, (b) middle level or coordination and scheduling activities, and (c) top level or executive functions. Both the theory and R&D findings of military psychologists indicate that since leader development is important to military operations, leadership training should consist of sequential and progressive development of increasingly complex skills required for the three levels of operations within military organizations.

A. Leadership in Small Units

Effective performance in combat is dependent on unit cohesion (i.e., the solidarity among the members of a military unit). Studies following World War II indicated that the most successful U.S. small combat units were those with supportive leaders who fostered group cohesion. Recent studies have found that U.S. Army platoon and company cohesion is strongly related to the confidence soldiers have in themselves and their leaders. The Army has developed a four-stage model for the development of unit cohesion. The model is based on a longitudinal study of the social-developmental processes of integrating individuals into units and how units develop over time. The model describes how inexperienced, fragmented beginning groups develop into highly skilled, cohesive, combat-ready small units. The Army Research Institute for the Behavioral and Social Sciences (ARI) has been a leader among military psychology R&D organizations in this area of work.

B. Executive Leadership

Starting in the mid-1970s, executive leadership models were developed to define three organizational domains—the production, organizational, and systems domains. Army military psychologists have adapted these models to reflect the general performance requirements for leaders at seven organizational levels, where the two highest levels (levels 6 and 7) were assumed to involve executive leadership.

During the mid-1980s, these Army psychologists conducted extensive and systematic R&D on leadership at the general-officer (executive) level. The result of interviews conducted with approximately two-thirds of the three- and four-star general officers in the Army indicated that most of the incumbents in four-star assignments had joint, unified, or combined-command responsibilities (i.e., multiservice, or multi-service and foreign-troop command responsibilities). These assignments were found to be extremely complex.

Other R&D has indicated that the majority of four-star general officer assignments consist of work that requires a multi-national perspective. In these assignments, consensus building and the ability to anticipate change have been found to be skills that must be mastered for the executive leader to be effective. Such skills have been found to develop only over an extended period of time, such as several decades. The R&D findings in this executive-leadership area have been implemented through policies that call for the assignment of military officers to increasingly complex positions at progressively higher organizational levels as they progress though the grades.

VI. INDIVIDUAL AND GROUP BEHAVIORS

Military psychologists have long known that the very act of measuring individual or group performances can alter the behaviors being measured. Thus, when conducting behavior R&D, one must consider the degree of reactivity and nonreactivity of the behaviors being measured. In many situations it is possible to determine performance levels for individuals and groups under simulated conditions. In other cases, the military psychologist can infer something about the knowledge, skill, and decision process of individuals and groups based on data obtained in operational settings—settings in which controls are not always optimum and even the experimental factors of interest may not be easily manipulated. The two important R&D areas discussed in this section (morale and cohesion, and organizational factors that affect individual and group behavior under stress) are particularly subject to these experimental limitations.

A. Morale and Cohesion

It has been accepted among U.S. Army military psychologists that a significant number of biological and psychological factors affect the morale of a military unit. These include good health, and adequate food, rest and sleep, shelter, clothing, equipment, and bathing facilities. During combat, most of these needs are not met, and the military commander is challenged to maintain the high levels of morale necessary for his unit to be effective. Most military psychologists believe that a clearly stated military objective or role is as important to morale as is training. Also important in this regard is the length of time that a military unit has been intact (i.e., stabilized, and generally with the same individual members).

Shared experiences are considered essential in the building of unit cohesion. To be successful, these experiences must provide the members of the unit with confidence in the ability and resolve of their leaders and their comrades to achieve a meaningful unit mission, and to protect them in combat. Questionnaires and surveys are typically used in R&D on unit morale and cohesion. Precombat attitudes, such as willingness for combat, confidence in physical endurance, and confidence in combat skills, are correlated with measurable events such as combat casualties. Traditionally, these methods of assessing morale have indicated that measures of high morale result in low incidence of combat casualties. Recent U.S. Army studies conducted in peacetime have indicated that measures of unit cohesion have also been highly correlated with measures of unit performance such as average physical training test scores, numbers of courts-martial, and operational readiness inspection scores.

B. Organizational Factors That Affect Individual and Group Behavior under Stress

As indicated previously, military R&D organizations have supported organizational psychology R&D since World War II. The Office of Naval Research and a variety of U.S. Army R&D organizations (especially ARI) have supported R&D in this area in military settings and at universities as well. Much of the R&D have been concerned with organizational behavior theory and how to develop more efficient organizations in military settings. However, particular interest has been devoted to R&D on the behavior of individuals and groups in the extreme situations that are relatively unique to military organizations. For example, situations such as combat where the individual and the group to which the individual belongs are exposed to conditions wherein the risk is perceived as high that individual personnel (one's self included) or unit will sustain injury or even death, or capture by the enemy and subsequent confinement as prisoner(s) of war.

Personnel taken prisoner during armed combat find themselves in a unique and threatening situation. During the 1970s, the U.S. Navy sponsored R&D in this area. One finding was that those who are prison authorities (guards and supervisors) can convert, sometimes unwittingly, to oppressors, and prisoners become oppressed. Lack of accountability, discipline, or humanity can often result in neglect and cruelty. When one considers military prisoner-of-war situations, in which personal statements from prisoners have substantive propaganda value, and could also provide leads or access to classified information, one can understand that the risk is substantial of abuse and intensive interrogation or even torture of prisoners of war.

The prisoner's daily routine and regime is substantially different from the previous military organizational structure with loss of support of comrades in arms. In many cases, their isolation, solitary confinement, unsanitary conditions, and restricted diets define standard living conditions. Among the successful contributions of military psychologists have been the results of their involvement in the development of training programs that permit individuals to develop and test in realistic simulated situations, the attitudes and skills that permit survival of prisoners of war regardless of the severity of their experiences in the situation. Military personnel assigned to combat zones are typically trained in escape and evasion techniques, as well as in survival training. An important, perhaps even necessary, part of this training is the use of a realistic confinement of each trainee, to provide a personal experience that better prepares the individual for the potential of captivity.

Finally, military psychologists are regularly involved as members of the teams established to debrief returning prisoners of war. Lessons learned by military psychologists from prisoners of war from the Korean campaign and the Vietnam War were similar. Those imprisoned by the North Koreans were subjected to systematic and lengthy periods of "brainwashing." Those in North Vietnam prisons suffered both psychological and physical abuse. Man's extreme inhumanity to man is readily apparent in the reading of these reports. [*See* BRAINWASH-ING AND TOTALITARIAN INFLUENCE.]

Bibliography

Defense Science Board (1976). ''Report of the Task Force on Training Technology.'' Department of Defense, Office of the Director of Defense Research and Engineering, Washington, DC.

Gal, R., and Mangelsdorff, A. D. (Eds.) (1991). ''Handbook of Military Psychology.'' Wiley, New York.

Jacobs, T. O. (1985). The airland battle and leadership require-ments. In ''Leadership on the Future Battlefield'' (J. G. Hunt and J. D. Blair, Eds.), Pergamon-Brassey's, New York.

Uhlaner, J. E. (1968). ''The Research Psychologist in the Army—1917 to 1967,'' Technical Research Report 1155. U.S. Army Behavioral Science Research Laboratory, Arlington, VA.

Wiskoff, M. F., and Schratz, M. K. (1989). Computerized adap-tive testing of a vocational aptitude battery. In ''Testing, The-oretical and Applied Perspectives'' R. F. Dillon and J. W. Pellegrino, Eds.). Praeger, New York.

Zeidner, J. (Ed.) (1986). ''Human Productivity Enhancement, Vol. 1–2. Praeger, New York.

MORAL DEVELOPMENT

F. Clark Power
University of Notre Dame

Glossary

Autonomy The capacity of self-governance according to reason.

Disequillibration The first part of the process of stage transition in which the equilibrium or balance achieved at a particular stage is disturbed.

Habituation Aristotle's approach to the learning of virture through guided instruction and practice.

Heteronomy The subordination of the self to an external authority, law, or source of influence.

Intentionality The child's ability to take into account intentions or motives in making judgments of praise and blame.

Longitudinal study A method that collects data on the same group of individuals over time.

Perspective or role-taking stages Stages that the describe the ability of children and adolescents to coordinate different viewpoints.

Structural wholeness The assumption in cognitive developmental theory that a stage is an organized pattern of reasoning that underlies more particular content considerations of moral choice and values.

Transformational model A model of stage development in which the lower stages are integrated by the higher stages.

MORAL DEVELOPMENT studies the acquisition of the attitudes, dispositions, sentiments, and cognitive competencies involved in the process of moral judgment and action. The nature and role of these components of the process depend on how morality is understood. Most contemporary moral psychologists distinguish morality from prudence or the pursuit of one's interests and from custom or etiquette. They generally agree that to be moral is to treat others fairly and with concern for their welfare without the anticipation of a reward or threat of punishment.

I. A HISTORICAL OVERVIEW

A. Introduction

How humans develop from impulse-governed infants to morally responsible adults has been a question of perennial concern and debate since the time of ancient Greece. Socrates, for example, believed that one's morality developed through rational inquiry into the nature of the good. He, therefore, challenged the youth of Athens to question popular views of morality and virtue, a practice that led to his being sentenced to death. Aristotle, on the other hand, emphasized the role of habituation over reasoning in moral upbringing. In his view, individuals learn how to be moral much the way apprentices learn their craft.

In the first half of the 20th century, the discussion of moral development took a more radical turn as psychoanalytic and behavioral psychologists called into question the very notions of universal morality, character, and virtue. The most significant of all the research at this time was Hartshorne and May's landmark study of deception, self-control, and service. They indicated that moral behavior does not depend on an individual's character or virtue but is a function of influences operating in the situation. Following Hartshorne and May, the psychological study of morality, as it has traditionally been understood, practically ceased, until in the 1960s, the cognitive developmental approach of Piaget and Kohlberg emerged.

B. Psychoanalytic Theory

Psychoanalytic theorists take their definition of what is moral from the norms and values of the existing culture. They describe the operation of becoming moral as the internalization of those cultural norms and values in the superego through a process of parental identification, which according the Freud culminates the resolution of the Oedipal conflict at age 5 or 6. In their research they typically look for correlations between early childhood parenting and behavior, and between the arousal of guilt and behavior. This paradigm presents the essence of moral functioning as following one's conscience in order to avoid guilt. Given the irrational nature of the superego, psychoanalytic theorists are concerned not only that cultural standards are upheld but also that the superego does not become excessively punitive. [*See* ID, EGO, AND SUPEREGO.]

C. Social Learning Theory

Social learning theorists tend to equate morality with societal norms and more broadly with other-oriented or altruistic actions. Like the psychoanalytic theorists, they maintain that individuals become moral through the internalization of those societal norms. In place of processes of parental identification, however, social learning theorists attempt to demonstrate that these norms are acquired through rewards and punishments. Children are in this view initially motivated to satisfy their own needs and desires. They are then shaped or socialized by environmental mechanisms to find satisfaction in socially approved and other-oriented actions. The test of a person's morality is thus whether she or he will adhere to a social norm or perform an altruistic action without the expectation of reward or punishment or at some personal cost.

D. Cognitive Developmental Theory

Cognitive developmentalists reject the assumption shared by psychoanalytic and social learning theorists that morality can be equated with culturally relative standards. Taking an explicitly philosophic stance, they maintain that morality is a process of adjudicating conflicting claims on the basis of universally recognized principles of justice and benevolence. Cognitive developmentalists see moral development as occurring through a sequence of stages in which individuals reason about moral problems in progressively more adequate ways. In contrast to psychoanalytic and social learning theorists, who view the child as being passively formed by environmental forces, cognitive developmentalists picture the child (and later the adolescent and adult) as developing a personal "moral philosophy" through interacting with the environment.

In general, as White has noted, psychological approaches serve as windows on reality, bringing clarity to aspects of human experience that have been largely obscure. As windows, however, these approaches provide only partial views, framed by their guiding assumptions and research methods. The cognitive developmental approach has succeeded in providing a penetrating analysis of the way in which individuals reason about moral problems; but moral reasoning is, of course, only a part, although perhaps the key part, of moral functioning. The other approaches sketched here provide different windows on moral experience, windows aimed more directly on moral feelings and observable behaviors.

Because Piaget and Kohlberg pioneered the field of moral development as we know it today, this article will focus on the major features of their theories. It will also attend to some of the major criticisms of their work as well as to some of the more promising extensions of cognitive development theory, particularly insofar as it relates to the relationship between moral reasoning and action. [*See* COGNITIVE DEVELOPMENT.]

II. PIAGET'S THEORY

A. The Moral Judgment of the Child

The study of moral development as we know it today drew its initial inspiration from Jean Piaget's seminal study, *The Moral Judgment of the Child;* it is the fifth of a series of books that Piaget published at the beginning of a highly productive career. Developmentalists either have focused directly upon these studies to elaborate, refine, and confirm their conclusions or, like Kohlberg, have used Piaget's ideas and methods as a springboard for their own theories. *The Moral Judgment of the Child* is subdivided into three empirical parts and a fourth theoretical part in which Piaget contrasts his views on moral development and education with those of other theorists, most notably the great French sociologist Emile Durkheim.

B. Heteronomy and Autonomy

In the first part of *The Moral Judgment of the Child*, Piaget examines the ways in which children from the ages or 3 to 12 understand and apply the rules of marbles and hopscotch, the most popular children's games in French-speaking Switzerland. Piaget believed that by studying children at play, he could penetrate into their own moral world, a world that they were attempting to understand and control on their own terms. Feigning that he had forgotten the rules of the game, he asked the children to teach him and let him play with them. He then proceeded to ask the children about the various shots in the game and how to determine the winner. All the while, he played the game as seriously as he could, letting the children beat him to sustain their sense of superiority but making an occasional good shot to avoid being dismissed as incompetent. Having determined children's ''practice of the rules,'' Piaget proceeded to inquire into their consciousness of the origins of rules by asking such simple questions as ''Can you make up a new rule?'' ''Would it be all right to play like that with your pals?'' ''Have people always played as they do today?''

Piaget found that young children (usually under the age of 8) typically believed that adults made the rules and the rules could not be changed. On the other hand, older children (usually over the age of 9) readily believed that they with their peers were authorized to make and change rules. Piaget theorized that children's belief in the creation of rules by adult authorities reflected a quasi-mystical, heteronomous respect for the rules, while older children's belief in their own power to make rules reflected a secular, autonomous respect. As is most evident in the final section of his book, Piaget's perspective was deeply influenced by Durkheim, whose views on the sociology of religion and moral education were highly influential at that time. According to Durkheim, respect for rules could be generated only if the rules were regarded as emanating from a power superior to the individual. Durkheim's historical studies led him to postulate that religion and morality were originally undifferentiated and that all rules were regarded as sacred because of their divine origin. With societal evolution rules became secularized, but, nevertheless, retained their power to elicit respect because of their transcendent, societal origin. In Durkheim's view, rules could only obligate if they were seen as issuing from a superior, quasi-

divine being. Individuals, therefore had to look beyond themselves to the collective being of society as the authority behind the rules.

Piaget's entire book may be regarded as an effort to respond to Durkheim by showing that children develop an alternative, autonomous morality through cooperative peer relationships. Unfortunately his preoccupation with Durkheim's view seems to have foreclosed his exploration of other types of moral reasoning, types later uncovered in Kohlberg's research. What Piaget's analysis loses in breadth, it gains, however, in depth by juxtaposing moral heteronomy with moral autonomy.

C. Egocentrism

Piaget found that children at the heteronomous stage flagrantly but unwittingly broke the very rules that they regarded as sacred and immutable. Piaget explained this paradox as a function of chidhood egocentrism. This term should not be confused with egoism or selfishness; it simply connotes children's apparent inability to distinguish their subjective perspective from the perspective of others. As Piaget and others have noted, egocentrism is a salient characteristic of children's speech and play. For example, when telling stories or making requests young children typically fail to take the needs of their listeners into account. They seem to assume that their listeners know what they are talking about. Similarly when young children play with each other, they tend to parallel play or play as individuals in the company of others.

Although young children tend to behave in egocentric ways, there is considerable debate over whether their egocentrism should be regarded as a stage of cognitive immaturity. Some research indicates that very young children are capable of altering their speech and actions to meet the needs of others, and Piaget himself had noted that even adults can be egocentric in expressing their opinions. There are other studies, however, that have reconceptualized the egocentrism construct to consist of stages of perspective or role taking. These studies show that young children's conceptions of the self, friendship, groups, and morality are limited by their ability to coordinate the perspectives of others.

Overlooked in this debate, as Youniss has noted, is the relational dimension of the egocentrism construct. Piaget consistently maintained that the unequal relationship that children have with adults fosters egocentrism by encouraging children to submit to the adult authority. On the other hand, the equal relationship that exists among peers encourages children to consider their perspectives in making reasonable decisions through mutual agreement. Piaget's relational perspective on moral development leads to the radical conclusion, elaborated in a provocative study by Youniss, that peers, not parents, play the decisive role in promoting moral development.

D. Intentionality

In the next section of the book, Piaget examined children's modes of moral evaluations with a focus on the origin of children's awareness of intentionality. The best known of his queries asks who was the naughtiest, a child who knocked over 15 cups accidently or a child who broke 1 cup in an act of disobedience. Piaget found that children below 8 or 9 years old typically based their judgments of culpability on the extent of material damage. The older children, however, recognized the moral relevance of the intentions of the actors. Conceding that objective responsibility may largely be a function of the way in which parents respond to children's clumsiness, Piaget observed that his own young children made spontaneous judgments of objective responsibility even though he and his wife were careful not to punish or blame their children for unintentional damage. Furthermore, Piaget found that when considering cases of stealing and lying, younger children tended to make judgments of objective responsibility that their parents would be very unlikely to make. For example, the younger children regarded lying as saying something untrue, whether or not the misstatement was made intentionally. The mere violation of the moral rule was a sufficient determinant of guilt. As in his discussion of egocentrism, Piaget attributed young children's failure to differentiate moral from physical laws (moral realism) and intentions from consequences partly to their immature thinking and partly to authoritarian child-rearing practices.

E. The Two Moralities of Childhood

In the third section of the book Piaget studied children's conception of punishment and distributive justice. Although his data indicated that development generally proceeds from heteronomy to autonomy, the many exceptions to this pattern suggested that heteronomy and autonomy are not sequential

stages but two irreducible types built on different relational foundations. For example, Piaget found that young children see expiatory punishment as fair only in the adult–child relationship, whereas, in the child–child relationship, children at all ages favor what Piaget called punishment by reciprocity, that is punishment aimed solely to make the transgressor aware of the undesirable consequences of his or her misdeed.

Post-Piagetian researchers, as indicated, have tended to view socio-moral development in a more cognitive and less relational framework than Piaget. Although this may have led many researchers to underestimate the effects of constraint and cooperation on socio-moral problem-solving, it also led to important break-throughs in the study of such topics as perspective-taking and intentionality. Furthermore, in the case of moral development, the cognitive developmental focus has led away from the two-morality hypothesis to a unitary process of stage development.

III. KOHLBERG'S THEORY

A. The Moral Domain

When asked to give his views on moral development and education, Lawrence Kohlberg was fond of citing Socrates' response to a similar request at the beginning of Plato's *Meno:* "You must think I am very fortunate to know how virtue is acquired. The fact is, far from knowing whether it can be taught, I have know idea what virture really is." Kohlberg, like Socrates, did not believe that one could address questions of moral psychology and education without first attempting to define in a philosophically justifiable way the nature of morality. Yet in the mid 1950s, when Kohlberg began his dissertation research on moral development, social scientists paid little if any attention to the philosophical presuppositions of their work.

Kohlberg was particularly distressed by the claim prevalent in social learning research and psychoanalytic theory that moral development reduces to the internalization of the rules and practices of one's society. Having become involved in the Hagganah's effort to smuggle European Jewish refugees into Israel following the Holocaust, Kohlberg was committed to an understanding of morality that transcends the status quo and provides a rational basis for responsible social criticism. He also questioned the assumption that morality can be reduced to culturally relative norms and values. Such an assumption, based on observed cultural differences, blurs an important distinction between morality and custom or social convention. Moral norms and values, such as prohibitions against causing physical injury, concern the rights and welfare of individuals in any societal arrangement. Customs or conventions (e.g., table manners), on the other hand, concern socially imposed rules that provide a certain order and decorum but are not recognized as obligatory in the same sense as moral norms.

In addition to differentiating morality from custom, Kohlberg also distinguished morality from personal and religious values or the right from the good. Underlying the distinction between the right and the good is a recognition that what is right or moral is obligatory, whereas what is good is left to individual choice, as long as it is in harmony with what is right. Kohlberg used this distinction to argue that moral education could be undertaken in the public schools without violating the separation between church and state or without indoctrinating personal values.

Following up on Kohlberg's philosophical attempt to delineate the moral sphere, Turiel and his colleagues have proposed that morality, convention, and personal values comprise three conceptual domains, each with its own developmental trajectory. Their research indicates that even very young children are capable of distinguishing moral violations from violations within the other domains. Such findings confirm the wisdom of Kohlberg's effort to base his research on a carefully defined conceptualization of morality, even as they call into question whether he consistently distinguished the moral from the conventional in his some of his stage descriptions.

B. The Moral Judgment Interview

Kohlberg's definition of moraltiy as justice, his emphasis on studying the development of moral reasoning, and his aim of charting moral development throughout the lifespan led him to construct a semiclinical moral judgment interview. His original interview posed 10 hypothetical moral dilemmas drawn, not from familiar episodes in the world of children (as were Piaget's) but from challenging problems in the world of adults. Kohlberg regarded the Heinz dilemma (slightly abbreviated here) as his best:

In Europe, a woman was near death from a special kind of cancer. There was a drug that could save her but the druggist was charging twice as much as the sick woman's husband, Heinz, could raise. Heinz pleaded with the druggist, but the druggist said, "No, I discovered the drug and I'm going to make money from it." Heinz has exhausted all other alternatives, should he steal the drug?

The Heinz dilemma puts subjects in the uncomfortable position of having to decide between his wife's claim to life and the druggist's legally sanctioned claim to property. The point of the interview is not to identify subjects' action choices but to examine the ways in which they justify their choices; therefore, interviewers are instructed to ask subjects to present, elaborate, and clarify their arguments.

C. Levels and Stages

Kohlberg's current theory describes a sequence of six stages grouped into three levels: The preconventional level (stages 1 and 2), the conventional level (stages 3 and 4), and the postconventional or principled level (stages 5 and 6). As the labels indicate, the levels are determined by the perspective taken on the moral expectations (rules, roles, norms, and values) of the conventional social order. The work "conventional" connotes simply what is commonly accepted and should not be confused with Turiel's use of the term to mean a nonmoral custom. At the preconventional level, conventional expectations are seen as external to the self. The obligation to follow such expectations comes not from their intrinsic worth or their place within the social fabric but from the mere fact that they are commanded or that noncompliance is punished. At the conventional level, conventional expectations are internalized. Conventional expectations are respected because individuals value their membership in society and want to be regarded as upstanding members of their communities. At the postconventional level, conventional expectations are subordinated to general, foundational principles. Conventional expectations are critically appraised according to such principles from a prior to society perspective, that is from the perspective of a moral agent aware of basic rights and values that all societies should recognize.

Like the levels, the structural core of the stages depends upon what Kohlberg calls the socio-moral perspective of the subject. At stage one, subjects are, to use Piaget's term, egocentric: they fail to differentiate their perspective from others, particularly those in authority who are valued for their superior size and power. As a consequence, those at stage one believe that rules are to be obeyed for their own sake or for the avoidance of punishment, which is seen as inevitable. For example, children at this stage often state that Heinz should not steal the drug simply because stealing is wrong or because his theft will be punished. At stage two, subjects are aware that individuals have concrete wants and desires and that such wants and needs can come into conflict. It is right to pursue one's interests as long as others are not prevented from pursuing theirs. Subjects at this stage sometimes justify Heinz's stealing simply by appealing to his wife's need or to the presumption that anyone in Heinz's situation would not want their wife to die or would automatically do what was necessary. Subjects will likewise justfy Heinz's not stealing by noting that the risk of punishment may not be worth it. Conflicts of interest are to be settled by making deals. For example, Heinz should steal the drug for his wife in return for what she has done for him or because he may need a favor from her sometime.

At stage three, subjects take a third person perspective and view themselves and others not only as individuals, but as members of relationships or small groups. They seek to uphold shared expectations for good behavior and value sympathetic and prosocial motives. For example, subjects will argue that Heinz should steal the drug because he loves her or because he is her husband. On the other hand, they will also argue that Heinz should not steal because stealing is selfish or takes advantage of the druggist who works hard. Subjects at the fourth stage take the perspective of the social system and respect its laws and legal processes as necessary for maintaining social order. Just as they see the need for consistency in society, they also see the need for developing individual character and respecting the dictates of conscience. Subjects at this stage sometimes maintain that Heinz should not take the law into his own hands by stealing. They will, however, also maintain that stealing may be justified in response to an idealized natural law that is higher than human law.

At stage five, subjects take a prior to society perspective and judge the moral worth of rules and values insofar as such rules and values are consistent with more fundamental considerations, such as liberty, the general welfare or utility, human rights, and contractual obligations. Subjects typically argue that Heinz should steal the drug because the right to life is more basic than the right to property. At stage six, subjects take a procedural or dialogical perspective on decision-making. What is right is what would be freely chosen by all interested parties who take each others' point of view into account and who respect others as equal and autonomous persons. Subjects at this stage make explicit appeal either to a procedure for adjudicating claims or to universal, regulative principles of justice.

The status of stage six is uncertain. Although stage six continues to be listed in the table of the stages, the current scoring manual provides only criterion judgments through stage five because no stage six examples were found in the longitudinal sample. The current formulation of stage six is embedded within the contractarian tradition in moral philosophy extending from Rousseau and Kant to Rawls and Habermas. Such a formulation and the fact that the few examples of stage six cited by Kohlberg come from individuals with philosophic training suggest that stage six may not be a psychological stage but a philosophical position.

D. Reliability and Validity

At the very heart of cognitive development theory are the assumptions of invariant stage sequence and structural wholeness. The test of invariant sequence is whether individuals develop through the stages in ascending order without skips or reversals. The test of structural wholeness is whether individuals respond to different kinds of moral dilemmas by using the same or adjacent stage reasoning. These assumptions have guided efforts over the years since Kohlberg's dissertation to refine the stage descriptions and methods for scoring interviews. The early definitions of and procedures for scoring were based on moral content, that is, the moral concerns and values typically associated with a particular stage. For example a simple statement of concern for law and order was scored as stage 4. At the 10th year of Kohlberg's longitudinal study, problems of regression and stage heterogeneity across the different dilemmas called the cognitive developmental assumptions of Kohlberg's theory into question. Case analysis indicated that regressions were occurring because content, like the law and order concern, was being coded as stage 4 regardless of its meaning in the larger context of the interview. Kohlberg thus revised both his stage definitions and scoring method to focus on structure rather than content. Because the structural scoring method required far greater interpretive judgment than the earlier method, inter-rater reliability suffered for a time, prompting critics to challenge the empirical foundation of the theory.

In response, Colby, Kohlberg, and their colleagues developed the present Standard Issue Scoring Manual, which supplements the structural scoring process by providing over 700 prototypes (criterion judgments) of common responses to nine dilemmas. Stage scores are assigned by matching arguments in the interview to these criterion judgments. This new method achieves high inter-rater reliability (from 88 to 100% agreement within a third of a stage) by eliminating much of the subjectivity in the structural coding method, while, nevertheless, providing guidance for distinguishing content from structure.

In addition to obtaining high inter-rater reliability, the new method also achieves substantial test–retest agreement over a 3- to 6-week interval (from 93 to 100% within a third of a stage), indicating the stability of the measure. A coefficient of internal consistency (Cronbach's alpha) in the 90s as well as factor analysis indicates that the interview taps a single construct. Some critics have dismissed the moral judgment measure as simply another intelligence test, yet correlations with IQ are only moderate (.37 to .59), indicating that moral development is related but not reducible to general intelligence.

The case for the validity of the measure is based on how well longitudinal data support the major theoretical assumptions of invariant sequence and structural wholeness. Three major studies, of U.S. males, of Turkish males from rural and urban areas, and of male and female adolescents from an Israeli kibbutz, were used to determine the validity of the construct. All of the studies show that development proceeds through an invariant sequence. There were no instances of stage skipping or stage reversal within the limits of measurement error (determined through test–retest instability). All of the studies also indicate that development proceeds as a structural whole. Individuals generally respond to different dilemmas using one or two adjacent stages (e.g., at stages 2 and 3). Cases in which three stages are used are infrequent (less than 10%). The data thus support Kohlberg's major theoretical claims as well the adequacy of the methodology.

E. Cross-Cultural Validity

Longitudinal studies in Turkey and Israel and cross-sectional studies in over 25 Western and non-Western countries, which include populations from both urban and traditional folk societies, generally support the universality of the moral stages. Although content differences were found, the interview responses were generally scorable with the new manual. The results displayed patterns of sequential stage development and structural wholeness similar to the United States longitudinal sample. Snarey and Keljo note, however, three discrepant cross-cultural findings of potential theoretical import. First, stage 5 was absent in traditional folk societies. Second, the rate of moral development was faster in urban than in traditional folk societies. Third, the current scoring manual does not have criterion judgments for responses typically found not only in traditional folk societies but in non-Western and communitarian societies. The first two of these findings do not necessarily indicate a problem with the theory. It is not surprising that individuals in small, relatively homogeneous traditional societies do not develop beyond the conventional stages and that the pace of their development is slower. The third finding, however, suggests at the very least that the scoring manual needs to be expanded. On the other hand, this finding may, as some critics have charged, be symptomatic of an underlying bias especially at the postconventional level in favor of the liberal, individualistic ideology of Western urban society.

IV. NEW DIRECTIONS

A. The Defining Issues Test

The Defining Issues Test (DIT) was developed by Rest as a practical alternative to the moral judgment interviewing and scoring procedures (for subjects at or above a 12-year-old reading level). It presents subjects with stage prototypic responses to six moral dilemmas and asks them to rate and then rank their preferences. Althought the DIT has been widely and successfully used as a proxy for the clinical moral judgment method (it correlates moderately well with the Kohlberg measure), it is an important measure in its own right. The DIT measures individuals' comprehension of and preference for preformulated moral arguments, while the moral judgment interview measures individuals' ability to produce spontaneously moral arguments.

Finding considerable rating and raking heterogeneity in the DIT and charging that Kohlberg's scoring procedures have tended to smooth over significant stage irregularities, Rest has suggested that an additive model of stage development may be more adequate than Piaget and Kohlberg's transformational or displacement model. Support for the additive model comes not only from DIT research but also from studies indicating considerable stage heterogeneity when comparisons are made between standard and certain nonstandard moral dilemmas and between hypothetical and real life dilemmas. Furthermore, most post-Piagetian psychologists, influenced by information processing, favor the additive model's more differentiated approach. The evidence favoring the holistic, transformational model comes from production tasks, like the moral judgment interview, which is designed to assess the moral reasoning competence and to facilitate the interpretation of discrete ideas into a more comprehensive framework. Perhaps both models (and others too) are necessary to elucidate different dimensions of the complex process of moral development.

B. Early Childhood Development

Kohlberg's longitudinal sample begins with 10-year-olds because the original intent of his research was to build upon Piaget's work. The nature of his moral dilemmas would have precluded his starting much earlier because they were specifically designed to describe how individuals develop the capacity to resolve moral problems in the adult world. Yet such dilemmas emphasize the limitations of children's thinking (as is evident in the punishment and obedience description of stage 1). Returning to Piaget's method of presenting children with familiar problems, Damon demonstrated that the socio-moral conceptions of young children (ages 4 to 9) in the areas of distributive justice, friendship, and authority develop through surprisingly varied and sophisticated developmental levels. For example, in describing the development of children's resolutions of distributive justice problems, Damon described a six-level scheme in which children based their judgments on the following sequence of considerations: their own desires, strict equality, merit, equity, and combinations of merit and equity that best serve the common good.

C. Gender and Development

Gilligan has since the mid-1970s charged that Kohlberg's stage theory is biased against women because it describes the justice and rights orientation favored by males, while it neglects the care and responsibility orientation favored by females. She attributed the one-sidedness of Kohlberg's approach to his embeddedness in the Western male philosophical tradition, his all-male sample, and his use of hypothetical moral dilemmas, which were better suited to males, who preferred abstractions, than to females who preferred context. Originally support for Gilligan's critique came from several studies showing women's moral judgment scores were, on the average, lower than those of men. Yet reanalyses of those studies indicated that once adjustments were made for education and occupation, differences between men and women disappeared. Gilligan has, nevertheless, persisted in her claim that an alternative theory is needed to describe women's moral voice. She maintains that Kohlberg has overlooked the dynamics of relatedness and interdependence, dynamics that require a radically new approach to moral psychology.

Gilligan's criticisms of Kohlberg's position seem more applicable to some of his philosophical statements than to the organization of the scoring manual. The scoring manual puts concerns about building relationships on the same footing as concerns about justice and rights. Furthermore, although Kohlberg's moral stages were based on an all-male sample, they are similar to Loevinger's stages of ego development, which were originally developed from an all-female longitudinal sample. In sum, there is little evidence to support the view that men and women follow radically divergent developmental paths. On the other hand, Gilligan's analyses suggest that men and women may tend to have somewhat different moral concerns and sensitivities.

D. Moral Judgment and Moral Action

Gilligan's work is one of the many projects broadening the field of moral development to include a wide array of affective and personality variables influencing decision-making and action. In an effort to organize this literature and to integrate relevant research in other fields, Rest has proposed that the internal processes leading to moral action be divided into four sequential components or phases: (1) interpreting the moral situation; (2) formulating the moral ideal; (3) choosing a course of action in the light of one's moral and nonmoral values; and (4) executing one's choice.

The process of moral action begins with a perception that one is in a situation that will likely require a moral response. Feminist ethicists have pointed out that key to this perception is what Weil and Murdoch have called attentiveness and what Noddings has called engrossment, a sensitive openness to and focused awareness of the needs, thoughts, and feelings of others. Their analyses point to the critical role that empathy plays in motivating individuals to become involved and in providing information about the source of the other's distress and how it may be alleviated. Hoffman's research elaborates such notions from a psychological perspective by showing how empathy develops from the quasi-instinctual reactions of infants to the deliberative responses of older children.

The second phase involves the reasoning and decision-making process that result in a moral judgment or in the determination of a moral ideal. The cognitive developmental approach has dominated the research in this area; yet it has only identified deep structures of moral reasoning. Such structures do not directly predict to behavior or even to action choices, yet moral judgment stages have been shown to be related to delinquency, altruism, resistance to the temptation to cheat, the clinical performance of medical interns, participation in the Berkeley Free Speech Sit-in, and a willingness to disobey in the Milgram experiment. In most studies, the higher one's moral stage was, the greater the likelihood that one would perform the putatively moral action. In order to obtain a fuller picture of the moral judgment process, psychologists need to attend to how particular beliefs, values, and life commitments influence the choice of one course of action over another. Here recent narrative and hermeneutical approaches that look at moral judgment within the context of an individual's life story may prove helpful.

In the third phase, individuals ascertain the extent to which they feel personally responsible for acting on their moral choices at the second phase. For example, many of those who participated in the Milgram experiment admitted that it was wrong to administer painful shocks, but, nevertheless, believed that they did not have a responsibility to quit the experiment because they were following the instructions of the psychologist authority. Blasi's research indicates judgments of responsibility develop in stages that roughly parallel the moral judgment stages. As individuals develop to the higher stages, they experience themselves as more autonomous, that is, as more personally responsible for their values, decisions, and actions. Judgments of responsi-

bility, while related to cognitive moral development, appear rooted in processes of identity and development through which adolescents making the transition into adulthood must determine the centrality of moral commitments to their self-definition.

In the fourth phase, moral aims become moral deeds. Many personality variables may play a role at this phase. For example, research by Krebs and Kohlberg indicated that stage 4 subjects with high ego strength were better able to resist the temptation to cheat than stage 4 counterparts with low ego stage. More recently research by Haan has shown that defenses and coping and self-assertion strategies play an important role in the way in which individuals interact in game simulated moral situations. [*See* DECISION MAKING, INDIVIDUALS; REASONING.]

E. Promoting Moral Development

Cognitive developmentalists generally explain stage change as the result of disequillibration brought about by experiences that are not readily assimilable within a person's existing cognitive structure. Such experiences are thought to lead to cognitive conflict, which in turn leads to the construction of a new stage. Experimental and educational research suggest that experiences fostering moral development provide at least one of the following conditions: (1) exposure to higher stage reasoning; (2) exposure to a conflicting opinion (at the same stage as one's own); and (3) perspective taking.

Relatively little attention has been paid to the role of families in promoting moral development. This is partly due to the research showing that moral development is not confined to early childhood as Freudians among others had posited but continues into adulthood. The lack of attention to the family may have also been influenced by Piaget's belief that the parent–child relationship tends to foster a heteronomous morality. Furthermore, the stages of parents and children are only modestly correlated and there is no evidence that parent's stage puts a ceiling on their children's development or that the children of higher stage parents necessarily develop to higher stages themselves. There is a growing body of research, however, that indicates that parenting style and the nature of family discussion play a significant role in stimulating moral development. Baumrind, for example, has found that the most effective parenting is neither authoritarian nor permissive, but authoritative. Authoritative parenting combines a high level of parent and child communication with control and realistic demands. Focusing on family discussions, Powers has identified that the patterns most conducive to moral development blend cognitive challenges with affective support. [*See* PARENTING.]

Considerable research has been conducted on educational applications of moral development theory. The most widely used approach based on cognitive developmental theory is the discussion of moral dilemmas. Hundreds of studies have found that moral discussions led by a teacher–facilitator employing Socratic questioning techniques promote modest (about a third of a stage) but significant stage change. Research by Berkowitz indicates that even leaderless discussion can promote stage change when the participants employ certain dialogical or transactional strategies, such as offering a countersuggestion, finding common ground, requesting a justification, and juxtaposing different arguments.

Kohlberg, Higgins, and Power have developed a more radical moral education strategy, the just community approach, which builds on Piaget's view that moral autonomy is fostered under conditions of equality and reciprocity. Just communities consist of a relatively small group of students (from 30 to 90) who take a core of courses together and who make and enforce their rules with their teachers in a direct participatory democracy. Research indicates that the just community approach not only promotes moral reasoning development but nurtures students' sense of responsibility and agency.

Key to the just community approach is an emphasis on building a positive moral culture. This culture has been described in terms of the extent to which norms and values expressive of a relatively high stage of fairness and group solidarity are shared and upheld by members of the program. A positive moral culture appears to provide both a motivating and a disequillibrating context for moral development. Students are attracted to a democratic group that they perceive as genuinely caring. At the same time, students are challenged by membership in a group with high expectations for responsible behavior.

V. CONCLUSION

The study of moral development emerged in the early 1960s as the seminal cognitive developmental studies of Jean Piaget and Lawrence Kohlberg captured the attention of developmental and social psychologists. The initial phase of cognitive developmental research focused on the description of stages of reasoning from childhood through adulthood. The current phase of research seeks to understand the relationship between moral reasoning and moral behavior by exploring dimensions of the self as well as the social environment.

Bibliography

Damon, W. (1988). "The Moral Child: Nurturing the Children's Natural Moral Growth." Free Press, New York.
Garrod, A. (1993). "Approaches to Moral Development: New Research and Emerging Themes." Teachers College Press, New York.
Gilligan, C., Ward, J. V., and Taylor, J. (1988). "Remapping the Moral Domain: A Contribution of Women's Thinking to Psychological Theory and Education." Harvard University Press, Cambridge, MA.
Kuhmerker, L. (1991). "The Kohlberg Legacy for the Helping Professions." Religious Education Press, Birmingham, AL.
Kurtines, W. M., and Gewirtz, J. (Eds.) (1991). "Moral Behavior and Development," Vol. I. Earlbaum, Hillsdale, NJ.
Kurtines, W. M. and Gerwirtz, J. (Eds.) (1991). "Moral Behavior and Development," Vol. II. Earlbaum, Hillsdale, NJ.
Power, F. C., Higgins, A., and Kohlberg, L. (1989). "Lawrence Kohlberg's Approach to Moral Education." Columbia University Press, New York.
Schrader, D. (1990). "The Legacy of Lawrence Kohlberg." Josey-Bass, San Francisco.

MOTIVATION

J. T. Newton

University of London

Glossary

Drive State of arousal resulting from a biological (or, occasionally, psychological) need.

Drive-reduction theory Theory of motivation that suggests that animals behave in ways which act to minimize or reduce drives.

Functional analysis Method for modeling the complex actions and interactions of variables in the determination of behavior. Data for the model are derived from many different sources, including direct observation, the observations of others, questionnaire data, etc.

Incentive An external stimulus which energizes behavior and/or gives it direction.

Instinct An innate biological force that predisposes an organism to act.

Need A state of deprivation, most usually associated with deprivation of a biological requirement such as food or water, but used to signify deprivation of a psychological or emotional nature (e.g., need for achievement).

PSYCHOLOGISTS have long been divided about the utility of the concept of motivation. This has been reflected in a plethora of definitions of the term. As popularly used, the term *motivation* refers to the cause or determinants of behavior. Such a definition would bring most current psychological research under the provence of motivational research; however, some researchers have used a similar definition. Young described the study of motivation as the "search for determinants . . . of human and animal activity." Perhaps the most commonly used definition has focused on motivation as those factors which energize behavior and give it direction. Others feel that motivation can only be used to account for the energizing aspects of behavior, with other mechanisms such as learning and cognition accounting for the direction of behavior. The notion of behavior as being motivated is a relatively recent historical phenomenon subsequent to the decline of rationalism, though the mechanistic thinking of the seventeenth and eighteenth century philosophers is implicit in many models of motivation which are used today.

An understanding of the ways in which motivation has been defined is important in understanding the models used by researchers to explain motivational phenomena. An extreme mechanistic view is the theory of *instincts*. An instinct is an innate biological force that predisposes the organism to act in a certain way. Animal behavior has long been explained in terms of instincts. The work of Darwin and Freud suggested that humans also were at the mercy of instinct (although these were unconscious, and their effects on behavior subtle if far reaching). The great problem of explaining behavior in terms of instincts lies in the circularity of the argument. Instincts, since they are not directly observable, must be inferred from behavior; the only evidence of their existence is that the behavior occurs.

Instinct theory later came to be replaced by the concept of *drives*. A drive is a state of arousal which results from some biological *need*. The state of arousal motivates the organism to remedy the need. Thus, humans and animals behave in order to reduce drives (the *drive-reduction* theory of motivation). Although drive, like instinct, is a hypothetical construct, it can be inferred from the presence of environmental and historical cues. For example, although we cannot measure whether someone is hungry, we can infer it from the length of time that has elapsed since he or she last ate. Needs can be defined, it is suggested, objectively and conditions specified for creating and eliminating them. A central assumption of this model is the concept of homeostasis, the body's tendency to maintain a stable internal environment. Motivation is seen as the process of maintaining homeostasis through behavior. This model suggests that motivation is largely the result of internal states.

Factors external to the individual may also act to energize behavior and give it direction. Such external stimuli have been referred to as *incentives*. Positive and negative incentives have been proposed; the former lead to approach, the latter to avoidance.

A selectionist approach to understanding motivation analyzes behavior in terms of the proximate factors influencing them at present and the ultimate factors that led to their evolution in the first place. In this analysis the greatest motivating force is natural selection—humans and animals engage in behavior (at least partly) because in the past these same traits increased the likelihood of that individual's genes surviving. This statement leaves us ignorant of the variables that cause behavior to be expressed in the present.

Alternatively, motivation can be seen as a learning process. Behavior is energized through discriminative stimuli which signal reinforcement or punishment. It is then given direction (shaped) by a process of systematic differential reinforcement or punishment. In this model, the term *motivation* is seen as a shorthand description of the multiple-discriminative stimuli and reinforcement contingencies which operate to both energize and direct behavior. This model has been applied in the understanding of clinically abnormal behavior, particularly in the field of learning difficulties.

I. MOTIVATION OF EATING BEHAVIOR

Eating behavior demonstrates many of the models of motivation which have been outlined above. Hunger, a drive state which we are motivated (generally) to reduce, arises from a need which we infer from the time since last we ate, how much we have eaten, and so on. Furthermore, the control of eating behavior appears to be under homeostatic control, certainly in the short term. Three major variables control immediate appetite: blood-sugar level, stomach fullness, and body temperature. The hypothalamus contains cells which respond to changes in glucose levels; cells in the ventromedial hypothalamus re-

spond to increased glucose levels, and cells in the lateral hypothalamus respond to lowered levels of glucose. These areas have long been suggested as areas controlling the eating function, since lesions of the lateral hypothalamus lead to decreased eating and stimulation of this area leads to the initiation of eating. Lesions of the ventromedial hypothalamus lead to increased eating and obesity in every species studied. Blood glucose as a method of controlling food intake in the short term suffers the disadvantage of being rather slow in responding to change; digestion is a relatively slow process. A more immediate signal is a full stomach. Experiments suggest that the ventromedial hypothalamus responds to distension of the stomach to inhibit eating, while the lateral hypothalamus responds to the periodic contractions produced by the empty stomach. Finally, the third factor controlling food intake in the short term is temperature. The mechanism by which cooling the brain results in increased eating is unclear. [*See* APPETITE.]

The long-term control of food intake is more complex in humans than most other species. Again, the hypothalamus appears to be involved in ensuring that the animal's weight remains stable over prolonged periods of time. As noted above, animals with lesions of the ventromedial hypothalamus overeat until they achieve obesity; however, they then maintain their weight at this new obese "set point." Similarly, damage to the lateral hypothalamus lowers the set point. Some biochemical correlate of body weight must act on the hypothalamus to determine food intake. There is some evidence to suggest that this may be levels of free fatty acids in the bloodstream. It seems likely that the hypothalamus exerts its control over food intake by the release of insulin into the bloodstream. This is a good example of a homeostatic model of motivation. [*See* HYPOTHALAMUS.]

An alternative model suggests that eating is controlled by learned responses. As we develop as individuals, we learn to associate a certain amount of eating (chewing, swallowing, etc.) with the physiological signs of satiety, such as stomach fullness and increased blood glucose. Thus we do not have to eat every meal until our stomach is full; instead, we come to learn how much we should eat before we are satiated. Furthermore long-term learning processes could explain how animals maintain a fairly stable weight over time and how specific hungers and conditioned taste aversions develop. Both people and animals show specific hungers that are strong preferences for certain foods. These result not only from ethnic and cultural differences but also from genuine nutritional deficits. For example, rats fed on a diet deficient in thiamin develop an aversion to the deficient diet and will avidly accept any new diet even if that also is deficient. They will continue this process until they are fed a diet which contains thiamin. An animal that becomes sick after eating a novel food will learn to avoid that food. Such conditioned taste aversions have obvious survival value. However, the mechanism by which they are acquired, and the nature of the aversion, have not yet been discovered.

Eating behavior in humans is under the control of many external cues such as the characteristics of the food, time of day, and the social context. Research suggests that individuals who are overweight are more sensitive to such cues than individuals of average weight. One study found that overweight subjects in comparison to individuals of average weight, ate more of an ice cream which they rated as tasting excellent and less of one if they disliked the taste. Similarly, obese individuals are more likely to eat if food cues are salient (e.g., if food is brightly lit or a vivid description of the food is given, or simply when it is time for a meal). Obese individuals are also more sensitive to internal cues to eating, and are more likely to interpret any physiological state of arousal as hunger.

One theory suggests that individuals may be described as either restrained or unrestrained eaters. Restrained eaters are those who conciously seek to restrain their eating, regardless of their actual weight. Their eating behavior resembles that which is generally found in obese individuals, (i.e., they are more sensitive to both external and internal cues). Furthermore there is some evidence to suggest that once restraint is broken, overeating may occur. This theory has been useful in explaining some of the behaviors that occur in bulimia nervosa.

II. MOTIVATION OF DRINKING BEHAVIOR

An organism which is suffering a deficit of water may respond in one of two ways; by drinking or by recovering water from the kidneys. The latter is a truly homeostatic mechanism; it is not a mechanism by which behavior is motivated. Drinking behavior is the result of both internal and external cues. It has been suggested that receptors in the mouth and throat appear to be able to detect the quantity of

fluid that has been drunk. Animals fitted with an esophageal bypass will drink a certain amount of water and then stop even though none has reached their stomach. However, such animals will subsequently drink again, indicating that there must be additional signals regulating water intake. Water deficit produces changes in the blood and fluids surrounding body cells, decreasing their volume and increasing the concentration of particular elements (primarily sodium). Current theories postulate two brain mechanisms for the control of water intake: osmoreceptors, which are sensitive to the concentration of elements within bodily fluids, and volumetric receptors, which are sensitive to the total volume of body fluids.

Osmoreceptors are located in the hypothalamus in the region immediately above the pituitary gland. They stimulate the release of ADH from the pituitary and thus trigger the reabsorption of water by the kidneys.

Loss of blood volume will motivate an animal to drink regardless of the concentration of bodily fluids (e.g., when there is blood loss following injury). Evidence suggests that renin secreted by the kidneys into the bloodstream is responsible for cuing drinking behavior in response to decreased volume of blood and body fluids. Renin causes the blood vessels to constrict, a homeostatic mechanism which reduces blood loss and increases blood pressure. It also acts as an enzyme on angiotensinogen (a blood protein), converting it to angiotensin I. As blood passes through the lungs, angiotensin I is converted into angiotensin II, which acts on specific receptors in the hypothalamus to induce thirst.

The mechanism by which organisms stop drinking is less well understood. Cellular rehydration is unlikely to act as a cue since it is relatively slow to change, and animals will usually stop drinking long before this can have taken place.

III. MOTIVATION OF SEXUAL BEHAVIOR

Sexual behavior, unlike eating and drinking, is unlikely to be controlled by a homeostatic mechanism. Freud suggested that sexual energy acts as a drive (the libido) and continually builds itself up until the time when it is released (catharsis). Such a model is not homeostatic; rather, it is a hydraulic model. Sexual behavior is governed by a combination of internal factors (hormones and brain mechanisms) and external factors (environmental cues and learning). [*See* SEXUAL BEHAVIOR.]

The development and functioning of sexual organs are the result of the release of hormones under the control of the pituitary gland. Pituitary hormones in females stimulate the ovaries to produce estrogen and progesterone. In the male, pituitary hormones stimulate the cells of the testes to manufacture and secrete a range of sex hormones called androgens, the most important of these being testosterone. The control exerted by sex hormones over sexual behavior decreases as study moves from lower to higher vertebrates, though the situation is different for males and females. Generally, castration of a sexually mature male primate or human will not result in a decline in sexual activity (castration before the start of puberty usually prevents copulation). In contrast, castration of the female usually results in the total cessation of sexual activity for all species except humans. The effect in humans is complicated by emotional and social overlays. [*See* HORMONES AND BEHAVIOR.]

Secretion of sex hormones is fairly constant in the male of most species, and sexual motivation is also fairly constant. In the female, hormones fluctuate cyclically with accompanying changes in fertility. Estrogen released during the first part of the cycle prepares the uterus for implantation and also tends to increase sexual interest in most animals. In humans, sexual interest in both males and females is most strongly influenced by social and emotional factors. Hormones influence sexual motivation not by eliciting sexual behavior but by increasing the probability that an animal will respond in the presence of certain stimuli.

IV. MOTIVATION OF AGGRESSIVE BEHAVIOR

Aggression has often been viewed as a basic instinct. Chief among these thinkers was Freud, who viewed the death instinct (thanatos) as building up within the individual, only to be released by overt or covert aggression. Later psychodynamic theorists rejected the idea that aggression was innate and instead suggested that it was a response to frustration. Frustration was defined as occurring when an individual's goals are blocked, leading to aggression (the frustration–aggression hypothesis). This drive is reduced by the expression of aggression. There is little evidence to support the idea of aggression as cathartic.

Studies of both adults and children generally show that aggression which is not punished is likely to be repeated. [*See* AGGRESSION.]

Stimulation (electrical or chemical) of certain regions of the hypothalamus appears to produce aggression in lower animals such as rats and mice. Aggression in higher mammals is under greater cortical control. For example, the effects of stimulation of the hypothalamus in monkeys depends to a great extent on the individual monkey's position in the dominance hierarchy as well as that of those in the vicinity of the monkey. The monkey may attack those who are below it in the dominance hierarchy but become submissive to those that are above it.

Social learning theory has viewed aggression as a learned response, rejecting the idea of an aggression drive. Just as with any other learned behavior, aggression can be learned through observation or imitation, increased by reinforcement, and controlled by the presence or absence of discriminative stimuli. Emotional arousal (of either an aversive or pleasant nature) increased the probability of an aggressive response in the presence of cues which suggest to the individual that such a response is appropriate. Thus the frustration–aggression hypothesis is incorporated within this model as a specific instance of a more general principle. The imitation of aggression and the effects of reinforcement of aggression were demonstrated strikingly by the famous ''Bo-bo doll'' experiments of Bandura and his team.

V. MOTIVATION AND THE FUNCTIONAL ANALYSIS OF BEHAVIOR

The functional analysis of behavior is a paradigm that seeks to identify those variables which maintain (and sometimes those which create) behavior. Emphasis is placed particularly on identifying variables from the environment surrounding the individual, as well as those within the individual. The use of functional analysis has been particularly common in the area of clinical psychology and behavior change, most notably in work with individuals with learning difficulties. The model is a hypothesis-testing one, the effects of changes in variables being assessed to determine their influence on the behavior in question. The data which form the basis of these hypotheses are usually taken from a wide variety of sources: direct behavior observation, self-report, the observations of others, etc. Some authors have used analogue situations to determine the impact of the environment on behaviors such as self-injury and stereotyped behavior. Such an approach, although time consuming, allows for the exquisite study of behavior.

The results of a functional analysis are normally represented as a diagram demonstrating the actions and interactions of those variables which determine the particular behavior under study. A functional analysis of behavior is usually specific to an individual person, general models of behavior being subject to more generalizations and limitations. It can be argued that in many ways the term *functional analysis of behavior* is synonymous with the term *motivation*—it is a way of describing those factors which energize a particular behavior and give it direction.

To conclude, motivation has generally been studied as an abstract concept which attempts to describe the way in which a general class of (complex) behaviors is energized and/or directed. This has led to the dissolution of the concept into a convenient shorthand description for biological states and envi-

ronmental circumstances. For example, in the discussion of the motivation of eating, motivation is seen as occurring when a certain time has elapsed since eating or certain levels of blood glucose have been reached. It is in this pragmatic sense of summarizing the effect of many variables that motivation as a term is perhaps most useful. However, it should be remembered that such a use is merely descriptive and not explanatory.

Bibliography

Cofer, N. C., and Appley, M. H. (1964). "Motivation Theory and Research." Wiley, New York.

Colgan, P. (1989). "Animal Motivation." Academic Press, Toronto.

Michell, G. A. G. (1987). "Behavior, Cogniton and Memory." Norton, New York.

Owens, R. G., and Ashcroft, J. B. (1982). Functional analysis in applied psychology. *Br. J. Clin. Psychol.* **21,** 181–190.

Satinoff, E., and Teitelbaum, P. (1983). "Handbook of Behavioral Neurobiology." Vol. 6: "Motivation." Plenum, New York.

Weiner, B. (1985), "Human Motivation." Wiley, London.

MOTIVATION, EMOTIONAL BASIS

Carroll E. Izard and Robert Eisenberger

University of Delaware

Glossary

Affect Emotions, drives, and emotion–drive interactions believed to be the basis of motivation by biosocial theorists.

Auto-shaping Phenomenon whereby cues for delivery of a reward produce approach tendencies of such strength that they interfere with responses that actually produce the reward. For example, an illuminated disc that precedes the automatic presentation of food elicits pecking by pigeons even though the pigeon's approach to the disc and the pecking response have no effect on food delivery.

Biosocial emotion theories Emphasize the origins of emotions in evolutionary–biological processes; a key assumption is that the emotions constitute the primary motivational system and that each discrete emotion has distinct organizing and motivational functions.

Cognitive emotion theories Emphasize the influence of cognitive processes on the generation of emotions; assume that emotion activation is a function of cognitive appraisal or evaluation.

Cognitive processes Processes involved in perception, learning, and memory.

Hedonic tone Status of one's feelings in terms of pleasantness–unpleasantness or pleasure–pain.

Homeostatic system Silent, automatic mechanisms for regulating physical processes like body temperature, respiration, and cardiac rhythmicities.

Learned industriousness theory Assumption that reinforcement of increased physical or cognitive performance classically conditions positive affect to the sensation of high effort, thereby reducing effort's aversiveness.

Muga Japanese method of expert training in which the performer of a skillful task is taught to eliminate self-awareness, allowing his energy to flow into the completion of the task.

MOTIVATION, EMOTIONAL BASIS The purpose of this article is to identify key differences and similarities between the concepts of emotion and motivation and then to demonstrate how the interaction of these two phenomena with each other and with cognition (e.g., plans, goals) can be used to explain animal and human behavior. Our challenge is to find a way of integrating findings from the seemingly parallel research efforts that focus on topics ranging from animal learning to the development of human personality and psychopathology.

I. EMOTIONS AND DRIVES

In his two-volume work on affect, cognition, and consciousness, Tomkins drew some distinctions between physiological drive states such as hunger and thirst and emotion states such as joy and fear. He began by noting that signals or information from drives (or drive systems) differ from the information transmitted within the homeostatic system (mechanisms for regulating body temperature, respiration, cardiac rhythmicities, etc.).

A. Homeostasis, Drives, and Emotions

The important difference between homeostatic processes and drives is that the homeostatic system operates silently and automatically, with the regulatory information remaining at the unconscious level, except in the case of emergencies. Thus, breathing goes on automatically until there is a dramatic change in the atmosphere. A room suddenly filling with smoke might lead to pain or an anticipation of suffocation, either of which could trigger fear, and the fear would motivate the postponement of automatic breathing and escape to a space with better air. That either the sensations of pain or the higher order cognitive processes involved in anticipating suffocation can trigger fear helps explain how rats and humans might experience the same motivational condition (fear) and behave in an essentially similar fashion—actions leading to escape. This example also sets the stage for understanding some fundamental properties of drives and emotions and how their interaction produces motivational conditions that are shared by different species. [*See* HOMEOSTASIS.]

B. Distinguishing Characteristics of Drives and Emotions

Tomkins maintained that physiological drive states differ from emotions in a number of important ways. An understanding of the differences between drives and emotions should help clarify the critical role of emotions in motivation. For example, drive states concern only a particular subsystem of the individual at particular times (e.g., when food or water is needed). To explain the functioning of the whole individual and to explain behavior when no drive is aroused, it is necessary to consider the emotions. They relate to the whole individual and they can be activated at any time. [*See* MOTIVATION.]

1. *The information inherent in a drive state relates to a particular organ or system and to specific responses, typically in a particular temporal cycle associated with biological changes.* Thus, the stomach and alimentary system complain when the animal (nonhuman and human) is hungry, and consummatory behavior is the only natural means of satisfying the drive. Drives are characterized by, or relate to, hedonic tone. Hedonic tone refers to the status of one's feelings in terms of pleasantness–unpleasantness or pleasure–pain. Strong, intense drive states may activate pain, as already noted, and drive satisfaction generates consummatory and postprandial pleasure.

An emotion may have none of the foregoing characteristics. Emotion relates to the whole animal, in humans to the self or what Erikson calls egoidentity, not to a particular organ or system. Although some emotions are characterized by an action tendency, an emotion does not normally *compel* a specific cognitive process (e.g., thought) or specific action. The act of eating to satisfy hunger has no

counterpart in behavior–emotion relations, at least at the level of specific responses. Thus, no specific sequence of responses (like consummatory behavior) will "satisfy" or ameliorate sadness, or any other emotion.

One might argue that escape is to fear as eating is to hunger. Both sets of responses (escape behavior and consummatory behavior) serve to reduce or eliminate the underlying motivational state (fear or hunger). However, there is a real difference in the range of responses in the consummatory set and the escape set. This is particularly easy to demonstrate in the case of human behavior. The consummatory responses are a set of well-defined motor acts. The escape responses may involve several different subsystems of the person. In some cases, perhaps the simplest ones in human societies, escape may be largely motoric in nature—moving away from danger. Most fear-eliciting situations, such as threat of loss of job or spouse, damage to reputation, or cancer, are not managed so simply. Any of these situations and the accompanying fear will evoke a complex array of responses that is likely to require the motor system, cognitive system, and the emotions system. In the cognitive response category alone, there is a great variety of possible responses ranging from careful planning to escape through denial or fantasy. Some fear-eliciting situations may eventually elicit an incompatible emotion, such as anger, which serves to ameliorate the fear. [*See* ANXIETY AND FEAR.]

According to Izard, joy, anger, and fear do indeed lead to different types of responses, but within each type there is a very wide variety of specific cognitions and actions. Furthermore, the effects on an emotion of any set of cognition–action sequences vary across situations and across individuals.

Finally, unlike drive states, emotions do not operate on a well-defined temporal cycle that relates to biochemical changes. There may be some cyclicity in moods (emotions of extended duration), but it is much more variable within and across individuals than is the case for drive states.

2. *Drive signals are more specific and time-bound than emotion signals.* As suggested in the two foregoing paragraphs, compared to the information in emotions, the information in drive signals is quite specific in identifying the system in trouble and in indicating when and what is to be done. As Tomkins put it: "The basic nature of this information is of *time*, of *place*, and of *response*—*where* and *when* to do *what* when the body does not know otherwise how to help itself."

The basic nature of the information in emotion signals differs in several ways from that in drives. Emotion information has great generality with regard to the when, where, and what of the response. A certain memory of a lost loved one might activate joy during the funeral service, but joy expression and joy-related behavior would be postponed. Retaliation motivated by insult-induced anger might take almost any form, at any place, and at any time in the future, or the memory of the insult may change over time and plans of retaliation may be completely abandoned.

II. COMPARATIVE PSYCHOLOGY OF EMOTION–MOTIVATION RELATIONSHIPS

Precursors of human emotion occur in animals and influence basic motivational processes. It is important to understand the emotional basis for animal motivation because humans, even with their evolutionary advance in emotional differentiation, are also influenced by the general experience of positive affect and negative affect. Moreover, classical conditioning in humans, as in animals, is an important mechanism by which basic emotions come to be elicited by new situations. Finally, all goal-oriented performance can be viewed as involving a trade-off between the positive affect resulting from greater reward and the negative affect produced by increased effort. [See CLASSICAL CONDITIONING.]

A. Emotion as a Motivator of Generalized Approach and Avoidance

The motivational effects of fear on animals have been studied for a long time. A classic theory of avoidance, suggested by Mowrer, holds that stimuli that precede aversive stimuli come to elicit fear and that animals learn to escape such stimuli through fear reduction. Consistent with this view, animals will learn a new response that allows them to escape or avoid a classically conditioned signal for fear. Thus, the emotion of fear motivates the acquisition and performance of responses that allow the animal to escape or avoid the fearful stimulus. Although additional factors besides the motivating effects of fear have been implicated in such learning, fear does seem to play an important contributory role.

In animals, as humans, emotions such as fear have generalized effects beyond simply increasing the strength of some consummatory response. B. F.

Skinner noted that the presentation of punishers, or of stimuli that signalled imminent punishment, disrupted the pursuit of positive reinforcers by animals and humans. For example, presentation of a light that has been paired with shock interferes with rats' lever pressing for food. Thus, fear reduces appetitive motivation.

Skinner's discussion of the motivational effects of fear has important conceptual and practical implications. But the generality of Skinner's analysis is limited by his failure to consider the emotional effects of positive reinforcers. Sources of positive affect are still not generally well understood, and some possible sources are not widely accepted or utilized in behavioral research. One such source that may have broad implications for motivation and learning is interest–excitement, conceived by Izard and Tomkins as an emotion. Remembering that interest–excitement is a positive emotion, it may account for the positive affect or motivation that drives curiosity and exploration.

Rats, monkeys, and other species engage in a variety of behaviors that reduce no biological drives, including visual exploration of novel stimuli, locomotor exploration of novel stimuli, unrewarded manipulation, and light-contingent lever pressing. Such activities often result in learning, as in the case of monkeys that solved complex puzzles without extrinsic reward. Interest–excitement may also be generally equivalent to what people sometimes describe as the ''fun'' of trying something new and different.

Recent evidence is consistent with the view that positive reinforcers, and signals for their impending occurrence, produce a positive central emotional state. The classical conditioning of positive emotional states serves the important adaptive function of motivating animals to anticipate and pursue biologically beneficial stimuli. This positive feeling state enhances the motivation to approach a variety of rewarding events, such as lever pressing for food. Correspondingly, aversive events may produce a negative central emotional state that motivates generalized avoidance of a variety of aversive events, such as climbing over a barrier to escape shock.

Several kinds of evidence support the view that rewards and aversive stimuli produce central emotional states that have broad emotional effects. Cues for the imminent delivery of a reward produce approach tendencies of such strength that they sometimes interfere with the responses that actually produce the reward. For example, an illuminated disc that precedes the automatic presentation of food serves to elicit pecking by pigeons; such generalized approach behavior occurs even though the pigeon's approach to the disc and the pecking response have no effect on food delivery. This well-established phenomenon is known as "auto-shaping." So strong is the effect of anticipated reward on generalized approach behavior that a pigeon will peck the signal disc even if pecking produces a delay in the presentation of food. Similar kinds of generalized approach behavior occur with rats when presented with stimuli that signal imminent presentation of food or water.

Central emotional states, elicited by a reinforcer, are assumed to become classically conditioned to stimuli that predict the reinforcer. Positive central emotional states, as elicited by a signal of reward, should enhance the animals' approach behavior toward signals for a variety of different kinds of reward. Thus, a tone that has been paired with food should enhance subsequent lever pressing that produces water.

Emotional reactions can be produced not only by the onset of rewards or punishers but also by the termination of these events. Stimuli paired with the termination of punishment evidently have positive emotional properties that are similar to the positive emotion produced by stimuli that have been paired with the onset of reward. For example, stimuli that previously signalled the termination of shock should enhance positive emotionality and invigorate lever pressing that produces food. Correspondingly, the termination of reward evidently has negative emotional consequences that are similar to the negative emotionality produced by signals for the onset of punishment.

The predicted generalized effects of stimuli paired with onset and termination of rewards and punishers are illustrated in Table I. The top of the table presents the positive or negative central emotional state hypothesized to result from the onset and termination of rewards and punishers. The left side of the table describes the two types of situations (instrumental performance to obtain reward or to avoid

punishment) that should be affected by the presentation of conditioned elicitors of the central emotional states. Eight different combinations are possible for the effects of stimuli, previously paired with the onset or offset of rewards or punishers, upon instrumental performance to obtain reward or escape punishment.

Consider for example, the positive emotional effect of a tone that has been paired with the termination of shock. This tone should become a conditioned elicitor of positive emotionality. As indicated in Cell 4 of the table, if the rat was subsequently trained to press a lever for food reward, presenting the tone should increase positive affect and motivate greater food-contingent lever pressing. The limited evidence now available is consistent with this prediction. Such *generalized* effects of classical conditioning upon ongoing performance support the view that the onset and termination of rewards and punishers influence central emotional states, with broad motivational effects.

Although not all of the cells in Table I have received intensive investigation, the results are generally consistent with the view that conditioned elicitors of positive affect and negative affect influence subsequent instrumental performance in new contexts. Such results seem to occur so long as the pairing of a stimulus with a reward or punisher does not result in the learning of specific approach or escape reactions that are inconsistent with the response required in the new context. These results and earlier research on the motivating effects of fear suggest that (a) rewards and punishers produce positive and negative central emotional states, respectively, (b) classical conditioning provides a mechanism by which emotional states come to be elicited by new stimuli, and (c) emotional states motivate approach and avoidance behaviors.

B. Emotional Impact of Required Effort

We have seen that positive and negative affect can influence a variety of generalized approach and

TABLE I

Effects of Classically Conditioned Stimuli on the Rate of Instrumental Behavior

Instrumental schedule	Reward		Punishment	
	Onset→ +emotion	Offset→ −emotion	Onset→ +emotion	Offset→ −emotion
+ Reinforcemt	1. Increase	2. Decrease	3. Decrease	4. Increase
− Reinforcemt	5. Decrease	6. Increase	7. Increase	8. Decrease

avoidance behaviors. The vigor with which a goal is pursued usually depends, even more strongly, on the trade-off between the positive affect produced by greater reward and the negative affect produced by greater effort. In most goal-oriented performance, the magnitude of reinforcement depends upon the amount of effort. The animal must choose between the pleasure of greater reward and the unpleasantness of increased effort. Models concerned with the ways in which animals manage their behaviors to maximize reward and to maintain activities at the preferred level do take into account the aversiveness of effort. These theories have been quite successful in predicting performance as a function of the amount of required effort. But they treat the aversiveness of effort as static, failing to consider the effects of prior experience.

Physical effort, as defined by English and English, involves "the subjective experience that accompanies bodily movement when it meets resistance or when muscles are fatigued" and has widely been considered to be aversive. According to Kahneman, a basic difference between the experience of effort and other experiences, such as those produced by drugs or loud noise, is that the performance the individual "invests at any one time corresponds to what he is doing, rather than what is happening to him."

Cognitive effort, according to English and English, denotes the "intensification of mental activity when it is obstructed in some way." The comparability of the experiences of cognitive and physical effort has long seemed self-evident. There may be a continuity of experience between physical effort and cognitive effort resulting, in part, from the dependence of both kinds of sensations on meeting performance criteria in goal-oriented behavior.

Moreover, prolonged physical performance and cognitive performance both produce fatigue, which refers to a response-produced decrement in the organism's capacity to continue to perform the same activity or similar activities efficiently. Although most research on fatigue concerns physical performance, extended cognitive activity similarly reduces cognitive performance. The negative affect associated with fatigue may enhance the perceived similarity of physical and mental effort. Thus, required high cognitive effort and physical effort may produce similar feeling states of negative affect.

Effects of learning on the unpleasantness of effort follow from the view that the sensation of effort, when paired with a satisfying state of affairs, takes on rewarding properties in the same way as pairing money with desired outcomes. According to the theory of learned industriousness proposed by Eisenberger in 1992, reinforcement of increased physical or cognitive performance would classically condition positive affect to the sensation of high effort, thereby reducing effort's aversiveness. Because different kinds of performance are assumed to produce similar qualitative experiences of effort, the degree of performance rewarded in one task would influence subsequent performance in other tasks.

In accord with this view, there is considerable evidence that rewarded high effort does produce a generalized increase in industriousness. For example, Eisenberger and his colleagues gave rats a choice between pressing a heavy lever for a large reward versus a light lever for a small reward. The number of selections of the heavy-lever, large-reward alternative was greater if the rats had previously been rewarded for every five trips in a runway, as opposed to reward for every trip. In humans, an increased degree of required performance involving one-or-more tasks raised the subsequent vigor and persistence of various other activities including card sorting by depressed mental patients, mathematics and handwriting by learning-disabled and regular preadolescent students, and manipulatory behavior, perceptual identifications, essay writing, anagram solving, and resistance to cheating by college students. Moreover, extended effort training with lower animals and humans produced long-term generalized effects. These results are consistent with the suggestion that repeated reinforcement of high effort may contribute to individual differences in human industriousness, and that industriousness is influenced by learned changes in the negative affect associated with high effort.

We have been discussing reductions in the aversiveness of effort that result from the performance and reward of difficult tasks. High effort might also lead to interest–excitement by increasing engagement with intrinsically pleasing aspects of many tasks. Shaping a rat to run in an activity wheel for food reward introduces the animal to an intrinsically rewarding activity. The rat will continue to run on a regular basis long after the food reward has been eliminated. Csikszentmihalyi has argued that humans (and, we may surmise, other higher organisms) find it innately rewarding to experience control over challenging tasks as they concentrate their total attention on maximizing performance.

The role of interest–excitement in promoting task performance is consistent with the Japanese concept of *muga*, a state of expert training in which self-consciousness is eliminated and the person's energy is said to flow into the task. In Japan, the expert is taught not to consciously *push* in carrying out a difficult task but, rather, to attempt to lose self-awareness in skillful performance. A visitor to Japan, D. E. Morley, described a woman kneeling on the floor and preparing a great supply of rice cakes for her family. She shaped the dough using quick, repetitive movements of such deftness that she seemed completely absorbed by the task. Morley noted, "As a personality in her own right, [the woman] was easily overlooked; perhaps the distinction was no longer possible. It was difficult to see how the woman could be separated from the function."

III. DIFFERENT THEORETICAL APPROACHES TO EMOTION

To put our position in perspective, we shall discuss the concepts of emotion, goal, and motivation as they are currently used in emotion theories that focus primarily on human behavior and personality. There are many such theories, but they can be loosely organized into two groups—biosocial and cognitive.

A. Emotions, Goals, and Motivation: A Biosocial View

Biosocial theories of emotions, like those of Izard and Tomkins, emphasize the origins of emotions in evolutionary–biological processes and inspire research on the functions of emotions. They conceptualize emotions as both reactive and proactive. Emotions are proactive in that they add selectivity to perception and focus to cognition and in these and other ways organize and motivate behavior.

A key assumption of biosocial theories is that the emotions constitute the primary motivational system and that each discrete emotion has distinct organizing and motivational functions. With this in mind, it is easy to see why researchers in the biosocial tradition look for relations among emotion, behavior, and personality in an effort to delineate the special functions of specific emotions.

Biosocial theories are also concerned with the activation of emotions and the role of cognition, but these matters are part of a much larger agenda that attempts to relate emotions to behavior, personality development and functioning, and psychopathol-

ogy. On the issue of emotion activation, for example, Izard conceives cognitive processes, along with spontaneous neural activity and sensorimotor and affective processes, as one of four emotion-activating systems.

To summarize, the biosocial position conceives motivation as a function of emotions and drives and the interaction of these with each other and with cognition. Emotions are considered the primary motivational system. However, drives may play an important role in behavior in some circumstances. Drives have motivational properties of their own, and high drive states typically activate emotions. When they do, drive–emotion interaction can produce powerful motivation. An example is the intense sex–emotion (sex drive plus the emotion of interest–excitement) motivation that occurs when a person long deprived of sexual pleasure finds herself in the company of a potential partner whose physical features are deemed attractive and whose personality is appraised as fascinating. Another example of drive–emotion interaction that produces powerful motivation is when a person learns that the pain he has been experiencing for some time has been diagnosed as cancer. In both these examples, cognition provides the directional component of motivation. This is the role of cognition in all cases in which plans and goals channel energy and action. Nevertheless, because biosocial theory views affect (emotions, drives, and emotion–drive interactions) as the real basis of motivation, *cognitive constructs such as plans, wishes, and goals are viewed as powerless abstractions until they activate affect.*

An important postscript to biosocial position qualifies the role of the drives and emotions as independent systems for organizing and motivating behavior. According to biosocial theory, emotions can function independently of drives. An example is a sated animal defending its territory, exploring new territory, or solving a puzzle, as in Harlow's experiments with monkeys. In contrast, we think the motivational power of a drive operating independently is weak relative to the power of that drive when amplified by emotion. The foregoing examples of drive–emotion interactions illustrate this point. This does not mean that drives are of little importance in motivation. As we noted earlier, drives frequently activate emotions, especially so for intense drive states. One could probably make a good case for Tomkins' argument that the pain and sex drives always recruit emotions that increase motivation and play a role in organizing subsequent behavior.

Emphasis on the centrality of emotions in motivation need not detract from the importance of learned motives and traits. Learned motives, including such affective-cognitive structures as values and goals, guide or influence many important kinds of behavior. These affective-cognitive structures are bonds formed through association between affects (emotions, drives) and cognition (images, symbols, thoughts) that occur in organism–environment transactions.

Organism–environment transactions include two independent sources of information. Human and nonhuman animals bring to their very first transaction with the environment a vast amount of information that was stored in the genes through natural selection during eons of evolution. As Mayr noted, the information coded in the genes represents the animal's capacities to adapt to its niche. For a considerable period in the history of psychology, researchers failed to appreciate the quantity and significance of gene-based or biological information. A new appreciation of biological information has been facilitated by work in ethology, genetics, and emotions. Lorenz has estimated that there are literally volumes of genetic information involved in the swift's first flight from its nest in a dark and narrow cave, a flight that includes navigating rugged, mountainous terrain, the capture of prey, and a safe landing in a totally strange location. Emotion researchers such as Ekman, Friesen, and Ellsworth, and Izard have shown that the expressive behaviors that signal basic emotions in humans are universal, and this and other evidence strongly suggest that the information controlling the development and spontaneous display of this complex array of signals is stored in the genes. Similarly, human newborns exhibit wide individual differences in expressive behavior and in neural and behavioral reactivity. This suggests that genes are significant determinants of emotion thresholds.

There is hardly a need to draw attention to the quantity and importance of information in the environment. This was demonstrated in the first half of this century by numerous researchers, including Hull, Thorndike, Tolman, and Skinner, and later by Gibson and Shepard, whose work contributed to our understanding of the interdependency of animal and environment.

The point of this digression on the vastness of the store of information both in genes and in environment was to lay the groundwork for appreciating the role of affects in individual–environment transactions. The motivational properties of drives and emotions and their power to influence and focus (or add selectivity to) perception, learning, and memory are required for individuals to steer their way through the jungle of environmental information and cope effectively.

These individual–environment transactions result in affective–cognitive structures. Through the interaction of affective motivation and cognitive processes, these structures become organized as learned motives and traits of personality. Izard and D. Watson and their colleagues have shown that measures of the frequency of discrete experiences are highly stable over time and significantly related to both broad dimensions and primary traits of personality. Particularly relevant to the issue of learning-influenced motives, they showed that both positive and negative emotions contributed to the prediction of trait achievement as measured by Jackson's Personality Research Form-E. The biggest emotion correlate of achievement was the positive emotion of interest, but positive correlations of achievement with shame and sadness approached significance. Taken together these studies of the correlates of personality strongly suggest that emotions play a significant role in the development of learned motives, goals, and specific traits.

B. Emotions, Goals, and Motivation: Cognitive Approaches

In addition to the biosocial theories of emotion, there are a group of theories that emphasize the role of cognition in the generation of emotion. There are several substantial variations among these cognitive theories of emotion. For example, within the cognitive theories of emotion, Averill's social construction theory explains emotions as socially learned roles, and Weiner and Graham's social–cognitive/attribution theory explains the activation of many, though not all emotions, in terms of the attributions ascribed to the causal agent. For example, if Student A asks Student B to lend him class notes because he (A) went to the beach instead of class, B might become angry, whereas if A needs B's notes because A had to attend his father's funeral, B is likely to feel sadness or pity. From the standpoint of a biosocial theorist, the differences among a number of the cognitive theories of emotion are not great, but each theory provides some insight on emotions, particularly on the processes by which they are activated. [See ATTRIBUTION.]

The important common denominator among these theories is the notion that emotions are dependent on cognitive processes, processes that are rooted in, or influenced by, learning and experience. The key role of cognition is especially apparent in the way these theories explain the activation of emotion activation. They explain emotion activation as a function of cognitive appraisal or evaluation. This means that the particular emotion, if any, that is activated depends on the way the individual *perceives* and *interprets* the stimulus event or situation.

Influenced by the theories of Lazarus, Weiner, Frijda, Scherer, Roseman, and others, investigators have done considerable research on the cognitive antecedents of emotions. Probably most of the research inspired by this group of theorists concerns emotion activation. This is consistent with another important distinguishing feature of this group of theories, namely, the emphasis on emotions as a response or response syndrome.

In his description of his cognitive–motivational–relational theory of emotions, Lazarus stated that "Emotions are first and foremost *reactions* to the fate of active goals in everyday encounters of living in our lives overall" (emphasis added). He does not give a formal definition of goal but implies that it is simply what an animal wants. He is more specific in describing a goal hierarchy as that "which provides the individual with a basis for evaluating personal harms and benefits." This suggests that he conceives a particular goal as a "want" to minimize harms and maximize benefits in a particular situation.

Lazarus sees "harms and benefits [to the self or ego-identity], actual or potential, real or imagined" as the stuff that is appraised during the cognitive processing that leads to emotions. Although he is not explicit on the matter, he seems to believe that motivation consists of the "wants" involved in accruing perceived benefits and avoiding perceived harms. Thus, a "fundamental role is played by motivation in defining the harms and benefits on which emotions depend."

Motivation is defined by Lazarus in terms of goals, particularly goal commitments and goal hierarchies, and these are developed through appraisals of personal harms and benefits that derive from person–environment encounters. Persistent goals become personality traits, and these, in turn influence appraisal. In this framework, the causal chain in behavior can be summarized as follows: Personality (or a set of long-term goals) → appraisals in terms of personality (or long-time goals) and imme-

diate harm : benefit ratio (short-term goals) → emotion → coping. Lazarus, like biosocial theorists, holds that the cognitions and actions involved in coping can influence or change the emotion. Careful study of the foregoing sequence of events leading to emotion and coping will show that Lazarus's position is that cognitive appraisal is the primary causal agent.

There are two reasons for distinguishing between cognitive and biosocial theories of emotion. First, cognitive theories do not have much to say about the functions and effects of emotions because they treat *emotions as reactive*. Thus, emotions are seen simply as reactions to stimuli. Biosocial theories consider emotions to be a continual source of motivation that *causes the individual to think and act,* not merely to react. Second, most cognitive theories view *appraisal, attribution, or some sort of cognitive process as the primary cause of behavior,* and they see personality traits or long-term goals (derived through cognitive processes) as playing a secondary, though often a more distal, role. In contrast, biosocial theories maintain that cognitive processes are only one of several types of phenomena that can activate emotions. They hold that spontaneous activity of the nervous system, feedback from expressive behavior, and affective states like pain or sexual pleasure can also activate emotions.

We hasten to add that in delineating differences between cognitive and biosocial theories of emotion we do not intend to highlight or create controversy. The differences are important to researchers and students of emotions, but they should not detract from the recent gains in knowledge about the emotions that were facilitated by both types of theory.

Both cognitive and biosocial theories have a common ground in the emotions as a subject of vital concern to psychology and the other behavioral sciences, and both types of theories are inspiring interesting research. Both biosocial and cognitive theories of emotions agree that emotions are of key importance to the processes of adaptation and adjustment. Both agree that cognitive processes such as appraisal and causal attribution frequently activate emotions. Both agree that once activated emotions influence subsequent perception, cognition, and action. Both include emotion in their explanations of the motivational processes that govern behavior.

IV. SUMMARY

This article delineated the key differences among homeostatic processes, physiological drives, and emotions, and showed how all of these interact with each other and with cognition in the processes of motivation. Although motivation was viewed as having several components, the central thesis of the article was that emotion is a primary basis of motivation. Emotions were distinguished from drives and homeostatic processes largely on the basis of their greater flexibility and generality, characteristics which make it possible for them to relate to cognition and actions in a great variety of ways. It is the flexibility and generality of the emotions as motivational processes that enable the individual to generate a wide variety of behavioral alternatives in coping with environmental contingencies.

The evolutionary basis for relationships between emotion and motivation is suggested by animal studies in which emotion serves to motivate generalized approach and avoidance. It has long been recognized that punishers, and stimuli that signal imminent punishment, disrupt the pursuit of positive reinforcers by animals and humans. More recent evidence indicates that positive reinforcers, and signals of their impending occurrence, produce a symmetrical effect, lessening the avoidance of aversive stimuli. More generally, contemporary learning theorists propose that signals for the onset of appetitive events and for the termination of aversive events produce similar kinds of positive central emotional states. Analogously, signals for the onset of aversive events and for the termination of appetitive events produce similar kinds of negative emotional states. Positive emotional states would enhance appetitively motivated behavior and reduce aversively motivated behavior; negative emotional states would enhance aversively motivated behavior and reduce appetitively motivated behavior. The evidence is generally supportive of the range of predictions made by this conceptualization. The general implications of the findings are that (a) positive and negative emotional states have a major influence on motivation, and (b) classical conditioning is an important mechanism by which new stimuli come to elicit emotional states.

The animal behavior literature suggests additional basic influences of emotion on motivation. Animals and humans engage in various kinds of exploratory/curiosity behaviors that seem to be intrinsically rewarding. One intriguing area for future investigation involves the possibility that novel stimulation elicits the emotion of interest–excitement.

Emotion may also play a key role in the organism's trade-off in goal-oriented performance between the positive affect resulting from greater reward and the negative affect produced by increased effort. Physical effort and cognitive effort appear to produce unpleasant feeling states that impair performance. According to learned industriousness theory, reinforcement of increased physical or cognitive performance classically conditions positive affect to the sensation of high effort, thereby reducing its aversiveness. Because different dimensions of effort are assumed to produce similar qualitative experiences of effort, rewarded high effort involving one task should reduce the subsequent aversiveness of effort in other tasks and thereby produce a generalized increase in industriousness. Considerable evidence with animals and humans demonstrates the broad motivational effects of reward for high effort. High performance that falls within the individual's capabilities might also enhance interest–excitement by increasing engagement with intrinsically satisfying components of many tasks and by promoting the experience of flow in which self-consciousness decreases and attention becomes dominated by the task.

The article presented an overview of the two broad sets of theoretical approaches to emotion. It elaborated on the key assumption of biosocial theories that the emotions constitute the primary motivational system and that each discrete emotion has distinct organizing and motivational functions. Motivation is constrained in important ways by the individual's genes and the ecology. Genes control such factors as emotion thresholds, intensity of reactivity, and general activity level—factors usually considered to be aspects of temperament or personality. The ecology and the social surround provide stimulus information and behavioral opportunities.

Biosocial theories view cognition as the source of plans and goals that provide the directional component of motivation. Goals are considered impotent until they activate affect. In this framework, a highly important research agenda item is the study of the development of emotion–cognition relations.

The cognitive theories of emotion place relatively more emphasis on study of the antecedents of emotion and a view of emotion as response or reaction. Appraisal and attributional processes are seen as critical in generating or mediating emotions. These theories have inspired a great deal of research that increases our understanding of the cognitive correlates of emotion.

Cognitive and biosocial theories of emotion agree on a number of important points. One of the most important of these is that emotions, once activated, influence subsequent perception, cognition, and action. Thus, virtually all experts in the field acknowledge the emotional basis of motivation and agree that emotions play a key role in driving cognition and action.

Bibliography

Averill, J. R. (1980). A constructivist view of emotion. "Emotion, Theory, Research, and Experience. Vol. 1. Theories of Emotion" (R. Plutchik and H. Kellerman, Eds.), pp. 305–339. Academic Press, New York.

Csikszentmihalyi, M. (1990). "Flow: The Psychology of Optimal Experience." Harper & Row, New York.

Domjan, M., and Burkhard, B. (1982). "Principles of Learning and Behavior," 3rd Ed. Brooks/Cole, Monterey, CA.

Eisenberger, R. (1992). Learned industriousness. *Psycholog. Rev.* **99,** 248–267.

Ekman, P., Friesen, W. V., and Ellsworth, P. C. (1972). "Emotion in the Human Face: Guidelines for Research and an Integration of Findings." Pergamon, New York.

English, H. B., and English, A. C. (1968). "A Comprehensive Dictionary of Psychological and Psychoanalytical Terms." David McKay, New York.

Erikson, E. H. (1950). "Childhood and Society." Norton, New York.

Frijda, N. H. (1986). "The Emotions." Cambridge University Press, New York.

Izard, C. E. (1971). "The Face of Emotion." Appleton-Century-Crofts, New York.

Izard, C. E. (1993). Four systems for emotion activation: Cognitive and noncognitive processes. *Psycholog. Rev.* **100**(1), 68–90.

Kahneman, D. (1973). "Attention and Effort." Prentice Hall, Englewood Cliffs, N.J.

Lazarus, R. S. (1991). Cognition and motivation in emotion. *Amer. Psychol.* **46.**

Lorenz, K. (1965). "Evolution and Modification of Behavior." University of Chicago Press, Chicago.

Mayr, E. (1988). "Toward a New Philosophy of Biology: Observations of an Evolutionist." Harvard University Press, Cambridge, MA.

Morley, D. E. (1985). "Pictures from the Water Trade." Atlantic Monthly Press, Boston.

Mowrer, O. H. (1947). On the dual nature of learning: A reinterpretation of "conditioning" and "problem-solving." *Harvard Educational Review* **17,** 102–150.

Schwartz, B. (1989). "Psychology of Learning and Behavior," 3rd. Ed. Norton, New York.

Tomkins, S. S. (1962). "Affect, Imagery, Consciousness. Vol.1. The Positive Affects." Springer, New York.

Tomkins, S. S. (1963). "Affect, Imagery, Consciousness. Vol. II. The Negative Affects." Springer, New York.

Watson, D., and Clark, L. A. (1992). On traits and temperament: General and specific factors of emotional experience and their relation to the five-factor model. *J. Personality* **60,** 441–476.

Weiner, B. (1985). An attributional theory of achievement, motivation, and emotion. *Psycholog. Rev.* **92,** 548–573.

MOTOR CONTROL

Stephan Swinnen
Catholic University of Leuven, Belgium

Glossary

Central pattern generator Network of neurons responsible for generating properly timed rhythmic output.

Closed-loop control Mode of control consisting of a reference mechanism (standard of correctness) against which feedback from the ongoing or completed response is compared to generate error.

Coordinative structures Group of muscles constrained to act as a functional unit; related terms are synergies and muscle linkages.

Degrees of freedom The least number of independent coordinates needed to describe the positions of the elements of a system.

Dynamics Branch of sciences that deals with changes in systems, expressing their existing and evolving states.

Feedforward As opposed to feedback, refers to the information used prior to executing a particular act, with the main advantage that the human movement system is prepared in advance of the movement and tuned to processing response-produced information.

Motor programs Central representation of movement containing abstract movement commands.

Open-loop control Mode of control that does not make use of error information but, instead, prepares instructions for actions in advance, without modifications on the basis of feedback.

Synchronization Phenomenon that refers to the (mutual) attraction of limb movements or body parts, often resulting in phase and frequency synchronization.

MOTOR CONTROL is a relatively young discipline of scientific inquiry that attempts to describe and explain how movement is accomplished with special reference to concomitant postural adjustments. It focuses on the organization and control of the motor apparatus. Moreover, it seeks to understand how sensory processes enter into action. This field of study has theoretical as well as practical relevance. After all, movement is at the heart of everyday life. Therefore, a better understanding of skilled performance in daily activities, sports settings, artistic contexts, and the workplace is desirable. This body of knowledge can be applied to the organization of practice with the goal of improving performance or restoring movement disabilities resulting from accidents, stroke, neurodegenerative diseases, etc.

The study of motor control has a pronounced interdisciplinary nature. It is an interface among the neurological, biophysical, kinesiological, and the behavioral sciences. The neuroscientific perspective tries to unravel how the brain and spinal cord bring about movement. The biophysical and kinesiological perspective seek to understand the physical principles to which the human body in action, consisting of limb segments with pendular characteristics and springlike muscles, obeys. The behavioral perspective attempts to describe and explain observable movement behavior and the various manipulations that affect it, leading to inferences about the design of the control system. Increasingly, these perspectives are merging into a unified approach for understanding human movement behavior. This article focuses on the behavioral analysis of motor control.

I. HOW DOES MOVEMENT TAKE PLACE?

Movement is so embedded in everyday life that one hardly thinks about this question. Control of movement can be understood as an interplay with the various forces of nature. On the one hand, movers exploit these forces to produce skillful actions (e.g., ground-reaction forces or elastic forces), generated through the springlike properties of muscles. On the other hand, living beings continuously fight against gravitational forces for their survival. Limbs have similarities to levers, designed to overcome these forces. Standing up against the laws of gravity, which takes several months in the newborn, is a primary accomplishment with survival value. Motor control research attempts to describe and explain movement as a complex combination of external and internal forces. On the one hand, mutual interactions between the mover and the (external) environment are a central focus of study. Action often leads to changes in the environment and changes in the environment bring about modifications in action. On the other hand, because the human body consists of a kinematic chain of interconnected body parts, various interactions exist among the respective segments. Even within a limb, interactions among the joints can be identified which are governed by various types of torque.

For voluntary movement to take place, two elements are required: muscles and a signaling system that makes muscles contract. Many centers in the brain are activated before, during, and after movement execution. Among them are various subcortical and cortical structures working together to control the final outputs from the brain to the spinal cord. An important question concerns how the information is encoded by these high-level systems, which are apparently far removed from the detailed peripheral events in the muscles. E. Evarts, who pioneered the recording of activity of single cells in the brain of awake animals, provided a major impetus to understanding the role of the motor cortex. He argued that activity of the nerve cells in the motor cortex was primarily related to the amount and pattern of muscular contraction rather than to the displacement that was produced by the contraction. Evarts also hinted at the tuning of the cortical cells to movement direction and this feature has been investigated intensively in subsequent years by Georgopoulos and colleagues. They found that cells have a directional preference even though they are only "broadly tuned" to movement direction. Movement in a specific direction is then represented as a weighted sum of the directions signaled by a population of cells in the motor cortex (the population coding hypothesis). The motor cortex is an important brain structure because it resides close to

final motor output. What happens next? Neural information from higher levels is relayed to motor neurons whose cell bodies are located in the spinal cord and whose axons terminate on the muscle-fiber membrane. At this site, neural events are translated into mechanical energy by generating a contractile force in the muscles. The properties of these muscles constrain the calculations of the central nervous system: The combination of muscle lengths and tensions are interdependent with the velocity of muscle shortening or lengthening.

To obtain an idea of the relationship between muscle contraction and the resulting physical events, an example of a horizontal forearm flexion–extension–flexion movement is depicted in Figure 1. The subject is instructed to flex the elbow toward the body midline, followed by two reversals in direction in between target zones (elbow extension), to finally move toward an endpoint in front of the body (elbow flexion) in the target time of about 500 msec. At the top is shown the angular displacement pattern, followed by its time derivatives, velocity and acceleration. This double-reversal movement is accomplished by activity of elbow flexors and extensors (i.e., those muscles that cause the elbow to flex, respectively extend). Activity in two of them, namely biceps and triceps, as registered by means of surface electromyography, is shown at the bottom. It is noteworthy here that many more muscles are activated to allow this movement to take place. Among them are those that serve to fixate the limb in reference to the trunk and to stabilize the whole body to ensure postural control.

Before any displacement is evident, the biceps muscle is activated; peak burst activity is even reached before movement onset. A second burst of biceps activity takes place before the second major elbow flexion is initiated. On the other hand, the triceps is marginally active before onset of movement but shows increased activity shortly after movement initiation to oppose elbow flexion and to prepare for elbow extension. A final major burst of triceps activity serves to position the limb at the endpoint, and some degree of biceps activity is evident as well to help accomplish this goal. Whenever displacement is recorded, transforming it to its time derivatives, velocity and acceleration, is useful. After all, acceleration requires force, which is the result of muscle activation. Accordingly, positive acceleration is mainly preceded by biceps activity and negative acceleration by triceps activity in the present example.

Three major points can be made from this example. First, the mechanical effects lag behind the elec-

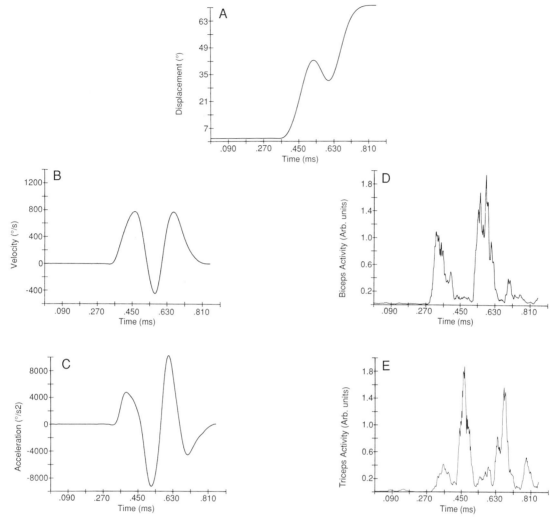

FIGURE 1 Displacement-, velocity-, and acceleration-time traces and rectified and smoothed electrical activity in biceps and triceps muscles for production of a horizontal flexion–extension–flexion movement. Note that when activity in one muscle is high, it is low in the other muscle. This is indicative of a key principle of reflex organization known as reciprocal inhibition.

trical changes that can be observed in the muscles. Second, some muscles allow movement to take place (the agonist); others oppose movement or cause movement to proceed in the opposite direction (the antagonist) and the latter need to be timed and organized as well. Third, movement is a complex combination of voluntary and reflex activity, and their rigid distinction is difficult to maintain. Note that biceps activity is low when triceps is activated and vice versa, a phenomenon known as reciprocal inhibition. Reciprocal inhibition is a key principle of reflex organization. Strong reciprocal inhibition allows the limb to be compliant whereas weaker reciprocal inhibition allows for cocontraction of opposing muscles, thereby stiffening the joint. Cocon-

traction is scarce in the depicted highly practiced trial but is usually more apparent at initial levels of practice. As will be pointed out later, many more reflexes operate during movement production. This intertwining of reflex and voluntary movement leads to a significant simplification of computational burdens for the higher levels of the motor control system.

II. GENERAL CONTROL MODES

A key issue that has dominated thinking in motor behavior for a long time concerns the locus of movement control. Competing ideas on this matter have formed one of the most persistent controversies throughout this century. On the one hand, the peripheral viewpoint argues that movement is controlled via some combination of feedback from the muscles and joints and the vestibular, auditory, and visual systems. The central perspective, on the other hand, assumes that commands are structured in advance and that feedback is not essential to produce patterned movement. These perspectives can be exemplified by two distinct modes of control, known as closed- and open-loop systems.

A. Closed-Loop Systems

Closed-loop systems (like home-heating techniques), usually consist of three parts. A central feature is the *reference mechanism*, which represents the goal of the system or something to be achieved (e.g., the thermostat setting at 20°C). Information from the environment is gathered to determine the value that the system seeks to regulate (actual temperature in the house), and this information is relayed to the reference, termed *feedback,* thereby closing the loop. Comparisons between a desired and actual state give rise to error detection. The *executive* level, informed about errors, takes action to reduce the error toward zero (e.g., the heater is turned on). Granted that slowly graded responses are being controlled in a closed-loop fashion, one is prompted to ask how very fast (ballistic) movements are produced.

B. Open-Loop Systems

In contrast to closed-loop control, strictly open-loop systems do not contain the feedback cycle and are not directed at nullifying error. Commands are structured in advance and are executed without regard to the effects they have on the environment. The major advantage of such a system is that it can act quickly, as it does not have to process incoming information. Its drawback is that it cannot adjust to changing environmental circumstances.

C. Representations for Actions

In the past decade, the conventional central–peripheral debate has waned, whereas discussions about the desirability to invoke central representations that are held responsible for the organization of action have gained attention. On the one hand (and similar to centralists), the so-called motor systems

perspective, backed by the information-processing approach, assumes that movements are centrally represented. Movement commands, specified in rather general or abstract terms, are said to be responsible for output organization. This perspective does not strictly adhere to open-loop control as feedback is argued to play a role in movement, depending on the type of task involved. The program is hypothesized to control when the muscles need to be turned on and off. Experimental observations showing invariant temporal relations between the muscle contractions underlying movement despite variations in overall speed are argued to be consonant with this viewpoint.

Conversely, the dynamical approach sets out a different strategy by minimal reliance on representations or central prescriptions for explaining order and regulation manifest in motor behavior. Instead, it is argued that order in action emerges as an *a posteriori* fact, or as a necessary consequence of the way the system is designed to function. The key question becomes what can be explained in movement organization "for free" (i.e., through universal biophysical laws) before burdening the central nervous system with computational and control problems. This approach is characterized by an emphasis on processes of self-organization, a feature inherent to complex biological and physical systems. The interplay of forces and mutual influences among the components of a system, tending toward equilibrium, is largely held responsible for order in movement. Dynamics is thus not to be understood in the strict traditional sense as the study of how objects move under the influence of forces. Rather, it is a more recent approach that resides at the interface between mathematics and the sciences and that is concerned with a description of changes in systems, their existing and evolving states. This perspective is committed to applying a rather universal language for describing both living and nonliving systems in which multiple components become collectively organized. It recognizes rhythmic movement as a cornerstone for a theory of coordination.

Although opposite schools of thought have initiated lively debates on major control issues in the past decades, this clash of doctrines has created the opportunity to appreciate the benefits of various modes of control which can be explored by the mover in response to the huge variety of existing task dimensions and environmental constraints. This paves the road for conceiving hybrid models of human motor behavior. Next, evidence for central and peripheral contributions to motor control will be discussed. This description goes beyond the formerly made sharp distinction between closed- and open-loop systems.

III. CENTRAL, SENSORY, AND PERCEPTUAL ELEMENTS IN MOTOR CONTROL

A. Central Contributions to Motor Control

As mentioned previously, the central perspective on motor control takes as a dictum that central commands are mainly responsible for organization of and order in movement. To strengthen this argument, various sorts of evidence have been collected to demonstrate that patterned movement can occur in the absence of peripheral feedback. Under conditions of feedback deprivation through deafferentation (severing the sensory nerves that carry information into the nervous system), monkeys have been shown to walk and climb, mice to display grooming patterns, and birds to sing even though portions of the song are eliminated by denervating one side of the vocal apparatus, etc. This has led some to argue that movement is mainly controlled via centrally stored movement commands, often called programs.

A motor program can be defined as a central representation of movement or skill. It is a cornerstone in many current motor control theories. Although it is generally argued that the program is represented centrally, where exactly it resides remains obscure. Task features may be of concern in resolving this matter. For example, in the case of learned movements, looking for a program in a well-defined location within the central nervous system might not be fruitful, as it may consist of several subprograms or command structures that are widely distributed in the nervous system and that involve many brain areas. On the other hand, programs for certain inborn rhythmic behaviors, such as locomotion, swimming, and scratching, have a more circumscribed location, taking the form of a network of neurons (called a neural oscillator or central pattern generator), responsible for generating properly timed rhythmic output. Timing of these repetitive movements is then regulated by intrinsic properties of the central nervous system. For example, the central pattern generator (CPG) for locomotion in certain animals is located in the spinal cord. CPGs drive the spinal motoneurons (innervating muscles) by rhythmically raising and lowering their membrane potentials, causing them to fire in bursts. The excitability of the CPGs is governed by locomotor centers in the midbrain and brain stem.

Although CPGs are mainly invoked for the generation of inborn interlimb cyclical actions, they may be critically involved in, or form the basis of, learned movements. S. Grillner, a pioneer in CPG research, has proposed that CPGs are made up of networks of smaller unit generators that may be of use in learning new motor acts that are far removed from locomotion. Think, for example, about the leg action in the breaststroke: Leg propulsion is accomplished by extending the hip and knees while dorsally flexing the ankle to maximize grip on the water. This is difficult to accomplish for the beginning swimmer because there is a natural tendency to flex and extend all joints simultaneously. It is reminiscent of the tight cooperation among joints which can already be identified in the kicking movements of the newborn. With practice, the ankle joint is dorsally flexed while extending the other joints, in other words, it appears that a recoordination of parts of the locomotor synergy has been obtained.

Whereas it has previously been assumed that a CPG consists of a well-defined assemblage of neurons, functionally distinguishable from others, recent work with invertebrates suggests that they may not be *immutable functional entities*. Instead, neurons from different circuits can be reconfigured into a new circuit that enables a different function. This selective dismantling of preexisting networks, and the building of new ones, provides us with important clues for a better understanding of the mysterious but enormous flexibility in motor coordination that can be found across the animal world. Additional research is required to demonstrate similar phenomena in the vertebrate nervous system where the neural networks are inherently more complicated.

B. Sensory and Perceptual Contributions to Motor Control

Even though the nervous system is capable of issuing stored motor commands without reference to peripheral feedback, this should not be taken to imply that feedback is unimportant for goal-directed motor performance and learning in animals and humans. As mentioned previously, some have argued that birdsong is represented centrally. However, experiments with birds reared from an early nestling stage without experience of their own species-specific song have underscored the learned contributions to development of the normal song template. These observations point to the important role of auditory experience in species-specific song development. Similarly, even though CPG networks can produce patterns of interlimb coordination in the absence of afferent information, it is equally the case that afference plays an important role in normal locomotion for grading the component movements to the specific environmental contingencies.

Research on deafferented humans is of critical importance to demonstrate the role of sensory information in human motor control. Two patients, showing severe losses of somatosensory modalities following episodes of sensory polyneuropathy, have been investigated intensively by a group of scientists in the United Kingdom (Marsden and collaborators) and in Quebec (Lamarre and Bard and their respective collaborators). Although these patients can perform many skillful activities with the help of visual information, they experience difficulties in producing fine manual skills, such as feeding, writing, and fastening buttons. Moreover, their recovery from unexpected disruptions or perturbations, that occur during movement production, takes longer than in control subjects. Interlimb and intralimb (intersegmental) coordination is disturbed as well. These observations point to the important role of sensory afferents in human motor control. Thus, whereas the peripheral and central viewpoints are incompatible at their polar extremes, their reconciliation is no longer a matter of doubt. The question can now be rephrased as to "how central commands and sensory information cooperate to produce skilled action." Next, the roles of sensory information will be dealt with more specifically.

Two important sources of information play a determining role in movement regulation: proprio- and exteroception. Proprioceptors provide information about body position in space, joint angles, and the length and tension of muscles. It is information about our own (proprio) movements. Exteroceptors inform us about the spatial coordinates of surrounding objects and the environment. A reciprocal relationship exists between sensory information and movement. Sensory information allows movement to proceed correctly as it tells the mover about the state of the body and environment; conversely, movement allows us to sense and perceive. For example, when holding a pen between your fingers for some time, you will experience a loss of sensation of the pen, and its presence fades from consciousness until you

move your fingers again, informing you that the pen is still there. In addition to the important role of sensory information in movement, it is also critically involved in the maintenance of posture. [*See* TACTILE PERCEPTION.]

1. Sensory Information and Postural Control

A variety of receptors contribute to the maintenance of posture. The vestibular apparatus in the inner ear contains receptors sensitive to deviations from the vertical and, more general, to the orientation of the body in space. In addition, receptors in the muscles (e.g., muscle spindles, golgi tendon organs) and joints (e.g., Ruffini endings, Pacinian corpuscles) provide information about muscle stretch, degree of muscle tension, and angle positions. Great effort has been spent in studying these ingenious receptor devices; nevertheless, their modes of operation are still a matter of debate. The muscle spindle is particularly interesting for movement control and has, perhaps, been studied most extensively. It signals changes in muscle length as well as in the rate at which these take place. Sometimes these changes occur abruptly, giving rise to an immediate response. [*See* SPATIAL ORIENTATION.]

For example, when standing upright in a driving bus that suddenly stops, you tend to fall forward, resulting in a stretch of muscles in the lower leg (e.g., gastrocnemius, soleus). The event is immediately followed by contraction of these muscles to maintain equilibrium. This response is mediated by the stretch reflex, which originates in the muscle spindle and causes muscles to increase tension (although not sufficient) as soon as 20 msec after detection of muscle lengthening. It is an example of a fast closed-loop control mode. Another negative-feedback servomechanism originates in the golgi tendon organ, which senses force rather than muscle elongation, resulting in the reduction of force. Postural control is not only an end but also a means to an end in that it participates in almost any action. When lifting the arm, leg muscles will be activated before onset of arm movement to secure body equilibrium during this focal act. Thus, posture can be regarded as a background upon which a picture of voluntary movement is "engraved."

In addition to these muscle-specific sensory devices, vision is a very dominant receptor system in the control of posture and movement. Close your eyes when balancing on one leg, and you will realize that visual information is indeed important for postural equilibration. Vision also provides information about the position and movements of objects in the environment, leading to decisions for action. But, it is a far richer source of information in that it also tells us about our own movements in relation to the environment (also called exproprioception, as distinguished from extero- and proprioception). Such information is mainly derived from the changing pattern of optical arrays, or the particular reflection of light by objects in the visual field. When the observer moves in the environment or when an object moves with respect to the observer, changes in the optical array occur, called optical flow. Thus, visual environmental information (e.g., texture, gradients, surface of objects) flows past us as we move around. The rate at which trees and houses become larger and pass by as we drive a car down a road, tells us about our speed and the time at which upcoming objects will be contacted (time-to-contact). Sometimes vision can be so powerful that it overrules the proprioceptive information: When waiting for the train to leave, the illusion of a starting train is often experienced (even though it remains immobile) when watching another train passing by. [See VISUAL PERCEPTION.]

Formal evidence for the powerful effects of vision in motor control has been provided by Lee and Aronson in a "moving room" experiment. Subjects stood on a stationary floor surrounded by walls that could be moved back- or forward together. When moving the wall a few centimeters toward or away from the subject, a loss of balance occurred. Apparently, moving the wall changed the optical array that was used as a source of information for postural control. The changes in the visual array were inappropriately interpreted as a loss of balance and produced a compensation. For example, moving the wall toward the subject induced the illusion of falling forward. The subject compensated with a backward movement, resulting in a disruption of posture.

2. Sensory Information and Movement

a. Role of Sensory Information before Movement

Information about the environment is gathered before actions are planned and executed. When throwing a ball, information is obtained about the location of the target to be hit and the position of the limbs and body. When enough time is available, this processing of information may occur at a conscious level. In other cases, as in suddenly avoiding obstacles, decisions for action need to be made so fast

that time-consuming processing stages are omitted. For example, D. N. Lee has argued that information derived from optical flow patterns enables the identification of important external temporal events (the time-to-contact objects), which can be used to control motor activity in humans and animals. This time-to-contact information is argued to derive directly from the rate at which retinal images of an object change in reference to their image size. It allows precise timing of actions without much conscious processing. This is supposedly the way plummeting gannets specify the time at which their wings have to be stretched backward before hitting the water or the way humans accurately strike the takeoff board and initiate the long-jump when running up the trackway. With the latter examples, the distinction between use of information prior to and during action has become blurred.

b. Role of Sensory Information during Movement

Ongoing movements can also be adjusted on the basis of incoming information that is fed back to a reference, as long as these movements proceed slowly enough. Examples of closed-loop control in human motor behavior are found in continuous tracking tasks such as driving an automobile, flying an airplane, etc. While driving an automobile, for instance, a major goal is to keep the vehicle on the right track without approaching the midline or side of the road too closely. This environmental information is used to guide steering behavior through a series of corrections. The motor system is directed at nullifying error in these tracking tasks.

c. Role of Sensory Information after Movement Completion

Sensory information can also be processed after movement has taken place, particularly when movements are performed rapidly. After completion of a golf swing, the information produced by this response (response-produced feedback information; e.g., the way the ball was hit, the sound produced at contact) is compared to some reference of correctness, providing information about the degree of correctness of the movement. Any discrepancy between the actual (what is) and expected (what should be) states leads to error-detection and decisions for error-correction that can be of use for the following trial. Of course, such comparisons can also take place during movement production.

This comparator function is hypothesized to reside predominantly in the cerebellum because central motor commands, as well as somatosensory, vestibular, and visual reports from the periphery, converge in this structure. One hypothesis concerning the mode of operation of this comparison process contends that signals are sent to certain neural centers, ahead of the response, to ready the human movement system for upcoming motor commands and for the receipt of feedback information. This advance information is also called corollary discharge (a related term is efference copy), and represents an example of what is called feedforward control. In contrast to feedback, feedforward control refers to sending information ahead of time to prepare for upcoming sensory information or for planned motor commands. It has the advantage that incoming information undergoes facilitated processing. Evidence for this viewpoint comes from experiments showing different sensory experiences in the case of passive or active movement production.

IV. MOVEMENT CONSTRAINTS: COMPUTATIONAL SIMPLIFICATION

A. Degrees of Freedom and Control of Movement

Considering all movements that can in principle be generated at one joint through various muscle combinations and reflecting on the numerous ways to combine the movements of many joints, our ability to control all these muscles for the purpose of goal-directed behavior is rather remarkable. Indeed, an enormously rich configuration of neuromuscular assemblages is theoretically conceivable in the human motor apparatus. This was identified by the Russian movement physiologist Bernstein as the "degrees-of-freedom problem." Roughly defined, "degrees of freedom" refers to the number of independent states or variables that must be controlled at the same time. The degrees-of-freedom problem can be conceptualized at various levels of the movement apparatus (e.g., joints, muscles, motor units). How the control and coordination of limb segments is accomplished has become a research matter of major interest in recent years.

There are various ways to address the degrees-of-freedom problem. One is to maximally exploit the biomechanical properties of the motor apparatus such as the length-tension characteristics of muscles or the external forces that act on movement (e.g., gravity). Another (related) way is to conceive of "efficiency" as a dominant criterion for shaping action. For example, it has been proposed that the minimization of mean squared jerk (the first time derivative of acceleration) is a primary efficiency constraint. Third, movement organization can be simplified by invoking larger units of behavior, such as preexisting synergies or reflex patterns. This latter issue will be touched on next.

In attempting to perform more than one motor task concurrently, limitations emerge that constrain our capability to perform different limb movements at the same time. Think for example how difficult it is to pat the head and rub the stomach simultaneously. A tendency for one movement to impose its pattern of activity on the other or a mutual synchronization of both action patterns becomes evident. Such constraints are common experience and are not limited to motoric dual-task performance. The study of these limitations is a long-standing issue in experimental psychology. I will limit the discussion to the particular case of discrete and continuous task coordination.

In a study on bimanual aiming tasks (pointing to different locations in space), Kelso, Southard, and Goodman showed that the laws governing unimanual performance do not necessarily apply to multilimb action. In order to better appreciate their findings, it is necessary to first elaborate on one of the most fundamental laws in motor behavior. When aiming at a certain target with the arm, more time is needed when the distance to be covered increases or when the target becomes smaller. This can be put in a formal mathematical relationship, known as Fitts' law:

$$MT = a + b[\log_2 (2A/W)],$$

where MT is movement time, a and b are empirical constants, A is amplitude of the movement, and W is target width. A combination of the two latter variables provides an indication of task difficulty. If the index of difficulty is increased, the movement will be performed at lower speed. Hence, there is a speed-accuracy trade-off. This law has proven very powerful in that it generally holds for a variety of aiming tasks, irrespective of whether one aims for a glass with the hand, types a keystroke with the finger, or positions the foot on the accelerator.

Given the strength of this lawful relationship for single effector performance, Kelso and collaborators wondered what would happen when making a short pointing movement to a wide target with one hand together with a long movement to a small target with the other hand. In the case of individualized control of the limbs, Fitts' law would predict both movements to be completed in different overall times because of their differential degree of difficulty. The findings, however, proved otherwise: The slow movement was sped up and the fast movement was slowed down, resulting in a rescaling of the movements toward a common underlying temporal structure. This was interpreted as evidence for interlimb control through a group of muscles constrained to act as a functional unit, i.e., a coordinative structure. These findings do not invalidate Fitts' law which was only conceived for unilimb motions. They show, however, that the laws governing multilimb actions are not necessarily linear extrapolations of those applicable to unilimb action. In other words, the whole is more than or is different from the sum of its parts.

Interlimb interactions not only appear in discrete movements but are also evident in cyclical movement production. In opposition to the former, the latter often display features of oscillators. The theoretical and experimental basis for this work was laid down by Von Holst some 50 years ago during his investigations of the coordination of fin movements in various anesthetized fish species. Two important principles of coordination were discovered, which have relevance for other species as well. First, each fin pattern tended to maintain its own frequency or speed of oscillation, referred to as the maintenance tendency (*Beharrungstendenz*). This frequency is interdependent with the lengths and masses of the segments to be moved. In other words, smaller segments (such as the human arm) are likely to display higher frequencies than larger segments (such as the leg). Second, Von Holst observed a tendency for one fin movement to impose its frequency on another, or for both fin movements to mutually affect each other. This (mutual) attraction was called the ''magnet effect'' (*Magnet effect*), often leading to a 1:1 temporal relationship between fins. These principles demonstrate that coordination arises as a result of the interplay between competitive and cooperative tendencies. Moreover, they exemplify how various modes of coordination are accomplished by lower centers through the combination of a few elementary principles. This reduces computational complexity through minimization of the degrees of freedom.

When humans perform cyclical limb movements simultaneously, similar phenomena can be ob-

served. Although this does not necessarily imply that the basic modes of operation are the same in both types of species, it is noteworthy from an evolutionary perspective that some general principles of coordination arise within the animal world. When making horizontal elbow flexions and extensions in both upper limbs simultaneously, a strong tendency becomes evident to synchronize the output patterns in a temporally compatible fashion (1:1 frequency ratio), similar to the magnet effect. Both arms are either flexed or extended simultaneously, or one arm extends whereas the other is being flexed (see Figs. 2A and 2B, respectively). The former type is called in-phase coordination and requires the simultaneous activation of homologous muscle groups. The latter type refers to anti-phase coordination, requiring the simultaneous activation of nonhomologous muscle groups. Phase refers to the point of advancement of the signal within a cycle, ranging from 0 to 360°. By subtracting the phase angles of both limbs, one obtains the phase difference or relative phase. Relative phase provides a measure or signature of the mode of interlimb coordination. Applied to the previous examples, in-phase refers to 0° and anti-phase to 180° relative phase. Alternative coordination modes, such as moving the limbs 90° out-of-phase with a 1:1 frequency ratio or producing a pattern with a 2:1 frequency ratio, are much more difficult to accomplish, requiring extensive learning to attain comparable degrees of stability (see Figs. 2C and 2D, respectively).

Overall, the previously mentioned observations point to a fundamental tendency for frequency and phase synchronization that is evident during the production of various coordination patterns. Stability during in-phase and anti-phase coordination is easily obtained and does not require any practice in adults, i.e., both are intrinsically stable coordination modes. Advocates of the dynamical perspective refer to these modes as *behavioral attractors*. The important behavioral implication is that alternative coordination patterns tend to converge to or are biased by these attractors.

When moving the upper and lower limbs in the sagittal plane, a similar set of preferred coordination modes can be identified: Moving the limbs in the same direction or in-phase (both limbs go up or down) is produced in a more stable fashion than moving in different directions or in anti-phase (one limb moves upward whereas the other moves downward, or vice versa). Again, the in-phase pattern is intrinsically more stable than the anti-phase pattern,

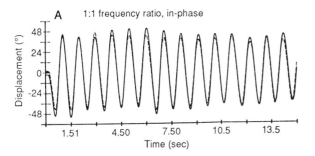

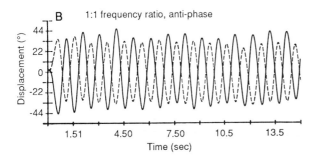

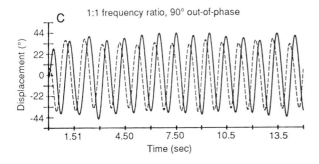

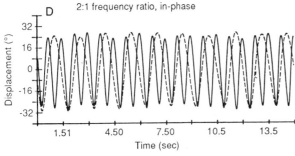

FIGURE 2   Some examples of preferred and nonpreferred coordination patterns, as produced by the upper limbs in the horizontal plane. (A) In-phase movements with a 1 : 1 frequency ratio, requiring the simultaneous activation of homologous muscle groups. (B) Anti-phase or 180° out-of-phase movements with a 1 : 1 frequency ratio, requiring the simultaneous activation of nonhomologous muscle groups. (C) A 90° out-of-phase movement with a 1 : 1 frequency ratio, requiring one limb to consistently lag with respect to the other. (D) A coordination pattern with a 2 : 1 frequency ratio. One limb moves twice as fast as the other and the relative phase goes alternatively through 0° and 180° relative phase at the reversal positions.

irrespective of the muscle groups that are used to generate these patterns. This points to the importance of the mutual direction of limb motions as a determinant of coordinative stability. In comparison to limb motions in the same direction, movements in different directions are also produced with more difficulty by hemiplegic patients and patients suffering from Parkinson's disease who often experience a transition to the same-direction pattern. So far, attention has predominantly been paid to the experimental investigation of in- and anti-phase coordination patterns with a 1 : 1 frequency ratio. A second round of research is now under way that focuses on more complex coordination patterns whereby the subcomponents move at different frequency ratios and/or the preferred interlimb phase patterns are abandoned (for some examples, see Figs. 2C–2D).

The previous sections have identified synchronization as a fundamental organizational property governing interlimb coordination and resulting in the exploitation of a restricted range of preferred interlimb relationships, irrespective of whether one deals with cyclical or discrete movements. It is now easier to appreciate the nature of errors or the interference that subjects experience when attempting more difficult or incompatible coordination patterns.

In summary, research on interlimb movements points to the necessity for investigating coordination as a distinct type of control problem with its own lawful modes of operation. In a more general way, global behavior of biological systems cannot always be understood by investigating its elemental units, because interactions among the units are responsible for emergent properties at the macroscopic level that cannot be deduced from knowledge of the individual components.

B. Significant Units of Motor Control

In recent years, systematic observation of coordination phenomena has prompted an animated discussion about the significant units of movement to be controlled by the human motor system. In this respect, the viewpoint has gained acceptance that cooperating groups of muscles, constrained to act as a functional unit, are preferably recruited. These are also referred to as muscle collectives, coordinative structures, or synergies. This mode of control has a number of potential advantages. First, it provides an economical solution to the aforementioned degrees-of-freedom problem in that a limited set of preferred modes of movement organization become apparent. Second, computational complexity in higher levels of the control system is reduced, as these muscle synergies constitute not only the external language of movement but also the internal language of the central nervous system. Although the synergy perspective provides a fruitful and economical way to theorize about the organization of action, it should not be taken to imply that individual muscles, or even motor units, cannot be controlled individually, or that a release from the constraints imposed by these coordinative structures would be impossible. This latter issue will be discussed in the next section.

What evidence has been advanced in support of the notion that the central nervous system preferably organizes movements by innervating groups of muscles? The strong tendency to synchronize patterns of motor output in the limbs for repetitive and nonrepetitive actions has already been reported. Another line of evidence is provided by the appearance of complete or fractionated reflex patterns in voluntary movement. For example, the tonic neck reflex, which arises in neck proprioceptors, gives rise to body and limb movements through a series of internally triggered reactions. The asymmetric tonic neck reflex, induced by turning the head sideward, is characterized by extension of the limbs on the side of face orientation and flexion on the other side. The symmetric neck reflex causes the upper limbs to flex and the lower limbs to extend when bending the head forward (ventriflexion) whereas the reversed pattern occurs when bending the head backward (dorsiflexion). As head movements also activate the labyrinth receptors, these reflex patterns often operate together with labyrinthine reflexes. Reflex patterns can be elicited rather easily in newborns or children with cerebral dysfunctions but more careful observation reveals that they are also evident in the skillful performances of athletes. Trainers of gymnastic skills have an intuitive knowledge of these triggered reactions. When performing a handstand, asking beginners to bend the head backward (trainer's hint: look at the floor) results in increased extension of upper limbs and trunk, thereby amplifying the support function of the upper limbs. During various somersaults, attention to head position often induces major improvements because it triggers the correct limb or trunk responses. These empirical observations are corroborated by experimental work that has shown actions in accordance with the tonic neck reflexes to confer additional strength. In addition, these reflexes have also been found to emerge during stressful activity to reinforce muscular contractions. Thus, genetically inherited reflex patterns appear to be part of the behavioral repertoire of the intact performer who integrates these patterns in the generation of voluntary movement. This viewpoint is not incompatible with a programming notion of movement control. Central commands may help orchestrate the possible role of these muscle synergies in movement and may incorporate fractions of it into the overall plan of action.

C. Acquiring New Patterns of Coordination

In the previous section, the property of synchronization was emphasized as a key organizational feature in the control and coordination of movement. This has a pitfall in that synchronization limits the kinds of activities that can be performed together. It is experienced as an obstacle whenever differing or incompatible limb movements have to be performed together, such as in producing polyrhythms, e.g., playing two different rhythms on the piano. Tapping rhythms with the fingers is not difficult when fingers move in synchrony (1 : 1), or when tapping in one finger is an integer multiple of the tapping rate in the other (2 : 1, 3 : 1). But, when the timing relationships are less compatible (3 : 2, 5 : 3), achieving the same degree of consistency in tapping rate is much more difficult. The degree of temporal incompatibility of the movements to be coordinated can then be considered an important criterion for determining task difficulty.

Luckily, the human motor control system has developed the capability to eliminate natural response tendencies (i.e., preexisting synergies, or other preferred coordination modes) to generate new task-specific forms of coordination. Therefore, it is as important for a theory of coordination to identify the restricted range of interlimb interactions as to provide insights into the way patterns of activity can be differentiated within a highly linked neural system, i.e., to dissociate constraints. The latter is not only a matter of selecting the appropriate action patterns but also of inhibiting or repressing unwanted or excessive motor activity. Shaping new forms of coordination requires a release from the constraints imposed by intrinsic muscle synergies to meet the general principle of minimal expenditure of energy.

Recoordination of action patterns sets in at an early age. In the newborn, reaching toward a visual target is initially accomplished by a tight coordination of elbow, wrist, and finger extension. This coordinative pattern evolves into a more differentiated organization of the joint movements in which the fingers can be flexed in anticipation of grasping an object while the arm extends; this is an example of intralimb dissociation. Nevertheless, dissociation of actions performed in different limbs can also be accomplished, as experienced musicians demonstrate. Imagine what would happen when attempting to perform a horizontal elbow flexion movement in the left arm together with a flexion–extension–flexion (reversal) movement in the right arm within the same time envelope. Swinnen, Walter, and colleagues addressed this question in a series of experiments.

Figure 3 shows the evolution of the displacement-time traces of one subject: The 10 initial and 10 final motion patterns of both limbs are displayed. At the start of bimanual practice (top), there is strong interlimb synchronization as shown by a tendency to perform a reversal pattern in both limbs. After 100 trials of practice (bottom), control of both disparate patterns of activation is gradually mastered and interference subsides, i.e., a smooth flexion movement is made in the left limb together with a correct reversal pattern in the right limb. The study of the

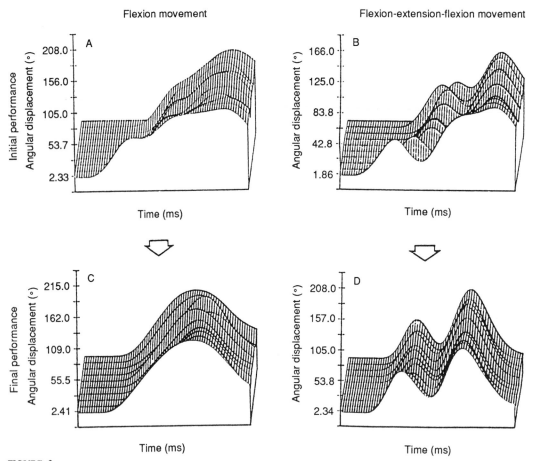

FIGURE 3   Displacement-time patterns of simultaneously performed right and left upper-limb movements with different spatiotemporal features. The first and final 10 trials of bimanual practice are shown in order to reveal the effects of training. The X axis represents time, the Y axis represents angular displacement in degrees and the Z axis displays 10 consecutive trials. At the start of practice (upper row), there is a strong tendency for interlimb synchronization as shown by the qualitatively similar displacement traces for the unidirectional and reversal movement. The unidirectional movement shows some discontinuities in the displacement profile (A). The reversal movement is roughly performed in accordance with the spatial requirements from the start of practice although trial-to-trial variability is initially large (B). At the end of practice (lower row), both limb movements are performed correctly and interference is no longer apparent in the unidirectional limb (C). The reversal movement is now produced with a high degree of consistency across trials (D). [From Swinnen, S. P., Walter, C. B., Lee, T. D., and Serrien, D. J. (1993). Acquiring bimanual skills: Contrasting forms of information feedback for interlimb decoupling. *J. Exp. Psychol. Learning, Memory, Cognition;* **19,** 1–17. Copyright 1993 by the American Psychological Association. Reprinted by permission.]

limitations in doing more than one thing at the same time has merit because features of complex systems become more readily apparent when they are overloaded. By observing and describing the nature of interference that occurs between the tasks, clues about the general principles of brain function become evident.

The previous example illustrates the possibility of overcoming synchronization effects to meet new task requirements. The examples of the learning of cyclical 1 : 1 coordination tasks with a 90° phase difference or 2 : 1 coordination tasks (see Figs. 2C and 2D) further support this contention. Learning does not appear to occur *de novo* but can thus be understood against the background of preexisting preferred coordination modes. How the dissociation of action is accomplished has yet to be determined. In this respect, a working hypothesis is that inhibitory neural networks are recruited that serve to harness patterns of activation to limit their spread, thereby sculpturing the movement plan. Inhibitory neurons are of fundamental significance to the operation of the central nervous system: They contribute to shape neural networks, as much as excitatory pathways do.

V. Motor Control Flexibility and Goal Accomplishment

Writing a computer program for analysis of one particular data set is easy. When it is to be used for various data sets, the job becomes much harder. Making an adaptive program or any other device to meet general-purpose requirements is indeed a thorny problem. Flexibility and adaptability are interesting properties of the human motor control system, favoring goal-appropriate behavior through various means. For example, when brushing your teeth, you can move your arm or your head or you can explore various ways to combine them. This is often referred to in the literature as motor equivalence.

Response equivalence is not unique to humans but can also be found in lower mammals as has become evident in conditioning studies. For example, a sheep is initially trained to lift his left foot off a grid floor when a tone sounds that signals an impending electrical shock. When the sheep is subsequently forced to lie down with its head on the grid floor, it will now lift its head and shoulders from the floor when the tone sounds. Thus, the animal

has not learned a stereotype response but a goal-directed action, i.e., it does whatever is needed to avoid the shock.

At least two types or levels of movement flexibility have received some attention in recent years. One type concerns adjustments to environmental circumstances through a rescaling of certain movement variables without affecting the basic structure of movement. A second type of adjustment is more invasive and occurs very fast. The former one may be more preplanned through evaluation of initial conditions, whereas the latter may appear rather suddenly during movement, or whenever attainment of action intentions is in danger.

A. Goal Accomplishment through Adjustable Parameter Specification

A favorite example to demonstrate that movement can be performed under a variety of circumstances without affecting its basic structure is that of handwriting. Handwriting skill is also a classic case for advocates of programmed control. If you do not believe that movements can run off in a clocklike (programmed) manner once initiated, try this: Write the words ''motor control'' at normal speed but try to omit the horizontal bar in the letters ''t.'' Although you intend to do so before movement initiation, modifying this particular aspect is difficult unless you slow down considerably. It leaves you with the impression that this action happens beyond voluntary control. But granted these strokes seem to be almost rigidly strung together into one unit, what evidence is there in favor of motor output flexibility? Suppose that you write the word ''skill'' under different circumstances and with different overall sizes and speeds. The basic question arises whether each variation is to be considered as a different movement or as another version of the same movement structure. Current evidence tends to support the second of both possibilities. Figure 4 shows the vertical acceleration patterns generated for writing the word skill on a digitizing board positioned horizontally (small and large size), with 45° inclination, and vertically (as in writing on the blackboard), respectively.

As shown in the figure, the word skill is written in different overall sizes: the word presented in graph A is two to five times smaller as the words in graphs B–D (see Fig. 4). The total duration for the smallest word is half that needed for writing the larger words, which require approximately the same overall time. Leaving aside these parameter differences, similari-

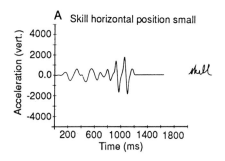

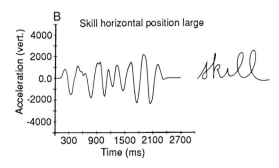

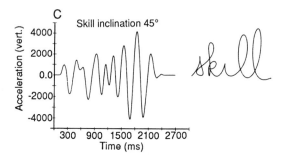

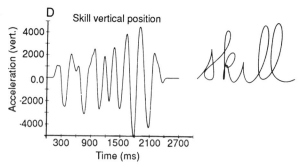

FIGURE 4   Vertical acceleration patterns produced for writing the word ''skill'' on a digitizer positioned horizontally, with 45° inclination, and vertically. On the left are shown the acceleration patterns that are roughly proportional to the forces produced in the vertical or upward direction. Note that the time basis in graph A is different from those in graphs B–D. Both upper traces differ from each other in letter size, as shown on the right. Letter sizes in C–D are also different from A although total duration is similar. [From Swinnen, S. P. (1991). Motor control. In ''Encyclopedia of Human Biology'' (R. Dulbecco, Ed.), Vol. 5. Academic Press, San Diego.]

ties among these variations are apparent. They reflect existing task constraints as well as the individual's particular writing style. Thus, although the absolute values of peak accelerations and decelerations differ among these written words, the general form of these acceleration patterns is very similar even though this word has never been written before under these varying conditions. The forms are not, however, exactly the same, and the distribution of ratios among chosen landmarks would probably not be fixed across these examples. This is probably due to the unique way movement commands unfold on every attempt, whereby unpredictable environmental circumstances have to be met, such as occasional random frictions in the pen–paper medium. It reminds us that each movement is unique and is never made in exactly the same way as before.

The consistencies or invariances across variations are noteworthy when realizing that the particular set of muscles used is unique for each example (due to shifts in writing posture, to differential effects of gravity, to the varying positions of the nonwriting hand, the size of writing, etc.). Consequently, the same program can thus be run off using entirely different muscle groups and with variations in overall size and timing. Whatever is represented in the program for writing this word must be coded in a rather abstract way and does not include information about the particular set of muscles involved; this is the responsibility of lower levels of the nervous system. This elaboration of commands, from general to specific, illustrates the hierarchical nature of the motor control system. It also marks current motor programming perspectives in that some features of movement are believed to be represented in the motor program (the invariant features), whereas others can be easily rescaled to produce variations in movement (in this case, overall size and speed). Thus far, experimental support for this distinction has predominantly been found in the temporal domain. Some studies have shown that acquired sequential movement patterns can be performed at different speeds (overall timing) without modifying the proportions of the times of each movement segment to overall time (relative timing). Thus, absolute timing is hypothesized to be a varying and relative timing an invariant feature. Accordingly, a one-to-one relationship between the program and movement does not exist; rather, programs govern all movements that belong to the same class. R. A. Schmidt therefore uses the term ''generalized motor programs.''

The separation of invariant features and adjustable parameters represents an economical account to human movement production in that movement can be tailored to particular environmental demands without compromising on its basic features.

B. Goal Accomplishment through Response Reorganization: Evidence for Motor Equivalence

In contrast with the previous example, the preservation of the movement goal in the face of disturbances sometimes results in a more invasive reorganization of movement control. When environmental circumstances happen to impede ongoing movement, the intended goal can often be accomplished by means of short-latency but set-dependent responses. Short-latency refers to the rapid character of these responses; set-dependence refers to their dependence on the performer's intention. Speech control research has been particularly productive in illustrating motor equivalence although it had also been observed in fine precision grip movements in humans and target directed arm movements in primates. There is mounting evidence that rapid reorganization of movements involved in speech is possible to achieve articulatory goals. For example, when upward movement of the mandible is impeded in the process of saying something that requires a labial occlusion (as in *p* or *b*), the upper lip increases its downward movement within 50 to 60 msec to achieve the articulatory goal. It is a case of feedforward open-loop control. These movements are unique in that they differ from voluntary responses that have much longer latencies. But they are also distinct from reflexes in that they are more adaptive in meeting the subject's goal and intentions. The details of the pathways, subserving these adjustments, have yet to be uncovered. These short-latency responses indicate that higher level parts of the control system are relatively unconcerned with the specific contribution of subsystems as long as the intended goal is met.

All together, these observations indicate that what is represented as a result of learning is not muscle-specific but consists of a rather abstract formulation of movement goals. By specifying general action goals or intentions at the highest levels and leaving the movement details to be fitted later in the process of organization at lower levels, the central nervous system is capable of producing the same effect over and over again, but never in exactly the same way. This is motor equivalence.

VI. SUMMARY

Recent concerns for the degrees-of-freedom problem on the one hand and for motor equivalence and output variability on the other hand illustrate that organizational and purposive issues in movement form basic tenets in current theorizing on motor behavior and movement control. Addressing such questions will eventually lead to a better understanding of the ingenious mechanisms that characterizes the human motor control system and will culminate in the development of appropriate learning settings to improve skillful behavior in a variety of contexts and to help restore movement disabilities.

The field of motor control is vivid and lively as ever before. It generates research at an accelerating pace and is marked with interesting discoveries that will result in the establishment of a solid body of knowledge on the functioning of the central nervous system and the great diversity of actions it generates. However, it is also a challenging area to work in for the practicing scientist in that information from various subdisciplines of science has to be brought together.

Bibliography

Kelso, J. A. S. (1993). Elementary coordination dynamics. In "Interlimb Coordination: Neural, Dynamical, and Cognitive Constraints" (S. P. Swinnen, H. Heuer, J. Massion, and P. Casaer, Eds.), pp 301–318. Academic Press, San Diego.

Magill, R. A. (1993). "Motor Learning: Concepts and Applications," 4th, ed. Brown & Benchmark, Madison, WI.

Newell, K. M., and Corcos, D. M. (1993). Variability and Motor Control." Human Kinetics, Champaign, IL.

Rosenbaum, D. A. (1991). "Human Motor Control." Academic Press, San Diego.

Rothwell, J. C. (1987). "Control of Human Voluntary Movement." Croom Helm, London.

Schmidt, R. A. (1988). "Motor Control and Learning. A Behavioral Emphasis," 2nd ed. Human Kinetics, Champaign, IL.

Stelmach, G. E., and Requin, J. (Eds.) (1992). "Tutorials in Motor Behavior II." North-Holland, Amsterdam.

Swinnen, S. P., Heuer, H., Massion, J., and Casaer, P. (Eds.) (1993). "Interlimb Coordination: Neural, Dynamical, and Cognitive Constraints." Academic Press, San Diego.

Turvey, M. T. (1990). Coordination. *Am. Psychol.* **45**, 938–953.

◆

MOTOR DEVELOPMENT

Jane E. Clark
University of Maryland at College Park

Glossary

Constraint A property of the organism, environment, or task that limits or sets boundaries on movement.

Coordination The spatial and temporal relationship between movement constituents.

Fine motor skills Manipulative skills that involve the small muscles of the hands (e.g., sewing).

Gross motor skills Motor skills that involve the large, force-producing muscles of the trunk, arms, and legs (e.g., kicking a ball).

Manipulative skills Motor skills in which the purpose is to act on or with objects in the environment (e.g., dribbling a ball, hammering).

Ontogenetic motor skills Those motor skills that are unique to an individual.

Phylogenetic motor skills Those motor skills that are common to all members of the species (e.g., walking).

Posture Maintenance of a desired orientation to the environment.

Transport task A movement task in which the body moves from one location to another.

MOTOR DEVELOPMENT is the change in motor behavior over the lifespan and the processes that underlie the change. Across the lifespan, our movement behavior is transformed dramatically. Compare the movement repertoire of the newborn who is barely capable of lifting her head with the Olympic gymnast who spins and twists through the air before landing on a 4-inch wide balance beam. In less than

20 years, the Olympic gymnast has developed from a helpless infant to a marvelously well-coordinated athlete. While we all do not become Olympic-level performers, the changes in our motor behavior from infancy to adulthood are nonetheless remarkable.

Motor development is that aspect of human development that focuses on an individual's movement behavior. Although the muscles and bones are important subsystems in determining how and why we move, movement behavior results from an interaction of many subsystems including perception and cognition. Understanding how and why movement behavior changes across the lifespan can be important to many fields. Indeed disciplines as diverse as kinesiology, psychology, and neurophysiology study motor development. And knowledge about motor development is applied by physical educators, physical and occupational therapists, early childhood specialists, and many other professions.

I. DEFINITION OF FOCUS

Broadly speaking, motor development encompasses all movement behavior. However in actuality it is *movement with a purpose* that is the focus of study. How do purposeful, goal-directed movements develop in our lifetime? How does the infant obtain a favorite toy or the adult steer a car on a snowy road? Across the lifespan, our ability to successfully achieve a variety of movement goals expands substantially. Ultimately some movement goals may be achieved optimally, that is, in the most satisfactory or desirable fashion. A movement goal achieved optimally is said to be *skillful*. A skillful movement can be characterized in a number of ways. First, skillful movement is efficient; in other words, the mover accomplishes the task with the least effort. Movement efficiency can be measured biomechanically, physiologically, and psychologically. Second, skillful movement is versatile in adapting to changing task demands. If the environment changes, a skilled mover quickly adjusts to the change. And finally, a skilled movement achieves its goal with maximum certainty. For the skilled mover, this means that the performance can be reliably repeated. Thus, the study of motor development focuses on purposeful movement that may evolve into skillful motor behavior.

As we examine the developmental changes in movement, three broad categories of movement purposes or goals emerge, these are: posture, transport, and manipulation. Postural tasks maintain the body in a particular orientation to the environment. For example, sitting on a chair or standing on one foot is a task that maintains the body's orientation in an upright position. Transport tasks include those movements that change the body's location. Walking and running are transport tasks as well as such actions as getting out of bed or swimming. In manipulative tasks, the movement's purpose is to act on or with objects in the environment. Examples of manipulative skills are throwing or kicking a ball, drinking a glass of water, and handwriting. Of course, a person may have more than one movement goal at a time. For example, a football quarterback throws as he is running and the train rider maintains her body's orientation as she writes or drinks her coffee.

II. DETERMINANTS OF MOTOR DEVELOPMENT

In the first year of life, the infant's motor repertoire displays an order and regularity that suggests strong maturational influences on motor development. However, while heredity may exert a strong force in infancy, we should not assume that motor development results from a genetic code that prescribes when babies rollover, sit up, and walk. While traditional accounts of motor development emphasized central nervous system maturation as a major determinant of motor development, today's contemporary explanations recognize the importance of a wide array of other constraints both within and surrounding the developing infant. These constraints are influences or factors that set the boundaries or limits on our development. Certainly the maturing central nervous system is an important source of constraints on behavior, but it is not the only source. Indeed constraints arise from three general sources: the organism, the environment, and the task that is to be achieved.

A. Organism Constraints

Constraints that arise within the organism include structural and functional constraints. Structural constraints refer to aspects of the individual's physical being, such as the body's size and shape. Functional constraints refer to the physiological state of the body's systems, including the nervous and cardiovascular systems. We can envision how constraints set boundaries on our movement behavior perhaps easiest by considering the organism's structural constraints. In humans, the knee is a hinge joint that permits forward–backward action over a specific range of motion. The knee's structure constrains the types of movements available to humans for locomotion. The universality of such structural constraints gives us many species-typical or phylogenetic motor behaviors. Thus, humans walk, run, and hop while snakes slither. The organism's functional constraints while arising from the organism's structure are influenced by experience and therefore provide a more individualistic developmental path. For example, while all humans have muscles, the strength and endurance of the muscles (i.e., their functioning) may be different because of their differing experiences.

Across our lifespan, there are clear changes in organism constraints. With increasing age, infants get taller and heavier and body proportions change. Every system from endocrine to circulatory will undergo changes that have the potential for influencing motor skill development. For example, at birth, the infant's head and neck comprise 30% of the body's length while the legs make up 15%. These proportions reverse with growth such that by age 6, the head and neck are 15% of the body's length and the legs are 25%, values comparable to adult proportions (i.e., adult's head/neck comprise 10% of the body's length while the legs are 30%). These changes in the body's proportions can influence our motor behavior. The baby's large head, short legs, and tiny feet create a structure that is mechanically very difficult for walking independently. In fact, there is evidence to suggest that infants with proportionately longer legs, and who are not overweight, walk earlier than infants with shorter legs. While the physical characteristics of the individual may be obvious constraints, other properties of the organism such as perceptual, cognitive, and emotional attributes also operate as organism constraints. For example, a child's perceptual abilities may limit catching a tossed ball or copying the alphabet. As we get older, our lack of knowledge about a particular sport might well limit our playing ability. Organism constraints, in other words, are those properties of the individual—both of structure and function—that shape the motor behavior we see across the lifespan.

B. Environmental Constraints

Environmental constraints arise outside the organism. The environment consists of the physical surroundings and the sociocultural milieu of the developing organism. Constraints in the physical environment would include such factors as gravity, ambient temperature, available light, and the supporting surface. An illustration of how the physical environment can influence motor behavior is seen in the disappearance of the walking reflex. At birth, if you hold an infant upright and over a surface you will elicit an organized walking pattern. This stereotypic motor response to the stimulus of pressure on the sole of the foot is referred to as the walking or stepping reflex. In normally developing babies, this reflex will ''disappear'' about 4 months after birth. This disappearance has been attributed to cerebral cortex maturation that inhibits lower central nervous system centers. However, experiments have shown that this reflex can ''reappear'' if the infant is placed in water. Changing the environment (i.e., the gravitational constraints) changed the behavior.

The environmental constraints found in society are more subtle, influencing the types of movement experiences that are available and practiced. For example, those societies that do not permit women to engage in athletic endeavors might restrict the level of motor skillfulness attained by women. Another example is found in the child-rearing customs of different societies. In societies that practice active, systematic handling of infants in which parents stretch and massage their infants as well encourage a diversity of movements, infants sit and walk earlier than infants of parents from societies with less active child-rearing customs.

C. Task Constraints

Task constraints are those requirements of the specific task or purpose that the mover seeks to accomplish. Although task constraints are in the environment, they are defined here as a unique source of constraints. They include the accuracy and speed requirements of the task, as well as when the task is initiated. In sport skills, task constraints can be imposed by the sport's rules. In diving, a $2\frac{1}{2}$ inward somersault in the tuck position has a very specific body configuration. To achieve the task successfully, the movement must conform to the task constraints imposed by the diving rules. Task constraints also can be much less confining. For example, there are any number of ways to travel across a room or sit in a chair.

Task constraints are found not only in the movement's goal but in the tools or equipment of the task. Riding a tricycle imposes different task constraints than riding a bicycle. Picking up a 1-inch vs 16-inch diameter ball constrains the arm and hand movements differently. Often young children cannot perform a movement like an adult because they are using adult equipment. If the equipment were scaled to their body size, their movements may well become more adult-like.

III. THE PROCESS OF DEVELOPING MOTOR SKILLS

How is it that humans develop motor skills? Amidst such a wide array of influential and continually changing constraints, what is the process by which we come to develop our motor skills? Contemporary theory explains motor development as a dynamic process in which a motor behavior emerges from the many constraints that surround that behavior. Behaviors are assembled to meet the task at hand against the backdrop of organism and environmental constraints. Changes in motor behavior occur because constraints change, not because there is a genetic code that prescribes the behavior's appearance.

Why do we see such similarity in performing some movements as well as incredible individuality in others? If movements emerge from constraints, then similarity in movements would suggest similarities in the organism, environment, and/or task constraints and for individuality, the converse. Thus, universally observed developmental sequences in which infants roll over, sit, crawl, and walk arise from similar constraints. Changing a critical constraint would change the sequence. For example, if an environmental constraint such as gravity were changed (i.e., we were born on the moon), we would not expect to see the same behaviors or the same developmental sequence.

IV. THE MAJOR PERIODS OF MOTOR SKILL DEVELOPMENT

From the beginning of our lives to the end, our motor behavior changes. Some of these changes are dramatic, others are more modest. To capture the major qualitative changes that occur in motor skill development across the lifespan, six major periods have been described. Starting with birth, these periods are (1) the reflexive period; (2) the preadapted period; (3) the fundamental motor skills period; (4) the context-specific motor skills period; (5) the skillful period; and (6) the compensation period. Progression from one period to another depends on changes in critical constraints. Skills and experiences acquired in the preceding period serve as a foundation for later skills. Although an age range for each period will be given, these are only estimates. It is the order of the periods, not the ages given, that is significant.

Finally, note that these periods characterize movement after birth. The human fetus can move from the second or third gestational month onward. Understanding the nature of these fetal movements has been difficult until recent advances in intrauterine recording. It is clear, however, that infants have a whole repertoire of movement behaviors practiced in the womb in anticipation of entering into the world.

A. Reflexive Period

The reflexive period of motor development begins at birth and lasts about 2 weeks. For the human fetus, birth is a major disruption. From the muffled dark viscous world of the womb, the infant emerges into a cold, noisy, and bright world in which gravity's pull is about two and a half times greater than it was in the womb. The cramped space of the womb that kept the infant in a flexed position has been replaced by a world that provides comparatively little support for its body and lots of room to move. Internal bodily changes occur as well. The circulatory system undergoes a remarkable transformation as the hole between the heart's auricles closes and the blood flow is redistributed from the placenta to the pulmonary system. The lungs, once filled with amniotic fluid are now filled with air. One marker that life outside the womb stresses the infant is the 6–9% weight loss experienced by the newborn in his first few days.

At birth, the neonate is capable of movement. However, the movement that we see during this 2-week period is primarily involuntary, and either *spontaneous* or *reflexive* in nature. Spontaneous movement is movement that appears to be elicited by no known external stimulus. A reflex, on the other hand, has a specific stimulus that evokes a stereotypical motor response. An example of a spontaneous movement would be "mouthing" as the infant sleeps. It is a well-organized movement of the lips and tongue for which there is no apparent stimulus. The palmar grasp is an example of a reflex. If the palm of the infant's hand is touched, the fingers will flex. This is a stereotypic behavior elicited by a specific stimulus.

The reflexive period does not last long—approximately 2 weeks. If it lasted any longer, it would be counterproductive. The infant needs to adapt to her environment with movements that are less stereotypic than reflexes. But this first period of motor development does serve a vital purpose. By having a repertoire of reflexes, the infant has a safety net of built-in responses that facilitate survival and, also, open a dialogue with the environment. The feeding reflexes are good examples of these early motor behaviors. These include the rooting, sucking, and swallowing reflexes. The rooting reflex is elicited by a touch to the baby's cheek around the mouth. In the newborn, the response to this stimulus is head turning in the direction of the stimulus followed by a turn away and then back again. Progressively the head-turning swings become smaller until the neonate's mouth is oriented toward the stimulus. The sucking reflex also is elicited by touch, but the touch must be to the lips. The response to this stimulus is a sucking action. Thus, as the mother brings the infant to her breast, the rooting reflex moves the baby's head into a position that affords nipple contact with the lips. Touch to the lips, then elicits the sucking reflex. In combination, these two reflexes offer the infant a set of behaviors that enable the infant to obtain nourishment. This helps the neonate make the drastic shift from the womb where the umbilical cord was the nourishment source to the world in which there is little time to learn to eat with the mouth.

In addition to their utility for survival, the reflexes also open a dialogue between the organism and the environment. The reflexes situate the infant in an interactive cycle in which the reflexive movements yield sensory consequences. The infant uses this sensory information to extend and refine her actions. For example, sucking will eventually show modulation, sucking faster or harder depending on the flow of milk. Reflexes are not simple on–off stimulus–response units that remain fixed, but behavioral patterns open to modification from experience.

Thus, from the beginning, the central nervous system provides a set of constraints that results in organized motor behavior (i.e., spontaneous and reflexive movements). These serve the newborn in several ways. First, they provide behaviors that are necessary for survival (e.g., sucking, swallowing). Second, these behaviors open a dialogue with environment—a necessary adaptive step. And third, they provide a movement organization that will provide an initial foundation for later movements.

Finally, reflexes are with us throughout our lives. The eye-blink and the knee-jerk are two common reflexes that can be elicited throughout the lifespan. The reflexive period is so named because it characterizes the principal types of movement observed during this period of life, not because it is the only time in the lifespan when we see reflexes.

B. Preadapted Period

The next period of motor development is characterized by what are called preadapted motor behaviors. These are behaviors that reflect a predisposition of the organism for certain actions. Indeed many have incorrectly assumed that they were predetermined behaviors. Careful study, however, has shown that while these are movements common to all developing humans, their appearance reflects species-typical organism and environmental constraints, not hard-wired fixed action patterns. Evolution, it seems, has found a compromise by providing the human species with a genetic repertoire that makes it highly likely that behaviors necessary for survival will appear, but still leaves the flexibility to change course if the environment demands different behaviors.

At birth, we are dependent on caregivers for our transportation (i.e., locomotion) and our feeding. To survive independently, we must acquire the abilities to transport and feed ourselves. If nature gave us too much freedom in how these behaviors develop, it could be detrimental to our survival. However, the diversity of environments in which human infants grow up requires that these behaviors be modifiable, not fixed action patterns. The compromise is a *preadapted* set of behaviors. That is, humans inherit a constellation of biological constraints (neuronal, muscular, skeletal, etc.) that give shape to our behaviors, but do not restrict us to only predetermined patterns of behavior.

To achieve the motor skills necessary for independent survival, the infant must solve three fundamental movement problems. One problem is how to move about in the environment (i.e., locomotion). Another problem involves how to act with and on objects in the environment (i.e., manipulation). To solve these problems, the infant must solve a third problem, namely how to achieve a desired orientation to the world (i.e., posture) so locomotion and manipulation can occur. The attainment of independent bipedal locomotion (i.e., walking) and independent feeding mark the solution of these movement problems. Indeed, it is when these two skills are achieved that the preadapted period ends—usually around 1 year when the baby takes her first steps having achieved independent reaching/grasping several months before.

The challenge for the infant in the preadapted period is to discover effective patterns of coordination within the existing constraints. Throughout the first year, the infant's movement behavior undergoes remarkable change as the infant progresses from a newborn incapable of lifting her head to the upright ambulating 1 year old capable of grasping those objects within her reach. The literature is filled with careful and detailed inventories of the motor behaviors changes in the first year of life. Figure 1 illustrates six developmental postural and locomotor milestones seen during the preadapted period. Also included are the average ages when these behaviors appear. These motor milestones mark dramatic changes in the infant's control and coordination of his various body segments (i.e., head, trunk, and limbs).

To achieve an orientation to the world that allows the hands to be free for manipulation and the legs to transport the body, the infant must learn to move her body in a gravitational world. Independent walking requires the infant to keep the head and trunk vertical. Coordinating various body parts (referred to as segments) with each other is also important. In walking, the legs must find a coordinated action that achieves forward propulsion without losing upright stability. Examining the motor milestones of this period reveals that the process of attaining independent walking is a slow process of building larger and larger units of action. How this developmental evolution occurs is illustrated by the motor milestones depicted in Figure 1.

At 2 weeks, the infant cannot lift her head off the support surface to gaze about the environment (Fig.

FIGURE 1 Six postural/locomotor milestones in the first year of life. Two weeks: prone position; three months: on hands; five months: sits alone; eight months: crawls; ten months: stands alone; twelve months: walks independently.

1). If we were to hold this infant vertically, such as at the shoulder, we would see that she cannot maintain her head vertically. Three months later, however, she not only can orient her head vertically, but also can push her upper trunk off the supporting surface and turn right and left (Fig. 1). The head and trunk move together as a coordinated unit. The arms too reveal an organization that enables the infant to push up and hold the head-up position. Indeed around this time, we see the arms and legs exhibit considerable coordination in arm banging and waving and leg kicks. In the next months, together with the head and trunk, these limb coordinations are assembled into units that span all the body's segments as the infant achieves sitting, crawling, standing, and walking.

Against this backdrop of changing postural and locomotor capabilities are the infant's expanding manipulative capabilities. At birth, the infant is ca-

pable of extending her arm and hand toward an object if her body is fully supported. Referred to as prereaching, these movements are infrequent, ineffective actions that rarely touch and never grasp objects. However, they represent a primitive coordination of the arm segments assembled in response to a visually fixated object. It is not until at least 4 months of age that the infant achieves a successful reach and grasp. These early successful reaches take place with considerable effort as the infant closely watches her hand move slowly toward the object. For a few months, most grasped objects end up in the mouth. Around the ninth month, infant reaches become more skill-like, displaying a degree of automaticity and effectiveness in goal attainment. Not everything goes to the mouth, but they are now capable of feeding themselves so long as forks and spoons are not required.

Thus, throughout the preadapted period, infants assemble, dissolve, and re-assemble coordinated actions. To achieve these changes in motor behavior, changes must occur in the constraints that surround the behavior. In the first year of life, most changes result from changes in the organism's constraints. In addition to the changes in the body's segmental proportions mentioned earlier, the infant will make rapid gains in weight and muscle strength. For the 2-week-old infant with muscles weak from their lack of movement in the womb, lifting a very large head while lying prone is impossible. Three months later when that infant easily lifts her head, constraints such as muscular strength may well be major contributors to the change. Similar strength changes occur in the muscles of the trunk, arms, and legs as the infant's own movements provide "weight training."

Other organism constraints that change in the first year that might contribute to the observed changes in motor behavior include such functional changes as increased sensitivity and understanding of perceptual information (such as vestibular, proprioceptive, and visual information), improved neuromuscular functioning, and expanding cognitive abilities.

C. Fundamental Motor Skills Period

With the achievement of independent feeding and walking, around the first birthday, the infant enters the next major period of motor skill development, the fundamental motor skills period. Lasting the next 6 to 7 years, this is a crucial period in the future attainment of skillfulness. Described as "building blocks,'' fundamental motor skills are the principal patterns of coordination that underlie later movement skillfulness. These fundamental or basic skills are apparent in a variety of sports, games, and other physical activities in which we engage. In baseball, for example, players run, throw, catch, strike, bend, and stretch. These skills are fundamental motor skills. Fundamental motor skills, however, are not limited to gross motor activities. The foundation for later fine motor skills also is established during this period. Manipulating implements such as feeding utensils, tools, writing instruments, and other graspable objects all provide the basic coordinations for later appearing fine motor skills such as those needed by graphic artists, surgeons, seamsters, or typists.

Thus, from about 1 to 7 years of age, children acquire the patterns of movement coordination essential to later skillfulness. During these years, children will greatly increase their motor behavior repertoire. The toddling infant finishes this period with such locomotor skills as running, galloping, hopping, jumping, and skipping. Acting on objects will include throwing, catching, and kicking balls, as well as the fine motor skills of writing and feeding with implements.

It should be stressed that while most children will acquire the fundamental motor skills, this achievement is not maturationally determined. In other words, getting older and growing bigger will not result in the attainment of the fundamental motor skills. Indeed, qualitative as well as quantitative differences are seen between children who have had rich and varied movement experiences that have encouraged the development of these skills and those children who have not had such experiences. Insufficient development of these fundamental patterns of coordination may well lead to later difficulties in acquiring skills that depend on these building block movements. For example, the mature pattern of coordination for throwing underlies the coordination used in tennis and golf. If youngsters do not acquire mature throwing patterns, their immature patterns will restrict their attempts to learn the tennis serve or a golf swing. This would not mean that they could not throw or they could not hit a tennis ball or golf ball. Rather, the movement patterns that they employed would hamper their achievement of a *skilled* performance.

1. Locomotor Skills

In humans, transportation overground usually is achieved in the upright posture and on two feet.

Around the infant's first birthday, the basic pattern of coordination for locomotion on two feet is successfully accomplished. First attempts at walking are unsteady; upright two-footed locomotion is a difficult challenge for the toddler resulting in many falls. In short order, however, the infant becomes a stable and versatile walker. Indeed 7–9 months after taking her first steps, the infant manages to run. To accomplish this feat, the infant must generate sufficient ground reaction force to propel the body off the ground (i.e., a flight phase). Creating this force while maintaining upright stability on two feet may be a major constraint limiting the emergence of running. Indeed since walking and running share the same interlimb pattern of coordination (i.e., the two legs perform alternating symmetrical actions that are 180° out-of-phase with each other), it would seem that running awaits the child's ability to generate and manage the additional force required in running.

Once running is established, infants begin to explore other patterns of locomotor coordination. For example, the next fundamental locomotor skill observed in toddlers is the gallop. This is an asymmetrical gait pattern in which one leg walks while the other runs. Around this time, infants demonstrate repetitive two-footed jumping (a sort of "bunny hopping"). A few months later, near the end of the second year or the beginning of the third year, children demonstrate the one-footed hop, the two-footed jump for distance (i.e., the standing long jump), and the jump for height (i.e., the vertical jump).

While the locomotor patterns are defined by their leg coordination, there also are clear developmental changes in the arm action used in locomotion. Freed from providing support for the body, the arms appear "frozen" at the onset of upright locomotion. Only later do they play a major role in maintaining postural stability or increasing force production in locomotion. In fact, it is not until the end of the fundamental motor skills period that most children exhibit a mature coordination between the arms and legs for these skills.

The last of the so-called fundamental locomotor skills to appear is the skip. The skip is a complex, symmetrical coordination in which the interlimb organization involves a step and hop on one leg followed by a step and hop on the other leg. Children have difficulty with this coordination, in part, because it requires the ability to hop on each leg sequentially. Skipping appears around 5 years of age, although there are many children who have difficulty with the pattern into late childhood.

Thus, in the 6 years following the onset of independent walking, the young child expands and elaborates the locomotor patterns of coordination to include asymmetric gaits (i.e., galloping, hopping), complex gaits (i.e., skipping), and body projection skills (i.e., jumping). Each skill requires the coordination of the arms and legs while maintaining the head and trunk in an upright orientation. However, each fundamental locomotor skill extends the range of coordinative relationships such that by the end of this period, the child has the foundation for the context-specific skills of our culture (e.g., ballroom dancing, the triple jump in track and field).

2. Play-Game Manipulative Skills

In the United States, two types of manipulative skills are fundamental to play-games and sports. These are object projection and interception skills. Object projection skills are those in which objects held in the hand or its extension are propelled away (i.e., a throw). Object interception skills are subdivided further into object deflection and reception skills. Object reception is defined as intercepting an object for the purpose of collecting the object (i.e., catch, trap). Object deflection also involves intercepting an object, but the purpose is to direct the object away (i.e., kick, strike).

Throughout the fundamental motor skills period, there are systematic changes in the development of play-game manipulative skills. Because these skills require the production and absorption of force, changes in the child's strength and balance are important constraints in the changing patterns of coordination. The manipulative play-game skills also place a serious demand on the perceptual capabilities of the young child, particularly for the interception skills. Motor skills such as throwing and catching balls require well-timed and spatially accurate movements. To achieve this level of perceptual-motor coordination requires considerable experience.

By the end of the fundamental motor skills period, children have acquired the basic coordination for object projection and interception that will serve as a foundation for their later refinement and elaboration into the specific sport and game skills of our culture. Children can now throw a ball with some degree of accuracy and, if distance is their goal, they can throw a small ball over 25 feet (or more than six times their height). Children are capable of catching different size balls that are thrown to them so long as the ball's speed is moderate. Small balls (such as a tennis ball) are much harder to catch, particularly if a one-handed catch is required. However, if the object is "clutchable," such as a beanbag, this task is managed more easily. Striking, kicking, and trapping balls also are included in the repertoire of fundamental motor skills achieved during this period.

3. Fine Motor Manipulative Skills

Manipulative skills that involve the small muscles of the hands are referred to as fine motor skills. Handwriting, sewing, and playing a musical instrument are fine motor manipulative skills. As with the gross motor skills, the fundamental motor skills period is the time-span when the patterns of coordination that form the bases for later emerging skills are established. Grasping patterns change as well as how the shoulder, elbow, and wrist are coordinated with each other. For example, during this period, the child first picks up implements (such as a crayon or spoon) so the implement lies predominantly across the palm (called a power grip). The fingers flex around the object, acting as a unit. Also early attempts to use the implement result in whole-arm movements that emanate from the shoulder. With increasing manipulative experience, these early holistic patterns of coordination evolve into more differentiated patterns both in the hand and between the hand and arm. By the time the fundamental motor skills period ends, the child has mastered the essential patterns of coordination needed for the fine motor skills of our culture, namely the use of tools for feeding and handwriting.

D. Context-Specific Motor Skills Period

Motor skill development after the fundamental motor skills period is, for the most part, more individualized. Indeed due to the strong influence of organism constraints, the fundamental motor skills have been classified as *phylogenetic* skills, that is, skills typical to the species. Context-specific motor skills, on the other hand, are classified as *ontogenetic* skills, those skills unique to the individual. Thus, motor skill development in the context-specific motor skills period is influenced more by the environmental and task constraints of the specific context than had been the case in the preceding periods. That is not to say that these constraints were not important, in fact they were very important in previous periods, particularly to the rate of development. But the attainment of hopping or galloping are skills that most members of the species acquire in almost all environments; whereas the acquisition of a tennis forehand or a gymnastics back walkover are dependent on opportunity and specific skill instruction. These context-specific skills emerge from *specific* task and environmental constraints.

Thus, the development of sport, dance, and fine motor skills are potentially nurtured and supported by the environment in which children grow up. For example, currently many children in the United States learn the keyboarding and joy-stick use associated with computers and computer games. Building on the fine motor skills of the fundamental motor skills period, these youngsters combine and refine their fine motor skills to achieve context-specific (or game-specific) skills. The context-specific motor skills period begins around 7 years of age and lasts until about 11 years of age or until the attainment of skillful motor behavior.

Performance improvements during this period coincide with changes in cognitive capabilities. Children entering this period have the fundamental motor pattern of coordination for moving a joy-stick, but knowing when and where to move the stick is dependent on knowledge. Children's knowledge base and their ability to retrieve such knowledges play an important role in the acquisition of context-specific skill. The context-specific motor skills also are dependent on the acquisition of context-specific knowledge. A child may well know how to throw a ball to another person, but in a baseball game knowing when and where to throw the ball is the critical factor in successful performance. Clearly improvement in context-specific motor skills requires context-based experience. Youth sport programs, for example, are designed to provide such experience for children.

However, the changes in motor behavior evidenced during this period are not due only to perceptual–cognitive changes. Most sports and games require specific skills within specific environments (i.e., a court or field of specific dimensions), performed with specific equipment (i.e., a racquet, bat, baseballs, basketballs) for successful participation. It takes time and practice within these context-specific environmental and task constraints to learn the motor skills necessary for successful participation. The fundamental motor skill patterns will be combined, elaborated, and refined to satisfy these specific constraints.

Fine motor skills also follow a developmental course through the context-specific motor skills pe-

riod. Consider the types of fine motor skills required by the society—handwriting, keyboarding, drawing, sewing, tool-use. Building upon their fundamental motor patterns for grasping and manipulating objects, children will slowly learn cursive penmanship that stays within the lines, draw pictures that look similar to the original, sew a simple pattern, and construct a simple structure with nuts and bolts. Indeed, many parents will spend hours teaching their children the hand-work skills that are passed from one generation to another.

In summary, the context-specific motor skills period is a transition period between the attainment of the fundamental motor skills and their eventual transformation into skillful motor performance. The transformation is driven by a motivation to be skillful in a particular context (albeit a videogame, a baseball game, or a handicraft). In any case, becoming skillful in the context requires considerable practice. Parental, societal, and peer support are critical to gaining the necessary practice time. Many children join a youth sport team or sign up for lessons, but without the encouragement provided by those around them, they fall far short of the time-on-task that moving to the skillful period of motor development requires.

E. Skillful Period

When a movement is performed efficiently, consistently, and with adaptive versatility, it is said to be performed skillfully. Achieving this level of motor performance is not easy. But somewhere around the age of 11, some children begin to evidence skillful motor behavior. However, as was true for the previous periods, the age this period is attained, or whether this period is ever attained, will depend on the individual. Becoming skillful is also context-specific; that is, skillfulness is specific to a game, sport, or context. Being skillful in one setting, such as basketball, does not necessarily imply you are skillful in other contexts, for example, in handwriting, piano-playing, or golf.

This developmental period does not depend upon being skillful in all motor behavior, rather it is characterized by the *potential* for skillfulness in a wide variety of movement contexts. Changes in the child's cognitive and emotional capabilities, along with increasing movement experiences, lead to skillfulness in specific contexts, but they also provide a basis for acquiring other new skills. For example, children may well have the navigational skills for driving a car as early as 7–8 years of age; however, becoming a *skilled* driver awaits the cognitive and emotional maturity necessary to make quick, accurate, and safe driving decisions.

This period also coincides with the onset of puberty in most children. The physical changes that accompany puberty offer a new set of organism constraints. After age 10, for example, both sexes double their body weight. For females, much of this weight gain is in subcutaneous fat; in males the weight gain is more likely to result from increasing muscle mass. Both sexes also have a height spurt as they achieve their full adult stature by the end of their second decade. For motor skill performance that is dependent on power, these organism changes can result in dramatic performance differences, particularly in males.

Continued practice and experience leads some individuals beyond the skillful level to what might be called *expertise.* Expertise is a level of motor skill performance that is exceptional. Olympic performers would be examples of individuals that have attained expertise. At the expert level, the skilled mover displays virtuosity and inventiveness, thinks of strategies rather than about the movement itself, sees meaning in patterns quickly and accurately, and always seems to move with an effortlessness that belies the difficulty of the skill. To become an expert mover requires years and years of practice. For example, despite the occasional early achiever, the average age of the U.S. tennis champion is well into the mid-20s. Similarly, golf, baseball, and football players are at their prime in their 20s, despite their early introductions to the sport.

But few individuals achieve expertise in movement. Indeed skillfulness itself is not easily attained. However, in motor skills that are repeated in our daily living, such as driving a car or writing, or those that are required for our employment, such as typing or carpentry, we achieve the time-on-task required to become skillful as well as to maintain or improve our performance level. Motor skills that are *recreational,* namely those done for our enjoyment, are more difficult to achieve and maintain because of the time demands of practice. As the participation statistics would support, however, adults continue to take part in recreational motor skills throughout their lifetime. And as scientific studies are now demonstrating, the physical activity that results from this participation may lead to a healthier life.

The skillful period is the culmination of years of movement experiences. It begins around the age of 11 and may be maintained throughout adulthood. And yet, it is not the final period of motor development. As we grow older, we begin to see decrements in our motor skills. We may not be as fast as we once were, or we may make mistakes we would never have made before. Because motor skills are produced by our bodies, changes in our bodies, especially those associated with aging, change our organism constraints. If these changes are great enough, they may lead to changes in our motor skill. And with the appearance of these changes comes the last period of motor skill development, the compensation period.

F. Compensation Period

Motor development is the change in movement behavior across the *lifespan.* From the reflexive to the skillful period, these changes are toward progressively more skillful behavior. However, at some point in our lives, changes in our body due to injury, disease, or the aging process will result in motor skill changes that may not lead to improved performance. An injury may restrict the range of motion in a jont, disease may leave us weak, and aging may slow our reactions. The compensation period of motor skill development is characterized by the need to *compensate* for such changes in organism constraints. Most individuals maintain their level of motor skillfulness throughout their adult years. However, with aging comes certain physical changes. For example, muscular strength and endurance and cardiovascular endurance decline. Diminishing physical capabilities, at some point, will diminish motor skill behavior.

With increasing age, there are often parallel declines in physical activity. If you do not exercise, no matter what your age, strength and endurance will decline. The lack of activity could explain part of the physiological changes; however, even with continued use, there are age-related declines. These muscular declines are not as marked if physical activity is maintained.

Other physical changes associated with aging that might affect the organism constraints for movement might include: sensory loss and slowed decision-making. Declines in the senses, particularly vision, balance, and touch may severely limit the amount and quality of sensory information available. The speed and accuracy of processing this sensory input as well as deciding what to do about it also are slow and often in error. Again disuse contributes substantially to these declines. Driving a car for the retired 70 year old, once a task done every day, may now be an infrequent activity. The quickness and accuracy of processing sensory information and making decisions fades with the lack of practice. Of course, these declines can be slowed or reversed with practice.

When organism changes take place, we respond by adjusting our motor behavior. In the compensation period, the older mover may employ compensatory strategies such as going slower, assuming a different posture, or reducing the range of motion. A level of skillfulness may be maintained, but not at a previous level; however, the movement may still be skillful. Organism changes associated with aging may affect some motor behaviors more than others. Especially vulnerable are the gross motor skills that depend on creating and managing quick forces such as those found in basketball or high jumping.

So while most of our lives, our motor skill performance improves, at some point organism constraints change such that our motor skill behavior declines. The extent of this decline depends on the nature of the constraint change. As with all motor skill development, it is the constraints that shape our behavior.

V. SUMMARY AND FINAL NOTE

From the reflexes of the newborn infant to the slow careful steps of an octogenarian, motor behavior changes. These changes and the processes underlying these changes are defined as motor development. Across the lifespan, these changes can be characterized in six major periods. While these periods describe the global changes, these periods fall short of capturing the individual differences apparent in motor behavior. Individuals differ in so many ways in their movement. We have distinctive walks, unique signatures, and favorite movements. Some individuals will win Olympic medals or dance on Broadway, many others will be happy keeping the ball in play or learning to waltz. So while we may globally describe motor skill development by six major periods over the lifespan, the diversity in the rate and the quality of development should not be forgotten.

Bibliography

Clark, J. E. (1988). Development of voluntary motor skill. In ''Handbook of Human Growth and Developmental Biology'' (E. Meisami and P. S. Timiras, Eds.), Vol. I, Part B, pp. 237–250. CRC Press, Boca Raton, FL.

Clark, J. E., and Whitall, J. (1989). What is motor development? The lessons of history. Quest **41,** 183–202.

Haywood, K. (1993). ''Life Span Motor Development,'' 2nd ed. Human Kinetics, Champaign, IL.

Thelen, E., and Ulrich, B. (1991). Hidden skills: A dynamic systems analysis of treadmill stepping during the first year. Monogr. Soc. Res. Child Dev. (Whole No. 223), **56**(1).

Wade, M. G., and Whiting, H. T. A. (Eds.) (1986). ''Motor Development in Children: Aspects of Coordination and Control.'' Martinus Nijhoff, Dordrecht, The Netherlands.

MUSICAL ABILITY

Rudolf E. Radocy
University of Kansas

Glossary

Ability Broadly, the quality of being able to do something. Musical ability encompasses skills in creating, perceiving, organizing, analyzing, and performing music.

Achievement Specific prior accomplishment. Musical achievement includes what a person already has accomplished regarding music.

Amusia Literally "without music," the term refers to some broad cognitive deficit regarding music, such as the inability to recall even the simplest tonal sequence.

Aptitude Potential for future achievement, based on genetic endowments and the results of informal training and experiences. Musical aptitude involves musically related skills which a person can demonstrate without benefit of musical training.

Audiation The ability to "hear" music mentally in the absence of an auditory stimulus.

Capacity A set of skills or potential for development present at birth. Musical capacity may include aspects of hearing sensitivity or physical traits lending themselves to vocal or instrumental performance.

Deep structure An underlying abstraction from which language and music develop in the context of genetically determined preconditions. Deep structure is more solidly established in language acquisition and processing than in music acquisition and processing.

Factor analysis A quantitative research technique where relationships among a set of variables are analyzed to determine underlying core variables or factors which explain the variability among the original variables. Music researchers have employed factor analysis in order to understand the possible components of musical ability.

Idiot savant A person of limited mental skill in most areas of knowledge who displays remarkable ability in one or a few relatively narrow areas. Some, who are retarded by any measure of intellectual ability, are able to perform prodigious feats of music memorization and performance.

Interval The physical or psychological distance between two musical tones. Physical distance is measured in scale steps or in cents (a musical octave contains 1200 cents). Psychological distance is a perceptual judgment; musicians learn to label certain characteristic distances, such as the octave.

Multiple regression analysis A technique to account for the amount of variability in some criterion variable, such as a measure of musical ability, that may be explained by a set of two or more predictor variables, such as measures of sensory discrimination and musical preferences.

Omnibus theory A theory that musical ability consists mainly of one general factor or overall musicality.

Scale A sequential set of tones ordered by steps (the distance exemplified by the space between two piano keys with one key between them) and half steps (the distance exemplified by two adjacent keys), selected for some musical purpose. Other than the distance requirements, the selection is quite arbitrary; there are no "natural" scales.

Specifics, theory of A theory that musical ability consists of a set of loosely related or unrelated individual components.

MUSICAL ABILITY encompasses the many skills people employ to create, analyze, and perform music. Such skills include recalling sonic sequences across time, singing or playing an instrument with accurate pitch and rhythm, judging the degree of similarity between two compositions, categorizing music stylistically and historically, composing new music and arranging old music in new ways, and detecting discrepancies between what appears in printed notation and what is heard. The component skills of musical ability are not understood fully, and a particular person may be quite skillful in one or more areas of music but rather unskillful in other areas. Musical ability may be defined casually as "ability to do things musical." Psychologists, musicians, and others do not agree formally regarding what constitutes musical ability. This article synthesizes diverse views and research.

I. MUSICAL ABILITY HAS DIVERSE DEFINITIONS AND CONNOTATIONS

Musical ability is a broad term, which one may interpret as the "ability" to accomplish musical tasks, regardless of the degree to which that ability results from prior achievement, formal musical training and education, informal musical experiences and enculturation, or genetic endowment. A procedure for measuring musical ability could be a melange of tasks requiring various degrees of musical experience and training; prior achievement may be the best predictor of success in a musical career.

Musical aptitude is a narrower construct, one which addresses what an individual might accomplish musically if given an opportunity for formal musical instruction. Aptitude results from informal experiences with music and whatever musical potential may be present at birth. That potential, occasionally called capacity, is conceived more narrowly than aptitude. Aptitude and capacity must be measured via a procedure that does not require reading music, recognizing particular musical styles, or any other procedure necessitating formal musical train-

ABILITY

APTITUDE

CAPACITY

(ACHIEVEMENT)

FIGURE 1   Relationships among ability, aptitude, capacity, and achievement.

ing. Capacity measures may be more addressed to a person's ability to detect slight differences in psychophysical stimuli (e.g., slight differences in pitch between two tones); aptitude measures may involve lengthier tonal or rhythmic sequences and memory for them.

Achievement means the specific result of formal instruction and study; musical achievements include composing a specific work, performing a particular composition in a recital, and analyzing the harmonic content of a recorded jazz improvisation. Music educators occasionally express great concern regarding the distinction between achievement and aptitude. In practice, the distinction may become blurred because, in the broad sense of ability, prior achievement is one predictor of future acahievement, just as aptitude may predict achievement.

In order from broadest to narrowest, then, one may arrange the terms *ability, aptitude,* and *capacity,* and one may place *achievement* off to the side (see Fig. 1). While this ordering seems logical and useful, exact definitions of the terms in musical and psychological contexts remain somewhat elusive, and distinctions may not always be clear-cut. The measurement and prediction of musical ability often require an *operational* definition, i.e., a definition in terms of how ability, aptitude, capacity, or achievement will be recognized in a particular musical setting.

II. ONE MAY VIEW MUSICAL ABILITY IN THE CONTEXT OF A SET OF INTELLIGENCES

Intelligence has diverse meanings. It may mean what the scores on some recognized intelligence test say it is; it may mean ability to adapt to the enviornment; it may mean ability to learn and develop skills. Historically, one view of intelligence holds that intelligence is a general aspect or factor of human ability, to which other aspects are related peripherally. Another view advocates existence of multiple intelligences, none of which is necessarily superior to or in control of the others. Recent developments in multiple intelligence theory, as exemplified in Howard Gardner's work, interest scholars of musical ability because multiple intelligence theory allows for a "musical" intelligence, which is substantiated via investigations of human musical deficits and superiorities. [See INTELLIGENCE.]

Musical deficits exist, as well as superior feats of musical achievement. There are cases of musical retardation, and there are cases of musical genius. Some individuals are unable to match individual pitches with their singing voices or recall simple melodies. Others are able to recall and notate intricate musical passages, even in the absence of any immediate auditory reference: Mozart's prowess was legendary. Some instrumentalists have remarkable ability to memorize music; just a few readings of the notes suffice. Others continually struggle to play anything without notation. Interestingly, musical genius, as in superior memorization skills, may occur in otherwise retarded individuals, as in some cases of *idiots savant*.

Musical deficits may be associated with traumatic events. Brain injuries may cause various types of amusia, in which one or more musical skills vanish. Amusia may or may not be accompanied by aphasia, a fact which lends support to views of musical ability or intelligence as being a separate cognitive entity.

As part of a set of intelligences, music may have its own modes of cognitive processing. Just as some theories of language acquisition involve an innate "deep structure" of language, to which "surface structures" in particular languages are related, some theories of music acquisition involve "deep structures" of music, into which the actual tonal/rhythmic sequences of music which a person hears are subsumed in evermore abstract hierarchical layers. Emerging studies of cognitive organization and processing suggest that an ability to create and organize music is a basic human cognitive potential.

Music may have some biological adaptive value and linkage to evolutionary processes. While the "need" for music may not be as readily apparent as the need for food, water, or shelter, researchers such as W. J. Dowling and John Sloboda point out that music provides a means for expression, especially through temporal organization, and that music facilitates social cohesion and cultural identity. If intelligence represents adaptation, music's facilitation of adaptation may be logical. While no one will ever explain with certainty just why music exists, anthropologists and sociologists have described musical functions in many cultures; all of the world's cultures possess music in some form.

III. THE STRUCTURE OF MUSICAL ABILITY IS NOT RESOLVED

Just as intelligence may be viewed as a set of loosely related set of skills, as in the L. L. Thrustone and J. P. Guilford tradition, so too may musical ability be viewed as a set of loosely related skills, as in the tradition of Carl Seashore. In such a view, occasionally called a "theory of specifics," musical ability is a group of more-or-less simultaneously developing sensory discrimination skills. Seashore's test battery, which asks for fine discriminations among paired tones, remains in print, despite criticism that musical ability must include more than rudimentary aural discrimination skills.

Musical ability may be predominantly a general aspect of a global property of "musicality," in accordance with the tradition of James Mursell. Such a view, occasionally called an "omnibus theory," is intellectually similar to the views of Karl Spearman. Rather than looking at separate sensory skills, a globally oriented procedure for assessing musical ability would include tasks based on intact musical passages, such as detecting whether the first or second performance of a passage was more appropriate or "musical" in accordance with customary performance practices.

Issues regarding the relative specificity or holism of musical ability might appear resolvable through factor analytic procedures. A researcher could administer numerous tests, all of which purport to measure some aspect of music ability, to many people and correlate the results. Techniques of factor analysis could enable the researcher to discover underlying factors or core variables that explain significant degrees of the overall variabilities in test scores; the resulting set of factors might illustrate what is really crucial in determining musical ability. In fact, different factor studies produce different results. Sometimes a general factor of musical ability is found; sometimes it is not. Since factor analysis depends on data collection instruments which are developed from different theoretical perspectives and there are diverse approaches to analyzing the correlations and isolating the factors, it is not surprising that factor analysis has not resolved the specifics versus generality issue. Attempts to measure and predict musical ability suggest clues to the psychological structure of musical ability, but the definitive structure is not yet determined.

IV. MANY ALLEGED INDICATORS OF MUSICAL ABILITY EXIST

As suggested earlier, the tasks from which musicians, educators, and researchers infer musical ability's existence may imply its definition. The way in which an investigator chooses to assess musical ability gives some indication of what the investigator believes about the structure of musical ability and the relative importance of particular structural components.

Sensory discrimination skills may indicate musical ability; this is the belief indicated in Carl Seashore's *Measures of Musical Talents,* originally developed in 1919, where the person under evaluation is asked to compare paired tones for small differences in the psychological tonal properties of pitch, loudness, duration, and timbre, and to make similarity judgments between paired brief tonal and rhythmic patterns. Other measures developed over the years also include tests of relatively simple sensory discrimination skills. Within the production and analysis of music, there certainly are occasions where minute differences in similar sounds are important: Tuning a musical instrument to meet a specific pitch standard and maintaining a steady beat in accordance with a conductor's imposed standard tempo are obvious examples. Detecting the difference between a performance in one scale mode as compared with another mode (i.e., pattern of scale tone intervals) may require fine aural discrimination. While music is by no means unavailable to hearing-impaired individuals, a certain amount of basic hearing acuity facilitates discriminating among musical sounds.

Essential though sensory discrimination skills may be for particular musical tasks, they obviously cannot encompass musical ability in its entirety. Music is structured in time; the time required for a musical experience is dictated by the performance. Sensitivity to musical form requires recalling previously heard material and comparing it with what

is presently heard. Consequently, the ability to recall tonal and rhythmic sequences across time may indicate musical ability.

The construct of *audiation,* developed and marketed by Edwin Gordon, refers to the ability to "hear" music in its absence. Gordon's series of tests of audiation present brief musical material, followed by other material; the listener must remember the original material and make a judgment regarding whether the following material is basically the same or different. Other tests, such as Herbert Wing's *Standardised Tests of Musical Intelligence,* include rather lengthy musical passages which the listener must recall while listening to later renditions of the passages to make a judgment regarding some performance aspect. The ability to identify musical styles, composers, and titles is facilitated by musical memory. Recall may be exceedingly exact, as it must be in the task of taking melodic or harmonic dictation (where one must transcribe heard music into written notation), or it may be an approximation, which may serve adequately for "name that tune" situations.

For many people, musical ability is an ability to perform, with an instrument or with the voice. While a person's musical education may not be sufficiently comprehensive if analytical and creative skills are not developed in addition to and along with performance skills, quality performance certainly indicates some ability. Performance may include performance which is rather creative, as in jazz improvisation, or performance which is rather *recreative,* as in the note-for-note prescribed performance which is characteristic of much art music.

Performance requires particular physical skills as well as an idea of how the performance should sound. Singers need to control their vocal folds (vocal "cords") and, for many styles of singing, the positions of their lips, tongues, and throats. Wind instrumentalists need control of their lips ("embouchures") and fingers. Orchestral string players practice diligently to control the bow, and players of plucked string instruments, such as guitar, develop considerable finger dexterity. Other instruments have their requisite needs for psychomotor skills. Advanced performers may reach a point where they do not have to be concerned consciously with psychomotor skills and the details of getting from one tone to the next: John Sloboda describes abstract performance plans somewhat analogous to the chess master's abstract reasoning applied to a long-term sequence of possible moves.

When performance is viewed as the primary manifestation of musical ability, the quality of performance of which a person is capable is the principal indication of his or her musical ability. The particular performance medium may interact idiosyncratically with a performer's skills; a fine pianist may be a terrible vocalist.

The creation of musical sounds, in composing or improvising, may indicate musical ability. Sequencing sounds in such a way that they "make sense" requires well-developed skills, although spontaneous creation of melodies and rhythms is quite natural in young children.

Thus, many skills may indicate musical ability. The skills may be simple sensory discrimination, more complex recall of musical sequences, psychomotor skills employed in musical performance, or skills employed in creating sequences of sounds. The particular mix and relative importance of musical indicators of ability will vary with philosophy and context. A comprehensive accounting of musical ability would need to consider all of the areas of music and musical problems. In addition, one must recognize that nonmusical or extramusical indicators of musical ability exist.

V. WHEN EVENTUAL "SUCCESS" IS THE CRITERION, MUSICAL ABILITY MAY INCLUDE NONMUSICAL ASPECTS

Music educators, guidance counselors, and parents often are interested in musical ability because they wish to recommend appropriate courses of study to students. In addition, music educators often wish to actively recruit students who will be successful in their bands, choirs, and orchestras. "Success" implies a mutually satisfactory experience in a structured program of music education; this requires the ability to prosper within a particular instructional setting as well as musical skills.

Academic ability, as demonstrated through success in literary and mathematical endeavors, may be related to musical ability. Research offers mixed evidence; some work indicates low correlations between measures of academic ability in the form of intelligence and musical ability. Other research suggests a relationship such that all highly musical people are highly intelligent, but not all highly intelligent people are highly musical. Multiple regression studies suggest that measures of academic ability or

achievement may be just as useful as measures of musical ability in predicting musical achievement. A theoretical independence of musical and other forms of intelligence in multiple intelligence theory should not prevent the use of academic ability and linguistic or mathematical intelligences in identifying potential music students.

In formal instructional settings, such as a music class in a public school system, self-discipline and conformity may relate to musical achievement. Music classes, as other classes, require a certain amount of paying attention, following directions, and, particularly in performance classes, subverting one's own musical ideas to those of a group, as imposed by the teacher or conductor. Highly creative students may cause exasperation for teachers and fellow students because of experimentation with divergent and even bizarre sounds. Students usually must practice to develop their performance and discrimination skills; rewards for practice are not always immediate. The student who cannot find and effectively manage practice time usually will have difficulty prospering in a traditional music instruction setting.

The presence of nonmusical indicators of musical ability points to the importance of taking them into account when making predictions and also shows how musical ability itself is elusive because of interactions with other conditions influencing eventual musical achievement.

VI. STUDIES SUGGEST DEVELOPMENTAL PATTERNS IN MUSICAL ABILITY

As do other types of human ability, musical ability proceeds through a developmental sequence. While music may be a "natural" part of being human, the presence of a nurturing and supportive environment greatly facilitates the development of musical ability. The literature regarding musical development is far from complete and is largely culture-bound, but enough research exists to demonstrate that a developmental sequene moves from initial perceptions to abstract musical reasoning. The exact nature of the sequential steps, the degree to which the steps are discrete, and their timing are not yet clear. The following discussion is largely based on the descriptions of Howard Gardner, W. J. Dowling and D. L. Harwood, and David Hargreaves and Marilyn Zimmerman.

Many infants repsond to musical stimuli. They may focus their attention toward the source of music and respond with apparent interest to a change in stimulus properties, such as father singing the song rather than mother. They make individual tone-like sounds and produce short babbling patterns with varying musical pitches. They vary pitch, loudness, and musical contour; i.e., the shape of the line which would be formed by connecting indications of sequential pitch levels.

At approximately 2 years of age, children begin to produce sequences of sounds which are separated by recognizable musical intervals from the scales employed in their surrounding musical culture. They proceed to active creation of spontaneous songs, and begin to mix their creative efforts with fragments from songs they hear around them—learned song. By the time children are around the age of 4, learned song generally has supplanted spontaneous song.

As the child approaches kindergarten age, he or she sings longer songs, with more stable tonal centers and steadier rhythm patterns. Children eventually learn that particular musical properties may change while other properties of a song remain the same (conservation), as in recognizing that melodic contour (the "shape" of a melody, indicated visually by connecting the individual notes on the musical staff) is invariate if the same song is sung at a faster or a slower tempo.

In learning a song, the words seem to be especially relevant, especially for children. Words or fragments of words may be learned prior to specific pitches. This may be related to rhythm. Research suggests that words are less important for older learners.

Into the early elementary school years, through about age 9, musical ability may develop quite adequately as a result of a child's immersion in the surrounding musical culture. Cultural indoctrination provides a wealth of musical materials, operating in accordance with stereotypical musical patterns, including scales, intervals, and harmonic conventions. For older students and adults, music which lacks sufficient similarity to what is usually experienced in the surrounding culture is likely to sound strange and unappealing—contemporary art music often has trouble finding an audience because it may be excessively atonal and lacking in any obvious basis for organization by the listener. Children, however, while forming their musical expectancies in accordance with what they hear, often are relatively open to unfamiliar music.

Formal music instruction generally is necessary to progress further, especially in music performance.

Unfortunately, music lacks a high instructional priority in many school systems in the United States. While some schools have quality music education programs, including the creation and analysis of musical sounds as well as performance, music often is relegated to a series of classroom activities of an entertainment nature. Talented instrumental or vocal performers may find nurturing, and private out-of-school instruction may be available, but, in general, there is no particular commitment toward musical literacy. Relatively few people develop their musical abilities beyond those present at about age 9.

Individuals who do pursue formal musical study into adulthood vary widely in the musical abilities they develop. Some become skillful performers; others become well-informed listeners. Some individuals become composers and arrangers, and a few become versatile in all fields of musical endeavor. Research suggests that people with extensive musical experience process music differently than other adults—they are more sensitive to organization around key tones (tonality), they hear more subtle relationships among tones, and they are better able to relate new musical experiences to former experiences. Physically, anyone with reasonably normal hearing *hears* the same acoustical stimuli as anyone else. As a function of musical training and experience, people vary greatly in what they *do* cognitively with the acoustical stimuli.

VII. MUSICAL ABILITY IS AN INTERACTION OF SENSATION, COGNITION, AND EXPERIENCE

Musical ability, present in varying degrees among many individuals in all cultures, requires sensation. People need to be aware of their auditory surroundings and discriminate among different acoustic stimuli. Those who are musically able can organize auditory inputs into meaningful patterns of unity and variety on the basis of commonalities and contrasts in tonal sequences. As a result of experience in hearing and describing music, people develop musical expectancies to use as a basis for organization.

While musical ability may not be defined easily, the interaction of sensation, cognition, and experience may be nurtured by providing young children as well as older listeners with a rich acoustical environment, filled with a wide variety of musical styles and structured guidance in experiencing them.

Bibliography

Boyle, J. D., and Radocy, R. E. (1987). ''Measurement and Evaluation of Musical Experiences.'' Schirmer Books, New York.

Butler, D. (1992). ''The Musician's Guide to Perception and Cognition.'' Schirmer Books, New York.

Dowling, W. J., and Harwood, D. L. (1986). ''Music Cognition.'' Academic Press, Orlando, FL.

Fiske, H. E. (1990). ''Music and Mind.'' Edwin Mellen Press, Lewiston, NY.

Gardner, H. (1983). ''Frames of Mind.'' Basic Books, New York.

Gordon, E. E. (1989). ''Learning Sequences in Music,'' 2nd ed. GIA Publications, Chicago.

Hargreaves, D. J., and Zimmerman, M. P. (1992). Developmental theories of music learning. In ''Handbook of Research in Music Teaching and Learning'' (R. J. Colwell, Ed.), pp. 377–391. Schirmer Books, New York.

Lerdahl, F., and Jackendoff, R. (1983). ''A Generative Theory of Tonal Music.'' MIT Press, Cambridge, MA.

Radocy, R. E., and Boyle, J. D. (1988). ''Psychological Foundations of Musical Behavior,'' 2nd ed. Charles C. Thomas, Springfield, IL.

Shuter-Dyson, R. (1982). Musical ability. In ''The Psychology of Music'' (D. Deutsch, Ed.), pp. 391–412. Academic Press, New York.

Sloboda, J. (1985). ''The Musical Mind: The Cognitive Psychology of Music.'' Oxford University Press, New York.

NARCISSISTIC PERSONALITY DISORDER

Salman Akhtar
Jefferson Medical College

Glossary

Narcissism Emotional investment into the self. When normal, it leads to sustained self-regard and mature aspirations. When pathological, it is accompanied by inordinate demands upon the self, excessive dependence upon acclaim from others, and deteriorated capacity for interpersonal relations.

Personality disorder A pervasive pattern of chronically maladaptive behavior which is a source of constant interpersonal problems. Personality disorders are ego-syntonic, i.e., such individuals are not aware of their own personalities as being deviant or abnormal. They suffer from the interpersonal consequences of their behavior but they do not recognize their own role in the origin and perpetuation of these problems. Such individuals are therefore unlikely to seek professional advice although they may consent to it if this is urged by others or forced by social repercussions of their behavior.

NARCISSISTIC PERSONALITY DISORDER is a newly recognized diagnostic entity in clinical psychiatry. It was introduced into "official" psychiatric nomenclature in 1980 with the publication of the third edition of the American Psychiatric Association's *Diagnostic and Statistical Manual of Mental Disorders* (DSM-III). There is, however, evidence that the concept had been evolving since the turn of the century beginning with Sigmund Freud's elucidation of the concept of narcissism.

Freud published his seminal paper "On Narcissism" in 1914. He defined narcissism as the concentration of libidinal interest upon one's ego and distinguished primary from secondary narcissism. The former was a normal phenomenon of infancy, the latter a result of withdrawal of interest from the outer world. Freud noted that human attachments are of two types: anaclitic and narcissistic. The former are evident when we are involved with those who nourish and protect us and the latter when we are involved with those who merely reflect us (the way we are, or were, or will be). In essence, the narcissistic relationship is nothing but thinly veiled self-affirmation. While avoiding character typology in this paper, Freud did refer to individuals who "compel our interest by the narcissistic consistency with which they manage to keep away from their ego anything that would diminish it." However, it was not until 1931 that he described the "narcissistic character type."

> The subject's main interest is directed to self-preservation: he is independent and not open to intimidation. His ego has a large amount of aggressiveness at its disposal, which also manifests itself in readiness for activity. In his erotic life loving is preferred above being loved. People belonging to this type impress others as being "personalities"; they are espe-

Encyclopedia of Human Behavior, Volume 3

cially suited to act as a support for others, to take on the role of leaders and to give a fresh stimulus to cultural development or to damage the established state of affairs.

This description is generally viewed as the pioneering portrayal of narcissistic personality disorder. The fact, however, is that a 1913 paper by Ernest Jones, one of Freud's distinguished pupils, also contained significant details regarding the phenomenology of this condition. Using the term ''God Complex'' for their condition, Jones portrayed such individuals as excessively admiring of themselves, having omnipotent fantasies, being exhibitionistic, and scornful of others. Such grandiosity is, at times, masked by caricatured modesty, pseudohumility, and a pretended contempt for materialistic aspects of life.

Over the subsequent decades, many other psychoanalysts contributed to the study of narcissistic personality. Prominent among these were Robert Waelder, Wilhem Reich, Christine Olden, Helen Tartakoff, and John Nemiah. These authors clearly recognized this condition though often without designating it as such. They noted that the central feature of this condition, grandiosity, is a defensive maneuver against feelings of inferiority which they traced to severe frustrations during early childhood.

In the 1970s the publication of two psychoanalytic books breathed new life in the study of narcissistic personality disorder: *The Analysis of the Self* (1971) by Heinz Kohut and *Borderline Conditions and Pathological Narcissism* (1975) by Otto Kernberg. The views of Kohut and Kernberg are summarized below. Suffice it to say here that their works stirred up considerable controversy and mobilized further interest in investigating the true nature of narcissistic personality disorder. Among those who made subsequent major contributions are Sheldon Bach, Ben Bursten, Mardi Horowitz, Arnold Modell, Arnold Rothstein, and Vamik Volkan.

Finally, when in 1980 the DSM-III included narcissistic personality disorder as a separate diagnostic entity, an official imprimatur was added to the evolving concept. The 1987 revision of DSM-III (DSM-III-R) retained the condition with only minor modifications of its diagnostic criteria.

I. MANIFESTATIONS

The cardinal feature of narcissistic personality disorder is heightened narcissism. Individuals with this disorder display grandiosity, intense ambition, and an insatiable craving for admiration. Their consuming self-interest renders them incapable of appreciating and understanding the independent motivations and needs of others. Consequently, they come across as cold, unempathic, exploitative, and having little concern for those around them.

The clinical features of narcissistic personality disorder involve six areas of psychosocial functioning: (i) self-concept, (ii) interpersonal relations, (iii) social adaptation, (iv) ethics, standards, and ideals, (v) love and sexuality, and (vi) cognitive style. In each of these areas there are ''overt'' and ''covert'' manifestations. These designations do not necessarily imply their conscious or unconscious existence although such topographical distribution might also exist. In general, however, the ''overt'' and ''covert'' designations denote seemingly contradictory phenomenological aspects that are more or less easily discernible. Moreover, these contradictions are not restricted to the individual's self-concept but permeate his interpersonal relations, social adaptation, love life, morality, and cognitive style.

Narcissistic individuals have a grandiose *self-concept*. They give an appearance of self-sufficiency and are preoccupied with achieving outstanding success. Covertly, however, they are fragile, vulnerable to shame, sensitive to criticism, and filled with morose self-doubts and feelings of inferiority.

Their *interpersonal relations* are extensive but exploitative and driven by an intense need for tribute from others. They are unable to genuinely participate in group activities and, in family life, value children over the spouse. Inwardly, they are deeply envious of others' capacity for meaningful engagement with life. They attempt to hide such envy by scorn for others; this may, in turn, be masked by pseudo-humility.

Capable of consistent hard work, narcissistic individuals often achieve professional success and high levels of *social adaptation*. However, they are preoccupied with appearances and their work is done mainly to seek admiration. The overly zealous vocational commitment masks a dilettante-like attitude, chronic boredom, and gnawing aimlessness.

Their *ethics, standards, and ideals* display an apparent enthusiasm for sociopolitical affairs, a caricatured modesty, and pretended contempt for money in real life. At the same time, they are often quite materialistic, ready to shift values to gain favor, irreverent toward authority, and prone to pathologic lying and cutting ethical corners.

A similar contradiction is evident in the realm of *love and sexuality*. Overtly, narcissistic individuals are charming, seductive, and given to extramarital affairs, even promiscuity. Covertly, however, they draw little gratification beyond physical pleasure from sexuality and are unable to have deep and sustained romantic relations. Moreover, they seem unable to genuinely accept the incest taboo and are vulnerable to sexual perversions.

Superficially, their *cognitive style* suggests a decisive, opinionated, and strikingly supple intellect. However, their knowledge is often limited to trivia (''headline intelligence'') and they are forgetful of details. Their capacity for learning is also compromised since learning forces one to acknowledge one's ignorance and they find this unacceptable. They are articulate but tend to use language and speaking for regulating self-esteem rather than communicating. [*See* SELF-ESTEEM.]

In sum, narcissistic personality disorder is characterized by a defensively inflated self-concept which is fueled by fantasies of glory, protected by being constantly admired for social success, and buttressed by scornful devaluation of those who stir up envy. Underneath this grandiose self-concept (not infrequently built around some real talent or special aptitude) lie disturbing feelings of inferiority, self-doubt, boredom, alienation, and aimlessness.

II. DISTINCTION FROM RELATED CONDITIONS

Individuals with narcissistic personality disorder have superficial resemblances to those with compulsive personality disorder. Both types of individuals display high ideals, great need for control, perfectionism, and a driven quality to their work. However, the compulsive seeks perfection while the narcissistic claims it. Consequently, the compulsive is modest, the narcissist haughty. The compulsive loves details that the narcissist casually disregards. The compulsive has a high regard for authority and strict inner morality, while the narcissist is often rebellious and prone to cutting ethical corners. [*See* OBSESSIVE–COMPULSIVE BEHAVIOR.]

Three other characterological constellations need to be distinguished from narcissistic personality disorder: borderline, antisocial, and paranoid personality disorders.

Both borderline and narcissistic individuals are self-absorbed and vacillating in their relationships.

Borderline individuals, however, show a greater propensity for disorganization into really regressed mental states. They are less tolerant of aloneness, more angry, and have a poorer capacity for sustained work than narcissistic individuals. [*See* BORDERLINE PERSONALITY DISORDER.]

Both antisocial and narcissistic individuals dream of glory and can lie, cheat, and indulge in ethically dubious acts to achieve success. However, in narcissistic personality such disregard of conventional morality is hidden, occasional, and cautious whereas in antisocial personality where it is open, frequent, ruthless and calculated. [*See* ANTISOCIAL PERSONALITY DISORDER.]

Both paranoid and narcissistic individuals are grandiose, emotionally stilted, envious, sensitive to criticism, and highly entitled. However, the paranoid individual is pervasively mistrustful and lacks the attention-seeking charm and seductiveness of the narcissist. The cognitive style of the two types of individuals differs in a striking way. The narcissist is inattentive to real events and forgetful of details. The paranoid, in contrast, has a biased but acutely vigilant cognition. [*See* PARANOIA.]

III. INTRINSIC NATURE

In the realm of probable causes and the intrinsic nature of narcissistic personality disorder the views of Heinz Kohut and Otto Kernberg form the two major, if sharply divergent, contemporary perspectives. According to Kohut, the origin of narcissistic personality disorder resides in faulty parental empathy with the child. Kohut posits that a growing child needs an enthusiastically responsive audience (''mirroring'') for his or her activities and achievements. When such mirroring is deficient, the child's ordinary pride and associated healthy need to be affirmed take on an insistent and unhealthy exhibitionistic quality (the ''grandiose self''). Kohut also proposes that, in addition to mirroring, the child needs the opportunity to idealize the parents and draw strength from this borrowed sense of importance. When parents either are truly not admirable or their weaknesses are prematurely or shockingly revealed to the child, the hunger for powerful figures goes unsatisfied and becomes a persistent feature of later, adult life. It is this paradoxical mixture of grandiosity and hunger to belong to prestigious others that forms the nucleus of narcissistic character. Inner fragility of self-esteem is hidden by these compensatory structures. Any threat to such self-regulation mobilizes shameful sense of imperfection and intense, vengeful anger ("narcissistic rage").

In contrast to Kohut, Kernberg regards narcissistic personality not as a developmental arrest but a specific pathological formation to begin with. Kernberg differentiates the normal narcissism of children (which retains a realistic quality and does not affect the capacity for mutuality) from the early development of pathological narcissism (which creates fantastically grandiose fantasies and impairs the capacity for mutuality). Kernberg agrees that narcissistic individuals were treated by their parents in a cold, even spiteful manner. However, he adds that they were also viewed as special since they possessed some outstanding attribute, e.g., talent, beauty, superior intelligence, etc. Using Kohut's term with a different formulation, Kernberg proposes that "grandiose self" is formed by the fusion of a highly idealized view of oneself (built around some truly good aspect of oneself) and a fantastically indulgent and admiring inner audience of imagined others. Such grandiose self is a defensive structure against the anger directed at the frustrating parents of childhood. Rage in narcissistic personality is therefore the inciting agent, not merely an epiphenomenon.

The views of Kohut and Kernberg differ in many other ways but their most important differences involve (i) a developmental arrest versus a pathological formation view of grandiosity, and (ii) the reactive versus the fundamental view of aggression in narcissistic personality disorder. These differences affect the techniques which the two theoreticians propose as being suitable to treat this condition.

IV. TREATMENT

The treatment of choice for narcissistic personality disorder is psychoanalysis, provided the patient is psychologically minded, has verbal facility, and is earnestly motivated for change. Within the psychoanalytic framework, however, the approaches outlined by Kohut and Kernberg (and developed further by their proponents) differ considerably. Kohut's approach aims at a full-blown reactivation, *in vivo*, of the frustrated childhood mirroring and idealizing needs. The analyst accepts the validity of such needs and helps the patient see their persistence as emanating from childhood deprivations. The patient's rage,

if it erupts in treatment, is interpreted as an understandable response to the inevitable empathic failures of the analyst. Such an experience is then shown to have connections with similar experiences caused by faulty parental empathy during childhood. Countless repetitions of feeling understood and seeing the present in the light of past gradually facilitate the relinquishment of grandiosity and idealizations.

Kernberg's approach differs. He emphasizes that the experiences of narcissistic patients in analysis are not readily traceable to the actuality of their childhoods. Instead, these are multilayered and include in them early wishes, defenses against those wishes, real experiences, and unconscious distortions of them. Kernberg notes that the patient's disappointments in the analyst not only reveal his or her real or fantasied frustrations of childhood, now being repeated in the treatment situation, but also dramatically reveal the patient's psychic readiness for hate and total devaluation of others. Kernberg does not view the patient's rage as a reaction to the analyst's failures but as an inevitable manifestation of the patient's pathology. At its core, this involves seething rage against real and imagined hurts from parents, a rage that is also used defensively to ward-off dependent longings. Empathy, for Kernberg, is not a therapeutic measure but a technical necessity. The mainstay of treatment is working through the patient's rage and mistrust, anxiety about dependence, and, in later phases of treatment, the guilt over having exploited, devalued, and hurt others including the analyst. With diminution of rage and dread of true attachment, there emerges a capacity to empathize with others, a reduction in self-centeredness, an ability to give, and a dawning awareness of life's complex emotional offerings in the context of genuine affective involvement with fellow human beings.

Bibliography

Akhtar, S. (1992). "Broken Structures: Severe Personality Disorders and Their Treatment." Jason Aronson, Northvale, NJ.
Akhtar, S. (1989). Narcissistic personality disorder: Descriptive features and differential diagnosis. *Psychiatric Clinics of North America* **12**(3), 505–529.
Bach, S. (1977). On the narcissistic state of consciousness. In "Narcissistic States and the Therapeutic Process." Jason Aronson, New York.
Kernberg, O. F. (1975). "Borderline Conditions and Pathological Narcissism." Jason Aronson, New York.

Kernberg, O. F. (Ed.) (1989). Narcissistic personality disorder. *The Psychiatric Clinics of North America,* **xii** (3).

Kohut, H. (1971). "The Analysis of the Self." International Universities Press, New York.

Kohut, H. (1977). "The Restoration of the Self." International Universities Press, New York.

Mahler, M. S., and Kaplan, L. (1977). Developmental aspects in the assessment of narcissistic and so-called borderline personalities. In "Borderline Personality Disorders: (P. Hartocolis, Ed). International Universities Press, New York.

Modell, A. (1984). "Psychoanalysis in a New Context." International Universities Press, New York.

Volkan, V. D. (1982). Narcissistic personality disorder. In "Critical Problems in Psychiatry" (J. O. Cavenar, and H. K. H. Brodie, Eds.). Lippincott, Philadelphia, PA.

NEGOTIATION

Peter J. Carnevale
University of Illinois at Urbana-Champaign

Glossary

Concession making Reducing one's demands or offers—that is, changing one's proposal so that it provides less benefit to oneself.

Contending Attempting to persuade the other negotiator to make a concession or an attempt to resist a similar effort by the other negotiator.

Integrative potential Existence of mutually beneficial options.

Issue Topic under consideration in negotiation that requires a joint decision by the negotiators. An issue entails two or more options, which are called "alternatives."

Limit Point at which a negotiator refuses to concede beyond; sometimes limit is the "best alternative to a negotiated agreement" or BATNA, which is often identical with the status quo, that is, the situation that would have obtained if negotiation had never taken place.

Problem solving Trying to locate and adopt options that satisfy both parties' goals or aspirations.

Strategy Plan of action that specifies broad objectives and the general approach that should be taken to achieve them. Some strategies must be translated into more specific tactics in order to be used.

Win–win agreement Outcome of negotiation that satisfies the major aspirations of all parties involved.

NEGOTIATION can be defined as collective deci-sion making wherein two or more parties talk with one another with the purpose of reaching an agreement on issues where they perceive that their interests are opposed. Opposed interests refers to the parties' belief that they have incompatible preferences among the set of available options. Negotiation is common in all areas of society: the workplace, marketplace, family, labor/management, and international relations. The parties to negotiation are frequently individuals, for example, buyers and sellers. Often, negotiators are representatives of groups, organizations, or political units such as nation states.

Negotiation governs much of the change that ocurs within society. It often occurs as a result of dissatisfaction with the status quo. Agreements in negotiation typically indicate new rules of behavior, new organizational forms, and new distributions of resources. Norms and social structures that guide society often have their roots in negotiation.

Negotiation is one of several procedures for dealing with opposed interests. Three other classes of procedures can be distinguished: (1) Joint decision making, which includes both negotiation and mediation. Mediation is a form of assisted negotiation in which a third party helps the negotiators reach an agreement. (2) Third-party decision making, which includes adjudication (going to court) and arbitration. These involve decision making by legitimate authorities. (3) Separate action, in which the parties make independent decisions. An example of separate action is struggle, which can take the form of physical combat (e.g., military battles, strikes), wars of words (e.g., shouting matches, accusations to the press), or political contests (e.g., vying for allies).

I. THE GENERAL NEGOTIATION PARADIGM

The behavioral approach to the analysis of negotiation seeks to develop and test predictive theory about the impact of environmental conditions on

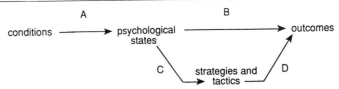

FIGURE 1   Causal sequence in the general negotiation paradigm that
guides behavioral research on negotiation.

negotiator behavior and the impact of these conditions and behaviors on negotiation outcomes. Most branches of the social sciences have contributed to and influenced the study of negotiation. For example, economists and game theorists have developed important mathematical models of rational behavior in negotiation. The behavioral analysis of negotiation has also been influenced by books and manuals that provide advice to negotiators written by practicing experts. The results of many behavioral studies of negotiation have practical implications as well as mathematical underpinnings.

Most behavioral studies of negotiation reflect a general paradigm or model of thought, which is shown schematically in Figure 1. Conditions that prevail at the time of negotiation, for example, characteristics of the social context, are assumed to have an impact on psychological states, such as motives and cognitions (path A in Fig. 1). Psychological states, in turn, have either a direct impact on negotiation outcomes (path B) or an impact that is mediated by negotiator strategies and tactics (paths C and D).

II. ISSUES AND OUTCOMES OF NEGOTIATION

A. Issues

The topics that negotiators discuss can usually be divided into one or more issues that require a decision. Each issue entails two or more options or "alternatives." Take for example the buying and selling of a car: The main issue is how much to pay for the car. The alternatives being considered include prices between $9000 and $11,000. A second issue is whether a package of accessories is installed in the car. The alternatives for this issue are installation versus noninstallation.

Divergence of interest between two negotiators can be precisely defined in terms of a "joint utility space," which is shown in Figure 2. The points in this space define the alternatives available for possible agreements for a set of issues. The solid points

define alternatives currently under consideration. The hollow points define alternatives that can be devised if the negotiators show some creative thinking. The axes of Figure 2 define the utility (subjective value) to each negotiator of the alternatives shown.

Figure 2 represents the car buying example mentioned above. Options 1 through 5 are prices between $9000 and $11,000. These options are arranged so that higher prices have greater utility to the dealer and less utility to the customer. In other words, the parties differ in their utility ordering for at least some of the options under consideration, which is divergence of interest.

Options 6, 7, and 8 are mutually beneficial options. For these alternatives, the dealer will throw in accessories that cost less than they are worth to the customer. They are shown as hollow points because they do not yet exist, that is, that parties have not thought of them at the start of negotiation. There is a divergence of interest among these three options as well. However, options 6, 7, and 8 have an advantage: they are better for both parties than some of the options that do not include the accessory package.

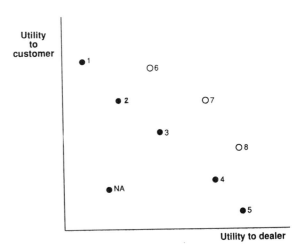

FIGURE 2   Joint utility space in car buying example. The following options are shown: NA = no agreement; 1 = $9000; 2 = $9500; 3 = $10,000; 4 = $10,500; 5 = $11,000; 6 = $10,000 plus options package (o.p.); 7 = $10,500 plus o.p.; 8 = $11,000 plus o.p.

These are mutually beneficial options. Thus, the negotiation illustrated in Figure 2 has integrative potential. Integrative potential refers to the existence of possible options that can integrate the interests of the two negotiators.

B. Outcomes

There are four basic kinds of outcomes that can end negotiation:

1. Victory for one negotiator, for example, in Figure 2, agreement on option 1 or 5.

2. A compromise, defined as agreement on some middle ground on an obvious dimension that connects the parties' initial offers. For example, agreement on option 2, 3, or 4 in Figure 2.

3. A win–win agreement (also called an "integrative agreement"), where the parties achieve higher joint benefit (collective utility) than they could with a compromise. For example, in Figure 2, agreement on one of the mutually beneficial options 6, 7, or 8. Win–win agreements can have a number of advantages over compromises: they are more likely to be complied with and are more beneficial to the relationship between the parties. A win–win agreement is "efficient" (sometimes called "Pareto optimal") in the sense that when the parties achieve the maximum joint gain position neither party can do better in an alternative agreement unless the other does worse.

4. Failure to reach agreement, which is shown by the point marked "NA" (no agreement) in Figure 2. Either party can drop out of negotiation and thus produce a failure to reach agreement, which is unlike the other options that require joint approval. Often the value of nonagreement is the utility of what has been labeled the "best alternative to a negotiated agreement" or BATNA. For example, a car buyer would have a BATNA of $10,000 if he or she knew that they could buy the same car from another dealer at that price. BATNA is usually identical with the status quo, that is, the situation that would have occurred if negotiation had never taken place. In Figure 2, no agreement is shown as a poor outcome for both parties. But this is not always the case: one negotiator may be advantaged by the status quo, making no agreement the same thing as victory for that negotiator (e.g., NA could be at point 1 or point 5 in Fig. 2).

Most negotiations take place in mixed-motive settings, which evoke both competitive and cooperative motives in the parties involved. The competitive motive arises because the players have opposing preferences (i.e., a divergence of interest) for some pairs of options. Thus, in the car buying example shown in Figure 2, the buyer prefers option 1 over option 2 and option 6 over option 8, while the seller has the opposite preferences. The cooperative motive arises because the players have similar preferences for other pairs of options. Thus, both of them prefer option 7 (one of the win–win options) to option 3 (the equal outcome compromise), and options 2, 3, and 4 to no agreement (NA).

The mixed-motive nature of negotiation can create a dilemma for negotiators. The competitive motive encourages negotiators to be contentious and to try to push the other party into making concessions that could mean a more favorable outcome. But the cooperative motive encourages negotiators to engage in problem solving, which might lead to better outcomes. The dilemma stems from the possibility that one's cooperative gestures might not be reciprocated but instead are exploited by a contentious opponent. [See SOCIAL VALUES.]

C. Research Tasks

Behavioral research on negotiation has been conducted in both laboratory and field settings. Field research often involves case studies of actual instances and questionnaire surveys where professional negotiators are the respondents. Laboratory studies usually entail undergraduate volunteers who are asked to negotiate with each other, a confederate, or a computer program. In laboratory studies, communication is sometimes face-to-face, sometimes by means of note passing, and sometimes between computer terminals. The tasks used in laboratory experiments usually involve stripped-down simulations of real-life negotiation. Two kinds of task are most common. The first involves negotiation about a single issue, for example, the price of a hypothetical used car. The second involves negotiation about two or more issues, such as the price of a car and the accessories to be mounted on it. The latter type of task provides the opportunity to study the development of win–win agreements.

III. STRATEGIES AND TACTICS

It is possible to distinguish five broad strategies that can be used in negotiation. A strategy is a plan of action for negotiation that specifies broad objectives and the general approach that negotiators should take to achieve them. Some of these strategies must be translated into more specific tactics in order to be used. The strategies include:

1. Concession making—reducing one's goals, demands, or offers. In other words, changing one's proposal so that it provides less benefit to oneself.
2. Contending—trying to persuade the other party to concede or trying to resist similar efforts by the other party.
3. Problem solving—trying to locate and adopt options that satisfy both parties' goals.
4. Inaction—doing nothing or as little as possible, for example, putting off meetings, talking around the issues, etc.
5. Withdrawal—dropping out of the negotiation.

A. Concession Making

There are three basic, interrelated findings about the effects of concession making on the outcome of negotiation. One finding is that if agreement is reached, a firm negotiator will often achieve a larger outcome. A firm negotiator has high goals, makes large initial demands, and resists concession making. For example, the car seller in Figure 1 starts with Option 5 and only extremely reluctantly makes a concession to Option 4.

A second finding is that negotiator firmness lengthens negotiation and makes agreement less likely. The more negotiators demand at first, and the slower they make concessions, the harder it will be for them to reach agreement. This unsurprising finding is true in most cases. However, there is a strange reversal when one negotiator is at the low (very soft) end of this dimension. If one negotiator makes a really low initial demand or makes very fast concessions, aggreement is less likely and takes longer to reach than if that negotiator had been a little more ambitious. This is because very fast concessions signal extreme weakness to the other negotiator, leading the other negotiator to expect more and thus stop making concessions. This makes agreement less likely.

A third finding is derived from the first two. Given that an agreement has value to a negotiator, there will be an inverted U-shaped relationship between negotiator firmness and negotiator outcome. Negotiators who demand too little may reach an agreement but they will achieve very low profits. Negotiators who demand too much will fail to reach agreement and thereby do poorly. Thus, the most successful negotiators, the ones who will maximize their outcomes in the long run, will be those who are moderately firm, who make moderate demands and moderate concessions.

B. Contending

There are many tactics that can be used to implement contending, including threats, positional commitments, and persuasive arguments. Threats are messages that indicate one negotiator will punish the other if the other fails to do what the first wants. Positional commitments are messages that indicate that one negotiator will not change their current position in the negotiation. Persuasive arguments are designed to change the target's attitude toward an issue.

1. Threats

Threats are effective to the extent that the penalty threatened has credibility. Credibility refers to the perceived likelihood that a threat will be carried out. Threat credibility goes up when threats have been regularly carried out in the past. It goes down when fulfilling the threat is costly to the threatener as well as the target. Credible threats can reduce the attractiveness of the no agreement option for the target to the threat. Credible threats can be successful at eliciting concessions. Sometimes they are the only way to get the other party to negotiate at all. However, threats have their down side: they tend to generate resentment and resistance, and they tend to be reciprocated, which can produce counter-threats and destructive conflict spirals.

2. Positional Commitments

Positional commitments (also called "irrevocable commitments") are often combined with a threat to break off negotiation if the other party does not accept an offer. They are only effective if failure to reach agreement is costly to the target. As with threats, positional commitments must be credible to be effective. They are not very credible if it is clear that their user will be badly hurt by no agreement. One way to demonstrate credibility is to show that one has a credible alternative to negotiated agreement (a favorable BATNA). But positional commitments can be hazardous: they can lock the negotiator into a position that is unworkable because it is completely unacceptable to the other negotiator—it exceeds the other's limit or minimally acceptable level of benefit. Negotiators can get around this hazard by hedging the commitment, indicating that it is not completely firm. Although this can endanger credibility, it allows a graceful retreat from the commitment if it is unworkable. Another approach is to delay making positional commitments until later in negotiation. There is evidence that experienced negotiators, in comparison to novices, will tend to delay positional commitments to the end of negotiation.

3. Persuasive Arguments

Social psychologists have long been interested in the effectiveness of persuasive arguments. In negotiation, persuasive arguments have the objective of convincing the target that one's proposal is in the target's best interests. [See PERSUASION.]

What effect do contentious tactics have on negotiation? Unequal use of contentious tactics can lead to an agreement that favors the heavier user. But such victories can be shortsighted when the negotiation situation has integrative potential. This is because contentious tactics often lead to low joint benefit and, when limits are high, to failure to reach agreement. Users of contentious tactics tend to focus on particular demands, which makes them unlikely to seek or discover new options. Contending creates a rigidity of thought that is incompatible with creativity. Contentious tactics are especially problematical when they are reciprocated by the other negotiator, when threats elicit counterthreats. Many studies have shown that reciprocated contentiousness is associated with failure to reach agreement in negotiation and poor long-run relations between negotiators.

However, despite their defects, contentious tactics can be useful as precursors to, or in conjunction with, problem solving. They can lead a reluctant adversary to the negotiation table and they can reduce a tough negotiator's goals to a realistic level that may then allow the discovery of an agreement. They may persuade an adversary that contentious tactics will not succeed, which might encourage them to shift to problem solving.

C. Problem Solving

There are very many problem solving tactics, including the provision of information about one's own priorities among the issues. Some problem solving tactics involve joint problem solving, in which the two parties work together to try to find a mutually acceptable alternative. Others involve individual problem solving, which has one or both negotiators act on their own. [See PROBLEM SOLVING.]

Problem solving can lead to win–win agreements, if there is integrative potential and the parties adopt ambitious but realistic goals. Win–win agreements can be reached in several different ways. Some win–win agreements are constructed by increasing the available resources so that both sides can get what they want, which is called expanding the pie. A second way to construct win–win agreements is for the negotiators, or a third party, to analyze the concerns that underlie the positions in the negotiation and then seek a way to reconcile these concerns. Alternatives that reconcile both negotiators' underlying concerns are called bridging solutions. Often bridging solutions are novel, as in the case of two people who were fighting over ownership of an orange. The problem was completely solved when it was discovered that one wanted the orange only for its pulp to make juice, and the other wanted only the peel for use in making a cake. Sometimes only one negotiator's underlying concerns need to be examined, because the negotiator will accept the other's demands if these concerns are handled. This type of win–win agreement is a solution by cost cutting.

A third way to construct win–win agreements is for negotiators to exchange concessions on different issues, with each negotiator yielding on issues that are of low priority to itself and high priority to the other party. Such concession exchanges are sometimes called "trade-offs" or "log-rolling," after the old-American tradition of helping neighbors roll logs into a pile for burning. Many laboratory studies of negotiation use multiple-issue tasks that provide the opportunity for trade-offs among the issues.

Sometimes negotiators are willing to speak directly about goals, priorities, and concerns, which is called information exchange. Information exchange is a crucial element of joint problem solving—a process in which the negotiators view their separate interests as a common problem and ponder possible alternatives for solving it. Both laboratory and field studies have confirmed that information exchange and joint problem solving are useful ways to achieve win–win agreements.

It can be argued that joint problem solving is the best approach in negotiation, since it can attenuate the rigidities and delays that are inevitable when negotiators develop their proposals before coming to the negotiation table. Unfortunately, information exchange and joint problem solving require a high level of trust in the other party, which is often lacking in negotiation. Without trust, negotiators tend to fear that the other party will misuse any information provided.

D. Inaction and Withdrawal

Both inaction and withdrawal are different from the other strategies in that they do not push negotiation toward agreement. Withdrawal means breaking off the negotiation. Inaction can take a number of forms such as not showing up for meetings or talking around the issues during negotiation. Inaction is sometimes a way-station in negotiation, prior to adoption of some other strategy. But if inaction goes on and on, it is essentially withdrawal. Negotiators who are advantaged by the status quo tend to opt for inaction.

IV. PSYCHOLOGICAL ANTECEDENTS OF NEGOTIATION STRATEGY

The psychological antecedents of negotiation strategy and outcomes can be roughly divided in two broad categories of processes: motivational and cognitive. These processes can influence the negotiator's choice of strategy, or they can have a direct impact on the outcome of negotiation (see Fig. 1).

A. Motivational Antecedents

The most comprehensive account of negotiator motives is the dual concern model. It asserts that negotiation strategies result from the conjunction of two independent motives: self-concern and other-concern. Self-concern and other-concern are regarded as independent dimensions. The model is shown in Figure 3.

The dual concern model predicts negotiator preferences among the strategies described above from combinations of high and low self- and other-concern. It makes the following four predictions: (1) High self-concern coupled with low other-concern encourages contending. (2) High other-concern and low self-concern encourages concession making. (3). High self-concern and high other-concern encourages problem solving. (4) Low self-concern and low other-concern encourages inaction. Of course, negotiator choice of strategy has

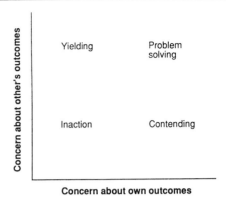

FIGURE 3   The dual concern model.

many other antecedents in addition to the two concerns specified by the dual concern model. But the model is one basis for making predictions about negotiator strategic preference.

The dual concern model can be viewed as a theory of personality, i.e., of individual differences in conflict style. Conflict style is the way a person most commonly handles conflict situations. There is a psychometric tradition of research on the dual concern model that involves scaling of the methods individuals use for dealing with conflict. Taken together, the data suggest that conflict style is a function of the strength of two nearly independent personality variables, concern about own interests, and concern about other people's interests, which are the two dimensions of the dual concern model.

The dual concern model also is a theory about the impact of changing conditions on strategic choice in negotiation. Some of these conditions affect concern about own interests; others affect concern about the interests of the party with whom one is negotiating. Combinations of these conditions can predict the strategy that will be chosen in a given circumstance. [See CONFLICT BEHAVIOR; CONFLICT COMMUNICATION.]

Self-concern in negotiation is a general reluctance to making concessions. This reluctance is often determined by the height and rigidity of limits and goals, and the strength of needs and principles that are linked to limits and goals. Higher limits tend to produce larger initial demands and greater resistance to concession making. Principles in negotiation, that is, convictions about what is proper or fair, are another source of goals and limits. This is because people aspire to, and are unwilling to concede beyond, benefits to which they feel entitled.

Other-concern is often enhanced by positive feelings toward and a perception of common group identity with the other negotiator. However, in negotiation, other-concern more often arises from instrumental considerations. Such considerations arise when people expect to be dependent on the other party in the future and wish to make a good impression now.

One way of looking at the dual concern model is that high other-concern leads to two different forms of cooperation, depending on the strength of self-concern: problem solving and concession making. When self-concern is strong, other-concern encourages problem solving. This implies that negotiators are likely to do their most creative thinking about the issues under circumstances that force them to try to reconcile both parties' interests. An example of such circumstances is when they are caught between a desire to please powerful constituents and a need to get along with the other negotiator in the future. But when self-concern is weak, high other-concern produces concession making. With no strong concern about their own outcomes, subjects develop weak goals which they easily abandon in the face of a strong desire to please the other negotiator. Hence, they do no work at satisfying both parties' interests. This suggests that concern about other people's interests—whether due to altruism or instrumental considerations—is usually quite desirable, but that it will lead to suboptimal results unless it is coupled with a healthy respect for one's own interests as well.

The dual concern model predicts a negotiator's preferred strategy. But if this strategy seems infeasible, he or she will shift to another strategy. Thus, high self-concern will lead to a preference for contending. But if contending seems infeasible, negotiators are likely to shift to problem solving as the next best approach to achieving their goals. Some conditions will influence the perceived feasibility of a given strategy. For example, time pressure encourages both concession making and increased use of contentious tactics. This is because the basic effect of time pressure is to reduce the feasibility of inaction, and thus to heighten the urgency of taking action to move toward agreement. Concession making is one form such action can take, contending is another; hence, time pressure can produce both reactions. Problem solving will also be abandoned if it seems infeasible, even when there is high joint-concern. For problem solving to seem feasible, it is necessary for there to be perceived integrative potential, that is, some basis for believing that one can find a win–win solution.

B. Cognitive Antecedents

The analysis of cognitive mechanisms in negotiation extend theory and research in social cognition, information processing in cognitive psychology, and decision theory, to negotiation. The root of the problem of suboptimal outcomes in negotiation is that negotiators have limited attention, limited capacity to store and retrieve information from memory, and limited capacity to process information.

As a result of cognitive limitations, negotiators consciously or unconsciously rely on heuristics and schemas. Heuristics are mental shortcuts and simplifying strategies that people use to help to manage information. Schemata are cognitive structures that contain information about aspects of a particular situation or a general class of situations. Schemata are thought to develop from prior observations of the phenomena to which they are relevant, and they lead people to construe situations in specific ways. Schemata tend to guide information processing, directing attention and memory, and thus cause some events to be noticed and remembered while others are ignored or forgotten.

A litany of cognitive effects and processes have been identified in negotiation. They include: the fixed-pie assumption, reactive devaluation, negotiation scripts, rigid thinking, overconfidence, availability, representativeness, and mood states.

1. The Fixed-Pie Assumption

An example of a schemata that is often found in negotiation is the assumption that the two parties' interests are directly opposed, that "your win is my loss." This fixed-pie (also called zero-sum or win/lose) assumption, which is tantamount to low perceived integrative potential, makes problem solving seem infeasible and hence encourages contentious behavior. For example, in multiple issue negotiation, the fixed-pie assumption implies that the other has the same priorities on the issues as the self. This is a faulty judgment that can block the discovery of a win–win solution.

2. Reactive Devaluation

Proposals and offers suggested by the opposing negotiator tend to be devalued in negotiation, simply on the basis of knowledge that the adversary has offered them. In one study, some negotiators rated the value of an opposing negotiator's concession before it was actually made and others rated the concession after it was offered. The results indicated that negotiators denigrated and misconstrued concessions offered by the opposing negotiator. Apparently, negotiators reason that whatever is good for the other must be bad for the self.

3. Negotiation Scripts

People hold intuitive theories about the process of negotiation, much like they do about procedures in any situation. These are called "scripts." Among other features, scripts usually include assumptions about the behavior that is fair or appropriate to expect from oneself and other parties. Negotiation scripts can have implications for attributions that negotiators make about one another's behavior. Attributions that negotiators make about the causes of the opposing negotiator's behavior are an important determinant of their reactions to that behavior. For example, confrontational negotiation behaviors will induce less retribution when they are attributed to the other's sincerely held beliefs rather than the other's selfishness. [See ATTRIBUTION.]

4. Rigid Thinking

Social conflict can promote rigid thinking, which involves a tendency to dichotomize information, to assign extreme values to objects or items, and not to see relationships among concepts in memory. Rigid thinking, in turn, tends to inhibit creativity and effective problem solving.

5. Overconfidence

Another cognitive source of suboptimal agreement in negotiation stems from the beliefs that negotiators have about their likelihood of success. Negotiators sometimes believe that the opposing negotiator will make greater concessions than they will. Also, sometimes, negotiators believe that the consequences of nonagreement are more favorable than they actually are.

6. Availability and Representativeness

Availability is the negotiator's use of the ease of recall of information as a cue for judgments about frequency or likelihood of occurrence, which in some circumstances can produce biased judgment. Information that is more available in memory, more salient, or more concrete and vivid may play a greater role in judgment than it should. Availability can lead negotiators to rely too much on salient information and therefore produce biased negotiator judgment. For example, negotiator behavior can be unduly affected by the salience of costs associated with failing to reach agreement.

Representative thinking can also bias judgment. This involves making judgments solely on the basis of the most obvious features of the object being judged and ignoring more subtle features that would permit a more balanced judgment. The object being judged may be the opposing negotiator, or it may include features of the negotiation context or issues.

Availability and representativeness may underlie the tendency for negotiators to rely too much on historical analogies. If a historical incident is highly memorable, or seems representative of a current situation, it may exert greater influence in the current decision than may be warranted. This may lead negotiators to miss other, possibly better, alternative outcomes, or other approaches to the negotiation. For example, in 1938 in Munich, negotiations between Neville Chamberlain and Adolf Hitler produced an agreement that resulted in British appeasement and unchecked Nazi aggression, with calamitous consequences. More than 50 years later, the statement, "If this aggression goes unchecked it will be another Munich," is sometimes used to justify the choice of struggle over negotiation. In this case, an historical negotiation is seen as representative of a current situation, when the current situation may in fact be quite different.

7. Mood States

Mood states such as positive affect—pleasant feelings that are typically induced by commonplace events such as reading a cartoon, hearing a joke, or getting a small gift or piece of candy—can have important effects in negotiation. For example, professional mediators have been known to tell humorous stories prior to and during negotiation in an effort to improve cooperation between negotiators. Positive affect diminishes hostile and contentious behavior and makes problem solving behaviors more likely. Positive affect also enhances concession making.

In addition to these effects, positive affect enhances cognitive functioning including the capacity for creative problem solving. The result is that positive affect can enhance the likelihood of adopting win–win agreements. In one study the subjects with positive affect were no more likely than the control subjects to exchange information during negotiation, but they were more likely to discover that the negotiators had complementary priorities among the issues, and hence, to discover win–win agreements. This was a sign of improved cognitive functioning.

V. SOCIAL ANTECEDENTS OF NEGOTIATION STRATEGY

Other antecedent conditions that affect negotiation (see Fig. 1) are social context variables, which include social norms, the nature of the relationships between the negotiators, and group processes.

A. Social Norms

Norms are shared beliefs about how people should behave. They are very often important in negotiation. They can affect the positions taken, the arguments and concessions made, and the agreements reached. Fairness principles are also particularly important, with the general finding that negotiators tend to be more concerned about fairness to themselves than fairness to the other negotiator.

Among the most important norms are principles of fairness (also called "distributive justice" norms), which govern distribution of resources. There are three broad classes of fairness principles: the equality rule, which specifies that everybody benefits or contributes equally; the equity rule, which specifies that benefit should be proportional to contribution (e.g., that pay should be proportional to work done); and the needs rule, which specifies that benefit should be proportional to need (e.g., that sick people should be taken care of). Each of these classes embraces a number of more specific rules, for example, the principle that both sides in a negotiation should make equal concessions as they move toward agreement. This reflects the reciprocity norm which is an adaptation of the broader equality norm. [See EQUITY.]

Norms often curtail social conflict: (1) They sometimes prevent conflict altogether, e.g., the principle of equal dues makes it unnecessary to debate the issue of whether some members should pay more than others. (2) Norms often regulate the way conflict is conducted, e.g., talking direcly first before taking the dispute to a third party. (3) Norms can help resolve a dispute by providing a solution once conflict arises, e.g., a dispute in which two friends are both trying to pay the entire restaurant bill may be solved by splitting the bill evenly.

Though norms often curtail conflict, they sometimes exacerbate it instead. This happens when they require one to challenge another person, for example to fight injustice or defend one's rights. This also happens when two or more parties disagree about which norms are applicable to their situation to how to interpret a norm that is clearly applicable.

In negotiation, agreement is more likely and is reached more rapidly when a single fairness principle can be applied compared to when no principle can be applied. There are two reasons for this. One is that both sides are likely to view fair outcomes as correct, and hence not quibble about them. The other is that both sides are likely to think that such outcomes are inevitable, because the other side cannot be expected to accept less than a fair outcome.

Even when there is a principle that clearly applies to the issues under consideration, agreement is not always reached. One reason for this is that the parties may disagree about how to interpret this principle or the nature of the evidence that pertains to it. For example, the principle of equal concessions is vulnerable to a partisan bias such that each party views the other's concessions as smaller than his or her own.

B. Relationships between Negotiators

Pre-existing relationships between the negotiating parties, especially aspects of power and trust, can have a great influence on how negotiation progresses.

Power in negotiation is usually viewed as the control of resources which, if used, will affect the other party's future welfare. One can reward the other or punish the other, and thus have a positive or negative effect. When viewed as an element of the relationship between two parties, there are two dimensions of power: relative power and absolute power. Relative power is the extent to which one party is more powerful than the other; for example, most supervisors have more power than their subordinates. Absolute (also called "total") power is the extent to which the parties have power over each other. Several studies have shown that, in the case of unequal power to punish the other negotiator, the party with higher power made fewer concessions than the one with lower power. This accounts, at least in part, for the better outcome usually achieved by the party with higher power.

The opposite of power is dependency. If A has power over B, B is dependent on A. In a study of bargaining in romantic couples, it was found that the party who was more in love achieved lower outcomes. This may have been because the party was the more emotionally dependent of the two. His or her partner had more power because of having less need for the relationship.

A mild discrepancy in power can put the negotiators at cross purposes, producing what is sometimes called a "power struggle." High power negotiators apparently expect to achieve more than their opponents, but low power negotiators were unwilling to accept this lower status and fought for equal treatment. The high power negotiators put up a return fight, creating an escalation that often wrecked the negotiation. Such a struggle did not occur when there was a large discrepancy in power, presumably because the low power negotiators realized that struggle was hopeless.

Several studies have looked at the impact of absolute power, finding that fewer threats were made and more agreements were reached when the two parties had high punitive power rather than moderate or low power.

Trust is the expectation that the other party will cooperate in the future. It is an aspect of the relationship between parties in that is deals with how the parties perceive each other. Trust has been shown to have many antecedents. Trust can be a personality variable—a general faith in humanity that is measured by a self-report inventory. Or it can be produced by environmental conditions, for example, when the other has cooperated with oneself, especially recently, or if the other is known to have cooperated with other people in the past. Several studies suggest that trust encourages the exchange of information about values and priorities, and makes it easier to reach agreement.

C. Group Processes

Negotiators often represent other people, who can be called their "constituents." When negotiators are a representative, they are motivated to make a positive and avoid making a negative impression on their constituents. In one study, negotiators representing a simulated helping agency were more likely to use an allocation rule they thought would please their constituent than a rule that would provide the most effective help to these constituents. If they believe that their constituent wants them to be contentious, negotiators will tend to make high demands and few concessions. But they will tend to make concessions if they believe their constituent favors cooperation and agreement.

Representatives are especially eager to please their constituents when they are accountable to these constituents. Accountability is the extent to which negotiators can be rewarded or punished by their constituents for their performance. It is produced by giving the constitutents power over negotiators' outcomes, or by making it clear that the constituents will receive information about the outcomes of the negotiation. Accountability has usually been found to slow concession making and enhance contending, making it harder to reach agreement. [See ACCOUNTABILITY AND SOCIAL COGNITION.]

Representatives are also especially eager to please their constituents when they feel insecure about their standing in the group. Negotiators are insecure when they have low status in their organization, or when they feel distrusted by their constituents. Representatives who have higher status in their group are not so tied to their constituent's views and thus are freer to make concessions than those with lower status. These findings suggest a paradox: Even though distrusted group representatives aspire to improve their relationship with their group, they often undermine their group's interests by failing to reach agreement with others outside the group. Constituent surveillance of the negotiation also tends to reinforce perceived constituent preferences.

In some cases, representatives can be more rational than their constituents, having a better understanding of the other party's priorities and hence being more realistic about success. Also, negotiation through representatives provides an opportunity for the use of tactical stratagems, such as the "black hat/white hat" routine. In this routine, the representative adopts a cooperative stance, while one of his or her constituents shows a tough stance. For example, the representative might say, "I'd like to give you this really good price on the car; but I can only do so if my manager approves it, and she's pretty tough about these matters." Such a strategy has been shown to be effective in eliciting concessions.

Sometimes negotiation is conducted by negotiation committee or teams, small groups of individuals whose responsibility is to negotiate on behalf of a larger group or organization. Team negotiation does seem to produce better outcomes compared to outcomes achieved by individuals. Negotiation teams are better at problem solving and discovering win–win agreements than are individual negotiators.

Group boundaries can also have a large influence on negotiation. Negotiators who deal with a member of their own group make more concessions and are more likely to adopt a problem-solving strategy than those who negotiate with a member of another group. Also, negotiations within a group are characterized by greater trust and greater concern that both parties should attain a good outcome.

Moreover, several studies suggest that within-group processes can have important carry-over effects on between-group negotiation. In one study, groups whose members engaged in a cooperative or competitive negotiation within their group adopted the same approach to a subsequent negotiation with an outgroup. Within-group cooperation made between-group cooperation more likely, and within-group conflict diminished the likelihood of between-group cooperation. This has implications for third parties in inter-group conflict. If they want to facilitate between-group cooperation, they should foster within-group cooperation prior to between-group negotiation.

VI. EXPANDING THE GENERAL NEGOTIATION PARADIGM

Current research on negotiation is largely devoted to expanding the field of vision beyond the general paradigm. For example, earlier work has largely lacked a time dimension, failing to come to grips with the stages of negotiation and the events that occur before negotiation starts and after it is over. In addition, earlier work has provided little information about why people choose negotiation rather than arbitration, struggle, or some other approach to resolving differences of interests. There are recent trends that indicate that future research in negotiation will focus on the cultural and institutional dynamics of negotiation, and how negotiation transforms relationships and organizations. These are but a few of the areas of inquiry that will advance theory and research in the behavioral analysis of negotiation.

Bibliography

Carnevale, P. J., and Pruitt, D. G. (1992). Negotiation and mediation. *Ann. Rev. Psychol.* **43**, 531–582.

Kremenyuk, V. (Ed.) (1991). "International Negotiation: Analysis, Approaches, Issues." Josey-Bass, San Francisco.

Lax, D. A., and Sebenius, J. K. (1986). "The Manager as Negotiator: Bargaining for Cooperation and Competitive Gain." The Free Press, New York.

Neale, M. A., and Bazerman, M. H. (1991). "Negotiator Cognition and Rationality." The Free Press, New York.

Pruitt, D. G., and Carnevale, P. J. (1993). "Negotiation in Social Conflict." Open University Press, Buckingham, England.

Putnam, L. L., and Roloff, M. E. (Eds.) (1992). "Communication Perspectives on Negotiation." Sage, Newbury Park, CA.

Thomas, K. W. (1992). Conflict and negotiation processes in organizations. In "Handbook of Industrial and Organizational Psychology" (M. Dunnette and L. M. Hough, Eds.), 2nd ed. Consulting Psychologists Press, Inc.

Thompson, L. L. (1990). Negotiation behavior and outcomes: Empirical evidence and theoretical issues. *Psychol. Bull.* **108**, 515–532.

NEOCORTEX

Barbara L. Finlay
Cornell University

Glossary

Cortical column The fundamental cellular grouping of the neocortex, a collection of cells extending perpendicular to the cortical surface, spanning all cortical layers, receiving and operating upon a common input.

Cytoarchitecture Description of the organization of a structure according to the types, sizes, and arrangements of its cells.

Lateralization The property that certain sensory, cognitive, and motor functions are represented preferentially on one side of the neocortex.

Modularity The property of the cortex that the circuitry for particular sensory, motor, or cognitive functions is kept physically and computationally separate from other sensory, motor, and cognitive functions.

THE NEOCORTEX is a layered sheet of cells covering the surface of the forebrain, the largest and most prominent feature of the human brain. Homologues of the cells that make up the neocortex can be found in the forebrain of all extant vertebrates, including fish, amphibians, reptiles, and birds, but only in mammals are these cells found arranged in the six-layered structure of repeating subunits that is termed the neocortex. The cortex's six layers consist of specialized zones for input, for communication with other areas of the cortex both locally and at a distance, and for output to noncortical structures. A column of cells arranged perpendicular to the cortical surface tends to perform a standardized computation on its input;

the input can vary greatly. Through this relatively uniform structure passes information for functions as diverse as recognizing faces, conversing, playing the piano, planning for the future, and adjusting emotional displays to the social context. Components of these capacities are represented in particular parts of the cortical surface, a property termed "modularity," and thus local damage to the cortex will cause disruptions of particular skills, and spare others entirely. The human neocortex is lateralized for some computations: in the great majority of individuals, the circuitry for language is located on the left side of the brain. [*See* BRAIN.]

I. EVOLUTION OF THE NEOCORTEX

A. Basic Questions

The neocortex is the single largest structure in the human brain, and because of its prominence and its importance for many capacities viewed as distinctly human, such as language and pronounced manual dexterity, there has been much inquiry into its origin. Three questions have been asked about the evolution of the neocortex. First, when does the neocortex first appear in vertebrate evolution, considering both the neurons that compose it and their organization? Second, what might explain the pronounced enlargement in volume of the cortex seen most notably in primates, but which has occurred independently in a number of mammalian radiations? Finally, in behavioral terms, is the enlargement of the neocortex best understood as the growth of a general learning device, or the accretion of a number of special structures for specialized skills like language and social cognition?

B. The Origin and Organization of Cell Types

In many classical textbooks, the cortex is presented as a structure that is found *de novo* in the mammalian

Encyclopedia of Human Behavior, Volume 3

brain. More modern anatomical explorations of vertebrate brains have demonstrated that this is not the case. All vertebrates possess a number of organized cell masses, termed nuclei, in their forebrains. Even in those extant vertebrates believed to have a brain organization most resembling the most primitive vertebrate condition, the lampreys and hagfishes (Class Agnatha), cell groups can be found that have, in part, the approximate location, types of input, patterns of connectivity, neurotransmitters, and neuromodulators that are characteristic of mammalian forebrain, and specifically, the neocortex. The characteristic mammalian pattern of layering is absent, and many aspects of the connections and organization vary. The neocortex of mammals, and the homologous forebrain structures in vertebrates should be viewed in much the same way the relationship between a human arm and bat wing might be viewed. The major bone and muscle masses have similar embryonic origins, similar topologic relationships and attachments, and similar gross functions.

However, the absolute and relative size of the components vary considerably; particular bone and muscle groups may be added, deleted, or combined, and details of the attachments of bone and muscle may change.

In reptiles, the structure thought to be homologous to the neocortex is called the dorsal ventricular ridge, and receives and integrates sensory input through the thalamus, and distributes this information to the midbrain and hindbrain, as does the neocortex. In birds, the laminarly arranged cells of the dorsal telencephalon, and also various divisions of cell masses of the forebrain area called the corpus striatum, are thought to be homologous to the neocortex. In that these areas receive and integrate the same sort of information that the mammalian neocortex does, functional homology is found as well as anatomic homology. For example, bird song, a complex communication system that involves auditory learning, elaborate sensory integration, and skilled motor performance, depends in part on the

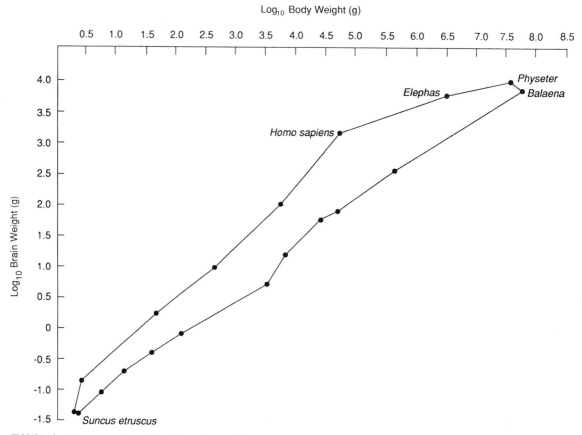

FIGURE 1   Convex polygon bounding the set of mammalian brain/body weight values. Logarithmic scale. Individual species identified represent a shrew, humans, the elephant, and two whales. [Reprinted with permission from Eisenberg, J. F. (1981). "The Mammalian Radiations," p. 227. University of Chicago Press.]

areas in its brain homologous to the neocortex in mammals and humans.

The difference in the developmental programs that produce a layered arrangement of cells rather than a collection of nuclear masses is not yet known, but a difference in the pattern of migration of cells during development is likely to be involved, which will be discussed below.

C. Change in Volume of the Neocortex across Mammalian Radiations

The entire brain shows striking differences in volume across the mammalian radiations, most pronounced in primates (Fig. 1). Some of this change in volume can be attributed to change in body size: unsurprisingly, bigger bodies are associated with bigger brains. However, at any particular body size, there is a residual variation of at least 10-fold in the relation of whole brain size to body size. The size of the neocortex, in turn, bears an exceedingly regular relationship to whole brain size (Fig. 2): the volume of the neocortex increases exponentially with whole brain size, so that larger brains are composed of an increasingly greater percentage of neocortex. The human brain does not

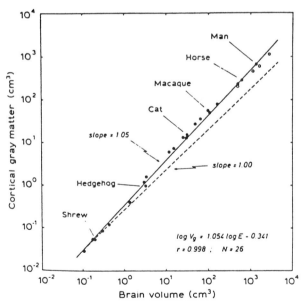

FIGURE 2   Volume of the neocortex (gray matter only) as a function of whole brain volume for a number of mammals. Logarithmic scale. The dashed line represents scaling of cortical volume by the first power, geometric similarity, and shows that the amount of cortex increases at a greater rate than that expected by geometric scaling alone. Dolphins and whales are indicated by open circles. [Reprinted with permission from Hofman, M. A. (1989). *Prog. Neurobiol.* **32,** 137–158.]

differ from all mammalian vertebrates in this respect. Humans have the largest brain to body size ratio of any vertebrate, and a great deal of this hypertrophy is accounted for by the neocortex. However, the amount of cortex in humans is the amount lawfully predicted from whole brain size.

II. FUNDAMENTAL STRUCTURE OF THE NEOCORTEX

A. Cortical Layers and Columns

Though many different schemes for the naming and ordering of the layers of the neocortex were proposed in the latter half 19th century when the anatomical organization of the cortex was first described, the one that has persisted is the six-layered scheme laid out by Brodman in his publications on cortical cytoarchitectonics in the period 1903–1920. The cortex consists of a number of distinct cell types and fiber bands, arranged in strata; variations in local areas of cortex are described as having condensations, omissions, or subdivisions of Brodman's fundamental six strata (Fig. 3). These layers are discussed not in their numerical order, but in the order information passes through them (Fig. 4).

The principal input to the cortex comes from the thalamus, a collection of nuclei in the diencephalon that receives information in turn from various sensory domains, from various areas from the midbrain to forebrain, and from the cortex itself. The input from the thalamus distributes to Layer IV, and to a lesser extent to the upper part of Layer VI. Layer IV is termed a "granular" layer, in that it is composed of small, relatively symmetric cells with radial dendrites, called stellate cells (Fig. 5). Several types of stellate cells can be further distinguished, as well as multipolar neurons associated with a variety of neuromodulators in this layer. The processes of cells from Layers V and VI also extend through this layer.

This information is then relayed up and down, to Layers II and III, and to Layers V and VI. The bulk of local interactions in the cortex are restricted to a column several cell diameters wide that extends perpendicularly from Layer IV to the cortical surface, and down to Layer VI. It is this local interaction and distribution of information that gives rise to the anatomical and physiological unit of the "cortical column." Layer I, the cell-free outermost fiber layer, is composed of the axons and dendrites of these cells engaging in local interactions. It should

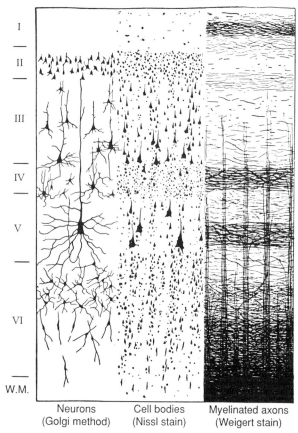

Neurons
(Golgi method) Cell bodies
(Nissl stain) Myelinated axons
(Weigert stain)

FIGURE 3 The layers of the neocortex, as described by Brodman. Cortical neurons and axons are arranged in six principal layers designated by Roman numerals. Three types of stains are represented, the Golgi method, which stains whole cells and all their processes; the Nissl stain, which shows only cell bodies; and the Weigert stain, which stains axons. [Reprinted with permission from Angevine, J. B., and Cotman, C. W. (1981). "Principles of Neuroanatomy." Oxford University Press, New York.]

be emphasized, however, that longer-range cellular interactions are also important in producing many of the characteristic features of cortical information processing.

Layers II and III are composed of pyramidal cells (Fig. 5), asymmetric cells with a profusion of dendrites at their base, and a long apical dendrite, all of which receive synaptic input. Multipolar neuromodulatory cells are also found in Layers II and III. Output from Layers II and III is long range and principally intracortical. Axons from these areas distribute to local cortical areas (for example, from primary to secondary visual cortex), to distant cortical areas (for example, from secondary visual cortex to visuomotor fields in frontal cortex), and across the corpus callosum to the cortex on the other side of the brain. The connections across the corpus cal-

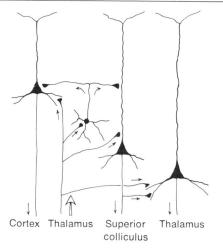

Cortex Thalamus Superior
colliculus Thalamus

FIGURE 4 Diagram of information flow through the neocortex. Principal input is from the thalamus to the stellate cells of Layer IV (see also Fig. 3). Cortical output distributes to the rest of the cortex, to the thalamus, and to many subcortical structures of which one, the superior colliculus, is shown here. [Reprinted with permission from Shepherd, G. M. (1988). "Neurobiology." Oxford University Press, New York.]

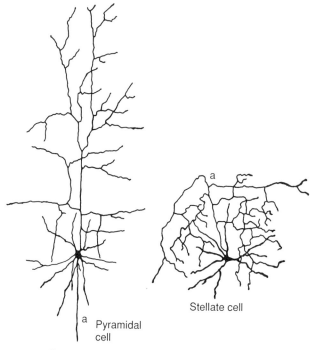

Stellate cell

a Pyramidal
cell

FIGURE 5 Drawings of a typical pyramidal cell and stellate cell. Pyramidal cells are especially abundant in Layers II, III, and V, and stellate cells are found in Layer IV. (a) designates the axon of each cell. [Reprinted with permission from Angevine, J. B., and Cotman, C. W. (1981). "Principles of Neuroanatomy." Oxford University Press, New York.]

losum can link both corresponding and noncorresponding cortical areas. These intracortical connections distribute principally to Layers II and III and Layer V.

Layer V also consists principally of pyramidal cells. These receive input from Layers II, III, and IV, and distribute their axons subcortically. These subcortical areas are quite diverse and include the basal ganglia and amygdala, the prominent nuclear masses of the forebrain; the superior colliculus, a midbrain structure concerned with attention and eye movements, and a variety of brainstem sensory and motor nuclei. Some giant neurons from the motor cortex, named Betz cells, send their axons as far as the spinal cord to terminate directly on motor neurons and associated interneurons.

Layer VI contains cells of a variety of morphologies. A principal output connection of Layer VI is a reciprocal connection to the area of the thalamus that innervates the same cortex.

This same organization of layers and repeating columns is found throughout the neocortex. Local subareas of cortex, which will be discussed below, are modified in such a way that reflects their specialization. Primary visual cortex, which receives a massive thalamic input of visual information, has a large number of cells in Layer IV. In motor cortex, Layer IV is almost absent, and the cells of Layer V, the subcortical output layer, are unusually large and prominent. These local differences can be employed to divide the cortex into "cytoarchitectonic areas," as Brodman did with his original maps (Fig. 6), the nomenclature of which is still in use today. These cytoarchitectonic divisions, based solely on the visualizable detail of the cellular organization of the cortex, have proved to typically correspond to functional divisions in the cortex as well.

B. Cortical Physiology

Electrophysiological recording from single neurons in the cortex, first undertaken by Mountcastle in the somatosensory cortex and by Hubel and Wiesel in the primary visual cortex, amplified and extended the neuroanatomical picture of columns and layers in the cortex. First, the best stimulus to excite single cortical cells was typically a complex transformation of the sorts of stimuli that best excite thalamic cells. In the case of the primary visual cortex, the best stimulus for a typical cortical cell would typically be a bar or edge in a particular orientation, in a specific location in the visual field (Fig. 7). Often,

cells would respond only to spatially congruent information with the right and the left eye stimulated together. The thalamic input to this area, however, is not binocular and the visual fields of thalamic neurons are spatially symmetric, not elongate. In the somatosensory cortex, a preferred stimulus would typically be a submodality of touch, like light touch or hot or cold, and cells would often be selective for a particular direction of stimulus movement. All of the neurons in a column perpendicular to the cortical surface had similar selectivity for the appropriate stimulus properties, like orientation, binocular integration, touch submodality, or location of the receptive field on the skin surface or visual field. Neurons in the different cortical layers vary systematically on some aspects of receptive field structure, for example, the degree of specificity for location in the visual field, but overall, all neurons in a column process the same type of input.

In areas of cortex that do not receive direct sensory input, the properties of single neurons are often complex combinatorial properties of neurons. These combinations can occur both within and between sensory modalities, and can involve aspects of both motor behavior and prior learning and cognition. For example, in the cortex of both monkeys and sheep, neurons have been described whose optimal stimulus is the face (or aspects of the face) of the animal's own species. In the area of bat cortex that processes information relating to echolocation, neurons will respond optimally to an auditory stimulus that is the bat's own call, and with a particular delay, the echo of that call, which thus specifies a target range. In the parietal cortex of monkeys, which is located between the visual and somatosensory/motor areas of the cortex and which receives input from both, neurons can be found that will fire only when a monkey is looking at and reaching for an object of interest. In the motor cortex, the response patterns of neurons can best be related to movements or limb positions that involve a number of muscle groups, and not a single muscle's contraction. In the frontal cortex, neurons have been described that fire only when the animal is attending to a stimulus that has previously been associated with reward, but which will not fire if the same stimulus is motivationally neutral.

C. Cortical Maps and Functional Modularity

1. Mapping

The dimensions of single neuron response properties described above are not found randomly distributed

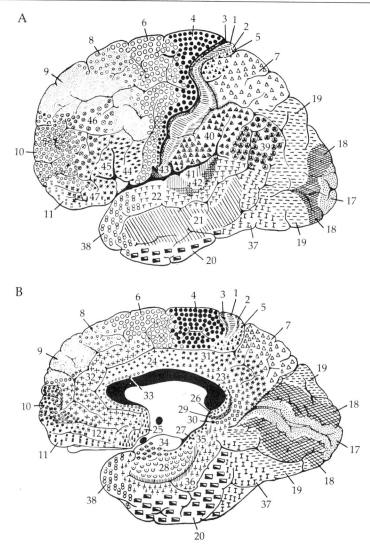

FIGURE 6   Cytoarchitectonic areas of the cortex according to Brodman (1909). Lateral (A) and medial (B) views of the neocortex are shown. The numbered divisions, based on the thickness, density, and cell size of the cortical layers, also correspond to functional specializations within the cortex. [Reprinted with permission from Angevine, J. B., and Cotman, C. W. (1981). "Principles of Neuroanatomy." Oxford University Press, New York.]

around the cortical surface, but are typically found as orderly dimensional maps laid out across the cortical surface. Neighboring cortical columns typically represent progressive changes in the mapped dimensions. The primary visual cortex is the best described example. In this cortex, the dimensions of location in visual space, preferred eye of activation, and preferred stimulus orientation are all laid out in an orderly way and these maps are superimposed. Location in visual space is represented once over the full extent in primary visual cortex, with the center of gaze represented at the occipital pole, and

the visual periphery buried in the medial cortex. For each mapped location in visual space, a full range of preferred eye activation (ocular dominance) is represented from left eye dominating to right eye dominating, changing in orderly sequence. For the same location in visual space, all possible stimulus orientations are also represented, also changing in an orderly way from a preferred angle of 0° to 180° across the cortical surface. These last two dimensional maps are arranged roughly perpendicularly to each other, such that for every location in visual space, every possible value of ocular dominance

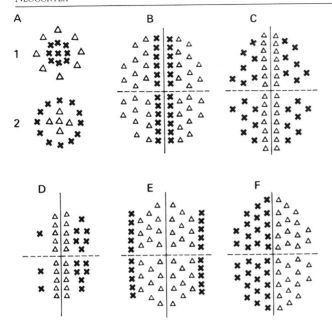

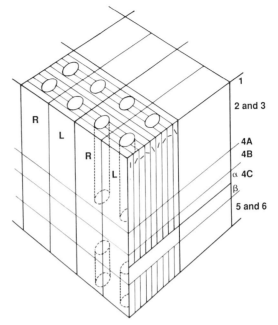

FIGURE 7   Comparisons of receptive fields of neurons in the retina (A1) and lateral geniculate nucleus (A2) with those of neocortical cells in the primary visual cortex (B–F). While the retinal and geniculate cells are symmetric, the cortical cells prefer elongate bars and edges as stimuli for maximal response. Both classes of neurons will respond to stimuli of light or dark contrast. X, excitatory response in the receptive field; triangle, inhibitory area. [Reprinted with permission from Kandel, E. R., and Schwartz, J. H. (1985). "Principles of Neural Science," 2nd ed. Elsevier, New York.]

FIGURE 8   A hypercolumn in the visual cortex, representing one location in the visual field. On the left-hand base axis, orderly alternation of perferred activation by the right or left eye is shown. On the right-hand base axis, orderly rotation in the preferred stimulus orientation is shown. On the vertical axis, the Brodman layers are numbered, with Layer IV broken into three subdivisions. Interposed in this regular array are cylinders, called "blobs," that are devoted to color processing. This processing unit is repeated over and over throughout the entire neocortex. [Reprinted with permission from Livingstone, M. S., and Hubel, D. H. (1984). *J. Neurosci.* **4,** 309–339.]

and preferred stimulus orientation is represented. A block of cortex that contains one full cycle of all the mapped dimensions has been termed a "hypercolumn" (Fig. 8). Finally, interposed in this regular map are "color blobs," islands interrupting the regular progression of the other dimensions, where calculations involved in color perception are carried out.

Similar maps can be found in other sensory and motor dimensions, such as the map of the body surface in somatosensory cortex, or changing values of best echo delay seen in the part of the bat auditory cortex devoted to echolocation. In many areas of cortex, the dimension that is mapped has remained elusive, but is suggested by the presence of orderly mapping in the neuroanatomical connections between related cortical areas.

While only the topographic maps of sensory and motor surfaces have been demonstrated directly in the human neocortex, the principle that the cortex represents complex properties of information as changing dimensions that can be mapped incremen-

tally across the cortical surface appears to be a general one. As such, this insight has guided modeling of the cortical mechanism of such particularly human functions as speech perception which cannot be directly investigated.

2. Relationships between Maps

The mapped stimulus dimensions described above for various stimulus dimensions are often represented multiple times in the cortex. For example, in both the monkey and human, the body surface appears to be mapped at least three times over, each representation emphasizing different features of this sensory array. In the monkey, the part of the cortex that analyzes visual information consists of not just one but many separate representations of the visual field (Fig. 9). Connections between these representations are both serial and parallel. For example, the representation of stimulus movement is kept separate from the representation of color through several remappings, and a common representation of

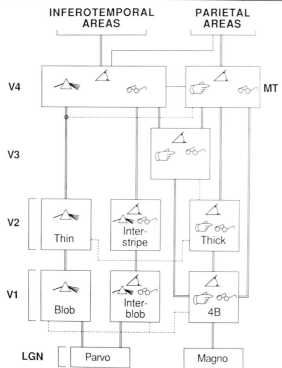

FIGURE 9 An example of serial and parallel connections between the multiple representations of the visual field (V1, V2, V3, V4, and MT) found in the visual cortex. Icons are placed in each compartment to symbolize a high density of neurons showing selectivity for color (prisms), orientation (angle symbols), direction of movement (pointing hands), and binocular depth (spectacles). The input from the thalamus, the lateral geniculate nucleus in this case, is shown with its principal divisions (parvo and magno). Inferotemporal cortex is thought to be involved in recognition and naming, and the parietal cortex with pointing reach and other operations in space. [Reprinted with permission from Shepherd, G. M. (1987). "Neurobiology." Oxford Universtiy Press, New York.]

the output of these two parallel systems is finally found only in the inferotemporal cortex, an area thought to be important for the identification and naming of objects.

3. Modularity

The property that the cortex keeps stimulus modalities and particular classes of computation physically separate over at least the initial stages of processing is termed modularity. It is this property that accounts for the often peculiar effects of localized brain damage, where, for example, an individual may have lost the capacity for language, but retain the ability to make the complex inferences required to play chess. These dissociations of function can also occur within sensory modalities; for example,

the ability to recognize faces can be lost with damage to a particular area of the parietal cortex while sparing the ability to read and navigate visually in the world. Or, an individual with damage to a subarea of the language cortex, Broca's area, might lose the capacity to appreciate grammatical relationships in sentences, but could fully understand and give the meanings of individual words.

The diversity of the functions that depend upon the uniform structure of the neocortex should be underscored. We have already discussed a number of the separable functions dependent on the visual areas of the occipital lobe: the sensory categorization of movement, color, and contour; the dissociability of locating objects for purposes of navigation versus naming those objects; and the specialized social skill of facial recognition and analysis of expression. Also represented in the cortex are the complex motor patterns for speech; the syntactic and semantic components of language itself; and aspects of the conceptualization, initiation, and execution of complicated learned motor acts like piano playing. In the frontal lobe are represented a number of dissociable complex capacities that are often difficult to describe. These include, but are not limited to, interrupting and taking account of one's past performance in planning new action; remembering in what context a particular fact was learned; adjusting emotional expression to the social context; and the execution of such social scripts as proper eye contact and the maintenance of appropriate interpersonal space. Overall, while excellent progress is being made in understanding the nature of cortical analysis in some sensory domains, the nature of the cortical analysis in cognitive and social domains has hardly begun to be understood.

III. LATERALIZATION OF THE HUMAN NEOCORTEX

The human neocortex has the relatively unusual property of showing lateralization for functions that bear no intrinsic relationship to the right or left side of the body. For most sensory and motor functions, the brain is lateralized: for example, left side of the brain receives sensation from the right side of the body and the right half of the visual field, and controls the motor functions of the right side of the body. However, in most right-handed people, language is represented on the left side of the brain. Damage to the left temporal cortex can cause complete loss of language ("aphasia") while damage to the corresponding area on the right will cause little or no change in language function. "Dexterity" itself is also lateralized; approximately 90% of individuals prefer the use of their right hand, and are more skilled using it for fine motor functions. The clear lateralization of these two prominent functions led to the characterization of the relationship between the hemispheres as "cerebral dominance," meaning the dominance of the left hemisphere for cognitive functions.

Later, however, Roger Sperry and his colleagues showed that the right hemisphere was dominant for some other functions, notably aspects of visuospatial understanding, particularly abilities that have a manipulation component such as drawing, arranging blocks, or recognizing something presented visually by feel. These functions are considerably less lateralized than language is, in that considerable visuospatial function remains after damage to the right side of the brain. This finding of some functions preferentially lateralized to the right side of the brain has led to a revision of the understanding of the relationship of the cerebral hemispheres, now termed "complementary specialization."

The reason for and genesis of lateralization are not well understood. In experimental situations, some primates will show evidence of lateralization for particular tasks, but not in the systematic way seen in the human brain. The most intriguing case of lateralization in animals is bird song, which is also controlled by the left half of the brain. The common feature of complex articulation in the case of bird song and language has led to the hypothesis that the genesis of lateralization might be found in the need for unitary, lateralized motor control of a midline organ, either the various organs of articulation in speech or the syrinx in song.

The left hemisphere is bigger in the language area than the right hemisphere in right-handed individuals. This anatomical asymmetry, and behavioral asymmetry is seen in human infants at birth, in the same proportion as there are right-handed individuals in the population at maturity. Ambidextrous or left-handed individuals show a greater likelihood of their language being bilaterally represented, or represented on the right, and their likelihood of an anatomic asymmetry is also less.

IV. DEVELOPMENT OF THE NEOCORTEX

The neocortex is one of the last structures to be formed in the human brain, with the final neurons composing it undergoing their last divisions and migrating into their mature position at about the sixth month postconception. Cells destined for the cortex are generated at a distant location from their adult position from precursor cells surrounding the lateral ventricles in the forebrain, and migrate on supporting glial guides to their position on the brain surface. The first cells generated form the innermost layer, Layer VI, and later generated cells bypass these cells and form Layers, V, IV, III, and II in turn. Cortical development is further marked by a large transitory population of neurons that are found on the white matter underlying the cortex, and in Layer I early in development, and which appear to die after the migration of neurons to the cortex is completed. The cortex will continue to increase in size well into early childhood by the growth of neurons and elaboration of their processes, but the full complement of neurons and their fundamental layering is established before birth.

Disorders of early cortical development are thus most likely to be caused by disorders of cell generation and migration, which is often visible as unusual cortical thinness, disorders of lamination, and mislocated clusters of cells that have failed to migrate ("ectopias").

V. CORTICAL PATHOLOGIES

Focal cortical damage, of the type caused by strokes, space-occupying tumors, and head trauma, was the first window into the nature of functional cortical organization. While there are a few deficits that appear to be common to all types of focal brain damage, notably an increased distractibility and inability to screen out irrelevant noise and activity while performing tasks, almost all focal brain damage is followed by inability to perform those particular tasks that correspond to the areas of damage. Particular deficits in sensory systems, language, visuospatial computation, and the like will result, and not a generalized decline in all cognitive functions. Therapy for such dysfunctions typically involves retraining the individual to substitute intact cognitive functions for the lost ones, for example, defining maps by verbal landmarks rather than by spatial relations for an individual with a spatial deficit.

Seizure disorders involve abnormalities in the ongoing electrical activity of the brain, and often involve the neocortex, particularly the temporal lobe. Normal electrical activity in the cortex is complex and asynchronous. The cortex has a number of recurrent and repeating circuits, however, that can produce rhythmic and synchronous activation when desynchronizing activity is removed, as normally occurs in sleep. In seizure disorders cortical activity becomes massively synchronized and rhythmic. Drugs, or in some cases removal of the area generating the abnormal synchrony, are employed as treatments for seizure disorders. [*See* EPILEPSY.]

Bibliography

Corballis, M. C. (1983). "Human Laterality." Academic Press, New York.

Felleman, D. J., and Van Essen, D. C. (1991). Distributed hierarchical processing in the primate cerebral cortex. *Cerebral Cortex* **1,** 1–47.

Jones, E. G., and Peters, A. (1984). "Cerebral Cortex," Vol. 2. Plenum, New York.

Peters, A., and Jones, E. G. (1984). "Cerebral Cortex," Vol. 1. Plenum, New York.

Peters, A., and Jones, E. G. (1988). "Cerebral Cortex," Vol. 7. Plenum, New York.

Sacks, O. (1970). "The Man Who Mistook His Wife for a Hat." Summit Books, New York.

NONVERBAL BEHAVIOR

Linda Tickle-Degnen
Boston University

Judith A. Hall
Northeastern University

Robert Rosenthal
Harvard University

Glossary

Channel Specific source of nonverbal behaviors: for example, those observed from the face, body, or tone of voice.

Decoding Detection or diagnosis of inner states or messages from observed nonverbal behavior.

Emotion Affective states including happiness, surprise, fear, sadness, anger, and disgust.

Encoding Display of nonverbal behavior that may be decoded or interpreted by others.

Expressiveness Clarity, extent, and frequency of an encoder's nonverbal behavior.

Leakage Nonverbal behavior that is manifested without intention or awareness.

Nonverbal skill Ability to encode and/or decode nonverbal behavior effectively.

Nonverbal style Individual differences in types and amounts of nonverbal behavior shown.

Social influence Process of one person's behavior affecting the behavior of another through subtle or obvious means.

NONVERBAL BEHAVIOR refers to virtually all behavior that is not specifically linguistic. It includes the many variables that can be observed from facial expressions, from body movements, and from nonvisual, auditory characteristics of speech and voice including pitch, pitch range, speech rate, rhythm, loudness, nasality, and many others.

I. AN INTRODUCTION TO NONVERBAL BEHAVIOR

A. The Relative Neglect of Nonverbal Behavior

Nonverbal behavior was not studied extensively until the 1970s. If so much of human behavior is nonverbal why is it that the extensive scientific study of nonverbal behavior is so new? Partly the answer is technological. With the development of motion picture, videotaping, and audiotaping equipment, it became easier to record nonverbal behavior for later, more leisurely, and more intensive study.

B. Approaches to the Study of Nonverbal Behavior

Three major approaches to the study of nonverbal behavior can be distinguished. The first of these, the structural approach, proceeds by trying to find the internal rules and units of nonverbal behavior much as a linguist might try to do for the case of language. This approach is descriptive rather than relational, leading to, e.g., a description of the regularly predictable phases of interpersonal greeting behavior.

The second approach is relational, in which the nonverbal behavior is seen as an antecedent or predictor of some other variables or as a consequence of some other variables. This approach looks for regularities in nonverbal behavior leading to conclusions such as ''warmer nonverbal behavior of teachers is associated with greater learning by their students,'' or ''more favorable expectations by teachers lead teachers to behave with more nonverbal warmth toward their students,'' or ''downturned mouths indicate sadness.''

The third approach is also relational in that nonverbal behavior is related to other variables but the emphasis here is not so much on the regularities in nonverbal behavior but on variations among groups or individuals in nonverbal behavior. This approach leads to conclusions such as "females are more accurate decoders of nonverbal behavior" or "depressed patients speak more slowly, with less animation, and with fewer hand movements."

In this article our emphasis will be on the latter two approaches, the relational approaches. In section II our emphasis is on the regularities of nonverbal behavior. In section III our emphasis is on individual differences in nonverbal behavior. Finally, in section IV, we focus on nonverbal behavior as "causes," "effects," and "explanations."

II. REGULARITIES OF NONVERBAL BEHAVIOR

We express our emotions, communicate our thoughts, develop and maintain relationships with others, and influence others through nonverbal behavior. In these four contexts—(a) emotion, (b) communication, (c) relationship, and (d) influence—nonverbal behavior demonstrates regularities, although specifics vary across individuals, genders, and culture.

A. Emotions and Nonverbal Behavior

1. Universal Expressions of Emotion

Charles Darwin linked emotional expressions in humans to genetic origins in evolutionarily selected non-human primate behavior. He argued that emotional expression signalled the approach of danger and strengthened the bonds between individuals, thus uniting these individuals against a hostile and predatory world and creating a favorable position for their survival.

At least six basic emotions are expressed in humans, and their expression emerges within the first year of life. These emotional expressions (as shown in Fig. 1) are happiness, surprise, fear, sadness, anger, and disgust. Of these, happiness, sadness, anger, and disgust are easily decoded by individuals of most cultures, regardless of the encoder's culture. Fear and surprise are often confused with one another when decoded, but still elicit relatively high degrees of accuracy.

The face is the most salient channel of emotional expression. Changes in emotion elicit changes in the mouth, eyebrows, movement of cheek and eye muscles, pupil dilation, amount and direction of gaze, and the skin color of light-skinned people. Head movements, such as head nodding or shaking, also convey emotion. [See FACIAL EXPRESSIONS OF EMOTION.]

The body, excluding the face, expresses emotion through arm and hand gesturing, trunk leaning, positioning of the arms and legs, and the erectness of posture. The expressions of the body may intensify, diminish, or even contradict the emotional messages given off by the face. A happy face and a tense, closed posture send a message quite different from a happy face with a relaxed, open posture.

The voice expresses emotion through pitch, pitch range, speed, volume, and rhythm. Individuals can detect negative emotions in the voice more readily than positive ones, possibly because the former set of emotions is accompanied by abrupt as opposed to smooth changes in vocal intensity and pitch. Information about the level of arousal of an individual is a primary feature of vocal cues.

2. Controlled Emotional Expression

Individuals may feel an emotion but not express it in a spontaneous, unrestricted manner. Three general reasons for individuals to control their emotional expression are to (1) conform to culturally defined display rules, (2) present oneself in a desirable manner, and (3) deceive someone.

Display rules are cultural norms that regulate what, when, and how emotions are expressed. Children are taught these rules, implicitly and explicitly, very early. They learn when they should and should not cry, and when and how to express happiness or anger. Cultures vary considerably in the content of display rules. Newcomers to a culture, who do not know these rules, will find themselves in situations where inhabitants perceive them to be behaving in an inappropriate or impolite manner.

Self-presentation occurs when an individual attempts to manipulate the impression that others are forming of him or her. Often this manipulation is done to create a favorable impression. The individual behaves in a manner that people find attractive, such as making eye contact and smiling (in mainstream American culture). The individual may want to demonstrate composure and happiness in situations that may be frightening, such as a job interview. Smiles, for example, are often used as an attempt to mask fear.

Deception differs from self-presentation only in degree and social acceptability. Deception occurs

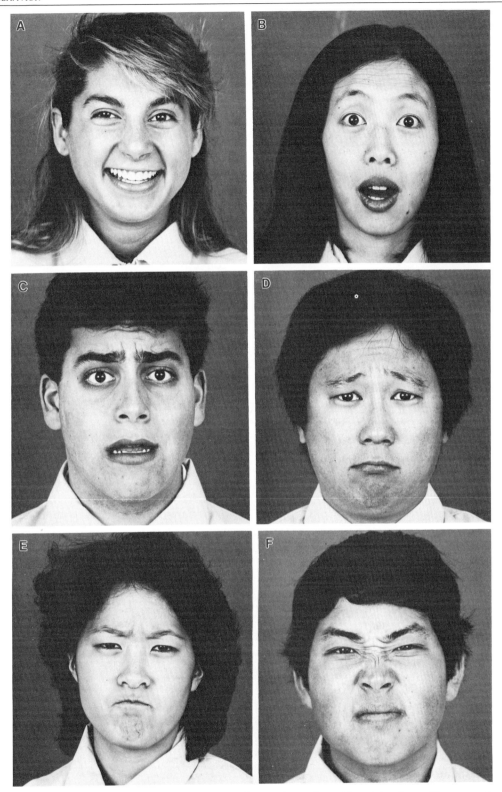

FIGURE 1   Basic emotional expressions: (A) happiness, (B) surprise, (C) fear, (D) sadness, (E) anger, and (F) disgust. [Courtesy of Matsumoto, D., and Ekman, P. (1988). *Japanese and Caucasian Facial Expressions of Emotions*. (Slides.) Intercultural and Emotion Research Lab, Department of Psychology, San Francisco State University.]

when individuals lie about their true beliefs or experiences, or when they clearly feel one way, for example, guilty, but want their audience to have an opposing impression, for example, innocent. Self-presentation types of deception are generally considered socially acceptable and are recognized as a necessary social skill. People recognize that a good job applicant should come across as confident despite feelings of fear. On the other hand, deception or lying is generally considered socially unacceptable.

Individuals who are highly motivated to lie overcontrol facial, head, and body movements by moving less than normal. In general, deceivers show more micromomentary facial expressions, lasting less than one-fourth of a second, and more mismatch in emotional expression between the various channels. Although the deceiver may be smiling, it may be more of a ''false'' than a ''felt'' smile. These two types of smile are distinguished by the facial muscles involved. During felt smiles, muscles around the mouth and eyes are activated, whereas during false smiles, muscular activation is primarily around the mouth. Behaviors also associated with deception are blinking, pupil dilation, direction of gaze, vocal pitch, speech hesitation, speech rate, and self-touching. The degree of motivation and amount of planning time a deceiver has affects nonverbal expression.

3. Emotional Leakage

The face is one of the most informative channels of emotion as well as the most easily controlled. Individuals are less able to control their bodily expression, and even less able to control their tone of voice. The degree of lack of controllability in the channels of expression relates to *leakage*. The most leaky channel is the voice, followed by the body, then by the face, and finally by speech content. Although there are markers of deception in all of the channels, deception may be the best detected if the observer focuses on leakier channels of communication, because these are least controlled by the deceiver.

4. Effect of Expression on Emotion

It makes sense that emotions give rise to expression. The reverse may be true as well. The hypothesis that expressions contribute to the feeling of the emotion is called the *facial feedback hypothesis*. People feel happier after smiling and more negative after frowning. Little is known about how expression affects emotion though there is evidence that changes in facial expression affect the autonomic nervous system. For example, heart rate and finger temperature increase when anger expression is posed. Possible mediators include changes in the activation of muscle receptors in the face or in breathing patterns that affect neurotransmitters.

There is a small amount of evidence that suggests bodily posturing also affects the feelings of emotions. For example, a tensed posture has been found to produce feelings of stress. Little to no research has examined the effect of voice on emotion.

B. Language, Speech, and Nonverbal Behavior

1. Clarification and Creation of Meaning

Nonverbal behavior may emphasize, clarify, supplement, or replace speech. A quick downward head motion, eye contact, pounding on the table, jumping up and down, and vocal emphasis are behaviors that can be used to emphasize the importance of a statement. A quizzical look or a rising pitch at the end of the sentence clarifies that someone's utterance is a question rather than a statement. Changing the position of the head, or body, and pointing while giving directions are used to supplement the verbal instructions given.

Speech is usually clarified or supplemented with *illustrators,* also called speech-related gestures. These help to depict the message by giving a visual picture or clarification, e.g., pointing to something being discussed. A person can communicate a message to another individual without using speech at all, but merely by using facial and bodily gestures. Gestures that have direct verbal translations and that can replace speech are called *emblems*. An example would be North Americans' shrugging of their shoulders to indicate uncertainty or indifference. [*See* GESTURES.]

If individuals are restricted in their nonverbal behavior during speech their communication suffers in complexity and fluidity. This phenomenon suggests that nonverbal behavior may not only help the listener to understand the communication of the speaker, but it may also help the speaker to encode speech (that is, put thoughts into words). The fact that nonverbal behavior as a communication form (as in pointing or pantomiming) emerges in infants as a precursor to speech suggests a neurological link between the two.

2. Regulation of Speech Turn-Taking

With nonverbal behavior, individuals signal one another, in a highly automatic manner, about their readiness to give up their speech or listening roles during conversation. A falling pitch in mid-utterance, a final drawl at utterance completion, returning gesturing hands to a resting position, and intensification of gazing at the other at the end of an utterance signal an end of the speaking turn. During a speaking turn, a speaker often pauses and turns the head toward the listener, presumably to receive *back-channel signals,* or feedback related to listener interest, understanding, agreement, or approval. The listener may respond with small head nods and smiles, behaviors which reinforce the speaker's behavior and tell the speaker to continue. A listener may signal the speaker that a speaking turn is desired by turning the head away from the speaker, starting to gesture, and using loud speech during an interruption.

During speech, there are behaviors that parallel and appear to mark the stream of speech. Punctuating movements and batonlike gestures with the arms keep in beat with the speech. Individuals who are interacting with one another appear to share a common rhythm, called *interactional synchrony.* The source of this rhythm may be related, in part, to speech and its timing.

3. Nonverbal Behavior and Language Development

Infants and their caretakers engage in nonverbal communication very early. By the end of the first month of life, the infant engages in mutual gaze with the mother, and by the third and fourth months, the infant and mother are mutually responsive to one another's smiles and vocalizations. The mother engages in pseudo-conversation with the child, in effect, teaching when to take a turn vocalizing and when to listen. Turn-taking occurs as early as 1 year of age between an infant and parent. Before speech emerges, the infant is able to communicate basic messages through nonverbal behavior.

Adult *baby talk* to the infant may have the effect of focusing the infant's attention on language, thus supporting language development. Adult baby talk consists of the use of simple words in short simple utterances. The nonverbal features of this speech register include a high pitch, great variability in pitch, a rising pitch at the end of utterances, vocal emphasis, and slow speech. Variations of this speech register may emerge when adults talk to lovers, pets, or plants, as well as to individuals perceived to have comprehension difficulties, such as foreigners, frail elderly, or individuals with brain damage.

C. Relationships and Nonverbal Behavior

Two general dimensions describe much of the quality of nonverbal behavior during social interaction: the *affiliative–withdrawn* and *dominant–submissive* dimensions. The affiliative–withdrawn dimension describes nonverbal behavior related to how much individuals like each other and how intimate or involved they are or want to become. The dominant–submissive dimension describes nonverbal behavior associated with assertiveness or the degree of power that individuals hold or attempt to hold in relation to one another.

1. Affiliation and Withdrawal

Affiliative nonverbal behavior decreases the subjective and objective distance between individuals. Research studies have shown that individuals communicate liking for one another, for example, when they smile and gaze at each other, nod their heads, orient and lean their bodies toward one another, and may match their arm and leg positions as an indication of involvement. They may also get closer to and may touch one another, and use a warm tone of voice. Withdrawn behavior involves less affiliative behavior, increased distancing between individuals, and behavior that signifies emotional distancing as well, such as gaze avoidance, or a rejecting tone of voice. The manner and context in which behavior is expressed is critical for determining its meaning. For example, smiling that is affiliative has a friendly as opposed to menacing quality. Affiliative eye contact is quite different from a glare. In part, the differences in the quality of expression are related to differing muscle activation in the face and body.

Affiliative–withdrawn behavior occurs early in infants and is reciprocated between infant and parent very early in life. Affiliative behavior is experienced as rewarding by the parent and is very important to the development of attachment between parent and child in this preverbal relationship.

Individuals regulate the intimacy of their interaction with one another through *reciprocation* and *compensation* strategies. When individuals are comfortable with the level of affiliation being expressed by partners, they will reciprocate that level of behavior. When they are uncomfortable, they will compensate for too much affiliative behavior by withdrawing, or for too little affiliative behavior by expressing more affiliation. The degree of comfort individuals feel with affiliative nonverbal behavior is related to a number of factors, including their emotional reaction to the partner and their perception of what type of nonverbal behavior is appropriate for a particular social situation. Other factors are also involved in reciprocation and compensation processes.

2. Dominance and Submission

Just as non-human animals establish dominance hierarchies through their behavior, so do humans. Higher status individuals gaze more at their lower status partners during talking, relative to while they are listening. They take up more space with their bodies and have a more relaxed body posture.

Individuals in lower status and submissive roles have more constrained and less flexible use of nonverbal behaviors than do dominant individuals. For example, they take up less space, touch less, interrupt less, and use a quieter voice. Individuals in a lower status position gaze more while listening, relative to while they are talking: the opposite pattern of that shown for dominant individuals. Although gaze can be used as a form of control by dominant individuals, people who are in a subservient position may use gaze to collect information about the more dominant partner. Such information might be useful for determining how one should be acting in relation to that more dominant individual.

D. Social Influence and Nonverbal Behavior

Individuals exert influence over one another in ways that range from subtle to dramatically evident. The subtle means of influence often occur through nonverbal behavior. Two types of influence in which nonverbal behavior plays a mediational role are *the expectancy effect* and *persuasion*.

1. Expectancy Effect

Individuals' expectations for others' behavior can bring about actual changes in that behavior. For example, people can facilitate or inhibit the successful performance of others merely by expecting them to succeed or fail. Interpersonal warmth and affiliation, expressed through such behaviors as smiling, head nodding, leaning forward, and a warm tone of voice, help to convey positive expectations. Individuals tend to act in an approving manner when they hold high expectations for another, and, thus, provide strong social reinforcement for improved performance. Individuals with lower expectations for another act in a cool or indifferent manner. They do not support improved performance through their

manner, and may inhibit another's successful performance by decreasing the other's sense of competency.

2. Persuasion

Individuals who are perceived as more credible tend to be more persuasive. They gaze more at the recipient of the persuasion attempt, have more facial activity, use more gestures and head nods, speak faster and louder, and speak with less hesitation. Nonverbal behavior may be more important than verbal content in some persuasion attempts. For example, politicians can gain popularity because of the credibility they portray with their nonverbal behavior despite questionable content in their arguments.

Affiliative behavior, such as a brief touch, enhances compliance to simple requests and advice. People have more favorable impressions of individuals who demonstrate affiliative rather than cool, withdrawn behaviors. They also are more satisfied with their interactions. [*See* PERSUASION.]

III. STABLE SOURCES OF VARIATION IN NONVERBAL BEHAVIOR

A. Nonverbal Skills vs Nonverbal Style

Previous sections describe how nonverbal communication is used to convey interpersonal messages, either as an independent communication modality or in conjunction with spoken language. In contrast to these message-specific functions, nonverbal communication can also be conceptualized as expressive style or communication skill, that is, as behavior patterns that persist over time and that may be associated with more enduring characteristics of a person, such as gender, personality, and culture.

Nonverbal skill is the term used to describe a person's ability to use nonverbal communication effectively in daily life. Two subskills are measured, *encoding skill* and *decoding skill*. Encoding skill refers to the ability to convey emotions or other desired messages through nonverbal cues, so that an observer can identify the meaning of the message. For example, you would be scored high on encoding skill if your face was accurately judged as showing "happiness" while you were trying to express this emotion through your face. Decoding skill refers to a person's ability to understand what others are communicating through nonverbal cues. Both encoding and decoding skill show considerable variation between individuals and are reliable over time.

Research has documented a number of correlates of nonverbal skills, some examples of which will be given. Better decoders tend to be better adjusted, more interpersonally democratic and encouraging, less dogmatic, and more popular, and are judged by others as more interpersonally sensitive. Greater encoding skill is associated with popularity, dominance, exhibition, and likability. (Other correlates of encoding and decoding skill are mentioned below.)

Individual differences also exist in nonverbal behavioral repertoire, or nonverbal style. For example, some individuals characteristically smile, gaze, touch, or gesticulate more (or less) than others do. One nonverbal style that has been extensively studied is *expressiveness,* or the extent and frequency of one's nonverbal expressions and movements. Expressiveness is sometimes measured while a person is unaware, as when watching a film alone; in this approach, individuals vary widely in how much their faces reveal about their moods or the stimuli being viewed. Individuals, including infants, who have more expressive faces are less physiologically reactive as measured by electrical activity of the skin. The terms *internalizer* and *externalizer* are used to describe individuals who have relatively unexpressive faces but more internal physiological arousal, or more expressive faces and less internal physiological arousal, respectively.

B. Developmental Aspects

A wide array of facial movements is made possible at birth by well-developed facial musculature. In infants, facial expressions suggesting happiness, surprise, disgust, interest, fear, and anger are evident, though it is difficult to assess the emotional or cognitive experiences accompanying these expressions. Newborns possess the ability to imitate others' facial expressions. Within the first year, infants show differential responses to others' facial expressions and movements. It is believed that observational learning and social reinforcement, combined with an innate repertoire of facial expressions for basic emotions and an innate ability to imitate, are the bases for the development of competence in the use of nonverbal cues.

Encoding and decoding abilities, as well as knowledge of display rules and social norms determining contextually appropriate usage, advance through childhood and adolescence. Some skills are easier to attain than others. One source of individual variation in nonverbal skills is *family expressiveness,* or the degree to which the home environment encourages or discourages free expression of emotion. There is evidence that a more expressive home fosters expressiveness and encoding ability in its children, while inhibiting the development of decoding ability, in theory because cues in a highly expressive home are very easy to read and are lacking in subtlety.

C. Gender

In keeping with popular stereotypes, males and females differ in both nonverbal skill and nonverbal style. Females are reliably more accurate as decoders of nonverbal cues, with the possible exception of anger cues. This overall difference has been found in many diverse regions of the world and also among children and adolescents. Females are also more accurate as encoders of affect cues, both "posed" (sent deliberately) and "spontaneous" (revealed without evident intent).

Females' faces are more expressive than males' faces are, and females have been found to smile, laugh, and gaze at others more during interaction, to stand closer and more directly toward others, to use their hands more expressively, and to touch themselves more. Males' body postures tend to be more relaxed and expansive, and they make more speech errors while speaking and use more filled pauses ("uh," "um," etc.). Some of these differences have been seen in children and infants as well as in adults.

Experts debate the explanations for nonverbal gender differences. Some see the differences as stemming from, and perpetuating, a lower-status social role for females. Others emphasize adaptive functions within same-gender groups; for example, nonverbal warmth and expressiveness is valued more in female than in male groups. Some nonverbal differences may reflect society's preparation for traditional adult roles (e.g., females may need nonverbal skill and an expressive nonverbal style in their role as mother). As gender roles become more fluid in our society, it will be interesting to see whether nonverbal gender differences undergo change as well.

D. Personality

1. Normal Personality

The best documented relations between nonverbal behavior and personality relate to introversion–extraversion. Extraverted individuals are more nonverbally expressive, are more skilled nonverbal encoders, have distinctive vocal style, and gaze more at others during conversation. People high on "self-monitoring" (the tendency to monitor closely one's impact on others and the social appropriateness of one's actions) have been found to be better nonverbal decoders and encoders. A personality characteristic known as "Type A" or "coronary prone personality" (associated with coronary heart disease) is defined partly by nonverbal expressive mannerisms. For example, Type A individuals have loud, explosive voices and they pause very briefly, if at all, at the end of another's speaking turn. Dominance as a personality trait is associated sometimes with more gazing at others during conversation; more dominant individuals also tend to gaze relatively more while speaking than while listening compared to less dominant individuals. [See EXTRAVERSION–INTROVERSION; TYPE A–TYPE B PERSONALITIES.]

2. Psychopathology

Mental disorders are associated with different nonverbal skills and styles. Mentally ill individuals have weaker abilities to decode and encode nonverbal cues. Depressed persons engage in less gaze during interaction, have slower speech with less pitch variation, pause more, and use fewer hand gesticulations.

E. Cultural Aspects

1. National Origin

Cultures differ in nonverbal cue usage. Emblems, which are mainly hand gestures denoting specific messages, vary widely from culture to culture; serious interpersonal misunderstandings can result from these differences, especially since many emblems convey sexual or insulting messages.

Some cultures are considered to favor more nonverbal immediacy during interaction—more gaze, more direct body orientation, more touching, and smaller interpersonal distances. (The study of how close people position themselves to others, both within a culture and across different cultures, is called "proxemics.") Southern European, Latin American, and Middle Eastern countries are considered to be such "contact" cultures in contrast to Northern European, North American, and Asian cultures (though such distinctions are not without exceptions).

Because of local customs relating to the use of nonverbal cues, both decoding and encoding accuracy are greater within than between cultures. For example, Mexican nationals would decode cues sent by other Mexicans better than Norwegian nationals would, and vice versa.

2. Race

Overall, black and Caucasian Americans do not appear to differ in nonverbal decoding skill, although, consistent with the above, accuracy is likely to vary with whether encoders and decoders are of the same or different races. Black American adults tend to gaze less and interact less directly, but touch others more, during conversation. Research indicates that black children interact more closely than white children do, but the reverse is true among adults. Observational research suggests that subcultural differences among blacks are associated with distinct poses and walking styles, especially among young black males.

3. Social Class

Not much is known about nonverbal differences that are specific to different socioeconomic groups. One clear finding is that the nonverbal decoding skill of higher social class individuals is greater than that of lower social class individuals, even when race is controlled for as a possible confounding variable. Lower social class children have been observed to engage in more interpersonal touch. In general, the confounding of social class and race in American society has made interpretation of research on these topics difficult.

IV. PERSPECTIVES ON NONVERBAL BEHAVIOR

A. Independent and Dependent Variables

It will help us better to understand nonverbal behavior in perspective if we recognize that nonverbal behavior can be studied as an independent variable, a dependent variable, and a mediating variable. An independent variable is one from which we can predict some subsequent behavior. For example, we learned that gender predicts accuracy in nonverbal communication. Thus, gender is the independent variable and accuracy of decoding nonverbal behavior is the dependent or outcome variable. Sometimes an independent variable is a causal variable but it need not be. For example, if we found that people who had received some training in decoding nonver-

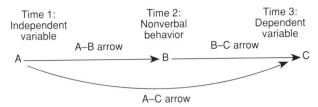

FIGURE 2   Nonverbal behavior as independent, dependent, and mediating variables. Nonverbal behavior (B) is a dependent variable relative to A, an independent variable relative to C, and a mediating variable serving to explain the A–C relationship.

bal behavior were more accurate decoders of nonverbal behavior we could state that training is predictive of performance. However, we could not state that training was the cause of increased accuracy because it is possible that more accurate decoders sought out more training than did less accurate decoders. The only way to be sure that training caused improved decoding would be to assign people randomly to the training condition or to the comparison condition of no training, i.e., so that each person had an equal chance of being assigned to either group.

When we considered training as an independent variable, accuracy of decoding nonverbal behavior was the dependent variable or outcome variable. When we try to predict the effectiveness of classroom teachers from the nonverbal teaching behavior shown in the classroom, the nonverbal behavior is the independent variable and the effectiveness of the teacher is the dependent variable. We illustrate these relations in Figure 2.

When we study the relationship of A to B, the A–B arrow, we are studying the nonverbal behavior as predictable from some preceding observation. When we study the relationship of B to C, the B–C arrow, we are studying the nonverbal behavior as a predictor of some subsequent observation. These B–C arrows are now being intensively studied because a recent series of analyses have shown that "thin slices" of nonverbal behavior lasting less than 30 sec can be used to predict such criteria as teacher effectiveness, teacher expectations, teacher status, the existence of deception, physician proficiency, patient compliance, success in the referral of alcoholic patients, the behavior of babies, and depression in patients.

B. Mediating Variables

We have examined the role of nonverbal behavior as independent and dependent variables. In this section we examine the role of nonverbal behavior as a mediating variable. A mediating variable is a variable that helps to explain the relationship between two other variables, one of which precedes and one of which follows the nonverbal behavior. For example, suppose that in Figure 2 the dependent variable (C) were students' intellectual functioning and the independent variable (A) were teachers' expectations for students' intellectual functioning. Also suppose that variables A and C were found to be substantially correlated such that when teachers had been randomly led to expect better intellectual performance from their students they actually obtained better performance from their students. Many experiments of this type have been carried out and they have shown that one person's expectations for another person's behavior can come to serve as self-fulfilling prophecy. That is an important finding but the fact that a relationship exists between the independent and dependent variable (an A–C arrow) does not explain how such a relationship comes about.

Nonverbal behavior has been found to be a variable mediating between the independent variable (A) of one person's expectation for the behavior of another person and the dependent variable (C) of that other person's actual behavior. To claim to have found a successful mediating variable (B) we must be able to show that a change in the independent variable (A) leads to a change in the mediating variable (B) and that a change in the mediating variable (B) leads to a change in the dependent variable (C). When both those conditions hold, the mediating variable (B) can be said to contribute to an explanation of the relationship between variables A and C.

Research shows two mediating variables (B) that have been found to help explain the effects of teacher expectations (A) on students' intellectual performance (C). One of the mediating variables, climate, is largely a nonverbal variable. Teachers treat students for whom they have higher expectations with greater nonverbal warmth. This warmth is predictable from the teacher's expectation and is predictive of students' performance.

The other mediating variable, input, is largely a verbal variable. Teachers teach more material and more difficult material to those students for whom they have higher expectations. This greater input of teaching material is predictable from the teacher's expectation and is predictive of students' performance. This actual example, summarizing scores of research studies, illustrates that nonverbal behavior and verbal behavior often serve as equally important mediating variables.

Because it is so often the case that nonverbal and verbal behaviors operate together, it does not seem useful to claim that either is more or less important in any absolute sense. In a given context either may be far more important than the other. But any effort to understand human social behavior would be incomplete if it did not consider both verbal and nonverbal behavior. However, the study of verbal behavior has been with us longer while the study of nonverbal behavior, in a relative sense, is still a new frontier.

C. The Future of the Study of Nonverbal Behavior

Much has been learned about nonverbal behavior over the past 20 years. The role of nonverbal behavior in emotional expression, communication, and interpersonal relations is better understood. We also are more aware of differences in nonverbal behavior and communication related to age, gender, personality, health status, culture, race, and social class. Finally, we are better prepared to predict how nonverbal behavior influences and is influenced by certain conditions.

Despite the advancement in knowledge about nonverbal behavior, the research is far from over. As methods for its study improve, as information accrues and is summarized, as more explanatory theories are developed, our understanding of nonverbal behavior will evolve. We will better understand how behavior relates to the diversity and similarity, to the cooperation and conflict of human beings across the world.

Acknowledgment

Preparation of this paper was facilitated by the Spencer Foundation, though the content of this paper is solely the responsibility of the authors.

Bibliography

Argyle, M. (1988). ''Bodily Communication,'' 2nd ed. Methuen, New York.

Blanck, P. D., Buck, R., and Rosenthal, R. (Eds.) (1986). ''Nonverbal Communication in the Clinical Context.'' Pennsylvania State University Press, University Park, PA.

Ekman, P. (Ed.) (1982). ''Emotion in the Human Face,'' 2nd ed. Cambridge University Press, New York.

Feldman, R. S. (1982). ''Development of Nonverbal Behavior in Children.'' Springer-Verlag, New York.

Feldman, R. S., and Rimé, B. (Eds.) (1991). ''Fundamentals of Nonverbal Behavior.'' Cambridge University Press, New York.

Hall, J. A. (1984). ''Nonverbal Sex Differences: Communication Accuracy and Expressive Style.'' The Johns Hopkins University Press, Baltimore, MD.

Knapp, M. L., and Hall, J. A. (1992). ''Nonverbal Communication in Human Interaction,'' 3rd ed. Holt Rinehart and Winston, Fort Worth.

Patterson, M. L. (1983). ''Nonverbal Behavior.'' Springer-Verlag, New York.

Rosenthal, R. (Ed.) (1979). ''Skill in Nonverbal Communication.'' Oelgeschlager, Gunn & Hain, Cambridge, MA.

Rosenthal, R., Hall, J. A., DiMatteo, M. R., Rogers, P. L., and Archer, D. (1979). ''Sensitivity to Nonverbal Communication: The PONS Test.'' The Johns Hopkins University Press, Baltimore.

Scherer, K. R., and Ekman, P. (Eds.) (1982). ''Handbook of Methods in Nonverbal Behavior Research.'' Cambridge University Press, New York.

Siegman, A. W., and Feldstein, S. (Eds.) (1985). ''Multichannel Integrations of Nonverbal Behavior.'' Lawrence Erlbaum Associates, Hillsdale, NJ.

OBEDIENCE AND CONFORMITY

Arthur G. Miller

Miami University

Glossary

Autokinetic effect An optical illusion involving perceived movement of light. Used by Sherif to investigate social influence.

Banality of evil Hannah Arendt's depiction of the "ordinariness" of the high-ranking Nazi, Adolf Eichmann. Consistent with Milgram's research documenting destructive obedience in large numbers of individuals not characterized by unusual hostility or harmful intent.

Conformity Displaying a behavior similar to one's peers as a result of social influence. Yielding to peer pressure may reflect normative or informational social influence. The focus of Asch's pioneering studies of individual responses to group pressure in the context of judgments of physical reality.

Fundamental attribution error A bias to perceive the causes of social behavior in terms of an individual's personality or moral character and to minimize the impact of external influences. This bias is contradicted in a particularly vivid manner by the research considered in this article.

Holocaust The Nazi extermination of Jewish women, men, and children. Interpreted by many commentators as reflecting, among a host of factors, the crucial role of obedience to authority on the part of large numbers of people. Milgram's experiments on destructive obedience have been regarded as having a unique explanatory significance regarding the role of authority in the Holocaust.

Obedience Behaving in line with orders from an authority. The focus of Milgram's influential experimental research on submitting to an experimenter's orders to inflict increasingly severe punishment on a protesting victim.

THE PHENOMENA of obedience and conformity illustrate the extraordinary degree to which people are susceptible to social influence. Conformity focuses upon the influence exerted by one's peers, whereas obedience considers influence directed from an authority. The classic research by Solomon Asch on conformity and by Stanley Milgram on obedience are featured in this article. Key theoretical processes underlying these phenomena as well as examples of current research are also discussed.

I. AN INTRODUCTION TO CONFORMITY AND OBEDIENCE

The guiding perspective of social psychology rests upon the extraordinary degree to which people are susceptible to social influence. To the lay observer, this influence is often unexpected, for we tend to believe intuitively that social behaviors—for example, acts of kindness or cruelty—are a reflection of an individual's personality or moral character. The role of situational pressures, even when these are unquestionably operative, may be discounted or ignored completely—a bias which social psychologists have termed "the fundamental attribution error." [See ACTOR–OBSERVER DIFFERENCES IN ATTRIBUTION.]

Many social behaviors are not primarily caused by factors unique to the individual, but rather by powerful, occasionally very subtle, external forces. Nowhere is this lesson more dramatically illustrated than in a consideration of the phenomena of conformity and obedience. Though originally conducted several decades ago, the pioneering experiments of Solomon Asch on conformity and Stanley Milgram on obedience to authority are, without question, two of the most influential research programs in the history of social science. In studies of conformity and obedience, the research participant must choose between remaining independent or yielding to social influence, perhaps at the expense of violating important values. How will the individual resolve this conflict? This is a question for which everyone wants a convincing answer, not only regarding what others might do, but also how we, ourselves, might act. The objectives of this chapter are (a) to present an overview of the definitive studies by Asch and Milgram, (b) to examine theoretical explanations for the phenomena of conformity and obedience, and (c) to consider contemporary research on these processes and some of their important implications.

II. THE ASCH CONFORMITY STUDIES

Solomon Asch was not the first social scientist to examine the influence of group opinion on individual judgments. Muzafir Sherif (1936) had shown earlier that individuals could be influenced in their perceptual judgments of the apparent movement of a point of light in a totally darkened room. Although the light spot was in fact stationary, people would typically experience an illusion of movement—from a few inches to several feet—known technically as the "autokinetic effect." Sherif's major finding was that when *groups* of individuals were placed in this setting, they came, in time but without any instruction or cuing, to a remarkable agreement as to the degree of motion of the light, forming what Sherif termed a "normative judgment."

That the judgment task in this experiment was extremely *ambiguous* is crucial. All estimates of the movement of light were, in a factual sense, *guesses*. The consensus that materialized in the group-judgment condition is thus understandable because upon hearing different judgments, subjects could reasonably say to themselves: "Perhaps the light did move more (or less) than I thought." A vital lesson from the Sherif studies was the *functional value of social comparison,* that in certain situations, we view other people as invaluable resources in the definition of physical reality.

A. The Asch Conformity Paradigm

Asch (1956) designed a powerful method to examine responses to group pressure. Groups of college students participated in what was described as a study in visual discrimination. In actuality, only one individual was a true subject; the others were assistants, set by prior arrangement to respond erroneously (and unanimously) on certain trials. The discrimination task involved a large card with one vertical line on the left and three comparison lines on the right. Participants were instructed to identify which of the lines on the right was identical to the line on the left. Judgments were made by each individual in the order of their seating position, the naive subject responding "next to last." There were a total of 18 trials, of which 12 were *critical trials* on which the group made an erroneous judgment.

1. Conformity and Reactions to the Group Pressure Situation

The typical subject conformed on slightly more than 4 of the 12 critical trials (37%). This finding is itself intriguing. If the average participant remained independent on a majority of the trials, why has this research always been regarded as so provocative? Why is Asch's research regarded as dealing with conformity rather than independence? (Not all commentators in fact take this position.)

One answer resides in the judgments of *control* subjects who indicated their judgments without knowledge of the estimates of other peers. These participants were invariably accurate. From this perspective, the observed conformity rate of 37% is dramatic. Unlike the ambiguous light-movement in Sherif's studies, the judgment task in the Asch paradigm was unequivocally objective, the equivalent of judging whether a ball tossed in the air would remain suspended or fall to the ground. On at least *one* of the 12 critical trials, over 75% of the subjects conformed, agreeing publicly with a judgment of their peers that blatantly contradicted physical reality—*a response they would never have made when alone.*

B. Factors Influencing Conformity

Asch reported numerous findings documenting situational influences upon conformity. For example, when the *size* of the group was varied (from 1 to 15), the maximum influence was observed with an opposition of 3 individuals, conformity not increasing substantially with larger groups. The *unanimity* of the group was of critical importance. When Asch arranged for one of the apparent subjects to depart from the group's erroneous judgment and give a correct response, conformity was reduced by almost 75%. The slightest break in the uniformity of the group's behavior thus released subjects from the pressure to conform. In yet another variation, the "deviating" subject initially gave correct line judgments but then changed and agreed with the group's erroneous estimations. Conformity increased noticeably as soon as the "ally" abandoned the subject. Personal factors were clearly in evidence as well, with a substantial number never conforming (approximately 25%) while almost one-third of the participants conformed on 8 or more of the 12 trials.

1. Reactions of Subjects

Asch observed, during the study itself and in extensive postexperimental interviews, pervasive signs of concern, embarrassment, temptation, even fear—some doubting whether they understood the instructions, whether there was an optical illusion in the experiment, whether their heads were tilted at the wrong angle, whether the group was following the first subject who, for some reason, was making mistakes. These accounts were essentially justifications or rationalizations for their submission to influence, because with an identical task but no group pressure (i.e., the control condition), judgment errors and displays of tension and doubt were nonexistent. One might presume that many subjects became suspicious. In fact, Asch reported minimal suspicion. Self-doubt was the modal response.

Thus, the decision to yield and agree with the group's verdict was *not* a reflection of "blind" conformity. Rather, subjects conformed to the group despite the presence of strong conflict and internal reservations. It is noteworthy that subjects in conformity experiments almost invariably *deny* (at least to the researcher) that they have been influenced, perhaps reflecting the social undesirability of conformity (or at least acknowledging one's reliance upon others) in this culture. From its very initial appearance, Asch's research became an instant "classic" because it raised a sobering question. If public conformity could be generated in the sterile confines of this laboratory paradigm, what might be the limits regarding our susceptibility to social influence in

other contexts with even more compelling social pressures?

2. Why Do People Conform?

Conformity reflects two distinct social concerns—our appearance in the eyes of others, and our need for information that others may provide. The concept of *normative social influence* is used to explain conformity that is driven by a person's anxiety about appearing deviant in the eyes of one's peers. There is vast research literature documenting the powerful connection between similarity and interpersonal attraction. Other things equal, we like those who are similar to us in attitudes and values. The perception that others share our view of the world is reinforcing. As logical as this may sound, there is an ominous consequence, for we may quite rationally anticipate that if we appear dissimilar to other people, *they may not like us*—an expectation that frequently proves to be valid. In a novel variation, Asch used a group of naive subjects with one participant being a paid assistant. Seated in the seventh position, this individual gave the same pattern of incorrect judgments that had been given by the group in the usual procedure. How did the group now react toward this deviating individual?

> At the outset they greeted the estimates of the dissenter with incredulity. On the later trials there were smiles and impromptu comments. As the experiment progressed, contagious, and in some instances, uncontrolled laughter swept the group. (Raven and Rubin, 1983, p. 575)

A departure from a group consensus may thus evoke *ridicule, embarrassment*, perhaps *rejection*, costs that many individuals are not prepared to accept. Needless to say, one's apprehension about appearing different (and thus one's motivation to conform) may increase substantially when the relevant "others" are personally significant, e.g., the parents of one's fiancee, one's employer, or one's friends.

A second explanation of conformity, *informational social influence*, recognizes that other people are frequently a primary source of valued information—as shown earlier in Sherif's autokinetic-effect studies. Consider such questions as, "What is the area in square miles of the United States?" "Is it fashionable to wear long dresses and skirts?" "How frightened should you be regarding an upcoming surgical operation?" On issues of this kind, although we may have personal views, we are likely to be susceptible to the opinions of other people. In fact, we are so accustomed to comparing our opinions with others and relying upon them for informational support, that it may seem bizarre even to contemplate ignoring the views of other people in many situations. "Ignoring others" is, of course, precisely what subjects in the Asch situation had to do to avoid conformity.

Is conformity in the Asch paradigm primarily normative or informational? Asch performed a variation in which the true subject arrived "late," making it infeasible to announce their line estimations out loud. Instead, they were to listen to the others' responses, record their own judgments *in writing,* and hand them directly to the experimenter. Conformity was significantly reduced, suggesting that a major component in this setting was normative influence. Nevertheless, there were more errors in this condition than in the control groups, suggesting that for some participants, there was informational influence operating in this experiment as well. Subsequent research has varied the nature of the judgment itself and the results are clear: Increasing the *ambiguity* of the task (relative to Asch's unambiguous line-estimation task) increases the rate of conformity because people become more informationally dependent.

What might occur if the existence of a "right answer" or undeniable "truth" was not as self-evident as the line-estimation task used by Asch? Conformity should be sharply reduced because the pressures of normative and informational influence would be diminished. Research involving judgments of "artistic preference"—for example, asking subjects to indicate which of two modern line drawings they prefer—in fact fails to indicate conformity. People thus appear to distinguish between situations calling for objective and subjective judgments. John Sabini has wryly observed in this context that "people are willing to be different; they just don't want to be crazy."

C. To Conform or Remain Independent: The Conflict in Conformity

Lee Ross and his colleagues (1976) suggest that the participant in Asch's experiment (and in many other potential contexts for conformity) must consider two important and disconcerting questions: (a) Why are the other subjects unanimously voicing judgments that are so clearly wrong and different from mine?

and (b) What will they think about *me*—and what will they infer regarding how I think about *them*—if I deviate from their judgments by responding correctly? To the first question, there is simply no obvious explanation, situational or dispositional, to account for their erroneous judgments. To the second, there is a decided risk: Dissenting from their judgments will make the subject appear foolish, incompetent, "crazy," etc., and, perhaps worse, will imply that she or he thinks that *they* are foolish, incompetent, and perhaps deranged. Such outcomes are, from the subjects' point of view, unacceptable, and as a result, a measure of conformity results.

Ross *et al.* verified their theoretical analysis in an ingenious variation of the Asch situation. They exposed subjects again to a unanimous group of peers clearly making errors on an objective task (estimating tone duration). In one condition, however, the participants (true subjects) were offered a reward for making the correct answer but were told that the other group members were given different instructions. Specifically they were led to believe that their peers would receive rewards if they guessed certain tones and if those guesses turned out correctly. Given this clarification regarding the *causes* of the peers' responses, conformity dropped sharply. Subjects could reason that the other group members—but not they—were driven by the prospect of a large reward and thus gambled by making ridiculously wrong guesses. Each subject also knew that the other members of the group would have a plausible interpretation to make regarding his or her own divergent responses, and that this response would not be an automatic indication that the subject viewed the other group members as incompetent.

According to Ross *et al.,* it is instructive to view an observed rate of conformity as the resolution of two competing forces—a pressure toward conformity and a pressure toward remaining independent. As the judgment task becomes more ambiguous or subjective, the pressure to remain independent is reduced because the individual can rationalize his or her yielding to the others' opinion on the basis of some hitherto unseen virtue of their position or in service of avoiding a confrontation, thus displaying good manners and keeping one's "cool." In the Asch situation, however, yielding to the group's opinion about the erroneous line is extremely disconcerting because there is no comforting rationale—the task is exceedingly objective. The conforming subject perceives himself or herself to be either weak and submissive or visually incompetent.

Thus, subjects in the Asch paradigm display a relatively *low* rate of conformity (37%). Despite the formidable situational pressures to conform (e.g., the presence of a large number of peers in unanimous agreement), there is a considerable counterpressure to remain independent (i.e., the completely objective judgment task, and the subject's self-esteem). There is, in short, a powerful *conflict,* resulting in tension and discomfort as well as a high incidence of *independence*. We will observe later, in conjunction with Milgram's obedience research, a strikingly analogous conflict.

D. Productive Conformity: Reducing the Expression of Racial Prejudice

Notwithstanding the pervasively negative connotation of conformity, might a socially *desired* outcome result from social pressure? The key is to identify a behavior in which individuals act in an undesirable manner *when alone*. Then, by exerting the social pressure to conform, might this behavior be changed in a significantly positive direction?

A recent study by Blanchard and his colleagues (1991) has suggested that conformity pressure may be instrumental in reducing prejudice. Their focus concerned student opinion about sending anonymous notes containing racial slurs and threats to black students. White undergraduate females were interviewed as they walked to class. While walking alone, they were approached by an interviewer who asked if they would agree to participate anonymously in a poll. White female confederates arrived at the same time as the true participant. The interviewer then read statements concerning how the administration should respond to anonymous racist notes (e.g., "The person who is writing these notes should be expelled"; "The college is making too big an issue of these incidents, thereby causing divisiveness on campus"; etc.). Five possible responses (lettered A through E), ranging from "strongly agree" to "strongly disagree" were to be given for each item, thus indicating a strongly antiracist or more racist reaction, or a more neutral opinion. Each participant (one naive subject) was to indicate their judgment orally after the confederates had responded, or in writing.

Each participant was randomly assigned to either a *favorable* or *unfavorable* condition consisting of the confederates using either the most racist or antiracist response alternatives. The major result was clear: *Subjects were strongly influenced by the social pressure in this study*. Participants conformed in either the anti- or pro-racist direction, depending upon the condition to which they had been randomly assigned. When the stated opinion of the peers was equivocal about the university's antiracism policy rather than strongly favorable or unfavorable, participants were influenced to express similarly neutral positions. Although the authors favor a simple normative influence interpretation, conformity effects were observed in the private as well as public response conditions, suggesting a degree of informational influence as well.

The power of the situation is shown in glaring terms. As the investigators conclude, "antiracist sentiment is malleable." Conformity pressures may thus alter behavior in a desirable direction without a prior change in the actor's private beliefs or opinions. The key, of course, is to locate or be fortunate to have present those few outspoken individuals who would take the lead and *provide the influence* to which other people are so unexpectedly responsive.

Having considered conformity, we turn now to a set of experiments that have had an unparalleled impact on social science. Stanley Milgram, a research assistant to Asch at Harvard and Princeton, was initially interested in examining the degree to which people would conform to others when the act involved a more socially significant event than estimating the lengths of lines, namely harming another person. A question was raised, however, in terms of the control condition. As noted earlier, Asch had used individuals making judgments without group pressure as his control. These data provided a crucial baseline for his subsequent analyses. Milgram similarly needed some indication of how far an individual might go in harming another person without group pressure. However, it was not clear what might induce an individual to harm another person without any group pressure. It was at that point that Milgram's interest turned from conformity to the question of obedience to authority:

> What would be the force that would get him to increase the shocks? And then the thought occurred that the experimenter would have to tell him to give higher and higher shocks. Just how far will a person go when an experimenter instructs him to give increasingly severe shocks? Immediately I knew that that was the problem I would investigate. (Evans, 1980, p. 189)

III. MILGRAM'S RESEARCH ON OBEDIENCE TO AUTHORITY

A short article with an innocuous title—"Behavioral Study of Obedience"—appeared in a 1963 issue of the *Journal of Abnormal and Social Psychology*. This was the first announcement of the results of a 3-year programmatic series of experiments by Stanley Milgram dealing with factors influencing obedience to authority. Contributing to the extraordinarily rapid visibility and controversial status of this research were its association with the Nazi Holocaust and the intense conflict experienced by many of Milgram's research participants. Milgram framed the obedience project in the context of the Nazi policy of genocide:

> Obedience, as a determinant of behavior, is of particular relevance to our time. It has been reliably established that from 1933–45, millions of innocent persons were systematically slaughtered on command. Gas chambers were built, death camps were guarded, daily quotas of corpses were produced with the same efficiency as the manufacture of appliances. These inhumane policies may have originated in the mind of a single person, but they could only be carried out on a massive scale if a very large number of people obeyed orders. (Milgram, 1963, p. 371)

A. The Research Program

More than 1000 individuals took part in a research program consisting of approximately 20 experiments. Participants, consisting primarily of males of diverse ages, educational backgrounds, and socioeconomic status, were recruited from advertisements announcing a research program on the "study of memory and learning" to be conducted at Yale University. The basic procedure consisted of two individuals appearing at each session, one of whom was an accomplice who, by a rigged random draw, chose the role of "learner." The actual subject always selected the role of "teacher" whose primary functions were to administer a learning task and to administer punishment for any errors. The task involved reading to the learner a list of word pairs (light–truck, fat–neck, etc.), and then to repeat the initial word of a pair. The learner's task was to recall the correct association and press a button that would activate an indicator light in front of the "teacher."

Punishment for errors consisted of administering a brief electric shock to the learner by pressing a lever on a shock generator. The learner was strapped into place, attached to (apparent) electrodes, etc.

The shock generator consisted of a row of 30 levers, each accompanying a designated voltage ranging from 15 to 450 V. Various switches, dials, indicator lights, and meters (and sounds) gave a highly authentic appearance. Verbal labels were also engraved at various levels, beginning with "slight shock" and proceeding to "extreme intensity," "danger: severe shock," and, finally, at the 450 V level, simply XXX. Subjects received a mild sample shock to convince them of the authenticity of the generator. Essentially every facet of this study was contrived. There were no actual shocks delivered by the "generator"; verbal protests (including screams, and the mention of a "heart problem") from the learner were in fact delivered by tape recorder.

B. The Manifestation of Authority

Milgram used the context of a psychological experiment with its "built in" hierarchical role structure. The role of "authority" was played by an experimenter, highly formal in appearance (white lab coat) and manner. Subjects were instructed to start at the first shock lever (15 V) and increase the punishment by one shock level for each of the learner's mistakes. In response to hesitation on the part of the subject, the experimenter responded, if necessary, with one of four increasingly strident prods or "commands" in the following order:

Prod 1—Please continue, or please go on.
Prod 2—The experiment requires that you go on.
Prod 3—It is absolutely essential that you continue.
Prod 4—You have no other choice, you must go on.

These prods are the most important methodological feature in Milgram's paradigm. Prods 3 and 4, in particular, distinguish this type of experiment from all other studies of social influence, for *these are literally commands or orders* which, if obeyed, ultimately resulted in the learner appearing to receive intolerable pain. Examined out of context, these statements are falsehoods and manifestly unenforceable. The fact that these prods influenced subjects to shock a protesting individual is, in a basic sense, the most intriguing finding of the study.

The psychological climate of the situation changed radically over time, from an initially uneventful phase (e.g., mild shocks, several correct responses from the learner) to a situation in which the experimenter would insist in the strongest manner that the subject inflict increasingly severe shocks to a protesting learner who, at various points, literally screamed in distress. In the baseline experiment, at the 20th shock level, the "victim" (in an adjoining room) pounded on the wall but no longer responded to the task by pressing a button to activate the light on the learner's panel. The experimenter nevertheless insisted that the subject treat the absence of a response as an error and continue shocking the (nonresponsive) learner.

C. Initial Findings

Two startling findings were cited in Milgram's initial report (1963). First, *65%* of the subjects obeyed all orders to the end of the shock series. No subject broke off prior to the 300-V level. Contributing to the impact of this finding was that it was so *unexpected*. Given a complete description of the laboratory situation, Milgram asked a variety of groups (undergraduates, psychiatrists) to predict the obedience rate of 100 hypothetical subjects. Invariably the estimations were that virtually *no* individual would continue to the 450-V level. Milgram's research thus constituted evidence of the most dramatic kind. Nobody expected what in fact occurred.

A second major finding was the intense stress in many participants, graphically reported by Milgram:

> I observed a mature and initially poised businessman enter the laboratory smiling and confident. Within 20 minutes he was reduced to a twitching, stuttering wreck, who was rapidly approaching a point of nervous collapse. He constantly pulled on his earlobe, and twisted his hands. At one point he pushed his fist into his forehead and muttered: "Oh God, let's stop it." And yet he continued to respond to every word of the experimenter, and obeyed to the end. (1963, p. 377)

Milgram interpreted his findings in terms of situational forces. A major theme was the *legitimacy* of the experiment in the eyes of his participants—the university setting, the scientific importance of the problem (allegedly) being investigated, the competence of the personnel conducting the research, the

voluntary basis of participation, the reassurances of the experimenter (at least initially). Milgram also emphasized the fact that for the typical subject, there was considerable *ambiguity* regarding the "prerogatives of a psychologist and the corresponding rights of his subject." Milgram had created a powerful *conflict* in which the subject was ultimately to face two competing forces—an authority figure instructing that he continue and a protesting peer demanding to be released. It is virtually certain that subjects had never been in a situation of this kind.

A major lesson from the obedience research is thus similar to that of the conformity studies: Under social pressure, many individuals will engage in behaviors which produce considerable personal distress—behaviors which they, in principle, consider themselves incapable of performing, and which, in fact, they would not perform without such influence. Milgram noted that "one might suppose that a subject would simply break off or continue as his conscience dictated. Yet, this is very far from what happened." Given the extraordinary influence exerted in this experiment, we need to ask why people underestimate obedience to authority? One answer is clear: As observers, we are prone to explain behavior, even in a circumstance of powerful influence, in terms of dispositional or characterological qualities—a "good, moral person would not obey the experimenter's orders" (i.e., the fundamental attribution error). Of course, this is essentially the *opposite* of what Milgram in fact observed.

D. A Note on Research Ethics

Shortly following the initial obedience report Diana Baumrind published an essay in the *American Psychologist* (1964) attacking the ethics of Milgram's treatment of his research subjects as well as the implications and value of the investigation. A rebuttal by Milgram (1964) appeared 5 months later. Their exchange was the impetus for a renaissance of sensitivity to ethical issues in human experimentation. The scholarship in this area is now voluminous. Although in many respects a highly unique form of psychological research, the obedience experiments have, for almost 30 years, been routinely featured in any serious discussion of ethical issues in research with human subjects. Aside from the particulars of the obedience research, Milgram's decision to pursue the study of destructive obedience in a rigorous controlled setting was extraordinarily valuable in raising important issues pertaining to the rights of both subjects and investigators. While many social psychologists are clearly on Milgram's side of this controversy, there is a considerable divergence of opinion, with a host of complex methodological and philosophical issues interwoven with the ethical dimensions. A common frame of analysis is to weigh the gains in knowledge provided by the obedience experiments against the costs incurred in terms of the tension and strain experienced by research participants.

With respect to Milgram's specific procedure, subjects were informed in a postexperimental interview of the deceptions involved and were introduced to the "learner" in a spirit of "friendly reconciliation." Milgram went beyond the usual debriefing procedure, mailing to each subject a thorough account of the basic research project. Although there is no documented evidence that any of his subjects experienced lasting psychological harm, Milgram clearly approached the limits in terms of ethical guidelines in human research, specifically in terms of respecting the participant's right to withdraw. He clearly challenged this right (see "Prods" above). What he learned in so doing has been of inestimable value in the eyes of countless scholars and social scientists. Whether he was ethical will depend, at least in part, on one's position regarding the cost/benefit analysis.

E. Situational Influences on Obedience to Authority

Milgram conducted an extensive research program consisting of situational variations in the basic paradigm, with 20 to 40 participants being studied in each. Brief titles of these variations and the level of observed obedience in each are shown in Figure 1. Each variation is numbered following Milgram's description. Experiments 1 through 4 varied the *proximity* of the subject (i.e., teacher) and learner. In Experiment 1 (described above), the learner was in an adjoining room. Vocal protests were introduced in Experiment 2. Experiment 3 placed the learner in the same room with the teacher. Experiment 4 involved the subject placing the learner's hand on a shock plate to receive the punishment. Obedience decreased as the physical closeness of the teacher and learner increased, suggesting the crucial importance of empathic identification with the victim. The physical distance between the participant and *experimenter* was examined in Variation

7. The experimenter was not physically present in the laboratory but gave instructions by phone. Obedience was considerably lower, approximately one-third of the baseline level. The physical presence and surveillance of the authority were thus of vital significance in the observed obedience.

Would subjects obey orders to *stop* shocking the learner? In Variation 12, Milgram devised a script in which the experimenter (at the 150-V level) instructed subjects to discontinue shocking the learner. However, the learner insisted that he was strong enough to continue. Obedience, in this instance, consisted of "not shocking the learner," and the findings clearly indicated that it was the authority who was obeyed, not the learner. Variation 14 required the experimenter to play the role of learner (the confederate assigned to the learner role expressed anxiety which the experimenter "relieved" by saying that he would assume the learner role initially himself). The subject was then ordered by the peer (confederate) to continue shocking the experimenter, but at the 150-V level, the experimenter instructed the shocks to cease. All subjects immediately obeyed these instructions. Thus, the key issue being examined in this research is *obedience to authority, not aggression*. Subjects are as willing to obey an order to stop shocking as they are to continue. A control condition (Variation 11), in which subjects were simply asked to select their own shock level without any directive from the experimenter, had also shown that subjects invariably chose the lowest shock levels.

1. Conforming to Disobedient Peers

Asch had shown that the most powerful inhibitor of conformity was a situation in which subjects had an ally who defied the (otherwise) unanimous group. An analogous variation (17) was conducted in which four (apparent) subjects arrived for an experiment on the effects of "collective teaching and punishment" on memory and learning. Only one of the individuals was a true subject. A rigged draw produced the learner and three teachers. The script called for the other "subjects" (assistants) to withdraw at the 10th level (150 V), and at the 14th level (210 V). This defiance of authority was an extremely powerful influence on subjects. Only 10% followed instructions to the 450-V level. Defiance was shown to be a concrete behavioral option, resulting in no harmful consequences and weakening the credibility of the experimenter's threatening prods (such as "you have no other choice").

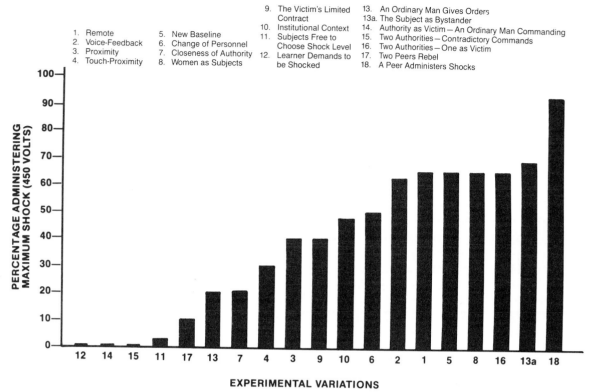

1. Remote
2. Voice-Feedback
3. Proximity
4. Touch-Proximity

5. New Baseline
6. Change of Personnel
7. Closeness of Authority
8. Women as Subjects

9. The Victim's Limited Contract
10. Institutional Context
11. Subjects Free to Choose Shock Level
12. Learner Demands to be Shocked

13. An Ordinary Man Gives Orders
13a. The Subject as Bystander
14. Authority as Victim—An Ordinary Man Commanding
15. Two Authorities—Contradictory Commands
16. Two Authorities—One as Victim
17. Two Peers Rebel
18. A Peer Administers Shocks

FIGURE 1   A profile of the experimental variations.

2. Additional Factors Influencing Obedience

Obedience does not require that the study be conducted at a prestigious university (Yale). Relocating the investigation in an office building in Bridgeport, Connecticut (Variation 10), yielded a marginally reduced obedience rate. Could an ordinary peer be as influential as the experimenter when placed in the role of authority? A scenario (Variation 13) was arranged in which the experimenter would be required to leave the laboratory momentarily, thereby creating a "need" for one of the subjects to perform the authority role. Obedience dropped sharply, indicating that the power of authority rests not simply upon duties and actions but also upon one's role status in an organization and mannerisms—the "style" of authority.

The experimenter's authority was challenged in one variation (9) by introducing a contractual agreement. The learner agreed to participate only if it was stipulated, in advance, that he would be released whenever he asked to do so. However, when the learner later asked to be released, the experimenter ignored the agreement and continued issuing orders to the subject. Obedience was reduced to 40%, still a sizable degree of compliance under such conditions. The power of the authority was thus intact even under conditions which might reasonably be viewed as delegitimizing.

How might an individual respond in this type of experiment if he or she was not instructed personally to shock the learner, but was assigned a subsidiary task (e.g., clerical recording) while *another person* was doing the actual lever pressing? When a peer (assistant) obeyed all orders, 37 of the 40 subjects in this variation (93%) remained in their role and *took no action* in terms of leaving the scene or rescuing the learner. In documenting the phenomenon of the "nonintervening bystander," this experiment (Variation 18) has been of particular interest to those who see important elements of the nature of "evil" in the obedience experiments. Milgram interpreted this important result in terms of *responsibility:*

> Any competent manager of a destructive bureaucratic system can arrange his personnel so that only the most callous and obtuse are directly involved in violence. The greater part of the personnel can consist of men and women who, by virtue of their distance from the actual

acts of brutality, will feel little strain in their performance of supportive functions. They will feel doubly absolved from responsibility. First, legitimate authority has given full warrant for their actions. Second, they have not themselves committed brutal physical acts. (1974, 122)

3. The Power of the Situation

In a widely circulated film produced by Milgram in 1965, a major segment is devoted to one participant who obeys all instructions to the 450-V level. Although this individual hardly appears sadistic or hostile—he makes repeated efforts to disengage himself, only to return to the shock generator upon the experimenter's prodding—it is virtually impossible not to think of this person's actions as reflecting his character—his lack of resolve, his weakness. Why then do social psychologists assert that it is *not the person but rather the "power of the situation"* that is the major lesson of these experiments?

The results of the *complete set* of experimental variations in Milgram's research program are extremely compelling evidence. As shown in Figure 1, in approximately half of the variations, the number of subjects proceeding to 450 V is 50% or less. In other variations, a clear majority obey to 450 V. For example, in Variation 18, virtually every subject was a willing bystander who refrained from leaving the experiment when another person was shocking the learner. It would be easy to explain such behavior as reflecting "callousness," "indifference," "uninvolvement," "a lack of empathy," etc. However, in condition 17, almost every subject disobeyed the experimenter if one or two peers first provided a model for disobedience. Logically, of course, the *same types of individuals* were involved in both variations (an assumption of random assignment to experimental conditions). Yet obedience was virtually absent in one situation, and at the bystander level, virtually total in the other.

Many readers have interpreted Milgram's *initial* obedience report as suggesting that people are intrinsically subservient to the dictates of malevolent authority. However, this was *not* Milgram's intended message. Rather, the primary conclusion is that people have a *repertoire of potential responses to social influence.* The option actually chosen—to yield or remain independent, to obey or to defy authority—is often a function of precise situational arrangements rather than intrinsic characterological traits of the person.

4. Disobedience in the Milgram Experiments

As is apparent in Figure 1, Milgram also observed considerable *disobedience* in many of his studies. In Variation 1, which reported the striking and unexpected 65% obedience rate, one-third of the participants defied authority. Thus, within the same physical situation, there were considerable differences among individuals in their behavior (similar to variations in conformity observed in the Asch paradigm). Clearly the role of the *person,* in addition to the situation, must be acknowledged. There must exist personal factors which, in principle, account for variations in obedience *within the same situation.* Milgram collected personality data on one group of subjects which suggested that persons relatively high in *authoritarianism* were more likely to be obedient. Level of moral development, as conceptualized by Kohlberg, has also been cited as a predictor of obedience. Evidence suggesting cross-cultural differences in obedience is also consistent with a focus upon personal factors. Unfortunately, research on the matter of individual differences has not been programmatic (as was Milgram's extensive series of situational variations) nor has it yielded solid information regarding specific predictors of obedience.

F. Milgram's Theoretical Analysis

Regardless of the specific situation, why did not people simply walk out of Milgram's laboratory once they surmised what was developing in terms of their inner moral conflict? Milgram identified critical factors that, in the aggregate, define a context which is conducive to obedience.

The *socialization* of obedience is of enormous significance. Put simply, from early childhood throughout our lives, we are taught to obey authority and are rewarded for doing so. Obedience becomes an unquestioned operative norm in countless institutions and settings, many of which are endowed with very high cultural status (what Milgram termed "overarching ideology")—e.g., the military, medicine, the law, religion, education, the corporate–industrial world. Successful outcomes in countless circumstances often reflect productive obedience to authority, whether it be a person's grades, health, promotions, medals, military victory, athletic performance, and recognition. We learn to *value* obedience, even if what ensues in its name is unpleasant. We also *trust* the legitimacy of the many authorities in our lives, even if abuses of this trust occasionally occur, for example in the domains of politics, corporate financial institutions, or child-care services. In this context, people become vulnerable to the dictates of *illegitimate* authority because they are habituated to presume legitimacy and are unpracticed in the act of defying authority when this is the appropriate response.

Reflecting the socialization of obedience is our *expectation* that someone will be in charge in whatever setting we encounter. Milgram's participants anticipated that the project would be directed by a knowledgeable authority in the person of a research psychologist. In the mind-set of research subjects, therefore, obedience was set into motion long before they actually arrived, before the experimenter's orders were issued and the learner was crying out in pain. A major lesson of social psychology is the power of preconceptions to influence perception and behavior so as to confirm those prior beliefs. Thus, contributing to the strain involved in Milgram's laboratory was the simple fact that people never expected to face the prospect of defying the experimenter.

1. Binding Factors

Once in the process of obeying an authority, it may be extremely difficult to extricate one's self from that situation. These difficulties may be largely *self-generated,* not a necessary reflection of the authority's use of coercion or threat. An important factor is the individual's prior *commitment* to the authority. The subject, having volunteered to participate, is "locked" into what will transpire:

> The subject fears that if he breaks off, he will appear arrogant, untoward, and rude. Such emotions, although they appear small in scope alongside the violence being done to the learner, nonetheless help bind the subject into obedience. . . . The entire prospect of turning against the experimental authority, with its attendant disruption of a well-defined social situation, is an embarrassment that many people are unable to face up to. (Milgram, 1974, pp. 150–151)

Notice the similarity of Asch's portrait of discomfort in many of his subjects (in the conformity studies) to Milgram's focus on embarrassment as an inducement to obedience:

> "I felt like a silly fool." "A question of being a misfit. They agreed—the idea that they'd think I was queer." "It made me seem weak-eyed or weak-headed, like a black sheep." "I felt conspicuous, going out on a limb, and subjecting myself to criticisms that my perceptions, faculties, were not as acute as they might be." (Asch, 1956, p. 31)

Why should anyone be concerned about being "impolite" to a brutal researcher (or about one's image of the eyes of peers making foolish judgments)? Such preoccupations would seem, on the surface, absurd. However, in the actual context of the situation, these concerns are influential. They *bind* the individual into the hierarchical structure of the relationship with authority. Thus, in addition to the explicit orders from the authority, there are *subtle,* self-imposed elements of many obedience situations that exert a pressure to remain in extraordinarily unpleasant situations.

2. The Psychology of Escalation and Entrapment

In the obedience experiment, the individual is never ordered to inflict, at the start, severe punishment. The question, rather, is the degree to which a person will *gradually escalate* the level of inflicted punishment under orders. Research on a phenomenon known as "the foot in the door effect" indicates that once an individual agrees to a relatively trivial request, he or she is far more likely to agree to a much more demanding request at a later time. As a result of the initial small-scale behavior, a change in self-perception occurs which facilitates subsequent compliance with the larger, more demanding request. Such action is then consistent with the individual's self-perception as "the kind of person who agrees to do such things." The "gradualness" factor is relevant to the generalizations which have been made from Milgram's findings to other contexts where the implications of engaging in immoral actions under authority are not realized at the start, but materialize after an individual becomes enmeshed in a bureaucratic chain of command. *Time,* therefore, is seen to be one of many important variables in obedience to authority. Even within the relatively small-scale confines of a psychological experiment, people can be changed, psychologically, by the situation they encounter. In this context, one reason why people underestimate the observed results in the obedience research is that they fail to appreciate the powerful but subtle self-perception changes that occur over the course of the experiment.

One might argue, however, that despite the transitions noted above, many subjects very obviously desired to leave the experiment. Matters were not, after all, entirely ambiguous in Milgram's study, for how subtle is a situation in which a peer is screaming in (apparently) intolerable pain and pounding on the wall as he demands to be released? This is precisely what subjects encountered in this study. Here, it is important simply to note that subjects were forced, by the design of the study, to invent their own means of defiance. It was, in essence, "messy," with each reservation of the subject met by an insistent researcher who, in his scripted role as a stoic, resolute scientist, never acknowledged the merit of the subject's compassion for the learner. In this context, Ross and Nisbett have noted a basic finding in social psychology, namely that people will often, for a variety of reasons, fail to behave in a manner consistent with their personal attitudes unless there are "channel factors" that facilitate action. Witnessing successful defiance on the part of a peer in Variation 17 would illustrate one such channel factor, and obedience was virtually absent in this condition. (Similarly, Asch found that conformity dropped sharply if one of the group members broke their consensus, even if this "ally" also made an erroneous judgment.)

3. Questions of Responsibility:
   The Agentic Shift

The central concept in Milgram's theoretical model of obedience is that of an *agentic shift,* a cognitive reorientation induced when a person occupies a subordinate role or position in a hierarchical social system or organization. The individual "no longer views himself as responsible for his own actions but defines himself as an instrument for carrying out the wishes of others." Inhibitions against certain acts can be effectively short-circuited. Matters of conscience are no longer the controlling force in a person's behavior. Rather, the individual becomes preoccupied with duty, with the task at hand.

The agentic shift was vividly portrayed in the Iran Contra hearings. When Lt. Col. Oliver North was asked, "Have you wondered why, if it was a good idea, that the President of the United States dismissed you because of it?" North's answer was a powerful documentation of a major lesson of Milgram's obedience experiments:

Let me make one thing very clear, counsel. This lieutenant colonel is not going to challenge

a decision of the Commander in Chief, for whom I still work. And I am proud to work for that Commander in Chief and if the Commander in Chief tells this lieutenant to go stand in the corner and sit on his head, I will do so. And if the Commander in Chief decides to dismiss me from the N.S.C. staff, this lieutenant colonel will proudly salute and say, thank you for the opportunity to have served, and go. And I am not going to criticize his decision no matter how he relieves me, sir. (*New York Times,* Aug. 4, 1987, p. A6)

From the perspective of Milgram's theory, the defense at Nuremberg (and many other places)—"I was following orders"—is a legitimate psychological position. A person accused of war crimes who claims "I was only following orders" may not be simply concocting an alibi or making excuses. Of course, this does not mean that the subordinate is not responsible for the consequences of his actions. Nevertheless, *from the subordinate's point of view,* it may be genuinely believed that one is carrying out orders because of one's role in a chain of command. Regarding the perspective of the person under influence, Milgram pointed to an interesting distinction between conformity and obedience, namely that subjects invariably deny being influenced in a conformity situation, but willingly acknowledge being influenced by an authority. This perception is, in a fundamental sense, very accurate, because a basic theme of this chapter is that people are, in certain circumstances, responsive to powerful social influences from peers and authorities. These influences, which can result in very undesirable acts, are in fact the major causes of their behavior (at least initially, prior to potentially significant changes in the individual which result from his or her behavior).

Oliver North's resolute commitment to authority reminds us of the association of an agentic shift to such ideals as loyalty, duty, honor, and discipline. Obedience can assume moral virtue. Typically, the issue of obedience is of no particular concern when there is a consensus that the authority is *legitimate.* In Milgram's obedience paradigm, however, the experimenter changes over the course of the experiment into an illegitimate authority. An important lesson of this research is that once the individual absolves himself or herself of personal responsibility, it can be extraordinarily difficult to regain a sense of personal autonomy and to act in terms of *one's own definition of the situation*—actions that are of great urgency when those in positions of authority are corrupt or evil.

G. Extensions to Milgram's Observations

A substantial research literature on obedience has evolved, stimulated by Milgram's provocative findings. Obedience to authority, in a variety of research contexts, is a highly reliable phenomenon. In this section, we highlight several illustrative studies by investigators other than Milgram.

How might one's position in a hierarchy determine obedience? The role played by Adolf Eichmann in the Nazi extermination policy is usually interpreted as an illustration of the middle-level bureaucrat, one who does not generate orders or establish policy but who is assigned the role of managing the execution of such directives. An investigation conducted in Australia concerned the degree to which a person would obey orders when not personally required to administer shocks to the learner but instructed, instead, to relay the orders to another person who would actually press the shock levers. Kilham and Mann assigned the true subject to either the transmitter or teacher role. Depending upon this assignment, the other roles (including the learner) were performed by assistants. The results clearly indicated that persons assigned (randomly) to be transmitters were significantly *more obedient* than were teachers. Males were also more obedient than females, regardless of role. Transmitters, when they defied the experimenter, did so at a considerably later phase in the experiment than did teachers.

The investigators relate their findings to the issue of responsibility: "Perhaps it is one of the characteristic effects of the role that with the passage of time, individuals who act as transmitters often begin to respond as machines, dehumanizing themselves and others." Hannah Arendt expressed a similar theme in her influential and highly controversial analysis of Adolf Eichmann. Arendt does not exculpate Eichmann, but she recognizes the plausibility of the transmitter function as a defense:

> In its judgment the court naturally conceded that such a crime could be committed only by a giant bureaucracy using the resources of government. But insofar as it remains a crime—and that, of course, is the premise for a trial—all the cogs in the machinery, no matter how insignificant, are in court forthwith transformed back into perpetrators, that is to say, into human beings. (Arendt, 1963, p. 289)

Thus, transmitters may see themselves as personally exonerated because of their role—they were, after all, not ordering the shocks nor delivering them. Arendt is saying, however, that their role does not provide a moral justification for their actions.

The precise identification and distribution of personal responsibility for destructive actions committed within hierarchically structured social systems can be extremely difficult. Kelman and Hamilton have written an informative analysis of the complexities involved in attributing responsibility to those committing what they term "crimes of obedience" in a variety of bureaucratic contexts. For example, it is not invariably self-evident when an authoritative command is or is not legitimate or moral. They also present evidence documenting clear individual differences among observers of crimes of obedience, for example with respect to the assignment of responsibility to Lt. William Calley for the My Lai Massacre during the Vietnam war. Kelman and Hamilton discuss a number of provocative, highly publicized cases of corruption or malfeasance in the domain of corporate–industrial organizations, including the production of cars with defective gasoline tanks and the marketing of insufficiently tested drugs. Assignment of responsibility in such cases can be extraordinarily difficult because of the lack of intentionality on the part of anyone in the hierarchical structure of the organization. Kelman and Hamilton note the subtle pressures often exerted on subordinates in such organizations to avoid "blowing the whistle," even when there is clear recognition for potentially destructive outcomes unless institutional changes are made. In this context, their analysis of the tragic explosion of the space shuttle "Challenger" is of particular interest. Although the engineers at the space administration clearly knew of the dangers of launching in cold temperatures and explicitly requested that the launch be delayed, they were overruled by higher authorities in the chain of command.

The use of electric shocks as the mode of punishment is a limiting feature of many obedience experiments, raising questions about the generality to other manifestations of obedience. In a study conducted at the University of Utrecht, Netherlands, subjects were instructed to purposely disturb another individual who had come to the laboratory to apply for a job (civil service position). Punishment consisted of administering remarks such as "if you continue like this you will fail" to the "job applicant" (actually an experimenter assistant) over an intercom. Negative remarks, in increasingly harsh form, were to be delivered as the applicant took a multiple-choice test. The applicant (as had Milgram's "learner") expressed increasingly strident protests to the subject's harassment. Resistance to the experimenter's orders was met by a series of prods (e.g., "you have no other choice, you must continue"), identical to those used by Milgram.

A critical feature of this experiment was its lack of ambiguity regarding the fate of the victim. In Milgram's research, it was somewhat unclear regarding how subjects interpreted the pain experienced by the victim, given the experimenter's reassurances regarding "no permanent damage." Before the experiment began, it was arranged that subjects would overhear the experimenter assure the applicant that the experiment was not connected with the job application and would not interfere in any way with the applicant's chances of obtaining the job. Thus, from the subject's perspective, the experimenter was *explicitly dishonest* in telling the applicant precisely the opposite of what he had told the true subject, i.e., that there *would* be adverse consequences to the stress remarks.

Obedience was extremely high. *Ninety-two percent* of the subjects made all of the required stress remarks. In a Milgram-type of control condition in which subjects were free to administer as many in the series of 15 remarks as they wished, no subject administered all of the remarks. Thus, the results in the experimental conditions were clearly attributable to the influence of authority. Two variations, modeled after those of Milgram, showed comparably reduced obedience—16% in "two peers rebel" (as in Variation 17) and 36% in "experimenter absent" (as in Variation 7). Postexperimental interviews suggested that the experimental procedure was convincing (to at least 80% of the participants) and that subjects had considered it irresponsible and unfair to treat the applicant in this manner. Despite these professed attitudes, there was virtually no opposition to the experimenter during the study itself. Unlike the agitation characterizing Milgram's subjects, the predominant mood in this study was that of aloofness. Thus, subjects were extremely obedient in performing actions of which they disapproved and which they knew, in advance, would cause the recipient "real harm" in terms of the loss of a desired job.

What will nurses do when receiving illegal instructions from a physician? Investigations of obedience in a *nonlaboratory setting,* in which the participants would not be aware that they were being studied, would be of considerable value in terms of extending the generalizability of Milgram's findings. A study conducted in a large hospital involved a scenario in which a physician called a nurse and told her to administer a drug, "Astroten," in four capsules to a patient on her ward. This order violated several hospital regulations (e.g., giving a medication order by phone, at twice the stated dosage limit, etc.). Unknown to the nurse receiving the call, an observer (actually a staff psychiatrist) was located on each ward unit and was prepared to terminate the experiment prior to the nurse's entry into the patient's room. This observer would also reveal the study's actual purposes to all participants.

Of 22 nurses receiving the illicit call, 21 (95%) would have in fact delivered the medication as ordered. Although the phone conversations appear to have been very brief with virtually no resistance displayed by the nurses, subsequent interviews indicated a clear acknowledgment that nonemergency telephone orders were inappropriate although not uncommon. When a control group of nurses were given a complete description of this study and asked to write down exactly what their responses would have been, they denied that they would have followed the physician's instructions. Once again, we see that people have, out of context, an idealized, morally correct view of what their behavior should be under circumstances of destructive obedience. *Yet, in their behavior, they fail to act on the basis of these ideals.* Note that the essential dynamics of a hierarchical social structure are captured in the physician–nurse–patient triad, analogous to Milgram's experimenter–teacher–learner structure. A follow up study by Rank and Jacobson varied the situation by having nurses free to discuss their situation with her supervisor and other nurses. Obedience under these circumstances was minimal. This finding reminds us of the important fact that in the obedience experiments, it was always a *solitary participant* who faced the prospect of defying authority. Research by Gamson *et al.* has shown that principled defiance of unjust authority is strongly facilitated by social support. *Groups* of individuals are, under certain conditions, far more able to defy authority than are individuals.

1. Obedience in Resolving an Ethical Dilemma

A study recently conducted by Arthur Brief and his colleagues illustrates the power of authority in a setting radically different from the strong influence contexts discussed in this chapter. Rather than ordering subjects to deliver punishment to a protesting victim, these investigators asked their subjects to play the role of a member of the board of directors of a drug corporation and to make a decision concerning the marketing of an antibiotic drug. The drug in question, on the market for several years and highly profitable, had come under scrutiny by the Food and Drug Administration (FDA) as suspect in terms of dangerous side-effects. Before making their recommendation as to how the company should respond to the proposed FDA ban, subjects were informed of the recommendation that had been given by the chairman of the board.

Subjects were randomly assigned to a condition in which the chairman had indicated a preference for resisting the ban by every legal and political means, or to a condition in which the chairman recommended an immediate recall of the drug in the interest of public health. The results indicated an extremely powerful influence exerted by the chairman's decision, with 76% of the subjects (in both conditions) recommending as their preferred course of action the decision that had been favored by the chairman. Interestingly, this effect was not significant when the chairman's views were not explicit but couched in more indirect terms regarding his philosophical values (humanitarian or self-interest). When his opinions were stated explicitly, however, subjects were strongly influenced to accede to his position. Evidence suggested that the personal view of most subjects was to resist the ban. Thus, the major impact of authority in this study was to induce subjects to resolve the ethical dilemma in the humanitarian direction.

An interesting result bears on the personal values of subjects in terms of humanitarianism or self-interest as measured prior to the actual study. These values were not related to their recommendation if they had been informed of the chairman's preference. Under a control condition, however, in which subjects were not informed of the chairman's view, their personal values did predict their resolution of the ethical dilemma regarding the proposed drug ban.

Thus, in a context of bureaucratic decision making, Brief *et al.* document, once again, the power of authority and how this influence can override matters of individual conscience.

IV. UNDERSTANDING THE HOLOCAUST AND EVIL FROM THE PERSPECTIVE OF THE OBEDIENCE EXPERIMENTS

The extermination of millions of Jewish men, women, and children by the Nazis has presented a monumental challenge for analysis. For decades, academic disciplines in the behavioral and social sciences and humanities have attempted to shed light on the simple question: How could people do this to other people? In this quest for understanding, many observers have interpreted the obedience experiments as having unique explanatory significance. Milgram's experiments have been closely identified with the Holocaust because obedience to authority is invariably cited as a crucial feature of the Holocaust. As noted earlier, Milgram, himself, made explicit reference to the Holocaust in his initial published report.

Although the "final solution of the Jewish problem" clearly reflected a pathological level of anti-Semitism in Hitler and a number of high officials in the Nazi hierarchy, it is generally conceded that the unparalleled mass murder involved in the Holocaust could not have occurred from the actions of these individuals alone. Submission to the dictates of authority was a critical factor. From this perspective, genocide is not convincingly explained simply in terms of vindictiveness, personal prejudice, or mental illness on the part of the perpetrators. One should note that "obedience," as considered here, refers not only to those who actually were engaged directly in the physical extermination of victims but also to millions of other individuals—both military and civilian—who engaged in various actions necessary for the "success" of the Holocaust or who refrained from protesting and intervening on behalf of victims because they feared the consequences from the Nazi authorities.

The Holocaust was thus made possible by the actions (and nonactions) of individuals who, by most standards, would be viewed as decent, good citizens—people who were well educated, who loved their families, who enjoyed the rich artistic and cultural life of Germany. Millions of German men were required to serve in the military and it is virtually certain that most of these persons were "ordinary" by any conventional definition. In a recent study of a German police battalion responsible for the shooting of almost 40,000 Jewish women, men, and children in Poland, Christopher Browning presents a striking portrait of the "normality" of these men. They were not committed Nazis, members of the SS, or racial fanatics, but drafted family men too old for combat service (workers, artisans, salesmen, and clerks). Making explicit reference to Milgram's obedience experiments, Browning observed that "many of Milgram's insights find graphic confirmation in the behavior and testimony of the men of Reserve Police Battalion 101." For example, he points out that "as in Milgram's experiment, without direct surveillance, many policemen did not comply with orders when not directly supervised; they mitigated their behavior when they could do so without personal risk but were unable to refuse participation in the battalion's killing operations openly." (This is in reference to Milgram's Variation 7, "experimenter absent".)

This account of the Holocaust is, of course, diametrically opposed to the bias of human observers to personalize the kinds of behaviors involved in destructive obedience, *to see evil deeds as inevitably a reflection of evil persons*. One motivation for this latter perception is readily apparent: The Holocaust requires that we find persons to blame, to find guilty, to attribute responsibility. But how can these ends be served if we conclude that many, perhaps most, of the actors involved in the Holocaust were in most respects innocent in terms of lacking personal motives and intent in the resultant killing?

Following the trial of Adolf Eichmann in Jerusalem, the philosopher Hannah Arendt wrote what was to be a stunningly controversial analysis of Eichmann (1963). Arendt depicted Eichmann, a high-ranking Nazi who had supervised the deportation of Jews to various concentration camps during the most intense phase of the Holocaust, as displaying the "banality of evil." In line with the premise of this chapter, Arendt claimed that Eichmann was notable in lacking the kind of motives, passions, or hostilities one might have expected, given the consequences of his behavior. Sabini and Silver, two of Milgram's students, agree with Arendt's position:

It is not the angry rioter we must understand but Eichmann, the colorless bureaucrat, replicated two million times in those who assembled

the trains, dispatched the supplies, manufactured the poison gas, filed the paper work, sent out the death notices, guarded the prisoners, pointed left and right, supervised the loading–unloading of the vans, disposed of the ashes, and performed the countless other tasks that also constituted the Holocaust. (1980, p. 330)

Although the comparison is obviously an analogy, the behaviors observed in Milgram's laboratory bear a startling resemblance to the "ingredients" of the Holocaust in the quotation above. Sabini and Silver then extend their reasoning to the Milgram obedience studies:

Subjects in the experiment did continue to shock even though the person they were shocking demanded to be released and withdrew his consent, even though the person they were shocking had ceased responding and might have been unconscious or even dead. Subjects in the experiment were induced to act in ways that we simply would not expect ordinary citizens of no obvious deficit of conscience to act. (p. 333)

In a recent social-psychological essay on the nature of evil, John Darley has emphasized the *dynamics of change* that occur once an individual has become involved in a setting conducive of evil or social destructiveness. He is particularly concerned with social organizations (e.g., military, governmental, and corporate bureaucracies) which may induce destructive actions in the context of powerful hierarchical authority structures. Darley acknowledges a major lesson of the obedience experiments, namely that under conditions of influence, "good" people—people who are not evil in any sense of that term, people without any malicious intent or deficiency of personality—can find themselves engaging in actions of unimaginable destructiveness. But Darley emphasizes that once engaging in these actions, particularly if in a relatively long-term, routine manner (as would be true in the context of a person's work role in an organization), people can change and become truly evil.

The critical factor here is the propensity that people have for constructing rationalizations and justifications for their action. Were subjects to remain in Milgram's laboratory for a protracted period of time, Darley suggests that they would have developed a stronger identification with the value of the project and a tendency to derogate the intelligence of the learner. A considerable amount of research in the areas of self-serving biases and cognitive dissonance theory supports this line of reasoning. Darley observes that "one can morally justify harmdoing, find euphemistic labels for the action, minimize the harmful consequences, and dehumanize and blame the victim. There are also the usual possibilities of displacing responsibility for the detrimental actions elsewhere in the system. These are the family of processes that seem to me to be involved in creating individuals who willingly do evil." Thus, a potentially crucial consequence of obedience to illegitimate authority is that a person may, in time, develop attitudes and emotions that are consistent with their actions. At this point, the individual is significantly changed, psychologically. Thus, it is not sufficient to simply observe that "good" people may behave badly under the pressures of conformity or authority. More critically, people may be profoundly altered by their exposure to such influence.

In conclusion, the phenomena of conformity and obedience reflect the extraordinary degree to which people are responsive to influences from other people. If we have portrayed this influence in a highly negative light, it is because the consequences of conformity and obedience are often undesirable and occasionally devastating. Although the research reviewed in this article is ample testimony for this conclusion, the possibilities of desirable, pro-social behaviors occurring as a result of conformity and obedience must not be overlooked. Milgram himself was explicit in investing the concept of obedience with moral neutrality, arguing that obedience could be life enhancing as well as destructive. However, the most appropriate conclusion for this article is seen in John Darley's recent analysis of the social organization of evil, where once again, we are reminded of the power of situations to override what we all too casually presume to be the critical determining forces in our behavior:

Evildoing is not confined to individuals who are evil at the time of committing the act. Each of us has the capacity to do evil actions if our surroundings press us to do so. The wonderfulness of our upbringings and the goodness of our personalities do not protect us from doing so. (Darley, 1992, p. 217)

Bibliography

Arendt, H. (1963). "Eichmann in Jerusalem: A Report on the Banality of Evil." Viking Press, New York.

Asch, S. E. (1956). Studies of independence and conformity: A minority of one against a unanimous majority. *Psychol. Monogr.* **70** (9, Whole No. 416).

Baumrind, D. (1964). Some thoughts on ethics of research: After reading Milgram's "behavioral study of obedience." *Am. Psychol.* **19**, 421–423.

Blanchard, F. A., Lilly, T., and Vaughn, L. A. (1991). Reducing the expression of racial prejudice. *Psychol. Sci.* **2**, 101–105.

Brief, A. P., Dukerich, J. M., and Doran, L. I. (1991). Resolving ethical dilemmas in management: Experimental investigations of values, accountability, and choice. *J. Appl. Soc. Psychol.* **21**, 380–396.

Browning, C. R. (1991). "Ordinary Men: Reserve Police Battalion 101 and the Final Solution in Poland." Harper Collins, New York.

Darley, J. M. (1992). Social organization for the production of evil. *Psychol. Inquiry* **3**, 199–218.

Evans, R. I. (1980). "The Making of Social Psychology: Discussions with Creative Contributors." Gardner, New York.

Gilbert, S. J. (1981). Another look at the Milgram obedience studies: The role of the gradated series of shocks. *Pers. Soc. Psychol. Bull.* **7**, 690–695.

Hofling, C. K., Brotzman, E., Dalrymple, S., Graves, N., and Pierce, C. (1966). An experimental study of nurse–physician relations. *J. Nervous Mental Dis.* **143**, 171–180.

Kelman, H. C., and Hamilton, V. L. (1989). "Crimes of Obedience: Toward a Social Psychology of Authority and Responsibility." Yale University Press, New Haven.

Kilham, W., and Mann, L. (1974). Level of destructive obedience as a function of transmitter and executant roles in the Milgram obedience paradigm. *J. Pers. Soc. Psychol.* **29**, 696–702.

Meeus, W. H. J., and Raaijmakers, Q. A. W. (1986). Administrative obedience: Carrying out orders to use psychological-administrative violence. *Eur. J. Soc. Psychol.* **16**, 311–324.

Milgram, S. (1963). Behavioral study of obedience. *J. Abnormal Soc. Psychol.* **67**, 371–378.

Milgram, S. (1964). Issues in the study of obedience: A reply to Baumrind. *Am. Psychol.* **19**, 848–852.

Milgram, S. (1974). "Obedience to Authority: An Experimental View." Harper and Row, New York.

Miller, A. G. (1986). "The Obedience Experiments: A Case Study of Controversy in Social Science." Praeger, New York.

Rank, S. G., and Jacobson, C. K. (1977). Hospital nurses' compliance with medication overdose orders: A failure to replicate. *J. Health Soc. Behav.* **18**, 188–193.

Raven, B. H., and Rubin, J. Z. (1983). "Social Psychology." Wiley, New York.

Ross, L., Bierbrauer, G., and Hoffman, S. (1976). The role of attribution processes in conformity and dissent: Revisiting the Asch situation. *Am. Psychol.* **31**, 148–157.

Ross, L., and Nisbett, R. E. (1991). "The Person and the Situation: Perspectives of Social Psychology." McGraw-Hill, New York.

Sabini, J. (1992). "Social Psychology." Norton, New York.

Sabini, J., and Silver, M. (1980). Destroying the innocent with a clear conscience: A sociopsychology of the Holocaust. In "Survivors, Victims, and Perpetrators: Essays on the Nazi Holocaust." (J. E. Dimsdale, Ed.), Hemisphere, New York.

Sherif, M. (1936). "The Psychology of Social Norms." Harper and Row, New York.

OBJECT RELATIONS THEORY

N. Gregory Hamilton
Oregon Health Sciences University

Glossary

Contain To internalize an emotional communication from another person, transform it, give it meaning, and return it to that person.

Countertransference The therapist's emotional response to a patient.

Ego A set of mental functions including differentiation, integration, balancing, and organizing in the realms of perception, memory, cognition, emotions, actions, and the demands of conscience.

Empathy (1) The mental act of looking inward as a method of understanding the emotions of another person, or (2) the communication of that emotional understanding back to the other person.

Internal object A conscious or unconscious fantasy or memory which is experienced as non-self and is invested with affect.

Object A person, place, thing, idea, fantasy, or memory invested with affect.

Object relations unit A self-image and internal object associated with an affect and an ego state.

Projective identification The attribution of an aspect of the self to an object with a simultaneous, partial, conscious, or unconscious awareness that the projected aspect pertains to the self, sometimes accompanied by an interpersonal attempt to make the object respond like the projected aspect of the self.

Self A conscious or unconscious mental representation which pertains to one's own person.

Self-object A self-image and internal or external object for which the boundary is not clear.

Selfobject An external object needed to sustain self-esteem or self-cohesion.

Splitting The active keeping apart of contradictory mental experience.

Transitional object Something which is neither self nor object, yet has the qualities of both.

OBJECT RELATIONS THEORY is a set of clinical concepts concerning how people internalize and externalize relationships. This psychodynamic theory holds that unconscious internal fantasies are equal in importance to external, social relationships. Many theorists consider the concepts of self, object, ego, and affect–sensation as inextricably intertwined object relations units. This notion, along with the mechanisms of splitting, projective identification, containment, and empathy, are becoming increasingly influential, not only in the realm of psychotherapy, but throughout the mental health professions.

I. INTRODUCTION

Personal relationships become a part of each individual and the history of those relationships influences the course of all future dealings with other people. Psychologically, human beings come to exist within and are thus limited, defined, and enriched by a personal context, even while they contribute to and change that context. This is the central theme of object relations theory.

Since this theory attends to both conscious and unconscious internal life, to the internal world as well as to external relationships, it is not merely a social theory. Neither do modern object relations understandings ignore or discount unfolding biologic processes, including sexual and aggressive impulses and needs, along with sensations such as hunger. The neurophysiologic organizing capabilities, which we call ego functions, are acknowledged as important. The psychological significance of these more mechanical processes, however, is seen as their role in establishing, channeling, and maintaining relationships.

II. SELF, OBJECT, EGO, AND OBJECT RELATIONS UNITS

In infancy, relationships seem fairly rudimentary and easily fractured into extreme, polar opposite experiences of the self and others. Various authors dispute whether these divided object relations come first in development or are breakdown products which occur when deprivation overcomes an original separate, but related, state. Most authorities agree, however, that at some point in childhood there is a reliance on primitive, dichotomized, and poorly integrated self-images and object-images. Through neurophysiologic ego development and the internalization of good enough relationships, these extreme, polarized experiences become modified and shaped into a cohesive sense of self in relation to others.

Because conscious and unconscious subjective experience is at times elusive and has subtle nuances, terminology must be attended to from the beginning. For Freud, the word "object" denoted a person, place, thing, idea, fantasy, or memory invested with emotion. Some clinicians feel that "object" is too impersonal. They would prefer the term "person." Since internal fantasies and external non-persons can be in meaningful relation to the self, however, and "person" denotes only an external human being, this word has its drawbacks, too. "Other" is a bit better. Within its meaning, other implies the existence of something which is non-other, that is, the self. Therefore, other suggests an inherent relationship. Although Freud originally used the word object at the turn of the 19th to 20th century in an attempt to be scientific and "objective," the term as used in psychoanalytic thinking has evolved into something with subjective meaning. An object is not an external thing observed with emotional detachment. It is not impersonal. On the contrary, it is something invested with emotional

meaning. In this chapter, object will be retained, because it is so widely used, despite its everyday meaning being less personal than its psychological meaning. Other will be considered synonymous with object.

Different theorists, in their attempts to understand object relations better, have also used the words "self" and "ego" in a variety of ways. Ego has been defined as an abstraction denoting the functions of differentiation, integration, balancing, and organizing in the areas of perception, memory, cognition, emotions, actions, and the demands of conscience. Self has been referred to as a set of internal representations which pertain to one's own person rather than to an object. Self, here, is an internal sense, not an agency. One shortcoming of this terminology is that it does not accurately describe the reflexive sense one has when looking inward or self-observing. This shortcoming can be accepted temporarily with the acknowledgment that it provides a false clarity, like that provided in physics by considering a particle in the isolation of a vacuum.

"The ego observes the self" does not accurately describe the experience of self-observation. The difficulty with a sharp distinction between self and ego, however, goes beyond this inaccuracy of subjective connotation. Such a terminological scission is also objectively inaccurate. While observing patients, clinicians have learned that self-images are so intimately connected with the state of ego functioning that they almost seem to be the same thing. The grandiose self-image, for example, is associated with ego functioning which is inspired, unmodulated, creative, and action oriented and is not thoughtful, modulated, perceptually accurate, or delayed in action. The activation of these later ego functions, thoughtfulness, modulation, perceptual accuracy, and postponement of action, invariably results in replacement of the grandiose self-image with a more tempered self-experience. On the other hand, a sudden change of self-image from grandiose to devalued, for instance, results in loss of the ego functions of activity and self-esteem maintenance. If a patient perceives himself or herself as incompetent, then the ego functioning of that person actually becomes less functionally competent. Residual capabilities continue to exist, but they are out of gear, so to speak. This intimate connection between ego functioning and self-experience can be observed introspectively and objectively.

Mr. A., a 35-year-old financial adviser, had extreme shifts in mood. Lithium carbonate helped stabilize these swings. When he stopped taking lithium, his mood would first become slightly elevated. His self-image became competent, insightful, certain, superior, and charming. His image of others was diminished. His clients seemed to him to be dependent, needing advice, lacking insight, and deficient in confidence. His marriage was stressed by his seeing his wife in the same diminished light as his clients. During such episodes, his ego state was overly active, intellectually astute, incisive, and outgoing. Needless to say, his sales of advice was very good during such times. His self-image and ego state were concordant. His self-image was a bit grand and his ego functioning was expansive.

He often made brilliant investments for himself during hypomanic episodes, but would sometimes get overextended. When his wife and colleagues complained enough, he would resume taking his medication. During long periods of stable mood, his self-image and ego functioning became more modulated, as did his views of others.

When he inadvertently learned that his wife had had several affairs, one with a good friend of his, he was crushed. He experienced himself as betrayed, helpless, alone, and inferior. As his self-experience shifted, so did his ego functioning. He lacked confidence and competence. He was indecisive and could not take action to the point where he would not return calls from clients or follow through on previous investment decisions. He wanted to die, but could not formulate a plan by which to kill himself. He became overly dependent on the advice of friends and the help of his psychiatrist. Fortunately, they were able to help him sustain his self-esteem until he recovered his more modulated ego functioning.

Otto Kernberg has dealt with this overlap and apparent interchangeability of ego function and self-image by suggesting that the word ego have both meanings, as Freud did. Heinz Kohut went the other direction by dropping the word ego as impersonal and mechanistic and retaining the word self to describe all the agencies and self-images of the mind. Other theorists retain both the words ego and self as distinguishable abstractions, with the added acknowledgment that they are intimately related and become more so with maturity. This terminological overlap or blurriness may be an accurate reflection of the subject studied rather than a theoretical shortcoming.

One way to use separate words, like self, object, and ego, and still recognize their relatedness, and to some degree overlap, is to employ the concept of object relations units. To some authors, these consist of a self-image and an object-image connected by a drive and its corresponding affect. It can be useful to add the state of ego functioning as an aspect of the object relations unit. In this system, self, object, and ego are all related to one another via the affects and sensations.

Throughout the object relations literature, the all-good and all-bad object relations units have been emphasized, stemming from Melanie Klein's description of the good breast and bad breast and from widespread interest in borderline disorders where all-good and all-bad units are so prominent. With increasing interest in narcissistic issues, the grandiose-devalued object relations unit deserves more emphasis.

As an example of the grandiose-devalued unit, the inflated self-image is related to a devalued object by contempt, triumph, or overexcitment. The ego functioning is creative, fanciful, active, and integrating at the expense of accurate perception, thoughtfulness, modulation, and differentiation. The grandiose self is always related to the devalued self which is split off, unintegrated, and projected onto the object-image. When the projection breaks down, the devalued self becomes dominant and is related to the devaluing object by the affect of shame. The ego functioning then becomes inactive, brooding, narrowly focused on perceived faults of the self, again at the expense of accurate perception of the external world, modulation, and differentiation, and also at the expense of creative fancifulness and integration.

This pair of object relations units for Mr. A. in the above example can be outlined as shown in Table I(a,b).

Because of the close connection between ego function and self–other relations, psychological growth involves not only the modulation of extreme self–other experiences, but also the actualization of residual ego capacities. It is the activation of these capabilities or aspects of ego functioning and the integration of them into the self-image, which are variously called the achievement of identity, an overarching self, or a cohesive self.

Not only are self and ego related concepts, so are self and object. Self-images and object-images are

TABLE I (a)
Grandiose Object Relations Unit

Grandiose self-image	+	Affect–sensation	+	Devalued object-image
Grand entrepreneur		Triumphant–exhilaration		Inferior competitors
Charming salesman		Amused–warmth		Admiring client
Seductive lover		Love–arousal		Responsive wife
Powerful manipulator		Contempt–cold		Innocent gull
Privileged person		Contentment–powerful		Appeasing public
		+		
		Ego functioning		
		Astute		
		Creative–outgoing–potent		
		Shrewd		
		Commanding		

TABLE I (b)
Devalued Object Relations Unit

Devalued self-image	+	Affect–sensation	+	Idealized object-image
Betrayed lover		Dejection–impotence		Seductive wife
Cuckold		Humiliation–weakness		Wife's lovers
Incompetent person		Self-doubt–shaky		Superior competitors
Business failure		Shame–empty		Disappointed clients
Suicidal patient		Hopeless–immobile		Competent psychiatrist
		+		
		Ego functioning		
		Impotent		
		Inactive		
		Indecisive		
		Unproductive		
		Brooding		

not always entirely distinguishable. There are a host of words to describe the process of boundary blurring or exchange. Introjection, identification, projection, projective identification, merger, fusion, empathy, and relatedness all describe slightly different nuances of self–other exchange or sharing. There are also words to describe different combinations of self and object, such as transitional object, selfobject, selfobject, and intersubjectivity. As with the overlap of self and ego, these complications may accurately describe the haziness of the subject studied.

III. SPLITTING

Whether it is inherent in early ego functioning or a reaction to trauma and neglect, splitting becomes a way of protecting and maintaining preferred object relations units.

Splitting is the active keeping apart of contradictory mental contents and states. For example,

Ms. B., a 32-year-old mother of three with a history of intense unstable relationships and episodic drug abuse, came to her first appointment with the complaint that her previous psychiatrist was cold and uncaring. She claimed he did not understand her, but she could tell right away that her new psychiatrist, a woman, was more caring. She seemed warmer and more empathic. Two weeks later, when the new psychiatrist would not prescribe a sedative to quell the patient's tirades at her children, but suggested she take a parenting class while she worked in therapy to better understand her frustration and feelings of help-lessness, the patient decided her new psychiatrist was rigid and controlling. She abruptly left treatment.

Like all human beings, both the psychiatrists probably had the capacity to be warm, caring, and empathic to varying degrees and also to be cool, analytic, and firm. The patient, however, seemed to have such a need for an omnipotently gratifying, caring relationship that she exaggerated. She split her experience into two separate object relations unit, which can be outlined as shown in Table II(a,b).

In practice, splitting is a term reserved for this kind of all-good, all-bad thinking, in which the self-image and object-image are both unwanted. Although it may be a related mental mechanism, idealization and devaluing usually separate the wanted and unwanted aspects of self- and object-images. Because there is a bit greater self- and object-differentiation, it is called by its own name, idealizing and devaluing, rather than called splitting, al-

though there is an active keeping apart of contradictory mental contents in both cases.

IV. PROJECTIVE IDENTIFICATION AND CONTAINMENT

Projective identification is a mental process by which splitting is both created and eventually overcome. It is defined as the attribution of an aspect of the self to an internal or external object and the simultaneous identification with the projected aspect. There is often an attempt to control or alter the projected quality in the other. These efforts can actually elicit a corresponding affect and self-image in another person. Thus, there is both an intrapsychic and an interpersonal aspect to projective identification. As an example,

Psychiatry residents frequently describe a particular kind of emergency room patient who

TABLE II (a)
Gratifying Object Relations Unit

Self-image	+	Affect–sensation	+	Object-image
Beloved child		Love–warmth		Caring mother
Understood patient		Contentment–satiated		Empathic doctor
Admired mother		Pride–full		Admiring children
		+		
		Ego functioning		
		Passively receptive		
		Excessively focused on good qualities		
		Ignoring unwanted qualities		
		Accurate memory sacrificed to omnipotent fantasy		

TABLE II (b)
Rejecting Object Relations Unit

Self-image	+	Affect–sensation	+	Object-image
Rejected, needy child		Dejection–cold		Rigid mother
Misunderstood patient		Indignant–hunger		Unempathic psychiatrist
Betrayed mother		Furious–blind rage		Bad, ungrateful children
		+		
		Ego functioning		
		Action oriented, fight–flight		
		Excessively focused on bad qualities		
		Ignoring wanted qualities		
		Accurate memory sacrificed to helpless fantasy		

comes in the middle of the night. The patient has a pressing need. It cannot wait until morning, the patient says. The doctor offers a suggestion, but the patient claims that the last time they tried such an approach an even greater calamity resulted. Yet, the problem must be taken care of immediately. The doctor makes suggestions, offers sympathy, asks the patient what he or she thinks is best, and interprets gently. Nothing helps. Soon, the resident feels helpless and angry. The doctor is stymied and wants to give up, but somehow cannot disengage.

Experienced clinicians have hypothesized that such patients behave in such a way as to elicit their own unwanted feelings of helpless rage in the doctor. This way of communicating so that the other not only perceives the subject's emotions, but actually experiences them, is projective identification. This is a difficult concept to use clinically, because it invites the clinician to attribute their own unwanted feelings to the patient. If the doctor is tired and irritable with a troubled patient, it does not always imply that the doctor's irritability derives from the patient's projective identification, but sometimes it does. The concept of projective identification is most useful as a way of considering what possibly may be taking place, rather than as a way of establishing fact.

People can use projective identification to divide or split both their internal world and their external relationships. This is most easily observed in inpatient settings.

Ms. C. was a 25-year-old woman with anorexia nervosa. She perceived two staff members on the evening shift as enlightened and understanding. She attributed to them all her internal fantasies of an omniscient and omnipotent, totally gratifying object. By treating the staff members almost as if they were goddesses, she elicited their feelings of specialness. They particularly enjoyed working with this interesting patient.

Ms. C. was equally convinced that two staff members on the day shift were rigid, unempathic, and controlling. She would not speak with them, would not cooperate with the group when they were near, and refused to follow ward routines during the day. This nurse and social worker gradually came to see the patient as manipulative, destructive, and spoiled.

The evening shift began to argue with the day shift about the patient's care. Evening shift staff members thought if the day staff were more understanding, the patient would not have to reject their food. The day shift members thought if the evening staff were to stick with the normal ward structure, the patient would stop using her eating disorder to manipulate the staff and would eat or not eat according to what her body required.

In conference with a consultant, members of the two shifts were able to hypothesize that through projective identification, the patient recreated her split internal object world outside herself. While the day shift personnel acknowledged that they were a bit more task oriented and the evening shift acknowledged that they were a bit more interested in understanding feelings than focusing on structure and tasks, neither group of people felt as extreme or polarized when Ms. C. was not involved. By projecting her harsh aspects into one group of people and her understanding, warm aspects into the other, the patient attempted to keep these contradictory experiences apart from one another and outside herself. When the clinicians were arguing, the patient always seemed serene.

In this example, projective identification was used to transform internal splitting into an interpersonal split. While projective identification is most often used to understand unwanted or negative feelings, in this example the patient also attributed special, good qualities to the evening staff members.

Wilfred Bion thought projective identification was not only a way of dividing experience, but also created an avenue for putting it back together. He thought that infants elicit their intolerable affects in their parents, who internalize the projections, transform them, psychologically metabolize them by giving them meaning, and return them to the infant in the form of holding or an understanding communication or gesture. He called this process containment. Not only is the transformed and modulated projection reintrojected by the infant, but the containment process itself is taken in and eventually becomes an ability of the child itself.

Some psychiatry residents have found that when they feel helplessly rageful with the kinds of patients described above, if they try to tolerate their overwhelming feelings and work to understand how the patient must be feeling, then let the patient know that they have some sense of how they must be feeling, the hopeless situation will soon be on its way to resolution. The doctor's containing function helps such patients mobilize their own resources.

Healthy groups can also perform a containing function for patients.

When the hospital staff members realized how their anorexic patient must feel torn between longings to be close and understood and fears of intrusive control, they were slowly able to resolve their own differences through open discussion. Just as the patient seemed to have projected her divided internal world into the staff members, she now seemed to introject or to reinternalize their more modulated functioning and to grow from the experience.

The containing function of the object is one influence which modifies object relations units in a more integrated direction. Another is a shift in ego functioning. As children mature neurophysiologically, their capacity to hold opposites in mind at the same time, to compare and contrast, and to modulate affect improves. Thus, some children with fortunate neurophysiologic endowment are able to grow psychologically despite a relative paucity of modulation and containment from the adults around them. With adults, too, effort and time to reflect can help them put extreme self and object experiences in perspective.

V. WHOLE OBJECT RELATIONS

As children mature, as their ego functioning becomes more complex, as they accrue benign and helpful experiences in the face of frustration or loss, their way of experiencing themselves in relation to others seems to become less extreme. The parent who frustrates them, who makes them wait for or work for something, is recognized as the same parent who gratifies and cares for them. Their psychological world becomes less split into all-good and all-bad, separate experiences. This is whole object relations.

With the loss of villains and monsters, the magic of idealization and fantasies of perfect love also dissipate. Most healthy adults retain a nostalgic longing for the clarity of a divided world. Within everyone, there seems to remain a capacity to let go of well-integrated, whole object relations and to call up the primitive experiences of split object relations, of total love and total hate. This ability allows for the passion of romantic infatuation and of battle. It is a dangerous ability to return to former functioning, which is both creative and destructive. The ability of the individual to determine when it is safe or necessary to relinquish whole object relations and integrated ego functioning temporarily is a sign of maturity, just as is the ability to retain whole object functioning in the face of adversity.

VI. TRANSITIONAL OBJECTS AND THE HOLDING ENVIRONMENT

Children not only develop increasingly clear and integrated self- and object-images, they create transitional objects. D. W. Winnicott used this term to describe something which is both self and object and yet neither. Often a blanket, stuffed animal, or similar soft object is invested with special meaning and represents or becomes the transitional object. There seems to be an unspoken agreement between parent and child that no one will ask the question, "Was this given to me or did I create it?" Transitional objects are not given up; they slowly lose meaning. Many authors believe that artistic, scientific, and spiritual interests are the adult equivalent of transitional experiences.

Originally, as Winnicott described it, transitional phenomena arise within the context of the holding environment and good enough parenting. After a search for what are the best parenting practices, students of child-rearing learned that this perfectionistic approach was counterproductive. What is needed for children is not perfectionistic parenting, but good enough parenting, given the constitutional requirements of a particular infant. This concept includes the provision of a holding environment whereby optimal parent–child distance sufficiently meets the child's security needs while also allowing for growing autonomy. The holding environment is related to the containing function of the parent, although Winnicott's concept of holding has more to do with actual physical closeness and distance and Bion's concept of containing has more to do with the intrapsychic experiences of parent and child.

VII. EMPATHY

The provision of a good enough holding environment and of containment requires an empathic capacity to sense what the child must be experiencing and needing. Empathy has been studied and discussed from many vantage points. Most current discussion in object relations and self-psychology literature emphasizes the receptive quality of empathy—that is, looking inward to understand another person emotionally. There is also an expressive quality, letting the other person know that their feeling is understood.

Most authors agree that empathic understanding by another person allows children to first use words for feelings. It also helps them feel valuable and valid and eventually cohesive. The importance of empathy as a growth-promoting factor in child development and psychotherapy forms the basis of Kohut's self-psychology, which is related to object relations theory in that both theories emphasize the internalization of relationships as important. Self-psychology, however, does not emphasize how relationships can be externalized, as does object relations theory.

Some authors distinguish between empathy and projective identification. These concepts seem to be related, but not identical. One could consider empathy the vehicle for projective identification, or alternately, projective identification the mechanism for empathic understanding. They seem similar in that they have to do with how emotions cross personal boundaries, but exactly how is not known. The behavioral and neurophysiologic correlates of empathy and projective identification have not been studied. Perhaps such studies would help elucidate these concepts. Perhaps such attempts to objectify complex intrapsychic and interpersonal experiences, however, would only make them disappear from the field of study. [See EMPATHY.]

VIII. TRANSFERENCE AND COUNTERTRANSFERENCE

Transference is another concept dealing with crossing interpersonal boundaries. Freud originally discovered that patients experienced their psychoanalyst as they experienced people earlier in life. That is, they transferred old object-images onto current perceptual images. Since Freud's viewpoint was that of a neutral, outside observer looking into the mind of the patient, he saw this as a transfer of images and energy within the mind of the patient. From a more relationship-oriented viewpoint, transference could also be considered a projection of an internal object-image onto an external object, the therapist. Because it is suspected that object-images always exist in the context of internal relationships, it can be hypothesized that transferences are accompanied by associated self-images and affects, as well as a characteristic state of ego functioning. Transference is therefore related to projective identification with the emphasis on object-images.

Since object relations theory considers relationships in their context, one of the contributions from this field has been the emphasis of countertransference, not just transference. Countertransference has been considered both an impediment and a tool in conducting psychotherapy. Freud originally described countertransference as the analyst's unresolved, unconscious, infantile emotional reaction to the patient's transference. As such, it was an impediment, which the therapist needed to overcome in his or her own personal analysis. More recently, however, this narrow definition of countertransference has been replaced by a broader definition. All the therapist's emotional reactions to the patient, including empathic understanding and experience of projective identifications, are now considered under the rubric of countertransference. This broader definition allows the therapist to use emotional reactions as a tool for more deeply understanding the patient. For example,

Mr. D., a 35-year-old man with obsessive compulsive disorder, who had significantly, but partially benefitted from serotonergic medication, told his psychotherapist how his obsessive self-doubt had interfered with all treatment efforts. It was now interfering with his persisting with the therapy and even with his job. He felt stuck. This had been going on his whole life.

The psychiatrist felt called upon to do something, but felt overwhelmed and stuck, too. He used his countertransference to convey in his words and facial expression how he understood the patient's feeling of being stuck. The patient seemed to relax when he felt understood. "When I was a boy," he said, "neither my mother nor father seemed to have time to notice how I felt, no less to sit there and feel stuck right along with me. I appreciate your doing that whether the therapy works or not."

In this example, the psychiatrist actually thought that the new experience of having someone tolerate his feelings of being stymied and with no place to go would provide a new emotional experience for the patient. Thus, his countertransference feeling of being stalemated became the key to his therapeutic technique.

IX. CHILD DEVELOPMENT

The central concepts of object relations theory described in the above paragraphs derived from clinicians listening to patients talk about themselves and from the introspection of theorists, both alone and in their own analyses or therapies. It has also been enriched by the observation of children alone and interacting with their parents. Kernberg, for instance, developed his concepts of development by observing borderline patients in psychotherapy and hospital treatment. He noticed that they seemed to progress from splitting and projective identification through integration and differentiation to the ability to tolerate internal conflict.

His conclusions must have also been influenced by his own self-observation in his own analyses, although he did not write about this contribution to his theories, keeping it appropriately private. It was later that he noticed a striking correspondence between his clinical observation of how patients grow and develop and Mahler's studies of the separation–individuation of infants in relation to their parents. Mahler's direct observation of children led Kernberg to alter the time frame of his clinical developmental theory, although it did not fundamentally change the sequencing of psychological processes as observed in psychoanalysis and psychotherapy. Similarly, self-psychology arose from Kohut's psychoanalytic observations and were only later put together with early infant studies by Daniel Stern and others.

Mahler's description of autism, symbiosis, separation–individuation, and developing whole object relations and Stern's delineation of emergent self, core self, subjective self, and verbal self are the two sets of developmental studies which have been most influential on American object relations theory. Although most clinicians have dropped Mahler's autistic phase, largely based on Stern's evidence, the clinical concepts do not rise and fall on developmental data alone. These two domains of study can be mutually enriching, but are not entirely compatible. Adult clinical studies rely on subjective experience and report in a therapy context and child studies rely on the empathic observation of parent and child dyads without the benefit of subjective report.

Object relations theories and self-psychology have both tended to look too exclusively at the relationship line of development and to ignore the unfolding of other lines of ego development such as cognitive, perceptual, and motor development. They have also overemphasized particular aspects of relationships, such as separation–individuation or development of a cohesive sense of self, to the exclusion of other important aspects of relationships, such as the development of a sense of conscience and duty or loyalty, or sense of belonging in a group or relating to institutions as well as to individuals. Object relations theorists, like most developmental theorists, overemphasize the continuity of development to the exclusion of attending to discontinuities in development. This emphasis seems particularly odd when clinical work so obviously deals with discontinuities, with sudden shifts of subject matter, of self-experience, and of transferential attitude to the therapist. Clinically, some memories and object relations units seem more like living fossils embedded in complex systems of relatedness than orderly unfolding phases of development to which the patient returns. The relationship between clinical observation, developmental observation, and clinical theory remains a wide-open area for future advances.

X. OBJECT RELATIONS PSYCHOTHERAPY

Object relations theory derived from observations made in the dynamic psychotherapy of severe disorders. As these ideas are becoming more widespread, they are influencing the practice of psychotherapy in general. This set of ideas has implications both for the psychological context of treatment and for specific interventions. [See PSYCHOTHERAPY.]

The emotional position of the therapist was once thought to be neutral and objective. Now, a whole new set of therapeutic stances are available—containing, providing a holding environment, empathic immersion in the patient's subjective experience, intersubjectivity. All these terms are much more experience-near and interactive than the old concept of the analyst observing the patient's unconscious through the lens of free association.

Providing a containing environment can be warm and empathic or cool and distant depending on the patient's needs. For example,

Mr. E. was a 33-year-old man whose daughter had sustained a severe head injury in an automobile accident. His wife, who was somewhat impulsive and entitled in her approach to life, had taken a 2-month trip to Europe with her mother to recuperate from the strain of caring for the daughter. Since her return, she would not help much with their daughter or their son. She rationalized that she needed to take care of herself. Mr. E. was attempting to provide for the family in a demanding profession, care for the children after work, and be supportive to his wife. As he recounted the facts, he seemed tense, anxious, and guarded, but he did not allude to his own emotions.

Hearing this story, the therapist felt a profound sadness on behalf of his patient, something which the patient did not show. He wondered if this dutiful man allowed the people around him to have his emotions for him—his wife, his children, his therapist. Perhaps Mr. E. feared he would be overwhelmed by grief and managed it through projective identification. Perhaps no one had ever valued him enough to hear his feelings, so he did not have words for emotions. "This must be very hard for you," the therapist said in a tone of voice which conveyed sadness or compassion.

"Yes, it is," Mr. B. acknowledged and seemed to relax a bit.

In this example, the therapist used his own countertransference grief to empathically understand his patient. He modulated the emotion and returned it to the patient in a simple comment. It was his tone of voice, suggesting to the patient that this grief was both meaningful and sustainable, which carried most of the message. This emotionally close form of containment eventually provided a context in which the patient could tolerate his own feelings, not just sadness, but the whole range, including anger, indignation, pride, and longing, particularly longing to run away.

Sometimes containing or providing a holding environment, however, requires more emotional distance. For example,

Ms. F. was a 43-year-old woman who came from a chaotic background with overcrowding in the home, sexual overstimulation, and violence. Since her mother had frequently beaten her, she had turned throughout her life to men for validation and protection. Her personal beauty and striking figure assured her at least the passing interest of numerous men. She had had multiple relationships and frequent drug and alcohol abuse. In a previous drug treatment program, she had had an affair with her counselor, which ended in her feeling both exploited and guilty. Her intelligence and work ethic were her greatest strengths and had allowed her a moderate degree of professional success, of which she was very proud.

Her story of passion and lust and betrayal aroused corresponding feelings in the doctor. If he empathized with her or even commented on her wishes for closeness and understanding, she became anxious and recounted previous seductions and rejections. In this case, the psychiatrist provided containment by adopting and sustaining an attitude of interested neutrality. Warmth and empathy would have been experienced by the patient as erotic or corrupt. Both her work life and relationships seemed to stabilize with this approach.

Providing a containing environment not only establishes a context for technical intervention, it actually performs an integrative function which helps patients overcome their need to rely so extensively on splitting and projective identification. By introjecting Mr. E.'s split off grief and self-image as overwhelmed, combining it with his own self-image as able to endure grief, and returning it to the patient in a comment touched with emotion, the therapist performed an integrative function for the patient, which the patient seemed to reinternalize. Thus, splitting and projective identification were modulated. With Ms. F., her passionate and compelling tales seemed to be a projective mechanism for externalizing sexually exploitive self- and object-images in an attempt to reenact or flee from the reenactment of her life story once again. By containing her projected affects and transforming them to clinical interest, the therapist performed an integrative function for the patient.

Within the context of containment, object relations psychotherapies still rely on the established technical interventions clarification, confrontation, and interpretation, as well as structuring and limit setting. Additionally, since this set of ideas pays careful attention to self–other boundaries, boundary clarification as a method of dealing with projective identification and juxtaposition of object relations units as a method of dealing with splitting have evolved. For example,

When Ms. F. became so anxious and hopeless about the therapy that her doctor began to worry about the outcome, he calmed himself, thought about similar cases which had improved, and said, "Sometimes you assume that I am as hopeless about the treatment as you are."

This simple statement clarified a boundary between the therapist and patient without abandoning her. It clearly implied that the patient's feelings were not the psychiatrist's feelings, yet he understood the hopelessness she felt. Such an intervention can interrupt unproductive projective identification and help the patient engage cognitive ego functions, which differentiate self from other and emotion from perception.

Ms. F.'s treatment also provided an example of juxtaposing split object relations units.

Some sessions, she would idealize her therapist and feel secure and understood in his presence. Her ego functioning was passive and receptive on such days. Other sessions, she would feel hopeless and overwhelmed with a corresponding perception of her therapist as ineffectual, uncaring, or abandoning. Her ego functioning seemed entirely directed toward confirming her pessimistic view of herself and others and demanding rescue. When the patient felt optimistic and understood in the therapy, the psychiatrist said, "Now that you are feeling hopeful and good about the therapy, can you remember the session last week when you were convinced all was lost and things would never get better?"

This intervention juxtaposed the split off all-good and all-bad object relations units. It also engaged her adaptive ego functioning of accurate memory

less colored by emotion, self-observation, and integration of self-images and object-images.

Object relations therapies have provided powerful tools for emotionally understanding patients and their relationships. They have tended to neglect, however, the appropriate assessment of ego functions and therapeutic techniques to elicit residual ego capacities which have lain dormant, because of unfavorable developmental circumstances. More thorough evaluation of ego functioning before and throughout therapies may help forestall or interrupt negative therapeutic reactions or unduly prolonged and unproductive therapies when the patient does not have the residual ego capacities to perform the integrative tasks required for psychological growth. This theoretical and clinical work remains for the future.

XI. NEW DEVELOPMENTS

Object relations concepts became widely known, initially, because they were useful in understanding and treating borderline and narcissistic disorders. As these ideas spread, the applications inevitably became broader. Individual psychotherapy, of course, has remained central to object relations theory. In this arena, Hamilton has discussed the application of object relations theory to healthier individuals and to combined psychotherapy–pharmacotherapy. David and Jill Scharff have elucidated an object relations approach to couples therapy based on the centrality of projective identification in intimate communications. Gabbard has built on the work of Kernberg and Burnham to address splitting in hospital treatment. He has also applied these concepts to the arts and letters, especially in film and theater.

XII. SUMMARY

Object relations theory is that aspect of psychodynamic thinking which deals with how people internalize and externalize their relationships. Psychologically, people begin to exist within a human context. Not only does this context take place externally in the social environment, but individuals also carry within them an internal object world, which is both conscious and unconscious. These internal relationships can be described in terms of object relations units, consisting of self-images, object-images, affects and sensations, and state of ego functioning. These internal relationships both color and structure actual, external relationships and also are changed by them in a reciprocal fashion. The therapies which have evolved out of object relations theory are becoming increasingly diverse as the theory matures. This set of clinical ideas does not claim to be a definitive explanation of human psychological life, but an important contribution to understanding how people grow and change in relationships.

Bibliography

Gabbard, G. O. (1990). ''Psychodynamic Psychiatry in Clinical Practice.'' American Psychiatric Press, Washington, DC.

Hamilton, N. G. (1988). ''Self and Others: Object Relations Theory in Clinical Practice.'' Jason Aronson, Northvale, NJ.

Hamilton, N. G. (ed.) (1992). ''From Inner Sources: New Directions in Object Relations Psychotherapy.'' Jason Aronson, Northvale, NJ.

Kernberg, O. F. (1976). ''Object Relations Theory and Clinical Psycho-Analysis.'' Jason Aronson, Northvale, NJ.

Scharff, J. S., and Scharff, D. E. (1992). ''Scharff Notes: A Primer of Object Relations Theory.'' Jason Aronson, Northvale, NJ.

OBSESSIVE–COMPULSIVE BEHAVIOR

Melinda A. Stanley
*University of Texas–Houston Health
Science Center*

Alisha L. Wagner
University of Houston

Glossary

Compulsion A ritualistic, stereotypic, or repetitive action generally performed to reduce anxiety associated with an obsession; a compulsion (or ritual) is generally perceived as excessive and irrational, although individuals find the behaviors very difficult to resist.

Obsession A thought, image, or urge that is intrusive, unwanted, persistent, and uncontrollable; an obsession generally is perceived as irrational, excessive, and distressful.

Obsessive–compulsive disorder A syndrome in which obsessions and compulsions occur with significant frequency, duration (at least 1 hr per day), or intensity such that social, occupational, or family functioning is impaired or significant psychological distress is experienced.

OBSESSIVE THOUGHTS and compulsive or ritualistic behaviors are a common part of everyday experience. In fact, 80–90% of individuals surveyed admit experiencing some type of obsessive ideation. Compulsive behaviors also are common among the general population. However, in some cases, obsessions and compulsions occupy a significant amount of time, create intense distress, and/or interfere with an individual's ability to function in social relationships, jobs, or family. In these cases, obsessive–compulsive disorder (OCD) may be diagnosed. Research suggests that symptoms in OCD differ from obsessions and compulsions in nonpatient populations primarily in a quantitative sense. In other words, the symptoms occur more frequently, last longer, create more distress, and are resisted more intensely in individuals diagnosed with the disorder. On the other hand, obsessive–compulsive symptoms in patients and nonpatients appear similar with regard to form and content. Thus, obsessive–compulsive behavior appears to lie along a continuum, with normal experience at one end, and a diagnosable psychiatric disorder at the other. The current review focuses on the latter end of the spectrum. Namely, the phenomenology and differential diagnosis of OCD in adults and children are reviewed, as are the epidemiology of the syndrome, etiological hypotheses, and common treatment approaches.

I. DESCRIPTION OF THE CLINICAL SYNDROME

A. Nature of the Symptoms

OCD, one of the most severe and chronic of the anxiety disorders, is characterized by the presence of obsessions and/or compulsions. Obsessions refer to persistent, recurrent ideas, images, or impulses that are unwanted, intrusive, and difficult to control. These phenomena generally are recognized as senseless products of the individual's own mind, and although they often are triggered by specific situations or events, the thoughts also at times appear to come from "out of the blue." At least initially, individuals attempt to resist obsessions with other thoughts or actions.

Obsessions can assume a variety of forms including images, urges, and fears. Obsessional *images* are vivid mental scenes that often involve violence, aggression, or sex (e.g., repetitive images of a loved one being killed). Obsessional *urges* are strong impulses to carry out a disruptive behavior (e.g., shout-

Copyright © 1994 by Academic Press, Inc. All rights of reproduction in any form reserved.

ing obscenities in a meeting), and obsessional *fears* are exaggerated concerns or worries involving "potential danger" (e.g., fears of contamination and disease, thoughts about the possible dangers of items such as razors or knives). The most common themes of obsessional ideation include dirt and contamination, aggression and violence, religion, and sex. Cross-cultural studies have found remarkable consistency in the nature of these themes across diverse cultures. Obsessions generally are perceived as "disgusting" or unacceptable by the patients who experience them, and thus they often evoke fear and anxiety.

Compulsions refer to repetitive, purposeful behaviors that are performed in a ritualistic, stereotyped manner or according to specific rules. Compulsions, or rituals as they are commonly called, are generally intended to neutralize or reduce the anxiety that frequently accompanies obsessional thoughts. Many rituals are performed in an effort to prevent a dreaded event from occurring (e.g., checking the stove 10 times to ensure the house does not burn down) or to restore safety to an environment perceived as dangerous (e.g., repetitive washing of clothing that may have been contaminated with disease-producing bacteria). Although individuals with OCD generally recognize that their rituals are excessive and unreasonable, they usually are unable to resist performing the behaviors. As a result, OCD patients often avoid various situations or events so as not to trigger the obsessional thinking and/or rituals.

The two most common types of compulsions are washing and checking. Compulsive "washers" engage in excessive cleaning or washing activities, with the intent to eliminate harmful germs and contamination. Common behaviors in this realm include excessive handwashing, repetitive or time-consuming showering, and extraordinary amounts of housecleaning. Some patients present with raw or damaged skin after having engaged in excessive handwashing or housecleaning for an extended period of time. Compulsive "checking" generally accompanies doubting obsessions, and typical behaviors include checking to see that doors are locked, faucets and stoves are turned off, and bills or work assignments are complete and without error. Many "checkers" feel that they cannot continue with other activities until they have checked a specific item a certain number of times. For example, a patient may need to check the stove 10 times before leaving home to be sure that it has been turned off.

Other common types of rituals include counting, needing to ask or confess, hoarding, or organizing things to obtain symmetry and precision. Rituals also can occur in the form of thoughts, rather than overt behaviors, that are aimed at undoing or neutralizing the original obsessive idea (e.g., repeating the thought "I'm okay" 10 times to reduce a fear that driving by a cemetery will lead to disaster). Like the overt ritual, cognitive rituals are intended to reduce tension or alleviate anxiety. [*See* ANXIETY AND FEAR.]

A diagnosis of OCD does not require the presence of both obsessions and compulsions; however, in 75–80% of cases both are reported. According to current nosological criteria, a diagnosis of OCD is warranted when symptoms cause marked distress, interfere with occupational or social functioning, or consume a minimum of 1 hr per day. In light of the latter criterion, most OCD patients report that they spend significantly more than 1 hr per day in obsessive and/or compulsive activity.

B. OCD Symptom Variations

Two variations of OCD symptomatology include primary obsessional slowness and OCD with overvalued ideation. Primary obsessional slowness is characterized by excessive amounts of time spent on normal, routine activities such as brushing teeth, combing hair, or dressing and undressing. In this condition, slow behaviors are usually not accompanied by obsessive thoughts, compulsions, or high levels of anxiety. As a result, it has been suggested that primary obsessional slowness may be more closely related to obsessive–compulsive personality disorder than OCD. Although most OCD patients recognize their symptoms as irrational, a subgroup characterized with overvalued ideation strongly believes that rituals are necessary to prevent future feared events. For example, a patient with overvalued ideation might believe strongly that a family member will become seriously ill if the house is not kept immaculate.

C. Associated Features

In addition to the defining characteristics of OCD, a variety of clinical features often are concomitant with the disorder. As noted above, social or occupational difficulties often accompany the symptoms of OCD. While it can be difficult to determine whether these difficulties precede or follow the onset of the disorder, studies indicate that the degree of social maladjustment is positively and significantly correlated with the severity of the symptoms. Patients with severe and very time-consuming symptoms also have a higher frequency of marital problems than patients who are more capable of controlling their symptoms and who do not involve the family with their rituals. In addition, recent research suggests that approximately one-half of OCD patients meet criteria for at least one personality disorder, defined as a long-standing pattern of problematic interpersonal functioning. This statistic is clinically relevant since the presence of certain personality disorders has been shown to have an impact on the efficacy of treatment for OCD. [*See* PERSONALITY DISORDERS.]

Most OCD patients also experience some degree of depression and generalized anxiety, with the majority meeting criteria for at least one or more secondary anxiety or mood disorder. More specifically, research has suggested that two-thirds of OCD patients will experience an episode of major depression at some point in their lives. Additionally, 20–50% of OCD patients meet criteria for a coexisting diagnosis of simple or social phobia. Given that OCD is so frequently accompanied by additional clinical symptoms, the differentiation of OCD from other disorders is an issue of great importance.

D. Differential Diagnosis

1. Other Anxiety Disorders

To differentiate OCD from other anxiety disorders, it is important to consider the centrality and pervasiveness of obsessional thoughts and ritualistic behavior. For example, patients with simple or social phobia also report anxiety and avoidance behavior when confronted with a specific feared object or situation. However, symptoms of phobia typically are absent when the object or situation is not present or imminent, unlike obsessional symptoms that can occur intensely in the absence of any overt environmental stimulus. In panic disorder with or without agoraphobia, anxiety-producing thoughts and avoidance behavior may be more pervasive than in simple or social phobia, but the symptoms still focus on the occurrence of panic and are therefore narrower in scope than is the case with OCD. Finally, although generalized anxiety disorder (GAD) is characterized by excessive or unrealistic anxiety and worry, it is not accompanied by behavioral rituals as in OCD. Moreover, although the obsessional style of thinking in GAD is similar to thought patterns in OCD, the GAD patient's thoughts are focused on more common and everyday concerns such as health, finances, and the family. This is in sharp contrast to OCD-related thoughts involving sex, contamination, and aggression. [*See* ANXIETY DISORDERS; PHOBIAS.]

2. Depression

Depression is the most common complication of an obsessional syndrome, and it has been posited that obsessive–compulsive symptoms are closely linked to changes in affect. Depression frequently occurs as a response to the social and occupational problems caused by OCD, and obsessive–compulsive symptoms also can occur in conjunction with a primary depression. Given this significant overlap of symptoms, it is necessary to determine which of the disorders is primary. Such a determination can be made based on which disorder had an earlier onset or which cluster of symptoms creates more significant subjective distress and/or functional impairment. In addition, affective illness usually has a slow or insidious onset, while OCD is often preceded by anxiety or fear and is characterized by a sudden onset. Further, the obsessions of depressed patients usually center on themes of aggression, suicide, and homicide whereas, as noted above, OCD patients experience obsessions focusing on contamination, religion, aggression, and sex. Finally, OCD tends to begin at a younger age, is more chronic, and has a lower ratio of female to male incidence (see Epidemiology of OCD).

Despite an apparent distinction between OCD and depression, some theorists have proposed that OCD may be a variant of depressive disorder. Support for this position comes from data attesting to the efficacy of antidepressant medication in the treatment of OCD and the presence of neurobiologic abnormalities thought to be distinctive of major depression. For example, similar to depressed individuals, OCD patients show an increased rate of nonsuppression on the dexamethasone suppression test, shortened rapid eye movement latency, and blunted plasma growth hormone response to intravenous administration of clonidine. Caution should be used in interpreting these studies, however, since OCD patients with secondary depression have sometimes been included and results generally have been confirmed only in subsets of OCD patients. [*See* DEPRESSION.]

3. Obsessive–Compulsive Personality Disorder

The distinction between OCD and obsessive–compulsive personality disorder (OCPD) also is an important one. Diagnostic criteria describe OCPD as a pervasive pattern of perfectionism and inflexibility characterized by the following: restricted ability to express emotion, excessive perfectionism and attention to detail, insistence that others conform to the patient's preferred style of doing things, excessive involvement in work, and indecision, tardiness, and procrastination. It was once believed that OCD was always precipitated by, or at least related to, the presence of OCPD and that the two disorders lie along a singular continuum. However, current personality research has indicated that OCPD is not present in all cases of OCD. In fact, prevalence rates have ranged from as low as 6% to as high as 55%. Compulsive personality traits, on the other hand, have been identified in many patients prior to the onset of OCD.

To differentiate OCD from OCPD, it is important to consider the presence of rituals (behavioral or cognitive) and the distinction between ego-syntonic and ego-dystonic disturbance. In particular, behaviors that characterize OCPD may be performed in a rigid, routine, and perfectionistic manner, but they generally are not performed repetitively as in OCD. In addition, symptoms of OCD typically are perceived as irrational and inconsistent with the patient's typical method of observing his/her environment. Conversely, symptoms of OCPD are perceived as consistent with the individual's behaviors and beliefs throughout life. As such, the behavior of OCPD patients often is more bothersome to those who must interact with the individual than to the person with OCPD.

4. Schizophrenia

The relationship between OCD and schizophrenia received much research attention in the 1950s and 1960s. Controversy existed over whether the two disorders were on a continuum (obsessional thoughts being an early sign of schizophrenia) or whether they were distinct entities. Contemporary research has not supported the overlap, indicating that the prevalence of schizophrenia among OCD patients ranges from 0 to 3%, which is no greater than the percentage of other neurotics who also develop schizophrenia. However, a subgroup of OCD patients are known to experience "psychotic-like" features as part of their obsessional symptomatology. For example, those patients with "overvalued ideation" experience their obsessions with an intensity that is characteristic of a delusion (see above). In addition, a certain percentage of OCD patients

exhibit schizotypal personality characteristics and report certain "psychotic-like" symptoms such as magical thinking or unusual perceptual experiences.

Although OCD patients may exhibit "psychotic-like" symptoms and schizophrenics may report obsessional or ritualistic patterns, the differentiation between the disorders usually is not difficult. Unlike schizophrenics, OCD patients do not exhibit hallucinations or symptoms of a formal thought disorder. Further, although the cognitive symptoms or delusions of the schizophrenic may appear similar to obsessions in OCD (i.e., both types of symptoms are highly intrusive and dominate the person's thoughts), differences are apparent in OCD patients' attempts to resist or neutralize the disturbing thought, their retention of insight (with the exception of overvalued ideation), and their feelings of responsibility for the symptoms. The schizophrenic patient typically does not attempt to resist the disturbing thought, does not retain contact with reality, and does not feel responsible for symptomatic thought patterns. Finally, ritualistic behavior in OCD generally is performed for a definite purpose, while rituals of a schizophrenic patient often are nonpurposeful or performed in response to paranoid thinking. [*See* SCHIZOPHRENIA.]

5. Impulse Control Disorders

OCD recently has been linked to the disorders currently classified as problems of impulse control. Specifically, it has been suggested that disorders such as trichotillomania, kleptomania, and pathological gambling may be variants of OCD given some symptom similarity. Like OCD, patients with impulse control problems perform certain behaviors repetitively, despite an apparent desire not to do so. Additionally, patients in both groups frequently report an increasing sense of tension or arousal before performing the behavior and a decrease in tension after engaging in the act. Unlike OCD, a certain degree of pleasure is often experienced while performing the impulsive act (e.g., hair-pulling, gambling, shoplifting), and the repetitive activities in impulse control disorders usually lack the clearly purposeful function of rituals in OCD.

The empirical literature addressing the overlap of compulsive and impulsive disorders is sparse, although the majority of attention has been directed at the relationship of OCD and trichotillomania (TM), a disorder characterized by repetitive hair-pulling. Empirical studies have suggested that serotonergic antidepressants effective in treating OCD also have benefitted patients with TM, and family history studies have indicated a higher than normal prevalence of OCD in the families of TM patients. Although these findings suggest some overlap between OCD and TM, studies comparing other clinical features of the disorders have identified substantial differences. First, TM patients report significantly fewer obsessive–compulsive symptoms than OCD patients. Second, OCD is often accompanied by pathological doubt and responsibility, obsessional slowness, and behavioral avoidance, while TM is not. Third, TM patients do not report the presence of generalized anxiety and depression that OCD patients commonly experience, and their daily functioning is significantly less impaired than is the case with OCD. [*See* CONTROL.]

6. Somatoform Disorders

Overlap between OCD and somatoform disorders has been suggested. In particular, patients with hypochondriasis exhibit a preoccupation or obsession with the fear of having a serious disease despite medical reassurance that a critical illness is not present. A parallel has been drawn between this disorder and OCD given the repetitive nature of the hypochondriacal patient's fears. Additionally, the hypochondriacal patient's repetitive visits to physicians can be conceptualized as ritualisitic behavior similar to the OCD patient's need to check something several times to reduce anxiety. OCD and hypochondriasis differ with regard to the nature of the obsessional thoughts in that an OCD patient may fear getting a serious illness but usually recognizes the bothersome thoughts as senseless, while the hypochondriacal patient fears having a serious illness and believes the thoughts are rational. In addition, despite the apparent overlap of symptoms, one research study has indicated that there is only a small percentage of lifetime prevalence for OCD (9.5%) among hypochondriacal patients.

Body dysmorphic disorder, also classified within the somatoform category, is characterized by a preoccupation with an imagined physical defect. Like hypochondriasis, it has been suggested that body dysmorphic disorder may be a variant of OCD given the concomitant obsessional thought pattern and the need to engage in repetitive checking of one's physical appearance. In addition, as in OCD, serotonin reuptake blockers have been efficacious in treating patients with this disorder. However, the relationship between OCD and body dysmorphic disorder

has received only slight research attention and clear conclusions await the completion of additional empirical work.

7. Eating Disorders

Bulimia nervosa (BN) is an eating disorder characterized by excessive concern about body shape and weight. These negative thoughts precipitate repetitive binge eating episodes, which are generally followed by extreme methods of weight reduction (e.g., vomiting, laxative use, starvation, or excessive exercising). The intrusive, recurring thoughts about food and body weight in BN parallel the obsessive thought pattern in OCD. Likewise, the drastic behavior that follows the binge episodes is similar to the compulsive rituals performed by the obsessive–compulsive individual (they occur repetitively and are designed to decrease anxiety and regain control). Anorexia nervosa (AN) is an eating disorder described as a refusal to maintain normal body weight and an intense fear of gaining weight or becoming fat. Again, intrusive and recurrent thoughts about food and body weight can be likened to obsessional ideation. However, a recent study examining the overlap between OCD and the eating disorders failed to support the position that eating disorders are a subtype of OCD. More research onthis topic is certainly necessary to elucidate the proposed overlap between OCD and the eating disorders.

II. EPIDEMIOLOGY OF OCD

Until recently, OCD was thought to be a rare syndrome affecting less than 1% of the general population. However, recent epidemiological surveys indicate that lifetime prevalence rates among adults are significantly greater than previously believed, with rates ranging from 1.9 to 3.3%. These figures suggest that approximately 4 million people in the United States will be affected by the disorder. Moreover, the statistics indicate that OCD may be twice as prevalent in the general population as schizophrenia or panic disorder.

A clear precipitant is reported to precede the onset of OCD in 60–70% of cases, with events such as pregnancy, childbirth, divorce, sexual issues, and death of a loved one commonly reported. Although stress alone does not cause OCD, it often exacerbates the symptoms. Onset generally occurs in early adult life, most often between the ages of 18 and 24 (see OCD in children and adolescents for a discussion of cases with an earlier onset). Approximately 50–70% of patients report onset prior to age 25, and less than 15% develop the disorder after age 35. Despite onset of the full-blown disorder during the late teens and early 20s, patients frequently experience subthreshold obsessional symptoms much earlier in life.

OCD is a chronic disorder that waxes and wanes in response to environmental stressors. Despite reduction of symptoms during less stressful periods, however, the symptoms generally do not remit without treatment. Furthermore, placebo response rate is unusually low, with only about 5% of patients showing improvement without active treatment.

Recent epidemiological data have demonstrated that males typically have an earlier onset of OCD than females. In particular, males seem to develop the disorder around puberty, while onset in females occurs most frequently between the ages of 20 and 24. This pattern contradicts earlier reports, however, and further clarification is necessary. Interestingly, there also appears to be an association between gender and primary type of rituals reported. Specifically, a recent study revealed that "washers" were six times more likely to be female, while "checkers" were almost equally represented by males and females. With regard to gender ratio, earlier studies have reported a slightly higher incidence of OCD among females, although more recent research indicates a relatively even distribution between genders.

OCD has been reported to be more common among unemployed, Caucasian, and divorced or separated individuals. Additionally, a high celibacy rate and single marital status are common among these patients. Although it was once believed that OCD patients possess higher than average intelligence, empirical data actually have revealed nonsignificant IQ differences between OCD patients and normal controls.

III. THEORIES OF ETIOLOGY

A number of etiological perspectives have been used to explain the onset and maintenance of OCD. The majority of literature in this arena has addressed biological and behavioral models, with theories positing genetic, neurochemical, neuroanatomical, and conditioning mechanisms. Each of these major perspectives will be reviewed, followed by discussion of a diathesis–stress or vulnerability model that incorporates both biological and behavioral components to explain the etiology of OCD.

A. Genetic Hypotheses

The role of genetic variables in the etiology of OCD has been examined using both family history and twin studies. Data from the former have provided some evidence of an increased incidence of OCD in the families of OCD patients relative to the general population. In addition, obsessional traits and general psychiatric distress are more common in the family members of OCD patients relative to normal controls. Although such data may be interpreted as supporting a genetic hypothesis, the design of these studies does not rule out the influence of environmental family variables (e.g., modeling) that may influence what appears to be genetic transmission.

Somewhat clearer data regarding genetic linkages are provided by twin studies which compare concordance rates (the percentage of time that both twins meet criteria for OCD) for monozygotic (MZ) and dizygotic (DZ) twins. The assumption underlying this methodology is that family environmental influences should be constant for both types of twin pairs, whereas increased genetic similarity occurs in MZ twins relative to DZ pairs. Early retrospective chart review studies supported this pattern for OCD, and the data have been confirmed more recently via interview studies with OCD patients and their twins. In the latter, a 33% concordance rate has been reported for MZ OCD twins compared to a 7% concordance rate for DZ pairs. Although such data support a role for genetics in the etiology of OCD, it is important to note that concordance rates for MZ twins are much lower that 100%, indicating that genetic variables alone are insufficient to account for the onset of OCD. Rather, it appears from these data that additional variables play an important role. Further evidence regarding the impact of genetic variables awaits completion of adoption studes which examine concordance rates for genetically similar twins reared in different family environments. To date, no such studies have been conducted for OCD. Furthermore, recent data from twin studies have suggested that differential concordance rates between MZ and DZ twins occur for anxiety disorders in general, suggesting that the role of genetic factors in the onset of OCD may not be unique to that disorder.

B. Neurochemical Models

The most popular and widely studied neurochemical model of OCD involves the role of the neurotransmitter serotonin. This model originated from early treatment studies demonstrating the efficacy of serotonergic antidepressants, in particular clomipramine, for the reduction of OCD symptoms. Because these drugs block reuptake of serotonin from the synaptic cleft, it was suggested that OCD may be caused or maintained by depletion of functional levels of serotonin at the neural synapse. Neurochemical studies have provided some support for this hypothesis, with early data indicating decreased serotonin in blood platelets of OCD patients. More recent research has demonstrated that serotonergic agonists such as *m*-chlorophenylpiperazine (mCPP) exacerbate obsessive–compulsive symptoms, and that this response is attenuated when patients are receiving concurrent treatment with clomipramine. Further, treatment outcome data have revealed positive correlations between levels of cerebral spinal serotonin metabolites and severity of obsessive–compulsive symptoms. Together these data provide support for some role of serotonin in the etiology and/or maintenance of OCD. However, it is important to note that results are not consistent across research reports and that a clear direction of causality cannot be ascertained from studies examining biological correlates in patients already diagnosed with a particular disorder. Nevertheless, the role of serotonin seems to be important and certainly deserves further empirical attention. [*See* SYNAPTIC TRANSMITTERS AND NEUROMODULATORS.]

C. Neuroanatomical and Neuropsychological Hypotheses

Neuroanatomical and neuropsychological theories regarding the etiology of OCD have been suggested given observed overlap between the symptoms of OCD and neurological disorders such as Tourette's syndrome, Sydenham's chorea, encephalitis, temporal lobe tumors, temporal lobe epilepsy, and head injuries. Neuropsychological studies have suggested that OCD is associated with difficulties in set-shifting, visuospatial tasks, and memory. Abnormalities in fine motor coordination and total number of neurological soft signs also have been reported. The possibility exists that some of these deficits may be associated differentially with various phenomeno-

logical subtypes of the disorder (e.g., the primacy of washing or checking rituals), and further research in this area is warranted.

As a result of the comorbidity, neuropsychological, and neuropsychiatric studies conducted to date, primary hypotheses in this realm have implicated frontal lobe, right hemisphere, and basal ganglia dysfunction in the etiology and/or maintenance of OCD. Studies investigating these neuroanatomical hypotheses have utilized electroencephalographic (EEG) measures, x-ray computed tomography (CT), positron emission tomography (PET), and nuclear magnetic resonance (NMR). EEG studies have reported abnormalities in 10–33% of OCD patients, but the data often have been collected from very small samples, and no clear and consistent patterns yet have emerged. Using CT, PET, and NMR procedures, other data have demonstrated bilateral abnormalities in the basal ganglia, smaller caudate volumes, and nonspecific changes such as ventricular enlargement or asymmetry in OCD patients. Despite the number of hypothesized neuroanatomical mechanisms, however, data in this area are relatively sparse. Significant advances in this aspect of the field are expected in coming years given continued development and refinement of relevant assessment technology.

D. Behavioral Learning Theories

Behavioral learning theories posit that the onset and course of OCD are mediated by environmental variables and various principles of conditioning. The role of environmental variables is implicated by data suggesting that onset of the disorder in adulthood typically occurs following a significant life event or change (e.g., marriage, childbirth, career or job change). In addition, an influence of environmental variables is indicated given that the course of the disorder fluctuates in response to environmental stressors.

With regard to the application of conditioning or learning principles, Mowrer's two-factor theory of fear acquisition appears relevant. This theory proposes that learning occurs via two steps: (1) a neutral stimulus acquires fear-producing properties through a process of classical conditioning; and (2) avoidance or escape behaviors performed in response to the fears persist and maintain the fear through a process of negative reinforcement. To apply this model to the acquisition and maintenance of obsessive–compulsive symptoms, compulsions or rituals are conceptualized as avoidance or escape mechanisms that serve to reduce the fear associated with obsessive thoughts. In opposition to other more specific phobias, these behaviors are less situation-specific given that feared stimuli (i.e., obsessive thoughts) are internal and thus become paired with multiple external stimuli, producing a myriad of possible escape or avoidance behaviors. Once a ritual is performed in response to an anxiety-producing obsessive thought, anxiety is reduced and the ritualistic behavior is then repeated whenever similar fear-provoking stimuli are encountered. Support for this pattern has been generated from studies demonstrating that subjective and physiological indices of anxiety increase in the presence of stimuli that precipitate obsessive thoughts and decrease following completion of ritualistic behavior.

More recent behavioral learning models of OCD have utilized cognitive theories which ascribe a central role to thoughts and perceptions. One of these, a bioinformational theory, suggests that fear is represented via a cognitive "network" of information about threatening events or situations, behavioral and physiological reactions to those stimuli, and the meanings attached to each. Other more general cognitive models propose that OCD is maintained by unrealistic perceptions of responsibility for obsessive thoughts and other dysfunctional beliefs about the meaning of those thoughts (e.g., "having a thought about an action is like performing the action").

In summary, behavioral models hold some promise for explaining the maintenance of obsessive–compulsive symptoms, and successful treatments have been derived from these principles as outlined below. However, the models alone do not explain why similar environmental stressors appear to precipitate OCD in some individuals but not others, nor do they address how obsessional thinking (which occurs frequently in "normal" populations, as noted above) develops into a dysfunction pattern for some people and not others. To explain these phenomena, we turn now to a discussion of a diathsis–stress or vulnerability model of OCD.

E. Vulnerability Model

The above reviews attest to the notion that no single biological or behavioral theory is sufficient to explain the development and maintenance of OCD. Rather, it appears that a vulnerability, or diathesis–stress, model is more appropriate. This type of model suggests that some individuals are predisposed to develop OCD given the presence of certain genetic, neurochemical, or neuroanatomical factors, but that onset of the full-blown disorder occurs only when these factors interact with specific environmental variables or patterns of learning.

One version of a vulnerability hypothesis has been proposed recently to differentiate the occurrence of "normal" and "abnormal" obsessive–compulsive symptoms. As noted in the introductory paragraph above, obsessional symptoms occur with a high frequency in nonclinical samples. In addition, there appears to be a high degree of similarity in the qualitative nature of obsessive–compulsive symptoms in clinical and nonclinical groups, although symptoms in the latter are more frequent, more intense, and cause significantly greater distress. To explain the differential development of these patterns, it has been noted that obsessional thoughts, increased anxiety, and perceptions of loss of control are common reactions to stressful situations in the general population. A pathological syndrome is predicted to occur, however, when this cluster of symptoms is perceived by the individual as unacceptable due to either biological or psychological vulnerabilities. If a typical reaction to stress is perceived as unacceptable, avoidance behaviors and rituals subsequently develop to reduce anxiety and restore a sense of control. Through a process of negative reinforcement, these behaviors are repeated and maintain themselves and the fear.

It has been suggested further in this model that the specific nature of obsessive thoughts and ritualistic behaviors is determined environmentally. Namely, it is proposed that early experiences teach the individual that certain types of thoughts or images are unacceptable. Thus, when these types of cognitions occur, ritualistic avoidance is likely. Some support for this proposal has been obtained from OCD patients classified as "washers" or "checkers" who describe their parents retrospectively as having differential styles of parenting, with the latter reporting that their parents were more meticulous and demanding. However, additional data collected in a prospective fashion will be necessary to support the validity of this model.

In summary, a vulnerability model appears to account most adequately for the etiology and maintenance of OCD given the inadequacy of any single biological or behavioral theory. However, the specific nature of such a theory and the specific roles of various mechanisms involved are far from clear.

IV. TREATMENT APPROACHES

As noted in the discussion of childhood OCD above, two primary modes of treatment currently are employed—pharmacotherapy with serotonergic antidepressants and behavior therapy, in particular exposure and response prevention. The empirical literature in each of these areas will be reviewed below.

A. Behavior Therapy

Behavioral treatment of OCD involves a process known as exposure and response prevention, an intervention considered by some to be the treatment of choice for this disorder. The approach consists of two components: (1) exposure to stimuli that provoke obsessive thoughts, and (2) prevention of ritualistic responses performed to reduce anxiety. This combination of components is based on Mowrer's two-factor theory of fear acquisition (see above). In particular, extensive exposure to feared stimuli allows for habituation of the fear response (defined by decreases in physiological, subjective, or behavioral indices of anxiety), and response prevention helps the patient to stop rituals, thus halting the negative reinforcement cycle that maintains the behavior and the concomitant fear.

Research has demonstrated that exposure and response prevention have differential effects. Namely, exposure leads to anxiety reduction, whereas response prevention reduces the frequency of rituals. Utilizing both components allows the patient to experience decreases in both anxiety and urges to perform rituals. Exposure and response prevention sessions typically last $1\frac{1}{2}$ to 2 hr to allow sufficient time for habituation of anxiety. Treatment also is often conducted in an intense fashion, with sessions held on a daily basis, to allow for rapid reduction of fear and the urge to ritualize. Throughout the course of treatment, it is important to observe habituation occurring both within and across sessions in order for the treatment to be effective.

Exposure sessions can be conducted in an imaginal or *in vivo* fashion. In the former, patients are asked to imagine feared stimuli and consequences (e.g., picturing themselves touching a contaminated object and passing germs on to a relative who then becomes ill). In the latter, patients are required to come into direct contact with the feared stimuli (e.g., being in an environment or touching an object perceived to be contaminated). Exposure and response prevention can be conducted in a gradual or rapid fashion, and the degree of involvement by the therapist varies depending on estimated severity of the disorder and the patient's ability to conduct exposure sessions independently. The goal of treatment is for the therapist to reduce his or her involvement over time as the patient assumes increased responsibility for self-treatment.

The earliest use of exposure and response prevention occurred in the 1960s. Since that time, a number of empirical studies have been conducted to examine the efficacy of the approach for the treatment of OCD. By the mid-1980s, over 200 patients (both inpatient and outpatient) had been treated in controlled trials. A review of these data suggested that 51% of patients were symptom-free or much improved at post-treatment (defined by at least 70% reduction in symptoms), 39% were moderately improved (30–70% symptom reduction), and 10% showed no treatment gains. By follow-up, which ranged from 3 months to 3 years, the failure rate had increased to 24%, but 76% of patients continued to show moderate to significant improvements.

More recent work has examined the role of spouse or family involvement in the implementation of exposure and response prevention, the utility of providing behavioral treatment in a group format, and comparison of treatment administered in inpatient and outpatient settings. In addition, studies have begun to examine the utility of exposure and response prevention for patients with obsessions only, a group previously thought to be refractory to behavioral interventions. First, data regarding the utility of family involvement have been mixed, with some studies demonstrating enhanced treatment outcome following inclusion of family, and others reporting no difference between treatment with and without family members. Second, preliminary data suggest that administration of behavioral treatment in a group format may be useful and cost-effective, although well-controlled trials have yet to be conducted. Third, very few differences in efficacy have been reported for behavior therapy conducted in inpatient and outpatient settings. Finally, reconceptualization of OCD patients with obsessions only has called for careful differentiation of obsessions and cognitive rituals in these individuals. As a result, effective exposure and response prevention programs have been developed for patients without overt ritualistic behavior.

In summary, exposure and response prevention appears quite effective in the treatment of OCD, and even may be considered the treatment of choice. However, it is time-consuming and anxiety-producing, and up to 25% of patients will not agree to participate in a behavioral program. In addition, data have suggested that patients with severe depression do not respond to this approach given that habituation within sessions does not occur. In these cases, pharmacotherapy should be considered.

B. Pharmacotherapy

As noted above, pharmacotherapy for OCD has focused primarily on the use of antidepressant medications that block reuptake of serotonin. These serotonergic compounds include two medications currently available in the United States—clomipramine and fluoxetine—and other drugs currently undergoing experimental trials (e.g., fluvoxamine and sertraline). By far, the majority of data in the area have involved the administration of clomipramine. A significant body of literature has demonstrated that clomipramine is more effective for the treatment of OCD than placebo and more effective than nonserotonergic antidepressants such as imipramine, amitryptaline, and desipramine. Across studies, patients report 30–70% improvement in symptoms following trials of clomipramine, with an average reduction in symptoms of 40%. Generally, such improvements are noted in 50% or more of patients studied. It also appears across the majority of studies that these reductions in OCD symptomatology are not due solely to decreases in depression, attesting to specific antiobsessional properties of the medication.

Similar results have been reported following pharmacotherapy trials with fluoxetine, fluvoxamine, and more recently sertraline. However, the data base with these medications is not nearly as large as the clomipramine literature. Initial comparisons of serotonergic medications with each other have suggested that clomipramine has a slight advantage over fluoxetine with regard to symptom reduction, but side-effect profiles created by fluoxetine are less severe.

Certainly, the results of these trials to date are encouraging. However, follow-up studies have demonstrated that relapse following discontinuation of medication is common, occurring in 23 to 89% of patients. Even when placebo is substituted following taper of active medication, symptoms reappear in 2–4 weeks. Long-term treatment with medication (in particular, clomipramine) does not appear to guard against relapse. In addition, medication side-effects (e.g., dry mouth, dizziness, fatigue, digestive problems, and genital–urinary dysfunction) are problematic and lead to discontinuation of treatment in 10–20% of patients, and serotonergic medications still are expensive given that they have been introduced into the market only recently. Thus, although medication can be of significant benefit in the treatment of OCD, response is well below 100% and drawbacks such as relapse and side effects need to be considered.

C. Combined Treatment and Prediction of Treatment Failure

Many researchers and clinicians have suggested that optimal treatment of OCD involves combined trials of medication and behavior therapy. It has been suggested that the addition of medication to a behavior therapy regimen makes the therapy easier to tolerate, and inclusion of behavioral interventions in a medication trial may help to reduce the probability of relapse. Initial controlled comparisons of behavior therapy, pharmacotherapy, and combined interventions have shown a slight advantage of combined treatment, and an advantage of behavior therapy over drug treatment at post-treatment and follow-up.

Despite the suggestion that optimal treatment includes a combined approach, available data indicate that up to 20% of patients fail to respond even when both interventions are utilized. Possible predictors of treatment failure include the presence of severe depression, overvalued ideation, or schizotypal personality traits. Severe depression and overvalued ideation have been targeted as predictors primarily when behavior therapy is conducted alone. In the former case, addition of an antidepressant medication is indicated; in the latter, addition of cognitive therapy to address delusional-type thinking has been recommended. Schizotypal personality disorder appears to predict poor treatment outcome for both behavior therapy and pharmacotherapy, and additional treatment components may be warranted to address interpersonal dysfunction in these cases.

V. OCD IN CHILDREN AND ADOLESCENTS

OCD symptoms in children and adolescents were first described in the early part of the 20th century.

At that time, and in fact until recently, childhood OCD was thought to be extremely rare given the infrequency with which such symptoms were reported in clinic patients. As a result, early scientific reports in the area consisted primarily of uncontrolled studies and case histories. In the last 10–15 years, however, larger surveys have suggested that the disorder is not as rare as was once believed, and empirical data have begun to address in a more systematic manner the nature and treatment of OCD symptoms in younger populations.

In general, the clinical picture of OCD in younger individuals is remarkably similar to that of adults. Cross-cultural similarities in the phenomenology of childhood OCD also have been noted across studies with children and adolescents in the United States, Denmark, Japan, and India. The most common themes of obsessional thoughts in these samples include contamination, responsibility for danger to oneself or others, symmetry, and scrupulous religiosity. Typical compulsions include washing (some form of which occurs in up to 85% of patients surveyed), repeating or arranging, checking, and avoiding. Within these broader categories, specific ritualistic behaviors also are similar to those observed in adult patients. For example, excessive handwashing or showering, use of chemicals such as alcohol or detergents for cleaning hands, repetitive checking of doors and lights, and repetitive walking in and out of doors are reported. For the most part, children and adolescents with OCD experience both obsessions and compulsions, although reports of rituals alone are more common than the experience of obsessions without compulsions. In fact, ritualistic behavior generally comprises the primary complaint when children with OCD are brought to psychiatric clinics.

As noted above, early reviews of clinical data revealed very low prevalence rates of OCD in children and adolescents. However, a more recent survey of over 5000 9th to 12th graders suggested a weighted lifetime prevalence rate of 1–2%, with onset between the ages of 7 and 18. Other studies with clinic samples, however, have reported an apparent bimodal distribution for age of onset, with initial symptoms reported either between the ages of 5 and 8 or during adolescence. Onset of symptoms appears to be gradual, with no precipitating events typically identified. However, assessment of such events has not been included in all studies to date, and identification of these may be difficult given that most children initially attempt to hide the symptoms from family members and peers. In fact, it has been estimated that symptoms may be present for 4–6 months before parents become aware of them. Teachers often are unaware of symptoms for an even longer period of time given stronger attempts on the part of the child to hide ritualistic behaviors in more public situations.

Gender distribution of OCD in the above-mentioned epidemiological survey indicated equivalent numbers of males and females. Data from clinic patients, however, have suggested that gender distribution may vary with age of onset such that a greater proportion of males are present in the earlier onset group. In addition, clinic data have suggested a higher percentage of OCD in first-degree relatives of patients with earlier onset, although prevalence rates for family members with OCD have ranged from 7 to 25%.

As is true with adult patients, the course of OCD in children and adolescents is fluctuating, with symptoms aggravated by increased stress, decreased activity level, and reduced environmental structure. In addition, up to 90% of young patients report changes over time in the nature of OCD symptoms, and one-third report some type of environmental trigger for onging obsessions or compulsions.

The majority of children and adolescents with OCD meet diagnostic criteria for at least one additional disorder. Affective disorders including depression and dysthymia appear to be the most common secondary diagnoses, although this phenomenon has not been confirmed cross-culturally. Secondary anxiety disorders including separation anxiety disorder, overanxious disorder, and simple phobia also are common, and eating disorders and obsessive–compulsive personality disorder have been noted in some reports. Overlap between OCD and neurological disorders such as Tourette's Syndrome and Sydenham's Chorea also have been noted and have contributed to etiological hypotheses implicating basal ganglia dysfunction [see Theories of Etiology]. Comorbidity data should be interpreted with caution, however, given that many studies of clinic samples have utilized exclusionary criteria that limit the ability to evaluate diagnostic profiles thoroughly.

With regard to treatment approaches for childhood OCD, it should be noted that once again there appears to be significant overlap between adults and younger individuals with the disorder. Namely, the two primary modes of treatment utilized with children and adolescents are pharmacotherapy, with a primary focus on the serotonergic antidepressants, and behavior therapy, in particular exposure and response prevention. Empirical data supporting the efficacy of these approaches in children, however, are significantly less voluminous than in the adult literature. Only two controlled pharmacotherapy studies have attested to the efficacy of clomipramine in the treatment of young patients with OCD. These studies have demonstrated that the effects of clomipramine are superior to both placebo and a nonserotonergic antidepressant, desipramine. With regard to the behavior therapy literature, no controlled experimental trials have been conducted with child or adolescent populations. It has been suggested based on clinical case studies that exposure and response prevention can be a useful intervention for children and adolescents with OCD, although adjunctive procedures often are included for these patients. In particular, some form of family therapy often is incorporated to assist in the implementation of exposure and response prevention, and operant programs including reinforcement for decreasing rituals and alternative contingencies for performing these behaviors frequently are added. However, firm conclusions regarding the utility of such programs await completion of adequately controlled experimental trials.

VI. SUMMARY

In summary, the past 20 years have produced significant advances in knowledge regarding the nature, etiology, and treatment of OCD, with the majority of work conducted within biological and behavioral domains. Overlap with other psychiatric disorders also has been examined, and the nature of symptoms in children and adolescents has been investigated. Despite the vast expansion in our understanding of this disorder, numerous important questions remain unanswered as noted throughout the text above. Hence, further research clearly is essential to maximize our ability to identify etiological mechanisms, and to diagnose and treat OCD with optimal effectiveness.

Bibliography

Barlow, D. (1988). Obsessive–compulsive disorder. In "Anxiety and Its Disorders: The Nature and Treatment of Anxiety and Panic," pp. 598–634. Guilford, New York.

Jenike, M. A., Baer, L., and Minichiello, W. E. (1990). "Obsessive Compulsive Disorders: Theory and Management," 2nd ed. Year Book Medical, Chicago.

Karno, M., Golding, J. M., Sorenson, S. B., and Burnam, A. (1988). The epidemiology of obsessive–compulsive disorder in five U.S. communities. *Arch. Gen. Psych.* **45,** 1094–1099.

Rachman, S. J., and Hodgson, R. S. (1980). "Obsessions and Compulsions." Prentice–Hall, Englewood Cliffs, NJ.

Stanley, M. A., and Prather, R. C. (1993). Obsessive–compulsive disorder. In "Psychopathology in Adulthood: An Advanced Test" (A. S. Bellack and M. Hersen, Eds.), pp. 164–178. Pergamon, New York.

Turner, S. M., and Beidel, D. C. (1988). "Treatment of Obsessive–Compulsive Disorder." Pergamon, New York.

Zohar, J., Insel, T., and Rasmussen, S. (Eds.) (1991). "The Psychobiology of Obsessive Compulsive Disorder." Springer, New York.

OEDIPUS COMPLEX

Eugene J. Mahon

*Columbia Psychoanalytic Center for Training and Research
and Columbia College of Physicians and Surgeons*

Glossary

Castration anxiety A child's neurotic fear, often persisting into adulthood, that sexual desire of the opposite-sex parent may lead to retaliation from the same-sex parent. The feared retaliation refers to loss of the penis.

Defense mechanism An unconscious psychological strategy whereby conflictual psychic products are disguised and rerouted so that consciousness does not have to deal with them directly. Defense mechanisms are ubiquitous. Adaptation or maladaptation refers not to their use, but to their abuse.

Identification A defense mechanism whereby one incorporates into the psyche what one is afraid of losing. A child, who fears losing his father's love, may put aside his rivalry with his father and identify with his father's authority instead.

Infantile amnesia At age 6, an amnesia for much of the psychological issues of the first 5 years of life develops.

Latency period A period of relatively quiescent development between the ages of 6 and 12 when the Oedipus complex is relatively repressed and the child can turn his attention to academic and other pursuits that ensure cultural and traditional inheritance.

Repression A defense mechanism whereby psychologically conflictual material is removed from consciousness. What is repressed may return, however, and other strategies may be required to deal with it.

Superego The intrapsychic regulator of morality which owes much of its authority to successful resolution of the Oedipus complex. Identification with the authority of parents, in particular, and societal values, in general, creates it and sustains it.

THE OEDIPUS COMPLEX, discovered by Sigmund Freud in October 1897 through self-analysis, refers to the psychological conflict that each human being struggles with when sexual desire for the opposite-sex parent awakens, usually between the ages of 3 and 5. The desire for the opposite-sex parent and rivalry with the same-sex parent is called the positive Oedipus complex. When the child tries to resolve his conflict unsuccessfully by wooing the same-sex parent, this is called the negative Oedipus complex. The complex is not resolved by either of these positive or negative maneuvers, but is eventually resolved by repression and identification with the assistance of cognitive maturity. At age 6 the Oedipus complex is usually repressed and replaced by identifications with the authority of the parents. These identifications lead to the formation of the superego. After a period of relative latency (ages 6–12), adolescence reawakens the Oedipus complex when conflicts have to be worked out again on a larger anatomical scale, so to speak, given the growth and development of the child into an adult. The adaptive resolution of the complex in adolescence leads to further maturity of psychic functioning and a reworking of family dynamics and points the adolescent appropriately toward the nonincestuous relationships out of which maturity and marriage will eventually ensue. Maladaptive resolutions of the Oedipus complex lead to neurosis in adult life.

I. INTRODUCTION

The Oedipus complex is a distinctly Freudian way of organizing human experience. It implies that the first 5 years of a child's life are full of genetic possibilities and developmental probabilities that, understood or not, will shape and determine future psychological outcomes.

The Oedipus complex refers to a period of psychological development (roughly ages 3 to 6) whereby a child's sexual desire for the beloved opposite-sex parent leads to conflict with the beloved same-sex parent. A child does not possess the psychological chutzpah to arrive at this heroic developmental point of view until certain pre-Oedipal issues have been addressed. Therefore, before we talk about the Oedipus complex some introductory remarks are necessary.

The psychoanalytic contribution to the study of human behavior rests heavily on the notion that what is manifest phenomenologically is not the whole psychological story. While consciousness may seem to set the behavioral world in motion, psychoanalysis suggests that there is a latent world of unconscious motivators that pull the strings behind the scenes. When Freud introduced this notion of a dynamic unconscious subtext that undermined a time-honored text called free will, he was fully aware that the world would not thank him any more than it had thanked Copernicus or Darwin for diminishing its narcissistic freedoms! To add insult to narcissistic injury Freud argued that at the core of this brave new unconscious world lay not rationality, but complex sexual forces that originated in zones of the body (mouth, anus, genitalia) that would take years of development to bend from their primitive goals of discharge toward socially acceptable forms of expression. This conflict between infantile sexuality and the social forces that attempt to shape and modify it has come to be known as the Oedipus complex since Freud believed that Sophocles' tragedy dealt with similar issues. If there had never been a Greek tragedy to name it by, the complex would probably have been called triadic developmental conflicts and their role in the genesis and maturation of infantile sexuality and its derivatives in the mature sexual behavior of adult life. (The Oedipus complex says it more succinctly and the name seems to have stuck!)

Human development is so complex, each human being so existentially unique, that it is difficult to speak in generalities without doing violence to the particulars that make no two people alike. Psychological blueprints can, however, be described and, if not taken too literally, can bring some clarity of focus to a topic as vast as the human mind itself and its growth and development.

When a child is born it is equipped with an endowment that will flourish in an appropriate facilitating environment. In current understanding of human development the old nature vs nurture controversy seems outdated as multi-disciplinary ecumenical research focuses its attention on nature *and* nurture and the complicated ways they influence each other. The facilitating environment usually consists of the family, a stable structure of consistent caregiving, usually provided by two caregivers, who imprint the structures with their beliefs and values. A child seems to have an innate apparatus of cognitive and sensorimotor abilities that the facilitating environment engages with and enhances. Human language, to choose one complex example, may seem to have its own prewired grammar as Chomsky has demonstrated, but it will not come to full fruition unless the seemingly meaningless cooing and babbling of the first year of life is given social meaning and turned into communication by the doting synergistic caregiver!

II. FIRST THREE YEARS OF LIFE

Before the Oedipus complex begins to dominate the psychological life of a child (roughly between 3 and 6 years of age), the first 3 years of life have preparatory tasks of great significance. In the beginning, a speechless infant has to develop other modes of communication to build a social life (mainly with mother and father in the first year of life). Sight, smell, rudimentary memory, crying, clinging, and smiling all cooperate to build communicative bridges and foster the growing complexity of first relationships. When Sigmund Freud, who discovered the Oedipus complex in October of 1897 through self-analysis, began to realize the psychological trove of pre-Oedipal experience that antedated his momentous discovery, he compared the two phases of development in archeological terms, as if the excavator of an ancient city unearthed an even more ancient city beneath the first, "like the discovery . . . of the Minoan-Mycenean civilization behind the civilization of Greece."

If the Oedipus complex refers to a child's conflict when he discovers it has two parents who not only love him but love each other as well, and have a private sexual relationship that excludes the child from the parental bedroom at nighttime, this conflict cannot be imagined until the mind has internalized significant learning experiences from the first 3 years of life. From an interpersonal point of view what the child internalizes is the conviction that his parents love him even when he is angry and has expressed some hatred toward his caregivers. This achievement has been called object constancy by Mahler and others, object in psychoanalytic parlance always implying the internal representation of the relationship with another human being. For a child to become convinced that love survives episodes of hatred and negativity, the first 3 years of psychological life seem crucial. In those first 3 years a child in an adequate facilitating environment (what Heinz Hartmann has called the "average expectable environment") can acquire these basic psychological convictions. Volumes could be written about the details of these achievements of the first 3 years of life, but for our purposes it is perhaps sufficient to set up in this rudimentary manner the psychological stage upon which the drama of the Oedipus complex will be enacted.

III. ONSET OF OEDIPUS COMPLEX

Sigmund Freud's classical descriptions of the Oedipus complex in boys and girls have been modified somewhat in the light of post-Freudian research, but the main points have stood the test of time and have been reaffirmed in the playrooms and consulting rooms of child analysts and adult analysts around the world. The major revision of Freudian theory has involved female sexuality and the Oedipal development of girls. Early Freudian theory and the later revisions will be addressed presently.

A boy's Oedipus complex is rife with castration anxiety since the child believes that his sexual desires for his mother and rivalrous feelings toward his father will surely meet with parental retaliation and that his offending organ (the penis) will, therefore, be taken from him. Eventually, the boy will resolve his dilemma by repressing these sexual desires toward his mother and identifying with his father's authority. Repression and identification are defense mechanisms and they are essential along with other defenses (sublimation) and psychological attributes (intelligence, frustration tolerance, etc.) if the child is to gain mastery over his instincts and resolve his conflicts in adaptive ways. The conflict, as described by Freud, is very complex, the child struggling to resolve it from a variety of angles. Freud described a positive Oedipus complex and a negative Oedipus complex to capture the complexity

of the struggle. The child's love for his rival, as well as his hate, makes the conflict virtually unresolvable. If the boy is loving toward his mother and rivalrous with his father (the positive Oedipus complex), he begins to feel anxiety that his rival could destroy him or guilt when he imagines destroying someone he also loves deeply. This developmental quandary can trigger a negative Oedipal approach to the dilemma in which the boy switches allegiances and contemplates loving his father (if only he could be a girl) and wresting his father away from the rivalrous mother! This strategy does not work either since the child also loves the mother deeply and cannot pretend to hate her for very long. Consequently, the negative Oedipal solution will be abandoned and the positive Oedipal strategy will set the cycle in motion once again. This is a time of excitement, passion, competition, and frustration for children, well-reflected in the boisterousness of playgrounds and schoolyards, as well as in the fantastic world of dreams and nightmares. Parents who are unconsciously or consciously aware of the complex psychological dramas of their "heroic" children do not squash the spirit of romance and rivalry in these burgeoning conflicts, but find ways to promote sexuality and aggression in statu nascendi without promoting incest and parenticide at the same time. Parenthood that foments child abuse or childhood incest obviously destroys the great potential the Oedipus complex has for promoting mental health, distorting developmental progress irrevocably, perhaps. [*See* DEFENSE MECHANISMS.]

IV. RESOLUTION

The eventual resolution of the Oedipus complex was first called a "dissolution" by Sigmund Freud. At age 6, approximately, an infantile amnesia sets in. This amnesia removes the whole developmental drama from consciousness until a later date when the return of the repressed in adolescence or adulthood can lead to conflict which may be resolved adaptively or maladaptively, depending on the quality of the psychic structures involved. What Freud called "dissolution" initially has been modified, since the complex is never really destroyed or put aside but continues to inform the mind and its conflicts throughout the life cycle. The relative resolution of the Oedipus complex at age 6 is brought about by repression and identification, mainly, though sublimation and other defense mechanisms obviously play a part, as does cognitive development. Repression and identification are crucial for psychic structuralization, the superego being the heir of this process. In other words, the child gradually relinquishes his sexual claim on the opposite-sex parent and aggressive rivalry with the same-sex parent and replaces his sexuality and rivalry with identifications. These identifications with parental authority lead to the formation of a structure of inner morality called the superego. The superego regulates the sense of pleasure or guilt each child experiences as he or she grapples with conflict and chooses adaptive or maladaptive strategies. From ages 6 to 12, approximately, in this relative "latency" period, Oedipal desire is set aside and replaced with what Erikson has called "a sense of industry." The industry Erikson refers to is the typical 7 year old's zealous interest in coins, stamps, baseball, skip rope, ballet, etc., an industry that allows the child the opportunity to imbibe the fruits of culture in a seemingly pacific manner. Adolescence will shake this pacific resolution to its roots, to be sure, when the Oedipus complex returns with hormonal and psychological fanfare. The 6-year respite called latency does however, seem to be necessary as the human organism develops and matures. The Oedipus complex needs to be digested slowly and incrementally, it would seem, throughout the vicissitudes of the life cycle.

The Oedipus complex of the girl, though comparable to that of the boy in many ways, has some distinctly gender-specific differences. Freud argued that castration anxiety eventually brought the boy's Oedipus complex to a close when the boy decides to relinquish his claim on his mother and identify with the authority of his father, an identification that will allow the boy as a grown-up to choose a wife unconsciously modeled on his mother. Freud argued that by contrast it was castration anxiety that triggered the onset of the girl's Oedipus complex, the girl's disappointment with her own and her mother's anatomy, steering her toward father and his more enviable anatomy. The anatomical distinction between the sexes is at the root of this Freudian theory, the penis and the vagina playing tricks on the imaginations of highly impressionable young children. The pre-operational animistic thinking of children ages 3 to 5 makes them especially vulnerable to neurotic distortions of perceptual information. If a boy, seeing the girl's anatomy for the first time, assumes that the penis was removed from it, a girl seeing a boy's anatomy for the first time wonders why her penis has not grown and considers ways of acquiring one. Her Oedipus complex begins with sexual longings for the man (father) who can perhaps give her what she lacks (the positive Oedipus complex). When the girl, fearing mother's retaliation or guilt-ridden about her negative feelings toward one she loves, turns her attention back toward her mother and away from her father, a negative Oedipal solution to the conflict is being tested. The ultimate resolution for the girl, as for the boy, is arrived at through repression and identification and the formation of a superego that will protect the industrious child from instinctual turmoil in latency. Freud has been criticized for his chauvinistic depiction of the girl's development and the developmental picture has been modified significantly by the post-Freudian research of the past 50 years. Whereas Freud implied that the psychology of a little girl was driven mainly by her lack of a penis, child analytic and child observational research on femininity has charted the pre-Oedipal components of a girl's identification with her mother long before the girl turns to her father in search of a penis. The superego development of women is another controversy that has undergone significant modification in post-Freudian analytic research. Whereas Freud argued that a girl's superego does not have to be so authoritarian or firmly established since her fear of castration is less than a boy's, continuing clinical research has shown that this theoretical implication does not have any clinical validity, the morality of girls being every bit as complex and intrapsychic as a boy's.

When boys and girls become adolescents after the 6 years of latency, the Oedipus complex returns with the renewed vigor provided by hormonal and anatomical development. Sexual desire for the opposite-sex parent takes on new meaning when one is taller, stronger, and capable of ejaculation and sexual intercourse, not merely in imagination but in actuality! The reawakening of the Oedipus complex in adolescence makes this phase of development psychologically stormy and socially precarious as children, who are no longer children and not yet quite adult, express their conflicts in action. Eventually, after years of adolescent turmoil, resolutions of the Oedipus complex will again be arrived at through repression and compromise and identification, and the superego will again benefit from the experience and become more "human" in the process. Adolescents, who at first rage against the stupidity of parents as they try to distance themselves from their incestuous longings, will eventually find nonincestuous outlets for their desires and form new, less extreme opinions of their parents in time.

V. CONCLUSION

While I have attempted to describe the Oedipus complex from a developmental point of view, charting its origins in prelatency, its relative disappearance in latency, and its reawakening in adolescence, one of the main interests in the Oedipus complex is its effects on the psychology of adults. Freud felt that the Oedipus complex was the cornerstone of his theory of neurosogenesis, by which he meant that maladaptive resolutions of the Oedipus complex accounted for much of the symptomatology and character pathology that is so ubiquitous in adult life. One could also argue, of course, that adaptive resolutions of the Oedipus complex give adult life its romantic zest and joie de vivre. In this regard, perhaps, it is fitting to give Oedipus himself the last word. He understood the meaning of the riddle of the Sphynx, "What when young walks on four feet, when grown walks on two feet, and finally walks on three feet?" to be a description of the stages of human development. He knew that, though life may begin helplessly on all fours and end rather feebly leaning on a stick, there is a glorious period in between called the Oedipus complex, when man carves his destiny out of guilt standing irrevocably on his own two feet.

Bibliography

Blass, R. (1992). Did Dora have an Oedipus complex? In "The Psychoanalytic Study of the Child," Vol. 47. Yale University Press, New Haven.

Blos, P. (1985). "Son and Father: Before and Beyond the Oedipus Complex." The Free Press, New York.

Brenner, C. (1982). "The Mind in Conflict." International Universities Press, Madison, CT.

Freud, S. (1931). "Female Sexuality: The Standard Edition of the Complete Psychological Works of Sigmund Freud," Vol. 21. Hogarth Press, Honolulu.

Lane, F. M. (1986). The genital envy complex: A case of a man with a fantasied vulva. In "The Psychology of Men" (G. I. Fogel, F. M. Lane, and R. S. Liebert, Eds.). Basic Books, New York.

Mahon, E. (1986). The contribution of adolescence to male psychology. In "The Psychology of Men" (G. I. Fogel, F. M. Lane, and R. S. Liebert, Eds.). Basic Books, New York.

Mahon, E. (1991). The dissolution of the Oedipus complex: A neglected cognitive factor. In "The Psychoanalytic Quarterly," Vol. LX, No. 4, Yale University Press, New Haven.

OPERANT LEARNING

W. F. Angermeier
Universität zu Köln, Germany

Glossary

Contingency Conditional probabilities relating the occurrence and nonoccurrence of events.
Discrimination Reliable difference in behavior in the presence of two or more stimuli.
Generalization Responding to similar stimuli in a similar fashion; responding to one stimulus event with similar reactions.
Ontogeny Lifespan of an organism.
Operant Behavior acting upon the environment.
Phylogeny Total time of development of all living things.
Punishment Aversive events which diminish responding.
Reinforcement Contingent event which increases responding.

OPERANT LEARNING can be defined as the more or less permanent changes in responding, associated with the consequences of behavior. These consequences may be positive, negative, or aversive. Correspondingly, the occurrence of the behavior may either increase or decrease.

I. BASIC PRINCIPLES OF OPERANT LEARNING

A. Phases of Operant Learning

1. Operant Levels

a. What Is It?

Operant level means the determination of the rate, frequency, or probability of the occurrence of be-

havior without any apparent reinforcement. If, e.g., we observe a person sitting on a park bench, to see how often he is scratching his nose, we would be determining the operant level for this particular behavior. In the laboratory, an animal (albino rat) is placed into a learning box, which is equipped with a lever and a food magazine. The determination of the operant level consists in this case of registering the number of times the animal depresses the lever without any reinforcement (food is not delivered after the lever-press) during a fixed time interval.

b. Advantages and Disadvantages

The advantages of operant level determination lie in the possibility to compare the frequency of a certain behavior when it is being reinforced with the frequency when it is not being reinforced. This comparison enables us to draw inferences about the effects of behavioral consequences, such as positive and negative reinforcement or punishment. The disadvantages are found when we study the number of responses within the time course given. Our own investigations showed that the animals *learn* to respond less and less as time goes on (45 animals responded during the first 3 min, and only 1 during the last 3 min of a 60-min operant level procedure). In addition to that, these animals took 180 min to learn lever-pressing (when that behavior was later reinforced with food) as compared to a second group, which was not exposed to the above procedure, and needed only 60 min to learn. Apparently, the first group had learned not to respond, since there were no adequate consequences to the behavior shown.

2. Acquisition

a. The Learning Process

Using a relatively simple model, let us stay with the learning box and the white rat. If we use food as reinforcement, we must first deprive the animal of food. This we can do by not feeding the rat for a period of 24 hr or by reducing its body weight to approximately 80 or 85% of its normal weight. Both methods have their advantages and disadvantages. We now place the animal gently into the learning apparatus and reinforce *every* lever-press with a small food pellet. This is called continuous reinforcement (CR) and absolutely necessary to establish learning. If we did not follow this procedure, the animal would not be able to associate the behavior with its consequences.

b. Beginning and End of Learning

The acquisition process begins with the first reinforced response and ends when the frequency of responding reaches a stable rate. In order to show the *development* of the learning process more clearly, it is advantageous to measure the time intervals between reinforced responses rather than to plot the responses in the form of cumulative curves (see Fig. 1.).

3. Maintenance

a. Performance

Performance begins after the learning process has been completed. This phase is characterized by stable and smooth responding (see Fig. 1). In general, operant behavior is better maintained through irregular (intermittent) application of reinforcement. Now, reinforcement is given according to certain prearranged schedules of reinforcement and changes behavior accordingly, as we shall see in section II.

4. Extinction

If we want to inhibit the behavior under consideration, we simply stop reinforcing it. Gradually or quickly, depending upon the mode of previous reinforcement, the behavior disappears—or is greatly reduced in its frequency. This shows, that it is not necessary to punish behavior in order to reduce its frequency; nonreinforcement has a similar effect (Fig. 2).

5. Spontaneous Recovery

After a certain time interval has elapsed following extinction, the organism will once again show the behavior although it is now not reinforced. This time, however, the frequency of it is greatly reduced. This indicates that extinction is a dynamic process, that one cannot simply eliminate reinforced behavior. One can readily see that spontaneous recovery (of undesirable behavior) is a problem in human psychotherapy.

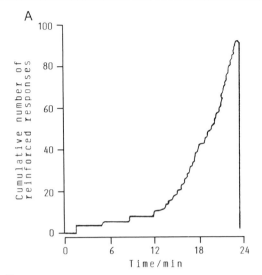

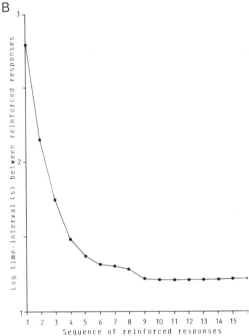

FIGURE 1   (A) Traditional cumulative curve of responding, and (B) time-interval curve of responding.

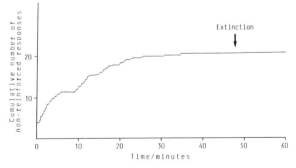

FIGURE 2   Curve of operant extinction.

6. Relearning

If we start to reinforce behavior following extinction, it will reach its once attained frequency very quickly. Although this process is generally called "relearning," it would be more accurate to speak of regaining previous levels of performance.

B. Variables Affecting Operant Learning

1. Distinction between Learning and Performance

It is very important to distinguish between learning and performance. The learning process is characterized, as we have seen in Figure 1, by a nonlinear reduction of time intervals between reinforced responses. This leads to a phase, we call performance, in which the time intervals between reinforced reactions are now more or less equal, and the behavior is smooth and stable. When we observe the changeover from the learning to the performance phase, we notice a great and nearly complete reduction of irrelevant behavior, as far as the learning task is concerned: the organism is now performing the required task without virtually any distraction by other stimuli or events.

2. Contiguity

In general, it is important that the chosen reinforcement follow the behavior immediately, so that the organism can associate the two events. If, the reinforcement is delayed, it might become associated with a different behavior, namely the one which immediately preceded it. In the human realm, we can bridge some time gaps with the help of verbal comments: "You can take the afternoon off because you did such a splendid job yesterday during the negotiations with . . . ." Such verbal statements should always be very precise, otherwise the danger exists that the reinforcement is associated with the "wrong" behavior.

3. Deprivation

Deprivation is a term that applies to need systems of various organisms. In animal investigations, we usually deprive the experimental subjects of food or water. But other needs are also evident, such as warmth, stroking, social contact in general and, among others, the opportunity to explore, play, etc.

Human needs are naturally more complex, and seem to be ever present, be it consciously or subconsciously. Such needs vary from person to person, between age groups, sexes, and members of different cultures. In a list of such human needs we would find, among others, physiological needs (such as hunger, thirst, sexual activity, activity, and rest), social needs (such as belonging, being appreciated, love, status), and individualistic needs (such as a sound comprehension of reality, growth and development of one's personality, control over environmental events, balance between success and failures, and personal independence). It is quite obvious that such needs are naturally present in our lives, so that deprivations need not be construed artificially.

4. Amount and Quality of Reinforcement

Our own research has shown that amount and quality of reinforcement *do not* influence the learning process, but greatly affect the performance of the learned behavior. Quite naturally, we prefer reinforcements which we specially like, be it more free time, more or less responsibility, money, power, status, etc. Again, our particular social involvement creates such needs and demands quite naturally.

5. Reinforcement Hierarchy

If we are in a leadership position and asked to guide human behavior properly, it is of utmost importance that we clearly recognize the "need structure" or—as it is called technically—the reinforcement hierarchy of the persons concerned. In a therapy situation, e.g., the therapist usually asks the client what kind of things, situations, and events he prefers most, very much, much, and less. From the answers to these questions he is able to construct a reinforcement hierarchy. It may look as follows:

1. Most preferred	—hiking in the mountains
2. Very much preferred	—fishing in the lake
3.	—watching professional sports
4. Much preferred	—going to parties
5.	—reading
6. Less preferred	—doing chores around the house
7.	—mowing the lawn
8. Least preferred	—straightening out problems with the neighbor, etc.

Since we all have different needs and preferences, no two reinforcement hierarchies are alike.

II. SCHEDULES OF REINFORCEMENT

A. Ratio Schedules

1. Fixed-Ratio (FR) Schedules

If we reinforce the behavior under consideration, let us say, every fifth time it occurs, we speak of a fixed-ratio (5:1) reinforcement. We find such FR schedules of reinforcement in situations where people, e.g., are being paid wages according to piece work. Since schedules of reinforcement are being used during the performance phase, it is important to work up *gradually* from a 1:1 reinforcement to a 10:1 or 20:1 reinforcement arrangement. If this is not done the behavior might be extinguished, i.e., disappear. This is especially true for young children, since their level of attention and endurance is affected by the intrusion of distracting events during periods of nonreinforcement. In such situations, we would, e.g., reinforce the said behavior maybe 10 times on a 2:1 FR schedule, then 10 times on a 3:1 schedule and so on. The advantages of FR schedules are the consistency of behavior and the reduced amount of reinforcement necessary to maintain behavior. Such behavior also extinguishes—after a burst of responding, caused by nonreinforcement—rather rapidly in time.

The disadvantage of FR schedules is that organisms come to expect the reinforcement after completing a certain amount of work (reactions, responses, etc.). Also, such schedules cannot be applied during the actual learning phase; behavioral frequencies would simply not increase and stabilize.

2. Variable-Ratio (VR) Schedules

If we reinforce behavior on the average every fifth time it occurs (4:1, 6:1, 3:1, 7:1, 5:1, etc.), then we are applying a variable-ratio schedule of 5:1.

The advantage of such a schedule over a FR schedule is that organisms cannot expect a regular occurrence of reinforcement. Behavior becomes even more predictable and less irregular. This is also true for the extinction phase following such schedules. Again, we have to take great care to introduce such a reinforcement arrangement gradually, otherwise it is counterproductive.

B. Interval Schedules

1. Fixed-Interval (FI) Schedules

Is the behavior under consideration reinforced after a certain time interval has elapsed, let us say, at the last day of each month, then we are using a FI schedule of reinforcement. The advantages of such schedules are similar to the FR schedules. The disadvantage is that organisms again come to expect the reinforcement at a certain point in time, and actually work less during the rest of the time period.

2. Variable-Interval (VI) Schedules

Analogous to the VR schedules, we can also arrange to reinforce behavior on the average after, e.g., 6 months (5 months, 3 months, 9 months, 4 months, 8 months, etc.). Again, organisms cannot expect a regular occurrence of reinforcement; behavior becomes very stable and regular. The same is also true during extinction following the application of such VI schedules. Some industries take advantage of the effects of such schedules and spread out salary increases and bonuses over varied periods of time.

C. Other Schedules

1. Differential Reinforcement of High Rates (DRH)

It is possible to reinforce a certain type of behavior only, if it occurs at a high rate. A secretary, e.g., is hired only if he can type 50 words/min.

2. Differential Reinforcement of Low Rates (DRL)

We can also decide to reinforce behavior when it occurs at a low rate. For example, in animal research, we select students to work in our laboratories who speak little while making observations. Politicians seem to prefer co-workers who disagree little with certain views of the boss. The schedules to follow now are not very common in the human realm, and will therefore only be defined briefly.

3. Tandem Schedules

If two or more different schedules of reinforcement follow each other, we speak of a tandem schedule. An example might be: FR 30:1–FI 3 min:1–FR 50:1.

4. Chained Schedules

The schedules are similar to tandem schedules, with the exception of a certain stimulus being given to indicate the change-over from one type of schedule to another.

5. Mixed Schedules

Here, a certain schedule, e.g., FR 50:1 is given for a period of 30 min, followed by a FI schedule, e.g.,

2 min : 1, applied for 30 min also. The change-over occurs without any application of a certain stimulus (discriminative stimulus).

6. Multiple Schedules

If we apply a discriminative stimulus to mixed schedules, we denote these as multiple schedules.

7. Alternative Schedules

If we choose two reinforcement schedules, e.g., FR 50 : 1 and FI 3 min : 1, and then give the reinforcement when the conditions of one or the other schedule are fulfilled, then we speak of an alternative schedule. For example, a teacher gives 20 math problems to his students (or lets them work for 10 min on these). The reinforcement consists of puzzle-solving as soon as they meet one or the other condition. The students who do well in math get their reinforcement quickly. Those who are slower also get their reinforcement, but somewhat later. These schedules can be used in situations where the work speed, etc., differs and individuality is of importance.

8. Concurrent Schedules

We can, e.g., reinforce one type of behavior according to a FR schedule, and another type according to a FI schedule. If we do this, we are using a concurrent schedule.

9. Conjunctive Schedules

If the conditions of two schedules have to be fulfilled before the reinforcement is given, we are applying a conjunctive schedule. For example, if the 20 math problems have to be solved within 10 min, reinforcement is attainable.

10. Aperiodic Reinforcement

In our times of computer control, it is possible to use a random generator to set, e.g., the delivery of

reinforcement at 2%. This means that 2% of all proper reactions will be reinforced. This makes it impossible to predict the occurrence of reinforcement, since it appears at random. Responses reinforced this way, are extremely difficult to extinguish.

Operators of lotteries and casinos have long been aware of the beneficial effects of such a schedule of reinforcement for their pocketbooks (Fig. 3).

III. GENERALIZATION AND DISCRIMINATION

A. Generalization: Stimuli and Responses

1. Stimulus Generalization

The question of stimulus generalization is a question of stimulus control. To what extent will a reaction, following a certain stimulus, also occur when other stimuli are perceived. If we sit in a car and wait for the green light to appear, that light controls our behavior. As soon as it comes on, we can drive on. Now, not all green lights have exactly the same physical properties. And yet, we react to them in much the same way. That is, nearly identical stimulus features lead to the same response. In animal experiments, a great many physical properties of stimuli have been investigated. The outcome is nearly always the same: the more alike the stimuli tested are, the more often the same reaction (kind, rate, strength, etc.) will be shown; and, conversely, the more differences exist along a dimension between stimuli to be compared, the more differences we also detect in the reactions (kind, rate, strength, etc.).

2. Stimulus Discrimination

Stimulus discrimination refers to a situation in which an organism reacts differently to two or more stimuli. Staying with our examples above, we would put on the brakes when the light is red, and push down the accelerator when it is green. Unless we are colorblind, we can clearly discriminate between the two colors. However, not all discriminations in our lives are that simple. Consider the situation of a young boy who gains approval when telling risky stories in the presence of his aunts and uncles, but not in the presence of his grandparents. Discriminative behavior, just like generalization or transfer, leads to reactions with positive consequences. In that respect they are alike, although the mechanisms

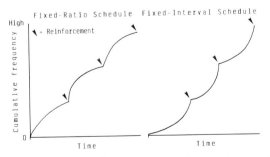

FIGURE 3   Typical cumulative curves of operant responding under fixed-ratio (left) and fixed-interval (right) schedules of reinforcement.

are—as one expert puts it—"loosely and symmetrically related."

3. Response Generalization

If we react to the same stimulus or stimulus situations with different responses, we speak of response generalization. Response generalization is a blessing in interpersonal relationships. It enables us to engage in vastly different conversations, helps us to solve the same problem in different ways, etc.

4. Response Discrimination

When we hammer a nail into wood with our right hand, we must let go of it with our left before we apply the final blow. Otherwise, it will probably be very painful for us. When we are in the presence of a certain person, we must phrase our verbal utterings in a certain way, otherwise we may be offensive. "Son of a . . ." may be a term of endearment to our basketball buddies, but not to the dean or the president of our company. When we master this art, we have learned response discrimination. Again, this process is largely controlled by the outcome or consequences of such behavior.

IV. ONTOGENY AND PHYLOGENY OF OPERANT LEARNING

A. Ontogeny

1. Tasks, Measures, and Results

When we look at results from animal investigations performed in our laboratories it is evident that the ability for operant learning apparently stays constant throughout the life of the organism. How can we reach such a conclusion? We tested 249 chickens, divided into 32 age groups (from 1 day of age to 1800 days of age) in a learning box, where a food-deprived animal had to peck a disc in order to obtain food. Figure 4 shows the results.

Figure 4 shows that, despite differences in number of reinforced responses to criterion, there is a constant factor, which we have called "K," which results if we divide the number of reinforced responses necessary to reach criterion by the number of reinfored responses the animal is capable of emitting within a certain time period (in our case 1 min).

Those age groups which need more reinforced responses in order to reach the learning criterion also emit more responses per minute. In a sense this means that the K factor is an indication how speed

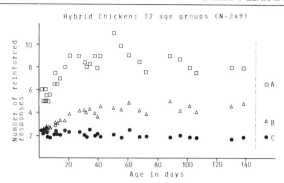

FIGURE 4   Relationship of A (number of reinforcements to criterion) to B (criterion performance/min) to C (K factor). The K factor for fishes was found to be 1, for birds 2, and for mammals 3.

of reinforced reactions is used for the formation of operant learning. In a speculative way we assume that it indirectly expresses the normal complexity of the organism (see also section B).

At the human level, things appear to be quite different. Here, much depends upon the development of language skills and logical reasoning. If, however, we assume that correct problem solving is rewarding—an assumption which has been shown to be true for many animals—the above categories of behavior can be correctly subsumed under the heading of operant learning. If we accept this, then the Piagetian model of ontogenetic development becomes relevant here, even with the restrictions and contradictions it contains. The key word in this theory is "invariance." What does it mean? We recognize invariance when we realize, e.g., that a belt stretched out is not longer than the same belt after we roll it up. An understanding of such relationships seems to progress from one- to two- to three-dimensional objects, i.e., from lines to areas to volumes. Even, considering the restrictions contained in these studies—they were done mostly with children in Swiss mountain villages—the results are nevertheless most interesting. A summary is presented in Figure 5.

2. Implications

Even those who are opposed to a strict deterministic interpretation of the effects of reinforcement or reward cannot deny its powerful influence upon behavior. They usually take offence to the notion that all behavior is to be explained in this way. The latter view pertains particularly to human behavior. It is quite obvious that aside from operant learning mechanisms, classical (Pavlovian) conditioning, observa-

Type of conservation	Dimension	Change in physical appearance	Average age at which invariance is grasped
Number	Number of elements in a collection	Rearranging or displacing the elements	6-7
Substance	Amount of a deformable substance (e.g., clay)	Altering its shape	7-8
Length	Length of a line or object	Altering its shape or displacing it	7-8
Area	Amount of a surface covered by a set of plane figures	Rearranging the figures	8-9
Weight	Weight of an object	Altering its shape	9-10
Volume	Volume of an object (in terms of water displacement)	Altering its shape	14-15

FIGURE 5   Piaget's concept of invariance.

tional learning (learning from models), and other cognitive learning processes play a decisive role in human behavior. Whenever there is, however, a confirmation of such behavior or behavioral tendencies, reinforcement is involved, and, thus, operant learning. Ultimately, it makes little difference whether we call such consequences confirmation, reward, reinforcement, or any other name. What is important is that we recognize that such consequences frequently come to *control* behavior and constitute an important aspect of adaptive behavior.

B. Phylogeny

When we consider phyletic comparisons of operant behavior, we find few systematic studies in the literature. This is particularly true of comparisons involving human subjects. The restraints are overwhelming.

In a series of studies, extending over nearly two decades, we have tried to circumvent these inherent difficulties through methodological considerations which allow such comparisons to be made. Time and space do not permit describing all of these, but here are the most important ones.

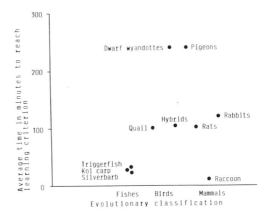

FIGURE 6   Learning time and evolutionary classification.

First, the task to be performed was an operant task, reinforced with food. The amount of food offered was approximately 1/300 of the daily need of the respective organism.

Second, the choice of organisms to be tested was primarily fishes, birds, and mammals. Within these classes, subclasses were selected which differed with respect to feeding behavior, socialization (precocial and altricial birds), and other variables.

Third, three measures of operant learning were taken: number of rewards to criterion, learning time, and percentage of animals learning the task at hand.

Fourth, the task was designed in such a way that the strength of activating the manipulandum did not take more than 3-5% of the animals body weight, usually much less.

Fifth, each animal defined its own learning criterion. That criterion was the average rate of reinforced responses shown after the responding had stabilized, e.g., after the intervals between reinforced responses stayed constant from minute to minute.

The results are shown in Figures 6, 7, and 8.

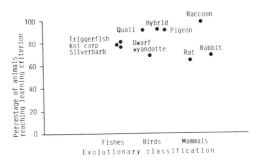

FIGURE 7   Percentage of learners and evolutionary classification.

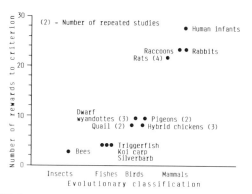

FIGURE 8 Number of rewards to criterion and evolutionary classification.

None of the variables investigated produced significant results except the *classes of animals used*. There, too, only *number of rewards to criterion* discriminated significantly between the various classes of animals. It is important to note that there were no differences within the classes of animals. What are the implications of these results?

The implications are that as far as simple tasks are concerned which are reinforced by the application of food, "lower" animals need fewer reinforced trials than "higher" ones. Why is this so?

There is no simple explanation or law to account for the results. We offer the following hypotheses to be considered *in toto* or various combinations to contribute toward an explanation of the findings.

Learning time varies unsystematically between classes of animals, probably because the adaptation to the apparatus and the general experimental conditions is not predictable. This means that animals are differentially affected by such conditions.

Percentage of animals learning is not significantly different between the classes of animals used. We interpret this to mean that the difficulty of task was the same for all animals.

Number of rewards (reinforcement) to criterion is the only dependent variable (measurement of behavior) which clearly discriminates between the classes of animals used here. We think this is because the learning task chosen was appropriate for the comparison made. Very difficult learning tasks lead to a meaningless *divergence* of results; very easy and primitive learning situations (such as reflexes or strong aversive conditions) lead to a meaningless *convergence* of results. Paradoxically, the "lower" organisms need significantly fewer reinforcements to reach a learning criterion then do the "higher" organisms. How can one explain this fact?

The percentage of instinctual and/or instinct-like behavior is considerably higher in lower organisms than in animals appearing later in evolution. This means that lower organisms have much less *irrelevant* behavior to suppress than higher organisms.

Next, corticalization greatly increases the behavioral repertoire. Thus, differences appeared in the behavioral skills of seeking, finding, and ingesting food. These differences led on the one hand—in higher organisms—to variability and on the other hand to restrictions in animal diets.

Another factor is the relationship between brain structures regulating food intake and mass of cortical tissue. The ratio between these two criteria is larger for lower organisms with respect to structures regulating food intake and smaller for higher organisms. This in turn would indicate a much higher probability of irrelevant types of behavior (in higher organisms) and hence a higher number of reinforced reactions to reach learning criterion (because more irrelevant behavior needs to be inhibited or suppressed).

The next hypothesis only applies in a limited fashion. Animals with a short lifespan and animals depending on a limited variety of food need to learn more quickly than those not so restricted. Other hypotheses possibly accounting for these differences are: the complexity of neural networks, the time, information remains within such networks, the ratio of instinctual to variable behavior (behavioral plasticity), the wealth of sensory inputs, the relationship of brain weight to body weight, metabolic factors (conversion of food to energy), possible negative feedback mechanisms which enable the animal to detect consequences of his operant behavior, and ecological factors, such as e.g., avoidance of poisonous substances (which is more important to an animal producing few offsprings than to an organism producing thousands).

Although, there are still many questions about operant behavior unanswered, it is nevertheless surprising how many answers we have found already.

V. MAJOR ISSUES IN OPERANT LEARNING

A. Reinforcement (Reward and Punishment)

At the beginning of this article, we gave a general definition of operant learning. We must now be more precise. It is difficult to give a definition of operant learning which incorporates long-term memory and which specifies the effect reinforcement has on responding, association, expectations, confirmations, or brain processes. All we can really define is the effect reinforcement has on behavior in terms of observable activities. Staddon's model is excellently suited for this purpose.

1. When the occurrence of a reinforcer is made to depend on the occurrence of a specific response, the response rate increases.

2. When the reinforcer is no longer presented or is presented independently of responding, response rate declines—often, but not necessarily, to zero (extinction).

3. . . . reinforcement must be reversibly selective for at least one pair of activities, that is, capable of strengthening reinforced activity A at the expense of activity B that is not reinforced, and vice versa.

Since these prerequisites also apply to human behavior, it means that:

1. Reinforcement must be contingent upon responding.

2. A lack of reinforcement leads to a decrease of responding.

3. When a certain type of behavior is reinforced, the response rate of another type or types of behavior declines (suppression of—what we called earlier—irrelevant behavior).

In order to produce these effects, a set of assumptions must be made as follows.

1. *Variability*. We assume that our model has at least two modes of behavior (activities), A and B. We represent the strengths of these two activities by two stochastic (random-in-time) variables, VA (t) and VB (t). That is, the strengths of A and B vary irregularly with time (t). This assumption is represented by variable E in our model.

2. *Competition*. The activity with the higher strength (V) is the one that actually occurs.

3. *Arousal*. We assume that the occurrence of a positive reinforcer produces an increase in the strength of both activities and that strength is directly related to their current strengths. In other words, positive reinforcers act like amplifiers, increasing the strengths of all tendencies to

action. This concept is represented by parameter b.

4. *Adaptation*. The strength increment caused by an individual reinforcer presentation dissipates with time. In other words, the boost the reinforcer gives eventually dissipates, which is crucial, although not necessarily at the same rate, for every activity. This idea is represented by parameter a.

From these assumptions follows a simple system of integrators.

Following nonreinforcement:

$$V(t + 1) = aV(t) + E,$$

where $0 < a < 1$.

Following reinforcement:

$$V(t + 1) = aV(t) + E + bV(t).$$

For human behavior, the implications of this model are clear. Reinforcement (or reward) must be contingent upon a certain type of behavior. The person must clearly be aware of what type of action is being reinforced. Statements such as "This is for being a good girl today," are nonsense. Much better would be, "This present is for you, because you helped your grandmother shop today!"

Reinforcement should follow the behavior; it is intended to modify, as quickly as possible (delay can be disastrous!). Reinforcement will not just affect the behavior it follows, but also other behaviors.

Behavior which is reinforced is much more likely to occur than behavior which is not reinforced (one aspect of reinforcing a specific behavioral act).

The effect of reinforcement dissipates in time. Some experts assume that this is caused by satiation, others think that competing responses interfere, etc. It is likely that a combination of several factors is responsible for this process.

Early researchers thought that the effects of punishment are diametrically opposed to those of reinforcement. Later, this assumption was dropped. Today, we think of punishment as when an aversive stimulus (event) is contingent upon a certain type of behavior (such as a slap on the hand, etc.) and reduces the frequency of occurrence of this behavior. Viewed in this manner, escape and avoidance are not to be subsumed under punishment, because both procedures lead to an increase in behavior (escape leads to flight, and avoidance to an increase of behavior when the aversive event is presented or signalled).

What then are the effects of punishment? The same factors in Staddon's model that were presented earlier in connection with reward also apply to punishment as follows.

1. When the occurrence of punishment is made contingent on a specific response, the rate of that response decreases.

2. When the punisher is no longer presented or is no longer response contingent, the rate of the response returns to its previous value (which is the procedural definition of extinction of punishment).

3. Punishment must be reversibly selective for at least one pair of activities: Suppressing punishment activity A relative to unpunished activity B, and vice versa.

From these assumptions, which are fairly well in accord with experimental data, follow the same integrator functions as previously presented for reinforcement.

In addition, we should perhaps state a few limiting conditions.

1. Punishment must be applied immediately after the negative behavior occurs.

2. Punishment must be sufficiently strong in order to be effective.

3. Some experts also consider the withdrawal or withholding of reinforcement as punishment, since it also diminishes the behavioral strength of certain reactions to which it is applied.

4. Punishment must be appropriate. It should neither be too harsh nor too mild.

5. Punishment, like reinforcement, is an effective way to modify behavior.

6. Dangers that exist are: using punishment exclusively and thus diminishing desired behavioral variability; using punishment to vent one's own anger and frustration; unfair punishment can lead to permanent negative interactions between persons and can actually cause physical harm.

B. Choice

Why do we select one type of activity rather than another? Why are some people crazy about professional football, and others prefer to read books or listen to music? Such questions relate to what psychologists call choice.

Some years ago, an expert psychologist asked the same questions that we posed above. The result of that inquiry was—and has since become known as—the Premack Principle. What does this principle entail? All activities have some value, but some activities have a higher value than others. It follows from this statement that activities with a higher value to the person will reinforce activities with a lower value. Thus, e.g., we can reinforce homework with the privilege of watching television, but not vice versa. Although, the early experiments on this problem did not provide all the necessary controls to rule out other interpretations, later studies generally confirmed this principle, if two or more activities are contingent upon one another. Shortcomings of this principle are obvious when we look at "strong" reinforcers, such as food and water, and not at preferences made without experimental restrictions of choice. Choice is more readily explained in terms of behavioral economics.

C. Behavioral Economics

Economics has to do with the availability of a commodity, its value, and its price, in short, with supply and demand. When goods are in short supply, the demand rises and with it the price. Generally speaking, we can transfer this principle also to operant performance: if an organism gets less and less reward (as, e.g., in a progressive fixed ratio schedule arrangement of 10:1, 20:1, 40:1, 60:1, 80:1, 100:1), he is also less willing to pay the "price," i.e., he works less and less, as shown in Figure 9.

Such a curve may be inelastic or elastic. We speak of an inelastic demand curve, e.g., when we have

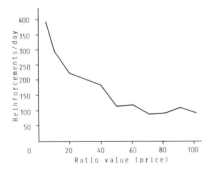

FIGURE 9   Ratio schedule performance plotted as a demand curve (closed economy).

to pay the higher price of medication, simply because we cannot live without it. An elastic demand curve is, e.g., when we are no longer willing to pay the ever-increasing price for cigarettes, and we quit. In the latter case, considerations about our health probably also play a major role in our choice. There is another point to consider, namely the labor–supply relationship. If the gain of work is low, organisms are not going to work much; as the gain rises, more work is performed. If the gain is very high, work drops again, supposedly because of a saturation process. Theoretically, such a curve will look like the one in Figure 10. Decisive for the shape of the curve is the question in what "type of economy" the organisms work. The data for Figure 9 were obtained from animals in a closed economy (24-hr access to the reinforcer). The data in Figure 10 represent results from an open economy, i.e., short work periods and supplemental feeding, if necessary. Thus, the question whether we deal with an open or closed economy becomes crucial for the type of responding we observe.

In a closed economy daily consumption depends on the amount of responding by the subject. When a subject works for essential commodities (things he cannot do without), responding tends to increase with rising prices; this will keep changes of daily intake to a minimum.

In an open economy, daily consumption of reinforcement is independent of the amount of total work. Here, responding tends to decrease with rising prices. As one expert puts it

In a closed economy elasticity of demand is controlled by the nature of the commodity un-

der study (reinforcement), the species of the consumer, and the availability of substitutes. The travel time to obtain a substitute is also an important determiner of the amount of interaction between two available sources of the same commodity. Substitutes, that are distant in time and space, will have relatively little impact on consumption of similar commodities in the current situation.

The effect an organism has to extend to gain a reinforcer can also influence the demand for an alternative commodity, this we term cross-price elasticity. The interactions may be a perfect substitution, an imperfect substitution, or complimentarity and independence. Investigations show that demand for a substitute increases with the price of another commodity, demand for complements decreases, and demand for independence is unaffected.

When income decreases (lower percentage of reinforcement) the consumption of "expensive" reinforcement decreases more than the consumption of "necessities." Delay of gratification, however, increases with reductions in income. These concepts show how complicated the effects of reinforcement are, the major factors which have to be considered in interpreting its effects upon behavior, and the wealth of new questions they can help us answer. At the same time, however, behavioral economics can help us in extending the analysis of behavior from the laboratory to real-life situations. [See ECONOMIC BEHAVIOR.]

VI. APPLICATIONS TO HUMAN BEHAVIOR

A. Behavioral Control

Many techniques of behavior modification depend upon the principles of operant learning as described in the previous sections. There should be no doubt about the powerful effects of reinforcement upon behavior. Such effects we may also term behavioral control. Aside from the mere sequence response–reinforcement, there are also stimuli which indicate to us the appropriateness of a response, i.e., whether to expect reinforcement. Such stimuli should not be underestimated, especially not in human behavior, where they can come to guide our reactions and expectations. Verbal promises of reinforcement to be given are examples of such stimuli. The same is

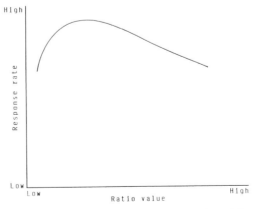

FIGURE 10 Ratio schedule performance plotted as a labor supply curve (open economy).

true of warnings and threats: "If you don't come home on time, you will not be allowed to spend the weekend with your grandparents."

At this point, we need to make another distinction, namely between positive reinforcement, negative reinforcement, and punishment. Positive reinforcement increases behavioral rate because of its "hedonic" effects (as one writer puts it); negative reinforcement also increases behavioral rate, but this time because the behavior aids in fleeing from or avoiding generally aversive conditions. Punishment diminishes behavioral rate, as we have seen earlier. One might say that it makes the behavior previously shown "unattractive" because of the pain it causes, psychologically (such as shame, fear, etc.) and physically.

Clinical applications, which consider punishment a viable alternative to positive reinforcement, usually stress the following points, some of which we already mentioned earlier:

1. Punishment must be applied immediately following the undesirable behavior.

2. Punishment must be applied consistently. Each undesirable action must be punished.

3. Harsh punishment works better than mild punishment.

4. It is wrong to increase the severity of punishment from occasion to occasion.

5. Possible alternatives to punishment consist of removal or lessening of the motivation for such undesirable behavior.

6. If the motivation for undesirable behavior cannot be diminished, it might be better to teach alternative behavior, which, of course, is not undesirable.

7. It might be advantageous to reinforce alternative reactions which are incompatible with the undesirable behavior.

8. The person to be punished must know why and how. When making decisions about the use of reinforcement or punishment, we must also consider the peculiar life circumstances of the person concerned, the age of the person, and, most of all, the consistency with which the behavioral control can be administered.

B. The Classroom

Good educators have been using operant control techniques in the classroom for decades, if not centuries. The difference between their use of these techniques and the "behavioral approach" is that usually the latter takes some form of baseline measures (to see how problematic the behavior is); analyzes the problem in behavioral terms (to make it amenable to behavioral procedures); selects appropriate behavior modification techniques (since not all problems are alike); and engages in follow-up evaluation (to check up on the success of the intervention). Sometimes, the establishment of a baseline alone is sufficient to eliminate the problem, because the children become aware of the attention which is being paid to the situation.

Educators recognized some time ago that sometimes children with behavior problems receive an inordinate amount of attention. This attention apparently serves as a reinforcer for that very inappropriate behavior, since adult attention is very much desired by children of a certain age. One way of correcting the problem could be to give adult attention only when the child shows appropriate (let us say cooperative) interaction with other children. In the course of time it frequently happens that this appropriate social interaction is sufficient for behavior to be maintained at a high level of frequency.

It should now be obvious why base-line measures of behavior are so valuable: the success of the intervention program can only be assessed realistically against such base-line measures. The intervention program consists of adult attention to appropriate behavior and ignoring inappropriate behavior. Control or improvement has been reported for the following behaviors:

attendance at school
paying attention during lessons
choice of playmate
cooperative behavior
excessive day dreams
hyperactivity
motor skills
regressive behavior

The same technique of behavioral management has also been successfully applied to classroom behavior. In addition to praise and ignoring, rules for the appropriate behavior were given to the class. Results show that here, too, behavioral intervention was successful in reducing inappropriate behavior and increasing the time used for studying.

Important, as mentioned several times before, is the contingency between the intervention measures and the children's behavior. The experts also recommend keeping written records of the children's progress or lack of progress. In this way, it is possible to identify possible shortcomings of the intervention program. Despite all good efforts, such programs do not succeed at times. One of the reasons may be the fact, that other influences upon the child are counterproductive: peers and parents.

In such cases, another intervention procedure has sometimes proved highly successful: the token system. Here, children receive tokens, such as checks on a chart, stars, poker chips, and the like for the desirable behavior. These they can exchange later for so-called "back-up reinforcers," such as money, free time, parties, etc. Again, in selecting these, the Premack principle should be taken into consideration. Thus, the back-up reinforcers can be adjusted to individual needs and preferences.

Among the punishment procedures used in the classroom, time-out and verbal reprimands rank foremost. In the time-out procedure, the child is either refused reinforcement or socially isolated for a short period of time. Both of these procedures are usually used only as a last resort (because of the negative connotation of punishment) for highly disruptive behavior.

Other classroom intervention procedures include peers as behavior modifiers, programs that evaluate sociometric behavior, and new techniques of maintaining the effectiveness of programs.

C. The Hospital

Many, if not most, of the principles described for the classroom management also apply to patients in a hospital setting. In addition to these intervention techniques, work with the family of patients and token economy programs have been most successful. Such work includes instruction to family members how to use reinforcement and punishment techniques and educating nurses to use the token system appropriately.

Ultimately, however, it is generally acknowledged that the situation of our mentally ill population will not improve significantly without comprehensive behavioral and psychiatric rehabilitation.

D. Experimental Communities

Ever since Skinner's *Walden II* was published, the idea of communal living has been in the minds of people, mostly in the young ones. Experts are quick to point out that many of the communes (estimates

go to 10,000 between 1965 and 1975) were quickly dissolved because agreements could not be reached by its members on work sharing and leadership. Experiments in the late 1960s and 1970s have shown, however, that some communal living projects were, indeed, successful. Because of limited space, a detailed exposition of these projects cannot be given here. What we will do, instead, is to summarize the problem of communal living and their behavioral solutions.

1. Worksharing

A list of all worksharing behavior was made. A team of members made the inspection to determine if the work was done properly (house-cleaning and cooking). Since this was the case, and credits could be given for the work, considerable savings ensued, and the savings were used to reduce the rent. The results indicated that when credits were given for cleaning, the amount of cleaning done was approximately twice as high as when no credits were given. Also, it made a difference when credits were made contingent upon inspection as compared to credits not being made contingent upon inspection. In the former case (part of an experiment), the average percentage of cleaning was nearly 40% higher than in the latter. Contingency—knowing what behavior is being reinforced—is a powerful variable in the control of behavior. The same is true of the immediate application of reinforcement.

2. Leadership Jobs

These jobs involve tasks, such as coordinating finances and work. Six important factors must be considered before a behavioral program in this realm is successful:

1. Specific job definitions
2. Evaluating job performance
3. Consequences of one's own actions
4. Training programs
5. Limited terms
6. Limited renumerations

Points 2 and 3 specifically fall under the heading of behavioral control, as can be readily seen.

It is at this time not quite clear whether such programs could also be applied to a larger framework of social living.

E. Sexual Problems

In this area too, operant learning techniques have been widely applied. Major emphasis is on changing the gender role, increasing heterosexual skills, and increasing heterosexual arousal, the latter usually done more with classical (Pavlovian) learning techniques.

When "deviant" arousal is being treated in the clinic, punishment is usually used, a treatment which was preferred during the 1960s and early 1970s.

Another method used is covert sensitization. Here, the client works in his fantasy progressively through all the aspects of the undesirable behavior and its aversive consequences; all this in a relaxed context. This latter method has also been used successfully in combination with aversive stimulation, usually in the form of electro-shock.

F. Social Skills

Many of us have problems when it comes to interacting with other people. We have problems in initiating contact with members of the other sex, in initiating and maintaining conversations, in talking too much or too little, etc.

Such problems cause us a great deal of anxiety, we are unsure of ourselves, we lack the appropriate social skills to be successful. Self-assertiveness training—thought to be based on the principles of reciprocal inhibition—is in conflict with existing anxieties, and leads to an inhibition of social anxiety, if successfully practised.

Such training guides the client (or patient) to express his emotions clearly and directly. The client also learns to articulate his emotions and opinions toward other persons. He learns to accept rewards and praise, and to give them. In other words, he learns to live more spontaneously, and not to have anxious misgivings about every step he takes.

In practical terms, the client has tasks to fulfill of increasing difficulty and gets praised (reinforced) by the therapist if they are completed successfully. Slowly, the client overcomes his difficulties, and the feedback from the success in his actions is sufficient reward for his efforts. Such treatment procedures are generally used in anxious and inhibited persons, but also work fairly well in mildly depressive patients.

Another method is "flooding." Here the patient is flooded with the anxiety-provoking stimuli or events. If the client, however, has never had the opportunity to acquire the appropriate skills, then the therapist can guide his behavior and teach him the new skills within the framework of behavioral rehearsal. This involves role-playing, and the thera-

pist's role is to reinforce appropriate action. This method is quite successful with most patients, since it can be tailored exactly to the needs of the person.

G. Alcohol and Drugs

Behavioral (operant) techniques can also be used to treat alcohol- and drug-related problems. They pertain mostly to reinforcement programs, aimed at decreasing the reinforcing effects of drugs, developing new behaviors, incompatible with drug and alcohol abuse, and restructuring the patients environment, so that incompatible or alternative behaviors are more heavily reinforced than the consumption of drugs and alcohol. Community self-help programs, which involve different dynamics, are also useful, such as the programs of Alcoholic Anonymous (AA).

To decrease drug and alcohol intake, aversive treatment techniques have been used, which are applied normally to the entire chain of such behaviors: settings, bottles, social interactions while drinking, etc. The aversive treatment is chemical, electrical, or verbal. Such treatment is usually most successful when it leads to self-control. A combination of chemical and verbal aversion seems to be most promising. [*See* SUBSTANCE ABUSE.]

H. Obesity and Smoking

Obesity and smoking create major problems for the individual's cardiovascular system. Although the various campaigns against smoking have greatly reduced the incidence of cardiovascular disease in the population of the United States, the problem nevertheless exists for millions of smokers.

As far as weight control is concerned, there is no other society in the world which offers as many diets and other weight-control measures as ours. And yet, the greatest problem is not so much weight control as the maintenance of a healthy body weight.

Two other vital factors have recently emerged as being important: genetic influences and early eating patterns.

A behavioral program to ensure weight loss should—according to the experts—include the following:

1. Positive reinforcement and aversive control
2. Control of the major factors leading to overeating

3. Self-monitoring, goal-setting, considering alternative behavior, analysis of life circumstances, and behavioral contracting

In addition, it is absolutely essential that the clients get all the information available about nutrition, calories, in-between-meal eating, proper exercise, etc.

Experience shows also that the therapist's skills in influencing behavior, communicating, and empathy are important variables for the success of such management programs. The major emphasis, finally, is not so much upon weight control as on changing undesirable eating behavior. Since that behavior is embedded in every imaginable human activity, it is of little wonder that is is so difficult to modify.

The last statement also applies to smoking. This means that motivation on the part of the client/patient is probably the decisive factor which determines success or failure.

This is what the experts say about quitting smoking. One should

1. Rapidly breathe in hot smoky air
2. Stop smoking at a predetermined date
3. Select alternative reinforcements

Attempts at quitting smoking gradually have been much less successful than quitting abruptly. This makes sense, since residual stimuli play a role in reinstating the undesirable habit. The results of various investigations show that most aversive procedures have been unsuccessful.

Behavioral treatment, including self-control techniques (such as developing a new hobby, engaging in distractive activities, and relaxation exercises), abrupt cessation of smoking, and support on the part of the therapist, are most promising. Finally, it is helpful if the client is prepared for the time after smoking before he quits.

I. Outlook

What we have seen in this section is far removed from the principle of operant behavior described earlier. The modern view of man sees persons not as stimulus–response machines, but rather as living beings, influenced by external events, but also by internal thoughts, emotions, and attitudes. Human behavior is also being viewed as an ecological factor, clearly adding to the quality or lack thereof of the physical and psychological world. Viewed in this manner, much remains to be done—and it is rather

doubtful whether behavioral management alone can be successful. Skinner's early warning comes to mind, which admonishes us that psychology should not think that it can solve all the problems put to it.

VI. ETHICAL CONSIDERATIONS

Behavioral methods have often been thought of as impersonal and mechanistic. A second fallacy is the thought that persons are controlled *in toto* by their respective environments. Either notion is fundamentally wrong. Behavioral methods are means toward a goal. They are administered by real people and are as humane or inhumane as the people using them.

Certainly, no one would argue that if a physician made a mistake in prescribing the wrong medication for an illness, he did so intentionally, and is therefore cruel and hateful. Stimuli do control our behavior. They do not exert less influence if we choose to negate this fact. But, indeed, we too have an influence upon our environments. Somewhat idealistically, we may view the behavioral approach to solving human problems as a process of making the afflicted persons aware of such undesirable environmental contingencies, and thereby ameliorating their conditions.

It is important to realize that during the process of therapy and intervention, responsibility lies with the therapist and the patient. As a matter of fact, therapy is an education toward responsible behavior. And intervention is always justified when the physical and mental health of the patient are at stake or when he becomes a menace to others.

If the treatment plan is not in accord with the patient's wish, periodic peer or advocate reviews are in order.

Those who say to let nature take its course are totally out of touch with reality, as far as the sheer number of behavioral disorders that we have to deal with.

Administered in a humane fashion, the behavioral approach to human suffering has great potential, if its advocates also are aware of its limitations. These methods can liberate persons from the restraints which environmental influences and, frequently, unfortunate combination of factors have wrought.

Bibliography

Cosmides, L., and Tooby, J. (1987). From evolution to behavior: Evolutionary psychology as the missing link. In "The Latest on the Best: Essays on Evolution and Optimality'' (J. Dupre, Ed.), Bradford, Cambridge, MA.

Ferster, C. B., and Skinner, B. F. (1957). ''Schedules of Reinforcement.'' Appleton-Century-Crofts, New York.

Rachlin, H. (1991). ''Introduction to Modern Behaviorism,'' 3rd ed. Freeman, New York.

Skinner, B. F. (1938). ''The Behavior of Organisms.'' Appleton-Century-Crofts, New York.

Staddon, J. E. R., and Ettinger, R. H. (1989). ''Learning: An Introduction to the Principles of Adaptive Behavior.'' Harcourt, Brace, Jovanovich, San Diego.

ORGANIZATIONAL BEHAVIOR

Karlene H. Roberts
University of California at Berkeley

Glossary

Context effects The influences of organizational contexts on individuals and groups in them. The influences of individuals and groups on their organizational contexts. The reciprocal influences of individuals, groups, and organizational contexts.

Human resource management Activities that help organizations attract, retain, and develop employees to meet current and future needs. These activities include selection, training, and performance appraisal.

Macro organizational behavior Approaches to gaining knowledge about organizations that examine organizations as entities, and account for their structures and reciprocal influences with their environments.

Micro organizational behavior Approaches to gaining knowledge about organizations which focus on internal characteristics and processes, particularly on the behavior of individuals and groups in organizations. Human resource management activities are often viewed as an aspect of these processes.

Organizational development A humanistic perspective on organizations that stresses change processes as strategies for solving organizational problems.

THE STUDY of organizations and behavior in them has its recent roots in psychology, sociology, and management. It is also influenced by anthropology, economics, political science, and psychotherapy.

The objects of study are everything from individuals and groups in organizations, to the organization as a whole, populations of organizations, and the relationship of organizations to larger social structures, such as the state and society.

The field is both interdisciplinary and rather young. As such, theoretically it is in a preparadigmatic state of development. New theories and concepts are introduced on a regular basis, but there is little agreement on appropriate substantive issues for and styles of inquiry.

The field typically divides itself into concern with "micro" issues, or those issues that focus on individuals and groups in organizations, and "macro" issues or concerns for organizations and groups of organizations. Between these two issues scholars have also given attention to change in organizations. Attention is beginning to be given to linking individuals and organizations to one another and to their contexts. This article describes the major research preoccupations in each of these areas.

I. MICRO ORGANIZATIONAL BEHAVIOR

The area of micro organizational behavior is concerned with the behavior of individuals and groups in organizations. There are two major subfields; human resource management and organizational behavior.

A. Human Resource Management

Issues concerned with personnel in organizations have been with American researchers since Hugo Munsterberg's first textbook in Industrial Psychology was published in the early 1900s. These issues received added push during both world wars when selecting, classifying, and training large numbers of men for the military were paramount.

The major research areas in human resource management are selection, training, and performance appraisal. To a somewhat lesser extent behavioral researchers are also concerned with equal opportunity and the law, compensation and benefits, and employee safety and health. Here we take up only the first three of these issues.

1. Selection

The major issue driving research is validity generalization, or the degree to which various selection devices predict accurately across organizations and groups. The statistical and methodological procedures of validity generalization appear to be sound.

A variety of predictors have been researched over the years. Aptitude and ability tests have long been a major focus of this research. Findings indicate that a number of tests make stable predictions over relatively long periods of time. Two major events have recently contributed to this research. Project A, funded at approximately $25 million, validated various predictors of hands on performance and other criteria in the U.S. Army. A National Research Council report on the Government Aptitude Test Battery (GATB) reaffirmed its validity and validity generalization. [See APTITUDE TESTING.]

Assessment centers have also been subjected to predictive validity research. A general finding is that assessment centers predict promotion better than they predict supervisory ratings. Despite the cumulative evidence for substantial validity, biographical data scales are still infrequently used in selection. A key assumption of this kind of selection device is that past behaviors (often behaviors far in the past such as high school activities) are good predictors of future behavior. Present behaviors are also shown to be good predictors of future behavior. [See PERSONALITY ASSESSMENT.]

For years personality measures and job interviews were considered among the poorer selection devices. Both are now judged more favorably. A number of studies support a five factor theory of personality; extraversion/introversion, agreeableness, conscientiousness, neuroticism, and intellect. Conscientiousness seems the best predictor of outcomes like job level. Recent research shows interviews to have higher validities than traditionally believed.

2. Training

While the importance of conducting thorough needs analyses before engaging in training is well accepted in the literature, little research has been done on needs analysis in the last few years. Research in job analysis and performance assessment has implications for assessing training needs.

A current issue in the literature is the importance of linking training and organizational strategy. Task analyses identify the tasks to be performed on the job and the knowledge, skills, and abilities (KSAs) required to perform those tasks. Evidence from task analysis studies shows that work requirements at all organizational levels are becoming cognitively increasingly demanding.

Considerable research has been done on the design of training. Within this domain learning principles underlying training have been the focus of considerable investigation. Recently this research has come into question because the learning principles identified have to do with short-term learning by college students, rather than the learning of complex skills required by many jobs. A number of guidelines for designing training are available.

A major issue in designing training is selecting training methods. The literature evaluating training methods is increasing. Simulations are widely used in both the civilian and military sectors. Aspects of simulations that may influence the success of the training include simulation complexity, scope of functional and environmental activities over short and long time frames, type of preliminary preparation and initial learning, type of feedback and debriefing, use of decision support systems and tutoring aids, and the quality of the simulation administration. Other high technology training methods (i.e., computer-aided instruction, interactive video discs, etc.) are increasingly used. Interest in behavior modeling is strong. Studies continue to evaluate it as one of the most effective training methods.

Training effectiveness is determined not only by the thoroughness of needs analysis and the quality of training design, but by other factors including trainee attributes. Trainability testing, in which a candidate is given a sample of the training material, predicts training success and job performance in most situations. From the selection standpoint it is valuable but it sheds no light on why training works or how to improve it. Trainee motivations, attitudes, and expectations also influence training success.

Researchers and practitioners generally agree that training evaluation is important. A great deal of information exists about how to evaluate training, but application is limited and employee reactions are most frequently relied upon to determine training effectiveness.

3. Performance Appraisal

Job performance is usually the criterion or outcome against which selection mechanisms and training efforts are evaluated. Most research on such outcomes has focused on job performance ratings. A number of kinds of quantitative ratings exist including the simplest, graphic rating scales, which list a number of traits and a range of performance for each one. Another quantitative method, the paired comparison method, ranks employees by making a chart of all possible pairs of employees for each trait and indicates which is the better employee in each pair.

Narrative methods include the critical incident method, wherein a supervisor keeps a record of the employees uncommonly good or undesirable work behaviors and reviews this list periodically with the employee. Behaviorally anchored rating scales (BARS) attempt to combine the benefits of critical incidents and quantified ratings by anchoring a quantified scale with specific narrative examples of good or poor performance. For example a number of performance dimensions might be identified for grocery clerks. One might be "knowledge and judgment." Within this dimension an example of extremely good performance might be "by knowing the price of items this checker would be expected to look for mismarked items," while an example of extremely poor performance might be "in order to take a break this checker can be expected to block off the check stand with people in line." Many writers state that too little is known about the constructs which underlie job performance.

B. Organizational Behavior

Early contributions to micro issues in organizational behavior have their roots in industrial and social psychology. Systematic research on small group phenomena began with Kurt Lewin's studies of leadership and the examination of small group processes at the Hawthorne works of Western Electric. Both of these activities occurred during the late 1920s and the 1930s.

For a number of years the major topics of interest to researchers in organizational behavior have been motivation, work attitudes, job design, turnover and absenteeism, and leadership. Studies of these issues usually ignore context effects.

1. Motivation

In the history of organizational research motivation and leadership have been the most frequently studied issues. The bulk of recent work focuses on two issues, goal setting and equity theory. Goal setting research has occupied the attention of researchers for over 25 years. The core findings of this research

are that goal difficulty is linearly related to performance; the establishment of specific and difficult goals is associated with higher performance than are instructions to do your best or the absence of specific goals; and goal commitment is crucial to the effectiveness of goal setting. [See MOTIVATION.]

Equity theory is concerned with an employee's perception of the association between his or her effort on the job and pay relative to his or her association of effort and pay for other employees. A core problem with the theory is that in emphasizing the results of reward allocation, researchers have ignored reactions people have to how the decision leading to the results was made. People may react differently to the same inequity depending on their beliefs about how the inequity was created. [See EQUITY.]

2. Work Attitudes

The second most frequently researched topic in organizational behavior is work attitudes, or positive or negative evaluations about various aspects of one's work. Much of the work is concerned with the development of attitudinal measures and the search for antecedents and consequences of work attitudes. Newer lines of research are exploring the basic nature of affect, the relationship of moods and work, and the expression of emotion at work.

Despite substantial evidence that job satisfaction is not consistently linked with performance it still remains the most frequently studied affect. One interesting debate is about the degree to which job satisfaction is dispositional. Some evidence suggests that affective responses to work are stable over time and jobs. This position is questioned by researchers who provide evidence that situational factors influence affect.

3. Job Design

Job design has long been a research topic in organizational behavior. In the 1970s interest in the topic solidified around the impact of five job characteristics (skill variety, task identity, task significance, autonomy, and feedback) on internal work motivation and job attitudes. In the 1980s an alternative view emerged, the social information processing (SIP) theory. Its proponents claimed that task perceptions and affective responses are functions of social cues. This alternative view sparked much research and discussion. Despite the fact that evidence for an integrated perspective is convincing, research continues on both sides of this debate. Outcomes other than motivation are largely ignored by organizational researchers, but are considered by researchers coming from other disciplines.

4. Turnover and Absenteeism

The study of turnover and absenteeism continues to be a popular research area. Recent investigations have attempted to do one of two things; predict turnover or absenteeism with arbitrary predictors or predictors drawn from some model of job withdrawal, or refine prediction through identifying variables that moderate the relationship of predictors and turnover/absenteeism.

5. Leadership

As the other most frequently researched topic in organizational research, leadership research originated in studies of supervision, first emphasizing traits, and then behaviors appropriate to various situations. Virtually all the behavioral theories introduce notions about the impact of authoritarian, task-oriented—versus democratic, people-oriented—leadership styles on subordinate satisfaction and performance. While people oriented styles have more positive impact on subordinate job satisfaction than do task oriented approaches, the differential impact of these styles on performance is not clear. [See LEADERSHIP.]

Because of this, later work closely examined superior–subordinate relationships, and that research continues. One research program looked at situational favorableness (defined as support by followers, structure of the group's task, and formal leadership power) as a determinant of appropriate leadership style. Another program was concerned with how the leader's behavior motivates or satisfies followers because of its impact on the followers perceptions of goals and paths available to reach those goals. Other approaches were also taken. This line of research continues today.

Recently interest has been directed to the broader construct of executive leadership and to the leader's influence on large numbers of followers, not just subordinates. With this framework there is a debate about whether leadership is a useful construct. One side of the debate suggests that leadership is more subjective than objective, and that the concept has a romantic and heroic quality unrelated to observable practices. The other side of the debate argues that executive leadership is an observable and influential process. Several characteristics of executive leadership have been identified. One approach differentiates transactional (centered on social exchange principles) and transformational (based on charisma, shared visions, and strong leader–follower identification) leadership.

II. ORGANIZATION CHANGE AND DEVELOPMENT

The field of organizational development (OD) now sees itself as moving on from its traditional issues and approaches to a larger strategic perspective, organizational transformation (OT). Human resource management, concerned as it is with the tools of managing, is and always has been rather static in its vision and accompanying research strategies. Likewise, until quite recently micro organizational behavior has also been rather static. Counter to these approaches, organizational development and transformation have always been concerned with process, and change is at their very hearts.

A. Organizational Development

OD often occurs in responses to modest mismatches of an organization or a part of an organization with its environment or an organization's desire to mesh well with some expected future environment. This usually leads to cognitive change and limited behavioral change.

In its early history OD was defined fundamentally by its philosophy, its set of beliefs and values about people and organizations. It celebrated the spirit and capacities of human beings and was part and parcel of the broader human potential movement. OD's humanistic perspective stressed people's potential to learn and grow in their work and to contribute and express themselves fully in organizations. These assumptions were treated as givens and OD's theories were elevated to moral imperatives.

OD also embraced a new set of beliefs and values about organizations. It was felt that bureaucratic models of organizations could not deal with problems of coordination, innovation, and commitment, posed by accelerating rates of social and economic change. OD offered an approach to organizing that was more fluid and adaptive.

Two techniques were invented for creating organizational change, both focusing most directly on individuals in organizations. The first was laboratory training, or providing settings in which small group exercises could "free up" people and "open" them to new ways to relate to one another. The assumption underlying these groups was that people had within them the capacity to become more complete and expressive. Feedback from others in a group would help them identify factors inhibiting their potential, and support would help them become more of whatever they had the capacity to become. The agents of change in OD are facilitators and their job is to facilitate change in people and organizations.

The second technique was "action research" which was aimed more directly at improving the workplace. This technique had groups identify problems in work relationships, diagnose factors contributing to those problems, and develop and implement solutions. The first model of action research was the conception that change proceeds through the phases of unfreezing, movement, and refreezing.

Later, conceptions of what OD is and could be were broadened. The field kept its focus on individual and group development but added more content to its intervention base with the development of life planning and transactional analysis. It also focused more on technical and structural forms of change. Early developments in survey feedback and an interest in organizations as "socio-technical" systems provided the field with diagnostic protocols and interventions. At the same time basic organizational research on job and organization design, reward systems, management practices, etc., entered the vocabulary and technology of the field.

As the newest of the human behavior in organizations subfields OD became fully delineated as a discipline in the 1970s. OD was legitimated as field of scholarship and as a form of professional practice. It became obvious, too, at this time, that simply emphasizing the power of human potential was not going to solve organizational problems. While the field still focused on promoting human identity in the workplace the notion of "quality of work life" was introduced. Thus, attention was now given to optimizing technical and social features of organizations through socio-technical work design.

At this time organizations found they had to do more than renew their originating spirit and cohesion. They had to address employee rights and confront structural barriers based on race, sex, class, and status. ODs function was to tackle those barriers. Recent OD research has focused on organizing arrangements, social factors, technology, and physical space.

B. Organizational Transformation

As organization strategy research took off in the 1980s OD embraced it as it had done many issues in human resource management and organizational behavior. OT was born. OT is an advancement over OD because of its focus on precipitating more profound changes in organizations. The variables targeted by OT affect a "deeper" level of the organization than those focused on by OD. They are components of organizational vision such as organizational beliefs, purpose, and mission.

Organizational level views of vision examine the processes through which organizations are able to change and learn. An underlying assumption is that organizational transformation depends on individuals radically changing their typical ways of thinking and doing. There are at least two distinct approaches to consciousness change; reframing and consciousness raising.

Reframing consists of organizational interventions that change a members perceptions of reality. Since the focus is on individual perception the organizational reality need not change. But change in perception leads to corresponding change in attitudes and behaviors that results in organizational transformation.

Consciousness raising makes the process of transformation visible to organizational members. Thought is viewed as the source of existing circumstances and change. Thus, people with more awareness of transformative processes should be better able to guide such processes. Techniques such as meditation and creativity exercises are intervention strategies using this approach.

Other work on organizational transformation focuses on creating organizations that understand how and when to initiate radical change and have strategies for doing so. One way to go about this is to engage in efforts to help improve an organization's ability to analyze and change current paradigms, as well as envision desired future paradigms.

Like OD, OT is planned and primarily directed at creating new vision. Its broader interventions, though, also foster more radical behavioral change.

III. CONTEXT EFFECTS

Presumably, the uniqueness of behavior in organizations is that the organizational context somehow shapes it. Yet, until recently these context effects were largely ignored. Where it does exist, the traditional approach to studying organizational context correlates perceptual measures of context with self-reported attitudes and intentions. It is difficult to know whether such relationships tell us more about the context or the respondent. Today some studies measure context more directly. Some research examines how contexts effect individuals and groups, some looks at how individuals and groups influence contexts, and some looks at the reciprocal relationships among contexts and people.

A. The Influence of Contexts on People and Groups

Research that examines the influence of contexts on people and groups takes three perspectives. Some work portrays context as an opportunity or constraint on behavior. Some considers elements of context as distal or proximate influences on behavior. Some examines the similarity or dissimilarity among people or groups and their organizations. Sometimes contexts do not influence behavior in them.

1. Contexts as Opportunities and Constraints

Sociologists portray contexts in terms of opportunities or constraints they provide for individuals or groups. Most organizational behavior researchers are unaccustomed to thinking of their work in this way despite the fact that the distinction between opportunities and constraints is often implicit in their view of organizations. For example, job enrichment techniques might be viewed as mechanisms for enhancing opportunities, while goal setting can be seen as a control device that constrains behavior.

A study of the role eunuchs played in administering the Ming Dynasty demonstrates how the interpretation of behavior can change when one's view of context changes. Castration has been thought about as a technique used by those in power to ensure civil servant loyalty and commitment. It was viewed as a control mechanism or constraint to eliminate competition with the interests of the emperor. The fact that castration was often voluntary suggests an alternative interpretation. Becoming a eunuch provided an otherwise unavailable avenue for upward mobility. The traditional path into the Confucian civil service included an expensive education. Poor men could attain powerful positions and wealth by becoming eunuch administrators, who were almost as powerful as Confucian scholars. Thus, a phenomenon commonly viewed as a constraint might alternatively be viewed as an opportunity.

2. Context as a Distal or Proximate Influence

Much organizational behavior literature examines relationships between very proximate variables (e.g., the relationship of leadership style and subordinate job satisfaction). However, relationships that exist across greater distance or time are inherently more interesting, and sometimes harder to believe, than relationships that occur more closely.

A study of how technological change influenced radiology illustrates different ways contextual proximity influences organizations. Computer tomography scanning changed individual skill levels, dyadic interactions, department structure, and organizational status. The technology was invented in the 1970s and slowly diffused into hospitals in the 1980s, with a series of reverberations.

It initially modified tasks, skills, and other nonrelational variables, which in turn shaped role relations. These altered role relations either changed or buttressed social networks that comprise occupational and organizational structures. Ultimately shifting networks either sustain or change institutions. A distal development, a new technology, had both distal and proximate influences on behavior. A temporal view of the situation across the 1970s and 1980s provides different insight than would have been provided by a cross-sectional study at either point in time.

3. Context as Similar or Dissimilar

Much recent research on social context focuses on the similarity or dissimilarity between individuals and their organizations as predictors of behavior in those organizations. Research on these effects falls into two camps; relational demography and individual–organization fit.

The observation that organizations are fundamentally relational entities encourages researchers to examine implications of similarity and dissimilarity between members of groups and organizations, or relational demography. However, demographic composition of groups and organizations has implications above and beyond average levels of group demographic characteristics. Relational demographic characteristics such as age, tenure, education, and gender influence outcomes such as employee turnover, social integration, supervisor–subordinate relations, and communication patterns.

The sociological approach to relational demography and the psychological theory of interpersonal attraction are complementary and lead to similar predictions. Relational demography is concerned with group and organizational explanatory variables such as homogeneity, cohesiveness, and interaction patterns. The attraction–selection–attrition theory of interpersonal attraction argues that the attraction to similar others leads to organizational homogeneity. The process of attraction, selection, and atttrition increases homogeneity in organizations because people are attracted to and tend to select others who are similar. Individuals who are dissimilar leave the organization. Thus, similarity with regard to psychological variables like personality, values, and interests leads to similarity in sociological demographic characteristics. [*See* INTERPERSONAL ATTRACTION AND PERSONAL RELATIONSHIPS.]

Individual–organization fit can be assessed. One study found that fit at the time of organizational entry was related to individual characteristics and to spending time with organizational members, while fit a year later was influenced by the socialization experiences of participating in work related social functions and time spent with a mentor.

B. The Influence of People and Groups on Contexts

Three means by which individuals or groups influence organizations are discussed in the literature. The first means is when autonomous people or groups pose as organizations by taking actions that reflect their preferences but claiming such actions reflect organizational policies. The second means is when powerful people (or groups) take actions that influence organizational structures, process, or performance. And the third means is through the aggregation of individual (or group) attributes that influence the organization as a whole.

We can all think of situations in which powerful leaders have influenced organizations by either successfully implementing their own agendas or through taking leadership actions that are more broadly based. Two general paths through which powerful leaders influence organizations are (1) making decisions that affect organizations and (2) shaping the thoughts, feelings, and actions of organizational members. Current research attention is being given to how leaders influence organizations and institutions. Leaders provide explanations, rationalizations, and interpretations of their organizations activities.

Psychological mechanisms are used to explain not only how individuals influence organizations, but how groups influence organizations. Aggregated cognitions and actions of individuals influence organizations. Other group influences on organizations have also been identified. For example, in the computer industry teams that made fast decisions were more effective than teams that made slow decisions. Fast decision-making teams used more information and compared more alternatives than their slow decision-making counterparts.

C. Reciprocal Relationships among Contexts, Individuals, and Groups

For a number of reasons little research has been conducted on the complex interplay among contexts, individuals, and groups. An example of the kind of research that has been done is an examination of the decision to build and operate the Shoreham Nuclear Power Plant by top management of the Long Island Lighting Co. The study shows how the interplay between top management actions and the organizational and political context created by these actions led the company to spend over 5 billion dollars on a plant initially estimated to cost 75 million dollars, and which never became fully operational.

D. When Context Does Not Matter

Sometimes contextual aspects of organizations have little influence on individuals or groups because they are buffered from or simply ignore them. An example is a study examining the relationship of work demands and stress symptoms among newcomers to organizations. The study found that stress symptoms found 9 months after entry were more strongly predicted by stress symptoms reported before organizational entry than by work demands 6 months after entry. Most stress research is cross-sectional, assessing relationships among measures taken closer together in time. If this research had failed to measure stress prior to organizational entry it may well have concluded what most stress research concludes—that stress is predicted by organizational demands. [*See* STRESS.]

IV. MACRO ORGANIZATIONAL BEHAVIOR

The predominant contributions to the macro perspective on organizations have been made by sociologists. These contributions are relatively new and might be dated back to the translation into English of Weber's, and to a lesser extent, Michel's analyses of bureaucracy in Europe. In 1947 the index of the *American Journal of Sociology* for the previous 52 years made no reference to "organization" or "formal organization" or "bureaucracy." Six years later the index of the *American Sociological Review* made no reference to "organization" and had only six entries for "bureaucracy." Since 1960 the growth of this area has been substantial.

As seen by macro organizational theorists the elements of organizations are social structure, participants or actors, goals, technology, and environments. Social structure refers to the patterned or regularized aspects of relationships among participants in organizations. Organizational participants are those people who make contributions to organizations for a variety of inducements. Goals are thought about as conceptions of desired ends and are among the most controversial of organizational components. Technologies consist of both machines and mechanical equipment and technical knowledge and skills of participants. Environment consists of specific physical, technological, cultural, and social aspects of the larger social system in which an organization resides. Early organizational analysts tended to overlook or underestimate the importance of organization–environment linkages, but recent work places great emphasis on these connections.

Three dominant perspectives of organizations emerged early in the life of the macro perspective. They are the rational system, natural system, and open system perspectives of organizations. Each of these perspectives informs more recent work on organizations.

A. Organizations as Rational Systems

From a rational perspective organizations are designed to attain specific goals. Rationality refers to the extent to which a series of actions is organized to lead to predetermined goals with maximum efficiency. The defining characteristics of this perspective include actions performed by purposeful and coordinated agents. They use language which connotes an image of rational calculation discussing information, efficiency, optimization, implementation, and design. This perspective also recognizes the cognitive limitations of the individual decision-maker and the effects of organizational contexts on decisions made in organizations.

Thus, these researchers talk about constraints, authority, rules, directives, jurisdiction, performance programs, and coordination. Rational systems theorists stress structure and goal specificity. Structure provides the tool for the efficient realization of goals. In a larger sense rationality resides in structure, rules, reward systems, and criteria by which participants are selected and promoted.

B. Organizations as Natural Systems

Rational systems theorists conceive of organizations as collectivities deliberately constructed to seek specific goals; natural systems researchers emphasize the collectivity aspect of organizations. These theorists acknowledge the existence of attributes identified by rational system researchers but argue that other characteristics are of greater importance. Natural systems researchers focus on complex interactions in organizations. They note the common disparity between stated and real goals and that even when stated goals are actually pursued they are never the only goals operating. The major thrust of the natural systems view is that organizations are not merely instruments for attaining goals but are also in the business of survival. Thus, the focus is much more on the informal organization.

C. Organizations as Open Systems

The newest of the three perspectives of organizations developed by macro researchers is the notion of organizations as open systems. This perspective emerged after World War II and is the result of initial efforts by a biologist to lessen the compartmentalization among various scientific disciplines. It was argued that many of the most important entities studied by scientists—nuclear particles, atoms, cells, organisms, groups, organizations, societies, etc.—are subsumable under the general rubric, systems. All systems are characterized by a combination of interdependent parts. Some systems are simple, others complex, with organizations being among the most complex.

Open systems theory not only loosens the more conventional views of structural features of organizations, it shifts attention from structure to process. Its emphasis is on organizing as opposed to organization. The process view is not only of the internal organization but of the organization itself as a system existing over time. The organization is not today what it was yesterday nor will it be tomorrow what it is today. The interdependence of the organization and its environment receives primary attention from this perspective.

D. Recent Work Combining These Perspectives

The three perspectives for analyzing organizations provide contrasting paradigms. Because of different assumptions underlying them, one may replace another but cannot disprove it.

Several authors have attempted to reconcile these perspectives by combining them into more complex models of organizations. Some see rational and natural systems models as complementary, focusing on conflicting tendencies present in all organizations. Some propose that all organizations are open systems, and that rational and natural forms emerge as varying adaptive structures in response to different environmental impacts.

Another way to combine these perspectives is to say they appeared in varying combinations over time and are applicable at different levels of analyzing organizations. Thus, the earliest models were closed rational models and dominated thinking between 1900 and 1930. Some were developed at the social psychological level and others at the structural level of organizations. From the 1930s through the 1950s a set of perspectives developed that combined the closed and natural systems assumptions. Again, some of these approaches were developed at the social psychological level and others at the structural level of organizational explanation.

Beginning in the 1960s open systems models largely replaced closed systems perspectives and analyses of ecological levels began to appear. During the 1960s open rational system models were dominant and during the 1970s open natural system models became dominant and continue to be dominant today. These models range from social psychological, through structural, and ecological approaches to organizations.

1. A Social Psychological Open Natural Systems Model

One model within this set focuses on learning as not outcomes but processes—that is, changes in organizational routines. This model sets aside assumptions of a single or unified decision-maker in organizations and focuses instead on the concept of loose and shifting coalitions. Processes of exchange, combat, compromise, and alliance supplement images of a hierarchy of goals or of means–ends chains linking participants throughout the organization. Decision outcomes are seen to be strongly influenced by their contexts.

2. A Structural Natural Systems Model

The socio-technical systems model proposes that the distinguishing feature of organizations is that they are both social and technical systems. Thus,

the relation between the non-human and human systems is at the core of this model.

Proponents of this approach developed a typology of organizational environments and speculated on their influences on organizational forms. The most resilient building blocks available to organizations as they respond to environmental demands are sets of semiautonomous groups, capable of self-regulation as cybernetic systems, and the larger networks of groups organized into primary work systems, that are functionally interdependent. Socio-technical researchers are interested in the creation of these groups.

3. An Ecological Natural Systems Model

The population ecology or natural selection model of organizations originated in biology with Darwin's work. This model differs from other approaches to organizations in that it applies to populations of organizations rather than to organizations as units. It is designed to explain why certain forms or types of organizations survive and multiply while others die. Central to the natural selection thesis is that environments differentially select organizations for survival based on the fit between organizational form and environmental characteristics.

Three processes are emphasized in evolutionary analysis. The first process is the creation of variety by some process, planned or unplanned. The second process is the selection of organizations for survival. The third process is the preservation of organizations through reproduction or duplication. The paradigm is thoroughly grounded in an open system view; the importance of the environment cannot be more strongly expressed than it is in the population ecology model of organizations.

Macro organizational researchers and theorists have come full tilt from thinking about organizations as closed, static systems to open, fluid systems. They have built increasingly complicated models to explain complicated phenomena.

V. CONCLUSIONS

That an increasingly complex world requires increasingly complex social and often organized social interaction is obvious. The organizational sciences are burgeoning as are organizations. A major challenge to the discipline today is tying together macro and micro phenomena. Small steps are being taken in this direction.

The existing streams of research continue. The old human resource management issues are being tied conceptually to organizational strategy, and practically extended and broadened through organizational transformation processes. Micro organizational behavior researchers are embracing notions of context and adopting open systems perspectives as have their macro colleagues. Macro theorists and researchers are taking ever more inclusive views of organizations and populations of organizations.

Increasingly, young organizational scholars are as comfortable working in both the macro as well as the micro arena. Until the 1970s micro researchers were trained primarily in psychology departments and macro researchers in sociology departments. The bringing of the social sciences into professional schools changed that. Today many new organizational scholars are trained by heterogeneous faculties in business schools. While these faculties may be rather insular in their own approaches to organizations, their students are increasingly less so. The early hopes of the open systems biologists are somewhat realized in these milieus in that the younger, more broadly trained organizational scholars bring their broader ideas to one another.

The 21st century may well be a heady era for social scientists. That social problems plague the world is clear from any perspective. That many of them are manifested in organizations and will be solved through organizational efforts is also clear. Thus, the ever-growing importance of organizations and organizing provides an impetus for greater knowledge development in the organizational sciences.

Bibliography

Aldrich, H. E., and Marsden, P. V. (1988). Environments and organizations. In "Handbook of Sociology" (N. J. Smelser, Ed.), pp. 361–392. Sage, Newbury Park, CA.

Mirvis, P. (1988). Organization development. I. An evolutionary perspective. In "Research in Organizational Change and Development." (W. A. Pasmore and R. W. Woodman, Eds.), pp. 1–58. JAI Press, Greenwich, CT.

Mowday, R. T., AND Sutton, R. I. (1993). Organization behavior: Linking individuals and groups to organizational contexts. In "Annual Review of Psychology" (L. W. Porter and M. Rosenzweig, Eds.), Vol. 44. Annual Reviews, Palo Alto.

O'Reilly, C. (1991). Organizational behavior: Where we've been, where we're going. In "Annual Review of Psychology" (M. R. Rosenzweig and L. W. Porter, Eds.) Vol. 42, pp. 427–558. Annual Reviews, Palo Alto, CA.

Pfeffer, J. (1985). Organizations and organization theory. In "Handbook of Social Psychology" (G. Lindzey and E. Aronson, Eds.), 3rd ed., Vol. 2, pp. 379–440. Random House, New York.

Porras, J. I., and Silvers, R. E. (1991). Organization development and transformation. In "Annual Review of Psychology" (M. R. Rosenzweig and L. W. Porter, Eds.), Vol. 42, pp. 51–78. Annual Reviews, Palo Alto.

Schmitt, N., and Robertson, I. (1990). Personnel selection. In "Annual Review of Psychology" (M. R. Rosenzweig and L. W. Porter, Eds.), Vol. 41, pp. 289–320. Annual Reviews, Palo Alto.

Scott, W. R. (1992). "Organizations: Rational, Natural, and Open Systems," 3rd ed. Prentice-Hall, Englewood Cliffs, NJ.

Tannenbaum, S., and Yukl, G. (1992). Training and development in work organizations. In "Annual Review of Psychology" (M. R. Rosenzweig and L. W. Porter, Eds.), Vol. 43, pp. 399–442. Annual Reviews, Palo Alto.

PAIN

Yair Lampl

*Edith Wolfson Medical Center, Israel
and Tel Aviv University, Israel*

Glossary

Hyperalgesia Increased sensitivity to pain stimulus with lowering of the pain threshold.
Neuralgia Peripheral nerve pain.
Nociceptor A receptor responding to harmful stimuli.
Noxious stimulus Harmful body tissue endangering stimulus.
Pain threshold Lowest level of sensitivity to pain.

PAIN is the most common symptom of human diseases. It is defined as an unpleasant experience which may or may not be primarily associated with tissue damage. Pain experience has two different components—the specific sensory discriminative components and the nonspecific emotional–cognitive components. Melzack and Casey divided the pain system into three dimensions: the cognitive or central control, motivation–emotional, and sensory discriminative dimensions.

In various cultures, pain has a different social meaning, in the Judeo-Christian cultures, for example, "the passion of the soul" (as Aristotelians define pain) has a close relationship to guilt and punishment. The word "pain" is derived from the Greek word *poine* and the Latin word *poene*, meaning pun-

ishment. In the Old Testament, the Hebrew word *Tsaar,* which means sorrow, was used to determine pain.

Although pain is usually combined with sorrow, fear, depression, or agitation, an intensive manifestation of the emotional modality can appear separately and independently from the discriminative modality. Our knowledge of psychiatric diseases has taught us that a pain reaction which is compatible to all pain criteria may not necessarily be accompanied by tissue damage. The different characteristics of acute, chronic, cutaneous, or visceral pain justify the assumption that pain is a result of a complex, multimodal mechanism. Knowledge of the different components of this system is essential for the understanding of this most important phenomenon of human disease.

I. ANATOMY AND NEUROCHEMISTRY OF PAIN

A. The Peripheral System

In the past, the question of pain origin was explained by two major theories—the summation theory or intensity theory and the specific theory. At the end of the 19th century, Goldsheider postulated that there were no specific pain receptors and that each sensory stimulus, with sufficient intense stimuli, produces pain sensation.

The specific theory suggested that pain, similar to thermal and mechanical stimuli, has a specific ascending tract with a specific pain center located in the brain. This theory which is postulated today, teaches that there is an intermediate position between both theories. The peripheral system is conducted through the skin, muscles, joints, and somaticovisceral stimuli from the periphery to the spinal cord through axons of the neural cells. The cell bodies are located in the dorsal root ganglia behind the spinal cord. At present, it is well established that two types of axons respond to transduce the pain sensation from the peripheral to the centers—the A_δ and C fibers. The primary afferent fibers are coated with sheaths of lipoid substances of different diameters known as myelin.

Generally, the peripheral axons are divided into three major groups (classified by Erlangen and Gasser): A, B, and C, according to the thickness of the myelin. Fiber group A is subdivided into another four subgroups: A_α, A_β, A_γ, and A_δ. The thickness of the myelin is directly proportional to the conduction velocity. The primary afferent fibers of the C group are covered by a very thin myelin layer measuring $0.1-1.5$ μm usually defined as unmyelinated C fibers characterized by a slow conduction velocity of $0.5-2.0$ m/sec. The thin myelinated A_δ fibers ($1-4$ μm) have a moderated conduction velocity of $12-20$ m/sec.

Pain has no specific receptor. Axon fibers detach themselves from their myelin sheaths and terminate as nerve endings in the skin. To date, there are five recognized types of afferent nociceptives which conduct the impulse of pain stimulation. (1) High threshold A_δ mechanoreceptors respond to moderated intense or noxious mechanical stimuli. (2) Myelinated A_δ mechanothermal nociceptives respond to noxious heat stimuli over 45°C and intense mechanical stimuli. (3) Pure heat sensitive A_δ nociceptive. (4) A_δ and C low-threshold cold receptors. (5) C-polymodal nociceptive afferents (CPN). This extremely important group of CPN consists of about 95–98% of the sensory C-units in the skin. They have a high threshold to intense mechanical stimulation (more than 1 g), a graded threshold to heat stimulus (between 38 and 49°C), and a sensitivity to mechanical stimulus. On repeated mechanical stimulation, the response of the CPN becomes fatigued and on repeated thermal stimulation, its response becomes sensitized.

The visceral nociceptive axons transduce pain stimuli characterized by an aching type of pain in the chest, abdomen, and pelvis. The visceral fibers contain a very high amount of C fibers compared to A_δ fibers (a ratio of 10 : 1 in the visceral nerve and only a ratio of 1 : 2 in the dorsal root). Only 10% of the dorsal root consists of visceral fibers which are connected to the sympathetic fibers.

B. Neurochemistry of the Peripheral System

Peripheral pain stimulation is caused by the releasing of endogenic chemicals when local tissue is damaged. The pain produces a substance that also has, besides a direct receptor stimulation, an influence on the vessel diameter and the permeability of the capillaries. These vascular changes influence the area of the nociceptive receptor and increase their sensibility.

Three groups of chemical substances influence the peripheral nociceptive receptors: (1) A chemical with a direct influence on the afferent nociceptive fibers of which bradykinin and potassium belong. The kinins, by-products of the clotting system found in the plasma, are released into the tissue and accept the direct pain which induces a reaction and have a vasodilatatory effect. (2) The second group consists of substances which enhance the reaction of the bradykinin. Prostaglandins, a product of polyunsaturated fatty acids (arachidonic type), also belong to this group. Although high doses of prostaglandins can produce mild pain, the main physiological effect is the potentiation of the kinin's reaction (especially PGE_1, PGE_2). (3) The third group, substance P (SP), was first described by Euler and Gaddun in 1931. It is synthesized in the spinal ganglions and has an antidromic peripheral effect (transmission in the cutaneal direction and not to the spinal cord). Substance P affects the veins by the extravasation of plasma and changing of the permeability of the capillaries and vasodilatation of the small vessels.

C. The Dorsal Horn

The primary afference of pain fibers reaches the spinal cord after transversing the tract known as the Lissauer tract. In the cord, the impulses are potentiated or attenuated within the different layers of the gray substance. The root contains the separation—myelin-poor fibers on the outside portion and myelin-rich fibers on the inside portion. Lissauer proved that partial separation resulted in the disappearance of pain in a selective interruption of the lateral part of the bundel. This finding is the basis for pain therapy by selective lateral rhizotomy. At the present time, we are aware of the theory that all sensory fibers that penetrate the spinal cord via the dorsal horn is incorrect. It was demonstrated that pain sensation can also be produced by a ventral tract stimulation. Thirty percent of the ventral fibers were found to be unmyelinated. It is presumed that the ganglion of the dorsal horn sends two processes—superficial and deep somatic projections. This finding is a reasonable explanation for the cutaneal distribution of deep visceral pain. Pain in the left shoulder and chest in heart attacks is a well-known example of this phenomenon. Most of the fibers terminate in the spinal gray matter of the same side, some extend contralaterally, and others reach one or two segments above or under the terminated segment. The gray matter was divided by Rexed into 10 laminae. Laminae 1–6 belong to the sensory dorsal horn; laminae 7–9 belong to the motor ventral horn; and lamina 10 contains interneuronal corrections building the area around the central canal of the cord. The pain fibers reach certain areas; the fine myelinated A_δ fibers travel into the medial portion of the dorsal horn and reach areas I, II, and V. A_δ and C visceral fibers terminate in areas I and V but also reach the laminae IV, VI, and VIII.

Three different kinds of neurons are found in the dorsal horn:

1. Neurons that respond to a mechanical and thermal input mode (LTT) with a low threshold to noxious and nonnoxious stimulation.
2. Wide dynamic range (WDR) neurons found partially in deeper layers: the WDR neurons respond to different inputs of thermal, mechanical, and chemical stimuli. The WDR activity range is wide and nonspecific. They consist of one-third to one-half of the neurons of the ascending system and are the most common neuron type in the deep V lamina.
3. Specific nociceptive neurons with an exclusive response to pain. These neurons were found in lamina I and also in lamina V. They contain specific small and large cells (Wahldayer) of different structure which are divided into two subgroups—cells activated only by mechanoreceptive A fibers and those activated by mechano- and thermoreceptors of A_δ as well as C fibers.

In examining these neuron groups, group 3 (NG) has a specific reaction to pain response. Group 2 (WDR) responds to pain and to other stimulations also, and group 1 (LTT) does not respond to pain at all. It seems that the WDR neurons have a central role in the modulation of the sensitivity of the nociceptive cells to pain stimulation.

It has been shown that WDR neurons can be inhibited by painful stimulation, a phenomenon known as "diffuse noxious inhibitory controls" (DNIC). This inhibition was suggested to be the main component of the pain signal function.

D. Ascending System

A pain message is transmitted from the periphery through the dorsal horn to the supraspinal structures almost entirely via the pathways of the anterolateral tracts. There are two types of ascending routes that characterize the ascending system and each one of them has a different anatomical physiological, and phylogenetical origin. One of the tracts, known as the neospinothalamic system, is characteristic in humans and primates containing the most important spinothalamic tract which transmits the nociceptive impulses to specific areas in the thalamus to the ventroposterolateral (VPL) nucleus. This stimulus is transmitted somatotopically via these pathways. Since the VPL nuclei are also divided somatotopically, it seems that this stimulation is responsible for the discriminative component of pain.

Similar to the spinothalamic tract is the trigeminothalamic tract which transmits pain message somatotopically from the face to the specific (VPM) nucleus in the thalamus. Another spinothalamic tract is the ventrospinal which is located in the anterior section of the spinal cord. This route was usually considered the only one for pressure and touch stimuli. It has been recently proved that the ventrospinothalamic tract is also involved in pain transmission explaining the occasional pain sensation that remains even after total dissection of the lateral pathways.

The second group of ascending tracts, known as the paleospinothalamic system, contains the medial part of the spinothalamic tract, known as the spinoreticular tract and the spinomesencephalic tract. These tracts are more paleogenetic in nature than the neospinothalamic system and transmit pain sensation into the nuclei of the brain stem and into the nonspecific thalamic nuclei—the medial and interlaminar nuclei which are nonsomatotopic in nature. Fiber projections to the limbic system and the hypothalamus transmit this message to the emotional and autonomical centers. It appears that the paleospinothalamic system is responsible for the creation of the effective–motivation component of pain. The stimulus that terminates in the hypothalamus is responsible for the autonomic reaction to pain, sweat, and increase in blood pressure and pulse. The spinoreticular tract projects the stimulus from neuron cells in laminae VII and VIII of the spinal cord to the reticular formation in the midbrain, pons, and medulla. It seems that this tract has a connection with the arousal and motivation of the reticular system. The spinomesencephalic tract originates in the cells of laminae I and V and transmits the stimuli to various nuclei in the brain stem especially to the periaqueductal gray matter. Its role is in the production of the emotional reactivity to pain and in the modulation of pain by the descending system.

We are aware of the fact that besides the neospinothalamic and paleospinothalamic system, there are other pathways that play a role in the transmission of nociceptive impulses. Their significance in the pain system is uncertain. One system, the propiospinal multisynaptic ascending system, is located almost entirely in the dorsal part of the spinal cord and presumably plays a role in chronic and visceral pain.

The dorsal columns, which are considered a completely propioceptive, nonnoxious system, contain almost 7% of nociceptive–anxious fibers.

E. Pain and the Supraspinal System

The spinothalamic, spinoreticularic, and spinomesencephalic tracts terminate in different nuclei in the brain stem and thalamus. The neospinothalamic bundle terminates in the specific thalamic nuclei while the paleospinothalamic system reaches the nuclei of the brain stem and the nonspecific medial and intralaminar nuclei in the thalamus.

1. Brain Stem Terminus

The paleospinothalamic system projects fibers of the nociceptive stimulus to the reticular formation in the medulla, pons, and mesencephalon. The periaqueductal gray matter is an important target of these fibers. The reticular formation is dissipated throughout the entire brain stem. It contains different kinds of neurons with short and long axons. A wide development of fibers with massive projection to the thalamus, subthalamus, and hypothalamus structure causes a rapid integrative response when stimulation occurs in this system.

The periaqueductal gray substance is the main terminating target of the spinomesencephalic tract. This structure is connected to the gigantocellularic substance of the reticular formation, the medial nuclei of the thalamus indirectly with the cortex (S$_2$ area) and the limbic system. It was demonstrated that the periaqueductal gray and the gigantocellularic cells are almost entirely responsive to pain sensations. The integrative function of these structures and the dense interneural connections intensify the efficacy of these structures in mediation of the effective emotional component of pain sensation.

2. Thalamus Terminus

The thalamus is the relay center for afferent sensory inputs, beginning in the periphery and ending in the brain. The primary afferent pain fibers reach two areas of the thalamus. The neospinothalamic system and the trigeminothalamic tract terminate in the VPL and the VPM nuclei. Most of the fibers originate in laminae I and V of the spinal cord and project into the subnuclei VPLo (oral) and VPLc (caudal) of the VPL group. The organization of the VPL and VPM is somatotopic and is transmitted to the primary and secondary cortex via thalamocortical fibers. These structures play the central role in the process of the specific discriminative aspect of pain. The paleospinothalamic tract terminates in the paleothalamic nuclei, the medial and interlaminar nuclei, and the nonspecific and nonsomatopic portion of the thalamus.

Some of the paleothalamic structures are exclusively sensitive to pain stimuli. Short nociceptive cells, which are activated by A$_\delta$ fibers, and long cells, responding to stimuli of C fibers, are found in the thalamus. The nonspecificity of this structure can be demonstrated by local electrical stimulation of the medial and interlaminar nuclei and a burning pain sensation, without exact anatomical localization, is produced. The projection from this nuclei reaches the cerebral cortex, mainly to the limbic system. The wide, diffuse connections are part of the nonspecific activation and modulation and the cognitive aspects of pain sensation.

3. The Limbic System and Pain

The limbic system, a paleogenetic section of the brain, plays the main role in the creation of affective and emotional expression. Wide reciprocal projections between the limbic system, cortex, brain stem reticular formations, and thalamus are responsible for modulating emotional and mood aspects of pain. A particularly important role in the creation of the pain process is played by the pathways between the brain stem reticular formations and the limbic forebrain structures especially the amygdala, hippocampus, cingulate cortex, and the septal area. The hippocampus and the related forebrain structures are the main influence on the modification of pain-related behavior. Stimulation of these areas produces an evoked response to pain. Electrical stimulations of other limbic system areas produce aversive pain behavior depending on the intensity of the stimulation. Disruptions of the cingulum bundle between the hippocampus and the frontal lobe diminish the negative effect and increase the pain tolerance. The central role in pain-related affective behavior is the amygdala. It seems that the nonsomatotopical projections between the brain stem, hypothalamus, thalamus, and limbic system create a dynamic system of behavior changes, motivation and emotional changes, according to the pain stimulus. [See HIPPOCAMPAL FORMATION; LIMBIC SYSTEM.]

4. Pain and the Cerebral Cortex

Contrary to the limbic system, the cerebral cortex receives inputs mostly from the specific thalamus nuclei (VPL, VPM), and to a lesser extent, from the postero- and ventrobasal thalamic groups. The majority of the somatotopical sensory fibers originated in the VPL–VPM, reach the primary sensory area in the postcentral gyrus. The primary sensory area (SI) has a typical somatotopic pattern (a specific representation for each part of the body). The secondary sensory area (SII) is located near the Sylvian fissure in the parietal lobe and has pathways from SI and the postero- and ventrobasal thalamic nuclei. The sensory cortex, together with the specific thalamocortical fibers, has a central role in adapting the discriminative component of pain stimulations. The importance of the anterior parietal area is controversial. It is widely accepted that there is no direct pain sensation in the anterior section of the thalamus. Nevertheless, studies which examined traumatic injuries in this area have proved there is a total disappearance of superficial pain and a partial decline in deep pain sensation. Vascular events and epileptic foci in this area are occasionally accompanied by severe pain. Intense pain, with the disappearance of superficial sensitivity, is known as "thalamic pain" (Dejerine-Roussy syndrome) in thalamic damages. Similar clinical features were described in cortico-parietal lesions. Dejerine and Mouzon described another parietal lobe syndrome as a pseudothalamic syndrome with the disappearance of all modalities of sensation including pain. The central role of this area in creating the discriminative pattern of pain is shown in the clinical picture of pain hemiagnosia. In this symptom, the paralytic patient reacts to pain stimuli on the same side only, with emotional and autonomic components, without even understanding the meaning of pain. It seems that this clinical feature is a result of selective activation only of the thalamolimbohypothalamic connections. In "asymbolic of pain," the inability to understand painful sensations in the body is accompanied by the disappearance of any adequate emotional or autonomic reaction. It seems that in such a symptom, the lesion is of the posterior parietal lobe with a disruption of the transcortical tracts.

Other cortical pathways having an important influence on the pain adapting mechanism are the frontal lobe tracts reaching the input from the nonspecific thalamic nuclei, the limbic system, and particularly the gyrus cingulate. Lesions of pathways projected to the orbitobasal area of the frontal lobe influence the personality and behavioral aspects of pain. Removal of the frontal lobe (lobotomy) as a surgical treatment for intractable pain results in the continuation of pain without, however, the subjective, negative, and emotional aspects; one may feel the pain but it does not disturb him.

The corticotemporal area also receives pain input mainly in connection with the amygdala and the hippocampus memory center. Its importance is probably in the emotional character and memory of pain experience.

F. The Descending Pain Control Mechanism

The existence of a pain modulating control system was suspected since Reinolds demonstrated a loss of sensation produced by electric stimulation of the periaqueductal gray. This theory has been confirmed in recent years and was the basis for understanding the pain mechanism. Electrical stimulation by implantation of microelectrodes in diverse structures of the diencephalon and the brain stem demonstrated a stimulation-produced analgesia (SPA) by inhibition of neurons in laminae I–V of the spinal cord. The following are the two most important centers that play a central role in the modulating pain system:

1. The periaqueductal gray has an intense connection to cortical, limbic, and thalamic structures. Reciprocal connections exist with nuclei of the reticular formation in the brain stem. The role of the periaqueductal gray in the pain modulating system is also proved by the increase of pain complaints in experimental local lesions.

2. The nuclei in rostal medulla, especially the nucleus raphe magnus (NRM) and the nuclei magnocellularis, are probably the most important relay centers of the descending modulating pain system. Electrical stimulation, injection of morphine, and direct input from other supraspinal structures, especially the periaqueductal gray, evoke pain depression. The inhibitory stimulus is transmitted along the tracts in the dorsal portion of the lateral fasciculus. The inhibitory input reacts mainly on cells in laminae I, II, and V.

Besides the modulatory effect of the mesencephalon and medulla, there are evidences of a direct depression effect on the cortex. Stimulation of primary and secondary sensory centers (SI, SII) may have a pain inhibitory effect. It seems that the inhibitory modulation is transmitted by motor fibers of the corticospinal tract and extrapyramidal system. Electrical stimulation of the medial part of the hypothalamus may also decrease the pain sensation by direct activation of the hypothalamospinal pathway or via activation of the periaqueductal gray.

1. The Neurochemistry of the Descending System and the Opioid Analgesia

Two main descending pain control systems play a role in pain modulation: norepinephrine-containing pathway and the serotonin-containing system. These systems are activated and react upon a number of peptides and monoamines, inhibitory and excitatory neurotransmitters. The epinephrine system transmits stimuli from the dorsolateral pontine nuclei to neurons in laminae I, II, IV–VI, and X in the spinal cord and have an inhibitory effect and an excitatory effect as well. The serotonergic descending system contains fibers from the rostroventral medulla which terminate in laminae I and II. Injections of epinephrine or serotonin antagonists given intrathecally may abolish the inhibitory effect and increase the painful sensation. Several peptides influence the descending modulating system. [See Synaptic Transmitters and Neuromodulators.]

A calcitonin gene-related peptide (CGRP) is localized in the dorsal root ganglion and in 5% of the lamina I cells. It is of therapeutic significance in cancer pain and nonmalignant bone pain, as in Paget's disease. The corticotropine-releasing factor (CRP) known as somatostatin and the ''gut'' peptide cholecystokinin (CCK) are other spinal neurotransmitters. The somatostatin was extracted for the first time from the hypothalamus. It is found in 10% of the laminae I and III cells, has an influence on the pinprick sensation test, and no effect on opiates. CCK is a very common neurotransmitter and is frequently accompanied by substance P (SP) without having any specific effect.

SP, which is located in the dorsal horn and in the periaqueductal gray as well, is a specific excitatory peptide having major importance in the pain pathway. It has a hyperalgesical effect (excessive sensitivity to pain) and is inhibited by opiates.

Neurotensin has a role in the pain control mechanism by acting in the hypothalamus, periaqueductal gray, and dorsal horn. Experimental intracisternal injection of neurotensin produces a comparable analgesia.

2. Opioid Analgesia

Opiates have a central role in the decline of pain sensation. Since Portoghese postulated the cellular receptors for morphine, five main groups of opioid receptors were discovered. The mu receptor is mostly activated by morphine and highly naloxone sensitive (morphine inhibitor). Other receptors are the kappa, sigma, delta, and epsilon. Mu receptors are heavily dissipated in the periaqueductal gray matter, brain stem, limbic system, and the dorsal spinal cord while other receptors are less active in the pain modulating system. Three groups of endogenous opioid peptides were found: enkephalin, highly concentrated in the spinal and supraspinal systems; dynorphine, found in the hypothalamus, periaqueductal gray matter, reticular formation, and spinal dorsal horn; and beta-endorphins, concentrated mostly in the hypothalamus. The opioids have a specific function in the dorsal horn and are concentrated in laminae I and II and also IV, V, VI of the spinal cord. They inhibit the releasing of SP, reduce the site of the peripheral receptive fields, and act on the excitatory postsynaptic potential (EPSP). Their effect is therefore pre- and postsynaptic. The pain transmitted C fibers are more sensitive to opioids than the A_δ fibers.

A new aspect in the neurochemistry of pain was postulated by researchers who found that the NMDA receptor—a subgroup of the excitatory neurotransmitter glutamate—contributes to hyperalgesia by intensifying the pain message in the spinal cord. It seems that NMDA inhibition blocks the overreaction of pain by leaving the normal sensation of pain intact. Due to the repeated pain messages after a tissue injury, the NMDA receptor probably sensitizes the spinal cord cells for the next signal. Another substance that may have a central role in pain message is GABA (γ-aminobutryic acid)—an inhibitory neurotransmitter. It probably reacts by the differentiation of sensory messages and prevents a mixture of pain sensation with other sensory inputs. The GABA is most likely active in the thalamus and dorsal horn.

tion of pain, and until the age of 7, there is no understanding of the linkage between pain and illness. These factors are responsible for the different aspects of pain response in children. Their total dependence on adults makes the role of parents highly important and the social and individual aspects extremely significant in the modulation of pain in childhood.

II. THE PSYCHOBIOLOGY OF PAIN

Acute and chronic pain are psychobiological experiences with essential effective and cognitive components which produce an intense alteration of emotions. Their intensity can also be modified by attention, mood, or changing of perception. Impressive examples of this modifying system are "pop out" and "spotlight," phenomena which define the ability to selectively choose different elements of pain and processing an interpretation. Autosuggestion and hypnosis are two clinical methods that use these phenomenon for pain therapy.

Fear and anxiety are greatly influenced by mood, motivation, and cognitive factors. Anxiety, as a warning signal prior to a familiar recurrent threatening situation (trait anxiety), is much more cognitive and emotionally dependent than the anxiety which appears during the pain itself (state anxiety). [*See* ANXIETY AND FEAR.]

Personal–individual and socioenvironmental factors significantly influence the sensitivity to pain—the subjective meaning of the unpleasant element, especially the threshold to pain (the least recognizable pain sensation of a subject). Lack of sufficient information, uncertainty concerning the personal circumstances, helplessness, and the loss of individual orientation influence the sensitivity of pain and suffering. Social and environmental factors also modify the interpretation of pain. Various cultures, races, and religions tolerate pain in different manners. The ceremonial torture ritual in primitive cultures and the maturity accompanying the adolescent to manhood are proposed to elevate the threshold of pain. The different comprehensions to the meaning of suffering in the Judeo-Christian and Far Eastern cultures are expressed by the different personal relations to pain.

In childhood, logical thinking is developed only at the age of 11 since any formal logical thinking in youth is impossible. In early childhood up till the age of 9 there is no clear understanding of the motiva-

III. THE THEORIES OF PAIN

Several theories, some incompatible with the physiological facts, were published during the last 200 years. The specificity theory, which indicated a specific pain receptor, pain pathways, and a pain center in the brain, contradicted the intensity theory which postulated the nonspecificity of pain sensation. According to this theory, every type of intense stimulation may be expressed as a pain sensation. Both theories contradict the Aristotelian hypothesis of pain as an affective aspect.

An extremely important development in the search for a unique concept was the gate theory by Melzack and Wall in 1965. The first step in this theory was the finding that in a decerebrated cat, stimuli of C fibers induce a positive potential in the dorsal root and the stimulation of the A_δ fibers induces a negative potential. This hypothesis postulates that the small (C) and the large (A_δ) fibers have a different and eventually contrary physiological activity in the dorsal horn. They presumed that both fibers activate a T transmission cell which transmits the stimuli toward the brain. Simultaneously with the T cell acitivity, the C and A_δ fibers have a contrary effect on the interneuron known as I inhibitory cell. These I cells depress the T cells and, therefore, suppress the transmission of pain. A_δ and C have opposite reactions on the I cells. A_δ inhibits, while C fibers increase their activity. The mechanism of both fibers reflects the inhibitory effect of the A_δ fibers on the T cells with a decrease in the pain sensation and an increase on the C fibers with intensification of pain. This hypothetical explanation of the pain mechanism explains several phenomenon but fails to explain other clinical observations. The findings of certain dorsal root neurons (WDR) which are powerful inhibitors of pain stimuli, and the phenomenon of "diffuse noxious inhibitory control," can be explained in connection with the gate theory.

Transcutaneous electrical nerve stimulation (TENS), a therapeutical method of using a high-frequency, low-intensity stimulation for diminishing pain sensation, can also be explained by the pain theory.

In 1968, Melzack and Casey modified the pain theory by including the role of the ascending system. They suggested there were three different aspects of pain—discriminative, motivation–effective, and cognitive—which ascend through different pathways—the paleospinothalamic, and the neospinothalamic tracts. In 1982, Melzack and Wall expanded this theory by also taking into consideration a cognitive control and descending brain stem inhibitory control system which modulates the pain system in the dorsal root. The involvement of endogenous opioids (opioid analgesia system) in the inhibitory interneural system must also be considered.

IV. CLINCIAL IMPLICATIONS OF PAIN

A. Acute Pain

Acute pain is produced by a sudden injury and ischemic damage to the skin or a visceral organ. Acute cutaneal pain is characterized by two different stages of pain known as "double response" (by Lewis). The first stage, which develops immediately after an injury and has a pricking sensation, is caused by the transmission of the pain signal via rapid myelinated fibers (A_δ). One or two seconds later, there is a burning, unpleasant pain which is characteristic of the second stage. This pain pattern is caused by transmitting the signal via slow unmyelinated fibers (C).

Acute visceral pain has an aching, sometimes sharp, penetrating character—"lightening pain," which also appears as a burning, unlocalized sensation, combined with referred pain. The diffuseness of this pain pattern is explained by the high proportion of C fibers which overlap the different receptive fields and wide innervation areas.

B. Chronic Pain

Chronic pain is a persistent painful sensation whose duration is longer than that of acute tissue injury. As a rule, the time limitation for this type of chronic pain is between 1 and 6 months.

Chronic pain is directly related to psychological aspects such as anxiety, especially the "trait anxiety state," isolation, feelings of loss and helplessness, emotions often accompanied with chronic pain.

These circumstances influence not only mood but perception as well.

The pain learning and initiation processes are emphasized more in chronic than in acute pain. The cultural and socioeconomical factors also severely influence the relation to prolonged pain. Since the meaning of suffering and pain varies according to the different cultures, chronic pain depends not only on the individual's cognitive and emotional condition, but also on the socioenvironmental aspects. Autonomical responses (sweating, increase in blood pressure and pulse, widening of the pupil) are very often accompanied by acute pain, and rarely by the chronic form.

C. Intractable Pain

Intractable pain is a permanent severe pain condition mostly uneffected by drug administration. It can be the result of a malignant or nonmalignant disease and also be associated with a psychiatric illness without any identifiable symptom. This type of pain (intractable cancer pain) in cancer patients is caused by the direct penetration of the tumor mass into the diverse organs by nonmalignant complications of cancer (pathological fractures), neoplastic remote symptoms, and as a complication of chemotherapy (for example, neuropathy) or radiation. The psychological condition of the cancer patient is a very important factor in the development of intractable pain. The hopelessness of the situation and the depressive stage can intensify the pain sensitivity and even decrease the threshold of pain.

D. Causalgia

Causalgia is a pain disorder of the peripheral nervous system having a sustained obstinate burning character. It can develop after a traumatic peripheral nerve lesion, such as complications of limb injuries which can occur from high-velocity missiles during warfare. The incidence of such a pain disorder in limbs of wounded soldiers is approximately 1.5–2%.

Causalgia is a very distressing and intense pain disorder which usually attacks patients severely during normal daily activities. It is usually combined with the median nerve injury in the upper limbs and the sciatic nerve in the lower extremities.

Emotional and behavioral factors can distinctly influence this pain either by aggravating or relieving its intensity. It is certain that dysfunction of the sympathetic nervous system plays the main role in this disorder. It has also been proved that hypersensation of the WDR cells in the dorsal horn and dysfunctioning of the C and A_δ activities are the physiological changes in causalgia. The main role of the sympathetic system is demonstrated by the complete abolishment of pain sensation by total disruption of all sympathetic fibers to the injured limb. This finding is the basis for effective therapy of surgical sympathectomy in causalgia.

E. Referred Pain

Referred pain is pain of somatic visceral origin which is projected to a fixed distant location. The best examples for this disorder are the projection of cardiac pain in the left shoulder and arm; pain in the right shoulder; pain in gallbladder diseases; and back pain in peptic ulcer. The explanation for the referred pain in a simultaneous activation of both processes of the dorsal root ganglian cells is the superficial skin branch and the deep somatic process. By stimulation of the visceral branch, the superficial branch activates and also depresses the activity of the visceral area. In the interaction between two different visceral pains (cardiac and gallbladder or pancreas and peptic ulcer pains), the fixed distant location moves in the vertical direction. This dislocation of the referred pain is known as "aberrant referred pain." It very often happens when there are other defects in the same area occurring simultaneously with referred pain. The "reflex paralysis" is a well-known combination of limb skin pain and muscle weakness in the same distribution. The close relationship between sensory and motor fibers explains this phenomenon.

F. Phantom Pain

Phantom pain, a postamputation disorder, is pain in the area of the body where a limb existed previously. This pain phenomenon is mostly associated with limb amputation but can also develop after nose, ear, tongue, breast, or penis excision. This type of pain has no particular identifying character and may present in a burning, throbbing, aching, or crushing form. Its intensity and duration also vary radically from patient to patient. Very severe intractable pain, a mild unpleasant sensation, or a sensation without a painful component (phantom) may be the presenting symptoms. Cognitive, emotional and behavioral factors play a role in the onset of this disorder. Patients suffering from emotional ridigity, in a depressive state, feelings of helplessness, and insomnia, are most likely to develop phantom pain, and possibly with even more intensity.

Theories concerning the importance of preamputation factors such as the last position of the leg before it was amputated, were previously reported. Currently, it seems that there is no relationship between phantom pain and preamputation conditions. The mechanism of phantom pain is uncertain. Peripheral, dorsal horn, supraspinal, and psychological causes were hypothesized. It seems that multifactoral causes are responsible for the development of this unusual disorder.

Medication (analgesics, antipsychotic, antidepressant drugs), surgical intervention, physio- and psychotherapy, hypnosis, and acupuncture are investigated but later were found to have only limited efficacy. The function of each of the therapeutical methods is individual and varies from patient to patient.

G. Pain and Psychiatric Diseases

Many psychiatric diseases are associated with long-standing chronic pain. The intensity of pain in psychiatric patients can become intractable without even any evidence of physical lesions.

In neurosis and hysteria, pain is of a somatoformic phenomenon, resulting from an emotional dysfunction. Forty percent of neurotic and hysteric patients, mostly males, complain of having pain. In its extreme form, pain can be the presenting symptom of a psychiatric disorder and may be totally unresponsive to analgesic medications. This condition is usually associated with anxiety, fatigue, depression, or irritability and sometimes with a neurological localized deficit such as paralysis or an atypical pricking sensation of the limb. The complaints, in contrast to organic physical pain, may be of a very localized character such as spot location in headache and the localized cardiac pain in cardiophobia. Prolonged, intractable pain often leads to medical misdiagnosis. In Briquet's syndrome (acute abdominal pain as a result of hysteria), many females, diagnosed as suffering from appendicitis, peptic ulcer, extrauterine gravidity, or even heart attack, may undergo unnecessary recurrent surgical intervention. Pain associated with muscle contractions which is characteristic of many of these cases, aggravates the somatoformic pain in neurotic hysteric patients.

Pain is very closely related to anxiety which decreases the pain threshold. On the other hand, anxiety can be induced by pain especially when it is of a visceral origin and associated with autonomic symptoms. In a situation of extreme stress with an overfunctioning of the sympathetic system, severe anxiety can be combined with the insensitivity and elevation of the pain threshold. War injuries, incurred at war during combat, mountain climbing, and road accidents, are examples of such stressful conditions.

Another, less common pain disorder in psychiatry is known as delusional pain which occurs in 2% of schizophrenic patients. In this case, it is difficult to differentiate between delusional pain and the extreme increase of the tolerance threshold to external pain stimuli. Schizophrenic patients with serious life-threatening medical conditions, such as heart attacks, perforation of the peptic ulcer, or multiple injuries from road accidents, may be free of pain. Neurochemical mechanisms, such as changing of the serotonin or bradykinin levels, were postulated as the cause of this phenomenon. Delusional pain is mostly a part of a complex psychotic picture and is treated by the administration of antipsychotic medication. [*See* SCHIZOPHRENIA.]

V. ASSESSMENT OF PAIN THERAPY

The management of pain therapy depends on the efficacy of therapy modality and the physical and psychological condition of the patient. Drug treatment, surgical intervention, physiotherapy, psychological management, including hypnotherapy and acupuncture, are categories of pain therapy.

A. Drug Therapy

1. Nonopioid Analgesics

These drugs contain acetaminophen, acetylsalicylic acid (aspirin), and nonsteroidal anti-inflammatory agents—NSAIDs (ibuprofen, naproxen, indomethacin, suprofen). The effect is mainly through their influence on the peripheral pain system. Most of the substances inhibit the prostaglandin synthetase enzyme and the kinin production. The central effect is also postulated but only with a limited clinical importance. These drugs are usually administered in muscle and joint pain, rheumatic complaints, inflammatory diseases associated with pain and headache, and some have a specific effect on migraine. This drug category does not induce tolerance, physical dependence, or influence mood and alertness.

2. Opioid Analgesics

Opioid analgesics are agents which eliminate pain by activating the "opioid analgesic system" in the spinal horn and supraspinal structure. The analgesic effect is induced by binding the externus opioid substances of different opiate receptors especially the mu receptor. Morphine, meperidine, methadone, codeine, and oxycodon belong to the exogenous opioids. Some of the drugs (pentazocine) have an agonist and antagonist effect on the system.

Opioid analgesics are very effective in severe, visceral, post-traumatic operation and cancer pain. Its efficacy on the peripheral nerve lesion with causalgia, phantom pain, and psychiatric disorders is less prominent. This drug category is associated with side effects such as vomiting, constipation, and even respiratory distress, and is characterized by the development of tolerance to the substance and addiction. Addiction to these opiates is highly individual.

3. Tricyclic Antidepressant

The tricyclic antidepressants (anitryptyline, dopexin, imipramine) are effective medications against peripheral–neuropathic pain and headache. The effect of these drugs is associated with the psychiatric, antidepressive, sleep-regulating and mood-stabilizing results with specific effect on the serotonic and norepinephrine turnover by preventing the reuptake into cell bodies.

4. Serotonin Agonists and Antagonists

Serotonin receptors play a central role in the pain mechanism, especially in migraine headaches. At least five different presynaptic and postsynaptic serotonin receptors (5HT receptors) are differentiated by dividing them into two major groups—$5HT_1$ and $5HT_2$. $5HT_{1B}$ or $5HT_{1D}$ agonists (sumatriptan) have a strong influence in the acute stage of migraine, while $5HT_2$ antagonist (pizotifen) has a preventive effect. α_2, H_3, μ opioid and somatostatin were found in the trigeminovascular fibers (fibers of the trigeminal nerve surrounding the cranial vessels) and may play a role in antimigraine therapy. Medications having a direct stabilizing effect on the membrane also belong to this group such as antiepileptic drugs (phenytoin, carabamazepine), local anesthetics, receptor blockers (propanolol), and calcium channel blockers (verapamil). These medications are useful in peripheral nerve pain and migraine. Valporic acid, another antiepileptic drug, also has an affect on the serotonin system in the brain stem.

B. Other Antipain Methods

Surgical intervention is a radical but nevertheless effective method in the treatment of severe, prolonged pain. Physiotherapy and psychological management are helpful in the elimination of aggravating emotional and cognitive–negative aspects of pain. Physiotherapy can help relieve muscle contraction and joint pain, which severely intensifies pain sensation from other origins. The use of TENS, a high-frequency, low-intensity stimulation, is effective in peripheral and spinal pain. This mechanism is independent of the opioid analgesic system and the effect is not reversible by administration of naloxone.

A prolonged inhibitory effect of TENS on the spinothalamic tract without abnormality in the peripheral nerve conduction and a spinal depressing activity by selective C/A fiber stimulus, according to the gate theory, are postulated as the mechanisms of TENS.

Acupuncture depresses pain sensation probably by activating the opioid analgesic system. A low-frequency, high-intensity stimulus has a similar effect; however, both physical therapies are partially reversible by naloxone administration. Hypnotherapy and biofeedback are other options in pain management. The relaxin–imaginary exercises may influence the autonomic system and induce self-regulation of pain by controlling cognitive and autonomic functions. Steroids and antipsychotic drugs can also be used in antipain treatment.

Bibliography

Aronoff, G. M. (Ed.) (1993). "Evaluation and Treatment of Chronic Pain," 2nd ed. Williams and Wilkins, Baltimore, MD.

Bonica, J. J. (Ed.) (1990). "The Management of Pain," 2nd ed. Lea and Febiger, Philadelphia.

Fields, H. L. (1989). "Pain Syndromes in Neurology." Butterworth, London.

Fields, H. L., and Besson, J. M. (Eds.). Pain modulation. In "Progress in Brain Research," Vol. 77. Elsevier, Amsterdam.

Kaas, J. H. (1990). The somatosensory system. In "The Human Nervous System" (E. Paxinos, Ed.). Academic Press, New York.

Wall, R. P., and Melzack, R. (1989) (Eds.). "Textbook of Pain," 2nd ed. Churchill Livingston, Edinburgh.

PANIC DISORDER

John A. Lucas
University of California, San Diego
and Department of Veterans Affairs Medical Center, San Diego

Glossary

Agoraphobia Avoidance (or endurance despite intense anxiety) of places or situations from which escape might be difficult or embarrassing, or in which help might not be available, in the case of a panic attack. Also known as phobic avoidance.

Anxiety A feeling of apprehension, uncertainty, or fear typically accompanied by increased physiological arousal.

Anxiety disorder A group of disorders in which the central features are anxiety and/or avoidance behavior which cause the individual significant distress and/or impairment in everyday functioning. These include panic disorder, agoraphobia, simple phobia, social phobia, obsessive–compulsive disorder, post-traumatic stress disorder, and generalized anxiety disorder.

Comorbidity The co-occurrence of more than one disorder in the same individual. Also known as dual diagnosis.

Diagnostic and Statistical Manual for Mental Disorders (DSM) A reference manual containing descriptions of the diagnostic categories used by mental health professionals to diagnose, communicate about, study, and treat various mental disorders. Currently in its revised, third edition (DSM III-R), the fourth edition (DSM IV) is expected to be published in spring 1994.

Epidemiologic catchment area (ECA) survey A survey sponsored by the National Institute of Mental Health (NIMH) in which approximately 3000 to 5000 people from each of five different cities across the United States were administered a structured clinical interview designed to yield diagnoses for mental disorders based on criteria from the third edition of DSM (DSM III).

Noradrenaline A neurotransmitter of the catecholamine family present within cells of the central and peripheral nervous system.

PANIC is an innate, phylogenetic mechanism designed to prepare an individual to overcome or escape a perceived danger or threat. Sometimes, however, this mechanism is triggered in the absence of any real danger. When this occurs repeatedly or is accompanied by significant distress, it may reflect a panic disorder. Panic disorder is a prevalent condition, characterized by discrete episodes of intense apprehension or fear that occur for no apparent reason. These episodes, called "panic attacks," are accompanied by multiple physiological symptoms, such as palpitations, sweating, shortness of breath, and dizziness, as well as cognitive symptoms, such as fears of dying, doing something uncontrolled, or going insane. Several aspects of panic and panic disorder will be discussed here, including clinical descriptions, prevalence estimates, etiological theories, and treatment considerations.

I. HISTORICAL BACKGROUND

The experience of sudden, unexpected fear has been described throughout the centuries; however, the clinical syndrome recognized as "panic disorder" today has held that name for only the last 10–15 years. The term panic is derived from the Greek god Pan, the half-man/half-goat deity who ruled over nature and the countryside. Startling or mysterious sounds were often attributed to Pan, and it was believed that he was capable of producing a scream so frightening that one could be scared to death by it.

Throughout much of medical history, panic symptoms were included among the many features of hysteria, a disorder characterized by physical complaints for which there was no apparent physical cause. Over the centuries, attempts were made to organize the various manifestations of hysteria, and by the late 19th century physicians had described several syndromes that included nervousness and unexplained physiological arousal as central features. These held a number of names, such as "irritable heart," "vasomotor congestion," "neurocirculatory asthenia," "nervous tachycardia," "nervous asthenia," and "effort syndrome."

At the end of the 19th century, Sigmund Freud separated out from the various nervous disorders those that were characterized by anxiety attacks, worry, and/or unrealistic fears (phobias). He believed that these disorders were the result of unconscious attempts to ward off forces within the individual that were threatening the sense of self (i.e., the ego) and its relation to the external world. According to Freud, the affect associated with threatening or unacceptable impulses (typically sexual or aggressive in nature) detached from its source and either attached to a neutral object or remained in a free-floating state. The former would manifest as phobic anxiety, while the latter would manifest as generalized anxiety or anxiety attacks, both of which Freud labeled "anxiety neurosis." [See ANXIETY AND FEAR.]

Anxiety neurosis (or the more general term "psychoneurosis") was included in the diagnostic nomenclature of the first two editions of the *Diagnostic and Statistical Manual of Mental Disorders* (DSM). In the 1960s, however, investigators demonstrated differential responses to medication treatment in patients with discrete anxiety attacks versus generalized anxiety. Studies such as these helped distinguish panic disorder as a separate entity and led to its official diagnostic status in both the third edition of DSM and the ninth revision of the World Health Organization's International Classification of Diseases (ICD-9).

II. DIAGNOSTIC CRITERIA

A. Current Diagnostic Criteria

The revised third edition of DSM (DSM-III-R), published in 1987, defines panic disorder as recurrent

attacks of intense fear or discomfort, with specific criteria delineating both symptom presentation and attack frequency. The symptom criterion requires that at least 4 of 13 characteristic symptoms be present in one or more attacks. These symptoms include

1. shortness of breath (dyspnea) or smothering sensations
2. dizziness, unsteady feelings, or faintness
3. palpitations or accelerated heart rate (tachycardia)
4. trembling or shaking
5. sweating
6. choking
7. nausea or abdominal distress
8. depersonalization or derealization
9. numbness or tingling sensations (paresthesias)
10. flushes (hot flashes) or chills
11. chest pain or discomfort
12. fear of dying
13. fear of going crazy or of doing something uncontrolled

The DSM-III-R frequency criterion specifies the number of attacks necessary to establish a diagnosis. According to this criterion, at least four panic attacks must occur within a 4-week period, or alternatively, one or more attacks must be followed by at least 1 month of persistent worry about having another attack.

To help distinguish panic disorder from other anxiety disorders and organic disorders that mimic panic symptoms, DSM-III-R specifies additional criteria. First, to rule out simple or social phobia, DSM-III-R requires that at least one attack be unexpected (i.e., must not occur in a situation that always provokes anxiety), and that attacks occur in situations other than when the individual is the focus of others' attention. To help rule out generalized anxiety, symptoms of at least one attack must develop suddenly and increase in intensity within 10 minutes after the first symptom is noticed. Finally, it must be established that the panic attacks are not initiated and maintained by organic factors, such as amphetamine intoxication or hyperthyroidism. [See ANXIETY DISORDERS.]

B. Proposed Diagnostic Criteria

Currently, the advisory committee for the revision of diagnostic criteria for anxiety disorders is considering changes for the fourth edition of the DSM

(DSM-IV). While the definition of panic and the symptom criterion will likely remain essentially unchanged, it has been proposed that the frequency criterion for panic disorder be revised. Instead of requiring four attacks in a 4-week period *or* one attack followed by at least 1 month of persistent worry, DSM-IV will require *both* recurrent unexpected panic attacks (number unspecified) *and* at least one attack followed by at least 1 month of (a) persistent concern about having additional attacks, (b) worry about the implications of the attacks or its consequences, or (c) a change in behavior related to the attacks. These changes reflect dissatisfaction with the relatively arbitrary assignment of specific attack frequencies used in the past, and the recognition that the fundamental feature of panic disorder is the presence of recurrent attacks that occur unexpectedly and cause apprehension about having more attacks.

III. CHARACTERISTICS OF PANIC ATTACKS

The experience of panic differs from individual to individual, and may also differ from one attack to the next in any one individual. Studies of the characteristics of panic reveal a variety of subtypes of attacks based on clinical presentation. These include distinctions in symptom quantification, attack frequency, diurnal distribution, and the presence or absence of an identifiable trigger.

A. Symptom Quantification

Patients with panic disorder typically endorse an average of seven to eight panic symptoms per attack, far more than the minimum number of four symptoms required by DSM-III-R. Panic attacks involving fewer than four symptoms, however, are not uncommon. These are typically less severe and of shorter duration than full symptom attacks, and are designated by DSM-III-R as ''limited symptom attacks'' (LSAs). It should be noted that some individuals report severe levels of intensity associated with LSAs. Moreover, at least one study found that patients suffering exclusively from LSAs were no different than patients with full symptom attacks on measures of anticipatory anxiety and phobic avoidance. Therefore, the consequences of limited and full symptom attacks may be essentially the same.

B. Panic Frequency

Some clinicians and investigators distinguish between panic attacks based on the frequency of occurrence. As noted previously, DSM-III-R allows for diagnosis of panic disorder based on one of two frequency criteria: either four attacks in a 4-week period, or one attack followed by at least 1 month of persistent worry. Studies of patients with panic disorder have shown no distinction between attacks which occur at least weekly and those that occur with less frequency on measures such as symptom patterns, duration of attacks, duration of illness, anticipatory anxiety or phobic avoidance. Data from these and similar studies strongly suggest that the frequency of panic recurrence does not necessarily reflect severity of panic disorder, and form the basis for the proposed changes in frequency criteria for panic disorder in DSM-IV.

C. Nocturnal Panic

Preliminary studies suggest that approximately 20% of patients with panic disorder also suffer from recurrent nocturnal panic attacks. These attacks typically occur during the first 2 hours of sleep, while the individual is in the stage of deep sleep. Patients with both daytime and nocturnal panic attacks typically report a significantly higher frequency of daytime attacks. Daytime attacks do not, however, differ from nocturnal attacks in terms of severity of attack, duration of attack, or the number of symptoms per attack.

D. Spontaneous versus Situational Panic

The experience of spontaneous (i.e., unexpected) panic episodes is a primary characteristic of panic disorder. When panic attacks occur only in specific situations or upon exposure to specific stimuli (e. g., public speaking, being in high places), a diagnosis of social phobia or simple phobia is made. Patients with panic disorder, however, frequently report having both spontaneous attacks and attacks that occur in the presence of readily identifiable triggers or situations. Research to date has suggested no significant differences between spontaneous and situational panic attacks on a number of characteristics, including severity or duration of the attack, frequency per week, or number of symptoms experienced per attack. Some have argued that although attacks may appear to be spontaneous to the patient, a trigger such as a physical sensation associated with panic (e.g., detecting an increase in heart rate) or a thought regarding the negative consequences of panic can always be identified.

IV. PREVALENCE

Most published epidemiologic studies of panic disorder have employed criteria from the third edition of DSM (DSM-III), published in 1980. Although the general description of panic has remained essentially the same, the frequency and exclusion criteria used by DSM-III differ substantially from those of the current and proposed diagnostic systems. Specifically, DSM-III required a frequency of at least three attacks in a 3-week period (see Section II for comparison). Moreover, panic disorder and agoraphobia were classified as separate disorders in DSM-III; if phobic avoidance was present, the diagnosis of panic disorder was excluded in favor of a diagnosis of agoraphobia. Since the publication of DSM-III, data have strongly suggested that agoraphobia is most frequently (albeit, not always) a consequence panic disorder (see Section V). This is reflected in DSM-III-R and DSM-IV (proposed) by the inclusion of agoraphobia as a subtype of panic disorder. Therefore, prevalence estimates based on DSM-III criteria may not reflect the same set of patients identified by current or proposed diagnostic criteria and may provide an overly conservative estimate of the prevalence of panic disorder. [*See* AGORAPHOBIA.]

The National Institute of Mental Health has estimated that approximately 1.5% of the U.S. population will meet criteria for DSM-III-defined panic disorder during their lifetime. The mean age of onset is approximately 24 years, with the incidence of panic disorder being significantly higher in persons ages 25–44 than in other age groups. Panic disorder is also significantly more prevalent in the separated and divorced, compared to other marital status groups. There is no consistent evidence of a relationship between panic disorder and race or education; however, at least one study reported that panic disorder is significantly more prevalent in the lowest socioeconomic level, compared to higher levels.

Several studies have found that patients with panic disorder are overrepresented in medical care settings. Compared to patients with other psychiatric and nonpsychiatric disorders, patients with panic disorder have significantly elevated rates of emergency room visits, health care utilization, and use of minor tranquilizers, sleeping pills, and antidepressant medications. In one study, 86% of panic disorder patients surveyed reported seeking medical attention for their symptoms at some time during their illness. Moreover, in 1991, the National Institutes of Health consensus development conference reported that many patients with panic disorder see more than 10 doctors before being given an accurate diagnosis.

Panic attacks, however, are not limited to patients suffering from panic disorder. On the contrary, panic is common among all anxiety disorders, as well as among other psychiatric disorders and nonpsychiatric medical disorders (see Table I). Panic episodes are also common among presumably healthy adults. In two separate surveys of college students, approximately 35% of each sample reported having had at least one panic episode within the year prior to the study. This figure reflects reports of both expected and unexpected panic. Based on community surveys and data collected from studies of college students, the percentage of individuals who report at least one *unexpected* panic attack in their lifetime ranges from approximately 8 to 14 %. Moreover, in a large, nonclinical sample of college students, approximately 2.4% of those surveyed endorsed all the necessary criteria to qualify for a DSM-III-R diagnosis of panic disorder.

The prevalence of panic disorder is frequently reported to be higher in females than males, at a rate of approximately 2:1. Some have suggested that this finding may be an artifact of societal norms,

TABLE I

Prevalence of Panic Attacks in Other Psychiatric Disorders

Diagnosis	Lifetime[a] (%)	Past 6 months[b] (%)
Social phobia	84	—[c]
Simple phobia	85	12–28
Generalized anxiety disorder	75	—[c]
Obsessive–compulsive disorder	83	23–35
Major depression	83	24–42
Schizophrenia	—[c]	28–63

[a] Percentage of patients in a mental health clinic who answered "yes" to the question "Have you ever had times when you felt a sudden rush of intense fear or anxiety or feelings of impending doom?" and reported at least four symptoms characteristic of panic (from Barlow, 1988).

[b] Range of percentages of respondents to the NIMH Epidemiologic Catchment Area Survey across five U.S. cities who meet psychiatric diagnoses other than panic disorder and report having at least one panic attack in the 6 months prior to the survey (from Boyd, 1986).

[c] Data not reported.

with women more likely to seek psychiatric help than men and thus more frequently coming to the attention of mental health professionals. This ratio, however, may also be an artifact of the diagnostic criteria used to define the disorder. Studies reporting a higher incidence of panic disorder among females have typically employed DSM-III diagnostic criteria. A study of nonclinical panic revealed that when DSM-III-R criteria are used, an interaction between gender and frequency criteria exists. When panic recurrence is used (e.g., four attacks in a 4-week period), a higher percentage of women satisfy panic disorder criteria. In contrast, use of the worry criterion (i.e., one attack followed by at least 30 days of persistent worry) yields a higher proportion of men than women meeting diagnostic criteria for panic disorder. These results may not generalize to clinical populations, but they do suggest that the higher prevalence of DSM-III-defined panic disorder in females may, at least in part, reflect the use of panic recurrence as the sole frequency criterion for diagnosis.

V. PHENOMENOLOGY OF PANIC DISORDER

Although specific diagnostic criteria for panic disorder may change over time, the general features remain essentially the same. These include the panic episode itself, the experience of anticipatory anxiety, and, for some individuals, the development of phobic avoidance. In addition, several other features are commonly associated with panic, including depression, substance abuse, medical disorders, and complaints of cognitive dysfunction.

A. Components of Panic Disorder

1. The Panic Attack

A panic attack is the activation of the body's protective mechanism, commonly called the "fight–flight" response. When faced with a dangerous or threatening situation, an organism can best protect itself by adopting one of two possible strategies: defend itself (fight) or attempt to escape (flight). Whichever course of action is taken, numerous physiological systems must be engaged and energy supplies must be diverted from nonessential functions to essential ones. Moreover, once the danger is gone, the body must return to a baseline level of functioning to con-

serve energy. These activities are controlled by the autonomic nervous system (ANS). The ANS has body-wide distribution, innervating organs of the circulatory, respiratory, excretory, endocrine, and exocrine systems. It comprises two principal subdivisions, the sympathetic and parasympathetic systems, which operate in an antagonistic fashion. Typically, if the signals sent along the fibers of one system stimulate an organ to begin or accelerate activity, the impulses sent along the fibers of the other system will stop or reduce activity.

The sympathetic division of the ANS is responsible for preparing the body for action. It acts upon all target organs at once, thus being quick and multifaceted in its presentation. Blood vessels in the skeletal muscles dilate, while those in the skin, mucosa, and abdominal viscera constrict. Cardiac, respiratory, and sweat gland activity increase, while gastrointestinal functioning is inhibited. The adrenal glands release epinephrine into the bloodstream, which reinforces the increased cardiac output and causes stored glycogen and fat to be broken down into more readily available energy sources (i.e., glucose and fatty acids). Functionally, these changes serve to improve energy delivery to the large muscle groups and vital organs, and prevent the body from overheating. These changes also lead directly or indirectly to the experience of physiological sensations presented earlier as symptoms of panic.

The parasympathetic division of the ANS restores homeostatic functions once the threat has passed by dilating blood vessels in the skin, mucosa, and viscera, decreasing heart rate, contracting the bronchioles in the lungs, inhibiting sweating, and stimulating gastrointestinal functioning. It cannot, however, counter the effects of the epinephrine that has been released in the bloodstream. Therefore, a heightened level of physiological arousal often persists despite parasympathetic activation.

2. Anticipatory Anxiety

Although panic is an adaptive response in the presence of an objective threat, it can be extremely frightening and maladaptive if it is experienced in the absence of a readily perceived danger. It is natural, for example, to experience the sudden onset of fear, palpitations, trembling, and sweating when confronted with a predator (e.g., a burglar in your house); experiencing the same symptoms while watching a favorite television show is not. When patients experience unexpected panic, they often develop anticipatory anxiety, which is characterized by excessive worry about having another attack. They become vigilant to indications that may signal the onset of an attack, and begin to develop a fear of fear.

3. Phobic Avoidance

The fear of having additional panic attacks may also prompt patients to limit their activities and avoid places or situations that they believe are associated with the attacks. This is known as phobic avoidance, or agoraphobia. Although the 10th revision of the International Classification of Diseases (ICD-10) continues to list agoraphobia and panic disorder as separate entities, studies estimate that up to 99% of patients with agoraphobia report panic symptoms predating their agoraphobic symptoms.

Research on the relationship between panic and agoraphobia suggests that the development of phobic avoidance is *not* a function of the duration of the disorder, frequency of attacks, or severity of attacks. Consequently, past hypotheses that agoraphobia is a more severe variant of panic disorder or the second stage of a two-stage illness (with the first stage being the development of panic disorder) do not appear valid. Although a significantly greater proportion of females than males with panic disorder reportedly develop severe agoraphobia, this estimate may be biased by factors such as those mentioned earlier in the discussion of gender differences in panic disorder (see Section IV). One possible predictor of agoraphobia is the presence of a comorbid Axis II (personality) disorder, which may represent an individual's characteristic style of responding to negative or aversive situations. Similarly, individual cognitive styles may play an important role in the development of phobic avoidance. Studies have shown that, compared to panic disorder patients without agoraphobia, those with phobic avoidance report more dysfunctional panic-related appraisals, such as anticipation of panic, perceived consequences of panic, and perceived self-efficacy of coping with panic.

B. Associated Features and Comorbidities

1. Depression

The comorbidity between panic disorder and depression is quite high. As many as 70% of patients with panic disorder report depressive symptoms, and up to one-third of patients with panic disorder with agoraphobia also meet criteria for a concurrent major depressive disorder. Moreover, several studies have documented that between 60 and 90% of patients with panic disorder develop a major depression at some time in their lives. The incidence of a past or concurrent panic disorder among patients with major depression is reported by one study to be approximately 21%. [*See* DEPRESSION.]

Although panic disorder and major depression tend to occur in the same patient population, the underlying etiologies of these two disorders are unclear. Some have suggested that there is a genetic link between panic disorder and depression; however, others have provided evidence that panic disorder is not associated with increased familial risk of depression. The development of secondary depressive symptomatology is understandable from a cognitive psychological perspective, in that patients with panic disorder often perceive having little or no ability to predict or control their attacks, and may be vulnerable to feelings of helplessness, hopelessness, and low self-worth. These feelings can be further exacerbated by phobic avoidance, which can isolate the patient from interpersonal contact and reduce the number of available pleasurable activities. Studies, however, have demonstrated that major depression frequently occurs independently in patients with panic disorder, and not merely as a secondary complication. One epidemiologic study, for example, reported that 44% of patients with panic disorder and a history of major depression suffered their first major depressive episode prior to their development of panic disorder. Thirty-three percent suffered from panic disorder prior to their first major depressive episode, while 22% reportedly developed both panic and major depressive symptoms essentially simultaneously. Clearly, additional, well-controlled family studies will be necessary to better understand the specific nature of the comorbidity of anxiety and depression.

2. Substance Abuse

Evidence suggests that the correlation between anxiety disorders and substance abuse is quite high. Several studies have shown that over half the subjects who enter alcoholism treatment programs have at least a mild, but identifiable anxiety disorder; studies employing more stringent diagnostic criteria place this estimate from approximately 25 to 45%. A recent study noted that over 50% of a sample of alcoholic patients participating in an inpatient treatment program reported having experienced a panic attack in the 3-week period prior to the survey, and over 80% of these subjects reported using alcohol to help relieve their anxiety. [*See* SUBSTANCE ABUSE.]

From the opposite perspective, the incidence of substance abuse in patients with anxiety disorders is estimated at approximately 10 to 25%. Looking specifically at panic disorder, data from the NIMH Epidemiologic Catchment Area survey reveal that approximately 26% of patients with panic disorder meet criteria for alcohol abuse, while 18% meet criteria for other substance abuse.

The question of which comes first, the anxiety or the substance abuse, is complex. For some patients, the experience of panic may be so unpleasant that they will use nonprescribed drugs or alcohol to help cope with their symptoms. In fact, empirical evidence suggests that in substance abusing patients who have panic disorder with agoraphobia, the onset of abuse most often follows the onset of panic. This relationship, however, is not found in studies of patients with uncomplicated panic disorder (i.e., panic disorder without agoraphobia). Therefore, the self-medication hypothesis may be valid only for the subgroup of panic disorder patients who also suffer from phobic avoidance.

Data from family studies suggest a genetic component to the relationship between alcoholism and panic disorder with agoraphobia. These studies report that first-degree relatives of patients with uncomplicated panic disorder are at no greater risk for alcoholism than those of normal controls. The first-degree relatives of patients with panic disorder with agoraphobia, however, are reportedly at three times the average risk for alcoholism. Again, additional studies are needed to better understand the common etiologic or causal associations between panic disorder and substance abuse.

3. Medical Disorders

In general, the comorbidity of panic disorder with chronic medical illness frequently causes exacerbation of the symptomatic complaints of the medical illness. This is typically due to a combination of factors, including an increased tendency to detect and report physical symptoms, and a worsening of the illness secondary to the increased autonomic nervous system arousal associated with recurrent panic. Studies of the association between panic disorder and specific medical illnesses have reported significantly higher rates of hypertension, peptic ulcer disease, and cardiovascular mortality in patients with panic disorder compared to clinical controls.

Early studies also suggested a higher rate of the cardiovascular condition known as mitral valve prolapse (MVP) among patients with panic disorder.

MVP is a disorder in which the cusps of the mitral valve of the heart slip out of place and into the left atrium during contraction of the ventricle, causing a mid to late systolic murmur. There may be no clinical symptoms associated with this condition; however, some patients experience nonanginal chest pain and discomfort, shortness of breath, palpitations, light-headedness, and fatigue. The early reports of the relationship between panic disorder and MVP fueled speculation that MVP may represent a biological marker for panic. Later studies, however, failed to find a higher prevalence of MVP in patients with panic disorder compared to the normal population, or a higher incidence of panic in patients with MVP compared to controls without MVP.

4. Cognitive Complaints

Clinically, patients with panic disorder frequently complain of cognitive difficulties, especially of poor concentration and memory. The cognitive psychology literature suggests that, in general, anxious patients tend to be more distracted by material that is related to their principal fears (e.g., words such as "dizzy" or "crash") than neutral material. Moreover, although anxious patients do not differ from normal controls in their ability to recall threat-related words, they demonstrate greater implicit memory for this information. For example, anxious subjects and normal controls may be presented a series of threat-related and neutral words with instructions to imagine themselves in a scene involving the word. If subjects are later asked to recall the presented words (i.e., explicit memory), groups will not differ in the number of threat words recalled. If, however, subjects are asked to complete word stems (e.g., MOT ____) by writing down the first word that comes to mind (e.g., MOTHER), anxious subjects will produce significantly more of the threat-related words to which they had been exposed previously than normal subjects (i.e., implicit memory). [See IMPLICIT MEMORY.]

Studies of panic disorder that have examined attentional capacity and memory functioning without experimental manipulation of the threat-related content of the stimulus material have yielded different results. Compared to normal and psychiatric controls, patients with panic disorder do not exhibit diminished span of immediate attention on an auditory–verbal digit span test, or impaired ability to sustain attention on a number cancellation test. Results from studies of memory functioning, however, have been mixed. One early study reported verbal memory deficits associated with panic disorder. Later studies, however, found greater impairment on tests of figure learning and recall in the absence of impaired performance on measures of verbal memory, attentional capacity, or visuospatial abilities. The presence of these deficits in patients with panic disorder may reflect abnormal functioning in the brain regions responsible for learning and memory (e.g., the hippocampal formation and related structures). [See MEMORY.]

Although additional study is needed, evidence suggests that these brain areas play an important role in both memory and panic. Patients with seizure disorders involving the amygdala and hippocampus frequently report panic-related fear and physiological sensations as primary symptoms. In addition, several case studies of patients with abnormalities in the medial temporal lobe have reported panic episodes as associated symptoms. Neuroimaging studies of patients with panic disorder also implicate temporal lobe abnormalities. A higher incidence of right temporal lobe abnormalities has been reported on magnetic resonance imaging (MRI) scans of patients with panic disorder compared to controls, and studies employing positron emission tomography (PET) have found abnormal metabolic activity in the temporal lobes of patients with panic disorder. Initial PET scan evidence also suggested lateralization of the abnormality to the right temporal lobe; this finding, however, has recently been called into question.

VI. ETIOLOGICAL CONSIDERATIONS

Most mental health professionals and neuropsychiatric scientists agree that biological, psychological, and sociocultural factors all play a role in the development and maintenance of panic disorder. The relative importance assigned to each of these factors, however, differs substantially depending on the theoretical orientation of the individual. The prevailing focus in recent years has been on the etiological importance of biological and cognitive–behavioral factors; however, psychoanalytic formulations have been present since Freud first described anxiety neurosis nearly a century ago. As noted earlier, Freud believed that the behavioral manifestation of what we would now describe as panic attacks reflected repressed, unacceptable sexual or aggressive impulses that had detached from their source and remained in a free-floating, intrapsychic state. Some

clinicians continue to conceptualize panic disorder within this framework, and focus their treatment plans accordingly. Over the past quarter century, however, our knowledge of the psychobiology of panic disorder has grown exponentially, and there is now compelling evidence of the etiological importance of biological and cognitive factors in panic disorder.

A. Biological Theories

1. Septohippocampal Theory

Guided primarily by studies of animal behavior, Jeffrey Gray hypothesized that environmental stimuli are continuously monitored by a "behavioral inhibition system" (BIS), which mediates behavioral output according to the type of stimuli detected. Stimuli that are novel or associated with species-specific danger or punishment activate the BIS and produce anxiety-related behavioral changes, including inhibition of ongoing activity, increased physiological arousal, and increased vigilance to the surrounding environment. Gray suggested that the neurological substrate underlying the BIS were the structures of the septohippocampal system (SHS).

The SHS is located medially in the cerebral hemispheres, and comprises the hippocampal formation, septal nuclei, and their interconnections. These structures are part of the limbic system, the phylogenetically older brain system that serves as a border zone between the brainstem and the cerebral cortex. The septal nuclei are located bilaterally in the basal forebrain, while the hippocampal formation is located bilaterally in the medial portion of the temporal lobes. The hippocampal formation consists of several structures, including the hippocampus proper, dentate gyrus, subiculum, entorhinal cortex, and several associated cortical areas, known collectively as the limbic neocortex. Fibers connecting the septal nuclei and hippocampal formation travel via two neural tracts: the fimbria and the dorsal fornix. [See HIPPOCAMPAL FORMATION; LIMBIC SYSTEM.]

The SHS receives sensory input and information regarding planned behavior from cortical association areas and prefrontal cortex. According to Gray, the SHS monitors and compares incoming stimuli with expected stimuli. If these match, the SHS allows behavioral control to remain in the currently functioning brain systems. If, however, incoming and predicted stimuli are inconsistent, or the predicted event is aversive, a "mismatch" occurs. When mismatch is detected, the process of generating predictions stops, the behavioral inhibition system is engaged, and the sensory stimuli, behavioral plans, and motor programs associated with the mismatch are tagged in memory as "important" and/or "aversive" for future reference.

As noted in the previous discussion of cognitive complaints, abnormalities have been found in the mesial temporal lobe of some patients with panic disorder, suggesting that dysfunction of septohippocampal structures may play a role in panic disorder. Hypothetically, dysfunction in the SHS may produce erroneous mismatches or inappropriately tag information as important or aversive, thus activating the BIS and causing an anxiety reaction unpredictably and in the absence of a valid threat cue. The complexities of the SHS and its role in pathological anxiety and panic, however, are not well understood, and other biological hypotheses have been advanced. One such theory posits that dysregulation of one of the brain's neurotransmitter systems, the noradrenergic system, is of primary etiologic importance to anxiety and panic.

2. Locus Ceruleus Theory

Over 70% of the brain's noradrenaline is produced by the locus ceruleus (LC), a collection of neuronal cell bodies found bilaterally in the pons. These neurons have extensive projections that innervate every major region of the central nervous system, including many of those associated with fear and panic. Lesion and electrical stimulation studies in nonhuman primates have suggested that the LC may hold a primary role in fear reactions, and some have suggested that the LC, rather than the SHS, is responsible for monitoring internal and external stimuli, and controlling anxiety-related behavioral and autonomic responses.

LC activity is regulated by several neuronal systems, including the benzodiazepine, endogenous opiate, epinephrine, norepinephrine, acetylcholine, γ-aminobutyric acid (GABA), substance P, and α-2 adrenergic receptor systems. Most of these systems have been shown to have important effects on anxiety and panic symptoms. In the majority of studies, administration of drugs that depress LC functioning (e.g., benzodiazepines, tricyclic antidepressants, opiates) produce powerful anxiolytic effects. Conversely, substances that increase activity in the LC (e.g., substance P, glutamate, acetylcholine, yohimbine) have anxiogenic properties.

Although the exact mechanisms are unknown, studies suggest that panic disorder may be the result of regulatory abnormalities at the level of the α-2 adrenergic receptor system or the GABA-benzodiazepine receptor system. These regulatory abnormalities are believed to cause indiscriminate initiation of the panic mechanism via LC connections to the hypothalamus and sympathetic nervous system neurons of the spinal cord.

3. Sodium Lactate and CO_2 Provocation

Numerous studies have demonstrated that patients with panic disorder are more likely to panic following infusion of sodium lactate than normal or psychiatric controls. The implication of these findings with regard to the etiology of panic disorder, however, is unclear. Some have suggested that the physiological arousal and uncomfortable body sensations produced by sodium lactate produce panic in patients because they have been conditioned to overreact to such stimulation. Sodium lactate infusion does not, however, provoke panic in all patients with panic disorder. This suggests that sodium lactate and its subsequent physiological effects are not panicogenic in and of themselves. Instead, it is believed that panic in response to sodium lactate infusion is most likely caused by an interaction between the effects of the substance and other variables, such as initial level of physiological arousal and cognitive expectancies.

Others have suggested that the mechanism responsible for lactate-induced panic is the conversion of sodium lactate to carbon dioxide (CO_2) and bicarbonate. Several studies report that patients with panic disorder are more sensitive to changes in levels of CO_2 than normal controls. When the percentage of inhaled CO_2 increases to a high enough level, however, normal controls demonstrate a similar frequency and severity of panic and anxiety symptoms as panic disorder patients.

Increased CO_2 in the blood is detected by receptors in the ventral medulla. These receptors, in turn, stimulate the LC in a dose-dependent fashion. If the level of CO_2 becomes excessive, hyperventilation is induced. Hyperventilation lowers the levels of CO_2 in the blood (a condition known as hypocapnea) and, paradoxically, results in a reduction in the amount of oxygen available to the body. This is often associated with physiological sensations, including increased heart rate, dizziness, paresthesias, and cold, clammy feelings in the extremeties.

Some have hypothesized that patients with panic disorder may have hypersensitive CO_2 receptors. To compensate for this, they may develop a mechanism of subtle, chronic hyperventilation to maintain lower levels of CO_2 in the blood and avoid triggering the receptors. Chronic hypocapneia leads to renal compensation and an accumulation of bicarbonate in the blood, a condition known as respiratory alkalosis. This, in turn, makes the individual vulnerable to small changes in respiratory physiology and blood chemistry, and provides physiological arousal cues for the initiation of panic in patients who are hypersensitive to such triggers.

B. Psychological Theories

1. Stress

The majority of patients with panic disorder cannot identify a precipitating event when asked about the cause of their first panic attack; however, systematic questioning about life events reveals that approximately 80% of these patients describe at least one negative life event preceding their first attack. Moreover, when compared to normal control subjects, patients with panic disorder report a higher frequency of severe life events, especially events involving danger and/or loss of a significant other. These and similar findings have led some to believe that stress is of etiologic importance to panic disorder. Stress has also been proposed as a precipitating factor in several other psychiatric and medical disorders. A common finding across many of these disorders, however, is that despite a clear association between stress and the onset of a disorder, a large proportion of individuals experience similar stress but do not develop the disorder. This suggests that the role of stress in the etiology of panic disorder is moderated by other variables, the most likely of which include genetic predisposition, family environment, personality characteristics, social support, and differences in cognitive appraisal. [See STRESS.]

2. Cognitive Theory

Most cognitive theories of panic disorder hypothesize that panic is a fear response in psychologically vulnerable individuals. This psychological vulnerability is made up of unconscious, automatic cognitive schemata of unpredictability and uncontrollability, which cause the individual to perceive the world as a dangerous place. Interactions between genetic predispositions and emotional experiences determine the degree to which an individual will scan and cognitively appraise his or her environment for signals of potential danger or threat. When stimuli related to a feared or threatening event are per-

ceived, physiological arousal and vigilance are heightened, and the emotion of fear is experienced.

Evidence suggests that the feared event in panic disorder is the physiological manifestation of the panic attack itself and/or the predicted consequences of the attack. This is a result of both a learned association between internal somatic cues and panic attacks, and errors in cognitive appraisal of the causes and consequences of the attacks. At first, attacks may be brought on by unexpected or unexplained physiological sensations that are incorrectly processed by the individual as signaling an immediate danger or threat. Thus, the body's fight–flight mechanism is evoked by a "false alarm" of danger. The individual may then begin to associate fear with the bodily sensations they experience at the time, as well as the situational context of the attacks. Consequently, false alarms of panic become conditioned or "learned alarms" in response to unexplained or misinterpreted physiological arousal and/or activities that induce similar somatic sensations.

Patients with panic disorder display a marked tendency to overestimate and exaggerate the negative consequences associated with physiological arousal and the probability that a feared event will occur. They also tend to underestimate personal coping resources and/or the availability of help from others. Agoraphobia develops when misappraisals regarding the causes and/or consequences of panic become frightening enough to prevent the individual from engaging in situations believed to be unsafe in the event of a panic attack.

As noted earlier, life stress may play an important role in the development of panic disorder in many cases. Cognitive models posit that the physiological arousal associated with stress may provide the first triggers for false alarms of panic. Stress associated with traumatic events, physical illness, and everyday concerns about work, home, school, and social responsibilities produces physiological arousal, as do positive life events, such as marriage or job promotions. According to the cognitive model, the presence of physiological sensations associated with stress will cause a panic episode if these sensations are misinterpreted by an individual as signaling danger; panic will not, however, ensue if the physical sensations are appraised as harmless. This may explain why some individuals develop panic disorder in response to stress and others do not. It may also explain why panic disorder is often exacerbated by life stress. A similar argument can be made to account for the fact that many nonstress-related, arousal-producing events, such as exercise, chronic hyperventilation, orthostatic hypotension, or the use of certain drugs (e.g., caffeine, marijuana) can also cause panic in some individuals but not others.

VII. TREATMENT CONSIDERATIONS

There are a number of treatments available for panic disorder. Because of the prominent physiological manifestation of panic, the majority of patients first present in medical settings. Even when presenting in nonmedical mental health clinics or pastoral counseling settings, however, the first course of treatment for suspected panic disorder is always to rule out the large number of medical disorders known to produce anxiety symptoms as secondary manifestations. These include disorders such as hyperthyroidism, cardiac abnormalities, hypoglycemia, temporal lobe epilepsy, pheochromocytoma, electrolyte or hormonal imbalance, pulmonary embolus, Cushing's disease, vestibular disturbance, hyperparathyroidism, and substance abuse.

Once the diagnosis (or comorbidity) of panic disorder is established, several effective treatment options are available, including pharmacological, cognitive–behavioral, and other psychotherapeutic interventions. Although any one of these may result in symptom relief and improved psychosocial functioning, many clinicians agree that some combination of all the aforementioned treatments is desirable.

A. Psychopharmacologic Treatment

The goal of psychopharmacologic treatments of panic disorder is to block spontaneous panic attacks. When attacks are successfully blocked, a reduction in anticipatory anxiety and phobic avoidance will likely ensue. One potential difficulty in such treatment, however, is the experience of physiological side-effects inherent to the use of psychotropic medication. These may exacerbate panic in patients who have become hypervigilant to such cues, especially before therapeutic levels of medication can be attained. Nevertheless, double-blind, placebo-controlled studies have demonstrated that three classes of psychotropic medications prove effective for blocking panic. These include tricyclic antidepressants (e.g., imipramine, desipramine), monoamine oxidase inhibitors (e.g., phenelzine), and high-

potency benzodiazepines (e.g., alprazolam). Unfortunately, studies report that anywhere from 30 to 90% of patients with panic disorder relapse within 1 year following "successful" pharmacotherapy. Although data from controlled studies are not yet available, some believe that this relapse rate may be attenuated by the addition of adjunct psychotherapy.

B. Cognitive–Behavioral Treatment

Cognitive–behavioral psychologists often attribute the high relapse rates associated with pharmacologic treatments to the failure of such interventions to address the faulty cognitive appraisals and learned alarms believed to be inherent to panic disorder. Recent studies of the relative effectiveness of cognitive–behavioral treatment compared to pharmacotherapy and/or no treatment appear to support these claims. One study by a group of investigators at Oxford University reported that 90% of patients receiving cognitive–behavioral therapy were panic free following treatment, compared to 55% of patients treated with impramine and 7% of patients receiving no treatment. At follow-up 1 year post-treatment, 80% of the patients receiving cognitive therapy were still panic free without having required additional treatment, while 50% of patients receiving imipramine treatment met similar criteria. A study at the University of Texas reported similar results, with 83% of patients receiving cognitive–behavioral treatment for panic disorder remaining panic free after 1 year.

The goals of cognitive–behavioral treatment are to correct faulty appraisal mechanisms and break the learned associations between normal physiological arousal cues and panic. This is accomplished by methods of cognitive restructuring and behavioral exposure. Treatment typically begins with an extensive educational component addressing the biological nature of panic and the cognitive model of panic disorder. Individuals are then taught how to dissect each attack and identify the thoughts and fears associated with their panic. Cognitive errors are identified and thoughts are restructured into more realistic and less threatening predictions. Relaxation techniques and breathing exercises are taught in order to build an arsenal of coping strategies and help ameliorate the effects of chronic hyperventilation, if present. Finally, patients confront somatic and situational cues that they have learned to associate with panic by means of interoceptive and *in vivo* exposure. Interoceptive exposure involves the reproduction of physiological sensations via specific exercises (e.g., rapid heart beat is produced by running in place), while *in vivo* exposure involves confrontation of specific external situations that trigger panic. In both cases, repeated exposure to feared stimuli without the feared consequence (e.g., exposure to rapid heartbeat without having a feared heart attack) breaks the learned fear associations. In addition, the use of newly learned coping strategies helps patients manage their symptoms and regain a sense of control. [*See* COGNITIVE BEHAVIOR THERAPY.]

C. Psychotherapy

Pharmacotherapy and cognitive–behavioral treatments produce impressive reductions in panic and phobic avoidance; however, it is often important to look beyond the individual patient and address the potential psychosocial disturbances that may be related to the onset, maintenance, and/or exacerbation of panic disorder. In addition, intervention at this level may aid in relapse prevention by identifying life stresses and appropriate coping responses. Issues that are addressed in psychotherapy vary from individual to individual, and may include interpersonal relationships, self-esteem, family of origin experiences, and possible characterological disturbance. [*See* PSYCHOTHERAPY.]

Acknowledgments

The author would like to thank Dr. Meryl Butters, J. Vincent Filoteo, and Mary Roman for their helpful comments on this article.

Bibliography

Barlow, D. H. (1988). Anxiety and Its Disorders: The Nature and Treatment of Anxiety and Panic. Guilford, New York.

Boyd, J. H. (1986). Use of mental health services for the treatment of panic disorder. *Am. J. Psychiatry* **143,** 1569–1574.

Eysenck, M. W., and Keane, M. T. (1990). Cognition, emotion, and clinical psychology. In "Cognitive Psychology: A Student's Handbook" (M. W. Eysenck and M. T. Keane, Eds.). Erlbaum, East Sussex, UK.

Lucas, J. A., Telch, M. J., and Bigler, E. D. (1991). Memory functioning in panic disorder: A neuropsychological perspective. *J. Anxiety Disorders* **5,** 1–20.

Margraf, J., Barlow, D. H., Clark, D. M., and Telch, M. J. (1993). Psychological treatment of panic: Work in progress on outcome, active ingredients, and follow-up. *Behav. Res. Ther.* **31,** 1–8.

National Institute of Mental Health. (1989). Panic disorder in the medical setting, by Katon, W. DHHS Pub. No. (ADM) 89-1629. Supt. of Docs, U.S. Government Printing Office, Washington, DC.

Telch, M. J. (1991). Beyond sterile debate. *J. Psychopharmacol.* **5,** 296–298.

Walker, J. R., Norton, G. R., and Ross, C. A. (Eds.) (1992). "Panic Disorder and Agoraphobia." Brooks/Cole, Pacific Grove, CA.

PARANOIA

Allan Fenigstein
Kenyon College

Glossary

Delusions Faulty interpretations of reality that cannot be shaken, despite clear evidence to the contrary, and that are not shared by other members of the community.

Ideas of reference The misperception of oneself as the target of others' thoughts and actions; for example, a person seeing others laughing might relate the event to himself, and see himself as the target of their laughter.

Paranoia A disordered mode of thought that is dominated by a pervasive, exaggerated, and unwarranted suspiciousness and mistrust of people, and a corresponding tendency to interpret the actions of others as deliberately threatening or demeaning.

Paranoid illumination The point at which the paranoid realizes that he has been singled out for mistreatment, and others are working against him; suddenly, everything begins to make sense.

Projection A psychological defense often associated with paranoid thinking, in which the individual attributes one's own unacceptable motives or characteristics to others.

Pseudo-community A delusional system in which the paranoid organizes a variety of unrelated persons into a structured group whose primary purpose is to engage in a conspiracy against him.

Self-focus A behavioral style characteristic of paranoia, in which the individual is especially prone to be aware of himself as an object of attention to others.

Therapeutic alliance A tactic frequently used in treating paranoids, in which the therapist acknowledges the patient's delusional beliefs as understandable, in an attempt to build trust.

PARANOIA, although originally referring (in Greek) to almost any kind of mental aberration or bizarre thinking, is currently used to describe a disordered mode of thought that is dominated by an intense, irrational, but persistent mistrust or suspicion of people, and a corresponding tendency to interpret the actions of others as deliberately threatening or demeaning. Because of the general expectation that others are against them or are somehow trying to exploit them, paranoid persons tend to be guarded, secretive, and ever vigilant, constantly looking for signs of disloyalty or malevolence in their associates. These expectations are easily confirmed: the hypersensitivity of paranoids turns minor slights into major insults, and even innocuous events are misinterpreted as harmful or vindictive. As a result, a pernicious cycle is set in motion whereby expectations of treachery and hostility often serve to elicit such reactions from others, thus confirming and justifying the paranoid's initial suspicion and animosity. Of all psychological disturbances, paranoia is among the least understood and most difficult to treat.

I. PARANOID SYNDROMES

Paranoid features are found in a variety of different psychological conditions. Although these conditions are often regarded as distinct, the criteria for distinction are not entirely clear and the practical utility of the distinction, in terms of etiology or treatment implications, has not been established. Thus, it may be useful to consider the different paranoid disorders as related syndromes existing along a continuum which varies in terms of the frequency and severity of paranoid thoughts, the degree to which reality is allowed to influence perceptions, and the extent to which functioning is impaired. The continuum extends from paranoid personality disorder, which is nondelusional, but where suspicion and its sequelae occur so regularly that work and family life are often disrupted; to delusional (paranoid) disorder, involving a chronic, dysfunctional delusional system, although apart from the delusion, reality testing is good and behavior is not obviously odd; and finally, to paranoid schizophrenia, a severe, incapacitating psychosis, involving a serious loss of contact with reality in which all thought is affected by the delusion.

A. Delusional (Paranoid) Disorder

The cardinal feature of this disorder is the presence of a delusion that is so systematic, logically developed, well-organized, and resistant to contradictory evidence, that others are often convinced by it. Delusions are faulty interpretations of reality that cannot be shaken, despite clear evidence to the contrary. Although the delusions in this disorder are nonbizarre (unlike those found in paranoid schizophrenia) and involve situations that may occur in real life, in fact they have no basis in reality, and are not shared by others in the culture. Delusional systems are usually idiosyncratic, but some themes or combination of themes are more frequently seen than others, and psychiatric diagnosis of this disorder is now specified by the predominant theme of the delusions present.

Delusions of persecution, in which the paranoid believes that "others are out to get me," are the most common form of this disorder. While those with a paranoid personality disorder may be suspicious that colleagues are talking about them behind their backs, persons with delusional disorder may go one step further and suspect others of participating in elaborate master plots to persecute them. They often believe that they are being poisoned, drugged, spied upon, or are the targets of conspiracies to ruin their reputations. Many of them tend to be inveterate "injustice-detectors," inclined to take retributive actions of one sort or another, and are constantly embroiled in litigation or letter writing campaigns, in an attempt to redress imagined injustices.

Persons with delusions of grandiosity have an exaggerated sense of their own importance. In some cases, these beliefs are related to persecutory delusions, in that the paranoid eventually comes to feel that all the attention he's receiving is indicative of his superiority or unique abilities. Such exalted ideas usually center around messianic missions, extremist political movements, or remarkable inventions. Persons suffering from delusions of grandeur often feel that they have been endowed with special gifts or powers and, if allowed to exercise these abilities, they could cure diseases, banish poverty, or ensure world peace. When these efforts are ignored or thwarted, as they almost inevitably are, the paranoid may become convinced of a conspiracy directed against him.

Another theme frequently seen is that of delusional jealousy, in which any sign—even an apparent wrong number on the phone or a short delay in returning home—is summoned up as evidence that a spouse is being unfaithful. When the jealousy becomes irrationally pathological, and the paranoid becomes convinced beyond all reason that his spouse is cheating and plotting against him in an attempt to humiliate him, he may become violently dangerous. [See JEALOUSY.]

An erotic delusion (also known as erotomania) is based on the belief that one is romantically loved by another, usually someone of higher status or a well-known public figure, although the other, presumably, cannot acknowledge it openly. Because of unrealistic expectations about the likelihood of living with the celebrity, these delusions often result in stalking or harassment of famous persons through incessant phone calls, letters, visits, and surveillance. When their love is not returned, these delusional individuals feel a sense of betrayal that may turn to rage and hatred. Although this disorder has been reported most often in women, it occurs in men as well (perhaps the best example being John Hinckley, whose erotomanic delusions involving the actress Jodie Foster led to his attempted assassination of then-President Ronald Reagan).

Those with somatic delusions are convinced that there is something very wrong with their bodies—that they emit foul odors, or have bugs crawling inside of them, or are misshapen. These delusions often result in an avoidance of others, except for physicians who, despite being accused of conspiring to deny the problem, are consulted continuously regarding the imagined condition.

The thinking and behavior of these individuals tend to become organized around the delusional theme in the form of a pathological "paranoid construction" that, for all its distortion of reality and loss of critical judgment, provides a sense of identity, importance, and meaning not otherwise available. The meaningfulness of delusions is also suggested by the fact that they often reflect the person's position in the social universe: Women and married men are most likely to have delusions with sexual content; foreign immigrants are most prone to have persecutory delusions; and people from higher socioeconomic levels are the most likely to have delusions of grandeur.

Once the basic delusion is accepted, other aspects of behavior, including emotional responses, may be described as appropriate and more or less conventional. Delusionally disordered persons do not suffer hallucinations or indications of other mental disorders, and their personalities do not change drastically; there are few exacerbations or remissions. There is a relatively high level of cognitive integration skills in areas that do not impinge on the delusional thought structure. Despite their mistrust, defensiveness, and fear of being exploited, they can sometimes function adequately, especially when their suspicions are limited to one specific area; for example, if they suspect poisoners everywhere, they may be satisfied if they can prepare all their own food. Their lives may be very limited and isolated, but they are just as likely to be regarded as harmless cranks than as someone requiring the help of a mental health professional.

Sometimes, however, the consequences of the delusions are debilitating and not so easy to manage; for example, a person suffering from delusions of persecution may assault an imagined persecutor or spend a fortune fleeing enemies and pursuing redress for imagined wrongs. In other instances, the disorder may be dangerous. In particular, paranoid delusional disorder may be overrepresented among fanatical reformers and self-styled prophets and cult leaders. These individuals may be especially attracted to an enterprise that encourages blaming others, regarding themselves as a victim, and putting themselves at the center of things. Especially in times of social cataclysm or uncertainty, their grandiosity and moralistic tendencies, as well as the logical and compelling presentation of their messianic or political delusions, can often attract disciples. In addition, their garrison mentality is quite capable of provoking events which then serve to confirm their apocalyptic prophecies.

Much of the difficulty involved in diagnosing paranoid disorders is because of the slipperiness of the concept of delusion. Even in the real world, it is not always possible to determine the truth or falsity of an idea: Does the government keep track of unsus-

pecting individuals? Is our air and water filled with unseen toxins? Does our boss really have our best interests in mind? Some ideas that are patently false are held with sincere conviction by many; and even when an idea is held as preposterous by the majority, that majority may be wrong. How, then, do we evaluate the irrationality of an idea, or decide whether clearly eccentric and convoluted thinking merits the designation "delusional?" Although it may be difficult to distinguish reality from illusion, particularly when the belief system develops around a potentially real injustice, other indications may be diagnostically helpful. An inability to see facts in any other light or to place them in an appropriate context, a glaring lack of evidence for far-reaching conclusions, and a hostile, suspicious, and uncommunicative attitude when delusional ideas are questioned usually provides clues of pathology.

B. Paranoid Personality Disorder

Anyone starting in a new situation or relationship may be cautious and somewhat guarded until they learn that their fears are unwarranted. Those with paranoid personality disorder cannot abandon those concerns. Although not of sufficient severity to be considered delusional, theirs is a rigid and maladaptive pattern of thinking, feeling, and behavior, usually beginning by early adulthood, that is built upon mistrust, vigilance, and hostility. The conviction that others "have it in for them" represents their most basic and unrelenting belief; they feel constantly mistreated, and have a high capacity for annoying and provoking others.

Seeing the world as a threatening place, these individuals are preoccupied with hidden motives and the fear that someone may deceive or exploit them. They are inordinately quick to take offense, slow to forgive, and ready to counterattack at the first sign of imagined criticism, even in their personal relationships. Disordered paranoid personalities see references to themselves in everything that happens. If people are seen talking, the paranoid knows they are talking about him. If someone else gets a promotion, that person's advancement is seen as a deliberate attempt to humiliate him and downgrade his achievements. Even offers of help and concern are taken as implied criticisms of weakness or as subtle manipulations of indebtedness. The constant suspicions and accusations eventually strain interpersonal relations to the point where these individuals are in continual conflict with spouses, friends, and legal authorities.

Given their hypersensitivity, any speck of evidence that seems to confirm their suspicions is blown out of proportion, and any indication to the contrary is ignored or misinterpreted. Trivial incidents become accumulated and unconnected "facts" are fit together to create false, but unshakeable beliefs regarding their mistreatment. Because of their conviction that others are undermining their efforts or ruining their achievements, they tend to see themselves as blameless, instead finding fault for their own mistakes and failures in others, even to the point of ascribing evil motives to others.

Those with disordered paranoid personalities also tend to overvalue their abilities, and have an inflated sense of their rationality and objectivity, making it extraordinarily difficult for them either to question their own beliefs or to accept or even appreciate another's point of view. Unable to recognize the possibility of genuine dissent, simple disagreement by others becomes a sign of disloyalty. The resulting obstinacy, defensiveness, and self-righteousness exasperates and infuriates others, and elicits responses that exacerbate the conflict and confirm the original paranoid expectations.

In addition to being argumentative and uncompromising, paranoids appear cold and aloof, and emotionally cut off from others. They avoid intimacy, partly because they fear betrayal, partly in an attempt to maintain total control over their affairs, and partly because of profound deficits in their capacity for joy, warmth, and nurturance. The resulting social isolation, by limiting the opportunity to check social reality and learn from others, only reinforces their egocentric perspective.

Compared to some other paranoid pathologies, those with disordered personalities tend not to progressively worsen, but rather reach a certain level of severity and stay there. They show considerably less disorganization of personality, and they do not develop the kind of systematic and well-defined delusions found in delusional disorders. However, the proverbial kernel of truth is often greater in the suspicions of disordered paranoid personalities than in those with delusional disorders; their accusations have more plausibility and their paranoid attitudes are more diffuse. Because of the complexity and pervasiveness of personality disorders, these individuals may have more impoverished lives, although some do manage to function adequately in society, often by carving out a social niche in which a moral-

istic and punitive style is acceptable or at least tolerated.

C. Paranoid Schizophrenia

This major mental illness is one of the most common types of psychotic disorders. Paranoid schizophrenics may be distinguished from those with delusional disorder on the basis of the extreme bizarreness of their paranoid delusions, such as the belief that their thoughts or actions are being controlled by external forces, and by the presence of hallucinations (e.g., hearing voices) and other indications of a serious break with reality. The delusions of schizophrenics are not organized and systematic, but fragmentary and unconnected. Although these individuals may be suspicious and very much threatened by outside influences, their reaction, unlike that of the disordered paranoid personality, is usually hesitant and confused; their anger has no concentrated intensity. The behavioral, cognitive, and perceptual disorders of paranoid schizophrenics are so dysfunctional that performance on the job or at home almost invariably deteriorates, and emotional expressiveness becomes severely diminished.

These individuals commonly suffer from delusions of persecution, wherein they are convinced that they are constantly being watched or followed, and that strangers or government operatives or even alien beings are plotting against them with fantastic machines, undetectable poisons, or extraordinary mental powers. Of course, given the exceptional cunning and duplicity of these diabolical forces, virtually anything—a look, a sound, a bodily sensation, for that matter, even the absence of anything, a particularly shrewd maneuver—is seen as confirmation of one's suspicions. When the schizophrenic experiences the "paranoid illumination," and recognizes that all this overwhelming evidence fits together, the sense of his own visibility and vulnerability is profoundly increased, as is the tendency to misperceive himself as the target of other people's stares, comments, and laughter. In some cases, persecutory beliefs are accompanied by delusions of grandeur: that they are the target of these forces is only because they are special or powerful or dangerous. They may recognize that others reject them and their message, but they interpret these negative reactions as persecution based on jealousy, hostility, or enemy conspiracies.

Some paranoid schizophrenics avoid detection for long periods because their extreme suspiciousness encourages them to keep their "precious knowledge" secret. Moreover, although these individuals are deeply disturbed and are subject to intense panic (given their sense of imminent danger) and extreme excitement (over their irrational "discoveries"), many of them are not overtly bizarre or belligerent. [*See* SCHIZOPHRENIA.]

D. Other Paranoid Disorders

Some paranoid thinking manifests itself in a less persistent form. Acute paranoid disorder, in which delusions develop quickly and last only a few months, sometimes appear after a sudden, stressful social change, such as emigration, prison, induction into military service, or even leaving a family home. Although these conditions are multifaceted, they all are associated with extreme social isolation, unfamiliarity with the appropriate customs and rules of behavior, a sense of vulnerability to exploitation, and a general loss of control over life, psychological factors which may play an important, albeit temporary, role in inducing episodes of paranoia.

Paranoid symptoms may also be a byproduct of physical illness, organic brain disease, or drug intoxication. Among organic illnesses, hypothyroidism, multiple sclerosis, Huntington's disease, and epileptic disorders, as well as Alzheimer's disease and other forms of dementia, are common causes of paranoia. In some people, alcohol stimulates a paranoid reaction even in small doses, and paranoia is a common feature of alcohol hallucinosis and alcohol withdrawal delirium. Chronic abuse of drugs, such as amphetamines, cocaine, marijuana, PCP, LSD, or other stimulants or psychedelic compounds, may produce some of the symptoms of paranoid personality disorder, and in high doses, may cause an acute psychosis that is almost indistinguishable from paranoid schizophrenia. These drugs may also exacerbate symptoms in persons already suffering from a paranoid disorder. [*See* DEMENTIA; SUBSTANCE ABUSE.]

II. PREVALENCE

It is difficult to estimate the frequency of paranoia in the general population because many paranoids function well enough in society to avoid coming to the attention of professionals, and because their suspiciousness and intellectual arrogance usually prevent them from volunteering for treatment. While clinical diagnoses of paranoid disorders are rare, a more realistic picture of its actual occurrence is suggested by the many exploited inventors, morbidly jealous spouses, persecuted workers, fanatical reformers, and self-styled prophets who are often able to maintain themselves in the community without their paranoid condition being formally recognized.

Estimates of prevalence are further complicated by the fact that almost everyone engages in paranoid thinking at one time or another. Most people can think of an occasion when they thought that they were being watched or talked about, or felt as if everything was going against them, or were suspicious of someone else's motives without adequate proof that such things had actually occurred. Recent studies have shown that for a significant number of people, these paranoid beliefs represent a relatively stable personality pattern. Such paranoid personalities—although characterized by suspiciousness, self-centeredness, scapegoating tendencies, and a generally hostile attitude—apparently are capable of functioning reasonably well in society.

III. CAUSES OF PARANOIA

A. Biological Bases

1. Genetic Contribution

Although there is little research on the role of heredity in causing paranoia, there is some evidence from twin studies indicating that paranoid symptoms in schizophrenia may be genetically influenced. In addition, family studies suggest that features of the paranoid personality disorder occur disproportionately more often in families with members who have either delusional disorders or paranoid schizophrenia, suggesting that these syndromes may be genetically related.

2. Biochemistry

No identifiable biochemical substrate or demonstrable neuropathology relates specifically to paranoid thought or delusions; that is, there is no brain system whose dysfunction would specifically produce the psychological characteristics associated with paranoia. Although the abuse of drugs, such as amphetamines, may lead to paranoid symptoms, thus suggesting a possible biochemical pathway, no such pathway has been identified; whatever drug effects have been found may be psychologically, and not biochemically, mediated.

B. Psychological Bases

In the absence of a clear organic basis or effective drug treatment for paranoia, most researchers have sought to identify the psychological mechanisms that explain how paranoid ideas become fixed in the mind.

1. Psychodynamic Theory

Of all psychological theories, Freud's is perhaps the best known, although it is increasingly challenged. He believed that paranoia was a form of repressed homosexual love. According to Freud, paranoia arises, at least in men, when a child's homosexual feelings for his father are preserved but driven into the unconscious, from which they re-emerge during an adult emotional crisis, converted into suspicions and delusions by projection—the attribution of one's own unacknowledged wishes and impulses to another person. That is, before reaching consciousness, the impulses undergo some kind of transformation that disguise their homosexual origin; for example, a man suffering from paranoid jealousy, unable to acknowledge that he himself loves another man, projects that feeling onto his wife and becomes convinced that it is his wife who loves the man.

Although Freud's theory of unconscious homosexuality has been largely discredited, projection is still recognized as a basic mechanism used by paranoids to defend against their feelings. Paranoids will explain their sense of helplessness by pointing to the control exerted by others; or self-critical ideas are transformed into the belief that others are criticizing them. Viewing others as hostile not only justifies the paranoid's feeling of being threatened, it may actually elicit the other's anger, thus confirming the paranoid's original assumption. As a result, paranoids are left feeling weakly vulnerable, but morally righteous. [See DEFENSE MECHANISMS.]

2. Faulty Development

Rather than emphasizing unconscious dynamics, other approaches have viewed paranoid thinking as the outcome of a complex interaction of personality traits, social skills, and environmental events, some of which may be traced to early family dynamics. Paranoids, even as children, were often described as aloof, suspicious, secretive, stubborn, and resentful of punishment. Rarely was there a history of normal play with other children, or good socialization with warm, affectionate relationships. Their family background was often authoritarian, and excessively dominating and critical. Paranoid persons may dread being watched and judged because, it has been suggested, that reminds them of their parents, who were distant, demanding, and capricious.

This inadequate socialization may have kept them from learning to understand others' motives and points of view which, in turn, may have led to a pattern of suspicious misinterpretation of unintentional slights. Social relationships tended to be suffused with hostile, domineering attitudes that drove others away. These inevitable social failures further undermined self-esteem and led to deeper social isolation and mistrust. In essence, these individuals emerged from childhood with deeply internalized struggles involving issues of hostility, victimization, power, submission, weakness, and humiliation. In later development, these early trends merged to create self-important, egocentric, and arrogant individuals, who maintained their unrealistic self-image and a sense of control by projecting blame for their problems onto others, and seeing weaknesses in others that they could not acknowledge in themselves. Their suspicion and hypersensitivity were made even more problematic by their utter inability to see things from any viewpoint but their own.

3. The Paranoid "Illumination" and the Paranoid Pseudo-Community

Other theorists have focused, not on early family history, but on the later emergence of a fixed, unyielding paranoid belief system. Given the paranoid's rigidity, self-importance, and suspiciousness, he is likely to become a target of actual discrimination and mistreatment; and ever alert to such occurrences, the paranoid is likely to find abundant "proof," both real and imagined, of persecution. The cycle of misunderstanding is then perpetuated by the paranoid's subsequent responses. The belief that others are plotting against him results in hostile, defensive behavior. This in turn elicits the others' anger and irritability in response to the paranoid's apparently unprovoked hostility, thus confirming the paranoid's original suspicion that they are out to get him. This cycle of aggression and counteraggression has also been offered as one explanation for the greater prevalence of paranoia among males than females. The paranoid's inability to consider the others' perspective—that the other may be operating out of defensiveness against the paranoid's antagonism and belligerence—only exacerbates the conflict. [*See* AGGRESSION; CONFLICT BEHAVIOR.]

As failures and seeming betrayals mount, the paranoid, to avoid self-devaluation, searches for "logical" explanations. He becomes more vigilant in his scrutiny of the environment, looking for hidden meanings and asking leading questions. Eventually, a meaningful picture, in the form of the "paranoid illumination," crystallizes and everything begins to make sense: he has been singled out for some obscure reason, and others are working against him. Failure is not because of any inferiority on his part, but rather because of some conspiracy or plot directed at him. With this as his fundamental defensive premise, he proceeds to distort and falsify the facts to fit the premise, and gradually develops a logical, fixed delusional system, referred to as the "pseudocommunity," in which the paranoid organizes surrounding people (real and imaginary) into a structured group whose purpose is centered on his victimization. As each additional experience is misconstrued and interpreted in light of the delusional idea, more and more events, persons, and experiences become effectively incorporated into the delusional system. Because the delusion meaningfully integrates all the vague, disturbing, amorphous, and unrelated "facts" of his existence, the paranoid is unwilling to accept any other explanation and is impervious to reason or logic; any questioning of the delusion only convinces him that the interrogator has sold out to the enemy.

4. Anomalous Perceptions

Another theory offers the intriguing hypothesis that delusions are the result of a cognitive attempt to account for aberrant or anomalous sensory experiences. For example, research has shown that persons with visual or hearing loss—because of both heightened suspiciousness and an attempt to deny the loss—may conclude that others are conspiring to conceal things from them. The experience of many elderly people, who are a high risk group for paranoia, provides a particularly good example of this phenomena. These individuals, because of physical disability or social isolation, often feel especially vulnerable. These realistic feelings may be converted to paranoia by an unacknowledged loss of hearing. That is, an awareness of oneself as a potential victim of greedy relatives or petty criminals, together with an increased sense that others are whispering, may contribute to a growing suspicion that others are whispering about them, or harassing

them, or perhaps planning to steal from them. When the others angrily deny the accusation, that only reinforces the conspiratorial delusion, and intensifies the cycle of hostility and suspicion.

The occurrence of paranoia in those with degenerative brain disorders, such as Alzheimer's disease, may be explained through a similar process. These diseases commonly involve a disruption of memory that victims may be unwilling to acknowledge. As a result, failures of memory become an anomalous experience that needs to be explained. For example, not being able to locate one's keys is transformed into the belief that someone else has stolen or misplaced them. This suspicion may then be incorporated with actual perceptions, such as seeing one's child speaking to the doctor, to produce the conviction that others are conspiring to confuse the patient in order to put them away. [*See* ALZHEIMER'S DISEASE.]

The general hypothesis that anomalous experience may be the basis for paranoia assumes that the process by which delusional beliefs are formed is very similar to the process that operates in the formation of normal beliefs; that is, delusions are not the result of a disturbed thought process, but arise because of abnormal sensory or perceptual experiences. Anomalous experiences demand an explanation, and in the course of developing hypotheses and testing them through observations, the delusional insight is confirmed through selective evidence. This explanation offers relief in the form of removing uncertainty, and the relief in turn works against abandonment of the explanation.

5. Stress

A related explanation may account for the often observed association between paranoia and stressors such as social isolation, economic deprivation, and abrupt situational changes. These conditions generally involve feelings of confusion, vulnerability, and a loss of control, suggesting that, in some ways, paranoid thought may serve to impose meaning and control in an otherwise uncertain and threatening environment. The paranoid belief that others are responsible for one's own misfortune, although threatening and irrational, may still be preferable to the belief that one is responsible for one's own misfortune or that such misfortune is a purely random event. In this regard, it is possible that the paranoid thinking which often develops as a result of acute drug intoxication (for example, amphetamine abuse), or aging (and its concomitant sensory loss and social isolation), or degenerative brain disorders (such as Alzheimer's disease) may be mediated by the confusion and vulnerability often found in these conditions. [*See* STRESS.]

6. Biases in Information Processing

Some of the approaches discussed thus far have emphasized the fact that, apart from the paranoid construction itself, the cognitive functioning of paranoids is essentially intact. In fact, given their delusional system, paranoid reactions are not unlike the biased tendencies of many individuals with strong belief systems, who are likely to exaggerate, distort, or selectively focus on events which are consistent with their beliefs. Once the paranoid suspects that others are working against him, he starts carefully noting the slightest signs pointing in the direction of his suspicions, and ignores all evidence to the contrary. With this frame of reference, it is quite easy, especially in a highly competitive, somewhat ruthless world, for any event, no matter how innocuous, to be selectively incorporated into the delusion. This, in turn, leads to a vicious cycle: suspicion, distrust, and criticism of others drives people away, keeps them in continual friction with others, and generates new incidents for the paranoid to magnify. [*See* INFORMATION PROCESSING AND CLINICAL PSYCHOLOGY.]

Although these information processing biases serve to maintain the paranoid's beliefs once they are established, they do not address the question of the origin of paranoid beliefs. The essence of paranoia is a malfunctioning of the capacity to assign meanings and understand causes for events. Ordinarily, these cognitive processes operate in a reasonably logical and objective fashion. In paranoia, such objective assessments are overwhelmed by judgments and interpretations that bear little relation to what actually happened, but instead are perverted in accord with the paranoid's own concerns and interests. The persistent misperception of oneself as the target of others' thoughts and actions, referred to as an idea or delusion of reference, is the hallmark characteristic of almost all forms of paranoid thought. Even when there is no basis for making any connection, paranoids tend to perceive others' behavior as if it is more relevant to the self than is actually the case as, for example, when the laughter of others is assumed to be self-directed, or the appearance of a stranger on the street is taken to mean that one is being watched or plotted against. Why does the paranoid consistently feel singled out or targeted by others?

a. Paranoia and Self-Focus

Part of the answer may lie in the characterization of paranoia as a very self-focused style of functioning. Recent studies have suggested that self-awareness, or the ability of an individual to recognize itself as an object of attention, heightens the tendency to engage in paranoid inferences. In essence, to see oneself as an object of attention, particularly to others, leaves a person susceptible to the paranoid idea that he is being targeted by others. Apparently, as a result of recognizing the self as an object of attention, the self is more likely to be interjected into the interpretation of others' behavior, thus transforming insignificant and irrelevant events into ones that appear to have personal relevance for the self. Self-focus not only relates directly to paranoid ideas of reference, it has important implications for other critical aspects of paranoid thought.

b. Personalism and Intent

Unfortunate things happen to everyone, and usually they are dismissed as random or chance events. But paranoids rarely accept the idea that bad things just happen; instead they are likely to believe that it is someone else's doing. Why? Because events that are taken personally or are seen as uniquely targeted toward the self, are more likely to be understood in terms of others' personal characteristics or intentions. For the paranoid, the negative event itself is evidence for others' malevolent intentions toward them. Eventually, the accumulation of such events constitutes evidence for a fundamentally irrational view of the world as a hostile and threatening place. Once the assumption of ubiquitous danger is accepted, the other manifestations of paranoia become comprehensible: suspicion and guardedness; selective attention and memory for signs of trickery or exploitation; misinterpretation of apparently harmless events as malevolent; and blaming others for all of one's difficulties. Moreover, when negative events are seen not as fortuitous occurrences, but as personally intended by others, hostilities become intensified and enemies are found everywhere.

c. Egocentricity

One of the critical elements of paranoid thinking is the utter inability to understand the motivations and perspectives of others. Not only are paranoids more likely to misinterpret the other's behavior, they are less likely to correct that misinterpretation by altering their point of view. The narrowness and rigidity of paranoid thought—the failure to examine events critically or in a broader context, the ability to fit anything into one's belief system, the unwillingness to consider ever changing one's mind—is, in large part, the result of being locked into one's own perspective. Although social isolation may account, in part, for this deficit in role taking, self-focused attention may also contribute to the self-centeredness of paranoids. Attention directed toward the self interferes with the ability to take the role of another or appreciate the existence of alternative perspectives. As a result, paranoids are likely to assume that others share their own view of events, and fail to appreciate the way in which their own actions are viewed by others. Thus, in a typical encounter, they are unlikely to consider how their own behavior provokes the hostility of others, but instead are likely to see themselves as the innocent victim of the other's hostility. Self-focus may also play a role in the egocentric tendency of paranoids to project their own characteristics onto others.

IV. TREATMENT OF PARANOIA

Treatment of paranoia is extraordinarily difficult for a number of reasons. First, little is known about the causes that presumably are to be treated. Second, it is difficult for the paranoid to recognize a problem when he is locked into his own perspective and is reluctant to accept another's viewpoint. Finally, it is nearly impossible for therapists to penetrate the barrier of suspiciousness. For all these reasons, paranoids are generally unlikely and unwilling to enter therapy; and once in therapy, their wariness often leads them to sabotage treatment, or break it off prematurely. Paranoids also generally refuse to take responsibility for their treatment, because the only problems they see are those created by the people intent upon harming them. In addition, the disclosure of personal information or other aspects of therapy may represent a loss of control, especially to male paranoids.

Mistrust obviously serves to undermine the therapeutic relationship. Any expression of friendliness or concern by the therapist is likely to arouse suspicion or be taken as confirmation that others are trying to humiliate them. Any questions or suggestions are likely to be seen as criticisms or attacks. Even if therapy improves other aspects of the paranoid's functioning, their delusional system is so strenuously defended, and so easily confirmed by "clues" detected in the therapeutic situation, that it often remains intact, yielding a highly unfavorable prognosis for complete recovery.

Because of the paranoid patient's guardedness and insistence on their own correctness, an effective therapeutic approach usually focuses on trust building rather than direct confrontation of the delusional beliefs. Perhaps the most powerful strategy is to establish rapport by forming a "therapeutic alliance" in which the therapist recognizes whatever kernel of trust exists in a paranoid system, and acknowledges the delusional beliefs as powerful, convincing, and understandable. The therapist can then try to identify the ways in which these beliefs may interfere with the patient's goals or create frustration for others as well as for the patient. The patient's paranoid reactions have usually driven others away or incited them to counterattack, heightening the cycle of suspicion and hostility. The therapist can sometimes bring about change by providing a different, empathic response that serves as a model of nonparanoid behavior. The task is then to help the paranoid become more competent at discriminating real threats from perceived ones, and the final step is the development of more adaptive responses to real or even ambiguous threats.

Behavioral theory assumes that paranoids have learned to be hypersensitive to the judgments of others and, as a result, they behave in ways that invite just the sort of reaction they anticipate and fear. As others begin to avoid them, they become socially isolated and develop increasingly elaborate suspicions that maintain the isolation. Behavior therapy tries to break the cycle by first using relaxation and anxiety management to teach the patient to be less sensitive to criticism, and then improving social skills by training the patient to act in ways that will not invite attack or avoidance. The patient can also be given help with recognition and avoidance of situations that produce or increase delusions. Paranoid thinking can in some cases be altered by aversive conditioning or the removal of factors that reinforce maladaptive behavior.

Bibliography

Akhtar, S. (1990). Paranoid personality disorder: A synthesis of developmental, dynamic, and descriptive features. *Am. J. Psychother.* **44,** 5–25.

Bentall, R. P., Kaney, S., and Dewey, M. E. (1991). Paranoia and social reasoning: An attribution theory analysis. *Br. J. Clin. Psychol.* **30,** 13–23.

Cameron, N. (1943). The development of paranoic thinking. *Psychol. Rev.* **50,** 219–233.

Fenigstein, A., and Vanable, P. A. (1992). Paranoia and self-consciousness. *J. Pers. Soc. Psychol.* **62,** 129–138.

Kaney, S., and Bentall, R. P. (1989). Persecutory delusions and attributional style. *Br. J. Med. Psychol.* **62,** 191–198.

Magaro, P. A. (1980). "Cognition in Schizophrenia and Paranoia: The Interpretation of Cognitive Processes." Erlbaum, Hillsdale, NJ.

Maher, B. A. (1988). Anomalous experience and delusional thinking: The logic of explanations. In "Delusional Beliefs" (T. F. Oltmanns and B. A. Maher, Eds.), Wiley, New York.

Shapiro, D. (1965). "Neurotic Styles." Basic Books, New York.

Williams, J. G. (1988). Cognitive intervention for a paranoid personality disorder. *Psychotherapy* **25,** 570–575.

Zimbardo, P. G., Andersen, S. M., and Kabat, L. G. (1981). Induced hearing deficit generates experimental paranoia. *Science* **212,** 1529–1531.

◆

PARENTING

Beverly I. Fagot
University of Oregon

Glossary

Attachment The process by which the child develops an internal model of the parent–child relationship.

Family management The process by which families manage children's behavior. The major components are discipline and monitoring.

Scaffolding The process by which an adult structures and models ways for a child to solve a problem.

Social learning A psychological approach emphasizing the importance of social interaction between individuals, especially family members, upon psychological processes.

PARENTING is a recent construct, not the act of taking care of children which is part of our role as mammals, but the idea that there is something unique and different about rearing children. The word *parent* comes to us from the Latin root meaning *to give birth*. However, today the word parent and the process we call parenting mean far more. It entails not only giving birth but providing for a child up to their adult years and beyond. It entails not only providing for the child's physical well-being, but also providing warmth and security to ensure good psychological adjustment, discipline for moral development, and stimulation for intellectual development. Society is harsh in its judgment of those who fail in any of these domains, yet dictionaries do not even define the word, and our society requires no training for parenting.

I. HISTORICAL OVERVIEW OF PARENTING

Modern day child specialists sometimes speak as if children and parenting were recent inventions. Yet for every culture about which we have any information, we have bits of information about parenting. Even for the cave painters of France about whose culture we know so little save the visual images left on the wall, we have tiny handprints left in the same caves, to remind us that these too were people who cared for their children and who kept them with them during important periods of their lives.

The care of children has always been important to philosophies and religions, and from all over the world we have fragments of concern about the rearing of children. Both Aristotle and Plato discussed appropriate rearing of children of various ages. Their concerns in some ways were very similar to those of parents today: How do we balance the necessity for teaching children to control their impulses and behavior with allowing them to explore the world enough to develop their skills? This problem of balance between too much and too little discipline echoes down through the ages, across the face of the globe, and is reflected today in modern theories and research studies, as well as in how-to-do-it books for parents.

Most early treatises on parenting were written by men, and they were concerned with the upbringing of boys more often than girls. While there is the occasional sensitive treatment of the necessity for providing love and warmth for the young child, most information on parenting emphasizes the importance of the child's mind, in terms of either what we call intellectual abilities or what we now call moral values. It is also clear that most discussion is about the training of the upper-class child, and we have little information concerning the rearing of the large majority of children.

One of the most complete treatises on child-rearing in modern Western culture was that of John Locke, *Some Thoughts on Education,* which is basically a practical guide to a father about raising a son. As might be expected from the culture of the time (17th century), much of the essay concerns the necessity of establishing early authority over the child. There are warnings about too much love, about the problems of material rewards, and the concern that children might be spoiled by servants. Yet there are surprisingly modern recognitions of individual differences in children, of the superiority of discipline through reasoning rather than corporal punishment, of the importance of parental role models, and the recognition that the best motivator for the child is the esteem of parents. As might be expected, Locke presents a very rational view of child-rearing, remaining above much of the turmoil of actual parenting, perhaps because Locke was a bachelor and himself had no children.

Approximately a century later (late 18th century), Mary Wollstonecraft wrote about the care of children. Her works are heavily influenced by John Locke's rational approach but also touch upon early care. There is a concern that mothers nurse their own infants, that young children need a warm, loving environment, and most of all, a concern for daughters. Her *Thoughts on the Education of Daughters* expressed a concern that girls were not taught to discipline their minds but allowed to grow without intellectual skills or moral discipline. Wollstonecraft's essays were very popular in her day, suggesting some influence and some concern on the part of parents that child-rearing was not simply the intellectual process suggested by Locke. However, most essays concerning the history of parenting and children have ignored the works of Wollstonecraft, and it is only within the last 20 years that copies of her work have become widely available.

Views on parenting and children have changed greatly in the 200 years since Wollstonecraft, yet it is interesting to note that she identified the two themes within the parenting literature of the last 50 years: the necessary balance, the inevitable tension, between parental warmth and parental control.

II. THEORIES OF PARENTING

Modern day theories of parenting have their roots in Freud's description of the family. Freud articulated very clearly family roles that mirrored the upper-middle-class European family structure during the late 1800s, with the mother providing love and warmth and the father rules and discipline. It is likely that such families were relatively rare, as upper-middle-class children were cared for by servants and the poor for the most part did not have the time to follow such strict roles. However accurate this characterization was in reality, it has had a profound effect on our thinking about parenting and about the roles of the mother and father within the family. Prior to Freud, most treatises on parenting emphasized the education and moral development of the child. With Freud's emphasis on the satisfaction of drives came a clearer articulation that the quality of early care would influence later development. While Locke and others emphasized the importance of helping the child to become a rational thinking human, and the Romantics emphasized the innocence and purity of the child, Freud placed human pathologies as firmly rooted in the child's early development. To some extent, the child's development as pictured by Freud is as seemingly unreasonable and irrational as many of his patients' later meanderings. Freud's influence on the modern mind should not be underrated, for we cannot really understand the theoretical and empirical literature on parenting since 1900 without understanding how Freud's views have permeated our thinking. Our emphasis on providing a sensitive caretaking environment during early childhood as well as our articulations of family roles are influenced either directly by or in opposition to Freudian thinking.

Parsons, writing in the middle of this century, articulated family roles and transformed these roles into gender traits. Women were more expressive, nurturant, and emotionally sensitive, and thus should be in charge of management of relationships, children, and the home. Men were more instrumentally competent, and should therefore be in charge of setting the rules, and be employed outside the home. According to Parsons, such roles are necessary for family life and child rearing. A good deal of empirical work on family relations and parenting has been done to refute the necessity or the benefits of such a rigid role structure. In fact, in one long-term study of successful men and women of the very generation most influenced by these ideas, regrets were expressed in old age by women because they had not used their talents in the world and by men because they had not spent enough time with their families in building relationships. Most studies suggest that both men and women have expressive and instrumental qualities and that they are happier when both are expressed. It is interesting to see feminist criticism bring back this rigid role structure, this time with more emphasis put upon the superior expressive qualities of women and their lack in men. The data for the current wave of such theorizing are as scant as for such theories of the past. [*See* FAMILY SYSTEMS; SEX ROLES; TRAITS.]

Robert Sears and his colleagues, writing in the middle of this century, attempted to rework Freudian theory within the framework of learning theory. For the first time in one theory, two qualities to parenting, *warmth* and *control,* were made explicit. However, Sear's concepts of parenting, influenced by Freud and Parsons, still made the assumption that mothers would provide warmth and emotional support, and fathers discipline and control. In fact, Sear's work, like most studies of the time, concentrated mostly upon the mother as informant, so that we had a view of the father filtered through the eyes of the mother. Throughout the 1950s and 1960s, there were tests of this supposedly optimal family role division, most of which found, first, that such families were in actuality few and far between and, second, that when they existed, they did not appear to be as functional as families in which both parents shared expressive and instrumental qualities.

Diana Baumrind published an extensive reappraisal of parenting in 1971 in which she concentrated upon the dimension of parental control to characterize three parenting styles. Parental control in Baumrind's work refers to the attempts of the parents to socialize the child into the family and society. Clearly all parents do this with more or less success. Baumrind found that children need a balance of control and warmth and are better off when both mothers and fathers can give both. She described three types of parenting in which the types of control varied. The first type of parenting she called *authoritarian,* in which the parent attempts to shape and control the child in accordance with a set standard of conduct. Such parents value obedience, believe in punitive measures to curb the child's self-will, and do not allow discussion about the correctness of the standard. *Authoritative* parents also believe the child should behave in accordance with their rules and standards, but within a context of rational discussion. Such parents encourage communication and share reasons for conduct with the child. The authoritative parents do not see themselves as infallible and are open to change as circumstances change. *Permissive* parents do not put as much emphasis on the child conforming to a set of rules; instead, the child is consulted, and self-regulation by the child is emphasized. The parent is

seen as a resource but not necessarily as the final word in setting external standards for the child's behavior. Within each of these parenting types, the parent can vary on warmth, and both the type of control and the use of warmth can influence the child's development. [*See* AUTHORITARIANISM.]

Baumrind argued strongly that authoritative parenting appeared to be a more effective style in that it produced a situation that gave the child a structure, but which was open to change. Much of the parenting work of the 1970s were attempts to validate Baumrind's categories and her suggestion that authoritative parenting would be the most effective style of parenting. There has been a great deal of support for this within the well-functioning, middle-class families favored by Baumrind for her research; however, recent work has suggested that in situations of high risk, such as an urban ghetto, boys in particular may benefit from authoritarian parenting. However, one problem with using Baumrind's typologies is that many parents do not fit the definitions, and within each type the variations are often greater than the differences between groups.

More recently, Eleanor Maccoby has used Sear's initial formulation of warmth and control and Baumrind's emphasis on style of control to attempt a reformulation of parenting which takes into account all these different components of parenting. Maccoby and her colleagues have used the social learning approach to reformulate parenting into two major divisions: *demandingness* and *responsiveness.* Parents can vary in their demandingness (that is, the number and types of demands they make upon the child) and in their responsiveness to the child's bids for attention. This framework has allowed Maccoby and other researchers to move beyond the types of families studied by Baumrind, into families of divorce, of differing ethnic groups, etc. In addition, families are no longer forced into categories that may not be a good fit to their individual styles. In her recent writings, Baumrind uses the categories of demandingness and responsiveness to define parental characteristics. Interestingly enough, present day theorists often sound very similar to John Locke in their discussion of the necessity for the parent to demand certain standards of behavior of the child while responding to the individual needs of the child.

III. METHODS USED TO STUDY PARENTING

At this point it would seem profitable to leave the area of theory and talk a bit about how information is gathered about parenting. Each method of study provides one view of parenting, so that it is important to understand the process from many points of view.

A. Self-Report

The most widely used method within the field of child and family studies is the use of self-report data. The parent, usually the mother, is asked about her parenting techniques. She may be asked to keep a diary of her responses to the child, or she may be interviewed about parenting practices, or she may fill out questionnaires concerning her parenting. Much of what we conclude about the effects of parents comes from this type of information. Such techniques use global measurements of variables yielding generalized and nonspecific descriptions of parents' skills. Clearly, parents themselves know the most about their individual parenting practices and are an invaluable source of information. However, parents are participants in the parenting process, and they may not be able to give objective answers to questions, or their stated attitudes may not match very well with their behaviors. Every experienced interviewer has had at least one parent tell them in an interview that they do not use physical punishment and then proceed to use such punishment in front of the interviewer. In addition, parents' answers are filtered through long experience in interacting with their child and colored by their feelings for the child. Consequently, we find that self-report measures have their limitations, and that while we get consistency from the one informant, very often the information contradicts other measures of both parenting procedures and child behaviors. Consequently, researchers have looked for other ways to study parenting. One technique that has evolved has been to train an impartial observer to code parenting behaviors.

B. Observation

The most common type of behavioral observation has been the social interchanges within the family in their home environment. This procedure forces an examination of the dual role of each subject as a reactor and as an initiator. Researchers who use these techniques believe that the day-to-day interactions between the parent and child underlie the way parents learn, maintain, and deploy different child management skills. Patterson, a pioneer in the use of behavioral observations since the early 1960s,

has shown that control processes studied through behavioral observation show that parents who use harsh punishment and noncontingent punishment have children who respond with similar techniques, and that such families become locked into coercive cycles, which are very hard for family members to end without escalation. A rigorous test of this reciprocity requires two kinds of investigation. First, it should follow that, for a dyad assessed over a series of days, coercion scores would covary. Second, it should be possible to demonstrate experimentally that an increase in coercive techniques by one member produces an increase in coercive reactions by the other. Such coercive cycles are found in families where both parents report a great deal of stress and poor marital adjustment. Observation has also been used to confirm that, within authoritative families, parents encourage reciprocal communication and do more listening, questioning, and reframing than in authoritarian families. However, observation techniques in naturalistic settings are very expensive and by their very nature are unstandardized, so that family researchers are making increasing use of family interactions in more standardized settings in a laboratory.

C. Laboratory Procedures

One of the currently more popular ways to study the outcome of parenting techniques with young children is the Strange Situation. This laboratory technique infers parenting procedures from a short standardized encounter. Developed by Mary Ainsworth in the late 1960s, this procedure examines the child's reactions to separation from the parent, usually the mother, in a strange environment. Children are brought into a laboratory for a 21-minute session in which mother and child first are together in a room with toys, then a stranger enters, the mother leaves the child with the stranger, the mother returns and the stranger leaves, the child and mother are alone together, then the mother leaves the child alone in the room, the stranger enters again, and finally the mother returns. Each episode takes 3 minutes. Individual differences in the way the child reunites with the mother are considered to be reflections upon the mother's sensitivity to the child's needs and demands.

Rogoff has used another type of laboratory study to understand parental instructional techniques. The parent and child are put together in a room and confronted with a task that requires the parent to help the child. The parent's behaviors are coded, and inferences are drawn concerning parenting skills in terms of helping the child in other situations.

Laboratory methods have many benefits. They place all individuals in the same situation and produce information that can be coded by someone other than the parent. They allow the researcher to manipulate variables so that they can observe the effects of changing certain aspects of information presented to the parent or child. However, like other methods of study, there are limitations. The behavior samples we get in the laboratory are influenced by many variables over which we have no control. Too often such studies manipulate trivial variables and leave more interesting variables unstudied simply because they are too difficult to control.

D. Child Reports of Parenting

Recently there have been attempts to examine parenting via the report of children. These have been conducted in two ways: either a child is interviewed about what his or her parents do in certain situations using a structured set of questions or the child is allowed to describe his or her family situation in an unstructured way. Child reports have all the same strengths and weaknesses of parent reports. In addition, it is more difficult to gain information from children, as they may be more easily influenced by the interviewer than adults, and young children often simply do not have the cognitive capacity to understand some questions.

There are no completely adequate ways to study parenting, but by using a combination of methods, one can begin to understand the different aspects of parenting. Below are reports of three differing concepts of parenting, all of which have developed through the use of multiple methods to study parents.

IV. COMPONENTS OF PARENTING

A. Family Management

Gerald Patterson has suggested four variables as crucial in effective parenting. He calls these variables together *family management*. First, some parents apply consistent and effective controls on problem behavior; other parents frequently threaten, scold, and natter but seldom back up their threats with effective action. The variable measuring this family management skill is called *discipline*. Second, some parents carefully track the whereabouts of

their children, while others do not note any but the most obvious changes in their children's behavior. The variable constructed to measure this skill is called *monitoring*. Third, some parents can negotiate, can solve problems, and can cope with crises arising inside and outside the family; others cannot. The variable that assesses these skills is termed *problem solving*. A fourth variable is *positive reinforcement* where the parent reinforces the child for those behaviors he wishes to maintain. By employing certain techniques in their own lives, parents inevitably foster these same techniques in their children, well or ill. Children learn to relate to others in part by watching adults relate, to help themselves by watching parents fend for themselves, and to work or learn by watching others do so. Patterson's theory focuses more upon the control or demand aspects of parenting, but has the advantage of very clearly defining what processes are behind the general concept of control. [*See* PROBLEM SOLVING.]

B. Scaffolding

In the early part of the 20th century, Vygotsky attempted to create a psychology of child development that included the social origins and influences on human cognitive functioning. For Vygotsky, the social world of the child channels development. He emphasized that development occurs in situations where the child's problem solving is guided by an adult who structures and models ways to solve a problem, a process he called *scaffolding*. Adults can arrange the environment so that children can reach a level beyond their present capabilities when working on their own. This is called the *zone of proximal development*, defined as the distance between the child's capabilities when working on a project independently and the child's capability when an adult or more capable peer has arranged the environment. The child's individual mental functioning develops through experience in the zone of proximal development. The structure provided serves as a scaffold for learning, providing contact between old and new knowledge. Thus, to understand development, we must attend to formal and informal instruction provided by the parents in the course of the child's daily activities. [*See* COGNITIVE DEVELOPMENT.]

Considerable work has been done in this area, first by Sigel and his colleagues, who examined the effect of what they label *distancing techniques* on the child's competence. Distancing techniques within this model are cognitive strategies parents use to help a child understand a problem. They can range from concrete (such as asking a child to label) to abstract (such as synthesizing new structures for the child). More recently, Rogoff and her colleagues have applied Vygotsky's principles to adults' attempts to provide scaffolds for children's problem solving. Again, the techniques studied have been cognitive strategies to increase the child's understanding of the problem and to help the child move to a new level of thinking. The work on scaffolding has focused upon the responsiveness aspect of parenting. The role of the parent as teacher is recognized, and the dimensions that go into this aspect of parenting have been more carefully defined, so that we have a better idea of the process behind this dimension of parenting.

C. Emotional Support

The third component of parenting that has received a great deal of attention in the research literature recently has been that of emotional support, but as noted in the historical review, this component of parenting does not have a long history. The Freudian point of view emphasized the importance of satisfaction of children's drives, but the discussion was mostly in terms of satisfaction of physical needs rather than satisfaction of emotional needs. In the 1960s, this began to change. First, Harry Harlow published his much cited work with infant monkeys and their surrogate mothers. Harlow paired a warm, soft surrogate mother who did not feed the infant monkey with a wire surrogate who fed the infant. If the Freudian view were correct, the infant should identify with the surrogate who fed him or her, but instead the infants went to the warm, soft cloth mother when they were distressed. At approximately the same time, John Bowlby began to publish his theory on the importance of attachment during the first year of life. Bowlby made the point that social responsiveness was necessary for development and that, without a caregiver that provided warmth and security, the child could not develop normally. Bowlby's second important point was that the child developed an internal working model of relationships from the early caregiving relationship. He called this whole process *attachment*.

Recent literature in the field of the child and family has emphasized the importance of the attachment relationship. Mary Ainsworth developed the Strange Situation to test individual differences in patterning of infant's attachment behaviors. This procedure allows one to classify the child in terms of security and in terms of reaction patterns toward the mother.

Work within the area has related the child's attachment relationship to maternal sensitivity, warmth, and intrusiveness. However, the most clear-cut findings with attachment are at the extremes of caregiving. Parents who are abusive or neglecting have children who show extreme avoidance or resistance in the Strange Situation. The classification system also has been used to predict the way that children will behave in new situations as they grow older. Again, the clearest findings are in terms of extreme behavior, but a growing literature suggests that children do approach new relationships in a manner similar to their attachment relationship.

V. DIFFERENCES IN PARENTING BY MOTHERS AND FATHERS

While the traditional view of the family is one of the mother providing warmth and caretaking and the father providing discipline and support for the family, these characterizations of family life do not appear to describe parenting today. While mothers do spend more time with their children than fathers, and this is as true of mothers who work outside the home as those who spend their days at home with the children, the roles of present day mothers and fathers appear to have evolved somewhat differently. Mothers do most of the routine caretaking, but the father's role is not the abstract disciplinarian that we see represented in many texts. Instead the father appears to have taken over many of the qualities of playmate. Michael Lamb found in one study that when fathers spent time with toddler-aged children, it was play time; whenever the child needed some type of care, then the child was given back to the mother.

Jeanne Block suggested that fathers will be more important to the sex-role development of children than mothers and that they will interact with boys and girls in very different ways whereas mothers will behave similarly to boys and girls. Boys will be sought out by the father and will be encouraged to take on an instrumental, independent style of behavior. Whereas both mothers and fathers are expected to encourage traditional sex typing, the father will make a greater distinction between sons and daughters. Recent articles from several researchers have found minimal support for the uniqueness of the father's role. While fathers in some studies played physically with boys more frequently than with girls and were more consistent in their encouragement of sex-typed toys, there was actually little support for a differential effect on other sex-role variables. Differences, when they were found, were more likely to occur with respect to reported attitudes about the differences between boys and girls rather than in differences in behavior toward boys and girls.

We do know, however, that mothers spend far more time with their children, do most of the caretaking, and if the family breaks up, are far more likely to raise the children as single parents. There is some movement within the middle class for more involvement of the father within the family; however, even in families choosing a equalitarian type of child-rearing in which both parents are employed outside the home, mothers continue to do most of the caretaking. Consequently, when one looks at parenting variables which predict future performance of the child in either the social or cognitive realm, mother variables in most studies tend to be stronger predictors than father variables. Father absence does predict problems for the child, but such studies tend to be highly confounded with economic well-being and social stress, so it is difficult to know whether it is father absence or other variables predicting negative outcome.

One thing that should be noted about the literature is that fathers are extremely understudied. Much of our information concerning the role of fathers comes from mothers. What we know directly from fathers is very biased toward well-educated fathers and concerns interactions in infancy and early childhood. The role of the father in the child's life after school entry and on into adolescence and adulthood remains a mystery.

VI. CHILD VARIABLES THAT INFLUENCE PARENTING STYLE

A. Age of Child

Parents report different levels of pleasure in their child at different ages. In one study in Fagot's laboratory, both mothers and fathers of 12 month olds appeared to be more comfortable with their roles than did parents of 18 month olds. Parenting an 18-month-old child, who is now quite mobile and starting to assert independence, calls for new skills, and it was clear that many of these parents were finding this transition a challenge. For instance, toddlers spend almost half of their time in communication attempts, and while a communication attempt may be considered a positive behavior, it also calls for an immediate response and can be extremely diffi-

cult for a busy parent. The tasks of parenting will change as the child grows. Parents use instruction and direction at much greater rates with 18 month olds than with 12 month olds. One consequence is that purely positive interaction decreases. Eighteen-month-old children require more management skills than 12 month olds, and this change is reflected both in the children's behavior and in the change of style of interaction seen in home observations. We need more studies which carefully define the parent's role as the child grows to understand the interaction between the age of the child and the parents' attitudes and behaviors toward the child.

B. Sex of Child

Whether parents provide differential socialization for boys and girls is a question that has been debated for a number of years. In the early 1970s, Maccoby and Jacklin reviewed the literature and declared that there were few differences in the socialization of boys and girls. Block questioned this finding. Specifically, she concluded that few of the studies dealt with fathers, who might be expected to provide stronger sex-role socialization than mothers, and that the studies were biased toward younger children. In the early 1980s, Block suggested several areas in which parental treatment might make a difference. Several subsequent attempts to examine parental differences in the treatment of boys and girls still have not yielded conclusive results.

Another of Block's contentions was that preschool-aged children were overrepresented in the literature, and she hypothesized that sex-role socialization should increase with age. However, recent reviews have suggested that preschool boys and girls are treated more differently than are middle-school children. There are very few studies concerning socialization of adolescent boys and girls, and many think that parents treat children of this age very differently.

Fagot's laboratory examined behavioral differences in mothers' and fathers' reactions toward boys and girls at three different ages: 12 months, 18 months, and 5 years of age. Home observations were chosen as the best method to look at socialization differences for several reasons. Home observations allow both the children and the parents to react more naturally than do more tightly controlled laboratory studies. There were some differences in mothers' and fathers' styles of interaction; for instance, mothers gave more instructions and directions than did fathers, while fathers spent more time in positive play interaction. There were also differences in parents' reactions to 12- and 18-month-old boys and girls; most differences were quite expected, with the exception that boys received more negative comments for attempts to communicate than did girls. There were no differences in the ways that parents reacted to boys and girls at age 5. Fagot argued that differences in parenting for boys and girls would occur at critical transitions in the child's life when it was important to the parent that the child behave in sex-stereotyped ways. For example, we see more differences at 18 months when the child is establishing a gender identity, and we should expect to see larger differences in adolescence when sex-role behaviors become very important.

C. Birth Order Effects

There is an old joke among parents that the first child should be considered a practice try and only later children should count in evaluating their skills as parents. Certainly, the effects of birth order exist. However, the first child in many ways appears advantaged, particularly in terms of achievement in school and in later career choices. Why might this be? The first child in general receives more parent attention during the early years, including attention to the child's language development. Parents, particularly mothers, talk to their first-born children more. However, the literature on birth order is sometimes difficult to follow, as the findings are not always the same. At this time, researchers think more in terms of the spacing of children and the adult–child ratio. Families in which children are more closely spaced seem to have more difficulties, perhaps because of the financial and physical stress on the parents. When children are spaced 4 or more years apart, the effects of birth order tend to disappear. [See BIRTH ORDER, EFFECT ON PERSONALITY AND BEHAVIOR.]

VII. CULTURAL INFLUENCES ON PARENTING

Clearly, the culture in which a child is raised has great implications for the child's well-being. Some cultures believe that children should be carefully nurtured and, because they do not yet understand the world, must be protected from harsh consequences. Other cultures seem to believe that children are born with evil tendencies and must be sharply curbed if they are not to grow up morally depraved. Some cultures cherish both boys and girls, while in others boys are of great value while girls are costly, and hence more likely to suffer infanticide. In some cultures, children are reared by many members of the community, while in others only the mothers participate in a child's upbringing. Humans seem to have an almost unlimited capacity to develop expectations and values about what is truly right. Some wish their children to be very communally oriented, and the children are trained never to be outstanding. Others, such as the United States, put a great emphasis on individual achievement, and the child is taught to try to stand out. Cultures are very effective at molding the types of individuals that are most acceptable to the culture. The medium by which this is done is the parenting process.

VII. FAILURES OF PARENTING

There is great concern today about the failure of the family and hence the failure of parenting. Certainly if one examines the rise in reported child abuse rate, there is cause for concern. It remains unclear whether such reports reflect a rise in child abuse or an increased awareness of child abuse. As recently as the 1950s, family violence was not widely recognized as a problem in American society. Since that time, the body of literature on child abuse and other forms of domestic violence has grown to be both extensive and diverse. A great deal of effort has been focused on understanding the causes and correlates of family violence. A rather diffuse field has developed, consisting of a number of indirectly related theories that focus on different aspects of family violence. Much of the literature of child abuse today suggests that many types of trauma in childhood lead to far-reaching problems, and often reactions to childhood trauma are considered in the same category as trauma suffered in wars and natural disasters. These reactions have come to be classified as post-traumatic stress syndrome. [See CHILD ABUSE; POST-TRAUMATIC STRESS DISORDER.]

Why do parents abuse their children? There are many theories, most of which can be grouped in one of three categories. Psychological theories propose that the violence arises from within certain individuals with deviant personalities and various forms of psychopathology. Social–interactional theories point to interpersonal, most often within-family, processes such as reciprocal reinforcement of aversive behavior as the origin of violence. Sociocultural theories suggest the etiology of violence may be found within general societal factors such as poverty, stress, and crowded living conditions, or within the values of a particular cultural subgroup. Each of these theories has contributed in important ways to our understanding of domestic violence. However, the solution to child abuse is quite different depending upon the theory. If the problem is psychological, then it might make sense to focus upon diagnosis of an abusing personality and work with that individual. However, if abuse originates in the social interaction of the family, then intervention with the family is called for. If child abuse is a result of societal pressures, then the solution would be best handled at the societal rather than the individual level. Many who work with abused children have adopted the social–interactional approach, not because they feel that societal conditions have no part in the cycle, but because they can do something about interactions within the family. They also find that most child abusers do not have recognizable forms of pathology. In effect, the tendency within the field has been to adopt educational approaches to failures of parenting.

IX. PARENT EDUCATION

The mother–child relationship has been a primary focus of both clinical and developmental investigations, and hence most of the parenting programs focus upon the mother–child relationship. Mothers may provide different social learning experiences for a child depending on the mother's style of interaction and the child's gender. Angry mothers typically have young children who display anxious and resistant behaviors, and this is particularly true for boys. Depressed mothers have been shown to spend less time taking care of their children, to use more physical punishment, and to be less affectionate. Comparisons of children's responses showed that daughters were more likely to display behaviors similar to mothers' depressive behaviors, especially during adolescence.

Studying the family has been given a prominent role in trying to understand both the antecedents of problem behaviors and healthy adjustment outcomes. Effective parents for both boys and girls have been characterized as nurturant, positive, and loving, as being sensitive to their children's individuality, and as having developed reasonable expectations and effective behavior management skills. How do we translate the research findings into effective treatment programs? At this point, there are several programs around the country that are developing prevention programs. Here the idea is that parents who are having difficulty or feel they may have difficulty are exposed to parenting programs. The components of such program usually include information on family management, on increasing the warmth and emotional support of the parent, and on teaching the parent to help the child learn new skills.

X. CHILDREN'S NEEDS VERSUS PARENTS' RIGHTS: A CHANGING EQUATION?

Biological parents are given a great deal of control over their children's lives. Perhaps this is due to the very root of the term parenting, meaning to give birth. There are some recent changes of this control; for instance, a boy in Florida was allowed to divorce his biological parents whom he claimed had neglected and abused him. However, the quality of parenting is rarely considered in placement of children in disputes, and the child continues to be at the mercy of his birth. As the process of parenting becomes better understood, perhaps in the future judgments of suitability will be made in terms of quality rather than biology.

Bibliography

Ainsworth, M. D. S., Blehar, M. C., Waters, E., and Wall, S. (1978). "Patterns of Attachment: A Psychological Study of the Strange Situation." Erlbaum, Hillsdale, NJ.

Baumrind, D. (1971). Current patterns of parental authority. *Dev. Psychol. Monogr.* 4(1, Pt. 2).

Maccoby, E. E. (1980). "Social Development: Psychological Growth and the Parent–Child Relationship." Harcourt Brace, New York.

Patterson, G. R., and Forgatch, M. (1987). "Parents and Adolescents: Living Together." Castalia, Eugene, OR.

Rogoff, B. (1990). "Apprenticeship in Thinking: Cognitive Development in a Social Context." Oxford University Press, New York.

Sears, R. R., Maccoby, E. E., and Levin, H. (1957). "Patterns of Childrearing." Row Peterson, Evanston, IL.

PATTERN RECOGNITION

William R. Uttal
Arizona State University

Glossary

Association The second stage of the pattern recognition process in which the represented image is connected to a name or category.
Elementalism A theoretical position stressing the precedence of the parts or local features of an object.
Holism A theoretical position stressing the precedence of the entire object or the arrangement of its parts.
Representation The first stage of the pattern recognition process in which the incoming image is transformed or coded for the subsequent association.
Stimulus equivalence The ability of the human to recognize objects in the face of severe transformations in shape, orientation, position, or size.

PATTERN OR FORM RECOGNITION, in the context of this article, is the process by which visually presented objects are identified, categorized, and named. In other words, the challenge of pattern recognition is to answer the question "*What* is it that I am seeing?" This is a different visual question than that asked in *detection*—"Is there anything there?"—or in *discrimination*—"Are the two things I see the same or different?" This definition of recognition specifically excludes the high cognitive processes by which the categories, inclusive concepts, or names of the objects are themselves created. Rather, the topic is treated purely as a problem in visual perception in this article. Two stages of processing can be distinguished: (Stage 1) The transfor-

mation and representation of the image into a form suitable for (Stage 2) the comparison or analysis that permits a concept, name, or category to be attached or associated with the image.

I. INTRODUCTION

The problem of visual form recognition is a classic one in visual psychology. From the time of the classic Greek philosophers until today it has been appreciated that the brain was capable of carrying out amazing feats of object recognition and identification. Despite its antiquity, the problem is still generally unsolved and a topic of active research in psychology, computer science, and, to an arguable degree, neurophysiology. As we shall see many controversies and uncertainties currently exist in this field.

It is clear now that two functional components—image representation and memorial comparisons or analyses—must be involved in the recognition process. The object, image, or scene must be represented in some way so that it can be either compared with an existing set of alternative stored categories or processed by some other kind of logic that allows naming or categorization to occur. It is important to appreciate that both possible means of categorization may exist—a structural comparison process, on the one hand, and a logical analysis, on the other—in different kinds of recognition. If there is any "law" of visual perception, it is that the visual system is capable of using many different strategies in meeting the challenges it confronts.

The true nature and complexity of the visual aspects of the human pattern recognition problem were not clarified until contemporary computer scientists such as D. Marr began to cope with the challenge of producing comparable image processing programs. The requirement that the computer program contain a precise statement of the necessary processing steps forced workers in this field to consider in detail the equivalent processes that are likely to be carried out by the human. In this context, we must appreciate that the study of pattern recognition is a thoroughly modern interdisciplinary issue that transcends psychology, neuroscience, and computer science.

A. The Whole versus Part Controversy

One of the major issues, if not the major issue, in developing a biologically valid theory of pattern recognition concerns the initial image processing strategy used by the viewer. The specific question is, *Is the image analyzed into its parts or is it examined as an organized whole during the recognition process?* All computer models and psychological theories are based on at least an implicit a priori judgment that pattern recognition is governed by either the *nature* of the parts or the *arrangement* of the parts. In contemporary fact, most modern theories are "elementalist" and assert that the *features* of which the image is constructed are precedent in recognition. A minority position—holism or Gestaltism—holds that the arrangement of the parts is more important than their nature.

The probable main reason for the predominance of "feature" theories is that pattern recognition research exists in a context of developments in other sciences. Contemporary theory and experimentation in neurophysiology, on the one hand, and computer technology, on the other, have both had an immense effect on the field. Modern neurophysiology is primarily a science of components and parts—the neurons of which the brain is made. Existing computer programming techniques force us to examine and manipulate the parts of an image detailed down to the individual feature or even the individual pixel. Conceptually, it "demagnifies" the problem down to one emphasizing elemental parts rather than global patterns. Unfortunately, there is no good equivalent algorithmic tradition for handling global arrangement per se.

Extraordinary successes in both of these cognate fields have led to many of their ideas being transferred to models of human pattern recognition as a natural result of communication in an interdisciplinary world. It also must be acknowledged that a major impetus toward the predominantly part or feature-based theory orientation in this field is that we do not yet have a satisfactory holistic theory of arrangement, a sufficiently powerful empirical methodology, or even a suitable mathematical tool to provide

the bases for a compelling theory of recognition based on global rather than local attributes.

The preponderance of perceptual experiments reported in the current scientific literature manipulate features or parts of the stimulus image. Data from such studies, therefore, also support theories of pattern recognition that are based on the nature of the feature or components of which the stimulus image is composed. The system is circular. Experimental designs are based on feature-based premises; the experiments then produce results that support the initial hypothesis.

Nevertheless, there is an increasing, though still relatively small, body of evidence that argues, to the contrary, that global or holistic strategies dominate human pattern recognition instead of feature-based ones. One kind of such evidence deals with the manifestation of the final phenomenal outcome itself—the exemplar demonstration or visual phenomenon showing the outcome of the entire perceptual process. Demonstrations (as opposed to parametric experiments) are all too often ignored by researchers in this field when it comes to generating theory. Nevertheless, this kind of "first-order" phenomenology should not be underestimated. Demonstrations reflect the overall nature of perception in a direct and immediate fashion and should set the stage for research and theory rather than being discarded as irrelevant. The work of V. S. Ramachandran, S. Antis, and N. Wade, among others, utilizing illusions as probes of recognition mechanisms, is especially notable in this regard.

One classic demonstration that is often used to illustrate the precedence of the global rather than the local attributes of pattern recognition is to be found in the work of the Italian artist Giuseppe Archimboldo (1527–1593). Upon first glance, the figure is just another portrait. However, the global "illusion" can be discerned to be composed of vegetable parts upon close scrutiny (see Fig. 1). Whatever local features are involved in the perception of the face are irrelevant; all that initially matters is the arrangement of this strange set of parts. This is what we mean by global precedence.

A more familiar set of arguments against a pure part or feature-based theory of pattern or object recognition is the fact that the specific features of which objects are composed often seem not to be very important in the recognition process. For example, the letters of the alphabet or chairs of various kinds can be recognized as exemplars of their general class (an "A" or a "Chair") regardless of the

FIGURE 1   A painting by Giuseppe Arcimboldo (1527–1593) demonstrating the precedence of global form over local features in our perception of objects.

font or specific shapes of the pieces of which they are made. Caricatures consisting of only a few well-chosen lines can be easily identified as representing a particular person. The essential fact is that no specific feature is necessary for the recognition of an object. The relationships of the features seem to be the keys to pattern recognition.

Another classic body of evidence that supports holistic or global precedence in pattern recognition can be found in the literature of Gestalt psychology. Many of their rules of the organization of visual perception, in particular the idea that forms have a certain fundamental unity or Pragnanz, speak strongly for the priority that the global, whole attributes of an image must have in many aspects of visual perception. Other experiments that deal with stimuli that are virtually free of any continuous features (for example, arrangements of dots or subjective contours) also support a holist point of view.

The ability to recognize an object from a vast number of viewing angles and under a vast number of distortions is referred to as *stimulus equivalence*. Stimulus equivalency reflects the extraordinary capacity of an observer to recognize an object (for example, a plate or a face) as an example of a particu-

lar class of objects even though the parts may be substantially distorted by the variations in the viewer's point of view or even partially occluded. It is also considered by many theoreticians to be strong evidence for a holistic interpretive process rather than one driven by local features.

Despite the vigor of the debate between the holist and elementalist theorists, a prudent review of the contemporary scene reveals that the issue is not yet resolved. Repeated demonstrations, experiments, and caveats have supported the precedence of *both* the arrangement of the parts into a meaningful global pattern and the specific nature of the parts. This may signal us that we cannot yet definitively specify which of these theoretical points of view best describes this powerful human perceptual skill. As in many human perceptual problems, it may be that there is no single all-inclusive answer to this conundrum. Rather, the method used by the human in each case depends upon a number of situational and experimental variables.

II. THEORIES OF PATTERN RECOGNITION

As noted earlier, contemporary theories of pattern recognition are mainly dedicated to answering two kinds of questions. The first concerns the initial transforms that are carried out on the input image. The foundation issue in this case is the nature of the *representation* of the image information. The second question concerns the process by which the transformed images are linked with a particular prototype name. The foundation issue in this case is the nature of the *association* between the incoming image, transformed and altered as it may be, and a name or category learned at some previous time.

A. The Representation Problem

Many modern pattern recognition theories that concentrate on the visual process take for granted that if the image is appropriately represented, the problem is essentially solved; the association of the appropriately represented image with a particular name being a trivial final step. (Of course, for those interested in the higher cognitive and linguistic processes, this second stage of the pattern recognition problem is central.) Much of the emphasis by pattern recognition theorists is, therefore, on image transformations and representations prior to the comparison process.

The image transformation process is by no means simple or immediate. It is, itself, a major challenge to explanatory theory. Human vision is wonderfully adaptive. At some stage, it seems that the human pattern recognizer normalizes the stimulus so that even when an object is rotated, translated, or magnified over wide ranges, it can still be recognized. (This invariance is another way of defining stimulus equivalence.)

Most computer models cum theories, as well as psychological models of perception, usually include some preliminary normalization to a canonical configuration or to an invariant representation. (This is especially true for connectionist or neural net models.) If the normalization is done properly, recognition is not dependent upon the particular situational properties of the stimulus and the model mimics human recognition invariance in a reasonably complete way. For example, simply transforming a stimulus to a polar, as opposed to a Cartesian, coordinate system is a means of establishing invariance to rotation and magnification. It is also possible to transform a stimulus to a completely different representational system such as a spectrum of spatial frequencies—for example, a Fourier or a Walsh transform—to provide another means of precluding any sensitivity to irrelevant spatial translations.

Whether or not such a standardization or canonical transformation of the stimulus actually occurs in human pattern recognition remains an unresolved question. At a behavioral level, human recognition skills exhibit a profound insensitivity to where an object is or what size it is. It is conceivable, however, that the analysis system is so powerful that this minor miracle can be accomplished without any image normalization of the kind to which theoreticians usually retreat. Such a preliminary modification of the image may merely be a convenience, if not a necessity, for the computer modeler or psychological theoretician because of our incomplete understanding of the later stages of processing. The difficulty of solving problems without some kind of a fixed frame of reference may be much less for the human visual system than for the computer program.

The mathematical problem of defining a canonical coordinate system to achieve good invariance to the various distortions and displacements is not trivial. However effortlessly the nervous systems seem to adjust to changes in stimulus position and shape, the general problem posed to the modeler or theoretician is profound, refractory, and clearly not yet solved.

There is, it should be noted, a major controversy currently raging concerning the ultimate resolvability of the problem of internal representation that may make all of these models interesting process descriptions rather than true reductive explanations. A number of psychologists have argued in recent years that the representation of the image within the visual system is not determinate through either behavioral or neurophysiological techniques. Behavior is not a satisfactory probe because it is neutral with regard to the internal mechanisms in a fundamental way; neurophysiology is not satisfactory because of the enormous complexity of the coding schemes used by the nervous system to represent spatio-temporal patterns beyond the peripheral portions of the sensory pathways. These arguments raise doubts about the utility of, for example, single-cell neurophysiological research for contributing to a satisfactorily complete solution of the human visual pattern recognition problem. Early studies which showed lateral inhibitory interconnections in simple peripheral structures such as the horseshoe crab eye may have been misleading harbingers for the future. While interneuronal inhibition may have been a good model of the Mach Band, most pattern recognition processes certainly take place at high and complex neural levels and are poorly served by explicitly neural models of this genre. A recent trend toward computational models led by the thoughtful contributions of computer scientists such as D. Marr, T. Poggio, and W. E. L. Grimson based on transforms, operations, and processes (rather than neural structures) seems more promising. Even the recent development of "neural" network or connectionist theories of pattern recognition are now appreciated to be process models describing interactions between symbolic nodes rather than between anything close to biologically realistic neurons.

B. The Association Problem

The next stage in the pattern recognition process following the initial image transformation and representation stage requires that the modified image be associated with a prestored name or category. This second stage is even more mysterious in terms of the specific underlying mechanisms than the representation stage even though it has been the object of considerable psychological research. There are, again, two major schools of thought concerning the nature of this second stage. In the first, the process is considered to be a simple correlational comparison with a library of templates, prototypes, or reference images. This type of comparison process depends upon at least a topological kind of isomorphic representation in which the geometrical relationships among the parts of the image are maintained. Depending upon the theoretician's proclivities toward a holist or elementalist approach to the first stage, the second stage may invoke (a) the triggering of a network in which decisions are made of the presence or absence of a feature or component until a final "recognition" occurs or (b) the comparison of the whole picture with the library of prototypes until a best fit is achieved. Preservation of the topological relations of the parts of the stimulus image, at least, is assumed in either case, if not the specific Cartesian geometry of the original image. That is, the image objects are assumed to be represented by a nervous system that preserves the spatial characteristics of the original stimulus. The match is made by a map-like superimposition, although on maps that may be very elastic. [See CATEGORIZATION.]

The second approach to name association (the second stage of the pattern recognition process) does not involve preservation of the topological and geometrical relations of the original image and its comparison with the prototypes in an isomorphic manner. Rather the process may be symbolic and the analysis carried as a series of logical decisions, analyses, or constructions. That is, an object may be represented in a nonisomorphic code that describes an object as a series of logical steps or in a descriptive language that specifies the rules that would allow the object to be reconstructed. From this point of view, the comparisons are not between maps that are at least topologically constant, but rather between symbol systems. This latter approach, in fact, does not require any kind of a comparison. It permits an alternative strategy in which the descriptive language or logical construction process acts as a decision tree directing the recognition process to a category or name for the object. Such a process is intrinsically faster than one that requires an exhaustive search (such as template matching) and can be implemented in a more economical manner than one requiring many multiple processes to be carried out in parallel.

A substantial body of work associated with pattern recognition utilizes the dichotomy of attentive and preattentive processes as an assay of recognition processes. The work of B. Julesz and A. Triesman

is especially notable. In each case they have distinguished between dimensions of a stimulus object that preattentively "pop out" and those that must be attentively scrutinized to become effective in the recognition process.

C. Some Contemporary Pattern Recognition Theories

Theories of pattern recognition come in many forms and stem from many different traditions. The best way to concisely include a broad range of pattern recognition theories in this article is to provide capsule descriptions of a number of sample theories. The brief descriptions presented here are based upon comprehensive taxonomies of pattern recognition methods suggested by J. T. Townsend, D. E. Landon, F. G. Ashby, S. Watanabe, S. Pinker, and the work of other contemporary theoreticians.

Townsend and his collaborators, Landon and Ashby, are mathematical psychologists and approach their taxonomies from the point of view of the human perceptual theories. All members of the four classes of recognition methods that these authors describe can be said to be *descriptive* in that no allusion to the possible physiological or cognitive mechanisms underlying the pattern perception process is made. They are also mainly based on statistical rather than deterministic kinds of mathematics.

Townsend and his colleagues divide pattern recognition theories into two major subdivisions. The first subdivision includes those pattern recognition theories that are "based on an internal observation." Members of this class of pattern recognition theories contend that each stimulus event is dealt with separately by the perceptual processing system. The probability of a correct recognition (i.e., a response with the correct name of the stimulus or the name of the appropriate category) depends, therefore, upon the evaluation of that stimulus item by a set of internal rules and criteria couched only in the terms of a particular stimulus presentation event. This class of theory attempts to describe the specific processes (e.g., feature detection) that are presumed to exist within the cognitive structure of the observer as an incoming image is processed.

The second major subdivision includes those theories that they designate "descriptive." In this case the role of the individual event is minimized. Instead, the process of recognition is modeled as a kind of guessing or choosing an item from a set of possible responses on the basis of probabilistic rules involving context properties that go far beyond the immediate event. Rather than processing the attributes of a single stimulus, as did the internal observation theories, this second class of models merely uses the stimulus as one of many influences leading to an appropriate guess or choice of the proper response by the observer.

The first major division made by Townsend and his colleagues—the "internal observation" category—is further broken down into two subdivisions—the *general discriminant* models and the *feature confusion* models. General discriminant models are characterized by decision rules and procedures that evaluate the attributes of a particular stimulus and calculate a numerical value or "discriminant" for all possible responses that could conceivably be associated with that stimulus. The largest numerical value associated with any possible response becomes the selection criterion leading to the emission of that correct naming response. Feature confusion models assume a matrix is actually constructed that tabulate the probabilities of confusing specific responses.

The second major kind of pattern recognition model described by Townsend and his colleagues—feature confusion models—is also divided into two subcategories. The first gathers under a single rubric called "sophisticated guessing type models," a number of different theories including the *sophisticated guessing* models themselves, *all or none* models, *overlap* models, and *confusion-choice* models. The second subcategory, which they designate the "choice category," includes but a single exemplar—the *similarity choice* model. All of these theories are completely descriptive—they make no effort to consider the neural or cognitive processes underlying the statistical formalities. Rather they involve the statistics of active decision making or choice behavior as their conceptual basis.

Engineers, of course, approach the problem of designing models of pattern recognition from a different point of view. They often invoke a number of different kinds of techniques that do not depend upon the peculiarities of human perception. Watanabe points out that techniques such as *entropy minimization, covariance diagonalization,* and *structural analysis,* are often used in that field. Interestingly, though the two traditions have grown up separately, inspection of the respective models indicates that there may be more similarities than the different names suggest. For example, the category of covariance diagonalization is hardly distin-

guishable from factor analysis, a method with which psychologists are more familiar. In a similar way, some of these methods are comparable to multidimensional scaling which also seeks to reduce large amounts of information to a smaller set of nonredundant measures. It is clear that there has been a vigorous cross-fertilization of pattern recognition models between engineering and psychology; data from psychology often leading to insights for the engineer and ingenious theories from the engineer providing the framework for psychological thinking about the pattern recognition process.

In this context of interdisciplinary interaction, it is interesting to note that most of the engineering methods are fundamentally feature-based. In some cases, such as the structural analysis method, the features are the same as the those defining the geometry of the image—the corners, sides, etc. But in others, such as discrimination and decision-making procedures, a list of geometrical features is not necessary—any collection of attributes, spatially absolute (e.g., "square") or relational (e.g., "larger") can be used to define a pattern. Patterns may even be dealt with in the abstract. That is, measurements of virtually any kind can be used to set up "vectors" or collections of measurements that can compare with each other or with stored nongeometrical (i.e., symbolic) prototypes to recognize patterns of other kinds.

Other theories of pattern recognition are intuitively more straightforward. For example, the classic template matching theory assumes that an incoming visual image is compared with a library of prestored dimensionally isomorphic images, each of which has a name already associated with it. Template theories are correlative—the best match of the incoming image with one of the stored library of templates determines which one will be associated with the incoming image. In their most basic form, template models are essentially global or holistic. The fact that they require enormous libraries of prestored images has always mitigated against them. Since the phenomenon of stimulus equivalence suggests that it is not even necessary to have previous experience with a particular view of a form (and thus to have a prestored image) for recognition to occur, it is not likely that template matching in its simplest version is a likely candidate to be the best model of pattern recognition.

A theory that models some kind of logical decision-making system is a more plausible candidate to explain human pattern recognition. That is, one that does not require exhaustive searching for the best match in an extensive library would be preferred over one in which the attributes of the incoming image direct the process through a decision-making tree to a final "recognition" point.

Many neural network type theories operate in this mode. One of the classic neural network theories was developed in 1959 by O. Selfridge. His *pandemonium* model assumed that an array of specialized form detectors, sensitive to local geometrical features of the stimulus, become active to the degree that the feature was present. The pattern of activity constitutes a "vector" of activity that directly determined which name will be associated with the stimulus. No correlation with prestored images was necessary—only the response names themselves which were located, in a conceptual sense at the end of the decision tree.

In recent years (after a hiatus stimulated by an important critique by M. Minsky and S. Papert in 1969) pattern recognition theories based on the operation of neural networks have become increasingly popular. This renaissance in network or connectionist type theories can be directly attributed to the extraordinary impact of the twin books on parallel distributed processing by D. E. Rumelhart, J. L. McClelland, and their colleagues. Some of these multilayer neural networks or *perceptron* (a term invented by F. Rosenblatt) type theories include training processes so that a particular output can be associated with a particular input by repetitive reinforcement as the network experiences incoming stimuli. The effect of reinforcement in this type of model is to modify the strength of connections between *nodes* in the network. (The nodes at various times have been conceptualized as either neurons or higher order symbol processing units.) The final outcome of this progressive change in the organization of the network is akin to the pandemonium model—logical routing from multiple alternate stimulus pattern inputs to appropriate singular response outputs. The distinctive properties of this type of model being the nature of the adaptive processes by means of which the weights between nodes can be modified. An equally influential, though conceptually quite different, approach has been proposed by S. Grossberg, whose prolific contributions in this field have also been enormously influential.

Most of the theories that have been considered so far use the features or attributes of the stimulus in the same space as originally presented. For example, an angle defined in a Cartesian (x, y) coordinate system is dealt with in the terms of that geometry. Currently, there are other very important theories of pattern recognition and vision that base their action on a significantly different foundation idea—spatial domain transformations. That is, these alternate models transform the stimulus from its original spatial representation to another one that has some other more general or useful property. For example, a stimulus originally presented in the familiar (x, y) coordinate space of the visual display may be transformed into a spatial frequency (u, v) space by means of a two-dimensional Fourier transform. This process would convert a pattern that is represented by a wide variety of unquantified features and attributes (such as angles and sides) into a spectrum of spatial frequencies.

There are two disadvantages of images in the x, y space. First, the original picture may be represented as a collection of component features that can only be laboriously transcribed or exhaustively tabulated. Second, the original picture is a multidimensional pictorial representation that is not quantified in a way that would permit calculations to be made on it. The Fourier transformed image, however, varies along only three dimensions—spatial frequency, phase, and amplitude. Therefore, this kind of transformation (which may produce a picture that may appear to be more complicated than the original one) also produces a numerically manipulable and computable spectrum or vector (of the frequency components) from the original unquantified pictorial representation. This is the main advantage and raison d'être of the Fourier technique; it takes geometrical forms that are not represented quantitatively and represents them in a form on which computations can be made.

Fourier transforms, or any of the many other similar transforms that are now available, are merely means of representing the image. Representation of an image in the (u, v) domain is a process that does not speak at all to the association problem, a matter that must be dealt with separately in a subsequent processing stage.

This is not unusual. Theories purporting to be theories of pattern recognition often turn out to be nothing more than methods for representing objects in psychologically significant or computationally useful parts. For example, there is a closely related field of computer vision called visualization. In this field, cognate to the pattern recognition field we have been mainly discussing, the task is to draw good images on a display. Theories of image representation aimed at solving this problem describe how complex geometrical forms can be reduced to simple standard shapes. D. Marr and H. K. Nishihara, as well as A. Pentland, have made major contributions to this field by suggesting ways in which images may be represented as sets of basic solid shapes or linear axes. Psychologists like I. Biederman have expanded upon this idea as a foundation for a theory of object recognition in which a small set of elemental three-dimensional components (Geons) provide the cues for visual pattern recognition.

III. EXPERIMENTAL RESEARCH

The prototypical and most definitive experiment in pattern recognition would be to manipulate the significant attributes or features of a stimulus pattern and determine the effect on some measure of recognition. Such an experimental paradigm is rare, however, and perhaps is realizable only in the form of an ideal "Gedanken" experiment. The reason for the scarcity of this kind of definitive experiment in pattern recognition research is that there is much uncertainty about what, in perceptual fact, are the salient attributes of a visual stimulus that determine what it will be called.

Perceptual experiments, therefore, tend to explore other issues than the fundamental one of determining the necessary and sufficient stimulus attributes for pattern recognition. The whole–part question is one that has had considerable attention in place of the essential issue. D. Navon, for example, has worked with stimulus patterns that are composed of two levels of features. The whole stimulus pattern defines one form while the parts of which it is composed consists of another (see Fig. 2). The question is, "Which level of processing dictates

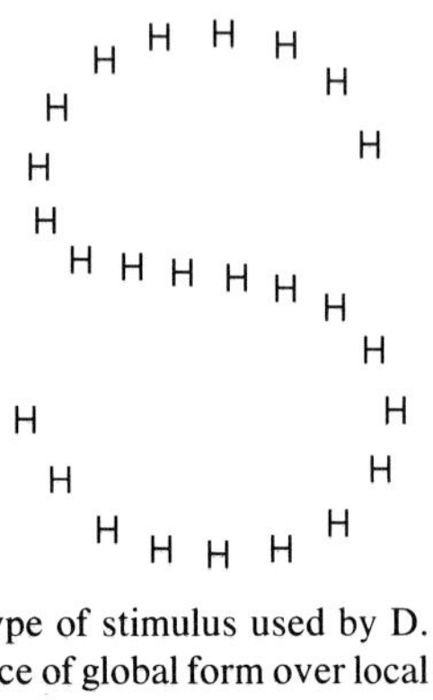

FIGURE 2   The type of stimulus used by D. Navon to demonstrate the precedence of global form over local features in character recognition.

what is recognized?" Navon's experiments, along with those of S. J. Lupker and H. Bouma, all support the idea that the global form is precedent.

Results with stimuli that varied in their degree of symmetry carried out by H. Pashler and B. Jenkins also speak for the holist theoretical point of view. This type of experiment typically showed that a symmetrical global arrangement of the parts of stimulus made for much more efficient recognizability. Since the same features were present in each case, once again arrangement is implicated the key variable in recognition.

The argument for holistic precedence is made even more profoundly when stimuli are chosen in which the features are not even present. This can be done if one uses dot patterns, a stimulus form in which there are no continuous geometrical features present, only arrangements of the featureless punctate component. In an extensive series of experiments, my colleagues and I have shown that the arrangement of the dots is critical in pattern recognition. Even more important was the fact that certain specific arrangements were shown to have particular perceptual potency. Specifically a general rule—*the law of linear periodicity,* which asserts that the best recognized arrangement is a straight line of evenly spaced dots—explained a very large number of different experiments.

Another class of experiment in which support for the holist point of view is obtained is generically classified as the *object* or *word superiority* paradigm. In this procedure, a comparison is made between the recognizability of a latter or an oriented line either isolated or in a context—a word or a stick figure. G. M. Reicher working with letters and words and N. Weisstein, M. C. Williams and C. S. Harris working with lines and outline objects all found that the lines and letters were better recognized when embedded in a relevant context than when isolated. It seems, therefore, that the arrangement of the stimulus and its context play primary, if not definitive, roles in the recognition process.

When the experimental paradigm is changed, however, results apparently supporting the opposite position in the whole–part controversy are obtained. Thus, for example, I. Biederman and E. E. Cooper, exploring the same issue, but using very different kinds of stimuli (complementary pairs of fractured outline figures) conclude something quite different than the "holists." They are among those who believe that their experimental findings support a "*recognition by components*" (i.e., feature) theory in which the parts are more important than the whole figure.

IV. CONCLUSIONS

This brief article has surveyed some of the theory and some of the empirical data in the field of pattern recognition. Obviously, this is a vital and exciting field of contemporary science that has much to gain from the interdisciplinary interaction of biological, psychological, and engineering sciences. Clearly, the generic problem of pattern recognition—how do we classify an incoming visual image?—has not been solved to the satisfaction of any one. We do have a number of interesting theoretical approaches and a smattering of human psychophysical research. We realize what some of the fundamental issues are, but have not yet been able to answer some of them.

It is also the case that the understanding of pattern recognition, as presented in this article, is not by any means complete. There are many other important research areas that could have been included if space permitted. We have made no mention of the one-dimensional patterns of speech that humans also recognize so effortlessly. Many other fields of science confront what are essentially pattern recognition problems. For example, the sequencing of the DNA molecule is a major pattern recognition problem as is the analysis of economic trends. Even in the context of visual perception, this article is not all-inclusive. We have not spoken of the problems of generating three-dimensional form from motion, stereoscopic vision, or textural changes—a very active field of inquiry in contemporary pattern recognition theory.

In conclusion, it does seem as if there is a contemporary contradiction between the theoretical models and the empirical work that attack the pattern recognition problem. We have seen how most theory is based upon feature analytic ideas. However, most parametric psychophysical studies of human pattern recognition and, even more strongly, most first-order demonstrations seem to suggest that the human observer recognizes pattern in a manner that is more sensitive to the global and holistic attributes of the incoming image. The resolution of this paradox is one of the major challenges facing this field in the future.

Bibliography

Anzai, Y. (1992). "Pattern Recognition and Machine Learning." Academic Press, San Diego, CA.

Bruce, V. (1988). "Recognizing Faces." Erlbaum, Hillsdale, NJ.

Grimson, W. E. L. (1990). "Object Recognition by Computer: The Role of Geometrical Constraints." MIT Press, Cambridge, MA.

Lockhead, G. R., and Pomerantz, J. R. (Eds.) (1991). "The Perception of Structure." American Psychological Association, Washington, DC.

Uttal, W. R. (1988). "On Seeing Forms." Erlbaum, Hillsdale, NJ.

Uttal, W. R., Bradshaw, G., Dayanand, S., Lovell, R., Shepherd, T., Kakarala, R., Skifsted, K., and Tupper, G. (1992). "The Swimmer: A Computational Model of a Perceptual Motor System." Erlbaum, Hillsdale, NJ.

PEER RELATIONSHIPS AND INFLUENCES IN CHILDHOOD

Kenneth H. Rubin, Robert J. Coplan, Xinyin Chen, and Jo-Anne E. McKinnon
University of Waterloo, Canada

Glossary

Friendship Reflecting the presence of a close, mutual, and dyadic bilateral relationship.
Peer An individual who may be regarded as equal with respect to some function (e.g., skill, educational level, age) or some situation (e.g., sociometric status).
Peer rejection The experience of being overtly disliked or isolated by a significant proportion of peer group members.
Popularity The experience of being liked or accepted by most members of a peer group.
Social competence The ability to achieve interpersonal goals in social interaction while simultaneously maintaining positive relationships with others over time and across settings.

PEER RELATIONSHIPS refer to the unique social context of children interacting with each other. Children spend an enormous amount of their time, both in and out of home, relating to and interacting with their peers. Assuredly, these peer relational experiences must carry with them some developmental benefits. Thus, the purpose of this article is to describe the nature and functional significance of children's peer relationships. It is our intention to argue that such relationships represent contexts within which a significant degree of adaptive development

occurs, and that without the experience of normal peer relationships, maladaptive development is likely to follow. We begin by providing a brief historical and theoretical overview of the literature on children's peer relationships.

I. PEER RELATIONSHIPS RESEARCH: HISTORY AND THEORY

At the turn of the 20th century, a number of influential investigators of human development wrote about the significance of peer relationships for children; however, it was not until the 1920s, when the first child welfare research stations blossomed throughout North America, that the empirical study of children's peer relationships and social skills gained a large and influential following. In these new research laboratories, investigators developed novel methodologies to examine developmental and individual differences in children's sociability, assertiveness and aggression, altruism, group dynamics, peer acceptance, and group composition. Although the exigencies of the second World War drove the study of children's social relationships to a virtual standstill, the topic regained new "breath" with the rediscovery of Jean Piaget's theory of cognitive and social-cognitive development, on the one hand, and with the preschool and day-care movements of the 1960s and 1970s on the other. Concerning the latter, children in North America are now entering organized peer group settings at earlier ages than ever before. Dual-income and single-parent families require that nonmaternal infant and early child care be made available. For the most part, such care is provided in out-of-the-home peer group venues. Furthermore, given the growing significance of education for life success, today's children remain with peers in age-segregated schools for more years than their cohorts of previous generations. From this applied perspective, it would be shortsighted to ignore the significance of children's peer group experiences and relationships for normal development and adjustment.

Theoretically, the significance of children's peer relationships is well described in the writings of Jean Piaget. In one of his first books, Piaget suggested that children's relationships with peers could be distinguished clearly, in form and function, from their relationships with adults. The latter relationships could be construed as being complementary, asymmetrical, and falling along a vertical plane of dominance and power assertion. Children normally accept adults' rules, not necessarily because they understand them, but rather because obedience is required. Alternately, adults are far less likely to follow the dictates of children.

On the other hand, children's peer relationships were portrayed as being balanced, egalitarian, and as falling along a more-or-less horizontal plane of power assertion and dominance. As such, it was within the peer context that Piaget believed children could experience opportunities to examine conflicting ideas and explanations, to negotiate and discuss multiple perspectives, and to decide to compromise with or to reject the notions held by peers. These peer interactive experiences were posited to result in positive and adaptive developmental outcomes for children. For example, positive outcomes included, among other things, the ability to understand *others'* thoughts, emotions, and intentions.

Armed with these new social understandings, children were believed able to think about the consequences of their social behaviors, not only for themselves, but also for others. The abilities to take into account the perspectives of others and to identify the potential consequences of one's social actions have long been posited to result in the production of socially competent behavior. The relative lack of such skills, conversely, has been thought to predict incompetent social behavior. These Piagetian derived notions have influenced a good deal of contemporary research concerning children's peer relationships. One of the principal off-shoots of this research has been the examination of relations among social-cognition (or how children think about their social worlds or about social issues), social behavior, and the quality of children's peer relationships. [*See* SOCIAL COGNITION.]

Several other authors have provided a rich perspective on the significance of peer relationships for normal development. For example, Harry Stack Sullivan wrote that the concepts of mutual respect, equality, and reciprocity developed from the "special relationships" that children developed with their chums. During the late elementary school years, children were thought to be able to recognize and value each other's personal qualities; as a consequence, peers gained power as personality shaping agents. Peers were thought to help each other understand the constructs of cooperation, competition, and social roles such as deference and dominance. Sullivan suggested further that during preadolescence, children gained a more complex understanding of social relationships as the concepts of equality, mutuality, and reciprocity became central to their own close friendships. Once acquired *between friends,* these concepts were thought to be extended to other relationships.

Like Piaget, George Herbert Mead emphasized the importance of the development of perspective-taking through peer interaction. Mead suggested that the ability to reflect on the self developed gradually over the early years of life, primarily as a function of peer play and social interaction experiences. Participation in rule-governed games and activities with peers was believed to lead children to understand and coordinate the perspectives of others with relation to the self. Thus, perspective-taking experiences led to the conceptualization of the "generalized other" or the organized perspective of the social group, which in turn led to the emergence of an organized sense of self.

Learning and social learning theorists have guided current research on children's peer relationships. It was suggested originally, and subsequently established empirically, that children learn about their social worlds, and how to behave within these contexts, through direct peer tutelage and indirect observation of peers "in action." From this perspective, peers are viewed as behavior control and behavior change agents for each other. Children punish or ignore nonnormative social behavior and reward or reinforce positively those behaviors viewed as culturally appropriate and competent.

Finally, ethological theorists have suggested that there is a relation between biology and the ability to initiate, maintain, or disassemble particular relationships. A basic focus of contemporary human ethological research has been the provision of detailed descriptions of the organization and structure of social behaviors and groups. For example, prosocial, playful, and aggressive displays have been examined within the contexts of parent–child attachment, and peer dominance and affiliative relationships. Those who have studied children's social behaviors from an ethological perspective have focused their attention on the organizational structure and functions of children's peer groups.

In summary, there is no shortage of theoretical and practical interest in children's peer groups. We turn now to the general functions of peer groups.

II. CHILDREN'S PEER GROUPS

A. Functions of the Peer Group

Generally, peer groups are characterized by participants who feel a strong desire to belong to a social unit, generate shared norms or rules of conduct beyond those maintained by society at large, and develop a hierarchical social structure of roles and relationships that govern their interaction with one another. The peer group serves several unique and significant functions for the growing child. For one, participation in peer groups teaches children how to engage in cooperative activities aimed at collective rather than individual goals. Such activities allow children to transcend the traditional egocentric or self-focused perspective traditionally attributed to young children. For another, participation in peer groups provides children with a venue in which control of hostile and aggressive impulses is socialized; when hostility is demonstrated, it is directed at members of other definable groups. Finally, through group membership, children gain first-hand experience with social structure, and are afforded the opportunity to practice skills associated with leadership and "followership." For example, there are times when members of the group must step forward and offer suggestions and solutions for the group to abide by. Furthermore, group participants must learn to accept and abide by the will of the collective, even if they are not in full agreement with a group decision. Given the significance of the peer group, it seems worthwhile asking how it is that groups are formed and how they look once formed. [*See* Leadership.]

B. Peer Group Formation

From classic social psychological research with children, the means by which groups are formed are well-known. When unfamiliar children are brought together, those children who display competencies in areas designated as important tend to acquire high status among peers. Oft-times the group has several leaders, each of whom takes on a particular role defined by his or her own areas of expertise. These leaders tend to set the norms for the group.

Once norms are established, members of peer groups develop a sense of belonging and a group identity. These affective components of group structure often result in competition (and in some subcultures, conflict) with other identifiable groups. Competition increases group solidarity and cohesion and adherence to norms. Thus, conformity to group norms is often intense and those who ignore the dictates of the peer group risk being rejected. Interestingly, there appears to be a developmental course of conformity to peer group norms. During *early childhood,* cognitive egocentrism, or the inability to understand the perspectives of others, often poses a problem concerning conformity to group norms; for example, preschoolers often follow their own sets of norms and they may shift rules in the middle of any given interaction in order to benefit themselves. With age and growth in social-cognitive understanding, from middle childhood through early adolescence, conformity to norms increases. Conformity to norms is greatest when the sources of influence are older or more competent than the child. [*See* Obedience and Conformity.]

C. Peer Group Hierarchies

Norms bind peer groups, and leaders play critical roles in determining norms for the group. But what determines group leadership? The most commonly investigated organizing principle in determining group structure is *dominance*. Dominance refers to an asymmetrical balance of power between two individuals in a social group. *Dominance hierarchies* represent a "pecking order" of individuals within a given group. Such hierarchies can be seen in groups of children as young as 3 years of age; they allow the prediction of who will prevail under various conditions of conflict or disagreement between any two group members.

Dominance hierarchies become increasingly stable during middle childhood and adolescence. These group structures serve the function of reducing aggression between group members; thus, even in preschool groups, overt acts of aggression diminish once a status hierarchy is established. When hostility does occur between group members, it is usually very restrained, often taking the form of playfully delivered verbal insults. As well, dominance hierarchies serve the adaptive function of helping to divide up tasks of labor and group resources. It is also often the case that "rank has its privileges"; lower status members typically assume most of the work and high status members benefit maximally from limited resources.

Although dominance represents a significant organizing function in children's peer groups, its role diminishes with age. Thus, by adolescence, group structures are less dependent on physical size and prowess, and more dependent upon characteristics that support a group's present normative activities. These characteristics include athletic ability, intelligence, and engagement in friendly or sociable behaviors. As such, since groups may vary in their normative orientations, social power among group members will be distributed differently in different social situations. There is also evidence that children's peer groups can be characterized along other dimensions, such as affiliation and attention. Thus, children's group structures are very complex and become increasingly so with the increasing age of its members.

In summary, it is clear that peer groups offer children a unique context within which they learn about themselves and others. Peer group membership affords children the opportunity to learn about common goals, normative behaviors, and the complexity of maintaining relationships. It is important to note, however, that within the child's peer group, "special relationships" may develop. These more intense, dyadic friendships serve their own distinct functions. Thus, we turn now to the literature on the significance of friendship.

III. CHILDREN'S FRIENDSHIPS

Friendship is defined by the presence of a close, mutual, and dyadic bilateral relationship that is built upon the principles of equality, mutuality, cooperation, and intimacy. During childhood, the constituent factors associated with friendship formation and maintenance change with age; in fact, the very meaning of friendship undergoes developmental change. In the following sections we discuss the functions of friendship, children's changing understandings of friendship, children's interactive behaviors in friend and non-friend peer groups, and the friendship formation process [See FRIENDSHIP.]

A. The Functional Significance of Friends

Developmental theorists have proposed that friendships in childhood serve a multitude of functions. For example, friendships in childhood serve to provide mutual validation of interests, expectations, and concerns; enhance one's feelings of personal worth; provide affection and opportunities for intimate self-disclosure; foster the growth of interpersonal understanding; and establish a foundation upon which later interpersonal relationships are built (e.g., romantic, marital, and parental relationships). Friendships are also thought to provide guidance and instrumental aid; offer significant sources of reliable alliance; provide companionship and excitement; enhance social perspective-taking skills; and offer a forum for the transmission of social norms and knowledge. Perhaps most important of all, friendships in childhood offer children an extra-familial base of security from which they may explore the effects of their behaviors on themselves, their peers, and their environments.

Recently, it has been proposed that friendships serve different functions for children at different points in development. In early childhood, friendship maximizes excitement and amusement levels in play, and helps to regulate emotions in the face of arousal (e.g., during conflict). In *middle childhood,* friendships assist children to learn those social skills necessary for successful self-presentation and impression management. These skills become crucial in middle childhood when anxiety about peer relationships develops. Finally, in *adolescence,* friendships serve to assist children in their quest for self-identity, and to help them integrate logic and emotions. [See ADOLESCENCE.]

B. Children's Conceptions of Friendship

It is one thing for theorists to posit the functions of friendship; it is quite something else to know how *children* think about the phenomenon. In the typical study, children are asked questions such as "What is a best friend?" or "What do you expect from a best friend?" It has been found that children's ideas about friendship progress through three broad stages. In the initial *"reward–cost"* stage (7–8 years), children characterize friends as companions who live nearby, have nice toys, and are willing to share them. In the *"normative stage"* (10–11 years), shared values and rules become important, and friends are expected to be cooperative, agreeable, and loyal. In the *"empathetic stage"* (11–13 years), friends are viewed as sharing similar interests, and as understanding, intimate confidants.

In summary, it is generally assumed that children's understanding of friendship becomes increasingly sophisticated and complex with age. Children's conceptions about friendship reflect their own transitions from the concrete world of the "here and now" to the more abstract world of the way things could or ought to be. What children may require and desire in a friendship develops as a function of their growing understanding of the world.

C. Factors Influencing Friendship Formation and Maintenance

Why is it that children are drawn into close relationships with each other? A facile first response is that observable characteristics such as racial/ethnic background, age, and sex are important magnets serving to pull children together. However, it is also the case that unfamiliar children who become friends are more likely to communicate clearly, self-disclose more often, engage in more positive interpersonal exchanges, and resolve conflicts more effectively than children who do not eventually become friends. Thus, childhood friendships form when partners are able to establish some sense of commonality and community.

Once formed, early childhood friendships are maintained because the partners direct positive affect to one another and share similarities in play preferences and cognitive sophistication. With increasing age, similarities in attitudes and aspirations aid in friendship maintenance.

D. How Children Play with Their Friends

Friends interact with each other differently than non-friends. Positive social exchanges and mutuality occur more often among friends than non-friends at all ages. Children as young as $3\frac{1}{2}$ years direct more social overtures, engage in more social and cooperative interaction, and play in more complex ways with their friends than with non-friends. Developmentally, it has been shown that altruistic or prosocial behaviors between friends increase with age until adolescence. [*See* PLAY.]

Interestingly, conflicts are not uncommon between friends. Friends not only engage in more positive interactions, but they also quarrel and engage in active (assaults and threats) and reactive (refusals and resistance) hostility more often than non-friends. Most likely, this seemingly contradictory finding can be attributed to the fact that friends spend much more time actually interacting with each other than do non-friends. Moreover, friends resolve their conflicts differently than non-friends. Friends, as compared with non-friends, have less intense conflicts; also, their conflicts are resolved more quickly. Friends are more likely to have equitable resolutions following conflict. Finally, following conflict resolution, friends are more likely than neutral associates to stay in physical proximity and continue to interact. [*See* CONFLICT BEHAVIOR; CONFLICT COMMUNICATION.]

E. Sex Differences in Children's Friendships

Children show a strong preference to play and be with same-sex peers; this tendency becomes stronger as children move from the preschool years through to middle childhood. The preference for same-sex playmates may emanate from children's increased awareness of culture's prescribed roles for males and females, and for the motivation to be included in the peer group.

The structural organization of friendships differs for boys and girls. For example, boys tend to have "extensive" (large) friendship networks, whereas girls' friendships are embedded in smaller, more "intensive" groups. Also, girls' dyadic relationships are more "exclusive" than those of boys. Boys are less likely to self-disclose and to share secrets with their friends than are girls. Finally, boys tend to be more competitive with their friends than girls.

F. Summary

In summary, friendships serve many important and changing functions for a child as he or she develops. Children's conceptions of friendship progress from the concrete to the abstract with age, and this change is reflected in their behavior with their friends. With age, children's friendships demonstrate more stability, more reciprocal altruism, and more intimate personal knowledge. Friends engage in qualitatively different types of interactions than non-friends at all ages, and the characteristics of these interactions can be used to describe and predict the friendship formation process. Children who are in the process of becoming friends are more likely to communicate clearly, self-disclose more often, and resolve conflicts more effectively than children who will not become friends. From the data extant, it would appear reasonable to conclude that childhood friendships play a highly significant role in social development. This being the case, it follows that children who lack friends are deprived of opportunities that enhance healthy social and emotional development. We examine this possibility below.

IV. PEER ACCEPTANCE AND REJECTION

The experience of being liked and accepted by the peer group is known as *popularity*. This construct reflects the view of the group vis-à-vis any given individual. Presumably, children who are not accepted by their peers experience some difficulty in their interactions with their peers. In the following sections, we examine the findings concerning the possible determinants of peer acceptance, and the outcomes that persistent difficulties with peers may entail.

A. Correlates and Determinants of Peer Acceptance and Rejection

Why is it that some children gain popularity amongst their peers while others are actively disliked? Most of the research extant concerning this question is purely descriptive; that is, investigators have provided a reasonable description of popular and rejected children. They have not, for the most part, focused directly on the causes of acceptance and rejection. Nevertheless, a review of the correlational database is revealing in that it provides reasonable hints about the determinants of peer reputations.

A wide range of variables, behavioral and non-behavioral, social and non-social, have been associated with acceptance and rejection. Although variables such as physical attractiveness, typicality of the child's first name, and minority group status have been found to be related to peer acceptance, it is clear that the strongest correlates of popularity are children's social behaviors. In general, it has been found that popular children are more socially competent than their rejected counterparts. That is, they are better able than rejected children to achieve their personal goals in social interaction in socially acceptable ways. They are generally more friendly, cooperative, and altruistic than their rejected counterparts.

There is no one set of characteristics that is associated with peer rejection. Some rejected children are unable either to take into account others' perspectives or to plan the solution of interpersonal dilemmas by taking into account the consequences of their actions for themselves and their social "targets." As a result, these children deal with their interpersonal problems by striking out against their social worlds; that is, they are aggressive. Needless to say, in studies concerned with the causes of rejection, the relatively frequent display of aggressive behavior is a well-worn route to isolation by the peer group. [*See* AGGRESSION.]

Other rejected children do not have difficulty thinking about the perspectives of others or about the most optimal solutions to interpersonal dilemmas. Rather, they appear to be anxious and wary of others, and as a result, they avoid interacting with their peers. By the mid-years of childhood, such passively withdrawn children gain negative reputations amongst their peers.

Interestingly, the relation between social competence and popularity appears to hold universally across cultures. The same may be said for the relations between aggression and peer rejection. However, in some cultures (e.g., Asia) wary or careful behavior in the peer group is encouraged by peers and parents; consequently, in these cultures, what is generally referred to in Western cultures as "passive-withdrawal" is associated with peer acceptance and not with rejection.

The distinction between aggressive-rejected and withdrawn-rejected children is important because it appears that these two groups carry with them different types of psychological problems—problems that appear to be associated with different "outcomes" or consequences for them during adolescence. For example, aggressive-rejected children do not think poorly of their social relationships; nor do they express feelings of loneliness or social anxiety. This may be explained by the findings that rejected-aggressive children do not report difficulties with the self-system. Although this group is generally disliked by classmates, rejected-aggressive children do tend to affiliate with others like them. Thus, the social support available to them, albeit from a deviant subgroup, may buffer them from developing negative self-perceptions and loneliness. On the other hand, withdrawn or socially anxious children who are rejected *do* think poorly of their own social prowess and of their social relationships; they are also more likely than aggressive-rejected children to acknowledge feeling lonely or depressed.

1. Summary

In this section we have described the characteristics of popular and rejected children. In general, only the rejected children appear to have substantive problems. They are unskilled socially and social-cognitively, and they think poorly of themselves and of their social relationships and skills. Rejected-*aggressive* children can best be characterized as behaviorally hostile and as having a limited social-cognitive repertoire insofar as their dealing with interpersonal problems is concerned. Rejected-*withdrawn* children can best be characterized as behaviorally submissive and as thinking and feeling poorly about themselves. Given these characterizations, it seems worthwhile asking whether peer rejection in childhood can predict negative psychological "outcomes" in adolescence or adulthood. We address this issue in the following section.

B. Outcomes of Peer Relationship Difficulties

Longitudinal research in which peer acceptance in childhood has been associated with adolescent or adult "outcomes" is only now beginning to emerge. The growing literature suggests that children who have difficulties in their peer relationships are "at risk" for having academic difficulties and dropping out of high school. The predictive connection between experiencing poor peer relationships in elementary school and academic difficulties later on makes a good deal of intuitive sense. Academia must assuredly lose its luster when many of a child's peers demonstrate and target their negative feelings toward her or him. This is likely to be the case, not only for the child who was doing poorly in school to begin with, but also for the intellectually competent child. Withdrawing via truancy or by dropping out may serve as the escape route for children who are consistently the target of peer rejection.

Rejected-aggressive children appear to be at further risk for engaging in delinquent and criminal activity. In a recent 7-year longitudinal study, it was reported that children identified as sociometrically rejected were twice as likely to be delinquent (35%) in adolescence than was the case for the sample base rate (17%).

Finally, researchers have yet to examine whether anxious withdrawn-rejected children are at risk for developing difficulties in adolescence and adulthood. On the basis of the concurrent correlational data described above, it is generally believed that these children will have particular problems concerning loneliness, social detachment, and depression.

Although the quality of children's peer relationships predicts later adolescent outcomes, it would be premature to suggest that either peer acceptance or rejection is the major "cause" of these consequences. In fact, it would appear as if the proximal "causes" of rejection (aggression; withdrawal) are better predictors of subsequent difficulty than the quality of the child's reputation in the peer group. For example, childhood aggression is the strongest predictor, by far, of adolescent crime and delinquency. Aggression in childhood also predicts academic failure and school drop-out. As well, childhood aggression is an antecedent of adult psychiatric problems, especially those of an externalizing nature (e.g., delinquency).

It has also been reported recently that passive withdrawal, at ages 5 and 7 years, predicts self-reported feelings of depression, loneliness, and negative self-worth, and teacher ratings of anxiety at age 11. In turn, social withdrawal at 11 years predicts *self-reports* of loneliness, depression, negative self-evaluations of social competence, feelings of not belonging to a peer group that could be counted on for social support, and *parental* assessments of internalizing problems (e.g., loneliness, depression) at 14 years.

In summary, children who have difficulty in their peer relationships appear to experience negative life-course outcomes. Although it remains unclear as to whether rejection actually "causes" later difficulty, it would appear safe to conclude that rejection must assuredly interact in a meaningful way with its own putative causes to determine negative life-course outcomes. One question that remains, however, is what it is that may lead a child to display those behaviors, or to think those thoughts, that lead ultimately to peer acceptance or rejection.

V. ORIGINS OF CHILDREN'S PEER RELATIONSHIPS

Given the contemporaneous and long-term significance of children's peer relationships, it seems reasonable to ask questions about their origins. Surprisingly, relatively little is known about this topic. The quality of children's peer relationships is probably multi-determined. For example, biological factors (e.g., temperament) may influence the quality of children's peer relationships; so too may the quality of parent–child relationships and parents' socialization practices.

A. Temperament and Peer Relationships

Despite the lack of research relating dispositional factors and children's peer relationships, it is not difficult to imagine how such factors may be influential. For example, *difficult* and *active* temperament in infancy and toddlerhood are associated predictively with developmental problems of undercontrol in early childhood (e.g., aggression); in turn, as we noted above, undercontrolled, impulsive, and aggressive behavior is characteristic and predictive of peer rejection. Similarly, infant inhibition predicts social withdrawal in early and middle childhood. Taken together, infant temperament may set the stage for the development of social behavioral profiles that ultimately predict the quality of children's peer relationships. [*See* INDIVIDUAL DIFFERENCES IN TEMPERAMENT.]

B. Parenting and Peer Relationships

Individual traits or dispositions do not develop *in vacuo;* children usually grow up living with their parents and one or more siblings. Moreover, their families bring with them societal and cultural expectations and values, and stressors and supports that must assuredly influence children's social repertoires. Thus, it should not be surprising to learn that researchers have investigated the relations between family factors and the quality of children's extrafamilial relationships. [*See* PARENTING.]

One relevant research stream focuses on the relations between the quality of parent–child and peer relations. Researchers have found a reliable association between the quality of the parent–infant relationship and (a) the child's subsequent demonstration of social skills in the peer group; and (b) the child's acceptance by peers. An insecure parent–infant relationship, however, predicts the production of incompetent social behavior and peer rejection in early and middle childhood.

A second research stream centers on the relations between parenting practices and children's peer relationships. For example, researchers have found that mothers of popular children are less demanding, less disagreeable, more feelings-oriented, and more likely to positively address their children when communicating, than mothers of less popular children.

Parental use of reasoning and explanations has also been associated positively with popularity.

In summary, there is, surprisingly, little research addressed to relations among parent–child relationships, parental behavior, and the quality of children's peer relationships. This is clearly an area in need of further study. There is a larger body of research concerning the relations between parenting behaviors and childhood *aggression*. Generally, it is found that physically punitive parents, and parents who are both critical and disapproving of their children, while also demonstrating too much permissiveness, have children who are aggressive in the peer group. In addition, it has been suggested that parental overcontrol, as evidenced in authoritarian patterns of socialization, is associated with social withdrawal in the peer group. Given that both aggression and withdrawal are predictive of peer rejection, these latter data appear especially relevent.

VI. CONCLUSION

In this article, we have reviewed literature concerning children's peer relationships. We have argued that peer group and friendship relationships play significant roles in social, emotional, and cognitive development. We also provided a description of the correlates and putative causes of peer acceptance and rejection. Thus, it is known that sociable and socially skilled behaviors lead to and maintain popularity among peers. From the earliest years of childhood, aggression is found to "cause" and maintain peer rejection. When passive, submissive, and withdrawn behavior becomes salient to the peer group (at around 7–8 years), it too becomes strongly associated with peer rejection. Interestingly, childhood aggression is found to forecast problems of an externalizing nature in adolescence (e.g., delinquency); recent longitudinal research suggests that withdrawal is predictive of internalizing problems in adolescence (e.g., loneliness, depression).

What we know about the correlates, causes, and outcomes of peer acceptance and rejection, however, is constrained by the cultures in which we study these phenomena. By far, the vast majority of the published literature concerned with peer relationships is derived from studies conducted in North America and Western Europe. There is virtually no consensus about the definition of social competence or incompetence in Western cultures, let alone in other cultures. We also do not know very much about the significance of peer acceptance, rejection, and friendship in non-Western cultures. Thus, one clear research agendum for the future should be the examination of the significance of peer relationships, their correlates, and their causes in cultures around the world.

Bibliography

Asher, S. R., and Coie, J. D. (1990). "Peer Rejection in Childhood." Cambridge University Press, Cambridge.

Hartup, W. W. (1992). Peer relations in early and middle childhood. In "Handbook of Social Development: A Lifespan Perspective." (V. B. van Hasselt and M. Hersen, Eds.), Plenum, New York.

Parker, J. G., and Asher, S. R. (1987). Peer relations and later personal adjustment: Are low-accepted children at risk? *Psychol. Bull.* **102,** 357–389.

Pepler, D. J., and Rubin, K. H. (1991). "The Development and Treatment of Childhood Aggression." Erlbaum, Hillsdale, NJ.

Rubin, K. H., and Asendorpf, J. (1993). "Social Withdrawal, Inhibition, and Shyness in Childhood." Erlbaum, Hillsdale, NJ.

Schneider, B., Atilli, G., Nadel, J., and Weissberg, R. (1989). "Social Competence in Developmental Perspective." Kluwer, Dordrecht, Netherlands.

Selman, R. L., and Schultz, L. H. (1990). "Making a Friend in Youth: Developmental Theory and Pair Therapy." University of Chicago Press, Chicago.

PERCEPTUAL DEVELOPMENT

Laura A. Thompson
New Mexico State University

Dominic W. Massaro
University of California at Santa Cruz

Glossary

Differentiation The active search for features of the environment that remain stable in a constantly changing world.

Distal stimulation Information about objects and events in the world which is incompletely specified by proximal stimulation.

Habituation The gradual waning of a response through repetitive stimulation. Dishabituation is a return to the original level of attentive responding.

Proximal stimulation The stimulation as it impinges on sensory receptors (e.g., the image produced in the visual system by a pattern of light).

HUMAN PERCEPTION involves the active pickup and coordination of sensory information via sensory channels such as vision, hearing, and touch, in order to understand, act on, and react to the world around us. Perceptual abilities are present even before birth and show rapid development during early infancy. More gradual improvements in perceptual understanding occur during childhood. Recent research findings on infant perceptual abilities are abundant and have broad implications for the nativist/empiricist debate. In the present article, selected research findings are set in the context of different approaches to the question of "What develops?" in perception.

I. THEORETICAL APPROACHES AND LEVELS OF ANALYSIS

A. Theoretical Approaches

1. Ecological Perception Approach

In the field of perceptual development, data are gathered and findings are interpreted within a particular theoretical perspective. Researchers are often forced to adopt a perspective before beginning their studies, because the selection of both stimuli and methodologies depends on which theoretical perspective is adopted. One of the reasons perceptual development is so interesting then, is that, lying beneath the surface of any "wow!-look-what-that-tiny-baby-can-do" finding is at least one controversial topic concerning the origin and nature of human thought. In current research, this tension is perhaps most apparent between those studying infant perception using the psychophysical approach, and those using the ecological approach. [*See* ECOLOGICAL PSYCHOLOGY.]

To the ecological perceptionist, the newborn infant's natural environment offers her plenty of opportunities for active, exploratory perception of complex stimuli which are important for her survival and for her normal development as a human being. There is an assumed richness of structure to the infant's perceptual world, a structure that is either inborn or discovered when there is a purpose to this discovery. Most important to the infant's survival are human beings, who, in their caregiving activities, present stimulation in many perceptual dimensions simultaneously, by cuddling infants close, communicating with their voices and facial expressions, and giving them tasty nourishment. Human voices, faces, and movements are examples of especially meaningful patterns of perceptually complex configurational information. Research has shown that newborns seek out and favor these patterns over patterns which are not inherently human-like.

One of the more controversial aspects of the ecological approach regards the level of perceptual representation which is innately given and accessible to infants. J. J. Gibson's premise was that people perceive information about objects and events (distal stimulation) directly, without accessing the stimulation initially given to the cortex from the receptor systems (proximal stimulation). Thus, *affordances,* or meanings of objects and events, are not constructed out of the more sensory elements of experience. The relevant question developmentalists must ask is, how does the distal perceptual experience of objects and events develop? How do infants learn to differentiate those relations among stimulus features that remain stable across many different situations from those that are not constant? Alternatively, perception can be construed as a matter of activating internal objects and events that are innately determined through adaptive change in human evolution.

2. Psychophysical Approach

The psychophysicist's approach to understanding perceptual development is to begin by precisely measuring and manipulating the primitive elements composing objects and events, such as the wavelength or the intensity of sounds or light. Often, stimulation is presented to the infant in a manner that is highly artificial and unlike the version of stimulation presented by the real world. However, some researchers adopt this reductionist approach because of its potential for uncovering more parsimonious explanations for behavior. The psychophysical approach sometimes identifies simple stimulus variables contained within more complex stimuli which alone can be used by the infant perceptual system. With a focus on the minimal stimulation required for detection, localization, discrimination, or identification, much is revealed about the infant's impressive perceptual abilities under optimal circumstances. [*See* PSYCHOPHYSICS.]

3. Piagetian Approach

Jean Piaget's contributions to the field of perceptual development bear some resemblance to his influential theory of cognitive development. To Piaget, the young infant perceived fleeting images that did not extend across time and space. He claimed that there were many characteristics of infant and toddler intelligence that prevented them from perceiving the world as adults know it. First, he thought that the ability to represent (hold an image in the mind when an object is not present) did not emerge until late in the second year of life. Second, infants could only perceive these passive perceptions as they related

to their perspective, that is, egocentrically. Third, perceptions and actions were independent processes, and gradually became coordinated. He also believed that vision, hearing, and touch began as independent perceptual experiences. After taking a long time to construct representations based on single modalities, Piaget thought that infants must learn to reconstruct their world to unify their previously separate perceptual experiences. And fourth, Piaget believed that perception was dependent on the cognitive abilities available to the child. For example, when a child matured enough to make perceptual comparisons by attending first to one stimulus dimension, and then another, perceptions could be "corrected" to be more like the adult form. Only gradually would children learn about object constancies, or be free of the deceptive influence of certain stimulus dimensions responsible for some visual illusions. [*See* COGNITIVE DEVELOPMENT.]

4. Information Processing Approach

The human anatomy that accomplishes perception is composed of living biological materials. The flow of information from the receptor surfaces through the nervous system is electrochemical, its structural and functional characteristics a culmination of tens of thousands of years of our species' biological adaptation to the ever-changing characteristics of the world. On the other hand, computer circuitry and the conductance of information from input to output or storage is electrical, not biological and not chemical. Yet, the analogy of the human as a computer-like system forms a productive approach to understanding perception and its development. Human perception is assumed to begin with the activity of taking in physical energy from the environment and subsequently translating the internalized input into an abstract code, that is, into objects and events we experience. People are like computers in that they are both fast symbol manipulation systems capable of operating at many levels in parallel.

Central to this approach is the distinction between information and information processing. *Information* is the code that is stored in long-term memory and it is also the code being accessed "on-line," that is prior to, and at the moment of, perceptual experience. Developmental change can occur in the representational code itself, due to neuroanatomical maturation, and also as a consequence of learning. *Information processing* is a descriptive analysis of what happens to the information as it flows through the perceptual and cognitive system. Developmental change can occur along several dimensions of information processing. One ubiquitous change involves the speed of information flow. As children mature, their faster information transmission rates allow for faster detection and recognition. Second, as children mature, they acquire knowledge. A third processing factor is apparent in developmental change in the efficiency of the selective attention mechanisms. Fourth, change occurs in the way information is segmented during perception. This factor is best understood using the example of learning to segment the stream of sounds in a second language. At first, the speech seems a continuous stream of unfamiliar sounds, and only after much intensive struggle are we able to parse the stream into meaningful words and phrases. Fifth, during the earliest moments of on-line processing, codes are transformed and integrated. These integration processes can undergo developmental change. Finally, there is developmental change in the strategies that are available to the child in directing attention to information that will ultimately result in veridical perceptual representations.

B. Multiple Levels of Analysis

1. Computational Theory Level

In 1982, David Marr outlined three levels of scientific understanding of information processing systems. At the highest level, the level of computational theory, scientific inquiry is focused on the problems needed to be solved by perceptual systems. Questions can be phrased in terms of needs, goals, and tasks. What does a person need to perceive to survive and, by surviving, what genetic codes and their behavioral manifestations are passed on to the next generation? What immediate goals is the individual attempting to fulfill by performing mental transformations on representations? How can information and information processing be better understood by looking at the physical laws of nature constraining the structural characteristics and behavior of objects and events humans perceive? The ecological perceptionist approach is aimed at undestanding perception at this level.

2. Representation and Algorithm Level

Marr recognized that the information-processing approach derives an understanding of perception at the level of representation and algorithm. The main questions asked about perception are, as Marr states, "How can this computational theory be im-

plemented? In particular, what is the representation for the input and output, and what is the algorithm for the transformation?" Many different types of representations and many different algorithms often tie for first place in the competition for the best theoretical explanation. Some theoreticians argue that there is as yet no justifiable method for determining the most accurate description of representations nor the algorithms relating sensory inputs to more abstract representational codes. The ecological perceptionist approach to studying infant perceptual development, with its nonconstructivist claims, seems to deny this level. However, the more gradual changes occurring through perceptual learning beyond infancy are viewed within the representational and algorithmic level of inquiry.

3. Hardware Implementation Level

In human vision, the eye, retinal ganglion cells, lateral geniculate neurons, and the neurons in the occipital lobe of the cortex together constitute most of the hardware of the visual system. Scientific inquiry at this level is focused on understanding their physiological and anatomical features. Development at this level can be shown to influence perception in infancy. However, as Marr warns us, ". . . trying to understand perception by studying only neurons is like trying to understand bird flight by studying only feathers: It just cannot be done. In order to understand bird flight, we have to understand aerodynamics; only then do the structure of features and the different shapes of birds' wings make sense." Thus, the most complete understanding of perceptual developmental change and stability is attained through consideration of factors affecting human information-processing systems at all three levels of scientific inquiry.

II. DOMAINS OF PERCEPTUAL PROCESSING IN INFANCY

A. Visual Perception

1. Perceptual Guidance System

Imagine for a moment that you had survived a horrible accident, yet were left completely paralyzed. Your legs could no longer transport you, your arms could no longer reach, your hands could no longer hold, your neck could no longer change your visual or auditory perspective. Without the ability to move, you would have minimal control over the stimulation available to your perceptual system. You would still have attentional control in that you could choose to "tune in" and out as you desire, but you would be at the mercy of the environment in offering you continual perceptual stimulation. This example illustrates the importance of action in perception. There is a dynamic interplay between perception and action such that they are entirely dependent on each other. For instance, muscle and joint movements are controlled by optical flow patterns interpreted by our perceptual systems which, in turn, guide action. Growth and development of the human system for action thus greatly affects our perceptual experiences.

Bennett Bertenthal recently proposed that infants are born with two distinct perceptual systems; one functions as a self-guidance system, the other functions to acquire and represent information about objects and events. To use shorthand, they can be referred to as the "where" and the "what" systems, respectively. Bertenthal claims that the two systems can be distinguished by their different courses of maturation and development. The what and where systems are also distinguishable by three processing differences. First, unlike the what system, the where system does not access fixed representational codes for objects. It does not need to look backward, because its purpose is to control bodily movements in the here-and-now, and to gather information so that movements can be planned ahead. Second, codes are accessed in both systems; however, the nature of the representational code is different. The what system uses representations that have been stored in a rather permanent, immutable form. Conversely, the where system uses representations that are continuously altered during the process of self-guidance and control. The third difference relates to the role of awareness. The control of perceptually guided action can often be attained without any conscious awareness, such as when you run along a desert path unconsciously leaping over rocks and dodging thorny bushes because you have your mind on last night's movie. However, conscious attention to the details of objects and events is a necessary component of perception for later successful discrimination or recognition (e.g., "Was that a rattle on the end of that snake's tail?").

There is much research evidence supporting the existence of a rudimentary perceptual guidance system in newborn infants, a system that is at first dependent on reflexive movements for looking, turning the head, sucking, and grasping. As Piaget so

carefully demonstrated, these initially reflexive actions become more finely tuned, and the reflexes become coupled with greater accuracy and intentionality as the infant matures. However, Piaget's claim that perception and action are independent and uncoordinated in infancy does not appear to be correct. At birth, for example, infants orient in the general direction of a sound. Newborns track moving objects and even attempt to reach for objects that are moving slowly. Undeniably, the perceptual guidance system undergoes considerable tuning in the early months of life. Tracking is performed with greater ease as infants learn to stabilize the head. Between 8 and 24 weeks of age, there is dramatic improvement in the ability to detect the direction that a sound is coming from, and to orient to the sound source. Within their first 6 months, they will be engaging their adult caregivers in "conversation" by taking turns in a babbling, cooing, "do-se-do," a perceptually guided language game with two players who want to have fun.

The link between visual perception and action in infancy is clearly demonstrated using an apparatus called the "moving room." An infant sits on the nonmoving floor of the apparatus while the walls and ceiling move in a way that the visual information would appear to move if he were actually falling. Many studies have shown that infants make compensatory postural movements of the head and trunk in response to this simulated visual flow information.

Development of locomotor ability affects the frame of reference used by infants in coding the locations of objects. Prior to crawling, an infant uses a spatial frame of reference which is centered on his own body. That is, the positions of objects are marked in relationship to where he is lying or sitting. While this method of spatial referencing may be adequate for the prelocomotor infant whose relevant world is contained within his nearby radius, he learns that it is not a reliable method once he is able to change his position in the environment on his own. For mobile infants, a nonegocentric (landmark) method of coding ensures that he can find the locations of objects when the spatial relationship between himself and the object have changed positions since he first encoded its location. Bertenthal tested two groups of infants who were of the same age, but some could crawl and some had not yet begun to crawl. An object was placed under one of two containers on a table, located on either the infant's right or left side. Then, the infant was moved 180°, to the opposite side of the table. They found that infants who had learned to crawl were much more likely to search for the object under the correct container than noncrawling infants. [*See* MOTOR DEVELOPMENT.]

Research has shown that infant action can also be directed by proprioceptive information, since glowing and sounding objects are successfully touched in the dark. Blind babies have been found to use echolocation in navigating around a room. Thus, vision is not the only perceptual modality that infants can use in guiding their actions. However, in the sunlit environment where we usually find ourselves, our visual system is the most dependable source of information for getting us to where we are going. An infant does not see the world exactly as we see it, but her perceptual exploratory system is matched to the demands of her environment. [*See* VISUAL PERCEPTION.]

2. Visual Object Recognition

Research conducted in the last two decades has revealed a number of immaturities in the newborn infant oculomotor system that together conspire to make it difficult for them to fixate on objects. Pupil dilation, the adjustment power of the lens, and muscular coordination of the eyes when fixating on objects at different distances all improve within the first few months after birth. Using sophisticated methods of testing, such as the corneal reflection method, three types of eye movements have been documented in infants by the age of 2 months: (a) infants make saccadic eyemovements toward a stationary target, but they usually undershoot it, (b) infants track a slowly moving object but they have difficulty keeping up with it, and (c) infants sometimes show an ability to make stabilizing eye movements, that is, they alternately use smooth and rapid eye movements when looking at something that interests them. Three additional maturational changes occur in the neuroanatomical system for vision. Retinal cells migrate along the receptor surface, potentially altering the mapping of spatial codes represented by the brain. The cone photopigments in the retina responsible for perceiving short (blue) wavelengths of light may not be fully developed until 3 months (although the other two photopigments are present at birth). Finally, as neuronal axons develop myelin sheaths during infancy, the speed of neural transmission becomes markedly faster. Thus, newborns develop rapidly at the level of hardware implementation.

Newborn infants cannot name the letters on the eyechart, but if they could, their acuity of between 20/200 and 20/600 would indicate the need for very thick lenses. In the first half year of life there is a substantial increase in spatial resolution, measured by the infant's ability to detect smaller and smaller black and white rings in a bullseye pattern. At birth, their contrast sensitivity, the ability to detect differences in brightness intensity between adjacent black and white rings, is approximately 1/10th of that measured in adults. These findings imply that great amounts of contrast in visual patterns are needed for the visual information to reach "decision centers" in the visual cortex. It is not coincidental that the types of patterns newborns fixate on are patterns with angles, edges, and high contrast.

The "externality effect" is an interesting and robust finding in newborn infants. Infants are shown a simple pattern, such as an outline of a square with a smaller square inside it. They are shown the pattern long enough to become habituated to it, in other words, to get bored with it. Habituation is indicated when, for example, sucking slows down to a slow and steady rate. When the inside square of the pattern is changed, 1-month-old infants do not dishabituate to the pattern unless the pattern moves. Four-month-old infants do notice a change in the internal elements of the pattern, even when the pattern is stationary. The newborn infant's predisposition to focus on high contrast areas of a two-dimensional picture, combined with the finding that he does not notice internal elements of a display unless the elements move, can help to explain why he seems to focus on the hairline of his caregiver's face and does not seem to make eye contact until the person holding him speaks.

Human faces have a special place in the visual world of an infant. At birth, infants will track moving schematic illustrations of faces further than faces with the same features in mixed-up positions (nose where the mouth should be, etc.). At 3 months, they show a preference for looking at nonmoving face patterns over "scrambled" face patterns. At this age, they can discriminate familiar faces from faces they have never seen before. Three months later, they are capable of recognizing faces from a different angle of orientation than their initial view of the picture. Also at 6 months, infants can classify photos by gender, and they even look longer at photos of faces that have been rated as attractive by adults, compared to unattractive faces. Across their first half year of life, increasingly realistic presentations of facial stimuli are required to capture and maintain their attention. [*See* FACE RECOGNITION.]

The environment of humans is a constantly changing one. As the sun rises and sets, the intensity of light reaching the eye changes. As people and objects move around us and as we move around them, their retinal images change size and shape. Yet, adults translate these varying forms of proximal stimulation into stable distal perceptions. This stable perception is called *constancy*. Do young infants have color, shape, and size constancy? There is some evidence that shape constancy exists in newborn infants. After habituating to a square, for example, 6-day-old infants dishabituate to a trapezoid, but not to a square that is rotated 90° from its original orientation along the frontal plane. Shape constancy does not hold for objects rotated in depth, however. Color and size constancy do not emerge until approximately 4 months of age. In one experimental test of size constancy, infants first habituated to a large mannequin head positioned 60 cm from their eyes. Then, they were tested in two different conditions to see if they would dishabituate. In one condition, the same large mannequin head was shown 30 cm from their eyes, which would produce a much larger retinal image (and would appear to an adult as the same object now closer). In the other condition, a smaller version of the mannequin was presented at the distance of 30 cm, so that the retinal image was the same as the mannequin at the 60 cm distance. Infants dishabituated to the smaller of the two mannequins, but not to the original mannequin brought closer, which shows that they have size constancy.

Information about depth is available from three sources, and is used by the infant at different points in her development. One source is kinetic information. Kinetic depth cues exist because velocities of objects change as they change location in depth and as the body changes location in space. Kinetic depth cues are used by 3-month-old infants. Infants will make eyeblink and startle responses when objects in space appear to loom toward them. Interestingly, they do not make these avoidance responses for the reversed form of this kinetic information, called "zooming" stimuli. A second source, available about 1 month later, is retinal disparity. Objects that are close to us create two separate retinal projections that are fused into a single, three-dimensional representation of the world. Infants adjust their reach to grab for the nearer of two objects when they are able to use both eyes. Binocular cues to depth are not always needed for depth perception, however. Six-month-old infants will avoid the deep side of a "visual cliff" when they are wearing an eye patch over one eye. In this case, infants use a third source, pictorial depth cues. Pictorial depth cues are the cues that artists use to create the impression of depth on a two-dimensional surface. They include texture gradients (objects far away have finer-grained textures than nearer objects), interposition (objects farther away are occluded by nearer objects), linear perspective (painting a trapezoid shape "up" the canvas to give the impression of a road projecting into depth), and shading. By the age of about 6 months, she can use all three sources of depth cues to help prevent her from falling off the bed, down the stairway, or even into the Grand Canyon. [*See* Depth Perception.]

Pictorial cues also provide information about the boundaries of objects; however, these cues would not be very useful to us if we had never learned to associate them with objects. Picture a small baby who is looking at the trunk of a tree. On the tree trunk is a very still moth. We know that moths have wings, they tend to be flat and their coloring usually camouflages them against the tree trunk. If an adult looked at the exact location on the tree, he might spot the moth but the baby would not, that is, not until the moth flies away. The 5-month-old infant knows that gaps between surfaces usually imply that those surfaces form the boundaries of different objects. If the surfaces of two objects touch, however, even if they are composed of very different colors and textures, they will perceive the two objects as one. Clever experiments have shown that young infants will reach for the closer of two objects if they are separated by a gap, although if the surfaces are touching, they reach for the further surface if it looks more "graspable."

Common motion of object surfaces is a dependable cue that parts belong to a whole, even if segments of the whole are occluded by the surfaces of other objects. Elizabeth Spelke and her colleagues tested 4-month-old infants in an experiment where they were shown a rod directly behind a rectangular block, the rod's surfaces protruding above and below it. When the rod parts touched the block and when they moved in the same direction and rate with each other and with the block, infants handled the rod and block as if they were one object. When the upper and lower parts of the rod moved in synchrony but the block remained stationary, they behaved as though the rod and block were distinct, by reaching for only one of them. When the upper and lower parts of the rod moved in different directions, they treated them as separate objects. A recent and related experiment showed that 3-month-old infants looked longer at a conically shaped object whose top half broke apart from the bottom and rose into the air, compared to when the entire object rose. [*See* VISUAL MOTION PERCEPTION.]

These findings and many similar ones led Spelke to the conclusion that young infants' perceptions of objects are guided by two processing constraints. The principle of cohesion is an understanding that *surfaces lie on a single object if and only if they are connected.* The principle of contact also helps them identify objects because they understand that *surfaces move together if and only if they are in contact.* A new area of research involves an attempt to determine if the perception of object motion is guided by a set of constraints based on the laws of kinematic geometry. The physical laws of nature governing object motion have not changed across human evolution; therefore, the visual system *may* be setup such that, at birth, the infant does not have to learn to predict object motion.

People form a special class of objects in motion. An extensive series of studies performed by Bertenthal and a colleague, Jeannine Pinto, shows that infants discriminate human walking (biological) motion from nonbiological motion. Their method for testing is to present two types of visual displays of points of light to the infant. Figure 1 illustrates the two types of displays shown to infants. In the canonical condition, the motion of the lights corresponds to the way they would move if they were attached to a walking person's head and joints, such as the

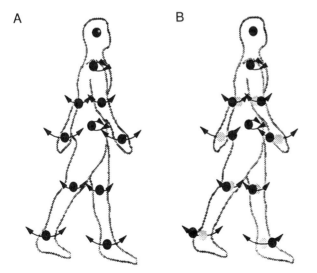

FIGURE 1 Point-light displays of a human walker in (A) canonical and (B) phase-shifted conditions (gray circles are canonical positions in phase-shifted displays).

knee and elbow. In a separate condition, the temporal patterning of the lights is phase-shifted so that the movement no longer could have been produced by a human walker. Three- and five-month old infants discriminate canonical from phase-shifted displays, and demonstrate a preference for the canonical displays. A salient difference between 3 and 5 month olds implicates the role of learning. Three month olds discriminate the two types of displays even if they are presented upside down, whereas 5 month olds do not. Perhaps in a period of 2 months, the older infants have learned to represent the abstract global structure of a human form in motion.

In sum, there are several processing constraints that infants use to guide their interpretation of higher-order perceptual structure. These constraints may be innate, but if not innate, they are acquired by the first half year of life. Object representations are formed through learning, and as such are defined with reference to the past.

B. Auditory Perception

At 25 weeks past conception, brain wave activity occurs in the human fetus in response to sounds. In the 28th week of fetal development, the fetus will clamp its eyelids tightly in response to a 110 dB sound. At birth, anatomical development of the ear is complete, and infants with normal hearing can detect sounds at most of the frequencies that adults are sensitive to. In fact, newborns are actually slightly more sensitive than adults in their detection of the higher range of frequencies given in human speech (speech extends between approximately 50 and 8000 Hz). Newborns' threshold for detection of a sound is only 10–20 dB higher than the adult detection threshold, which is about the amount of decrement we experience when we have a cold with fluid in our ears. Infants can respond to acoustic differences in loudness, pitch, duration, and timing at birth, and these abilities improve with age. For example, adults can discriminate pitch changes on the order of 1% whereas the 5- to 8-month-old infant requires 2% pitch change to notice a difference. Also present at birth is the ability to locate the general direction where a sound is coming from. However, the localization response disappears at approximately 3 months, emerging again at 4 to 5 months. This nonmonotonic developmental pattern implies the existence of an initial reflexive mechanism which later becomes an exploratory mechanism as subcortical activation becomes linked to cortical functioning in the fourth month of life. [*See* EARS AND HEARING.]

It is easy to overlook one very important environmental context for learning, yet some recent provocative studies suggest that speech-based learning begins at the source—in the womb. This possibility is apparent in the preferences infants show at birth, preferences that could only exist if the stimuli were familiar to the infant. Newborn infants will go to some trouble to listen to their mothers' voices. In one experiment, infants learned that their rate of sucking on a nipple activated a tape recorder. Infants "played" their mothers voice more often than a strange female's voice. Using French and Russian languages, newborns were found to prefer the prosodic components (stress, rhythm, timing) of the language spoken by their mothers compared to the nonnative language. Even more remarkably, newborn infants can distinguish between two different Dr. Seuss stories, a task that is challenging to some adults. Twice a day, mothers in their last trimester of pregnancy read passages from *The Cat in the Hat* to their babies. This prenatal exposure enabled the infants to extract from the passages an overall story melody, and it was on this basis that they discriminated the familiar from the unfamiliar story passage when they were just 2 days old.

Equipped with excellent auditory resolution and a capacity for learning specific sound patterns, infants are quickly assimilated into the language game. Each language has a unique set of speech segments that differ from one another in subtle ways. These differences allow the segments to be discriminated from one another. Infants are capable of distinguishing these distinctions from all languages at the age of 6 months. However, adults have trouble distinguishing segments of a new language that they are learning. One classic example is the difficulty that native Japanese speakers have with the segments /r/ and /l/. On the other hand, 6-month-old Japanese infants have no trouble making this discrimination. An early conclusion from this research was that learning a spoken language involved a *loss* in the ability to discriminate nonnative contrasts. However, additional research revealed that adults could discriminate nonnative contrasts to some extent, and that they were capable of learning the new contrasts to a high degree of accuracy. This research, carried out by Janet Werker, David Pisoni, and others, prompted investigators to think about other explanations for why perceivers better distinguish contrasts in their own language relative to other nonnative

languages. These new hypotheses included explanatory concepts such as attention, perceptual tuning, and cognitive mediation.

Although the exact mechanism cannot be specified at this time, it is clear that perceivers become tuned to the important distinctions of their language. One way to think about this is in terms of the psychophysical approach. The infant's auditory system (and visual system) makes available a set of primitive sound qualities during language processing. These qualities necessarily become associated with different meanings. With extensive experience, the infant learns which sensory qualities are important in signifying specific meanings. Given that meaning is where the action is in the language game, the child learns to attend to those qualities that are significant in his or her language. This process can be interpreted within the ecological approach by the infant learning to differentiate those sensory properties and their relationships that are consistently associated with meaningful distinctions. As monolinguals, we learn the distinctions unique to our language. Confronted with another language, we must learn anew the distinctions important in that language because they will necessarily differ from our native language. Insights into the exact nature of learning to perceive speech will be facilitated by the information-processing approach because it can specify the memory representations and psychological processes that occur.

C. Intermodal Perception

Distinct physical forms of energy are efficiently used by the separate sensory systems; likewise, the brain has separate areas for processing and storing the information made available by the separate modalities. However, the "divide and conquer" design does not capture the essence of most human perceptual experience. Fortunately, nature, in its infinite wisdom, endowed infants with a way to put back together what the sensory modalities take apart.

The capacity for intermodal representation in infancy was long debated by developmental psychologists, including Piaget, who believed in the gradual coordination of separate modality-independent perceptions. However, in the last two decades, the results of many informative studies reveal that Piaget's interpretation was an underestimation of infant perceptual abilities. In one study, 1-month-old infants suckled on a pacifier with either a nubby or a smooth surface. Shortly after this tactile exploration period, they were shown pictures of the two pacifiers. Infants looked longer at the pacifier that they had suckled, showing that they could match object properties specified visually and tactually. Four-month-old infants will look longer at a video image of an event that looks like it should be making the noise they are hearing. In one experiment, they were presented two different films, side-by-side, on screens in front of them. The sound source was directly in the middle of the two screens. A kangaroo on puppet strings jumped into the air and hit the ground on one side, and a donkey did the same on the other, but the two animals moved at different rates. The sound (a thump or a gong) was synchronous with the impact of one of the animals. Infants looked longer at the video image that matched the tempo of the sound that was playing through the central speaker. Further experimentation revealed this preference even when the sound occurred in synchrony with the moment that the animal reached its highest point and began to fall. Thus, any abrupt change in the direction of the object's movement was sufficient for the infant to connect sight and sound.

Infants also coordinate sights and sounds when the objects to be coordinated between modalities are faces and voices. Infants prefer to look at a picture of a female over a picture of a male when a female voice is playing, and vice versa. If they hear one of their own parent's voices, but look at snapshots of both parents simultaneously, they look longer at the face whose voice it is they are hearing. They also detect the correspondence between the visual and auditory modes of conveying emotion at least by the age of 6 months. Adult strangers appeared on side-by-side films talking in either a "happy" or an "angry" manner. The sound track, coming as before through a centrally located speaker, was from only one of the films. By now, it is easy to predict the findings: Infants looked for longer periods of time at the film consistent with the emotive content of the monologue they were hearing.

The previous experiments are convincing in their demonstration of a general intermodal perceptual ability in infancy, but they do not inform as to how finely tuned the ability is. Patricia Kuhl and Andrew Meltzoff have conducted an extensive series of studies on 4- and 5-month-old infants, which clearly show that infants detect auditory and visual correspondences in speech. In their experiments, infants sat in a seat facing two screens. A speaker presented speech sounds directly in front of them and between the two screens. An infrared camera filmed them from above. The film showed an adult repeatedly making the vowel sounds /i/ (as in *peep*), or /a/ (as in *pop*). Infants looked longer at the matching visual speech display. The experiment was carefully controlled so that there could not have been temporal characteristics in the sound stimuli that were associated with the phonemic contrasts. In this study, infants were engaging in *lip-reading*. They recognized that /i/ sounds are made with retracted lips and that /a/ sounds come from open mouths. Kuhl and Meltzoff discovered another important aspect of the intermodal organization of speech, specifically, the infant's capacity for vocal imitation. When infants heard pure tones that were vowel-like, but were not speech, they gurgled, squealed, and grunted. In contrast, when they heard /i/ and /a/, they produced speech sounds. Phonetically trained listeners found that infant productions matched the presentations of the different vowels. Relating speech sounds with the visual articulatory movements necessary to produce them is an early and impressive human language achievement. The infant's tendency to speak when spoken to will entice her caregiver to provide ample spoken language input, and will also help to maintain their communicative bond.

III. PERCEPTUAL DEVELOPMENT BEYOND INFANCY

Oddly enough, relative to the voluminous literature on infant perceptual development, there is comparatively little research in childhood populations above the age of 2. Certainly one factor that can account for this differential emphasis is theoretical focus. Those interested in the question of what perceptual capacities are innate simply must conduct their investigations with infant populations. However, as the remainder of the chapter will show, perceptual growth continues during childhood and across the lifespan.

One of the themes that has emerged in recent research is that children and adults use similar perceptual mechanisms, but they process information at different rates. One experiment of our own illustrates this point. We employed a visual search task which had previously been used to test a theory of attention in adult populations. The theory, proposed by Anne Triesman, states that recognition of objects during visual search is accomplished in two stages. In the first stage, primitive elements, or features, of objects are accessed in parallel across the visual field. In the second stage, features are fused using a "spotlight" of attention into the wholistic percepts that we are aware of seeing. The first stage is accomplished automatically, without demanding cognitive resources. When searching for a target that has a different feature from the rest of the objects in the visual field (feature search), the target "pops out" immediately, no matter how many objects are present. The second stage is resource-demanding, and is evident in a different pattern of data. Specifically, the amount of time it takes people to find targets should be a linearly increasing function with display size (conjunctive search). Figure 2 shows the search data for 5-year-old children and young adults. Since children in our experiment showed the pattern of results predicted by the theory, we concluded that children and adults used the same processes of object recognition during visual search. However, children were different from adults in that they conjoined features more slowly in the second stage of processing. Many studies comparing children and adults show that children become faster processors of information as they develop into adolescence.

We have also studied adult–child similarities and differences in pattern recognition processes used to understand the perception of speech by ear and by eye. The youngest age group we have tested was 4 years of age and the oldest group were individuals in their 70s. The fundamental processes involved in understanding visible speech (articulatory movements of the face and mouth) and auditory speech appear to be the same across age groups. That is, features of the auditory and visual stimuli are first evaluated, and then integrated in a process of matching the percept with a representation held in long-term memory. In a final stage of understanding, a decision is made as to the best category for the auditory–visual speech event, in comparison to all possible relevant alternative categories. However, there were significant differences in the informational value of auditory and visible speech as a function of age. The adults discriminated the auditory and speech categories better than children. Furthermore, children did not lip-read as well as adults. This factor can explain why the influence of visible speech in auditory–visual speech understanding was diminished in children compared to adults. Results from several of our own studies lead us to the conclusion that the prototype descriptions of the distinguishing characteristics of speech increase in resolution during childhood.

If there is one guiding principle that can be used to conceptualize perceptual development across the lifespan, it is differentiation. According to the ecological perceptionists, human perception is guided by a search for order and invariance in a highly fluctuating environment. It is a lifelong nonexistential search for meaning. Sometimes, our search ends almost instantaneously. For example, you might be searching for a face in a crowd and pass right over it, but when your friend next to you says, "Over

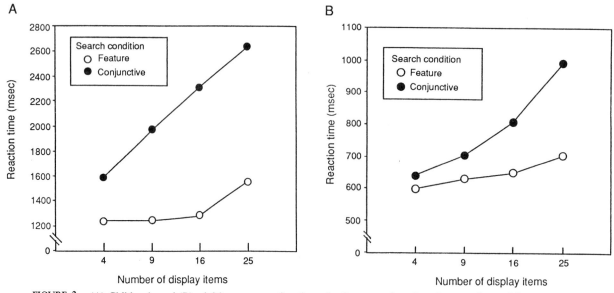

FIGURE 2   (A) Children's and (B) adult's mean reaction times for feature and conjunctive search conditions.

there, the one with the red glasses!'' the face pops out at you, and you can no longer see that mirage of faces without seeing the one you were looking for. Or, the search for meaning can be long and frustrating, like when you learn to understand the words of a new language. Research shows that young children have difficulty finding simple forms which are embedded in larger pictures, while older children easily find much more complicated forms within embedded figures. Thus, much of perceptual development can be described as a constant process of learning what to look or to listen for. During learning, representations are formed that aid us in subsequent similar perceptual experiences.

In summary, the equipment in our perceptual system is up and running at birth, and functions superbly by the age of 4 months. Perceptual development beyond infancy involves five basic phenomenon. First, representations are built at the level of sensory primitives and at the level where they are bundled into the ''wholes'' that define the objects and sounds we are aware of seeing and hearing. Second, these representations increase in resolution with experience. Third, although not specifically addressed in this article, the ability to selectively attend, to focus on the relevant and filter out the irrelevant, does improve with age. Fourth, children become generally faster at processing information, so that objects are detected and recognized with less time across development. And finally, with experience we accumulate knowledge, which is perhaps our best source for constructing meaning from the multiple and rich sensory experiences we actively seek from our world.

Bibliography

Aslin, R. N. (1987). Visual and auditory development in infancy. In ''Handbook of Infant Development'' (J. D. Osofsky, Ed.), pp. 5–97. Wiley, New York.

Aslin, R. N., and Smith, L. B. (1988). Perceptual development. *Ann. Rev. Psychol.* **39**, 435–473.

Gibson, E. (1987). Introductory essay: What does infant perception tell us about theories of perception? *J. Exp. Psychol. Hum. Perception Performance* **13**, 515–523.

Kellman, P. J. (1988). Theories of perception and research in perceptual development. In ''Perceptual Development in Infancy: The Minnesota Symposia on Child Psychology'' (A. Yonas, Ed.), Vol. 20, pp. 267–282.

Smith, L. B. (1989). A model of perceptual classification in children and adults. *Psychol. Rev.* **96**, 125–144.

Thompson, L. A., and Massaro, D. W. (1989). Before you see it, you see its parts: Evidence for feature encoding and integration in preschool children and adults. *Cog. Psychol.* **21**, 334–362.

Thompson, L. A., and Massaro, D. W. (1986). Evaluation and integration of speech and pointing gestures during referential understanding. *J. Exp. Child Psychol.* **42**, 144–168.

PERSONALITY ASSESSMENT

Paul T. Costa, Jr., and Robert R. McCrae
National Institutes of Health

Glossary

Five-factor model An organization of personality traits in terms of the broad factors of neuroticism versus emotional stability, extraversion, openness to experience, agreeableness, and conscientiousness.

Objective test An assessment device that can be scored clerically, without the need for clinical interpretation.

Projective technique A method of assessment in which responses to ambiguous stimuli (e.g., inkblots) are thought to reveal aspects of the respondent's personality.

Reliability The consistency with which an assessment instrument gives the same results.

Validity The accuracy with which an assessment instrument measures its intended construct.

THE TERM PERSONALITY is used by different theorists in widely different ways, and the practice of personality assessment is correspondingly varied. Nevertheless, most definitions of personality refer to features that characterize an individual and distinguish him or her from others, and most assessment procedures attempt to measure these features, usually in comparison to the average person. Different approaches to personality assessment differ in the variables they measure, in the source of information about the individual, and in the way information is evaluated. This article reviews the most common approaches to personality assessment (projective techniques, self-report questionnaires, observer ratings, and laboratory measures) and their status in contemporary psychological science and practice.

Personality variables are pervasive and enduring, and thus can be expected to have an impact on a variety of areas in the individual's life—for example, the prototypic extravert has a wide circle of friends, speaks out in class, does well in enterprising occupations, enjoys competitive sports, and has an optimistic outlook in life. In consequence, personality assessment is important in many applied areas. Psychiatrists who need to diagnose psychopathology, counselors who want to suggest meaningful vocational choices, and physicians concerned with behavioral health risk factors may all turn to personality assessment. Personality variables are important in forensic, developmental, educational, social, industrial, and clinical psychology, as well as personality psychology, the discipline which seeks a scientific understanding of personality itself. For all these purposes, accurate assessment of personality is crucial.

Personality is also of great importance to laypersons in everyday life and in such significant decisions as whom to vote for or marry. Lay evaluations of personality are in some respects unscientific and susceptible to many biases; in other respects they are extremely sophisticated interpretations of observed behavior. Much (though not all) of personality assessment consists of knowing how to systematize the information laypersons have about themselves and each other in order to capitalize on the strengths and reduce the limitations of lay perceptions of personality.

The scientific study of individual differences in personality can be traced to the work of Sir Francis Galton in the 1880s, and it has occupied many of the brightest minds in psychology since. During the 1950s and 1960s, personality assessment underwent a period of crisis, based in part on humanistic objections to the depersonalizing labeling that much assessment seemed to foster, and in part on real (although exaggerated) technical problems with assessment instruments. Considerable progress has been made in the past 30 years in both personality theory and test construction, and today personality assessment is once again assuming a central role in psychology.

I. ASSESSMENT METHODS AND INSTRUMENTS

A. Projective Techniques

The single most influential theory of personality is psychoanalysis, a complex system developed by Sigmund Freud and elaborated by a host of his followers. Briefly, psychoanalysis sees human personality as the result of conflict between the individual's sexual and aggressive impulses and society's demand for their control. In the course of early development, people evolve characteristic ways of resolving these conflicts which guide their adult behavior, particularly their interpersonal relationships. Because the underlying conflicts are psychologically painful and threatening, both the impulses and the defenses against them are repressed from consciousness. From this perspective, individuals never really know themselves and hide their most important features from those around them.

Thus, psychoanalytic theory poses formidable problems for personality assessment. The central information is not merely unavailable; it is systematically distorted. The analyst must make elaborate inferences on the basis of free associations, dreams, and slips of the tongue. But patients may not recall dreams or make revealing slips, and psychoanalysts need a dependable source of information that can be gathered as needed. Projective tests were designed to fill this need.

Rorschach's inkblots are a series of 10 cards shown to the patient or subject, who is asked to explain what he or she sees in them. The basic premise is that these abstract blots, having no meaning of their own, will act as a screen onto which the inner conflicts, impulses, and emotions of the patient will be projected. They will of course still be disguised—otherwise they would be censored by the patient's defenses—but they can be interpreted by the knowledgeable analyst just as an X-ray can be read by a skilled radiologist.

The projective technique is an ingenious approach to the problem of assessing unconscious conflicts, and the window it promises into the depths of the mind is extremely appealing. The Rorschach continues to be one of the most widely used instruments in personality assessment, and dozens of variations (including the Holtzman Inkblot Technique) and scoring systems have been developed.

It is therefore more than a little unfortunate that the scientific basis of these instruments—and of psychoanalysis itself—is highly questionable. Different interpreters draw very different conclusions from the same set of responses, and few rigorous studies have demonstrated that inkblot scores predict important external criteria. While clinical psychologists still rely heavily on the Rorschach, academic personality researchers have almost entirely abandoned it. A search of abstracts in the personality research field's most important publication, the *Journal of Personality and Social Psychology*, showed that of over 4000 articles appearing between 1974 and 1992, only four studies employed the Rorschach. (Rorschach studies do still appear regularly in more clinically oriented journals.)

All projective techniques use responses to relatively unstructured, ambiguous stimuli on the assumption that these will elicit spontaneous expressions of psychologically important features. This general approach to assessment is not limited to psychoanalytic theories of personality, but can also be applied to better supported theories about needs, motives, or traits. The Thematic Apperception Test, or TAT, shows a series of drawings about which individuals are asked to tell stories. The responses can be scored in a relatively straightforward fashion—for example, a story about overcoming obstacles in pursuit of a goal is scored as evidence of a need for achievement—and when so scored they typically show somewhat better evidence of scientific validity.

Note that these approaches do not assume that the characteristics they assess are repressed. When asked, people who tell stories about achievement or intimacy often report that they are high in achievement striving or nurturance. These projective tests apparently do not reveal a level of personality from which self-reports are excluded.

B. Objective Tests: Self-Reports

Projective tests are usually contrasted with *objective tests,* typically questionnaires in which subjects are asked to describe themselves by answering a series of questions. For example, a measure of conscientiousness may ask 10 questions such as ''Do you always keep your desk clean?'' and ''Are you devoted to your work?'' The test is considered objective because it can be scored directly, without the need for clinical interpretation: The number of conscientiousness items to which an individual responds *true* is that individual's score, and higher scores indicate higher levels of conscientiousness.

That basic paradigm—asking a standard set of questions and scoring responses with a predetermined key—has been used in thousands of assessment applications. Intelligence tests, vocational interest inventories, mood indicators, and measures of psychopathology as well as personality scales have adopted this model. Its scientific appeal lies in the fact that it can be repeated at different times and with different subjects, and consequently its accuracy can be evaluated. A whole branch of statistics, *psychometrics,* has been developed to analyze responses, both for what they tell us about the individual and for what they tell us about the quality of the test. Psychometric analyses provide information that can allow researchers to improve the quality of the test by changing the questions or the response format or the interpretation of the results.

If psychoanalysis formed the theoretical basis of projective tests, then trait psychology must be considered the basis of objective personality tests. Briefly, trait psychologies hold that individuals differ in a number of important ways that are usually thought to be continuously and normally distributed. Just as a few people are short, a few tall, and most average in height, so some people may be very agreeable, some very antagonistic, and most intermediate along this psychological dimension. Unlike moods, traits are enduring dispositions; and unlike specific habits, they are general and pervasive patterns of thoughts, feelings, and actions. Scores on trait measures should therefore be relatively constant, and scale items measuring different aspects of the trait should go together. These theoretical premises are the basis of the psychometric requirements of retest reliability and internal consistency in personality scales. [*See* TRAITS.]

Among the most important personality questionnaires in current use are the Minnesota Multiphasic Personality Inventory (MMPI), developed in the 1940s to measure aspects of psychopathology; the Sixteen Personality Factor Questionnaire and the Eysenck Personality Questionnaire, representing the personality theories of Raymond B. Cattell and Hans J. Eysenck, respectively; the Myers-Briggs Type Indicator, which is based on C. J. Jung's theory of psychological types; the California Psychological Inventory, a set of scales intended to tap folk concepts, the personality constructs used in everyday life; and the Personality Research Form, a psychometrically sophisticated measure of needs or motives. The NEO Personality Inventory is a more recent addition, based on new discoveries about the basic dimensions of personality. In addition to these omnibus inventories which all measure a variety of traits, there are a number of individual scales that are widely used in personality research, such as the self-monitoring scale and the locus of control scale.

C. Objective Tests: Observer Ratings

The vast majority of personality assessments are made on the basis of either projective tests or self-reports, but observer ratings provide a powerful alternative that is increasingly used in both research and clinical contexts. The clinical interview is a kind of observer rating, because the clinician not only asks questions, but also observes the reactions of the patient to the interview process. With a few exceptions (such as the Structured Interview for the Type A Behavior Pattern), these observations are not standardized, and thus they share with projective tests potential problems of unreliability.

There are, however, assessment methods that are both objective and observer based. These methods apply the same psychometric principles used in self-report questionnaires to ratings from informants. One simple and effective way to do this is by rephrasing questions in the third person. Instead of asking the individual, "Are you devoted to your work?" we could ask her spouse, "Is she devoted to her work?" One advantage of observer ratings is that we are not limited to a single respondent. It is possible to obtain ratings from friends, relatives, and neighbors, and there is evidence that aggregating or averaging several ratings yields better information on the individual.

Ranking methods provide an alternative to observer rating questionnaires. In these methods, all the members of a group rank each other on a series of characteristics. For example, all the members of a fraternity may be asked to decide which fraternity members are most and least *talkative,* and rank order all the other members between them. In the assessment center method, a group of expert raters (typically psychologists) interacts with a group of subjects over a period of a few days, observing them in both standardized and unstructured situations. They then make personality ratings, perhaps by checking descriptive adjectives.

The advantages of these different forms of gathering information from observers are still debated, as are the relative merits of self-reports versus observer ratings. Fortunately, however, many recent studies have shown general agreement between many different objective methods of assessing personality. This consensual validation of observations about personality traits forms an essential basis for scientific personality psychology.

D. Objective Tests: Laboratory Procedures

Researchers dedicated to objectivity have often hoped that personality could be assessed by laboratory tests that did not depend on the judgments of individuals. Quantity of salivation in response to a drop of lemon juice, perspiration as measured by the galvanic skin response, and dilation of the pupil have all been proposed as measures of personality attributes. This approach to personality assessment has been of limited value; physiological responses typically have shown only modest and inconsistent relations to personality variables.

Yet accumulating evidence on the heritability of most personality traits suggests that there is some genetic and presumably physiological basis for many traits. Increasing sophistication in our understanding of the brain and new techniques such as magnetic resonance imaging may one day lead to discoveries about personality/brain relations with implications for assessment. At present, however, our best source of information about personality is the individual and those who know him or her well. [*See* BEHAVIORAL GENETICS.]

II. EVALUATING ASSESSMENT METHODS

A. Reliability and Validity

Although well-constructed objective measures of personality are valuable scientific tools, it should not be assumed that all objective measures are well-constructed. Psychometricians have, however, established a series of criteria by which scales can be evaluated. It is traditional to divide these into *reliability* criteria and *validity* criteria, although the distinction between the two is somewhat artificial. In essence, both require that the scale perform in ways that are consistent with its intended theoretical interpretation.

The two most common forms of reliability are *internal consistency* and *retest reliability*. If each of the items in a scale is considered to be an indicator of the same underlying trait, it seems reasonable to require that they all agree with each other. Cronbach's coefficient α is a commonly used measure of this internal consistency of scale items. Internal consistency can be increased by discarding items that show limited agreement with other items, or by adding more items of the same kind (longer scales are more reliable because the errors introduced by individual items tend to cancel each other out in the long run).

For narrow constructs, the higher the internal consistency, the better. For broad constructs, however, higher internal consistency is not necessarily better because it may be purchased with a loss of generality. For example, a measure of general psychological distress that consisted of the items, "I am fearful," "I am nervous," and "I am anxious" would probably have high internal consistency, but it would offer a very narrow measure of distress focused exclusively on anxiety. Depression, frustration, shame, and other aspects of psychological distress are omitted. By including items to measure them, we would probably produce a scale with lower internal consistency but higher fidelity to the broad theoretical construct of psychological distress.

Test–retest reliability refers to the reproducibility of scores on different occasions. We would not expect major changes in personality over a 2-week period, so if individuals score very differently when they complete the questionnaire twice over this interval, it suggests that there are problems with the test.

In essence, questions about reliability ask whether the scale elicits responses that are consistent across items and across time. Without some minimum of reliability, it is hard to argue that the scale measures anything meaningful, so reliability is often taken as a prerequisite to validity. *Validity* refers to the degree to which a scale actually measures the construct it is intended to measure. A spelling test might have excellent internal consistency and retest reliability, but no validity at all if it were intended to be used as a measure of extraversion.

The central problem in establishing the validity of a test is that we rarely have completely satisfactory external criteria. A good measure of agreeableness–antagonism would separate agreeable from antagonistic people, but—without giving the test—how do we know who is agreeable and who is antagonistic? No single answer is usually sufficient, so we rely on a pattern of evidence in evaluating the construct validity of a scale. We may correlate it with other scales that measure similar constructs, (e.g., scales measuring trust and altruism), or we may see if it distinguishes between known groups that should differ on the dimension (e.g., social workers versus convicted felons), or we may compare self-reports with ratings on the same scale made by spouses or peers.

All of these studies would give information on the *convergent validity* of the scale, but they would not necessarily speak to its *discriminant validity*. The criterion of discriminant validity requires that scales be *un*related to scales which measure theoretically different constructs. If a test is designed to measure agreeableness, it should not be strongly related to intelligence, because intelligence is theoretically independent of agreeableness. In order to establish discriminant validity, a scale must be related to a series of other measures, especially those with which it is apt to be confounded. The strongest designs for construct validity usually require that multiple methods be used for assessing multiple traits, and that stronger correlations be seen for measures of the same trait obtained from different methods than for measures of different traits obtained from the same method.

Table I gives an example of convergent and discriminant validity across instruments and observers. Five basic dimensions of personality—neuroticism, extraversion, openness to experience, agreeableness, and conscientiousness—are measured by self-reports on adjective rating scales, and by peer ratings on a questionnaire measure, the NEO Personality Inventory. The convergent correlations (given in boldface) show substantial agreement—far greater

agreement than would be expected by chance. By contrast, the discriminant correlations (e.g., between peer-rated neuroticism and self-reported openness to experience) are much smaller and generally do not exceed chance. Such data provide evidence that both instruments measure the intended constructs with considerable success.

B. Sources of Error and Bias; Response Styles

Most personality questionnaires consist of a series of statements that the respondent must answer either *true* or *false* or rate on a scale (e.g., from *strongly disagree* to *strongly agree*). As anyone who has taken such a test knows, the items are often ambiguous and sometimes of dubious relevance. The question, "Are you devoted to your work?" might be interpreted in several ways. Some respondents might compare their devotion to work with their commitment to family. Some might compare their own devotion to that of their co-workers. Retired or unemployed respondents might not know how to respond. Even with the sincerest cooperation, respondents may not give the response the test developer intended.

Further, some respondents may not be sincerely cooperative. They may respond carelessly or at random simply to be finished with the task. Or they may wish to present a flattering picture of themselves to the tester. One of the most troubling discoveries of personality psychology was that laypeople are exquisitely sensitive to the social desirability of items and can, if so instructed, fake most personality tests.

Another common problem is acquiescent responding. It was discovered long ago that individuals differ in the tendency to agree with statements,

TABLE I

Convergent and Discriminant Validity of Measures of Five Basic Dimensions of Personality

Mean peer rated NEO Personality Inventory domains	Self-reported adjective factors				
	N	E	O	A	C
Neuroticism (N)	**.44*****	−.03	.00	−.03	−.15*
Extraversion (E)	.06	**.45*****	.16**	.00	.06
Openness to experience (O)	.07	.08	**.45*****	.13*	−.07
Agreeableness (A)	−.06	−.11	−.15*	**.45*****	−.10
Conscientiousness (C)	−.11	−.05	−.10	−.09	**.39*****

Note. $N = 267$. Convergent correlations are given in boldface. Adapted from McCrae and Costa (1987). *J. Pers. Soc. Psychol.* **52,** 81–90.
* $p < .05$. ** $p < .01$. *** $p < .001$.

regardless of content. So-called yea-sayers interpret items in ways that allow them to endorse most of them; nay-sayers find something in most items to which they object. If all the items are keyed in the same direction—that is, if *true* or *agree* responses are always indicative of the trait—then scale scores will confound measurement of the trait with measurement of acquiescent tendencies. Two such scales might show a positive correlation even if they measured very different traits, because both might also measure acquiescent tendencies.

This particular response style can be controlled quite effectively by creating scales with balanced keying: Half the items are scored in the positive direction, half in the negative. For example, we might measure conscientiousness by including the item "I often fail to keep my promises," and giving points for conscientiousness if the respondent *disagrees*. In responses to a balanced scale, acquiescent tendencies cancel themselves out, leaving a purer measure of the trait.

Similar strategies have been developed for dealing with other response styles. For example, random responding can be detected by including a set of items that virtually no one would endorse if they were paying attention and cooperating (e.g., "I keep an elephant in my basement"). Endorsing several such items would suggest random responding, and test results should be considered invalid. Cooperative respondents, however, may find the inclusion of such "trick questions" offensive. An alternative way of detecting one common form of random responding is by looking for a string of identical responses on an answer sheet, which may indicate thoughtless, repetitive responding merely intended to finish the questionnaire. This is an unobtrusive measure of random responding.

The greatest attention has been paid to the problem of socially desirable responding. Many scales have been devised in the hopes that they could identify individuals who responded on the basis of the desirability of an item rather than its accuracy as a description of their personality. Researchers routinely include such scales in construct validity studies to estimate the discriminant validity of the scales of interest from socially desirable response tendencies. Unfortunately, however, no good measure of desirable responding per se has yet been developed, and most research suggests that attempts to correct for social desirability do more harm than good.

The root of the problem is that statements have both substantive and evaluative meanings. Anyone who wished to appear in a good light would endorse the item "I always try to do my best"—but so would highly conscientious individuals who are scrupulously honest in their responses. It is impossible to determine from the response alone whether the individual really has desirable characteristics or is presenting a falsely favorable picture of him- or herself.

Two general strategies appear to be useful for dealing with this problem. First, in most cases it appears that respondents are more truthful than psychologists anticipated. Even though they *can* endorse desirable items when instructed to do so, test takers normally do not, when asked to be honest and accurate. Research volunteers have little incentive to distort their responses, and clients in counseling and psychotherapy should be convinced by the assessor that accurate responding will be in their best interest. Mutual respect and trust between test administrators and test takers is usually the best basis for assuring valid results.

However, in some cases there may be good reasons for mistrusting self-reports. The responses of prison inmates who describe themselves as saints when being evaluated for parole should be regarded with considerable skepticism. In these cases, the most appropriate tactic may be to obtain observer ratings from knowledgeable and impartial informants. The current availability of validated observer-rating questionnaires (such as Form R of the NEO Personality Inventory) makes that approach feasible.

None of these approaches to scale construction or administration eliminates all the limitations of personality assessment by questionnaire. The inevitable ambiguity of items and respondents' imperfect knowledge of themselves or the individuals they rate mean than personality measures lack the precision that we admire in the physical sciences. The data in Table I show that our assessments are on the right track, but they can also be interpreted to show that our measurements are far from perfect. Both self-reports and observer ratings are useful tools that give valuable information about personality, and either is acceptable for use in research on groups. For the intensive understanding of the individual (e.g., in psychotherapy), it is desirable to obtain both self-reports and informant ratings, and all inferences about personality traits should be considered provisional, subject to revision or refinement as new information becomes available.

C. Content and Comprehensiveness in Personality Questionnaires

Psychometric theory gives general guidelines for constructing and evaluating measures of psychological characteristics, but it gives little guidance about *what* should be measured. For decades, one of the central problems in personality psychology was the proliferation of hundreds of scales measuring aspects of personality that some researcher or theorist thought important in understanding human beings. Many of the most eminent personality psychologists were those who offered a system, a model of personality structure that specified the most important aspects of personality and thus brought some kind of order to the chaos of competing ideas.

Factor analysis has frequently been used as the statistical technique for studying personality structure. Factor analysis is a mathematical procedure which condenses the information about intercorrelations among many variables by detecting groups of variables that covary separately from other groups. These groups of variables define a factor, a dimension along which individuals can be ranked. For example, the individual traits of trust, straightforwardness, altruism, compliance, modesty, and tender-mindedness covary to define the broad dimension of agreeableness.

In the days before computers, a factor analysis might consume months of computational labor, and it is not surprising that early factor analysts tended to defend whatever structure they first uncovered. As a result, for many decades disputes raged about whether there were 2 basic factors, or 3, or 5, or 10, or 16. Failure to resolve this issue lowered the credibility of the field, and paralyzed much personality research: How could we study personality and aging, say, unless we knew which aspects of personality we needed to measure as individuals aged?

In 1961 two Air Force psychologists, Ernest Tupes and Raymond Christal, factored data from several different studies and concluded that five, and only five, major factors seemed to recur. Their work was largely ignored during the next 20 years, but around 1980 interest in the five-factor model revived. Initially, these five factors were seen as the basic dimensions underlying trait adjective terms used by laypersons and encoded in the natural language—terms such as *nervous, enthusiastic, original, accommodating,* and *careful.* Questionnaire measures, including the NEO Personality Inventory, were then developed to measure these five factors (see Table I for names of the factors). Subsequent research showed that the same five factors were also found in most of the theoretically based questionnaires that had previously been constructed. For example, the four scales of the Myers-Briggs Type Indicator correspond to four of the five factors (introversion–extraversion to extraversion, sensation–intuition to openness, thinking–feeling to agreeableness, and perception–judgment to conscientiousness).

The same basic dimensions have been recovered in cross-cultural analyses of personality (including studies conducted in Hebrew, German, and Chinese), in self-reports and observer ratings, in men and women, and in young, middle-aged, and older adults. Although disagreements remain over the precise nature and scope of the factors, there is a general consensus that these five represent basic and universal features of personality. (Intelligence, another fundamental dimension of individual differences, is generally considered to be outside the realm of personality proper.) The five-factor model thus provides a general answer to the question of what personality traits should be measured: A comprehensive assessment must include measures of all five factors.

However, the five factors themselves are too broad to give a detailed picture of the individual. Anxiety and depression are both aspects of neuroticism, and in general, people who are anxious also tend to be depressed. But some anxious people are not depressed, and some depressed people are not anxious, and it is extremely important to clinical psychologists to determine whether a patient is anxious, depressed, or both. A global measure of neuroticism would not provide that information; instead, more specific scales are needed to provide the details. The same could be said for all five factors. [*See* ANXIETY AND FEAR; DEPRESSION.]

While most personality psychologists see the need for assessment of personality at this more specific level, there is no consensus about which specific traits should be measured, or even how to go about identifying the most important specific traits. Advocates of circumplex models suggest that we expand the five-factor model by measuring traits that represent combinations of pairs of factors. For example, friendliness is related to both extraversion and agreeableness, so it might merit separate assessment.

Other researchers believe that there are a large number of important traits—perhaps 100 or

TABLE II
Global Domains and Specific Facets in the Revised NEO Personality Inventory

Neuroticism	Extraversion	Openness	Agreeableness	Conscientiousness
Anxiety	Warmth	Fantasy	Trust	Competence
Angry hostility	Gregariousness	Aesthetics	Straightforwardness	Order
Depression	Assertiveness	Feelings	Altruism	Dutifulness
Self-consciousness	Activity	Actions	Compliance	Achievement striving
Impulsiveness	Excitement seeking	Ideas	Modesty	Self-discipline
Vulnerability	Positive emotions	Values	Tender-mindedness	Deliberation

more—that should be separately analyzed; the five-factor model could then be used primarily to organize the results. In the Revised NEO Personality Inventory, 30 separate traits identified from an analysis of the psychological literature are measured by facet scales, and global domain scales are formed by summing groups of six of them, as shown in Table II. This scheme encourages hierarchical personality assessment at both the more specific and more general levels.

III. PERSONALITY ASSESSMENT AND PERSONALITY THEORY

Human beings have always tried to understand themselves and the people around them; scientific psychology has made real, if slow, progress in this endeavor over the past century. Theories of test construction and validation and psychometric techniques have provided the technical basis for developing sound measures, and the five-factor model specifies which aspects of personality should be measured. As usual in science, there is a continuing interaction between theory and measurement: The more we know about human personality, the better our techniques for measuring it, and the better we measure it, the more we are able to refine our theories.

Psychoanalysis, behaviorism, and humanistic psychologies in turn dominated personality psychology, and each led to serious problems for personality assessment. Self-reports about thoughts, feelings, and actions were considered trivial by psychoanalysts, who believed that the important psychological variables were unconscious, and unscientific by behaviorists, who preferred observation of behavior in laboratory settings. Humanistic psychologists sometimes opposed assessment on principle, because they believed that rating individuals on a fixed set of dimensions was depersonalizing.

Trait psychology has always coexisted with these other schools, but has rarely been dominant. But personality assessments based on the principles of trait psychology have shown themselves to be scientifically defensible and useful in applied contexts. For these reasons, trait psychology and the five-factor model appear poised to be the dominant paradigm in personality psychology in the next century.

Bibliography

Briggs, S. R. (1992). Assessing the five-factor model of personality description. *J. Pers.* **60,** 253–293.

Funder, D. C. (1991). Global traits: A Neo-Allportian approach to personality. *Psychol. Sci.* **2,** 31–39.

Kline, P. (1993). ''The Handbook of Psychological Testing.'' Routledge, New York.

McCrae, R. R., and Costa, P. T., Jr. (1990). ''Personality in Adulthood.'' Guilford, New York.

Wiggins, J. S., and Pincus, A. L. (1992). Personality: Structure and assessment. *Annu. Rev. Psychol.* **43,** 473–504.

PERSONALITY DEVELOPMENT

Kevin MacDonald

California State University at Long Beach

I. Research on Temperament in Childhood
II. Personality Development in Later Childhood and Adulthood
III. Evolutionary Approaches to Temperament and Personality

Glossary

Factor analysis A statistical technique which is used to find clusters of measures which intercorrelate with each other and thus define a dimension of personality or temperament. For example, a personality questionnaire may consist of several items such as "Has many friends," "Enjoys working with others," "Avoids being alone," etc., which correlate together and define a dimension labeled by the researcher as "sociability."

Heritability Individual variation in traits is understood to be the result of both variation in genes between individuals as well as variation in the environments individuals are exposed to. Heritability is the proportion of the variation of the trait which is due to genetic variation.

Personality dimension Personality is a more inclusive term than temperament (see below). Personality theory attempts to develop a set of individual difference dimensions consisting of all the ways in which individuals differ from each other. Although there has been much research on the biological basis of some personality traits, there is no implication that these traits are biologically influenced, as is the case with temperament. Nor is there any implication that personality dimensions must appear early in life.

Stability A trait is stable if individuals maintain their relative position in a distribution between two points of measurement. For example, the trait of height (or sociability) is stable if individuals measured as relatively tall (or sociable) at one time remain relatively tall (or sociable) when measured at a second time. Notice that stability does not imply that there is no change. Thus, height could be a stable trait because tall individuals measured at age 5 are still relatively tall at age 10, even though all of the children grew substantially during the time interval. In the case of personality, the stability of individual differences is a major issue. However, researchers are also interested whether there are average developmental changes in personality traits over time, so that, for example, individuals become less prone to taking risks in later adulthood than during adolescence.

Temperament dimension Individual differences which appear early in life, are of a reasonably enduring nature, and underlie the typical manner in which an individual either reacts to stimulation or regulates his or her behavior in order to approach or avoid stimulation. Temperament is thus usually applied to differences in emotion, attention, and activity. These individual differences are viewed as rooted in biological differences between individuals, and are often viewed as influenced by both environmental and genetic sources of variation.

RESEARCH ON personality development is concerned with individual differences in a wide ranging set of traits which are important in describing and evaluating human social behavior. For example, some people are highly sociable and enjoy interacting with others. They enjoy an occupation in which there is a great deal of contact with other people and they may be more likely to be sought after as friends and associates. Others would find high levels of social interaction to be aversive. They prefer to be alone and could be expected to seek a fairly solitary occupation in which socializing with others is unimportant. Notice that when we say that a person is sociable, we are implicitly saying that the person has a tendency to behave in a sociable manner in a wide range of situations which are conducive to sociability (e.g., parties, attitudes toward meeting new people, etc.), although we certainly do not expect such a person to behave sociably in all situations (e.g., being interrogated by the police). Moreover, we also suppose that if a person is sociable, then he or she will more than likely continue to be sociable for a prolonged period of time. Being sociable is not simply an ephemeral mood, but a relatively stable aspect of one's behavior. If change occurs at all, it is expected to be gradual and over a fairly prolonged period of years, while one's mood can change quite quickly. The extent to which personality changes over time is an important area of developmental research on personality.

In developmental research on children, the field of personality research is closely intertwined with research on temperament. Like personality research, temperament is concerned with individual differences in behavioral tendencies, but there is the understanding that these individual differences are present very early in life. For example, some infants may react with a great deal of distress even at very low levels of stimulation, whereas another infant may react to the same stimulation in a very positive manner, and yet another infant may show very little response at all. [See INDIVIDUAL DIFFERENCES IN TEMPERAMENT.]

For several theorists, there is an explicit understanding not only that temperament traits are influenced by biological systems, but that temperament traits by definition are traits which have a genetic component. Thus, several theorists have defined temperament as including only those traits which show significant heritability (i.e., traits for which individual differences are at least partially due to genetic differences between individuals). For these theorists, infants and children vary on these behavioral traits, and at least some of that variation is due to genetic variation. However, these researchers also accept the idea that not all variation in temperament is due to genetic variation. Children are exposed to different environments as well, and these different environments are also viewed as influencing the child's temperament. [See BEHAVIORAL GENETICS; TRAITS.]

For many researchers, therefore, temperament research involves understanding the biological basis of a variety of behavioral traits which appear early in life. As in the case of personality, temperament traits are of obvious relevance to social behavior, and they are viewed as fairly stable across time and characteristic of individuals in a wide range of situa-

tions. However, it should be noted that there is continuing research, summarized below, on the extent to which temperament and personality traits are stable over time.

The field of temperament research uses several methods for measuring temperament. Temperament traits may be studied at a behavioral level (such as observing individual differences in negative emotional response in a laboratory situation), or they may be studied from a biological perspective (such as attempting to find individual differences in neurotransmitter level associated with negative emotional responding). By far the most widely used technique is parental ratings of the child's behavior in response to questions developed by the researcher. The responses are then subjected to factor analysis in an attempt to discover independent dimensions of temperament. Personality and temperament dimensions are independent of each other in the sense that an individual's status on one dimension is not highly correlated with his or her status on another dimension. Thus, if sociability and emotional reactivity are temperament dimensions, knowing that a person is sociable tells us little or nothing about that person's emotional reactivity.

I. RESEARCH ON TEMPERAMENT IN CHILDHOOD

The field of temperament research is far from settled territory. However, despite continuing lack of agreement on such basic issues as the correct set of temperament dimensions, the following is a set of temperament traits based on a fairly broad convergence of findings obtained by a number of researchers in the field. Moreover, the stability of temperament traits during childhood, and especially during infancy, although significant, is not very robust. Between-age correlations for temperament traits in childhood are in the .3 to .4 range, and therefore explain only 10–25% of the variation. While some of this lack of stability is undoubtedly due to the unreliability of the measurements, the data available at present suggest that there are important environmental influences on temperament in childhood.

A. Reactivity

Children differ in the extent to which they become aroused by particular levels of environmental stimulation. As a general rule, children respond positively to low levels of stimulation. At intermediate levels of stimulation there are also positive responses, but in addition there is the onset of negative, inhibitory responses which result in a tendency to withdraw and function to protect the child from overstimulation. At very high levels of stimulation, the response tends to be overwhelmingly negative and inhibitory and the child withdraws. Individual differences in this system define the temperament trait of reactivity.

Children who are highly reactive respond very strongly to stimulation, and are conceptualized as having a very low threshold for arousal. These children are often viewed as having a weak nervous system in the sense that they are easily overstimulated. In the presence of high levels of stimulation, these high-reactive individuals inhibit their responding and tend to withdraw from the source of stimulation. On the other hand, they respond very intensely to even low levels of stimulation. Low-reactive children, on the other hand, may be said to have a relatively strong nervous system in the sense that they have a relatively high threshold of stimulation and do not become aroused by stimulation which would overwhelm a high-reactive individual. These low-reactive individuals are thus more likely to be found in highly stimulating environments, although at extremely high levels of stimulation, even these individuals begin to inhibit their responding and withdraw from stimulation.

As can be seen in these comments, the concept of reactivity really involves two separate ideas. The first is the idea of threshold of responding (low versus high threshold for arousal) and the second involves the onset of inhibitory (withdrawal) tendencies. There is some evidence that individuals with a low threshold for arousal also tend to show inhibition at relatively low levels of stimulation. On the other hand, individuals with a high threshold for arousal (relatively insensitive) begin to inhibit their responding only at very intense levels of stimulation.

It should also be noted that there are individual differences in the extent to which individuals show reactivity depending on the modality of the stimulation—the concept of *modality specificity*. Thus, a child may be highly reactive to tactile stimulation, but much less reactive to vestibular stimulation.

The trait of *negative emotionality* is often distinguished as a temperament trait closely linked to reactivity. Children who are high on the trait of negative emotionality are prone to negative emotional response to stimulation (irritability), including distress

and anger. Individual differences in negative emotionality can be observed in the newborn period, and there are important cross-cultural differences in this trait beginning during the newborn period, with Chinese-American infants and other Mongoloid infants being less prone to distress than Caucasian-American or African American infants. There is also some evidence for general developmental shifts in negative emotionality, with peaks around age 2 (perhaps accounting for the "terrible twos") and during adolescence.

B. Positive Emotionality and Sociability

This cluster of traits essentially measures individual differences in behavioral approach. Even in the newborn period there are individual differences in the extent to which infants will approach rewarding stimulation, such as sweet foods or interesting visual patterns. At around 4 weeks of age behavioral approach is accompanied by smiling and other indications of positive affect in both social and nonsocial situations. Children who are high on the trait of positive emotionality are prone to positive emotional response, including smiling, joy, and laughter available in rewarding situations, including the pleasant social interaction sought by sociable children.

As a result, sociability is intimately linked with the trait of positive emotionality. Sociable children tend to seek and enjoy social contact with others. Positive emotionality and sociability may thus be seen as *appetitive* traits in which the child regulates his or her own behavior in a manner which results in positive emotional response. There is some indication of sex differences in behavioral approach tendencies, with boys being more prone to behavioral approach than girls. Later in childhood sociability has been linked to the more general trait of extraversion, and such a relationship continues during adulthood (see below).

C. Behavioral Inhibition

Children who are high on behavioral inhibition respond negatively to new people and other types of novel stimulation. This trait has been subjected to considerable research, and the results will be presented in somewhat greater detail than for the other temperament dimensions. Unlike the other temperament traits discussed here, behavioral inhibition is not observable at birth, but becomes established in the second half of the first year. The predominant emotions of the behavioral inhibition system are fear and anxiety, and children are typically tested for differences in this trait by placing them in unfamiliar situations, and especially with unfamiliar people. Approximately 10–15% of normal, healthy 2-year-old children will react to these unfamiliar situations by becoming quiet, vigilant, and subdued. They cling to their mothers and attempt to withdraw from the novel situation. Longitudinal research indicates considerable stability for this trait: children who were behaviorally inhibited at age 2 also tended to be behaviorally inhibited at age 7½ when placed in a group of other unfamiliar children. During the play sessions the children made few spontaneous comments and tended to remain apart from the group.

Physiological research on behaviorally inhibited children indicates that these children generally have a more responsive sympathetic nervous system. This sympathetic dominance can be seen by the finding that behaviorally inhibited children tend to have a high and stable heart rate in unfamiliar situations, indicating that these children are highly aroused by the unfamiliarity. This sympathetic dominance can also be seen in the tendency for behaviorally inhibited children to have greater muscular tension and arousal, especially in the larynx, as well as greater pupillary dilation. Finally, behaviorally inhibited children have been shown to have higher levels of the stress hormone cortisol. The indications are that behaviorally inhibited children have a very strong emotional response to novel situations, and in particular, they tend to be highly prone to tension, anxiety, and fear in these situations.

D. Attention Span, Distractibility, and Focused Effort

By 3 months of age there are clear differences in distractibility and persistence among infants as indicated by differences in the length of time infants will attend to visual and auditory stimulation. In early childhood, this trait is manifested in differences in gaze shifting and in duration of orienting toward objects such as toys. This trait is linked to individual differences in the development of effortful, persistent behavior in a pursuit of a goal, since such effortful performance requires inhibiting responses to other stimuli in the environment. There is a general trend in development such that older children have longer attention spans, are less distractible, and are better able to effortfully pursue a goal.

E. Activity

Activity refers to the degree of energy expenditure characteristic of the child. Active children are "on the go," and they tend to engage in frequent and intense bouts of motor activity. Individual differences in activity level can be observed from early infancy and throughout childhood. There is some indication that activity is positively associated with the positive emotionality dimension mentioned above and thus with Factor I on adult personality dimensions described below.

These temperament traits are of great importance in understanding the social development of children. A commonly held view in the area of social development is that children have significant effects on their social and nonsocial environments, and these temperament traits are an important means by which the child affects the world around him or her. Children are viewed as actively influencing the world around them and choosing environments which are conducive to their temperament. For example, a sociable child actively seeks social contact with others and in a sense creates his or her own world. A child who enjoys fast-paced high energy motor activities seeks out opportunities to engage in this type of activity and selects friends who have similar interests.

Moreover, children with different temperaments evoke different responses from their environment. For example, children with a short attention span have difficulty sustaining the prolonged attention and effort required at school, and this behavior in turn is likely to result in negative responses from teachers. As another example, there is evidence that extremely withdrawn, behaviorally inhibited children can become rejected by the peer group. Children who begin life high on temperamental behavioral inhibition and continue to exhibit this trait tend to be less mature, less assertive, and more compliant or deferential than their more sociable peers, and some extremely withdrawn children tend to be victimized by the peer group.

Finally, despite the conceptualization of temperament as a set of biological systems, there is very good evidence that temperament can be influenced by the environment, especially during infancy and childhood. For example, many premature infants as well as infants whose mothers have taken drugs such as cocaine, are very high on negative emotionality. They are thus very difficult to interact with, and such babies are at significantly higher risk for child abuse, at least partly because their intense negative emotionality is very aversive to caregivers.

II. PERSONALITY DEVELOPMENT IN LATER CHILDHOOD AND ADULTHOOD

One of the unfortunate aspects of writing in the area of personality development and temperament is that, despite some very obvious commonalities, there has been little research which formally establishes the linkages between these areas. Research on adult personality has been dominated by the Five Factor Model of personality. This model has emerged consistently as a result of factor analytic studies of personality questionnaires performed over the last 50 years. In the following, I briefly describe the five factors, link them with the research on temperament in childhood, and provide an overview of the development of these systems in adulthood.

Factor I is generally labeled extraversion. Individuals high on this factor are described as talkative, assertive, active, energetic, outgoing, dominant, forceful, enthusiastic, and adventurous, while individuals who are low in this factor are described as quiet, withdrawn, and retiring. At a more general level, this dimension may be viewed as encompassing individual differences in what may be termed a set of "GO" systems underlying behavioral approach, impulsivity, and attraction to reward, and is therefore linked with the "positive emotionality and sociability" and "activity" dimensions found in temperament studies of childhood. [See EXTRA-VERSION–INTROVERSION.]

Although at a general level the GO systems can be viewed as a single dimension, there are a several semi-independent traits characteristic of behavioral approach in addition to sociability as discussed above. For example, sensation seeking is a trait which involves attraction to novelty, danger, and excitement, and is phenotypically and genetically correlated with sociability. The trait of sensation seeking peaks in late adolescence and young adulthood, followed by a gradual decline during adulthood. There is also some evidence to support the view that extraversion and sociability decline in adulthood, although the evidence is mixed and the declines are minor. These trait dimensions have been observed cross-culturally and show an important sex difference: Males tend to be higher in these "GO" trait dimensions.

Factor II is often termed agreeableness or warmth. Individuals high on this trait are described as sympathetic, affectionate, warm, generous, trusting, and unselfish, while those low on this trait are described as cold, unfriendly, hard-hearted, cruel, and stingy. This trait has been hypothesized to underlie the development of close affectional relationships in the family, including especially romantic attachments. This trait is not found among the temperament dimensions of childhood described above, but there is some evidence that individual differences in warmth and affection observable in early parent–child relationships, including secure attachments, are linked with this dimension later in life. There is an important sex difference in this trait throughout development, with females tending to be higher than males. In addition, there is some indication that this trait increases during adult development, concurrent with decreases in aggression and hostility, although the change is minor and there are conflicting data.

Factor III is often termed conscientiousness. Individuals high on this trait are described as thorough, planful, efficient, dependable, reliable, responsible and deliberate, while those low on this dimension are described as careless, disorderly, frivolous, and irresponsible. Individual differences in this trait can be found as early as age 5, and this trait is highly correlated with academic success. While formal research is lacking, this trait has been linked to the temperament trait of attention span and distractibility described above as a temperament trait in infancy and early childhood. Like the other dimensions of personality and temperament described here, the trait is moderately stable through childhood. While we have noted that there is a developmental increase in attention span and persistence during childhood, this trait has not been found to change significantly during adulthood.

Factor IV is often termed neuroticism or emotionality. Individuals on one extreme of this factor are described as tense, anxious, fearful, emotionally unstable, and nervous, while individuals on the other extreme are described as calm, stable and unemotional. This factor appears to be related to both the childhood temperament dimensions of behavioral inhibition (as indicated by the emphasis on fear and anxiety in this dimension) and high reactivity (especially negative emotionality, as indicated by the importance of intense, negative emotional response for this dimension). Based on cross-sectional studies with adults, there are no age differences in neuroticism.

Factor V is often termed intelligence, intellect, or openness to experience. Individuals high on this dimension are intelligent, have a wide range of interests, are curious, open to new experiences, inventive, and original, while those low on this dimension are described as having narrow interests, and commonplace, shallow ideas. Research on this dimension as a personality trait in childhood is lacking (although there is much research on intelligence of children as it relates to academic success), but the trait has been found consistently in studies of adult personality. No age differences in this trait during adulthood have been found. [*See* INTELLIGENCE.]

III. EVOLUTIONARY APPROACHES TO TEMPERAMENT AND PERSONALITY

The general conclusion is that there is very good evidence for a set of basic personality traits which show some stability beginning in infancy and persisting throughout the lifespan. While stability as assessed by correlations between ages is fairly low during childhood, ranging between .3 and .4 even over a span of a few years, there is considerable evidence that adult personality is quite stable. Several studies have found correlations in the range of .7 to .85 for adult personality over periods as long as 12 years, indicating a very high level of stability indeed. However, despite some evidence for changes in traits related to extraversion and agreeableness, there is relatively little evidence for changes in the average level of personality traits over the lifespan.

While traditional personality and temperament research emphasizes individual differences, recent evolutionary approaches to this field emphasize the idea that these individual differences should be thought of as individual variation in discrete biological systems with particular evolved functions. There is evidence that all of the personality dimensions reviewed here are significantly heritable, indicating that genetic variation is an important source of individual differences for the trait. Moreover, while only the physiological data relevant to behavioral inhibition are reviewed here, there is increasing evidence that all of these personality/temperament systems have important physiological roots.

From an evolutionary perspective, the evolved function of the GO systems described as being central to Factor I in adult personality research is proposed to be that of motivating the individual to ac-

tively engage the environment. Individuals high on the GO systems actively seek out rewards and a variety of other sources of environmental stimulation, including other people (sociability). At the extreme end of this dimension, individuals high on this trait engage in high levels of risk-taking and impulsive behavior—what one might term a high-risk evolutionary strategy. On the other hand individuals who are low on this dimension are implicitly adopting a more cautious strategy in which there are lower payoffs as well as lower risks.

The behavioral inhibition system which is central to Factor IV, on the other hand, is proposed to function as a mechanism for protection and the inhibition of behavior in the face of threat. This system is viewed as a biological STOP system which responds to perceived threat with behavioral inhibition and the initiation of fight or flight behaviors.

The proposed evolved function of Factor II (agreeableness) is to provide a mechanism for facilitating close personal relationships within the family. The high level of altruism and generosity characteristic of individuals who are high on this dimension is proposed to function to facilitate transfer of resources within close, intimate human relationships such as family relationships, including care of children.

Finally, the evolutionary functions of Factors III (conscientiousness) and V (intellect) are perhaps obvious. Both are correlated with academic success, with the former underlying the ability to make effortful, persistent, and careful behavior in pursuit of a goal, and the latter underlying the ability to process information and solve problems creatively.

From the evolutionary perspective, personality dimensions may thus be thought of as discrete, independent systems which are differentially recruited in particular life situations. In a situation of personal threat, personality systems underlying fear and anxiety (Factor II) may predominate, while at a party, sociability and positive emotionality are more likely to be exhibited (Factor I). Individuals thus not only have a characteristic level of a particular personality dimension which is highly stable, at least during adulthood, but are also able to finely tune their behavior in response to particular environmental contingencies, so that a person who is generally low on behavioral inhibition may show fear and anxiety in a situation of extreme threat to his or her interests. An individual's personality is thus flexibly responsive to environmental contingencies rather than uniform across all possible situations.

The basic design of the biological basis of children's (and adults') temperament and personality is finely tuned to be able to both approach the world and engage in enthusiastic interaction with it (the GO systems), but also to be able to inhibit behavior in the face of threat (neuroticism or behavioral inhibition), conscientiously and persistently pursue important goals (conscientiousness), and engage in close, affectionate relationships with others (agreeableness). Evolution, like a good engineer, designed children (and adults) with both a powerful engine (the GO systems) and a good set of brakes and monitoring systems (the STOP system and conscientiousness). All of these systems have important functions, but the field of temperament and personality research shows that there is enormous variation in the power and salience of these traits among individuals.

Clearly evolution did not result in the an "optimum" or "ideal" personality profile for all humans. Instead evolution appears to have resulted in a broad range of individual differences in approach and avoidance, affiliation and conscientiousness, and even for such traits as creativity, originality, and intelligence. It is quite possible that this variation in personality and temperament serves to enable humans to occupy a wide range of possible niches and occupations in the human and non-human environment. Several different personality combinations may function equally well in many human environments, while a personality which is ideally suited to one type of environment (working as a military officer) may be poorly suited to another (working in a library). The result is the fascinating kaleidoscope of diversity which is an endless source of fascination to both researchers and laypeople alike.

Bibliography

Buss, A. H., and Plomin (1984). "Temperament: Early Developing Personality Traits." Erlbaum, Hillsdale, NJ.

Digman, J. M. (1990). Personality structure: Emergence of the five-factor model. *Annu. Rev. Psychol.* **41,** 417–440.

Goldsmith, H. H., Buss, A. H., Plomin, R., Rothbart, M. K., Thomas, A., Chess, S., Hinde, R. A., and McCall, R. (1987). Roundtable: What is temperament? Four approaches. *Child Dev.* **58,** 505–529.

Halverson, C. F., Kohnstamm, G. A., and Martin, R. P. (Eds.) (in press). "The Developing Structure of Temperament and Personality from Infancy to Adulthood." Erlbaum, Hillsdale, NJ.

Kagan, J. (1989). "Unstable Ideas: Temperament, Cognition, and Self." Harvard University Press, Cambridge.

Kohnstamm, G. A., Bates, J. E., and Rothbart, M. K. (Eds.) (1989). "Temperament in Childhood." Wiley, New York.

MacDonald, K. B. (1988). "Social and Personality Development: An Evolutionary Synthesis." Plenum, New York.

McCrae, R. R., and Costa, P. T. "Personality in Adulthood." Guildford, New York.

Pervin, L. A. (Ed.). (1990). "Handbook of Personality." Guildford, New York.

Rubin, K. H., LeMare, L. J., and Mills, S. (1990). Social withdrawal in childhood. Developmental pathways to peer rejection. In "Peer Rejection in Childhood" (S. R. Asher and J. D. Coie, Eds.), pp. 217–249. Cambridge University Press, New York.

PERSONALITY DISORDERS

Robert G. Meyer
University of Louisville

I. Personality Types and Disorders
II. Treatment Relationships and the Personality
   Disorders
III. Summary

Glossary

Paranoid pseudocommunity The conspiracy network of persons a paranoid perceives as against him or her.
Personality disorder Chronic disruptive adjustment patterns, found as a formal diagnosis on Axis II of the DSM system
Personality type Patterns of behavior found in normals that operate as a predisposition to a personality disorder.
Underlying beliefs The cognitive beliefs that help to generate, and maintain, a personality disorder.

PERSONALITY DISORDERS are chronic, cognitive–behavioral patterns, generated from an early age, that the individual has developed in order to cope with his or her particular problems of living. These disorders are not so clearly bizarre as the psychoses, nor do they include the clear anxiety patterns of the neuroses. However, they are severely maladaptive, because (1) the psychopathology is pervasive and thoroughly integrated into the personality, (2) the patterns are chronic and often recognizable by the time of adolescence or earlier, and (3) such persons usually avoid treatment and are difficult to treat if for some reason they do enter treatment. Thus, a personality disorder describes a pattern of behavior, or lack of behavior, that is troublesome to others or whose pleasure sources are socially defined as either harmful or illegal.

I. PERSONALITY TYPES AND DISORDERS

The various personality disorders are generated because they are effective, at least in the short run, in coping with that person's individual environment. Of course, the more distorted or disturbed that environment is, the more likely it is that a distorted coping pattern will emerge and become reinforced. Within this perspective, a personality type (a behavior pattern seen as within the normal range of adjustment) is a way-station on the developmental road toward a full-blown personality disorder. Table I describes common personality types (which we all manifest to some degree), along with the personality disorder they are most likely to develop, if they are exaggerated and crystallized.

The DSM-III-R personality disorders have traditionally been grouped into three clusters in the DSM's. The first includes the paranoid, schizoid, and schizotypal personality disorders, as these are denoted by peculiar or eccentric behavior. The second cluster focuses on dramatic and emotionally labile behavior: It includes the histrionic, narcissistic, antisocial, and borderline personality disorders. The last cluster, which emphasizes chronic fearfulness and/or avoidance behaviors, includes the avoidant, dependent, obsessive–compulsive, and passive–aggressive personality disorders.

The following is a discussion of each individual personality disorder, from the perspective of both behavioral patterns and the more recently articulated cognitive patterns.

A. Paranoid Personality Disorder

The paranoid personality disorder can be thought of as anchoring the other end of the continuum of paranoid disorders from the most disturbed and fragmented pattern, paranoid schizophrenia. However, since there is neither thought disorder nor even a well-formed delusional system in the paranoid per-

TABLE I

Personality Types and Correlated Traits and Disorders

Correlates	Personality types									
	Controlling	Aggressive	Confident	Sociable	Cooperative	Sensitive	Respectful	Inhibited	Introverted	Emotional
Typical behaviors	Manipulative, demanding	Bold, initiating	Poised, distant	Animated, engaging	Docile, submissive	Erratic, responsive	Organized, formal	Watchful, preoccupied	Passive, quiet	Energetic, engaging
Interpersonal patterns	Authoritarian	Intimidating	Unempathic	Demonstrative	Compliant	Unpredictable	Polite	Shy	Withdrawn	Provocative
Thinking styles	Calculating	Dogmatic	Imaginative	Superficial	Open	Divergent	Respectful	Repressed	Vague	Distracted
Mood-affect expression	Disappointment, resentment	Anger, distrust	Calm, unconcerned	Dramatic, labile	Tender, fearful	Pessimistic, hurt	Restrained, content	Uneasy, wary	Bland, coolness	Intense, frenetic
View of self	Unappreciated	Assertive	Self-assured	Charming	Weak	Misunderstood	Reliable	Lonely	Placid	Interesting
Probable personality disorders	Passive-aggressive, sadistic, paranoid	Antisocial, sadistic, paranoid	Narcissistic, paranoid, antisocial	Histrionic, borderline narcissistic	Dependent, compulsive, avoidant	Passive-aggressive, borderline avoidant	Compulsive, paranoid, passive-aggressive	Avoidant, schizotypal, self-defeating	Schizoid, schizotypal, compulsive, avoidant	Borderline schizotypal, histrionic, narcissistic

Source: Adapted in part from T. Millon and G. Everly, 1985, *Personality and Its Disorders*, Wiley, New York.

sonality disorder, it is not listed under the DSM paranoid disorders and is not a psychotic condition. Like the other personality disorders, it is a chronic, pervasive, and inflexible pattern of behavior that typically has been in evolution since childhood and is already recognizable in adolescence. Modeling of parental or other significant others is possibly even more important in this disorder than in the psychotic paranoid conditions. [See PARANOIA.]

1. Behavioral Patterns

Paranoid personalities manifest hyperalertness toward the environment and have a chronic mistrust of most people. They see themselves as morally correct, yet vulnerable and envied, and see others as far less than perfect. As a result, their information base is continuously distorted and their affect is constricted. Consequently, they find it difficult to adapt adequately to new situations or relationships, which is paradoxical because of their hyperalertness to their environment. Paradoxically, they will frequently be correct in assuming that other people are against them. Yet the paranoia is usually a disabling overreaction to a low initial level of scrutiny by others.

Unless these individuals have almost absolute trust in another person, they cannot develop intimacy and are continually seeking various ways to be self-sufficient. They avoid the emotional complexities of working out a meaningful relationship and tend to be litigious. For example, they may write negative letters to public figures or bring lawsuits on minimal grounds. It is rare for them to come into therapy without significant coercion from others. The disorder is more common in men.

Both Nero and Robespierre displayed characteristics of the paranoid personality pattern. As with other individuals in this classification, these important historical figures were suspicious and oversensitive about the behavior and intentions of other people. Each was very manipulative in his relationships so that the other person could not gain the advantage. Nero was a Roman emperor during the first century, and Robespierre was a leader of the French Revolution; each man had considerable power over large numbers of people. Unlike most paranoid personalities, therefore, their paranoid reactions had a significant impact on a great many lives; and their delusions or misperceptions may have caused them to unjustifiably imprison or execute many innocent people. Although most paranoid personalities are not dangerous or physically injuri-

ous, they are at best perceived as a nuisance, e.g., through perennial complaints and lawsuits against other persons.

In order to relate to, or even treat the paranoid personality, it is essential to gain their trust through empathy, but not through participation in the disorder patterns. It is especially necessary to empathize with and articulate the consequences of such an individual's behavior, such as the sense of being isolated and not understood or the interpersonal rejection that appears unfair to the paranoid.

The underlying beliefs that paranoids often struggle with are (a) I am unique and others are jealous; (b) others will exploit my mistakes; (c) it always pays to be wary, accusatory, and adversarial (some paranoids do make good trial lawyers); (d) people who are trusting or content are fools, i.e., I can't be that way; (e) negative events are generated purposefully by others.

The concept of the paranoid pseudocommunity holds that the paranoid is unable to communicate freely with other persons and has a pattern of finding fault with others as a result of inadequate social development. This inability creates a problem when the paranoid is under stress, because he cannot corroborate his perceptions with those of other persons or cannot assume the perspectives of other individuals. Relying on his own devices, he continues in his misperceptions and reconstructs reality to make it consistent with them. The culmination of this behavior is the paranoid's conception of himself as the center of a community of persons who are in a conspiracy against him. Because the situation does not exist as the paranoid perceives it, he is said to be living in a pseudocommunity.

B. Schizoid Personality Disorder

The essential feature of this disorder is impairment in the ability to form adequate social relationships. As a result, schizoid personalities are shy and socially withdrawn or, as novelist Joan Didion states in *The White Album* (p. 121), "only marginally engaged in the dailiness of life." They have difficulty expressing hostility and have withdrawn from most social contacts. But, unlike agoraphobia, the behavior is ego-syntonic, i.e., the individual is at least minimally comfortable with the behavior.

1. Behavioral Patterns

In contrast to the personalities who relate to the environment, the schizoid personality is particularly characterized by distancing behaviors and alienation. The schizoid individual reacts to disturbing experiences and conflicts by apparent detachment from the environment rather than by manifesting normal coping responses. The schizoid personality is described in DSM as shy, oversensitive, seclusive, often eccentric, and likely to avoid close or especially competitive relationships.

Walter Mitty is the schizoid hero of James Thurber's novel and the movie *The Secret Life of Walter Mitty*. Mitty is essentially detached from his environment and is much more absorbed in his elaborate, heroic fantasies. Given the situation of an idle moment or a disturbing experience, he plunges into his imaginings, rather than utilizing normal coping mechanisms. Most schizoid persons are considered to be cold and withdrawn because they do not seem to respond to their environment. Walter Mitty, however, seems more warm and likeable, although no more reachable, than other schizoid personalities.

2. Cognitive Patterns

Like the person with an avoidant personality disorder (discussed later in this article), the schizoid has inadequate interpersonal relations. But unlike one with an avoidant personality disorder, the schizoid does not care, so therapy is quite difficult.

Characteristic underlying cognitive assumptions are (a) any disruption of my emotional routine (however minimal the emotions are) is scary and messy—in that sense they are analogous to the obsessive–compulsive's fear of disruption of external routines; (b) I can survive alone (maybe not optimally, but at least predictably), and need space to do that; (c) it's necessary to be free and independent—other people are like Brer Rabbit's "Tar Baby"; if you relate to them, you get stuck to them.

C. Schizotypal Personality Disorder

The reader is referred to the previous category, the schizoid personality disorder, since many of the features of that disorder are found here. The essential difference is that in addition to the disturbances in social functioning, the schizotypal personality manifests peculiarities in the communication process. Schizotypal individuals are much more likely than the schizoid to show dysphoria and anxiety, and because of the odd thinking patterns, they are more likely to have developed eccentric belief systems and become involved in fringe religious groups. The schizotypal personality is also more likely to be emo-

tionally labile, overtly suspicious, and hostile of others than is the schizoid. Many schizotypal individuals also appear to meet the criteria for the borderline personality disorder. Any therapist's attention must be directed not only toward the interpersonal withdrawal processes, but also to the emergent disturbances in affect and thinking that are common.

D. Histrionic Personality Disorder

These persons seek attention and are overreactive, with the response being expressed more dramatically and intensely than is appropriate—hence, the term "histrionic." This category has traditionally been labeled the "hysterical personality." However, "hysteric" wrongly suggests a disorder that parallels the causes and symptoms of what has been traditionally labeled "hysterical neurosis."

1. Behavioral Patterns

Histrionic personalities may elicit new relationships with relative ease, as they appear to be empathic and socially able. However, they turn out to be temperamentally and emotionally insensitive and have little depth of insight into their own responsibilities in a relationship. Even though they may be flirtatious and seductive sexually, there is little mature response or true sensuality. If one accepts the apparent sexual overture in the behavior, the histrionic individual may act as if insulted or even attacked.

There has been a continuing controversy as to whether this disorder occurs with any frequency in males. But, it is clear that this disorder is found in males, but because the symptoms are a caricature of the traditional role expectations for women, it is more common in women.

An excellent behavioral example of a histrionic personality pattern is seen in the character of Martha in Albee's play *Who's Afraid of Virginia Woolf?* The stormy relationship between Martha and her husband, George, alternating between wild physical and verbal abuse and tender affection, is not fiction created for the stage, as many couples live in what can be termed a "conflict–habituated" marriage. In such a marriage, there is private though sometimes unverbalized acknowledgment by both husband and wife as a rule that incompatibility is pervasive, that conflict is ever-potential, that an atmosphere of tension permeates the relationship; nevertheless, the relationship will continue. It seems likely that at least one of the partners in this kind of marital situation would be labeled as a hysterical personality, and often, as is the case with the character George in *Who's Afraid of Virginia Woolf?*, the other partner is a passive–aggressive personality. Such people do not often seek treatment. Rather, they maintain the core around which the pretense and the conflict revolve, much as Martha and George maintained her fantasied pregnancy as well as their mythical child.

2. Cognitive Patterns

Histrionics quickly avoid blame for any difficulties of interpersonal relationship and, in that sense, show a degree of the projection that is characteristic of paranoid disorders. Common underlying beliefs in histrionics are (a) being responsible or attending to details means the loss of "zest for life"; (b) rejection is disastrous; (c) people won't love me for what I do but what I pretend to be, or what I present to entertain/entice them; (d) being "special" means never having to say "I'm sorry" (or at least I don't have to feel it or mean it).

E. Narcissistic Personality Disorder

This category, which was new in the DSM-III-R, centers on individuals who are to a degree products of our modern social-value systems. No doubt, such people have always existed, but it appears that this pattern has become more common recently. It is not a surprising development when there are advertisements about "The Arrogance of Excellence" and self-help seminars unequivocally urging people to live out the axiom "I'm number one" (with little evidence that there is much room for a number two or three close behind). [*See* NARCISSISTIC PERSONALITY DISORDER.]

1. Behavioral Patterns

Narcissistic personalities are "flattery-operated"; more specifically, they manifest an unrealistic sense of self-importance, exhibitionistic attention seeking, inability to take criticism, interpersonal manipulation, and lack of empathy resulting in substantial problems in interpersonal relationships.

Narcissistic personalities are similar to antisocial personalities, except that they are not so aggressive or hostile and their value systems are more asocial and hedonic than antisocial. The prognosis for major change is moderate at best.

In 1984, Otto Kernberg introduced the subdiagnosis of *malignant narcissist*. It was first applied to people like Adolf Hitler and Joseph Stalin, and more recently it has been suggested as fitting Sad-dam Hussein. The four characteristics of this pattern are (1) a strong suspiciousness, occasionally to the point of paranoia; (2) an extremely inflated sense of self, often grandiose; (3) sadistic cruelty (which in some individuals is turned inward as self-mutilation—"for a higher goal"); and (4) an utter lack of remorse.

There are numerous *productive narcissists* in society. One night while we were on a fishing trip, my friend and I had dinner at a fine Chinese restaurant. The restaurant was named after the owner, an aging but still attractive Chinese woman. The walls were totally covered with formal photographs of her, there was a bulletin board filled with candid shots from throughout her life, the restaurant's cards had a photo of her as a young woman, and you could even purchase postcards with various pictures from her life. A short conversation with her quickly revealed her narcissism, but it should have been evident to any customer. She was not especially offensive (it was a short conversation); however, by narcissistically including her restaurant as a part of her "self," she had turned it into an excellent operation that she groomed as carefully as her hair. Certain media-created stars, "personalities," and politicians are also examples of extreme but at least occasionally productive narcissism.

2. Cognitive Patterns

Underlying beliefs common to this disorder are (a) I am special, unique, elite; (b) I like to challenge or compete with others, but because of both "a" and the fact it is psychologically necessary for me to prevail, I may play by other rules (usually known only to me); (c) any defects I have come from my bad parents and/or background; (d) recognition, admiration, and respect are necessary and others exist to provide it, and indeed, promote it; (e) sharing, serving others, or selfless behaviors are signs of weakness and signal disintegration of my self.

F. Antisocial Personality Disorder

The antisocial personality is an interesting category that deserves special consideration in light of its evolution as a concept. In the early 1800s Prichard suggested the term "moral insanity" or "moral imbecility" to designate persons who did not fit the psychiatric categories of that time. The first reference to the classic notation "psychopathic" occurred in 1891 with the introduction of the label "psychopathic inferiority." This classification was an attempt to place the disorder with other disturbances, such as retardation, that were believed to be congenital. Caesare Lombroso's classic conception of the criminal as showing consistent and significantly different facial characteristics was also a popular view. The *Zeitgeist* of that period therefore maintained that the psychopathic disorder was the result of genetic or hormonal defects rather than learning or environmental factors.

Eventually, the term "psychopathic personality" was used, but in such a way that there was much confusion about the concept. In time the term "sociopathic personality pattern" was also adopted by the American Psychiatric Association for DSM-I (to emphasize, now apparently inaccurately, that this pattern is largely a result of social conditioning) and became the broad category under which several problematic social behaviors, such as sexual deviations, alcoholism, and drug addiction, were listed.

Hervey Cleckley, a pioneer in this area, has described the antisocial personality (more specifically, psychopathy) as having a "mask of sanity," or the absence of the usual indicators of insanity. These are persons who discard meaningful relationships, goals, and success for reasons that others cannot understand. Cleckley's list of the following 16 indicators of psychopathy has been influential through the ensuing years:

1. Superficial charm and good "intelligence"
2. Absence of delusions and other signs of irrational "thinking"
3. Absence of "nervousness" or psychoneurotic manifestations
4. Unreliability
5. Untruthfulness and insincerity
6. Lack of remorse or shame
7. Inadequately motivated antisocial behavior
8. Poor judgment and failure to learn by experience
9. Pathologic egocentricity and incapacity for love
10. General poverty in major affective reactions
11. Specific loss of insight
12. Unresponsiveness in general interpersonal relations
13. Fantastic and uninviting behavior, with drink and sometimes without
14. Suicide rarely carried out
15. Sex life impersonal, trivial, and poorly integrated
16. Failure to follow any life plan

Although the DSM-III-R discusses only the overall category of antisocial personality, there is good evidence that it can be further subdivided, e.g., into categories of primary psychopath and secondary psychopath. [*See* ANTISOCIAL PERSONALITY DISORDER.]

G. Borderline Personality Disorder

This disorder was a confusing entity in the original DSM-III-R drafts, but now it seems to be more clearly defined. At first glance, it may seem to overlap with the schizotypal personality disorder, as both imply an easy transition into a schizophrenic adjustment. However, individuals with borderline personality disorder are neither as consistently withdrawn socially nor as bizarre in symptomatology as are schizotypals, and the borderline diagnosis covaries most commonly in inpatients with a diagnosis of histrionic personality disorder. [*See* BORDERLINE PERSONALITY DISORDER.]

1. Behavioral Patterns

Though the DSM does not specifically mention it, this category seems to be a resurrection of an old term at one time much favored by clinicians: "emotionally unstable personality." Persons in the borderline personality disorder category do show significant emotional instability, are impulsive and unpredictable in behavior, and are irritable and anxious. They also often show "soft" neurological signs, and avoid being alone or experiencing the psychological emptiness or boredom to which they are prone. There is some evidence that as these individuals improve, they show more predictable behavior patterns, yet this is combined with increasingly evident narcissism. Glenn Close's character in the movie "Fatal Attraction" is a good example of this disorder.

2. Cognitive Patterns

Borderlines are intense and labile emotionally and cognitively, and are draining to significant others (and therapists). Yet, paradoxically, they need to understand that they fear facing their own intense negative emotions over time, and so find it hard to grieve the many relationship losses they generate. They maintain a facade of competence and independence, yet desperately want various types of help, and then react negatively when it is not forthcoming.

The following beliefs are common: (a) I'm afraid I'll be alone forever, as no one who really gets to know me will want to love me; (b) If I ignore my own needs, I can entrap some people into relationships, but, since I can't control my feelings, and I need the relationships, I'll be very unhappy; (c) though I need people, they will eventually hurt or reject me, so I must protect myself; (d) I deserve any bad things that happen to me; (e) my misery (and/or "badness") is how people recognize me as a unique self.

H. Avoidant Personality Disorder

These individuals are shy and inhibited interpersonally, yet at the same time desire to have interpersonal relationships, which distinguishes them from those with the schizotypal or schizoid personality disorders. They also do not show the degree of irritability and emotional instability seen in the borderline personality disorder. This is a common secondary diagnosis in inpatient populations.

1. Behavioral Patterns

A major feature of this chronic disorder is an unwillingness to tolerate risks in deepening interpersonal relationships. These persons are extremely sensitive to rejection and seem to need a guarantee ahead of time that a relationship will work out. Naturally, such guarantees are seldom available in healthy relationships. Thus, the friends they manage to make often show a degree of instability or are quite passive.

In many ways, this disorder is close to the anxiety disorders, since there is a degree of anxiety and distress, and low self-esteem is common. However, the behaviors that produce the distress are relatively ego-syntonic. Their depression and anxiety are more related to the perceived rejection and criticism of others. This common disorder is seen more often in women. Any disorder in childhood that focuses on shyness predisposes one to the avoidant personality disorder.

2. Cognitive Patterns

Avoidant personalities are extremely sensitive to rejection and seem to need an advance guarantee that a relationship will work out—a relationship with an attached warranty. Thus, they resonate negatively to the refrain form W. B. Yeats: "Only God, my dear / Can love you for yourself alone / and not for your yellow hair."

Other cognitions common to the avoidant personality include (a) if people really got to know me,

they would see how inadequate (or odd) I really am, and they would reject me; (b) I am unable to cope with unpleasant people or situations; (c) not thinking about a problem or unpleasant situation or not trying to cope with it may allow it to go away; (d) you'll never leave me because I'll make sure I leave you first; (e) nothing ventured, nothing failed.

I. Dependent Personality Disorder

In one way, dependent personality disorders can be seen as successful avoidant personality disorders. They have achieved a style that elicits the desired relationships, though at the cost of any consistent expression of their own personality. They show elements of agoraphobia, not crystallized, and they lack any real self-confidence. [*See* DEPENDENT PERSONALITY.]

1. Behavioral Patterns

People with the dependent personality disorder have a pervasive need to cling to stronger personalities who are allowed to make a wide range of decisions for them. They are naive and show little initiative. There is some suspiciousness of possible rejection, but not to the degree found in the avoidant personality disorder.

Since this is an exaggeration of the traditional feminine role, it is not surprising that it is far more common in women. If the individual is not in a dependent relationship, anxiety and upset are common. Even if enmeshed in a dependent relationship, there is still residual anxiety over the possibility of being abandoned.

Dependent personalities may be getting many rewards for their behavior, in the midst of the negatives that may have led them into therapy, e.g., abusive relationships. Very often significant others only want very circumscribed changes, so once changes begin, they will likely subvert things. At the same time, the eventual termination of any therapy is always threatening with these clients.

2. Cognitive Patterns

Underlying cognitive systems that are often included are (a) I am perpetually at risk of being alone in a cold and dangerous world; (b) I'm not able to cope with and/or enjoy life without a supportive other; (c) a loss of self is a fair price to pay in order to obtain a relationship with a supportive other, even if they periodically abuse me in some fashion; (d) I need constant access to this other, with as much intimacy as I can elicit, so I'll be as subservient and inoffensive as I need to be.

J. Obsessive–Compulsive Personality Disorder

This disorder is occasionally confused with the obsessive–compulsive disorder (which is an anxiety disorder), but there are significant differences between the two syndromes. First, the obsessive–compulsive personality seldom becomes obsessed about issues. Second, for the obsessive–compulsive personality the term *compulsive* refers to a lifestyle in which compulsive features are pervasive and chronic, but it does *not* refer to a specific behavior such as persistent hand-washing. Third, the person with an obsessive–compulsive personality disorder is not upset, anxious, or distressed about his or her lifestyle, whereas anxiety is generic and often obvious at times in the functioning of the obsessive–compulsive disorder. [*See* OBSESSIVE–COMPULSIVE BEHAVIOR.]

1. Behavioral Patterns

According to Sigmund Freud, their essential characteristics are that they are "exceptionally orderly, parsimonious and obstinate." Obsessive–compulsive personalities are preoccupied with rules and duties, are unable to express warmth and caring except in limited situations, are highly oriented toward a lifestyle marked by productivity and efficiency, are temperamentally and emotionally insensitive, and are generally distant from other individuals. They are inclined to be excessively moralistic, litigious, and hyperalert to criticism and perceived slights from others. They can be described as workaholics without warmth.

The extent to which the ritualistic and conforming behavior is generalized throughout the person's life and, more importantly, the degree to which it is functional must be taken into consideration before a diagnosis is made. For example, a pilot develops rituals for determining that his plane is safe before takeoff. If a part of the ritual is omitted by a copilot, the pilot may experience considerable distress and may actually risk alienation by insisting on the performance of the ritual. The pilot's insistence on carrying out a ritualistic check of the instruments makes him appear obsessive, but it also keeps him alive.

Captain Queeg, in the novel and movie *The Caine Mutiny,* may be regarded as an obsessive–compulsive personality. Queeg continually insisted on order, cleanliness, and obedience; disruption of routine panicked him. However, because Captain Queeg's symptom pattern also included paranoid features, he does not completely fit the obsessive–compulsive category.

2. Cognitive Patterns

It is true that a degree of compulsivity is effective, particularly in our society. It becomes a problem when it overwhelms the rest of the personality. Paradoxically, obsessive–compulsives are often indecisive in their thinking and poor planners of their time, a result of their narrow focus and concern with precision, even when precision may be irrelevant.

Typical underlying beliefs such as (a) to err, or worse, to fail, is anxiety-provoking, will allow others to criticize me, and makes me feel less than a whole person; (b) to lose control is anxiety-provoking; (c) my obsessiveness and/or compulsivity are powerful enough to avoid errors, failure, or finding myself with nothing to do, yet; (d) as regards meaningful decisions, rather than "Better to have tried and failed than to never have tried at all," my motto is "Better to have not tried at all, than to have tried and failed"; (e) details are important, i.e., if you can see trees, no need to look for the forest; (f) I am responsible for myself and others; (g) I hate others when they don't follow "the rules," i.e., my rules, and especially if they get by with it.

K. Passive–Aggressive Personality Disorder

Most parents have had the experience of a child pushing them to the limit of their control and then backing off. Like that child, the passive–aggressive becomes acutely sensitive to such limits and is consistently able to go so far but no further. When this pattern becomes an integral part of a social and vocational lifestyle, a passive–aggressive personality disorder exists. Although these patterns are commonly modeled and learned in childhood, such a family usually reaches a state of mutual détente. The pattern then causes severe problems when it is transferred into any new intimate, consistent contact relationship, such as marriage.

1. Behavioral Patterns

The passive–aggressive pattern is characterized by pouting, procrastination, stubbornness, or intentional inefficiency that is designed to frustrate other people. The essential condition in this category is that there is a social context in which something has been requested from the individual exhibiting passive–aggressive behavior. The individual is apparently capable of complying with what is requested but does nothing. This inaction results in severe frustration for the observer rather than for the passive–aggressive individual. Typically, there is no overt opposition from the individual such as a blatant refusal to comply. Rather, there is an apparently cooperative attitude but no resulting action. For example, there may be stubborn insistence on procedural detail that effectively renders any actual achievement impossible. The classic example of this behavior pattern is seen in the character of Schweik in *The Good Soldier Schweik* (Hasek, 1930), the model for the cartoon character Beetle Bailey, who managed to infuriate his military commanders by carrying out each order to the ultimate detail, thereby revealing its absurdity.

The passive–aggressive personality disorder often takes the standards and the belief system of significant others and turns them around to immobilize the others effectively. The strategy (which is not thought to be a conscious behavior) is to present the "enemy" (often a person depended on) with a choice that forces one either to capitulate or to violate an individual belief system. That person is thus immobilized, with no adequate reason to justify retaliation.

2. Cognitive Patterns

The automatic thought "I don't have to get there on time—nobody can tell me what to do" is common to passive–aggressives. Thus, they are inclined to be late for payments, sessions, etc., so clear contracts with detailed consequences are necessary.

Passive–aggressives are also often late within a much longer perspective—the developmental tasks of life, e.g., establishing a career, or getting married or having children. This stems not only from their sense "You (in this case, society) can't make me do it . . ." but also from an impaired inability to tie responsibilities to time, and the fact that responsibility per se is often aversive because it is interpreted as a "society should." Analogously, there is often a passive refusal to accept the discipline and sacrifice needed to develop either vocational or interpersonal "careers." Attaining the required credentials and "putting in your time" in order to attain the payoff of an accrual process is seen as too restricting and demanding.

In addition to the beliefs embedded in the prior points, beliefs common in the passive–aggressive are (a) I know I can really be self-sufficient, but I apparently do need others, at least now, and I resent that; (b) any control by others is aversive; (c) while I apparently have to accept some subjugation of my desires and/or loss of control, they'll pay a price for making me do so; (d) if the conditions were right (and/or I really tried), I would be outstanding; (e) following rules, expectations, deadlines, etc., makes me less of a whole person; (f) no one, including me, really deserves to have authority.

L. Sadistic Personality Disorder

The term "sadistic personality disorder" does not officially appear in the DSM's, though it is made available in an Appendix of the DSM-III-R as an optional diagnosis for clinicians to add when they find it helpful. In any case, the concept has a long history. Kernberg (1984) terms the sadistic personality the "malignant narcissistic" and places it between the antisocial and the narcissistic personalities on this continuum. The personality might also be thought of as an antisocial pattern, though with better socialization and a more prominent quality of revenge. See the prior description of those disorders for the relevant cognitive patterns, as they are an amalgam of those two, combined with the cognitive schemata "Not only does pain in others not generate empathic emotions, it may result in pleasure or an enhanced sense of self for me."

The proposed DSM criteria are (1) uses violence or cruelty to establish a dominance relationship; (2) demeans or humiliates people in the presence of others; (3) takes pleasure in physical or psychological suffering of other humans or animals; (4) has, with unusual harshness, disciplined someone under his or her control; (5) has lied with the goal of inflicting pain or harm; (6) uses intimidation, or even terror, to get others to do what he or she wants; (7) restricts the autonomy of someone with whom he or she has a close relationship; or (8) is fascinated by weapons, martial arts, injury, torture, or violence in general. The dominant trend is a love of cruelty and an absence of remorse.

There is a noteworthy distinction between sadism, which is a paraphilia and thus appears on axis I of a DSM-III-R diagnosis, and the sadistic personality disorder, which is an axis II diagnosis. While sadistic sexual patterns are common in the sadistic personality disorder, it is not a necessary part of the pattern. In essence, the sadistic personality disorder is marked by a very assertive lifestyle based on power motives, commonly accompanied by gender dominance, the inflicting of pain for pleasure, and extreme aggression with or without sexual motivation. Yet, the sadistic behavior is well rationalized, and the individual may even present a very self-righteous air.

M. Self-Defeating Personality Disorder

This is a second disorder which was newly proposed in the DSM-III-R, yet it hearkens back to the "inadequate personality" disorder that appears in earlier DSM's. Self-defeating behaviors can be defined as any behavior one employs to achieve a desired consequence or goal that paradoxically inhibits the attainment of that desired goal. Self-defeating behaviors can be observed in all persons to some degree. Such behaviors may be recognized by the person even though they are continued. In other cases, the individual may be unaware that her actions are self-defeating, similar to the "oppositional" child who may long for closeness with her parents but distances herself through hostile and rebellious behaviors. In all instances, self-defeating behaviors are dysfunctional and bring dissatisfaction and discomfort to the individual. These behaviors are paradoxical in that they are at one and the same time self-perpetuating and self-defeating—thus, the traditional term "neurotic paradox." Indeed, the self-defeating personality disorder seems as much akin to some of the more "neurotic" diagnoses as it does to the personality disorder diagnoses. [*See* SELF-DEFEATING BEHAVIORS.]

Proposed criteria are (1) chooses situations and/ or people, even when better options are evident and available, that lead to disappointment, failure, or mistreatment; (2) rejects or subverts the efforts of others to help him or her; (3) responds with guilt, depression, and/or pain-producing behavior (e.g., accident-proneness) to positive personal events; (4) incites rejecting or anger responses from others, then feels devastated; (5) rejects opportunities for pleasure or has difficulty acknowledging that he or she is enjoying himself or herself; (6) subverts or fails to accomplish tasks critical to personal objectives; (7) engages in excessive self-sacrifice that is unsolicited by the intended recipient; or (8) rejects or is uninterested in people who consistently treat him or her well.

II. TREATMENT RELATIONSHIPS AND THE PERSONALITY DISORDERS

Modern theorists point out that treating the personality disorders, particularly those with antisocial, narcissistic, or borderline components, requires a rethinking of what are often termed transference issues. They note that such individuals often elicit an "objective counter-transference." This is usually a response of anger and frustration, even hate, but in some cases can be a type of protective affection.

The important point is to recognize that these emotional reactions of the therapist are reasonable, and based on good data. This is in contrast to the traditional conception of the therapist's reactions to neurotics. In the latter instance, such feelings would be seen as indicative of emotional blocks in the therapist, which would signal a need for more analysis for the therapist and/or a transfer of the patient to another therapist.

However, in the "objective counter-transference" to the personality disordered client, the therapist needs to (a) recognize and "metabolize" such feelings, i.e., not act out toward the client in response to such feelings; (b) gradually let the client know that such reactions are ocurring; (c) relate them to the eliciting behaviors; and (d) thus let the client know they can and are being controlled. Therefore, rather than allowing the client to project "onto" the therapist, as with a neurotic type in more classical analysis, this type of client is allowed to project "into" the therapist. Most such clients seem to use this as a means of communication, as well as control, almost as if it is the only way another can ever know the level of pain they went through.

III. SUMMARY

Personality or character disorders, unlike other mental disorders, are manifested primarily in a social context. They are more like "us," and we would rather not think so. These disorders trouble society, over time, more than they trouble the individual. Rarely do such individuals experience the crippling anxiety that is characteristic of the neuroses, the loss of functioning due to thought disorder characteristic of the schizophrenic process, the incapacity of organic brain syndromes, or the consistently manifested extremes of mood found in the affective disorders. Instead, one finds an apparently intact organism, with little evident symptomatology, whom is unable to organize his or her behavior and relate interpersonally in an effective manner. These disorders present a life-long problem for the individual, the treater, and society as a whole.

Bibliography

Beck, A., Freeman, A., *et al.* (1990). "Cognitive Therapy of Personality Disorders." Guilford, New York.

Cleckley, H. (1982). "The Mask of Sanity," 5th ed. Mosby, St. Louis.

Kernberg, O. (1984). "Severe Personality Disorders: Psychotherapeutic Strategies." Yale University Press, New Haven.

Meyer, R. (1993). "The Clinician's Handbook," 3rd ed. Allyn and Bacon, Boston.

Meyer, R. (1992). "Abnormal Behavior and the Criminal Justice System." Lexington Books, Lexington, MA.

Millon, T. (1981). "Disorders of Personality. DSM-III Axis II." Wiley, New York.

Oates, W. (1987). "Behind the Masks." Westminster, Philadelphia.

Turkat, D. (1990). "The Personality Disorders." Pergamon, New York.

Widiger, T., and Frances, A. (1985). The DSM-III personality disorders: Perspectives from psychology. *Arch. Gen. Psych.*, **42,** 615–623.

PERSUASION

Michael Winkler
University of North Carolina at Asheville

Stanley Krippner
Saybrook Institute

Glossary

Attitude An agreeable or nonagreeable evaluation reaction toward something or someone, displayed in people's beliefs, attitudes, feelings, and behavior.

Attitude inoculation Presenting weak attacks against someone's attitudes, which makes people more resistant to stronger attacks that follow.

Channel of communication The medium in which messages are delivered—whether face to face, television, periodicals, or in some other form.

Credibility A credible communicator is one who is viewed as both expert and trustworthy.

Cult Groups which isolate themselves from mainstream society and direct their devotion to a charismatic person believed to embody or represent a diety and his or her teachings.

Demand characteristics Unexpected cues in an experiment which reveal to the participant what behavior is expected.

Door-in-the-face technique The inclination for people who have initially turned down a large request to comply with a small request following.

Foot-in-the-door technique The inclination for people who have first agreed to a small request to submit to a larger request following.

Persuasion Language or nonverbal behavior intended to change people's beliefs, opinions, attitudes, and/or behavior.

Sleeper effect A delayed effect of a message that has been remembered over a period of time, but not its source.

Two-step flow of communication An influence which occurs through opinion leaders, who in effect influence the general public.

PERSUASION is one of the most powerful forces within the realm of social behavior. It can be utilized in many different ways and for many different purposes—for both benevolent and malevolent reasons, to influence a single individual, or to wield control over an entire nation. From the persuasive influence that Dr. Martin Luther King had on American civil rights and desegregation in the United States, to the control that Jim Jones used to sway hundreds of people to move to Guyana only to be ordered to drink poisoned Kool-Aid and have their Utopian dreams shattered. As these examples demonstrate, persuasion takes a variety of forms which intrinsically are neither good nor bad but nonetheless can produce change and consequences, both subtle and drastic.

I. INTRODUCTION

On a daily basis everyone comes into contact with persuasive forces. Whether it is with friends, family members, or co-workers, elements of persuasion can be found in almost any social interaction. Although most people would argue that they are responsible for their attitudes and beliefs, social scientific theory and research has yielded a large body of evidence that does not support this notion. Within the United States and other developed nations, the media present powerful persuasive forces in the form of consumer advertising, political campaigning, and the dissemination of general news and information that, by and large, play a crucial role in the development of opinions, beliefs, and attitudes of individuals and groups.

Due to the widespread use of persuasive communication in advertising, marketing, politics, academics, and so on, social psychologists have, in recent years, studied the effects of persuasion and its ability to strengthen existing attitudes and beliefs or to change them completely.

Persuasion has often been defined as an act of human communication that has the specific goal of influencing the beliefs, opinions, and attitudes, and/or behavior of others. In many instances this definition does not describe the full range of conditions under which persuasion takes place. Specifically, when receiver factors are taken into account one message may be a clear example of persuasive communication to a specific audience or individual, while presented to another it may simply validate existing beliefs and opinions and thus fail to present a clear distinction of persuasion. Furthermore, instances of coercion can be misconstrued as acts of persuasion since there is a fine boundary between forced change and persuasive change. For practical purposes, we will focus on the more salient instances of persuasion and contrast them with examples that are not as distinct.

Within the large body of theory and research on persuasion the concept of *attitude* has received a great deal of attention since it is closely linked to the success of persuasive communication. The mental state of the receiver is an important part of persuasion and in many instances the ultimate goal of the persuader is to bring about some form of attitude change. Furthermore, in many cases attitudes are the precursors to behavior, and many theories of persuasion involve the concept of attitude. [*See* ATTITUDE CHANGE; ATTITUDE FORMATION; ATTITUDE STRENGTH.]

II. FACTORS OF EFFECTIVE PERSUASION

A. Source Factors

Persuasion researchers have focused a great deal of attention on the communicators' characteristics that play a role in how persuasive their messages are delivered. Although there are a number of different factors that make a given individual more persuasive, the communicator's *credibility* and *liking* seem to be the two most important factors in persuasibility while similarity, attractiveness, and other source factors play minor roles.

1. Credibility

Credible communicators are looked upon as experts. That is, they display a degree of competence

in their field and are commonly viewed as knowledgeable and experienced. Furthermore, receiver judgments of competence are significantly influenced by the communicator's level of training, occupation, and experience. This value judgment made on the part of the receiver is important in whether the message is accepted or rejected. If the receiver believes the communicator has displayed a high degree of competence, then it is much more likely that the message being conveyed will have an impact. In addition to this, a communicator's degree of trustworthiness is also assessed by the receiver. If a communicator is viewed as being truthful then the message will seem much more reliable and acceptable. On the other hand, if a persuasive message is remembered but not its source, then the influence of a communicator of high credibility may have a diminishing effect over time. However, low-credibility communicators may receive a beneficial gain in this situation which would result in having a more persuasive response to their message after a period of time has passed. This is a phenomenon known as the *sleeper effect* that occurs under circumstances in which the receiver remembers the message but not reasons that may discount it. For example, a receiver may remember factual information from a message but forget about the credibility of the communicator and other source factors which we normally rely upon to judge information. In addition, practical issues that may influence the credibility of communicators include their rate of delivery and the degree of confidence in their tone. A communicator is viewed as more credible if his or her speech contains no hesitations and is delivered at a rapid pace.

2. Liking

A related source factor which is closely linked to credibility involves the receivers' liking of the communicator. Although the effects of liking tend to be weaker than those of credibility factors, they still play a dominant role in persuasibility. There are two general rules to this source factor; one of these rules is that when a receiver is highly involved in an issue, influences such as liking are greatly reduced. In this case, receivers tend to actively process the message and pay less attention to peripheral cues such as liking. On the other hand, if a receiver is not highly involved in the issue then he or she is more likely to rely on simplistic cues such as liking to develop opinions about the message. In some cases disliked communicators are more effective than liked communicators. This has been shown to occur when other characteristics of the communicator, such as credibility factors, produce a compensation effect. Furthermore, disliked communicators are more persuasive in cases where the receiver has paid more attention to the message content than to the communicator's personal characteristics.

3. Similarity

Although the relationship between similarity and persuasive effects are much more complex to determine than connections between credibility and persuasion, there seem to be some common instances where similarity facilitates persuasion. For example, in instances where messages contain information concerning matters of personal taste and value, similar communicators tend to be more effective. On judgments of fact, however, dissimilar communicators tend to be more persuasive in confirming beliefs.

4. Attractiveness

The frequent use of endorsements from entertainers and athletes to sell products is a common element in advertising. Most people are fully aware of the fact that these people are not experts on the products but nevertheless are attracted to them and through this identification process are led to believe their opinions are credible. Furthermore, attractiveness leads to liking, and liked communicators are more effective than their disliked counterparts. There is, however, an exception to this rule in which attractive communicators are less effective in persuasion. In instances where an attractive communicator persuades individuals to agree to do something that is troublesome or unpleasant they explain their behavior by their purported liking of the individual and not because they wanted to do the task. On the other hand, when an unattractive person gets someone to perform a similar task, they cannot justify their actions to the liking of the person so they attribute it to their desire or wanting to comply with the request. Subsequently, they experience dissonance when trying to justify their reasons for conforming to the communicator's request so they develop the belief that they wanted to engage in the behavior.

B. Message Factors

Along with factors involving the communicators own personal characteristics, structural components of the message contribute to effective persuasive communication also. There are a number of important questions to consider concerning the content of persuasive messages. For example, should the message arouse emotion or highlight well-reasoned examples to support your ideas? Should you use one- or two-sided appeals? And lastly, how much discrepancy should the message contain in light of the audience's own existing opinions and beliefs? These issues will be examined closely.

1. Appeal to Reason versus Emotion

In cases where existing audiences are composed of well-educated people, messages that have objective and rational appeals tend to be much more persuasive than those containing fearful or emotional appeals. Likewise, highly motivated and involved audiences are equally as responsive to rational appeals. On the other hand, audiences that may be less analytically oriented or not personally involved in the message content will be motivated more by the liking of the communicator than the content of the message.

Moreover, emotional appeals have been found to be quite effective, especially when they are incorporated with factual information. For example, the American Lung Association's antismoking campaign and the driver education programs in high schools that show horrible traffic accidents both share a common element of fear with the intention to persuade. Research suggests that fearful and emotional appeals that are successful in producing greater fear will, in fact, strengthen the messages' effectiveness. The degree of fear appeals in a message and the amount of fear evoked in an audience are prime determinants of successful persuasion. However, if a message contains an extremely high degree of fear it may persuade an audience but it might also deter their attention away from the message content, producing an opposite effect.

It has been found that the amount of fear experienced in any given audience is variable and complex. Even in carefully controlled experimental designs the inducement of fear is variable across individuals. In general, research shows that fearful persuasive appeals may or may not be effective.

2. One-Sided versus Two-Sided Appeals

When presenting an argument one must consider whether opposing arguments should or should not be addressed. As a general rule, presenting two-sided arguments is more effective because the audience tends to believe that the communicator is offering objective and unbiased information. Moreover, well-informed and well-educated audiences are more receptive to two-sided appeals as opposed to one-sided arguments. Although there are instances in which recognizing opposing arguments may obscure the communicators message and fail to sway people's opinions, the vantage point is still more robust with a two-sided appeal. However, in instances where the audience is in full agreement with the message of the communicator a one-sided appeal is more effective. Speculation has it that factors which influence peoples' persuasibility to one- as opposed to two-sided arguments are dependent upon their educational level and their acquaintance with the issue.

3. Discrepancy

Persuasive communicators commonly have an idea of how much they wish to modify a given audience's attitudes and opinions. Some communicators may defend a position strongly discrepant to that held by the audience, while others may possibly advocate a position which is only somewhat discrepant from the audience's initial opinion. Overall, research shows that with both excessive and conservative usage of discrepancy a communicator's effectiveness is diminished. The instance where discrepancy works best is when the message of the communicator is only slightly different from the opinions held by the audience. As one would guess, moderate levels of discrepancy work best when the message is delivered by a credible communicator. In some cases, messages with extreme levels of discrepancy seem to have positive results when given by a credible communicator. Additionally, when a receiver maintains a high degree of involvement with a message the communicator's range of discrepancy is greatly reduced. As may already be apparent, a receiver who has a personal acquaintance with an issue may become more intolerant against strongly discrepant points of view.

4. Foot-in-the-Door Technique

A skillful persuasive strategy that is commonly used to strengthen personal commitments is known as the *foot-in-the-door technique*. The strategy consists of making an initial request of a receiver which is granted and then later on making a larger request. The assumption is that if the communicator is able to obtain a small request on the part of the receiver then he or she is much more likely to commit to the larger following request. Research suggests that this strategy is useful under certain conditions. First of all, the strategy works best when the requester is a

nonprofit organization that is benefiting charitable organizations or the community. Second, the initial request should be large enough for the second more crucial request to be granted. And finally, the initial request should not be justified by any other means such as a payment or compensation.

Explanations for this technique's effectiveness have been, for the most part, based upon self-perception theories. For instance, when people make public commitments and perceive that they are responsible for their commitment, then they begin to believe more strongly that they are helpful and cooperative. Moreover, their enhanced self-perceptions should, in fact, make them more likely to comply with the second request.

5. Door-in-the-Face Technique

A second type of strategy which involves requests similar to those of the foot-in-the door strategy but is arranged in the exact opposite order is the *door-in-the-face technique*. This strategy involves initially making a large request that the receiver does not grant and then making a second small request. It is assumed that once the receiver does not comply with the first request then he or she will feel responsible for granting the second smaller request. This strategy seems to work some of the time but only under conditions where the receiver turns down the first request, and when the time interval between the two requests is limited. In many cases this strategy will only work under conditions where the two requests are asked of the receiver with no time delay at all.

There have been several explanations for the effectiveness of the door-in-the-face strategy. Two of the more useful explanations rest upon two general factors. One is that after the receiver has been asked to grant a large request and subsequently turns it down, the second smaller request appears to be a negotiation. In a sense, receivers are put in a position in which they assume the communicator has lowered their request to a more reasonable degree so they may feel a need to reciprocate with a similar action which results in granting the favor. A second reason may be a contrast effect between the two requests. Since the first request is very large it tends to distort the size of the second. In short, the second request does not appear as large as it normally would if asked by itself and thus it becomes easier to grant.

C. Context Factors

It is probably apparent that the *channel of communication* can play a critical role in persuasive messages. Whether the message is delivered personally, in writing, videotape, or audiotape it is a fact that persuasive effects will vary with each of these channels. In conjunction with this, our active participation plays a critical role in determining our beliefs and attitudes while passive reception plays a secondary role.

1. Personal versus Media Influence

Perhaps the most effective influence upon peoples' beliefs and attitudes is through their daily interactions with people. Our direct contact with people is more influential by far than information gained from sources such as television, radio, and periodicals because they represent an interactive medium whereas the latter are examples of noninteractive media. As a general rule the order of effective persuasiveness seems to be live, videotaped, audiotaped, and written. There is, however, some contrary evidence that more complex messages are more persuasive when in written form; it is speculated that this allows the receiver to control the pace of the message presentation which leads to better comprehension. Furthermore comprehension is one of the precursors to persuasion.

The general point is, peoples' attitudes and beliefs typically have their roots in direct experience with others. Attitudes that are formed out of direct experience have more stability than ones gained from passive reception. Nevertheless, the media's influence is extremely pervasive and should not be underestimated. For instance, those who have direct impact upon people's beliefs, attitudes, and opinions develop these from source factors as well. Some persuasion researchers have theorized that media's influence follows a *two-step flow of communication* through opinion leaders to the general public.

2. Active versus Passive Variables

Both active experience and passive reception are used to shape people's behavior. Media messages, billboards, sermons, and product packaging are all examples of passive appeals. Attitudes based on experience are more stable and less vulnerable than those formed passively. Therefore, passively received appeals must be presented with clarity and conviction in order to elicit attention and produce long-lasting results. Furthermore, passively received appeals are more likely to be effective on minor issues (such as which brand of product to buy) than on major issues (such as racial attitudes in which up-bringing and personal experience have already solidified a person's position).

3. Persuasion and Psychotherapy

The role played by persuasion in psychotherapy is an important and controversial topic. Psychotherapy attempts to produce enduring changes in persons who seek relief from some form of distress, demoralization, or disability. Some forms of psychotherapy use overtly persuasive techniques, purportedly for benevolent purposes. Other forms of psychotherapy claim to avoid overt persuasion, but there are experimental data that indicate that covert means of influencing client's opinions, attitudes, beliefs, and behaviors frequently occur. As a result it is important that psychotherapists be aware of their own belief system and construct guidelines that will govern their use of persuasive techniques.

This phenomenon can also be present in social science experiments, even those claiming to be "objective." However, just as a client may be influenced by the covert actions of a psychotherapist, a research participant may be influenced by the behavior of the experimenter. *Demand characteristics* of an experiment are the cues which communicate what is expected of a research participant and what the experimenter hopes to find. They are closely related to *interpersonal expectancy effects* in which the interaction between experimenters and research participants shapes the outcome of a study in ways that belie its purported "objectiveness."

Examples of these phenomena can be found in studies of teacher–student interaction in the classroom, the behaviors of purportedly "hypnotized" subjects, and even the laboratory performance of rats and other animals. These expectations are transmitted in many ways, both verbal and nonverbal, e.g., the way research participants are greeted when they arrive, the tone of the experimenter's voice while giving instructions, and perceived emphasis toward positive or negative bias.

D. Receiver Factors

The receiver or audience is made up of a single individual or group whose attitudes the communicator is trying to modify. Successful persuasion is dependent upon a number of factors regarding the make-up of a given audience or individual. For the most part, there are no direct relationships between an individual's personality and attitudes which can be attributed to degrees of susceptibility to persuasion. However, there are some clear instances where receivers may be more or less vulnerable to persuasive messages depending upon specific factors.

1. Forewarning

It has been noted that forewarning about a persuasive message inoculates receivers against its potential effectiveness. Two particular ways of forewarning an audience are to either give specific information about the message or simply state that a message will contain persuasive elements. In cases where audiences are told detailed information about a persuasive message they will have more time to develop counterarguments against it which will decrease the likelihood of the messages effectiveness. On the other hand, if an audience is only given warning of a persuasive message they will not be able to develop counterarguments. But even in this case, receivers are less vulnerable to persuasive messages and will be more prepared to defend their own opinions. However, in cases where receivers are not highly involved in the issue, sometimes forewarning has little or no impact on the judgment of the message.

2. Distraction

A communicator's persuasiveness can be raised by catching the receiver's attention with something long enough to restrict counterarguments from developing. This technique is useful only in instances where the distraction does not prevent the audience from receiving the message. The reasoning behind this approach is that the less counterarguing occurs the more persuasion increases. This technique is frequently used in advertisements and political ads.

3. Involved versus Uninvolved Audiences

Receivers vary to the extent in which they engage in elaboration on an issue. Those who are highly involved in a message will stimulate ideas and critically analyze a message. In short, they elaborate beyond the actual information given and are influenced by the thoughts they develop. However, some receivers may be less interested in the message and draw their conclusions based on peripheral cues such as liking and attractiveness of the communicator. The *elaboration likelihood model* states that persuasion can take place in both of these cases described. Nevertheless, persuasion will occur differently for involved audiences as oppose to uninvolved audiences. For instance, a central route to persuasion occurs when receivers are engaged in elaboration upon a message. While a peripheral route to persuasion results when receivers elaboration with the message is very low. These two routes of persuasion represent the two extremes of the elaboration likelihood model while moderate levels of

both can occur as well. Factors which influence a receiver's elaboration upon a message are his or her ability and motivation to elaborate upon a message.

III. DEVELOPING RESISTANCE TO PERSUASION

A. Cult Indoctrination

In democratic and pluralistic countries, such as the United States, a variety of religions and philosophical belief systems exist for peoples' allegiance. Persuasion researchers have focused attention on those organizations regarded as "cults" and the techniques by which they appear to indoctrinate their followers. The term "cult" is generally used to refer to groups that isolate themselves from mainstream society and direct their devotion to a charismatic person believed to embody or represent a deity and his or her teachings. This definition is, of course, malleable because today's cult may become tomorrow's mainstream religion.

Cult leaders seem to realize that a commitment that is voluntarily chosen, and that is publically declared, is likely to become internalized. Converts are brought into the organizations' fund-raising and recruitment activities and their identities as cult members are constantly reinforced. Jim Jones initially accepted volunteer monetary offerings, then 10% of one's income, followed by 25%, and eventually 100%. This "foot-in-the-door" technique was a gradual process. As a charismatic leader, Jones' techniques of persuasion ranged from counterfeiting paranormal abilities to offering emotionally charged messages. Eventually Jones' People's Temple separated its members from their customary support groups producing "social implosion" in which a group collapses inward, losing its access to counterarguments. Threats and physical punishment intimidated group members, and the promise of spiritual rewards strengthened the group's positive attitude toward Jones and his message.

These techniques of social influence are often used in modified, supposedly more benevolent forms in mainstream churches, fraternal groups, college sororities and fraternities, and sales organizations. Malevolent uses of persuasion characterize terrorist and totalitarian groups, as well as by many individuals who abuse people sexually, physically, or emotionally for their own personal gratification. If indoctrination has been successful, the cult member, the abuse victim, or the member of a totalitarian group will react to outside criticism with increased commitment!

B. Attitude Inoculation

Persuasion research has shown that when people are exposed to weak attacks upon their beliefs, that they will become even more committed to their attitudes and are less likely to be swayed by opposing arguments. As was stated earlier, forewarning can drastically alter an audience's reception of a persuasive message. Whether an audience is warned about an intent to persuade or specific information regarding the persuader's position, both seem to stimulate counterarguing.

1. Counterarguing

In the event an audience has been given topic-specific information concerning the persuader's position, then they will be able to anticipate counterarguments. Moreover, if an audience is only given a warning of an intent to persuade they will not have a chance to make anticipatory counterarguments but will develop them during the delivery of the persuasive message. In both cases, research has shown that either will stimulate counterarguments but will vary greatly depending on the degree of the receiver's involvement.

2. Critical Thinking

Developing the capacities for *critical thinking* is an important means of empowering people who might otherwise be vulnerable to indoctrination. The ability to analyze data, evaluate proffered evidence, and construct counterarguments can bolster mature, independent decision-making on the part of various age groups.

3. Peer Pressure

Various types of persuasive techniques are used by one's peers to initiate or reinforce various behaviors. *Peer pressure* can assist in maintaining the social order (e.g., obeying prescribed rules, roles, and laws) but it can also be disrupting (e.g., encouraging shoplifting and other illegal activites, acts of violence, high-risk behavior). Peer confrontation techniques have been useful in reducing inappropriate classroom acts among behaviorally disordered adolescents; direct peer modeling appears to play a major role in the development of preventive health beliefs and practices among college students; peers norms have been found to be a major influence in both substance abuse and its avoidance.

Large-scale inoculation programs have been developed in recent years in an attempt to prevent children and adolescents from becoming addicted to alcohol, tobacco, and illegal drugs. These programs often use role playing as a way to develop counter arguments against peer pressure. Research has shown that relatively short-term inoculation programs decrease the likelihood of smoking, that resistance training strategies decrease middle grade students' vulnerability to pressure from their peers to drink alcohol, and that the use of peer influence can be a major factor in avoiding the use of illegal substances.

Peer pressure increases its power as students grow older, and is a focus of considerable research in developmental and cross-cultural psychology. It is a key factor in social ecology models of behavior and, itself, is multi-dimensional in nature. Involvement with peers interacts with school and family involvement in the adolescent socialization process. [*See* PEER RELATIONSHIPS AND INFLUENCES IN CHILDHOOD.]

IV. CONCLUSION

The study of persuasion dates back at least to the time of the ancient Greeks, who distinguished between "noble" and "base" rhetoric. Aristotle added that the rhetorician seeks to influence listeners by evoking their confidence, engaging their emotions, and providing truth by argument. Recent theory and research on persuasion have indicated its pervasive influence in social interactions; it is both intrinsically benevolent and malevolent, and can produce a powerful impact on beliefs, attitudes, opinions, and behavior through verbal and nonverbal communication. This topic assumes major importance in an era where mass communication techniques can be employed persuasively by political, economic, and religious institutions. The investigation of compliance-gaining messages and the means of critically evaluating them, as well as the ethical issues involved on the part of communicators of these messages, represent some unexplored territory and key theoretical frontiers for the students of human behavior.

Bibliography

Andreoli, V., and Worchel, S. (1978). Effects of media, communicator, and message position on attitude change. *Public Opinion Quart.* **42,** 59–70.

Cialdini, R. (1988). "Influences: Science and Practice." Scott, Foresman, Glenview, IL.

Eagly, A., and Chaiken, S. (1984). Cognitive theories of persuasion. In "Advances in Experimental Social Psychology" (L. Berkowitz, Ed.), Vol. 17, pp. 267–359. Academic Press, New York.

Frank, J. (1973). "Persuasion and Healing: A Comparative Study of Psychotherapy." The Johns Hopkins University Press, Baltimore.

Hovland, C., Janix, I., and Kelly, H. (1953). "Communication and Persuasion." Yale University Press, New Haven, CT.

O'Keefe, D. (1990). "Persuasion: Theory and Research." Sage, London.

Petty, R., and Cacioppo, J. (1986). "Communication and Persuasion: Central and Peripheral Routes to Attitude Change." Springer-Verlag, New York.

Simons, H. (1986). "Persuasion: Understanding, Practice, and Analysis," 2nd ed. Random House, New York.

PHOBIAS

John H. Riskind
George Mason University

Mary Ann Mercier
George Washington University

Glossary

Alarm reaction Physical and cognitive mobilization, usually in the form of preparing for a fight or to flee, in the face of a life-threatening event.

Avoidant personality A personality style beginning in early adulthood which is characterized by a pattern of feeling socially uncomfortable, fearing negative evaluation, and feeling timid.

Cognition The process of knowing and perceiving.

Cognitive An approach relying on empirical or factual validation. For example, cognitive psychotherapy focuses on the way in which humans process information and on correcting any distortions in perceptions by means of empirical validation.

Exposure-based treatments In psychotherapy, exposure-based treatments are those that involve some direct experience with a feared object whether by imagining being in close proximity to, or touching the feared object; actually entering into the feared situation either alone or with a therapist; or observing a model enter into the situation or approaching the feared object.

Panic attacks Discrete periods of intense fear which appear to come from "out of the blue," and which are accompanied by a number of symptoms such as shortness of breath, dizziness, palpitations, trembling, choking, depersonalization, and a fear of dying, fear of going crazy, or fear of losing control.

Panic disorder (PDA) To meet the American Psychiatric Association's current diagnostic criteria (DSM-III-R) there must be four panic attacks within a 4-week period, or at least one attack in 4 weeks followed by persistent fear of another attack for at least 1 month.

Vasovagal Pertaining to blood vessels.

A PHOBIA is defined as an intense, persistent, irrational, or exaggerated fear of an object or situation of sufficient potency to result in a strong desire to avoid the phobic object or situation despite the knowledge that the fear is unreasonable.

I. OVERVIEW OF PHOBIAS

A. History of Phobias

The term "phobia" comes from the Greek word *phobos,* meaning dread or fear, after the Greek god Phoebus, who so frightened his foes from afar that only his parents could endure being with him. Although the term can be traced from Roman times, phobias were considered personal idiosyncrasies until the 19th century when they were first studied clinically and given Greek and Latin names.

B. Prevalence

Epidemiological studies suggest that phobias may be the most common psychiatric disorders in the community, more common than alcohol abuse, dependence, or major depression.

C. Types of Phobias

Three types of phobias are currently delineated by the American Psychiatric Association in their diagnostic manual (DSM-III-R): simple phobia, social phobia, and agoraphobia without a history of panic disorder. Although they will be described separately, two or more of these phobia types can coexist; e.g., a person may be a social phobic, agoraphobic, and have a simple phobia.

1. Simple Phobia

Simple phobias are a persistent fear of a specific object or situation in which any exposure to the feared stimulus almost always provokes immediate anxiety. The object or situation is either avoided or endured with intense anxiety. This fear (or avoidant behavior) either interferes with one's normal functioning or causes marked distress. The fear is recognized as exaggerated or unreasonable. [See ANXIETY AND FEAR.]

There are hundreds of simple phobias; in fact there are at least 25 whose names begin with the letter A alone! Phobias range from the most common fears such as the fear of snakes to such obscure ones as the fear of the Northern lights. Some involve an exaggerated fear of things that most people fear to some degree such as disease and fires, but others involve situations that most people do not find frightening. The most common phobias for which people see treatment are claustrophobia (fear of closed places); blood, injury, or injection phobias; dental phobia, and small-animal phobias.

Simple phobias are distinguished from agoraphobia by their earlier age of onset, lower rates of fluctuation in galvanic skin response, greater response to desensitization treatment, and nonresponse to imipramine.

2. Social Phobia

Social phobia is a persistent fear of a situation(s) in which a person feels exposed to possible scrutiny by others and fears that he or she may be humiliated or embarrassed. As with the simple phobias, exposure to the specific phobic stimulus almost always provokes immediate anxiety, the phobic situation is either avoided or endured with intense anxiety, the avoidant behavior interferes with normal functioning, and the person recognizes that his/her fear is excessive.

Some of the most common problems that social phobics experience are difficulties in public speaking, urinating in crowded public rest rooms, writing or signing one's name in front of others, and eating in a public restaurant.

3. Agoraphobia without a History of Panic Disorder

The word "agoraphobia" means the fear of open spaces. It is really a misnomer, as agoraphobia actually is the fear of being in a situation (1) from which either one cannot escape or escape would be embarrassing; and/or (2) in which help may be unavailable if incapacitating symptoms such as dizziness, cardiac symptoms, loss of bowel control, or depersonalization suddenly develop. Usually these symptoms are associated with panic attacks, and the majority of agoraphobics present with either a current or past history of panic attacks (see panic disorder with agoraphobia). However, in agoraphobia without a history of panic disorder, the origin of these symptoms is less clear. Unlike the simple and social phobias, in agoraphobia, fear is not necessarily viewed as unreasonable. Common agoraphobic situations include being outside of one's home alone, standing in a crowded line, crossing a bridge, and traveling by car, bus, train, or subway. [See AGORAPHOBIA.]

II. DEFINITIONS AND CASE EXAMPLES

A. Simple Phobia

1. Defined

A simple phobia is a persistent fear of a specific object or situation.

2. Case Example

Beatrice, a 38-year-old woman, first reported experiencing a fear of elevators after seeing the movie *The Towering Inferno*. Whenever she thought of getting on an elevator, she would see an image in her mind of the elevator cable fraying and her being inside an elevator car hanging perilously above the ground. She would then fear that the cable would break entirely and that she would plunge to her death. Initially she was able to ride an elevator as long as it was a very short ride, and she would experience great relief from her anxiety once she exited the elevator. However, Beatrice lived in a major metropolitan city where many buildings were skyscrapers and found herself unable to even consider riding an elevator in these buildings.

B. Social Phobia

1. Defined

Social phobia is a persistent, irrational fear and compelling desire to avoid a situation in which the person may be exposed to possible scrutiny by others.

Heterogeneity exists in social phobia, and a recent distinction has been drawn between a nongeneralized and a generalized variant of social phobia. The former subtype is restricted to specific situations in which the person may be observed by others—such as eating in public or using a public lavatory—while the later subtype involves a generalized social apprehension.

2. Case Example

Anna is a 31-year-old employee in a local utility company. She is respected for her conscientious approach to her job and is being considered for promotion. Yet, Anna dreads this possibility almost as much as she keenly looks forward to it. She becomes markedly uneasy when she has to give presentations in front of others, particularly when she has to hold slides or write on a blackboard. She dreads, too, any situation where she must eat in public because of her fear that her hands will shake and cause others to see her as psychologically inadequate or unbalanced. Despite Anna's desires to rise in her career, she suffers from terror of being in the spotlight and being humiliated or making a fool of herself. She suffers more generalized social apprehension that she might do this but particularly in situations in which people may scrutinize the shaking of her hand.

C. Agoraphobia without a History of Panic Attacks

1. Defined

Agoraphobia is not simply the fear of wide open spaces, but rather is the fear of being in a situation in which escape is difficult or embarrassing or without help if incapacitating or embarrassing symptoms suddenly develop. Other names have been suggested for this disorder that more accurately describe the syndrome, including *platzschwindel,* which refers to the sensation of dizziness in public places, *phobic anxiety-depersonalization syndrome,* and *panphobia,* after the Greek god Pan, who would scare people to death when he jumped out of bushes.

2. Case Example

Shirley is a 41-year-old woman with irritable bowel syndrome who has bouts of abdominal pain, cramping, and diarrhea, and who has no history of panic attacks. One day, she was traveling with friends on her way to a restaurant, when she experienced a particularly severe bout of cramping and diarrhea in the car. Although her friends were very understanding, she felt humiliated by this experience. The next time her friends wanted to get together, she suggested an activity unrelated to going to a restaurant, for she found that even thinking about going out to eat would cause her to have cramping. Once she would decide not to go, the cramping would diminish. Despite the fact that she never again had such severe cramping or diarrhea when out in public, nor did she ever develop panic attacks, she feared that she would have these symptoms and slowly began to confine her outings to those places where she knew she could readily reach a bathroom, if that became necessary.

III. TYPICAL CLINICAL PICTURE

A. Simple Phobia

The essential features of a simple phobia are that the feared stimulus (object or situation) is specific; anticipatory anxiety leads to avoidance of the feared stimulus; and exposure to the stimulus results in intense anxiety. The fear is usually not of the object itself, but the predicted outcome. For example, claustrophobia is not really the fear of an enclosed space, but rather of suffocation; acrophobics (heights) fear falling; and snake phobics fear being bitten or otherwise harmed. Simple phobics may also fear having panic attacks to the feared stimuli.

There are three types of anxiety symptoms: physiological (e.g., increases in heart rate and respiration), behavioral (fleeing or freezing), and the subjective appraisal of the danger due to exposure to the feared stimulus. Physiological and neuroendocrine changes due to exposure to the feared stimulus have been documented. However, the phobic's subjective experience of these changes is greater than the actually documented changes.

Diagnosing a simple phobia is not as straight forward as one might think because people rarely seek treatment only for a simple phobia; rather, most may have multiple problems. What appears as a simple phobia may be part of an obsessive–compulsive disorder, or a major depressive episode. (*See* DEPRESSION; OBSESSIVE–COMPULSIVE BEHAVIOR.]

Although all simple phobias are classified together, there may be a good deal of heterogeneity in this category. At the time the DSM-III-R criteria were developed, there were insufficient data to subtype simple phobias, but this is being considered in the next revision of the criteria. The *blood/injury/injection phobias* appear to be well differentiated from other simple phobias in terms of the biphasic physiological response involved. After a brief initial increase in heart rate, blood pressure, and activation, there is then a reverse process in which there is a vasovagal slowing of the heart rate sometimes to the point of fainting. Second, some believe that *animal phobias* should also be a separate subtype due to their early age of onset, chronicity, and possible genetic component. Third, *situational phobias* such as claustrophobia and the fear of flying or driving resemble panic disorder with agoraphobia (PDA) with limited or moderate avoidance. Research suggests that situational phobias and PDA have similar age of onset, progression of events, and predictability of panic. Support for subtyping of phobias also comes from a factor analytic study of common phobic fears which suggests four subtypes: interpersonal events or situation; death, injury, illness, blood, and surgical procedure; animals; and agoraphobic fears.

B. Social Phobia

The key element in social phobia is a persistent, irrational fear and compelling desire to avoid a situation in which the person may be exposed to possible scrutiny by others. A fear also is felt that the individual may behave in a manner that will be humiliating and embarrassing. The fear is thus not just a fear of being observed but of the perceived risk of personal humiliation.

Individuals who are social phobic become pressured and fearful in ordinary social situations in which other people show little vestige of fear. They may experience threatening thoughts and feelings they cannot quell in situations that could involve scrutiny by others. The most typical domain of social circumstances that triggers anxiety in social phobics is one that requires formal speaking and interaction. The most typical situation feared across the subtypes of social phobia is the fear of public speaking, which occurs in over 70% of social phobics.

The DSM-III-R distinguishes a nongeneralized and a generalized variant of social phobia. Most social phobics fall into the generalized subtype and experience anxiety in more than one type of social situation. Some social phobics experience anxiety in only one kind of situation, however, such as in public speaking situations, or eating in public. This nongeneralized group of social phobics may present with both a later age of onset and lower symptoms of generalized anxiety, depression, and avoidance than the generalized group.

Despite the fact that difficulties with interaction with others may be a widespread concern in the general population, the category of social phobia is the extreme endpoint of such difficulties. Social phobia is a severe extreme along a continuum of social anxiety of milder forms—such as shyness, stage fright, dating anxiety, or audience anxiety. Unlike other anxiety disorders where females predominate, social phobias may be equally common in males and females.

Social phobia can be hard to diagnose because its features can be seen in a number of clinical syndromes. In addition, it can occur in people who have multiple problems. For example, fear and avoidance behavior of particular social situations—such as parties or meetings—are experienced by patients with other anxiety disorders; however, the greatest disruptiveness occurs for social phobics. From a third to a half of social phobics may have other anxiety disorders including agoraphobia and generalized anxiety disorder. [*See* ANXIETY DISORDERS.]

Social phobics may also be distinctive in terms of their demographic characteristics, typical cognitions, and behaviors. Social phobics are less likely to be married and have an earlier age of onset in life (between the ages of 15 and 20 years) in comparison to agoraphobics. Social phobics also tend to be of higher social class and attain higher educational status than other phobics. They have a later age of onset than animal phobics or blood phobics.

In addition, fears can arise from different cognitions in social phobics and other phobics. For example, the cognitions or thoughts of social phobics show more concerns with the fear of negative evaluation by others or fears of visible blushing. In contrast, agoraphobics report more cognitions concerned with the fear of losing bodily control, experiencing physically catastrophic events such as having a heart attack or dying.

In their behavior, social phobics exhibit more blushing, sweating, trembling, and muscle twitching, than agoraphobics, as well as palpitations. Agoraphobics seem to exhibit or report greater complaints with dizziness, breathing difficulties, weakness in limbs, buzzing or ringing in the ears, and fainting episodes. Agoraphobics also deal with anxiety by seeking out others, whereas social phobics tend to avoid interactions with others. Thus, social phobics attempt to reduce anxiety in very different ways than agoraphobics.

Another diagnostic difficulty concerns the distinction between social phobia and avoidant personality disorder. Although these categories have many similarities, it would appear that social phobics tend to make efforts to confront their fears or to enter feared situations. On the other hand, avoidant personalities may usually adopt avoidance as an unsatisfying lifestyle and have little desire to actually confront their fears. Approximately 20% of social phobics may also have avoidant personality disorder.

Social phobics and patients with avoidant personality disorder can be discriminated in part by differences in social skill. Many social phobics are not generally less socially skillful than other individuals yet have trouble using their skills. But the individuals with avoidant personality disorder seem to be generally less skillful and have greater social avoidance and distress.

C. Agoraphobia with History of Panic Disorder

It is difficult to present a typical clinical picture of the agoraphobic patient who has no history of panic disorder because few clinicians have ever seen patients in whom there is not a report of an initial panic attack. In fact, the committee that worked on the development of the APA's DSM-III-R criteria arrived at the present name for this disorder after deciding that it was premature to call it "agoraphobia with limited symptom attacks," even though this may have been correct in most cases. [See PANIC DISORDER.]

Consequently, one would expect the clinical picture to look very similar to that of PDA. First there are some unexplained and unpredictable symptoms which a person then fears will recur, leading to anticipatory anxiety and apprehension about another attack, and finally avoidant and dependent behavior. The attacks are associated with the situations in which they occurred and thus those situations are avoided in hopes of preventing another attack.

There is research to suggest that avoidance behavior is not related to frequency of panic, such that low incidence of panic symptoms would not necessarily correspond with mild avoidance. Degree of avoidance may be more related to availability of coping strategies for dealing with anxiety, job requirements, tolerance of others for the behavior, and gender.

IV. PREVALENCE AND AGE OF ONSET

A. Simple Phobia

Epidemiological studies suggests that between 5% and 10% of the population have fears severe enough to be considered phobias. Simple phobias appear to be more common in women.

Situations arousing intense fear are not necessarily phobic situations. For example, the fear of snakes is the most common fear, but not a common phobia, as snakes are fairly easily avoided without interference with everyday functioning. Likewise, fear of enclosures occur in 50 per 1000 persons, yet less than 5% of phobics are claustrophobic. The most common phobia is an illness/injury or blood phobia, with 42% of phobic persons having a phobia of this type. The next most common phobias are storm phobias (18%) and animal phobias (14%), agoraphobia (8%), fear of death (7%), fear of crowds (5%), and fear of heights (acrophobia, 5%).

Simple phobias have an earlier age of onset than either social phobia or agoraphobia. Animal phobias develop earlier (average age of onset, 7 years of age) than blood phobias (average age of onset, 9 years of age) or dental phobias (average age of onset, 12 years). Claustrophobia, on the other hand, tends to develop over a broader range of ages, with average age of onset of 20 years, which is more similar to that of agoraphobia (average age at onset, 27 years).

B. Social Phobia

Epidemiological studies suggest that approximately 2% of the population are socially phobic. However, these estimates may underestimate the extent to which people have severe social fears. For example, between 30 and 40% of individuals describe themselves as shy; nearly 22% of the general population report strong fear of social interaction situations, which include becoming very nervous as a result of fear of criticism or embarrassment. Nevertheless, many of these individuals are able to prevent significant disruption of their lives by avoiding the feared situations. They do not fully meet criteria for diagnosis because they are able to avoid confronting the feared social interaction situations in their lives. Thus, there is a direct analogy to people who are terrified of snakes but who do not qualify as snake phobics because they can avoid snakes.

C. Agoraphobia

Between 2.8% and 5.8% of the population are agoraphobic, with epidemiologists suggesting that 25 to 50% of these have agoraphobia without a history of panic attacks. Nevertheless, in one epidemiological study nearly half of patients who met criteria for agoraphobia without panic disorder actually had panic-like symptoms which did not meet criteria for panic disorder (e.g., limited symptoms, frequency too low, etc.); approximately a third had a major depressive episode leaving only 1% with "pure agoraphobia." In another study some of the agoraphobic patients had a somatic problem which was of an unpredictable nature, e.g., epilepsy or colitis.

Several explanations have been offered to explain this discrepancy between epidemiological and clinical samples, including (1) differences in definition of agoraphobia, (2) faulty memory of interviewees regarding infrequent panic attacks or limited symptom attacks that do not meet criteria for panic disorder, and (3) agoraphobics without panic may not seek treatment, a hypothesis at least partly supported by the fact that panic with agoraphobic avoidance is one of the leading reasons why people seek treatment. Those agoraphobics without panic also appear to have fewer comorbid anxiety disorders.

Although the relationship of panic and gender is nearly a one to one ratio, nearly 75% of all agoraphobics are women, a finding that is consistent around the world. There are a number of hypothesis regarding this higher incidence of agoraphobia in females, two of which suggest that the gender difference is an artifact: (1) the apparent gender differences may really be due to a difference in reporting symptoms, as it is culturally more acceptable for females to express fear, or (2) women may cope with their anxiety via avoidance, whereas men cope by other means, such as the use of alcohol. Also, there are two hypotheses suggesting that the gender differences are real: (1) women may be more avoidant due to endocrinological changes, or (2) males are taught to endure their anxiety.

Agoraphobia usually develops in early adulthood or late adolescence with the peak years being in the 20s.

V. CAUSES

A. Simple Phobia

The cause of simple phobias is not known. Several theories seek to explain the etiology and means of transmission of simple phobias.

1. Psychoanalytic

According to Freudian psychoanalytic theory, phobias are the result of unconscious conflicts related to an unresolved childhood Oedipal situation and thus castration anxiety is prominent.

2. Biological

More biologically based theories suggest that some stimuli have a greater probability of becoming phobic stimuli than others, and that these stimuli are objects or situations that may be potentially dangerous such as thunderstorms, illness or injury, heights, or small animals; thus, they are biologically "prepared" stimuli.

There is evidence which suggests that phobic fear, like depression, may be related to hemisphere preference such that right hemisphere preference is more highly associated with both depression and phobic fear.

3. Genetic

The transmission of simple phobias does appear to have a familial component. In one study, more than 30% of the relatives of simple phobics received a simple phobic diagnosis sometime in their lives; whereas only about 10% of the relatives of normal controls developed severe phobic anxiety sometime in their lifetimes. Simple phobia seems to have a genetic basis and does not seem to transmit an increased risk for other phobic disorders. Genetic studies suggest higher concordance rates among monozygotic (MZ) than dizygotic (DZ) twins in fears, especially animal fears.

Another theory based on a study of the interrelationship of environmental and genetic risk factors suggests that simple phobias result from a modest (30–40%) genetic vulnerability and phobic-specific traumatic events in childhood. According to this theory, situational phobias are considered more closely related to animal phobias than to agoraphobia. Also, maternal, but not paternal, separation was associated with an increased risk of phobias.

4. Cognitive–Behavioral

Early behavioral theories held that simple phobias were classically conditioned, and subsequent avoidance of the phobic stimulus led to a prevention, or reduction, of anxiety thus ensuring continued avoidance. This "two-factor" theory cannot account for the fact that many cases of phobias are not preceded by a traumatic incident, nor can it account for the specificity of phobias, or for the evidence that fears can be acquired by vicarious conditioning; i.e., the acquisition of a fear simply by the process of observation. Thus, the etiology of simple phobias appears to be far more complicated.

Later theories are more cognitive–behavioral as well as more complex. For example, some tend to see phobias as stemming from a biological vulnerability to anxiety along with a psychological vulnerability due to early experiences with uncontrollability. Central to one such theory are true and false danger signals or alarms, learned alarms, anxious anticipation, and biological prepared stimuli. The cognitive element of anxious apprehension is crucial, as a phobia cannot develop without anxious cognitions about the possibility of another alarm or traumatic event. The addition of false alarms accounts for conditioning in the absence of a traumatic event (true alarm), which, like a true alarm, can then lead to learned alarms. Such real and false alarms appear to play an important role in claustrophobia, as conditioning experiences are reported in a high percentage of cases. However, less than 50% of animal and blood–injury phobics report conditioning experiences. Real alarms are also experienced by those whose phobias appear to be the result of vicarious learning.

Recent studies have interviewed or given questionnaires to simple phobics to examine the pathways that have led to their fears. Aversive conditioning experiences in childhood or later appear to play a more frequent role as factors than pathways that involve indirect acquisition experience. For example, simple phobics are more likely to report having had a direct frightening encounter with a dog than a vicarious experience in which they learned of someone else's suffering. However, vicarious learning experiences also seem to serve as pathways, and many phobias are based on a combination of different pathways to fear.

5. Cognitive

A cognitive model of phobias suggests that the dread or fear arise from exaggerated expectations of being overmatched by threats or situations that can leave one suffering and helpless. A result of the faulty cognitions is that the person tends to automatically exaggerate the probability and consequences of harm, attentionally scan the environment for threats, and interpret ambiguous situations as likely to turn into the worst possible case scenarios. The phobic person may also exaggerate the extent that feared stimuli (e.g., spiders or dogs) can put him or her into danger by looming or moving forward.

6. Claustrophobia

Another theory suggests that in those claustrophobics who later develop agoraphobia, it may be that these persons have partial (embryonic or formes frustes) panic attacks in which symptoms begin but do not peak which act as an unconditioned stimulus interacting with biologically prepared stimuli. This is in keeping with the notion of false alarms as an initial trigger for the development of a phobic fear.

7. Blood–Injury Phobias

Blood–injury phobias appear to have an evolutionary, genetic, and physiological basis. Blood–injury phobia usually starts in childhood and appears to have a familial link. In some studies, estimates of between 27 and 67% of the blood–injury phobic patients also reported that family members had like problems. A strong link also exists between blood–injury phobia and the fainting experience. In some studies more than a third of people who reported having fainted to blood–injury stimuli reported having family members who fainted, compared to only slightly more than 10% among nonfainters. In a recent study, more than 66% of a group of blood–injury fainters had at least one parent who reported a similar history of fainting to blood–injury stimuli. This suggests the possibility of a hereditary component in the tendency to faint in response to blood–injury stimuli.

B. Social Phobia

A number of theoretical perspectives have attempted to account for the causes of social phobia. The principal explanations have been phrased in terms of classical conditioning, skills deficits, and cognitive factors.

1. Conditioning

Conditioning theories suggest that people who are socially phobic have experienced an aversive social encounter or interaction which has conditioned them to become anxious in similar settings in the future.

2. Skills Deficit

Skills deficit theories suggest that social phobics lack social skills or are unable to put their repertoire of skills into practice. A body of research exists which indicates that socially anxious individuals lack social skills, as does other research which indicates no differences between them and other individuals. One possible explanation of these findings is that there are two groups of socially anxious individuals, one with a deficit in social skills and the other without this deficit.

3. Cognitive

Cognitive theories suggest that social phobia is a result of faulty cognitions. For example, the person tends to automatically exaggerate the probability and consequences of humiliation in social encounters, or perceives the self as lacking the ability to sustain a desired social impression on others, while having unrealistically high standards. Research suggests that socially anxious individuals make more negative self-evaluations of their social performance (such as ''I looked like a fool''), and make more negative self-statements before and during social interactions (such as ''I'm boring, and not doing a good job''). They also report more irrational beliefs (such as ''If other people don't approve of me, I'm worthless''), lower expectations for their performance, and selectively exhibit better memory for negative versus positive information about their social performance. Social phobics also exhibit heightened self-consciousness and focus greater attention to how they may be regarded by others.

4. Genetic

Family studies suggest that there may be a genetic component to social phobia.

5. Social/Environment

Social phobics may differ from other individuals and agoraphobics in aspects of their experiences of parental rearing. Some studies suggest that social phobics rate their parents both as having been rejecting and lacking warmth and as having been overprotective. In contrast, agoraphobics may primarily regard their mothers as having been rejecting, although they see both parents as having lacked emotional warmth. Individuals with avoidant personality disorder may regard their parents in similar ways as do social phobics, but not rate their parents as having been overprotective.

C. Agoraphobia without History of Panic Disorder

The cause of agoraphobia is not known. Several hypotheses have been put forward. None are considered definitive.

1. Psychoanalytic

Freud did not distinguish between types of phobias, and some learning theorists also do not distinguish between agoraphobia and simple phobia. Hence, the psychoanalytic and some learning theories of the etiology of agoraphobia are the same as for simple phobias.

2. As Related to Panic Disorder

Other theories view agoraphobia in relation to panic attacks or panic disorder. One such theory suggests that PDA is a complication of panic disorder.

Some suggest a relationship between separation anxiety in child and adult panic disorder, and agoraphobia; however, there is more disconfirmatory than supporting evidence for this theory.

Learning theorists who do distinguish between simple phobias and agoraphobia also point to the role of panic attacks in the etiology of agoraphobia.

There are also a number of theories about avoidance in the absence of panic including the absence of safety signals (situations in which the person feels safe), bereavement, and an agoraphobic or dependent personality. However, there is not strong support for any of these theories.

It may be that there simply is not enough information about this type of agoraphobia. It may be that this is a heterogeneous group, with some persons experiencing limited symptom attacks, and others not. There is some evidence that phobic avoidance is no less in those with limited symptom attacks than it is in those with full-blown attacks.

VI. TREATMENT

A. Simple Phobia

1. Psychoanalytic

Psychoanalytic treatment aimed at uncovering and analyzing unconscious conflicts is not helpful to a majority of phobic patients. Even Freud realized that exposure to the feared stimulus was essential.

2. Pharmacotherapy

Pharmacotherapy (drug treatment) is not considered to be effective in the treatment of simple phobias. It may be, however, that with subtyping of simple phobias, the role of pharmacotherapy may be further investigated and more may be learned about various subtypes.

3. Cognitive–Behavioral

Various behavioral and cognitive–behavioral treatments have been developed all of which involve some type of exposure to the feared stimulus as a crucial element, such as in desensitization, modeling or participant modeling, and flooding. There continues to be debate as to which method of exposure is best. [*See* COGNITIVE BEHAVIOR THERAPY.]

It remains to be seen if different techniques may produce different results with different types of simple phobias. For example, treatments for panic may be helpful in situation phobias to the extent they resemble PDA.

4. Treatment for Blood Phobia

Due to the physiologically different processes in blood phobias, traditional *in vivo* exposure therapy has been modified. The tendency to faint early during exposure therapy can be reduced by lying down and tensing the muscles, a technique called "applied tension." The induction of anger during exposure can also reduce the tendency to faint early. Interestingly, in one treatment study, 10 of the 16 patients who completed treatment went on to become blood donors.

B. Social Phobia

1. Exposure-Based Treatments

As with the simple phobias, some type of exposure to the feared stimulus seems to be a crucial element in treatment for social phobia. Exposure-based treatments are effective at reducing anxiety and avoidance in social phobics.

2. Social Skills Training

Some theorists have suggested that social skills deficits are a cause of social anxiety. Research has as yet presented scant evidence that social skills training is more effective than other treatments or even than no treatment. Such skills training may be most appropriate when social phobic patients actually have deficiencies in their skills.

3. Cognitive–Behavior Therapy

Cognitive–behavioral techniques have been shown to be effective in the treatment of social phobia. The precise mechanisms by which they produce positive outcomes, however, are not clear. Nonetheless, a cognitive–behavioral approach has not been shown to be superior to behavioral treatments including applied relaxation, exposure, or social skills training. An apparent advantage of a cognitive–behavioral approach, though, is that treatment gains not only tend to be maintained after the termination of

treatment, but in some cases, there may be continued improvement.

4. Pharmacotherapy

The role of drug treatment or pharmacotherapy in social phobia is not fully defined. Tricyclic antidepressants, which are of benefit in panic disorder, do not appear useful in the treatment of social phobia. The beta-blocker drugs may reduce anxiety in limited situations in which temporary experiences of social anxiety are felt, but are not considered useful in the generalized type of social phobia. For example, they may reduce anxiety in situations (such as when individuals bowl or play musical instruments) where fine motor coordination is vital and may be disrupted by peripheral arousal in the limbs or hands.

Recent studies have demonstrated that phenelzine, a monoamine oxidase inhibitor type of antidepressant, and perhaps some other newer MAO inhibitors have positive effects in reducing social anxiety, and particularly that of generalized social phobia. The roles of fluoxetine (Prozac) and benzodiazepines (e.g., Xanax) are being investigated and preliminary results look promising.

C. Agoraphobia without History of Panic Disorder

1. Exposure-Based Treatments

Exposure is currently considered the best treatment for agoraphobia without panic. However, as has been demonstrated, this category of phobics is quite heterogeneous. Those who meet criteria for this phobic type may have panic attacks that fall below the threshold for criteria for panic disorder or may have a physical ailment which produces unpredictable symptoms. Those persons who have panic-like symptoms may benefit from treatments designed for PDA including cognitive–behavioral therapy either along or in combination with pharmacotherapy.

2. Cognitive–Behavioral

Cognitive behavior therapy (CBT) for agoraphobia alone, without the adjunctive use of exposure, is not as effective as exposure alone. However, when cognitive therapy is added to exposure treatments, the results are better than for exposure alone. Thus, the combination appears to more effective than either treatment by itself.

The results of studies of CBT of panic disorder in comparison to control groups are quite impressive. It seems reasonable to expect that such treatment would also be useful for persons with limited attacks. It is unclear whether the addition of exposure treatment to cognitive treatment is of any benefit.

3. Pharmacotherapy

Pharmacotherapy studies suggest the efficacy of the tricyclic antidepressant medication, imipramine, in the treatment of panic disorder. The role of benzodiazapines, such as Xanax, in the treatment of panic are currently being investigated, as well as the relative efficacy of both of these pharmacologic treatments. Although their role in cases of limited attacks has not yet been demonstrated, they may be of benefit.

Bibliography

Arrindell, W. A., Pickersgill, M. J., Merkelbach, H., Ardon, A. M., et al. (1991). Phobic dimentions. III. Factor analytic approaches to the study of common phobic fears: An updated review of findings obtained with adult subjects. Adv. Behav. Res. Ther. 13(2), 73–130.

Barlow, D. H. (1988). "Anxiety and its Disorders: The Nature and Treatment of Anxiety and Panic." Guilford, New York.

Chambless, D. L., and Gillis, M. M. (1993). Cognitive therapy of anxiety disorders. J. Consult. Clin. Psychol. 61(2), 248–260.

Edelmann, R. J. (1992). "Anxiety: Theory, research, and Intervention in Clinical and Health Psychology." Wiley, Chichester, England.

Fyer, A. J. (1987). Simple phobia. In "Anxiety" (D. Klein, Ed.). Karger, Basel.

Fyer, A., Mannuzza, S., Gallops, M. S., Martin, L. Y., et al. (1990). Familial transmission of simple phobias and fears: A preliminary report. Arch. Gen. Psych.. 47, 252–256.

Katerndahl, D. A. (1990). Infrequent and limited-symptom panic attacks. J. Nervous Mental Dis. 178(5), 313–317.

Kendler, K. S., Neale, M. C., Kessler, R. C., Heath, A. C., et al. (1992). The genetic epidemiology of phobias in women: The interrelationship of agoraphobia, social phobia, situational phobia, and simple phobia. Arch. Gen. Psych. 49(4), 273–281.

Kendler, K. S., Neale, M. C., Kessler, R. C., Heath, A. C., et al. (1992). Childhood parental loss and adult psychopathology in women: A twin study perspective. Arch. Gen. Psych. 49(2), 109–116.

Last, C. (Ed.) (1993). "Anxiety across the Lifespan: A Developmental Perspective." Springer, New York.

Last, C., and Hersen, M. (Eds.) (1988). "Handbook of Anxiety Disorders." Pergamon, Elmsford, NY.

Liebowitz, M. R. (1991). Psychopharmacologic management of social and simple phobias. In "The Clinical Management of Anxiety Disorders" (W. Coryell and G. Winokur, Eds.). Oxford University Press, New York.

Marks, I. M. (1988). Blood-injury phobia: A review. Am. J. Psych. 145, 1207–1213.

Merckelback, H., De-rutter, C., Van-den-Hout, M. A., and Hosktra, R. (1989). BRAT. 27, 657–662.

Zinbarg, R. E., Barlow, D. H., Brown, T. A., and Hertz, R. M. (1992). In "Annual Review of Psychology" (M. R. Rosenzweig and S. W. Porter, Eds.). Vol. 43. Annual Reviews, Inc., Palo Alto.

◆

PHONETICS

Pamela Case and Betty Tuller
Florida Atlantic University

Glossary

Allophone A variant of a phoneme; different sounds within a group which convey the same meaning.

Articulation Speech production; the postures and movements of the speech organs in speech production.

Coarticulation The overlapping of articulatory gestures in the production of adjacent speech sounds.

Formant A vocal tract resonance; relationships between formants characterize vowels.

Fundamental frequency The lowest frequency of a periodic wave; in speech, fundamental frequency corresponds to the rate of vocal fold vibration.

Phone A speech sound or segment.

Phoneme A minimal contrastive unit of speech; the smallest unit of speech which conveys meaning.

Prosody Phonetic aspects of speech that apply across segments, such as stress and intonation.

Source-filter theory A theory of speech production that quantifies the relationship between articulation and the acoustic output of the vocal tract.

Spectrogram A visible record of speech which provides information regarding frequency, intensity, and time.

PHONETICS is the study of speech sounds. It involves description of the possible sounds of the languages of the world, investigation of how the human vocal tract produces those sounds, and the attempt to understand how such sounds are perceived. His-torically, phonetics was taken to be the study of speech sounds without regard to their linguistic function. Contemporary phonetics is increasingly concerned with the aspects of sound that are necessary to convey meaning from the speaker to the listener, with explanations for the patterns of speech sounds used within and across languages, as well as with the changes that occur in those patterns over time. While the latter concerns have been considered exclusively the domain of phonology (the study of how sounds are organized into systems used in languages), it is becoming apparent that speech production and perception influence and are influenced by linguistic function.

I. WHY STUDY PHONETICS?

Henry Sweet was a 19th century phonetician on whom George Bernard Shaw's Professor Henry Higgins of *Pygmalion* was based. He considered phonetics to be the foundation of all study of language, applied or theoretical. At the applied or practical level, phonetics is useful for teaching pronunciation to non-native speakers of a language or to the deaf. Actors, politicians, broadcast journalists, and others may wish to acquire or eliminate an accent or affect a dialect. Teachers of reading can benefit from a thorough knowledge of phonetics to better understand the relationship between written and spoken language. Speech pathologists who diagnose and treat speech disorders must be able to describe disordered speech accurately, to understand how that speech is being produced, and to determine appropriate courses of correction. Engineers who design speech transmission devices, speech recognition systems, or speech synthesizers must have knowledge of phonetics. Linguists use phonetics to describe and catalog the sounds of the languages they study, patterns of sound change in the historical development of a language, and the sequence of events in language acquisition. [*See* PHONOLOGICAL PROCESSING AND READING.]

On a theoretical level, phonetics relates the physical aspects of how speech sounds are produced and perceived with their function in language. Phonetic theory should account for the sounds observed in human languages and the relative frequency with which they occur. It should make sense of the data acquired by linguists who phonetically describe the observed sequence of events in language acquisition and the types of sound changes which occur in languages. In addition, it should be able to account for the effects of physical damage to or deformities in the speech organs, as well as neurophysiological deficits.

II. A BRIEF HISTORICAL PERSPECTIVE

Phonetics had its beginnings in the work of the Sanskrit grammarian Panini in the 4th century B.C. Sir William Jones brought the Sanskrit work to light in the West in 1786. In the Indian writings, phonation and articulation were understood to be distinct processes, and the larynx was known to be the site of phonation. Places of articulation were used to classify speech sounds.

In the second half of the 18th century, phonetic science focused on how the different sounds in speech could be produced by the vocal apparatus. C. G. Kratzenstein developed one of the earliest speech synthesizers in order to obtain a prize offered by the Imperial Academy of Sciences of St. Petersburg for explaining the physiological differences between the five vowels of the Russian language. Wolfgang von Kempelen also produced an early speech synthesizer, or "talking machine," built primarily of wood and leather with the vocal cords represented by a reed and the airstream supplied by a bellows. C. J. Ferrein sought a physiological explanation for how the vocal cords produced phonation.

In the mid-19th century, the relationship between physiology and phonetics was still at the forefront of phonetic science, culminating in Johannes Müller's source-filter theory of speech production which still guides much phonetic research. Also, influential was A. M. Bell's *Visible Speech,* a system of speech classification designed for use in teaching the deaf to speak. In addition, Bell established the notion of cardinal vowels to serve as reference points for the articulatory description of vowels. Henry Sweet elaborated on Bell's visible speech, producing a

speech classification system which ultimately served as the basis for the International Phonetic Alphabet.

Into the early 20th century, Jean Pierre Rousselot produced a body of experimental work designed to obtain measurements of articulatory positions and to create permanent records of speech sounds. Jan Baudouin de Courtenay pointed out the distinction between a *phone,* or speech sound, and a *phoneme,* or group of speech sounds which have no significant differences in meaning in the language under study. During this time period, phonetics began to be treated as a science separate and distinct from phonology, or in Baudouin's terms, psychophonetics. Phonologist Ferdinand de Saussure contributed to this view with his notions of "*parole*" vs "*langue.*" He believed although speech (*parole*) was the substance of language (*langue*), it was essentially unrelated to linguistic function just as the substance of which chess pieces were made was unrelated to the game of chess. In a different vein, the work of R. H. Stetson in the early 1900s introduced the notion of motor phonetics with studies of speech as a set of "audible movements" rather than sounds produced by movements. He defined the syllable as being delimited by a chest pulse, contrary to the prevailing view of his colleagues that syllables were bounded by points of minimum sonority. His work anticipated the contemporary interest in the relationship between speech production and perception.

Since the 1950s, improvements in the technologies used to quantify the production and perception of speech have allowed empirical tests of traditional phonetic theory. Results from the studies converge on the notion that phonetics and phonology overlap, i.e., that the perception and production of speech are intimately linked with each other as they are with linguistic function.

III. PRELIMINARIES TO THE STUDY OF PHONETICS

One aspect of a phonetician's job is to understand what happens when human beings speak, which includes understanding how the speech sounds are produced and what the acoustic characteristics of the speech sounds are. Articulatory phonetics is the particular branch of phonetics concerned with the description of speech sounds in terms of postures and movements of the speech organs. Acoustic phonetics is concerned with how articulatory positions and movements shape speech sounds, and how speech sounds may be classified on the basis of acoustic characteristics. In order to study phonetics, it is necessary to have some knowledge of (1) the anatomy and physiology of the speech organs, (2) basic acoustics, and (3) the instrumentation and methods used to describe and analyze speech. The next three sections are devoted to these topics.

A. Anatomy and Physiology

The speech production apparatus is typically divided into three physiological components: (1) the respiratory system, which furnishes the airstream that powers speech, (2) the larynx, or voice box, which is the source of sound energy, and (3) the supralaryngeal vocal tract, which consists of air-filled cavities that act as an acoustic filter (see Fig. 1).

The respiratory system consists of the lungs and respiratory musculature. The muscles involved include the internal and external intercostals, the diaphragm, and abdominal muscles. The external and most of the internal intercostal muscles are involved in inhalation, while some internal intercostals and the abdominal muscles can act during exhalation to maintain steady air flow from the lungs. In quiet respiration, exhalation lasts about as long as inhalation. During speech, the duration of exhalation is markedly increased and is determined by the length of utterance. The steady air flow generated by the lungs during exhalation essentially powers speech.

The second physiological component, the larynx, is a cartilaginous group of structures which contains the vocal cords (more accurately called the vocal folds) and the glottis. The vocal folds are, literally, folds of ligament attached to the arytenoid cartilages on each side of the larynx. During normal breathing the arytenoids are quite far apart, but for speech, they move closer together to narrow the glottis. The glottis is the name given to the opening between the vocal folds. When the vocal folds are in complete contact the glottis disappears. Phonation, or voicing, occurs when the vocal folds adduct (move together) and subglottal air pressure builds up sufficiently to push them apart. Air rushes through and the vocal folds again come together as a result of their elasticity and the suction (Bernoulli force) generated by

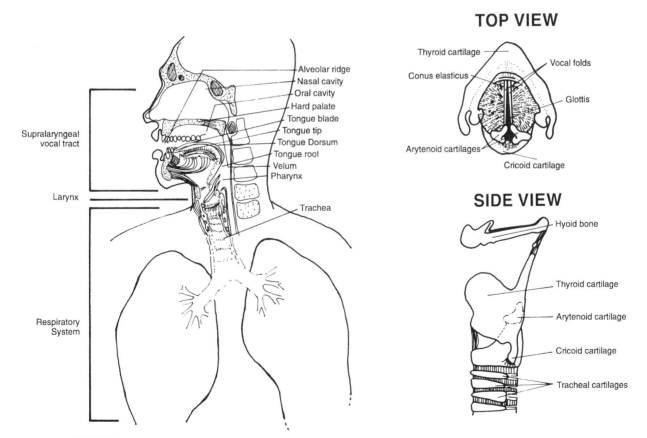

FIGURE 1   Major anatomical components of the speech production system with top and side view of larynx.

the air flow through the narrow glottis. Thus, the larynx acts as a valve to change the steady air flow from the lungs into a series of quasi-periodic pulses of air.

The third component is the supralaryngeal vocal tract (henceforth, the vocal tract). It encompasses the structures above the larynx, including the nasal cavity, oral cavity, and pharynx, and it acts as a variable acoustic filter on the source of acoustic energy to produce the characteristic resonances of speech sounds. The oral cavity serves as a resonating chamber with highly variable size and shape. The nasal cavity is actually partially filled and divided into several smaller cavities by membranes; thus, it is a relatively poor resonator. The pharynx, or throat, is a resonating cavity behind the oral cavity and above the larynx.

Anatomical structures of the vocal tract which are important for classifying speech sounds with respect to articulatory position are shown in Figure 1 (left side). The *lips* are used to close, constrict, or change the length of the oral cavity. The *teeth* are a point of constriction for some speech sounds. The *tongue* is a mass of muscles. Its base is attached to the hyoid bone which, in turn, is connected by a membrane to the top of the larynx. Although phoneticians generally divide the tongue into several functional regions including the tip (or apex), blade, dorsum, and root, the boundaries between regions are not anatomically distinct. The flexibility of the tongue allows significant manipulation of the shape and size of the oral cavity. The *hard palate* is the hard, bony part of the roof of the mouth. An important landmark on the hard palate is the *alveolar ridge,* the rough-textured ridge directly behind the upper front teeth. The *velum,* or *soft palate,* is at the back of the roof of the mouth; it can be raised to close the nasal cavities off from the rest of the vocal tract, or lowered to open the velic port and introduce nasal resonance.

B. Basic Acoustics

Sound results when a vibrating source first compresses nearby air molecules creating a region of increased air pressure. Then as the source moves back past its resting position, it pulls the disturbed air molecules back along with it resulting in an area of low air pressure or rarefaction. In other words, the local air molecules vibrate with the source. Each vibrating air molecule disturbs the molecules near it to produce the alternating high- and low-pressure areas which set up the wave motion of sound. Note

that the molecules themselves only oscillate and disturb the next molecules; they do not themselves travel along the sound wave.

To illustrate the important characteristics of wave motion, sine waves are shown in Figures 2a–2c, which graph the air pressure of sound waves at a point some distance from the sound source measured repeatedly over time. The physical characteristics of each wave include its amplitude and wavelength. Amplitude corresponds to the air pressure or strength of disturbance, and wavelength is the space occupied by a single cycle of the wave. The temporal dimensions of sound waves include the period, frequency, and propagation velocity. The period of a wave is the duration of time it takes to complete one cycle. For the wave in Figure 2a, the period is 0.01 seconds. Frequency refers to the number of cycles per unit time, usually cycles per second, or hertz (Hz). Thus, the frequency, which is the inverse of the period, is 1/0.01 or 100 Hz. The speed of propagation of a wave varies directly with the density of the medium through which it travels; thus, a wave travels faster through solids than gases. Propagation speed of a sound wave is about 1100 feet (or 35,000 cm) per second through air at sea level, and is independent of the frequency. Waves may be periodic (each cycle of the wave having the same period) or aperiodic (each cycle of the wave

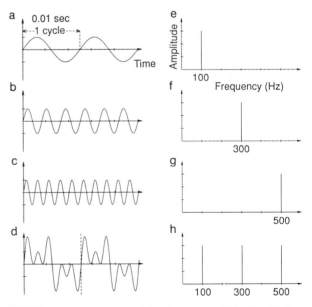

FIGURE 2   (a) Sine wave with a frequency of 100 Hz. (b) Sine wave with a frequency of 300 Hz. (c) Sine wave with a frequency of 500 Hz. (d) The sum of the three components in (a–c). (e–h) Corresponding amplitude spectra.

having a different period). An aperiodic wave may be characterized by the range of frequencies of its components, a fact which is important for acoustic classification of fricatives.

The three sine waves in Figures 2a–2c may combine to form the complex periodic wave in Figure 2d. Any complex periodic wave can be fully described as the sum of a number of sine waves, or Fourier components, of different amplitudes, frequencies, and phases. The frequency of the lowest frequency component of a complex wave corresponds to the fundamental frequency (f_0) of the complex wave. Notice that the period of one cycle is the same for the lowest frequency component wave in Figure 2a and the complex wave in Figure 2d. The frequency of each higher frequency component of the complex wave is an integer multiple of f_0. These components are referred to as the second, third, etc., harmonics (f_0 is the first harmonic). Figures 2b and 2c represent the second and third harmonics of the complex wave. In speech, f_0 corresponds to the rate of opening and closing of the vocal folds, and harmonics arise due to the elastic nature of the vocal folds. The amplitude spectra specify the frequencies and amplitudes of each of the component sine waves (Figs. 2e–2h). Phase of the components does not influence phonetic perception.

The sound source produced by the vibrating vocal folds is shaped by the vocal tract into resonant speech sounds. The laryngeal source of quasi-periodic pulses of air provides a set of spectral components (fundamental frequency and harmonics) that, on its own, produces a weak, buzzing sound. When the laryngeal source passes through the vocal tract, resonance properties of the vocal tract act as an acoustic filter, amplifying some frequencies of the source and suppressing others. Resonance refers to the propensity of an object undergoing forced vibration to oscillate with greatest amplitude in response to applied frequencies near its own natural frequency. Strike a tuning fork and it will vibrate at its natural, or resonant, frequency. (To strike a tuning fork is to apply a mechanical force containing many frequencies.) Place the vibrating tuning fork near another tuning fork which has the same resonant frequency, and the second fork will begin to vibrate. However, the two tuning forks must have the same (or very close to the same) natural frequencies for this resonance to occur. The irregularly shaped, air-filled cavities of the vocal tract also act as resonators amplifying their natural frequencies. The resonant frequencies of the vocal tract are called formants.

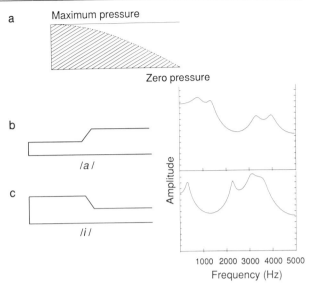

FIGURE 3   (a) Quarter-wave resonator. (b) The two-tube model of the vocal tract configuration associated with the vowel /α/ and the corresponding output spectrum. Peaks in the output spectrum represent formants. (c) Model of the vocal tract configuration and output spectrum for the vowel /i/.

The preceding description essentially summarizes the source–filter theory of speech production first postulated by Johannes Müller in 1848. Source–filter theory, which continues to be developed, accounts for much current data and allows for the quantification of the relationship between articulation and the acoustic output of the vocal tract. To examine source–filter theory more closely, consider the simplest model of a vocal tract as an air-filled tube open at one end and closed at the other (see Fig. 3a). Such a tube is called a quarter-wave resonator because there is maximum air pressure at the closed end and zero air pressure (relative to atmospheric pressure) at the open end. From point of maximum pressure to point of zero pressure is one-quarter of the total sine wave. The tube resonates to frequencies given by $(2k + 1)v$ times $\frac{1}{4}$ the length of the tube, where v is the velocity of propagation (35,000 cm per second through air at sea level) and k is an integer. If the length of the tube is 17.5 cm, which is about the length of the average male vocal tract, then the first three resonances (formants) are

$$\frac{(2 \times 0 + 1)35,000}{4 \times 17.5} = 500\,\text{Hz} = \text{F1}$$

$$\frac{(2 \times 1 + 1)35,000}{4 \times 17.5} = 1500\,\text{Hz} = \text{F2}$$

$$\frac{(2 \times 2 + 1)35{,}000}{4 \times 17.5} = 2500\,\text{Hz} = \text{F3}.$$

F1, F2, and F3 are the symbols which correspond to the first, second, and third formants, respectively. Resonant speech sounds have characteristic formant patterns. The particular formants calculated above are the formants of the schwa vowel (the initial sound in *about*), which is produced with a vocal tract configuration that is essentially a single uniform tube. The fact that the actual tube, the vocal tract, is curved has little effect on the formants. If the tube, or vocal tract, is longer, the denominators in the equations above increase and the resonance frequencies are lower and closer together.

In this simple model, the tube has a uniform cross-sectional area everywhere along its length, which accounts for the even spacing of the formants. However, the human vocal tract is flexible; its length (e.g., by protrusion or retraction of the lips) and shape are changeable, resulting in unevenly spaced formants. Thus, the vocal tract is able to produce many sounds with many different formant patterns. For example, consider the vowel /ɑ/ as in *father* which can be modeled as a two-tube resonator. The "tubes" correspond to the vocal tract cavities in front of and behind the major vocal tract constriction. Each cavity is effectively a quarter-wave resonator because the cross-sectional area of the back cavity is so much smaller than that of the front. For the vowel /i/ as in *deed,* the vocal tract can also be modeled as a two-tube resonator, but in this case the cross-sectional area of the back cavity is large relative to that of the front, so that the back cavity effectively has two closed ends, making it a half-wave resonator, while the front is a quarter-wave resonator. (A half-wave resonator has maximum air pressure at both ends, so that it resonates to integer multiples of half a sine wave.) The configuration of the vocal tract determines which of the frequencies in the signal produced by the laryngeal source will be amplified and which will be effectively suppressed. Figure 3 (b and c) illustrates the two-tube configurations and the output spectra associated with /ɑ/ and /i/.

To summarize, in source-filter theory there is a clear separation of the glottal source of sound energy and the filtering of the sound by the vocal tract configuration which amplifies sound energy at certain frequencies and attenuates others. The resonant frequencies are the formants associated with voiced speech sounds which determine, to a great extent, perception. A major strength of source-filter theory is that it provides a means of quantifying the relationship between articulatory postures and acoustics.

C. Instrumentation and Methods

1. Descriptive Methods: Phonetic Transcription

Phonetic transcription is a tool for describing the sounds of speech. One level of phonetic transcription, broad transcription, is concerned primarily with the functional distinctions between sounds. A *phone* is a speech sound, and a *phoneme* is a group of speech sounds which have no significant differences in meaning in a particular language. For example, the *p* in *pat* and *spat* are two different phones, but not different phonemes, in American English. Only the first is accompanied by unvoiced airflow (aspiration) on release of the lip constriction. The *p* in *pat* versus the *b* in *bat* are different phonemes; they are two different sounds which convey different meanings. When transcription is for the purpose of noting phonemes, or how sounds convey meaning, a simple set of symbols placed between slashes (/ /) is used. For example, the *p* in *pat* and in *spat* are both indicated as /p/ in a broad transcription. The small differences in pronunciation of the *p* are ignored. Another level of phonetic transcription, narrow transcription, specifies articulatory details of the production of speech sounds. Narrow transcription has different symbols that are placed in square brackets ([ ]) for each allophone, or variant, of a phoneme. A narrow transcription of the *p* in *pat* is [pʰ], indicating that the *p* is produced with aspiration. A narrow transcription of the *p* in *spat* is [p]. Narrow transcription is particularly useful when transcribing an unknown language or disordered speech.

The most commonly used set of symbols for phonetic transcription is the International Phonetic Alphabet (IPA; see Fig. 4). The first version of the IPA was published in 1888, and was based on the premise that there should be one symbol for each speech sound possible without regard to language. Many of the symbols are taken from the Roman alphabet, with other letters and diacritics (marks added to a symbol to modify its value) used as necessary. For example, the raised *h* in [pʰ] is a diacritic which signifies aspiration, and the colon in [a:] indicates a longer duration. A word of caution regarding the IPA is that because it was developed in Europe using the Roman alphabet as its basic symbol set,

CONSONANTS

	Bilabial	Labiodental	Dental	Alveolar	Postalveolar	Retroflex	Palatal	Velar	Uvular	Pharyngeal	Glottal
Plosive	p b			t d		ʈ ɖ	c ɟ	k ɡ	q ɢ		ʔ
Nasal	m	ɱ		n		ɳ	ɲ	ŋ	ɴ		
Trill	ʙ			r					ʀ		
Tap or Flap				ɾ		ɽ					
Fricative	ɸ β	f v	θ ð	s z	ʃ ʒ	ʂ ʐ	ç ʝ	x ɣ	χ ʁ	ħ ʕ	h ɦ
Lateral fricative				ɬ ɮ							
Approximant		ʋ		ɹ		ɻ	j	ɰ			
Lateral approximant				l		ɭ	ʎ	ʟ			
Ejective stop	p'			t'		ʈ'	c'	k'	q'		
Implosive	ɓ ɓ			ɗ			ʄ	ɠ	ʛ		

Where symbols appear in pairs, the one to the right represents a voiced consonant. Shaded areas denote articulations judged impossible.

VOWELS

Front   Central   Back

Close   i • y ——— ɨ • ʉ ——— ɯ • u
ɪ ʏ   ʊ
Close-mid   e • ø ——— ɘ • ɵ ——— ɤ • o
ə
Open-mid   ɛ • œ ——— ɜ • ɞ ——— ʌ • ɔ
æ
Open   a • ɶ ——— ɑ • ɒ

Where symbols appear in pairs, the one to the right represents a rounded vowel.

OTHER SYMBOLS

ʍ Voiceless labial-velar fricative
w Voiced labial-velar approximant
ɥ Voiced labial-palatal approximant
ʜ Voiceless epiglottal fricative
ʢ Voiced epiglottal fricative
ʡ Epiglottal plosive
ɕ ʑ Alveolo-palatal fricatives
ɺ Additional mid central vowel

⊙ Bilabial click
| Dental click
! (Post)alveolar click
ǂ Palatoalveolar click
‖ Alveolar lateral click
Alveolar lateral flap
ɧ Simultaneous ʃ and x

Affricates and double articulations can be represented by two symbols joined by a tie bar if necessary.
k͡p t͡s

SUPRASEGMENTALS

ˈ	Primary stress	ˌfoʊnəˈtɪʃən
ˌ	Secondary stress	
ː	Long	eː
ˑ	Half-long	eˑ
˘	Extra-short	ĕ
.	Syllable break	ɹi.ækt
		Minor (foot) group	
‖	Major (intonation) group	
‿	Linking (absence of a break)	

TONES & WORD ACCENTS

	LEVEL			CONTOUR
e̋ or ˥	Extra high		ě or ˩˥	Rising
é ˦	High		ê ˥˩	Falling
ē ˧	Mid		e᷄ ˧˥	High rising
è ˨	Low		e᷅ ˩˧	Low rising
ȅ ˩	Extra low		e᷈ ˧˩˧	Rising-falling etc.
↓	Downstep		↗	Global rise
↑	Upstep		↘	Global fall

DIACRITICS

◌̥	Voiceless	n̥ d̥	◌̹	More rounded	ɔ̹	◌ʷ	Labialized	tʷ dʷ	◌̃	Nasalized	ẽ
◌̬	Voiced	s̬ t̬	◌̜	Less rounded	ɔ̜	◌ʲ	Palatalized	tʲ dʲ	◌ⁿ	Nasal release	dⁿ
◌ʰ	Aspirated	tʰ dʰ	◌̟	Advanced	u̟	◌ˠ	Velarized	tˠ dˠ	◌ˡ	Lateral release	dˡ
◌̤	Breathy voiced	b̤ a̤	◌̠	Retracted	i̠	◌ˤ	Pharyngealized	tˤ dˤ	◌̚	No audible release	d̚
◌̰	Creaky voiced	b̰ a̰	◌̈	Centralized	ë	◌̴	Velarized or pharyngealized	ɫ			
◌̼	Linguolabial	t̼ d̼	◌̽	Mid-centralized	e̽	◌̝	Raised	e̝ (ɹ̝ = voiced alveolar fricative)			
◌̪	Dental	t̪ d̪	◌̩	Syllabic	ɹ̩	◌̞	Lowered	e̞ (β̞ = voiced bilabial approximant)			
◌̺	Apical	t̺ d̺	◌̯	Non-syllabic	e̯	◌̘	Advanced Tongue Root	e̘			
◌̻	Laminal	t̻ d̻	◌˞	Rhoticity	e˞	◌̙	Retracted Tongue Root	e̙			

FIGURE 4 International phonetic alphabet revised for 1989. [From International Phonetic Association; reprinted by permission.]

it has a built-in Western bias. Currently, phoneticians are attempting to recast IPA symbols into those readily available in computer fonts.

2. Analytic Instruments and Methods

The sound spectrograph, first introduced in the 1940s, is an instrument that provides a visual record of sound called a spectrogram. Spectrograms, including their computerized digital versions, display time from left to right on the horizontal axis, frequency on the vertical axis, and amplitude on a gray scale (or, less often, on a color scale) with greater amplitude producing darker marks. In the spectrogram of a production of *stop now* in the bottom of Figure 5, the formants associated with the vowels can be seen as dark bars. They remain steady while formant frequency is constant, and bend up or down as the configuration of the vocal tract changes over time, indicating the dynamic nature of speech. Fundamental frequency can be observed in the vertical striations which occur during voiced sounds. Blank spaces in the spectrogram indicate the absence of sound energy, as during vocal tract obstruction for the unvoiced stop consonants /t/ and /p/. Frication, as for the /s/, is indicated by relatively intense energy spread over a broad range of frequencies. The nasal sound /n/ is indicated by a dominant low frequency formant with several higher frequency, very low amplitude formants.

Digitized speech waveforms (top of Fig. 5) display the amplitude variations in the acoustic signal over time, and permit fast, accurate measurement of duration and amplitude of speech. The flexibility of computerized digital speech signals allows the speech scientist to choose any segment of an utterance for further analysis. Speech processing software permits editing of the waveform or spectral components for experimental purposes. For example, silent gap duration associated with a stop consonant can be increased or decreased, and the resulting waveform played to listeners. Effects of such manipulations provide a window into the nature of speech perception. Attempts to edit waveforms underscore that speech is not merely a string of discrete segments. Because of the effects of coarticulation (overlapping articulations, see Section VI), any selected segment of speech is colored by its context. A fundamental problem for speech scientists is that the same utterance spoken by different people with different vocal tracts producing different acoustic output can be understood by listeners to be the same utterance, but the common aspects among the acoustic signals have not been found. The search for acoustic commonalities is motivated by the desire to understand how human beings perceive a speaker's intended message and to produce computer-based speech recognition devices. Until there is a better understanding of what information in the speech signal is essential to maintain phonetic identity, it is unlikely that machines will recognize multiple speakers producing a corpus of speech that approximates the size recognized by human beings.

The development of speech synthesizers has made it possible to control almost any speech feature of interest, and thus to test hypotheses regarding the importance of the feature for perception. Two basic types of speech synthesizers use either an articulatory or acoustic level of control. Articulatory synthesizers are based on models of the vocal tract, and acoustic synthesizers are based on acoustic models of the speech signal. The earliest speech synthesizers, such as those of Wolfgang von Kempelen and C. G. Kratzenstein in the 1800s, were mechanical models of the vocal tract. The Vocoder, developed by Homer Dudley in the 1930s, first analyzes input speech, then reconstructs the acoustic signal. A later development, the use of operator-specified control signals instead of input speech, made the Vocoder more suitable for use in experi-

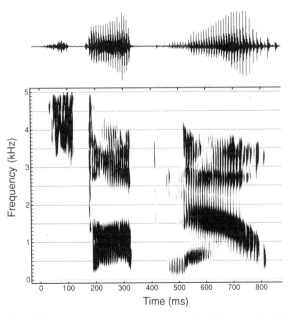

FIGURE 5   (Top) The speech waveform of a digitized production of *stop now*. (Bottom) A spectrogram of the same production. See text for details.

mental phonetics. A significant improvement in speech synthesis occurred with the development of the Pattern Playback at Haskins Laboratory in the 1950s. The Pattern Playback is an acoustic synthesizer that uses hand-painted patterns, usually formant tracks, on transparent acetate that are scanned with a beam of light and converted to an acoustic signal. Manipulation of the number, duration, and frequencies of the formants provided much new data regarding the acoustic information for speech perception. With digital computers, both acoustic and articulatory synthesis have become more rapid and flexible. Of the two basic types of synthesis, acoustic synthesis is less complicated and efficiently produces relatively high quality speech. Articulatory synthesis is particularly useful for testing hypotheses about articulation directly. However, it is limited by our knowledge of vocal tract activity, which is largely hidden. Much of the current data regarding the vocal tract are from cineradiographic, and other X-ray techniques. Such techniques have limitations, including the harmful effects of radiation, which severely restrict the number of speakers studied and the generality of the findings. More recent noninvasive technologies, such as magnetic resonance imaging (MRI), ultrasound, and alternating magnetic field devices, have great potential for enhancing the articulatory models on which synthesis is based.

IV. ARTICULATORY AND ACOUSTIC CLASSIFICATION SCHEMES

In this section, we describe classification schemes for the two major classes of speech sounds, consonants and vowels. Although both articulatory and acoustic classification schemes have been devised relatively independently, here we depart from tradition and intertwine the two in order to highlight the intimate relationship between articulation and the acoustic characteristics of speech sounds. While most of the examples are from English, the principles apply across languages.

A. Consonants

Consonants are produced with a degree of obstruction of the vocal tract. They are typically described according to place of articulation (the place of the major vocal tract constriction), manner of articula-

tion, and presence or absence of voicing. Table I lists and describes significant places of articulation and provides selected examples of phonemes produced in those places.

Manner of articulation refers to the way in which the airstream is obstructed. The categories of manner of articulation include stops, nasals, fricatives, affricates, and approximants (glides and liquids), as well as flaps, taps, and trills.

Plosives are a type of stop consonant. A plosive occurs when the velum is raised to block the passage of air through the nasal cavity and a complete closure is formed at some point in the oral cavity. Air pressure builds up behind the closure and is released explosively when the articulators are opened. Examples are /p t k b d g/, the initial sounds in *pad, tad, cad, bad, dad,* and *gad.*

Acoustic characteristics of stop consonants include a silent period of about 50–100 msec duration, a transient burst of energy of no more than 40 msec duration on release of the vocal tract occlusion, and formant transitions. When the stop consonant is in syllable-initial position, the release burst may or may not be accompanied by aspiration. Aspiration is a breathy noise generated as air passes through the partially closed vocal folds and into the pharynx. It typically sounds like the glottal fricative /h/ as in *hop.* Stop consonants in word-final position may or may not be released. The common articulatory feature for word-final stops is a period of closure which shows up as a gap in the acoustic signal. Release results in a short burst of acoustic energy; when the stop is not released, no burst is evident.

Stop consonants may also be categorized according to their voicing characteristics. The time

TABLE I
Some Places of Articulation

Place	Description	Examples
Bilabial	Made with two lips	p, b, m
Labiodental	Lower lip to upper front teeth	f, v
Dental	Tongue tip to upper front teeth	θ, ð
Alveolar	Tongue tip to alveolar ridge	t, d, n, s, z
Retroflex	Tongue tip to back of alveolar ridge	r
Palatoalveolar	Tongue tip to post-alveolar palate	ʃ, ʒ
Palatal	Tongue dorsum to hard palate	j
Velar	Tongue dorsum to soft palate	k, g, ŋ

interval between the release of the stop and the onset of vocal fold vibration is called voice onset time (VOT). Voiceless stops are characterized by a 25- to 100-msec VOT. Voiced stops have VOTs which extend over a small range around zero. In some cases there may be a slight lead when voicing begins before the release burst occurs. Thus, the range of VOTs for voiced stops is about −20 to +20 msec. In English, the voiceless stops have aspirated releases except when they follow /s/. Consider the earlier example of the aspirated stop in *pat* versus the unaspirated stop in *spat*. Voiced stops are typically unaspirated in English. Aspiration of stops is not phonemic in English, although it is in some languages. For example, in Thai [pàak] means *mouth* while [pʰàak] means *forehead*.

When stop consonants are in syllable-initial position, stop release entails a rapid change in vocal tract shape resulting from movement away from the place of articulation of the stop. This articulatory transition (the rapid change in resonator shapes) is associated with transitions in the acoustic signal. Such formant transitions are a very important source of acoustic information for speech perception. In Figure 6, the formant transitions for /d/ followed by several vowels are illustrated. Notice that formant transitions for /d/ are different for syllables with different vowels. This provides an example of the lack of segmentability of speech at the acoustic level. There is no acoustic segment for /d/ that always represents a /d/ in every context.

An additional stop is the glottal stop /ʔ/ which is used by many English speakers in the production of *unh-unh*, an expression for *no*, or as the sound before the /l/ in the London Cockney pronunciation of *bottle*. Acoustically, glottal stops do not usually have the marked formant transitions observed in other stops. In word-initial position they are characterized by a brief release burst of energy that is spectrally like the following voiced sound.

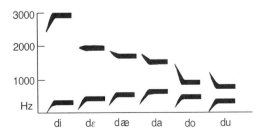

FIGURE 6   Stylized formant patterns (F1 and F2) for /d/ followed by indicated vowels.

Nasals occur when there is a closure at some point in the oral cavity and the velum is lowered to open the velic port to permit passage of air through the nasal cavities. The nasal stops in English are /m, n, ŋ/, as in the initial sounds of *map* and *nap* and the final sound in *sing*. When the velic port is open, allowing air passage through the nasal cavity, the vocal tract is a relatively long tube from the larynx to the opening at the nose with a side branch in the oral cavity. Since longer tubes are associated with lower frequencies, nasal consonants typically have a dominant low frequency resonance of about 300 Hz called a nasal murmur. The higher frequency formants are highly damped due to the absorption of sound energy in the nasal cavity.

Fricatives result from narrowing the vocal tract at some point by the close approximation of articulators. As the airstream moves through the narrow constriction, turbulence occurs producing the "noisy" quality associated with aperiodic waves. Fricatives may be voiced or voiceless. Voiceless English fricatives include /s ʃ f θ/, the initial sounds in *so*, *show*, *fin*, and *thin*. The corresponding voiced fricatives are /z ʒ v ð/ as in *zoo*, *pleasure*, *view*, and *the*. Fricatives have relatively long noise duration, which varies with place of articulation and presence or absence of voicing. For example, frication noise for the labiodental /f/ is longer than for the alveolar /s/. Voiced fricatives tend to have shorter noise segment durations than voiceless fricatives. For example, frication noise for /v/ is shorter than for /f/. Voiced fricatives have two sources of energy (the laryngeal source and turbulence), while voiceless fricatives have only the turbulent source. Thus, voiced fricatives tend to have greater amplitude than their voiceless counterparts.

Affricates are combinations of a stop consonant and a fricative having the same place of articulation as the stop. The initial sounds in *chair* and *jump* are examples of English affricates which result when /t/ and /ʃ/ are combined and /d/ and /ʒ/ are combined, respectively. Frication noise tends to be shorter for affricates than for fricatives. An important acoustic cue distinguishing affricates from stops or fricatives is rise time of turbulent noise energy. Rise time is the time it takes for the amplitude of an acoustic signal to reach its maximum value. Stops have the most rapid rise time, followed by affricates, then fricatives.

Approximants are sounds made when articulators are moved into approximation, but not so close as to produce the turbulence associated with a fricative.

They are divided into glides, or semivowels, and liquids. There are only two English glides, /w/ and /j/ as in *wet* and *yet*. They are distinguished from vowels by the rapid motion toward or away from an articulatory position corresponding to a vowel. For example, the /w/ in *wee* is described as having the same place of articulation as /u/, but there is a rapid movement away from that position toward the place of articulation for the following /i/. The transitions associated with glides are relatively longer than transitions in stop-vowel syllables and shorter than transitions between two vowels. For example, the transition for /w/ is longer than that for /b/ and shorter than the transition from the vowel /u/ to another vowel sound, as in *buoy*. The formant frequencies for all three sounds start and end at similar values. The major distinction among them is duration of the transition. Note, however, that speaking rate affects perception of transition durations. When sounds that have transition durations which at a normal speaking rate would indicate a stop consonant are heard in the context of a faster speaking rate, they are perceived to be glides. Relative duration, not absolute duration, is the important acoustic cue.

The liquids in English include /l/ as in *led* and /r/ as in *red*. Liquids are also classified as approximants since they involve approximation of vocal tract structures without complete closure. Liquids have well-defined formant structures like those of glides and vowels. As is true for stops, the articulatory movements associated with liquids are quite rapid, resulting in relatively short acoustic transitions. The transition associated with /l/ is even shorter than that associated with /r/. The F1 for both sounds begins with a steady state. The F1 for /r/ has a relatively short initial steady state and longer transition, and for /l/ has relatively long initial steady state and shorter transition. Onset frequencies for F2 and F3 are relatively low for /r/ compared to /l/. The acoustic description given here is specific to liquids in syllable-initial position, and does not take into account the fact that /r/ and /l/ have many allophones, or variants. Consider, for example, the difference between the /l/ sounds in *leaf* versus *feel* or the /r/ sounds in *reef* versus *fear*.

A flap, or tap, can be heard in the medial sounds of *latter* or *ladder*. It is made with a very rapid movement of the tongue tip to and away from the alveolar ridge. The primary acoustic feature is its brief duration compared to distinctive production of /d/ or /t/. A trill is produced aerodynamically; air passes through a constriction formed by a relaxed articulator. The resulting Bernoulli forces cause an oscillation of the articulator toward and away from the point of constriction. This series of brief occlusions imposes periodic modulation on the acoustic signal. In Spanish, there is a phonemic contrast between the flapped [ɾ], as in *pero* which means *but,* and the trilled [r], as in *perro* which means *dog.*

The sounds that have been described so far have all been produced with a *pulmonic egressive* airstream mechanism. *Pulmonic* refers to the lungs, and *egressive* means that the air flows outward. There are a number of speech sounds in a variety of languages that are produced in other ways, with an inward air flow (*ingressive*), by moving the closed glottis up or down (the *glotallic* airstream mechanism), or by raising or lowering the velum to move the column of air in the oral cavity (the *velaric* airstream mechanism). For example, one class of such sounds, ingressive velaric clicks, is common in North American Indian and South African languages. The *tsk-tsk-tsk* sound of disappointment or admonition is a series of such clicks.

B. Vowels

Vowels are characterized by a relatively open vocal tract and vibrating vocal folds. In general, none of the articulators come in close contact, and the airstream is relatively unobstructed. Acoustic classification schemes for vowels are based on formant patterns which are shaped by the relative positions of the articulators along several dimensions: (1) the front-to-back position of the highest point of the tongue, (2) the relative height of the tongue body, and (3) the degree of lip rounding. In general F1 varies inversely with tongue or vowel height, so low vowels such as the /ɑ/ in *father* typically have higher F1s than high vowels such as the /i/ in *feed*. In addition, tongue root advancement, which is characteristic of high vowels, has the principal acoustic effect of lowering F1. Thus, the distinction between high and low vowels is signalled primarily by differences in F1. F2 and the difference between F2 and F1 vary with front–back position of the tongue. Lips can be rounded, neutral, or spread. In /u/ as in *food* the lips are rounded, in /i/ as in *feed* the lips are spread, and in /ə/ as in the initial vowel sound in *about* the lips are in a neutral configuration. In general, lip rounding has the effect of lengthening the vocal tract, thus lowering the formant frequencies. However, there are interaction effects, and F3 is lowered relatively more for front vowels while F2 is lowered relatively more for back vowels. Lip rounding is often associated with back vowels, while spreading is associated with front vowels. Thus, distinctions between vowels are not typically made on rounding alone. There are exceptions to this rule, and some languages do make use of (1) front rounded or (2) back spread vowels. For example, the /y/, as in *tu* in French is a front, rounded vowel, and can be demonstrated by trying to pronounce /i/ as in *feed* while rounding the lips.

Four vowels, /i u α æ/, represent the extremes of the articulatory positions, and form the vowel quadrilateral. When the vowel /i/ as in *feed* is produced, the tongue is in the extreme high, front position with the lips spread. When /u/ as in *food* is produced, the tongue is in the extreme high, back position, and the lips are rounded. The /α/ sound as in *father* is made from the extreme low, back position with the lips in a neutral configuration. The /æ/ as in *fad* is a low, mid-front (the tongue cannot move as far forward in a low position as when it is in a high position) vowel with lips spread. There is a set of eight reference vowels defined along the periphery of the quadrilateral called the cardinal vowels. The front cardinal vowels (/i e ɛ a/) are equidistant from each other, as are the back cardinal vowels (/u o ɔ α/). The schwa is a mid, central vowel produced with the tongue in a relatively neutral or resting position; it is represented near the center of the vowel quadrilateral. (Figure 7 illustrates relative articulatory position of the vowels of the vowel quadrilateral, the cardinal vowels, and the schwa in a vowel space.) The first three formants are sufficient

to identify a given vowel (see Figs. 8 and 9 for schematic representations of the formant patterns and articulatory postures, respectively, associated with the vowels /i I ɛ æ α ɔ U u/ in *heed, hid, head, had, hod, hawed, hood,* and *who'd*). Of course, the specific formant values and articulatory positions of vowels in the space are for canonical vowels. Much variability occurs when the vowels are actually produced, even in isolation, although the relative values and positions are assumed to be maintained.

Certain pairs of vowels share most of the same articulatory features, but differ primarily in tongue root position, or in tenseness of tongue muscles. These are the tense–lax pairs, and include /i/ as in *beet* versus /I/ as in *bit,* /u/ as in *food* versus /U/ as in *good,* and /e/ as in *bait* versus /ɛ/ as in *bet.* As the tongue root is moved forward, the pharynx widens to produce tense vowels. Tense vowels are characterized by lower F1, higher F2 and F3, and longer duration than their lax counterparts.

Examples of a rhotacized, or r-colored, vowel are found in *bird, herd, purr,* or *pearl.* This single-vowel sound is called the *schwar,* and it can be produced in several ways. The front of the tongue can be retracted, the back of the tongue can be bunched, or the tongue root can be retracted into the pharynx. The primary acoustic characteristic of rhotacized vowels is the lowering of F3.

Nasalized vowels occur when the velic port is open, as is often the case when a vowel precedes a nasal consonant, e.g., in the word *bond.* As with consonants, nasalization of vowels results in a low frequency nasal formant. In English, there is no vowel distinction based on nasalization. However, such distinctions are made in other languages. For example, in French, *mon* (meaning *my*) pronounced [mõ] contrasts with *mot* (meaning *word*) pronounced [mo].

Two aspects of formant patterns besides formant center frequencies are of interest, bandwidth and

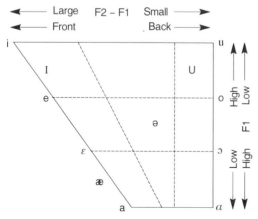

FIGURE 7   The relative articulatory positions and acoustic relationships of the vowels of the vowel quadrilateral (/i æ α u/), the cardinal vowels (/i e ɛ a α ɔ o u/), and the schwa (/ə/) in a vowel space.

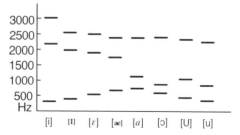

FIGURE 8   Schematic representations of the formant patterns (F1, F2, and F3) for indicated vowels.

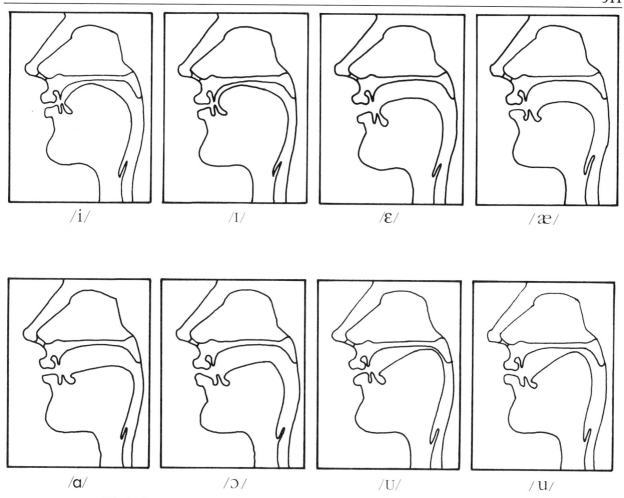

FIGURE 9   Schematic representations of the articulatory patterns for the vowels shown.

amplitude. Bandwidth is related to damping; damped sounds die out quickly as energy is quickly dissipated. When there is little damping, sound is sustained. Since the human vocal tract has soft walls, there is considerable damping. In general, formant bandwidth increases with formant number; higher formants have larger bandwidths. Bandwidth has little effect on vowel identification, but a significant effect on how natural a vowel sounds. Nasalization has the effect of increasing bandwidth, and makes vowel sounds less distinctive. Formant amplitude is generally inversely related to bandwidth when acoustic energy from the larynx is constant. The relative amplitudes of the formants in a vowel are determined by the formant frequencies, the bandwidths of the formants, and the energy available from the source. Formant frequency pattern affects formant amplitude because formants interact. Two formants that are close together reinforce each other and their amplitudes increase.

Diphthongs are like vowels in that they are produced with a relatively open vocal tract and have well-defined formant structures. In general, they cannot be adequately characterized by a single vocal tract shape or single formant pattern. The diphthong /ai/ as in *eye,* for example, begins with the formant structure for /a/ and ends with the formant structure for /i/. The rate of frequency change may be an important characteristic of diphthong identification in English.

V. PROSODY AND SUPRASEGMENTALS

Phonetic aspects of speech that apply across segments, such as stress, pitch, and timing, are referred to as suprasegmentals or prosodies. Vowels and consonants are the segments of speech which combine to form syllables. While people intuitively know what a syllable is, there is no entirely adequate objective definition of the term. Syllables are usually defined as a pulse of air, bounded by either (1) the production of a consonant as in the syllables *pop, op,* or *pa* or (2) a self-imposed reduction of air flow as in the string of syllables *ah-ah-ah.* However, while this allows for general agreement on the number of syllables in such words as *phone* (one), *phoneme* (two), *phonetic* (three), and *phonological* (five), it does not account for the disagreement for words such as *pool* or *fear,* which may be considered to have either one or two syllables.

Stress can be defined as giving emphasis to one or more syllables in a word or phrase, and it is most commonly associated with, but not equivalent to, variations in loudness. In general, stressed syllables will be louder, longer in duration, higher in pitch, less subject to modification by context, and contain a more distinct vowel than unstressed syllables. In unstressed or weakly stressed syllables, the vowel tends to be reduced toward the schwa. In English, stress can play a grammatical role, indicating whether a word is being used as a noun or a verb. Consider *to construct* versus *a construct.* In the case of the verb, primary stress is on the second syllable, while for the noun, primary stress is on the first syllable. Stress can also serve a contrastive function as in the sentence "*I have a DOG, not a cat.*"

Variations in pitch are used to convey both linguistic and nonlinguistic information. Absolute values of pitch convey nonlinguistic information regarding the speaker's gender, age, and emotional state. It is the relative changes in pitch which convey linguistic information at the phrase or sentence level (intonation) or the word level (tone). Although English and most other Indoeuropean languages are not tone languages, a majority of the world's languages are. In tone languages, differences in pitch can signify different words. For example, in Chinese, the word *ma* spoken with a rising pitch means *hemp,* and spoken with a falling pitch means *to scold.* In some tone languages, differences in the pattern of pitch changes within a word can convey syntactic information, such as tense or possession. Most languages, including English, use an intonation pattern of falling pitch to signal the end of a grammatical unit. A variation in that pattern signifies a change in meaning. For example, in the declarative sentence "*She ate squid,*" pitch falls, signifying the end of the sentence. However, when pitch rises at the end of the same sentence, it signifies a question: "*She ate squid?*"

Timing variations may also convey linguistically relevant information. For example, the vowel in *cab* is longer than the vowel in *cap.* In general, vowels are longer when they precede a voiced consonant as opposed to a voiceless consonant. In addition, there are many languages in which variations in duration of vowels and/or consonants result in semantic differences. In Italian, *papa* means *father* and *pappa* means *porridge.* The two words are distinguished on the basis of the longer double consonant or geminate. In English, such distinctions based on geminates occur across, but not within, word boundaries, as in the phrase *cite Ed* versus *cite Ted.* Timing variations in the pattern of relationships among syllable durations determine the rhythm of a language. For example, English is a stress-timed language, which means that the duration between stressed syllables tends to be (loosely) the same. Compare "The boy ate the peanut" and "The elephant ate the peanut." *Elephant* has more segments than *boy,* yet the time from stressed syllable to stressed syllable is about the same in each sentence. In syllable-timed languages such as French, the duration of syllables rather than stress groups remains relatively constant.

In general, it is the relative values of stress, pitch, and timing which contribute to the semantic and/or syntactic information conveyed by the speaker to the listener. Inappropriate application of the suprasegmentals by non-native speakers of a language, the deaf, or those with speech disorders results in perceptual errors and speech that does not sound natural.

VI. COARTICULATION

The articulatory and acoustic classification schemes that have been described may lead to the misconception that conversational speech is a collection of distinct segments strung together like beads. However, speech is a dynamic process. It is not made up of static postures corresponding to phonemes with movements simply connecting one phoneme posture to the next. Speech sounds, as they are produced, are modified by the phonetic context in which they occur. For example, "I want to go home" is usually produced more like "I wanna g'home," and "I have to go home" is usually produced more like "I hafta g'home." In the modification, or coarticulation, of *want to,* the stop consonants are completely assimilated, and the /u/ in *to* is reduced to the schwa vowel. In the case of *have to,* the voiced labiodental becomes voiceless, the stop consonant is only partially assimilated, and the /u/ in *to* is reduced to the schwa. The coarticulations involve the overlapping of articulatory gestures due to the requirements for rapid production and processing of speech and exhibit the tendency of speakers to expend the least amount of articulatory effort necessary to convey the message. Factors such as stress, rate of speaking, and formality of the situation in which speech occurs affect the degree of coarticulation, but even in the most precise productions the sounds are coarticulated.

VII. EXPERIMENTAL/PERCEPTUAL PHONETICS

Thus far the articulatory basis of speech sound production and the acoustic consequences of articulation have been examined. However, speech communication also includes the listener's perception of the speaker's message. What the listener perceives and how it is perceived are issues that cannot be ignored. The obvious, but ultimately superficial response is that the listener perceives the acoustic signal produced by the human vocal tract.

One theory of speech perception, feature detection theory, was based on the distinctive feature theory proposed by Roman Jakobson, Gunnar Fant,

and Morris Halle in 1963 that is still recognizable in the phonetic descriptions of sounds in Section IV above. Jakobson, Fant, and Halle recognized that speakers of any language use only a subset of all possible speech sounds. For example, the first sound in *think,* /θ/, is a common speech sound in English, but is not used in French. Clicks are common in some American Indian and South African languages, but not in English. Yet, despite many such differences in the inventories of speech sounds used in the various languages of the world, there are regularities within and among languages. Jakobson, Fant, and Halle proposed that all speech sounds in all languages could be described by the presence or absence of 12 features. Noam Chomsky and Morris Halle, in their 1968 book *The Sound Pattern of English,* extended the list to more than 30 distinctive features (see Table II for some of the Chomsky-Halle features and their descriptions).

The notion that each abstract linguistic unit could be described as a unique "bundle" of distinctive features led to the hypothesis that neurons in the auditory nervous system were selectively responsive to each feature, as instantiated in the acoustic signal. Feature detection theory was appealing because it provided a physiological mechanism devoted to speech, which could account for the fact that speech is rapidly processed (human beings produce and perceive about 20 phonemes per second) and that infants seem innately predisposed to per-

TABLE II

Some Chomsky-Halle Features for Classifying Segments

Features indicating	Feature name	Description
Place of articulation	Anterior	Obstruction in front of palatoalveolar region
	Coronal	Blade of tongue raised from neutral
	Distributed	Constriction extending in the direction of air flow
	High	Tongue body above the neutral position
	Rounded	Narrowing of lip orifice
Manner of articulation	Tense	Deliberate, maximally distinct gesture
	Nasal	Lowered velum, open nasal passage
	Lateral	Lowered mid section of the tongue at one or both sides
	Strident	Acoustically noisy sounds
	Continuant	Accompanied by little or no turbulence
Phonation	Voiced	Vocal cords in position for spontaneous voicing
Major sound classifications	Consonantal	Radical obstruction in the midsagittal region of the vocal tract
	Vocalic	Produced in the oral cavity, constriction not greater than for high vowels, and vocal cords in position for spontaneous voicing
	Sonorant	Spontaneous voicing possible

ceive phonetic categories. While feature detection theory was generally abandoned because it failed to account for the finite number of features or the relative importance of acoustic and phonetic features, distinctive features continue to be useful for describing speech sounds.

A second influential theory, postulated in the 1970s, K. N. Stevens' quantal theory, explains how articulatory system constraints influence the acoustic patterns associated with speech sounds, leading to some insights regarding the finite number of sounds used in the languages of the world. Potentially there are an infinite number of places of articulation, yet only a relatively few places of articulation are needed to describe existing speech sounds. The term "quantal regions" refers to areas in the vocal tract for which small changes in articulatory postures have very little effect on resulting acoustic patterns. In effect, less precision of articulation is required to make speech sounds produced within such a region. At the boundaries of these quantal regions, even small articulatory changes result in significant differences in the acoustic signals produced. Thus, the infinite number of possible sounds is limited to a finite number of stable sound categories. Likewise, perceptual system constraints are demonstrated by the phenomenon of categorical per-

ception which refers to the ability to discriminate between speech sounds only to the extent that they can be identified or labeled. Experimental evidence indicates that speech continua are heard in categorical fashion, which implies that there are perceptual limits regarding the number and closeness of speech sounds that may be used in various languages. Together these articulatory and perceptual constraints provide a possible basis for the finite inventory of speech sounds and the phonetic features sufficient to describe them.

Bibliography

Catford, J. C. (1988). "A Practical Introduction to Phonetics." Clarendon, Oxford.

Denes, P. B., and Pinson, E. N. (1993). "The Speech Chain: The Physics and Biology of Spoken Language," 2nd ed. Freeman, New York.

Kent, R. D., and Read, C. (1992). "The Acoustic Analysis of Speech." Singular, San Diego.

Ladefoged, P. N. (1992). "A Course in Phonetics," 3rd ed. Harcourt Brace Jovanovich, Orlando.

Lieberman, P., and Blumstein, S. (1988). "Speech Physiology, Speech Perception, and Acoustic Phonetics." Cambridge University Press, Cambridge.

MacKay, I. R. A. (1987). "Phonetics: The Science of Speech Production," 2nd ed. College-Hill, Boston.

Smalley, W. A . (1989). "Manual of Articulatory Phonetics," revised ed. University Press of America, Lanham.

PHONOLOGICAL PROCESSING AND READING

Joseph K. Torgesen and Stephen R. Burgess
Florida State University

Glossary

Phoneme The smallest unit, or variation, in sound that makes a difference to the identity of a word.

Phonological awareness Sensitivity to, or awareness of, the phonological structure of words in one's language.

Phonological coding The primary process by which verbal information is represented in verbatim form in working memory.

Phonological processing The use of the sounds of one's language in processing written or oral language.

Reading-related phonological processes Mental operations that make use of the phonological, or sound structure, of oral language when learning how to decode written language.

Speech-related phonological process The rules or processes which map mental representations of phonemes into their phonetic representations in speech.

THE CONCEPT of phonological processing is central to our understanding of development and individual differences in both speech and reading skills. However, the concept is used to refer to very different processes by those who study speech, as opposed to those who are interested primarily in reading. This article focuses on reading-related phonological processes, which include phonological awareness, phonological coding in working memory, and visually stimulated access to phonological information in long-term memory. The nature of each of these processes, as well as their relationship to one another and to reading, provides the content of this article.

I. DEFINITIONS AND DISTINCTIONS BETWEEN SPEECH- AND READING-RELATED PHONOLOGICAL PROCESSES

Most of the words defined in this section are derived from the Greek word *phone,* which means "sound," or "voice." At its most general level, the term *phonological processing* refers to the use of the sounds of one's language in processing written or oral language. However, the processes that support the production and perception of speech are quite different than those that have been identified as important to the acquisition of reading skills. The manner in which the concept of phonological processing differs for speech/language clinicians and scientists as opposed to teachers and researchers interested in the acquisition of reading skills will become clear as we define the important terms related to the phonology of language and reading.

A. Phones, Phonemes, and Systematic Phonemes

At the first level of analysis, speech consists of continuously variable waves of acoustic energy. When displayed visually by a spectrograph, the speech stream displays little of the segmentation that we perceive in spoken language. For example, one cannot determine from a spectrographic representation of the word "dog," that it contains three separate sound segments, each of which is critical to the identity of the word.

At the next level of analysis, speech may be described in terms of its phonetics. Speech at this level is represented by *phones,* which include all the speech sounds in a given language. An example of a phone is the sound associated with the letter "k" in the word "kite." The sound associated with the same letter in the word "park" is a different phone because the speech sounds represented by the letter are different when it occurs at the beginning and ending of words. When words are described at the phonetic level, the attempt is made to capture as much as possible about the unique way that each part of the word is pronounced.

Although speech can be described at the phonetic level, differences at this level are not usually perceived in everyday speech. That is, in ordinary speech perception, the distinction between the sound of "k" in "kite" and "park" is usually not perceived because it makes no difference to the meaning of the words. The sound differences that are perceived, and that do make a difference to the identity of a word, are referred to as phonemes. A *phoneme* can be defined as the smallest unit, or variation, in sound that makes a difference to the identity of a word, and each phoneme has a number of different *phonetic* representations depending upon its location, and the surrounding phonemes, in a given word. Another way to define a phoneme is as a distinctive unit of speech that maintains its inherent identity despite slight pronunciation differences resulting from word context. The individual phones that can be grouped together as representing a single phoneme are called *allophones* of that phoneme. For instance, the sounds represented by the letter "n" in "no," "bunny," and "on" are allophones of the English consonant phoneme /n/. Allophonic differences between words never make a difference in their identity. Although the number of phonemes in the English language varies somewhat according to the way they are counted, most accounts place the total number between 39 and 45 (with numbers of consonant phonemes varying between 24 and 29, and vowel phonemes varying between 15 and 16).

At a more theoretical level, phonemes are thought to exist in the mind as *systematic phonemes.* Modern linguistic theory suggests that words are represented in our lexicons as strings of systematic phonemes. Phonemic representation at this level is abstract,

because groups of words that are related to one another by meaning (e.g., heal, health, healthy) may have only one lexical entry (/he/). Speech requires the use of phonological rules, or phonological processes, to transform abstract, or systematic phonemes, into surface phones, which are instantiated through the articulatory gestures that produce speech.

B. Phonological Processes in Speech

As indicated in the preceding paragraph, we have now introduced the way that the concept of phonological processing is used by those interested in development and individual differences in speech. For speech and language therapists, or for scientists who study speech and language as a content area, phonological processing refers to the rule-guided mental activities which map underlying representations of phonemes (systematic phonemes) into their phonetic representations in speech. As children develop, not only do they become aware of important contrasts at the phonemic level that make a difference to word meaning, but also the processes they use to translate between the underlying representation and its phonetic equivalent in speech become more sophisticated. Incorrect pronunciations of words by very young children are attributed to the use of general simplifying processes that affect entire classes of sounds. For example, simplifying processes tend to reduce all words to basic CV syllables (e.g., deletion of final consonants, reduction of clusters to one segment, deletion of unstressed syllables).

For older children with speech production difficulties, the goal of treatment is often to identify a single phonological process that is responsible for patterns of errors in a child's speech, and then to focus on remediation of that process. For example, instead of conceptualizing errors involving the substitution of [b] for [v] or [d] for [z] as independent of one another, they are recognized as being the result of a single erroneous process that involves making voiced fricatives into stops.

To further illustrate the way in which the concept of phonological processing is used within the field of speech/language/communication disorders, consider the tasks that are used to assess phonological processes on two popular tests. The Test of Language Development (TOLD), which is perhaps the most widely used measure of language development in the public schools, has two measures of phonological development in children. One of the measures, Word Articulation, assesses the ability to correctly pronounce words that broadly sample English phonology. The other measure, Word Discrimination, assesses children's ability to discriminate phonemic contrasts by asking them to indicate whether two words varying in one phoneme are the same of different. Children do not have to identify which phonemes are different, but must simply indicate whether the words sound the same or different overall. In contrast to the TOLD, which is a broad measure of language development that also assesses semantic and syntactic development, The Assessment of Phonological Processes-Revised (a test used widely by speech and language clinicians) focuses exclusively on the categorization of articulation errors into 10 varieties that are thought to be the result of different phonological processes. Examples of these processes include syllable reduction, consonant singleton omissions, or deficiencies in pronunciation of such classes as stridents, glides, or nasals.

The concept of phonological processing is much older in speech science than in the study of reading. In addition, there is probably a wider consensus about their critical role in speech than in reading. As both speech and reading science continue to develop and perhaps to interact, it may become important to routinely distinguish which types of phonological processes are being discussed in a given context. At the very least, those working within the speech and reading fields should be aware that others, working in a closely related field, are using similar terms to mean very different things. We turn now to a discussion of reading-related phonological processes.

II. PHONOLOGY AND READING

Reading is an extremely complex activity that involves many different processing operations, and these processing operations change as reading skills develop. Since phonological processing is of primary importance to only a subset of reading skills, it is necessary to make a number of distinctions among reading processes in order to establish a proper context for our discussion. First, it is important to distinguish between word identification and comprehension skills in reading. Word identification skills are used to identify individual words in printed form, while comprehension skills are involved in con-

structing the meaning of the passage being read. As currently conceptualized, phonological processing skills are most critical to word identification, and they affect reading comprehension primarily in an indirect way through their influence on word level reading skills. Thus, this discussion of phonological processes and reading focuses on the way that these processes are involved as children learn to translate between written and oral language. Though not established with certainty, phonological processing skills are likely to be most heavily utilized when reading skills are being initially acquired, rather than after they have become fluent. [See READING.]

Another distinction that is helpful in understanding the specific impact of phonological skills on reading involves variations among word identification processes themselves. At least two different kinds of information are commonly used to identify words in text. For example, readers sometimes use information obtained from their understanding of what they are reading as an aid to identifying words. That is, words are more easily recognized when they are consistent with expectations derived from context. Processes that rely on understanding of context are referred to as meaning-driven word identification processes. Although important during the reading of novel or difficult texts, these meaning-driven word identification processes are not the primary way that words are identified during reading. Recent research has established that the most important source of information about the identity of words in print are the printed visual symbols on the page, as opposed to information derived from the context of the passage being read. Thus, a major task in becoming a good reader is to learn to efficiently utilize the printed spellings of words as the primary clue to their identity, and it is in this domain—the ability to identify words on the basis of their printed visual symbols—that phonological processing skills play their most important role.

However, since words can be identified from print in several different ways, one final distinction is important. Current models of word identification suggest that the information involved in identifying words from print falls within two broad domains: phonological and orthographic. Within the phonological domain, words can be identified because of correspondences between the written representation and the word's phonological structure. In the English language, our alphabet represents words at the level of phonemes, rather than directly at the level of meaning, or specifically at the phonetic level.

With words represented at the phonemic level, writing is related to the sound of a word being identified, but with inconsistencies and compromises that are frequently related to the word's meaning. Our alphabetic system is an optimal way of representing our spoken language if we assume, as outlined in an earlier section of this paper, that words are represented in our mental lexicons by strings of systematic phonemes. Thus, with a number of important and frequently confusing exceptions, our writing system represents words in terms of the same units by which words are represented in our mental dictionaries.

Older discussions of the relationships between the phonology and orthography (alphabetic representation) of words suggested that learning to read involves learning to use a set of grapheme–phoneme correspondence (GPC) rules to construct the sequences of phonemes in individual words. However, recently proposed connectionist models of word identification have shown that readers do not have to follow explicit GPC rules in identifying the phonological elements of words. Rather, the phonology of words can be identified simply because of statistical regularities in the covariance of graphic and phonological representations of words. Although the finer points of these word identification models are still the subject of much debate, the basic point is that one source of information about the identity of words in print arises from the systematic relationships between the visual and phonological representations of words.

In contrast to phonological knowledge and skill, which utilizes statistical regularities in phoneme/grapheme relationships across words, orthographic processes in word recognition are much more word specific. Orthographic knowledge involves memory for specific visual/spelling patterns that identify individual words, or word parts, on the printed page. Orthographic knowledge is acquired by repeated exposures to words until a stable visual representation has been acquired. The question of whether high levels of orthographic knowledge allow the reader to bypass a word's phonology and go directly to meaning is a subject of considerable controversy in the research on word identification.

Models of the acquisition of word identification skills describe at least three stages of growth. First, children recognize many words by using a logographic strategy. At this stage, words (often those appearing frequently in the child's environment) are identified on the basis of visual features that are not

necessarily letters. Thus, the child might be able to read the word ''McDonald's'' when it appears in yellow next to a set of golden arches but be unable to read it when printed in black and white block letters.

The second level of word reading skill is usually referred to as the alphabetic stage. At this point, the child learns to utilize phonological information in identifying words. Specific letters and letter order become important, and the child gradually learns to utilize all the letters in the word as part of the identification process. At the same time that children are becoming facile in using an alphabetic strategy to identify words, they are also acquiring a vocabulary of words that they identify as wholes. If alphabetic reading is successfully mastered, children gradually move into the final stage of word identification and begin to rely on orthographic processes to identify more and more words. The analytic knowledge about words that is acquired in the alphabetic stage contributes importantly to the attainment of full orthographic skills, because orthographic word identification processs rely on information about individual letters and letter order in words. Orthographic recognition processes are much more analytic and systematic than logographic recognition.

As can be inferred from the foregoing discussion, phonological processing skills have their most important impact on the acquisition of alphabetic reading skills in young children. Thus, they are particularly important in the early stages of learning to identify printed words. However, since alphabetic reading skills continue to be used to identify unfamiliar words even in adults, theses processes undoubtedly continue to play an important supporting role even after word identification processes have become fluent. We will now consider each of the three major types of reading-related phonological processes in turn, beginning with an explication of the process itself, and then considering its relationship to the acquisition of word reading skills in young children.

III. THREE READING-RELATED PHONOLOGICAL PROCESSES

A. Phonological Awareness

The first skill to be considered, phonological awareness, is actually not a process at all, but a type of knowledge that children acquire about language. Although mental operations are certainly involved on tasks used to measure phonological awareness, it is more properly thought of as a type of knowledge or understanding about the phonological structure of words, rather than as a dynamic process. It is frequently referred to as metalinguistic knowledge, because it is knowledge about language that is more explicit, or conscious, than that required when words are used in speaking or listening. Phonological awareness can be formally defined as sensitivity to, or awareness of, the phonological structure of one's language.

A beginning level of phonological awareness is manifest in the ability to recognize that despite subtle changes in their acoustic signals (allophonic differences), the initial sounds in "cat" and "cot" are the same. It also implies a beginning recognition that words can be divided into segments at the level of the phoneme, as well as the ability to direct one's attention to a specified part of the phonological structure of a word. A child with a slightly deeper level of phonological awareness would be able to indicate that the word "cat" comprises three different "sounds," rather than only one. Finally, a child with fully explicit awareness would be able to separately pronounce the individual sounds in "cat" (albeit with some distortion of the sounds), or indicate what word is left if the /l/ sound is deleted from the word "slit." On average, children can respond reasonably well to tasks that measure beginning levels of awareness in kindergarten, but fully explicit phonological awareness usually develops only after reading instruction begins.

Phonological awareness develops slowly in young children because, as was pointed out earlier, the phoneme is an abstract concept: phonemes are not distinct from one another in the actual sounds we hear when words are spoken. For example, the word "dog" has three phonemes—it differs from "log" in the first, from "dig" in the second, and from "dot" in the third—but when it is spoken, these phonemes are merged into a single pulse of sound so that it is impossible to separate the phonemes without some articulatory distortion. Because of our natural capacity for language, it is not necessary to be consciously aware of the phonological structure of words in order to speak or understand words in oral language. The phonological processes that translate between the underlying structure of the word in the mental lexicon and its instantiation in speech operate outside of conscious awareness.

However, in order to make sense of the alphabetic system we use in our written language, in order to understand that letters map to words at the phonemic level, children must become aware that words actually are composed of segments at the phonemic level.

Isabelle Liberman and her colleagues at Haskins Laboratories in New Haven, Connecticut, most completely developed the early theoretical basis for research on phonological awareness. They recognized that speech and reading both involve phonological processing, and they sought to determine why speech was so easy for most children to master with no explicit instruction, while at the same time reading was so hard for many children, even with explicit instruction. Their initial answer, which has been supported in subsequent research, was that reading requires an " . . . awareness of the phonological structure of the words of the language, an awareness that must be more explicit than is ever demanded in the ordinary course of listening and responding to speech."

A large research literature now supports the idea that children with higher levels of phonological awareness find it easier to learn to read in the early elementary grades. Studies have shown that good readers do better than poor readers on a wide variety of phonological awareness tasks, even when the effects of intelligence and social class are controlled. Performance on phonological awareness tasks (such as those mentioned earlier that assess beginning levels of awareness) before reading instruction begins is an excellent predictor of reading success in the first grade. Correlations between performance on phonological awareness tasks in kindergarten and word reading skills at the end of first grade usually fall within the range of .4 to .6.

Causal modeling studies using longitudinal–correlational designs have verified that individual differences in phonological awareness prior to the beginning of reading instruction actually have a causal influence on the rate at which early reading skills are acquired. Importantly, these studies have also shown that reading instruction itself contributes to the further development of phonological awareness. Thus, the relationship between phonological awareness and reading is actually reciprocal: early development of phonological awareness facilitates the acquisition of alphabetic reading skills, while instruction in reading contributes to further development of phonological awareness.

Many studies have also shown that specific training in phonological awareness can have a positive impact on success in early reading. Although a few studies have shown that training in phonological awareness as an oral language skill, by itself, can positively influence rate of reading acquisition, most studies show that combining phonological awareness training with training in letter–sound correspondence is most effective in accelerating the rate of growth in reading skills. The conclusion from the training studies thus far is that most children may require instruction designed specifically to help them generalize their newly acquired phonological awareness to the task of reading. In addition to the studies showing that early instruction in phonological awareness can accelerate reading growth in young children, evidence is also beginning to show that systematic instruction in phonological awareness may be a helpful precursor to instruction in alphabetic reading skills for children with specific reading disabilities, or dyslexia. [*See* DYSLEXIA.]

B. Phonological Coding in Working Memory

Phonological coding in working memory is the process by which exact sequences of verbal information are retained in memory over brief periods of time. Coding processes translate sensory input into a representational form that can be efficiently stored in memory. When an individual is required to retain a short sequence of verbal items in the correct order, these items are represented in working memory in terms of their phonological features. Coding is involved because the entire acoustic signal for each item is not retained, but rather codes that utilize each item's distinctive phonological features are used to represent the item in working memory.

Developmentally, phonological representations for verbal items are gradually constructed as the items are processed (heard, spoken) on repeated occasions. Eventually, these codes, or representations, acquire sufficient distinctiveness, accessibility, and permanence that they enhance processing on many different kinds of verbal tasks. Hearing or seeing an item on a short-term memory task engages processing operations that activate the code stored in long-term memory. This activated representation is then "read off" during recall. A substantial amount of converging evidence indicates that the codes used to represent verbal information on tasks that require immediate, verbatim, and ordered recall are composed primarily of the phonological features of the stimuli.

Phonological codes can be activated in two different ways. When information is presented visually, phonological codes are activated through sub-vocal speech. This is freuquently referred to as articulatory coding. In contrast, when information is presented aurally, phonological codes are activated directly by the acoustic stimuli without articulatory processes. However, even when material is presented aurally, sub-vocal articulation is frequently used to enhance the strength of the phonological code.

Children with phonological coding difficulties can be expected to have problems acquiring alphabetic reading skills because these coding difficulties make it hard to utilize knowledge of letter–sound correspondences in decoding words. Specifically, phonological coding inefficiencies make it difficult to perform the simultaneous, or rapidly sequential identification, comparison, and blending processes that are required to identify words by phonological/analytic strategies.

In fact, difficulty remembering exact sequences of verbal information over brief periods of time is one of the most frequently reported cognitive characteristics of children with severe reading disabilities. The tasks most often used to demonstrate this difficulty are called memory span tasks. These tasks typically involve recalling sequences of random digits, words, or letters immediately after a single auditory or visual presentation. Recently, another type of task has been used to assess phonological memory. This task involves the repetition of complex nonwords or nonword phrases.

Evidence for the relationship between individual differences in phonological coding efficiency and learning to read has been obtained in comparisons between good and poor readers, and in several longitudinal–correlational studies. Most comparisons between groups of normal and reading disabled children find significant differences in memory span between the groups, as long as the material to be remembered is verbal in nature. If memory for nonverbal material (i.e., visual designs that are not easily named) is examined, there are usually no differences between groups. Evidence from longitudinal–correlational studies indicates that phonological coding processes are causally related to the acquisition of word reading skills, although the relationships found are uniformly weaker than those for phonological awareness.

In contrast to phonological awareness, no one has seriously proposed that reading skills might be improved by training on memory span tasks. The reason for this is that memory, per se, is not the problem. The problem involves the lack of availability, or accessibility, of good representations for phonological information. Thus, children might be taught various strategies (cumulative rehearsal, or chunking) to improve their performance on memory span tasks, but this would not necessarily affect the underlying coding problem. In addition, it seems unlikely that elaborate strategies for improving verbatim storage of phonological material would be useful during reading, given the speed at which reading processes must operate, as well as the overall complexity of the task. [*See* CHUNKING; MEMORY.]

C. Visually Stimulated Access to Phonological Information

Children's ability to easily and rapidly access phonological information that is stored in long-term memory has typically been assessed in the reading literature by rapid automatic naming tasks. This type of task was first introduced as a way of predicting and understanding individual differences in reading ability by Martha Denkla and her colleagues, and typically requires the child to name, as rapidly as possible, a series of 30 to 50 items (digits, colors, letters, or objects) printed on a page.

Theoretically, rapid naming tasks are linked to reading because they are thought to measure the speed of processes that are intrinsically related to processes involved in word identification. In utilizing alphabetic reading skills for example, the child must rapidly access, store, and interpret strings of phonemes represented by letters in words. If access to the phonological information represented by letters occurs rapidly and easily, the entire complex string of mental operations will be facilitated.

Evidence for the role of rapid naming processes in reading acquisition is similar to that reported in the previous section on phonological coding processes, although the evidence is generally stronger than for coding processes as assessed by memory tasks. That is, longitudinal–correlational studies have shown that individual differences in naming rate are causally related to growth in reading skills, and performance on rapid automatic naming tasks is generally slower for children with reading disabilities than for children who read normally. However, the relationships between rapid naming skill and reading are complicated by methodological differences among

naming tasks, and by developmental changes in the relationships between naming and reading.

It is possible to measure naming speed using either a continuous naming or discrete trial procedure. Continuous naming tasks were described in the first part of this section. Discrete trial tasks involve individual presentation of the items to be named on a tachistoscope or computer, with response time being measured by a voice key and timer. Typically, performance on continuous naming tasks is more strongly related to word reading skill than is performance on discrete trial tasks. This pattern of results can be explained by considering that the continuous naming format actually represents a better match to the processing requirements of reading than does the isolated naming format. That is, the continuous naming format demands access to phonological information in a context that also requires rapid scanning, sequencing, and processing of serially presented items. Another feature of continuous naming tasks that they share with reading is the opportunity to identify items while simultaneously engaging in the identification of other items. Thus, the continuous naming format provides the opportunity to demonstrate a level of automaticity in the naming response that is not provided by the discrete trial format.

Developmentally, relationships between rapid naming tasks and reading appear to change in two ways. First, naming rate for almost anything in kindergarten (digits, letters, colors, objects) is significantly related to both word identification skills and reading comprehension in second grade. However, if naming rate is measured concurrently with reading in second grade, only naming rate for digits and letters is significantly related to reading. Further, relationships of second grade naming rate to comprehension are much weaker, and are accounted for entirely by the relationships between naming rate and word identification skills. These changing relationships are accounted for by the fact that, as children grow older, the processes used to access names of graphological symbols like letters and digits begin to diverge from those used to access names of colors and objects. As compared to colors and objects, naming of graphological symbols becomes a more automatized process with development, so that, by second grade, only tasks which involve naming of digits and letters continue to assess common processes with reading.

Many studies have shown that children with severe developmental reading disabilities (dyslexia) have much slower response rates on rapid automatic naming tasks than do children who learn to read normally. These differences not only are present during the period of initial reading acquisition, but also they have been found in adult samples. One study showed that the naming rate of a sample of adults who had significantly improved their reading skills as a result of intensive remediation was still different from average adult readers and not dissimilar to a group of dyslexics with much lower reading skills who had not received remedial help.

IV. RELATIONSHIPS AMONG READING-RELATED PHONOLOGICAL PROCESSES

Over most of the brief history of research on reading-related phonological processes, they have been studied in relative isolation from one another. Individual differences on measures of each processing skill have been found to be significantly, and sometimes very strongly, associated with individual differences in reading acquisition. However, until very recently, the question of whether these three phonological constructs represent different sources of reading-related individual differences, or whether they are simply different names for the same underlying construct, has been left unanswered.

A. Separate but Correlated Abilities

Thanks to several recent large scale studies, we now have relatively clear answers to questions about the relationship of the three phonological constructs to one another, and to reading. First, when a large sample of the tasks used in this research domain is administered to the same sample of children, they appear to assess five separate but correlated abilities. These abilities are (1) *analytic phonological awareness*—ability to identify or manipulate constituent phonemes within whole words (i.e., "Which word, 'cat,' 'boat,' or 'dot' begins with the same first sound as 'car'?" Or "What word is left if you say 'card' without saying the /d/ sound?"); (2) *synthetic phonological awareness*—ability to blend together separately presented phonological segments into whole words (i.e., "What word do the sounds, /b/-/i/-/t/ make?"); (3) *phonological coding in working memory*—ability to repeat verbatim strings of verbal material (i.e., repeating a sequence such as 8-5-9-2-6 when the digits are presented orally at a rate of two per second); (4) *serial naming rate*—rate

of naming for verbal items that are available simultaneously and named serially (i.e., a sequence of letters, digits, objects, or colors that are printed on a card or page); and (5) *isolated naming rate*—rate of naming for verbal items presented one at a time on discrete trials (i.e., items such as letters, digits, objects, or colors that appear one at a time on a computer screen or tachistoscope).

In samples of very young children, measures of analytic phonological awareness and phonological coding in working memory appear to assess the same construct, but these abilities undergo differentiation with development. Their early unity as a single construct might stem from their mutual dependence on the quality of the child's phonological representations for words. We know that impoverished or degraded phonological representations impair performance on memory span tasks, and these same impoverished representations may also limit the child's ability to acquire the kind of linguistic knowledge about spoken words that is measured by analysis tasks at an early age. This argument implies that the type of phonological awareness assessed by analysis tasks is more complex or subtle than that measured by synthesis tasks, which is consistent with the fact that synthetic skills emerge earlier in development, and are easier to train in young children.

Although analytic awareness and phonological memory do differentiate from one another with development, overall there is also remarkable stability in the structure of these abilities between preschool and the early elementary grades. In addition to stability in their overall structure, there is also remarkable stability in the pattern of individual differences for each ability with development. For example, when latent variables are used to stand for each of the constructs (latent variables represent the common variance among several different measures of the same construct so that they provide measurement uncontaminated with task specific, or error variance), the correlations between measures of each construct given in kindergarten and first grade obtained in one large study were: .87, .71, 1.0, .78, and .81 for analysis, synthesis, phonological memory, isolated naming, and serial naming, respectively. The correlations between kindergarten and second grade testing for the same variables were .66, .49, 1.0, .65, and .62.

This remarkable stability in the face of dramatic changes in reading skills taking place during the same period of time suggests that reading-related phonological processing abilities are not simply an alternate expression of reading knowledge and skill. Both their relationships to one another and to themselves are not overwhelmed by the large variations in reading growth, experience, and instruction that take place in the early elementary grades. Rather, the data available at this point suggest that these phonological processing skills should be considered important individual difference variables in their own right, comparable to those measured on other tests of intellectual ability such as measures of general intelligence.

B. Relative Rates of Growth in Young Children

Patterns of individual differences on the reading-related phonological processes we have been describing suggest that, although they are clearly correlated, they also have a substantial degree of independence from one another. Examination of the growth rates for each of the constructs provides additional evidence of their relative and increasing divergence from one another with development. One large study, for example, examined growth in each construct (using variables obtained by combining standardized scores from several different measures for each construct) across the period from kindergarten to second grade. These results are displayed in Figure 1. Analysis showed that the growth rates for all variables were significantly different from one another, with the single exception of that between phonological synthesis and isolated naming. For comparison purposes, if the growth in a measure of verbal intelligence were plotted on the same graph, it would fall directly on the line for phonological

memory, and if growth in word identification skills were plotted, it would be identical to that for serial naming through first grade, but then would diverge in a positive direction between first and second grade.

C. Simultaneous Relationships with Reading Acquisition

Although each of the reading-related phonological processes has been shown to have a significant causal relationship with reading when considered by itself, it is important to know if these relationships to reading are independent from one another, or are redundant. The best information available at this point suggests that they are largely redundant with one another in their effects on early reading acquisition. For example, in one large scale longitudinal study that used latent variables for each phonological construct (measured in kindergarten) and included a measure of verbal intelligence and previous reading skills (measured in kindergarten) in the causal equation, the only two variables that emerged with significant independent causal paths to first grade reading were analytic phonological awareness (causal coefficient = .75) and previous reading skills (causal coefficient = .35). In other words, all of the significant reading-related variance among the phonological processing measures was essentially captured by the analytic awareness construct, with none of the other measures having a significant unique causal relationship with later reading skills. A similar finding was obtained when the causal contributions of phonological processing and reading skills in first grade were examined in relationship to second grade reading. This time, however, synthetic awareness skills captured all the reading related variance of the phonological measures (causal coefficient = .22). As might be expected, this analysis also showed that reading skills in first grade made a strong causal contribution (causal coefficient = .47) to reading in second grade.

As was mentioned in an earlier section, while clear evidence exists that phonological processing skills are causally related to individual differences in the rate of growth of early reading skills, it is also true that reading growth has a causal impact on the subsequent development of phonological processing skills. However, at least for the early elementary grades, the causal impact of reading growth on phonological processing is not as powerful as the influence of phonological skills on reading. Furthermore, the influence of reading on phonological skills is

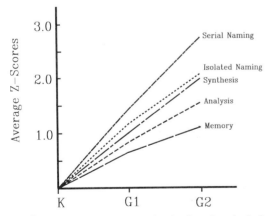

FIGURE 1 Rates of development for the five phonological processing abilities. [From Wagner, R. K., Torgesen, J. K., and Rashotte, C. A. (in press). *Dev. Psychol.*]

strongest for phonological awareness, marginally reliable for naming rate, and nonexistent for phonological memory.

V. ETIOLOGY OF INDIVIDUAL DIFFERENCES IN READING-RELATED PHONOLOGICAL PROCESSES

Large scale twin studies have produced convincing evidence that a substantial proportion of the variation in phonological skills among children is due to genetic factors. However, the relative strength of genetic vs environmental factors in producing individual differences in phonological skill does vary with the type of skill being considered. For example, almost all variation in phonological memory can be accounted for in terms of genetic factors, while for phonological awareness both heredity and environment appear to play a role, albeit with the stronger factor being the genetic one. The relative strength of genetic factors for rapid serial naming tasks appears to be intermediate between that of phonological awareness and phonological memory.

Consistent with the role of genetic factors in producing individual variability on reading-related phonological processes is the finding that, relative to orthographic reading skills, individual differences in alphabetic reading skills are much more strongly determined by genetic factors. For example, in a population of twins, some with severe reading disabilities, and some with normal reading skills, the coefficients for genetic and shared environmental factors for alphabetic reading skills were .75 and .11, respectively. When orthographic (reading words on basis of stored visual image) reading skills were assessed, the genetic and environmental coefficients were .41 and .41.

The finding that variation in phonological skills is primarily caused by genetic factors should not be used to conclude that these skills, phonological awareness at least, cannot be productively trained in young children. Phonological awareness does vary with overall social class and language experience, and training studies have consistently shown that specific training experiences can improve this awareness in young children. However, the strong influence of genetic factors is consistent with the conceptualization of reading-related phonological skills as coherent and stable dimensions of individual difference that comes from longitudinal studies of their early development.

Bibliography

Goswami, U., and Bryant, P. (1990). ''Phonological Skills and Learning to Read.'' Erlbaum, London.

Liberman, I. Y., Shankweiler, D., and Liberman, A. M. (1989). The alphabetic principle and learning to read. In ''Phonology and Reading Disability: Solving the Reading Puzzle'' (D. Shankweiler and I. Y. Liberman, Eds.). University of Michigan Press, Ann Arbor.

Lundberg, I. (1988). Preschool prevention of reading failure: Does training in phonological awareness work? In ''Prevention of Reading Failure'' (R. L. Masland and M. W. Masland, Eds.), pp. 163–176. York Press, Parkton, MD.

Stanovich, K. E. (1990). Explaining the differences between the dyslexic and the garden-variety poor reader: The phonological-core variable-difference model. In ''Cognitive and Behavioral Characteristics of Children with Learning Disabilities'' (J. Torgesen, Ed.). PRO-ED, Austin, TX.

Torgesen, J. K. (1993). Variations on theory in learning disabilities. In ''Better Understanding Learning Disabilities: New Views from Research and Their Implications for Education and Public Policies.'' (G. R. Lyon, D. B. Gray, J. F. Kavanaugh and N. A. Krasnegor, Eds.). Brooks, Baltimore.

Wagner, R. K., Torgesen, J. K., Laughon, P., Simmons, K., and Rashotte, C. (1993). The development of young readers' phonological processing abilities. *J. Educational Psychol.* **85,** 83–103.

Wolf, M. (1991). Naming speed and reading: The contribution of the cognitive neurosciences. *Reading Res. Quart.* **26,** 123–141.

PLANNING

Ellin Kofsky Scholnick
University of Maryland at College Park

Glossary

Goal The desired outcome of a task and sometimes the purpose for performing it. The final goal may be decomposed into intermediate goals called subgoals.

Precondition A necessary condition for performing an action. Achieving a subgoal may be the precondition for achieving a later goal.

Representation An individual's cognitive model of stimuli.

Semantic network A means of representing knowledge. Networks are composed of nodes, which contain basic concepts, and links between nodes that vary in strength. External stimuli activate relevant nodes and activation spreads along the links.

PLANNING involves thinking out acts and purposes beforehand in order to act effectively. Planning requires marshalling cognitive resources in order to meet goals. Therefore, the study of planning is central to attempts to explain the interplay of motivation and cognition in intelligent behavior. Problem solving and motivated action are themselves rich and complex processes. So the meaning of the term, the explanation of the mechanisms underlying planning, and the settings in which it is studied have been diverse. A survey of the various meanings and different approaches to planning is provided, followed by a detailed examination of four accounts of planning in different settings. Each of these accounts was intended to describe adult planners but the survey will incorporate data on developmental changes in planning skill. Because these accounts focus on the cognitive components of planning, the final section includes a brief discussion of motivational factors.

I. THE MANY MEANINGS OF PLANNING

A. Syntactic Issues

"Plan" is both a noun and a verb. The noun refers to a design that guides action and the verb refers to the acts creating the design. As a noun, "plan" can refer to the completed design that governs behavior and to the knowledge used to construct the design and to interpret the plan-guided behavior of others. The nature of the design is of interest to those who investigate human representational competence. When "plan" is used to refer to interpretation, the study of planning encompasses an intuitive psychology of goal-directed behavior. The verb framework emphasizes various aspects of the act of planning. Because observers only see the implementation of the plan, not its construction, the verb, "plan," has been employed in diverse ways. Some accounts simply describe the execution of a strategy to achieve a goal, but others emphasize the anticipatory processing responsible for that strategy. Additionally, planning has been characterized as (a) the product of retrieval of past knowledge and as the construction of novel strategies; (b) a forecast of a future course of action and as a mixture of anticipation and spontaneous reactions; and (c) an activity directed toward the accomplishment of brief tasks and as the attainment of long-term goals.

B. Scope

Descriptions of planning also vary in scope. Neuropsychologists view planning as a general executive skill that regulates cognitive processing and that can be measured by global performance on specific tasks such as the Tower of Hanoi (TOH). The opposite stance is that skill in planning is domain-specific and reflects the planner's knowledge of the task and awareness of the changing circumstances that unfold as a plan is enacted. The choice of perspective determines whether planning is thought to be present when infants show their first anticipations of events or whether planning is thought to emerge gradually in different contexts.

Moreover planning is not always viewed as a unitary skill, but as a set of component processes. Plans may begin with accessing or constructing a representation of the situation. The planner makes a causal analysis of the situation to determine the relevant preconditions and constraints on anticipated actions that will provide a representational framework for planning. A second component of planning is selection of the goals, namely the desired outcomes of the plan and the purposes those outcomes serve. Particular representations of the environment narrow the choice of feasible goals and particular goals influence the contents of the representation. The third component in planning is making the decision to plan. A planner who has ample time and intellectual resources, confronting a stable world with limited external resources, is likely to plan. Chaotic external conditions or limits on internal processing capacity may inhibit planning. Highly valued goals and confidence in the ability to achieve them also foster planning. A commitment to planning leads to a search for an appropriate strategy. This fourth step, choice of a plan, leads to the fifth, enactment, and the sixth, monitoring implementation. The final, seventh step, is learning. Planning tests the validity of knowledge. When plans must be modified, knowledge about the situation and about the art of planning is modified, too.

The diversity of views about planning may arise because each definition emphasizes different facets of planning at the expense of others. Models that define plans as designs for action emphasize representation, but models that equate plans with strategies focus mainly on execution and strategy choice. Consequently explanations of the situational factors that influence planning and the course of development of planning skill will also differ.

C. Disciplinary Perspectives

Planning has also been studied from several disciplinary frameworks. Planning is a central construct in the field of artificial intelligence (AI). The AI approach is characterized by detailed analyses of the various knowledge structures and processing steps implicated in planning. The validation of those analyses rests on their successful computer implementation. AI researchers have proposed explanations of human and robot problem solving in restricted domains such as moving blocks. Other computer simulations are designed to accomplish everyday planning tasks, to comprehend narratives relating goal-directed actions, and to account for learning.

Cognitive psychologists have studied planning of humans engaged in the same tasks, problem solving, running errands, and interpreting texts. This research is designed to delineate the internal factors that influence planning, such as the planner's knowledge, representational capacity, processing resources, and forebrain functioning. The role of external factors, such as task instructions and problem complexity, has also been examined. Like the AI research, cognitive analyses focus mostly on representation and computational processes. [See PROBLEM SOLVING.]

Cognitive psychologists assume a ''standard'' problem solver who is willing to plan and is invested in planning. However, cultural norms and family practices influence the frequency of planning and the situations where planning takes place. Certain populations lack the self-control or motivation to deal with tasks planfully rather than plunging into action. Some developmental psychologists supplement cognitive explanations with discussions of the motivational factors that influence the choice of goals and engagement in planning. The concern with personal motivational issues and goals also permeates diverse research on strategic, long-term planning in managerial settings, and on the setting of life goals, such as vocational success or satisfying retirement.

D. A Syntactic–Task Taxonomy

Consequently models of planning differ on several dimensions. One distinction captures the noun and verb uses of ''plan.'' Some models emphasize the choice and enactment of procedures while others emphasize the kind of knowledge that underlies comprehension and production of plans. Of course, there are no pure cases. Knowledge-based models include inherent processing components to account for accessing and selection of plans, and conversely, procedural accounts assume knowledge of those procedures and of the conditions under which procedures are implemented. A second dimension contrasts explanations of planning of well-defined problems and planning in the more unpredictable social environment of human interaction. Four types of models of planning and research relevant to them will be described: procedural planning in (a) constrained and (b) naturalistic environments, and knowledge-based accounts of planning for actions in (c) constrained and (d) natural environments. Because each model describes an expert and well-motivated planner, the validity of the model for less knowledgeable and younger planners will be discussed.

These four categories are more than a convenient system for describing research on planning. The psychological study of planning originated in procedural accounts of strategy choice and implementation in constrained problem-solving tasks. Then interest shifted to the construction of strategies for daily life tasks and to knowledge-based accounts of constrained problem-solving tasks. Knowledge-based accounts of planning in natural environments first took the form of programs enabling computers to understand stories of human action. Knowledge-based accounts of production of daily plans are very recent and these AI models are largely untested in psychological research.

II. PROCEDURAL PLANNING IN CONSTRAINED PROBLEM SPACES

A. Planning as a Test for Goal Satisfaction

The pioneering model of planning was introduced by Miller, Galanter, and Pribram. Although their explanation was applied to phenomena as diverse as brainwashing, memorizing nonsense syllables, and hammering nails, their analysis was inspired by work on problem solving and much of the work on planning has followed this tradition. Miller and his colleagues suggested that intentional behavior consisted of images and plans. Comparatively little attention was paid to the image that encoded knowledge of a problem. Instead they focused on the plan, which was composed of test–operate–test–exit (TOTE) units. Whenever problems arose, the indi-

vidual used the image to project its solution, which constituted a *test* goal. Individuals *operated* (or acted) to meet the test and the results of their action were *tested* against their goal. If an action produced a goal, the person *exited* from the plan. Otherwise the plan recycled.

Most plans contain several TOTE units because the goal cannot be achieved directly. Some preconditions which are necessary for goal attainment are absent. For example, boarding a plane requires a ticket. Plans must be designed that will either create the preconditions or reduce the difference between the current circumstance and the desired one. The traveler might go to the bank to withdraw the money for purchasing a ticket. This strategy, called means–end analysis, is achieved by a process of sequential subgoaling. Boarding a plane requires a ticket which requires the money to obtain it.

B. The Tower of Hanoi as a Measure of Planning

Many problems require subgoaling. One such task is the Tower of Hanoi, which has come to be regarded as an important measure of planning. A typical TOH task uses three pegs. The first peg contains several rings stacked in size order from the smallest ring on top to the largest ring on the bottom. The goal is to duplicate the stack on the third peg in the fewest moves without violating certain rules. Only one ring can be moved at a time and it can only be moved to another peg. The size order must be preserved. A large ring can never be placed above a smaller one.

The optimal subgoaling strategy can be illustrated with two stacked rings. The main goal is to move both rings to the goal peg. But the large ring must be free to move from its present site to a legal destination. Although the goal peg is vacant, the small ring prevents the transfer. So a subgoal is created to remove the obstacle. Transferring the small ring to the vacant middle peg allows the large ring to be moved directly to the goal peg. Then the small ring can be placed on the large one. The rebuilt tower requires three moves.

The number of moves required for task completion depends on the number of rings and the starting and ending configurations. Each plan retains, however, the same structure, removing obstacles to destinations which will not impede other transfers. TOH problems have been classified by the minimum number of moves to build a given configuration. Planning skill is gauged by the most demanding problem the planner can complete in the optimal number of moves.

The TOH task makes heavy computational demands on the problem solver who must decompose the goal into subgoals and coordinate them. The repetitive application of the same strategy of obstacle removal in an impoverished task environment makes it difficult to keep track of progress and to remember the end goal of the task. Hence, the TOH task is very sensitive to differences in intellectual, developmental, and neurological status. Task conditions that lessen memory load improve performance. More complicated problems can be solved when young children are allowed to implement their strategies rather than simply verbalize them and when they are presented with a separate model of the end-goal state.

Although the TOH task is viewed as requiring processing capacity, it also taps representational skill. The task occurs in a novel problem space defined by a small number of rules and permissible moves. The problem solver must understand how these rules and moves fit together and influence strategy choice. Young children perform poorly on the task because it is arbitrary, boring, and repetitive. They may lack the motivation and knowledge to produce a coherent, workable task representation. Klahr had to adapt the TOH task in order to make it comprehensible to preschoolers. He created a story that justified the goal of the task and the rules for stacking the items. He also made the items more discriminable.

The ordering of subgoals and goals also contributes to the difficulty of the task and to developmental changes in performance. Errors arise when a move that physically puts the planner nearer to the goal is inefficient. In the two-ring problem, the smaller ring should not be placed directly on the goal peg, but on the middle peg, until such time as the larger ring has been moved to the goal peg. Additionally, when the final TOH configuration contains rings on more than one peg, it increases the difficulty of coordinating subgoals for movement.

TOTE units account for strategy assembly and implementation. However, in discussing strategies for remembering, Miller and his colleagues mentioned a higher-order strategy, or *metaplan,* which encoded the intention to be planful by adopting a strategy for learning. But they provided little information to explain the choice of goals or the decision to be planful. In Klahr's adaptation of the TOH task, he provided a rationale. The child was plotting the

moves of copycat monkeys desirous of imitating the goal monkeys. But usually it is simply assumed that problem-solving tasks automatically evoke planning. People have complete control over the necessary physical resources and over the outcome of their plan. Task instructions stressing efficiency imply the need to plan. The task is posed as an intellectual challenge and researchers assume that their subjects accept the challenge and strive to meet it by planning. Variations in performance are thought to reflect variations in planning ability rather than variations in willingness to plan or variations in achievement-related beliefs that might affect investment in planning. However, differences in motivation and belief may account for individual and developmental variability in performance.

III. PROCEDURAL PLANNING IN THE NATURAL ENVIRONMENT

Laboratory problem-solving tasks with constrained problem spaces, logically ordered rules, and logically constrained moves provide simplified settings for analyzing task representation, strategy construction, implementation, and learning. But these environments bear little resemblance to daily life where the tasks of ordering goals and of coordinating knowledge, needs, and external conditions to build a plan are much more complex. Psychologists who generated procedural models of planning in the natural environment therefore posited a more complex internal structure than TOTE units. They also took advantage of advances in explanations of cognitive processing.

Hayes-Roth and Hayes-Roth proposed a model of errand planning that has inspired several studies of planning across the lifespan. Their model describes how people plan to run a set of errands in a downtown area during a short time period in which it was impossible to complete every errand. The errands differed in their importance, location, and time constraints on them. The planner was given instructions, errands, and a map of the area complete with projected travel times from some locations to others, and was asked to think aloud while selecting and sequencing errands.

The model differs strikingly from the TOTE structure. Planning is described as opportunistic rather than completely anticipatory. Individuals chart a sequence of errands, but because the environment is complex and constantly changing, they may suddenly notice new opportunities. Thereupon they alter or interrupt their plans to take advantage of the new data. TOTES are homogeneous structures describing sequential subgoals. Instead this model presupposes that planning is carried out by categories of planning specialists, each of whom, under appropriate conditions, proposes a decision. An executive selects one of these proposals to implement and writes it on a blackboard. Each specialist scans the blackboard looking for a change in conditions that will provide the chance to go into action and propose a new decision. Five categories of specialists, residing on separate planes of the blackboard shown in Figure 1, are responsible for various facets of planning.

Specialists on the *executive* plane allocate resources among the multiple planning processes and goals. Three functions, each delegated to a unique specialist, are carried out: (a) the establishment of general priorities or principles of operation, such as attention to proximity relations; (b) determination of attentional focus on particular parts of the blackboard; and (c) scheduling of decisions.

The *metaplan* plane constitutes the planner's overview of the problem. One specialist creates a problem definition that includes the goals, the resources available, the constraints on their achievement, and possible action alternatives. The problem definition resembles Miller, Galanter, and Pribram's image. A second specialist decides on the problemsolving models or modes of attack, such as annotating the map. A third decision specialist sets policies for evaluating strategies using criteria like efficiency and importance. A fourth specialist projects the outcomes of any strategy and evaluates its risks and likelihood of success. The metaplan plane can potentially account for individual differences in approaches to planning and in goal definition.

The first two planes govern the cognitive system and construct a framework for planning. The other three planes create the plan. The *plan abstraction* plane lists general directives. The *knowledge base* supplies information about the task and the environment relevant to these directives. The *plan* plane uses these data to select the actions the planner will take. When the intention in the plan abstraction plane is to do important errands, the knowledge base supplies errands with imminent deadlines, and then the plan plane designates specific errands to complete. Each plane has specialists at four parallel levels of abstraction. For example, after the *outcome* specialist on the plan plane chooses the set of errands, at a lower level of specificity, a *design* specialist selects the first spatial cluster of errands to be performed, a specialist or the *procedures* level decides the order of errands in that cluster, and the specialist on the *operations* level generates routes between errands.

Judges of plan statements can distinguish levels of abstraction in planners' think-aloud protocols. Planners often engage in opportunistic planning with flexible switching between levels of abstraction. People who create plans that maximize spatial efficiency and errand importance are most flexible in switching levels of abstraction. They also employ more forethought. Their planning protocols contain more decisions on the executive and metaplan plane. When they use the three plan production planes, they operate more often at abstract levels. During childhood there is an increase in the amount of forethought and analysis in planning protocols.

However, even the best planners overestimate what they can accomplish in a given time. People whose occupations require chore management, such as housekeepers, do better in scheduling. Problems in time estimation may also arise from differing interpretations of the task. Some planners use a traveling salesman strategy that minimizes distance, but others emphasize time-scheduling constraints. Planners who work with errands they deem important underestimate the time needed to complete them more than when the errands are of lesser importance. Time stress also results in overestimation of what might be accomplished. Planners also often fail to prevent anticipated problems from occurring because the failures serve other aims. Shoppers might enjoy wandering around even when they do not finish errands. The impact of these and other motivational factors needs to be explored and the model expanded to account for them.

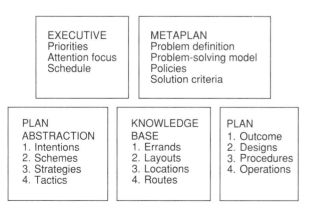

FIGURE 1   The five planes of the planning blackboard.

The Hayes-Roths' model describes an adult planner who understands the task environment and the need to set priorities and choose efficient strategies. The hypothetical planner is inclined to anticipate as well as to act directly upon the environment. Young children's errand planning is not like this. Preschool and early school-age children who are assigned a list of errands show representational problems. They have difficulty reorganizing lists into spatial or conceptual clusters that will generate efficient plans, sometimes because their categorical structure differs from that of adults. Decisions about planning change during development. Older children are more able to differentiate circumstances where advance planning is useful from those where it is not helpful. Older children understand the distinction between planning and doing and they know the specific mental processes employed in constructing a plan, but younger children do not.

As childhood progresses, children search for more background information about tasks, generate more alternative actions, and include more contingencies and steps in their plans. The gap between the intended plan and actual behavior narrows. Young children often forget goals and fail to monitor progress, particularly when they must coordinate diverse goals into the same plan, such as shopping for a party and breakfast, simultaneously.

The blackboard model enriches our understanding of planning by including decisions about the policies and priorities that govern choice of goals and strategies and the immediate knowledge people use in planning. But the model was not designed to explain the origin of those factors. The errand planning task is also idealized. Isolated planners select actions with fairly predictable outcomes. They do not contend with shortages of goods or money or with uncooperative vendors. Hence, the model does not give sufficient weight to the role of task interpretation, increasing experience in planning, and the complex motivational and social factors that permeate every aspect of planning.

IV. KNOWLEDGE-BASED PLANNING IN CONSTRAINED PROBLEM SPACES

A. Expertise and Planning

Building the Tower of Hanoi or scheduling errands in an unfamiliar town requires creating a new plan. But people often possess plans to deal with familiar situations which they merely need to adapt to current circumstances. In this case planning makes fewer demands on processing capacity. There are many familiar well-structured tasks like computer programming where past knowledge greatly simplifies planning.

Planning plays a crucial role in the performance of experts, people with extensive knowledge and skill in a task. Compared to novices, experts devote more time to anticipatory planning and rely more on long-term memory for solutions to problems. Experienced geometricians also use the strategy that Newell and Simon called planning. When first approaching a task, they create an abstract representation that ignores certain distinctions. They use this simplified model to recognize the pattern a problem exemplifies and then they search for similar problems they have encountered rather than developing a solution from scratch. They use old plans and modify them. In forging their representation they rely heavily on integrative mental models such as charts and diagrams. These models emphasize the relational structure of the situation, enable the generation of familiar inferential schemes, and facilitate monitoring of progress. A geometric sketch of a figure might enable the recognition of congruent angles which could be annotated on the diagram. Hence, experts are more likely to work forward planfully from their representation of the problem to the solution rather than working backward from the solution. Finally, many of the steps for solving problems are accessible as prepackaged routines. The knowledge base of an expert enables the formation of the integrative models of the world that enable planful problem solutions. It is assumed that experience and practice in a domain automatically precipitate the anticipatory, integrated representations we call plans.

B. A Construction–Integration Model of Planning

Studies of expertise show the impact of knowledge on planning performance. Some theoretical approaches account for the nature of that knowledge and the means by which it is accessed during planning. For example, Mannes and Kintsch proposed and simulated a construction–integration model that enables a computer to plan to generate the steps to complete an elementary computing task based on understanding the task's instructions. The model was adapted from prior work on text comprehension. They assume that the planner is knowledgeable about computers and programming commands. The planner's task is merely to use that knowledge to select the appropriate behaviors in a task. The content of knowledge is represented by a semantic network of plan elements. A plan element consists of a command, the preconditions for its use, and the outcome. A network links elements. Plan elements sharing common constituents, such as preconditions, are connected, as are those that have common roles in a causal sequence. Links vary in strength based on how frequently elements have been connected in the past.

The first phase of planning is interpretation, namely bringing past experience to bear on the problem. Before the problem is presented, all the task elements in the network are inactive. When a task instruction is presented, the network automatically activates the plan elements mentioned in a request, such as "list file," and specifies the objects to which the request refers (list file x). These elements then activate some of the other elements that are linked to them to enrich interpretation of the task. The spread of activation through the network leads to the choice of the plan element the network *wants* to enact. But the determination of this most strongly activated element is not yet influenced by the actual task conditions. The subsequent integration stage refines the plan to remedy this flaw. A parallel network of *can*-do elements, which is governed by situational input, changes the activation of the proposed plan element by testing to see if it is feasible. If not, some other plan element is chosen. The selected step, once activated and enacted, will produce a result that changes the current situation and may make other plan elements feasible to enact. Then the network recycles to select the next step in the plan until such time as enactment of an element produces the outcome that was stipulated in the task instructions.

The Mannes-Kintsch model is a knowledge-based account of the planning of tasks which are amenable to serial ordering of steps or subgoals. Their model elaborates the test–operate–test–exit paradigm by specifying how particular operations are accessed, enriched, and tested. The TOTE cycle is replaced by a semantic network that assembles and tests a plan.

Mannes and Kintsch made certain assumptions about the network based on their interviews of experienced computer programmers. The model assumes that the planner: (a) formats plan elements in terms of preconditions, actions, and outcomes; (b) chooses

the right items for each constituent; (c) knows all the required commands; and (d) links plan elements appropriately. But more knowledgeable programmers might have as planning elements routines comprising several steps rather than single steps. Novices might be unaware of the constituents of each plan element. At present, the model fails to account for planners who misinterpret the task situation, and therefore need to revise their approach because of erroneous selections of plan elements. It neglects the impact of learning which could result in adding elements and reorganizing the network. The Mannes-Kintsch account suggests that the major hurdle for the young or inexperienced planner is constructing a causal model of the workings of a domain. Once this is constructed the individual will automatically test the model for feasibility and use it in planning. But research on children's strategy choice suggests that skill in evaluating plans and awareness of the need to evaluate the feasibility of a plan develop slowly even in simple tasks like memorizing lists of words or stories.

The choice of task also constrains the explanation. Each plan element has a fixed precondition, action, and outcome. The actions are performed in sequence after having been selected by a solitary problem solver. The model cannot explain planning in the less predictable and less cooperative environment of the ordinary problem solver for whom the setting of priorities about goals, the decision to invest effort in planning, and the persuasion of people to cooperate constitute major issues in planning.

V. KNOWLEDGE-BASED PLANNING IN THE NATURAL ENVIRONMENT

A. Comprehending Plans

Some of these deficiencies are remedied in the fourth approach to planning, which is based on AI attempts to characterize a knowledge system that could be used by computers, and presumably by humans, to decode narratives about human actions. Essentially stories relate the history of a protagonist's plans to attain desired ends. Hence, Schank and Abelson embedded their descriptions of planning in a proposal for what ordinary people know about the links among the goals, actions, and outcomes that constitute plans. Schank originally suggested that plans are knowledge structures containing information about how actors achieve particular goals. Several types of plans were analyzed. For example, the plan for using an object requires knowing its location, gaining proximity to it, gaining control over it, and preparing for its use. Thus, the model of planning incorporates motivation but it serves as a part of the knowledge base.

Schank later suggested that plan knowledge was hierarchical. The top level contained abstract knowledge of the "universal" structure of plans. All plans contain the conditions motivating the plan, the strategy, the preconditions necessary for the success of the strategy, the side conditions produced by the strategy, its predictable results, and the aftermath. Plans to gain possession and use of an object were subcategorized into specific types and linked with routine means of goal attainment. These routines were tagged with information about failed attempts. Thus, planning is an integral part of Schank's theory about the contents and structure of human event memory. Text interpretation is based on prediction of plans. Failures of prediction produce a refinement of plan knowledge.

Accounts of text interpretation also describe goal selection. Protagonists in a story are not confined to decomposing goals and sequencing the resulting subgoals. They combine, interrupt, abandon, and substitute goals, and they persuade others to be agents in the search for goal fulfillment. Readers try to detect various kinds of goal conflicts within and between individuals and to track the plans used to resolve conflicts. Preschoolers have difficulty detecting goals and monitoring attempts to achieve them, particularly in narratives with many episodes.

B. Making Plans

Accounts of text interpretation describe what people know about authors' descriptions of planful behavior and motivation, not how people employ their understanding to generate their own plans or how people are motivated to comprehend. Researchers, therefore, have adapted the work on text comprehension to examine active planning. These analyses use a narrower definition of plans, specific strategies to achieve goals. The basic premise is that people know how to plan, want to plan, and have a repertoire of plans. A satisfactory model therefore needs to explain how people choose goals and select and modify familiar plans to handle the novel situations confronting them.

For example, Hammond claims that planning is remembering. Plans are created by accessing past successful plans to deal with a situation. These remembered cases are often tagged by the problems that have arisen in past plan implementations and the ways these problems have been avoided. Planning begins with setting a goal, such as traveling to Seattle or cooking a meal. The model contains a series of four boxes that carry out the key functions that will produce a viable plan (Fig. 2). The role of the *anticipator* is to analyze the situation, guided by past experience, to detect those features that warn of impending obstacles. The anticipator produces a set of instructions, "Search for a plan that satisfies the following goals in a particular situation but avoids particular problems." For example, "Find a plan to fly to Seattle without stopping in Chicago."

These instructions are handed to the *retriever*, which searches memory for specific plans that have been used in the past to accomplish goals and circumvent problems. Hammond supposes that the very guidelines that provoke planning—the search for a way to achieve a goal in a given type of setting without encountering problems—are the features that organize plan memory. Often there are no exact matches between the content of memory and search criteria. Then the retriever chooses a plan based on how many goals can be accomplished. In making the decision, the retriever compares the similarity of goals achieved in an old plan to the new goals. Plans are also weighted by the importance of goals they achieve and the critical nature of the problems avoided. So a successful trip to Boston might be a better candidate plan than a flawed Seattle trip.

The chosen plan is then retooled by the *modifier* in order to add neglected goals, eliminate goal conflicts, and adapt the plan to fit the current circumstances. The modifier relies on knowledge of a set of general rules for changing plans such as adding, substituting, and reordering steps. Two critics sup-

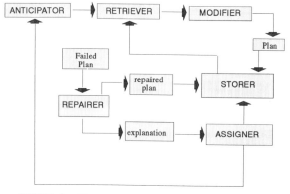

FIGURE 2   The components of case-based planning.

ply information about the specific objects in the task environment to which the plan must be adapted and a general framework of aims that accomplishment of each new goal must not violate. The modified plan is then enacted. If the results are successful, the plan goes to the *storer* which tags the plan by its goals, circumstances of enactment, and problems avoided. The storer deposits the plan in memory for future use.

But planners are fallible. Their understanding of the situation may be incomplete or the plan might have unintended side effects. The *repairer* handles the consequences of failure. It begins by diagnosing the problem using extensive knowledge of the task domain. This knowledge enables it to find the unsatisfied goals that index a failure such as, "The car would not start when I put the key in the ignition." It then detects the relevant conditions at the time the goal failure occurred and the steps in the plan producing the failure. The diagnosis is achieved by working step by step through the plan and then evaluating how the outcome of each step affected the achievement of desired goals. In some fields, we delegate diagnosis to specialists like auto mechanics, but experienced travelers and chefs can produce their own causal explanations of the steps and conditions that contributed to a fiasco.

After making a diagnosis, the *repairer* uses a second knowledge base containing repair methods. These are organized in memory by kinds of goal failure. Each kind of failure indexes a set of repair strategies that remedy it. For example, a plan may go awry when implementing one step interferes with the precondition for a later step. One repair known to fix this problem is reordering the steps. This strategy is then adapted to the particular problem. The resulting modified plan is enacted. If successful, the plan is stored in memory tagged by the goals it meets as well as the problems it has resolved.

The diagnosis that enabled the repair also explains the failure. The explanation is handed to an *assigner* which extracts the situational cues that signal impending problems. This knowledge is used by the anticipator. When it encounters a similar situation, the anticipator is reminded of the problem conditions that any plan relevant to that condition must handle. For example, if a car does not start because of cold weather, the anticipator will access plans for a winter car trip that include checking the antifreeze and the battery.

Case-based planning requires an impressive array of knowledge. Memory houses tested plans, indexed by their goals, circumstances of evocation, and warning signals. The modification of plans requires understanding how new objects affect a strategy. Diagnosis of failure is based on an informed causal analysis of action and a set of inference rules that track the steps in goal attainment. Recovery from failures requires access to abstract repair strategies and storage. Case-based planning also requires skillful decision making to order goals by priorities and candidate plans by their utility during the course of plan selection. The psychological validity of the model rests on an empirical assessment of the contents, organization, and use of individuals' knowledge base during planning to determine if actual planning fits the model. Although there have been few direct tests of the model, it does provide a framework for understanding developmental research which reports increasing understanding of the causal structure of plans and increased knowledge of the obstacles and repair strategies available. For example, the Kreitlers document how children increasingly structure their explanations of the meaning of events into a temporal and causal framework. They show that developmental differences in adoption of that framework are related to differences in the number of alternatives and contingencies children generate while planning.

However, Hammond's work is designed to enable computer generation of plans. He describes an ideal system effortlessly engaged in extensive analysis of the situation and of personal goals before searching for a plan. The system never decides to plan or to search memory. It simply plans. Its processors are automatically critical of the plans that are retrieved, modified, and repaired. Affect only enters in when the knowledge domain is interpersonal problem-solving. The affect is produced by the protagonist, not the planner. The case-based model, designed to enable computers to plan, is an incomplete description of human planning.

VI. COMPARISONS AND PROSPECTS

Four approaches to planning were described, dealing with well-structured and ill-structured domains and focusing primarily on knowledge and computation. The approaches differ in the richness of the explanatory model that accounts for planning knowledge and processes, as well as the forms of representation of knowledge and processing. Some of those differences reflect the state of the field at the time the models were proposed. Other differences reflect the tasks set for the planner. Goal conflicts, probabilistic outcomes, and social constraints loom larger in determining planning to accomplish daily tasks.

The explanatory models are idealized descriptions of mature competence rather than actual performance. The learning of plans is discussed, but not other developments in planning that may permit learning and implementation of plans. Models which focus on representation and computation necessarily presuppose a theory of the origin and growth of these fundamental processes, but many contemporary models ignore development.

A universal model of cognitive processing in standard task environments fails to capture the richness of planning. Introducing experiential components and metaplan knowledge into models of planning increases their explanatory power. Most analyses of planning also neglect the factors affecting the decision to plan and investment in planning. The cognitive literature on planning is often artificially divorced from the literature on decision making although retrieval of plans, evaluation of plans, and implementation of planning and plans involve a set of choices. Social and cultural norms influence planning. It is socially appropriate to plot strategies in the Tower of Hanoi task but not the course of a romance. Parents and educational systems teach children what, when, and how to plan. Motivation also influences the decision to plan. The consequences of failing to plan should outweigh the effort required for planning. Beliefs about personal capacities and attributions about the reasons for success or failure can influence engagement in the construction and implementation of plans. There is extensive research on the effects of these beliefs on academic performance, but little research to date on the role of these beliefs on planning to perform academic and other tasks. Beliefs about the power of fate and the prevalence of chaotic conditions dampen efforts at planning. Behavior may be goal-directed without being plan-directed.

Bibliography

Friedman, S. L., Scholnick, E. K., and Cocking, R. R. (1987). "Blueprints for Thinking: The Role of Planning in Psychological Development." Cambridge University Press, New York.

Hammond, K. J. (1990). Case-based planning: A framework for planning from experience. *Cog. Sci.* **14**, 385–444.

Scholnick, E. K., and Friedman, S. L. (1993). Planning in context: Developmental and situational considerations. *Int. J. Behav. Dev.* **16**, 145–167.

Vere, S. (1987). Planning. In "Encyclopedia of Artificial Intelligence" (S. S. Shapiro, Ed.), Wiley, New York.

Welsh, M. C., and Pennington, B. F. (1988). Assessing frontal lobe functioning in children: Views from developmental psychology. *Dev. Neuropsychol.* **4**, 199–230.

Wilensky, R. (1983). "Planning and Understanding: A Computational Approach to Human Reasoning." Addison-Wesley, Reading, MA.

PLAY

A. D. Pellegrini and Lee Galda
University of Georgia

Glossary

Ecological context Three levels of context include microsystem (face-to-face interaction), macrosystem or two different microsystems (e.g., school vs home), and exosystem (social economic status).

Exploration Deliberate, information-seeking behavior that characterizes encounters with new/novel stimuli.

Fantasy Simulative, or make-believe, behavior.

Rough-and-tumble play Play fighting and chase behaviors.

Scaffolding Support/guidance provided by adult for children's learning.

Thematic fantasy play Make-believe play around supernatural themes.

Transformation Changing the definition of object or situation in play.

WHAT IS PLAY? This may seem like a simple enough question, answerable by lay people and students of play alike. Indeed, at a gross level most people can reliably differentiate certain forms of children's play from nonplay. Partially for this reason, some think a formal definition of play is not necessary. The need for such a definition becomes more understandable when observers try to explicate, specifically, what it is they mean by play and the fit between these attributes and examples of play and nonplay. Further, the need for detailed definitions is important in examinations of the developmental and educational functions of play. In such ventures one must ask what, specifically, about play is responsible for educational and developmental effects. That is, to document developmental and edu-

cational functions of play we must pair specific aspects of play, such as reciprocal role-taking or nonliterality, with theoretically related outcome measures, such as perspective-taking and writing, respectively. After all, different forms of play have many dimensions: these dimensions are often shared with other types of behavior not typically considered play.

I. DEFINING PLAY

A. Structural

In trying to define play in this section, we first and briefly examine structural dimensions. Structural definitions address the specific behaviors that are considered playful, for example, play face and chase.

Structural definitions of play use physical appearances and features of behavior. Structural definitions, however, attempt to differentiate play from nonplay; they do not relate play behaviors to other outcome measures. Common structural dimensions of play include: play face (e.g., laughing), exaggerated movements (e.g., giant steps), exaggerated voice (e.g., deep, adult-like voice), and reciprocal roles (e.g., alternating between bully and victim).

Pretend play has been defined structurally to include: decontextualized behavior (i.e., taking a familiar behavior, such as eating movements, out of context, such as eating invisible food), self–other relationships (i.e., children treat themselves, first, and then other objects as fantastic, such as enacting mother–child roles with a doll), substitute objects (children invest realistic objects, such as dolls, first with fantasy characteristics, and then do not rely on objects to make transformations, such as declaring a space to be a doctor's office), and sequential combinations (i.e., where play episodes move from a single enactment, such as feeding a doll, into embedded themes, such as feeding a doll, and then bathing, reclothing it, and putting it to bed). Research into these components of pretense documents the progression toward more differentiation of the components, but has not addressed the definitional aspects of these components.

While such structural definitions have intuitive appeal, in that a list of observable behaviors exists, they are problematical. First, and foremost, structural aspects of play may also exist in nonplay categories; for example, play face can be observed in many nonplay areas, such as an adult reading a ridiculous claim of scientific fact; exaggerated movements are often observed in real aggression, without play face. Second, and relatedly, no one structural dimension distinguishes play from nonplay. Consequently, a polythetic definition of play, or defining play according to numerous criteria, seems most plausible. While even this is problematic, it may be a useful way in which observers can agree among themselves on what is "play."

B. Multiple Criteria

Defining play according to multiple criteria assumes that behaviors containing more of the hypothesized components should be considered more playful than those with fewer components. Further, certain components may be more important than others in discriminating play from nonplay. A recently conceptualized definition of play utilizing multiple criteria has been put forth to include the following criteria: nonliterality, intrinsic motivation, attention to means, What can I do with it? vs What can it do?, freedom from external rules, and active engagement. It has been argued that behaviors should be considered more or less play, not as play or nonplay, according to the number of criteria met. The assumptions behind this definition for *preschool* children's play were tested and supported; nonliterality was the most potent criterion, especially when combined with either positive affect or flexibility, while intrinsic motivation was not associated with play, and the means/end distinction was minimally associated. The importance of nonliterality in defining play in this study was probably an artifact of the age of the sample: The paradigm case of play among preschool children is fantasy play, in which nonliterality is crucial. Further research should be directed at other periods of childhood. This method has also been applied to preschool elementary school and middle school children's rough-and-tumble and the ways in which it differs from aggression.

II. PLAY THROUGH CHILDHOOD

In this section we describe the forms of play enacted from infancy through the primary school period. Such descriptions are important in that there may be a positive relation that should exist between resources allocated to an activity, in this case, time and energy, and any potential function, or outcome: The more time and energy expended, the larger the benefits. The organization of this section is such that the most common forms of play of infancy, preschool, and primary school children is described. Additionally, antecedent factors for these forms of play, such as infants' attachment status or preschoolers' gender, are outlined as are the consequences of these behaviors; for example, a consequence of primary school children's rough-and-tumble play is social affiliation. Children's constructive activities are not reviewed in this article because they are not play in the sense used here. From a Piagetian perspective, construction is more accommodative than assimilative and it, generally, does not vary with the age of the preschool child.

A. Infancy: Exploration

Infants, that is, children from birth to 1 to $1\frac{1}{2}$ years of age, commonly engage in exploration behaviors. While not play as defined above, it is an important precursor to play. In an attempt to integrate the play and exploration literatures, exploration is examined here. Infants spend most of their time exploring their environment. Exploration initially involves single objects, until children are about 9 months of age, and then multiple objects, until about 18 months of age; combinations of two objects, that is, putting two objects together is rather uncommon during this period. Where combinatory acts are observed, they tend to follow, within the same observation period, children's exploration of single objects.

Exploration can be solitary or social with the latter typically involving a parent or other adult. Infants' exploration is more complex in the adult context than in the solitary context to the extent that they exhibit more diverse and combinatorial behaviors in the former than in the latter. These results are consistent with Vygotsky's notion of the social origins of cognition whereby children's thought is a result of their interaction with a more competent other. Adults structure, or scaffold, children's interactions so as to facilitate their competence at a level higher than is possible alone. Infants, it seems, attend to those parental suggestions that are relevant to tasks that they are in the process of mastering and ignore comments relevant to skills already mastered or beyond their capabilities.

The extent to which adults serve this scaffolding function for infants should, of course, vary in relation to the quality of their relationship, an antecedent factor affecting exploration. A common, as well as a valid, indicator of parent–child relations is attachment status, as defined by interactions in the Ainsworth Strange Situation or with, the correlated, Q-sort methodology. Coordinated interaction around objects between adult and infant should reflect a relationship in which the participants' interactions are also coordinated. Securely attached infants, compared to anxiously attached infants, are more successful at initiating certain types of interaction around toys, such as toy exchanges, because these mothers are responsive to their infants. Further, the tenor of the interactions of securely attached infants is more positive, e.g., more positive tone and less distressed infant vocalizations. The nature of the attachment relationship, then, is an important antecedent of infant exploration. Securely attached children are more likely than anxiously attached children to explore their environments and gather information in that environment because they have a safe base from which to explore their world. This secure base, further, results in securely attached children engaging in longer and more complex forms of fantasy. This latter point will be explicated in the section on fantasy.

Other factors also affect the ways in which infants explore objects. Because of space limitations, these will only be listed. They include the temperament of the infant and the fit between his or her temperament and that of the playmate, gender of child and playmate, and the props around which they interact. Of course, these mediators of play may have independent effects, but it is more likely that they have interactive effects, e.g., fathers play with boys differently around blocks than they do with their daughters around the same props.

Consequences of infants exploration are increased knowledge of the objects being explored, boredom with one object and corresponding motivation to play with that object, and then to search the larger environment for other objects to explore. In short, exploration results in infants coming to know their environment, mastering the methods used in exploration, and practicing novel recombinations of that knowledge and those methods.

Social learning may be another consequence of prop-related exploration for young children. It is well documented that parents provide male and female infants with sex-role appropriate toys. Further, fathers tend to use toys less when interacting with infant sons than with infant daughters and the interaction between fathers and sons is more physically vigorous than between fathers and daughters. These antecedent conditions, it is argued, result in children developing same-sex toy and play preferences. These preferences then, the argument goes, predispose children to play in gender segregated groups. Play with peers in these groups further reinforces sex-role stereotypic behavior. [*See* SEX ROLES.]

B. Childhood: Fantasy

Children begin to engage in fantasy during the second year of life. Like other forms of play, fantasy play follows an inverted-U developmental function, increasing in frequency of occurrence for the next 3 to 4 years and then declining. Interestingly, the frequency of occurrence of fantasy, relative to other forms of play, is rather limited: 10–17% for preschoolers and 33% for kindergarten children. This statistic is interesting because it suggests that different forms of play co-occur within developmental periods and that it accounts for a relatively small amount of children's behavior. Of course, it may be that the contexts which give rise to these statistics do not support fantasy, but the question still is worth consideration.

Fantasy play can, generally, be defined as nonliteral activity, or activity where one thing represents something else. Further, fantasy can be social, with an adult or peer, or solitary. Earlier in this article, we noted that fantasy had the following structural components: self–other relations, decontextualized behavior, substitute objects, and sequential combinations. Suffice it to say here that self–other relations move from self-referenced, e.g., the child drinks an imaginary cup of milk, at about 1 year of age, to other referenced, e.g., the child gives his doll an imaginary drink, at $1\frac{1}{2}$ years of age, and that these acts develop from initially independent forms to integrated themes. Decontextualized behavior relates directly to the nonliteral dimension of play. A behavior is decontextualized when it is removed from its appropriate context, e.g., a nonliteral reenactment of a tea party.

Substitute objects involve children's substituting one thing for another. Initially, when children are between 1½ and 2 years of age substitutions are dependent upon realistic props, e.g., a doll. Children progress from such transformations to using less realistic props (both cases of object transformations) and then to using no props at all, e.g., rocking an invisible baby and proclaiming, "She's tired." Within this most abstract level of substitutions, i.e., ideational transformations, are included role and situation transformations, whereby children, mainly through the use of language, transform their roles and those of their peers and situations from the real to the fantastic. While 3 year olds are very capable of making ideational transformations we have argued that children must use explicit language in order to convey the meaning of ideational transformations to their peers. Without such explication meaning could not be conveyed because of the lack of correspondence between the symbol and its referent; e.g., How is a child to know that his friend walking in long strides, with a grimace on his face signifies his transformation into a solider unless the "solider" conveys it verbally?

Sequential combinations involve moving from single, unrelated acts of fantasy, to inter-related series of acts. Children's play episodes move from single unrelated schemes to well-integrated narrative-like themes. As in the case of object substitutions, the ability to generate an integrated play theme is dependent upon children's ability to use language to encode the theme.

Children's ability to engage in fantasy play is affected by a number of contextual factors such as social economic status, gender, and group composition. Cultural–ecological theory is useful in describing these relations. Children's play, like other dimensions of their behavior, in this system is affected at the microsystem level, by boys or play partners; these microsystems are further affected by the more general macro- and exosystems in which they are embedded. Our discussion will begin at the exosystem level and move to the microsystem.

The effects of two dimensions of the exosystem (school and public policy toward play and socioeconomic effects) on play are discussed. First, the attitudes of the public at large and school personnel, specifically, have an important impact on children's fantasy play. At the level of preschool policy, the role of fantasy play for preschoolers seems, for the moment at least, well established. Slogans such as "Play is children's work," the NAEYC (1987) guidelines for developmentally appropriate curricula, and the general "play ethos," suggest that play generally

and fantasy specifically, for preschoolers, is important. Consequently, home and school settings try to encourage fantasy play for preschool children's education and development. This encouragement may come in the form of providing time, materials, and space for fantasy, as well as allowing children to engage in the fantasy themes of their choice. The recent debate over the "appropriateness" of children's fantasy with war toys and play guns is relevant to this fantasy theme choice issue.

The effect of socioeconomic status (SES), an aspect of the exosystem, on preschool and kindergarten children's fantasy play has a long and interesting history. Indeed, the seminal studies of children's fantasy are studies of SES and fantasy. The impetus for studies in this genre came from Smilansky in 1968 who suggested, without the presentation of quantitative evidence, that the fantasy of lower SES Israeli children was less frequent and less diverse than their middle-class counterparts. This stimulated numerous studies examining class differences in play, as well as other aspects of child development and educational attainment. These studies generally concluded, like Smilansky, that the fantasy play of lower SES preschool and kindergarten children was less complex, frequent, and varied than that of middle-class children.

McLoyd's concise critique of these studies, however, raises serious questions with their results. She points out, first, and most importantly, that economic class and race are typically confounded. Ethnographic work illustrates the different ways in which LSES black and white children interact with parents and peers; thus, the need to separate race and economic status.

A second problem with the extant play literature relates to the failure to control classroom and school variables. As will be explicated below, children's play, both verbal and nonverbal is extremely sensitive to classroom variables, like teacher presence, type of peer group configuration, types of toys, etc. Most of the studies in the literature were observations of children's free play in classrooms. Consequently, observed differences may have been due to either class or classroom variables. Relatedly, experimental studies which manipulate children's play with toys do not always circumvent this problem. The toys in these experimental playrooms, and indeed the playrooms themselves, are more familiar to mainstream culture children than to nonmainstream children. As a consequence, nonmainstream children, compared to their mainstream counterparts, may spend their time exploring toys and the environment and less time engaging in symbolic play. The spurious conclusion may be made that the fantasy play of these children is deficient.

Microsystem level variables are also related to children's fantasy play. In this section, we outline ways in which mother–child relationships and specific aspects of classrooms and playgrounds relate to and affect children's fantasy play. An important consideration here is the way in which different levels of contexts are embedded in other levels. So to with the microsystem, which is embedded in larger macro- and exosystems. An example of this embeddedness was provided in the discussion of SES: Nonmainstream culture children play with props differentially, depending on familiarity. The larger influences should be kept in mind when reading this subsection to the extent that the research reported herein was conducted, for the most part, in university lab school classrooms and experimental play rooms.

In the previous section on exploration we noted that the quality of the child's attachment to his or her mother related to the ways in which the child explored the environment. There are also relations between attachment status and toddlers' symbolic play to the extent that securely attached children, at 20 months, compared to anxiously attached children, engage in longer and more complex symbolic play bouts. These results are consistent with a number of theories. First, like the explanation given above for exploration, securely attached children may be better able to engage in symbolic play because they are less concerned with mothers' emotional and physical availability. Second, the origins of symbolization may lie in the dyadic interaction of mothers and young children. Consistent with this position, mothers' actual involvement in children's play episodes seems to be a particularly important dimension of the interactive process.

Regarding studies at another microsystem level, the preschool classroom, the research strategies involve observing children in their classrooms and describing variation in children's play with different toys and with different social group compositions or to take children into an experimental playroom and manipulate exposure to props and peers. Not surprisingly, more fantasy is observed when preschoolers play with doctor props than when they play with blocks. More interesting, however, was the interaction among age, props, and gender composition of the groups. With age (i.e., 3, 4, and 5

years of age), children's play conforms to sex-role stereotypes. For example, in mixed-gender dyads boys are more dominant than girls, in terms of initiating fantasy topics and issuing commands, with both male-preferred and gender-neutral props. Gender socialization can certainly be considered an exosystem variable that affects play at the microsystem level. An interesting outcome of these findings that children's play behaviors vary according to age, gender, props, and group composition is that context seems to be defined differently by children at different periods. For example, a blocks context for girls would have different meaning, in terms of demand characteristics, at 3 years of age than at 5 years of age. Context, then, is not a unidirectional force of the environment on children; it is a transaction between children and their environment.

Other research has examined the extent to which play props effect specific aspects of verbalized fantasy, substitute objects, and sequential combinations. Regarding object substitution, we find children are quite capable, by 4 years of age, of making ideational transformations; indeed, almost half of their transformations take this form. This may explain why functionally ambiguous (e.g., blocks and styrofoam shapes) and functionally explicit (e.g., doctor kits) toys were equally successful in eliciting ideational transformation.

When we look at children's ability to weave these individual transformations into a theme, i.e., sequential combinations, we also find prop effects during the preschool period. Generally, thematically related sequences become more integrated across the preschool period but they are still rather fragmented and short. Children also seem to have a more difficult time generating integrated themes around functionally ambiguous props than around explicit props. It may be that children at this age expend most of their cognitive resources on verbally encoding individual transformations and consequently have fewer resources left to integrate verbally these transformations.

Children also engage in fantasy on the playground. Generally, boys, more than girls, choose to play outdoors and correspondingly, exhibit more complex behavior while outdoors. So the "effects" of playground variables may be mediated by gender. That aside, 7-year-old children engage in more fantasy play on a creative playground, e.g., climbing structures, swings, and a house-like structure, than on traditional playgrounds, e.g., see-saws, swings, slides.

In this final subsection addressing children's fantasy play, we will discuss some of the consequences of fantasy play. Consequence, as noted above, can be deduced by specific temporal relations between fantasy and outcome measures. That is, play is antecedent to some consequence. Longitudinal or experimental manipulations are necessary, then, to make causal inferences. In this section we review selected longitudinal and experimental studies which are post–Rubin *et al.* (1983). In the first series of studies to be reviewed, we discuss relations between fantasy and language and literacy. Next, studies which make causal attributions about fantasy in relation to creativity and problem solving are presented.

Structural dimensions of symbolic play were thought to provide the basis for the production of similar linguistic structure. Longitudinal work suggests that symbolic play and language production co-occur at 20 months, but not at 28 months. It may be more fruitful to examine relation between fantasy and language comprehension because Piagetian and Vygotskiian theories stress the meaning or control functions of language, rather than the production functions. While we have contemporaneous correlation support for the relation between fantasy and language comprehension, not production, longitudinal research is needed in this area.

In another, short-term longitudinal study (6 weeks), examining relations between play and language production, the ways in which a 3-year-old Korean girl (SooJong) used a specific form of fantasy, role playing, to help her learn a second language, English, was examined. SooJong initially used English narrative discourse in solitary fantasy play. In these play episodes she practiced school-relevant dialogues, symbolically transformed toys, and play roles and situations. She then used English in social play to set goals and transform settings and roles. Like her monolingual playmates, SooJong was motivated to comprehend and produce stretches of discourse because she enjoyed playing. When she experienced difficulty in cooperative play, she would go back to solitary doll play in Korean and, with the help of her mother, practice her English while "reading" to her doll. In short, play provided a safe environment in which to learn and practice a new language.

Consequence can be inferred from experimental manipulation of play treatments, as well as longitudinal research. Experimental studies have examined the extent to which thematic fantasy play training

facilitated children's (grades k, 1, and 2; k and 2, respectively) story comprehension and production. In these training studies the concern was with identifying specific aspects of thematic fantasy which might be responsible for corresponding narrative competence. The first aspect of the thematic play paradigm which must be considered as having a possible impact on development and/or learning play tutoring, or the extent to which adults' coaching of children's play is responsible for observed gains. Studies have shown that there are no between-group differences for tutored and nontutored thematic play groups.

The second interesting finding in one of these studies was the treatment × grade interaction, whereby play was more effective for kindergarten children than for older children. However, it has also been found that play training with third graders was affective. Their results suggest that play training can be useful in facilitating the story comprehension of children identified as poor comprehenders. It seems that play training interacts with children's level of competence. Clearly more research examining such interactive effects is necessary.

Next we will examine the effects of play on associative fluency, an aspect of creativity, and problem solving. The theoretical orientation of most of these studies is that the assimilative nature of unstructured fantasy is responsible for the novel uses assigned to conventional stimuli. Specifically, the assumption is made that play facilitates creativity, both in terms of novel uses for objects and in novel problem solutions, because preschool children are concerned with the means of activities and not ends. Further, the suspension of reality allows children to recombine behavioral routines in novel ways. The empirical support for the effects of preschoolers' play on associative fluency and problem solving has been widely cited.

More recently, however, these claims have been questioned. The results favoring play conditions in the earlier experiments in both genres related to experimenter bias. First, regarding associative fluency, the effects attributed to play may have been due to experimenter bias; when experimenter bias was eliminated, differences favoring play groups were not found.

The problem-solving tasks are based on the seminal work of Wolfgang Kohler in 1925 involving the problem solving of chimpanzees. In the play experiments, children are given sticks and clamps and exposed to play, modeling, or, in some cases, control conditions. Criterion measures included the number of hints needed from a tester and the duration needed to solve a lure-retrieval task. The general problems with most of these studies was experimenter bias and lack of an adequate control group. [*See* PROBLEM SOLVING.]

C. Early Primary School: Rough-and-Tumble Play

When children move from preschool to primary school they enter an institution which places little value on play, the implication of which is that we have fewer opportunities to study primary children's play. When we choose to study it, we are often relegated to the playground. Also as noted above, the study of play on the playground is a skewed view of play to the extent that it is a male-preferred setting and the play behaviors observed there are typically male. In this section we discuss one well-researched form of play that boys exhibit on the playground, and in other spacious areas, rough-and-tumble play (R & T). Indeed, as the frequency of fantasy play decreases, at the beginning of the school years, the frequency of R & T increases. R & T seems to represent an intermediary between fantasy and games with rules. R & T and games, such as tag, share design feature such as chase, hit-at, and alternating roles and strategies. Further, the gender differences observed in R & T are also observed in games with rules. Games with rules are not discussed in this chapter because it is not often observed in children's spontaneous play. As in the previous sections of this article, R & T is first defined; second, antecedents to it are presented; and third, consequences of R & T are outlined.

In studies of children's social behavior R & T was found to be a empirical factor, independent of aggression, composed of the following behaviors: play face, run, chase, flee, wrestle, and open hand beat. Structurally, R & T is typified by reciprocal role taking; for example, children often alternate between victim and victimizer. Like other forms of play, R & T, too, follows an inverted-U developmental function whereby it accounts for about 5% of the free play of preschoolers, increases to about 10–17% in early elementary school, and declines to 5% again in middle childhood.

1. Contextual Effects on R & T Have Been Most Clearly Documented at Exosystem and Microsystem Levels

The exosystem variable that is considered is, again, school policy. The aspect of school policy that are relevant to R & T is the role given to recess in the school curriculum. An important policy variable that affects R & T is the amount of time that children are "confined," or kept in their classrooms with little physical activity, before recess. Experimental research with preschoolers and primary school children suggests that the longer children are confined the more vigorous is their outdoor play.

2. There Are Microsystem Level Variables That Affect R & T

We discuss gender, social/spatial density, locations within playgrounds, and peer group composition. First, regarding gender. Boys, more than girls, engage in R & T. This finding is incredibly robust to the extent that it seems to be a cross-cultural truth. Gender differences may be due to hormonal and/or socialization factors, both of which are considered.

First regarding hormones, the dominant theory in this area, androgen theory, suggests that sufficient amounts of androgen sex hormones are necessary if the fetus is to display male-typical behavior, like R & T. Low levels of androgens are associated with less active behavior. In natural experiments whereby mothers experiencing pregnancy difficulties are given androgens, their female offsprings are more active and engage in more R & T than other female controls. These data, in conjunction with the animal data, suggest that males have a biological predisposition to engage in R & T.

Males also seem to be socialized to engage in R & T more than girls. Fathers, more than mothers, engage in physical play with their children, especially boys, from infancy through early childhood. Parents also provide children with sex-role stereotyped toys which, in turn, elicit different levels of activity. Children, from the toddler period onward, prefer to play with such gender appropriate toys. The male-preferred toys seem to elicit more active play than the female-preferred toys.

The preference for active play may also be related to the peer groups in which R & T occurs. Specifically, boys' preference for rough and active play results in their playing with other boys, not girls. Correspondingly, girls' dislike for this type of play results in their playing together and not with boys. The result of all this is that boys tend to engage in R & T with other boys who are of similar dominance and sociometric status.

The last microsystem variable affecting R & T to be discussed is the playground. Not surprisingly, we find that R & T is more likely to occur on soft, grassy areas than on hard surfaces. Further, children need space to engage in R & T. Consequently, more spacious areas, compared to less spacious areas, will elicit R & T.

3. R & T Also Has Important Consequences for Children's Development

These consequences may be related to aspects of the microsystem, children's sociometric status, and their R & T playmates. When boys engage in R & T with other popular or rejected boys they have different opportunities to observe, imitate, and practice prosocial and antisocial behaviors and social strategies. Indeed, we find that when popular elementary school children engage in R & T it typically moves in to games with rules, e.g., chase turns into tag. Additionally, our longitudinal work also shows that popular children's R & T in year 1 predicts games with rules in year 2. For rejected children, on the other hand, R & T moves into aggression and does not relate to prosocial behavior either contemporaneously or longitudinally.

III. CONCLUSION

In this article we have tried to provide an updated review of the research on children's play. We stated that clear definitions of play are necessary if we hope to explicate relations between play and various outcome measures. The reasoning here was straightforward: The category play has numerous dimensions, some of which co-occur with other nonplay categories. To identify the extent to which play per se is responsible for specific consequences, we must explicate empirical relations between theoretically related design features.

We also described commonly observed forms of play for three periods of childhood: exploration in infancy, fantasy in preschool, and R & T in primary school. The intent here was to provide normative information. We were also concerned with possible functions of play. Our conclusion was that play in some cases was functional and in others it was no more effective than other conditions.

We suggest future research should try to explicate theoretically important dimensions of play as a first step in any examination. Next, relations between these dimensions and specific outcome measures should be tested. Because play is a broad and sometimes ambiguous construct such a strategy is necessary. Other important research implications relate specifically to research methodology. There is a real need for longitudinal research. In our review we were amazed by the paucity of longitudinal designs. If we are to understand the ways in which children develop this is the most appropriate strategy.

Another methodolgical issue involves the locus of our studies. The time has come to study children in the laboratory, the classroom, and in the home. Such a strategy is necessary if we are to understand the ways in which children develop. Research restricted to the laboratory often tells us what children are capable of doing whereas studies of children in their natural ecologies tell us what they actually do.

Acknowledgments

A. D. P. acknowledges the support of the H. F. Guggenheim Foundation and the Fogarty Center of N.I.H. for supporting the work on this article.

Bibliography

Belsky, J., and Most, R. (1981). From exploration to play: A cross-sectional study of infant free-play behavior. *Dev. Psychol.* **17,** 630–639.

Blurton Jones, N. (1972). Categories of child interaction. In "Ethological Studies of Child Behavior" (N. Blurton Jones (Ed.), pp. 97–129. Cambridge University Press, London.

Bronfenbrenner, U. (1979). "The Ecology of Human Development." Harvard, Cambridge.

Bruner, J. (1972). The nature and uses of immaturity. *Am. Psychol.* **27,** 687–708.

Fagen, R. (1981). "Animal Play Behavior." Oxford University Press, New York.

Garvey, C. (1977). "Play," 2nd ed. 1990. Harvard, Cambridge.

Kohler, W. (1925). "The Mentality of Apes." Harcourt Brace, New York.

Martin, P., and Caro, T. (1985). On the functions of play and its role in behavioral development. In "Advances in the Study of Behavior" (J. Rosenblatt, C. Beer, M. C. Busnel, and P. Slater, Eds.), Vol. 15, pp. 59–103. Academic Press, New York.

McLoyd, V. (1982). Social class differences in sociodramatic play. A critical review. *Dev. Rev.* **2,** 1–30.

Pellegrini, A. D., and Boyd, B. (1993). The developmental and educational roles of play during early childhood. In "Handbook of Research in Early Childhood Education" (B. Spodek, Ed.). Macmillan, New York.

Piaget, J. (1962). "Play, Dreams, and Imitation." Norton, New York.

Rubin, K., Fein, G., and Vandenberg, B. (1983). Play. In "Handbook of Child Psychology: Socialization, Personality and Social Development'' (E. M. Hetherington, Ed.), Vol. IV, pp. 693–774. Wiley, New York.

Saltz, E., Dixon, D., and Johnson, J. (1977). Training disadvantaged preschoolers on various fantasy activities: Effects on cognitive functioning and impulse control. *Child Dev.* **48,** 367–387.

Smilansky, S. (1968). ''The Effects of Sociodramatic Play on Disadvantaged Preschool Children.'' Wiley, New York.

Smith, P. K. (1982). Does play matter? Functional and evolutionary aspects of animal and human play. *Behav. Brain Sci.* **5,** 139–184.

Vygotsky, L. (1978). ''Mind in Society.'' Harvard, Cambridge.

PORNOGRAPHY, EFFECTS ON ATTITUDES AND BEHAVIOR

William A. Fisher
University of Western Ontario, Canada

Glossary

Correlational research on pornography effects Research which systematically measures exposure to pornography and assesses its association with phenomena of interest (e.g., antiwoman attitudes or behavior), often conducted in "real world" settings.

Ecological validity Degree to which research procedures provide valid representation of "real world" situations.

Experimental research on pornography effects Research which systematically manipulates exposure to pornography and assesses its causal relationship with consequences of interest (e.g., antiwoman attitudes or behavior), often conducted in laboratory settings.

Pornography Sexually explicit material; legal definitions and content-based definitions appear in entry.

Subject awareness effects Subjects in pornography research may become aware of the hypothesis under study, and may modify their responses in light of the perceived purpose of the study.

PORNOGRAPHY, a Greek term originally used to refer to the writings of harlots, is at present employed to denote the general category of sexually explicit materials. Pornography has been the focus of much public controversy in recent years, and

social scientists have produced theoretical analyses and empirical investigations which have helped to inform pubic debate on this issue. The present discussion focuses on definitions of pornography and on theoretical views of how it may affect attitudes and behaviors, and on currently available information concerning the prevalence and effects of such material.

I. DEFINING PORNOGRAPHY

A definition of pornography that is clear and objective is a prerequisite to the scientific study of sexually explicit material. Definitions of pornography have focused on both legal characteristics and content characteristics that may be involved in classifying material as pornographic.

A. Legal Definitions

Legal definitions of pornography (or obscenity) are present in many Western societies, but they have provided relatively little clarity in defining pornography for legal reasons, and less clarity still in defining pornography in a fashion that facilitates scientific investigation. For example, U.S. law stipulates that obscenity exists when:

(a) . . . the average person, applying contemporary community standards, would find that the work, taken as a whole, appeals to the prurient interest . . . ; (b) . . . the work depicts or describes, in a patently offensive way, sexual conduct specifically defined by the applicable state law; and (c) . . . the work, taken as a whole, lacks serious literary, artistic, political, or scientific value. (*Miller v. California*, 1973)

Canadian law specifies more simply that ". . . any publication a dominant characteristic of which is the undue exploitation of sex . . . shall be deemed to be obscene" (Criminal Code of Canada, Section 163.8).

From a legal standpoint, the subjective nature of the factors on which these definitions turn (does the work appeal to prurient interest? have serious artistic value? unduly exploit sex?) has resulted in the need for lengthy legal actions to determine whether particular materials are obscene, and in largely ineffective efforts to suppress such materials. From a scientific standpoint, these definitions lack the objectivity necessary for systematic classification and study of pornographic material, and they provide no conceptually meaningful account of the factors that unify such material or why it might affect our attitudes and behavior.

B. Content-Based Definitions

Content-based definitions of pornography have been proposed by social scientists in recent years. From a scientific standpoint, content-based definitions represent an advance over legal definitions for two reasons. First, the objective of content-based definitions is to provide a clearer indication of the characteristics which make material pornographic than is true of legal definitions. Second, content-based definitions conceptualize content, at least by implication, as the characteristic of pornography that determines its effect on attitudes and behavior.

Violent pornography has been defined as sexually explicit material that portrays or endorses sexual aggression, or material that fuses sexual content and aggressive content. Violent pornographic portrayals of sexually aggressive acts (e.g., sexual assault) or of the fusion of sexuality and aggression (e.g., sexual activity followed by brutal aggression) typically involve violent acts committed by men against women. The content-based definition of violent pornography raises the possibility, at least by implication, that exposure to such material might encourage the development of sexually aggressive attitudes or behaviors toward women.

Degrading pornography has been defined as sexually explicit material that dehumanizes people, usually women, or sexually explicit materials that reduce individuals, usually women, to sex objects that are portrayed as sexually nondiscriminating, automatically sexually responsive, and of little use for other purposes. Such materials might include dehumanizing portrayals of sexual activity that focus ex-

clusively on genital detail and exclude personifying information, and portrayals of sexually nondiscriminating and euphorically responsive women. The definition of degrading pornography raises the possibility that exposure to such material might encourage the development of degrading or dehumanizing beliefs and behaviors with respect to sexuality and women.

Erotica has been defined as sexually explicit material that is nonviolent, nondegrading, and consensual in nature. Such material could include portrayals of sexual activity between participants who have mutual sexual or affectionate motives. The definition of erotica raises the possibility that exposure to such material might encourage the development of nonviolent, nondegrading, and consensual attitudes and behaviors concerning sexuality.

C. Summary and Critique

From a scientific perspective, content-based definitions of pornography represent an advance over legal definitions of such material, but content-based definitions remain limited in a number of significant ways.

First, content-based definitions remain heavily subjective. While it is relatively easy to objectively define sexually violent portrayals, it is not easy to objectively define demeaning or erotic portrayals. Does a nude photograph debase an individual and reduce him or her to the dehumanized status of a sexual object, or is a nude photograph an erotic portrayal that is in fact nonviolent, nondegrading, and consensual?

Second, content-based definitions provide no basis for dealing with cases in which themes from different content-based categories directly conflict. Is the portrayal of consensual but physically and genitally focused, impersonal, and anonymous sexual activity considered to be degrading because of the depersonalized focus of the portrayal, or is it deemed to be erotic because of the participants' mutual desire for the exclusively libidinous activity that is portrayed?

Third, content-based definitions of pornography fail to acknowledge the fact that sexually explicit materials evoke powerful sexual arousal and emotional responses in observers. Beyond the content factors that may define pornographic material, the degree to which it evokes sexual arousal, enjoyment, or abhorrence seems highly likely to moderate its effects.

Finally, content-based definitions of pornography fail to recognize the fact that mentally active individuals perceive and interpret and idiosyncratically alter sexually explicit stimuli and construct personalized representations of such material that may be quite distant from the objective portrayal presented. Over and above the content of pornographic material, individuals' perceptions and interpretations of such material are also likely to influence their reactions to it.

While definitions of pornography are subject to many criticisms, there still seems to be something to be learned from attempts to define such material. Specifically, the present analysis suggests that it is important to focus on the content of pornographic stimuli, and on individuals' perceptions of such stimuli in seeking to understand effects of pornography on attitudes and behavior.

II. PREVALENCE OF PORNOGRAPHY

A. Prevalence of Violent Pornography

It is believed by many that violent pornography is prevalent in Western societies and that such material is on the increase. Numerous studies conducted over the past 20 years support this view, showing that violent pornographic imagery is relatively common in sex magazines, videotapes, and adult bookstore materials, and is increasingly common across time. As is often the case in research on pornography, however, other studies show precisely *opposite* findings and indicate that violent pornographic imagery is *uncommon* in sex magazines, videotapes, and adult bookstore materials, and is on the *decline*. Such opposite findings for the prevalence of violent pornography are often based on investigations of similar or identical media over similar or identical periods of time, and satisfactory explanations for these striking contradictions are often not apparent. It should be noted that despite inconsistencies in research findings for the prevalence of violent pornography, results typically show that such imagery comprises a relatively small porпортion of sexually explicit materials overall.

B. Prevalence of Degrading Pornography

The definition of degrading pornography has only recently been proposed, and this definition is a heavily subjective one. Consequently, little research has specifically focused on the prevalence of degrading pornography. Some research that has examined the prevalence of degrading pornography, as defined at present, has studied X-rated videotapes, and confirms the impression that the proportion of depersonalized and dehumanizing images is considerable in this genre, at least according to some definitions of these terms. Sexually explicit imagery in mass-selling sex magazines, which emphasize solitary nude photographs with focused genital displays, would also qualify as degrading pornography according to some definitions of this term, but not according to others. If characterized as degrading pornography, the prevalence of mass-selling explicit sex magazines would support the conclusion that degrading pornography is common in Western societies.

C. Prevalence of Erotica

Because erotica as recently defined involves sexually explicit material that is nondegrading and nondehumanizing, and because of the subjectivity of this characterization, little research has investigated the prevalence of erotica as defined at present. Research on this topic would require clear definitions of whether, for example, depersonalized and purely libidinous but consensual sexual portrayals, as are common in X-rated videotapes, comprise degrading pornography or erotica, and would require clarification of whether solitary nude photographs would be deemed to be degrading pornography or erotica.

D. Summary and Critique

The prevalence of violent pornography has been studied intensively over the past several decades, but findings are contradictory and inconsistencies difficult to explain. The prevalence of degrading pornography and of erotica has been studied but little, owing to the recency of these classifications and to the subjectivity inherent in these definitions. The subjective nature of the definitions of these categories of sexually explicit material would seem to make it difficult to conduct research to investigate prevalence or trends in these areas.

Several points can be made in relation to the prevalence of sexually explicit materials, despite the ambiguities of this research area.

First, it seems obvious that there is more sexually explicit material available to the public at present than ever before. However, it is unclear what proportion of this material involves violent pornography, what proportion involves degrading pornography, and what proportion involves erotica.

Second, observers have noted the obvious fact that the amount of *nonsexual* violence in the media is far greater than the amount of sexual violence in the mass media. Related to this observation, it appears that violent pornographic imagery comprises a relatively small proportion of sexually explicit imagery in general.

Third, it is clear that advances in research on the prevalence of degrading pornography and erotica must await more objective definitions of these categories of sexually explicit material.

Finally, for these reasons, it must be emphasized that when we discuss possible effects of violent pornography, degrading pornography, and erotica, we do so without knowing with precision whether we are examining effects of relatively common or relatively rare stimulus events.

III. EFFECTS OF PORNOGRAPHY: THEORETICAL VIEWS

Pornography has been the subject of considerable public concern because it is presumed to have negative effects on attitudes and behavior. The possibility that pornography may have prosocial effects (e.g., be educational, lower anxieties) has received little public discussion or research attention. During much of the present century, public fears centered on the likelihood that pornographic representations of sexual activity would encourage sexual promiscuity in society. During the past two decades, public fears have centered on the possibility that pornographic representations of sexual violence and degradation will encourage men to develop antiwoman attitudes and to commit antiwoman acts.

Social science conceptualizations have been developed to account for presumed effects of sexually explicit material on attitudes and behavior. While various formal and informal conceptualizations have been proposed, most employ a number of the components and relationships that are included in a generic model of effects of sexually explicit material that is presented in Figure 1. It can be seen in Figure 1 that exposure to sexually explicit materials, the socialization process, and personality factors jointly affect an individual's sexual dispositions, which include his or her sexual attitudes, beliefs, norms, and arousal patterns. In the presence of facilitating

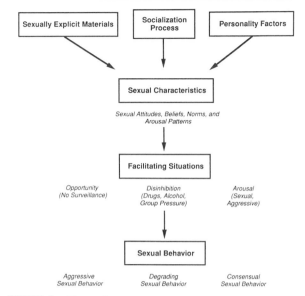

FIGURE 1   Theoretical analysis of effects of pornography on attitudes and behavior, embodying concepts common to several theoretical approaches (see, for example, Malamuth and Briere, 1986, and Fisher and Barak, 1989).

situational circumstances, such sexual dispositions are thought to determine sexual behavior in its social and antisocial forms.

Using the constructs presented in Figure 1, different theorists have reached different conclusions concerning hypothesized effects of pornography on attitudes and behvaior.

A. A Theory of Strong Negative Effects of Pornography on Behavior

In the view of a majority of theorists of the 1980s, exposure to violent or degrading sexually explicit material works together with socialization patterns that teach and reinforce antifemale attitudes and behaviors, and with predisposing personality factors such as poor self-control and low intelligence, to produce antiwoman attitudes and antiwoman acts. Specifically, exposure to violent or degrading pornography, socialization patterns that favor misogyny, and predisposing personality characteristics are thought to facilitate acceptance of the antiwoman messages of violent and degrading pornography. Acceptance of the explicit and implicit messages of violent and degrading pornography is hypothesized to result in individual sexual dispositions that include antiwoman sexual attitudes (e.g., positive evaluations of sexual aggression), beliefs (e.g., perceptions of the instrumentality of sexual aggression), norms (e.g., perceptions of the social acceptability of sexual aggression), and arousal patterns (e.g., sexual arousal in response to sexual aggression). Such sexual attitudes, beliefs, norms, and arousal patterns, in the presence of facilitating circumstances such as chemical disinhibition or group pressure, are thought to determine sexual behavior that involves antiwoman aggression and antiwoman degradation.

B. A Theory of Null or Weak Effects of Pornography on Behavior

From the perspective of an emerging minority of theorists in this area, an entirely different set of outcomes is predicted from the same conceptual base. In this emerging view, the values of violent and degrading pornography are *so profoundly* at variance with the values that an individual has learned during a lifetime of socialization that contact with pornography will have no influence or an exceptionally weak influence on his or her attitudes and behavior. In this line of reasoning, violent pornography is seen to advocate sexual violence against women, and degrading pornography is seen to communicate that women are sexually insatiable, nondiscriminating, and perennially available to anyone at all. Most individuals have socialization and learning histories that repeatedly teach and repeatedly reinforce completely opposing messages, and this lifetime of learning experiences to the contrary should lead the individual to reject the messages and values of violent and degrading pornography. For example, most males have been socialized and reinforced for human decency to the extent necessary to prevent them from sexually assaulting a struggling, weeping female victim. Most males are also aware that the physical assault of a woman to obtain sexual gratification is regarded by society as a profoundly *unmasculine* act that will cost much of one's masculine image. Most men have managed to learn that women are not sexually nondiscriminating and always available to any partner in proximity. Intermittent exposure to violent or degrading pornography is hypothesized to have little or no influence on sexual dispositions such as attitudes, beliefs, norms, or arousal patterns, because the message of violent and degrading pornography is at such profound variance with the remainder of the individual's learning history. Moreover, these theorists propose that the extremity of undersocialization or of predisposing personality characteristics that would be necessary to

facilitate acceptance of the message of violent or degrading pornography would be so great as to render the individual vulnerable to virtually *all* antisocial messages. This analysis would designate the individual, and not pornography per se, as the social problem in such instances.

C. Summary and Critique

The theoretical constructs that have been invoked to explain effects of pornography on attitudes and behavior do not possess a logic that compels one to accept a particular conclusion about the occurrence of such effects. Focusing on identical constructs, theorists have reached the conclusion that pornography will have consistent effects, or no effects, on attitudes and behavior, depending upon assumptions that are made about the content of socialization in our society and on the weight this socialization has as a determinant of behavior. Research findings may eventually help clarify which set of theoretical assumptions is the more tenable one.

IV. EFFECTS OF PORNOGRAPHY: RESEARCH FINDINGS

A. Effects of Violent Pornography

Violent pornography portrays and endorses sexual aggression, usually committed by men against women. Theoretical cases can be made to suggest that violent pornography will work with, or clash with, other factors and have a strong or a weak effect on attitudes and behavior. Research findings concerning effects of violent pornography on attitudes and behavior may help to confirm one or the other of these views.

During the past decade, research has repeatedly found that exposure to violent pornography can have fairly dramatic negative effects on men's attitudes and behavior toward women. Research has routinely indicated that even exceedingly brief, one-time exposure to as little as 5 minutes of violent pornography can cause men to fantasize about raping a woman, to become more accepting of the rape of a woman, and to engage in physical aggression against a woman in a laboratory setting. Violent pornography which portrays female victims who eventually seem to ''enjoy'' their victimization seems especially likely to have negative effects. Moreover, there is some evidence that individuals who possess certain preexisting personality characteristics (e.g., psychoticism, relatively high self-rated likelihood of raping a woman) are especially likely to be affected by violent pornography in laboratory settings. The view that violent pornography has reliable negative effects on men's attitudes and behaviors toward women has gained wide currency over recent years, has been endorsed by some (but by no means all) government commissions of inquiry that have investigated this area, and has figured prominently in legal proceeding that have sought to punish purveyors of violent pornography and to limit its availability.

During the past several years, and in contrast to "common wisdom" in this area, highly critical reviews of the literature, alternative conceptual analyses, and failures to find or to replicate expected effects of pornography have appeared in the literature. Each of these sources has raised serious questions about the likelihood that brief exposure to violent pornography can cause otherwise normal men to adopt attitudes and behaviors that are at profound variance with fundamental social norms and values. These critiques have posed significant empirical, methodological, and conceptual challenges to research that seems to support the view that exposure to violent pornography causes men to develop antiwoman attitudes and to commit antiwoman sexual aggression. [*See* VIOLENCE, OBSERVATIONAL EFFECTS ON BEHAVIOR.]

1. Empirical Limitations

Critics of the proposition that violent pornography causes men to develop antiwoman attitudes and antiwoman behavior have emphasized that research support for this assumption is far from consistent. First, there are experimental studies that have failed to find any effect of exposure to violent pornography on antiwoman attitudes and antiwoman aggression. To cite extreme examples, although there are experiments that have found that exposure to 5 minutes of violent pornography is sufficient to produce antiwoman attitudes and antiwoman acts, there are other experiments that have found that exposure to 5 *hours* of violent pornography has no effect on these outcomes. Second, there are numerous correlational studies that have found no association between violent pornography use and the actual performance of sexually aggressive crimes. While we might be concerned that individuals with certain preexisting personality characteristics seem especially vulnerable to effects of violent pornography in laboratory

settings, individuals who have actually committed sex crimes appear by and large to have no increased likelihood of contact with violent pornography.

2. Methodological Limitations

Critics of the presumption that violent pornography causes antiwoman attitudes and antiwoman acts have pointed out that some of the research that appears to support this position has serious methodological flaws.

First, it has been asserted that some research which appears to support a link between exposure to violent pornography and antiwoman attitudes and acts suffers from subject awareness effects. Specifically, in many experimental studies in this area, subjects are shown violent pornography, and then their attitudes or behaviors toward women are assessed. Despite the transparency of these procedures and the likelihood that subjects are aware of how they are expected to respond, and the likelihood that many comply with these expectations, the identification and elimination of aware or suspicious subjects in this research line is rare. In these cases, it seems likely that subject awareness of the experimenter's purpose—and not violent pornography per se—may be responsible for the results observed.

Second, research which supports the hypothesized link between violent pornography and antiwoman outcomes may suffer from the selective attrition of subjects who are intolerant of violent pornography. For example, in one study of repeated exposure to violent pornography, about one in seven men who were repeatedly exposed to violent pornography dropped out of the study across repeated exposure sessions. No one in the comparison group, which met for only one session, dropped out. It seems probable that many men who dropped out of the violent pornography condition of the experiment did so because the violent pornography was repugnant to them. This selective attrition would have left remaining in the violent pornography condition only men who were relatively tolerant of violent pornography and who had relatively negative attitudes to women *before* the study began. At the end of the experiment, results seemed to show that men who had been repeatedly exposed to violent pornography had developed more negative attitudes toward women than men in the comparison group. However, it seems quite possible that selective attrition of subjects, and not violent pornography, may be responsible for the "effects" observed.

Third, experimental procedures which seem to support the hypothesized link between violent pornography and antiwoman behavior may be ecologically invalid. In effect, critics have asserted that the experimental procedures used in some of the most influential research on violent pornography and aggression may be so unrepresentative of natural settings that they tell us little about the relation of violent pornography and antiwoman aggression in the "real world." At the same time as these ecologically invalid procedures fail to model the "real world" faithfully, it is asserted that these procedures increase the likelihood of showing "effects" of violent pornography as well. For example, in influential research on violent pornography and aggression, male subjects are angered by a female who gives them a negative performance appraisal and sends several painful electric shocks to them. Next, male subjects see 5-minute film clips of either violent pornography or erotica or nonsexual material, and then they are instructed by the experimenter to send electric shocks to the female who provoked them earlier, every time she errs on an experimental task. In general, male subjects who have seen violent pornography choose to send higher levels of electric shock to the female than do male subjects who have seen comparison stimuli. However, critics have pointed out that these experimental procedures are ecologically invalid and that it is by no means clear that *any* male subject would have aggressed if any *nonaggressive* response option had been open to him. In effect, critics assert that these experimental procedures are ecologically invalid because they fail to provide a fair model of "real world" settings in which angered men who have seen pornography are not forced to aggress and indeed have nonaggressive response options open to them. These ecologically invalid procedures both fail to inform us about the relationship of pornography and aggression in natural settings, where multiple response options are open to men, and at the same time they *guarantee* that exposure to violent pornography will be followed by some level of antiwoman aggression.

3. Conceptual Challenges

Conceptual challenges of assumptions guiding research on violent pornography effects have been reviewed in the preceding discussion of theory in this entry. Essentially, critics have taken serious issue with the notion that exposure to violent pornography will alter individuals' attitudes and behavior in a direction that is greatly at variance with their

lifetime socialization histories and well-entrenched values. Such critique has led to the hypothesis that intermittent exposure to violent pornography will have little or no influence on attitudes and behavior.

4. A "Second Wave" of Research on Violent Pornography

Critiques that have emphasized empirical inconsistencies, methodological limitations, and conceptual reservations concerning research on violent pornography have begun to stimulate a "second wave" of research on this topic in recent years. This research line questions whether brief and transitory exposure to violent pornography can move men to antiwoman attitudes and antiwoman acts that are at variance with lifetime socialization and learning histories to the contrary, and seeks to correct some of the methodological limitations that critics have identified in work in this area. One "second wave" research line has emphasized the creation of experimental situations for studying violent pornography and antiwoman attitudes and antiwoman acts that are less prone to subject awareness problems and more ecologically valid representations of the choices available to men in natural settings.

One study in this research line permitted males to *choose,* in an ecologically representative fashion, whether or not to view violent pornography or comparison stimuli. Findings showed that the vast majority of men chose to view stimuli *other* than violent pornography. These findings suggest that we may have to temper our assessment of research on effects of enforced contact with violent pornography with the understanding that most of the individuals under study would not have chosen to see it.

A second study in this research line involved an initial experiment in which men were exposed to brief segments of violent pornography or to comparison stimuli. The initial experiment then ostensibly ended, and the initial experimenter turned the subjects over to a second experimenter who was conducting a supposedly different study of perceptions of women. Subjects were then asked to indicate their attitudes toward a number of women's issues, including acceptance of rape myths and acceptance of interpersonal violence against women. The "separate experiments" ruse was used to try to minimize subjects' awareness of the link between exposure to violent pornography and the measures of their attitudes toward women. Results showed *no* measurable effects of exposure to violent pornography on measures of attitudes toward women.

Still other research in this line has studied the behavior of males who have been provoked by a female, and who have seen violent pornography in which a female appears to eventually enjoy being assaulted. The males are then given both aggressive *and* nonaggressive response options, in order to improve the ecological validity of the research procedures. Findings showed that when given a choice, men in this situation overwhelmingly choose *nonaggressive* response options, even after they have seen violent pornography, and even after they have been provoked by a female.

Taken together, "second wave" findings suggest that there may be some truth to conceptual criticism of the view that men can be relatively easily moved to antiwoman attitudes and antiwoman acts by simple exposure to violent pornography. These findings suggest that there may be some truth as well to methodological criticisms of the procedures of research in this area and to the suggestion that findings for violent pornography—aggression links may be partly the result of methodological shortcomings in research on this topic.

B. Effects of Degrading Pornography

Degrading pornography promotes the view that women are sexually nondiscriminating, easily arousable, and always willing partners. As mentioned earlier, a theoretical case can be made to suggest that exposure to degrading pornography will work together with other factors in society which promote these views and have strong effects on attitudes and behavior. However, a theoretical case can also be made to suggest that degrading pornography is so profoundly at variance with the rest of an individual's experience that it will have little or no effect on attitudes and behavior.

Research on degrading pornography per se has been undertaken only in recent years, since the definition of this material as a distinct category is a fairly recent occurrence. Such research has focused primarily on the impact of degrading pornography on attitudes toward women, although some information that is indirectly relevant to the effect of degrading pornography on antiwoman aggression is available as well.

Research concerning effects of degrading pornography on attitudes toward women has had mixed results. On one hand, experimental studies have shown that repeated exposure to degrading pornography is associated with decreases in punitiveness regarding rape, decreases in support for the women's liberation movement, decreases in subjects' satisfaction with their sexual partners, and increases in self-rated likelihood of raping a woman and appetite for uncommon and violent pornography. Some research in this area has also suggested that individuals with certain predisposing personality characteristics (e.g., psychoticism) may be especially likely to show effects of exposure to degrading pornography. On the other hand, there are numerous experimental studies that have simply failed to find effects of exposure to degrading pornography on views about rape, support for traditional sex roles, perception of women as sexual objects, self-rated likelihood of raping a woman, and related outcomes. In addition, numerous correlational studies have measured the association of people's use of sexually explicit materials that embody characteristics of degrading pornography and their attitudes toward women, and have found little or no evidence for a link between the two. Finally, a number of the experimental studies which have found effects of exposure to degrading pornography on attitudes toward women appear to be subject to subject awareness and other methodological problems similar to those discussed in relation to violent pornography.

With respect to effects of exposure to degrading pornography on antiwoman aggression in laboratory settings, studies that have specifically investigated the impact of degrading pornography are not available. However, research on effects of exposure to "standard-fare" sexually explicit materials which embody some characteristics of degrading pornography, but which was conducted prior to the definition of this category of material, is of at least indirect relevance. Research findings on the effects of these sexually explicit materials have been weak and inconsistent. One study in the literature reports that a single exposure to this material produced increased aggression against a same-sex other, while repeated exposures to such material produced decreased aggression against a same-sex other, presumably because repeated exposures to such materials results in less arousal and presumably less motivation to aggress. Several other experimental studies of nonviolent sexually explicit materials have failed to show aggression-facilitating effects (in terms of male aggression against women) of such stimuli.

C. Effects of Erotica

Erotica, by definition, portrays nonviolent, nondegrading, consensual sexual activity. From the theoretical perspective proposed earlier, the case could be made that erotic stimuli may encourage such activity and that together with other factors in our permissive society and with any predisposing personality traits, erotic stimuli should encourage promiscuous and perhaps novel sexual activity. From the theoretical perspective proposed, the case could also be made that erotic stimuli will encourage nonviolent, nondegrading, consensual sexual activity that takes place within the guidelines already set down by an individual's socialization history and present social circumstances. In the latter view, erotica would be expected to activate preexisting patterns of sexual activity rather than to result in promiscuous or novel sex activities.

Research that focuses specifically on effects of erotica as defined at present has been a recent phenomenon, since the definition of erotica, as distinct from degrading pornography, is a relatively recent occurrence. However, some early research on the effects of sexually explicit material, undertaken in the 1960s and 1970s, seems to employ stimuli that would approximate erotica more closely than degrading pornography. Such research provides at least an indirect indication of the effects of erotica on sexual behavior. In general, findings support the notion that exposure to erotica leads to transitory increases in *preestablished* patterns of sexual behavior, but not to novel sexual performances. For example, married couples who see erotica have been found to have an increased likelihood of marital coitus on the night of viewing the erotica, and they report that they do not incorporate anything new in terms of positions or techniques into their lovemaking. By the same token, following exposure to erotica, unmarried individuals report brief elevations in masturbatory activity or in sexual activity with an established partner, but they do not appear to engage in novel or promiscuous behavior. These effects appear to be similar for males and females who are exposed to erotica.

D. Summary and Critique

Research findings for effects of violent pornography indicate that such material encourages the development of antiwoman attitudes and antiwoman behavior. At the same time, numerous findings directly contradict this conclusion, methodological and conceptual critiques of the literature have strongly questioned the relationship of violent pornography and antiwoman outcomes, and research that has sought

to improve methodological quality and ecological validity has failed to find effects of exposure to violent pornography. Research findings for effects of degrading pornography are also quite mixed: some studies report negative effects of such stimuli on attitudes and behavior, while some do not. Research findings for effects of erotica-like stimuli seem to be more uniform, suggesting that exposure to such material causes brief activation of patterns of sexual activity that persons are already accustomed to engage in. Overall, conceptual limitations, definitional ambiguities, methodological shortcomings, and empirical inconsistencies would seem to preclude strong conclusions concerning effects of violent and degrading pornography at the present time. Many of these same limitations affect our ability to form conclusions about the effects of erotica, but to a somewhat lesser extent. [*See* ATTITUDE CHANGE; ATTITUDE FORMATION.]

V. WHAT WE KNOW AND WHAT WE NEED TO KNOW

The scientific study of pornography effects receives its impetus from public and political concerns about the impact of exposure to such material. To address these concerns with scientific consensus, however, it will be necessary to conduct further, scientifically more credible research on the question of pornography. It will be necessary to catalogue the sizable body of inconsistent findings in this area and to try to conceptualize what the inconsistencies mean, to improve conceptual and methodological approaches to the study of this important topic, and to reconcile the results of experimental research, which often shows effects of exposure to pornography, and correlational research, which often does not show effects. While society is exceedingly concerned about the problem of sexual violence, and this concern is entirely proper and urgent, improved research will be necessary before deciding whether pornography, or other factors is a significant cause of the tragic level of sexual violence our society produces. In coming years, it will also be crucial to examine significant but understudied questions, including the impact of pornography and erotica on women's sense of self, trust, and well-being, and to factor such findings back into public debate on pornography. Finally, it should be possible to introduce further legal and educational measures to directly reduce

POST-TRAUMATIC STRESS DISORDER

Richard Katz
CIBA-GEIGY Corporation and Rutgers University

Glossary

Avoidance Activity (cognitive, behavioral, motivational) with an intended outcome of reduced or eliminated exposure to stimuli previously associated with trauma.

DESNOS Disorder of extreme stress, not otherwise specified. An extreme variant of PTSD characterized by an motivationally complex pattern of traumatization and extreme personality and somatic changes beyond those routinely seen in PTSD.

Intrusion The reexperiencing of aspects of a prior traumatic encounter via images or thoughts, including the virtual reliving of a prior trauma.

PADS Phobic anxiety depersonalization syndrome. A psychiatric response to moderate to extreme physical or psychological trauma that produces immediate and possibly chronic anxious avoidance coupled with feelings of unreality or loss of personal coherence.

Post-traumatic stress disorder A complex chronic psychiatric disorder which follows traumatic exposure and results in intrusive thoughts or images, avoidant behaviors, and arousal disturbances, all of which impede coping and functioning.

Psychic numbing A loss of loving and other positive feelings, such that the patient's emotional repertoire is restricted to at most painful or hostile emotions.

Trauma One or more stimuli with harmful potential of extreme or severe intensity which produce fear, helplessness, or horror upon exposure.

Before I speak, with a shadow's friendship
And I remember that we who move
Are moved by clouds that darken midnight
At This Moment in Time, Delmore Schwartz

POST-TRAUMATIC STRESS DISORDER (PTSD) is a chronic reaction to extreme stress. It occupies a unique place in current psychiatry. It is the only psychiatric diagnosis with an identifiable and proximate cause. In this sense it is a disease of civilization (or more accurately its lapses), recognition of which demands further consideration of an even broader spectrum of stress-induced disability. PTSD also is a psychiatric tertium quid. It uniquely and necessarily entwines significant aspects of affective disturbance, phobic avoidance, paroxysmal anxiety, and obsessional intrusive imagery which comprise the majority of psychiatric diagnoses. This inherent comorbidity has potentially significant ramifications for differential diagnosis, severity, prognosis, and therapeutic intervention. Arguably because recognition of PTSD as a unique diagnosis is recent, it represents the least studied major psychiatric disorder and our ignorance is as significant as our understanding. We review both the evolution of the PTSD concept, our understanding, and our current limitations.

I. HISTORIC AND LITERARY ANTECEDENTS

While the specific recognition of PTSD as a syndrome is less than a decade old and resides in DSM

(American Psychiatric Association's *Diagnostic and Statistical Manual of Mental Disorders*) conceptualizations, early recognition of the emotionally toxic effects of trauma may be found in a variety of historic and literary sources. Abraham's binding of Isaac, recounted in the Biblical book of Genesis, embodies a life-threatening event, human sacrifice, prevented at the last moment through divine intervention. Following this near fatality the intended victim Isaac virtually disappears from the further flow of events. Moreover, his few subsequent appearances (e.g., an arranged marriage to Rebecca at age 40, disputes over the wells of Esek and Sitnah) are brief, limited, and characterized by social avoidance and passivity. In his withdrawal and demoralization Isaac demonstrates some of the cardinal sequelae of traumatic exposure. It is telling that the name used to describe God in this section of the Bible uniquely is subject to alternate translation either as fear or as kinsman (Genesis 31:42, 53).

Pepys' account in his diary of the great fire of London of 1666 indicates he personally suffered insomnia, intrusive dream imagery, anger, and anxiety while the fire may well have led others (i.e., Kate Joyce's husband) to commit suicide.

Shakespeare's *Henry IV* opens with news of the warrior Hotspur having engaged in bloody battle and lost a kinsman as a battle hostage. His wife, Lady Percy, subsequently described Hotspur:

In thy faint slumber I by thee have watched
And heard thee murmur tales of iron wars
Speak terms of manage to thy bounding steed.
Cry "Courage! To the field!" and thou hast talked
Of sallies and retires, of trenches, tents
Of palisades, frontiers, parapets
Of basilisks, of cannon, culverin
Of prisoners' ransom, and of soldiers slain
And all the current of a heady fight.
Thy spirit within thee hath been so at war
And this hath so bestirred thee in thy sleep
That beads of sweat have stood upon thy brow . . .

(Henry IV, Part I)

This description includes significant aspects of reexperiencing and arousal disturbance. It is particularly telling that Lady Percy previously had spoken also of Hotspur's melancholy, musing, and social isolation. Shakespeare remains one of the keenest psychologists, and his observations indicate an appreciation of Hotspur's disorder.

II. MEDICAL RECOGNITION— NINETEENTH AND TWENTIETH CENTURY ANTECEDENTS

DaCosta's observations of Civil War combatants noted a syndrome of anxiety, tachycardia, and respiratory difficulty, which was viewed as possibly of cardiac origin. However, empirical evidence for cardiac dysfunction was not evident. Janet independently in *L'Automtisme Psychologique* acknowledged two potentially relevant syndromes—these being a hysterical dissociation of feelings and memories, and psychasthenic reexperiencing. He also noted "vehement emotions" might produce long-term maladaptive psychological sequelae including autonomic arousal and psychic numbing. Kraepelin significantly recognized "schrenkneurosen" as emotional responses to disasters such as accidents, train derailments, and fires. Thus, a specific cause–effect relationship was hypothesized for traumas on the one hand and psychiatric disability on the other; nonetheless, recognition in 19th century psychiatry was relatively fragmented.

The major impetus to broader recognition of a link of stress and disability in this century was war trauma. During the first World War, British physicians referred to a state of acute confusion and disorientation following bombardment as "shell shock." This term reflected the then current notion of a physiogenic basis for symptoms. However, following the war, Freud argued strongly against an organic basis for war neurosis to an Austrian Medical High Commission. He further suggested that war neurosis was a consequence of adult trauma, and recommended psychoanalytic therapy as treatment. It should be further recognized that Freud's initial, although later-modified, general theory of neurosis was predicated upon childhood sexual seduction. This subsequent emphasis upon actual onset in an adult after trauma suggests a long standing concern, which spanned much of Freudian theory.

World War II brought further medical recognition of combat fatigue as an acute stress reaction, and saw the further recognition of long-term consequences of trauma in World War I veterans. In particular, Kardiner's studies of combat stress identified a pathophysiological complex he termed physioneurosis. The syndrome included many of the stigmata of PTSD including exaggerated startle, autonomic disturbances, irritability, dream disturbances, and dissociative episodes. Personality changes also were noted. Kardiner significantly acknowledged a role for traumatic conditioning in establishing a maladaptive biological response. [*See* STRESS.]

Sir Martin Roth's recognition of a phobic–anxiety depersonalization syndrome (PADS) significantly extended the range of possible triggers to illness and provided a diagnostically more fully realized syndrome. It also postulated possible pathophysiological overlap with organic states. PADS was defined by its eponymous core clinical features—depersonalization and phobic anxiety were considered both its most consistent and resistant features. While specific forms of trauma were recognized, the general causal rubric included overwhelming anxiety, based upon an individual vulnerability. Roth additionally noted a frequent depressive coloration and obsessional features, albeit with a content atypical for pure obsessional neurosis.

III. DSM CONCEPTIONS

DSM-I, the initial manual for diagnostic standardization of American psychiatric practice, recognized a category of gross stress reaction; however, this was regarded as a phasic response unique to combat. This category was removed from the succeeding version, and combat stress reactions were subsumed under stress reactions. Efforts by Lifton, Shatan, and others led to the recognition of a post-combat syndrome in returning Vietnam veterans. This reaction and related responses to extraordinary circumstances (e.g., rape, assault, natural disaster) were recognized as a separate and unique maladaptive syndrome and was termed post-traumatic stress disorder (PTSD).

The diagnosis of PTSD was based upon a constellation of symptoms. The clusters of symptoms necessary for the diagnosis included reexperiencing/reliving, psychic numbing, and trauma-related responses to the stimulus aspects of the event. Implicit in the initial and subsequent DSM conceptions is the recognition of a potentially widespread vulnerability to the disorder. Prevalence is limited since most people are not exposed to precipitating circumstances; however, given exposure, PTSD is a predictable psychiatric outcome.

IV. STRESSOR CHARACTERISTICS

The universe of traumatogenic stimuli has been variously described. DSM-III posits a stressor which is recognizable, and which would evoke significant symptoms of distress in anyone. While stressors such as marital conflict and business loss are excluded in the extended definition, a discontinuity with normal experiences is implicit rather than explicit.

DSM-III-R refers to an event outside the range of usual human experience, and includes as examples threats to one's life or physical integrity, serious threats to significant others, and various forms of violence (see Table I). While the examples are adequate, their normative status again may be misleading, as the definition fails to account for high base rates of urban violence, or assaults against women (20% lifetime risk of sexual assault). ICD-10 describes an exceptional mental or physical stressor; thus, the nature of the stimulus is demarcated, and its modal occurrence is less emphasized. This proposal has been forwarded for DSM-IV as well.

V. PHENOMENOLOGY

Table I provides the current (i.e., DSM-III-R) diagnostic criteria. Seventeen symptoms or symptom clusters are listed, and 6 of 17 items must be endorsed for a full diagnosis, with a distribution across categories as indicated in the table. Reexperiencing, the intrusion of distressing thoughts and images, includes actual memories, thoughts, or images. It can also include dream imagery, the actual partial or complete reliving of an event (awake or asleep), or conditioned responses to relevant cues. In the most extreme form of reexperiencing, patients may lose touch with actual current circumstances and feel they have returned to the trauma situation.

Avoidance cluster items include avoidance of distressing thoughts or feelings, avoidance of relevant actions, cues, or stimuli, amnesia for significant aspects of the event, social avoidance, and withdrawal, feelings of social separation, avoidance of former sources of gratification, and absence of loving feelings, and a marked absence of futurity—in essence all planning is derailed by the inability to sustain positive images of the present or future. Avoidance may involve some aspects of affective blunting but generally is not a true melancholic depression. Present gratification may be bracketed, but remain partially present and the mood disorder may be responsive to circumstances.

Arousal disturbances include insomnia, anger, and loss of focused attention, often leading to a fail-

TABLE I

DSM-III-R Diagnostic Criteria for 309.89 Post-Traumatic Stress Disorder[a]

A. The person has experienced an event that is outside the range of usual human experience and that would be markedly distressing to almost anyone, e.g., serious threat to one's life or physical integrity; serious threat or harm to one's children, spouse, or other close relatives and friends; sudden destruction of one's home or community; or seeing another person who has recently been, or is being, seriously injured or killed as the result of an accident or physical violence.

B. The traumatic event is persistently reexperienced in at least one of the following ways:
  1. recurrent and intrusive distressing recollections of the event (in young children, repetitive play in which themes or aspects of the trauma are expressed)
  2. recurrent distressing dreams of the event
  3. sudden acting or feeling as if the traumatic event were recurring (includes a sense of reliving the experience, illusions, hallucinations, and dissociative [flashback] episodes, even those that occur upon wakening or when intoxicated)
  4. intense psychological distress at exposure to events that symbolize or resemble an aspect of the traumatic event, including anniversaries of the trauma

C. Persistent avoidance of stimuli associated with the trauma or numbing of general responsiveness (not present before the trauma), as indicated by at least three of the following:
  1. efforts to avoid thoughts or feelings associated with the trauma
  2. efforts to avoid activities or situations that arouse recollections of the trauma
  3. inability to recall an important aspect of the trauma (psychogenic amnesia)
  4. markedly diminished interest in significant activities (in young children, loss of recently acquired developmental skills such as toilet training or language skills)
  5. feeling of detachment or estrangement from others
  6. restricted range of affect, e.g., unable to have loving feelings
  7. sense of a foreshortened future, e.g., does not expect to have a career, marriage or children, or a long life

D. Persistent symptoms of increased arousal (not present before the trauma), as indicated by at least two of the following:
  1. difficulty falling or staying asleep
  2. irritability or outbursts of anger
  3. difficulty concentrating
  4. hypervigilance
  5. exaggerated startle response
  6. physiologic reactivity upon exposure to events that symbolize or resemble an aspect of the traumatic event (e.g., a woman who was raped in an elevator breaks out in a sweat entering any elevator)

[a] Reproduced with permission of the American Psychiatric Association.

ure to complete tasks and exaggerated vigilance and startle responses, both normally and in response to relevant cues. For example, patients may complain of "jumping out of my skin" or "hitting the dirt" in response to stimulation similar to gun shots. While there is some overlap with panic, the arousal disturbance is provoked rather than spontaneous, potentially more chronic, and experienced less as a near-fatal physiologically cataclysmic occurrence.

The diagnostic criterion sets for DSM-III-R and those proposed by DSM-IV are close. In both systems reexperiencing, avoidant behavior, and increased arousal must be commonly present. These three clusters each are defined by the same 17 items. The major change is a possible inclusion of physiological reactivity upon reexposure to relevant cues, previously considered an arousal response, within a reexperiencing cluster. Clearly this item partakes of both clusters and may be considered relevant to each. In addition, based upon required endorsement frequency there is a reduction of the emphasis upon avoidant behavior.

VI. MORBIDITY OF PTSD

The most significant attendant morbid risk of PTSD is suicide. Elevated rates of attempted suicide equivalent to or greater than those seen with major depressions have been reported in studies of Vietnam veterans (approximately 20% had attempted), studies of childhood sexual abuse victims (up to 39% attempters), adult rape victims (20–25% attempters) and one study of battered women (42% attempters). While depression is a common short-term consequence of trauma, it also is a self-limiting response, and typically it is not present beyond 4 months. Therefore, it probably cannot account for these figures which reflect a chronic risk. However, demoralization, guilt, and other comorbid pathology all may exacerbate risk. Increased morbid risks of drug and alcohol abuse have been reported. There appears to be some increase in risk for other Axis I and Axis II disorders. Social phobia, eating disorders, avoidant personality, generalized anxiety, and dysthymia are not uncommon in affected women; depression, anxiety, panic, and phobic disorders may be seen in affected men. To some degree these morbid states may be seen as increasingly autonomous and elaborated extensions of core PTSD features. [*See* DEPRESSION; SUICIDE.]

Increased medical problems for physical illnesses including hypertension, cardiovascular disease, bronchial asthma, and peptic ulcer disease have been reported in association with a PTSD diagnosis.

It also should be recognized that early victimization doubles the risk of adult abuse, including rape, harassment, and sexual battery. This has been called a "sitting duck syndrome." As noted below, hypochondriasis, while not central to the PTSD, is nonetheless a frequent concomitant. PTSD patients may use somatization expressively—headache, gastrointestinal distress, sweating, and chill may be anticipated, and should be considered as relevant aspects of the disease.

VII. PSYCHOLOGICAL PERSPECTIVES OF PTSD

Post-traumatic stress disorder may be variously conceived from a psychological point of view. Lifton describes its genesis in terms of the symbolic imagery of life and death. Ronnie Janoff-Bulman offers a cognitive reappraisal theory, and finally the DSM criteria themselves may be examined for their motivational significance.

For the psychohistorian Robert J. Lifton, immersion in near-death circumstances such as war, Nazi death camps, or the nuclear bombing of Hiroshima engender five survival-related themes, these being the death imprint, survivor guilt, psychic numbing, the questioning of true vs false nurturance, and a need to reestablish personal meaning. The death imprint represents a morbid intrusion of death imagery into one's personal psychology. It is an immediate and signal violation of personal and cultural symbolism that threatens core values of continuity in life. Because the threat of annihilation is immanent in everyday thoughts and images, the world becomes filtered through a screen of death. Overshadowing death images in turn engender a psychic claim upon the survivor, who comes to ask why he or she survived, while others perished? Cruelly, the guilt attendant upon an atrocity is thereby internalized, becoming personal. Insofar as the death imprint is incorporated personally it creates a state of death in life, a psychic numbing, as a response to unbearable pain and absurdity. The failure to resolve guilt con-

flicts can further evolve into a mental paralysis, depression, and fixed ruminations. Thus, the survivor is faced with the task of personal reconstruction. Yet, given a world already tainted with betrayal and death, he or she faces a further conflict between authentic and false nurturance. Prior destruction and violation of the human web needs must lead to a first questioning of all nurturance as counterfeit. Moreover, immersion in the death experience may have left a stigma that must be overcome to rejoin a community of the living. These conflicts reduce the capacity for love and require a need to reestablish interpersonal continuity. To regain feelings the survivor must find a transforming act or image that allows continuity with the future.

Janoff-Bulman places less emphasis on images and more on cognition. She argues that PTSD arises from a violation of deeply held expectations about the world and our place in it. Most individuals implicitly maintain a world view characterized by notions of security, safety, and predictability, and a view of the self as worthy, efficacious, and at least relatively invulnerable. Such core assumptions are both adaptive and deeply ingrained, and therefore resistant to change. A traumatic event poses an immediate challenge to these views and demands a restructuring of one's personal universe. By this view, the threat to one's psychological integrity, a terrifying and disabling outcome of exposure, is basic to the evolution of PTSD. The destruction of the assumptive world creates anxiety, demoralization, and pessimism. The cardinal symptoms of PTSD—denial, numbing, and reexperiencing—represent attempts to integrate the traumatic event into previous assumptions, and to acknowledge a tragic universe.

For Janoff-Bulman at least to some degree the nature of the trauma may inform the reconstituted view of the world. For example, personally victimized individuals such as rape victims may develop more negative self-appraisals and greater pessimism, while victims of natural disasters may become more concerned about randomness. For Janoff-Bulman a successful resolution involves a cognitive restructuring providing a revised and functional world view. The world may be darker, but it is not dark.

Functional autonomy theory is less concerned with the genesis than the maintenance of a persistent state of disability, and in that sense it is complementary to both the above hypotheses. It suggests the long-standing and refractory nature of PTSD may reflect the self-reinforcing nature of a closed system.

In counterdistinction to most psychiatric disorders which are characterized by a single axis of disability, PTSD necessarily is characterized by three sets of symptoms which potentially may reinforce each other. In essence, it is an inherently comorbid disorder.

Examples of potentially synergistic pathology include interactions within and across B, C, and D criteria sets. For example, the C criteria define depression and phobic avoidance, while the D criteria define intense paroxysmal anxiety, which while not panic per se may reach panic-like proportions. Depression and phobic avoidance characterized by panic are more persistent and treatment refractory than corresponding panic free states. Likewise, one also might imagine that reexperiencing associated with stage II sleep might contribute to arousal disturbances which include poor sleep continuity. Even within the D criteria hyperarousal, exaggerated startle, and anger might reduce a capacity to maintain sleep. Figure 1 illustrates some of the reinforcing connections inherent in a complex diagnosis such as PTSD.

At least three consequences are predicted from the model. One is motivational stability—the syndrome reinforces its own disease status. A second prediction concerns severity. Finally, one may predict the form of comorbid processes. Once all criteria sets are satisfied PTSD should appear full-blown and in extreme form. Few mild cases are expected given the fact that any of the three axes might activate a fear structure and reinforce the severity of

the remaining two. Symptoms might multiply their own significance via frequent reexperiencing, phobic avoidance, and biased sensitivity to even an innocent environment. Finally, since a motivational structure supports a persistent disability with links to other disorders, one might predict the eventual development of autonomous anxious and depressive features in severe chronic cases.

VIII. COMPLEX PTSD—THE DESNOS CONCEPT

PTSD itself may be considered a highly complex response to a traumatic pathogen. Further complexity in presentation may follow more extreme, chronic, and emotionally significant forms of traumatization. Concentration camp or slave labor camp experiences, hostage situations, or chronic childhood abuse all of which carry complex and long-standing interpersonal abuse may produce a multiplicity of personality changes and psychiatric symptoms which incorporate PTSD symptoms but go beyond them. Personality changes following extreme stress include fugue-like and dissociative states, which may evolve to multiple personalities. Borderline personality disorder may result. Victims concomitantly may feel certain parts of themselves are dead, or that they have irretrievably lost a part of their former selves. A failure to feel may lead to drug abuse, self-mutilation, and extreme passivity. Moreover, certain life experiences may be compartmentalized to a point of psychic insignificance. Victims may regard parts of their lives as closed chapters, or as having happened to someone else. Affective flattening, depression, suicidal urges, and labile rage are common. In addition, DESNOS may entail somatic responses. Damage to the self may be expressed as physiological changes. Insomnia and nightmares are common and so are cardio-respiratory and gastrointestinal complaints, including tension headaches, pain, nausea, dizziness, choking, and palpitations. Object relations may be severely disturbed. The Stockholm syndrome of aggressor identification may occur in captivity situations, and chronically the ability to sustain or accept love may be lost. [See DISSOCIATIVE DISORDERS; BORDERLINE PERSONALITY DISORDER.]

The DESNOS concept suggests that PTSD is a continuum stress disorder, and extreme aspects may engender greater and less tractable disability. In par-

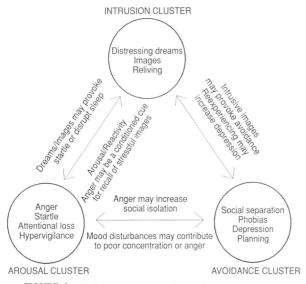

FIGURE 1 Reinforcing connections inherent in PTSD.

ticular it represents a fundamental destruction of the integrity of the self.

IX. NEUROBIOLOGICAL THEORIES OF PTSD

The biological dysfunction of PTSD represents a complex and highly ramified state of sympathetic/pituitary–adrenal hyperactivity consistent with D criteria arousal disturbance. For example, in comparison with other veterans, veterans with PTSD who are exposed to combat sounds demonstrate significantly increased cardiac responses. Yehuda and co-workers examined the stress–hormone system. They suggest that the pattern of overresponsiveness extends also to pituitary–adrenal hyperresponsivity to an endocrine challenge. Also within the opiocortin response modulatory system, a system for the control of pain and coping, it appears that veterans may show enhanced analgesia when exposed to combat-related stimuli. This response may represent a direct concomitant of psychic numbing. The interested reader is referred to Friedman (1991) for a more detailed review of the neurobiology of PTSD.

X. THERAPEUTIC APPROACHES

Numerous therapies have been proposed for the treatment of PTSD symptoms; however, at present, no one therapy enjoys broad acceptance. Therefore, treatment options should be combined with sensitivity to the individual sufferer. Insofar as a stress response can be identified as acute, crisis intervention is indicated. The likelihood of full PTSD may be reduced in part via intensive initial support and good debriefing. The two major classes of therapeutic intervention for the established syndrome are cognitive–behavioral therapies and pharmacotherapy. Behavioral therapies include variants of exposure regimens including systematic desensitization, flooding, and modeling. The danger of abreaction particularly with implosion and flooding suggests it should be used cautiously. Some patients appear to have benefitted from cognitive therapy. Some success has also been obtained with a modified 12-step program. [*See* Cognitive Behavior Therapy.]

Pharmacological management has been most typically employed with war trauma. Initial approaches are based upon the management of acute anxiety, particularly via minor tranquilizers, and upon fur-

ther treatment of PTSD core symptoms. Tricyclic drugs including amitriptyline have been employed with some success. Amitriptyline may benefit avoidant symptoms preferentially whereas other tricyclic antidepressants may be of greater benefit upon intrusive symptoms. The monoamine oxidase inhibitor, phenelzine, has been used in several trials with generally good outcome. Again there is some, albeit limited, evidence that intrusive symptoms may be preferentially improved. Because MAO inhibitors may themselves pose health hazards particularly in drug abusers, they should be used with caution. Fluoxetine has been employed, and appears to benefit the cluster of symptoms associated with reexperiencing and with explosive hostility. Because agitation is countertherapeutic dose should be carefully monitored for any serotonergic drugs. Other treatments, of unproved benefit, include neuroleptic drugs and clonidine. These findings, as well as a thorough review of the methodological complications inherent in PTSD pharmacotherapeutic trials, are summarized in Davidson *et al.* (1990).

Supplemental therapies to be considered include family therapy, which might help significant others cope with the apparent suffering, rejection, and refusal to communicate that may occur, and group therapies. Discussion of common problems and sharing common grief may protect against atomization and may help restore confidence.

Treatment of any sort for PTSD must be appropriately sensitive to the sufferer. Torture victims will be particularly mistrustful of medical garb if it was previously present in a torture situation. Bright lighting, linoleum flooring, or other institutional trappings may provoke extreme anxiety. Victims who have experienced medical support of their torture via instruments (e.g., drugs, dental drills), resuscitation, or aftercare may also feel anxiety facing white coats and crash carts. They also may resist injections or physical examination for related reasons. Vietnam veterans may have strong reactions to Asian physicians. Women who have been sexually assaulted may respond more readily to a female than to a male physician. Finally, if the sufferer has been a victim of political terror there may be a general fear of being questioned by any authority, in which case there is a need to establish and maintain a trusting relationship.

XI. LONG-TERM OUTCOME

Functioning and well-being are not equivalent measures, and their differences may be particularly acute in PTSD. The sociologist William Helmreich conducted a survey of Holocaust survivors approximately 30 years after the end of the second world war. In comparison with a matched sample of Jewish Americans the survivors appeared to have enjoyed greater success on a number of measures, including marital stability, an absence of criminality, a reduced likelihood of seeking psychiatric help, and a variety of other traits. Other studies have further pointed to one high level of economic achievement and community involvement. Any number of factors may contribute to these outcomes ranging from the selective survival of a more adaptive cohort, to associative mating, particularly with respect to marital stability, to learned persistence and tenacity.

Findings of economic and sociological success belie psychiatric well-being even in the well motivated. Symptoms may persist covertly for an indefinite duration and it is not uncommon to find such long-term sequelae as frequent, sometimes daily, reexperiencing, emotional withdrawal, suspiciousness, and pessimism about the future, nor is it uncommon to find intrusive dream imagery, dream anxiety, and nightmares. Survivors may manage to bracket significant aspects of their past with some success; clearly, however, this is at some psychic cost. Given its relatively recent disease status more studies of outcome are necessary, with particular attention to the nature of initial traumatization.

XII. CONCLUSION

PTSD is a prevalent disabling condition of considerable complexity. Its roots can be traced at least to the 19th century, and current concepts are quite recent. The PTSD concept doubtless will undergo further refinement, and may lead to additional recognition of a broader spectrum of stress responses.

Nonetheless, the current diagnostic triad of intrusion, avoidance, and arousal is unlikely to change radically, and further change may represent refinements of current concepts. Our century will be known as much for its brutality as for its triumphs and as much for its lapses as for its leaps. Particularly in this century PTSD demands recognition of some of our darkest impulses—the existance of therapeutic optimism may provide some countervailing glimmer of light.

Bibliography

Davidson, J. R. T., Kudler, H., Smith, R., Mahorney, S. L., Lipper, S., Hammett, E., Saunders, W. B., and Cavenar, J. O. (1990). Treatment of posttraumatic stress disorder with amitriptyline and placebo. *Arch. Gen. Psychiatry* **47,** 259–266.

Des Pres, T. (1976). ''The Survivor.'' Oxford, New York.

Eldrige, G. T. (1991). Current issues in the assessment of posttraumatic stress disorder. *J. Traumatic Stress* **4,** 7–24.

Friedman, M. (1991). Biological approaches to the diagnosis and treatment of posttraumatic stress disorder. *J. Traumatic Stress* **4,** 67–92.

Janoff-Bulman, R. (1992). ''Shattered Assumptions—Towards a New Psychology of Trauma.'' McMillian, New York.

Kulka, R. A., Schlenger, W. E., Fairbank, J. A., Hough, R. L., Jordan, B. K., Marmar, C. R., and Weiss, D. S. (1990). ''Trauma and the Vietnam Generation: Report of Findings from the National Vietnam Veterans Readjustment Study.'' Brunner/Mazel, New York.

Litron, R. J. (1979). ''The Broken Connection.'' Simon and Shuster, New York.

March, J. (1990). The nosology of posttraumatic stress disorder. *J. Anxiety Disorders* 61–82.

Pynoos, R. S., Nader, K., and March, J. (1991). Posttraumatic stress disorder. In ''Textbook of Child and Adolescent Psychiatry.'' pp. 339–348. American Psychiatric Press, Washington, DC.

Scott, W. J. (1990). PTSD in DSM-III: A case in the politics of diagnosis and disease. *Soc. Problems* **37,** 294–310.

Vandenbos, G. R., and Bryant, B. (1987). ''Cataclysms, Crises and Catastrophes, Psychology in Action.'' American Psychological Association, Washington, DC.

Van Der Kolk, B. (1987). ''Psychological Trauma.'' American Psychiatric Press, Washington, DC.

PREFERENCE JUDGMENTS

David A. Houston
Memphis State University

Steven J. Sherman
Indiana University

Glossary

Direction of comparison When comparing the features of two alternatives, whether item A is compared to item B, or item B is compared to item A.

Referent of comparison The item used as the target of a comparison. For example, if item A is compared to item B, then item B is the referent of comparison.

Status quo bias The tendency (often a nonnormative tendency) to choose the option that one already has, rather than to trade it or give it up for another, perhaps even better option.

Subject of comparison The item used as the starting point of a comparison. For example, if item A is compared to item B, then item A is the subject of comparison.

MAKING CHOICES between competing alternatives is a ubiquitous social and psychological process. Every day we are faced with a variety of choices, from the mundane (which shirt should I wear?) to the consequential (should I quit my current job and accept a new position?). The most obvious inputs into judgments of choice are the subjective preferences of the person making the judgment. Arriving at our preferences, however, can involve more than a rational assessment of the pluses and minuses of each of the choice alternatives, and the selection of the best alternative on the basis of such an assessment. Various factors can influence our assessment of the alternatives, apart from merely their perceived value. Factors such as the context of the choice, the composition of the set of choice alternatives, previous experience with one or more of the alternatives, and current ownership of one of the alternatives are just some of the things that can influence a choice. Predicting and measuring the impact of these factors has been the primary interest of psychological theories of choice.

This article briefly reviews some of the more prominent contemporary psychological models of the choice process—elimination by aspects, the status quo bias, and the comparison of overall or global evaluations of the alternatives. The majority of the article then deals with one specific model of the comparison process as applied to preference judgments—the feature mapping model, which involves a feature-by-feature comparison of choice alternatives. Following the extended discussion of the feature mapping model, we briefly compare the various models of choice reviewed, pointing out relations among the models, and indicating when each is most likely to be applicable.

I. ELIMINATION BY ASPECTS

Many choice dilemmas present the individual with a confusingly wide range of alternatives. In buying a new car, for example, a person is confronted with literally hundreds of makes, models, and options. A common first step in dealing with such a dilemma is to try to eliminate some of the alternatives, and thereby arrive at a more manageable set of available options.

Accordingly, in preparing to buy a car, a person could first determine a set of features or aspects that he or she wants the car to have. Those features are then ranked in order of their overall importance to the decision. For one person, the three most important features may be price, appearance, and mileage. For another person, the features to be considered first may be road handling, safety, and price. Starting with the most important aspect, the potential buyer eliminates all cars that do not possess that aspect. For example, the first aspect selected might be a $15,000 price limit. All cars whose price exceeds that limit are eliminated from consideration. The next aspect selected may be air-conditioning, thereby eliminating all models without air-conditioning. This process can then continue until either all cars but one are eliminated or the set of alternatives is at least narrowed down enough to allow a more individualized assessment of the remaining options. This process is termed "elimination by aspects."

Elimination by aspects is a convenient and time-saving way in which large numbers of options can be quickly eliminated from consideration. Accordingly, it is probably best if used early in the choice process, as a way of trimming down a large choice set. Obviously, it works best if the person making the choice can clearly identify and rank order a set of aspects that the to-be-chosen item "must" possess. If choice alternatives are eliminated because they do not possess a rather unimportant feature, the person making the choice runs the risk of rejecting good, potentially satisfying alternatives.

One of the implications of the elimination by aspects process should be pointed out. If an aspect under consideration happens to be included in all currently available alternatives, no alternatives will be eliminated. For example, if a price below $15,000 is a key aspect and if all car models under consideration are priced below $15,000, the alternatives cannot be distinguished on the basis of the price criterion. Thus, aspects shared by all available alternatives do not aid a person in making a choice among those alternatives. As we shall see in our discussion of the feature-mapping model, aspects or features shared by choice alternatives, because they cannot distinguish between those alternatives, will tend to drop out or be canceled during the choice process.

A curious property of the elimination by aspects process is that features that may have been important and even *necessary* for an alternative to get past the preliminary elimination stage may drop out of consideration in the decision process, once a manageable set of alternatives is constructed. For example, considering only automobiles that cost below $15,000 and have gas mileage estimates above 28 miles per gallon, leaves one with a very reduced set of options. However, in *now* choosing among those options, perhaps on the basis of a careful compari-

son, price and mileage drop out of the evaluation process because *all* available options share the same price range and mileage estimates.

II. STATUS QUO BIAS

The status quo bias is relevant to only a special and limited kind of choice situation. It applies to analyses of preference situations that involve a choice between an already owned or endowed object and some new alternative. Thus, the status quo bias would be an applicable principle when one is deciding whether to leave one's current job for a new offer, or when one is deciding whether to trade one collectible for another. Status quo bias does not apply, however, when one is choosing between two novel alternatives, as when a student is deciding whether to attend college A or college B.

Status quo bias refers to the tendency to prefer the current state of affairs rather than a new or changed situation. This bias thus represents a form of conservatism in judgment and preference. As a model of choice, it predicts a tendency (often a nonnormative tendency) to choose the option that one already has, rather than to trade it or give it up for another, perhaps even better option. Such a preference bias means that one will generally demand more money for selling an owned object than one would be willing to lay out to buy the very same object. Thus, in certain circumstances, one would be unwilling both to buy an object at a given price or to sell the object (if owned) at that same price.

There have been a number of quite simple demonstrations of the status quo bias. In one experiment, some subjects were given a coffee mug and were later asked how much they would sell it for. Other subjects, who were not given a mug, were asked what they would spend in order to buy such a mug. Buyers were willing to spend only $2.87, whereas sellers demanded $7.12. In another demonstration, half the people in a room were given a mug as a gift. The other half were given a pen. All subjects were then given the opportunity to trade their gift for the other gift. Assuming random assignment of the mugs and pens to mug-preferrers and pen-preferrers, rational economic theory would predict that 50% of the subjects would choose to switch gifts. In fact, only about 10% of subjects chose to trade for the non-owned item, demonstrating a strong status quo bias.

There have been two major explanations for the tendency to stick with the status quo. The first is a mere ownership explanation. This account proposes that an item will suddenly take on added value as one gains ownership of it. In other words, we raise the value of what we have. The other explanation is a loss aversion account. It maintains that the mere ownership of an item in and of itself adds no value to the item. However, consideration of potential gains and losses becomes important when one is faced with a choice that involves giving up an owned object for some new alternative. At that point, the current state of affairs (the status quo) acts as a reference point, and the features of the other options are judged as gains and losses from this reference point.

However, a loss is more important psychologically than its equivalent gain. That is, losses are given greater psychological weight than comparable gains. This greater weight given losses relative to gains gives an advantage to the current state of affairs over its alternative. In other words, the value "lost" from having the gift mug to not having the mug is greater than the value "gained" from not having the gift pen to having the pen. There is experimental evidence for both the mere ownership and the loss aversion explanations of the status quo bias, indicating that this may well be a multiply determined preference strategy.

III. COMPARISON OF GLOBAL EVALUATIONS

Often, when faced with a choice, the chooser has had some previous experience with one or more of the choice alternatives. In such a case, it is possible that general attitudes toward those choice alternatives have already been formed and stored in memory. Accordingly, a choice could then be based upon the person's global attitudes toward or overall evaluations of the alternatives, rather than upon novel, attribute-by-attribute assessments of those alternatives. A person could simply use and compare his or her preexisting global attitudes toward the alternatives, and select the alternative with the most favorable attitude. Even if the person has had no previous experience with one or more of the choice alternatives, an independent assessment of the overall goodness of each alternative could be made during the decision process. A choice could then be made based upon a comparison of the global evalua-

tions of the alternatives. Each alternative would be evaluated as a whole, without reference to the other alternatives, and the overall "best" item would then be selected.

It is important to stress that this process consists of *separate* and *global* assessments of each of the choice alternatives, with little or no comparison of the competing alternatives and their features at the time of the global evaluations. Because overall evaluations are based upon the person's assessment of the choice alternatives as discrete and complete items, *and* are made without explicit reference to the features of the competing alternatives, basing a choice on a comparison of such global evaluations can be thought of as a major alternative to a feature-by-feature comparison of the alternatives, as is contemplated by the feature mapping model discussed in the next section. As we shall see, such a feature-based comparison accentuates direct comparison of the individual attributes of the choice alternatives under consideration, rather than a comparison of independently formed global evaluations. It may be helpful to keep in mind the possibility of comparison of global attitudes toward the alternatives as the feature mapping model is presented.

IV. THE FEATURE MAPPING COMPARISON PROCESS

We now take up the model that is the primary focus of this article, the feature mapping model of comparison for choice.

A. Comparison for Choice: Shared and Unique Features

Objects can be characterized as sets of features or attributes. These features may correspond to specific components of the object (such as eyes for a face), concrete properties such as size or color, or abstract attributes such as quality. Our total knowledge about a particular object may be rich in content and complex in form. When faced with a particular task concerning an object (choosing one for example), we extract from our total data base of that object a limited list of task relevant features. Thus, our working feature list for any object could vary, depending on the task at hand.

Many of our most basic judgments about novel people, places, and things begin with comparisons of the features of those people, places, and things.

A comparison is necessary to determine both the similarities and differences among items. In turn, judgments of similarity and difference are often necessary for such fundamental decisions as the proper categorization of an item or the relative preference of a set of items. Such comparisons of features are thus clearly involved with preferences and choices between competing objects, such as buying a car or choosing a college to attend. Although the process of matching features is theoretically applicable when many items are available for choice, we shall limit our discussion of this process to the case of a choice between two alternatives.

The comparison of the features of objects for the purpose of making a choice would seem to be a rather straightforward matter—line up the features of each object and note the differences and the evaluative implications of those differences. However, the precise way in which the features of the alternatives are called to mind, weighed, and compared can vary greatly depending upon a number of factors.

It would be natural to presume that in comparing the features of two objects to each other, the features of each object would be mapped onto the other in a bidirectional way. Similarities and differences between the characteristics of the two items would then determine the result of any comparison process. However, the current model assumes that most comparisons are made in a unidimensional way. Either the features of item A are mapped onto the features of item B, or the features of item B are mapped onto the features of item A.

Furthermore, it would seem reasonable to assume that the results of any comparison process would be the same regardless of the direction of the comparison (compare A to B, or B to A). In fact, this is not the case. For example, in judging the similarity of two objects, X and Y, people will often judge the similarity of X and Y as different from the similarity of Y to X. People faced with a choice between alternatives exhibit similar inconsistencies in judgment. That is, people will not always make the same choices under seemingly similar conditions. Thus, B may be preferred when A is compared to B, but A may be preferred when B is compared to A.

The feature mapping comparison process stresses the importance of specifying which object is made the starting point, or subject, of the comparison and which is the target, or referent, in the comparative judgment. In this view, when comparing items for the purpose of a preference judgment, people engage in the comparison or mapping of the features of

the subject onto those of the referent. By using the subject as the starting point of the comparison, people are attuned to its features, and the features of the referent are recruited, reviewed, and evaluated only in reference to those of the subject. To the extent that the referent's features are also present in the subject (i.e., the features are shared by both alternatives), they will be noted by such a comparison. However, features unique to the referent will not emerge in the comparison process as the subject's features are used as a kind of checklist. On the other hand, features unique to the subject will be especially highlighted by this kind of comparison, and will play a significant role.

Figure 1 shows a feature mapping comparison. The comparison begins with the features of the subject. As these are mapped onto the features of the referent, those features shared by both alternatives (features, 1, 2, and 3) will be noted. Features unique to the subject (features 4, 5, and 6) will be emphasized in the comparison, while features unique to the referent (features 7, 8, and 9) are likely to be neglected.

The feature mapping model of choice has two major components. First, the model specifies the role of the shared versus the unique features of the choice alternatives. Whereas shared features can be important in some comparison tasks (such as judgments of similarity), they provide no distinguishing information between choice alternatives—regardless of which item the individual chooses he or she will end up with the shared features. Accordingly, features identified in the comparison as shared by both items should cancel out during choice process leaving the choice to be made on the basis of the unique features of the paired items. Note that this process stands in opposition to a process in which the two alternatives are separately and globally evaluated and then compared. "Shared" and "unique"

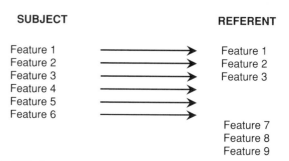

FIGURE 1   The features of the subject are mapped onto the features of the referent.

features have meaning only in the context of a direct comparison of the attributes of the choice alternatives. Furthermore, features can be identified as "shared" or "unique" only if the person engages in a feature-based comparison of the alternatives.

The second component of the feature mapping model involves the importance of the object that is focused on as the starting point of the comparison process. Because the feature mapping process emphasizes the importance of the unique features of the subject of comparison, the direction of comparison will determine which unique features of the alternatives are recruited and are thus emphasized in the comparison process. The features of the subject control the agenda of the comparison. Its features become more important to the comparison than those of the referent. This focusing process has the effect of increasing the influence of the unique features of the attended alternative (the subject of comparison), while decreasing the influence of the unique features of the unattended alternative (the referent of comparison).

This feature mapping model, with its cancellation of shared features and focus upon the unique features of the subject of comparison, has implications for many aspects of the choice process, from predicting which alternative is likely to be chosen, to experienced feelings of prechoice conflict and postchoice satisfaction or regret.

B. Implications of the Feature Mapping Model

1. Predicting Which of Two Items Is Preferred

As indicated, the feature mapping model proposes that, in making a choice between two items, the features of the subject of comparison will be the important starting point for the comparison and the unique features of the subject of comparison will play the biggest role in determining which item is chosen. The relative preference for the subject of comparison or the referent of comparison should thus depend on whether the unique features of the subject are evaluatively good features or evaluatively bad features.

Consider two items that share all their bad features. In addition, each item has several good features. These good features are different (unique) for each item, but they are equally good (for an example, see the two automobiles in Fig. 2). According to the model, whichever automobile is used as the subject or starting point of the comparison, its unique fea-

tures (in this case good features) will weigh most heavily in the decision. In Figure 2, these are the features in boldface. The shared (bad) features will cancel out and the unique (good) features of the referent of comparison (in Fig. 2, the features in italic) will play a relatively minor role in the choice. Thus, *whichever* of the two automobiles is used as the starting point of the comparison should be preferred because of its unique good features. When items share bad features and have unique good features, the subject or starting point of the comparison will have an advantage in the choice process.

Now consider two items that share all their good features. In addition, each item has several bad features. These bad features are different (unique) for each item, but they are equally bad (for an example, see the two automobiles in Fig. 3). Once again, the unique features of the subject of comparison (in this case bad features) will weigh most heavily in the decision. In Figure 3, these are the features in boldface. The shared (good) features will cancel, and the unique (bad) features of the referent of comparison (in Fig. 3, the features in italic) will play a relatively minor role in the choice. In this case, the unique bad features of the subject or starting point of the comparison will drive the chooser away from it and toward the other object (the referent). Thus, when items share good features and have unique bad features, the referent of comparison will have an advantage in the choice process.

These predictions have been tested and confirmed in several different laboratories. When items have unique good and shared bad features, the subject of comparison is generally preferred. When items have unique bad and shared good features, the referent

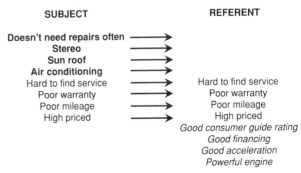

FIGURE 2 A pair of automobiles with shared bad features and unique good features. The positive features unique to the subject of comparison (indicated in boldface) will be emphasized in the comparison. However, the positive features unique to the referent (shown in italics) will be likely to be neglected. The negative features shared by the alternatives will cancel each other out.

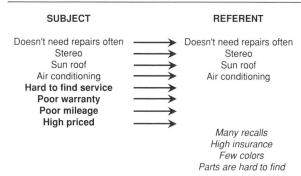

SUBJECT   **REFERENT**

Doesn't need repairs often ⟶ Doesn't need repairs often
Stereo ⟶ Stereo
Sun roof ⟶ Sun roof
Air conditioning ⟶ Air conditioning
Hard to find service ⟶
Poor warranty ⟶
Poor mileage ⟶
High priced ⟶

Many recalls
High insurance
Few colors
Parts are hard to find

FIGURE 3   A pair of automobiles with shared good features and unique bad features. The negative features unique to the subject of comparison (indicated in the boldface) will be emphasized in the comparison. However, the negative features unique to the referent (shown in italics) will be likely to be neglected. The positive features shared by the alternatives will cancel each other out.

of comparison is generally preferred. It is important to note that the items involved in these choices are typically equal in their overall evaluation. It is the value of the unique features plus the direction of comparison that determines which of these objectively equivalent items will be preferred.

It is also important to note that this model predicts preference reversals—a different item will be preferred depending on whether one compares item A to item B or compares item B to item A. Consider a car buyer deciding between a Honda and a Toyota. Imagine that the two cars have the very same bad features and unique (but equally positive) good features. If the Honda is compared to the Toyota, the good features of the Honda will be the focus of the comparison, and, accordingly, the Honda will be preferred. Suppose, however, that the Toyota is compared to the Honda (thus reversing the direction of comparison). Now the focus of the comparison is the good features of the Toyota, and it is the Toyota that will be preferred. In this type of choice, the subject of comparison is always preferred, regardless of which item is the subject.

The same kind of preference reversal is seen for items with unique bad and shared good features. Imagine a voter choosing between two candidates, Smith and Jones. They share all their good attributes and have unique (and equally negative) bad features. If Smith is compared to Jones, Smith's bad features are the focus of the comparison, leading to a preference for Jones. However, when Jones is compared to Smith, Jones's bad qualities become the focus of the comparison, and Smith is preferred. Thus, we again see a preference reversal, but in this case it

is the referent of comparison that is always chosen, regardless of which item is the referent.

A purely rational model of choice would maintain that the direction of comparison should play no role in preference decisions. Such a rational model would require that all features of both items be given the same level of consideration. The feature mapping model should be considered a short-cut kind of decision model, one that makes the decision process easier by focusing on only some of the available features, but one that does not take into account all the relevant information in making a choice.

2. Shared Features and the Comparability of Choice Alternatives

Suppose that a person has a choice between a Caribbean cruise or a trip to London. Let us further suppose that he or she is equally likely to choose either alternative. That is, the probabilities of his or her choosing either the Caribbean or London are both equal to 1/2. If the person is then offered a new alternative, which consists of a Caribbean cruise with a $5 bonus (we will call this Caribbean+), he or she will undoubtedly prefer it over the original Caribbean cruise, so that the probability of selecting Caribbean+ as compared to the original Caribbean cruise is equal to 1. Now, given that our person treated the original choice between the Caribbean and London as a choice between equivalent alternatives, and he or she will *always* prefer Caribbean+ to Caribbean, does it follow that Caribbean+ will *always* be preferred to London? Such a result would be counterintuitive. If our person could not easily decide between the Caribbean and London, it seems unlikely that such a relatively small bonus would completely resolve the conflict and change a 50% choice probability into a certainty.

This example demonstrates an important aspect of shared features in comparisons for choice. Choice probabilities reflect not only the person's evaluation of the alternatives, but also the ease or difficulty in comparing them. Thus, extreme choice probabilities (those close to 0 or 1) can result either from large differences in their subjective evaluations (e.g., a classical music lover choosing between listening to a Beethoven symphony or a heavy metal album) or from an easy comparison, as in the case of the two cruises to the Caribbean, that differ in only one clear-cut aspect.

In the latter case, a comparison of Caribbean+ to the original Caribbean cruise reveals that the two alternatives share all of their features, *except* the addition of the $5 bonus. Because this is the only unique feature between the alternatives, the comparison is simple and the choice dilemma is easily resolved in favor of the alternative possessing the single, unique positive feature. However, a comparison of a Caribbean cruise (with or without the $5 bonus) to a trip to London reveals a far smaller set of shared features than the comparison of the two Caribbean cruises. Further, each of these alternatives possesses a large number of distinct, unique features, making this a much more difficult and elaborate comparison, and, accordingly, a much more complex choice dilemma to resolve—one essentially unaffected by the $5 bonus.

This example establishes some important points about comparisons for choice: aspects or features shared by choice alternatives will have little effect upon choice decisions; aspects or features that are unique to one or more of the choice alternatives are highlighted by the comparison process, and will drive the choice that is made; and the ease or difficulty in comparing alternatives can affect the probabilities of choosing one of those alternatives.

3. Predecisional Conflict

Making a choice between competing alternatives (as in buying a house or choosing between job offers) is a dynamic process, with the potential for much internal conflict. However, the degree of conflict is likely to be different depending upon the attributes of the candidate items. Obviously, if one of these candidate items is clearly better than the other, there will be little conflict, and the decision can be made quite quickly and easily. However, even when the items are equivalent in overall value, there may be a degree of predecision conflict that varies from very large to very small, depending upon the specific features of the items involved.

Consider again a choice between two objects that have unique good features but share all their bad features (as in Fig. 2). As indicated by the feature mapping model, the shared (bad) features will be canceled, and they will play little role in the choice process. In addition, the unique features (in this case good features) of the subject of comparison will become the focus of attention and will play the predominant role in the choice process. When these unique features are good, they will attract the chooser toward the subject of comparison once they are focused upon, and the decision should then be made quite easily and without much vacillation.

However, the same comparison process should produce a very different outcome when the items share good features but possess unique bad features (as in Fig. 3). In this case, it is the unique bad features of the subject of comparison that carry most of the weight in the decision. As the chooser focuses on one item, the shared (good) features will cancel out. The unique (bad) features of the subject of comparison will become prominent, and this item should, accordingly, become less and less appealing. This, in turn, will cause attention to be shifted to the alternative item. This alternative now becomes the starting point of the comparison, and its unique (bad) features will become prominent. Now the alternative item will become less and less appealing, and attention will again switch to the original starting point of the comparison. In this way, there should be much vacillation between alternatives, resulting in a slow and difficult choice process.

In fact, when choice alternatives have unique good and shared bad features, the decision time has been shown to be very fast, and the process relatively stress free. On the other hand, for items that share good features and have unique bad features, the decision process is generally slow and stressful.

4. Overall Satisfaction with One's Choice

Once one chooses between alternatives, there is a certain amount of satisfaction or dissatisfaction that one feels with respect to the chosen option. How happy is one likely to be with the chosen option? The feature mapping model has something to say about this level of satisfaction. The analysis that has been provided above indicates that there are two general reasons for choosing an item. That item might be chosen because of its unique and special good qualities, or it might be chosen because the unique bad features of the other alternative has pushed one away from this other alternative. The first of these reasons for choosing an item corresponds to the case where bad features are shared and good features are unique. The second reason corresponds to the case where good features are shared and bad features are unique. These two instances are experienced very differently psychologically, and this has important implications for one's satisfaction level.

When the candidate items have unique good features and shared negative features, these negative features are canceled and play no role in the choice. The choice is thus experienced as a selection between the good attributes of the items—''Do I want this unique set of positive attributes or that unique set of positive attributes?'' Even the number of shared negative attributes that were in the candidate items is relatively unimportant. These shared features recede into the background, and the unique positive attributes become the foreground and the focus of the choice process. Accordingly, such a choice is experienced as an approach–approach conflict, a win–win situation in which the decision maker will inevitably end up with a set of unique positive attributes. In the extreme, even if both items have predominantly negative features (all of which are shared) and only a couple of unique positive features (nice color versus attractive style, for example), the choice will still be experienced as expressing a preference between two sets of positive features. This kind of choice is generally psychologically satisfying and pleasant.

However, when the candidate items have shared positive features and unique negative features, it is the positive features that are canceled and thus play no role in the choice process. This, then, becomes a choice between negative alternatives—"Do I want this set of bad features or that set of bad features?" Now it is the positive features that recede into the background, and the choice is experienced as an avoidance–avoidance conflict, a lose–lose situation in which the decision maker will inevitably be stuck with a set of unique negative attributes. This kind of choice is generally psychologically unsatisfying and unpleasant, and as a result, the chosen alternative is not fully appreciated.

Research has indicated that satisfaction is significantly higher among those choosing between pairs of items with unique good features than among those choosing between pairs of items with unique bad features. The general happiness level is higher in the former case, and both the chosen and the rejected items are rated better from unique good pairs than from unique bad pairs. In fact, it is sometimes the case that a rejected item from a unique good pair is rated as high or higher than is a chosen item from a unique bad pair.

This implication of the feature mapping model for satisfaction can be seen most strikingly when considering choosers' satisfaction with and liking for exactly the same item—in one case when this item is selected against an alternative with which it shares bad features and each has unique good features; in the other case when it is selected against an item with which it shares good features and each has unique bad features.

Consider automobile A in Figure 4. In the upper panel, automobile A is paired in a choice situation with automobile B. Automobiles A and B share neg-

Automobile A	Automobile B
Stereo	Good financing
Sun roof	Good acceleration
Air conditioning	Powerful engine
Poor warranty	Poor warranty
Poor mileage	Poor mileage
High prices	High prices

Automobile A	Automobile C
Stereo	Stereo
Sun roof	Sun roof
Air conditioning	Air conditioning
Poor warranty	Many recalls
Poor mileage	High insurance
High prices	Few colors

FIGURE 4   When automobile A is selected over automobile B, the comparison for choice focuses on the *good* features of automobile A (shown in boldface in the top panel). However, when automobile A is selected over automobile C, the comparison for choice focuses on the *bad* features of automobile A (shown in boldface in the bottom panel).

ative features and have unique positive features. Accordingly, because the shared negative features cancel out, the focus of the choice will be on deciding which set of positive features is most desirable, and then selecting the automobile that possesses them. Thus, the person who chooses automobile A over automobile B, bases his or her choice upon automobile A's good features (indicated in boldface in the upper panel of Fig. 4). However, in the lower panel, automobile A is paired in a choice situation with automobile C. Automobiles A and C share positive features and have unique negative features. Here, it is the shared positive features that cancel, putting the focus of the choice on deciding which set of negative features is most objectionable, and then rejecting the automobile that possesses them. Here, the person who chooses automobile A over automobile C, bases his or her choice upon automobile A's bad features (indicated in boldface in the lower panel of Figure 4). Studies have found that those people who select automobile A over automobile B report that they like automobile A more and are happier with their selection than those who select automobile A over automobile C.[1]

---

[1] Because automobiles A and B form a shared-bad, unique-good pair, automobile A would have been the *subject* of comparison for most of the people who selected it over automobile B. However, because automobiles A and C form a shared-good, unique-bad pair, automobile A would have been the *referent* for most of the people who selected it over automobile C.

Thus, the very same automobile (automobile A) will be rated very differently, depending upon the automobiles that are being considered along with it as alternative choices. Psychologists have known for a long time that the context of a judgment affects decisions about a stimulus. The same tepid water will be judged as hot after dipping a hand into cold water, and will be judged as cold after dipping a hand into hot water. Armed robbery will be judged as a much more severe crime if it is evaluated after thinking about shoplifting and embezzlement, than when it is evaluated after considering rape and kidnapping. However, in the present choice analysis, *all* the candidate automobiles in Figure 4 are equivalent in terms of overall evaluation. They do not differ in objective value. It is only because shared features are canceled during the choice process that the unique features of the candidate automobiles, be they positive or negative, are brought into the foreground, and become the basis for making the choice. When the choice is made on the basis of unique positive features, both the eventually chosen and rejected automobiles are compared and evaluated in terms of their strengths. When the choice is made on the basis of negative features, both the eventually chosen and rejected automobiles are compared and evaluated in terms of their weaknesses. This variation in focus during the choice process then produces very different ratings of satisfaction for both alternatives.

5. Postdecision Regret and Satisfaction

We have considered the immediate level of satisfaction that is experienced when an item is chosen and the alternative is rejected. In addition, feelings of satisfaction and regret with one's choice are likely to be experienced at various times subsequent to the initial decision. People often look back at old choices and either congratulate themselves on their earlier decision or feel considerable regret over this previous choice. What determines the degree to which a chooser will experience satisfaction or regret after making a choice? This is an important question because people's general feelings of well-being depend greatly on the extent to which they are satisfied with their life choices and do not feel regret for the decisions that they have made.

Some psychology theories propose that, in general, people will be satisfied with their choices. For example, cognitive dissonance theory proposes that, initially, people may experience regret after a decision as they consider the positive features of the alternative that they rejected and the negative features of the item that they chose. Such thoughts bring internal conflict (referred to as cognitive dissonance). Fortunately, people have learned to reduce such feelings of cognitive conflict by changing certain beliefs and attitudes. Thus, after an initial short period of postdecision regret, people will focus on the positive features of what they chose and on the negative features of the item that they rejected. This will lead to a reevaluation of the alternatives such that the chosen item increases in subjective value and the rejected alternative decreases. Interestingly, this process is presumed to occur *after* the choice has been made rather than during the predecision phase.

In addition to the general tendency to become more satisfied with our choices over time, postdecision feelings of regret and satisfaction may vary to some extent over time, and this variation may depend on certain aspects of the original choice and on the postchoice focus of attention. The feature mapping model makes some very specific predictions in this regard. Consider once again a choice between items that share negative features and have unique positive features. Let us assume for the moment that these items are automobiles. As we have seen, the unique (positive) features of the subject of comparison become the focus of attention, and this item is thus likely to be chosen. How is one likely to feel some time after the decision? It should depend on where one's focus of attention happens to be. As one looks out at the driveway and sees the chosen automobile, its unique positive features will again be highlighted, and one ought to feel very satisfied with the decision. However, if one is driving along the highway, and the model of car that was rejected approaches, suddenly the unique positive features of this rejected alternative will be momentarily highlighted. At that moment in time, regret is likely to be experienced, as the good things that were bypassed are brought to mind. Later, back in one's own driveway, satisfaction should reemerge, as the focus shifts back to the good qualities of the chosen automobile. Thus, in choices involving items with shared bad and unique good features, it is best, subsequent to the decision, to focus on the item that was chosen and to avoid or ignore the item that was rejected.

Once again, the situation is reversed for choices that are made between items that share positive features and have unique negative features. Here, as the unique negative features of the subject of comparison are focused on, the chooser is pushed away from the subject of comparison and selects the referent of comparison. How one will feel subsequently will again depend on whether one is focusing on the automobile that was chosen or on the automobile that was rejected. As one looks out onto the driveway, the unique negative features of the chosen automobile will be highlighted, and one should feel regret over the decision. However, while driving along the highway and seeing the rejected model, the unique negative features of this rejected alternative will become apparent and one should suddenly feel more satisfied about the prior decision. Thus, in choices involving items with shared good and unique bad features, it is best, subsequent to the decision, to avoid as much as possible focusing on or thinking about the item that was chosen (primarily by default). Rather, one will feel better and will feel less regret if the rejected item, with its unique negative features, is focused on.

Of course, *avoiding* focusing on the *chosen* alternative, which of necessity is the alternative most often encountered subsequent to the choice, can be a difficult matter in the real world. We drive the car we chose to buy; we go to work at the job we accepted. This is the alternative that the individual making the choice will continue to encounter, and it is likely to be the focus of attention for most evaluations of satisfaction. Accordingly, regret will be most commonly and frequently experienced when we are forced to live with the outcome of a choice between unique bad alternatives. Indeed, there is experimental evidence that the lowest levels of postchoice satisfaction are reported by people who have had to choose between unique bad alternatives, and who are then focused upon the chosen alternative. These people in fact reported far lower levels of satisfaction than people who chose between two unique good alternatives who were focused upon the rejected alternative. This finding, taken together with the results discussed in the previous two sections, clearly shows that choosing between two alternatives with unique negative features is a psychologically difficult and unpleasant task—before, during, and after the time at which the choice is made!

6. On the Generality of the Feature Mapping Model

In our discussion of the feature mapping model, we have focused on choices involving *either* alternatives where all shared features are bad and all unique features are good, *or* alternatives where all shared features are good and all unique features are bad.

Obviously, in the real world, such "pure" cases are relatively rare. In most choice situations, the alternatives will share a mix of good and bad features, and will possess some unique good and some unique bad features. Keep in mind, therefore, that the key factors in the feature mapping model of choice are that shared features are canceled out (as irrelevant to the choice) and that the weight of the choice will fall on the unique features of the subject of comparison. What will determine the nature of the choice and the feelings about the alternatives, then, is whether the unique features of the starting point of the comparison are primarily, not purely, positive or negative. The "pure" cases were used as examples in our discussion to demonstrate the model in its simplest and strongest application, not to imply that the model is applicable only to such "pure" choices.

In summary, the feature mapping model gives us a simple but powerful way to make predictions about the choice process. Not only does the model aid in the prediction of which item will be chosen and which will be rejected, but it can also make predictions about the ease or difficulty of the predecision process and about the levels of satisfaction and regret that immediately follow the choice and are likely to occur even at later times.

V. CONCLUSION

As we have seen in this review, there are a number of contemporary psychological models of choice. All of the models discussed have been demonstrated experimentally, and all clearly help in understanding the various ways by which people make choices.

There are aspects of the choice process that more than one of these models highlights. Both elimination by aspects and the feature mapping model note that aspects or features shared by choice alternatives will not allow the decision maker to distinguish between those alternatives. However, each brings its own perspective to the nature of features shared by the choice alternatives, directing our attention to different factors in the choice process. Thus, from the perspective of elimination by aspects, aspects or features shared by all remaining members of the pool of choice alternatives may represent those features that the decision maker regards as absolutely necessary for the chosen alternative to possess. From the perspective of a feature mapping comparison, though, once it is determined that all remaining alternatives possess a specific feature, that feature should drop out of consideration in the decision process, because the chooser will obtain that feature no matter which of the choice alternatives he or she selects.

The example of shared features, as seen from the perspective of different models of choice, demonstrates one of the ways in which all of these models can be compatible with one another. Because these processes can be used at different stages of the choice process, a person could make use of more than one of these strategies in making a single choice. For example, a prospective car buyer could use elimination by aspects to arrive at a manageable set of alternatives. Then, he or she could make a global evaluation of each of the remaining alternatives to select the two overall "best" cars. Finally, now that the choice has been narrowed down to two alternatives, the decision maker could engage in a detailed, feature mapping comparison of the two final contenders before making his or her choice.

These models are, therefore, not competing versions of how people always will make choices. Rather, they present a range of choice processes, all of which are sometimes at work. Thus, some of the models are most applicable to certain times in the choice process. Elimination by aspects is most useful when the decision maker is faced with a large number of alternatives, and the first task is trimming down the number of competing choices. The feature mapping process, although usable with more than two competing alternatives, is probably most useful when dealing with a dichotomous choice. Other models are applicable to only certain kinds of choices. The status quo bias explains only choices involving the possibility of choosing to replace an existing choice with a new alternative. Accordingly, much of the current psychological research being conducted in this area is aimed at determining when and under what conditions each of these various choice models is most likely to operate.

Bibliography

Houston, D. A., Sherman, S. J., and Baker, S. M. (1989). The influence of unique features and direction of comparison on preferences. *J. Exp. Soc. Psychol.* **25,** 121–141.

Houston, D. A., Sherman, S. J., and Baker, S. M. (1991). Feature matching, unique features, and the dynamics of the choice process: Predecision conflict and postdecision satisfaction. *J. Exp. Soc. Psychol.* **27,** 411–430.

Kahneman, D., and Tversky, A. (1982). The psychology of preferences. *Sci. Am.* **246,** 160–173.

Samuelson, W., and Zeckhauser, R. (1988). Status quo bias in decision making. *J. Risk Uncertainty* **1,** 7–59.

Thaler, R. (1980). Toward a positive theory of consumer choice. *J. Econ. Behav. Organization* **1,** 39–60.

Tversky, A. (1972). Elimination by aspects: A theory of choice. *Psychol. Rev.* **79,** 281–299.

PREJUDICE AND STEREOTYPES

Werner Bergmann
Technical University of Berlin

Glossary

Attitude System of evaluation of social circumstances that is relatively continuous, object-related, learned, behavior effective, and structured.
Discrimination Behavior aimed at limiting or denying social, political, economic, or other opportunities to certain individuals or groups of people, although they are technically entitled to equal rights.
Prejudice Predominantly negative attitude toward members of some outgroup.
Stereotype Set of beliefs about the personal attributes of a group of people.

THE CONCEPTS of prejudice and stereotypes are closely related. All types of theories assume that the attitude toward a group is closely related to the attributes perceived as dominant traits of that group and with the positive or negative evaluation of these attributes. But the theories differ in their assumptions about the direction of causality: (a) a person's attitude toward an outgroup may result from the stereotypes she holds about the group, or (b) an attitude change can lead to changes in a person's belief about the group. There is empirical evidence for both assumptions.

Prejudice, defined as a negative attitude toward an outgroup, is normally connected with a negative group stereotype, i.e., the distinction between prejudice and stereotype parallels the common distinction between attitudes and beliefs. In the traditional three-component view of attitude (and prejudice), which is in use to this day, stereotype stands for the cognitive component. Alongside the cognitive component there is a differentiation of an affective component of prejudice (dislike) and a behavioral or conative component (discriminatory behavior). The concept of prejudice, which up to the 1960s was seen as a negative attitude based on irrational beliefs (stereotypes are seen as rigid, overgeneralized, incorrect, and biased beliefs), has included a value-laden, normative aspect, since it is bad or wrong to have prejudices. However, for epistemological reasons a clear distinction cannot be drawn between an adequate or an inadequate judgment, since an objective ascertainment of reality, as it actually is, is not possible. To the same degree there exists no sharp difference between positive and negative prejudices. A definition of prejudice as a negative attitude is still prevalent in research, but there are of course also positive intergroup attitudes. Since the late 1960s in the cognitive approach (Tajfel), which dominates today, there is a tendency to regard stereotyping as a normal psychic process of categorization. Stereotypes, seen as frames of references, enable people to predict, rightly or wrongly, how members of an outgroup will behave in a given situation. The presence or absence of motivational biases and exaggerations in stereotyping is open to empirical investigation and is not part of the concept of stereotype. From the concept of prejudice too, the cognitive psychology removed the features of psychopathology and irrationality.

I. A SHORT HISTORY OF THE RESEARCH ON PREJUDICE AND STEREOTYPES

With the age of the great journeys of discovery, the Eurocentric view of life and the secure confidence in customs and convictions were shaken. One's own way of thinking was found to be relative and faulty.

At the present, since the ideological criticism of the Enlightenment of the 18th century, three central questions have been formulated which affect research on prejudice to this day: the question of whether prejudices are actually the result of an "insufficient exertion of the abilities to understand"; the question of correspondence between judgment and reality—expressed otherwise as the question of the defectiveness of prejudice; and the assumption of the utility of prejudices for asserting certain interests.

Academic research on prejudice and stereotypes began in the 1920s. The conceptual scheme of Walter Lippmann and the methodology developed by Emory Bogardus with his social distance scale since the 1920s and then by Daniel Katz and Kenneth W. Braly with their adjective checklist in the 1930s have marked the research for decades. Psychological research between 1920 and 1940 was concerned almost exclusively with the direct or indirect measurement of attitudes; little or no theoretical research on prejudice was done during this period. The turn toward theory, which was dominated in the 1940s and early 1950s by a personality theory view of prejudice, had already been anticipated in the theoretical synthesis of John Dollard *et al.*, who—in their frustration–aggression theory of 1939—brought together existing anthropological and sociological explanations of intergroup hostility with Freud's psychodynamic insights. This approach received attention in the field of research on prejudice and was elaborated in the late 1950s and early 1960s (e.g., in the work of Leonard Berkowitz), when the concept of the "authoritarian personality" began to lose its attraction. During the 1960s the group psychological orientation within social psychology brought about an increasing influence of sociological research design on prejudice and minorities. Purely psychological and especially psychopathological patterns of explanation were dropped and social structural models were adopted in which problems of power and intergroup conflict took center stage. The rise of cognitive psychology in the 1970s has led to a re-evaluation and re-definition of the concepts of attitude, prejudice, and stereotype, in that the patterns of data processing and the cognitive function of stereotypes—as an acquired pattern of interpreting social reality—have been given priority. Comparing the chapters on prejudice in the three editions of the famous "Handbook of Social Psychology" (1954, 1969, and 1985) one can observe a reduction in theoretical perspectives: The approach to prejudice and stereotypes from multiple theoretical perspectives—as given below—has been reduced in 1985 to only one perspective: the cognitive approach. But recently critics as Wolfgang Stroebe and Chester I. Insko proposed to broaden the limited perspective once again and to review whether some of the other approaches to the field of intergroup relations such as the "authoritarian personality," the "realistic conflict theory," the work on the "social identity theory," and others can contribute to our understanding of prejudice and stereotypes. So the following chapter gives a more comprehensive treatment of the theoretical traditions of research on prejudice.

II. THEORETICAL TRADITIONS

A. Conceptions of Prejudice Based on Individual Psychology and the Theory of Personality

The individual psychological and psychodynamic theories of personality analyze, above all, the affective components of prejudice and inquire about their function for the psychic stability of the individual. They trace prejudices ultimately back to an internal psychic conflict so that the expression of prejudices or even a disposition toward prejudice is interpreted as a symptom of underlying personality conflicts. The individual develops prejudices (projections) and tends toward discrimination against others (displacement of aggression) in order to resolve his internal conflicts and tensions. Prejudices are thus, at the same time, results of and resolutions for internal psychic conflicts and therefore need not necessarily stand in close relation with the target of prejudice.

1. Psychoanalysis

As varied as the psychoanalytic interpretations of prejudice from individual authors may appear, nonetheless they are in agreement that prejudices result from a neurotic form of conflict resolution. That means that with prejudices, problems are expressed in a compulsive manner, problems which have their origins in other contexts, for example, in an Oedipus conflict, in social, economic, or religious crisis experiences, or in a constitutional potential for aggression (aggression drive). Despite the varied sources of conflict, the psychodynamic model for resolving them remains, nonetheless, the same. It is assumed that the normal psychodynamic relations between the psychic authorities ego, id, and superego are disturbed in the case of a personality filled with prejudice. The ego of this personality is so weakly developed that it is incapable of successfully integrating the demands of authority figures or of social groups, or it is too weak to cope with its own driving impulses, with the demands of the id.

The conflict between the ego and the superego, i.e., between their external representatives (father, God, social groups), leads to the so-called Oedipal conflict, which is characterized by a feeling of ambivalence. The fears of being destroyed, the disappointments and pain experienced through conflict with the authority are transformed into aggression and feelings of hatred toward this authority. These feelings must, however, be frequently repressed or transferred, either because the originator of the fear is too powerful and aggression against him would be punished, or because he is regarded with ambivalent emotions, meaning that, for example, one fears one's father but also loves him. These inhibited aggressions and emotions press with the defense mechanism of displacement to vent themselves against persons or groups from whom no sanctions and no resistance are to be expected because of their powerlessness. With this thesis of displacement (scapegoat theory), it can be explained why just ethnic or social minorities represent preferred victims for discharging aggression. [*See* ID, EGO, AND SUPEREGO; OEDIPUS COMPLEX.]

The conflict between ego and id arises when the ego attempts to fend off libidinous and aggressive driving desires. The weak ego defends itself against the awareness and existence of its own drives, which it considers as dirty and sinful, by projecting them on others who are then correspondingly stigmatized as sexually active and criminal. An example of this form of projection is to be found in the strong sexually tinged anti-Semitism of the "Stürmer" of Julius Streicher, where the Jews are presented as seducers and criminals.

In both conflict constellations, prejudices clearly serve the function of defending and relieving the weak ego. Since this weak ego has its source in early childhood problems with creating an identity, the psychoanalytic view is that a predisposition for a prejudiced personality arises very early. A prejudice can be used individually as well as collectively to guard against unconscious fears; as a form of defense it is comparable with the neurotic and psychotic defense mechanisms. [*See* DEFENSE MECHANISMS.]

2. The Frustration–Aggression Theory

The frustration–aggression theory creates—often unexpressed—the basic model for sociological and historical analyses of group conflicts and is thereby used to explain the development of prejudices. This theory, in which psychoanalytical, learning theoretical, and behavioristical, but also social psychological and culture anthropological, findings are assimilated, can explain the development of an affective readiness to form prejudice and to discriminate. The classic frustration–aggression hypothesis, as developed at the end of the 1930s, consists of four basic assumptions: (1) frustration is always followed by aggression, i.e., no aggression without frustration; (2) there is a quantitative relation between frustration and aggression: the stronger the frustration, the stronger the consequent aggression; (3) acting out an aggression serves a cathartic, relieving function; and (4) if the possibility of release is blocked at one point, a displacement of aggression takes place, by the choice of another external target (scapegoat), by the direction of aggression toward oneself, or by indirect forms of reaction (criticism, a bad mood). [*See* AGGRESSION.]

This classic model has been subject to diverse criticism. As a result, the supposition of a deterministic and proportional relation between frustration and aggression had to be qualified in favor of an inducement hypothesis, meaning that frustration stimulates aggression, but does not determine it. Thus, by no means must frustration always lead to aggression. The catharsis hypothesis also had to be differentiated, since aggressive acts may reduce aggression, but also may aggravate it (positive reinforcement). The ethological theory emphasizes the drive-reducing, i.e., the releasing, effect while learning theory stresses the reinforcing effect of aggressive acts: they are learned through application, when they are not sanctioned. That means that the readiness to discriminate against a group can result from an actual frustration and its displacement, but it can, however, be a matter of socially "normal" aggressive action carried out against a certain group, where definite prejudices exist, without actual frustrations having to be present. Learned, negative attitudes play an important role in the choice of the scapegoat. Other determinants in the choice of a substitute target are the expectations of resistance associated with him, the similarity with the perpetrator of the original frustration, and the visibility of the target, among other things.

The frustration–aggression hypothesis offers explanations for the development of an affective readiness to form prejudices and to discriminate; no evidence is to be found relating to the cognitive dimension.

3. The Theory of the Authoritarian Personality

The theory of the authoritarian personality, developed at the end of the 1940s, proceeded from the following basic assumptions: an individual's political, economic, and social convictions often form a coherent pattern. This is an expression of deep-lying personality traits. With this arise three conclusions for the theory of prejudice: (1) the same attitudes and values are to be expected from one person in respect to different objects, for example, minorities; that means that ethnocentrism, anti-Semitism, and racism appear as expressions of one and the same pattern. (2) These attitudes rest upon a few basic personality characteristics, so that personality types can be accordingly distinguished, for example, a tolerant and an authoritarian, prejudiced character. (3) These structures are the result of early childhood rearing in the family. The authoritarian character is, as in the psychoanalytic theory of prejudice, determined by its ego weakness. The origin of this lies in a disturbed parent–child relationship, in parental rejection of the child, or in a relation marked by authoritarianism. The weak ego, which lives permanently in conflict with its own drives and urges and its conscience, tends toward conformity, a rigid structuring of its environment (thinking in terms of black and white) and shows limited tolerance of frustration. Belonging to the components of the attitude pattern of the "authoritarian personality" are characteristics which favor the development of prejudices: conventionality, submission to authority, superstition, and proclivity to stereotyping, projectivity. As in psychoanalysis and frustration–aggression theory, the theory of the authoritarian personality also postulates a displacement or projection mechanism by means of which aggressions and feelings of guilt can be projected on alien groups which lie outside the conventional morality of one's own group. Because of their authoritarian fixation on strength and dominance, authoritarian figures choose weak objects as victims. Despite their weakness, these objects are felt to be threatening because the sense of threat is fed by the person's own internal psychic conflicts and therefore needs no anchor in reality. Psychic problems and needs are decisive in creating prejudice and hatred toward minorities. On the other hand, developments within the structure of the family and in the educational process cannot be ignored in regard to their social consequences. These studies about the authoritarian personality have triggered a discussion for decades, and it still continues. Aside from criticism of the scales (see below), it is primarily the correlation with the cognitive dimensions, i.e., the rigidity of thought, which has remained controversial. This led Milton Rokeach to the development of his dogmatism and belief congruence theory. [See AUTHORITARIANISM.]

4. Dogmatism

The dogmatism concept developed by Rokeach, which is similar to the emotional–perceptual personality variable (intolerance of ambiguity) already described in 1949 by Else Frenkel-Brunswik, is, in variance with the affective authoritarianism concept, a cognitive theory where the structural characteristics of information processing are responsible for the formation of prejudice. Dogmatism—earlier Rokeach had spoken of a generalized mental rigidity or narrow-mindedness—refers to resistance against changing a complete, relatively closed belief system containing a dualistic structure of beliefs and disbeliefs, through whose use the surroundings are judged. The dogmatic personality is centered on convictions in regard to an absolute authority which create a frame of reference for intolerant patterns of attitude and behavior toward others. Dogmatism or, more generally, the belief–disbelief system furnishes the person with compulsory, socially polarized categories for classification of other persons or groups. In contrast to the authoritarian concept, which regards prejudicial thought and intolerance as a problem of the political right, the dogmatism concept as generalized authoritarianism should be independent of the right/left dimension. In the following period, this dogmatism theory and the dogmatism attitude scale developed from it have been increasingly judged with scepticism by psychology.

B. Group Psychological Theories

In the 1950s and 1960s the concepts of depth psychology and personality theory were taken over by group psychological explanations which trace prejudices as coming from specific forms of relations between the ingroup and the outgroup. As early as 1906, the American ethnologist Sumner, with his thesis of ethnocentrism, had pointed out the functional significance of a negative assessment of other groups for the integration of one's own group. The ethnocentric overestimation of the ingroup increases the homogeneity of the group, facilitates decisions and friendly relations, generates motivation to work for the group, and promotes learning of group norms. In regard to the outgroups, ethnocentrism leads to a distorted perception, to heightened preparedness for conflict, and to a lesser ability of the group to learn from external influences.

This thesis of a universal, quasi-natural ethnocentrism has been extensively criticized. Research has shown that there are certain conditions, for example, the size ratio of both groups, the objective, internal crises, etc., which determine the perception of and behavior toward other groups. That means that the form and substance of the relations between groups determine the extent and the content of prejudice and behavior.

1. Realistic Conflict Theory

Conflicts theorists (Muzafer Sherif, Donald T. Campbell) see the existence of real conflicts of interest and/or the presence of hostile, threatening, and competitive outgroups as essential prerequisites for the development of prejudice and discrimination against these groups. The real or perceived threat affects not only the feeling and the perception of members of the outgroup, but also increases ingroup solidarity, the tightness of group boundaries, and the rejection of defectors (ethnocentrism). [*See* CONFLICT BEHAVIOR.]

In their famous robbers cave experiment, Muzafer Sherif and his colleagues show that two groups of children who did not know each other tended, in a competitive situation, to respectively view the other group more negatively and to overestimate the achievement of their own group. The same effect appeared when one group was divided, cutting across existing friendships, into two groups. That means that the competition for limited resources led to the formation of prejudices and tendencies toward discrimination. When both groups then had to cooperate to attain a common goal, the hostile approach continually diminished. According to this theory the form of the group relation is decisive for the perception and emotional evaluation of the outgroup. In the so-called "minimal group experiments" Henry Tajfel and his colleagues challenged the hypothesis that intergroup conflict, whether real or perceived, is a necessary and sufficient cause of group antagonism and prejudice.

2. Relative Deprivation Theory

In this theory, which links to the frustration–aggression theory and develops it further on a group psychology basis, the rejection of minorities is explained by experiences of deficiency resulting from the comparison of one's own position with that of members of other groups. It is not a question of absolute deprivation, for example, the experience of great poverty, unemployment, etc.; it is rather a matter of experience of lack or depreciation in relation to reference groups. With this approach, the continually observed connection between social mobility and prejudice can be explained. Whoever declines socially, be it individually or as a member of a declining class, tends to form prejudices against reference groups to whom he attributes the responsibility for his decline. In this process, the interpersonal comparison plays a lesser role than the group-oriented comparison; that means that for the formation of prejudices, the sheer personal fate is not so decisive, but rather it is that of the group to which one sees himself belonging. The determining factor, then, is not the objective status of the ingroup, but the individual perceptions of group members concerning the position of their group in comparison with other groups. With these perceptions it is a matter of affectively charged cognitions since it is a matter of self-value and social identity. As with frustration generally (compare the frustration–aggression hypothesis), relative deprivation also leads to discriminating, aggressive behavior.

3. Social Identity Approach

In the social identity approach, essentially developed by Henri Tajfel and his colleagues in Bristol, three cords of the psychological theory are systematically bound together: the theory of social categorization, the theory of social identity, and the consideration of the emotional significance of comparison, as also developed, for example, in the relative deprivation theory. The theory thus has a threefold structure:

♦ The social environment is grouped into discrete social categories (e.g., man/woman, black/white), and whenever an individual is classed into a category, it is said that the individual identifies himself with the category because it defines the person to a certain degree.
♦ The set of social affiliations defines the social identity of a person as part of the self-concept

through the systematic inclusion and exclusion of certain other categories.

◆ Social identity emerges in relation to other groups, and is thus the result of continuous comparisons.

From the perspective of this approach, prejudices are the result of intergroup differentiations. Since the beginning of the 1970s, Tajfel and his colleagues have found in the famous "minimal group experiments" that competition for material resources or real interest conflicts are not required for the development of hostile tensions and prejudices between groups. Arbitrary—and also recognizable as such for the test persons—group classifications were much more sufficient in generating mutual discrimination and resentments. In the meantime, these results have been confirmed and refined in numerous experiments on ingroup favoritism. These surprising results led Tajfel and Turner *et al.* to the development of the theory of social identity which assumes that a part of the self-concept (self-categorization) of a person is defined by his group affiliation(s), thus by his social identity. The evaluation of one's own group arises from comparison with outgroups, whereby certain groups can gain particular significance as reference groups. The theory now supposes that the group members want to derive a positive social identity from their membership. This essentially occurs through the process of positively contrasting their group with the reference groups by degrading them. Thus, the self-image is gained through contrast with a negatively accentuated outgroup stereotype. As a result, differences between in- and outgroups are overemphasized. Prejudices then arise from the attempt to preserve or upgrade one's own identity. Today the social identity approach is the most broadly developed group psychological concept. It gains its central importance in prejudice and stereotyping research through attempting to tie together theoretical approaches stemming from the various psychological traditions.

C. Theories of Social Cognition and Learning

1. The Cognitive Approach

The cognitive turn in social psychology has led to a new interpretation of the concept of prejudice. Prejudice and stereotypes are seen as the results of the normal cognitive processing of social perceptions. This means that cognitive psychology analyzes the courses of information processing (percep-

tion, storage, and organization of memory and of recall) and the functional rank of category information for an orientation toward individuals and social groups. The cognitive dimension of prejudice and stereotyping shifts to the foreground but more recently researchers have addressed the role of affective or emotional factors in prejudice (e.g., moods, feelings of ambivalence, unconscious needs). It has been shown that both emotions and symbolic beliefs (i.e., beliefs that groups violate or uphold shared values) had better predictive power for global evaluations and social distance than stereotypic beliefs about groups.

In the process of social categorization, mechanisms are in operation which, on the one hand, come to a typified, extreme, and negative perception and evaluation of outgroups and, on the other hand, lead to an intensification of ingroup/outgroup differences. Here some of the most important findings shall be briefly presented.

The theory of illusory correlation assumes a purely cognitive act of the development of stereotypes, where the perception of the co-occurrence of two distinctive events leads to the creation of a close, but illusory relation between characteristics. Thus, members of a minority, with whom there is less frequent contact than with the majority, are placed in a closer relation with forms of behavior which also appear less frequently. The consequence is that the groups are perceived quite differently, although there is no informational basis for such differential perception.

If a stereotype already exists, that is, if there are associative expectations regarding the relationship between group membership and attributes, then information which fits to the stereotype is seen more often and remembered better than that which bears no relation to the stereotype (confirmatory bias). Such a perceptional bias has the consequence of perpetuating stereotypic conceptions even in the absence of confirming evidence. Other researchers have formulated the cognitive bolstering process which, as with reconstruction, suits the past to existing prejudices. The expectations of behavior direct the interactions with members of ethnic groups in such a manner that they may constrain the other's behavioral options in a way to produce actual behavioral confirmation for the own beliefs about the target.

Characteristics are not attributed to persons or groups absolutely, but rather always in relation with others, meaning that in the evaluation the (positive) autostereotype of one's own group mostly serves as the standard. This comparison can, as in the case of anti-Semitism in Germany, be intensified to such an absolute contrast so that the alien group is seen as nothing short of an antithesis of one's own group.

This heterostereotype attained by comparison need not be continually developed anew, but rather it is stored as a group concept, a general schema, which embraces evaluating and descriptive traits. This leads to a de-individualization of the outgroup. It is interesting for prejudice research that with homogeneous groups (e.g., in a circle of friends, in the family) it is primarily the deviant forms of behavior which are noticed, whereas with large nonhomogeneous groups, such as nations and ethnic minorities, it is rather the consistencies which are remembered and the differences are forgotten as being irrelevant. That means, we attain a more strongly typified, undifferentiated picture about ethnic groups per se, in that we mostly store only abstract information about the groups as a whole—information which is indirectly taken based on prototypical members of the outgroup. If the information is negative, then individual members are also negatively evaluated according to the group concept, totally irrespective of their own behavior. Deviations are flexibly regarded as "exceptions" from the rule. Behaviors of ingroup and outgroup members also were encoded and communicated quite differently: desirable behaviors by ingroup members and undesirable behaviors by outgroup members were encoded on a more abstract level (in terms of traits) than undesirable behaviors of ingroup members and desirable behaviors by outgroup members.

The picture of the outgroup is, however, not only more strongly typified, it also presents more extreme traits. Individuals have a more complex picture of their own group. Cognition psychology has found a connection between the differentiation of a picture and its evaluation: the more simplified the picture is, the more extreme is the positive or negative judgment about ways of behavior or characteristics. The collection of persons into a group is mostly based on their correspondence in external characteristics (language, skin color, sex, etc.). Due to this classification these persons seem to us to have more similarity with one another than they may in fact have. This classification leads to an overestimation of similarities among group members, while the differences between groups are overstressed (similarity or difference accentuation). This accentuation of intragroup similarity and intergroup difference is partic-

ularly strong when the corresponding social categories are differently evaluated and when, along with the purely cognitive function of a simplification and systematization of the social situation, the accentuation also fulfills the function of protecting the own system of values. Psychology has experimentally established the tendency to favor the ingroup, i.e., the effort to accentuate the differences between the ingroup and the outgroup so that the ingroup is better evaluated.

As early as 1960 with his concept of belief congruence Milton Rokeach pointed out the significance of the perceived similarity or dissimilarity of beliefs as determinants for ethnic attitudes. It could be empirically demonstrated in cases without social pressure that perceived belief congruence on topics of high emotional importance is a more significant determinant of social distance than ethnic differences. Belief congruence may be granted very great importance for intergroup relations, particularly in cases of attitudes between religiously or ideologically defined groups, but that perceived similarity of beliefs should be the most important determinant for the character of ethnic relations must be doubted. Today the "weak version" of the belief congruence theory is accepted, meaning that in situations without external social pressure, differences in beliefs have a greater discrimination effect than ethnic differences, but the strong version, where racial effects are supposed to play no role, is rejected.

When observing persons or groups, one searches for the reasons for their behavior. In that, one has the choice of tracing behavior either back to external factors or to characteristics of the person/group itself. Therefore, in psychology one makes a distinction between external and internal attribution. Now it is of interest for research on prejudice that, concerning members of outgroups, behavior is more often attributed to internal dispositions. Thomas Pettigrew called this an "ultimate attribution error," whereby attribution processes reinforce negative stereotypes of minorities. The special concentration of Jews in business and trade, for example, is ascribed to the inborn "Jewish shopkeeper mentality." In contrast to this, when members of the ingroups are concerned, attributions are directed more externally, meaning that their behavior is rather explained as personal fate, difficult external circumstances, etc. The cognitive mechanisms played out here function, so to say, "behind the back of the subject," i.e., they remain unrecognized for the perceiver. In cognitive psychology stereotypes appear both as necessary results and as a prerequisite for social perception and categorization processes. [*See* CATEGORIZATION.]

2. Social Learning Theory

In contrast to conflict or frustration theories the theory of learning need not assume motives for prejudice toward other groups, because prejudices and stereotypes either can be based on one's own actual observations or may be taken over from the parents, the peer group, the school, or the mass media. Taking on definite social roles or social structural differences can lead to the fact that the interaction with certain groups is limited to a few typical situations where similar forms of behavior and characteristics appear time and again. Since contacts between ethnic groups are determined in part by class and power differences, ethnic stereotypes can very strongly reflect class stereotypes and prejudices. While stereotypes and prejudices as probabilistic beliefs are not changed by singular, contradictory pieces of information, but rather possess a certain stability, it is to be assumed that changes in the social relations between groups are only slowly reflected on the level of stereotypes. That means that today's prejudices mostly reflect social constellations which are already past.

Prejudices are, however, for the most part not developed but adopted. Children not only learn prejudices and stereotypes from their parents, other adults, or the mass media, they also learn about typical forms of interaction with members of outgroups. Through the regulation of contacts between their children and other children, parents particularly further the adoption of their own prejudices and emotions. Research on the adoption of prejudices in the process of socialization show that children learn racial, ethnic, and gender stereotypes already at a very young age. In the adoption of ethnic prejudices, three overlapping phases are distinguished: Ethnic awareness occurs by the age of 3 or so. At this age, the child has developed an awareness of his own ethnic identity and is becoming aware of the ethnic identities of others. Between the ages of 4 and 8 the child has learned many of the terms and concepts which are used to describe members of other ethnic groups, but at this age he has not generalized these concepts to all members of an ethnic group. By the age of 8 or so the child develops an "adult" ethnic attitude with quite definite patterns of preferences. In the prejudiced child a full picture of stereotyping and hostility can be observed.

III. PREJUDICE AND DISCRIMINATION

Discussions have been carried on for decades now about the problem of "attitude and behavior," and they are still going on. The relation of prejudice to discrimination is one aspect of this general connection. Attitudes as hypothetical constructs attributed to personality systems cannot be used readily as predictors for overt behavior. In a very early field experiment, Richard LaPiere found that hotel managers, who generally rejected guests of Chinese origin on the telephone, accepted them without any hesitation when he appeared with them personally in the hotel. Research has confirmed that prejudice and discrimination are only loosely connected with each other. Personal, social, and situational factors may prevent prejudiced persons from discriminating against members of other groups, and conversely, discrimination need not always be the result of prejudice but can be brought about by pressures to conform to group norms and by a high degree of public exposure. To reinforce the predictive value of attitudes/prejudice psychologists, who postulate a general connection between attitude and behavior, add other personality and situational variables to their models, e.g., earlier experience, strength of personal involvement, beliefs, group norms, role requirements, reference group influence, degree of commitment, social constraint, social distance, etc. Already in the early 1960s Donald T. Campbell introduced the concept of the "situational threshold" to explain the observed inconsistencies between attitudes and behavior. Various attitudes have to overcome thresholds of differing heights for their conversion to behavior.

In recent years, attempts to more exactly define and measure the relations between attitude and behavior have led to substantial correlations. Attitude and behavior must be measured on the same level of specificity, meaning that one cannot employ a general attitude toward an ethnic group as a predictor of behavior in a specific situation. Therefore, in their influential model called theory of reasoned action Martin Fishbein and Jcek Ajzen placed a specific behavior in relation to an equally specific behavioral intention. This intention is made of two psychological factors: the attitude toward the specific behavior and the subjective norms which apply to the situation, or stated otherwise: the beliefs about the normative expectations of significant others. The strength and the clarity with which an attitude is held as well as the knowledge about one's own attitude and its relevance for one's own behavior are additional important predictors for the correspondence between attitude and behavior.

In his theory of planned behavior Ajzen adds to his model perceived behavioral control as a third predictor for behavioral intentions, which operates independently from attitudes and subjective norms. Others argued that behavioral expectations are better predictors than behavioral intentions, because they take into account the successful completion of the action in question. New methods for measuring specific attitudes and behaviors, e.g., the development of multidimensional measurements of behavior, also improved the predicatability of attitudes.

But as social psychology has proven, the effects of behavior on attitudes (attitude follows action) are greater than the other way around. For example, in cases of dissonance between attitude and action people are motivated to change their attitudes thus reducing the inconsistency between them. Especially if prejudice is weak or ambiguous individuals tend to infer these inner states (attitude or emotion) from knowledge about their overt behavior (theory of self-perception). Techniques of reducing prejudice use this behavioral effect in interethnic relations (cooperation, jigsaw classroom, etc.) to bring about changes in attitudes (see below). [See COGNITIVE DISSONANCE.]

IV. METHODS OF RESEARCH

Research on prejudice historically started with the development of measurement methods. Both theory and empirical studies concentrated on the search for reliable standards with which to measure prejudice. From the 1930s on, the social distance scale of Emory Bogardus and the adjective checklist developed by Daniel Katz and Kenneth Braly dominated research until the late 1960s, later supplemented by the much criticized, but often used, fascism, anti-Semitism, and ethnocentrism scales developed by Theodor W. Adorno and his colleagues in the 1940s. The most influential was the practical method of the adjective checklist. With its assistance, stereotypical attitudes about ethnic groups could be easily determined. The test persons received a checklist with 84 adjectives and were asked to pick out characteristics for each of 10 national groups. In a second step, they were asked to pick out the five words that seemed the most typical of each group. Using this method the basic lines of group stereotypes (images)

and the distinctiveness of stereotypes can be measured. A high degree of agreement among subjects on a small number of traits considered typical indicates a high degree of definiteness of the stereotypes. This Katz/Braly paradigm, which was modified and expanded by other researchers, has been subject to multifarious criticism. Fundamentally, it was doubted whether the naming of traits can be considered stereotyping since it remains unclear whether the traits are considered true or false and are used for negative generalized images of the group in question. In other words, the relation to the affective and cognitive aspects of prejudice remains unclear. Other points of criticism were the presentation of traits, which restricted the choice available, the omission of relevant traits from the list, etc. To correct these shortcomings, less restricted forms were used, such as free association techniques, sentence completions, the use of visual stimuli in ethnic identification or descriptions of actual life situations to identify characteristic traits of other nationalities.

Another technique for empirically determining group stereotypes is the percentage technique, which seeks to determine the prevalence of a set of traits in a given group. The respondents should indicate the percentage of members of a given group who possess each trait. Those traits perceived to be possessed by the highest percentage of group members constitute the group stereotype. A third technique which has achieved acceptance is the diagnostic ratio technique. The respondents are asked to indicate (a) the percentage of people in general and (b) the percentage of members of a given group who possess each of a list of traits. A diagnostic ratio is showing the degree to which this group is perceived to differ from the "people in general." The stereotype consists of those traits reaching the highest ratios.

Two other cognitives techniques used more recently are based either on research on prototypes or research on the structure of information in memory. The "prototype" refers to category information about the typical characteristics of a group. Respondents are asked to indicate the traits possessed by a typical member of the group in question. The second technique, the pathfinder technique, assesses the links between nodes in a network by asking respondents to judge how closely related or how similar the items in the nodes (e.g., each pair of traits in a checklist and the group label) are. A stereotype thus consists of those traits which are related most closely to the group label. A recent empirical comparison of the five techniques mentioned reveals that they—with the exception of the diagnostic ratio technique—produced remarkably similar findings.

In order to measure the social or affective proximity to another group, Emory Bogardus developed a social distance scale which consists of seven statements by which social distance can be ordered: (1) I would admit to close kin by marriage; (2) would admit to my club as personal chum; (3) would admit to my street as neighbor; (4) would admit to employment in my occupation; (5) would admit to citizenship in my country; (6) would admit only as a visitor to my country; (7) would exclude from my country. The response indicating the smallest degree of distance is taken as a measure of social distance toward a certain target group. This scale has the known limitations of the Thurstone scales: the intervals between the points on the scale are uneven, the scale lacks coherence and is multidimensional instead. The criticism of the scale led to a further development by Harry C. Triandis and Leigh M. Triandis. With their behavioral distance scale, they set up a 7-point scale ranging from agreement to rejection, splitting the one-dimensional Bogardus scale into five specific areas of distance: formal acceptance, acceptance as a friend, acceptance as a marriage partner, social distance (neighbor status), and subordination. In addition they distinguished various areas where distance was from time to time expressed, for example, with race, religion, nationality, and profession. Thus, they created complex stimuli, as, for example, with "Swedish physician, white, same religion," or "civil engineer, black, different religion, French." By using factor analysis, it could be determined what influence the various factors had on the expression of social distance. Since the meaning of race, religion, etc., varies with different cultures and groups, a universally applicable distance scale cannot be constructed. To this day the affective dimension of prejudice is mostly measured with a sympathy/antipathy scale which ranges from a very negative value, e.g., -5, over a point of indifference, zero, to a very positive value, e.g., $+5$. In the 1930s H. H. Grice and H. H. Remmers had already developed a similar 11-point scale using a neutral point of 6 with their scale for measuring attitudes toward race and nationalities.

In the late 1940s Daniel J. Levinson and R. Nevitt Sanford developed an anti-Semitism scale consisting of 52 degrading statements in order to measure prejudices against Jews. The items were in part intended to reveal the subject's opinion of Jews and in part

his idea on how to behave toward Jews, in order to link stereotype with intended behavior. With the help of this scale, it was hoped not only to assign a precise numerical value to "degree of anti-Semitism" (from $+3$ = strong agreement, to the -3 = strong disagreement), but to clarify the entire range of anti-Jewish ideology. This anti-Semitism scale and the other scales developed by the same research group—the fascism scale (F-scale) and the ethnocentrism scale (E-scale)—were conceived as personality scales and were widely used through the 1960s for prejudice research when it was intended to identify authoritarian and prejudiced test persons for experimental situations. Today, in a less systematic form, opinion surveys (interviews or questionnaires) about stereotypes and prejudices toward ethnic groups work with similar statements and ad-hoc structured scales, which, however, do not measure personality structures, but rather the stereotypical views and emotional attitudes toward specific groups.

In group psychology primarily the field experiments of Muzafer Sherif and his colleagues have become famous (robbers cave experiment). Here groups of children were observed in competitive and cooperative situations (see above). Later group experiments, for example the equally famous minimal group experiments of Tajfel and his colleagues and continuing on to newer investigations about ingroup favoritism, are artificial laboratory experiments where attitudes and behavior (e.g., distribution of rewards) of test persons toward members of ingroups and outgroups are investigated. Moreover, other known measurement methods have found their way into group psychology, for example, the social distance scale and sociometric methods, which test the degree of identification with one's own group and the outgroup.

According to Stuart A. Cook and Claire Seltiz, five sorts of measurement methods can be distinguished in attitude psychology: (a) self-report measures, in which the test person is asked for oral or written agreement or disagreement with certain items, using attitude scales or standardized questionnaires. (b) Techniques which measure attitude with reference to actual behavior, whereby the willingness to act (realistic action commitment) or actual behavior can be measured, e.g., the willingness to let oneself be photographed with a black person, behavior in role playing, sociometric choices, etc. (c) Techniques which reveal attitudes through reaction to, or interpretation of semi-structured stimulus situations, for example, sentence completion tests, description of pictures. Here also belong the projective tests developed in the tradition of psychoanalysis. (d) Techniques which require that the test person solve certain "objective" problems, e.g., choosing between programs for the improvement of ethnic relations. (e) Physiological techniques measuring involuntary physical reactions, such as pupil responses or other reflexes revealing positive or negative feelings toward certain statements.

All these methods have been criticized, for example, because the test persons respond in a socially desired direction, because the test situation deviates from real situations (ecological validity), because they refer to nonexistent attitudes, and so forth. The objection, which is probably of the most importance and which touches on practically all methods of measuring prejudice, concerns its reactive character. The test persons respond in a defined test situation and can accordingly adjust their behavior. One recent trend in racism research today is the use of experiments on helping behavior, aggression, and nonverbal communication involving hidden manipulations and unobtrusive measures of prejudice and discrimination in alone or group conditions.

V. REDUCING PREJUDICE

Different procedures in reducing prejudice are favored depending on the underlying concepts of prejudice. Following Yehuda Amir and Rachel Ben-Ari one can differentiate between three major models dealing with change in intergroup relations: the psychodynamic model, the contact model, and the information model. Psychodynamic theories which see internal conflicts and problematic parent/child relations as the main source of prejudices regard forms of psychotherapy and changes in educational styles as being appropriate. Concepts arising from social psychology expect prejudice reduction from intergroup contact. Research on the contact hypothesis has shown that these contacts must satisfy certain requirements, especially cooperative interaction, equal status between the members of the interacting groups, support of authority figures, and contact of an intimate nature, in order to reduce tensions and change attitudes. These requirements are inherent not only in the program of desegregation (the *Brown v. Board of Education* decision of 1954), supported scientifically by leading social psychologists, but

also in the jigsaw or in the scripted cooperative learning for fostering positive ethnic or racial attitudes in desegrated classrooms. If the contact does not occur under the conditions specified above, it may even lead to a further polarization of intergroup attitudes.

Besides desegregation, other state undertakings could also be considered, as for example affirmative action or anti-discrimination laws, which have an influence on the social position of groups and make discrimination more difficult. There is a consensus that these affirmative action programs, equal employment opportunity laws, court rulings, etc., have led to an improvement of black occupational status in the United States and to a process of eroding formal and open racial discrimination. Although the goal to alleviate formal barriers to inclusion of minorities is widely accepted, affirmative action methods remain controversial, even among the intended beneficiaries. Besides the accusation that these programs are unfair and promote reverse discrimination, more recent research is concentrating on the problems arising from the structure of the new interracial job situation (the solo role of a black in a working group, the token role) and the operation of anti-black prejudice and discrimination in its modern, more subtle forms (tokenism), since white resistance to ethnic change has evolved from "dominative racism" and overt bigotry to more indirect "modern," "aversive," or "symbolic" racism, because the civil rights movement gave overt anti-black prejudice a disreputable image. Another objection of affirmative action centers on the fact that accentuation of social categories (e.g., race, sex) can in the long run lead to the association of negative expectancies with those category labels among prejudiced people and thus may perpetuate disadvantage through a process of a self-fullfilling negative prophecy. Cognitive theories, which make certain cognitive mechanisms responsible for the formation of negative stereotypes, would preferably rely on better education, rational instruction, persuasive communication, and role-playing where the lifestyle and the perspectives of the other groups can be learned and emotionally understood. The main assumption of this information model is that lack of information and ignorance of the modus operandi of stereotype-based judgments are the basis for the development of prejudice and tensions between groups. Nisbett *et al.* suggest programs in which simple probabilistic models and statistical heuristics will be incorporated into everyday reasoning. An understanding of the rules of information gathering and processing would improve human judgment and decision making. The possibility of attitude change depends on the strength with which an attitude is held. Strong prejudices serving as important sources of a persons' identity and exerting strong effects on perception and behavior will resist most attempts at change. It seems obvious that one has to specify what it is one wants to change. Different goals, e.g., changing the readiness for social acceptance, changing attitudes and stereotypes, learning about the culture and lifestyle, etc., require different methods for their attainment. So all three models discussed above have their field of implementation.

Bibliography

Bar-Tal, D., Graumann, C., Kruglanski, A. W., and Stroebe, W. (Eds.) (1989). "Stereotyping and Prejudice: Changing Conceptions." Springer Verlag, New York.

Bergmann, W. (Ed.) (1988). "Error without Trial. Psychological Research on Anti-Semitism." De Gruyter Verlag, Berlin/New York.

Dovidio, J. F., and Gaertner, S. L. (Eds.) (1986). "Prejudice, Discrimination, and Racism." Academic Press, New York.

Hamilton, D. L. (Ed.) (1981). "Cognitive Processes in Stereotyping and Intergroup Behavior." Erlbaum, Hillsdale, NJ.

Mackie, D. M., and Hamilton, D. L. (Eds.) (1992). "Affect, Cognition, and Stereotyping: Interactive Processes in Group Perception." Academic Press, New York.

Miller, A. G. (Ed.) (1982). "In the Eye of the Beholder. Contemporary Issues in Stereotyping." Greenwood Press, Westport, CT.

Miller, N., and Brewer, M. B. (1984). "Groups in Contact: The Psychology of Desegregation." Academic Press, Orlando, FL.

Stephan, W. G. (1985). Intergroup relations. In "Handbook of Social Psychology" (G. Lindzey and E. Aronson, Eds.), Vol. I, 3rd ed. Random House, New York.

Taylor, D. M., and Moghaddam, F. M. (1987). "Theories of Intergroup Relations: International Social Psychological Perspectives." Praeger, New York.

Zanna, M. P., and Olson, J. M. (Eds.) (1993). "Psychology of Prejudice: The Ontario Symposium," Vol. 7. Erlbaum, Hillsdale, NJ.

PREMENSTRUAL SYNDROME

Margaret L. Moline
The New York Hospital–Cornell Medical Center

Glossary

Affective symptoms Symptoms related to emotion or mood, such as depression, irritability, anger, etc.

Follicular phase The section of the menstrual cycle from the onset of menstrual bleeding until ovulation.

Late luteal phase dysphoric disorder (LLPDD) A severe form of PMS where the prominent symptoms are related to mood (depression, mood swings, anger). The symptoms must have a substantial impact on a woman's ability to function in the home or workplace.

Luteal phase The section of the menstrual cycle from ovulation to the onset of menstrual bleeding.

Menses The section of the menstrual cycle when menstrual bleeding occurs.

Premenstrual phase/late luteal phase/premenstruum Generally the 5–7 days preceding the onset of menses, when women with PMS experience their symptoms.

Premenstrual syndrome (PMS) A condition of women when physical, behavioral, and/or mood symptoms appear regularly in the late luteal phase of the menstrual cycle and disappear during menses. PMS is commonly used to describe syndromes that may be of mild, moderate, or severe intensity.

Psychotropic medication Prescription drugs that are used to treat psychiatric illnesses and symptoms such as depression, anxiety, and mania.

Retrospective history A report of symptoms based on a woman's recollection that needs to be substantiated by prospective assessment.

PREMENSTRUAL SYNDROME (PMS) is a condition related to the menstrual cycle that is characterized by mood, behavioral, and/or physical symptoms that appear in the week to 10 days before menses and remit during menses. When symptoms are of severe intensity, the woman may experience difficulties with relationships or functioning and therefore be considered as suffering from a disorder. Women with predominantly affective symptoms as well as those with severe physical symptoms can all receive a diagnosis of PMS. The timing, number, and severity of symptoms are important in making the diagnosis. The cause of PMS is not yet known, and there is no one symptom management technique for all women with the syndrome.

I. HISTORY OF PREMENSTRUAL SYNDROME RESEARCH

The modern era of research on PMS began in 1931, when the term was first used to describe women who regularly experienced symptoms in the latter half of the menstrual cycle. Early theories as to the cause of PMS included excess estrogen, deficient progesterone, allergies to hormones, and nutritional deficiencies. Each of these theories spawned treatment studies and management techniques, some of which are still used although they remain unproven.

There have been over 20 proposed etiologies and more than 80 treatment techniques published since 1931. Much of that research suffered from design flaws that limit the interpretation of the data. These problems are related to diagnostic methods, rationale, placebo responses, and safety.

The diagnosis of PMS is made after other medical or psychiatric illnesses that could potentially cause similar symptoms have been ruled out. The methods for diagnosing the syndrome will be described in detail under Section IV. Research has established that having a retrospective history of premenstrual symptoms alone is not sufficient to make the diagnosis. Many more women believe that they have PMS than can be confirmed through the use of prospective daily ratings. Prospective daily ratings require that a woman rate her symptoms every day for at least one complete menstrual cycle. This usually is done after an initial consultation with a treatment provider or researcher (see Fig. 1).

Much early research in PMS used subjects who reported premenstrual symptoms only retrospectively; these subjects were not required to keep prospective daily ratings. It is therefore likely that some research subjects who were thought to have PMS did not actually have the disorder. The number, type, and severity of the symptoms that were required to be included as a subject (see Section II) were also not consistent across studies. As a result of these methodological problems, findings from studies before the late 1980s (and even some con-ducted in the present) must be viewed with skepticism.

Women with predominantly affective symptoms and women with primarily physical symptoms can all receive a diagnosis of PMS. In some research, women with particular types of symptoms were selected, making the data from such studies hard to generalize to women with PMS in general. Some of this diagnostic heterogeneity has been overcome in recent years. In 1987, a new diagnostic category appeared in the Research Appendix of the *Diagnostic and Statistical Manual of Mental Disorders* 3rd Ed., Revised (DSM-III-R), describing a subgroup of women with PMS whose severe *mood* symptoms seriously interfered with their relationships with others and/or their ability to function at home or at work. This subtype of PMS was called late luteal phase dysphoric disorder (LLPDD), a name that reflects the timing of symptoms, the affective nature of the problem, and the severity of the condition. This diagnosis has become increasingly important over the years since researchers have begun to use the tools of modern psychiatry to study the etiology and treatment of this subgroup in particular. However, just as it is difficult to apply the findings from

Code #_____	Menstruating	Yes____ No ____	Temperature	_____	Date _____
Scale: 1 = None	2 = Minimal	3 = Mild	4 = Moderate	5 = Severe	6 = Extreme
Less productive (job, home), inefficient 1 2 3 4 5 6	Mood swings 1 2 3 4 5 6	Increased appetite 1 2 3 4 5 6	More sleep, naps, stay in bed 1 2 3 4 5 6	Increased enjoyment in living 1 2 3 4 5 6	Depressed, sad, low, blue, lonely 1 2 3 4 5 6
Headaches 1 2 3 4 5 6	Sensitive to rejection 1 2 3 4 5 6	Decreased interest in usual activities 1 2 3 4 5 6	Anxious, jittery, nervous 1 2 3 4 5 6	Breast tenderness or swelling 1 2 3 4 5 6	Difficulty concentrating 1 2 3 4 5 6
Abdominal bloating, swelling, or heaviness 1 2 3 4 5 6	Low energy, tired, weak 1 2 3 4 5 6	Crave foods 1 2 3 4 5 6	Irritable, angry, impatient 1 2 3 4 5 6	Stay at home, avoid social activity 1 2 3 4 5 6	Decreased appetite 1 2 3 4 5 6
Trouble with relationships 1 2 3 4 5 6	Back, joint, muscle pain 1 2 3 4 5 6	Difficulty sleeping, disturbed sleep 1 2 3 4 5 6	More productive (job, home), efficient 1 2 3 4 5 6	Feel overwhelmed, can't cope 1 2 3 4 5 6	Feel out of control 1 2 3 4 5 6

FIGURE 1   Typical daily rating form. In the morning, the woman records her basal body temperature and whether she is menstruating. In the evening, she uses the 6-point scale to rate each symptom. The average of ratings from the follicular phase are compared to the average of ratings from the luteal phase to determine if a symptom is present. Five or more positive symptoms are commonly required before a menstrual cycle would be considered positive for PMS.

a study of a treatment for a physical symptom like breast pain to treatment of emotional symptoms, it would be premature to assume that what works well for women with LLPDD (who have severe affective symptoms) should be prescribed for all women with PMS (who may or may not have milder affective symptoms). One could ask at this point whether it would be more sensible to study individual symptoms rather than the syndrome. This would not be feasible since symptoms tend to cluster (appear together), especially mood symptoms.

Another problem with PMS research has been that many women with PMS tend to respond quite well to any kind of treatment, including to placebos, at least for one or more cycles. High placebo response rates do not mean that a syndrome is imagined by the patient. Some attribute the high response to placebo in PMS to factors related to support and validation of the woman's condition which can help her symptoms to seem more manageable. One does need to take into account the initial tendency to respond to any treatment by designing one's experiment carefully, either by increasing the length of treatment so that the placebo response rate decreases or by excluding subjects who respond to the placebo.

Safety has also been an issue in PMS treatment research over the years. One of the first proposed treatments for PMS was irradiation of the ovaries. Such therapy was considered safe in the 1930s. The harmful effects of such treatments were not appreciated until much later, when much more experience had been accumulated. More recently, concerns over the consumption of megadoses of vitamin B_6 for PMS have emerged, since high doses of this vitamin can cause nervous system damage. In addition, many psychotropic or other medications must be taken daily over long periods in order to be effective. One must weigh any risk to the patient from chronic use of such treatments against the benefit of the treatment.

Thus, although in the past 60 years many possible causes and treatments of PMS have been studied, much research remains to be done, using adequate experimental design and considering the risks and benefits to the patient with PMS.

II. SYMPTOMS OF PREMENSTRUAL SYNDROME AND LLPDD

As mentioned earlier, PMS symptoms can be emotional, behavioral or physical. The common symptoms are listed in Table I. Some additional "symptoms" related to productivity, ability to concentrate, and so on are frequently measured and have been studied. However, there has not been a definitive study demonstrating premenstrual impairment of cognitive function in women with PMS.

Both the timing of symptoms and their severity are key factors in PMS. Symptoms can begin at any time in the luteal phase. There can also be an emergence of symptoms around ovulation followed by symptoms during the late luteal phase. In either case, by definition, symptoms must remit during the week of menses. Women who have some symptoms all month long would not receive a diagnosis of PMS. Women who have a psychiatric or physical disorder such as depression or migraine headaches that worsens during the late luteal phase also would not be considered to have PMS. If those women had new symptoms during the late luteal phase in addition to their chronic problem, then they would be diagnosed with PMS as well.

There is no guideline for the number of symptoms needed or the severity required for the diagnosis to be made. Most research groups consider a symptom as present based on a quantitative difference between symptom ratings in the luteal phase and the follicular phase of the same menstrual cycle. Often a research group will use a 30% change rule, which means that the luteal symptom ratings must be at least 30% higher than those of the follicular phase. Others use an absolute severity criterion, requiring a symptom to be rated as "severe" or "extreme" during the luteal phase and as "absent" or "mild" during the follicular phase.

TABLE I
Common Symptoms of Premenstrual Syndrome

Psychological symptoms	Physical symptoms
Anger	Bloatedness, edema
Anxiety	Breast swelling and tenderness
Depression	Fatigue, low energy
Decreased self-esteem	Food cravings, overeating
Impulsive behavior	Gastrointestinal complaints
Irritability	Headache, migraine
Lethargy	Joint and/or back pain
Malaise	Muscle pain
Mood swings	Weight gain
Moodiness	
Sleep disturbances	

The diagnostic criteria for LLPDD are more specific than those for PMS; they require that five symptoms show a marked change in the luteal phase *and* that one of these five be an affective symptom. Physical symptoms are much less important in this diagnosis. The LLPDD criteria also require that symptoms be present during a majority of the menstrual cycles in the past year and that they have a severe impact on the women's relationships or ability to function. Thus, it is clear that these criteria should only be applied to a subgroup of women with PMS.

It is commonly held that 20–40% of all women experience some premenstrual symptoms and that 5% report some significant impact on their work or lifestyle. These figures probably represent the prevalence of premenstrual *symptoms,* not PMS. To date, no large epidemiological study of women receiving either the diagnosis of PMS or LLPDD has been published. There are few data on the incidence of PMS or LLPDD in different cultures. Without such studies, one can only make informed guesses about how common these disorders are.

A role of heredity in the development or severity of PMS is supported by research, but has not been conclusively demonstrated. Some evidence from survey studies suggests that daughters of mothers with PMS are more likely to complain of the syndrome than daughters of mothers who are symptom-free. The incidence of PMS in twins has also been studied. The concordance rate (if one twin has PMS, the other does as well) for monozygotic twins was significantly higher (93%) than for fraternal twins (44%) or siblings (31%). These data suggest that there may be a hereditary component to PMS, but research would need to be performed to identify such factors.

While PMS can begin anytime after menarche, women usually seek treatment for their symptoms beginning in their late 20s and 30s. Symptoms disappear with menopause and with any other condition, such as pregnancy or breast feeding, that interrupts regular menstrual cycling. Symptoms may occur in the absence of menstrual bleeding if a woman has had a hysterectomy that leaves her ovaries intact.

III. POTENTIAL ETIOLOGIES

Since 1931 many suggestions have been put forth in the research literature to explain the cause of PMS. These proposals were based on biological or nutritional bases, on psychological rationales, or on a combination of causes. However, to date, the etiology of PMS remains incompletely understood.

A. Biological Etiologies

Potential biological causes of PMS range from hormonal disturbances, alterations in neurotransmitters, and poorly timed biological rhythms to changes in prostaglandin secretion.

1. Hormonal Causes

A variety of hormonal systems have been proposed as the culprits in PMS, including ovarian steroids, prolactin, aldosterone, thyroid hormone, and insulin. [*See* HORMONES AND BEHAVIOR.]

a. Ovarian Steroids

Over the years, researchers have measured estrogen and progesterone concentrations in the blood to determine whether there are abnormalities in women with PMS compared with normal healthy women. There are apparently no differences between groups in levels of these hormones in the blood across the menstrual cycle. However, there are some reasons to believe that progesterone may be a factor in the appearance of symptoms. First, the timing of symptoms is in the luteal phase after progesterone has been secreted. Second, when postmenopausal women received continuous estrogen replacement therapy and intermittent progesterone, symptoms appeared in some women when the progestin was administered. Despite the lack of evidence for a progesterone deficiency, and some data in support of a role for increased progesterone in *generating* symptoms, progesterone still is widely prescribed for PMS treatment. This will be discussed under Section IV.

b. Prolactin

Prolactin, a pituitary hormone responsible for milk production in women, has been postulated as a cause of PMS in part due to its role in fluid balance and the frequency of bloating as a premenstrual complaint. There do not appear to be differences in prolactin secretion between women with PMS and control women, so prolactin is not a likely cause of PMS.

c. Aldosterone

This hormone produced by the adrenal cortex is involved in fluid balance, and, like prolactin, was investigated in women with PMS because of the physical symptoms related to bloating and weight gain. Neither this hormone nor the renin-angiotensin system, also part of the fluid balance system, appears to be the causal agent in PMS.

d. Thyroid Hormone

There are some similarities between symptoms of patients with hypothyroidism and with PMS: fatigue, lethargy, irritability, anxiety. While there may be differences in the endocrine responses of women with PMS to challenge (stimulation) tests involving the thyroid axis, not enough data are available to know whether this hormonal system has a role or an association in PMS. However, a thyroid disorder, like other medical problems, should be treated before a diagnosis of PMS is given.

e. Insulin and Glucose Metabolism

Some symptoms of PMS (irritability, nervousness, sugar cravings, and fatigue) are also symptoms of hypoglycemia. Research has not shown any difference in glucose tolerance or insulin secretion across the menstrual cycle in women with PMS compared to control women. A hypoglycemia diet is, nevertheless, frequently recommended as a management strategy for women with PMS.

2. Serotonin

Serotonin, a brain neurotransmitter, has been studied in women with PMS since serotonin has been implicated both in depression and in disorders of impulse control. Studies of blood platelets, which provide a model for the physiology of serotonin in the central nervous system, suggest that women with PMS are different from control women across the entire menstrual cycle, not just in the symptomatic luteal phase. This finding is interesting since it implies that there may be trait differences in women with PMS (i.e., consistent differences) regardless of whether the women who suffer from PMS are having their symptoms at any particular moment. Trait differences in sleep and other parameters have also been noted in people who suffer from other disorders such as depression. Although the data do not conclusively show how serotonin may be involved in PMS, additional evidence that it plays a role comes from recent treatment studies of drugs that alter serotonergic functioning in the brain. Antidepressant drugs that release and/or block serotonin re-uptake into brain cells have been shown to be effective for women with LLPDD. Although this does not prove that serotonin is the cause of PMS, it does suggest that future research on serotonin as well as other

brain neurotransmitters could be very important. [See SYNAPTIC TRANSMITTERS AND NEUROMODULATORS.]

3. Circadian Rhythms

Some researchers have been interested in whether biological rhythms that repeat daily (circadian rhythms) are involved in PMS. There are abnormalities in certain hormone rhythms, temperature patterns, and sleep characteristics in depressed people. One research group has data that suggest that women with PMS are warmer at night than healthy normal women across the menstrual cycle, again a potential trait difference. There have been reports of differences in sleep characteristics in women with PMS, especially in deep (slow wave) sleep and dreaming (rapid eye movement) sleep, that are related to mood. Melatonin rhythms are also different in women in PMS. Taken together, these findings suggest that abnormalities in several biological rhythms are associated with PMS. It is unlikely that these abnormalities directly cause the symptoms of PMS. They may provide valuable clues as to the actual cause or causes of the disorder.

4. Prostaglandins

Prostaglandins have been studied as a factor in PMS since they influence hormonal actions in peripheral tissues (e.g., uterus), neurotransmission in the central nervous system, and pain. Both an excess prostaglandin theory and a prostaglandin deficiency theory have been proposed and are the bases for treatments. However, the role of prostaglandins is not yet clear.

B. Nutritional Etiologies

1. Vitamin B₆ (Pyridoxine)

Vitamin B_6 has been investigated extensively in women with PMS since the 1940s. There were several reasons why a relative pyridoxine deficiency could cause symptoms. Vitamin B_6 has a role in hormone metabolism, in neurotransmission with dopamine and serotonin, in prostaglandin synthesis, and in carbohydrate metabolism. None of these roles has been proven, and women with PMS do not appear to have a Vitamin B_6 deficiency. Yet despite the lack of supportive data, this vitamin is frequently prescribed for the treatment of PMS.

2. Calcium

Calcium supplements have been shown to be effective in treating symptoms of PMS. This research does not mean that low calcium intake is the cause of PMS. More research is required to fully elucidate the role of calcium in this disorder.

3. Magnesium

There are conflicting reports of differences in magnesium in blood or blood cells between women with PMS and control women. Whether magnesium plays a role in the disorder will probably be determined in the near future, but it has already been proposed as a supplement.

4. Caffeine

There has been some research on the association of caffeine with premenstrual symptoms, but little on women with PMS. Greater consumption of caffeinated beverages such as coffee and tea has been associated with more symptomatic menstrual cycles.

5. Daily Diet

One research group studied the daily intake patterns of women with PMS compared to control women and developed a classification system based in part on their food selection patterns and purported nutritional deficiencies. Their studies need to be replicated and additional research needs to be performed to determine whether food intake can alter mood, as has been suggested by work in other subject populations.

C. Psychosocial Causes

Stress of many types has been implicated as a factor in PMS. More frequent stressors or undesirable life changes have been associated with the number and severity of PMS symptoms. Additional work suggests that social support is also quite important in ameliorating negative life experiences. A women with low social support may experience her symptoms as more problematic.

Some researchers have suggested that women may report physical or emotional discomfort premenstrually because they expect or are conditioned to have symptoms. The problem with this theory is, however, that women with hysterectomies and intact overies still can experience "premenstrual" symptoms, even though there is no longer any physical marker (menses) of the phase of the menstrual cycle. This does not rule out a role for expectation entirely, but suggests that it cannot explain the presence of symptoms in all women with PMS.

D. Miscellaneous Causes

1. Allergies

An early theory about the cause of PMS was that women were hypersensitive to their own hormones or metabolites. This theory has not yet been substantiated, but antihistamines remain component parts of several over-the-counter preparations for PMS that are available today.

2. Yeast and Uterine Infections

Some research on the role of yeast infections and uterine infections has been performed. However, such medical problems should be treated first, before a diagnosis of PMS is made.

E. Summary

The conclusion from this section is that the etiology of PMS remains unknown. Future research needs to address possible different etiological bases for women with LLPDD and women with predominantly physical symptoms of PMS.

IV. DIAGNOSTIC PROCEDURES

A complete diagnostic evaluation requires not only a history of premenstrual symptoms, but a medical history and examination, a psychiatric history, a blood chemistry screen, complete blood count, and at least 2 months of prospective daily ratings of common menstrual cycle symptoms (Table II).

Women who are seeking immediate treatment may be less than enthusiastic about delays in treatment. However, the daily ratings are necessary since they are visual representations of the symptom patterns from the individual patient. Not all women with retrospective histories of PMS will ultimately receive the diagnosis.

TABLE II

Steps in a Diagnostic Evaluation

Medical and psychiatric history
Physical, gynecological and psychiatric evaluation
Blood tests
Two months of prospective daily symptom ratings

At the end of the 2 months of symptom charting, a diagnosis of PMS can be made. The diagnosis is based on (1) ruling out another physical or mental illness, and (2) demonstrating the appearance and severity of symptoms in the late luteal phase, and their disappearance in the follicular phase. The daily ratings will show that some women indeed have PMS or LLPDD. Others will have a pattern that is consistent with a chronic mood disorder such as dysthymia, that may or may not worsen premenstrually. Still others will have a persistent problem like dysthymia and new symptoms that appear premenstrually. Those women would receive two diagnoses. The last group of women will not have a pattern consistent with PMS or a psychiatric disorder. The management of these groups is discussed under Section V.

V. TREATMENT OPTIONS: RATIONALES AND SUGGESTIONS FOR MANAGEMENT

As mentioned earlier, over 80 different substances or methods have been proposed to treat the symptoms of PMS. Many of these treatments stem from the research on etiology regardless of whether the putative cause actually had empirical support. Others were suggested after a woman being treated for a different disorder reported that her premenstrual symptoms had also improved. The various treatments can be classified as follows: nonpharmacological techniques, using drugs to alter the menstrual cycle, modifying other hormones, altering prostaglandins, promoting diuresis, changing nutritional intakes, using psychotrophic medications, and miscellaneous treatments.

A. Nonpharmacological Techniques

Lay articles and many clinicians often recommend several initial steps for women with PMS to take before pharmacotherapy is begun. These steps include restricting salt, limiting caffeine, exercising, and eating frequent small meals. The problem with these interventions is that none has strong support from the research literature. It is possible for a woman to follow such a regimen assiduously yet continue to have symptoms, with the risk of decreased self-esteem as a result. The salt restriction suggestion is intended to decrease bloating and other symptoms related to water retention. No research study has been performed that can uphold this view,

but decreasing salt intake is a generally healthful suggestion. Since caffeine can cause irritability and nervousness, and these are symptoms associated with PMS, women are advised to limit their intake of caffeinated beverages such as coffee, tea and colas. Some research suggests that women who consume more caffeine have more severe symptoms. However, prospective research will be needed to confirm that this advice makes a difference for women with PMS.

Exercising aerobically is another healthful suggestion that may help women with physical symptoms related to water retention. However, more research on women with PMS is required to validate the recommendation. Eating frequent small meals stems from the view that some symptoms of PMS are similar to those of hypoglycemia. As discussed under Section III, PMS is not the result of impaired glucose tolerance. However, if a woman's primary complaint is food craving, then a dietary program may be helpful. Several groups have recommended relaxation therapy or other methods that can relieve stress and help women with PMS to rechannel negative thoughts. This research is in the early stages and needs to use more stringent experimental techniques to show that the behavioral interventions can be useful. More traditional psychotherapy has not been shown to be effective.

In summary, there is no reason that a women should be discouraged from trying any or all of the simple behavioral modifications once she has been diagnosed with PMS or LLPDD. However, she should bear in mind that they may not help her with all of her symptoms and that further intervention may be required. Support groups and education about PMS may also help symptoms seem more manageable.

B. Treatment Modalities That Alter the Menstrual Cycle

Since premenstrual symptoms occur during intervals of regular menstrual cycling and not when a women is pregnant, lactating, postmenopausal, or prepubertal, many researchers have used different techniques to modify the menstrual cycle. It is commonly held that ovulation is necessary for a particular cycle to be symptomatic, but this point has not been well-studied. Ovulation can be blocked through the use of oral contraceptives, estradiol patches, synthetic anti-estrogens, and gonadotropin releasing hormone (GnRH) agonists.

Oral contraceptives are not usually recommended for women with PMS since some women become depressed after starting them. Survey studies, while suffering from design problems due to their retrospective nature, do suggest that women taking oral contraceptives tend to report fewer and less severe symptoms than women using other forms of birth control. Estradiol patches such as those used to treat postmenopausal symptoms of estrogen deficiency can also block ovulation. Periodically, a woman needs to take some form of progesterone to avoid overstimulating uterine tissue. This dual-hormone regimen has been shown to be effective in treating the major symptoms of PMS, but the research needs to be replicated before the treatment regimen can be endorsed without reservations.

A synthetic androgen (male steroid hormone), danazol, can also block ovulation. It has been studied in PMS by several research groups and has some efficacy in symptom management. The drug has side-effects such as masculinization when given at higher doses that may limit its tolerance by the patient.

Drugs that mimic the action of gonadotropin releasing hormone (GnRH) block the menstrual cycle by interfering with the timing of the release of pituitary hormones that are responsible for ovulation. When menstrual cycles cease by this method, it is analogous to menopause in that ovarian steroid hormone (estrogen and progesterone) production is very low. If such drugs are used for long periods, the patient might be susceptible to symptoms of menopause and risks of osteoporosis or cardiovascular changes. While these drugs can demonstrate whether a break in menstrual cycling would be helpful to the patient, more chronic use would also require hormonal supplements like estrogen and progesterone replacement. While the use of GnRH agonists appears viable in the limited number of studies to date, more research will be required to determine the most effective therapeutic regimen.

Women sometimes undergo surgery to remove their ovaries and uterus to treat their symptoms. While this technique eliminates menstrual cycling and premenstrual symptoms, it is clearly irreversible. It may be appropriate for some older women with severe PMS that has not responded to less invasive methods of symptom management (i.e., hormonal manipulation).

C. Other Hormonal Treatment Techniques

1. Progesterone

Luteal phase progesterone therapy is one of the oldest yet controversial treatments for PMS. Its use stemmed originally from the theory that progesterone was deficient in the luteal phase relative to estrogen. As discussed under Section III, there does not appear to be such a deficiency in women with PMS.

Open trials of progesterone, where both the patient and clinician knew what she was taking, reported its effectiveness as a treatment. However, well-designed, double-blind placebo-controlled studies were not able to show that progesterone is more effective than placebo. In a double-blind study, neither the clinician nor the patient knows which drug the patient is taking. Thus, progesterone cannot be recommended as a treatment option for PMS even though it is widely used as such.

2. Bromocriptine

Bromocriptine is a drug that decreases the release of prolactin. It was tested in women with PMS since one theory held that prolactin levels might be elevated in PMS. Double-blind studies have not supported its use to treat mood symptoms. Bromocriptine is not well tolerated and many only be helpful for breast pain. Therefore, it should not be used to treat PMS.

3. Thyroid Hormone

Due to similarities in symptoms between PMS and hypothyroidism, thyroid hormones have been studied as a treatment. Despite initial enthusiasm from an open trial, a more carefully designed study with placebo controls could not show that thyroid hormone was any more effective than placebo. A thyroid disorder should be looked for and treated before PMS is diagnosed.

D. Treatments Related to Prostaglandins

Since there are theories about excessive and deficient prostaglandins as the causes of PMS, it is not surprising to find both prostaglandin inhibitors and precursors as treatment recommendations.

1. Prostaglandin Inhibitors

Mefenamic acid, a prostaglandin inhibitor, has been shown to be more effective than placebo in treating some symptoms of PMS. The problem is that the symptoms that improved were not consistent across studies, including such major ones as depression and irritability. Naproxen has also been studied for women with PMS. Only symptoms related to pain improved more with active drug than with placebo. Taken together, the results of these studies suggest that prostaglandin inhibitors may be useful for the treatment of physical symptoms of PMS related to pain.

2. Prostaglandin Precursors

Free fatty acids are prostaglandin precursors. A rich source is evening primrose oil, which has been recommended for women with PMS. However, well-designed studies have not shown that evening primrose oil is more effective than placebo. Therefore, it should not be recommended.

E. Treatments That Alter Fluid Balance

Over the years, many different types of diuretics have been tested for PMS. The results of these studies suggest that bloating and weight gain can be minimized, but that other symptoms of PMS may not improve. Further, only women who actually gain weight during the premenstruum may benefit. Thus, diuretics should be reserved for women whose predominant symptoms are related to fluid retention.

F. Treatments Related to Nutrition

1. Vitamin B_6

Vitamin B_6 is frequently recommended as a therapy for PMS. The research literature is contradictory on its usefulness. Many of the reports were either open or had experimental or analytic design flaws that hamper their interpretation. Another problem with Vitamin B_6 as a treatment is related to safety. It is established that large daily doses of Vitamin B_6 can cause damage to the peripheral nervous system. There appears to be a dose versus time relationship, which means that larger daily intakes can cause neurological problems sooner. Women with PMS do not appear to be deficient in this vitamin. Since the research literature is mixed on its efficacy and since the underlying rationale for its use is weak (Section III), Vitamin B_6 is not recommended as a treatment for PMS.

2. Calcium

Calcium supplements (1000 mg/day) have been shown to be effective in treating women with PMS. Whether calcium deficiencies can lead to symptoms remains to be determined. Women should be encouraged to obtain the recommended daily intake of calcium before a diagnosis of PMS is made.

3. Tryptophan

Before tryptophan was removed from the over-the-counter market, this amino acid precursor of seroto-nin was sometimes recommended for the treatment of PMS symptoms. There has not been a controlled trial of tryptophan alone, and a study of Vitamin B_6 plus tryptophan did not indicate that the combination was effective. Therefore, tryptophan cannot be recommended to treat PMS.

4. Vitamin and Mineral Supplements

There are specific combination vitamin and mineral supplements that have been formulated to treat PMS. The research, while apparently favorable, suffers from design or statistical problems. Further, the recommended dose of the combination supplement would provide high levels of Vitamin B_6. These supplements are not recommended for women with PMS.

G. Psychotropic Drugs

Even though affective symptoms are quite often the most troubling symptoms that lead women to seek treatment, studies of antidepressant drugs have only recently begun to appear in the literature. One of the reasons why studies of these drugs may have lagged behind is the need to have a patient take medication every day of the menstrual cycle for most of these drugs to be effective. If a woman experiences symptoms for only a few days per month, the benefit to her may not exceed the risk of side effects. Another reason could be that women with PMS may be reluctant to seek help from a mental health professional because of the perceived stigma of mental illness, even though mental health specialists have specific expertise in the use of psychotropic drugs. However, with the new diagnostic classification LLPDD, more treatment trials are being performed with that specific population. The drawback is that the results will not be generalizable to women with milder affective premenstrual symptoms.

1. Alprazolam

Alprazolam is an anxiolytic (anti-anxiety) drug that has been shown to be effective for the treatment of irritability, depression, and anxiety when given during the symptomatic luteal phase. This drug is sedating and can cause tolerance and dependence. Therefore, a clinician must be familiar enough with his/her patient to know whether the drug can be safety prescribed for her.

2. Fluoxetine

Fluoxetine is an antidepressant drug that has been shown to be effective in women with LLPDD. While this drug appears to be promising for LLPDD, additional research should be performed to determine long-term safety and efficacy as well as its applicability for women with less severe PMS.

3. Clomipramine

Clomipramine is a tricyclic antidepressant that has been studied for the treatment of irritability and dysphoria. It also appears promising, but additional research should indicate whether other symptoms may be improved by this treatment modality.

4. Fenfluramine

Fenfluramine is an anorectic (appetite suppressing) drug that has been used successfully to treat women with premenstrual depression and carbohydrate craving. Its usefulness for women with PMS featuring other symptoms is not clear, so it cannot be recommended for PMS at this time.

5. Lithium

Lithium, a drug that is used to treat mania, prevent depression, and serve as an adjunctive antidepressant, has been evaluated in open trials and in placebo-controlled studies. It has not been shown to be more effective than placebo for PMS.

H. Miscellaneous Treatment Modalities

1. Over-the-Counter (OTC) Medication

There are a number of OTC products that are combinations of a diuretic, an antihistamine, and an analgesic. The use of an antihistamine is interesting since one of the early theories about the cause of PMS was related to allergies. There has apparently not been a controlled trial of those drugs in combination published in the research literature, and thus, they cannot be recommended. Other OTC medications contain nonprescription diuretics. These products also lack research support.

2. Bright Full-Spectrum Light

One research group compared bright full spectrum light exposure in the evening and in the morning for the treatment of women with PMS. Light treatment is currently the treatment of choice for seasonal affective disorder, a depressive disorder characterized by dysphoria (dysphoria refers to chronic low mood), sleep disturbances, carbohydrate craving, and subjective cognitive complaints that are reminiscent of PMS. The long-term effectiveness of light

TABLE III
Recommended Nonpharmacological
Management Techniques for PMS and LLPDD

Education about PMS using results of symptom ratings
Limited caffeine
Regular physical exercise
Good sleep hygiene
Adequate calcium intake

treatment compared with placebo is needed to validate this therapeutic modality.

VI. SUMMARY

Recommendations for symptom management are summarized in Tables III and IV. Simple behavioral changes may help some women with PMS. Most women with more severe symptoms will probably need additional symptom management using medication. Women with psychiatric diagnoses with or without additional premenstrual symptoms should be referred to an appropriate mental health professional. Women who come for an evaluation believing that they have PMS, but whose symptom patterns show that they do not, may need counseling or a referral as well.

Despite decades of research, investigators have yet to discover the etiology and treatment for PMS.

TABLE IV
Pharmacological Managements Techniques
with Support from the Research Literature

For women with PMS and LLPDD: Agents that alter the menstrual cycle
GnRH agonists with steroid hormone replacement
Estradiol patches with intermittent progestin
Danazol
For women with LLPDD: Psychotropic medication
Fluoxetine
Clomipramine
Alprazolam
For women with predominant, severe physical symptoms
Breast pain—bromocriptine, tamoxifen, danazol
Premenstrual headache or migraine—standard analgesics
Water weight gain—diuretic

It is fair to say that more is known about what PMS is *not* than what it is. More research is needed that differentiates between women with physical problems and those with LLPDD. Based on recent treatment and etiology studies, that appears to be the trend.

Bibliography

Severino, S. K., and Moline, M. L. (1989). "Premenstrual Syndrome: A Clinician's Guide." Guilford, New York.
Spitzer, R. L., Severino, S. K., Williams, J. B. W., and Parry, G. L. (1989). Late luteal phase dysphoric disorder and DSM-III-R. *Am J. Psych.* **146,** 892–897.

PROBLEM SOLVING

Richard E. Mayer
University of California at Santa Barbara

Glossary

Computer simulation Programming a computer to solve a problem as a human would.

Deductive reasoning Applying the rules of logic to premises in order to generate a conclusion.

Heuristics General strategies for problem solving; also called weak methods.

Inductive reasoning Inferring a rule based on a series of instances or examples.

Insight The act of mentally restructuring a problem.

Means–ends analysis A problem solving heuristic in which a problem solver recognizes obstacles and selects means for eliminating them.

Problem Any situation in which a problem solver has a goal but does not know how to accomplish it. Well-defined problems have clearly described given states, goals states, and allowable operators whereas ill-defined problems do not. Routine problems can be solved by applying a procedure that the problem solver already knows whereas nonroutine problems cannot.

Problem representation Cognitive processing that transforms a presented problem into an internal mental representation of the problem. Problem translation refers to encoding each sentence or unit of the problem and problem integration refers to building a unified mental model of the situation described in the problem.

Problem solution Cognitive processing that devises and carries out a plan for solving a problem. Solution planning is devising and monitoring a plan; solution execution is carrying out the plan.

Problem solver A person, animal, or machine engaged in problem solving activity.

Problem solving Cognitive processing directed toward achieving a goal, including problem representation and problem solution.

Problem space A description of the problem that includes the given state, goal state, and all possible intervening states.

Strong methods Specific problem solving procedures that apply to a limited set of problems.

PROBLEM SOLVING is cognitive activity directed toward achieving a goal. Consider a physician who is given information about a patient and must make a medical diagnosis, a shopper who must determine which of two jars of peanut butter is the better buy, a chess player who must generate the next move in a game, a student trying to solve a homework problem in physics, or a scientist who wishes to test a theory about the flow of electricity. These situations are examples of problem solving. The physician, the shopper, the chess player, the student, and the scientist are each problem solvers.

I. WHAT IS A PROBLEM?

A *problem* exists when a problem solver has a goal but does not know how to accomplish it. A somewhat more precise way to express this definition is to say that the problem is in a given state, the problem solver wants the problem to be in the goal state, and there is no obvious way of changing the problem from the given state to the goal state. For example, for the physician, the given state is the patient information, such as the results of heart tests as well as the patient's descriptions of chest pain, and the goal state is a description of the patient's ailment, such a defect in a specific valve in the heart. This is a problem because the path from the given state to the goal state is not obvious. In contrast, for the shopper, the choice of best buy would be obvious if the market listed the unit price of each item on the shelf.

Problems can be classified as routine or nonroutine. In a routine problem the problem solver knows a procedure to solve the problem. For example, the need to multiply 378 by 15 is a routine problem for someone who knows how to carry out long muliplication. In this case, the problem solver does not immediately know the answer but does know how to produce it. In contrast, a nonroutine problem occurs when the problem solver does not know a procedure that is certain to generate an answer. For example, the need to create an experiment to test a new theory about electricity is a nonroutine problem because the problem solver does not possess a pre-existing technique for solving the problem. In general, complex human problem solving involves non-routine rather than routine problems.

Problems can also be classified as well-defined or ill-defined. A well-defined problem has a precise given state, goal state, and set of allowable operations. For example, finding the value of X in the equation $X^2 + 2X + 4 = 0$ is a well-defined problem because the given state is precisely presented (i.e., $X^2 + 2X + 4 = 0$), the goal state is precisely presented (i.e., find a value for X), and the allowable operators are precisely given (i.e., use the rules of algebra and arithmetic). Ill-defined problems lack a clearly presented given state, goal state, and/or set of operators. For example, the problems of how to end an economic recession or how to choose a spouse are ill-defined. In general, complex human problem solving involves ill-defined problems.

II. WHAT IS PROBLEM SOLVING?

Problem solving is cognitive activity aimed at changing a problem from the given to the goal state. In short, problem solving refers to directed cognitive processing. Problem solving is directed because the problem solver is motivated by a desire to achieve a goal; problem solving is cognitive because it occurs within the problem solver and can only be inferred from the problem solver's actions. Problem solving is a process because information is mainpulated or operated upon within the problem solver. This definition is broad enough to encompass making medical diagnoses, determining best buys, generating chess moves, solving physics problems, and discovering scientific theories, but does not include nondirected thinking such as daydreaming.

The term "problem solving" sometimes can be used interchangeably with thinking and cognition. Inductive and deductive reasoning can be seen as subcategories within the broader category of problem solving. Inductive reasoning refers to inducing a rule based on a series of instances or examples. For example, solving a series completion problem such as 2–4–6–___ involves inducing the rule "add 2 to the number." Deductive reasoning involves applying the rules of logic to premises in order to generate a conclusion. For example, if Alice is taller than Betty, and Betty is taller than Carmen, then deductive reasoning can be used to conclude that Alice is taller than Carmen. In inductive reasoning, the problem solver cannot be sure that the conclusion is correct because not all possible examples are given. In deductive thinking, if the premises are correct and the rules of logic are correctly applied, then the problem solver can be certain that the conclusion is correct. Both inductive and deductive reasoning are involved in many problem-solving situations. [*See* DEDUCTIVE REASONING; REASONING.]

Problem solving methods can be classified as weak or strong. Weak methods are general problem-solving techniques that can be applied to a wide array of problems, such as finding a related problem, breaking a problem into parts, or working backward from the goal to the givens. Weak methods can be called heuristics—general rules of thumb that provide direction but do not guarantee an answer. In contrast, strong methods are specific procedures that apply to a specific domain of problems, such as using the long multiplication procedure to solve a multiplication problem. In general, experts use strong methods whereas novices use weak methods to solve problems in a given domain, such as physics professors and beginning students solving physics homework problems. However, in some cases, even experts must use weak methods, such as experienced physicians confronted with a difficult case of medical decision making.

III. WHO IS A PROBLEM SOLVER?

A problem solver is an intelligent being who recognizes that a problem exists. A situation that represents a problem for one problem solver may not be a problem for another. For example, a particular chess move in a game may be a problem for a novice but not for an expert who has memorized a ready-made move for that situation.

Although this article focuses on human problem solving, there is reason to suspect that problem solving is not confined to our species. One issue concerns whether non-human animals think. There is ample evidence that some animals form hypotheses, make inductions, and solve problems both in the laboratory and in the field. A second issue concerns whether machines think. Evidence is increasing that computers can be programmed to become creative problem solvers, including programs that can make medical diagnoses or play chess at a competitive level.

IV. PHASES IN PROBLEM SOLVING

The process of problem solving can be analyzed into problem representation and problem solution. Problem representation occurs when the problem solver transforms the presented problem into an internal mental representation of the problem. This phase involves understanding the problem. For example, consider the representation of a word problem such as, "Gas at ARCO costs $1.13 per gallon. This is 5 cents less per gallon than gas at Chevron. If you want to buy 5 gallons of gas at Chevron, how much will you pay?" To represent this problem, the problem solver must encode each sentence—a subprocess that Mayer calls problem translation–and build a unified mental model of the situation being described in the problem—a subprocess that Mayer calls problem integration. Problem translation includes being able to translate each of the three sentences into other forms of representation such as, "ARCO = 1.13," "Chevron − .05 = ARCO," and "5 × Chevron = ____." Problem integration includes the recognition that gas at Chevron costs more than gas at ARCO.

Problem solution occurs when the problem solver devises and carries out a plan for solving the problem—subprocesses that Mayer calls solution planning and solution execution, respectively. For example, a student's plan for the ARCO problem might be to determine the cost of a gallon at Chevron and then to determine the cost of 5 gallons at Chevron, yielding a two-step problem. In executing the plan the student must be able to carry out the arithmetic operations of addition of decimals, such as $1.13 + .05 =$ ____, and multiplication of decimals

and whole numbers, such as $5 \times 1.18 =$ ____. The problem solver also must monitor his or her solution plan to make sure it is working.

V. APPROACHES TO THE STUDY OF PROBLEM SOLVING

The history of scientific research on problem solving, which is less than 100 years old, has been influenced by three competing approaches—associationist, gestalt, and cognitive science. The associationist approach views thinking as a chain of mental associations, in which one idea is associated with another and so on. The associationist approach motivated the earliest research on problem solving, including Thorndike's studies of how cats learn to get out of a puzzle box that has a trap door. According to Thorndike's theory, the problem solver possesses a set of responses associated with any problem situation based on past experience. When confronted with a problem situation, the problem solver tries the strongest response associated with the situation; if it works the association is strengthened and if it does not work the association is weakened. Although associationist theories are useful in describing problem solving in familiar situations, their value in explaining creative problem solving has been criticized.

The gestalt approach, which developed in the 1920s through the 1940s, viewed problem solving as mentally restructuring the problem, that is, as seeing the problem in a new way. The act of restructing a problem is called insight and often involves overcoming previous experience which blocks new ways of seeing the problem. For example, Kohler observed an ape in a cage with crates on the floor and bananas attached overhead and out of reach. To solve the problem of getting bananas that are out of reach, the ape had to view the crates as a potential staircase rather than as containers; this insight provided a restructuring of the problem in which the crates could be used to reduce the distance between the ape and the bananas. The gestalt approach to problem solving emphasizes the creation of a novel solution, but the theory has been criticized for lack of precision.

The cognitive revolution, which began in the late 1950s, offers the most recent approach to problem solving. Cognitive science views thinking as a series of mental operations (or computations) that are applied to knowledge in the problem solver's memory.

For example, Newell and Simon produced computer simulations of human problem solving, that is, they programmed computers to solve problems in the same way as humans. Successful problem solving requires domain-specific knowledge as well as general strategies for how to solve problems. Problem solvers must build a problem space—a representation of the given state, goal state, and all possible intervening states—and must use a strategy such as means–ends analysis to find a path through the problem space from the givens to the goal. In means–ends analysis, the problem solver works on one goal at time by continually asking, "What do I need?" and "How can I get what I need?" The cognitive science approach, with its emphasis on thinking as making mental computations, is precise; however, it has been criticized for its lack of attention to practical problem solving in realistic social contexts. Finally, human problem solving occurs within the human brain and nervous system, so recent advances in cognitive neuroscience (the study of the biological bases of cognition) can contribute to a fuller understanding of problem solving.

VI. PAST AND FUTURE RESEARCH TRENDS

Traditionally, research on problem solving has focused on how people solve puzzles and games in controlled laboratory situations. For example, in the Tower of Hanoi problem, the problem solver is given three pegs and three disks as shown in the top of Figure 1, and the problem solver's task is to move the three disks to the third peg as shown in the bottom of Figure 1. However, the problem solver is allowed to move only the disk on top of the pile on any peg to the top of the pile on another peg and may never place a larger disk on top of a smaller one.

In contrast, recent research has focused on problem solving in more realistic situations. Research on

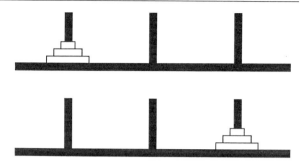

FIGURE 1   The given and goal state of the Tower of Hanoi problem.

expertise examines differences between expert and novice problem solving in professions such as computer programming, medicine, and science. Research on everyday thinking examines how people solve problems that occur naturally at work or in shopping. Research on analogical reasoning examines how people use previous problems to solve new problems. Research on intelligence seeks to understand intellectual abilities and disabilities in terms of the underlying cognitive processes. Research on teaching of thinking examines how to help people become more effective problem solvers. [*See* ANALOGICAL REASONING.]

Bibliography

Gilhooly, K. J. (1988). "Thinking; Directed, Undirected, and Creative," 2nd ed. Academic Press, London.
Lave, J. (Ed.). "Cognition in Practice." Cambridge University Press, Cambridge, England.
Mayer, R. E. (1992). "Thinking, Problem Solving, Cognition," 2nd ed. Freeman, New York.
Newell, A., and Simon, H. A. (1972). "Human Problem Solving." Prentice-Hall, Englewood Cliffs, NJ.
Osherson, D. N., and Smith, E. E. (Eds.) (1990). "Thinking, An Invitation to Cognitive Science," Vol. 3. MIT Press, Cambridge, MA.
Sternberg, R. J., and Smith, E. E. (Eds.) (1988). "The Psychology of Human Thought." Cambridge University Press, Cambridge, England.
Wertheimer, M. (1959). "Productive Thinking." Harper & Row, New York. [Reprinted by University of Chicago Press.]

PSYCHOLOGICAL PREDICTORS OF HEART DISEASE

Howard S. Friedman
University of California at Riverside

Glossary

Coronary heart disease Blockage and hardening of the coronary arteries which supply the heart, due to build-up of fatty plaques on the artery wall.

Fight or flight response The body's physiological response to significant challenge, involving activation of the sympathetic nervous system and the release of stress hormones.

Self-healing personality A psychosocial reaction pattern that leads to good physical health, characterized by an enthusiastic, positive emotional style, an alert, energetic motivation, and secure, constructive interpersonal relations.

Social support Emotional, informational, or tangible resources provided by family or friends.

Type A behavior pattern An emotional and behavioral style characterized by a chronic, aggressive struggle to accomplish more and more in the shortest possible time period.

THERE IS substantial evidence that psychological factors predict heart disease and premature mortality. What is less clear are the causal pathways and causal mechanisms. Many people assume that stressful patterns of psychological reaction and associated unhealthy habits can increase the likelihood of heart disease—a blockage (occlusion) of a coronary artery or an irregular heartbeat (arrhythmia). There is relatively little surprise among observers when a heart attack victim is a hard-working 50-year-old obese businessman who is known for chain-smoking cigarettes and compulsively devouring doughnuts while screaming into two telephones that he wants that shipment "YESTERDAY." The scientific difficulty comes in separating fact from stereotype—that is, in discerning which if any behavioral patterns are solid predictors of increased likelihood of heart disease.

There are three basic kinds of relations between psychology and heart disease. First, psychological factors can play a direct causal role in increasing the likelihood of disease. That is, physiological stress reactions and unhealthy habits can dramatically increase one's risk. Second, underlying (third) variables like genetic abnormalities can produce both distinctive psychological profiles and elevated disease risk. In such cases, psychological patterns are associated with disease but interventions to affect the psychological factors may or may not have any effect on the likelihood of disease; the relation may be spurious. Third, psychological correlates of disease may be the result of the disease process. For example, depression may follow a heart attack. In such cases, psychological interventions obviously will not affect health risk unless the factors are also tied through other pathways. All of these three sorts of ties between psychological factors and heart disease have been shown to exist, thus making simple explanation and simple amelioration problematic. Nevertheless, much is known about healthier and unhealthier psychosocial living patterns.

I. HISTORICAL PERSPECTIVE

Psychological predictors of heart disease have been noted since ancient times. There are biblical proverbs on this matter, such as "Gladness of the heart is the life of a man, and the joy of a man prolongs his days" (Apoc. 30:22). The ancient Greeks were especially keen observers of the relations between psychological factors and illness. They were good at describing nature, but not so good at causal mechanisms. Their idea of essential bodily fluids or "humors" was intriguing but of course erroneous. The four bodily humors—black bile (or melancholy), blood, yellow bile (or choler), and phlegm—were said to lead to proneness to depression and degenerative disease, or to a sanguine and ruddy disposition, or an angry (choleric), bitter and unhealthy persona, or to a phlegmatic, cold, apathy. As this humoral explanation of physiology was found to be incorrect, it was gradually discarded over the centuries. Unfortunately, so too was the scheme of the four emotional aspects of personality that so influenced medical practice for 2000 years. Hostility, cheerfulness, depression, and apathy are indeed useful patterns for understanding psychology and health. The ancient Greeks had correctly observed psychosocial correlates of disease but their causal mechanisms were wrong.

In the first half of the 20th century, there was again considerable interest in the psychological predictors of heart disease. The influential medical educator Sir William Osler proposed a link between high-pressure activity and coronary heart disease; and the well-known psychiatrists Karl and William Menninger asserted that heart disease is related to repressed aggression. Psychosomatic theorists developed and applied the psychoanalytic notions of Sigmund Freud to their patients, looking for repressed conflict as a cause of chest pain and heart disease. Psychological treatments often proved helpful. These physicians were all trying to account for the dramatic rise in coronary heart disease that was occurring in the 20th century. Since the 20th century was also a time of rapid social and technological change, it made sense to look for explanations in the pressure and demands of modern-day life. However, most of this work was clinical and speculative. It was not until the 1950s that the idea of a Type A person was proposed and led to substantial controlled empirical research.

The Type A behavior pattern was proposed by two cardiologists—Ray Rosenman and Meyer Friedman—who noticed that their patients possessed a distinctive constellation of psychological characteristics. Since traditional risk factors like high blood pressure hardly did a complete job in accounting for heart disease risk, the cardiologists began a systematic search for psychosocial and behavioral predictors of heart disease. These efforts led to three decades of intensive research, upon which our current understanding rests. [*See* TYPE A–TYPE B PERSONALITIES.]

Current research indicates that certain people are psychologically vulnerable or resilient due to a combination of temperament and early socialization. When vulnerable people encounter psychosocial environments that are a poor match for their needs, chronic negative emotional patterns often result. These reactions are accompanied by physiological disturbance—high levels of sympathetic activation and cortisol, and possibly other hormones. And, unhealthy behaviors such as substance abuse may also occur. Finally, these disturbances interact with disease-proneness caused by heredity (e.g., proneness to the build-up of plaque in the coronary arteries) and environment (e.g., high fat diets). The resulting increased risk of illness is comparable in size to that of many other commonly noted health risks.

II. DISEASE-PRONE PERSONALITIES

There is strong reason to believe that stress, chronic negative emotions, and poor social relations can play a role in the development or triggering of cardiovascular disease and heart attacks, and in impairing postsurgical recovery. The evidence is as strong as or stronger than the findings usually trumpeted about concerning the effects of diet, environmental pollution, body weight, exercise, and similar health factors. Unfortunately, this psychosocial evidence often goes mostly unnoticed by a biomedically oriented health care system. For an acute, life-threatening illness like a heart attack, doctors in their super-high-tech medical centers often work miracles. Yet there is a hefty percentage of the population heading for expensive and dangerous coronary bypass operations (or the newest high-tech equivalent), while psychosocial preventive measures are sometimes ignored.

Originally (in the 1960s and 1970s), research on the Type A behavior pattern focused on individuals who are aggressively involved in chronic struggle to quickly achieve more and more in less and less time. But many active, expressive people often tend to work hard and hurry around like Type A people but are not at all coronary-prone; on the contrary, they are especially healthy! In addition, many so-called

"Type B" people (supposedly stress-free) are not really calm and healthy, even though they look superficially like Type B's; rather their emotional conflicts are repressed. The Type A concept has therefore been deemed inadequate to capture the richness of individual differences in emotional response. It often is too imprecise to predict heart disease. Rather than being "wrong," the Type A construct has inspired research that has led to its being surpassed and encompassed. Subsequent research suggests that hurrying around or working hard is not necessarily unhealthy. Rather, hostility and aggressive or cynical struggle seem predictive of disease.

Use of the statistical technique called meta-analysis (which is a sophisticated kind of statistical average, across different studies) has allowed investigators to address the broad issue of psychological predictors of heart disease and to help us look at how big an effect is; it also points us toward specific patterns of findings, rather than just vague general impressions. The degree of consistency in the overall findings is remarkable. Results consistently indicate significant relations between chronic emotional disturbance—namely, hostility and depression—and coronary heart disease. These associations are similar in size to those of other risk factors such as diet and lack of exercise.

III. SOCIAL INTEGRATION

A variety of sociological and epidemiological investigations indicate that people who are well-integrated into a stable community are less likely to develop heart disease or die prematurely. It appears that when faced with life change and the stress experienced as a result of it, the support of family and friends can significantly aid one's coping. (Social support comes from the friendly ties an individual has with family, associates, neighbors, and the community.) Conversely, the sudden loss of social ties seems to have a dramatically negative effect. Community studies have consistently shown effects of social ties on cardiovascular health—people with fewer community ties are more likely to become ill and die. [See COPING; SOCIAL SUPPORT.]

How does social support work? First of all, social support can sometimes influence an individual's coping by affecting how stressful events are appraised. For example, if one knows other people who have gone through the same challenging experience, the experience may be seen as less stressful.

More importantly, social support may help one deal with the emotional consequences of stress. (Not surprisingly, this is termed emotional social support.) Social support can also help the stressed individual develop new coping strategies by providing information about how to deal with the stress. This informational support often goes hand in hand with emotional support, but sometimes it comes alone in the form of written materials about how to deal with the challenge. Finally, social support may also operate by providing tangible resources. This is called instrumental support. Instrumental support might sometimes be harmful if it made the recipient feel inadequate, indebted, or unduly manipulated. Social support is especially important when a person faces a severe challenge such as the challenge of chronic cardiovascular illness.

Social integration may also protect against heart disease by providing an opportunity for self-disclosure. Scattered lines of evidence suggest that it is healthy to be able to discuss one's feelings and self-image with at least one intimate friend or companion. The degree of importance and the generality of this phenomenon are not yet known.

Hostile and cynical people are likely to have interpersonal disputes, due to their suspicious, competitive, irritating style. This may lead to poor health in three ways: by interfering with social support, by exacerbating any tendencies toward physiological hyperreactivity, and by placing the individual into more stressful situations—an onslaught of major and minor hassles. In short, although there is good evidence that people who live in stable families and in stable communities are more protected from heart disease, it is not yet well understood how these factors are related to the other relevant psychosocial influences on health.

IV. CAUSAL MECHANISMS

Efforts to identify a coronary-prone personality or a coronary-prone behavior pattern focus on two sorts of mechanisms or pathways through which psychological factors can help bring about disease. These are nervous system and hormonal mechanisms, and behavioral mechanisms.

A. Psychophysiological Mechanisms (Nervous System and Hormonal)

Most often implicated are physiological disturbances involving high sympathetic (and sometimes parasympathetic) activation. This activation is commonly summarized as the "fight or flight" response—the immediate internal bodily response to danger. However, some people are quite frequently in this state of agitation. The links to sudden death via autonomic nervous system-induced arrhythmias of the heart are documented: when psychological stress, such as seeing a shocking scene of mutilation, or when physical stress such as shoveling heavy snow becomes too great, the heart may beat uncontrollably and irregularly and soon fail. But such fatal events are relatively rare, especially as compared to chronic but slow artery obstruction. It is also the case that such irregular, fatal heartbeats are much more probable when there is partial pre-existing heart disease.

The links to atherosclerotic disease—the major type of heart disease in which fatty plaques build up on the arteries that supply the heart with blood—are necessarily more problematic. Sympathetic nervous system arousal has numerous effects, including increased physical stress on the arteries and changes in lipid (fat) metabolism. It appears that both the physical stress of high blood pressure and the metabolic effects on blood lipids (fats) promote plaque formation.

Experimental studies demonstrate that social stress promotes atherosclerosis among monkeys straining to maintain a position of social dominance. When the composition of monkey groups is changed by the experimenter, those monkeys struggling for dominance face ill health. Further, those animals with the greatest heart-rate reactivity show the most coronary artery damage and act more aggressively, again suggesting the relevance of the "fight or flight" physiological response. These experiments confirm clinical studies of humans regarding aggressiveness and struggle. Since this artery damage in monkeys can be prevented by a beta-blocker (Propanolol), the evidence again points to harmful effects of excessive activation of the sympathetic nervous system, by social struggle. Everything else being equal, the modulation of sympathetic arousal is likely to promote physical health, in both monkeys and people.

Less well understood are hormonal effects. Both nervous system arousal and other forms of psychophysiological imbalance such as depression alter the usual complement of bodily hormones. For example, stress, helplessness, and depression are linked to high cortisol levels; and stress, anger, and frustration are linked to high levels of catecholamines (such as of norepinephrine). Increasing attention is turning

to the possible links between such matters and heart disease. Other stress-related or stress-influenced hormones such as thyroxin, testosterone, and other hormones have also been shown to play a significant role in stress-related homeostasis and physical health. No study has yet followed the whole process, showing for example that hostile people develop certain psychophysiological disturbances that impair metabolism and thereby bring on heart disease. [See HORMONES AND BEHAVIOR; STRESS AND ILLNESS.]

There is weak but accumulating evidence that the repression of thoughts or feelings, partly genetically based, is a form of stress that is accompanied by detrimental psychophysiological arousal similar to that of the other disease-prone states. Speculation has centered on chronic autonomic arousal. Ongoing research will shed light on the complex issues of emotional self-regulation; it is unlikely that a simple hydraulic model of "bottling-up" versus emotional "discharge" will prove relevant. Indeed, the issue of whether to repress or express negative emotion may be somewhat of a red herring; the problem seems to arise from having the chronic imbalance in the first place.

B. Behavioral Mechanisms

Personality-based behavioral patterns likely have an independent effect as well as interacting with stress-related psychophysiological influences on cardiac health. For example, a major problem in medical care is the patient's failure to cooperate with treatment. A host of individual and psychosocial characteristics affect whether a patient will take medication, follow a low-fat diet, return for follow-up, and so on. The patient's sense of self-efficacy and confidence that success is achievable is one dimension often found to relate to healthy behavior. Relatedly, failure to take prophylactic measures may be associated with sensation-seeking, low conscientiousness, hostility, low self-esteem, or other traits. Tendencies toward denial or excessive optimism may result in a deadly delay in seeking treatment. [See SELF-EFFICACY; SELF-ESTEEM; SENSATION SEEKING.]

Regarding substance abuse, there is evidence that hostile and neurotic people are more likely to smoke, drink to excess, and/or use drugs, thereby increasing their risk of heart disease. There is also evidence that people low in ego strength, that is, low on conscientiousness, are similarly at risk. Surprisingly, there is very little prospective study of such potentially important relations of personality, unhealthy behavior patterns, and subsequent health. [*See* SUB-STANCE ABUSE.]

Depression (and possibly repression) is clearly associated with a whole host of behavioral risk factors for disease including disturbances in eating and sleeping, impaired social relations, as well as substance abuses. Here again, however, little is known of the causal pathways. Prospective clinical studies of depression and of substance abuse could prove especially informative if they also included psychophysiological measurement, general assessment of health behaviors, and heart disease outcomes. [*See* DEPRESSION.]

V. NONCAUSAL EFFECTS

Some of the association between psychological variables and heart disease is due to noncausal pathways. The development of heart disease can produce dramatic psychological and social changes in the patient's life. Heart attack victims (who survive) may become angry at the world for their plight. Or they may become depressed about the new limitations on their activities. They may lose their job or may be treated differently by their employers or their colleagues. Sexual relations with one's partner may change, as fear, fatigue, or resentment enters the relationship. In all of these cases, psychological and behavioral patterns are a result rather than a cause or predictor of heart disease. (Nevertheless, these factors or patterns may then predict or contribute to further deterioration, through the causal mechanisms described above.) Interestingly, some disease predictors may act differently following a heart attack. For example, anxiety that contributes to the development of disease may prove helpful after the attack if it leads the patient to cooperate more fully with medical treatment. We should not expect the same factors to predict disease and recovery from disease, although this error of inference is often made.

Spurious relations between psychological variables and heart disease may result from underlying third variables that produce both the psychological characteristics and the disease. For example, men are less likely to be nurturant than are women, and men are more likely to die prematurely from heart disease; but it is not likely that nurturance is a key causal factor. Similarly, various genetic patterns affect both personality and health, but interventions to change these aspects of personality would not necessarily lead to improvements in health.

A final type of noncausal association between psychological variables and heart disease results from methodological artifacts. A common artifact here is a selection artifact or bias. For example, consider the case of neuroticism, angina, and angiography. Neurotics are more likely (than nonneurotics) to persistently seek out medical care, even when there is little or no discernable organic disease. When such patients are referred by their cardiologists for angiography (a picture of their coronary arteries), an interesting relation emerges. Neuroticism is found to be inversely related to arterial blockage, since only the neurotics (with clean arteries) and nonneurotics (with true blockage-caused pain) are in the sample. This artifact might obscure a true causal relation between neuroticism and the development of disease, and so such artifact-laden studies should not be undertaken. Analogously and more simply, a high percentage of cardiology patients may be found to be neurotic; the explanation is a selection artifact.

VI. SELF-HEALING PERSONALITIES

In the field of medicine, it is too often assumed that health is simply the absence of disease. In medicine, a negative test result is good news—it means the disease is not there. But little attention is paid to the positive, proactive elements of good health. In fact the word "health" itself is often corrupted. To speak about people who stay healthy and resist disease, the awkward term "wellness" must be used. However, despite a few polite nods toward behavioral science, most medical students do not take serious courses on wellness after their pathology course. This problem is not the fault of individual health care providers, but rather is a systemic flaw. That is, the medical care system is designed mostly to fix illness problems, not to prevent health problems. What is a healthy psychological pattern?

Briefly stated, a good way to characterize the self-healing personality is in terms of enthusiasm. The word enthusiasm literally means "having a godly spirit within." Enthusiastic people are alert, responsive, and energetic although they may also be calm and self-assured. They are curious, secure, and constructive. There are several good clues that indicate emotional balance and an inherent resilience. Enthusiastic, sanguine people tend to infect others with their exuberance. They are not ecstatic but rather are generally responsive and content. They are people one likes to be around. They are not downcast or shifty-eyed. They smile naturally—the eyes, eyebrows, and mouth are synchronized and unforced; there is usually no holding back of expression of pleasant feelings. Such enthusiastic people have smooth gestures, that tend to move away from the body; they are less likely to pick, scratch, and touch their bodies. They are not apt to make aggressive gestures with their hands. Emotionally balanced individuals not only walk smoothly, they talk smoothly. They are inclined to show fewer speech disturbances such as saying "ah," and their speech is modulated rather than full of sudden loud words. Their voices are less likely to change their tone under stress. Obviously, there are exceptions to these rules: A single nonverbal gesture does not tell us much. Still, lab research has shown how valid information can be gathered about a person's healthy emotional style from just a few episodes of social interaction.

A sense of continual growth and resilience is also relevant. Dr. Walter Cannon, who developed the ideas of homeostasis upon which modern notions of self-healing are built, emphasized that the body has developed a margin of safety. By this Cannon meant that the body has allowance for contingencies, that we may count on in times of stress. The lungs, the blood, and the muscles have much greater capacity than is ordinarily needed. In other words, the body naturally prepares itself for the rare "extra" challenge, and self-healing people do what they can to increase these margins of safety. William James, who anticipated much of our modern scientific understanding of emotional responses, summed up this idea succinctly when he advised, "Keep the faculty of effort alive in you by a little gratuitous exercise every day. That is, be systematically ascetic or heroic in little unnecessary points, do every day or two something for no other reason than that you would rather not do it, so that when the hour of dire need draws nigh, it may find you not unnerved and untrained to stand the test" (*Principles of Psychology,* 1890, Chapt. 4).

Self-healing personalities have often been described by existential and humanistic psychologists, although they usually thought they were describing only mental health, not physical health. For example, Abraham Maslow pointed out that healthy people first need to achieve balance in their basic biological needs, and then affection and self-respect. But he emphasized what he called self-actualiza-

tion—the realization of personal growth and fulfillment. People with this growth orientation are spontaneous and creative, are good problem-solvers, have close relationships to others, and have a playful sense of humor. They become more concerned with issues of beauty, justice, and understanding. They develop a sense of humor that is philosophical rather than hostile. They become more ethical and more concerned with the harmony among members of the human race. These characteristics of the self-healing personality are not merely the opposite of such disease-prone characteristics as suspiciousness, bitter cynicism, despair and depression, or repressed conflicts, but are positive, meaningful motives in their own right. Similarly, Viktor Frankl, the existential philosopher and therapist who developed his theories of a healing personality as an inmate in a Nazi concentration camp, noted that survival was more likely for those who tried living in a meaningful way, even in dire straits.

Like much of social and behavioral science, psychosocial prescriptions for good cardiovascular health often sound like "common sense," until the matter is examined more closely. In actual fact, it is very difficult to walk the fine line between narrow-minded biomedical views of the nature of health that exclude psychosocial factors, and the unscientific touchy-feely health gurus who proclaim oversimplified and overgeneralized prescriptions for good health.

VII. INTERVENTIONS

In the practice of medicine, and to a lesser extent in the practice of public health, the relevant question that always jumps to the forefront is "What psychosocial interventions can be made to reverse, prevent, or stop the progression of heart disease?" Given that cardiovascular disease is by far the greatest cause of premature mortality, and given that the social and economic costs of heart disease are overwhelming for both families and society, what can be done? Unfortunately, various sorts of unsubstantiated advice are often given based on scanty evidence. Since the various elements of a self-healing (or a disease-prone) personality are usually intercorrelated, teasing out the causal pathways is a major challenge, one that has been given relatively little research attention or funding.

There is good evidence that lifestyle changes affect the incidence of heart disease. Most of this evidence is epidemiological and anthropological, showing that when people move from one country or one cultural group to another, their heart disease rate can change dramatically. There is also some experimental evidence indicating that dramatic lifestyle changes can improve aspects or correlates of cardiovascular health. A serious problem with this work is that little is known about which components of the healthy, self-healing lifestyle are the necessary causal elements.

For example, consider Japanese immigrants entering America. They leave a close-knit, well-ordered society with an Asian diet and Asian recreation patterns, and they (or their children) enter an individualistic, heterogenous American society with very different social and recreational patterns and a hamburger stand on every corner. If heart disease rates rise, what is to blame? We simply do not know. Nutritionists may point to fish oils or fat intake; religionists may point to meditation patterns; sociologists may point to family structure; psychologists may point to stress reactions. There is evidence that some or all of these points may be valid.

What about specific recommendations that are often heard regarding individuals at risk for an initial or recurrent heart attack? For example, is it really healthy to retire and get away from the stresses of the workplace? In fact, retiring may be very stressful and unhealthy, or it may be helpful. It all depends upon the particular individual and the particular situation. Retiring has been shown to be unhealthy if it results in a diminution of social ties, inadequate financial resources, and psychological states of uselessness or boredom. On the other hand, retirement may be healthy if it reduces the psychosocial stress of the workplace and increases opportunities for healthy habits. In addition, changing societal reactions to retirement can be extremely important—in terms of social security programs, health insurance, laws that prohibit age discrimination, opportunities for educational and social activities, and so on.

Can heart disease be reversed by meditation? Meditation is now being used in several popular programs, in combination with diet and exercise to reduce stress. This is sometimes even covered by medical insurance. Is stress a risk factor for heart disease? Yes. Has it been shown through controlled study that increasing the incidence of meditation is key to reducing the incidence of heart disease? No. Meditation is wonderful for some people, but others may find it stressful or silly. And, there is no good evidence that meditation is superior to other forms of systematic relaxation.

Is it healthy to be optimistic and look on the bright side? Although it seems to be the case that a sense of willpower and positive hopes for the future can help us through difficulty, it is also the case that optimism can lead us to be shocked by reality or to avoid taking necessary prophylactic measures. It makes sense, as has been found, that for a heart disease surgical patient, optimism is helpful. It does not, however, make sense to assume that optimism will prove helpful to a chain smoker or an ice cream addict. The emphasis on optimism without sufficient regard to context is an example of the search for the psychosocial equivalent of a "miracle drug" that can cure all disease.

Are societal pressures encouraging jogging the key to protecting one's heart? It is very clear that a cigarette-smoking obese person who cannot walk up a flight of stairs is at markedly increased risk of heart disease; and this often has led to the incorrect belief that being in shape means the ability to run 6 miles each morning. In actual fact, the benefits of aerobic exercise rapidly reach an asymptote. A brisk walk or swim for 30 minutes every other day seems to do it. People struggling miserably each morning to get "in shape" may be harming their health.

Is it unhealthy to work long hours? In actual fact there is no evidence at all that it is unhealthy to be a "workaholic" if all the other elements of self-healing are in place. That is, hard work and long hours themselves have never been shown to be a risk factor. On the contrary for example, many powerful or influential executives, leaders, artists, and scientists work exceedingly long hours and live long and healthy lives. This is an illustration of where an overgeneralized stereotype of Type A behavior leads to an inaccurate conclusion about behavior and health.

Is all this information common sense? Do physicians and others commonly accept that psycho-emotional reactions can affect cardiovascular health and recovery. Not at all. There are regularly major reports published which break the "news" that some medical researchers are now urging that psychological and emotional reactions of patients be taken into account. Such considerations generally still lie outside the traditional medical model of disease that focuses primarily on pharmaceuticals and surgery.

VIII. CONCLUSION

Contrary to some common conceptions, most of the past increase in adult life expectancy in the developed countries has come not from high technology medicine but rather from infection control techniques, low-cost inoculations, improved sanitation, nutrition, and other public health improvements. Antibiotics have also made a significant difference, but visits to super-specialized cardiologists at university hospitals produce limited impact overall when the big picture is considered. This is not to say that a heart disease patient would not be wise to seek out such a specialist, but only that the overall public health benefit of such high-cost cardiology care is relatively small. However, there is reason to suspect that dramatic (and low-cost) improvements can be realized if we put our knowledge of self-healing to good use. Societal and lifestyle changes may be the psychosocial equivalents of improved sanitation, nutrition, and infection control.

The scientific evidence for self-healing—prevention of and recovery from heart disease—is much stronger than many skeptical doctors imagine, but different from what many health gurus proclaim. Individuals who learn their own psychosocial needs and develop appropriate techniques of self-regulation can maximize their potential for good health. And these psychological styles can be significantly complemented by societal structures that promote healthy reaction patterns and behaviors.

Bibliography

Friedman, H. S. (Ed.) (1990). "Personality and Disease." Wiley, New York.

Friedman, H. S. (1991). "The Self-Healing Personality: Why Some People Achieve Health and Others Succumb to Illness." Henry Holt, New York.

Friedman, H. S. (Ed.) (1992). "Hostility, Coping & Health." American Psychological Association, Washington, DC.

Houston, B. K., and Snyder, C. R. (Eds.) (1988). "Type A Behavior Pattern: Research, Theory, and Intervention." Wiley, New York.

Matthews, K. A., et al. (Eds.) (1986). "Handbook of Stress, Reactivity, and Cardiovascular Disease." Wiley, New York.

Miller, T. Q., Turner, C. W., Tindale, R. S., Posavac, E. J. and Dugoni, B. L. (1991). Reasons for the trend toward null findings in research on Type A behavior. Psychol. Bull. 110(3), 469–485.

Sarason, B. R., Sarason, I. G., and Pierce, G. R. (Eds.) (1990). "Social Support: An Interactional View." Wiley, New York.

Schneiderman, N., McCabe, P., and Baum, A. (Eds.) (1992). "Stress and Disease Processes." Erlbaum, Hillsdale, NJ.

Schneiderman, N., Weiss, S. M., and Kaufmann, P. G. (Eds.) (1989). "Handbook of Research Methods in Cardiovascular Behavioral Medicine." Plenum, New York.

Siegler, I. C., Peterson, B. L., Barefoot, J. C., and Williams, R. B. (1992). Hostility during late adolescence predicts coronary risk factors at mid-life. Am. J. Epidemiol. 136(2), 146–154.

PSYCHOLOGY AND PSEUDOSCIENCE

I. W. Kelly and D. H. Saklofske
University of Saskatchewan, Canada

Glossary

Astrology A pseudoscience based on the belief that strong correlations exist between the positions of constellations and planets and their relationships with terrestrial affairs.

Birth chart A grouping on paper of information obtained from the heavens. These "birth maps" are interpreted by astrologers to allegedly provide information about the subject.

Pop psychology Popular psychology of the marketplace. It relies on testimonies and experiences of the writers rather than reflection and research. Testing of essential claims is not conducted. Negative cases and alternative conceptions are typically ignored or insufficiently considered.

Pseudoscience A theory or approach that portrays itself as a science but falls short in a number of essential aspects. A pseudoscience is usually not based on diverse supporting evidence from well-conducted studies and the conceptual structure of the theory has not been refined over time adequately in response to research findings. In addition, it has not contributed research to new areas, nor is it compatible with well-supported theories in related domains.

Psychology The scientific study of human behavior, including overt behavior and mental processes.

Science An approach using a diverse set of methods to understand the natural world. A central component of science is its reliance on testing or demonstration of claims rather than reflection alone or appeals to authority.

THE MAIN GOAL of psychological science is to fit our theories about ourselves to the social and physical world. Such knowledge can be used to explain, understand, predict, and even change human behavior. Unlike other disciplines or perspectives that also claim to contribute to our knowledge about ourselves and the world (e.g., religion, philosophy), science relies in a central way on the testing and demonstration of the very claims it makes. In contrast to commonsense, personal beliefs, or pseudosciences, this is accomplished by the development of paradigms or research traditions. Of course, the term pseudoscience implies that there exists a contrast, namely science proper. The distinction is not always clear and at times it is difficult to determine if some description of human behavior is a scientific or pseudoscientific one. However, pseudosciences are approaches that *pretend* to be something they are not. They suffer from deficiencies both in experimental findings and in the rigor of the research methods employed that would allow them to claim to be a science.

I. PSYCHOLOGY: THE SCIENTIFIC STUDY OF BEHAVIOR

Psychology is a science that studies behavior, not only overt or observable behavior but also mental processes such as thoughts, attitudes, and feelings. As a science, psychology employs systematic and controlled procedures for obtaining and analyzing information. Attempts to organize the observations and findings often result in theories. While a theory may attempt to explain particular findings, it also generates new ideas or hypotheses that can be tested. Thus, a theory is not so much right or wrong as it is either more or less useful as a tool for studying human behavior.

Psychologists create hypothetical constructs to aid in discussing human behavior. Thus, concepts such as intelligence, extroversion, anxiety, achievement motivation, sensation seeking, and self-concept describe hypothesized internal conditions of the individual, while concepts such as social support and classroom climate refer to external features of the psychological environment. Many of these concepts are referred to as variables since they are not static or fixed. For example, psychologists have demonstrated that intelligence has a strong genetic basis. The measured IQ between identical twins is much more similar than between fraternal twins, siblings, half siblings, cousins, and finally, unrelated individuals. However, research has also shown that the environment impacts on the development and expression of intelligence. Culture, family factors, and educational opportunities can all influence measured intelligence. Thus, intelligence is not a fixed or static concept but one that varies as a result of particular conditions. [See INTELLIGENCE.]

Once psychologists have put forward these variables, they begin to examine the possible relationships among them in order to create principles. Thus, psychologists may not only study arousal (those reactions that cause a person to be alert and attentive) but also observe the effects that arousal has on performance such as solving mathematics problems of varying degrees of difficulty. Through carefully controlled studies, it may be observed that a moderately high level of arousal promotes better performance on very simple tasks. However, when more complex problems are presented, lower levels of arousal are related to better performance in contrast to higher levels which tend to detract from or interfere with performance. Another example is the Premack Principle. By carefully observing the different effects that naturally occurring rewards, such as commonly engaged in activities, have on an individual's behavior, it was suggested that any highly preferred and engaged in activity (e.g., playing computer games, working at a favorite hobby) could be used as a reinforcer to increase less frequently occurring but desirable activities (e.g., cleaning your room; completing homework on time).

II. THE ROLE OF THEORY IN SCIENCE

As research findings accumulate about these concepts and principles, theories are created to attempt to pull them together into a more coherent, organized, and logical system. In the process, these theories then allow for the generation of hypotheses or predictions that may either be confirmed through rigorous testing or suggest that the theory is less

useful for explaining the very phenomenon it was designed for. If the former holds true and consistently strong support emerges for these hypotheses, the theory, in turn, is supported. Alternatively, a lack of confirmation or support for the hypotheses generated by the theory requires either that the theory be modified, restricted in application, or that it be abandoned in favor of alternative theories. For example, Hans Eysenck's original theory of extraversion relied very heavily on Pavlovian views of inhibition and excitation but the results of various research investigations suggested the initial theory was inadequate. Thus, Eysenck refined his theory so that introversion and extraversion are now hypothesized to be related to differences in cortical arousal associated with the ascending reticular activating system (ARAS). [See EXTRAVERSION–INTROVERSION.]

While scientists and research psychologists seem to be able to patiently test ideas and cope with the various different theories put forward to describe human behavior, this can be very confusing and irritating to the general public. Thus, while psychologists debate the intricacies of human memory or argue whether reinforcement is necessary in learning, the general public wants answers. Parents who refer their child for learning problems are not interested in discussions about the various causes of learning disabilities but rather what can be done to improve their child's situation in school. Of course, we all wish for a complete understanding of the cause(s) of AIDS and more importantly a cure, but in the meantime we must continue to actively research the disease and use all of our current knowledge to assist HIV-infected individuals. Wishful thinking and pop remedies (some of which are fraudulent and only intended to benefit the seller) will not cure this horrible disease. The same applies to the study of human behavior; pop psychology and pseudopsychology may have great surface appeal to many people but in the final analysis, they bring us no closer to the "truth" about human behavior.

III. SCIENTIFIC METHOD

Psychology's claim to being a science is grounded in the use of systematic observation and data collection with the attempt to minimize bias as the basis for gaining increased understanding about human behavior. Various research methods are used to gather information and to test hypotheses and generate new findings. Correlational research is designed to explore the extent that two or more variables are related. Information is carefully collected through questionnaires measuring particular psychological variables (e.g., IQ, anxiety, self-concept, attitudes), naturalistic observations (e.g., observing the frequency of occurrence of inattentive behaviors exhibited by an ADHD child), interviews (e.g., "how do you most effectively cope with job stress?"), and other techniques. Through such research, it may be determined that, for example, IQ scores of children are highly correlated with such home factors as parental encouragement to achieve and the opportunity for language development. IQ scores also show a moderate relationship with school achievement. While these findings are only correlational and therefore do not imply a causal relationship, they do describe and can be used to predict behavior. Thus, IQ scores are quite reliable predictors of elementary school achievement as suggested by correlational studies. As always, the results need to be replicated and the studies must be carefully conducted in the first place. The saying respecting computer data, "garbage in–garbage out" also applies to psychological research. Like scientists from other disciplines such as physics and biology, psychologists are most interested in discovering causal or cause-and-effect relationships among variables. While the chemist knows that a mix of hydrogen and oxygen produces water, the psychologist is interested in addressing questions such as can intelligence be raised by creating more stimulating environments for children? Does cognitive–behavioral therapy result in greater improvement for depressed patients than other therapies? Does viewing TV violence result in increased aggression among children and adolescents? Whenever possible, psychologists are interested in conducting *experimental* studies to investigate these questions. [*See* COGNITIVE BEHAVIOR THERAPY; VIOLENCE, OBSERVATIONAL EFFECTS ON BEHAVIOR.]

The intention of an experiment is to impose the necessary controls that will allow the researcher to determine what factors are responsible for any changes observed. Often there is one or more 'treatment' groups and even a control group that receives no treatment. Participants are carefully assigned to groups so as to ensure there are no pretreatment conditions or characteristics unique to one group that could affect the results. Once assignment to the experimental or control groups has occurred, the treatment(s) is administered and the effects are carefully observed, measured, and recorded. The treatment variable or the one believed to be responsible for any observed changes is called the independent variable. The dependent variable is the one that changes because of the treatment. A simple example should assist in clarifying the nature of a psychological experiment, although it should be remembered that most experiments are extremely complex.

Let us say that a university professor is concerned about the lack of participation and involvement by students registered in a first-year psychology course. Despite the professor's request for students to ask questions or respond to questions posed in class, there is very little student participation. Further, the professor is convinced that greater student interaction in class should have a positive effect on student grades. Since the professor teaches several sections of introductory psychology where students are randomly assigned to a given class, a study is created whereby group 1 is verbally reinforced ("thank you for such a good question, Cameron," or "that was a great answer, Genevieve; you have quite correctly outlined the purpose of the clinical interview") for questions asked and answered, or information sharing on an appropriate topic. Group 2 is told that up to a 5% bonus mark will be awarded to students who volunteer answers, ask questions, or volunteer content-related information in class (average of 1 question/answer/comment per class = 1% up to 5 or more questions/answers/comments per class = 5%). Group 3 receives only the usual request to participate in class. A graduate student is asked to record the class participation on a specially designed data sheet. At the end of a 3-week unit on memory and forgetting, a carefully constructed objective test is administered to the three classes. The results suggested that the average participation rate per person and exam mark, respectively, for group 1 was 2.9 and 78%, for group 2 the results were 2.5 and 76%, while the results for the control group were 0.6 and 70%. Group 1 and 2 were very similar in achievement and participation and certainly more active and higher achieving than group 3. Further, the results comparing the two treatment groups with the control group were found to be statistically significant ($p < .05$). Thus, the professor concludes that even though these were all university students and quite intelligent, learning could be enhanced through the use of strategies designed to promote more active participation in class.

A question that is often asked by psychologists is "are the groups really different, or did the results occur by chance?'' The above example indicated the probability that the differences between groups was due to chance is unlikely; if this study was repeated 100 times, such a difference would occur less than 5 times if only chance was operating. If the differences between the groups are very unlikely due to chance, then the psychologist will conclude that there is likely a difference worthy of further investigation. Other psychologists will then try to successfully replicate the results and extend the study using other designs or variables to further increase our knowledge base.

Psychology is the scientific study of human behavior, but other scientific and nonscientific claimants also profess to further our understanding of humankind. For example, cultural anthropology, philosophy, history, and sociology are all alternative ways of conceptualizing human behaviors ranging from aggression to altruism. While these disciplines vary along the scientific continuum and may even, as in the case of philosophy, be a more reflective approach, they all employ critical analyses and/or rigorous testing procedures of their claims and applications. The results of inquiry in turn modify the tenets of that discipline. In contrast, other efforts to characterize human behavior fall short with respect to a critical, reflective usage of their own tenets and findings and can in the extreme case be considered a pseudoscience. We will use astrology as an example of the latter type of enterprise.

IV. ASTROLOGY: AN EXAMPLE OF A PSEUDOSCIENCE

Astrology contends that there is a strong relationship between particular planetary and stellar configurations in the heavens and terrestrial affairs. More specifically, the birth time and place on earth of an entity (person, animal, country, company, etc.) allows the contruction of an astrological chart for the frames of reference provided by the astrologically significant indicators such as signs, houses, and planetary aspects. On the basis of the interpretation of the birth chart, astrologers claim that they can obtain information about a particular individual's character and life.

Astrology is based on several principles. One is ''as above, so below,'' implying an association (not necessarily a causal relationship) between terrestrial events and heavenly configurations. Another principle is ''the stars incline, they do not compel.'' This states that the relationship between the heavens and human behavior is one of tendency and is not simple cause and effect. A third principle is that ''the whole is more than the sum of its parts,'' namely that the astrologically significant indicators such as signs, houses, and planetary aspects cannot be viewed in isolation. Rather, they interact and modify each other.

Astrological practitioners contend that the tenets of astrology are based on ''practical'' research or clinical observation, rather than on the findings of experimental studies. In other words, these tenets have allegedly been arrived at by the ''critical'' observation and discussion among astrologers of case studies of clients (including presumably, countries, companies, and pets).

A. Astrological Theory: A Critique

Theories can be evaluated according to their track record of past successes and their research potential. These involve an examination of a theory's empirical/conceptual performance over a specified interval of time. Some considerations here are the success of the theory's problem-solving ability in its domain, and whether the theory has opened up new areas of investigation or extended fertile problem-solving resources without the resort to ''face-saving'' ad hoc hypotheses. The track record of a theory can also be evaluated on the elaboration and progress of its conceptual resources in helping us understand the social/natural world. Not only should the conceptual structure of a theory become more refined over time in response to research, but the conceptual changes should direct and facilitate empirical research.

The conceptual/empirical performance of the field of astrology is extremely unimpressive. There is little or no understanding by astrologers of the kinds of biases in judgment that plague clinical observation in all areas of inquiry, including psychology and medicine. The reason controlled studies and experiments are used in psychology and disciplines such as biology in the first place was to rule out as much as possible memory, perceptual, and reasoning biases as well as alternative explanations. While case studies may play a role in generating hypotheses, they are too fraught with error to be convincingly used as methods of confirmatory research.

If the claims of astrologers were based on observation then they would have been confirmed long ago by statistical tests, which basically do what any astroler does (that is, look for correspondences) only with a much greater sensitivity. But they do not.

The claim that astrological interpretations developed as a result of clinical observation is like claiming to know the effect of each of 20 chemical elements on every feature of every plant in your garden. Any reader who has tried to interpret a four-way interaction in an analysis of variance (ANOVA) will appreciate the problem if 15 to 20 or more factors are involved! The problem of examining the relationship between many variables has led to the development of sophisticated research tools in psychology such as LISREL, path analysis, and multivariate statistical models.

Astrology has an unimpressive track record. Its problem-solving ability in the domain of understanding human behavior is noteworthy by its lack of success. Well over 100 controlled studies of signs, aspects, whole charts, and so on now exist, and indicate that overall the effect sizes (the impact of the variables in questions) are, at best, trivial. Moreover, there is nothing hinting at the sort of internal consistency that would arise if it was all real, like the effect size for whole charts being bigger than for parts. A meta-analysis (a statistical method of combining the results from many research investigations) on studies involving a number of prominent astrologers clearly showed that astrologers (even world famous ones) tend not to agree on an interpretation of birth charts.

B. The Work of Michel Gauquelin

Astrologers have made much of the research conducted by the late Michel Gauquelin of France and colleagues. His empirical research into astrology was conducted over a 40-year period. Gauquelin's negative results regarding zodiac signs, planetary aspects, and tests of astrologers are seldom mentioned by astrologers or are explained away. Instead, astrologers have claimed, and misinterpreted, Gauquelin's positive findings as support for astrology.

Gauquelin forwarded three findings that are relevant to astrological theory. The first is that there is a relationship between planetary positions in the sky at the birth of *eminent* people in *some* occupations. For example, Mars tended to occur more often in certain sectors of the sky at the birth of outstanding athletes in some (but not all) sports. The planetary relationships did not hold with ordinary people or less eminent sportsmen. The effects were also very weak, needing large sample sizes for detection. In addition, there are nonastrological explanations for the occupation–planetary link. For example, Arno Muller in Germany has pointed out that in ancient times (Babylon and before) being born under a particular planet conferred a *social advantage* related to the astrologically symbolized planetary nature (e.g., Mars = warriors). Over the generations, Muller suggests this advantage may have led to the inheritance of a planetary sensitivity, which can still be detected today among the elite.

Hence, Muller explains the Gauquelin planetary–occupation relationships by a sort of self-attribution. Geoffrey Dean has modified Muller's suggestion by pointing out that the notion of a development of "planetary sensitivity" is problematic and the same self-attribution explanation occurs by substituting "the faking of birth times" for "the inheritance of planetary sensitivity." Hence, even if Gauquelin's hypothesis of a relationship between planetary position at birth and elite performance in some professions is reliable it may not be related to astrology except peripherally, since it could be ultimately a socially/culturally constructed relationship. When astrologers cite the Gauquelin research as supporting astrology they neglect to inform people that Gauquelin only found planetary relationships at the birth of *eminent* individuals and not the rest of us. Second, Gauquelin only found some of the planets were associated with eminence, namely, the moon, Venus, Mars, Jupiter, and Saturn. He uncovered no relationship with the astrologically important sun, Mercury, Uranus, Neptune, and Pluto, and no relationship between zodiac signs or planetary aspects and the occupations of eminent or ordinary people. Third, the relationships uncovered by Gauquelin were very weak; there was little overall difference between effective and ineffective planets. Hence, while the results would be of theoretical interest, they would have no practical benefit for astrological practice.

Gauquelin later offered two other claims, partly to explain the link between eminent individuals in some occupations and planetary positions at birth. One of these was to suggest a relationship between planetary position at birth and temperament. Gauquelin later claimed that the underlying link between occupation and planetary position was temperament. The stronger the traits, as exhibited by top individuals in certain fields, the stronger the relationship uncovered. For example, Mars is associated with strength and violence, and individuals outstanding in careers needing those traits should have, more often than those less eminent, Mars in certain sectors of the sky at their birth. However, Suitbert Ertel, a German psychologist, has found substantial biases on the part of Gauquelin regarding the temperament (trait) hypothesis, and has published a number of papers on this topic. Gauquelin's trait research was based on trait extractions from the biographies of famous individuals. Ertel found that, using the same biographies as Gauquelin, the latter extracted more "typical" traits for the relevant planets than did extractors who were "blind" to planetary position. When coupled with other biases found by Ertel, it seems likely that Gauquelin's planetary–trait hypothesis will be, at best, severely weakened, and at worst, demolished.

The combination of an occupation/trait link to planetary position suggested a third hypothesis to Gauquelin, namely that the planetary relationships might be linked to hereditary factors. An initial study by Gauquelin with 24,961 parents and children showed that children tended to be born with the same particular planets in certain sectors of the sky as their parents. However, a replication by Gauquelin himself with 50,942 parents and children in 1988 found no relationship. This leaves the reality of the Gauquelin heredity effects also in doubt.

The British astronomer Percy Seymour has written several books on astrology that have received media attention. Like Gauquelin, Seymour rejects much of astrology, including zodiac signs. Seymour's entire case for astrology rests on the Gauquelin data, which as we have seen, is now far less solid, at least in regards to his trait and heredity hypotheses than it was a decade ago. Seymour has attempted to explain Gauquelin's findings in terms of geomagnetic activity which induces currents in an individual's neural network by resonance. Seymour fails to answer the most important question of all, how does the fetus connect with the relevant planets in the first place? In addition, the planetary frequencies Seymour refers to are so microscopically weak that it seems doubtful to say the least that any organism could respond to them. Finally, Ertel in Germany found no evidence of geomagnetic influences in his reanalysis of Gauquelin's data which in effect, nips Seymour's theory in the bud. The reader should also notice that any *physical* explanation put forward for astrology creates other problems for astrologers. Astrologers will produce not only a birth chart for people and animals but anything that has a "moment of birth," including a company or a country. How could a physical force imprint itself on the nature of a company or country at its "moment of birth?"

C. Astrological Practice: A Critique

Astrological *practice* has also not produced concrete evidence of its efficacy. When astrologers are asked to produce evidence of the validity of astrological practice they usually cite testimonials or case histories. Popular astrology books contain case studies involving the birth charts or horoscopes of famous individuals which after the fact invariably show a close connection between the interpretation of these individual's birth charts and their significant personality characteristics and life events. These case studies, however, should not be persuasive because of the large number of components in a birth chart which allow the interpretation of a birth chart to be made to fit almost any individual's life. As an example of this, at a British conference dealing with research into astrology, Geoffrey Dean showed that British singer Petula Clark's horoscope matched her biographical details exactly; the horoscope was then revealed to be that of U.S. murderer Charles Manson.

Counselling success with clients carries the most weight with astrologers. The assumption here is that a horoscope based on an individual's true birth date would be more accurate and informative than one based on wrong birth dates or someone else's birth date. This assumption which lies at the heart of astrology is not supported by the evidence. Let us briefly consider reasons to support this skepticism. First of all, astrologers themselves do not seem to be able to distinguish between correct and incorrect horoscopes for well-known individuals. There are a number of published horoscopes that are based on *in*correct birth data but purportedly describe the people involved perfectly. The German astrologer Peter Niehenke came across three different astological publications, each containing a different horoscope of the late ex-Beatle John Lennon, each based on a different birth time, and each indicating "definitely" the time of Lennon's tragic death. Second, most investigations of the validity of personality interpretations based on horoscopes have found that people or clients of astrologers were unable to distinguish between authentic interpretations and false interpretations. In other words, wrong horoscopes are accepted as readily as right horoscopes.

The "remarkable correspondences" that astrologers find between horoscopes and the lives of their clients are therefore unpersuasive. Every system from phrenology to three-cycle biorhythms can produce similar "remarkable correspondences." One should also keep in mind that startling coincidences should be expected to occur in such situations, given the length of the typical horoscope, the number of astrological elements involved, the leeway in interpretation of the statements contained in the horoscope, and the human tendency to concentrate on successes and ignore failures. Astrologers have failed to provide evidence that clients would find more startling correspondences in birth charts based on an individual's correct birth data rather than incorrect birth data. In reference to Peter Niehenke again, he produced a horoscope for a client who was thrilled at its accuracy. The client told him that she had received horoscopes (based on accurate birth data) from several other astrologers and that his was the most thorough and accurate of all of them. Niehenke's pride was diminished when he discovered that the horoscope he produced was based on incorrect birth data—twenty years earlier than the client's actual birth date!

In a related vein, a number of studies have addressed the ability of astrologers using the complete horoscope to match individual horoscopes and various personal qualities, life events, handicaps, and so on. Some initial tests were made by the psychologist Vernon Clark. He carried out three tests, and each gave weak but positive results in favor of astrology. The studies by Clark are important because they have been widely cited as evidence for astrology. One problem with the studies is that no follow-up was conducted to measure the astrologers' skill again in a second test along the same lines or to extend the study in new areas. Also, equally competent astrologers from other countries (e.g., France) who tried Clark's tests failed and there was no evidence that the professional French astrologers had abilities inferior to those from other countries. In a rigorous study conducted by Geoffrey Dean in Australia, individual's horoscopes were altered to make them as opposite in meaning to the authentic horoscopes as possible: thus extraverted indications were substituted for introverted, stable for unstable, tough for tender, ability for inability, and so on. It was found that reversed interpretations were accepted as accurate just as readily as authentic interpretations. In another set of studies Dean tested whether astrological theory or astrologers could predict two of the most important personality factors, namely, extraversion and emotionality in ordinary people. To this end, subjects with extreme

scores on the Eysenck Personality Inventory were selected from over 1000 people. The average pair of opposite extremes used in the test was roughly equivalent to the two most extreme persons in a random sample of 15 adults. In the first experiment, Dean tested whether computer analyses of astrological factors such as tropical signs, elements, sidereal signs, aspects, Gauquelin plus zones, angularity, and so on, both individually and in combination, could predict extraversion and neuroticism (emotionality) in extreme subjects. None of the astrological factors, either singly or in combination, performed better than chance. In a second experiment, Dean tested whether 45 astrologers using the entire chart could predict extraversion and emotionality in ordinary people. He found that the well-known astrologers did no better than chance. In addition, there was no relationship with the astrologer's experience, sex, personality, or technique.

Fourth, and most importantly, Dean found (as in other studies) there is poor agreement among astrologers regarding what astrological factors should predict various personality characteristics and even astrologers using the same technique show little agreement. This suggests that each astrologer's technique and interpretation are highly individual. In other words, the results of Dean's study showed that astrologers do not usually agree on what a chart (horoscope) indicates, even when using the same factors! In practice, this means that a client visiting equally competent astrologers is unlikely to get similar horoscopes. Yet the client is likely to be satisfied with either horoscope. This is strong evidence that factors other than astrological ones are responsible for the perceived success of astrology.

V. CONCLUSION

Science is characterized by an emphasis on the demonstration of its claims. To this end, theories are constructed, refined, tested against alternatives, and re-constructed and refined. Theories exist on a continuum regarding quality and usefulness. These attributes reflect the track record of past successes and the theory's research potential. A good theory has success in its own domain, has opened up new areas of successful research, and has been conceptually modified in light of research findings. Theories can also be evaluated on the basis of their promise or research potential. While the past track record of a theory is relevant to the consideration of a theory's promise, other indices might be the production of analogies that direct researchers to examine problems in a new way, the introduction of new fruitful procedures for solving outstanding problems in an area, and the theory's consistency with well-established findings/theories in related domains.

As many of the expository articles in the *Encyclopedia of Human Behavior* show, psychology is a thriving, creative discipline. Many of the theories in psychology cannot yet duplicate the precision of those in the natural sciences—the sheer complexity, newness of many areas of psychology, and conceptual problems in the field mitigate against this, yet the field has advanced both conceptually and empirically over the last 100 years.

The reader will be able to contrast the expositions given in other parts of the *Encyclopedia of Human Behavior* with the pseudoscience of astrology. If we appraise astrology's present status we find a theory that has a very poor record of success in terms of studies obtaining positive evidence and, even less support once effect sizes are taken into account. Present day astrology has not opened up new areas of research. While some astrologers have written books on the position of astrology in medicine, politics, crime, economics, and so on, the books are notable more for their authoritative postures than research studies and calculations of effect sizes.

Astrology does not appear to have any prospect in sight for providing a plausible mechanism that would explain human behavior. Instead, astrologers have resorted to many face-saving hypotheses; for example, that the relationship between an individual's planetary positions at birth exhibits patterns that are acausally related (synchronicity) to that individual's earthly activities, or that astrology is only involved in subjective human experiences that involve individual perceptions. These are precisely the situations where misinterpretation of data and biased evaluations of ambiguous data are most likely to occur.

Astrological claims (albeit not the Gauquelin effect) are readily explained by the perceptual, inferential, and small-sample biases to which people in general are quite prone. For example, knowing that Scorpios are supposed to be secretive, our observations will invariably confirm it, simply because everyone is secretive at times and we are disinclined to test non-Scorpios.

Lest the reader come away with the impression that all that is put forward in the name of psychology is scientific, in contrast to other pretenders such as astrology, numerology, Tarot, and so on, we would caution the reader that there exists within psychology the same continuum. In psychology there exists areas of developed theory, confirmed laws, well-conducted replicated studies, in contrast to areas that are on a par with astrology. As an example of the latter, we would classify much of what could be termed pop psychology. Many pop-psychology books are million sellers and involve New Age (now misleadingly called "New Science") psychobabble regarding "co-dependency," "spirituality," "the adult child," "addictions," and a host of "recovery programs." These books and articles involve poorly articulated theory, the use of testimonials instead of clinical research, appeals to authority, the neglect of alternative explanations, and contradictory assumptions. In the final analysis, a useful understanding of human behavior will be best achieved by the development of rigorous testable theories that can be improved upon by careful analysis and evaluation in both laboratory and real-world settings. Psychology is committed to this ideal.

Bibliography

Dean, G. A. (1987). Does astrology need to be true? *Skeptical Inquirer* 9, 166–184, 257–273.

Dean, G. A. (1993). Review of "Astrology's Complete Book of Self-Defence" and "The Case For Astrology." *Skeptical Inquirer* 18, 42–49.

Ertel, S. (1992). Update on the "Mars effect." *Skeptical Inquirer* 16, 150–160.

Gambrill, E. (1992). Self-help books: Pseudoscience in the guise of science? *Skeptical Inquirer* 16, 389–399.

Gilovich, T. (1991). "How We Know What Isn't So: The Fallibility of Human Reason in Everyday Life." The Free Press, New York.

Hines, T. (1988). "Pseudoscience and the Paranormal." Prometheus Books, Buffalo.

Kaminer, W. (1992/1993). "I'm Dysfunctional, You're Dysfunctional: The Recovery Movement and Other Self-Help Fashions." Vintage Books, New York.

Kanitscheider, B. (1991). A philosopher looks at astrology. *Int. Sci. Rev.* 16, 258–266.

Kelly, I. W., Culver, R., and Loptson, P. (1989). Arguments of the astrologers. In "Cosmic Perspectives" (S. K. Biswas, D. C. V. Malik, and C. V. Vishveshwarda, Eds.). Cambridge University Press, New York.

Kelly, I. W., Dean, G. A., and Saklofske, D. H. (1990). Astrology: A critical review. In "Philosophy of Science and the Occult" (P. Grim, Ed.), 2nd ed. State University of New York Press, Albany.

Mueller, A., and Ertel, S. (Eds.) (1993). Astrologisches zuordnungsexperiment mit aerzte-horosckopen. *Zeitschritt fuer Parapsychologie und Grenzgebiete der Psychologie* 35.

Whitt, L. A. (1992). Indices of theory promise. *Philos. Sci.* 59, 612–634.

PSYCHOLOGY AND RELIGION

Ralph W. Hood, Jr.
University of Tennessee at Chattanooga

Glossary

Extrinsic religiousness Religious commitment based upon utilitarian motives.

Intrinsic religiousness Religious commitment based upon religion as an ultimate end in and of itself.

Myth Explanations as to the origin, meaning, and ultimate nature of life accepted as authoritative within a tradition. Some view religions as myths or at least as having mythical components. Others view some psychologies as also mythical or containing mythical components.

Parapsychology The study of a range of experiences, such as telekinesis, clairvoyance, mediumship, and apparitions, whose existence is disputed by some but a serious object of study by others. Many consider at least some parapsychological phenomena to be religious phenomena.

Postmodern A generic term referring to the multiplicity of perspectives and methodologies that coexist simultaneously. Postmodernism does not consider any one method or perspective ultimately more valid than another.

Psychedelic drug A generic term referring to drugs that facilitate a variety of states of consciousness that many see as either identical or similar to certain religious states.

Quest religiousness Religious concern based upon the questioning of existential concerns.

Reductionism The explanation of complex phenomena in terms of simpler phenomena. In psychology and religion this often means the explanation of religious phenomena by psychological processes.

Spiritual Referring to phenomena typically described within religious traditions that claim to transcend the corporeal or material.

Transcendent Referring to the ultimate object of religious participation.

PSYCHOLOGY *OF* RELIGION takes religious phenomena as objects of inquiry to be either described or explained by principles of psychology. Psychology *and* religion assumes equality between both disciplines, neither exhaustively explaining the other. Relationships between psychology and religion are complicated by the fact that little consensus exists on the meaning of either of these terms.

I. PSYCHOLOGY AND RELIGION

A. Religion Defined

Religion has proven notoriously difficult to define leading some to suggest that religion is a broad umbrella term having no consensually agreed upon common core. More promising have been phenomenological efforts to find common structures that traditions identified as religious might have in common. Under the influence of the philosopher Wittgenstein, the family resemblances of phenomena classified as religious have been sought. Typically these include (1) a concern with transcendent reality (whether or not conceived in personal terms); (2) a sense of intense seriousness or of ultimate concern; (3) a shared consensus rooted in faith concerning interpretations of transcendent reality; and (4) an imperative to act in the context of such shared concerns. Religions can be diverse in content and in their objects of worship, but few would accept as religious any tradition that was devoid of all four of the criteria just noted. When all criteria are present religion is acknowledged as unique and a permanent part of human culture.

B. Psychology Defined

As with efforts to define religion, any definition of psychology has its opposition. Most historians of the discipline note that psychology is less a unified science with a set of consensually accepted methodologies than a discipline of loosely knit and sometimes incompatible schools. Most schools of psychology can be identified by the methods of investigation they accept or refuse to accept as legitimate. All schools of psychology attempt to describe and explain phenomena with a consistent set of methodological assumptions. Methodological pluralism accounts for the varieties of psychology that currently exist. It is this lack of consensus as to what constitutes appropriate methods for psychology that leads us to discuss varieties of psychology and their relationships to varieties of religion. At best we can confront what particular psychologies have to say about particular religions.

II. HISTORY OF PSYCHOLOGY AND RELIGION

As a permanent aspect of culture, religion is at least as old as recorded history. Similarly, as an effort to describe or explain phenomena based upon methodological assumptions, psychology has a long and perhaps undateable origin. Yet, psychology as a natural science emerged in the 19th century as largely an American phenomena. The roots of scientific psychology had been laid by philosophical developments utilizing natural science assumptions to explain widely diverse phenomena in light of principles based upon observation and experimentation. By the middle of the 19th century European scientists had begun to measure the speed of nervous transmission and to conduct psychophysical experiments. Psychology as a natural science had its uneasy origins in such activities. Often psychology textbooks date the origin of scientific psychology with the official founding of a psychology laboratory at Leipzig in 1879 by the German scientist Wilhelm Wundt. Yet scientific psychology was seen as a limited set of assumptions applicable to some phenomena but not to others. Psychological interest in religion, even by these founders, often utilized different methodological procedures amounting to different psychol-

ogies. Especially in America, psychology and religion in both the popular and scientific mind were at odds and neither could be explained by the other. Methodological appeals rooted only in the natural sciences failed to meaningfully confront some religious phenomena. In America, William James was most articulate in exposing this dilemma. It is one that continues to characterize psychology and religion today as it did then.

A. American Psychology and Religion

The emergence of psychology as a natural science found fertile soil in America. William James had a laboratory in the basement of Harvard University a few years before Wundt's formally founded laboratory at Leipzig. Spiritualism was a powerful force in late 19th century America and associated in the popular culture with psychology, largely to distinguish it from established religions and their spiritual claims. In Europe the Society for Psychical Research was founded in 1882 to investigate paranormal phenomena, including mediumship, apparitions, telepathy, telekinesis, and clairvoyance. These were associated in the popular culture with psychology. James helped found the American Society for Psychical Research (ASPR) in 1884. Disputes arose quickly as to the commitment of investigators to the reality of the phenomena studied. Many early members [who were to also be founders of the new American Psychological Association (APA), whose first annual meeting was held in 1892] assumed that a scientific psychology would dispel the reality of psychic phenomena in favor of naturalistic explanations. Several of these members quit the ASPR when the organization was perceived to support the reality of spiritual claims. Thus, phenomenal growth of psychology as a discipline in America was due to a curious alliance of unwitting supporters. On one hand, there were psycholgoists who took as their task the establishment of the validity of psychology by debunking spiritualistic claims. On the other hand, there was popular cultural support for psychology that was based upon the assumption that psychologists were establishing the reality of spiritualist claims. This uneasy alliance still characterizes the study of psychology and religion, especially in America.

1. Hall, Starbuck, and Leuba: The Clark School

G. Stanley Hall was the first president of the APA and one of those who quit the ASPR. He also founded the first journal of psychology of religion (*The American Journal of Religious Psychology and Education*) and established the only school of psychology of religion in America, the Clark school. Two members of that school illustrated the tensions between psychology and religion noted above.

Edwin Starbuck utilized questionnaires to study religious development. He utilized simply quantitative procedures to determine the age at which conversion was most common. His sympathy to religion, particularly evangelical Protestantism, was evident. He was careful to avoid reductionistic explanations of religious development; he was content to simply chart its path.

In contrast, the other famous member of the Clark School, James Leuba, provided clinical assessments of mystical experiences that assumed their pathological nature. He offered reductive physiological explanations for what the religiously devout assumed to be experiences of union with God. This initiated the long tradition of psychological threats to at least some religious claims.

2. James and Pratt: The Descriptive Tradition

William James, a founding member of ASPR and twice president of APA, illustrates another uneasy alliance between psychology and religion. James' Gifford Lectures, published as *The Varieties of Religious Experience,* has proven to be the one undoubted classic in the field. It has been continuously in print since first published in 1902 and is the text most often quoted in the contemporary study of psychology and religion in America. The APA's division of Psychology of Religion gives an annual William James award for research in the psychology of religion. In the *Varieties* James painstakingly described extreme cases of religious experience in sympathetic fashion.

James Pratt, a student of James, extended his mentor's work in an extensive study of common religious experiences. His text *The Religious Consciousness* (1920) is second only to James' *Varieties* in the number of reprintings. Neither James nor Pratt utilized methods of the newly emerging scientific psychology. The popularity of their work (and James' today) rests largely upon their rich descriptive nature and their openness to the validity of religious experience.

By the end of the 1920s American psychology was firmly established and interest in the study of religion quickly waned. The emergence of behaviorism and the banishment of mental phenomena from scientific psychology left little room for the study of religion. Not until the early 1960s would the psychology of religion reemerge as a popular concern of psychologists. When psychology of religion did re-emerge as a concern its early roots would once again bear similar fruits. The study of religion by psychologists continues to focus primarily upon varieties of American Protestantism. Apologists for religion and the religiously faithful are as easily identified as those seeking purely naturalistic explanations. Whether, and if so, how, to include transcendent reality in a science of religion is still debated. The same disputes would emerge. We will confront these issues shortly as they continue to characterize the psychological study of religion.

3. Classical Psychoanalysis and Religion: Freud

We have emphasized that there are varieties of psychologies associated with various schools. There are also psychologies so different in aim, scope, and methodology as to be rival traditions. Psychoanalysis, founded by Sigmund Freud, emerged from the medical tradition and from a concern with pathology. As with analytic and object relations psychology to be discussed shortly, psychoanalysis was of largely European origin. Yet, it was quickly accepted in America. Psychoanalysis as a uniquely human science developed parallel to, but independent from, academic psychology. Psychoanalysis quickly gained wide cultural and medical appeal, despite severe criticisms from academic psychologies. It also provided powerful reductive explanations claiming to debunk religion. Psychoanalysis has been widely criticized as postulating its own myths of early childhood drama, especially experiences focusing upon the father in what has become the cornerstone of classical psychoanalysis, the Oedipal drama. Avoiding the methods of most schools of psychology, the psychoanalytic tradition developed a unique set of methods rooted in ultimately uncovering unconscious mental processes. Such processes were systematically and coherently utilized by Freud and his colleagues to provide naturalistic (albeit distinctively psychoanalytic) explanations of religious truths. Ultimately, Freud saw religion as delusory, a falsification of reality rooted in illusion or the hope that the world will conform to one's personal wish. God was interpreted as a projected idealized father, derived from the Oedipal drama. With this claim, classical psychoanalysis set itself firmly at odds with Christian religion. While American academic psychology of religion lay largely dormant from 1930 through 1960, psychoanalysis in its classical Freudian variety produced literally thousands of articles and books describing virtually every aspect of religion in reductive terms. The popularity of psychoanalysis continues to be extremely strong among those seeking a naturalistic, reductive explanation for religion, not merely a psychologically sympathetic description of it. Curiously, psychoanalytic theories of religion have been extensively tested by more traditional psychological methodologies and (not surprisingly) often found inadequate. Whether theories based upon radically different psychologies can be tested by a single set of methodological criteria remains problematic. Furthermore, there are contemporary psychoanalysts who utilize classical Freudian theories to support traditional religious beliefs. Psychoanalysis is no longer interpreted to be necessarily hostile to religion. This parallels the phenomena already noted with other American psychologies.

4. Analytic Psychology: Jung

Among Freud's most famous early followers and one of the few non-Jewish psychoanalysts was both the hand-picked successor to Freud and eventually his greatest rival in the study of religion, Carl Jung. Jung quickly rebelled from the reductive explanations psychoanalysis offered for religion and developed his own analytic psychology which gave religious experience a central and prominent place. Jung's interpretations of religious material place his psychology in direct, often contentious, dialogue with religious traditions. Jung's work utilizes materials from the widest range of religious traditions including occult traditions largely ignored by most psychologists. Analytic psychology is seen by many academic psychologists as more akin to literary analysis or even an alternative to classical religion than a legitimate psychology. On the other hand, religious studies have been extensively influenced by analytic psychology and its powerful interpretative tradition.

5. Object Relations Theory

Within dynamic psychology, continued interest in religious experience has been maintained by object relations theorists. The term comes from the focus upon the objects of early infantile experiences, including those pre-Oedipal experiences, largely ignored by classical psychoanalysis. Such experiences demand more focus upon the mother rather than upon the father. Not surprisingly, object relations explanations of religious phenomena permit more sensitivity to gender issues, since many religious phenomena are seen as based upon infantile, pre-Oedipal maternal experiences. While diverse in their views, object relations theorists are commonly united in sharing sympathetic descriptions of religious phenomena as at least revealing legitimate psychological experiences. [*See* OBJECT RELATIONS THEORY.]

6. Transpersonal Psychology

Interest in integrating spiritual phenomena directly into psychology is explicitly the domain of transpersonal psychology. Heavily influenced by dissatisfaction with major schools of psychology, including both scientific psychologies and their dynamic counterparts, transpersonal psychology focuses upon the study of experiences traditionally the domain of religion. Tending to reject traditional religious explanations, transpersonal psychologists are developing a psychology that integrates spiritual and scientific approaches to the study of persons that are as unique as they are difficult to classify. Despite the success of *The Journal of Transpersonal Psychology,* founded in 1969, efforts to establish a division of transpersonal psychology in the APA have repeatedly failed. Transpersonal psychology so uniquely mixes scientific and religious approaches to the investigation of spiritual phenomena that it is seen by many as an emerging religious psychology rather than a psychology of religion or an effort to relate psychology and religion.

B. The Dominance of American Psychology

The success of psychology in America has always been associated with its rapid development as a profession. Major journals sponsored by the APA assure the world dominance of American Psychology. Divisions of specialty within the American Psychological Association absorb the widest possible range of differences under the umbrella of one organization. A division of Psychology of Religion both reflects interest in and assures the continued study of religion by American psychologists. There is a recently formed counter-organization to the APA, focused more upon research than the practice of psychology as a profession, the American Psychological Society (APS). The APS allows the identification of psychology of religion as a specialty. While neither the APA nor the APS formally sponsors a journal in the psychology of religion, numerous journals more or less directly concerned with the psychology of religion exist. The Religious Research Association has published a journal since 1959 (*Review of Religious Research*), while the Society for the Scientific Study of Religion has published a journal since 1961 (*Journal for the Scientific Study of Religion*). More recent is *Research in the Social Scientific Study of Religion,* a journal not affiliated with any society. While none of these journals are purely psychological journals, all publish social scientific studies of religion by psychologists. Two journals specifically focused upon psychology of religion have recently emerged. *The International Journal for the Psychology of Religion* published its first issue in 1991, while in 1992 *The Journal of the Psychology of Religion* published its first issue. These specifically psychological journals compliment long-established journals focused upon psychology of religion within specific religious traditions such as *The Journal of Psychology and Theology* and *The Journal of Psychology and Christianity*. The fact that some journals are associated with religious commitments and others are not continues the dilemma of the field where psychology and religion have tenuous relationships, with some making the scientific study of religion their priority and others placing more emphasis upon a faith commitment of those who study religion.

C. Psychology and Religion in Global Perspective

With the emergence of *The International Journal for the Psychology of Religion* the global dimensions of psychology and religion have been emphasized. While still primarily focused upon the Christian tradition, the psychology of religion in the European and Continental cultures has been fairly substantial. Largely associated with the emergence of the psychology of religion in America in the 1960s and in most European and Continental traditions the study of religion have a short history and do not reflect a re-emergence of the discipline that characterizes the American pattern. Furthermore, European and Continental traditions have been more receptive to phenomenological and dynamic studies than has American psychology of religion. Australia, Canada, Israel, and the Scandanavian countries all have recent histories of psychology and religion. Asian and Eastern studies are not as common, largely due to the minimal influence of American psychology in these cultures. Furthermore, psychologies from these cultures are less distinct from both philosophy and religion than American psychology. They are beginning to find an audience among American psychologists and promise to broaden even more the range of methodologies acceptable to a field long dominated by American psychology.

III. MAJOR METHODOLOGICAL STANCES IN PSYCHOLOGY AND RELIGION

Various psychologies of religion are characterized by what procedures investigators consider legitimate and preferable in the study of religion. Within American academic psychology, insistence has been placed upon the demand for a scientific study of religion. However, there is little consensus as to exactly what constitutes science or if psychology should strive to model itself after the natural sciences. For those who see psychology as a purely scientific discipline, the focus is upon research that is experimental or at least quasi-experimental. For others, psychology is respectably scientific if it employs measurement in correlational investigations. Whatever the ideal, most scientific psychology of religion is characterized by measurement and correlational research. Few true experimental research designs have been employed. Phenomenological and hermeneutical methods are common, although many would not refer to them as legitimately scientific.

A. Measurement Studies

Many psychologists consider the ability to assign numbers to phenomena an essential characteristic of scientific psychology. Religious phenomena are no exception in this view insofar as their scientific study requires the ability to be measured. Questionnaires and scales have been developed for the widest possible range of religious phenomena, from beliefs about God, to reports of religious experience, to motivational bases for religious involvement, to fears and anxieties about death. All measurement studies are ultimately rooted in paper and pencil self-reports. Self-report measures require cautious interpretation, but no more so than other observable phenomena such as behavior.

B. Correlational Studies

The most common scientific studies in psychology of religion are correlational, relating one measured phenomena such as religious belief to something else, such as gender or age. Modern sophisticated statistical techniques also allow for multivariate research in which several variables can be simultaneously related. While correlational studies do utilize measurement, the fact that correlation cannot establish true causation has made it very difficult to establish a body of consensual findings even among scientifically oriented psychologists of religion. Thus, this is the major reason there are no generally agreed upon psychological theories of virtually any religious phenomenon.

C. Experimental and Quasi-experimental Studies

Closely associated with measurement is the demand that a truly scientific psychology of religion utilize experimental methods. In experimental methods, participants are randomly assigned to experimental and control groups such that true variations between groups can be assessed as due to a factor or factors under the control of the experimenter and hence known to be operating only in the experimental group into which they were introduced. By the very nature of religion, true experimental studies are rare and some would argue ultimately impossible. The few truly experimental studies in the psychology of religion have been on drug-induced experiences, an area of controversy in the psychology of religion.

Quasi-experimental studies randomly assign persons already assessed on some measurement scale to experimental conditions. These measured characteristics are not produced in persons by the experimenter and hence are not true experimental studies. Quasi-experimental studies by psychologists of religion have focused upon religious beliefs and their effects upon helping behavior and religious orientations and their relationship to reports of religious experience, and the effects of drugs on reports of religious experience.

D. Phenomenological Studies

Phenomenological methods have not been widely accepted within American psychology. Yet within psychology of religion, many classic works are phenomenologically based. Such studies focus upon careful description of the content and structure of consciousness. Phenomenological studies of religion have focused upon religious experience, including studies claiming there is a unique religious experience. An interface between phenomenological and measurement studies has characterized much of the contemporary study of mysticism, with scales to measure mysticism developed from phenomenological studies of mystical experience.

E. Hermeneutical Studies

Hermeneutical studies include a variety of psychologies that seek to interpret the meaning of phenomena. Many dynamic and object relations psychologies focus not only upon causal investigations of religious phenomena, but seek to interpret the meaning of religious phenomena as well. Typically hermeneutical approaches in the psychology of religion seek to understand religious claims in light of systems of meaning derived from psychological theories. Both Jungian and Freudian theories have spawned a wide literature interpreting religious beliefs and rituals in terms far removed from the language and concepts of the faith traditions within which they emerged. Psychologists employing hermeneutical methods have studied more than just the Christian tradition. Many psychologies reject hermeneutical methods as not legitimately scientific to which hermeneutical psychologies often respond with their appeal to a uniquely human science of psychology necessarily demanding interpretation and not simply causal analysis.

IV. MAJOR CONTENT AREAS IN PSYCHOLOGY AND RELIGION

Since its American re-emergence in 1960, the psychology of religion has been characterized by a limited number of content areas that have been investigated by a combination of methods discussed above. While typically investigators using correlation, measurement, and quasi-experimental studies read, share, and quote one another's literature they largely ignore the hermeneutical and phenomenological literatures. Likewise, they are unlikely to read or reference dynamic or object relation researchers. This creates a series of discrete literatures associated with various psychologies but does not permit a single psychology of religion to emerge. Therefore, even within specific content areas it is difficult to state a consensus opinion and still be fair to the varieties of methodologies and hence psychologies that claim to possess knowledge or insight into religious phenomena.

A. Religious Experience

Since the time of William James, psychologists have focused upon religious experience. Included in this area are the widest range of experiences that individuals claim to be religious or to have religious importance. On the positive side, psychologists from a variety of methodological perspectives have shown that individuals of a devout orientation derive specific experiential awareness from their religious commitments. Not only do they interpret phenomena within the concepts derived from their religious traditions, but to do so makes their experience of the world a religious one. Particularly within the hermeneutical methodologies, religious experience is identified as finding a transcendent meaning within experience that causal investigations can only identify in terms of proximate origin. A more drastic claim made by psychologists sympathetic to religious truth claims is that certain experiences provide the legitimate empirical basis from which to infer religious truths. In the latter case, mystical experience is often cited as a human experience that suggests the validity of language and concepts protected within religious traditions. Among specifically religious practices,, some forms of prayer have been investigated as producing a unique experiential awareness of the world that is both meaningful and productive of personal contentment. The availability of a religious language has been shown to facilitate the report of religious experience, and for some theorists, to be necessary for the experience to occur. Others have provided data and argument to show that both religious and not religiously commited persons may have similar experiences which they simply differentially interpret. Typically, women report more religious experience than men. However, the widest variety of religious experiences are documented to be common in modern cultures for both men and women. Crisis conditions, including near death experiences are especially likely to produce experiences for which religious interpretations seem meaningful. Often such experiences confirm religious commitments for those previously only nominally religious.

B. Conversion

As with religious experience, the re-emergence of the psychology of religion in America once again focused upon the study of conversion. Both sudden and gradual conversions have been studied with sudden conversions apparently demanding more psychological explanation, especially from dynamic perspectives. Here, "sudden" is seen as simply the moment at which long operating unconscious factors come to fruition. Gradual conversions are seen as involving more intentional and conscious decision to adopt beliefs or lifestyles associated with faith traditions for a wide variety of psychological motivations. Sudden conversions are sometimes due to weakness or deficiencies within the individual for which religions provide functional solutions. Probably more typical are gradual conversions in which the deficiency is seen more in light of seeking a more meaningful existence than that which converts had prior to their conversion. In addition, psychologists have documented the routine adoption of religious beliefs based simply upon socialization in which children are raised within a faith tradition they learn to accept. In addition, many conversions are as simple as a new mate adopting the religion of their partner.

C. Religious Development

Theories of religious development have long dominated the dynamic literatures. Several theories of religious development have been popular, including Freud's social psychological theory that religion is merely a stage in the development of both individuals and cultures, fated to be abandoned once maturity is reached. Others have proposed that religion is an essential characteristic of individual development, fated to be sophisticatedly developed along with other characteristics such as intelligence. Several of these stage theories have been developed both within and across different schools of psychology. None have clear empirical support, partly due to the paucity of true longitudinal studies in which individuals with religious commitments are followed over their lives and their pattern of religious development is charted. In addition, stage theories implicitly contain evaluations that higher, later developed stages are better, healthier, or more mature and this places them in contention with particular religions. No consensus as to either a hierarchical stage of normal religious growth or a normative sequence of religious development through such stages exists within or across various school of psychology. However, many have been proposed. Recently, psychologist have begun to investigate empirical correlates of early infant attachments, especially to the mother, and patterns of latter religious development without proposing stages of development. Efforts to purely descriptively trace religious development across age groups in Western cultures tend to indicate that religious commitment of whatever form rises to a peak in adolescence, declines, then emerges strong once again in late life.

D. Psychopathology

From its origin, much of the psychology of religion has been controversially involved in claims as to the psychopathology of either particular religions or religion itself as a generic form. Early Freudian claims that religion may be analogous to collective neurosis and that many religious rituals are analogous to individual compulsions have been contested by modern dynamic theorists that see the presence of healthy religious practices. Even among Freudians, theorists sympathetic to religion have emerged. Likewise, object relations and Jungian theorist have developed theories of psychological processes that tend to be inherently religious or spiritual in nature. The more scientific psychologies have tended to rely upon studies in which various definitions of psychopathology are differentially related to forms of religious commitment. The immense complexity in this area of research is rooted in the fact that neither claims to psychological health nor pathology is strictly speaking capable of objective determination. Thus, the ideological basis of research in this area has been exposed with a massive set of literature defending and documenting which religions may elict, foster, or facilitate behaviors, thoughts or feelings seen as psychopathological by particular psychologies. The contentious basis of this research is reflected in current debates which tend to identify fundamentalist religions of whatever sort as falling short of what most psychologies see as fostering healthy psychological development. Yet the effort of psychologies to define optimal psychological functioning, especially in religious terms, has been questioned repeatedly as reflecting neither a special competence of psychology as a science nor a position capable of merely objective articulation outside of implicit or explicit evaluations.

E. Coping

Closely related to the study of psychopathology is the study of coping. By coping psychologists refer to the strategies by which persons adjust to difficult situations. Religion and coping have been a controversial area of research for similar reasons already noted for religion and psychopathology. Early psychologists, unsympathetic to religion, tended to view religious participation per se as an avoidance of reality, although one that was collectively supported. Among contemporary psychologists, how particular religious beliefs are related to forms of coping have been empirically investigated. Perhaps most consistent is the finding that religious belief may do less to alter harsh realities than to provide a meaningful framework within which to view such realities. The psychological assessment of the value of such a framework often varies with the compatibility of the religiously sanctioned framework with the psychological perspective of the investigator. For instance, psychologists who propose stages of faith development tend to identify higher stages of development that can be empirically measured once defined, but the definition itself remains perpetually problematic. Psychologists tend to value open systems of meaning within a pluralistic framework and tend to be unappreciative of closed systems claiming absolute authority. Hence, psychological measures, including assessments of psychopathology and coping, tend to reflect these values. Overall measurement data most clearly support the subjective well-being of religious individuals whose commitment is sincere, regardless of the religion in question. [See COPING.]

F. Religion and Social Psychology

Among psychologists who study religion in universities, next to clinical psychology, social psychology is perhaps the most frequent specialty in which the investigator has her or his degree. It is fair to say that the revival of the psychology of religion as a research specialty in America has its roots in the study of religion and prejudice by social psychologists. This quickly spread to closely related studies of altruism, and the phenomena of sects and cults.

1. Prejudice

American interest in the study of prejudice was accentuated by the aftermath of World War II. Clinical and social psychologists united in an effort to understand anti-Semitism in particular and prejudice in general. A persistent finding was that a particular form of religion was related to prejudice. Worried that psychologists tended to see religion in general as related to prejudice, the American psychologist Gorton W. Allport distinguished between a religious faith which he identified as intrinsic and an instrumentally oriented religious faith which he identified as extrinsic. The focus of his research was to demonstrate that while extrinsic faith related to prejudice, intrinsic faith did not. From this simple research finding evolved what undoubtedly been the central concern in the contemporary academic and scientific psychology of religion in America. First, was a continual revising and clarification of the psychometric nature of Allport's scales to measure intrinsic and extrinsic religion and the correlation of these scales with other religious and psychological phenomena. Second, was a focus upon identifying healthy or mature religion (intrinsic) and less healthy or immature religion (extrinsic). The empirical debate over research with these scales as well as the conceptual debate over healthy vs unhealthy religion has dominated the last three decades of the psychology of religion in America. Until recently a consensus had emerged that intrinsic religion related to a wide variety of healthy and positive psychological phenomena, such as effective coping, lack of prejudice, altruistic behavior, and a wide variety of positive religious experiences. More recently, researchers have suggested that intrinsic religion may reflect a social bias to appear unprejudiced when, in fact, that is not true. Another dimension of religion discussed below (quest) has recently been proposed as relating to a lack of prejudice. Confounding this entire research tradition has been debate concerning the evaluation of behaviors mandated by religious beliefs and whether such religiously sanctioned evaluations can be meaningfully defined as prejudice. [See PREJUDICE AND STEREOTYPES.]

2. Altruism

Altruism in general and helping behavior in particular have long been a central concern in social psychology. From the study of religion and prejudice a gradual movement to the study of religion and helping behavior occurred. While psychologists have generally found that intrinsic religion relates to altruism, some investigators have argued that a newly added dimension to Allport's intrinsic/extrinsic distinction, a quest orientation, relates most meaningfully to helping behavior in actual quasi-experimental studies. Quest is defined and measured to reflect less commitment to a set of religious beliefs than a concern with existential questions such as death and human finitude. The debate over quest religion and its relationship to other forms of religion (especially intrinsic and extrinsic) occupies much of the contemporary psychology of religion in

America. It is the one area of research in the psychology of religion dominated by quasi-experimental studies, especially by investigators committed to investigate quest religiosity. [See ALTRUISM AND HELPING BEHAVIOR.]

3. Sects and Cults

Among the more sociologically oriented psychologists extensive debate and research into religious groups have utilized a classification system of sect, cult, and denomination. Denominations are socially acceptable religious groups within the larger culture. Sects are defined as religious groups at odds with the cultures in which they exist. Sects are often formed by breaking away from established denominations either to progressively advance in terms of cultural mores or to repressively return to forms of religiosity now at odds with the culture. Cults represent religious innovation, often occurring *de nova* and led by a charismatic figure. Both sects and cults, since they are at odds with the dominate culture are similar to deviant groups. Some psychologists tend to offer pathological interpretation of cult leaders and sect leaders and to suggest metaphorical processes such as "brainwashing" for reasons individuals might joint cults or sects. More balanced studies suggest that wide diversity in processes by which persons both join and found sects or cults. While some religious groups use various degress of coercive persuasion, such processes are common in a wide variety groups and do not differentially characterize either sects or cults. Noncoerceive psychological processes, including the seeking of alternative lifestyles and dissatisfaction with existing religious groups, account for much of both sect and cult formation. However, as with religion and psychopathology, research into cults and sects is heavily confounded by evaluative claims and the inability of any psychology to define what constitutes a legitimate religion in other than evaluative contexts. [See BRAINWASHING AND TOTALITARIAN INFLUENCE.]

V. CONTROVERSIAL ISSUES IN PSYCHOLOGY AND RELIGION

Since psychology and religion are so problematic one is tempted to define the entire field as controversial. Yet two areas especially justify being labeled controversial; psychedelic drugs and parapsychology.

A. Psychedelic Drugs

The literature on psychedelic drugs is vast and much of it truly experimental, giving it an especially firm scientific basis. However, with respect to religion, the claim that psychedelic drugs might produce or at least facilitate religious experience has generated controversy. Social scientists had long documented the use of drugs in religious rituals, inducing the peyote cults of Native Americans. With the revival of interest in psychology and religion a few quasi-experimental studies of drugs and the report of religious experience became widely quoted. Further complicating the situation is the fact that early research into psychedelic drugs was associated with major American universities and became part of a cult movement within America led by formerly renowned research psychologists. These studies still occupy a prominent place in virtually every current textbook in the psychology of religion. While no longer capable of legal study in the United States, it does appear that a wide variety of what generally became known as psychedelic drugs, including LSD-25, psilocybin, and peyote can elicit states of awareness similar to independently defined religious states. Similarly, studies of persons in isolation tanks and under conditions of sensory restriction also elicit reports of religious experience. Perhaps most fair is the claim that when persons with an appropriate religious set and in an appropriate setting alter their bodies in any manner to foster new awareness, experiences long defined as religious become more likely. Studies also suggest that the experience per se is less crucial than what one does or how one reacts to the experience within the context of their life. Many mainstream religions have opposition to drugs so that incorporating drug-facilitated experience into these traditions is unlikely.

B. Parapsychology

As noted above, the very founding of psychology was linked in the popular mind with parapsychological phenomena. Most psychologists reject evidence of parapsychology not only because most claims are inadequately scientifically established but because parapsychological phenomena trouble most psychologies on purely conceptual grounds. However, survey studies continually reveal that persons who report religious experiences also report parapsychology phenomena. Likewise, parapsychological phenomena are conceptually identified with many more literal religious beliefs, creating a problem for psychologists of religion who take it as their task to explain religious phenomena in natural scientific terms. Parapsychology is not widely accepted as purely spiritual or as scientific fact, producing a bridge between psychology and religion that is neither a scientific explanation of religion nor a religious claim to transcend science in purely spiritual terms. Once again, the popularity of parapsychological claims, especially among those who identify with new religious sect and cult movements, is creating a tension among those who would defend and define the boundaries between various definitions as to what constitutes legitimate psychology.

VI. FUTURE PROSPECTS

Psychology and religion promise to continue to be an area of investigation filled with tensions. In a postmodern perspective, simple claims as to what constitutes science and affirmations to adhere to a single or limited set of methodologies are difficult to sustain. The widest variety of methodologies are being sustained and created to look afresh at all that the broad umbrella of the term religion covers. It is unlikely that other than a narrowly defined psychology can offer much in the way of exhaustive explanation of religious phenomena. The American preoccupation with a limited range of methodologies, with which they study a limited number religious traditions, focusing upon even more limited range of religious phenomena, will surely be broadened. The descriptions of psychological process operating within religions, as well as the content of religious belief they validate, will continue to be useful as long as the variety of the psychologies and the methodologies by which they are defined are respected. Both religious and psychological pluralism undoubtedly will continue to be the rule in the future.

Bibliography

Beit-Hallahmi, B. (1994). "The Psychoanalytic Study of Religion: Critical Assessment and Annotated Bibliography." Greenwood Press, Westport, CT.

Coon, D. J. (1992). Testing the limits of sense and science: American experimental psychologists combat spiritualism, 1880–1920. *Am. Psychol.* **47,** 143–151.

Gorsuch, R. L. (1988). Psychology of religion. *Ann. Rev. Psychol.* **19,** 201–221.

Hood, R. W., Jr. (Ed.) (1994). ''Handbook of Religious Experience: Theory and Practice.'' Religious Education Press, Birminghan, AL.

Kirkpatrick, L. A., and Hood, R. W., Jr. (1990). Intrinsic-extrinsic religious orientation: The boon or the bane of contemporary psychology of religion? *J. Sci. Study Religion* **29**, 442–462.

Preus, J. S. (1987). ''Explaining Religion.'' Yale University Press, New Haven, CT.

Roth, P. A. (1987). ''Meaning and Method in the Social Sciences: The Case for Methodological Pluralism.'' Cornell University Press, Ithaca, New York.

Stevens, J. (1988). ''Storming Heaven.'' Harper & Row, New York.

Wulff, D. M. (1991). ''Psychology of Religion: Classic and Contemporary Views.'' Wiley, New York.

Zollschan, G. K., Schumaker, J. F., & Walsh, G. F. (Eds.) (1989). ''Exploring the Paranormal.'' Prism Press, Great Britain.

PSYCHOPATHOLOGY

Keith S. Dobson and Dennis Pusch
University of Calgary, Canada

Glossary

Diagnosis The process of applying consistent labels to patterns of abnormal functioning.

Insanity A legal term, meaning that a person is not legally responsible for his or her actions.

Mental health The absence of psychopathology, and the positive aspects of subjective well-being, development and use of abilities, social adaptation, and achievement of goals.

Mental illness Largely synonymous with psychopathology, although implying an underlying disease or illness process.

Psychopathology An aberrant or dysfunctional way of functioning, defined in terms of behavioral, interpersonal, emotional, cognitive, and psychophysiological patterns.

THE DEFINITION of psychopathology has long been a matter of theoretical and practical importance to individuals involved in the mental health movement. It is primarily psychiatric and psychological professionals who have been involved in the conceptualization and definition of psychopathology. At the theoretical level, debates have centered around such issues as whether humans or their behavior is disordered or "ill," the different approaches that can be taken to define health and pathology, and the moral implications of defining some individuals as having a pathological condition. At the practical level, there have been extensive discussions about how best to conceptualize and assess abnormal behavior, and how to minimize the potentially negative influences of labeling.

I. DEFINITIONAL ISSUES

A. Normalcy versus Abnormalcy

Within the overall frame of reference of psychopathology a number of related concepts must be defined and distinguished. As a term, *psychopathology* refers to an aberrant or dysfunctional (i.e., pathological) way of functioning, where functioning is defined in terms of behavioral, interpersonal, emotional, cognitive, and psychophysiological patterns. Whether a particular way of functioning is aberrant can be judged by a number of criteria. Included in such criteria is whether that functioning causes personal distress, causes others in the person's social sphere to become distressed, falls outside of accepted social norms or values for functioning, falls within certain criteria for abnormal functioning, or is a statistically rare functional pattern. Each of these approaches to establishing an aberrant pattern of functioning has advantages and disadvantages. It is due to the presence of these approaches that different approaches to conceptualizing psychopathology exist.

Mental illness is a term that is largely synonymous with psychopathology, although it carries the implication that the unusual or aberrant patterns of functioning seen in these conditions reflect some form of disease or illness. The medical model reflected in the illness term is rejected by some psychopathologists, as an inappropriate model for either all or some forms of psychopathology. Another term that is considered synonymous with psychopathology is *abnormal behavior*. This term is equally descriptive as psychopathology, as neither implies a belief in the cause of the unusual or aberrant patterns of functioning, but is more focused on the behavioral component of the dysfunction.

A term that is sometimes confused with psychopathology is *insanity*. Although such terms as insane, mad, and lunatic were once used in much the same way modern society uses the terms psychopathology and mental illness, insanity has taken on a much more narrow definition. Specifically, insanity is a legal term that addresses the question of whether a particular person can be held criminally responsible for his or her actions. Several different tests of insanity exist, but in every case the decision as to whether a person is legally insane is made by a judge or jury, and is made with respect to the crime they are alleged to have committed. It is the case that many different forms of abnormal or psychopathological behavior do not meet the criterion for insanity. Further, it is possible that a person can be legally insane (i.e., not legally responsible for their actions) when they have no discernable form of psychopathology, as defined by mental health practitioners.

A term that has relevance to psychopathology is *mental health*. While one can imagine mental health as the absence of psychopathology, it is also possible to conceptualize mental health in terms of its positive attributes. The World Health Organization has defined mental health as "inner experience linked to interpersonal group experience," and is associated with such characteristics as subjective well-being, optimal development and use of mental abilities, social adaptation, and achievement of goals.

In summary, psychopathology is a concept that is similar to mental illness and abnormal behavior, but is distinct from insanity. Mental health can be conceptualized as the absence of psychopathology, but also has other positive components not related to the concept of psychopathology.

B. Conceptual Approaches to Psychopathology

There are a large number of theoretical approaches to psychopathology, and these have steadily evolved over the centuries.

One dominant belief about the cause of abnormal behavior is that of possession; which is the idea that evil spirits or demons possess the mind and body of the person in question and cause them to behave in an aberrant fashion. There is fossil evidence that early humans believed in demonic possession as a cause of abnormal behavior, as there are skulls dating from prehistoric times which shown purposeful cutting of the skull, or trephination. Trephination is often explained as an effort to release pressure in the skull, which may have been conceptualized by early humans as possession by an evil sprit. The idea of demonic possession as an explanation for abnormal behavior continues to persist (for example, the Roman Catholic Church still has procedures for exorcism as part of its accepted canon, and voo-

dooism is still practised in some parts of the world today), but it has largely been supplanted by other explanations of abnormalcy.

One early alternative model to possession was the humoral theory promoted by Hippocrates. The humoral model proposed that four humors, or fluids, are in the body, and that each is associated with a particular attitude and time of life. Blood, for example, is associated with growth, optimism, and good health, while black bile, or melancholia, is associated with death, depression, and darkness. The humoral theory was a prominent one in medicine for centuries, but has been since shown to be false.

Contemporary conceptions of psychopathology can be broken down into the two major categories of categorical and dimensional types. Categorical conceptions of psychopathology view abnormal behavior as discontinuous with normal behavior; as something that has a qualitatively different sense to it. Such conceptions are apt to include ideas of illness or disease processes, as these processes are those that distinguish normal from abnormal functioning. Categorical approaches to psychopathology are consistent with the practise of diagnosing or labeling dysfunctional patterns of functioning. The categorical approach to psychopathology is very heavily subscribed to because diagnosis is often considered to be necessary prior to the provision of treatment in psychiatric settings.

Dimensional approaches to psychopathology view aberrant functioning as falling on a continuum, with some types or levels of functioning being more or less dysfunctional than others. Within a dimensional approach diagnosis and labeling are less accepted, except to the extent that labels are applied to individuals at agreed upon points along a continuum. For example, if a person bites his or her nails more than three times a week, we might label that as "abnormal"; less than three times a week might be considered "normal." Dimensional approaches are often used in combination with statistical conceptions of what is "average" or normal, and abnormalcy is defined as being atypical or highly different from the "average" person.

II. CATEGORICAL MODELS OF PSYCHOPATHOLOGY

A. Historical Precursors to the Diagnosis of Psychopathology

The labeling of abnormal behavior has taken place for centuries. In ancient Greek society, such disorders as melancholia (what we would today term depression), mania (agitated or excited behavior), and phrenitis (most other forms of psychopathology, including severe forms of thought and behavior dysfunction) were distinguished. Models for the onset (etiology) of these disorders were established, and these disorders had differentiated treatment programs.

After the Dark Ages, the Renaissance and Enlightenment periods of Western civilization saw a renewed and more sophisticated approach to the diagnosis of psychopathology emerge. With the creation of asylums, large institutions designed for the holding and treatment of persons with mental illness, came the ability to study, differentiate, and more carefully assess abnormal conditions. Different systems for diagnosing psychopathology began to emerge, with different labels being proposed, debated, and either accepted or rejected. By the end of the 19th century, the number of divergent systems for diagnosis was recognized as a serious problem for the credibility and acceptability of any diagnostic system.

The approach to diagnosis and labeling that has been generally accepted was formalized by a German physician, Emil Kraepelin, in 1883. Using an approach comparable to that used in the rest of medicine, his approach included the assessment of different symptoms that formed cohesive patterns called *syndromes*. These syndromes, once identified, could then be labeled. In the original Kraepelinian diagnostic system there were a relatively small number of syndromes and diagnoses, but each was conceptually distinct and had its own specific symptoms.

B. The International Classification of Diseases

The World Health Organization (WHO) adopted Kraepelin's system for diagnosing psychopathology, and has listed mental disorders as potential causes of death since 1939. The list of mental disorders included in the WHO directory has been revised a number of times, and the 1969 revision in particular received some acceptance. In 1979 the WHO published the ninth revision and the current version of the *International Classification of Diseases* (*ICD*). There are a total of 30 major categories of mental disorders in the ICD-9 (see Table I). As many of these categories contain more specific forms of psychopathology, there are a total of 563 diagnostic categories in the ICD-9.

One of the principle features of the ICD is that it distinguishes organic from nonorganic forms and

TABLE I

Major Mental Disorder Diagnostic Categories from the International Classification of Diseases

A. Organic psychotic conditions
 1. Senile and presenile organic psychotic conditions
 2. Alcoholic psychoses
 3. Drug psychoses
 4. Transient organic psychotic conditions
 5. Other organic psychotic conditions

B. Other psychoses
 1. Schizophrenic disorders
 2. Affective psychoses
 3. Paranoid states
 4. Other nonorganic psychoses
 5. Psychoses with origin specific to childhood

C. Neurotic disorders, personality disorders, and other nonpsychotic mental disorders
 1. Neurotic disorders
 2. Personality disorders
 3. Sexual deviations and disorders
 4. Alcohol dependence syndrome
 5. Drug dependence
 6. Nondependent abuse of drugs
 7. Physiological malfunction arising from mental factors
 8. Special symptoms or syndromes, not elsewhere classified
 9. Acute reaction to stress
 10. Adjustment reaction
 11. Specific nonpsychotic mental disorders due to organic brain damage
 12. Depressive disorder, not elsewhere classified
 13. Disturbance of conduct, not elsewhere classified
 14. Disturbance of emotions specific to childhood and adolescence
 15. Hyperkinetic syndrome of childhood
 16. Specific delays in development
 17. Psychic factors associated with diseases not elsewhere classified

D. Mental Retardation
 1. Mild mental retardation
 2. Other specified mental retardation
 3. Unspecified mental retardation

causes of abnormal behavior. For example, a major distinction is made between "organic psychotic conditions" and "other psychoses." This distinction has been severely examined in the diagnostic literature as potentially lacking validity. For example, it is sometimes the case that what appears to be the same type of abnormal behavior may have different etiological bases; it is often impossible, however, to know with certainty which of the different etiological possibilities is the correct one. A diagnostic system that requires the diagnostician to make etiological judgments may therefore force false decisions.

Another aspect of the ICD is that it distinguishes "psychotic" from "nonpsychotic" (also referred to as "neurotic") conditions. The psychotic–neurotic distinction within the ICD is also problematic. For example, depressive conditions are found listed both as psychotic (major depressive disorder) and neurotic (depressive disorder) conditions, but the distinction between these two hypothetically distinct types of depression is not clear.

Despite some problems with the ICD system for diagnosing mental disorder, it is a widely subscribed to international model for diagnosis. It is the dominant approach used in Europe, as well as countries that have been under European influence. The World Health Organization is currently at work on the *ICD-10*.

C. Diagnostic and Statistical Manual

Due to problems with earlier versions of the ICD, the American Psychiatric Association developed its own system for diagnosis. Referred to as the *Diagnostic and Statistical Manual* (DSM), the system was first published in 1952, and has since been updated and republished three more times. The current DSM is the third version—revised (DSM-III-R), which was published in 1987 (although DSM-IV is scheduled for release in 1994).

The first two editions of the DSM had many similarities to the ICD. Distinctions were made between psychotic and nonpsychotic disorders, for example, and the diagnostic system included many etiological terms in the diagnoses. In 1980, with the publication of DSM-III, the American Psychiatric Association made a major departure from this approach and deleted, as much as possible, all references to putative causes of disorder. Instead, the DSM-III was a more descriptive system that attempted to label disorders solely on their objective features, with as little inference as possible about the cause of the disorders.

In addition to the more descriptive nature of the DSM-III, an additional feature was that it was multi-axial. The multi-axial nature of the DSM-III meant that it examined different axes or dimensions of functioning within the person being diagnosed at a single time, in order to achieve a more rounded assessment of the person and their functioning. The publication of DSM-III was widely applauded in psychiatric and psychological circles as a major step forward from the diagnostic systems found in earlier versions of the DSM and are still found in the ICD to a large extent.

DSM-III-R has continued the basic descriptive approach, as well as the multi-axial form, of the DSM-III. Its publication was largely due to changes in some of the diagnoses in the field, as well as a desire by the American Psychiatric Association to have a bridge between DSM-III and DSM-IV (currently in development). The DSM-III-R, as was true for the DSM-III, has five major axes. The first two DSM-III axes are those most analogous to the ICD diagnostic system. Axis I comprises the major psychopathology diagnoses (see Table II), while Axis II is used to diagnose personality disorders in adults and developmental disorders in children. Axes I and II comprise a total of 253 specific diagnoses. Axis III is used to diagnose physical disorders and conditions. Some of these disorders or conditions may be relevant to the other psychopathology diagnoses, as malnutrition may be to anorexia, for example, whereas other medical disorders or conditions may simply help to round out a picture of the person's current problems. Axis IV of the DSM-III-R is used to rate the severity of psychosocial stressors, ranging from 1 (none) to 6 (catastrophic), whereas Axis V consists of a global assessment rating of the individual's functioning for the past year, ranging from 1 (worst possible functioning) to 90 (highest possible functioning).

In order to diagnose a person using the DSM-III-R, information should be provided on each of the

TABLE II

Major Mental Diagnostic Categories from Axis I of the *Diagnostic and Statistical Manual-III-R*

1. Disorders usually first evident in infancy, childhood, or adolescence
2. Organic mental disorders
3. Organic mental syndromes
4. Psychoactive substances use disorders
5. Schizophrenia
6. Delusional (paranoid) disorders
7. Psychotic disorders not elsewhere classified
8. Mood disorders
9. Anxiety disorders
10. Somatoform disorders
11. Dissociative disorders
12. Sexual disorders
13. Sleep disorders
14. Factitious disorders
15. Adjustment disorder
16. Psychological factors affecting physical condition
17. Conditions not attributable to a mental disorder that are a focus of attention or treatment

five axes. Thus, whereas only Axes I and II are comparable to the ICD's diagnostic labels, the DSM system is more comprehensive than the ICD, and provides more of a complete context in terms of the patient's medical and psychosocial issues.

D. Future Issues and Developments

A large number of conceptual, research, and ethical issues are relevant to the categorical approaches to psychopathology. At the conceptual level, issues of validity (i.e., accurate portrayal of reality) have been raised. These issues have taken a number of forms. For example, the fact that over time the total number of diagnostic categories has been increasing, and the fact that the ICD and the DSM systems have different numbers and types of diagnoses, leads to the question about which (if either) system best reflects the real range of psychopathology. Ideally, diagnostic systems should be both comprehensive (that is, include all potential diagnoses) and distinctive (that is, each diagnostic category should be distinct and minimally overlapping with other categories). It is not clear at present that either existing system meets these criteria. Nor is it easy to imagine how they could demonstrate that they are both comprehensive and distinctive.

Another validity issue that has been raised with regard to the two major diagnostic systems is the extent to which a categorical system best represents psychopathology. This issue has been particulary raised in the case of the personality disorders, where it has been argued that rather than being discrete disorders they represent the extreme ends of personality dimensions. According to this view, rather than diagnosing personality disorders such as dependent personality disorder, psychopathologists should speak about the relative strength or weakness of certain personality dimensions such as dependency.

Although the issue of whether disorders are dimensional or categorical in nature is most acute in the case of personality disorders, it is also clear that in other disorders judgments must be made about when a given behavioral pattern or other symptom falls outside the range of normal. Consider, for example, the diagnosis of anorexia nervosa (see Table III). Within that diagnosis are a number of judgments that a diagnostician would have to make, including what is an "expected body weight," when a fear of being overweight is "intense" and when thoughts about body size are "disturbed." While at the extremes of such judgments there would likely be high

TABLE III
Diagnostic Criteria for Anorexia Nervosa

A. Refusal to maintain body weight over a *minimal normal* weight for age and height, e.g., weight loss leading to maintenance of body weight 15% below that *expected;* or failure to make *expected* weight gain during period of growth, leading to body weight 15% below that *expected.*

B. *Intense* fear of gaining weight or becoming fat, even though underweight.

C. *Disturbance* in the way in which one's body weight, size, or shape is experienced, e.g., the person claims to "feel fat" even when emaciated, believes that one area of the body is "too fat" even when *obviously* underweight.

D. In females, absence of at least three consecutive menstrual cycles when otherwise *expected* to occur (primary or secondary amenorrhea). (A woman is considered to have amenorrhea if her periods occur only following hormone, e.g., estrogen, administration.)

Source: Adapted from the *Diagnostic and Statistical Manual-III-Revised.* Italics not in the original.

agreement across diagnosticians, less extreme fears and disturbances are more difficult to judge with certainty. Put otherwise, some of the symptoms are themselves not dichotomous, but reflect dimensions of disturbance, which are identified only if they cross some imaginal "line" of dysfunction. Decisions about how to recognize where that line has been crossed require some agreement among diagnosticians about what that line is, and how to recognize it is being breached.

Similar arguments have been made with respect to most forms of childhood disorders, as these disorders are typically conceptualized in terms of extreme forms of behavior (for example, too much aggressive behavior) that might better be seen as extremes on a continuum rather than discrete forms of psychopathology.

A third issue about diagnoses has been that to some extent they do not reflect the real world of psychopathology, but rather society's beliefs about and experience of abnormal behavior. Critics of diagnosis have pointed out that the "emergence" of new disorders and deletion of others reflect changing societal values, rather than scientific advances that could validate such changes. For example, the diagnosis of homosexuality has had an interesting history within the DSM system. In the DSM-II, published in 1968, homosexuality was defined as a psychopathology diagnosis. By the time DSM-III was published in 1980 the system had changed, such that only ego-dystonic homsexuality (i.e., sexual preference for a same-sex person, but where the individual felt that this preference was inconsistent with their own wishes) was a recognized disorder; instances where the homosexual patterns were ego-syntonic (consistent with the persons's wishes) were not considered abnormal. Homosexuality has been totally deleted as a diagnostic label in the DSM-III-R (ICD continues to include homosexuality). It has been pointed out that this evolution of approaches to homosexuality mirrors a growing recognition and acceptance of homosexuality in Western society. It has been argued, therefore, that the changing diagnoses related to homosexuality do not reflect changes in the scientific basis of that diagnosis, but rather reflect changes in the attitudes and biases that the developers of diagnostic systems share with society at large. It has been similarly argued that other disorders, such as anorexia nervosa, reflect societal beliefs and awareness about specific behaviors, rather than necessarily reflecting the ''true'' nature of psychopathology. [See SEXUAL ORIENTATION.]

At the scientific level, the major issues that face categorical systems of psychopathology are those related to the internal consistency and reliability of diagnostic categories. If a perfect diagnostic system existed, then every person with psychopathology should be captured in the system, and every trained diagnostician should recognize an individual's unique diagnoses in a manner consistent with other diagnosticians. Research on these issues suggests that our current systems, although better than their precursors, do not closely approximate these goals. Clearly, further research and development are needed to clarify why consistency and reliability have been elusive.

Finally, there have been ethical arguments raised against the practice of diagnosis. It has been argued, for example, that diagnosis involves an artificial process of labeling people, and that once these labels are applied they become more than descriptions of the individual's current functioning, but become long-term crosses for the individual to bear. These abuses of the diagnostic process have been used as a basis for arguing that the utility of diagnosis is more than offset by its costs, and should be abandoned.

Despite the above issues and criticisms of diagnosis, it is clear that the Kraepelinian model of psychodiagnosis has been extremely popular, and is not likely to be supplanted. DSM-IV is currently in the development stages, and has proceeded from literature reviews of the adequacy of certain existing and other proposed diagnostic categories, through to field tests of the proposed system. The American Psychiatric Association is preparing its final texts in late 1993, with the publication of DSM-IV planned for 1994 or 1995. One important aspect of this review has been the collaboration between the APA and the WHO. It is anticipated that DSM-IV and ICD-10 will be closer to each other than previous versions. Perhaps at some point in the future they will merge and a universal diagnostic system for psychopathology will exist.

III. DIMENSIONAL MODELS OF PSYCHOPATHOLOGY

Dimensional models view psychopathology as deriving from underlying dimensional constructs that explain both normal and abnormal functioning. For example, it is possible to imagine a construct called interpersonal dependency. At one end of this construct is extreme dependency, as would be marked by such thoughts as being insufficient without others, having to have others around to feel comfortable, and marked by such behavior as constantly seeking out others to be with, talking to others, etc. At the other end of this construct is extreme interpersonal independency, which would be marked by such thoughts as never needing others, having to be alone to feel comfortable, and such behaviors as spending time alone, not starting conversations with others, etc. A person functioning at either of the extremes on this dimension would be considered dysfunctional or psychopathological; between these two extremes lies a wide range of normal dependency–independency options.

Research has shown that most constructs are more common at their middle range, and less common at their extremes. As such, if those constructs related to personality or behavior that are related to psychopathology could be identified, then it would be possible to identify those points along the continua where abnormal or extreme patterns could be identified. For example, using the dimension of interpersonal dependency–independency, it might be possible to identify a point along that continuum where the person is either so dependent or independent it causes distress and/or interpersonal problems for the person. It would be at those points we would talk about the person crossing an imaginary line from normal to psychopathological functioning (see Fig. 1).

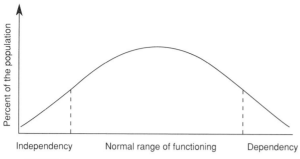

FIGURE 1 A dimensional approach to dependency.

A. Trait versus Symptom Approaches

Dimensional models of psychopathology can be viewed as typically being one of two major types. Some dimensional models focus on underlying theoretical dimensions or traits that might explain abnormal behavior, while other focus more on the range of symptoms or descriptive features of the dysfunctional behaviors themselves. Trait approaches are more theoretical than symptom approaches, and typically have an associated theory of normal personality as well as psychopathology, while symptom approaches focus more on the elements of psychopathology alone. [*See* TRAITS.]

There are a number of trait approaches to psychopathology, and all cannot be described here. The work of Hans Eysenck is a good example of this approach, however, and will be used to provide an example. In Eysenck's earlier research, he identified two basic dimensions to normal and abnormal behavior. One of these was the dimension of introversion–extroversion, which had extremes of being highly introverted (shy, retiring, isolated) and highly extroverted (outgoing, sociable), while the other was neuroticism (which had two extremes of stable versus unstable patterns; where instability is marked by such attributes as anxiety, physical complaints, moodiness, etc.). According to Eysenck's research these two personality dimensions were unique from each other. An individual's placement on each dimension, according to Eysenck, reflects a basic disposition on the part of the individual which likely could be seen in different situations that the person finds him/herself in, and also lasts across time. [*See* EXTRAVERSION–INTROVERSION.]

Within Eysenck's model of functioning, psychopathology is identified at the extremes of each dimension. Thus, a person who is "too" extroverted could be said to be dysfunctional; similarly, a person "too" high on neuroticism could be said to be dys-

functional. Eysenck developed questionnaires to measure these dimensions which allowed clinicians to identify how much of these dimensions were represented by an individual, and thereby identify if the person was in the normal range of functioning or not.

A later addition to Eysenck's theory was a third dimension, referred to as *psychoticism*. This dimension was theoretically distinct from the other two, and reflected an underlying tendency toward more extreme forms of abnormal behavior, including insensitivity toward and lack of caring about others, and opposition of accepted social customs.

A mental health professional using Eysenck's system to describe psychopathology would not talk about a given individual as "extroverted," "neurotic," or "psychotic," but would rather talk about an individual as being high on these dimensions. The mental health professional would know that certain forms of thought, emotion, and behavior are related to these dimensions, and would explain psychopathology in terms of these underlying trait dimensions.

As stated previously, Eysenck's is just one of a number of trait approaches to psychopathology. One of the major issues that has been addressed by theorists who use these models has been that of trying to develop a comprehensive and exhaustive system. In recent years, there has been considerable discussion about what are referred to as the "Big Five" personality traits that might explain most human behavior. These five factors include neuroticism, extraversion, openness, agreeableness, and conscientiousness. While we will not discuss the adequacy of this model here, it is important to note two elements: first, that many theorists are beginning to converge on the importance of these five factors in personality, and second, that one of these dimensions—neuroticism—is explicitly oriented toward identifying abnormal behavior of a neurotic type (anxiety, physical complaints, nervousness, edginess, etc.).

As opposed to trait models of psychopathology, there are symptom dimensional approaches. One prominent example of this type of approach has been with regard to the personality disorders. Within the DSM-III-R, there are 11 recognized personality disorder diagnoses. As is true for other diagnostic categories, DSM-III-R lists the descriptive features of these disorders, and presents them as unique (although a given individual could have more than one diagnosis simultaneously). An alternative perspective to conceptualizing types of personality disorders is to conceptualize personality as having a number of dimensions, which at their extreme represent dysfunctional patterns of interpersonal relating. Such an alternative approach would view personality features in terms of their symptoms, as well as in terms of the severity of these symptoms. [*See* PERSONALITY DISORDERS.]

Symptom-based approaches, as seen in the area of personality disorders, can be imagined for most types of psychopathology. In the area of depression, for example, one can imagine that rather than diagnosing an individual as depressed or not based upon whether they meet certain diagnostic criteria, a psychopathologist could describe the severity or depth of depression. Such an approach would require a psychopathologist to determine the key symptoms of depression, to evaluate the severity of each of these symptoms, and then determine the overall depth or severity of depression for a given individual. The fact that the end result is a index of severity, though, means that an underlying dimensional, rather than categorical, approach has been used to conceptual and describe depression. [*See* DEPRESSION.]

Dimensional approaches to most forms of psychopathology exist. Typically, the assessment of psychopathology using such approaches relies on questionnaires, which are self-report means to determine the number and severity of different symptoms the person may be experiencing. A large number of trait and symptom questionnaires have been developed, predominantly by psychologists working in the fields of personality and psychopathology. A listing of all published questionnaires and psychological tests can be gained by examining the *Mental Measurements Yearbook,* which is an annual publication of the Buros Institute.

B. Models of Psychopathology

Psychopathologists are not content with conceptualizing and describing categorical and dimensional aspects of psychopathology. Another key activity of psychopathologists is to develop theoretical models than can potentially explain the cause, course, and required treatment of these disorders as well. A large number of theoretical models have been developed to attempt to explain psychopathology, many of which are very complex and well beyond the scope of this article. An excellent starting reference for interested readers is *Abnormal Psychology,* by Davison and Neale (1991).

Models of psychopathology fall into several major categories. One major dimension which can be used to think of these models is whether their focus is on factors that are external or internal to the person. Models that focus on external factors might place an emphasis on such issues as early childhood experiences, family dynamics, traumatic experiences, and even social and cultural issues that might lead to different forms of problematic behavior. These models are likely to focus on the need for changes external to the individual to correct psychopathology, including marital and family therapy. Some theorists who adopt this type of environmental or social perspective also focus on the need to change societal or cultural variables to lower the likelihood of some forms of psychopathology. For example, it has been argued that some eating disorders are encouraged by the value that society places on thinness, and that by changing societal values, we may actually be able to lower the future likelihood of some eating disorders.

Theorists who focus on factors internal to the individual typical adopt either a biological or a psychological perspective. Biologically oriented theorists might focus on genetic contributions to psychopathology, structural problems in the nervous system that cause abnormal behavior, or neurological processes that can be disordered and lead to psychopathology. These theorists are likely to focus on biological treatments to psychopathology, including psychoactive medications. A large number of medications for treating psychological disorders exist, many of which have documented benefit.

The third major theoretical approach to psychopathology is psychological in nature. Such approaches focus upon psychological models of both normal and abnormal personality, and try to explain psychopathology in terms of these processes. Within the psychological approaches are a number of discrete models, including psychoanalytic, behavioral, cognitive, humanistic, and other theoretical approaches. While all of these models share the assumption that there is something within the individual at the psychological level that explains abnormal behavior, the specifics of each model vary dramatically, as do the therapies they promote.

In summary, psychopathology researchers not only classify, diagnose, and assess abnormal behavior, but also are interested in the causes, course, and treatment of these conditions. Different models are used in the effort to explain psychopathology. While some models appear to be better suited for some forms of abnormal behavior, others may be more appropriate for other conditions. It is also possible that a given form of psychopathology, such as anxiety, may have multiple causes, which may vary from person to person having that disorder. Humans are extremely complex, and the large number of approaches helps to encompass that complexity in the way psychopathologists conceptualize their subject field.

IV. FUTURE ISSUES IN PSYCHOPATHOLOGY

As the above reveals, psychopathology is an intricate and often perplexing field of study. Although there are a large number of issues that face the field, major issues include the future of categorical and dimensional approaches, theoretical models, and treatment issues. Each is discussed in turn below.

A. Categorical and Dimensional Approaches

Both of the categorical and dimensional approaches to psychopathology face the issues of comprehensiveness and distinctiveness. How many diagnoses or dimensions, respectively, adequately account for the range of human dysfunction? Are these distinct diagnoses and dimensions, or is their overlap such that they call into question the theoretical basis for the approach to psychopathology?

Another question that both approaches face is how best to assess psychopathology. As has been stated, each of these approaches has its own methodology for assessment. Categorical approaches lend themselves to diagnoses, which are typically constructed as a result of interviews with individuals, and the decision as to whether the given individual qualifies for one or more diagnoses. Dimensional approaches are most often assessed using questionnaires that assess one or more dimensions of psychopathology, using traits or symptoms as the conceptual basis for assessment.

Interview and questionnaire assessment strategies are not necessarily contradictory, and many psychopathologists believe that using both leads to a more comprehensive understanding of the individual in question. It remains for the field to adequately ad-

dress which strategy or strategies are best within each approach, and how best to integrate these two types of assessment.

B. Theories of Psychopathology

Theories of psychopathology, as is true for all scientific theories, are tested against their explanatory power. Within psychopathology, many research methods exist to test theoretical models, including the ability to discriminate groups with different types of psychopathology, or the correlation between certain theoretical constructs and the severity of psychopathology. The field of psychopathology is rich with research questions.

Psychopathology research is notoriously difficult to conduct for a number of reasons, including the large number of definitional, assessment and theoretical perspectives already discussed. Further, it is often difficult to easily obtain large numbers of research subjects that clearly have a distinct form of psychopathology, and for ethical reasons it is often not possible to conduct the experimental types of studies that might best test different theories of psychopathology. Finally, a good number of different forms of psychopathology need time to develop (indeed, sometimes it is the course of different disorders that itself is the object of scientific study), which requires long-term research funds and geographical stability of both researchers and research objects. Such control is not easy to obtain in the real world.

Despite the above problems, research in the field of psychopathology is increasingly driven by strong theoretical questions, and the answers to these questions are slowly being accumulated. The field has begun to contrast competing theories, and the overall adequacy of some theoretical models is beginning to become clear. It can be expected that over the next decades some "best models" for different forms of psychopathology will emerge.

C. Treatment Issues in Psychopathology

Many psychopathologists enter the field because of a desire not only to understand, but also to help people with behavioral problems. One hope is that with accurate assessment and diagnosis, treatment options may become clarified. Although there does not yet exist a clear correspondence between different forms of psychopathology and treatments, the field has advanced considerably in this direction.

For a given disorder there likely are several viable treatments, some of which may have better success rates, but all of which have some potential for helping an individual in distress. With increasing sophistication of assessment, diagnosis, and conceptualization, it is likely that treatment of psychopathology will become an even more complex and successful enterprise in the future than now.

Bibliography

American Psychiatric Association (1987). ''Diagnostic and Statistical Manual-III-Revised.'' Washington, DC.

Buros Institute (1992). ''Mental Measurements Yearbook.'' Gryphen, Highland Park, NJ.

Davison, G., and Neale (1991). ''Abnormal Psychology,'' 5th ed. Wiley, New York.

World Health Organization (1979). ''International Classification of Diseases,'' 9th ed. Geneva, Switzerland.

PSYCHOPHYSICS

Michael H. Birnbaum
California State University at Fullerton

Glossary

Absolute judgment Task in which subject is asked to judge stimuli using "absolute" standards. Important finding is that absolute judgments are relative: they depend on the context.

Birnbaum's subtractive theory Judgments of "differences" and "ratios" are both governed by subtraction, but "differences of differences" and "ratios of differences" are governed by two operations on the same scale of sensation.

Choice task (comparison) Subject is asked to compare two stimuli and judge a psychological relation between the two (e.g., choose which weight is heavier). Dependent variables can include proportion of choices and time to make the choice. Comparison task can also involve judgments of quantitative relations between stimuli.

Context The context includes all features of the environment that affect the judgment of a stimulus besides the value of the stimulus itself. The judgment of a given stimulus depends, for example, on the set of other stimuli also presented for judgment.

Cross-modality Task in which stimuli from different psychological modalities or dimensions are to be matched, compared, or combined. For example, a subject might be asked to adjust the loudness of a tone to match the heaviness of a lifted weight.

"Difference" task Subject is asked to compare two stimuli and estimate the psychological "difference" in psychological values. (Quotation marks are used to remind the reader that "difference" judgments may or may not be governed by subtraction.)

Fechner's law Subjective value is a logarithmic function of physical value, so equal physical ratios produce equal psychological differences.

Just noticeable difference Value of smallest difference that can be detected. Usually defined as the physical change in the comparison stimulus that would be required to change the proportion of judgments that the "comparison is greater than the standard" from 0.5 to 0.75.

Magnitude estimation Task in which subject is asked to assign a number to represent the strength of sensation using an unbounded scale.

Point of subjective equality (PSE) Value of comparison stimulus that is judged greater than the standard 50% of the time.

Rating Subject assigns a number to a stimulus to represent the strength of its sensation using a numerical scale that is bounded at both ends.

Recognition Subject reports that a stimulus is the same as a previously presented stimulus.

Scaling The process of assigning measurements to psychological values, developing a numerical scale.

Signal detection theory Stimuli are represented by distributions, as in Thurstone's law. The subject will report a "signal" if the momentary sensation produced by a stimulus exceeds a criterion that is established by decision processes.

Standard Stimulus against which a comparison or variable stimulus can be judged.

Stevens' law Subjective value is a power function of physical value, so equal physical ratios produce equal psychological ratios.

Encyclopedia of Human Behavior, Volume 3

Threshold Absolute threshold is the value of smallest stimulus that can be detected. Difference threshold is the smallest difference that can be detected. The exact definition of "threshold" changes in different theories of detection and discrimination.

Thurstone's law of comparative judgment Theory that each physical value produces a distribution of subjective values. Judge reports that the comparison exceeds the standard whenever its momentary sensation exceeds the sensation produced by the standard.

Weber's law Physical size of just noticeable difference is a constant proportion of the value of the standard for a given dimension.

PSYCHOPHYSICS is the study of the relationships between the physical and the psychological worlds. Corresponding to physical weight and sound energy, for example, it is assumed that people have sensations of heaviness of weights or loudness of sounds. Psychophysics includes the study of thresholds, discrimination, recognition, and scaling. It deals with such questions as "What is the weakest stimulus that can be detected?" "What is the smallest difference in stimuli that can be discriminated?" "How does a person recognize another presentation of the same stimulus?" "Can we assign numbers to represent the strengths of psychological sensations in a meaningful way?" Psychophysical methods, theories, and empirical findings have proven valuable in many fields of psychology in which stimuli, responses, or intervening psychological constructs are measured quantitatively. Psychophysics has had important influences on the study of perception, sensation, social psychology, memory, judgment, and decision making.

I. INTRODUCTION

Psychophysics is the oldest area of psychology and probably the most controversial. Regarded as "mad" and "moonshiney" by some and as the foundation of scientific psychology by others, the field has continued to provide new and interesting problems to each generation of psychologists. Psychophysics had its origin on October 22, 1850, the morning when Gustav Fechner lay in bed contemplating problems in the philosophy of mind and body.

Fechner initially thought that psychophysics would resolve age-old controversies in philosophy. However, by 1860 (when he published *Elements of Psychophysics*), Fechner realized that psychophysics could be accepted as a new field of study, independent of its philosophical interpretations.

Fechner proposed that corresponding to the physical world there is a psychological world. In the physical world, material objects can be measured in physical units, and in the psychological world, sensations can be measured in psychological units. Based on ideas of D. Bernoulli and E. H. Weber, Fechner concluded that psychological sensations (Ψ) are a logarithmic function of physical values (Φ). Fechner's mathematical interpretation of Weber's results and his derivation of the logarithmic psychophysical law are presented in simple form below.

II. WEBER'S LAW

Weber's law states that the increase in a stimulus that is just noticeably different is a constant proportion of the stimulus. In a typical experiment, illustrated in Figure 1, the judge lifts a standard weight, followed by one of several comparison weights and judges whether the comparison seems "lighter" or "heavier" than the standard. The proportion of "heavier" judgments is plotted as a function of the comparison stimulus in Figure 1. [Quotation marks

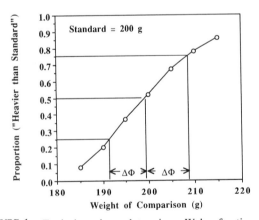

FIGURE 1   Typical results to determine a Weber fraction. The subject lifts the standard weight (200 g), followed by one of the comparison weights, and reports whether the sensation produced by the comparison exceeds that of the standard. In this case, it takes an increase ($\Delta\Phi$) of about 10 g to increase the proportion of judgments from 0.5 to 0.75, so the Weber fraction $k = 10/200 = 0.05$. If the standard were increased to 400 g, for example, Weber's law implies that the $\Delta\Phi$ would be 20 g to produce the same change in choice proportion.

are used in this article to distinguish subject's judgments from actual or theoretical statements. In this case, Figure 1 shows that when the comparison stimulus is 190 g (actually lighter than the standard), the subject judges it "heavier" than the standard 20% of the time.] The point of subjective equality (PSE) is defined as the value of the comparison that is judged "greater" than the standard 50% of the time. The difference between the standard and the PSE is defined as the time order error. In this case, there is a negative time order error because the subject tends (more than half the time) to judge the 200-g weight to be "heavier" than the standard of the same value.

The just noticeable difference (JND) is defined as the change in the stimulus required to increase the percentage of "greater" judgments from 50 to 75% (or some other arbitrary level). Weber found that this change in physical value ($\Delta\Phi$) is a constant fraction of the standard,

$$\Delta\Phi = k\Phi, \qquad (1)$$

where k is the Weber constant for the continuum and the particular definition of a JND. For example, in this case the just noticeable difference at 200 g is a change of 10 g, so $k = 10/200 = 0.05$. According to Weber's law, it should take an increase of 20 g to make one JND from a 400-g standard, or an increase of 40 g to produce one JND from a standard of 800 g.

III. FECHNER'S LAW

Fechner theorized that if Eq. 1 held for any value of the standard, and if it would hold in the limits for any definition of a JND (for tiny changes in detection probability, $\Delta\Phi \rightarrow \delta\Phi$), and if all just noticeable differences are psychologically equal, then Weber's law implied:

$$k\,\delta\Psi = \delta\Phi/\Phi, \qquad (2)$$

where $\delta\Phi$ is the physical differential value and $\delta\Psi$ the psychological differential. Integrating both sides,

$$\int k\,\delta\Psi = \int \delta\Phi/\Phi, \qquad (3)$$

which reduces to Fechner's law:

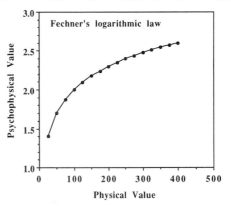

FIGURE 2   Fechner's law, illustrated for lifted weight.

$$\Psi = a \log \Phi + b, \qquad (4)$$

where a and b are constants that reflect the value of the Weber fraction (k), the constant of integration, and the base of the logarithm.

A logarithmic relationship is illustrated in Figure 2, which shows Fechner's law applied to lifted weights. According to the logarithmic function, when stimuli bear the same physical ratio, the psychological differences will be equal, i.e., $\Phi_1/\Phi_2 = \Phi_3/\Phi_4$ implies $\Psi_1 - \Psi_2 = \Psi_3 - \Psi_4$. For example, $100/200 = 200/400$, so weights of 100, 200, and 400 g are equally spaced psychologically, according to Fechner's law.

IV. CATEGORY RATINGS

In the method of category rating, the subject is instructed to assign integers to stimuli to represent categories of sensation. When subjects are asked to sort the heaviness of weights into categories, category ratings of heaviness appear to fit Fechner's logarithmic law fairly well.

Fechner's law seemed to connect discrimination and judgment, because category ratings (judgments) seemed to be a linear function of the logarithm of physical value. For example, the ancient astronomer Hipparchus (c. 150 B.C.) rated the brightness of stars on a six-category scale, from stars of the first magnitude (brightest) to stars of the sixth magnitude (faintest). When modern astronomers measured the intensity of light from the stars, the scale of Hipparchus was found to be approximately logarithmically related to intensity, consistent with Fechner's law. [*See* Categorization.]

V. LIMITS OF SENSATION

Some stars are too dim to be seen by the naked eye. Sensory psychologists have been concerned with the thresholds of sensation, values below which judgments would be random guesses. The average adult can reliably detect a candle flame from 30 miles on a clear night, he or she could reliably hear the ticking of a watch in a quiet room from 20 feet, feel the wing of a bee falling on the cheek from 1/2 in., taste a teaspoon of sugar in 2 gallons of water, or smell a drop of perfume diffused in a classroom. Psychophysical studies of thresholds have led to useful procedures for studying sensory deficiencies.

At the other extreme, there also may be an upper threshold. In summary, as one increases the physical measure of sensation below the lower threshold, psychological value does not change; above the threshold, sensation increases with increases in the physical magnitude. Finally, as the stimulus exceeds the upper threshold, becoming painful, sensations on the original dimension are unaffected by further increases.

VI. THURSTONE'S LAW

L. L. Thurstone realized that the basic idea of discrimination could be used to scale stimuli without physical measures. If each stimulus produces a normal distribution of values on a subjective, discriminal continuum, and if the subject says "stimulus i exceeds j" whenever the momentary sensation of stimulus i exceeds the momentary sensation produced by stimulus j, then the probability of this judgment, $p(i, j)$, will be given by the following equation:

$$p(i, j) = \mathbf{N}[(\Psi_i - \Psi_j)/\sigma_{ij}], \qquad (5)$$

where Ψ_i and Ψ_j are the means of the distributions of subjective values on the discriminal continuum, $\mathbf{N}$ is the cumulative normal distribution function, and σ_{ij} is the standard deviation of difference between the momentary sensations. Special cases of Eq. 5 provided testable theories that allow one to construct a scale of sensation that can be checked for internal consistency and independently tested against Fechner's law.

For example, if all of the σ_{ij} are equal, we can set the value of σ_{ij} to 1. Suppose there are three stimuli (A, B, and C); suppose $p(A,B) = 0.84$ and $p(B,C) = 0.84$, then we know that the interval from

A to B and from B to C are both 1 [because $\mathbf{N}(1) = 0.84$]. Therefore, the interval from A to C is 2, so $p(A,C) = 0.98$ [because $\mathbf{N}(2) = 0.98$]. As Thurstone put it, if an experimenter obtained a matrix of choice proportions and one of the entries were erased from the matrix, the missing value could be reproduced by knowing the other values and the theory.

VII. THEORY OF SIGNAL DETECTION

Signal detection theory developed from a premise similar to that in Thurstone's law, that each stimulus produces a distribution of values. The classical problem studied in the theory of signal detection is how to interpret the subject's report that a "signal" has been detected. (Quotation marks distinguish the subject's response from the actual event.) For example, the subject might be asked to listen to auditory stimuli which consist of either a burst of white noise (Noise) or a 1000-Hz tone (Signal) embedded in white noise. The subject's task is to report "signal" or "noise" to identify the two types of trials. We can classify the outcomes in a two by two table as in Table I.

Figure 3 illustrates the basic tenants of signal detection theory. The distributions represent the variability of sensation produced by the two stimuli. When the sensation exceeds the limen, shown in the figure, the subject reports that a "Signal" occurred. The probabilities of hits and false alarms are the areas under the Signal and Noise curves to the right of the limen, shown as shaded regions in Figure 3.

If each stimulus produces a normal distribution on a sensory continuum, and if there is a limen (boundary, or decision criterion) to decide whether each experience should be classified as a "Signal" or a "Noise" then we can represent the hit rate (conditional probability of saying "Signal" given a Signal was presented) and the false alarm rate (con-

TABLE I
Classification of Events in Signal Detection

Actual stimulus	Response	
	"Noise"	"Signal"
Noise	Correct rejection	False alarm
Signal	Miss	Hit

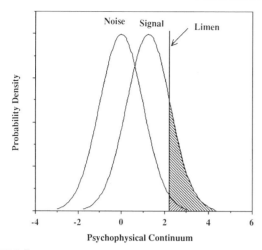

FIGURE 3   Illustration of a simple theory of signal detection. In this theory, each stimulus produces a normal distribution of subjective experiences. When the momentary experience exceeds a criterion, or limen, the subject reports the experience as a "signal." The probability of hits (saying "signal" given signal) and of false alarms (saying "signal" given the stimulus was actually noise) are shown as shaded areas to the right of the limen. Discriminability (d') is the difference between the means, divided by the standard deviation, which in this case is 1.25.

ditional probability of saying "Signal" given Noise was presented) as follows:

$$p(\text{"Signal"} \mid \text{Signal}) = \mathbf{N}[(\Psi_j - t_k)/\sigma_{jk}] \quad (6)$$

$$p(\text{"Signal"} \mid \text{Noise}) = \mathbf{N}[(\Psi_i - t_k)/\sigma_{ik}], \quad (7)$$

where $\mathbf{N}$ is the cumulative normal distribution, Ψ_j and Ψ_i are the mean strengths of sensation for the Signal and Noise, t_k is the limen (criterion to report "Signal" rather than "Noise"), and the standard deviations of the differences between the momentary values of the stimuli and the limen are σ_{jk} and σ_{ik}. In a simple special case, all of the standard deviations are assumed to be equal. In this case, the difference between the stimuli, $\Psi_j - \Psi_i$, in standard deviation units, is defined as d', the measure of discriminability. The criterion (or limen) is sometimes called the "bias" parameter. A scale of sensation can be constructed by cumulating successive differences between stimuli.

For example, suppose an experiment were performed in which the subject is paid \$1 for every hit and penalized \$20 for every false alarm. In this case, the judge would avoid saying "signal" because of the high cost of a false alarm. Suppose the data are

as in Table II. The hit rates and false alarm rates are 0.198 and 0.018, respectively. In a table of cumulative normal probabilities, these values correspond to -2.1 and -0.85, yielding a difference, or d' of 1.25. These values correspond to the situation depicted in Figure 3. Considering the experiment and its results, the next logical question is to ask, "What would happen if the incentives for hits and false alarms were changed using the same stimuli?"

A large variety of rival detection, threshold, and choice theories have been developed to answer such questions. Some of these theories also have testable implications for decision times and the relations between decision times and response probabilities under different conditions of bias. An important graph for analyzing theories and data in signal detection experiments is a plot of hit rate against the false alarm rate obtained under various experimental conditions. This plot, called the ROC (receiver operating characteristic), could be used to compare different theories of signal detection and to examine the consequences of experimental manipulations.

Equations 6 and 7 imply that the ROC curve should be concave downward, if only the bias parameter (the limen) were affected by an experimental manipulation. Experiments that varied only the probability of a signal or the payoffs for hits and false alarms produce concave downward ROC curves that are consistent with the theory that the value of d' stays constant and that the motivational factors affected only bias. However, changes in the signal intensity affect d'. Thus, by increasing the signal intensity or by decreasing the level of noise, it is possible to increase the hit rate while holding false alarm rate constant. In contrast, changes in motivational factors such as payoffs produce correlated changes in both the probability of a hit and the probability of a false alarm.

Figure 4 illustrates two ROC curves. The higher curve illustrates the value of d' of 1.25 that is de-

TABLE II
Hypothetical Detection Results

Actual stimulus	Response	
	"Noise"	"Signal"
Noise	0.982	0.018
Signal	0.802	0.198

Note: Each entry shows the proportion of each response, conditioned on the presentation of the stimulus.

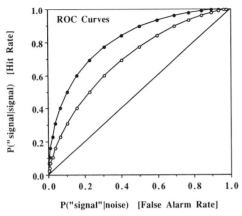

FIGURE 4   ROC curves. Filled circles show ROC curve for distributions in Figure 2 (d' is 1.25); different points represent hit rates and false alarm rates as the limen is moved across the scale. Open circles show ROC curve for a smaller value of d' (0.75).

picted in Figure 3. Points along this curve would be produced by changing the value of the category limen, t_k, in Eqs. 6 and 7, holding the value of d' (the separation between the distributions in Fig. 3) fixed. The lower curve illustrates the ROC curve for a smaller value of d'. Chance performance would fall on the identity line in Figure 4.

The study of signal detection, especially its distinction between discriminability and bias, has had important influences on basic and applied problems in psychology. The distinction is important to the analysis of recognition memory, social influences on memory, and the analysis of credibility of eyewitness testimony. Signal detection analysis has also proven very important in the study of such problems as medical diagnosis, weather forecasting, and the military problem of distinguishing "friendly" or "enemy" forces.

VIII. STEVENS' LAW

Stevens argued that the approaches of Fechner, Thurstone, and signal detection are "indirect" because they define ability to discriminate among stimuli as the basic unit of sensation. Stevens asked subjects to "directly" assign numbers to stimuli to represent the magnitudes of their sensations. In one variation of the magnitude estimation procedure, a standard stimulus is assigned a fixed number (called the modulus) and subjects are instructed to assign numbers to the comparison stimuli so that ratios of numbers would match psychological "ratios" of

sensation [again, quotation marks distinguish judged "ratios" from actual or theoretical ratios].

Stevens and his associates found that magnitude estimations could be fit as power functions of physical value for a variety of continua. Stevens' power law of sensation can be written as follows:

$$ME = \alpha\Phi^\beta, \tag{8}$$

where ME is the average magnitude estimation, β is the exponent of the power function (which depends on the physical dimension), Φ is the physical value, and α is a constant that would depend on the modulus and standard. For example, for lifted weight, the exponent was reported to be 1.5. Thus, according to Fechner, the subjective difference in heaviness between 300 and 200 g is less than the subjective difference between 200 and 100 g, but according to Stevens, the differences in heaviness have the opposite order, getting larger as one moves up the scale. Stevens' power law is illustrated in Figure 5.

According to the power function, equal physical ratios produce equal sensation ratios, not equal sensation differences (i.e., if $\Phi_1/\Phi_2 = \Phi_3/\Phi_4$, then $\Psi_1/\Psi_2 = \Psi_3/\Psi_4$). Stevens introduced a new task, called cross-modality matching, in which the subject was instructed to report the sensation produced on one continuum by adjusting the value of a stimulus on another dimension whose sensation matched in intensity. For example, to express the heaviness of a lifted weight, the subject could adjust the loudness of a tone so that the loudness matched the heaviness. If subjective values are power functions of physical values on all continua, then cross-modality matches should be power functions of one another, with ex-

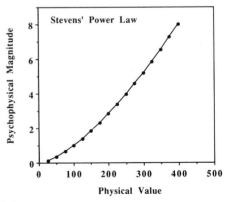

FIGURE 5   Stevens' power law, illustrated for lifted weight.

ponents predictable from the ratio of exponents determined by the method of magnitude estimation.

IX. CONFLICTS OF SCALES

Although cross-modality matches can be predicted from magnitude estimations, scales derived from different procedures do not agree. Compare Figures 2 and 5 for lifted weight. Because the two "laws" do not agree (Eq. 4 vs Eq. 8), Stevens said, "honor Fechner, but repeal his law." Magnitude estimations are not a linear function of category ratings, nor scales based on Thurstone's law, nor are they linearly related to scales based on the subtractive signal detection theory. Instead, magnitude estimations tend to be approximately an exponential function of category ratings. This conflict of scales caused much disagreement in psychophysical scaling.

The relationship between the two scales depends on the stimulus range, spacing, and frequency distribution and on other contextual features of the study. Some psychophysicists concluded that the conflicts of scales might be due to contextual effects, because the exact results for either category ratings or magnitude estimations could be altered by changing the procedures and stimuli used in the experiment.

X. CONTEXTUAL EFFECTS

Although magnitude estimations appear to be a power function of physical value when data are obtained with certain methods, the results can be strongly affected by the stimulus range and distribution, and the response range and distribution. The power function exponent can be predicted from the assumption that subjects match a fixed response range to the stimulus range that the experimenter will likely present. The greater the stimulus range, the lower the exponent.

Even though the subject is free to use an unbounded range of responses, the range of example responses used to illustrate the task has a powerful effect on magnitude estimations. For example, subjects who are instructed to judge the "ratio" of two stimuli are willing to call a certain "ratio" 4 : 1 when the instructions mention a "ratio of 4" as the largest example. Other subjects receive the same stimuli and instructions, except a "ratio of 64" is mentioned; these subjects are willing to judge the same "ratio" 64 : 1.

H. Helson, E. C. Poulton, A. Parducci, and others demonstrated the effects of many contextual variables and proposed theories to explain them. Their research shows that absolute judgments, category ratings, magnitude estimations, and direct judgments obtained with other procedures all depend on the context.

The same stimulus can receive different judgments, depending on the distribution of other stimuli presented for judgment. Range-frequency theory, developed by Parducci, gives a good account of contextual effects in category ratings as a compromise between the subject's tendency to make responses linearly related to the subjective value of the stimuli relative to the end stimuli and the subject's tendency to use equal portions of the response range with equal frequency.

Some investigators saw contextual effects as a threat to the establishment of measurement, whereas others considered contextual effects to be lawful properties of quantitative judgments that could themselves be used to measure psychophysical magnitudes.

XI. COMPOSITION OF FUNCTIONS

In psychophysics, it is important to make clear distinctions between the physical measures of stimuli, the physiological events produced by the physical stimuli, the corresponding psychological sensations, perception of the object that produced the sensations, and the overt responses (judgments or decisions) made by the subject. For example, a subject lifts a lead weight with a mass of 400 g, nerves and muscles fire, events occur in the brain, and the subject says the weight is "heavy."

The problem for "direct" scaling from magnitude estimations or category ratings is that the data can be represented as a composition of a psychophysical function and a judgment function, as in the following equations:

$$\Psi = \mathbf{H}(\Phi) \qquad (9)$$

and

$$R = \mathbf{J}[\Psi], \qquad (10)$$

where R is the overt response to stimulus Φ, $\mathbf{H}$ is the psychophysical function, and $\mathbf{J}$ is the judgment function that assigns responses to sensations. Scales based on "direct" measurement implicitly assume that the **J** function is known. Within the context of "direct" measurement, it is not possible to disentangle the functions, because responses are a composition, $R = \mathbf{J}[\mathbf{H}(\Phi)]$. Thus, the disagreement between category ratings and magnitude estimations could not be pinpointed to **H** or **J**, nor could the locus of contextual effects be determined. Some argued for category ratings and others defended magnitude estimations as the "true" measures of sensation, but the disputes could not be resolved in the framework of so-called "direct" scaling. Nevertheless, they could be resolved, if subjects could judge two different operations on a common scale of sensation.

XII. "RATIOS" AND "DIFFERENCES"

In principle, judgments of "ratios" and "differences" allow one to derive a scale of sensation that would be unique to a ratio scale, and to analyze the **H** and **J** functions, if the following equations held:

$$R_{ij} = \mathbf{J}_R[\Psi_j/\Psi_i] \qquad (11)$$

$$D_{ij} = \mathbf{J}_D[\Psi_j - \Psi_i], \qquad (12)$$

where R_{ij} and D_{ij} are the judgments of "ratio" and "difference" between stimuli with sensations Ψ_i and Ψ_j; $\mathbf{J}_R$ and $\mathbf{J}_D$ are strictly monotonic judgment functions for "ratios" and "differences," respectively. This two-operation theory implies that judgments of "ratios" and "differences" will not be related by a function, but instead will show particular order relations. For example, $2/1 = 4/2$ but $2 - 1 < 4 - 2$; similarly, $3 - 2 = 2 - 1$, but $3/2 < 2/1$.

TABLE III
Predictions of Two-Operation Theory of "Ratios" and "Differences"

Row stimulus	"Differences": Minuend stimulus				"Ratios": Numerator stimulus			
	1	2	3	4	1	2	3	4
1	0	1	2	3	1	2	3	4
2	−1	0	1	2	0.5	1	1.5	2
3	−2	−1	0	1	0.33	0.67	1	1.33
4	−3	−2	−1	0	0.25	0.5	0.75	1

Note: Entries are calculated from Eqs. (11) and (12), using successive integers for scale values. These are actual ratios and differences and therefore are not related to each other by a monotonic function.

Table III illustrates two-operation theory using identity functions for $\mathbf{J}_R$ and $\mathbf{J}_D$, and using successive integers for the values of Ψ. The left half shows differences (column values minus the row values) and the right half of the table shows ratios (column values divided by row values).

W. Garner and W. Torgerson found results that they explained as inconsistent with the theory that subjects were using two operations on a common scale. Instead, they asked, what if subjects are doing the same thing despite the experimenter's instructions? Torgerson noted that if subjects only have one way of comparing two stimuli, it might be impossible to discover what that one operation is.

XIII. ONE-OPERATION THEORY

Judgments of "differences" and "ratios" are monotonically related in many studies for different continua such as heaviness of weights and loudness of tones. In these cases, it appears that subjects use the same operation to compare stimuli, despite instructions. These results can be represented by the following equations:

$$R_{ij} = \mathbf{J}_R[\Psi_i \otimes \Psi_j] \qquad (13)$$

$$D_{ij} = \mathbf{J}_D[\Psi_i \otimes \Psi_j], \qquad (14)$$

where $\otimes$ represents the (single) operation for both tasks.

For a variety of continua, it has been found that judgments of "ratios" and "differences" are indeed monotonically related, as predicted by Eqs. 13 and 14, rather than showing two orders as would be predicted by the theory that subjects use both operations. The data are consistent with the theory that if the common operation is subtraction, $\mathbf{J}_R$ is exponential and $\mathbf{J}_D$ is linear; on the other hand, if the common operation is a ratio, then $\mathbf{J}_R$ is a power function and $\mathbf{J}_D$ is logarithmic.

Table IV illustrates one-operation theory under the assumptions that the operation is subtraction and $\mathbf{J}_R$ is an exponential function. For simplicity, let $D_{ij} = \Psi_j - \Psi_i$ and $R_{ij} = 2^{[\Psi_j - \Psi_i]}$. Thus, judgments of "ratios" and "differences" are monotonically related.

XIV. BIRNBAUM'S SUBTRACTIVE THEORY

M. Birnbaum theorized that when the subjective scale is inherently an interval scale, subjects use the

TABLE IV
Predictions of One-Operation Theory of "Ratios" and "Differences"

Row stimulus	"Differences": Minuend stimulus				"Ratios": Numerator stimulus			
	1	2	3	4	1	2	3	4
1	0	1	2	3	1	2	4	8
2	−1	0	1	2	0.5	1	2	4
3	−2	−1	0	1	0.25	0.5	1	2
4	−3	−2	−1	0	0.125	0.25	0.5	1

Note: Theory of Eqs. (13) and (14). In this case, $R_{ij} = 2^{D_{ij}}$. Thus, "ratios" are an exponential function of differences, and do not show two rank orders characteristic of actual ratios and differences. See also Figure 6.

subtractive operation for both "ratios" and "differences" but that they indeed can use two operations as instructed when the ratio operation is meaningful on the subjective scale. Intervals of stimuli form a ratio scale even when the original scales are intervals; therefore, subjects should be able to use two operations to judge "ratios of differences" and "differences of differences." For example, it may not be meaningful to judge the "ratio" of the *easterliness* of Philadelphia to that of San Francisco because the stimuli may be represented as points on a mental map, rather than as magnitudes. However, even with such a map representation, it is meaningful to ask, "what is the ratio of the *distance* from San Francisco to Philadelphia relative to the *distance* from San Francisco to Denver?" because distances between stimuli have a well-defined zero, even when the stimuli themselves are defined on an interval scale.

Experimental tests of this theory have so far confirmed two orders for these more complex tasks, even when the simple "ratio" and "difference" tasks have yielded evidence of one order. Table V

shows the predicted order for the more complex, four-stimulus task.

In Birnbaum's theory, magnitude estimations form an exponential function of subjective differences when the examples are geometrically spaced and the subject is asked to judge simple "ratios" of most continua. Figure 6 illustrates the theory of the J_R function for magnitude estimation. In this theory, nominal "ratios" form a category scale on which a "ratio" and its nominal reciprocal are equidistant from zero. In addition, if the examples are geometrically spaced, the subject treats them as equally spaced on a category scale of differences.

Indeed, manipulation of examples appears capable of changing "ratio" judgments drastically. For example, in an experiment on prestige of occupations, the median judged "ratio" of the prestige of a *doctor* to that of a *trash collector* was either "4" or "64" depending on the range of examples in the instructions. Similar results have been obtained with lifted weight and other continua.

In summary, experiments favor the subtractive theory of psychophysical comparison, which resolves the conflict between scales by theorizing that different procedures have different **J** functions. The **J** function for category ratings is nearly linear, but will take on different forms in different contexts, as predicted by range-frequency theory, as the frequency of presentation of the stimuli and spacing of the stimuli are varied. The **J** function for magnitude estimations can take on a roughly exponential form, and this function appears to be malleable, depending on the examples given to illustrate the task as well as the range and distribution of the stimuli.

XV. PSYCHOPHYSICAL PERSPECTIVES

Although its core ideas are still under debate, psychophysics has developed as a cumulative science.

TABLE V
Predictions of Subtractive Theory of "Ratios of Differences" and "Differences of Differences"

Row difference	"Differences of differences": Minuend difference				"Ratios of differences": Numerator difference			
	(3,2)	(3,1)	(5,2)	(5,1)	(3,2)	(3,1)	(5,2)	(5,1)
(3,2)	0	1	2	3	1	2	3	4
(3,1)	−1	0	1	2	0.5	1	1.5	2
(5,2)	−2	−1	0	1	0.33	0.67	1	1.33
(5,1)	−3	−2	−1	0	0.25	0.5	0.75	1

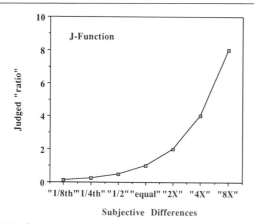

FIGURE 6   Theoretical judgment function, J_R, for magnitude estimation, including "ratio" judgment. In this theory, subjective differences are mapped into judged "ratios" by the examples, which form a category scale. If the examples are geometrically spaced, the function is an exponential function.

New data have forced old theories to be abandoned in favor of new ones.

Psychophysics seems to provide an ideal, simple psychological paradigm for investigating complex questions such as, "how can we measure a psychological value?" and "What produces a happy life?"

The techniques and theories of psychophysics are inherent in many areas of study in psychology, including those fields in which the investigator uses numbers to represent the psychological values of stimuli or uses numerical dependent variables to measure psychological reactions. People who use the results of psychophysical studies include people studying sensation, physiological mechanisms, individual differences, perception, memory, and social psychology. Ideas from signal detection have important interconnections to studies of judgment and decision making, in memory research, and in analyses of the reports of courtroom witnesses. [*See* DE-CISION MAKING, INDIVIDUALS; EYEWITNESS TESTIMONY; MEMORY.]

Many areas of psychology have debated whether it makes sense to discuss intervening variables that refer to internal psychological events. Modern psychophysics provides the best affirmative answer to this basic question of any field of psychology, but it will continue to remain controversial until a more complete, coherent system of measurement has been developed.

Bibliography

Birnbaum, M. H., Anderson, C. J., and Hynan, L. G. (1989). Two operations for "ratios" and "differences" of distances on the mental map. *J. Exp. Psychol. Hum. Percep. Perform.* **15,** 785–796.

Bolanowski, S. J., Jr., and Gescheider, G. A. (Eds.) (1991). "Ratio Scaling of Psychological Magnitude: In Honor of the Memory of S. S. Stevens." Erlbaum, Hillsdale, NJ.

Geissler, H.-G., Mueller, M. H., and Prinz, W. (Eds.) (1990). "Psychophysical Explorations of Mental Structures." Hogrefe & Huber, Toronto.

Gescheider, G. A. (1988). Psychophysical scaling. *Annu. Rev. Psychol.* **39,** 169–200.

Green, D. M., and Swets, J. A. (1966). "Signal Detection Theory and Psychophysics." Wiley, New York.

Guilford, J. P. (1954). "Psychometric Methods." McGraw-Hill, New York.

Link, S. W. (1992). "The Wave Theory of Difference and Similarity." Erlbaum, Hillsdale, NJ.

Luce, R. D., and Krumhansl, C. L. (1988). Measurement, scaling, and psychophysics. In "Stevens' Handbook of Experimental Psychology" (R. C. Atkinson, G. Lindzey, and R. D. Luce, Eds.), Vol. 1, pp. 3–74. Wiley, New York.

Poulton, E. C. (1989). "Bias in Quantifying Judgments." Erlbaum, Hillsdale, NJ.

Stevens, S. S. (1986). "Psychophysics: Introduction to Its Perceptual, Neural, and Social Prospects." Transaction, New Brunswick, NJ.

Torgerson, W. S. (1958). "Theory and Methods of Scaling." Wiley, New York.

Wegener, B. (Ed.) (1982). "Social Attitudes and Psychophysical Measurement." Erlbaum, Hillsdale, NJ.

◆

PSYCHOSOMATIC ILLNESS

R. Sergio Guglielmi
Lake Forest College

I. Historical Overview of the Mind–Body
   Relationship
II. Psychosomatic Medicine: A Challenge to the
   Biomedical Model
III. Terminology: Evolution of Psychiatric
   Nomenclature
IV. Stress
V. Assessment in Behavioral Medicine: Measurement
   of the Stress Response
VI. Psychoneuroimmunology

Glossary

Behavioral medicine The interdisciplinary field that focuses on the contribution of psychological and social factors to disease.

Biopsychosocial model The view that physical illness is multifactorial in origin and that psychosocial determinants, in addition to biological ones, are important contributors to its onset and progression. This approach to medicine developed in reaction to the reductionistic single-factor conception (known as the biomedical model), which viewed illness simply as the result of biochemical abnormality.

Pituitary-adreno-cortical system (PAC) This system is activated in response to stress and enhances the organism's resistance by supplying corticosteroid hormones which have widespread effects on the body.

Psychoneuroimmunology The emerging interdisciplinary field that investigates the intricate interactions among psychosocial factors, neuroendocrine mechanisms, and immune function.

Social readjustment rating scale (SRRS) A scale developed by Holmes and Rahe to measure stress as a function of life change. It has been widely used to examine the relationship between stress and the development of physical illness.

Sympatho-adreno-medullary system (SAM) This system mobilizes the organism's energy reserves

in response to stress. Together with the PAC system, it provides the neuroendocrine resources necessary to cope with and adapt to a stressor.

Type A behavior pattern A personality style, also known as coronary-prone behavior pattern, first described by Friedman and Rosenman who proposed it as a risk factor for coronary heart disease. It is characterized by excessive competitiveness and need to achieve, time urgency, impatience, and hostility.

THE CONCEPT of psychosomatic medicine rests on the fundamental assumption that social and psychological factors, in addition to biological ones, play a very important role in determining vulnerability to disease and in modulating its progress and symptomatic expression. An evident corollary of this assumption is that physical illness cannot be effectively treated without attending to both its physiological and psychological determinants. Although some early formulations of psychosomatic medicine appeared to restrict the designation of psychosomatic disorders to a relatively small number of illnesses, the generally accepted view today is that all human disease is psychosomatic inasmuch as the initiation, maintenance, course, and outcome of all disease are influenced by psychosocial factors.

I. HISTORICAL OVERVIEW OF THE MIND–BODY RELATIONSHIP

A. Early History

Interest in the relationship between emotional state (psyche) and bodily function (soma), as well as debate about whether psyche and soma are independent entities or interacting ones, have a very long history. Our Stone Age ancestors apparently viewed disease as a result of demonic possession. In many areas of the world, archeologists have found neo-lithic skulls with circular holes believed to have been intentionally produced with sharp stone instruments. In the absence of written records, it is tempting to speculate that this "surgical" procedure, known as trepanation or trephination, was used by the medicine man, or shaman, to make evil spirits leave the head and thus liberate the patient from their pathogenic influence. The Stone Age conception of disease, suggested by this reconstruction, obviously postulates an interaction between body and spirit.

Many ancient civilizations, including Egyptians, Babylonians and Assyrians, Hebrews, and early Greeks, continued to hold a spiritual/supernatural view of disease. Generally, illness was considered the result of invasion of the body by demons or punishment by a deity for one's wrongdoing. In either case, the spiritual nature of the disease required spiritual healing in the form of exorcism, prayer, magic, libations, and animal sacrifice. This intimate connection between medicine and religion blended the role of the priest and the role of the healer which were typically assumed by the same individual.

Hippocrates (460–377 B.C.), widely acknowledged as a founding father of modern medicine, was an early believer in the holistic view, the idea that psyche and soma are inextricably related. He conjectured that the human body contains four fluids, or humors: blood, black bile, yellow bile, and phlegm. He regarded human disease not as the product of divine or demonic encroachment into human affairs, but rather as a disturbed fluid balance. According to his humoral theory, both somatic and psychological processes emanate from the same physiological substratum; alterations in bodily fluid equilibrium explain not only health problems but also the emergence of specific psychological characteristics. Predominance in the body of one of the four humors listed above would be associated with a particular temperament: sanguine, melancholic, choleric, and phlegmatic, respectively. What is most valuable and revolutionary about Hippocrates' contribution is obviously not his physiologically naive theoretical proposal, but rather a view of medicine that emphasized natural instead of supernatural explanations. He also moved medicine closer to the scientific approach and stressed the importance of clinical observation in understanding health problems. A *bona fide* harbinger of behavior therapy, Hippocrates advocated dietary and lifestyle modification as a way to obtain an optimal emotional and humoral balance.

Hippocrates' humoral theory of illness was further elaborated by Galen (A.D. 130–200), a Greek physician who lived and practiced in Rome. In the Hippocratic tradition, Galen maintained a focus on the interplay between physiological and psychological factors, and his study of the nervous system through animal experimentation betrayed considerable sensitivity to the value of scientific methodology.

B. Middle Ages

Superstition, demonology, and a supernatural conception of disease returned in full force during the Middle Ages along with the mystical revival, spiritualism, and religious zealotism and intolerance that characterized this period. Once again, illness and even pestilence were accepted as God's punishment for personal or collective sins. Witches and demons were also believed to cause disease. Accepted therapeutic practices included exorcism, penance, corporal punishment, as well as torture which was believed to drive the demons out of the body. Medical knowledge, as was true for all knowledge, was patrimony of the Church, and the priest again became the healer.

C. Renaissance

The cultural rebirth that came with the Renaissance was accompanied by a sharp reaction against the theological conceptualization of medicine that, during the Middle Ages, had ignored the somatic basis of disease in favor of spiritual interpretations. A pervasive theme running through the Renaissance was the struggle to liberate reason and critical thinking from any dogma and from theological shackles. This effort not only led to great rejuvenation in the humanities, political thought, economics, philosophy, arts, and sciences, but also produced renewed interest in the physical world and in the study of natural causes of illness. The practice of autopsy, which had been previously restricted on religious grounds, significantly advanced knowledge of human anatomy as reflected in the work of the great Renaissance masters. Leonardo da Vinci is perhaps the embodiment of this new thinking that challenged the restrictive doctrine of the past and placed high value on direct experience, observation of nature, mathematical reasoning, logic, and a creative connection between art and science. An unfortunate by-product of the shift of interest from spiritual matters to the study of natural phenomena through observation and experimentation was a growing neglect of the psychological contribution to physical illness. Since emotions cannot be directly observed and empirically investigated, inquiring about the relationship between mind and body was repudiated as unscientific. On the other hand, through laboratory investigation great strides were made toward understanding the somatic basis of disease. The study of the body and its pathology was the province of medicine, while understanding the mind and the soul was left to the philosopher and the theologian.

D. Descartes and the Emergence of the Biomedical Model

During the 17th century, this mind–body schism obtained its clearest expression in the rationalism of French philosopher and mathematician Rene Descartes (1596–1650). His distinction between *res cogitans* (thinking substance) and *res extensa* (material substance) juxtaposed the mind and the body, the spiritual world and the material world, as distinct and nonoverlapping spheres. The mind operates freely while the body is subject to a rigid mechanistic determinism. Stimulated by William Harvey's insightful account of the circulatory system, Descartes viewed the body as a machine reducible to simple mechanical operations and impenetrable to the influence of the mind. This Cartesian dualism, and particularly the reductionistic view of the body as a machine, exerted a powerful influence on the direction taken by medical science during the subsequent 300 years. The introduction of the microscope, the remarkable advances made in microbiology and biochemistry, and the vast medical knowledge acquired during the 18th and 19th centuries further solidified the mind–body dichotomy by establishing organ pathology and cellular pathology as the necessary bases for disease and as the foundation for medical treatment. The model that finally emerged, often referred to as the *biomedical model*, explains disease as malfunction of the machine originating from discrete organic/biochemical abnormalities. Although the biomedical model has been enormously successful in explaining the body-machine and in eradicating illness, especially the infectious diseases that plagued humanity until the 20th century, its reductionistic single-factor conception excludes the contribution of psychosocial and behavioral variables

and cannot be easily reconciled with the multifactorial etiology of the chronic diseases that kill us today.

II. PSYCHOSOMATIC MEDICINE: A CHALLENGE TO THE BIOMEDICAL MODEL

A. Sigmund Freud

The foundations of the biomedical model were shaken by Austrian neurologist Sigmund Freud (1856–1939), who called attention to the critical role played by emotions in the development of both psychological and somatic disorders, and whose seminal work opened the modern era of psychosomatic medicine. Freud insightfully observed that physical symptoms (e.g., paralysis, convulsions, blindness, loss of speech, etc.) can occur in the absence of demonstrable organ malfunction. He concluded that such symptoms are the result of a process whereby repressed (unconscious) psychological conflicts are converted into somatic manifestations. This condition is known as conversion hysteria. The proposed psychogenic origin of manifestly physical afflictions unambiguously bridged the gap between psyche and soma.

B. Early Contributions to Psychosomatic Medicine

After the turn of the century, interest in psychosomatic medicine grew at an extremely rapid pace and remained heavily dominated by Freud's psychoanalytic theory. In time, the study of the relationship between emotional factors and somatic illness came to encompass cases in which physical symptoms existed in the absence of organic pathology (conversion hysteria), as well as conditions in which tissue damage was present (e.g., peptic ulcer and ulcerative colitis). In 1939, this growing interest culminated in the creation of the journal *Psychosomatic Medicine*, followed 4 years later by the formation of the American Psychosomatic Society whose members were mostly psychiatrists. The early period of this burgeoning field was dominated by "specificity" theories which postulated a rather simplistic relationship between specific psychological variables (e.g., unresolved conflicts or personality characteristics) and specific disorders, so that each disorder could be described in terms of a particular psychological make up. Flanders Dunbar (1902–1959), for example, maintained that patients suffering from the same psychosomatic illness share the same personality profile. Franz Alexander (1891–1964), a Chicago psychoanalyst who became the most influential figure of this period, on the other hand, submitted that vulnerability to a particular psychosomatic disorder is related to a specific unconscious emotional conflict, or conflict constellation. Hypertension, for example, is presumably linked to an unconscious conflict between passive–dependent and hostile–aggressive impulses, whereas asthma could be traced to unresolved dependence upon one's mother and to a suppressed impulse to cry. The pathogenic effect of these unresolved conflicts is independent of personality characteristics since different character types may exhibit the same conflict.

In fairness to Alexander, he acknowledged that genetic liability plays an important role in determining which organ is targeted by the disease process. This would explain why frustrated dependency needs may result in hypertension in one case and in peptic ulcer in another. Unfortunately, however, it was his specificity hypothesis that attracted the greatest interest and inspired a rather sterile and conceptually naive search for the psychogenic origins of various physical disorders. Heavily grounded in psychoanalytic theory, these efforts often deteriorated into unsupported dogmatic pronouncements about the psychological etiology of physical symptoms and into unscientific, albeit colorful, interpretations such as the assertion that urticaria (hives) symbolically represents weeping from the skin. Not surprisingly, controlled research has failed to validate the specificity hypothesis, and even those who believed in it often obtained contradictory results, so that different psychological profiles were reported for the same psychosomatic disorder. The work by Alexander and his followers, and generally the psychosomatic research conducted by psychodynamically oriented psychiatry during this early period, were beset by serious methodological flaws. The inability to operationally define concepts such as conflict constellation makes it impossible to test the specificity hypothesis. If unconscious conflicts cannot be empirically defined and measured, how can one determine whether the presence of such conflicts predicts the occurrence of the disorder? The excessive reliance on self-report, on single-case studies, and on clinical intuition, the retrospective reconstruction of psychological characteristics after

the physical disorder has been diagnosed (as opposed to assessing first the psychological dimension and then prospectively determining whether it predicts the outcome), and the lack of elementary control procedures characteristic of this research cast serious doubt on its conclusions. The unbalanced emphasis placed on the psyche side of the psychosomatic equation was probably responsible for the lack of interest demonstrated by this early research in the role of mediating variables. If psychological factors lead to physical symptoms, how is this relationship mediated? What are the neurobiological pathways that explain how the psyche causes the soma to malfunction?

C. Contemporary Psychosomatic Medicine, Behavioral Medicine, and the Biopsychosocial Model

The study of mediating mechanisms has now become an integral component of contemporary psychosomatic medicine and has led to exciting new developments such as the area of psychoneuroimmunology. In the past, psychosomatic medicine was dominated by psychiatry. Today, the field is interdisciplinary in nature and includes other medical specialties as well as psychology. The almost exclusive hegemony of the psychoanalytic model has been replaced by the influx of alternative psychological perspectives, especially behaviorism, which have stressed the need for rigorous scientific methodology and empirical validation of hypotheses. With the declining influence of psychoanalysis, the term "psychosomatic medicine" has lost its popularity and is now typically used to refer to the historical contribution made by psychodynamic psychiatry. *Behavioral Medicine,* instead, has gained favor as it designates the interdisciplinary field that includes different specialties and different theoretical models. Also, the term "psychosomatic disorders" as a diagnostic category has been officially replaced over the years with different descriptors (see terminology section below). As the scientific bases of psychoanalytic formulations were challenged, the research focus gradually shifted away from the concept of unconscious conflict and moved toward the concept of stress and its contribution to somatic problems, often referred to as "stress-related disorders." During the 1950s and 1960s, the list of psychosomatic disorders was significantly expanded from the original "holy seven" group (bronchial asthma, peptic ulcer, neurodermatitis, ulcerative colitis, migraine headache, hyperthyroidism, and rheumatoid arthritis). Today, as noted earlier, all disease is believed to be influenced by psychological, social, and behavioral factors.

Despite the challenge by early psychosomatic medicine, the biomedical model stood its ground and remains popular today. However, a growing appreciation for the importance of emotions, social environment, behavior, and lifestyle in understanding and managing the diseases that ravage humanity today (e.g., coronary heart disease, cancer, AIDS) has created increasing insufference with the dualistic/reductionistic view and has spawned more inclusive proposals. In 1977, George Engel published a landmark paper in *Science* titled "The Need for a New Medical Model: A Challenge for Biomedicine." In it, Engel reviewed the limitations of the biomedical model and called for the adoption of a biopsychosocial paradigm that would preserve the advantages of the biomedical model but would also acknowledge the role of psychosocial determinants. According to him, the onset of an illness, its course, the patient's response to it, such as the decision to seek treatment, as well as the patient–physician relationship are the result of a complex interaction among multiple factors, including genetic susceptibility, biochemical aberration, emotional, cultural, and environmental elements. This multifactorial conception and the recognition of the need to consider the patient as well as the illness have become the basic framework which has inspired exciting research activity and the clinical practice of behavioral medicine in the last 15 years.

III. TERMINOLOGY: EVOLUTION OF PSYCHIATRIC NOMENCLATURE

The official psychiatric nomenclature and classification of mental disorders parallel, to a great extent, the conceptual evolution sketched in the previous pages. Early psychodynamic contributions often referred to "organ neuroses" to describe the relationship between somatic dysfunction and psychological factors, and the term *psychosomatic disorders* could be found in the titles of many publications and also in diagnostic classification systems. The first edition of the Diagnostic and Statistical Manual of Mental Disorders (DSM-I), published in 1952 by the American Psychiatric Association, however, introduced the diagnostic descriptor *psychophysiologic autonomic and visceral disorders* "in preference to 'psy-

chosomatic disorders,' since the latter refers to a point of view on the discipline of medicine as a whole rather than to certain specified conditions" (p.29). In the second edition (DSM-II), published in 1968, this designation was retained but was shortened into *psychophysiologic disorders.*

DSM-III (1980) and its revised edition (DSM-III-R, 1987) offered the new diagnostic label *psychological factors affecting physical condition.* Consistent with the current view that all disease is psychosomatic, this open-ended category was introduced to designate "any physical condition to which psychological factors are judged to be contributory. It can be used to describe disorders that in the past have been referred to as either 'psychosomatic' or 'psychophysiological'" (DSM-III, p. 303). Outside the official diagnostic nomenclature, the term *stress-related disorders* is frequently found in the professional and popular literature, reflecting the enormous interest in the contribution of psychosocial stress to physical illness.

IV. STRESS

Probably the concept of stress has been the most heuristically powerful in behavioral medicine. It has generated a tremendous amount of research activity and it has stimulated the development of therapeutic interventions which are now solidly established procedures in clinical practice. Furthermore, the study of stress and of its physiological effects has contributed to a healthy shift away from a simplistic acceptance of a causal relationship between ill-defined unconscious psychological determinants and physical illness and toward a focus on the neurobiological mechanisms that mediate the psyche–soma interaction. [*See* STRESS.]

A. The Neurobiology of Stress

1. Walter Cannon: A Pioneer

The great American physiologist Walter Cannon (1871–1945) significantly contributed to our understanding of the bodily changes that accompany emotions. Cannon elaborated Claude Bernard's idea of "milieu interieur" into the concept of homeostasis, which he used to refer to the maintenance of a constant and optimal internal environment. The preservation of homeostasis (literally "steady state") is a function of the autonomic nervous system which, through its sympathetic and parasympathetic divisions, controls the internal visceral organs such as smooth (involuntary) muscle, cardiac muscle, and glands. A familiar example of homeostatic control is temperature regulation. Unless you are ill with a fever, your body temperature is maintained fairly constant, despite large variations in ambient temperature. When the body begins to deviate from the steady state, autonomic mechanisms are activated to restore the equilibrium. The analogy between this precise regulatory system and a thermostat is an apt one. In the presence of a warm environment, normal body temperature is maintained through vasodilation and sweating which allow heat loss. Conversely, when heat needs to be preserved in a cold environment, peripheral vasoconstriction and shivering prevent heat loss. Autonomic control over glands and blood vessels makes these homeostatic reactions possible. [*See* HOMEOSTASIS.]

The sympathetic and parasympathetic branches of the autonomic nervous system cooperate in maintaining homeostasis. Many visceral organs are innervated by both sympathetic and parasympathetic fibers which have antagonistic functions. The parasympathetic nervous system is an anabolic system which facilitates conservation and restoration of the organism's energy stores. Some of its effects on the body include stimulation of digestive functions, bronchila constriction, and cardiac deceleration. The sympathetic nervous system, on the other hand, is a catabolic system which is massively activated in emergency situations requiring expenditure of energy. The physiological changes that occur when the organism is confronting a threat were called by Cannon the "fight or flight" response. Whether the choice is to attack the threat or to flee from it, the body's resources need to be mobilized. As a result of sympathetic activation, heart rate, blood pressure, and respiration increase; the liver accelerates its conversion of stored energy (glycogen) into usable energy (glucose); activities that can be deferred, such as digestion, are inhibited; the peripheral blood vessels constrict in order to channel blood flow to vital organs and especially to the skeletal muscles that are needed to fight or to flee. Cannon provided a detailed account of the sympathetic changes that occur during the fight or flight reaction. He also discussed the synergistic function of the adrenal medulla which promotes further mobilization and expenditure of energy. This gland, which is directly innervated by preganglionic sympathetic fibers (splanchnic nerves), secretes the hormones *epinephrine* (adrenaline) and *norepinephrine* (nor-

adrenaline). These catecholamines potentiate and prolong the effects of sympathetic stimulation. Although the sympatho-adreno-medullary (SAM) system described by Cannon has obvious survival value, as it quickly prepares the organism to face the threat, a prolonged state of activation in response to chronic stress can lead to health problems. In the presence of what Cannon called "critical stress" levels, the homeostatic mechanisms fail, the steady state cannot be restored, and the organism may die. Cannon argued, for example, that voodoo death can be explained in terms of homeostatic failure induced by intense fear.

2. Selye's Biological Stress Model

Without doubt, the most influential and prolific contributor to stress research has been the late Canadian physician and physiologist Hans Selye (1907–1982), whose work on the subject spanned nearly half a century. He greatly expanded our understanding of the neuroendocrine correlates of stress, proposed a model that explained the development of stress-related disorders, and more than anyone else popularized the concept of stress by reaching the nonprofessional audience with his books *The Stress of Life* and *Stress without Distress*. As it is true of many great contributions, Selye's interest in stress began serendipitously. In the process of studying a new ovarian hormone at McGill University, he observed that when rats were injected with extracts of ovarian tissue, they would reliably exhibit a sequence of pathologic changes consisting of: (a) enlargement and hyperactivity of the adrenal glands, which secrete the stress hormones; (b) shrinkage of the thymus and of other lymphatic structures, which serve important immune functions; and (c) bleeding gastrointestinal ulcers. Furthermore, Selye found that this same response triad could be elicited not only by injecting different hormones and irritants but also by a variety of noxious stimuli including overcrowding, exposure to heat or cold, infection, trauma, and hemorrhage. He called these stimuli "stressors," and defined stress as "the nonspecific response of the body to any demand made upon it."

In 1936, Selye briefly reported his findings in a *Nature* article titled "A Syndrome Produced by Diverse Nocuous Agents," and later elaborated these observations into a theoretical model of stress that he called the General Adaptation Syndrome (GAS). Selye's GAS consists of a series of neural and hormonal changes that are triggered by any stressor and that allow the organism to defend itself and to adapt to the stressor. It involves three stages: alarm, resistance, and exhaustion. During the alarm stage, the body mobilizes its defensive resources. This stage is reminiscent of the fight or flight response described by Cannon and it is indeed characterized by activation of the SAM system. Selye, however, pointed out that an endocrine component, the pituitary-adreno-cortical (PAC) axis, plays a critical role in resisting the stressor and in promoting adaptation. The contribution of the PAC system will be reviewed after completing this outline of Selye's triphasic model.

Once the physiological defenses are in place, the organism enters the stage of resistance, during which it attempts to cope with the threat. This effort is often successful and it leads to adaptation. If the stressor is sufficiently severe and prolonged, however, the organism's finite supply of "adaptation energy" becomes depleted, further resistance proves impossible, and the coping effort fails. At this point, the organism is in the stage of exhaustion, a defenseless state during which the neuroendocrine system can no longer supply the physiological resources needed to sustain the resistance. If the stressor continues, or new ones are introduced, adaptive energy cannot be restored and the result may be the development of "diseases of adaptation" (ulcers, hypertension, arthritis, immune deficiency), and even death. [See STRESS AND ILLNESS.]

As noted earlier, in Selye's model resistance to stressors is made possible by the mobilization of two physiological systems, the neural (SAM) and the endocrine (PAC) components. The following section reviews the contribution of the PAC system.

3. The Pituitary-Adreno-Cortical System

The pituitary gland or hypophysis (literally meaning undergrowth) is a pea-size oval structure located at the base of the brain just above the roof of the mouth. It is composed of an anterior lobe and a posterior lobe which are embryologically and functionally distinct. The posterior lobe, also called neurohypophysis, is primarily composed of neural tissue and is really an outgrowth of the hypothalamus, by which it is richly innervated. The neurohypophysis does not synthesize any hormones of its own but it secretes two hormones manufactured by hypothalamic cells. One is antidiuretic hormone (ADH), which helps regulate the body's fluid balance, and the other is oxytocin which has many interesting functions, including sperm transport, initiation of labor, and ejection of milk when the lactating breast is stimu-

lated by the suckling infant. [See HORMONES AND BEHAVIOR.]

Of much greater importance to the organism confronting a stressor is the anterior pituitary, or adenohypophysis, which makes up about 75% of the gland and is composed of glandular tissue. The anterior pituitary manufactures and secretes six hormones: prolactin, growth hormone, two gonadotropins (luteinizing hormone and follicle-stimulating hormone), thyrotropin, and corticotropin, also called adrenocorticotropic hormone (ACTH). The last four are referred to as tropic (stimulating) hormones because they control the secretory activity of other endocrine glands. For the purpose of understanding the physiological effects of stress, the most important pituitary hormone is ACTH. Although it is customary to characterize the hypophysis as the "master gland," it is now clear that the master is under hypothalamic control. The hypothalamus either stimulates or restrains the hormonal output of the anterior pituitary by means of releasing hormones (or releasing factors) and inhibiting hormones (or inhibiting factors). Once released by the hypothalamus, these regulatory hormones reach the adenohypophysis via local circulatory connections. ACTH-releasing factor (ACTH-RF) from the hypothalamus initiates the release of ACTH from the anterior pituitary. ACTH, as the name would suggest, in turn stimulates the adrenal cortex to secrete its hormones.

Our body has two adrenal glands, one above each kidney, which explains why they are also called suprarenal glands. Each adrenal gland is composed of two separate parts differing in origin, structure, and function. The inner core, or medulla, makes up 10 to 20% of the gland. The adrenal medulla developed from sympathetic ganglion cells and is an integral part of the SAM system. Its hormonal production (epinephrine and norepinephrine), as noted earlier, is under sympathetic control and is not regulated by the pituitary gland. The second component of the pituitary gland is the outer region, or cortex, which makes up the remaining 80 to 90% of the gland. When ACTH is carried through the blood to the adrenal cortex, the cortex synthesizes and secretes three groups of steroid hormones, or corticosteroids.

1. Gonadocorticoids, or sex steroids. The adrenal cortex produces both androgens and estrogens in amounts, however, that do not compare to the production of sex hormones by

the gonads. These steroids have marginal biological significance and are not believed to play a major role in promoting adaptation to stress.

2. Mineralocorticoids. The major function of these steroids is the regulation of water and electrolyte balance. Aldosterone, the principal mineralocorticoid, stimulates active retention of sodium by the kidney, at the expense of potassium and hydrogen ions which are excreted in the urine. Active sodium retention, which under stress compensates for the sodium lost through sweating, is accompanied by passive water retention and consequent increases in blood volume and in blood pressure.

3. Glucocorticoids. Effective resistance to stress is critically dependent on the availability of these steroid hormones. Total adrenalectomy (complete surgical removal of the adrenal gland) cannot be survived without glucocorticoid replacement therapy. Cortisol is the most abundant and the most important hormone in this group. The primary function of cortisol, essential when confronting a stressor, is the mobilization of energy resources in order to meet the metabolic needs of the organism. As suggested by the physiological effects of glucocorticoids to be described next, this catabolic function operates synergistically with the effects of SAM activation as it assures that sufficient energy is available to fight and resist the stressor.

Cortisol produces a sharp increase in blood sugar level (hyperglycemia) by promoting the conversion of glycogen into glucose or, when glycogen stores are low, by facilitating conversion of amino acids into glucose (gluconeogenesis). Cortisol also stimulates the mobilization of fatty acids from fat depots. At the vascular level, glucocorticoids intensify the peripheral blood vessels' sensitivity to vasoconstricting agents such as norepinephrine. This increase in peripheral resistance elevates blood pressure; an adaptive response should the encounter with the stressor result in significant blood loss. Finally, glucocorticoids have a marked anti-inflammatory and immunosuppressive action. The anti-inflammatory properties of glucocorticoids are exploited in the management of arthritic conditions, rheumatic disorders, collagen diseases, allergic states, etc. The immunosuppressive effects of corticosteroids have also found medical applications and have been used to prevent rejection of transplanted organs. Interestingly, there is suggestive evidence that this steroid-

induced inhibition of immune function may help explain the observed relationship between stress and reduced resistance to infections, impaired surveillance against cancer cells, or progression of HIV infection. Other known effects of glucocorticoids that have been related to the development of stress-related disorders include atherogenesis, hypertension, menstrual irregularities, and increased risk of peptic ulcer.

The neural (SAM) and the endocrine (PAC) responses do not unfold independently but are integrated and coordinated by the hypothalamus and are ultimately under cortical control. Complex SAM-PAC interactions have been described. The release of ACTH from the anterior pituitary, for example, is stimulated by the catecholamines, while catecholamine biosynthesis in the adrenal medulla is affected by the corticosteroids. The hormonal production of both systems is regulated by precise feedback mechanisms. Selye suggested that the biochemical correlates of the stress response can be used to precisely quantify the otherwise elusive stress concept. He maintained that although the stress response is nonspecific, that is, not dependent on any particular stimulus, it cannot be considered vague since levels of stress hormones can be accurately measured. We will return to the issue of stress measurement later.

B. The Psychology of Stress

1. Psychological Stress Models

Although Selye conceded, in response to critics, that stressors are not necessarily physical and that emotions and cognitions can trigger stress reactions, his model clearly paid insufficient attention to the contribution of psychological factors. He acknowledged that his nonspecificity assumption had to reckon with the critical issue of how so many different noxious agents could lead to the same physiological outcome. He recognized the need to investigate the "first mediator," that is, the mechanism that initiates the hypothalamic response to stressors. Although he admitted that the precise identity of the mediator remained undetermined, he believed it to be biochemical in nature.

a. John Mason

John Mason was among the first to challenge Selye's nonspecificity hypothesis. He argued that different aversive stimuli elicit a similar pattern of neuroendocrine activation because they all produce emotional arousal. For Mason, then, the first mediator is the psychological meaning of the stimulus to the organism. In other words, a stimulus is a stressor, capable of triggering the physiological cascade of events, only to the extent that it is perceived as stressful by the organism. The ubiquitous but often unrecognized psychological mediation, according to Mason, probably affected the results of Selye's research on physical stressors. Mason reviewed experimental evidence indicating that when the psychological meaning is removed, physical stimuli cannot activate the hypothalamic-pituitary-adrenocortical axis.

b. Richard Lazarus

The critical role of psychological appraisal in mediating the physiological stress response was fully elaborated by Richard Lazarus. He conceptualized stress as a transaction between the individual and the environment "that is appraised by the individual as taxing or exceeding his or her resources or endangering his or her well-being." The appraisal process, which fundamentally determines the outcome of our transactions with the environment, moves through two stages. During the *primary appraisal,* according to Lazarus, the person tries to answer the question "Am I O.K., or am I in trouble?" Primary appraisal, in other words, involves evaluating the meaning of the event and determining whether the event is irrelevant, benign, or stressful. A stressful interpretation is made if the event is considered to be potentially harmful, threatening, or challenging. Irrelevant or benign appraisals obviously do not create stress. When divorce is interpreted as relief from pain and suffering and freedom from conflict, for example, it will be far less stressful than when it is seen as abandonment and betrayal by someone we still love.

After a stressful interpretation is made during the primary appraisal stage ("I am in trouble"), the *secondary appraisal* process answers the question "What can I do about it?" Secondary appraisal, then, refers to the process of reviewing the available coping options, as well as the cost, benefit, and likely outcome of different strategies. Divorce, again, is made more stressful by the belief that we do not have the skills to find someone else and that we are going to spend the rest of our lives alone and unloved.

The next step in the process of dealing with stressful transactions is *coping,* which refers to the actual implementation of the options reviewed in the previous stage. According to Lazarus, coping can take two forms. *Problem-focused* (or *direct action*) coping involves efforts (typically behaviors) that deal directly with the source of stress and aim at terminating the stressful transaction that is harming, threatening, or challenging the individual. Loneliness following divorce, for example, can be directly coped with by seeking friends, dating, and initiating other social contacts. *Emotion-focused* (or *palliative*) coping, on the other hand, serves to reduce the subjective distress and mitigate the negative emotions associated with the stressful transaction, but does not deal directly with the problem at hand. Coping with loneliness, anxiety, or depression by using alcohol or drugs is a good example of palliative coping.

Lazarus' transactional mode of stress represents a radical departure from Selye's conception. For Selye, noxious stimuli are inherently capable of stressing the organism which is viewed as a passive recipient of environmental insults with little control over stressors and their effects. For Lazarus, stress is not a property of stimuli or events but is in the head of the perceiver. In the absence of a stressful appraisal, events cannot produce stress. This explains why the same event (e.g., skydiving) can elicit different emotional and physiological responses in different people, or why the same event can evoke different reactions in the same person at different times. In fact, the exquisitely human capacity for imagination, misinterpretation, mental reenactment, and cognitive distortion can create stress even in the absence of a physical stimulus. A Swedish research group lead by Marianne Frankenhaeuser, for example, has repeatedly found that marked sympatho-adrenal activation, as measured by catecholamine levels, can be produced by purely psychological stressors, such as boredom, conflict at work, and taking exams. Lazarus' cognitive conception of stress, and particularly its emphasis on appraisal and coping processes which are essentially modifiable, leaves the door open to the possibility of therapeutic interventions. Procedures such as stress management, cognitive restructuring, stress inoculation, and cognitive–behavior therapy rest on the fundamental assumption that if one's catastrophic/unrealistic perception of events can be changed and more effective coping strategies can be developed, the severity of stress and of its psychological and physiological correlates can be mitigated.

The concept of stress and the theoretical formulations outlined above have stimulated an extraordinary amount of research. In particular, a great deal of work has focused on the factors that influence the severity of stress and the coping effort; the psychological and physiological measurement of the stress response; and the relationship between stress and the immune stress.

2. Coping with Stress: The Role of Moderator Variables

Cognitive appraisal is not the only factor that determines the impact of a stressor on the individual. Some of the other moderator variables that facilitate or interfere with the coping process are predictability, perceived control, social support, and personality characteristics.

a. Predictability

Many studies have found that the ability to predict the occurrence of a stressor usually reduces its perceived severity as well as its physiological impact, even if the organism has no actual control over the stressor and no possibility of escaping it. This appears to be the case for both animals and humans. Jay Weiss, for example, found that rats exposed to unpredictable shock developed more extensive and severe ulcers than rats exposed to the same shock made predictable by a warning tone. Given a choice, people also prefer predictable to unpredictable stressors. In a 1985 study by Katz and Wykes, subjects perceived predictable shocks as less aversive compared to unpredictable shocks of the same intensity. Moreover, emotional arousal and autonomic activation were lower during the warning period preceding predictable shocks than during the period preceding unpredictable shocks. Research has consistently shown that providing patients facing surgery with information about the procedure and about the pain and discomfort associated with it significantly improves their postoperative adjustment. Patients who receive preparatory information are typically found, postsurgically, to be less psychologically distressed, and to require less pain medication as well as a shorter hospitalization period. The positive effecs of predictability are probably mediated by the opportunity to develop effective coping strategies when adequate preparation for the stressor is made possible.

b. Perceived Control

Perceived control refers to the belief, realistic or illusory, that one has the ability to influence events and outcomes. A large body of animal and human literature has indicated that perceived control can significantly attenuate the severity of stressors. In Jay Weiss' classic "executive rat" study, rats that had control over the electric shock and could escape it by pressing a lever (the executive group) suffered significantly fewer gastric ulcers compared to a second group of rats, yoked to the first, that had no control over the stressor but received the same shock as the executive group. Other rat studies have found that uncontrollable shock results in marked immunosuppression.

Human research on perceived control has yielded similar findings. When allowed to choose, people consistently prefer self-administered noxious stimuli (electric shock, bursts of loud noise) over experimenter-delivered ones, even though the intensity and duration of the stressor is identical. Frankenhaeuser's work on job stress indicates that self-paced work is far less stressful than work paced by a machine or by other people. In a variety of settings and for a variety of stressors, personal control, even if only perceived, has been found to produce significantly less emotional and physiological arousal, better health outcomes, and better performance on poststress tasks requiring attention and concentration (e.g., proofreading). These findings have stimulated the development of control-enhancing interventions to reduce, for example, the alienation and the mental and physical deterioration of nursing home residents, or to improve the emotional and medical response of patients undergoing uncomfortable therapeutic (e.g., chemotherapy) or diagnostic (e.g., endoscopy) procedures.

Animal and human research conducted by Martin Seligman and his collaborators over the last 20 years has indicated that repeated exposure to uncontrollable stressors that, despite one's efforts, cannot be escaped or avoided eventually leads to giving up and to *learned helplessness*. This outcome is particularly likely in people who tend to view their failure to control events as the result of their own idiosyncratic, enduring, and pervasive ineptitude rather than the consequence of external factors. Learned helplessness has been found to breed reduced motivation, impaired performance on problem-solving tasks, and depression. At the medical level, patients who perceive their illness as uncontrollable are more likely to exhibit poor health practices and a hopeless noncompliance with their therapeutic regimen. Interestingly, a relationship has been found between depression and immunosuppression, and a hopeless attitude has been reported to increase susceptibility to infectious diseases and even to cancer. [*See* LEARNED HELPLESSNESS.]

c. Social Support

Emotional and tangible support from friends and family has been repeatedly found to be an important buffer against stress. The Alameda County Study was a longitudinal investigation of the relationship between health practices and overall mortality in a sample of 6928 Alameda County, California, residents who returned a questionnaire. As part of this study, Berkman and Syme developed a Social Network Index to measure the availability of supportive relationships. At follow-up, 9 years later, they found that mortality from all causes was strongly associated with social isolation, which was as good a predictor as cigarette smoking and a better predictor than obesity. The investigators determined that the relationship between social isolation and mortality rate was not mediated by differences in initial health status and health practices. Another prospective community study, the Tecumseh Community Health Study, obtained very similar findings. Confidence in the results was significantly strengthened by the use of physical examinations, rather than self-report, to assess health status at the beginning of the investigation. Although the correlational nature of this research does not permit the establishment of a causal relationship between social support and health outcomes, and although contradictory findings have also been reported, the preponderance of the large literature published to date fairly consistently suggests that a supportive social network is associated with lower morbidity and mortality rates, improved ability to cope with chronic disease, and faster recovery when illness does occur. Social support has also been found to mitigate the negative effects of various psychological and physical stressors. While the mechanisms through which social support exerts its beneficial effects remain to be elucidated, it seems plausible that the encouragement, advice, and prodding received from someone who cares can be effective in motivating people to use health services, adhere to therapeutic regimens, improve health practices, and abandon unhealthy ones. [*See* SOCIAL SUPPORT.]

d. Personality Characteristics

The modern interest in the notion that specific personality traits mediate the risk of developing particular illnesses can be traced back to the early psychosomatic work of Flanders Dunbar. Since her contribution, the study of personality as a variable that could explain the observed individual differences in susceptibility to specific stress-related disorders has generated intriguing proposals about the existence of an ulcer-prone personality, an asthmatic personality, a diabetic personality, a Type C (cancer-prone) personality, etc. Despite its evident

appeal, however, the hypothesized contribution of personality patterns to the etiology of those diseases has not been substantiated by methodologically adequate research.

More recently, Type A personality, also known as Type A behavior pattern or coronary-prone behavior pattern, has attracted a great deal of attention and has generated a tremendous amount of research. The concept was originally developed by two cardiologists, Meyer Friedman and Ray Rosenman, who in 1974 published a popular account of their observations, *Type A Behavior and Your Heart*. The key characteristics of this behavior pattern include: (a) an excessive competitive drive and need to achieve; (b) a chronic sense of time urgency; and (c) diffuse impatience and hostility. Type A individuals are hard-driving and ambitious, find it difficult to relax, tend to become impatient and angry when faced with delays, and push themselves to achieve more and more in less and less time, often finding it necessary to engage in multiple activities at the same time. At the other end of the personality spectrum, there is the Type B individual who is easygoing, is not in a hurry, and finds it easy to relax. [*See* TYPE A–TYPE B PERSONALITIES.]

A great deal of research has reported that Type A behavior intensifies the psychological and physiological impact of stressors and that it increases the risk of coronary heart disease (CHD). Heightened physiological reactivity to stressors (increased heart rate and blood pressure, elevated plasma catecholamine and cortisol levels), reportedly exhibited by Type A individuals, has been proposed as the likely pathogenetic mechanism that makes these people vulnerable to CHD. The association between Type A behavior and CHD has been reported by many retrospective and prospective studies, including some large-scale ones. The Western Collaborative Group Study (WCGS) involved 3154 initially healthy men and found that people identified as Type A at the beginning of the study were more than twice as likely as Type B individuals to have developed CHD 8.5 years later. The Framingham Heart Study, also a prospective investigation of initially healthy subjects, showed that Type A behavior was a strong independent predictor of CHD in both men and women. Under the impetus of a growing body of converging evidence, the National Heart Lung and Blood Institute appointed an eminent panel of biomedical and behavioral scientists to critically examine the evidence implicating Type A behavior in the development of CHD. In its final report, published in 1981 in the journal *Circulation*, the panel unambiguously accepted "the available body of scientific evidence as demonstrating that Type A behavior . . . is associated with an increased risk of clinically apparent CHD in employed, middle-aged U.S. citizens. This risk is greater than that imposed by age, elevated values of systolic blood pressure and serum cholesterol, and smoking and appears to be of the same order of magnitude as the relative risk associated with the latter three of these other factors" (p.1200).

Despite these strong conclusions, however, many recent studies have failed to support the Type A–CHD relationship. Perhaps the most persuasive refutation of the Type A hypothesis came from the Multiple Risk Factor Intervention Trial (MRFIT), a large prospective clinical study of middle-aged men who, although initially healthy, were at risk for CHD because of smoking, high blood pressure, or high serum cholesterol levels. A 7-year follow-up revealed no differences in the incidence of CHD between Type A and Type B subjects. More recently, an extended follow-up of the WCGS paradoxically seemed to suggest that Type A behavior pattern may actually play a protective role. Of the original participants in the WCGS, 257 were identified as suffering from CHD at the time of the 8.5-year follow-up. Ragland and Brand examined the relationship between Type A behavior and the 22-year survival among these 257 men. Surprisingly, they found that coronary mortality was lower among Type A than Type B subjects.

These and many other studies that have failed to corroborate the Type A–CHD association have recently prompted a reexamination of the Type A concept. It has been suggested that the predictive power of the global Type A construct may be attenuated by the possibility that not all of its defining characteristics actually increase the risk of CHD. Accordingly, the research interest has recently shifted toward isolating the more toxic components. This new approach has yielded suggestive evidence that anger and hostility, especially when coupled with a cynical and mistrusting attitude, are strong predictors of atherosclerosis and CHD, even in cases in which the global Type A measure is not. Interestingly, some studies have shown that anger and hostility are associated with greater neuroendocrine reactivity to stressors, a likely mediator of the increased coronary risk. There is, of course, always the possibility that Type A behavior, or its more malignant components, may be a consequence rather than the cause of the heightened physiological

reactivity to stressors. The typically correlational nature of the evidence provides no clue about the direction of the relationship, assuming that a causal relationship exists.

While Type A personality is presumably a characteristic that enhances the impact of stress, some investigators have been interested in identifying personality attributes that may insulate or protect the individual from the pathogenic effects of stress. Suzanne Kobasa has introduced the term *hardiness* to describe a personality constellation characterized by: (a) control, the belief that one can influence events, as opposed to helplessness; (b) commitment, a sense of purpose and involvement, as opposed to alienation; and (c) challenge, a perception of change as an opportunity for growth, as opposed to threat. Although Kobasa and others have found that hardiness is an effective protection against stress and its adverse effects on health, this research has been challenged on conceptual and methodological grounds. Additional work appears necessary to clarify the role of hardiness as a stress buffer.

IV. ASSESSMENT IN BEHAVIORAL MEDICINE: MEASUREMENT OF THE STRESS RESPONSE

The impact of a stressor can be inferred by measuring its psychological and biological effects on the individual.

A. Psychological Measurement

Psychological measurement focuses on the emotional, cognitive, and behavioral correlates of stress. Two different strategies have been used. The objective assessment approach involves experimentally evaluating the *aftereffects* of a stressor on observable or quantifiable behaviors. This strategy is illustrated by the work of Glass and Singer who conducted an elegant series of studies on the aftereffects of noise as a stressor. These investigators found, for example, significant performance decrements on a proofreading task following exposure to unpredictable and uncontrollable noise.

A more subjective, and methodologically weaker, assessment strategy has relied on self-report and on correlational designs to determine the relationship between stress and its negative effects. This commonly adopted research approach has been used primarily to investigate the extent to which stress can predict the development of physical illness. The best known example of this methodology is the work of Holmes and Rahe. These researchers conceptualized stress in terms of life change. According to them, any life change, desirable or undesirable, requires some adjustment; the greater the change, the greater the adjustment necessary and the more severe the resulting stress. In 1967, Holmes and Rahe published a scale, called the Social Readjustment Rating Scale (SRRS), which was developed by asking a large number of subjects to rate 43 life events on a 100-point scale in terms of the degree of readjustment each required. Marriage was given an arbitrary value of 50 and was used as the anchor. On the basis of these ratings, each life event was assigned a value ranging from 11 for "minor violations of the law," to 100 for "death of spouse." The scale includes undesirable events (divorce, being fired from work, sex difficulties) as well as desirable ones (vacation, outstanding personal achievement, marital reconciliation). When taking this self-administered scale, the individual simply checks those events that occurred in the recent past, usually the previous 6–24 months. The total stress score is easily obtained by adding the checked values. Countless studies have used the SRRS to explore the relationship between life stress and illness. Some ill-advised but catchy adaptations of this scale have even appeared in the popular media with the ludicrous suggestion that a total score of 150 gives you a 50–50 chance of developing an illness, while a score of 300 or more makes the likelihood of disease virtually a certainty.

Despite its considerable heuristic value, the life events research pioneered by Holmes and Rahe has encountered widespread and serious criticism. A compelling account of the methodological, conceptual, statistical, and psychometric problems associated with this research can be found in a 1976 *Science* article by Rabkin and Struening titled "Life Events, Stress, and Illness." The major issues can be briefly summarized as follows:

◆ Holmes and Rahe's assumption that the desirability or undesirability of the event is irrelevant has not been supported by research which instead has consistently found that desirable change is unrelated to illness.

◆ Very modest correlations have been reported between SRRS scores and subsequent illness. The typical correlation is in the neighborhood of .12, while some of the highest correlations are about .30. Thus, under the best conditions, life change scores account for only 10% of the variance in illness. In simpler words, these correlations are practically insignificant and life events scores predict future illness very poorly.

◆ Too many studies that showed a relationship between life change and illness have used retrospective designs and have relied exclusively on self-report. As Rabkin and Struening pointed out, a major problem of this type of research is *retrospective contamination,* the tendency to exaggerate or distort past experiences in order to find antecedents of current illness, especially if the respondent believes in the stress–illness connection and/or is eager to confirm the researcher's hypothesis.

◆ SRRS research fails to take into account the critical role of cognitive appraisal in the experience of stress. Divorce is the second highest event on the SRRS and contributes 73 points to the score of anyone experiencing it, despite the fact that its impact is obviously dependent on the person's perception of it.

◆ Important moderator variables (e.g., availability of social support and of other coping resources, personality traits, perceived control) can modify the experience of stress. Life events research, instead, assumes a simple relationship between stress and illness and ignores the contribution of possible buffers.

◆ If stressful events are causally related to illness, they must be experienced before the illness occurs. It has been noted, however, that 29 of the 43 events on the SRRS (e.g., change in sleeping habits, sex difficulties, even divorce) can be consequences rather than causes of illness. If the necessary temporal relationship cannot be established, a causal relationship cannot be claimed. Particularly vulnerable to this criticism is research that has examined the impact of life events on some chronic diseases in which the pathogenic process starts long before the illness is finally diagnosed. Many studies have reported an association between loss of an emotionally important relationship and cancer. The neoplastic process, however, may require as long as 20 years before the malignancy becomes clinically apparent and symptomatic. Confidence in a causal relationship between loss of spouse and breast cancer diagnosed a year later should be strongly tempered by these considerations. The same reasoning applies to the development and growth of atheromas that may eventually culminate in a myocardial infarction.

◆ Finally, the reliability and validity of the SRRS have been seriously questioned. Content validity is particularly problematic. The SRRS appears to overrepresent events and concerns of young adults. The relevance and appropriateness of its 43 items to different ethnic, cultural, and socioeconomic groups is highly questionable.

Efforts to address these and other weaknesses of the SRRS have resulted in the development of alternative life events scales (e.g., the Life Experiences Survey by Sarason and his colleagues). Some investigators, on the other hand, have suggested that the wear and tear associated with minor but frequent life stressors (*daily hassles*) are more taxing than the major but less common life events. Accordingly, Richard Lazarus and his collaborators have developed a Hassles Scale which includes 117 common and seemingly trivial annoyances such as misplacing or losing objects, planning meals, and getting stuck in a traffic jam. Recent research has found daily hassles to be a better predictor of psychological and medical problems than major life events. Lazarus and his colleagues have also investigated the potential benefits of minor positive experiences (*daily uplifts*). Scores on their Uplifts Scale, however, have not yet been found to predict health outcomes.

B. Physiological Measurement

As noted earlier, stress is accompanied by marked neuroendocrine changes involving SAM and PAC systems. A rapidly growing body of research has also found a solid association between stress and immune function. Thus, the impact of a stressor can be inferred by measuring: (a) urinary or plasma concentrations of stress hormones (biochemical methods); (b) the activity of various organs innervated by the autonomic nervous system (psychophysiological methods); and (c) the response of effector cells in the immune system (immunological methods).

1. Biochemical Methods

The secretion of catecholamines (epinephrine and norepinephrine) by the adrenal medulla and of corticosteroids (cortisol) by the adrenal cortex in response to stress can be precisely quantified. These objective indices have been employed in many animal and human studies that have examined the biochemical correlates of various physical and psychological stressors. Despite marked individual differences in the hormonal response to stress, researchers have been able to identify specific excretion profiles for different stimulus configurations. Frankenhaeuser's group, for example, found that subjects under stress exhibit different hormonal patterns depending on whether they experience effort with distress, effort without distress, or distress without effort. Timing, duration, and type of stressor are also important determinants of the neuroendocrine picture.

2. Psychophysiological Methods

As noted earlier, activation of the sympathetic nervous system has striking effects on a number of visceral organs. Stress-induced changes in the activity of these organs, and of other structures that are not under sympathetic control, can be measured with a polygraph. Although generalizations are made difficult by the existence of significant individual differences in physiological reactivity, exposure to a stressor typically produces the following changes:

◆ Cardiovascular activation, as measured by sharp increases in arterial blood pressure and in heart rate.
◆ Reduced peripheral blood flow (vasoconstriction). This can be measured with a thermistor registering the temperature of the skin, which increases as blood flow increases, or with a plethysmograph which detects changes in blood volume.
◆ Increased activity of the sweat glands, which decreases the electrical resistance of the skin. This electrodermal activity, formerly called galvanic skin reflex, can be assessed by measuring skin conductance, skin resistance, or skin potential.
◆ Rapid and shallow respiration with a predominantly thoracic, as opposed to diaphragmatic, pattern.
◆ Increased activity of skeletal (voluntary) muscles, as recorded by electromyography.

3. Immunological Methods

The body's specific immune functions are carried out by lymphocytes, which respond to particular antigens (foreign substances that trigger an immune reaction). There are two types of specific immune mechanisms: antibody-mediated (humoral) immunity whose effector cells are the *B-cells,* and cell-mediated (cellular) immunity whose lymphocytes are called *T-cells.* The thymus is particularly important for the maturation and development of T-cells. Interactions between these two arms of the body's defense system allow for reciprocal regulation. The antagonistic functions of *helper T-cells* and *suppressor T-cells,* two subtypes of T-lymphocytes, for example, serve to coordinate cellular and humoral responses. Communication in the immune system and integration of different functions are made possible by chemical messengers (*lymphokines* and *interleukins*). Stress can alter these immune functions and a growing body of research that has examined the relationship between stress and disease has used immunological change as the dependent variable.

VI. PSYCHONEUROIMMUNOLOGY

Recent evidence of complex interactions among psychological factors, neuroendocrine mechanisms, and immune processes has promoted the development and rapid growth of an emerging interdisciplinary field known as *psychoneuroimmunology.* The demonstration by Robert Ader and his colleagues that immune responses can be classically conditioned has provided compelling evidence that the brain can modulate immune function. Less than 20 years ago, these investigators reported that when the immunosuppressive drug cyclophosphamide (the unconditioned stimulus) is paired with a saccharin solution (the conditioned stimulus), rats injected with antigens reliably show significant immunosuppression when exposed to the saccharin solution alone (conditioned response). These findings are very robust and have been replicated in a number of independent laboratories on different animals and under precise control conditions. There is also evidence that classical conditioning can be used to elicit more vigorous immune reactions to antigens (conditioned immunoenhancement). The potential applications of this research can be easily imagined.

The demonstration of a connection between brain and immunity provides the necessary premise for investigating the effects of stress on the immune system. A great deal of animal and human research has persuasively established that a variety of physical and psychological stressors can significantly compromise the immunocompetence of the host. Janice Kiecolt-Glaser, Ronald Glaser, and their associates, for example, have conducted an impressive series of studies on the immunological effects of stress in medical students. Comparison of blood samples taken during examinations with baseline samples taken 1 month before showed that examination stress was associated with marked immunosuppression, as indicated by reduced helper T-cell levels; impaired proliferative response of lymphocytes to antigens; lower levels of *natural killer (NK) cells,* which have a powerful antiviral and antitumor activity; and lower levels of *interferon,* a lymphokine with important immunoregulatory functions. Interestingly, students who obtained a high score on a measure of loneliness exhibited the largest impairment of NK cell activity. Similar evidence of immunosuppression has been reported for stressors such as living near a damaged power plant, separation or divorce, spaceflight and splashdown, caregiving, unemployment, poor marital relationship, and bereavement, to name a few. There is always the possibility, of course, that behavioral changes associated with stress (e.g., sleep problems, dietary changes, smoking, drinking), rather than the stressor itself, may be responsible for the observed immunosuppression. The results of abundant research with animal models which allow precise experimental control, however, generally support the stress-induced immunosuppression hypothesis. Despite the fact that important issues remain to be elucidated, the vast human and animal literature, considered *in toto,* warrants the conclusion that stress impairs the host's immune resistance. Immunological status, then, can be used as an index of the stress response.

But if stress alters immune function, the existence of pathways that permit this interaction must be substantiated. In addition to the persuasive demonstration of conditioned immunosuppression, there is other suggestive evidence of direct and reciprocal influences between the brain and the immune system:

◆ Lesions and stimulation of hypothalamic areas have demonstrable effects on immune activity. Communication appears to be bidirectional since alterations in immune function change the firing rate of hypothalamic cells.

◆ It has been established that the thymus and other lymphoid tissues receive autonomic innervation. Immune function is inhibited by sympathetic stimulation and is enhanced by chemical sympathectomy (drug-induced suppression of sympathetic activity).

◆ Lymphocytes have surface receptors for a number of stress hormones and neurotransmitters (including the catecholamines) and for β-endorphin, one of the brain's opioid peptides released under stress. Again, the arrangement seems to be reciprocal; receptors for interleukins have been discovered on some brain cells.

There is very solid evidence that immunomodulation by the brain also utilizes endocrine pathways, especially the catecholamines and corticosteroids which, overall, have a marked immunosuppressive effect. The inhibitory action of corticosteroids on immune function had already been delineated by Selye who observed involution of the thymus and of other lymphoid structures as a major component of the nonspecific response to stress. Corticosteroids have been repeatedly found to decrease total lymphocyte count, by inhibiting their proliferative response, and to interfere with many other immune functions. These effects have been demonstrated at physiological doses, comparable to the levels produced by stress. The catecholamines, and other hormones for which receptors on lymphocytes have been found, also play an important immunomodulatory role. Epinephrine, for example, has been reported to increase suppressor T-cell levels and decrease helper T-cell population.

This sketchy overview of neuroendocrine immunoregulation admittedly oversimplifies a very complex situation. While the above conclusions are strongly supported by sifting an enormous literature, they also conceal the fact that the effects of neuroendocrine manipulations often vary with the type of immune response studied and are dependent on many variables such as hormonal concentration and timing of administration, as well as on important host factors. The picture that emerges from the large psychoneuroimmunological literature is one of intricate interactions, multiple opposing forces, bidirectional regulatory loops, and feedback mechanisms. The central nervous system, directly and through endocrine pathways, modulates all these influences

and keeps them in balance. When the delicate orchestration of synergistic and antagonistic forces is disrupted, the immunological status of the host is compromised and disease may develop. Figure 1 shows how some immune disorders may be related to immune imbalance.

Within this model, stress can be viewed as one of the factors that can disrupt immune function and increase susceptibility to illness. Conceptually consistent with the immunosuppressive effects of stress discussed earlier, is the sizeable parallel literature demonstrating that stress also makes the host more vulnerable to a number of medical outcomes, including upper respiratory infections, recurrence of herpes simplex lesions, influenza, tuberculosis, poliomyelitis, infectious mononucleosis, and numerous other infectious diseases. There are remarkable individual differences with respect to progression of HIV infection. The possible contribution of psychosocial factors to the evolution from asymptomatic seropositive status to full-blown AIDS has recently been the object of much research interest. Finally, there is also a very large body of literature on the relationship between psychosocial factors and cancer. In the past, this research limited its focus to the study of personality variables, emotions, and life events as predictors of neoplastic disease. Methodological limitations and lack of attention to the immunological mediators had precluded sustained progress. Psychoneuroimmunology has given new impetus to this area of research and has equipped it with more precise and hopefully fruitful investigative tools.

The interaction of behavior, psychosocial elements, and host factors is critical to understanding and managing today's leading causes of morbidity and mortality (e.g., coronary heart disease, cancer, diabetes). These chronic diseases have a multifactorial etiology that includes genetic susceptibility and biological factors, but also psychosocial, behavioral,

	Immune system	
	Overactive	Underactive
Exogenous antigens	Allergy	Infection
Endogenous antigens	Autoimmune disease	Cancer

FIGURE 1   Immune imbalance and immune disease. [Adapted with permission of the Society of Behavioral Medicine from M. Borysenko (1987). The immune system: An overview. *Ann. Behav. Med.* **9**, 3–10.]

and lifestyle determinants. As the emphasis in medical practice is finally shifting from treatment of disease to prevention, the potential modifiability of behavioral risk factors has attracted increasing attention. While it is not feasible, at least at the moment, to change one's biogenetic predisposition to heart disease, for example, it is possible to modify the remaining leading risk factors, all of which are grounded in behavior and lifestyle: smoking, consumption of saturated fat and cholesterol, sedentary lifestyle, uncontrolled high blood pressure, obesity, and a tendency to respond with anger and hostility to frustration and stress. Behavioral and cognitive–behavioral therapy, stress management, relaxation training, biofeedback, and stress inoculation are effective tools in the therapeutic armamentarium of the behavioral medicine practitioner who attempts to modify the behavioral and lifestyle risk factors as well as the psychosocial mediators of disease.

Bibliography

Ader, R., Felten, D. L., and Cohen, N. (Eds.) (1991). "Psychoneuroimmunology," 2nd ed. Academic Press, San Diego.

Baum, A., and Singer, J. E. (Eds.) (1987). "Handbook of Psychology and Health," Vol. V. Erlbaum, Hillsdale, NJ.

Field, T. M., McCabe, P. M., and Schneiderman, N. (Eds.) (1985). "Stress and Coping." Erlbaum, Hillsdale, NJ.

Gentry, W. D. (Ed.) (1984). "Handbook of Behavioral Medicine." Guilford, New York.

Krantz, D. S., Grunberg, N. E., and Baum, A. (1985). Health psychology. *Ann. Rev. Psychol.* **36**, 349–383.

Matarazzo, J. D., Weiss, S. M., Herd, J. A., Miller, N. E., and Weiss, S. M. (Eds.) (1984). "Behavioral Health: A Handbook of Health Enhancement and Disease Prevention." Wiley, New York.

Matthews, K. A., Weiss, S. M., Detre, T., Dembroski, T. M., Falkner, B., Manuck, S. B., and Williams, R. B., Jr. (Eds.) (1986). "Handbook of Stress, Reactivity, and Cardiovascular Disease." Wiley, New York.

Monat, A., and Lazarus, R. S. (Eds.) (1991). "Stress and Coping: An Anthology," 3rd ed. Columbia University Press, New York.

◆

PSYCHOTHERAPY

Dennis Pusch and Keith S. Dobson
University of Calgary, Canada

Glossary

Eclecticism A recent therapeutic approach which involves integrating various elements of previously existing models of therapy.

Psychotherapy The treatment of mental and emotional disorders by any of a variety of methods which occurs in the context of a relationship between a trained professional and a patient.

Resistance Conscious or unconscious efforts of the patient to thwart the progress of therapy.

Self-actualization The lifelong process of fulfilling one's capabilities and achieving one's total potential.

Unconscious The sum of all thoughts, feelings, memories, and impulses of which an individual is not aware, but which influence emotions and behavior.

PSYCHOTHERAPY, generally defined, is any form of treatment for mental illnesses, behavioral maladaptations, and/or other emotional problems, in which a trained person deliberately establishes a professional relationship with a client for the purpose of removing, modifying, or retarding existing symptoms and/or behavior problems, and of promoting positive personality growth and development. Given the breadth of this endeavor, it is hardly surprising that tremendous diversity currently exists in the way that psychotherapy is conceptualized and practiced. This diversity does not naturally lend itself to brief presentation, and as a result, any discus-

sion of specific issues presented here will necessarily be introdutory in nature.

I. INTRODUCTION

One of the factors responsible for the rich diversity in the field is the fact that therapists can currently receive their training in a variety of fields of study. Some of the fields of study which prepare people to become therapists include

◆ clinical psychology
◆ counseling psychology
◆ psychiatry
◆ educational and school psychology
◆ marriage and family therapy
◆ clinical social work
◆ nursing
◆ pastoral psychology
◆ child and adolescent psychology
◆ community mental health services
◆ human services

Each of these areas offers its own unique advantages in terms of training, and no one area corners the market when it comes to the ability to produce qualified and competent therapists. Therapists can also come to the profession with a variety of degrees, licenses, and credentials, reflecting their status as either professionals or paraprofessionals. Regardless of background training, the common denominator between all psychotherapists (and all forms of psychotherapy) is that they employ the relationship established between the client and the therapist to influence the client to modify maladaptive responses and to adopt better ones.

There has been considerable discussion about the difference between psychotherapy and counseling. In many ways it is difficult to make a distinction between the two terms. Counselors and psychotherapists are both trained to use a special kind of relationship to help people with their problems, and students taking courses which include either ''counseling'' or ''psychotherapy'' in the title would likely encounter much of the same material as is presented in the following sections of this entry. However, many people working in the mental health field perceive a difference between counseling and psychotherapy, and some have suggested that the distinction lies in the types of problems which are dealt with in the helping relationship. While considerable overlap certainly exists in the types of problems encountered, a distinction at this level does appear to be warranted. As a general rule of thumb, counseling often implies work with clients who present with less serious problems or very specific problems which do not include significant personality disturbance. Psychotherapy usually implies work with more seriously disturbed individuals, and is more likely to occur in a medical setting. Some advanced training is generally required of all mental health workers, but is especially necessary for psychotherapists, given the severity and range of problems they are expected to treat. As a result, the average psychotherapist is more likely than the average counselor to have earned advanced degrees and have achieved professional status.

Despite the perceived differences between counselors and psychotherapists, the areas of overlap between the two disciplines are probably much larger than the areas of divergence. The term ''psychotherapy'' is used throughout the following discussion, but the reader should be aware that most of the theories and techniques presented are shared by psychotherapists and counselors alike.

II. RECIPIENTS OF PSYCHOTHERAPY

During psychotherapy's formative years, roughly 1900 to 1950, the recipient of therapeutic intervention was almost invariably an adult who was treated in one-on-one sessions with the therapist for a period of months or years. Although individual adult clients are still the most frequent recipients of therapy, there has been a successful movement toward offering therapy to other populations, such as groups, families, and children. This broadened approach reflects the diversity of theory and practice which has been a hallmark of psychotherapy over the past four decades. The percentage of American and Canadian therapists who offer treatment to these various pop-

TABLE I

Percentage of American and Canadian Therapists Who Conduct Therapy with Specific Populations

Type of therapy	American therapists (%)[a]	Canadian therapists (%)[b]
Individual therapy	99.0	
Adult		86.4
Child/adolescent		59.1
Marital/couples therapy	73.7	60.2
Family therapy	53.6	46.6
Group therapy	45.8	
Adult		21.6
Child/adolescent		10.2

[a] Adapted from Prochaska, J. O., and Norcross, J. C. (1983). *Psychother. Theory, Res. Practice* **20**(2), 161–173.

[b] Adapted from Hunsley, J., and Lefebvre, M. (1990). *Can. Psychol.* **31**(4), 350–358.

ulations in the course of their practice is presented in Table I.

A. Individuals

The fact that nearly all therapists regularly conduct therapy with individual clients reflects the widespread belief that a one-on-one therapeutic relationship offers unique advantages over and above other types of therapy. Perhaps the strongest argument in favor of individual therapy is that it allows for an intensive focus on the subjective world of the client. Most clients who come for therapy do not want to talk exclusively about other people or the world in general, but rather their own subjective experience of those people and that world. Developing a meaningful relationship with a therapist gives many clients a feeling of security which allows them to disclose material which they might be reluctant to reveal if other people were present. In individual therapy the client has the chance to consider issues of personal growth without outside distractions, and can expect to leave with the feeling of having been uniquely attended to, heard, and understood.

Individual therapy is especially indicated for those clients whose chief complaints are personal in nature, and whose complaints are such that the person has the power to do something to improve the situation. Individual therapy is also warranted for persons trying to come to terms with troublesome issues in the near or distant past, where the inclusion of other parties involved in the situation is either impossible or ill-advised (e.g., child abuse, death, a painful divorce). Of course, involvement in individual therapy presupposes a certain motivation on the part of the client to change, as well as a sufficient fund of personal insight to make the therapeutic process useful.

Individual therapy may also be contraindicated in some cases. For example, if the client displays a tendency to become overly dependent upon the therapist, it may be appropriate to suggest group therapy, where the likelihood of such a dependency developing is lessened. Group therapy may also be a viable option for clients who have already dealt with some of their personal issues in individual therapy, but need more work in the area of interpersonal relationships. Individual therapy is also contraindicated in those cases where the therapist believes that the client's larger system is responsible for causing or maintaining the presenting problem. For example, it would be unacceptable to treat a child for enuresis if the child was incontinent as a defense against the possibility of sexual molestation during the night.

B. Groups

Group therapy has risen dramatically in popularity over the past 50 years, largely as the result of increasing pressure on mental health professionals to treat growing numbers of patients. Therapists have found that group therapy can have a dramatic impact on individual participants, yet also allows therapists to provide service to more people than could reasonably be treated otherwise. However, the advantage of group therapy is not simply logistical. While it is true that members of a group usually do not have the luxury of exploring personal issues in the same depth that they would in individual therapy, they are rewarded in return with an expanded understanding of group dynamics and increased efficacy in interpersonal relationships.

Group therapy is unique in that it involves combinations of individuals occupying the patient or the therapist roles. In its most typical form, group therapy includes one therapist and six to eight patients. However, many variations of this model are offered, with common variants including multiple therapists and smaller or larger groups.

Experience has shown that just about any type of patient can benefit from group therapy, and some heterogeneity among group members in terms of age, gender, and presenting problem is often considered desirable. At the same time, the group process is likely to be compromised if members represent too broad a range of functioning. The therapist must be careful in screening potential participants, keeping in mind both the characteristics and needs of the individual and the goals of the group. The therapist must also be prepared to modify the approaches and techniques normally used with groups of relatively healthy patients when forming groups consisting of patients with more severe pathology, as such groups are naturally more modest in their goals.

Three phases of group process have been identified. In the first phase, members are concerned with matters of inclusion (i.e., "Will I be accepted?"; "Can I become a member of this group?"). The goal of the first phase is for members to cease to function as isolated individuals, and to take on an identity as part of the group. In the next phase, group members begin to reassert their autonomy. The individual's need for independence arises, and issues regarding the distribution of power in the group are raised. Finally, the group moves into a phase where members are able to accept and appreciate each other as individuals and express real affection and support.

Therapists who take on the role of leader in group therapy need to be flexible in that role. The therapist with an advanced understanding of group dynamics will know that at times it is useful to be more or less active. An active therapist will serve to reduce the group's anxiety, which can be advantageous, especially in the early life of the group. However, too much activity on the part of the leader may promote the belief that the most important dynamics occur between individuals members and the therapist, rather than among all the participants collectively. A less active therapist may cause more group anxiety, but can also force a group to develop a strength and identity of its own more quickly. The most effective group therapist is one who understands the changing needs of the group and is able to adapt his or her leadership style to meet those needs. Therapists must also be particularly aware of their own character traits and personal weaknesses, since it is not uncommon for therapists to adopt a leadership style based on their own needs at some point in the group process (e.g., the need to be in control, or the need to appear perfect).

C. Families

Family therapy began to gain prominence as an alternative form of therapy in the 1950s, essentially as an antiestablishment movement. The era was characterized by a growing dissatisfaction among some therapists with traditional forms of therapy, which tended to look at psychiatric symptoms in isolation, resulting in the conclusion that the individual must be defective in some way. The unique contribution of family therapists was their focus on understanding people's behavior in light of their familial context. Problematic behaviors viewed as part of a larger context suddenly seemed more reasonable, if not inevitable, as a result of the way the family had evolved.

There are a few core assumptions and foci shared by family therapists, regardless of the specific model to which they adhere, which distinguish them from other therapists. One of these assumptions is that psychopathology serves a function in families. For example, consider a family where the mother and father habitually fight and one daughter develops an eating disorder. A typical family therapy formulation would see the eating disorder as serving the family's needs by forcing the mother and father to refocus their attention on their daughter's dangerous behavior rather than on their dissatisfaction with each other, thereby reducing the possibility of the dissolution of the family. The daughter's behavior would likely continue as long as it seemed to meet the family's unspoken need, and the removal of the behavior without a concomitant change in the family system would only encourage someone else to develop a problem.

Another key concept of family therapy is circularity. This concept was emphasized as a reaction against therapists' tendency to think linearly (i.e., to think that there is a specific cause for a specific effect). In family therapy, problems are seen as part of an ongoing, circular sequence of behavior wherein Behavior A results in Behavior B, which in turn strengthens Behavior A, and so on. Assessment in family therapy involves trying to identify the negative circular patterns which augur against healthy family functioning, and in therapy the therapist will encourage family members to speak directly to each other and change their usual interactions in order to break those patterns. The therapist will also contribute to breaking the patterns by ''reframing,'' or restating, the family's problems or issues in a new light, which allows the family to consider new possibilities, which will it is hoped lead to the establishment of new, healthy circular patterns.

D. Children

While child therapy could legitimately be included under the rubric of individual or family therapy, the subject warrants a discussion of its own due to the unique needs and characteristics of this population of clients. These needs have been highlighted by researchers, who have made important advances in the understanding of the nature and etiology of various forms of child psychopathology. The challenge which faced child therapists was to combine this growing knowledge base with the existing knowledge of developmental psychology in order to arrive at effective assessment and treatment methods for use with children. An element of urgency was added to this challenge by related research findings which underscored the importance of early detection and treatment of psychological problems in children. It is now clear that adverse outcomes in later life can often be attenuated or avoided by prompt and effective tretment at the first signs of trouble.

The techniques chosen for use in therapy with children take a number of forms, depending on the age and comprehension level of the child. ''Talking'' therapy is generally more effective with older children and adolescents. Play therapy is often used with younger children, or older children who may have difficulty discussing troubling issues with an unknown adult. In play therapy, the therapist and child spend time together in a play room, often moving from one activity to another (e.g., painting, puzzles, doll houses, etc.). The therapist usually makes inferences about the child's functioning on the basis of how the child plays, and what the child says during the play time. The therapist also looks for ''teachable moments,'' which can be used to promote therapeutic insight.

Therapy with children has been found to be effective in the treatment of many problems. Child therapists routinely treat children who are depressed, have excessive fears, have been abused, have physical or mental handicaps, or have poor self-confidence. Specific problem behaviors, such as bed-wetting, biting, and temper tantrums are also treated, although the treatment in these cases usually involves the establishment of a system of rewards and/or punishments for the child, and the therapist's role mainly involves teaching the child's caregivers how to administer the specially designed behavior modification program.

Therapists who intend to work with children, regardless of their theoretical orientation and the specific treatment goals, must be mindful that children are undergoing rapid developmental changes, and that problem behaviors often wax and wane at different ages. Many problems will disappear over time as a function of the child's development, even in the absence of intervention. The therapist must also be aware that many behaviors which may be indicative of severe maladjustment or emotional disturbance (e.g., lying, destructiveness) are also relatively common in most children. In general, it behooves the therapist to avoid jumping to conclusions on the basis of one or two pieces of behavioral evidence. Responsible therapy requires a thorough understanding of the child's situation, which implies a multi-method assessment approach. Such an assessment might include some or all of the following: child interview; parent interview; teacher interview; tests of cognition, personality, and academic achievement; behavioral observation in the home, at school, and at play.

III. BASIC ISSUES IN PSYCHOTHERAPY

A. Assessment and Therapy

Individuals who seek help from a therapist often have trouble pinpointing exactly what is troubling them. In order to make the best use of the therapeutic time, the therapist conducts a thorough assessment of the patient and the nature of their difficulty. The data gleaned from the assessment allow the clinician to arrive at a case formulation, and provide specific directions for the therapy itself.

Although assessment is an ongoing component of therapy, it is often the case that the first one or two sessions with a new client will focus especially on assessment. Adequate assessment at this stage will include obtaining the client's description of their chief complaint (e.g., depression, marital discord, addiction, etc.). The therapist should establish when the present problem began, previous occurrences of the problem, the duration of episodes, and specific symptoms. Any history of prior treatment should be investigated, including any medications that have been taken, as well as any knowledge of a precipitating event that may have led to the current difficulties.

An assessment of the client's past history is likely to provide significant data for understanding and helping the client. Areas which are often discussed include birth history, early development and attainment of milestones (e.g., walking, talking), relationships with parents and siblings, educational history, social contacts and leisure activities, occupational history, and marital status.

As part of the assessment process, therapists often administer one or more standardized psychological tests. These tests come in a variety of formats (e.g.,

verbal or nonverbal responses, fill-in-the-blank or complete sentences, timed or untimed, etc.) and are designed to measure a variety of aspects of psychological functioning (e.g., personality, intelligence, mood, aptitude). Established population norms are available for these tests, allowing the therapist to see how the client compares with his or her peers on any given measure of functioning. Given the possibility of misinterpretation of statistically based data, therapists are ethically bound to administer and interpret only those tests for which they have received the requisite training. [*See* CLINICAL ASSESSMENT; PERSONALITY ASSESSMENT.]

Depending on the nature of the case, the therapist may also seek additional data from outside sources. Potentially useful information can be provided by spouses, parents, teachers, physicians, or previous therapists. Of course, the release of such information requires the consent of the client or their legal guardian.

B. The Therapeutic Relationship

When one considers the strength of the arguments which are raised in favor of one theoretical orientation over another, and the conviction with which they are raised, it would be easy to conclude that theoretical orientation is the most important variable affecting the outcome of psychotherapy. The literature on psychotherapy outcomes clearly indicates that this is not the case. It has consistently been demonstrated that the most important predictor of therapeutic outcome is the quality of the relationship between the therapist and the client. Rather than being an indictment against theories, the evidence simply suggests that therapists would be wise to pay close attention to the development of positive relationships with clients. Good therapeutic rapport will encourage clients to lower their defenses in the belief that they will not be judged or rejected, and this lowering of the defenses is a necessary prerequisite for therapeutic change. The chance of meeting therapeutic goals is generally not good (even if the therapist has developed a perfect case formulation) if the quality of the relationship is poor.

The helping relationship is a very unique kind of relationship. It is not formed for social reasons, but rather to help clients achieve specific goals. The relationship is one-sided in that it is designed to meet the needs of the client, not those of the therapist. To be effective, the therapist must develop the ability to lay aside personal needs in favor of those of the client.

A successful therapist will do several things to establish a good relationship with a client. Most importantly, the therapist will communicate an understanding of what the client is saying and feeling. Clients should feel that they have been heard, that their pain and frustration have been understood, and that they have been accepted despite their deficiencies. The therapist also needs to be honest with the client, thereby demonstrating care and respect. An important part of honesty involves the ability to communicate feelings and intentions without distortion or facade. Such congruence between what the therapist feels, says, and does serves to establish trust, and provides a model for the client to follow. The therapist should be patient, and not press for the exploration of difficult issues before the client is ready to discuss them. The relationship will also be facilitated if the therapist recognizes and acknowledges the client's strengths as well as weaknesses, and involves the client in decision-making whenever possible.

An important caveat to the concept of establishing a good relationship is that the pursuit of comfort in the relationship as an end in itself can be counterproductive. Therapists can be deceived into thinking that real progress must be occurring if the relationship remains harmonious. But the goal of the relationship is not just to keep the encounter pleasant. The ultimate goal of therapy needs to be kept in mind. Shying away from the real purpose of therapy because the client finds the process painful is not doing the client a service.

C. Resistance

It is to be expected that roadblocks to progress will occasionally occur during the course of therapy, with the most common obstacle being a resistance to change on the part of the client. Resistance may be expressed in a number of ways. The client may habitually show up late for appointments, or may fail to arrive at all. Homework assignments may be neglected. In the session itself, the client may deny the existence of unwanted thoughts or feelings, or may derail the therapist's efforts to move to deeper levels of exploration by continually switching the discussion to trivial details or unrelated topics. Whatever form it takes, resistance can leave the therapist feeling stymied, especially since resistance sometimes occurs in the wake of important therapeutic gains.

Therapists have tended to interpret the meaning of resistance in two ways. One group of therapists

has argued that the concept of "resistance" is nothing more than an elaborate rationalization which therapists use to explain away their treatment failures (i.e., "if treatment is not working, there must be something wrong with the client, rather than something being wrong with my therapeutic ministrations"). Advocates of this position suggest that what is often labeled resistant behavior is merely an indicator that something about the way the therapist has structured the therapy is not meeting the client's needs. In such a case, it becomes necessary for the therapist to move back to the assessment stage to ascertain if the correct target for intervention was originally identified. The therapist must also evaluate if sufficient trust and rapport have developed between him- or herself and the client, or if there is something about the client's social network which is serving as an impediment to change. The therapist should also question if incorrect techniques are being used to combat the problem, or if correct techniques are being incorrectly applied. In general, resistance is seen as a function of the limitations of the therapist's knowledge and methods, and to the extent that these problems can be dealt with, the resistance will dissipate.

The second, more traditional, view of resistance sees it as an instinctive opposition displayed toward any attempt to expose a person's unconscious conflicts (i.e., conflicts that are so deeply rooted that the person is unaware that they even exist). Resistance is not viewed as an interpersonal problem between the patient and the therapist, but rather as a predictable demonstration of how invested the client is in trying to guard against the possibility of further pain in a vulnerable area of his or her emotional life. In other words, resistance occurs when the possibility of change becomes so real that the client's anxiety is aroused. Resistance thus serves as a natural signpost, telling the therapist that the therapy is probably moving down the right road. The therapist's job is not to tackle the resistance directly, but to use the quality of the therapeutic relationship to generate an imbalance that favors progress rather than maintenance of the status quo. The client will naturally abandon resistant behavior when the perceived advantages of moving forward outweigh the natural anxiety associated with moving into uncharted territory.

D. Length of Therapy

The number of sessions devoted to a given client in a therapeutic relationship has undergone a substantial shift in recent years. Earlier therapeutic approaches, which were often largely based on the theoretical assumptions of Sigmund Freud, usually aimed at the resolution of unconscious conflict and the alteration of personality. Practitioners did not expect that these ambitious goals could be rapidly attained, and as a result, patients often spent a number of years in therapy.

The current emphasis on therapy of shorter duration can be attributed to several factors. First, after World War II therapeutic approaches began to evolve which tended to focus on specific problem behaviors or moods. Therapists who moved away from personality reconstruction as the fundamental goal of therapy found that positive changes could be realized in more limited areas of a client's functioning in much shorter time frames. This position was bolstered by a growing empirical research literature which began to validate the use of specific interventions to combat specific problems. This trend, coupled with ongoing refinements in the theories of psychopathology, resulted in a realization on the part of therapists that effective therapy could perhaps be accomplished more quickly than previously thought possible.

The move toward shorter therapy was also spurred on by the attitudes of the consumers of mental health services. Many of today's clients are either unwilling or unable to devote several years and thousands of dollars to psychotherapy. As the general population becomes more psychologically sophisticated, mostly due to the influence of the media, their expectation for prompt, effective service rises. This attitude is especially prevalent on the part of third-party payers (e.g., government agencies, the legal system, and insurance companies, all of whom are involved in paying for psychological care at various times). Third-party payers are increasingly forcing therapists to work within limited time frames as a cost-saving measure. Given the current cost of psychological care and the growing demand for mental health services, it is unlikely that the trend toward short-term therapy will be reversed in the near future.

Despite the movement toward brief therapy, it should be noted that a tremendous range of therapy durations still exists. Those who practice in the Freudian tradition, though more willing to consider the viability of short-term therapy, continue to assert that personality change is far from being an overnight endeavor. Thus, modern psychotherapy can require anywhere from one to hundreds of sessions. On average, though, most therapeutic relationships involve between 15 and 40 meetings. The variables which are most likely to affect the eventual duration of therapy include the theoretical orientation of the therapist, the nature and severity of the presenting problem, and the willingness/capacity of the client to pay for the treatment.

E. Ethical Considerations

Ethical considerations play an important role in the way that therapists conduct therapy. There is general agreement that therapists are in a position to wield considerable influence in their relationships with clients. To protect against potential abuses of this power, and to help clinicians make ethical decisions in specific situations, a number of ethical codes have evolved.

The diverse educational backgrounds and current affiliations of therapists have rendered it impossible to develop one ethical code which is binding upon everyone who practices therapy. As a result, various professional organizations have published their own ethical guidelines; *Ethical Principles of Psychologists*, by the American Psychological Association (APA, 1992); *Ethical Standards*, by the American Association for Counseling and Development (AACD, 1981); *Ethical Guidelines for Group Leaders*, by the Association for Specialists in Group Work (ASGW, 1980); *Standards for the Private Practice of Clinical Social Work*, by the National Association of Social Workers (NASW, 1981); *Code of Ethics for Certified Clinical Mental Health Counselors*, by the American Mental Health Counselors Association (AMHCA, 1980); *Code of Professional Ethics*, by the American Association for Marriage and Family Therapy (AAMFT, 1991).

While the specific details of the various ethical codes may vary somewhat from specialization to specialization, there does seem to be almost universal agreement on a number of basic principles which should govern a therapist's conduct. First, therapists must be competent to practice by virtue of training and experience, and only provide services and use techniques for which they are qualified. Second, therapists must respect the confidentiality of all information obtained from others in the course of their work. Information may only be revealed with the consent of the client or his or her legal guardian, except in those unusual cases where failure to reveal information would result in a clear danger to the client or someone else (e.g., suicide, homicide, child abuse). Third, therapists must avoid any action that will violate or diminish the legal and civil rights of clients. This principle also implies that therapists must adhere to government laws and institutional regulations. Fourth, therapists make every effort to ensure that their services are used appropriately. It is considered unethical for clinicians to engage in professional relationships which limit their objectivity or create a conflict of interest. Fifth, therapists do not use their influence to exploit clients. Sexual intimacies with clients are definitely unethical. Also, financial arrangements should be made with clients in advance of therapy, and therapy should be terminated when it is reasonably clear that the client has achieved the therapeutic goals established at the outset, or when the client is no longer benefitting from therapy.

While efforts to regulate the practice of therapy through the development of ethical codes are laudable, it should be recognized that breaking ethical codes does not necessarily imply legal malpractice. Specific codes are only binding upon members of a given association, and infractions of those codes generally involve sanctions (e.g., reprimand or expulsion) from that association. The consequences of unethical conduct by a professional, such as a psychiatrist or psychologist, are considered somewhat more serious, in that a license to practice that particular profession may be revoked. However, there are no laws which prevent any unethical practitioner from adopting the generic title of "counselor" and continuing to see clients. Legal proceedings through the civil courts can be brought against therapists who demonstrate unethical conduct only if their behavior is deemed illegal according to state law.

IV. THEORETICAL ORIENTATIONS

As has already been intimated, therapists have adopted a wide variety of theoretical stances. There are dozens of separate approaches to psychotherapy today, and the techniques utilized by advocates of these approaches number in the hundreds. For the sake of brevity and clarity, five influential approaches—psychoanalytic/psychodynamic, behavioral, cognitive, humanistic, and eclectic—will be presented here. Table II presents the percentage of American and Canadian therapists who identify themselves according to these theoretical orientations.

A. Psychoanalytic/Psychodynamic

Psychoanalysis is the oldest recognized approach to explaining and treating psychological illness. The

TABLE II
Theoretical Orientations of American and Canadian Psychotherapists

Orientation	American (%)[a]	Canadian (%)[b]
Psychoanalytic/dynamic	29.2	19.3
Behavioral	5.6	21.6
Cognitive	8.3	25.0
Humanistic	14.1	14.7
Eclectic/integration	30.2	47.7

[a] Adapted from Prochaska, J. O., and Norcross, J. C. (1983). *Psychother. Res. Practice* **20**(2) 161–163. The total equals 87.4%, with the remainder of therapists polled in this study endorsing other, lesser known models of therapy.

[b] Adapted from Hunsley, J. and Lefebvre, M. (1990). *Can Psychol.* **31**(4), 350–358. The total exceeds 100% because some respondents reported more than one theoretical orientation.

procedure, designed by Viennese neurologist Sigmund Freud, entails investigating mental processes by means of free association, dream interpretation, and interpretation of resistance and transference manifestations. The approach is predicated upon the assumption that unconscious mental processes exist, and sees the role of the analyst as being to interpret and point out the nature of the patient's hidden conflicts, in order to produce insight and make the conflicts conscious. Once the conflicts become conscious, the patient is encouraged to "work through" them, which eventually culminates in the alteration of the patient's inner psychological structure. Psychoanalysis generally requires a commitment of several years before the process is considered complete.

In the therapeutic session itself, the patient is encouraged to talk about whatever he or she wishes. The therapist then asks the patient to describe any thoughts, fantasies, or feelings associated with the material given (free association). It is expected that the patient will exhibit any of a number of defense mechanisms (e.g., denial, repression, projection) in the course of therapy, all of which serve to protect the patient against the perceived danger associated with their long-hidden impulses and affects being brought to conscious awareness. Use is also made of the patient's unconscious emotional response to the therapist (transference). For example, the patient may unconsciously respond to the therapist as a father figure or mother figure. It is the analyst's role to interpret and point out the nature of the transference, thereby facilitating understanding of the patient's unconscious feelings toward their own father or mother.

Psychodynamic psychotherapy is a direct offspring of psychoanalysis. Most of the fundamental assumptions of psychoanalysts are shared by psychodyanmic therapists (e.g., the importance of bringing unconscious conflicts to light). However, there are also some significant differences. For instance, while psychodynamic therapy places some emphasis on dealing with the past and its effect on the patient, it is much more concerned with the person's current personality dynamics and interpersonal functioning. Therapy aims at symptom reduction and the adaptive functioning of the patient, and not necessarily core personality reconstruction. The therapist often takes a more active role than the psychoanalyst, and therapy is often completed in fewer sessions.

B. Behavioral

A dramatic shift in the theoretical underpinnings of psychotherapy began to take place in the 1940s and 1950s. Based on emerging results of studies with animals, a view of neurosis developed which suggested that all maladaptive behavior is learned through normal learning processes. Behaviorists denied the concept of free will, suggesting rather that all behaviors are simply predictable responses which are contingent upon antecedent events, with the likelihood of a given behavior being repeated being directly related to the reinforcement received by the person for performing the behavior. For example, a parent may learn to yell at a child at the slightest provocation if the yelling is quickly reinforced by the child's compliance. As behavior came to be understood in this way, the goal of behavior therapy became the modification of specific stimulus–response connections, which was often achieved via the alteration of the reinforcement schedule.

The role of the behavior therapist is to help the client reverse maladaptive learning through the learning of new, appropriate responses. Behaviorists value the therapeutic relationship, but do not see it as a sufficient cause for change. More emphasis is placed on the therapist's role as a scientist and teacher. Part of that role involves very structured history-taking and behavioral assessment by the therapist in order to determine which of the client's behaviors are maladaptive, as well as the circumstances in which they occur. In addition to the specific behaviors and their antecedents, behaviorists also scrutinize the real and perceived consequences of the behavior, since these are believed to maintain the problem. Interventions are designed to break these antecedent–behavior–consequence patterns, with the evaluation of therapeutic outcomes usually being characterized by a rigorous adherence to scientific method.

Among the more well-known behavior therapy techniques are systematic desensitization, assertiveness training, and aversive conditioning. Systematic desensitization is often used to help people overcome fears and phobias. The procedure involves relaxation training and a gradual exposure of the person to the feared situation, first in the person's mind and then in real life. By alternating between relaxation and approaching the feared situation/object, the person learns that their worst fears about the situation/object are not confirmed, and the power of the pattern is broken. Assertiveness training has been used to help clients gain control over social situations which tend to evoke their problematic behaviors. A given training program may include modeling, therapist coaching, group feedback, behavioral rehearsal, and repeated practice, which together teach patients a variety of skills for coping effectively with high-risk situations. Aversive conditioning involves the pairing of a problem behavior with an unpleasant punishment which is specifically designed to replace a positive reinforcement which maintained the behavior in the past. For example, chemical agents may be given to alcoholic clients to induce vomiting immediately after taking a drink. Before long, the very thought of taking a drink will make these clients feel sick to their stomachs. Although outcome data support the use of aversive techniques, these methods are often seen as rather undesirable from an ethical standpoint, and are generally only used after other attempts at intervention have failed.

C. Cognitive

As the applications of behavior therapy spread, it became evident that the behavioral model was unable to account for all psychological distress, and the therapeutic pendulum, which had swung away from Freud's heavy emphasis on internal processes, began to swing back. However, rather than pointing again to unconscious conflicts, many theorists began to emphasize the way in which a person's conscious thoughts contributed to their psychological difficulties. Cognitive therapy, which aimed to intervene in a person's life primarily at the level of thinking, developed as a natural by-product of the cognitive model of behavior.

The main assumption of cognitive therapists is that a person's feelings or behavior in response to a given situation is not predicted by the situation itself, but rather by the person's interpretation of the situation. Thus, a person could feel either relieved or despondent in the face of the death of a loved one, depending on whether the accompanying thought was "I'm glad that his pain and suffering are finally over" or "I don't know how I can live without him."

Researchers have been able to demonstrate convincingly that certain types of psychopathology (e.g., depression and anxiety) are often associated with certain types of irrational thoughts and faulty interpretations. These cognitions, which seem to surface automatically in people who are prone to them in the face of certain life events, are believed to reflect the person's core self-schema. The self-schema contains a person's basic beliefs about the self, which are usually based on childhood experiences. If the childhood experiences are sufficiently injurious or trauamtic, the self-schema may take on a decidedly negative flavor, containing ideas like "I can't do anything right" or "I'm unlovable." The negative self-schema provides a filter through which events are interpreted throughout the course of a person's life. For example, a woman with a negative self-schema who is passed by a friend on the street without a wave or greeting may jump to the conclusion that the friend no longer likes her, which in turn strengthens the negative self-schema and results in subjective feelings of depression.

Cognitive therapy is a collaborative endeavor in which the therapist and client join forces in investigating and challenging the thoughts which give rise to the client's actions and emotions in everyday life. Homework assignments are often used to help clients identify their negative thoughts and to test the assumptions on which they are based. Childhood issues are discussed to help clients gain insight into the source and content of their negative self-schema. This exploration can be a very painful process, but is usually seen as a necessary step toward the alteration of the self-schema. The ultimate goal of cognitive therapy is to help clients realize that the negative beliefs about the self which were formed in childhood are no longer accurate, thus freeing them to respond to both good and bad life events in a healthy and realistic manner.

D. Humanistic

Humanistic therapies arose as a reaction against the determinism which is characteristic of both psycho-

analysis and behaviorism. Rather than adopting a view which sees people's behavior as being primarily determined by their childhood experiences or external rewards and punishments, humanistic therapists focus on the ultimate freedom which people have to make choices which affect their lives. People are viewed as inherently good, and the therapist's role is to create a therapeutic environment which allows the client's innate tendency toward growth to surface. Although many humanistic approaches exist, only two of them, client-centered therapy and gestalt therapy, will be discussed here.

Carl Rogers' client-centered therapy is the best known of the humanistic therapies. Rogers believed that individuals have problems in living because others impose conditions of worth on them. As people learn that they are expected to act, feel, or think in certain ways in order to be acceptable to others, they begin to conform themselves to those expectations. This conformity occurs at the expense of the person's own true feelings and impulses, resulting in an impediment in the individual's natural process of growth and self-actualization.

The main function of the client-centered therapist is to demonstrate unconditional positive regard for the client. As the client experiences this unconditional acceptance, they are freed to clarify their true feelings and come to value who they really are. The therapist maintains a nondirective stance throughout this process. The therapist strives to display empathy by accurately reflecting the client's thoughts and feelings, ultimately resulting in the client's increased self-understanding and renewed growth as an individual.

Gestalt therapy, developed by Fritz Perls, is based on the idea that psychological problems arise from unresolved and repressed conflicts, and that these conflicts must be uncovered and worked through in order for a person's inherent potential for growth to be released. However, rather than dwelling on the past, emphasis is placed on the client's immediate thoughts and feelings (i.e., their experience in the "here and now"). Clients are encouraged to express themselves openly, and to take responsibility for their feelings and actions. Awareness of important psychological conflicts may be heightened by having a client stage a conversation between opposing parts of the self, or by conversing with an emotionally significant person who is not actually present. In order to help clients become even more aware of their experience in the present, gestalt therapists consider not only what is said, but also how it is said—including voice inflection, posture, gestures, breathing patterns, etc.

E. Eclectic

As evidenced in Table II, the majority of therapists today do not align themselves with one particular theoretical orientation, but prefer to think of themselves as eclectic in their practice. "Eclectic" does not imply that therapists, overwhelmed by the diversity of the approaches available to them, resort to a random hodgepodge of techniques in psychotherapy. Rather, therapists are increasingly aware that there are strengths and weaknesses inherent in all models of therapy, and are endeavoring to include those specific models and techniques in their practice which have demonstrated efficacy in dealing with certain types of problems and populations. As the popularity of this approach to therapy grows, it will become important for eclectic therapists and theorists to build models of systematic eclecticism which are empirically valid and clinically useful.

V. DOES PSYCHOTHERAPY WORK?

The historical pattern of new therapeutic approaches arising to challenge and supplant more established models has naturally led some critics to question the validity of the entire therapeutic enterprise. Unfortunately, the question "Does therapy work?" does not lend itself to an easy answer. The most accurate answer is that some therapies work for some people sometimes. Outcome studies comparing the efficacy of different types of therapy have certainly demonstrated that some types of therapy are better for treating specific problems than others. For example, cognitive therapy has been shown to be especially effective in the treatment of major depression, while behavioral approaches are probably the best for dealing with phobias. These same studies have also consistently revealed that groups of subjects who undergo psychotherapy experience greater symptom reduction than control group subjects who receive no treatment at all. It should be noted, though, that these conclusions are based on statistical probability, and the truth is that a minority of people who undergo therapy will not achieve their therapeutic

goals. Given that therapy usually involves therapists trying to help clients whom they have never met with problems that they have never experienced, and given that clients come to therapy with widely ranging levels of motivation, insight, and commitment to change, it is highly unrealistic to expect that therapy will ever be able to help everyone.

The current limitations of psychotherapy suggest some natural directions for therapists and theorists to move as we enter the 21st century. Further refinements of existing theories are necessary within the discipline, and an increased emphasis on the integration of theories will likely prove to be fruitful. There is also a need for increased communication and research across disciplines. For example, the interaction between biological and psychological factors in the onset and maintenance of mental disorders requires further examination. Finally, as results in these areas of theory and research are reported, steps must be taken to ensure that the gap between research and practice is bridged. This can occur by encouraging more therapists, who understand the unique demands of the therapeutic situation, to become involved in theory construction and research. Also, an insistence on continued education for all therapists would be beneficial, and efforts to disseminate current knowledge via academic journals, seminars, and workshops, both within and across disciplines, should continue. To the extent that these goals are met, we will move forward in our ability to match specific interventions to specific problems in light of the unique needs of individual clients. It is our conviction that as this progress occurs, the minority of people whose psychological needs cannot be met by psychotherapy will continue to decrease.

Bibliography

Cottone, R. R. (1992). "Theories and Paradigms of Counseling and Psychotheray." Allyn and Bacon, Boston.
Dobson, K. S. (Ed.) (1988). "Handbook of Cognitive–Behavioral Therapies." Guilford Press, New York.
Egan, G. (1990). "The Skilled Helper: A Systematic Approach to Effective Helping," 4th ed. Brooks/Cole, Pacific Grove, CA.
Mahoney, M. J. (1991). "Human Change Processes: The Scientific Foundations of Psychotherapy." Basic Books, New York.
Prochaska, J. O. (1984). "Systems of Psychotherapy: A Transtheoretical Analysis." Dorsey, Homewood, IL.